THE APPLIED NEW TESTAMENT COMMENTARY

The Applied New Testament Commentary

THOMAS HALE

WITH GENERAL ARTICLES CONTRIBUTED BY

STEPHEN THORSON

KINGSWAY PUBLICATIONS

EASTBOURNE

First published in Great Britain 1996
Reprinted 1997, 1999

ISBNs
0 85476 508 5 – Kingsway
1 5647 6675 6 – Victor Books

Published in the USA by Victor Books, an imprint of ChariotVictor Publishing, a division of Cook Communications, Colorado Springs, Colorado 80918

For more information about Victor Books, write to them at 4050 Lee Vance View, Colorado Springs, Colorado 80918

Published by
KINGSWAY PUBLICATIONS
Lottbridge Drove, Eastbourne, BN23 6NT, England.
E-mail: books@kingsway.co.uk

Designed and produced for the publishers by
Bookprint Creative Services, P.O. Box 827, BN21 3YJ, England.
Printed in Great Britain.

CONTENTS

ACKNOWLEDGEMENTS

This commentary is not intended to be biased toward any particular denomination. It is hoped that Christians of all denominations will be able to use it. Where true Christians have differing opinions on certain subjects, these are presented side by side in the commentary without partiality. This is done throughout the commentary, but especially in the General Articles.

In writing this commentary, great help has been obtained from four main sources: 1) *The New International Commentary of the New Testament,* Eerdmans, 17 Volumes; 2) *The Expositor's Bible Commentary* [New Testament], Zondervan, 5 Volumes; 3) *New Bible Commentary: Revised,* Eerdmans; 4) *Matthew Henry's Commentary, Abridged,* Zondervan. In addition to these four main sources, the writings of Martyn Lloyd Jones, Andrew Murray, John Stott, and others have been most helpful. The work of selecting and writing the material in this commentary has been done by Thomas Hale, M.D., F.A.C.S.

All but the last four General Articles have been contributed by Stephen Thorson, M.D., F.A.A.P. M.A. (Theological Studies). The General Article entitled "Summary of the Old Testament" has been contributed by Rebecca Thorson. The General Articles are based on material taken from many sources, including the following major creeds and confessions of the Christian church: the Apostle's Creed, the Nicene Creed, the Augsburg Confession, the Formula of Concord (Lutheran), the Westminster Confession (Calvinist Reformed), and the Thirty-nine Articles (Anglican-Episcopalian). The works of Martin Luther (Lutheran), John Calvin (Reformed), Jacob Arminius (Arminian), John Wesley (Methodist), and several Anabaptist and Baptist writers have also been used, as well as many other sources.

All Bible quotations are taken from the *New International Version* and are printed in bold type. This commentary accepts the decisions of the NIV translators without debate. Occasionally, alternative translations of disputed passages are mentioned in a footnote.

In the commentary, an effort has been made to minimize the inclusive use of the masculine words "man" and "men", but it has been impossible to eliminate such usage completely. This commentary has followed the NIV in this regard, since it is based on the NIV text. In each case the inclusive meaning is evident from the context. Such usage is employed in the interest of clarity and of compatibility with the NIV text. The patience and understanding of the reader are requested.

INTRODUCTION

How To Use This Commentary

This commentary has been written to help people study the Bible. It should not be read in the same way that one reads an ordinary book. First, the reader should read and prayerfully meditate upon the portion of scripture that begins each section of the commentary. After doing that, the reader should study each verse together with its corresponding comment, proceeding verse by verse. It is important to understand the meaning of every verse in the Bible as fully as possible. The commentary will help the reader do this. Finally, after understanding the meaning of each verse, the reader should go back and read the entire scripture portion again. Together with understanding the meaning of each verse, it is also necessary to understand the context and meaning of the entire scripture portion as a unit. To understand the full spiritual meaning of the Bible text, it is necessary above all to ask for help from the Holy Spirit. The Bible is God's living word. Whenever we read from the Bible, we must always pray this prayer: "Lord, open my mind; speak to me through your word."

Following this introduction there is a Word List, which gives the meaning of fifty-one important words. These words are used many times throughout the New Testament. In this commentary the first occurrence of one of these fifty-one words in any of the chapters is printed in small capitals. In order to understand the meaning of any verse in which one of these important words occurs, it is first necessary to understand the meaning of that word.

Following the Word List there is a series of General Articles. These articles give help in understanding a number of very important subjects. Therefore, when a comment on a verse relates to one of these subjects, very often at the end of the comment there will be written: "(see General Article: . . .)" By referring the reader to these General Articles, the commentary avoids repeated explanations of the same subject, and thus much space is saved.

In many of the comments in this commentary the reader is advised to refer to some other verse or verses. Sometimes only the name and number of the verse is given; for example: "(Matthew 5:22)." Sometimes the word "see" is added; for example: "(see

Matthew 5:22)." Whenever the word "see" is added in this way, it means that it is necessary to look up that verse in order to fully understand the verse being studied. Sometimes the words "and comment" are added after the verse number; for example: "(see Matthew 5:22 and comment)." When this is written, it is necessary to look up both the other verse and its corresponding comment in order to understand the verse under study. By referring the reader to other comments in this way, the commentary does not have to repeat the same comment over and over for many different verses, and thus much space is saved.

Sometimes a Bible verse is not commented upon; instead, the reader is referred directly to another verse and its comment. When this happens, it is because that other verse and the verse being studied are almost identical. In this commentary, when two or more New Testament verses are almost identical, only one of them is commented upon. Again this is to save space and avoid repetition. The reader will encounter this situation especially when studying the Gospels of Matthew and Luke, because many of the verses in those two Gospels are also found in the Gospel of Mark. Thus to read the comments on those verses, the reader must refer to the corresponding verses in Mark's Gospel. Similarly, many verses in Luke are referred to the equivalent verses in Matthew.

In this commentary, some books and some sections of the New Testament are given more lengthy and detailed comments than others. Therefore, for one studying the New Testament for the first time, it is advisable to study these books and sections early in the course of one's study. Examples of such sections and books would be: Matthew Chapters 5–7, Mark, John, Romans, 1 Corinthians, Galatians, and Ephesians.

WORD LIST

Abraham Abraham was the first Jew (see Word List: Jew). He was born about two thousand years before Christ in a place called Ur, which is now modern Iraq. God told Abraham to go to another country (Genesis 12:1), a country which God promised to give to Abraham's descendants (Genesis 12:7). That country was Israel. God told Abraham that He would make Abraham's seed a great nation, from which all the world would be blessed (Genesis 12:2–3). That nation was the Jewish nation. The great blessing which came from that nation was Jesus Christ, the Savior of the world, who was a descendant of Abraham (Matthew 1:1).

Abraham was a man of great faith (see Galatians 3:6; Hebrews 11:8–12 and comments). The Jews took great pride in being descendants of Abraham according to the flesh. However, all those who believe in Christ are the true spiritual descendants of Abraham through faith (see Galatians 3:7–9 and comment).

Abraham's life is described fully in Genesis Chapters 11–25.

Adoption Through faith in Christ, we become an adopted child of God. This is one aspect of our salvation in Christ (see Word List: Salvation).

Initally we all were slaves of sin and of Satan (see Word List: Satan). We were not in God's family. God is the Creator of all men, but He is not the Father of all men. He is the Father only of those who believe in Jesus. Only when we receive Christ's righteousness through faith does God accept us into His family.

Any adopted child receives the full inheritance of the person who adopts him. Even though he is not a natural son according to the flesh, legally he is considered a son, and receives the full privileges of sonship. In the same way we, who were once by nature sinners, now through Christ become true sons and daughters of God spiritually. And in heaven we shall receive our full inheritance. (see Romans 8:15–17; Galatians 4:3–7; Ephesians 1:4–5 and comments).

To become an adopted child of God is one of the greatest blessings of our salvation. It means that God's nature enters into us through the Holy Spirit. It means that we are in close fellowship with God, as a child is with his earthly father. It also means that we must live like children of God. To be a child of God is a great privilege and joy; it is also a great responsibility.

Angel An angel is a heavenly or spiritual messenger. Angels are spirits created by God (Psalm 148:2–5; Colossians 1:16; Hebrews 1:14). They are higher beings than humans (Hebrews 2:6–7). They were created before humans were created (Job 38:7).

Though angels have no earthly bodies as men do, they can still appear to men in bodily form (Luke 1:11,26–27; Acts 12:6–7). Angels do not marry, and they do not die (Luke 20:34–36).

All angels were created as holy beings. However, some angels rebelled against God and fell from their holy state. These fallen angels have become demons or evil spirits (see Word List: Demon). The chief of the demons is Satan (see Word List: Satan).

God has given angels various kinds of responsibilities to fulfill. Some angels stand in the presence of God and worship Him (Hebrews 1:6; Revelation 5:11). Other angels assist and protect God's people (Genesis 19:11; Psalm 91:11; Daniel 3:28; 6:22; Acts 5:19; 12:6–7).

Angels ministered to Christ after His temptation in the wilderness (Matthew 4:11). An angel strengthened Him in the garden of Gethsemane (Luke 22:43). An angel rolled the stone away from His tomb (Matthew 28:2–7).

Many Christians believe that each believer in Christ has a special guardian angel who stands in God's presence and watches out for that believer (Matthew 18:10).

Apostle An apostle is a person appointed, sent, and inspired by the Holy Spirit to preach the Gospel and to establish Christ's church.

In the beginning only Jesus' twelve main disciples were called apostles. But later others also were called apostles, such as Paul and James (1 Corinthians 15:7), Barnabas (Acts 14:3–4), Silas and Timothy (1 Thessalonians 2:6–7), and Andronicus and Junias (Romans 16:7).

The main work of the apostles was to faithfully pass on the teachings of Christ, and to establish His church. In Ephesians 2:20, the apostles are called the church's foundation.

Atonement Atonement is a special action which is performed in order to escape God's wrath against sin or to avoid punishment for sin. In the Bible this action is usually some kind of blood sacrifice, called a propitiation.

All men have sinned and deserve to receive God's judgment and punishment (see Numbers 14:18; Psalm 7:11; Romans 1:18; 3:10 and comments). But God in His mercy has provided a means for men to escape that punishment. In the Old Testament, the Jews sacrificed animals to divert God's wrath. God's wrath fell upon the animal instead of the man (Leviticus 4:27–31; 16:20–22). In addition to the ordinary sacrifices, God also established one day each year as a "day of atonement," when the Jewish high priest would carry out a special sacrifice to atone for the sins of all the people (Leviticus 16:1–34).

However, after Jesus Christ came into the world, these Old Testament sacrifices for sin were no longer necessary. Because Jesus Himself, God's own Son, was sacrificed for our sins. He Himself is our propitiation, or **sacrifice of atonement** (see Romans 3:23–25; 1 John 2:2; 4:10 and comments). His sacrifice is once and for all. When we place our faith in Jesus and in His sacrifice (His death on the cross), we then no longer need any other sacrifice for sin (see Hebrews 9:26,28; 10:10,14 and comments). Our sins are all forgiven, because Christ took our punishment. He is our propitiation for removing God's wrath against us.

In order to remove God's wrath and receive forgiveness for sins, a living sacrifice is necessary. Blood must be shed. . . . **without the shedding of blood there is no forgiveness** (Hebrews 9:22). Christ Himself was that living sacrifice. He shed His blood on the cross (see Word List: Cross). Nails were driven through His hands and feet, and a spear was driven into His side from which blood flowed (John 19:34; 20:24–27).

Paul wrote that **we have now been justified by his blood** (Romans 5:9). This means we have been justified by Jesus' death (Romans 5:10). It is not Jesus' blood alone that saves us: it is Jesus' death. The punishment of sin is death (Romans 6:23). Jesus had to die in order that we might live.

Baptism Baptism in the Old Testament means washing or cleansing (Exodus 30:17–21; Leviticus 11:25). John the Baptist preached a baptism of repentance, so that men and women would be prepared to meet Jesus (see Mark 1:4 and comment). Jesus baptized believers with the Holy Spirit and with fire (see Matthew 3:11; Mark 1:8 and comment).

In the New Testament, baptism is the application of water (by sprinkling, pouring, or immersion) in the name of the Father, the Son, and the Holy Spirit. Baptism is a sign of the believer's repentance, of his forgiveness from sin, and of his cleansing from sin (Acts 2:38). Baptism is also a sign of the believer's union with Christ (Galatians 3:26–27). When the believer is baptized, he partakes in the death of Christ. He dies to sin and to his old sinful nature. At the same time, the believer partakes in Jesus' resurrection. Through faith he receives new spiritual life (see Romans 6:3–8 and comment). Finally, baptism is a sign that we have become members of the body of Christ (see 1 Corinthians 12:13 and comment). In short, baptism is a sign that we have received salvation (see Word List: Salvation). All these blessings of baptism we receive through faith in Christ.

Many Christians, however, believe that baptism is more than just a sign of having received these spiritual blessings. They believe that baptism is also a means by which believers receive these blessings. They believe that baptism is a means by which God puts our old sinful self to death and raises our new spiritual self to life. But all Christians acknowledge that the ceremony of baptism does nothing by itself; true faith in Christ is always necessary to receive any of the blessings of baptism. For a further discussion of this subject, see General Article: Water Baptism.

It is not necessary to be baptized in order to be saved (Luke 23:39–43). Salvation comes only through faith. But if a person refuses to be baptized, it shows that his faith is not real. The New Testament commands believers to be baptized. If we refuse, we are disobeying Christ. Those who deliberately remain in disobedience to Christ do not have true faith. Therefore, all Christians should be baptized at the first suitable opportunity.

There is another special kind of baptism called Holy Spirit baptism. For a further discussion of this subject, see General Article: Holy Spirit Baptism.

Church The church, in simplest terms, is believers united together in Christ.

The church can be thought of in two main ways: first, the local church—that is, a congregation of believers in a particular locality; and second, the universal church—that is, the spiritual fellowship of Christians worldwide. In the New Testament, the word "church" is used in both these senses; in any verse, the sense can be determined by the context.

The local church is the visible manifestation of the universal church in a particular locality. The local church is considered by some Christians to be the highest authority for believers who are members of that church. According to this opinion, each local church is completely autonomous and self–governing.

Among other Christians, however, bishops have the highest authority, not the local churches. According to this system of church government, one bishop exercises authority over a number of local churches together (see General Article: Church Government).

The church (both the local church and the universal church) is the body of Christ (1 Corinthians 12:27–28; Ephesians 4:11–12). The members of the church are therefore members of Christ's body (Ephesians 5:30). The head of the church is Christ Himself (Ephesians 5:23; Colossians 1:18).

The church can also be described as **God's household** (Ephesians 2:19). It is like a "living structure," into which believers are **built together** and whose **chief cornerstone** is Christ (see Ephesians 2:20–22 and comment). Peter describes the church as a **spiritual house**, built up of members who are **like living stones** (1 Peter 2:5).

The main purpose of the church is to be a witness to Christ, to be a light in the world. The church is necessary for corporate worship and for the nurture and teaching of Christians; but its main purpose is to reach out to the world and draw men and women to Jesus Christ. This, then, is the mission of the church (see General Article: Purpose of the Church).

The church of Christ is the most important thing in the world, because through the church God lives and works in the world today to accomplish His eternal purposes (see Ephesians 3:10–12 and comment).

Circumcision Circumcision is the cutting off of the excess skin at the tip of the penis. God commanded Abraham and all of his descendants to be circumcised. This was to be a sign of the covenant which God made with the Jewish nation (Genesis 17:9–14). All Jewish males are required to be circumcised on the eighth day of life. Circumcision is the outward sign of being a Jew.

However, for receiving salvation circumcision gives no advantage (see Galatians 5:6 and comment). In fact, outward circumcision of the flesh is not even a sign of being a true Jew (see Romans 2:28–29 and comment). Therefore, it is not necessary for Gentile Christians to be circumcised (Acts 15:5–11).

Covenant A covenant is an agreement between two individuals or two parties. In the Old Testament, God made a covenant with the Jews. He promised to bless them (Genesis 15:18; Exodus 19:5–6; 2 Samuel 23:5). But the Jews, on their side, had to obey God's law (see Word List: Law).

In the Old Testament, the Jews did not keep God's law perfectly. They did not fulfill their part of the covenant. Therefore, God withdrew the promise He had made to them. Instead, God established a new covenant with men. He promised salvation to all who would believe in His Son Jesus. This new covenant is described in Jeremiah 31:31–34 and Hebrews 8:6–13.

In the Old Testament, a covenant was ratified by the shedding of blood. An animal was sacrificed and the parties agreeing to the covenant would walk between the pieces of the animal. In doing this, they were, in effect, saying: "Let it happen to whoever breaks this covenant as it has happened to this animal" (Genesis 15:17–18; Jeremiah 34:18–20). The shed blood of the animal was called the **blood of the covenant** (Exodus 24:5–8).

In the same way, Jesus' shed blood became the blood of the new covenant between God and man (see Mark 14:24; 1 Corinthians 11:25; General Article: Lord's Supper). God agreed to put the punishment for our sins upon His Son Jesus. God's part in the covenant was to sacrifice His Son. Our part in the covenant is to believe in Jesus and to obey Him. And this covenant between us and God has been ratified by Jesus' blood.

Cross In the New Testament, the word cross means a wooden post with a crosspiece. In the time of the Roman Empire, the cross was used by the Romans to execute criminals. The criminal was hung on the cross either with ropes or by means of nails driven through his hands and feet. Often it took two or three days for a criminal to die. To hasten death, the criminal's legs were often broken.

Jesus was condemned to death by the Romans, and was hung on a cross to die. Therefore, the cross is a sign for all Christians of Jesus' death and sacrifice for man's sin. By dying on the cross, Jesus bore the death penalty for sin in our place (see Mark 10:45 and comment).

The cross is also a sign of the suffering that each Christian must be ready to endure for Christ's sake (see Mark 8:34 and comment). It is also a sign of the death of our old sinful self (see Romans 6:6; Galatians 2:20; 5:24; 6:14 and comments). The cross is also a sign of the Christian's glory, because if we suffer with Christ, we shall also be glorified with Him (Romans 8:17).

David David was the greatest king of the Jews. He was born in 1040 B.C., and his reign lasted from 1010 to 970 B.C. (40 years).

David established the Jewish capital at Jerusalem. During his rule, the Jewish nation, Israel, gained great power. David also wrote seventy–three of the Psalms in the Old Testament. Jesus Himself was descended from David (see Matthew 1:1,20; Luke 1:26–27, 32–33 and comments).

David's life is described beginning in 1 Samuel Chapter 16 and continuing through 1 Kings Chapter 2.

Demon In the Bible, demons are also called evil or unclean spirits. These spirits are not the spirits of dead people. They are spirits who were created by God but who later rebelled. The chief demon is Satan (see Word List: Satan).

These demons or spirits have no body of their own. Therefore, they desire to live within someone else's body. Demons are intelligent and powerful. They can take control of men, and can cause blindness (Matthew 12:22), dumbness (Matthew 9:32), and insanity (Mark 5:1-5; 9:20–22).

In the world demons have great power (Ephesians 6:11–12). But the power of the Holy Spirit is greater (1 John 4:4). Christians must keep away from anything that is connected with demons, especially idol worship. An idol itself is nothing, but when people worship an idol, they are, in fact, worshiping a demon (see 1 Corinthians 10:19–21 and comment).

For a further discussion of demons, see General Article: Healing and Deliverance.

Discipline Discipline is any kind of trouble or pain which leads ultimately to our improvement or welfare.

Parents discipline their children in order to train them and teach them how to lead good lives. In the same way, God trains and disciplines believers in Christ. All of us have weaknesses and defects in our characters, and God wants to remove these weaknesses and defects and to make us perfect. Therefore, He allows trouble and persecution to come upon us in order to test us and to strengthen our faith and correct our faults.

God Himself does not send evil or temptation. But He allows the devil, Satan, to tempt us. In addition, our own sins bring trouble upon us.

When we are disciplined by God we should rejoice, because such discipline is proof that we are indeed the children of God (see Hebrews 12:5–12; James 1:2–4; 1 Peter 1:6–7 and comments).

Egypt The Egypt mentioned in the Bible is the same as the modern nation of Egypt located in northeast Africa. The Jews were held in bondage in Egypt for many generations, until they were set free by Moses in about 1400 B.C.

Eternal Life Eternal life is spiritual life that has no end. Eternal life begins as soon as one believes in Jesus and is born again (see John 3:3,5 and comment). Eternal life is eternal fellowship with God. This fellowship begins here on earth when we believe, and continues in heaven after our bodies die. Therefore, believers in Jesus need have no fear of death, because believers do not really die. Their spirits live forever (John 11:25–26). Not only that, believers will receive a new spiritual body in heaven (see Word List: Resurrection).

Eternal life is the main part of our salvation (see Word List: Salvation). All of the stages of salvation—forgiveness, justification, adoption—all end in joyful and glorious eternal life for every true believer in Christ. Eternal life is not just living forever; it is living joyfully in the presence of God forever. Life here on earth is not worthy to be compared with eternal life in heaven (Romans 8:18; 2 Corinthians 4:17).

Evil Spirit (See Word List: Demon)

Faith The word faith in the New Testament means faith in God, faith in Christ. Faith is also a firm belief that Christ's teachings are true, and that through His death we are saved.

Faith is not just a strong thought. It is placing complete trust in Christ. It is placing ourselves in dependence on Him. For example, say we come to a bridge. Perhaps we are sure it is strong. But if we are afraid to cross the bridge, we have no faith. Faith is crossing the bridge.

In the New Testament, the word "faith" is used to describe different degrees of belief in Jesus. Some people had faith in Jesus' power to heal (Matthew 8:10). Some people believed He was a prophet (Mark 8:27–28; John 9:17). But true faith, saving faith, means to believe that Jesus is the Son of God, the Savior (Mark 8:29; John 9:35–38). This is the usual meaning of the word "faith" in the New Testament.

We are saved through faith (see Ephesians 2:8 and comment). We receive all spiritual blessings through faith. . . . **without faith it is impossible to please God** (Hebrews 11:6). . . . **everything that does not come from faith is sin** (Romans 14:23).

Faith is not a kind of "work" that we do. Rather faith is accepting the work that Christ has done for us on the cross. Faith is a gift from God (Romans 12:3).

However, after we believe, there will always be a change in our lives, in our behavior. When we believe, the Holy Spirit comes into our lives. We begin to do good works (Ephesians 2:10). We are not saved by these works; we are saved only through faith. However, good works are the visible proof that our faith is true. If our faith does not lead us to love and obey God and to do works of love, then our faith is false, it is dead. Such "faith" will not save us (see Matthew 7:21; Galatians 5:6; James 2:14–17 and comments).

Flesh Depending on the translation used, the word flesh in the New Testament can have two meanings. Which meaning to apply in any verse can be determined by looking at the context of that verse.

First, flesh can mean body. For example, "body" is the meaning intended in Romans 8:10–11; 12:1,4.

Second, flesh can mean sinful nature. Our bodies themselves are not sinful. But Paul often calls our sinful nature "flesh." He does this, for example in Romans 7:5,18,25; 8:3–9,12; 1 Corinthians 5:5; Galatians 5:13,16–17,19,24; 6:8. (The *New International Version* actually uses the expression "sinful nature" instead of flesh in all verses where this is the meaning called for.)

These two meanings of flesh are very different. When flesh means body, there is no evil connotation intended. There is nothing evil or sinful about our bodies. We are made in God's image (Genesis 1:27).

But what is evil is our sinful nature, our sinful desires. These desires are what cause us to sin (James 1:14–15). Therefore, when flesh is used to mean our sinful nature, its meaning is very different from body. Our sinful nature is evil; our bodies are not.

When the Holy Spirit controls our body, we will act rightly. When our sinful nature controls our body, we will act sinfully (see Romans 6:12–13).

Gentile In the Bible, all who are not Jews are called Gentiles. The Jews despised the Gentiles, because in Bible times most Gentiles did not believe in the one true God. They believed in many false gods and worshiped idols. The Jews considered the Gentiles to be impure.

Jesus Christ came to save not only the Jews but the Gentiles also—the whole world. The Apostle Peter gave the Gospel to the Gentile Cornelius and his family, and they became the first real Gentiles to believe in Christ and be saved (Acts 10:44–48). The Apostle Paul was appointed to be a special apostle to the Gentiles to bring them the Gospel of Christ (Acts 9:15; 22:21; Galatians 2:9).

Gospel The word Gospel in the New Testament means the good news about Jesus Christ—His life, His death, His resurrection. The Gospel is the good news that Jesus is the Savior of the world and that He has come to earth to save sinners. The Gospel is the good news that the kingdom of God has come near in Jesus Christ (see Mark 1:14–15). The Gospel is the good news that the only thing a person has to do to be saved is to believe in Jesus.

Grace Grace is the love and mercy of God toward man. God gives grace to men freely. Men do not deserve to receive God's love and mercy, because they are sinful. But even though man is not deserving of God's love, God still loves man. Even while we were sinners and enemies of God, He sent His own Son Jesus to save us (Romans 5:8).

Because of God's grace, we receive salvation (Ephesians 2:8; Titus 2:11). By God's grace we live our Christian lives. All blessings man has ever received, both material and spiritual, have come because of the grace of God. Because of grace, God sent His Son Jesus to save us. Because of grace, God sent His Holy Spirit to make us holy. Because of grace, believers in Christ will live with God forever.

Holy Spirit The Holy Spirit is God Himself. **God is spirit** (John 4:24). The Holy Spirit is one of God's three forms or modes of existence. God is Father, Son (Jesus), and Holy Spirit: one God in three persons.

The Holy Spirit lives in believers (John 14:17; 1 Corinthians 3:16; 6:19; Ephesians 2:22 and comments). The Holy Spirit teaches believers (John 14:26). He bears witness to Christ (John 15:26). He inspired and directed the writers of the Bible (Acts 1:16; 2 Peter 1:21). To have the Holy Spirit is essentially the same as having Christ, for when we accept Jesus we receive the Holy Spirit (Romans 8:9–12). Since Jesus and God are one (John 10:30), the Holy Spirit is also Jesus' Spirit.

The Holy Spirit gives believers great power (Acts 1:8; 2:1–4 and comments). The Holy Spirit gives special gifts for service (1 Corinthians 12:7–11 and comment). But most important, the Holy Spirit helps us lead holy lives and produces in us the nine fruits of the Spirit (see Galatians 5:22–23 and comment). We cannot live a Christian life for one minute without the help of the Holy Spirit.

For a further discussion of the Holy Spirit, see General Articles: Holy Spirit, Holy Spirit Baptism.

In Christ To be "in Christ" is a common expression used by the Apostle Paul. To be "in Christ" means first that we believe in Him. Then having truly believed in Christ, we become united with Him; that is we have fellowship with Him, we know Him, we obey him and we are blessed by Him. All of our spiritual blessings are **in Christ** (see Ephesians 1:3 and comment). When we are "in Christ" we become a new creation; we receive new life (see 2 Corinthians 5:17 and comment).

Israel In the New Testament, the usual meaning of Israel is the Jewish nation; that is, all the descendants of Abraham. But Paul sometimes uses the word "Israel" to describe those who are true spiritual children of Abraham through faith (Galatians 6:16).

In the Old Testament, Abraham's grandson Jacob was given the name Israel by God (Genesis 35:10). Jacob had twelve sons, from whom came the twelve tribes of Israel (Genesis 35:23–26).

Today Israel is the name of a nation in the Middle East located on the eastern shore of the Mediterranean Sea. This modern nation was established for the Jews in 1947 on the same land that God had first promised to give to Abraham's descendants (Genesis 12:4–7). Its main city is still Jerusalem, which was the capital of the Jewish nation in New Testament times.

Israelite (See Word List: Jew)

Jew A Jew (or Israelite) is a descendant of Abraham, the father of the Jews (see Word List: Abraham).

God made a promise to Abraham saying: "**I will make you into a great nation**" (Genesis 12:2). God established a covenant (see Word List: Covenant) with Abraham and his descendants. God said to Abraham: "**I will establish my covenant as an everlasting covenant between me and you and your descendants after you for the generations to come, to be your God and the God of your descendants after you**" (Genesis 17:7–8). In this way God chose the Jews to be His special chosen people (Exodus 19:5–6). But God demanded that the Jews obey Him and worship only Him; that was their part of the covenant.

In Old Testament times, the Jews were the only race that worshiped the one true God. However, they fell away many times and disobeyed God, and God sent them prophets to call them to repent and turn from their evil ways.

God chose the Jews to be a blessing to all the peoples of the earth (Genesis 12:3). The main blessing to come from the Jews was Jesus Christ, the Savior of the world, who was Himself a Jew, a descendant of Abraham (Matthew 1:1). Through Jesus Christ, the promise God made to Abraham was fulfilled.

It was possible for Gentiles (see Word List: Gentile) to become Jews by being circumcised (see Word List: Circumcision) and by carefully following the Jewish law (see Word List: Law). Gentiles who converted to the Jewish religion in this way were called Jewish proselytes.

Judgment In the New Testament the word judgment has three different meanings; that is, it is used in three different ways.

The first meaning is the judgment of men against each other. Jesus said that we must not judge each other (see Matthew 7:1 and comment). Man's judgment is never completely true, because no man can ever know the full truth about another man. Only God knows everything about each person. Therefore, only God can truly and fairly judge.

The second kind of judgment mentioned in the New Testament is the punishment that God gives to evil doers. This punishment comes upon both believers and unbelievers (1 Corinthians 11:29–34 and comment). The purpose of this kind of judgment is to turn sinners to God and to correct and purify men's lives.

The third kind of judgment mentioned in the New Testament is God's final judgment, which will occur at the end of the world. God has given the final authority to judge mankind to Jesus Christ (John 5:22). Every man must stand before the judgment seat of Christ (see 2 Corinthians 5:10 and comment). Christ's judgment will be without partiality. His judgment on that day will not be like the judgments of men in this world; it will be completely true and fair. Those who have believed in Christ in this world will be saved and go to heaven. Those who have not believed in Christ in this world will be condemned and go to hell (John 3:18,36). After the last judgment, there is no possibility of appeal. Therefore, a person must believe in Jesus in this life in order to receive salvation; there is no other way (Acts 4:12).

Kingdom of God The kingdom of God is not any particular place; it is not like an earthly kingdom. The kingdom of God is a spiritual kingdom in which God rules with complete authority. In one sense, God's kingdom is everywhere. But in the New Testament, the kingdom of God usually means the spiritual "kingdom" where men and angels worship and obey God. Therefore, in accordance with this meaning, the earth is not yet in God's kingdom; it is in Satan's kingdom. Satan is the prince of this world (see John 12:31; 16:11 and comments).

However, in another sense, Jesus brought the kingdom of God to earth. All who believe in Jesus are immediately delivered from Satan's kingdom, the kingdom of darkness, and brought into God's kingdom. Christians live in God's kingdom even while still here on earth. We are citizens of God's kingdom; God is our ruler. Through His Holy Spirit He helps us to overcome Satan. And after our bodies die, we will continue to live in God's kingdom in heaven.

Therefore, when we are in Christ through faith, we enter God's kingdom. In a sense the kingdom enters us—God's rule enters us (see Luke 17:20-21 and comment). The main message that Jesus preached was: "**The kingdom of God is near. Repent and believe the good news!**" (see Mark 1:14-15 and comment).

Kingdom of Heaven (See Word List: Kingdom of God)

Law In the Bible when the word law is used, it usually refers to the Jewish law. The main part of the Jewish law is the ten commandments, which God wrote on two tablets of stone and gave to Moses to give to the Jews (Exodus 20:3–17; 31:18). In addition to the ten commandments, God gave Moses many other laws for the Jewish people, which are written in the books of Exodus, Leviticus, Numbers, and Deuteronomy. There are over six hundred other rules in the Jewish law which the Jews have to obey. All these together are known as the law. Sometimes the first five books of the Old Testament are also called the Law, or the Law of Moses.

The Jews believed that if they carried out these laws and commands completely they would thereby obtain salvation. However, the New Testament teaches and human experience confirms that no one can obey the law completely all the time (see Galatians 3:10; James 2:10 and comments). Thus no one can be justified or saved by the law (see Galatians 2:15–16 and comment). The law doesn't save men; it condemns them. Indeed, Christ came to free men and women from the bondage of the law and to show them the true way to salvation—that is, Christ Himself (see Romans 8:1–4 and comment).

Christ camc to fulfill the law (see Matthew 5:17 and comment). He Himself obeyed the law perfectly. Christ fulfilled the law not only by obeying it; He also fulfilled it in another way. The law demands the death penalty for sin; the law condemns all men to death, because all men are sinners (Romans 3:10–12). So Christ came to die in our place for our sins. In this way He fulfilled the demand of the law for the death penalty. Because Christ died, the law can now no longer condemn those who put their faith in Him. We are saved from the punishment of the law (eternal death) by our faith in Christ.

Lord's Supper Jesus and His disciples celebrated the first Lord's Supper on the day before Jesus died (see Mark 14:22–24 and comment). Jesus Himself commanded Christians to celebrate the Lord's Supper in memory of His death (see 1 Corinthians 11:23–26 and comment).

During the celebration of the Lord's Supper, Christians eat bread and drink wine or some other drink. When believers gather to commemorate the Lord's death, the bread in some way represents Christ's broken body, and the wine (or other drink) represents Christ's shed blood. Concerning the bread, Jesus said: "**. . . this is my body, given for you**" (Mark 14:22). Concerning the wine, He said: "**. . . this is my blood of the covenant, which is poured out for many**" (Mark 14:24). By Jesus' blood, a new covenant has been ratified between man and God (see Word List: Covenant).

When we celebrate the Lord's Supper, we in a way participate in His death and in His resurrection life. When we eat the bread and drink the wine, we are in a special way, through faith, united with Christ. Many Christians believe that when we partake of the bread and wine, we receive anew through faith the spiritual blessings that have come from Christ's death and resurrection—that is, forgiveness of sins, cleansing, and new life.

Only believers can partake of the Lord's Supper. Before eating the bread and drinking the wine, the believer must have repented of all known sin and be walking in obedience to Jesus. Before partaking, each believer must carefully examine himself (see 1 Corinthians 11:27–29 and comment).

For a further discussion of the Lord's Supper, see General Article: Lord's Supper.

Moses Moses was the greatest leader of the Jewish people. He was born about 1500 B.C. He led the Jews out of bondage in Egypt. He received the ten commandments from God and delivered them to the Jews, so that they might walk in God's way. He led the Jews for forty years in the Sinai desert. He wrote the first five books of the Old Testament. The description of Moses' life can be found in the books of Exodus and Numbers.

Peace In the Bible the word "peace" has many meanings. In the Old Testament, "peace" is often used as a greeting. Peace can also mean the absence of war. It can also mean inner peace of mind.

In the New Testament, the word peace usually means complete well-being in body, mind, and spirit. But more important, it means peace with God. When we were unrepentant sinners, we were enemies of God. Now, through faith in Christ, we can make peace with God. We are no longer His enemies; we are His children (see Romans 5:1 and comment).

Passover The Passover festival was celebrated each year to commemorate the release of the Jews from bondage in Egypt. The festival lasted for one week, during which time the Jews were to eat only unleavened bread. The Passover festival, therefore, was also called the Feast of Unleavened Bread. On the first day of the festival, the Passover feast was eaten, and the Passover lamb was sacrificed (Leviticus 23:4–8; Deuteronomy 16:1–8).

The word "passover" means a passing over. On the last night the Jews were in Egypt God determined to kill all the firstborn living creatures in Egypt, because the Egyptian ruler, Pharaoh, had refused to let the Jews go free. But first God instructed the Jews to sacrifice a lamb and put some of its blood on the doorposts of their houses. Then, when the destroying angel came and saw the blood, he would know not to destroy the firstborn in those homes (Exodus 12:1–14,21–30; Hebrews 11:28).

In the same way, Christ is like a **Passover lamb** (see 1 Corinthians 5:7). Through Christ's blood (His death on the cross) we are set free from bondage to sin and death. Therefore, it was completely fitting that Christ Himself should die right at the time of the Passover festival (see Mark 14:1,12 and comment).

Christians, therefore, do not celebrate the Jewish Passover festival itself—that is, the Feast of Unleavened Bread. Instead, Christians celebrate the death and resurrection of Jesus. The celebration of His death is called Good Friday, and the celebration of His resurrection is called Easter.

Pentecost The word "pentecost" comes from the Greek language and means the "fiftieth day." Thus the Jews celebrated the day of Pentecost on the fiftieth day after the Passover feast. The day of Pentecost was also called the **Feast of Weeks** (Exodus 34:22; Deuteronomy 16:9–11). It was also called the **day of firstfruits** (Numbers 28:26), because on that day the Jews offered the firstfruits of their harvest to God.

The day of Pentecost is especially important to Christians because on the first Pentecost after Jesus' death, the Holy Spirit came upon the disciples of Jesus with great power. At that time the disciples were filled with the Holy Spirit, or baptized with the Spirit (see Acts 2:1–4 and comment; General Article: Holy Spirit Baptism).

Pharisee The Pharisees were a sect of the Jews. The word "pharisee" means "separated one." In Christ's time the Pharisees' influence was very great among the Jews. They were a strict sect, who carefully tried to follow each detail of the Jewish law (see Word List: Law). They considered themselves righteous; but, in fact, in Christ's time they were only outwardly righteous. Inwardly they were evil; they were hypocrites (see Matthew 23:13–32).

However, not all Pharisees were hypocrites. Nicodemus and Gamaliel were upright men who were also Pharisees (John 3:1; Acts 5:34). The Apostle Paul himself was a Pharisee (Acts 26:5; Philippians 3:5).

Prophecy Prophecy, according to its usual biblical usage, is a word coming directly from God that is spoken by men. Those who speak God's word in this way are called prophets (see Word List: Prophet).

Prophecy can also mean the gift of prophecy—that is, the gift of speaking God's words (1 Corinthians 12:10).

Prophecies can take many forms. They can be predictions of future events. They can be warnings from God. They can be important teachings that God wants to impart.

In every case, however, the prophecy is not something that originates with man; rather, a true prophecy always originates with God.

There are false prophecies, of course, which do not come from God. The men who utter them are called false prophets. We are told to beware of them (Matthew 7:15; 1 John 4:1).

The Old Testament prophets were sent by God to the Jews to rebuke them for their disobedience and to remind them of God's will. The Old Testament prophets also gave many prophecies concerning the coming of the Savior Jesus Christ.

In the New Testament, there are also prophets. The gift of prophecy was very important in the New Testament church (1 Corinthians 12:28; 14:1; Ephesians 4:11). The entire New Testament book of Revelation can be considered a prophecy about the end of the world.

Prophet One who speaks prophecies is called a prophet (see Word List: Prophecy). The true prophets of the Bible received words from God and then spoke them to the people. They were God's spokesmen. They were not simply tellers of the future.

The largest number of prophets referred to in the Bible are the Jewish prophets of the Old Testament. These Old Testament prophets carried out two special functions. First, they admonished the Jews concerning their repeated disobedience to God's law. And second, they announced the coming of the Savior Jesus Christ.

Propitiation (See Word List: Atonement)

Redemption Redemption means the regaining possession of something by paying a price. It could mean the repurchasing of some article that was sold. Or, in the case of a slave, it could mean the purchasing of his liberty that was lost. But in the New Testament, redemption means the "purchasing" of our deliverance from the penalty of sin by paying a ransom or offering a sacrifice. Christ gave Himself as a ransom, or sacrifice, for us (see Mark 10:45 and comment). The payment for our deliverance was Christ's own blood. Paul writes: **In him** (Christ) **we have redemption through his blood** (Ephesians 1:7).

Redemption is one aspect of our salvation. In some New Testament verses, the words "redemption" and "salvation" can almost be used interchangeably (see Word List: Salvation).

Repentance To repent means not only to feel sorry for and ashamed of one's sin, but it also means to turn from that sin. Confessing our sin is not enough; we must also stop sinning. When a person truly repents, his actions, thoughts, and desires will be changed. If a person says "I have repented" but there is no improvement in his life, then his "repentance" is false.

To repent is an essential step in receiving salvation. Without repenting, it is impossible to be saved (see Matthew 5:3–4; Mark 1:4,15; Acts 2:37–38; 20:21; 2 Peter 3:9 and comments).

Resurrection Resurrection is a return to life after dying. Jesus has the power to raise the dead to life (John 5:24–25). He raised the son of the widow of Nain (Luke 7:11–17); He raised Lazarus, who had been dead for four days (John 11:38–44). He Himself overcame death and rose to life; therefore, through His power, others will overcome death also (see 1 Corinthians 15:20–23 and comment). Among those on earth, believers in Christ will be the first to be raised when He comes again at the end of the world (1 Thessalonians 4:16–17). But all men will be raised in the end, both good men and evil. The resurrection of believers will be in heaven; the resurrection of unbelievers will be in hell (see John 5:28–29; Acts 24:15; Revelation 20:4–15 and comments).

When our body dies our spirit continues to live, but we will not immediately receive a new body. We will receive our new body only when Jesus comes again at the end of the world. Paul calls this the **redemption of our bodies** (Romans 8:23). Believers in Christ will receive their new bodies in heaven. These new bodies will never die. They will be glorified bodies. They will be like Christ's resurrected body (see Luke 24:36–43; Philippians 3:21; 1 John 3:2 and comments).

The most important event in the history of the world was the resurrection of Jesus Christ (see Mark 16:8 and comment). By His resurrection from the dead Jesus proved to men that He was indeed the Son of God, the Savior of the world (Romans 1:4). Because of His resurrection, we too have the hope of eternal life (John 11:25–26). Jesus said: "**Because I live, you also will live**" (John 14:19).

Righteous To be determined righteous (that is, to be justified) is one of the main parts of our salvation (see Word List: Salvation).

No unrighteous person can come into God's presence. . . . **without holiness no one will see the Lord** (Hebrews 12:14).

Since this is so, how then does a person become "righteous" in God's sight? One cannot become righteous through his own effort, by good works. He can only become righteous by repenting of his sin and turning to Christ in faith. When we believe in Christ, Christ takes away our guilt, our punishment. Our guilt is placed on the innocent Christ, and thus we become "righteous" because of Christ. Through faith we receive Christ's righteousness. Christ brings us before God and, in effect, says to God, "I have died for this person's sins. Therefore, he no longer needs to be punished. He can now be considered innocent." And God will then declare us righteous in His sight and accept us into His family (see Mark 10:45; Romans 3:24–26; Galatians 2:15–16 and comments).

Therefore, when God justifies us (declares us righteous), He frees us from the punishment of sin. He forgives our sin completely. We have peace with God (see Romans 5:1 and comment). We are no longer condemned (see Romans 8:1 and comment).

Righteousness Righteousness in the Bible means God's righteousness. We can tell what the righteousness of God is by studying God's law, especially the ten commandments (Exodus 20:3–17) and the two great commands to love God and to love our neighbor (Mark 12:30–31). The law and commandments are God's standard of behavior for all people.

No one has righteousness in himself (Romans 3:10). In God's eyes, **all of us have become like one who is unclean, and all our righteous acts are like filthy rags** (Isaiah 64:6). Only Christ was completely righteous. When we believe in Him we receive His righteousness, and therefore become acceptable in God's sight.

There are two steps to receiving righteousness. First, we receive Christ's righteousness through faith and are declared righteous by God (see Word List: Righteous). Second, through the work of the Holy Spirit (see Word List: Holy Spirit) Christ's righteousness becomes more and more manifest in our behavior and actions. We become more and more holy and righteous in our daily lives.

Rome Rome today is the capital of the modern European nation of Italy. In the time of Jesus, Rome was the capital of the Roman Empire (see Word List: Roman Empire).

Roman Empire The Roman Empire was established in 31 B.C. and lasted for over four hundred years. In Christ's time the Romans controlled most of the countries surrounding the Mediterranean

Sea, including Egypt, Israel, Syria, Turkey, and Greece. They also controlled much of Europe as far north as England.

In New Testament times, the countries of the Roman Empire were divided up into provinces which were placed under the control of Roman governors. The Romans gave the local citizens of each province a certain amount of authority over local matters. In the beginning they allowed the people of each province to follow their own customs and to practice their own religion. But in Paul's time, the Roman Emperors began to demand that all people throughout the entire Empire worship the emperor as a god. The Jews and Christians refused to do this. Therefore, the Romans began to persecute them. The Apostle Paul spent the end of his life in a prison in Rome, the capital of the empire (Acts 28:16,20). And in 70 A.D. the Roman armies completely destroyed the Jewish capital, Jerusalem, and killed all the Jews that were there.

However, in spite of persecution, the Christian church grew. Thousands of Christians were killed by the Romans. The Romans even fed Christians to lions, and for entertainment watched the lions eat them. Those Christians who weren't killed outright the Romans turned into slaves. Nevertheless, the number of Christians kept growing. Finally, in about 310 A.D., the Roman Emperor Constantine himself became a Christian. After that, Christianity became the official religion of the Roman Empire and subsequently spread all over the Middle East and Europe.

Sadducee The Sadducees were an important Jewish sect at the time of Christ. Most of the Jewish chief priests were Sadducees. The Sadducees did not believe in the resurrection of the body or in eternal life. Like the Pharisees, they opposed Christ and His disciples.

Saint In the New Testament, believers in Christ are called saints. The word "saint" means "holy or separated one." In the Bible, to be holy means to be both "righteous" and also "set apart" for God. Thus Christians are those people who through faith have received Christ's righteousness and through the Holy Spirit have begun to live holy lives. Such people are truly "set apart" for God. They are separated from sin and from the power of Satan.

Salvation In the New Testament, salvation has a broad meaning. In short, it means to be delivered from God's judgment and to receive eternal life (see Word List: Redemption).

All spiritual blessings are included in the word salvation. First, salvation is deliverance from sin, from both the power of sin and the punishment for sin, which is eternal death (Romans 6:23). When a person is saved, he receives forgiveness for his sins and is cleansed from sin. Thus he becomes righteous, or justified, in God's sight (see Word List: Righteous). He becomes a member of God's family (see Word List: Adoption). He becomes sanctified and glorified (see Romans 8:30 and comment). But the greatest of all the blessings of salvation is eternal life with God and Christ in heaven (see Word List: Eternal Life). We receive all of these blessings in Christ when we are saved (Ephesians 1:3).

There is only one way to receive salvation, and that is through faith in Jesus Christ; there is no other way (see General Article: Way of Salvation).

Sanhedrin The Sanhedrin was the highest governing council of the Jewish nation. The leader of the council was the Jewish high priest. During New Testament times, the Sanhedrin had authority over all local and religious matters of the Jewish people. However, the Sanhedrin was not allowed to do anything in opposition to the Romans. Neither were the Jewish leaders allowed to carry out the death sentence against any criminal. This is why Jesus was put to death according to the order of the Roman governor, Pontius Pilate.

The Sanhedrin had seventy members, plus the high priest. These members were chosen from among the leaders and elders of the Jewish nation.

Satan Satan is the chief of all evil spirits, or demons (see Word List: Demon). He is the chief enemy of God and men. Satan is a fallen angel; his main sin was pride. He tried to make himself like God, but God banished him from heaven (Isaiah 14:11–15; 1 Timothy 3:6).

Satan's main work is to lead men into sin, that is, into disobedience to God. He does this mainly by deceiving men, by stirring up men's evil desires, and by weakening men's faith.

Satan has many names in the New Testament. He is called the **devil** (Revelation 12:9) and the **accuser of our brothers** (Revelation 12:10); he is called an **enemy** and a **roaring lion** (1 Peter 5:8). He is called **Beelzebub** (Mark 3:22), the **tempter** (Matthew 4:3), the **father of lies** (John 8:44), and the **prince of this world** (John 12:31).

Although Satan is very powerful, he is still under God's control. He can only do as much as God permits him to do (Job 1:12; 2:6; Luke 22:31).

Through the help of the Holy Spirit, we can overcome Satan. If we resist him, he will flee (see James 4:7 and comment). He has already been defeated by Jesus on the cross (Hebrews 2:14–15), but he still has much power in this world. However, at the end of the world, when Christ comes again, Satan will be completely destroyed and cast forever into a lake of fire (Revelation 20:7–10).

Temptation In the Bible, the word temptation (or trial) has two meanings. In each verse where temptation (or trial) is mentioned, it is necessary to determine which meaning to apply by looking at the context of the verse.

The first meaning of temptation is a test or trial. God examines and tests His people in order to improve, strengthen, and discipline them. He does this by allowing various difficulties to come upon them, or by putting them into difficult situations. In the Old Testament, God tested Abraham by telling him to sacrifice his only son, Isaac (Genesis 22:1-19). God's testing of Job is described in detail in the book of Job. Job said concerning God: **"When he has tested me, I will come forth as gold"** (Job 23:10). In this same way, God tests and disciplines all Christians (see 1 Corinthians 11:32; Hebrews 12:4–11; James 1:2,12; 1 Peter 1:6–7 and comments). In all of these examples, God tests us for our spiritual good, that we might become more holy. In testing us, God Himself does not send evil upon His children, but He does allow Satan to do so.

The second meaning of temptation found in the Bible is a desire to do evil, a desire to sin. These evil desires arise in man's sinful nature or heart (see James 1:13–15 and comment). Satan is always trying to stir up these evil desires in our hearts in order to make us sin and turn from God. Satan is called a **tempter** (Matthew 4:3; 1 Thessalonians 3:5). Satan tempted Eve (Genesis 3:1–6). He tempted Christ (Matthew 4:1–11), but he could not lead Christ into sin (see Hebrews 2:18; 4:15). This second kind of temptation (the temptation to do evil) never comes from God, and it is never for our good. These temptations to do evil always come from Satan. These are the temptations that we must pray to be saved from: Lord, **lead us not into temptation** (Matthew 6:13).

The first kind of temptation, the trial or test, we must endure with patience. The second kind of temptation, the desire to sin, we must resist and overcome.

GENERAL ARTICLES

INTRODUCTION TO THE GENERAL ARTICLES

There are some things that every Christian must believe. These are called the "cardinal doctrines," meaning the major central doctrines that must be accepted by everyone in order to be a true Christian. These have been listed in several different creeds. Every Christian believes the following:

1. There is one God—Father, Son, and Holy Spirit—three persons in one God.
2. There is one Father Almighty, maker of heaven and earth.
3. There is only one begotten Son of the Father, our Lord Jesus Christ, who was eternally one with the Father, but was manifested in the flesh for our salvation, becoming completely man while remaining completely God.
4. Jesus Christ was conceived by the Holy Spirit, born of the virgin Mary, and died on the cross shedding His blood for our sins.
5. Jesus rose again in His body from death and ascended into heaven, but will come again to judge the living and the dead.
6. The Holy Spirit is with us always, convicting the world of sin, and strengthening the universal church, which is the body of Christ on earth.
7. All men and women are by nature sinful and in need of forgiveness of sins through the atonement of Jesus Christ and in need of regeneration by the Holy Spirit. All this is freely offered by God's grace through faith.
8. The Bible is the inspired word of God, containing all things necessary for salvation, and is the ultimate standard of our faith.
9. The bodies of all believers will be resurrected for eternal life with God forever.

However, in addition to the above nine cardinal doctrines, there are other secondary doctrines about which true Christians have disagreed. These secondary doctrines do not change our central belief in **Jesus Christ and him crucified** (1 Corinthians 2:2). These secondary teachings are about the ceremonies and practices of the church, and about the meaning of certain passages of Scripture.

True Christians have believed differently about these secondary doctrines.

Some may say: "Why don' t we simply look at the Bible? Why not write just what the Bible says?" But that is exactly the problem! What does the Bible say? True Christians have drawn different views from the same verses. Nor does the Bible answer all the questions we can ask. On many of these subjects it is impossible to be certain which is the correct view. If the Bible was perfectly clear on these secondary issues, there would not be so many different opinions among Christians. It is not honest or fair to the serious Bible student to keep him in ignorance of ideas that many true Christians believe are correct. This commentary is a Bible study aid, not a catechism or statement of faith for a particular church or denomination.

The majority of the General Articles that follow deal with these secondary doctrines, about which true Christians have had differing opinions.[1] In these articles, the Bible student should focus on the text of the Bible above all. Thus, in each of the controversial articles, the main Bible verses related to that subject are presented first. Then there is an explanation of the problem, followed by a brief description of the main viewpoints held by different Christians. Each Bible student should also go to his or her pastor or teacher for further instruction regarding his own church' s practices and beliefs.

Some may fear that discussing these questions will bring division. On the contrary, remaining in ignorance of these matters increases the risk of division. When there is ignorance of the views of other Christians, misunderstandings and ill feelings easily arise, and divisions result. The entire history of the Christian church shows that it is ignorance or intolerance of others' beliefs that has split churches.

A major principle of these articles is that a person can be a true spiritual Christian in spite of having differing beliefs on these secondary matters. When that principle is accepted, then ill feeling and accusations will cease. Mature Christians have learned to accept differences of opinion on these matters. In many churches and organizations, Christians with widely different beliefs have learned to walk in fellowship, and they worship, pray, and work together for the glory of God.

None of us is perfect in all that we think or do, but we should keep on pressing toward that goal. **All of us who are mature should take such a view of things. And if on some point you think differently, that too God will make clear to you. Only let us live up to what we have already attained** (Philippians 3:15–16).

---

[1] A few of the articles, however, deal with non-controversial cardinal doctrines—in particular, the General Articles entitled Jesus Christ, The Way of Salvation, and The Holy Spirit.

JESUS CHRIST

Jesus Christ—Who Is He?

Jesus has many names or titles. The name "Jesus" itself means the "one who saves." We usually add the term "Christ" after His name. The word "Christ" is a Greek word and means the same as "Messiah," a Hebrew word. Both "Christ" and "Messiah" mean the "anointed one" or the "one whom God has anointed for service."

The Jews had been looking for the "anointed one" for hundreds of years when Jesus finally came into the world. The prophet Isaiah had written about the promised Messiah as one who would bear the sins and sorrows of the people (Isaiah 53:1–12). Isaiah even said that this Messiah would be called the **Mighty God**, the **Everlasting Father**, the **Prince of Peace** (Isaiah 9:6). However, the Jews were looking for a king who would lead their nation into political victory over ROME; they did not believe that the Messiah would be God Himself come to earth as a man, or that their Messiah would die on a CROSS.

The terms "Son of God" and "Son of Man" are other terms used for Jesus (see Mark 2:10; John 1:14,18,34; 5:25–27 and comments). The term "Son of God" usually emphasizes Jesus' deity. The term "Son of Man" usually emphasizes His messianic role. In the Old Testament, the Messiah was called the "Son of Man" (Daniel 7:13–14). Although this messianic "Son of Man" comes from heaven and accepts divine worship, Jesus often used the term "Son of Man" when emphasizing His own humanness (Matthew 8:20; 11:19; 17:22–23). The terms are used interchangeably in Matthew 26:63–65.

We must remember two things about Jesus Christ: first, Jesus is completely man; and second, Jesus is also completely God. Jesus is both man and God (Romans 1:3–4).

Jesus Is God

Jesus has characteristics that are divine. He is eternal, having always been with God (John 1:1–2; 17:1–5). Jesus was involved in the creation of the world (John 1:3; Colossians 1:16–17; Hebrews

1:2). God was in Jesus, and Jesus was in God (John 14:10; 17:21,23). Jesus is called the **one and only Son** or **firstborn** of God (John 3:16,18; Colossians 1:15,18; Hebrews 1:6).

More specifically, the Bible states that Jesus has shown us the Father (John 1:18; 14:9), and that He is the **image of the invisible God** (Colossians 1:15), and the **exact representation of his being** (Hebrews 1:3). Elsewhere the Bible states that Jesus is one with God (John 10:30; 17:11,22), or equal with God (Philippians 2:6). Indeed, Jesus is actually declared to be God (John 1:1; Romans 9:5; Hebrews 1:8). Jesus is not just partly God, but He is the **fullness of the Deity** (Colossians 1:19; 2:9). Jesus is fully God.

Jesus Is Man

But Jesus is also fully man. Although He was conceived by the HOLY SPIRIT, He had a human mother and was born as a baby into this world (Matthew 1:20; Luke 1:34–35). Although Jesus was God, He was **made in human likeness** (Philippians 2:7). He was seen and touched by men (1 John 1:1–2), and He was tired, hungry, and thirsty like other men; He wept like a man. Jesus was **tempted in every way, just as we are** (Hebrews 4:15). Like us, Jesus expressed ignorance of the future when God had not revealed it to Him (Mark 13:32).

It is important to believe that Jesus became fully man. John makes it a test of the true Spirit, saying that deceivers and false prophets would deny that Jesus came in the flesh (1 John 4:1–2).

Heresies About Jesus

From the very beginning, the church faced trouble from those who taught false doctrines about Jesus. Even today there are those who continue to be led astray by false teachings about Jesus. These false teachings can be divided into three main ideas.

The first false idea is that Jesus was just a man, not God at all. Those who believe this agree that Jesus was a great moral teacher, and that God blessed Him, but they deny that Jesus was God.

The second false idea is just the opposite; namely, that Jesus was God but not man. Some say that Jesus was only a spirit, that He did not have a body like other men. Some say that Jesus' spirit was not a man's spirit but was God's own Spirit in a human body. But this is also untrue, because Jesus was a complete man with a human body and a human spirit (Hebrews 2:17–18).

The third false idea is that Jesus was a god, but less than God the Father. Those who believe this say that the body is impure and sinful, and that the true God would never appear in a human body. Therefore, they say that Jesus is only a lesser god sent from the

Father, but is not actually God Himself. These people (not true Christians) point to verses where Jesus said that the Father was greater than Himself (John 14:28). But Jesus had referred to the Father being greater than Himself only as it related to His role as the incarnate Son. Elsewhere Jesus said, "**I and the Father are one**" (John 10:30). "**Anyone who has seen me has seen the Father**" (John 14:9). John said clearly that Jesus **was with God from the beginning** and that He **was God** (John 1:1).

Therefore, Jesus is both fully God and fully man, as we saw above.

The Work of Jesus Christ

Jesus is both the creator and preserver of the world (John 1:3,10; Colossians 1:16–17; Hebrews 1:2–3). Jesus did not stay in heaven, but He left the glory that He had there (John 17:1–5) and became man. There were two important reasons for this incarnation of Jesus as man.

The first reason for the incarnation is that by looking at Jesus we can see what God is like. No one has seen God the Father at any time (John 6:46). But Jesus showed the Father to us (John 12:45; 14:7–9). For example, by looking at Jesus and at what He said and did, we can know not only that the Father is good and loving and that He forgives our sins, but also that He is concerned about all our needs and problems as well.

The second reason for the incarnation of Jesus was His death and resurrection for our SALVATION. The Bible speaks of Jesus being our "redeemer," meaning the one who redeemed us from sin and the curse of the Law (see Mark 10:45; Galatians 3:13 and comments). Jesus did not pay the price for our freedom with silver or gold, but with His own precious blood (1 Peter 1:18–19). This ransom **rescued us from the dominion of darkness and brought us into the kingdom of the Son** (Colossians 1:13–14).

A holy God must reject and punish sin. But Jesus took our sin and its punishment upon Himself by His death on the cross. Therefore, Jesus is said to be our PROPITIATION, meaning that Jesus satisfied the just demands of a holy God (Romans 3:25; 1 John 2:2). Jesus' propitiation allows God to forgive sinners and yet remain holy, because He has punished sin instead of ignoring it. Because of our sin we were separated from God, but **God reconciled us to himself through Christ** (2 Corinthians 5:18) and His blood (Romans 5:1,9–11; Colossians 1:20–22).

By Jesus' death on the cross and His shedding of blood, we obtain forgiveness of sins, meaning not that God merely ignores our sins, but that God removes our sins (Colossians 2:13–14; Hebrews 10:17) and cleanses us (Hebrews 9:14,22; 1 John 1:7–9). By His death on the cross, Jesus drove out and destroyed the devil (John 12:31; Hebrews 2:14–15). Many Christians believe that Jesus also carried our diseases on the cross, thus providing healing for our bodies and deliverance from evil spirits (see Isaiah 53:4–5; Matthew 8:16–17; Mark 1:27; General Article: Healing and Deliverance). By His own RESURRECTION Jesus gives us bodily resurrection and ETERNAL LIFE (John 6:54,58; 11:25–26; 1 Corinthians 15:20–22).

All of the above blessings Jesus obtained for us by His death on the cross. But Jesus has an ongoing work as well. Jesus sent the Holy Spirit to empower the church on the first day of PENTECOST (John 14:16–17; 15:26–27; Acts 2:1–4), and Jesus still sends His Holy Spirit (see Mark 1:7–8; General Article: Holy Spirit Baptism). He has promised to be with us always through the Holy Spirit (Matthew 18:20; 28:20; John 14:16–18). Jesus is our intercessor and helper in heaven, praying on our behalf (Romans 8:34; 1 John 2:1). Jesus remains as the "head" of the church (Ephesians 5:23; Colossians 1:18), and the ruler of all things (Matthew 28:18; Ephesians 1:20–22; Philippians 2:9–11).

The Uniqueness of Christ

Jesus is not like other religious leaders or founders of religions. Most other religious leaders have been considered either divine or human, but not both. Other religious leaders who were considered human have died and no one has claimed that they rose again.

Jesus is God's true incarnation. Some people think that Jesus is only one incarnation, or avatar, among other incarnations. But this is not true. The true living God has only one incarnation: namely, Jesus Christ. A true incarnation should live a fully human life, yet show by his life that he is fully divine (Romans 1:3–4). A true incarnation should live a life without sin. Only Jesus lived a fully human life, yet **without sin** (Hebrews 4:15; 1 Peter 2:22). Other so-called incarnations were not both fully God and fully man, but a little of each.

Jesus is a true mediator between God and man, because He is both God and man (Hebrews 9:15). Jesus had to be truly man in order to make atonement on behalf of man (Hebrews 4:14–15), and he had to be truly God in order to live the perfect life needed to make an atonement sacrifice acceptable to God (Hebrews 9:14). And Jesus had to be truly God in order to defeat Satan on behalf of man (Hebrews 2: 14–17), and in order to be powerful enough to defeat Satan and his evil spirits (Colossians 2:15; Revelation 19:11–21).

Jesus was not only a guide to the way of salvation, but He was also the actual way Himself (John 14:6). Jesus was not only a preacher encouraging us to live right; He also gave us the power to live right. He gave us the power to be righteous. Through the power of the Holy Spirit, Jesus gave us freedom from the bondage of sin. Jesus not only gave us good teaching; He also gave all believers eternal life.

Jesus is the only true way to God. Jesus said: "**I am the way and the truth and the life. No one comes to the Father except through me**" (John 14:6). The Apostle Peter said: "**Salvation is found in no one else, for there is no other name under heaven given to men by which we must be saved**" (Acts 4:12).

THE WAY OF SALVATION

Man's Condition

All men and women are by nature sinners (Romans 3:10–12). The first man and first woman sinned (Genesis 3:1–6), and since then every man, woman, and child has sinned (Romans 3:23). The result was physical death (Romans 5:12) and spiritual death (Romans 7:11; Ephesians 2:1) for every man. Unsaved people are slaves to sin, forced to obey evil (Romans 6:17–21), and are enemies of God (Romans 8:7). Many people try to become righteous by doing good deeds. But Isaiah said that our own good deeds are **like filthy rags** (Isaiah 64:6), of no help for obtaining salvation. Others try to become righteous by following the rules of God's LAW written in the Old Testament, but this also will not work (see Galatians 2:15–16; 3:11 and comments).

Men and women cannot be saved by their own desire or works (Romans 9:16); they can be saved only by the GRACE and mercy of God (see Ephesians 2:8–9; Titus 3:4–7 and comments).

God's Work

God has done everything necessary for our salvation. In Romans 8:29–30, the Apostle Paul lists in order what God has done for us in salvation. Before the world began, God had predestined us, by His foreknowledge, to be like His Son (Romans 8:29; 1 Peter 1:2). He also called us, justified us, and glorified us (Romans 8:30). All of these words and a few others decribe what God has done for us in the inclusive word "salvation."

God has "called" us. The Bible says that no one can come to Jesus unless the Father draws him (John 6:44). And we can not know the Father unless the Son reveals Him to us (Matthew 11:27). Man in his sinful condition can not even understand the things that come from the Spirit of God (1 Corinthians 2:14). The call of God is necessary, or else no one would be able to turn to Him (see General Article: Salvation—God's Choice or Man's Choice?).

God has also "justified" us. This term does not mean that God, in fact, makes us righteous, but only that He "declares us RIGHTEOUS." It is a judicial act of God, by which He forgives our sin **freely by his**

grace on the basis of redemption by Jesus Christ on the CROSS (Romans 3:24). God cannot ignore sin. He must punish sin. In Christ, God Himself atoned for the sin of man. This allows Him to forgive us and "declare us righteous" (see Romans 3:25–26 and comment; General Article: Jesus Christ).

God not only declares us righteous, but He also gives us a new nature that is able to be righteous. This is seen in the word "regeneration." We are dead in sin, but can be made "alive" in Jesus Christ (Romans 8:10–11; Ephesians 2:1,5). Jesus said we must be **born again** (see John 3:3,5–7 and comment. We are born again **through the living and enduring word of God** (1 Peter 1:23). When we are saved, our old nature isn't merely reformed; rather, we receive a new spiritual nature that is able to obey God (Ephesians 4:22–24), and we become a **new creation** (2 Corinthians 5:17). Some Christians believe that this "new birth" is connected with water BAPTISM (see Titus 3:5; General Article: Water Baptism).

However, God not only declares us righteous and gives us a new nature able to be righteous, but He also helps us to actually become righteous. He "sanctifies" us or makes us "holy"; that is, He gives us His holiness. Jesus not only rescues man from the punishment due to sin, but cleanses His people **from their sins** also (Matthew 1:21; Romans 6:22). In one sense, we are already made holy by the one-time finished sacrifice of Jesus Christ (Hebrews 10:10); we are already called "saints," or "holy ones" (Ephesians 1:1; Philippians 1:1). But in another sense, we often do not experience holiness in our daily lives. So the Bible talks about the continuing work of the Holy Spirit to make us holy (see Romans 7:24–25; 8:10–11; Galatians 3:3; General Article: Holy Spirit).

God also "glorifies" us (Romans 8:30). The word glorification refers to the RESURRECTION of our bodies and to our eternal life. Jesus prayed that we might see His glory with the Father (John 17:24), and Paul said we would share that glory (Romans 8:17). Our present bodies will be changed into glorious bodies (1 Corinthians 15:42–44), and death will be conquered (1 Corinthians 15:54–57). Paul pointed out that our salvation is not only in this life, but also in the life to come. The bodily resurrection is central to our hope (1 Corinthians 15:12–20). We have been promised eternal life (see John 3:16; 10:28).

There are other words in the Bible to describe our salvation. For example, we are "redeemed" in Christ (Ephesians 1:7). Redemption (or ransom) means "to deliver by paying a price." Jesus Christ redeemed us from sin (Titus 2:14) and the curse of the Law (Galatians 3:13), purchasing us for God (Acts 20:28; Revelation 5:9). We were **bought at a price** (1 Corinthians 6:20), the price of His own blood (1 Peter 1:18–19).

Using another word to describe our salvation, we are "adopted" as the children of God. God the Father **predestined us to be adopted as His sons** through the work of Jesus Christ (Ephesians 1:5), and through our receiving the Holy Spirit who makes us sons (Romans 8:14–17; Galatians 4:5–7). At present we have only received a deposit guaranteeing our inheritance. But Paul also wrote about a future full ADOPTION when our bodies will be resurrected and we will receive our full right as sons and daughters (Romans 8:18–25; Ephesians 1:13–14).

We see, then, that salvation is a word that is used in three tenses: past, present, and future. We have been saved (Ephesians 2:5,8; 2 Timothy 1:9), we are being saved (1 Corinthians 1:18; 2 Corinthians 2:15; Philippians 2:12–13), and we will be saved (Romans 13:11; 1 Thessalonians 5:9; 1 Peter 1:5). To put it in the terms used above: in the past we have been "justified", "redeemed" and given a "new nature"; in the present we are being made "holy"; and in the future we will receive our complete "adoption" and our bodies will be "glorified."

Man's Response

Men and women can not save themselves. They can only be saved by the grace and mercy of God. But that does not mean that man has no part in his salvation. Although Jesus took away the sins of the world on the cross (John 1:29), not all have been saved. For us to receive the salvation offered by God, only one thing is necessary: FAITH in Christ (John 3:16–18; Acts 16:31).

Faith in Christ not only means believing that Jesus is the Christ, the Son of God (John 8:24); it also means receiving Jesus into one's heart and life (Matthew 10:40; John 1:12; Revelation 3:20), and placing complete trust in Him (2 Timothy 1:12). Faith is not just knowing Jesus; it is commitment to Him in our hearts. Having true faith means that we will confess our sins (1 John 1:9) and will repent, or turn from our sins (Luke 13:3,5; Acts 2:38). If we truly have faith, we will confess the Lord Jesus openly with our mouth before men and not hide the fact that we are Christians (Matthew 10:32–33; Romans 10:9–10). We will also obey the command of Jesus to be baptized (see Matthew 28:19–20; Mark 16: 15–16; Acts 2:38; General Article: Water Baptism).

Although salvation is God's work for us through the death of Jesus Christ on the cross, we must believe in and trust in that salvation. But we are not the source of our salvation; God is the source and gives it to us freely by grace. We do not obtain salvation by our own power or effort, nor earn it by our good works (Romans 9:16). But neither do we earn it by our faith. Faith is not a work or something we do to make our own salvation; it is simply trust in God and His gift of grace (Romans 4:5).

This is why Paul says that salvation and all its blessings are obtained **by grace through faith** (Ephesians 2:8). In other passages Paul writes "by faith" as a short form of writing "by grace through faith." By or through faith we are declared righteous (Romans 3:27–28; Galatians 2:15–16). By faith we become holy (Acts 26:18; Galatians 3:1–5). By faith we are born into God's family (John 1:12–13). But faith itself is a gift of God: there is no room for any boasting on our part (Acts 3:16; Ephesians 2:9; Philippians 1:29; 2 Timothy 2:25). Jesus Himself is the originator of our faith, and he will preserve and perfect it to the end (Hebrews 12:2).

The example of a window can help us understand the relationship between grace and faith. We receive sunlight into our room through a window, but having a window does not make the sunlight! Grace is like the sunlight, and faith is like the window. We receive God's grace through faith, but we do not make or earn God's grace because we believe. We are able to cover up our window in unbelief so that God's grace cannot enter. Belief and trust in God is a necessary condition for salvation, but not the source of our salvation.

Faith and Works

Other religions of the world teach that man earns salvation by doing good works. The followers of other religions think that Christians also do good works in order to obtain salvation, because they see them doing so many good deeds. Therefore, many people say that there is no difference between Christianity and other religions.

But the people who say this are mistaken. The difference between Christianity and other religions is very great. Christians receive salvation first, and only after that are they truly able to do good works. We don't do good works in order to obtain salvation; we do good works because we have already been saved.

But here even some Christians make a big mistake. They suppose that, having been saved, they then must do good works in order to keep their salvation. But just as people cannot earn their salvation by their own effort and work, so also they cannot keep their salvation by their own effort and work (Galatians 3:3). From beginning to end, our salvation is by God's grace, and is received through faith.

However, even though this is true, Christians must obey God and do works that please Him. If our life shows no good works or good behavior, it means that our faith is false. Good works always accompany true faith (see James 2:17 and comment).

If we take the example of a tree, we will be able to understand the relationship between faith and works. To produce fruit (that is, good works) we first have to be alive. But those who don't believe and have not received salvation are still dead! They don't have the power to do good works that are pleasing to God. Just as a dead tree cannot produce fruit, so those people who are dead in sin, who have not been saved, cannot do true good works, that is, works that arise out of unselfish love for God and other men. They are still trusting in their own work to save them, rather than in God's work (Romans 4:4–5). True good works are not for our own good, but for the good of others, and show our love for God (John 14:21).

On the other hand, a living fruit tree must produce fruit. If a fruit tree bears no fruit, we know it's just like a dead tree, or like one about to die. If we say that we believe but do not show good works, our faith is false (Matthew 7:21; 1 John 2:4). Good works are the proof of our faith. True faith always gives birth to good works.

According to other religions, then, people are like dead trees which hope to receive life by producing fruit. But according to the Christian religion, we must first receive life; only after that will we be able to produce fruit.

We see, therefore, that we must "use" our faith by forsaking our sins and obeying God. If we have true faith, our behavior will be completely different (Romans 8:13; 1 Corinthians 6:9–11; Galatians 5:19–26). But all this is only possible for us because God has already given us the power to do these things. He gives us a new life, a new mind, and a new nature; because of this we are able to live a life pleasing to Him. **Therefore, my dear friends . . . continue to work out your salvation with fear and trembling, for it is God who works in you to will and to act according to his good purpose** (Philippians 2:12–13).

SALVATION–GOD'S CHOICE OR MAN'S CHOICE?

Main Verses

Joshua 24:15 . . . **choose for yourselves this day whom you will serve.**
Matthew 23:37 **I** (Christ) **have longed . . . but you were not willing.**
John 7:17 **If any one chooses to do God's will, he will find out whether my teaching comes from God.**
John 15:16 **You did not choose me, but I chose you.**
Acts 7:51 **You always resist the Holy Spirit.**
Acts 13:46 **Since you reject it** (God's word) . . . **we now turn to the Gentiles.**
Romans 8:29–30 **For those God foreknew he also predestined . . . called . . . justified . . . glorified.**
Romans 9:10–24 According to His own will, **God has mercy on whom he wants to have mercy, and he hardens whom he wants to harden.**
Romans 11:32 **God has bound all men over to disobedience so that he may have mercy on them all.**
Ephesians 1:4–5 **For he chose us . . . before the creation of the world.**
1 Timothy 2:4 [God] **wants all men to be saved and to come to a knowledge of the truth.**
1 Peter 1:2 [Christians] **have been chosen according to the foreknowledge of God the Father.**
2 Peter 1:10 . . . **make your calling and election sure.**

The Problem

Jesus in John 8:34 and Paul in Romans 6:14–18 both clearly stated that unbelievers are slaves to sin. Unbelievers, without help, cannot even understand the things of God (1 Corinthians 2:14). They cannot choose RIGHTEOUSNESS by their own power. No one can come to Jesus unless the Father draws him (John 6:44). And no one can know the Father unless the Son reveals Him (Matthew 11:27–28).

We see examples of God opening people's hearts to see and understand in Luke 24:45 and Acts 16:14.

Both Jesus and Paul said that unbelievers can be set free from slavery to sin (John 8:36; Romans 6:17–18), and Paul stated that believers become slaves to righteousness. This salvation is not a result of human work, but is a free gift of God (see Romans 6:23; Ephesians 2:8–9 and comments).

Jesus said that the disciples did not choose Him, but that He chose them **to go and bear fruit** (John 15:16). Paul said that God **chose us in him before the creation of the world** (Ephesians 1:4), and that He **predestined us to be adopted as his sons** (Ephesians 1:5,11). Our election is according to God's foreknowledge (Romans 8:29–30; 1 Peter 1:2). In Romans 9:16, Paul emphasizes that God's choice does not depend on man's effort or desire, but on God's mercy.

All Christians believe that SALVATION comes by God's grace and mercy alone, and that we cannot work to earn our salvation. But a problem arises. Does this mean that we have no choice at all in our own salvation? Are REPENTANCE and FAITH things we choose to do, or are they things that God chooses to produce in us? Does man have the power to resist God's GRACE and say "No" to God?

Does Man Have a Choice in His Salvation?

Different Christians answer this question differently. Some Christians believe that only God chooses who will be saved; man cannot choose because he is a slave to sin. They believe that God chooses only some people, not everyone, to be saved; God chooses the rest to be destroyed. These Christians point to Jesus' statement that **many are invited, but few are chosen** (Matthew 22:14), and to Paul's statement that certain vessels are prepared for destruction while others are prepared for glory (Romans 9:22–23). In Romans 9:18, Paul writes: **God has mercy on whom he wants to have mercy, and he hardens whom he wants to harden.** Elsewhere, some people are mentioned as being **appointed** to eternal life (Acts 13:48), and others as being appointed to stumble and disobey (1 Peter 2:8). These Christians believe that God chooses who will be saved, and then gives the ability to repent (2 Timothy 2:25) and believe (Philippians 1:29) only to those who are chosen. The chosen ones have no choice themselves and cannot say "No" to salvation.

Many other Christians believe that God's choice is not the only thing involved in our salvation, but that we also have a part. The Jewish people in the Old Testament, although chosen by God through no merit of their own, apparently were given a choice whether to follow God or not (Deuteronomy 30:19; Joshua 24:15). In the New Testament, Jesus said that if anyone **chooses to do God's will,** he will recognize God's teaching (John 7:17). We are commanded to repent (Acts 2:38) and to believe (Romans 10:9–10) in order to receive salvation. These Christians believe that God first calls us, but that we can resist God's call and salvation.

Some of this second group of Christians believe that God takes the unbeliever who is a slave to sin and frees him just enough to be able to make a free choice again. If the freed person chooses God, he is saved; if he chooses SATAN, he falls again into slavery to sin and is damned. Others, however, believe that men and women are so bound in sin that they will never choose God. Therefore they believe that God does all the choosing for salvation, but man does all the choosing for damnation. In other words, if God chooses someone to be saved and that person does not resist God, he is saved. But if he resists, God will not force him to be saved, and thus he will be damned by his own choice.

But are we able to resist God in this way? Many Christians point out that God is all-powerful. Who are we to resist the creator? (Romans 9:19–21). But in spite of that, many other Christians believe that God has given us freedom of choice. They point to passages which speak of people resisting God's desires for them (Matthew 23:37; Acts 7:51; 13:46), and to other passages which warn us not to resist God (2 Corinthians 6:1; Hebrews 3:8,13; 12:25).

Therefore, we see that Christians have given three main answers to this question: 1) man has no choice in his salvation or his damnation; 2) man has a choice in both; 3) man cannot choose salvation, but after God calls him he can then resist God's call and choose damnation.

These three main ideas about whether we have a choice in our salvation can be described by the following illustration. Picture a boy tied by the side of a road. He represents the unbeliever bound in slavery to sin. A man comes along with an oxcart. He represents God, who wants to bring us to salvation. The man with the cart can do one of three things. 1) He can leave the boy still tied up, but place him in the cart and take him away. This represents the viewpoint of those who believe we have no choice in our salvation nor power to resist God. 2) The man can untie the boy and ask him if he wants to be taken away or not. If the boy chooses to be taken away, the man places him in the cart and drives off. This represents the viewpoint of those who believe that God first frees us so that we can make the choice for either salvation or damnation. 3) The man can untie the boy after placing him in the cart. Then the boy can jump out if he wants to do so. If the boy does nothing, he will be carried off. This represents the viewpoint of those who believe that God chooses us and will do all the work for salvation, but that we may resist and reject God's work.

In summary, according to the first viewpoint, God does all the choosing for both salvation and damnation. According to the second viewpoint, God gives man the freedom to choose both salvation and damnation. According to the third viewpoint, God does all the choosing for salvation, but man can resist and choose damnation.

Does God Call All Men?

Does God want every single person to receive salvation, or only some? In Matthew 22:14 Jesus said that **many are invited but few are chosen**. It is clear that Jesus is the Savior of the world (John 4:42; 1 John 4:14), and that He died to take away the sins of the world (John 1:29; 1 John 2:2). Furthermore Paul said that God wants **all men** to be saved (Romans 11:32; 1 Timothy 2:4–6; 2 Peter 3:9). What does the phrase "all men" mean?

Some Christians think that "all men" means "all kinds of men," meaning that God calls or chooses some individuals from all groups of people. They believe that God wants the good news of Christ spread to the whole world, but that He gives the gift of faith only to a few from each group. But other Christians think that "all men" means "every single person." Although God calls all men, only believers can properly be called "chosen." (Both meanings are possible in the Greek[1] text.)

What about those who have never heard about Jesus? Can they be saved? Most Christians think they cannot. All men are sinners by nature. All are worthy of death (Romans 3:10–12; 6:23). There is no other way to be saved except by Christ (John 14:6; Acts 4:12). Therefore, in Romans 10:13–14 Paul writes: **"Everyone who calls on the name of the Lord will be saved." How, then, can they call on the one they have not believed in? And how can they believe in the one of whom they have not heard? And how can they hear without someone preaching to them?** It is possible that God may show mercy to those who have never heard about Jesus (Luke 12:47–48; Romans 2:12), but that is God's own decision. The Bible does not clearly state what God will do to those who have never heard. However, the Bible does state clearly that it is our responsibility to tell others about Jesus Christ.

Summary

The questions asked in this article are hard ones. The Bible does not give an unequivocal answer to them. God's will is such a mystery! How deep is His wisdom and knowledge! (Romans 11:33–36). Perhaps all of these opinions are true in part. John wrote: **We love**

---

[1] The New Testament was originally written in the Greek language.

because he first loved us (1 John 4:19). Perhaps we could also say: "We chose God because He first chose us." Salvation is God's work, but it appears that we have a part also. Paul points out these two thoughts when he writes: . . . **work out your salvation with fear and trembling, for it is God who works in you to will and to act according to his good purpose** (Philippians 2:12–13).

CAN WE LOSE OUR SALVATION?

Main Verses

John 6:39 **I shall lose none of all that he has given me.**
John 10:28 **. . . no one can snatch them out of my hand.**
Romans 8:38–39 **. . . neither death nor life . . . neither the present nor the future . . . will be able to separate us from the love of God.**
Ephesians 1:13–14 **Having believed, you were marked in him with a seal, the promised Holy Spirit, who is a deposit guaranteeing our inheritance.**
Philippians 1:6 **. . . he who began a good work in you will carry it on to completion.**
2 Timothy 1:12 **. . . he is able to guard what I have entrusted to him for that day.**
1 John 2:19 **. . . if they had belonged to us, they would have remained with us.**

Luke 8:11–15 **They believe for a while, but in the time of testing they fall away.**
John 15:2 **He cuts off every branch in me that bears no fruit.**
Romans 11:22 **Consider therefore the kindness and sternness of God . . . kindness to you, provided that you continue in his kindness. Otherwise, you also will be cut off.**
Galatians 5:1–4 **You . . . have been alienated from Christ; you have fallen away from grace.**
1 Timothy 4:1 **The Spirit clearly says that in later times some will abandon the faith.**
Hebrews 6:4–6 **It is impossible for those who have once . . . shared in the Holy Spirit . . . if they fall away, to be brought back to repentance.**
Hebrews 10:26–27 **If we deliberately keep on sinning after we have received the knowledge of the truth, no sacrifice for sins is left, but only a fearful expectation of judgment.**
Hebrews 10:29 **How much more severely do you think a man deserves to be punished who has . . . treated as an unholy thing the blood of the covenant that sanctified him.**
1 John 2:24 **See that what you have heard from the beginning**

remains in you. If it does, you also will remain in the Son and in the Father.

The Problem

Before we believed in Jesus, we were slaves to sin and to SATAN, (Romans 6:17). After we believed, we became slaves to righteousness (Romans 6:18). Does this mean that it is impossible for us to reject God's GRACE and lose our SALVATION?

Many Christians think that believers are not able to lose their salvation. These Christians say that believers can sin and appear to fall away, but God will always bring them back to His grace. They call this "eternal security." They say, "Once saved, always saved."

Many other Christians, however, think that believers can indeed reject God and lose their salvation. God will try to bring them back, but if they persist in rejecting Him, God will not force them to accept salvation again. (See General Article: Salvation—God's Choice or Man's Choice?)

Security in the Bible

Scripture does not give a clear answer to this question of eternal security. Some verses of the Bible seem to say we cannot lose our salvation, while other verses seem to say that we can.

Those Christians who think that believers cannot reject God or lose salvation point to the many verses that speak of God giving eternal and everlasting life (see John 3:16; 6:54; 11:26). Jesus said that He gave His sheep eternal life, and that "**they shall never perish; no one can snatch them out of my hand**" (John 10:28). Jesus said that He will **never drive away** those who come to Him, and that He will not lose any that the Father has given Him (John 6:37,39). Paul said that nothing would be able to separate us from the love of God (Romans 8:38–39), and that we have been marked with the HOLY SPIRIT who is a **deposit guaranteeing our inheritance** (Ephesians 1:14). God **who began a good work in you will carry it on to completion until the day of Christ Jesus** (Philippians 1:6). God is able to keep what we have given to Him (2 Timothy 1:12), rescue us from temptation (2 Peter 2:9), and keep us from falling (Jude 24). From these verses we can see the believer's security.

But those Christians who think that believers can lose their salvation point to all the warning passages, such as: **he who stands firm to the end will be saved** (Mark 13:13). They also point to 1 Corinthians 15:1–2; Colossians 1:21–23; Hebrews 3:6,12; 10:35–36. They point to Jesus' words in John 15:1–6 that anyone who does not abide in Christ is **like a branch that is thrown away and . . . thrown into the fire**. Paul said in Romans 11:22 that the GENTILES who did not continue in God's mercy and grace **will be cut off**. Paul told the Galatians that those believers who were returning to the Old Testament LAW had **fallen away from grace** (Galatians 5:1–4). Jesus Himself, while explaining the parable of the sower, said that some "**believe for a while, but in the time of testing they fall away**" (Luke 8:13). Paul noted that **some will abandon the faith** (1 Timothy 4:1). The writer of Hebrews pointed to the danger facing those who **have shared in the Holy Spirit** or who have been **sanctified** by the blood of Christ but who later reject Christ (Hebrews 6:4–6; 10:28–29,39). The New Testament gives other similar warnings (2 Peter 2:20–21; Revelation 3:5; 22:19). These Christians ask why these warnings were given if it were not possible to lose our salvation.

John wrote that the antichrists of the church age **went out from us, but they did not really belong to us . . . their going showed that none of them belonged to us**—that is, none of them belonged to the church (1 John 2:19). Those who think that believers cannot lose salvation say that none of those who later fall away were ever true believers to begin with. Those, on the other hand, who think that believers can lose salvation say that some who fall away were previously true believers and some were not; those who were true believers later rejected Christ and no longer **belonged to us**. We must be careful about judging who is a false Christian and who is a true Christian (Matthew 7:1–2). And we must not be proud and say that we ourselves will never fall. Paul says that **if you think you are standing firm, be careful that you don't fall** (1 Corinthians 10:12). John also wrote: **See that what you have heard from the beginning remains in you. If it does, you also will remain in the Son and in the Father** (1 John 2:24).

Thus we see that some verses in the New Testament support the idea that a believer cannot lose his salvation, and other verses support the idea that he can lose it. Surely we must be seeing here two sides of a great truth, which our human minds cannot fully grasp. God's wisdom is greater than ours.

Someone has said that believers need to hold in balance both of these truths. But for the believer who is anxious about his salvation, one should emphasize the truth that his salvation is secure. Whereas for the believer who is overly confident that he cannot fall, one should emphasize the truth that he can indeed fall. Here again, we can see the depth and richness of the Bible. The Bible meets the needs of every man and woman.

What Is the "Sin Unto Death"?

In 1 John 5:16–17, we are instructed not to pray for a brother (a Christian) who has committed a **sin that leads to death**. John may be referring to spiritual death. However, he could be referring instead to the physical death of a sinning Christian brother whose spirit will not be lost (see 1 Corinthians 5:5). If John is referring here to spiritual death, then this verse would support those who think that a believer can lose his salvation. But John does not say what that kind of sin actually is.

It could be that this "sin that leads to death" is blasphemy against the Holy Spirit, which Jesus said will not be forgiven (Mark 3:28–29). Notice that Jesus did not say whether or not a Christian can commit this sin. However, the writer of Hebrews talks of the possibility, at least, that a former true believer (one who has **shared in the Holy Spirit**) can reject God and publicly disgrace the Lord. **It is impossible . . . if they fall away, to be brought back to repentance** (Hebrews 6:4–6). Later, in Hebrews Chapter 10, the writer says: **If we deliberately keep on sinning after we have received the knowledge of the truth, no sacrifice for sins is left** (Hebrews 10:26). He then points again to former believers who have been **sanctified** by Jesus' blood and who have **trampled the Son of God** and **insulted the Spirit of grace** (Hebrews 10:29). It would seem, then, that whoever rejects God's Spirit and keeps on sinning will not be able to listen to God's voice in the end, and his chance for salvation will be lost forever. When men keep on sinning after knowing better, their hearts become hardened. They not only cannot hear the voice of God; God may stop calling to them as well.

Many Christians think that a believer also can fall away and keep on rejecting the call of Christ until the same state is reached, and they further believe that these verses (Hebrews 6:4–6; 10:26–31) warn of that possibility. But other Christians think that true believers will not reach that final lost state; rather, they will always repent and fully believe again before they die.

Summary

All Christians believe that we are saved only by the grace and mercy of God through FAITH in Jesus Christ (Ephesians 2:8–9). All Christians also believe that we are able to continue in that faith only by the help of the Holy Spirit (Galatians 3:3). However, from New Testament times until now, Christians have had different opinions about whether or not a true believer can lose his salvation. The Bible does not give an unequivocal teaching on this subject. Therefore, whatever view we hold, we must not allow our opinion to separate us from our Christian brothers and sisters who may think differently on this question. We can see these two opinions about losing our salvation expressed side by side in Jude. In verse 21 Jude writes: **Keep yourselves in God's love as you wait for the mercy of**

our Lord Jesus Christ to bring you to eternal life. In verse 24 Jude points to God **who is able to keep you from falling and to present you before his glorious presence without fault and with great joy.**

THE HOLY SPIRIT

The Holy Spirit—Who Is He?

The Holy Spirit is God Himself. He is one of the members of the Triune God. All Christians believe that God is one in substance, but always has three forms or modes of existence, all fully God: our Father in heaven; the Son, who also became a man on earth; and the Holy Spirit, who lives in believers' hearts. Jesus Christ and the Holy Spirit are not parts of God; they are completely God Himself. This is difficult to understand, but it is taught to us in Scripture. For example, after Jesus was baptized in water, the Holy Spirit descended on Him in the form of a dove, and the Father spoke from heaven, "**You are my Son**" (Mark 1:9–11). Jesus told us to baptize **in the name of the Father and of the Son and of the Holy Spirit** (Matthew 28:19). The Apostle Paul gives us the benediction: **May the grace of the Lord Jesus Christ, and the love of God, and the fellowship of the Holy Spirit be with you all** (2 Corinthians 13:14). The three members of the Godhead are constantly mentioned together (Ephesians 2:18; 4:4–6; Jude 20–21).

All three—Father, Son, and Holy Spirit—are distinct (John 14:16–17,26; 16:7–15; 1 Corinthians 12:4–6; 1 Peter 1:2). But they are also equal. All three are called "God" (John 6:27; Hebrews 1:8; Acts 5:3–4). All three give life (John 5:21; Romans 8:11). All three receive divine honor (John 5:23; 2 Corinthians 13:14). All three are said to be eternal (John 1:1; Hebrews 9:14).

The Holy Spirit can be quenched (1 Thessalonians 5:19). However, the Holy Spirit is not just a kind of power or energy; He also is a person. Like the other members of the Trinity, the Spirit is personal in His relationship with us. He speaks (Acts 13:2), He can be grieved (Isaiah 63:10; Ephesians 4:30), and He can be insulted (Hebrews 10:29). Speaking against the Holy Spirit is considered blasphemy, and is a sin which will not be forgiven (Mark 3:28–29).

The Holy Spirit is one with the Father and the Son. We can see this in Romans 8:9–10, where "Holy Spirit," "Spirit of God," "Spirit of Christ," and "Christ" are interchangeable words and all mean "God." This oneness does not mean that the Father, Son, and Holy Spirit are identical. The Son is not the Father, but is begotten by Him (John 3:16); and the Holy Spirit is not the Father or the Son, but is sent by the Father and the Son (John 15:26). But the three have a oneness of mind, desire and purpose, as well as oneness of nature.

The Triune God has been thought of as similar to an egg with its three parts: the shell, the white, and the yolk. But God does not have three parts, since God is one substance. The Triune God has also been thought of as similar to water in its three forms: water, ice, and steam. This is a slightly better comparison, since the substance is the same in all three forms. But the problem is that water cannot be in all three forms at the same time, whereas God is three persons at one and the same time (Mark 1:10–11).

It is better to think of God the Father as a writer writing a drama. The drama represents the world we live in. The writer places a character in the drama exactly like the writer himself. This character exactly like the writer is Jesus. The writer's spirit is also involved throughout the drama influencing every character and giving power to one and taking it away from another. This is like the Holy Spirit, who is active in the world.

The Holy Spirit is "God in the world." Jesus said that He would leave the world (John 14:2–3), but would send the Holy Spirit to be with us (John 14:16–20,26). The Holy Spirit is God Himself in action, God working in the world.

What, then, does the Holy Spirit do?

The Holy Spirit—His Work

First of all, the Holy Spirit was active in the creation of the world (Genesis 1:1–2). He is involved in giving the breath of life to man (Genesis 2:7; Job 33:4). Second, the Holy Spirit is the One who inspired the writers of the Bible, directing them to write exactly what God wanted to say (Acts 28:25; Hebrews 9:8; 10:15; 2 Peter 1:21).

The Holy Spirit was active in the Old Testament, both teaching (Nehemiah 9:20,30) and coming on God's people to give them power and gifts (Numbers 11:17; 27:18; 1 Samuel 19:20–24; 2 Kings 2:9–14). However, DAVID feared that God would take His Holy Spirit away from him (Psalms 51:11). Therefore, it may be that during Old Testament times the Holy Spirit did not dwell within every believer, but only came on certain persons for special ministry at special times.

Jesus was conceived by the Holy Spirit (Matthew 1:20), and anointed with power by the Spirit (Mark 1:10; Luke 4:18; Acts 10:38). Jesus needed the help and power of the Spirit just as we do, because Jesus was fully human. Jesus laid aside His divine power and glory while He was here on earth (John 17:5; Philippians 2:7), although He remained divine in nature.

In John Chapters 14–16, Jesus promised a new age of the Spirit when He and the Father would send the Holy Spirit to His disciples

(John 14:26; 15:26). But the disciples already knew the Spirit because He already lived with them (John 14:16–17). This new "sending" of the Spirit did not mean that the Spirit had not been present in the world beforehand. But in the New Testament, the Holy Spirit came into the world in a special way to do some new things.

The Holy Spirit came in a special way to establish the church, the body of Christ (Ephesians 1:22–23; 5:29–30). The Holy Spirit is the source of our unity and fellowship (1 Corinthians 12:13; Ephesians 4:3). The Spirit empowered the church on the day of PENTECOST (Acts 2:1–4), an event that was also prophesied in the Old Testament (Joel 2:28–29; Acts 2:17–18). The Spirit gives special gifts to help the church (Romans 12:6–8; 1 Corinthians 12:8–10). He guides the church in choosing those for ministry (Acts 13:2), and He sends His word to the church through prophecies, dreams, and revelations (Acts 10:9–16; 16:9; 21:9–10; 1 Corinthians 14:26–32; 1 Timothy 4:14; Revelation 1:1).

But the new age of the Spirit was not just for the church as a group. The Holy Spirit became more closely involved with every individual believer. It is the Holy Spirit who convicts men of their sin (John 16:8–11). Ezekiel prophesied that God would put His own Spirit within us (Ezekiel 36:25–28). Jesus had promised that the Holy Spirit would not just live with the disciples, but that He would soon be living inside them (John 14:17). Before His ascension to heaven, Jesus breathed on His disciples and said, **"Receive the Holy Spirit"** (John 20:22). The Holy Spirit lives in all Christians (Romans 8:9; 1 Corinthians 6:19; Galatians 4:6). When we believe, we are born of the Spirit (John 3:3–6; 1 John 5:1), and the Holy Spirit bears witness with our own spirits that we are God's children (Romans 8:16; 1 John 5:6–8). The Holy Spirit gives us the right to call God "our Father" (Romans 8:15; Galatians 4:6). Jesus promised that the Spirit would teach us (John 14:26; 15:26; 16:13–14) and guide us (Mark 13:11). We see examples of this in Acts 15:28 and 16:6–7. The Spirit also helps us to pray according to the will of God (Romans 8:26–27).

The Holy Spirit lives within every Christian (Romans 8:9); however, He works in different ways in different believers. Paul says that we are sealed with the Spirit when we believe (Ephesians 1:13–14), but he also tells us to **be filled with the Spirit** (Ephesians 5:18). The disciples received the Spirit in John 20:22, but were **filled with** the Spirit in Acts 2:4, and then filled again in Acts 4:31. The Spirit can come in special ways for special ministry as well (Acts 13:2–4; 1 Timothy 4:14). Paul tells us not to **put out the Spirit's fire** (1 Thessalonians 5:19). Timothy is told to **fan into flame the gift of God** given to him by the laying on of Paul's hands (2 Timothy 1:6). We see that we can either allow the Spirit to work more and more in our lives, or we can stop the Spirit from working. We can either be **filled with the Spirit**, or we can **put out the Spirit's fire**.

What does this "filling with the Spirit" mean? What works of the Spirit are not present equally in all Christians' lives? They can be divided into two groups: the special gifts of the Spirit, examples of which are given in 1 Corinthians 12:8–10; and the fruits of the Spirit, which are listed in Galatians 5:22–23. For a further discussion of the gifts and power of the Spirit, see General Article: Holy Spirit Baptism. The fruits of the Spirit, or "holiness," will be discussed below.

Holiness, or Sanctification

What is holiness, or sanctification? Briefly, it is Christ-likeness. It results in love and in the other fruits of the Spirit (1 Corinthians 13:1–13; Galatians 5:22–23). It involves separation from sin and from the world. But it also involves being set apart for God, whereby all our abilities and opportunities are given to God.

God views us as already being holy (Hebrews 10:10). But we see unholiness in our lives. How can we understand this? There are two meanings of holiness in the Bible. In the first sense, God as judge considers us to be holy or blameless. Jesus Christ is our holiness (1 Corinthians 1:30), and we are called "saints," or "holy ones" (Ephesians 1:1; Philippians 1:1). In God's view this is our position in Christ.

But the second meaning of holiness in the Bible is the actual degree of holiness in our experience, in our lives. When we look at our lives, do we see perfect holiness? No, we do not. Christians are declared RIGHTEOUS when they receive SALVATION, but they are still sinners and need to become holy. This is an ongoing work of the Spirit whereby we can become truly holy in our daily lives (2 Thessalonians 2:13; 1 Peter 1:2). God calls us to live a holy life (Ephesians 1:4; 1 Thessalonians 4:3–7; 1 Peter 1:15–16), and Jesus commands us to be holy, or **perfect** (Matthew 5:48). But it is the Holy Spirit who actually makes us holy, or sanctifies us.

Sanctification is included in our salvation (2 Thessalonians 2:13). Without holiness we cannot see God (Hebrews 12:14). Holiness is not something we must have in order to be saved; it is something that becomes possible because we are already saved (Romans 6:22). We cannot become holy through our own efforts alone. The Holy Spirit helps us. It is by the Spirit that we put to death the sins of our sinful nature (Romans 8:13). Paul was concerned that the Galatians were beginning by accepting salvation as a free gift of God, but were then going back to human efforts to be made perfect or holy (see Galatians 3:3; General Article: Way of Salvation).

It is only through the Holy Spirit that we can become holy. But this does not mean that we have no part in the process. We must accept God's discipline (Hebrews 12:9–11). We must train our bodies in holiness (1 Corinthians 9:24–27; 1 Timothy 4:7). We must "throw off" all sin of body or spirit that may hinder us (2 Corinthians 7:1; Hebrews 12:1–2), and we must offer our bodies and minds to God (Romans 6:13,19; 12:1–2). We should read the Bible (2 Timothy 3:16), memorize verses (Psalm 119:11; 2 Peter 1:4), and then allow the Scriptures to change our behavior. We can receive help from the leaders God has placed over us (Ephesians 4:11–13). In addition to all this, we need to pray for God's help (Colossians 1:9–10; 1 Thessalonians 3:12–13; 5:23) or we will fail.

Some Christians believe that there is another step, a separate special experience of being sanctified. They believe that after much prayer and seeking God we can receive sanctification in a special experience and can know for sure that we have received it. They call this experience of sanctification a "second work of grace." (The first work of grace is our salvation.) These Christians teach that initial salvation results in our being born again, separated from the world (1 John 5:4), and indwelt by the Spirit (Romans 8:9). We become **infants** in Christ (1 Corinthians 3:1). But the "second work of grace," sometimes called the "second blessing," results in our being sanctified, separated from self (Galatians 2:20), and filled with the Spirit (Ephesians 5:18). We then become **mature** (Ephesians 4:13), and God's love is made **complete** in us (1 John 4:12,17). Many of these Christians believe that we can be completely sanctified, so that we will no longer continue to sin knowingly or voluntarily (1 John 3:9). They believe that the latter part of Romans Chapter 7 gives a picture of the immature Christian, while Romans Chapter 8 gives a picture of a mature Christian who has had this "second blessing." They point to the filling of the Spirit in Acts 2:4 and 9:17 as examples of this holiness experience (see General Article: Holy Spirit Baptism).

Most Christians, however, believe that sanctification is a slow process that takes time and will not be finished even when we die. They do not believe that there is a separate experience required for holiness. They point to verses which say we "are being" made holy (Galatians 3:3; Hebrews 10:14; 12:10–11), or which say that we are to keep on in the race and to continue to struggle against sin (Hebrews 12:1–4). Many verses in the New Testament tell us to "train" our bodies, "offer" ourselves, "run" the race, or "fight," and because of such verses it appears that we have not become completely holy yet. Paul himself said that he had not been made perfect, but was still striving for perfection (Philippians 3:12–14), even though he included himself among the **mature** (Philippians 3:15). Some point to 1 John 1:8, where John says that if we claim to be without sin we are not being honest. The more we become "mature" in Christ, the more we realize our own sin and imperfection. At the end of his life, Paul said that among sinners he was **the worst** (1 Timothy 1:15). Christians holding this second opinion usually believe that the latter part of Romans Chapter 7 refers to the Christian in his daily struggle against sin. They believe that a Christian may gradually come to experience more and more the victorious life described in Romans Chapter 8, but that in this world he will never completely end his fight against his old sinful nature.

Every Christian's experience is different. Many Christians say that they have received this "second blessing" or special filling of the Holy Spirit. Some Christians experience sudden periods of increased holiness coming in addition to a more gradual experience of sanctification. God works in each life in different ways. We must not confine the workings of the Holy Spirit to our own limited individual experience.

Whatever we believe about a holiness experience, our responsibility is clear: we are commanded to be holy. Peter wrote: **. . . be holy in all you do** (1 Peter 1:15). **Make every effort to live in peace with all men and to be holy; without holiness no one will see the Lord** (Hebrews 12:14).

HOLY SPIRIT BAPTISM

Main Verses

Mark 1:8 . . . **he** (Jesus) **will baptize you with the Holy Spirit.**
Luke 24:49 . . . **stay in the city until you have been clothed with power from on high.**
John 14:16–17 **I will ask the Father, and he will give you another Counselor.**
John 20:22 . . . **he** (Jesus) **breathed on them and said, "Receive the Holy Spirit. . . ."**
Acts 1:5 . . . **in a few days you will be baptized with the Holy Spirit.**
Acts 1:8 **But you will receive power when the Holy Spirit comes on you.**
Acts 2:1–4 **All of them were filled with the Holy Spirit and began to speak in other tongues.**
Acts 2:38–39 **Peter replied, ". . . you will receive the gift of the Holy Spirit. . . ."**
Acts 8:14–17 **Then Peter and John placed their hands on them** (the Samaritans), **and they received the Holy Spirit.**
Acts 10:44–48 **The Holy Spirit came on all who heard the message. The . . . gift of the Holy Spirit had been poured out even on the Gentiles.**
Acts 19:1–6 **When Paul placed his hands on them, the Holy Spirit came on them** (the Ephesians), **and they spoke in tongues and prophesied.**
1 Corinthians 12:7–11 **Now to each one the manifestation of the Spirit is given for the common good. To one there is given through the Spirit the message of wisdom, to another the message of knowledge . . . to another faith . . . gifts of healing . . . miraculous power . . . prophecy . . . ability to distinguish between spirits . . . ability to speak in different kinds of tongues . . . interpretation of tongues.**

What Is the Baptism of the Holy Spirit?

The baptism of the HOLY SPIRIT was first mentioned by John the Baptist (Matthew 3:11; Mark 1:8; Luke 3:16). John said that his

BAPTISM was **with**[1] (or in) water but that Jesus would baptize believers **with** (or in) the Holy Spirit and fire. For water baptism, a pastor baptizes the believer with (or in) water; for Holy Spirit baptism, Jesus Himself baptizes the believer with (or in) the Holy Spirit. Jesus used the term also in Acts 1:5, distinguishing between John's baptism with water and the baptism with the Holy Spirit. Jesus also described baptism with the Holy Spirit as a time when the Holy Spirit would "come on" His disciples and they would **receive power** (Acts 1:8). In Acts 1:4 and Luke 24:49, Jesus told His disciples to wait for this power.

The disciples did wait and did receive this baptism of the Holy Spirit on the day of PENTECOST (Acts 2:1–4). They began to speak in **other tongues** by the power of the Spirit. Later, we can see the power and gifts of the Holy Spirit being used by the APOSTLES and deacons in the early church (Acts Chapters 3–9). Throughout the New Testament we read about people who have received special gifts and power from the Holy Spirit (1 Corinthians Chapters 12–14; 2 Corinthians 12:12; 1 Timothy 4:14; 2 Timothy 1:6).

The question is whether the Holy Spirit's power and special gifts are available for us today. And if they are available, when and how may we receive them?

Experiences of the Holy Spirit's Power

The Bible teaches clearly that the Holy Spirit is within all believers (Romans 8:9; 1 Corinthians 6:19; Galatians 4:6), but He may be active in different believers' lives in different ways. John the Baptist was filled with the Spirit from his mother's womb (Luke 1:15,41–44). The Spirit descended upon Jesus in the form of a dove after Jesus' water baptism (Mark 1:10; John 1:32–33). During His ministry on earth, Jesus gave power and authority to heal diseases and drive out demons both to His original twelve disciples and again to seventy-two other disciples (Luke 9:1–2; 10:1,9,17–19). He later promised that the Holy Spirit would be not only with them but also in them (John 14:16–17). Before the day of Pentecost, Jesus had already breathed on His disciples and said, **"Receive the Holy Spirit"** (John 20:22). But He told these same disciples to wait for the Holy Spirit to come on them with power, that is, to wait for the baptism of the Holy Spirit (Luke 24:49; Acts 1:4). Their receiving of the Spirit for power and gifts in Acts Chapter 2 marked the beginning of the church age. They preached everywhere, making disciples, baptizing them with water, and encouraging them to

[1] The Greek word **with** in Matthew 3:11 and Luke 3:16 can also mean "in." Whichever word is used, the meaning is the same.

receive the Holy Spirit for power and special gifts (Acts 8:14–17; 9:17; 19:1–6; 1 Corinthians 12:8–10).

There are many words in the Greek[2] language used in Acts to describe this experience of Holy Spirit baptism. We have already seen the terms "baptism with the Holy Spirit" (Acts 1:5; 11:16), "receiving power" (Acts 1:8), and the Holy Spirit "coming on" (Acts 1:8; 8:16; 10:44; 11:15; 19:6). There are also the terms "being filled with the Holy Spirit" (Acts 2:4; 4:31; 9:17), the Holy Spirit "being poured out" (Acts 10:45), and "receiving the Holy Spirit" (Acts 8:15; 10:47; 19:2). Notice that the same disciples who received power and gifts in Luke 9:1–2; 10:9,17–19, and who "received" the Spirit in John 20:22, again "received" Him in Acts Chapter 2 (see Acts 10:47). Those same disciples who were "filled" with the Spirit in Acts 2:4 were "filled"' again in Acts 4:31. It can be seen that different kinds of experiences may be given the same name, and one kind of experience may be given two or three different names.

Not only that but in Acts the same experience happened at different times and in different ways. The experience sometimes occurred: 1) after conversion and after receiving the Holy Spirit in some way (John 20:22; Acts 2:4; 4:31); 2) after conversion and some days after water baptism (Acts 8:9–17); 3) at conversion and before water baptism (Acts 10:44–48); 4) after conversion and a few minutes after water baptism (Acts 19:1–6). For some, the Holy Spirit came when hands were laid on them (Acts 8:17; 9:17; 19:6; 2 Timothy 1:6); and for others, the Holy Spirit came without special laying on of hands (Acts 2:4; 4:31; 10:44).

Therefore, from these verses we see that the Holy Spirit can come and work in a believer in different ways. The Holy Spirit is free; we should not make our own rules for Him. The important thing is whether the power of the Holy Spirit is evident in our lives. We should pray for that power to be evident (Acts 8:14–17; 9:17). In whatever way the Holy Spirit works in a Christian's life, we should praise God and thank Him for that work.

The Power of the Holy Spirit in the Church

All Christians believe that the Holy Spirit is with each one who believes in Jesus (Romans 8:9; Ephesians 4:30). Many Christians also believe that we receive the Holy Spirit in a special way at water baptism and at the LORD'S SUPPER (1 Corinthians 10:2–4; 12:13; Titus 3:5). Many others believe that the Holy Spirit can be received in a special way for special ministry, such as that of a pastor, deacon or missionary (Acts 6:6; 13:2–3; 1 Timothy 4:14; 2 Timothy 1:6), or for repeated power and encouragement (Acts 4:31).

---

[2] The New Testament was originally written in the Greek language.

The early church believed that Christians received the Holy Spirit in a special way for power and gifts when the leaders of the church laid hands on them, similar to the situation described in Acts 8:14–17. The early church believed that this was an experience separate from conversion and water baptism. This was the general belief for the first several hundred years of church history.

However, through much of subsequent church history, most Christians did not show evidence of special power or gifts of the Holy Spirit, such as those described in 1 Corinthians 12:7–11. For example, most people never saw anyone healed by divine power. Many began to suppose that God had given this special power and these gifts only to the early church. Today, some Christians believe that many of the gifts are no longer available to us in this age. They point to 1 Corinthians 13:8–10, where Paul states that **prophecies** and **tongues** and **knowledge** will all **cease** when **perfection comes**. These Christians think that "perfection" refers to the finished New Testament, which was completely written within one hundred years after the death of Christ.

But many other Christians believe that all the gifts are still available for us today, and furthermore, they claim they have experienced them. They believe that in 1 Corinthians 13:8–10, Paul is referring to a future time when we shall see Jesus **face to face** (1 Corinthians 13:12). They point out that all through church history, the Holy Spirit's power and gifts have appeared from time to time and place to place. Indeed, from the beginning of this (20th) century the gifts and power of the Spirit have been increasingly seen. These Christians point to the great promises of special signs and gifts for believers recorded in Mark 16:17–18; John 14:12; Acts 2:17–18.[3]

---

[3] 1 Corinthians 12:13 is another verse that relates to this difference of opinion. There are two different views concerning the meaning of this verse. Some believe that the verse should read: **For we were all baptized** [in] **one Spirit into one body**. If this is correct, the verse is most likely referring to Holy Spirit baptism only, not to water baptism. Therefore, some Christians teach that all believers have been baptized in the Holy Spirit, but that this is not an experience of receiving power and gifts from the Spirit; rather, it is only a term used for our spiritual birth when we believe in Jesus.

However, most translators believe that the verse should read: **For we were all baptized** [by] **one Spirit into one body**. For this reason, most Christians believe that the verse is referring mainly to water baptism. Many of these Christians conclude, therefore, that being baptized "in" the Holy Spirit (in other verses) does not merely refer to our new spiritual birth, but mainly refers to an experience of receiving power and gifts. Thus these Christians say that the power and gifts of the Holy Spirit are available to the church today.

These two opinions arise from the fact that the Greek word translated "by" in English translations can have two meanings. In some places in the Bible it clearly means "in" (Matthew 3:6; 1 Corinthians 10:2; 11:25; Ephesians 1:11). But in other places it clearly means "by" or "through" the work of someone (Romans 5:9; 1 Corinthians 12:9; Ephesians 2:13).

How and When Do We Receive This Power?

Among those Christians who believe that the gifts and power are available to the church today, there are many different opinions as to how and when they are received. Many believe that the "baptism of the Holy Spirit" is received by all believers at conversion, as described in Acts 10:44, but that it may be years later that the gifts begin to appear in a believer's life. A second group of Christians believe that the "baptism of the Spirit" comes at water baptism, pointing to Jesus' water baptism described in Matthew 3:16–17, and to Acts 19:5–6 where the Holy Spirit came shortly after water baptism. Both these groups believe that the rest of the verses in Acts on Holy Spirit baptism actually describe exceptions to the usual manner of receiving the Spirit, which they believe normally occurs at conversion or at water baptism. Since the power and gifts received at that earlier time may not appear for many years, these Christians believe that we may have to pray and ask God to show them forth in our lives.

A third group of Christians believe that the Acts passages show that the power and gifts may be received at any time, but that usually they are received at a time separate from conversion and water baptism (Acts 2:4; 8:17; 1 Timothy 4:14; 2 Timothy 1:6). They believe that the Holy Spirit's power will come if one asks and prays for it. It is available to all who ask, they say. They also believe that to receive this power it helps to ask the leaders of the church to lay on their hands and pray (Acts 8:17; 19:6).

Another question arises here: How important is the gift of tongues in our lives? Those holding the three views expressed above all agree that the gift of tongues is one of the many signs of having received the Holy Spirit. The gift of tongues is the ability to speak in a special language given by the Spirit, one not previously learned (1 Corinthians 12:10; 14:1–5). In the New Testament, almost all those who received the baptism of the Holy Spirit did, in fact, speak and praise God in another language (Mark 16:17; Acts 2:4; 10:46; 19:6; 1 Corinthians 14:18). But there are different opinions as to whether this gift is for all believers or for only a few.

Some Christians believe that God desires only a few people to speak in a special tongue. It is a fact that many spiritual Christians have not received this gift. Paul himself said, **Do all speak in tongues?** (1 Corinthians 12:30). Paul's meaning is that all do not speak in tongues. Christians holding this view may believe that it is right to ask God for the gift of tongues, since many blessings can be received through this gift. But they point out that it is not written clearly in the Bible that all are, in fact, required to speak in tongues.

However, other Christians believe that the main sign or proof of the baptism of the Holy Spirit is the ability to speak in a special language. They point out that Paul also wrote that he wanted all the Corinthians to speak in another tongue (1 Corinthians 14:5). Therefore, these Christians believe that there are two kinds of tongue speaking gifts: the first, a gift of speaking God's message to others in public, which is given only to a few and should be accompanied by the interpretation (1 Corinthians 14:1–5,13,26–27); and second, a personal worship gift of praising and praying to God oneself, which is given to all believers (1 Corinthians 14:2,15–17). In their opinion, 1 Corinthians 12:30 refers only to the first "message-giving" kind of tongues. In other words, in a church service only a few will be called to give a special message to the congregation by speaking in another tongue. However, according to these Christians, all should be able to praise and pray "to God" in another tongue without interpretation (1 Corinthians 14:2,28), and to receive blessings through this personal gift.

Other Christians hold to a third view that although God does give the ability to speak in this personal kind of tongue at the time of the baptism of the Holy Spirit, not everyone will use it right away. Some may not know about this gift; others may not use it for some other reason. These Christians do not believe that tongues is the only sign of the baptism of the Holy Spirit; any gift of the Spirit can be a sign that the Spirit's power has come into our lives. This third view agrees with the first view that everyone is not required to speak in tongues, but agrees with the second view that God desires everyone to have the personal gift of tongues for prayer and praise.

Summary

However we think about the power and gifts of the Holy Spirit, we must remember: 1) the power and gifts were given for the common good (1 Corinthians 12:7; 14:3) and for power to witness to others (Acts 1:8); 2) they must be used in love and in a controlled manner, or they are worth nothing (1 Corinthians 13:1–3; 14:40); 3) they are to be desired and should not be forbidden (1 Corinthians 12:31; 14:1,39); 4) they should not divide us (1 Corinthians 12:4–6). In spite of different beliefs about the gifts of the Spirit, we are brothers and sisters in Christ. In Christ we are **one** (1 Corinthians 12:13; Galatians 3:28).

WATER BAPTISM

Main Verses

Matthew 28:19–20 . . . **make disciples . . . baptizing them in the name of the Father and of the Son and of the Holy Spirit.**

Mark 16:16 **Whoever believes and is baptized will be saved.**

John 3:5 . . . **no one can enter the kingdom of God unless he is born of water and the Spirit.**

Acts 2:38 **Repent and be baptized . . . so that your sins may be forgiven.**

Acts 22:16 . . . **be baptized and wash your sins away, calling on his name.**

Romans 6:3–4 **We were therefore buried with him through baptism.**

Galatians 3:27 . . . **all of you who were baptized into Christ have clothed yourselves with Christ.**

Ephesians 5:25–26 **Christ loved the church . . . cleansing her by the washing with water through the word.**

Titus 3:5 . . . **he (Christ) saved us through the washing of rebirth and renewal by the Holy Spirit.**

Hebrews 10:22 . . . **let us draw near to God . . . having our hearts sprinkled to cleanse us from a guilty conscience and having our bodies washed with pure water.**

1 Peter 3:21 . . . **this water** (the water of the flood in Noah's time) **symbolizes baptism that now saves you also. . . . It saves you by the resurrection of Jesus Christ.**

What Is Water Baptism?

Water baptism is the application of water to a person by sprinkling, pouring, or immersion **in the name of the Father and of the Son and of the Holy Spirit** as commanded by the Lord Jesus in Matthew 28:19.

The Old Testament Jews practiced a ceremony similar to baptism. This was CIRCUMCISION of the male child's foreskin on the eighth day of life (Genesis 17:10–14). Paul said that believers in Christ do not have to practice physical circumcision (Acts 15:1–29; Galatians 5:2). Most Bible scholars believe that the meaning of Colossians

2:11–12 is that water baptism has replaced physical circumcision and is related to our "spiritual circumcision" by Christ Himself, in which our old sinful nature is "cut off" and thrown away.

John the Baptist practised a **baptism of repentance for the forgiveness of sins** (Mark 1:4), but this was not Christian baptism. After Jesus' death and RESURRECTION, John's baptism was not considered adequate for Christians (Acts 18:25), and the Ephesians who had previously received John's baptism were rebaptized **into the name of the Lord Jesus** (Acts 19:1–7). However, there is only one Christian baptism (Ephesians 4:5).

Jesus Himself was baptized by John in the Jordan River (Matthew 3:13–17). Although without sin and without the need for repentance, Jesus was baptized **to fulfill all righteousness** (Matthew 3:15). Indeed, after His water baptism, the HOLY SPIRIT descended on Jesus, empowering Him for service and ministry (Mark 1:10).

Jesus described His death on the CROSS as a "baptism" (Luke 12:50). Jesus' baptism of death and His resurrection is the basis for our baptism, the reason we are able to be baptized (Romans 6:3–4; Colossians 2:12; 1 Peter 3:21).

From the very beginning, the church has followed Jesus' command and baptized new believers. Notable examples of Christian baptism in the New Testament are found in Acts 2:41; 8:12; 8:38; 10:48; 16:15; 16:33; 19:1–5. In many of these verses, water baptism followed immediately after profession of faith in Christ. Several were baptisms of entire households (Acts 10:48; 16:31–33).

Baptism is not unique to the Christian religion. Before the time of Christ, non-Jewish converts to the Jewish religion were often baptized in water. And some of the Greek "mystery" religions at the time of Christ required baptism, sometimes with blood being allowed to drip over the recipient instead of water.

Why Do We Baptize With Water?

Jesus commanded us to baptize new believers (Matthew 28:19). In all cultures and countries, water baptism has been viewed as the act of conversion from one's old religion to Christianity. It is one of the initial steps in SALVATION (Acts 2:38). Jesus also connected the promise of salvation to baptism (Mark 16:16). In the history of the church, there have been many different opinions about how salvation is connected with baptism.

Many Christians believe that baptism is one of the "means of grace," one of the ways God's GRACE is given to us. The most important means of grace is the word of God (Romans 10:17; 1 Peter 1:23). These Christians believe that God's grace comes to us through water baptism also. Even in water baptism the important thing is

God's written word (Ephesians 5:26). These Christians talk of baptism as having an outward and visible sign (the water) and an inward and spiritual gift (union with Christ's death and resurrection, forgiveness of sins, and membership in the church through the Spirit). These Christians believe that through baptism, received in faith, our life is truly buried and resurrected with Christ (Romans 6:3–4; Colossians 2:12) and clothed with Christ (Galatians 3:27). Since in Acts 2:38 Peter calls us to be baptized **so that** [our] **sins may be forgiven**, these Christians believe that through water baptism we receive forgiveness of sins in a special way. In 1 Peter 3:21, Peter wrote of a **baptism that now saves you also. . . . It saves you by the resurrection of Jesus Christ**. Peter said that this baptism was not a **removal of dirt from the body**, but rather a spiritual washing that results in a **good conscience**. Therefore, these Christians say that in baptism our sins are actually "washed away" and our consciences are truly "cleansed" (Acts 22:16; Ephesians 5:26; Titus 3:5; Hebrews 10:22). In their view, baptism actually is our spiritual circumcision, our **putting off of the sinful nature** (Colossians 2:11–12). Jesus said, "**. . . no one can enter the Kingdom of God unless he is born of water and the Spirit**" (John 3:5). These Christians believe that "water" in this verse refers to baptism. The water alone has no effect, but baptism is water used as God commanded with His word of promise (Mark 16:16; Ephesians 5:26), and for this reason it becomes effective.[1] In baptism God offers and gives His grace, but this grace must be received by faith. Without faith in God's word of promise, we receive no benefits. Water baptism itself strengthens our faith in God's word of promise.[2]

Many other Christians do not believe there is any special grace available in water baptism. Since many verses in Scripture only mention faith in Jesus (John 1:12; 3:16; Romans 10:9–10) or faith in the word of God (Romans 1:16; 10:17; 1 Peter 1:23) as the way to receive God's blessings, these Christians believe that the word of God is the only "means of grace." Hearing the word of God and believing in Jesus is all we need to receive salvation. These Christians believe that water baptism is only a sign or symbol of what happens when we believe. In their view, baptism does not truly cleanse us or bring forgiveness in a special way. It is only a symbol of our death with Christ, of being clothed with Christ, and of being circumcised by Christ (Romans 6:3–5; Galatians 3:27; Colossians 2:11–12). It is only an outward sign of what takes place when we believe. Some believe that being **born of water** in John 3:5

---

[1] The Jordan River had no healing power in itself for Naaman, but when used in obedience as God had commanded, Naaman was healed (2 Kings 5:9–14).

[2] Some of these Christians say that baptism is a "means of grace" because baptism is a special way to increase our faith.

refers to physical birth; others believe **water** refers to the word of God. Some of these Christians also say that baptism is a witness to the world of one's faith in Christ; therefore, it must be done publicly, not privately. Some of these Christians believe that baptism is a sign of God's COVENANT with His people as a group, just as circumcision in the Old Testament was a sign of God's covenant with the JEWS. They point to Colossians 2:11–13 to support this view.

Concerning the meaning of baptism, some true spiritual Christians have believed one view and some the other. All believe that they are following the teaching of the Bible. Whichever view we hold, we should not judge and condemn one another.

Related to this, several further questions arise regarding the necessity and the permanence of baptism. The first question is: What happens if a believer dies without being baptized? The Bible does not say for sure. Almost all Christians believe that that person is saved. According to Mark 16:16, it is unbelief that damns a person, not lack of baptism. And the dying criminal in Luke 23:40–43 was promised **paradise**, even though he had no chance to be baptized. However, the church has always believed that one who refuses baptism is in a dangerous position. Does that person have true faith? If we knowingly continue to refuse Christ's command, we will not enter the kingdom of heaven (Matthew 7:21). Therefore, when the church leaders are ready to baptize someone, that person should not delay, but take the first opportunity to receive baptism.

A second question is this: If a baptized believer rebels against God and lives a life of sin but later repents and returns to Christ, does he need to be baptized again? The church has always answered "No." There is only one baptism (Ephesians 4:5). After God has made us His children, we may rebel and lose the benefits of being a child of God. If we later repent, we do not need to be readopted, but only forgiven (Luke 15:11–24). God is faithful, even if we are unfaithful (Romans 3:3; 11:29; 2 Corinthians 1:20).

There is a related question: When we have been baptized in one church, do we need to be rebaptized when we join another church? The answer is no. There is only one Christian baptism (Ephesians 4:5). A believer who has been baptized **in the name of the Father and of the Son and of the Holy Spirit** (Matthew 28:19) does not need to be baptized again.

Baptism of Children

Different customs related to the baptism of children have been followed in the church. In church history, the earliest recorded discussions of baptism mention infant baptism and claim it was a tradition handed down by the apostles. By 250 AD, it was the universal custom in the churches. However, after the Protestant

Reformation in the 1500s, some of the Protestant churches believed that baptism should only be given to adults and older children. Many churches today follow this practice. Christians in these churches point out that there are no clear examples of infant baptism in the Bible. They believe baptism should be only for those who can be taught about Christian beliefs and can confess with their mouth that **Jesus is Lord** (Romans 10:9–10). Repentance should be first, followed by baptism (Acts 2:38). They call this "believer's baptism" (Acts 8:37). They believe that infants can neither repent nor have true faith; therefore, small children are not eligible for baptism. In most of these churches the earliest age for the baptism of believing children is around ten or twelve years. A few churches will baptize as early as age five or six, if the child can declare his faith clearly. Most of these churches that do not baptize infants have developed an infant dedication ceremony in place of baptism.

However, many other Protestants continue to baptize infants of believing parents shortly after birth. These Christians point out that the Bible contains no examples of an infant dedication rite in the early church. Nor is there any reference to a child of Christian parents coming later to be baptized. They note that entire households were baptized, and it would be a rare household that did not include children (Acts 16:15; 16:33; 1 Corinthians 1:16). They believe that baptism is similar to the circumcision of males in the Old Testament, which was for both Jewish infants and also adult converts to Judaism. When parents brought their newborn **babies** and **children** to Jesus, He said, **"Let the little children come to me . . . for the kingdom of God belongs to such as these"** (Mark 10:13–16; Luke 18:16–17). Therefore, these churches believe that Jesus' command to make disciples, **baptizing them in the name of the Father and of the Son and of the Holy Spirit**, refers not only to baptizing adult converts but also to baptizing infants and children (Matthew 28:19; Acts 2:39).

The question centers around the meaning of baptism itself. Does infant baptism fit in with the meaning of baptism? Those Christians who believe baptism is a way to receive God's grace usually practice infant baptism. Some of these believe that infants also can (and do) have faith (see General Article: Children and the Kingdom of God). Others believe that the parents' faith is enough (as the Jews believed in the case of circumcision in the Old Testament). However, after becoming an adult, the baptized person must have faith in Christ in order to have salvation. Those churches which believe baptism is only a symbol may or may not baptize infants. If they believe that New Testament baptism has replaced Old Testament circumcision as a sign of the covenant God makes with a group of people, they usually practice infant baptism. If they believe that baptism is a public witness to the world of one's personal faith, or that one must be able to confess faith in Christ with one's mouth, then they will wait until one is old enough to declare his faith in Jesus.

Which Method of Baptism Is Correct?

There are three main methods of baptism: immersion, sprinkling, and pouring. In most churches sprinkling or pouring of water on the head of the recipient is practiced. If infants are baptized, sprinkling or pouring is usually used, although infant immersion has been practiced in the past. For adults, all three methods have been used. Very ill adults or those in unfavorable habitats of the world, such as deserts and ice-locked lands, usually do not receive baptism by immersion. However, in one place or another, all three methods have been practiced since the days of the early church.

The Bible itself does not state exactly how baptism should be performed. Baptism in the New Testament usually was done in rivers (Mark 1:5), or where there was **plenty of water** (John 3:23). Baptism by immersion would have been easy in such places, and probably was the usual practice. But at times, immersion would have been very difficult. For example, the Ethiopian was baptized in a desert place (Acts 8:36–38). The Philippian jailor and his household were baptized in the middle of the night between washing Paul's wounds and giving him food (Acts 16:33). And three thousand converts were baptized at one time on the day of Pentecost (Acts 2:41). Because of the difficulties, many Bible scholars believe that in these cases the water was either sprinkled or poured.

The Greek[3] word for baptism itself has several meanings. The most common meaning is "immersion." The symbol of our death and burial with Christ (Romans 6:3–4) is most clearly portrayed by immersion. Therefore, many churches baptize only by immersion. However, "immersion" is not the only meaning of the word "baptism." The ceremonial washing mentioned in Mark 7:3–4 is described using the Greek word for baptism and the Greek word which means "sprinkling " (see Luke 11:38–39). The "baptism of the Holy Spirit" (Acts 1:5) that the Gentiles also received is described as a "pouring out" of the Spirit (Acts 2:17–18; 10:44–45). The Bible also talks of **having our hearts sprinkled to cleanse us from a guilty conscience** (Ezekiel 36:25; Hebrews 10:22), which many Christians believe refers to water baptism. Therefore, many churches baptize by sprinkling or pouring.

---

[3] The New Testament was originally written in the Greek language.

Summary

Three major questions related to baptism have been discussed in this article: 1) What is the meaning of baptism—is it a means of receiving grace, or is it only a symbol? 2) Is baptism for infants also, or only for older children and adults? 3) Are all three methods of applying the water equally valid, or is only immersion valid? Only after studying the Scriptures involved should we decide any of these questions. And whatever we decide, we should not judge or condemn other Christians if they should decide differently. The Bible does not give unequivocal answers to these questions. Our own beliefs about baptism should not separate us from our brother or sister for whom Christ died. **There is one body and one Spirit—just as you were called—one Lord, one faith, one baptism, one God and Father of all, who is over all and through all and in all** (Ephesians 4:4–6).

THE LORD'S SUPPER

Main Verses

Matthew 26:26–29 Jesus' last feast, the first Lord's Supper.
Mark 14:22–25 Jesus' last feast, the first Lord's Supper.
Luke 22:17–20 Jesus' last feast, and the first command to observe the Lord's Supper.
John 6:48–59 Jesus' body and blood for us to eat and drink.
1 Corinthians 10:16–17 Participation in the body and blood of Christ.
1 Corinthians 11:17–34 Partaking of the Lord's Supper in a worthy manner.

What Is the Lord's Supper?

The Lord's Supper, or Communion, was first celebrated by our Lord on the day before He died. It was the PASSOVER meal of the Passover festival, which took place during the last week of Jesus' life. God had commanded the Jews to observe the Passover every year as a remembrance and celebration of their deliverance from EGYPT (Exodus 12:1–20). God commanded that only unleavened bread be eaten during the Passover festival. In 1 Corinthians 5:7, Paul states that Christ became our Passover sacrifice. Therefore, Christians celebrate the Lord's Supper instead of Passover itself.

Jesus commanded us to observe the Lord's Supper. In the Gospels this command is recorded only in Luke 22:19. But Paul emphasizes this command in 1 Corinthians 11:23–25. The first Christians celebrated the Lord's Supper frequently (Acts 2:42; 20:7).

Looking at all four accounts of the first Lord's Supper in Matthew, Mark, Luke, and 1 Corinthians, we can see that none of them records all of Jesus' words. But we can make a composite record by combining the four accounts as follows:

> **Take and eat; this is my body, given for you; do this in remembrance of me. This cup is the new covenant in my blood [or] this is my blood of the covenant, which is poured out for many for the forgiveness of sins. Drink from it, all of you . . . do this, whenever you drink it, in remembrance of**

me (Matthew 26:26–29; Mark 14:22–25; Luke 22:17–20; 1 Corinthians 11:23–25).

Many different ways of observing the Lord's Supper have been practiced throughout the history of the church. In many churches today, the Lord's Supper is celebrated every week. Many other churches today observe the Lord's Supper three or four times a year. Many churches use an unleavened bread and an actual wine, as was the custom during the Jewish Passover feast of Jesus' time. But many other churches use a leavened bread and a non-fermented juice instead. There is usually a time of confession of sin beforehand. Many churches serve the elements in the front of the church, while in other churches the elements are served where the partakers are sitting. Many large churches use individual small cups, while other churches prefer to use one or more common cups, as in the first Lord's Supper. A few churches even practice foot washing beforehand (John 13:1–17).

The Body and Blood of Jesus

Jesus said, "**This is my body. . . . This is my blood**." Christians have different opinions about what this means. Many Christians believe that Jesus' actual body and blood becomes present in or through the bread and wine in a supernatural, spiritual way. These Christians point to 1 Corinthians 10:16, where it says that the bread and cup are a **participation** in the body and blood of Jesus. They also point to 1 Corinthians 11:27,29, where Paul says that we are **guilty of sinning against the body and blood of the Lord** if we eat in an unworthy manner. Jesus said, "**For my flesh is real food and my blood is real drink. Whoever eats my flesh and drinks my blood remains in me, and I in him**"[1] (John 6:55–56).

Many other Christians do not believe that Jesus' actual body and blood are present at the Lord's Supper. Since Jesus had not yet died on the cross when He first instituted the Lord's Supper, they believe that Jesus meant, "This represents my body," and "This represents my blood." These Christians believe that John 6:55–56 does not refer to actual eating of Jesus' body and blood but to believing in Jesus. In John 6:35, Jesus says: "**He who comes to me will never go hungry, and he who believes in me will never be thirsty**." These Christians, then, say that to partake of Jesus' body and blood is the same as to **believe** in Him.

[1] Some of these Christians believe that Jesus' physical body and blood are actually "present" for us in the bread and wine. Others believe that in communion the Holy Spirit makes believers "present" to Jesus' physical body and blood in heaven.

Why Do We Celebrate the Lord's Supper?

Jesus commanded us to celebrate the Lord's Supper. But there are times when a person should not participate in it. In 1 Corinthians 11:27, Paul tells us we must not partake of the Lord's Supper **in an unworthy manner**. Since none of us in ourselves are worthy of Jesus' death and forgiveness, how do we partake in a "worthy manner"? The answer is that we must first examine ourselves, confess our sins, and repent. Only then should we partake in the Lord's Supper (1 Corinthians 11:28–31; 1 John 1:9).

Therefore, a person who is living in a state of unconfessed sin should not join in the Lord's Supper. If he does, he is **guilty of sinning against the body and blood of the Lord** (1 Corinthians 11:27). Such a person **eats and drinks judgment on himself**, and this can result in weakness, sickness, or even death (1 Corinthians 11:29–30). This is a serious matter. Many churches do not allow a member living in unconfessed sin to partake in the Lord's Supper, since it would cause him to bring judgment on himself. Although it is dangerous to partake in the Lord's Supper without repentance, it is even more dangerous to refuse to repent! If we have sinned, we need to confess, repent, and then to come to the Lord's table.

All Christians believe that the Lord's Supper is a time of remembering Christ's death with confession and repentance, because Jesus asked us to remember His death when we eat and drink at His table (1 Corinthians 11:24–25). In celebrating the Lord's Supper, we not only remember Christ's death, but we also proclaim to others the grace that comes from His death. Paul wrote that **whenever you eat this bread and drink this cup, you proclaim the Lord's death until he comes** (1 Corinthians 11:26). Because of Christ's death, we receive forgiveness and eternal life; by partaking in the Lord's Supper we show our gratitude for these blessings. But we also look forward to Christ's second coming, since we will keep on celebrating the Lord's Supper **until he comes** (1 Corinthians 11:26).

Many Christians call the Lord's Supper "Holy Communion." This is in recognition of our fellowship with Christ. Jesus said, "**Whoever eats my flesh and drinks my blood remains in me, and I in him**" (John 6:56). However, this fellowship is not only with Christ but with our fellow believers also. We share in Christ's body; therefore, we also share in each other. There is one loaf—that is, Christ Jesus—and although we are many, **we . . . are one body, for we all partake of one loaf** (1 Corinthians 10:17).

In addition, many Christians believe that the Lord's Supper is also a "means of grace," one of the ways by which God's GRACE is given to us.[2] Just as we can receive real judgment through the Lord's Supper (1 Corinthians 11:27–32), so we can also receive real blessings. These Christians believe that in the Lord's Supper we receive forgiveness of sins in a special way. Jesus said, "**This is my blood of the covenant, which is poured out for many for the forgiveness of sins**" (Matthew 26:28). Jesus also said, "**Whoever eats my flesh and drinks my blood has eternal life**" and "**remains in me, and I in him**" (John 6:54–56). Therefore, these Christians believe that in the Lord's Supper God gives us His grace in a special way; this grace consists of forgiveness of sins, union with Christ, and eternal life. They say that the bread and wine are outward and visible signs of an inward and spiritual grace. Partaking of the bread and wine alone does nothing; it is partaking through faith that we receive the inward grace of the Lord's Supper. If we partake without faith, we do not receive grace; rather, we receive **judgment** (1 Corinthians 11:27–32).

Many other Christians do not believe there is any special grace available in the Lord's Supper. They believe God's grace is available to us only through the written word of God; they do not believe God gives His grace through special means or ceremonies. When we believe in Jesus by faith, we are then "eating His body and drinking His blood" in a spiritual way, not physically. They believe that the Lord's Supper is special only in the sense that we as a church body come together to remember Christ's death; it is only an act of corporate worship and witness.

Summary

Christians should make up their minds on these questions after studying the verses involved. There are two main questions. First, do we receive Jesus' actual body and blood during the Lord's Supper, or not? Second, we remember Christ's death and confess our sins when we partake in the Lord's Supper, but do we also receive God's forgiveness in a special way? Whatever we decide on these questions, we should not condemn our brother or sister if they have a different belief from ours. We all celebrate the Lord's Supper. Our own beliefs about its meaning should not separate us from our brother and sister for whom Christ died. Many believe that in 1 Corinthians 12:13 Paul is referring to water baptism and the Lord's Supper when he says that we are **one body**, having been **baptized . . . into one body** and made to **drink** of **one Spirit**. The Lord's Supper should bring us together, not separate us.

---

[2] These Christians believe that water baptism also is a means of grace. But other Christians believe differently (see General Article: Water Baptism).

Whether or not the blood of Christ is actually present in the Lord's Supper, Jesus asked us to remember His death and all it did for us. We cannot begin to count all that Jesus' death—His blood—has done for us: justification (Romans 5:9), redemption and forgiveness (Ephesians 2:13; Colossians 1:20), cleansing of conscience (Hebrews 9:14), access to mercy (Hebrews 10:19), purification from sins (1 John 1:7), and an overcoming victory (Revelation 12:11). The blood of Christ—what a precious thing!

CHURCH GOVERNMENT

Main Verses

Acts 6:1–6 The apostles and the first deacons.
1 Corinthians 12:28 Ministries in the church: **God has appointed first of all apostles, second prophets, third teachers, then . . . those able to help others, those with gifts of administration. . . .**
Ephesians 2:20 The church is **built on the foundation of the apostles and prophets, with Christ Jesus himself as the chief cornerstone.**
Ephesians 4:11–13 Christ gave to the church **apostles . . . prophets . . . evangelists . . . pastors and teachers.**
1 Timothy 3:1–13 Qualifications for bishops and deacons.
1 Timothy 5:17–20 The work, pay, and discipline of elders.
Titus 1:5–9 Qualifications for elders and bishops.

The Church

The word "CHURCH" in Greek means a "gathering" or "assembly" of people who are "called out" for a special purpose. The Christian church is "called out" by God to be a people for Him (1 Peter 2:9–10). The word "church" can refer to a gathering of believers in a local area, and also to the entire company of believers throughout the world. Wherever three or four believers gather together, there is a local church. All the believers of the world make up the universal, spiritual church. Those who profess to believe in Jesus and are baptized in His name become members of a church (1 Corinthians 12:13), but only God can know who truly believes (Matthew 13:24–30,36–43).

The church was established on a foundation laid by the apostles and prophets, with Jesus Christ as the chief cornerstone (Matthew 16:18; 1 Corinthians 3:11; Ephesians 2:19–22; 1 Peter 2:4–8). It was founded by the Holy Spirit (Acts 2:1–4,36–41). The Holy Spirit indwells the church; the church is God's temple (1 Corinthians 3:16; Ephesians 2:22). Elsewhere, the church is called the "bride of Christ" (2 Corinthians 11:2; Ephesians 5:22–32; Revelation 19:7). The church is also called the "body of Christ" (Romans 12:4–5;

1 Corinthians 12:27), with Jesus Christ as the **Head** (Ephesians 4:15–16; 5:23; Colossians 1:18).

Jesus Himself gave leaders to the church: apostles, prophets, evangelists, pastors and teachers (Ephesians 4:11). God appointed the many ministries in the church (1 Corinthians 12:28), and the Holy Spirit gave His special gifts and power to enable the work to be done (1 Corinthians 12:7–11).

However, we read in the Bible of deacons, elders, bishops, and councils as well. How did all these leaders or groups work together? How has the church been governed?

Church Leadership in the Bible

In Ephesians 4:11, Paul writes of several kinds of leaders, the first of which are APOSTLES. The word "apostle" in Greek means simply "one who is sent." The original twelve apostles were chosen by Jesus (Mark 3:13–19). They were special, having been witnesses of Jesus' ministry, death, resurrection, and ascension (Acts 1:21–22). Paul defended his apostleship on the basis of his having seen the risen Christ (1 Corinthians 9:1–2; 15:5–11). These apostles often moved from place to place founding many new churches. They provided the church with much of the New Testament Scriptures, and had final authority in the church. However, the Bible also calls certain other people "apostles," such as Barnabas (1 Corinthians 9:5–6), James, the brother of Jesus (Galatians 1:19), Silas and Timothy (1 Thessalonians 1:1; 2:6–7), and others (Romans 16:7; Revelation 2:2).

Second in Paul's list of leaders in Ephesians 4:11 are PROPHETS. Like the Old Testament prophets, they gave the word of God, which they had received directly from Him (1 Corinthians 14:30). This included exhortation for encouragement, strengthening, and comfort (Acts 15:32; 1 Corinthians 14:3,31), as well as prediction of the future (Acts 11:28; 21:10–11). Prophecy is listed as one of the gifts of the Holy Spirit to believers in 1 Corinthians 12:8–10. Paul taught that their "word" must be subject to the judgment of others in the congregation (1 Corinthians 14:29–33). There were many such prophets in the early church, both men and women (Acts 11:27–28; 13:1; 15:32; 21:9–10; 1 Corinthians 11:4–5; 1 Timothy 4:14).

Third in Paul's list of leaders in Ephesians 4:11 are **evangelists**. The term means "one who tells the good news." Philip, one of the first seven deacons (or helpers), was also called an evangelist (Acts 21:8). He was especially able to bring the good news, or GOSPEL, to new areas and people (Acts 8:5–8; 8:26–40). Although called an "apostle," Timothy was commanded to **do the work of an evangelist** (2 Timothy 4:5).

"Pastors" and "teachers" are mentioned last, and refer to the shepherding, counseling, preaching and teaching leaders in the church.

The church has sent out missionaries from the very beginning (Acts 13:1–3; 15:22,32; 18:27). Since the word "apostle" means "one sent," some Christians believe missionaries are actually apostles, especially those missionaries who establish new churches. But other missionaries seem to be more like evangelists or teachers; perhaps missionaries constitute a different office altogether (see General Article: Purpose of the Church).

The term "elder" was first used to refer to the leaders in the Jerusalem church (Acts 11:30). Their responsibility was to rule and lead a particular local church. At the end of their first missionary journey, Paul and Barnabas appointed elders in each church they had founded earlier (Acts 14:23). The apostles were included among the elders in Jerusalem, and both Peter (1 Peter 5:1) and John (2 and 3 John) call themselves elders. Therefore, the word "elder" did not exclude other functions. The elders were to direct the affairs of the church (1 Timothy 5:17), shepherd and guard the church (Acts 20:28–31; 1 Peter 5:1–4), anoint the sick with oil (James 5:14), and some were to teach and preach as well (1 Timothy 5:17).

"Bishop" was a term used by Paul in his later letters. The term means an "overseer." Paul refers to bishops in the Philippian church (Philippians 1:1), and lists the qualifications for bishops in 1 Timothy Chapter 3 and in Titus Chapter 1.

Many Christian scholars believe that the words "elder" and "bishop" refer to the same office. They believe that the term "elder" refers to the position, and the term "bishop" refers to the ministry or work done by persons in that position. They point to Acts 20:17,28, where Paul speaks to a group of elders and calls them "bishops," and to 1 Peter 5:1–2, where Peter asks the elders to serve as bishops.

Many other Christian scholars believe that elders and bishops already had separate functions in the early church. They point to the two lists of qualifications in Titus Chapter 1, a short one for elders and longer one for bishops, both lists starting with **blameless** (see Titus 1:5–9). They also point to the separate discussions of bishops and of elders in 1 Timothy 3:1–7 and 5:17–20. Only some elders taught (1 Timothy 5:17), but all bishops were supposed to be **able to teach** (1 Timothy 3:2). These Christians believe that all bishops were elders, but that not all elders were bishops. In other words, some of the elders were given the office of bishop, and the rest of the elders were assistants to the bishop.

There were also "deacons" in the church (1 Timothy 3:8). The first deacons are mentioned in Acts 6:1–6. The term "deacon" means "one who serves." Deacons were chosen to administer the worldly affairs of the church and to look after the poor and the sick. Paul listed the qualifications for deacons in 1 Timothy 3:8–13. Although they did the more normal daily work and service of the church, they were chosen on the basis of both their wisdom and their filling by the Holy Spirit (Acts 6:3). For example, Stephen (Acts 6:5,8–10) and Philip (Acts 6:5; 8:4–8) were two deacons who had great spiritual ministries.

We should remember that although the leaders of the church are given special authority and responsibility, all the church members should be continually witnessing about Christ to others and, when needed, helping in God's work.

Church Government

There have been four main types of government in the history of the church. They may be described on the basis of who is actually ruling or in control. The ultimate authority may rest 1) with a bishop who watches over a number of local churches, or 2) with a group of elders who watch over a single church or a group of churches, or 3) with a single pastor who runs his own church, or 4) with the entire congregation as a group. All four types of church government are based on various New Testament verses and each can be said to follow a Biblical pattern.

Christians of those churches in which authority rests with a bishop claim they are continuing the system of church government begun by the apostles. The apostles took responsibility to oversee many churches and the elders of those churches (Acts 8:14–17; 14:23), even to the point of "judging," "commanding," and using "authority" (1 Corinthians 5:3; 9:1–2; 2 Corinthians 10:1–11; 2 Thessalonians 3:14; Titus 1:5). These Christians point to the bishop-like role of Timothy and Titus, who were chosen by Paul to have authority over the churches in Ephesus and Crete (1 Timothy 1:3; 5:19–22; Titus 1:5; 3:10). They also note the importance of the church councils in Jerusalem (Acts Chapters 11 and 15), with Peter and James leading and passing judgment. Under the authority of the bishop, local churches have their pastors, elders, and deacons, but the main authority is in the hands of the bishop.

Christians of those churches in which authority rests with a group of local elders believe that the apostles were given to the church for the first century only, and that the system of elders was intended to be the permanent form of government in the church (Acts 14:23; Titus 1:5). They consider the terms "elder" and "bishop" to refer to the same position. In these churches some are "ruling elders" and some are "teaching elders" (1 Timothy 5:17). There may be a group of deacons as well. Many of these churches are part of an organizational structure in which a larger group of elders have authority over a number of churches at one time, or in which the elders of many churches meet together and decide issues that affect all of their churches.

In the third form of church government, authority rests with a single elder or pastor. These churches emphasize the autonomy of the local church. They do not believe anyone outside the local church can rule over it. Although these churches may have a group of elders and deacons to help the pastor direct the church, the final authority rests with the pastor. These churches point to the authority Paul exercised in local congregations, when he stopped on his missionary journeys and spent several years preaching and teaching in one church. Paul did this more than once (Acts 18:11; 19:10; 20:31). Timothy probably acted as this kind of pastor at Ephesus as well (1 Timothy 1:3; 4:11–14).

The fourth form of church government places the authority of the local church in the hands of the entire membership of the church. Although these churches share in the opinion of the third group above that the local church is independent, they differ in that they believe no single person is in a position to rule over other believers. Christians who hold this opinion point to the fact that Christ alone is the "head" of the church (Colossians 1:18), and that Jesus commanded us to call no one "master," "father," or "teacher" (Matthew 23:8–10). All believers are to be considered "priests" (1 Peter 2:9; Revelation 5:10). These Christians also point to verses which show the entire church involved in choosing leaders (Acts 6:3), teaching (1 Corinthians 14:26), and in discipline **by the majority** (Matthew 18:17; 1 Corinthians 5:4–5; 2 Corinthians 2:6). Therefore, these churches have general meetings in which all the members vote on every important issue. These churches may have a single pastor who does most of the preaching and teaching, but such a pastor does not have authority over the congregation. Some of these churches do not have any specific leadership, but divide the preaching and teaching responsibilities among the members of the congregation who are able to perform those functions.

Selection of Leaders

The qualifications for bishops, elders, and deacons are listed in 1 Timothy 3:1–13; Titus 1:5–9; Acts 6:1–6; and so they will not be discussed here. For discussion of those qualifications see the comments on the above passages. But here something must be said on the subject of how to appoint leaders.

During the time of the original apostles, the elders in new churches were appointed by the apostles themselves (Acts 14:23) or by their fellow workers, such as Timothy and Titus. The deacons mentioned in Acts 6:1–6 were chosen by the people, and Paul and Barnabas were selected by the Holy Spirit through His prophets

(Acts 13:1–3). On one occasion the church cast lots to decide who should replace the betrayer, Judas (Acts 1:23–26). The early church often fasted and prayed about appointing people to different offices or work, and then laid their hands on the ones chosen (Acts 6:6; 13:1–3; 14:23; 1 Timothy 4:14; 5:22). Frequently a prophecy preceded or accompanied this laying on of hands for service (Acts 13:1–3; 1 Timothy 1:18; 4:14).

Since the passing away of the original apostles, different churches have followed different customs. In those churches which are ruled by bishops, special study is required in order for one to become a church leader. In these churches, only the bishops may ordain new leaders, and they do so by prayer and by the laying on of hands.

Those churches which are ruled by a group of elders usually allow the congregations to have some choice in the selection of leaders for ministry, but only the elders may ordain, again often by prayer and the laying on of hands. They usually require special study as well.

Those churches which are ruled by a single pastor have usually been founded by that pastor. Often he has already studied and been ordained elsewhere. Such pastors usually choose their own assistant pastors, or their own succesors when they move on, but the advice of the congregation is often sought.

Those churches which are ruled by the entire membership may have a single pastor for preaching and teaching, but he is chosen by vote of the congregation at their general meeting; if his work is inadequate, he may be removed by the congregation as well. However, these churches may not have any special leaders at all, but only ordinary members who are chosen by the congregation to oversee some of the affairs of the church.

Summary

The Bible is not definite about which form of church government is best. If it had been definite, perhaps these different forms would not have arisen. Maybe all four forms of church government mentioned above are acceptable, and Christians merely need to use which one suits their individual circumstances the best. Whatever our belief about church government, however, we must not condemn our brother or sister for having a different opinion from our own. Let all churches govern in their own way, but let fellowship and cooperation continue between all of them, regardless of which form of government they choose.

The Bible is clear that whatever form of leadership we have, the members have a responsibility to respect their leaders (1 Thessalonians 5:12), to submit to them (1 Peter 5:5), and to obey them (Hebrews 13:17). The teaching of the leaders may be tested or judged (Acts 17:11; 1 Corinthians 14:29; 1 John 4:1; Revelation 2:2), but an accusation against a leader must be rejected unless raised by two or three witnesses (1 Timothy 5:19). Finally, if necessary, we must financially support our leaders (Matthew 10:9–13; 1 Corinthians 9:3–11; 1 Timothy 5:17–18).

WOMEN IN THE CHURCH

Main Verses

Judges 4:4 Deborah, a prophetess, the leader and judge of Israel.
Acts 1:14; 2:1–4,16–18; 21:8–9 The Holy Spirit and the gift of prophecy is for women also.
Romans 16:1,7 Phoebe, a deacon? Junia, an apostle?
1 Corinthians 11:3–16 (especially verse 5) Women praying and prophesying.
1 Corinthians 14:26–40 (especially verses 26, 34–35) Women disturbing the service.
Galatians 3:26–28 Men and women are equal before God.
1 Timothy 2:11–15 Women are not to teach or have authority over men.
1 Timothy 3:11–13 Women as workers in the church.

What Is the Work of Women in the Church?

Throughout most of church history women have not been allowed to lead the church. The preachers, teachers, and pastors of the church have usually been men. Even so, in certain parts of the world, women have occasionally led or taught the church. In the past few hundred years there have been increasing numbers of women involved in the preaching, teaching, and pastoring of churches. This has happened at the same time that many societies of the world have allowed more freedom to their women.

What does the Bible say about women leading the church? It is not very clear. Many churches do not allow women to preach or to be a pastor, although most of these churches allow women to preach and teach as missionaries. On the other hand, many other churches today allow women to preach, teach, and even to be pastors and bishops.

Women Praying and Prophesying in the Church

In Galatians 3:28, Paul clearly wrote that men and women are **one in Christ Jesus**. We are all sinners in need of God's grace. Indeed, Galatians 3:28 was the most important verse supporting the fight against slavery by Christians in Western countries. However, even though men and women are one in Christ, this does not mean that they are identical in every respect. Men and women are equal before God, but their roles in the church may be different. Similarly, although husband and wife are both to submit to each other, their roles in a marriage may be different (see Ephesians 5:21–23; General Article: Christian Marriage).

Acts Chapters 1 and 2 make it clear that both men and women were present at PENTECOST when the HOLY SPIRIT descended upon Jesus' disciples to empower them. Peter quoted the prophet Joel, who stated that God would pour out His Holy Spirit on **both men and women** and that both **sons and daughters** would prophesy (Joel 2:28–29; Acts 2:16–18). There were many women prophets in the Old Testament (Exodus 15:20; Judges 4:4; 2 Kings 22:14; Nehemiah 6:14; Isaiah 8:3). In the New Testament, Philip the evangelist had four daughters who prophesied (Acts 21:8–9).

In 1 Corinthians 12:11, Paul also agreed that the Holy Spirit will give His gifts to all, not just to men. And in 1 Corinthians 11:5, Paul talked about women who were praying and prophesying in the church service in Corinth. When Paul said that women who prayed and prophesied in the church service must wear a veil on their head, he clearly implied that it was proper for women to pray and prophesy in the service. Paul said that all may participate and share in the church meeting (1 Corinthians 14:26), and this certainly included women.

Women As Deacons and As Fellow Workers

Many people believe that women can be deacons in the church. In 1 Timothy 3:8–13, Paul wrote about men and husbands. Verse 11 also mentions women. There are two possible kinds of women referred to in verse 11, either "wives" or "women deacons," and it is not certain which kind Paul meant. We do know that in Romans 16:1, Paul praised a woman named Phoebe and called her a servant or "deaconess." (The word is translated as "servant," but in the Greek[1] it is the same word as "deacon.")

In Romans 16:3,6,12 and Philippians 4:2–3, Paul greeted many other "fellow workers" who were women. Priscilla and her husband Aquila are always mentioned together and appear to have shared a teaching ministry (Acts 18:18,26). In addition, many scholars believe that in Romans 16:7 Paul is referring to "Junia," a woman, not to "Junius," a man. (The Greek word can be either masculine or feminine.). If the word refers to a woman, then Paul called a woman an "APOSTLE."

---

[1] The New Testament was originally written in the Greek language.

Women Leaders

Even if women may be deacons, the question remains whether or not women may lead the church in a pastoral role. The Bible does not give a completely clear answer to this question, and as a result, different churches today follow different customs. Many Christians point to 1 Corinthians 14:33–35 and to 1 Timothy 2:11–15, where women are told to be **silent** and not to **teach or to have authority over a man**. These verses say this very clearly, and many churches allow women to teach children and other women, but do not allow them to teach men. Almost all of these churches allow women to pray or share testimonies in church meetings, and most allow women missionaries to preach and to teach men in new churches.

Other Christians interpret these same Bible verses differently. They point out that at the same time Paul wrote these verses to the Corinthians saying that women must be silent, he also in the same letter wrote that when women pray and prophesy they must cover their heads (1 Corinthians 11:5). Therefore, these Christians believe that the meaning of 1 Corinthians 14:34–35 cannot be "complete silence"; rather it must mean "disturbance" or "speaking out loud" during the church service. In Paul's day it is possible that many women were accustomed to ask questions or call out to their husbands right in the middle of the service.[2]

Similarly, in 1 Timothy 2:11–15, this second group of Christians believe that Paul is telling Timothy that untaught women should not take authority away from men, but to be submissive and learn. They believe that the church may decide to give authority to a woman who has herself been taught and is a good teacher. Deborah in the Old Testament book of Judges was an example of a prophetess who led the Jews by God's will (Judges 4:4).

A third group of Christians believe that Paul's words were intended only for Timothy and the Corinthian and Ephesian churches of the first century. These Christians believe that Paul never intended his rules to apply to churches of today with their markedly different cultures. They point to the example of Paul who sent back a slave to his master but surely did not approve of slavery, since he implied that Philemon should free his slave (Philemon 17–21). Paul commanded everyone to **submit to one**

---

[2] An alternative interpretation of 1 Corinthians 14:34–35 is that it is a quotation from the Corinthians themselves. In many places in 1 Corinthians, Paul quoted the Corinthians' own ideas and then refuted them (1 Corinthians 1:12; 3:4; 6:12–13; 7:1; 8:1; 10:23). According to this interpretation, 1 Corinthians 14:34–35 would be a statement of the Corinthians referring to the normal rules in Jewish congregations. If this is so, verse 36 would be Paul's denial of their idea. In fact, in the Greek language, the "you" in verse 36 refers to the masculine gender. Therefore, Paul was asking the men: **Did the word of God originate with you** [men]**? Or are you** [men] **the only people it has reached?** In the Greek language, these questions are written in such a way that they demand a negative answer.

another out of reverence for Christ, not that women only should do so (Ephesians 5:21). These Christians point out that Jesus broke down cultural barriers and brought freedom to all. Unbelievers will not take offense at women leaders if their particular society has already given freedom to women. Therefore, these Christians believe that the church also should give leadership positions to women.

The matter is not as clear as it may seem at first when looking at only two or three verses. Whatever we decide, we should not allow our own custom to separate us from our brother and sister who may follow a different custom. **There is neither Jew nor Greek, slave nor free, male nor female, for you are all one in Christ Jesus** (Galatians 3:28).

CHILDREN AND THE KINGDOM OF GOD

Main Verses

Genesis 17:10–14 . . . **every male among you who is eight days old must be circumcised.**

Psalm 22:9–10 . . . **you made me trust in you even at my mother's breast.**

Psalm 51:5 **Surely I was sinful at birth, sinful from the time my mother conceived me.**

Matthew 18:2–6 . . . **a little child . . . one of these little ones who believe in me.**

Matthew 21:15–16 **From the lips of children and infants you have ordained praise.**

Mark 10:14–16 **He** (Jesus) **said to them, "Let the little children come to me . . . for the kingdom of God belongs to such as these."**

Luke 1:15 . . . **he** (John) **will be filled with the Holy Spirit even from birth.**

Acts 2:38–39 **The promise is for you and your children and for all who are far off.**

The Question

The Bible clearly states that we must believe and be baptized to be saved (Mark 16:16). We are commanded to repent and to be baptized so that our sins may be forgiven (Acts 2:38). We are told to believe in our heart and to confess with our mouth (Romans 10:9–10). And, of course, we are told in John 3:16 that whoever believes in Jesus will have eternal life.

The question arises: What happens to infants and children who are too small to speak? Can they truly repent, or believe, or confess with their mouth? If not, how do they receive salvation? Related to this, then, is a further question: If a small baby dies, where does it go? To heaven or to hell? These are hard questions, because the Bible does not give definite answers to them. There are only a few verses that relate to the question of children and the kingdom of God, and many of these are only indirectly related.

Children in the Bible

The Bible says that all have sinned (Romans 3:23; 5:12). The Psalmist says that he was not only **sinful at birth**, but was **sinful from the time** [his] **mother conceived** [him] (Psalm 51:5). Job says similar things (Job 25:4). Thus the Bible says that all of us, even newborn babies, have natures that are sinful and set against God. Every human being needs God's GRACE to be saved from sin and to be made RIGHTEOUS.

The Bible says that by God's help and grace even newborn babies can place their trust in God (Psalm 22:9–10). Jesus called a little child to stand before Him and talked about the **little ones who believe in me** (Matthew 18:6). Jesus also quoted from Psalm 8:2, which says: **From the lips of children and infants you have ordained praise** (see Matthew 21:16). It was promised that John the Baptist would be filled with the Holy Spirit **even from birth** (Luke 1:15,41–44). Therefore, at least some babies seem able to have a kind of faith in God.

Jesus commanded His disciples to let the little children come to Him, and He prayed for and blessed them (Mark 10:13–16). This even included little babies (Luke 18:15). He said that the kingdom of God belonged **to such as these** (Mark 10:14). God looks kindly on children. . . . **their angels** always stand in God's presence (Matthew 18:10). But it is not written here whether all children have angels in heaven or only some children, namely, those who "believe" in Jesus (Matthew 18:2–6; Mark 9:42).

In the Old Testament, God told the Jews to CIRCUMCISE all male infants in order to bring them into the family of God. This had to take place at eight days of age, and was a sign of the COVENANT between God and the Jews (Genesis 17:10–13). God even declared that if a male infant was not circumcised, that infant would be **cut off from his people**, because he had broken God's covenant (Genesis 17:14). There is no mention of female infants, nor of what happened to them in regard to the covenant.

The New Testament makes it clear that we are free from the Old Testament LAW. To be in God's family, physical circumcision is not necessary. We are made children of God through faith, not through the Jewish law. **You are all sons of God through faith in Christ Jesus** (Galatians 3:26).

Children in the Church

Little children and even newborn **babies**[1] are able to have some kind of FAITH by God's power and grace, and are able to be in God's kingdom (Psalm 22:9–10; Luke 18:15–16). But is this true of all children, or only some? And how can this be true? Throughout church history scholars have given many different answers to these questions.

Many Christians believe that water BAPTISM replaced circumcision as the means by which children are brought into the family of God. They think that water baptism is the "circumcision of Christ" (Colossians 2:11–13), by which our sinful nature, through faith, is cut off and thrown away and we come into God's family. Jesus commanded that the children be allowed to come to Him (Mark 10:14), and promised that whoever **believes and is baptized will be saved** (see Mark 16:16; General Article: Water Baptism). Some of these Christians think that infants can believe in Jesus. Others think that the parents can believe for the baby and that God accepts the faith of the parents (1 Corinthians 7:14). Then, when the child is old enough, he must accept or reject Jesus for himself.

Many other Christians believe a second view. According to this view, God does not choose all people to receive salvation, but only some (see John 15:16,19; Romans 9:18; General Article: Salvation—God's Choice or Man's Choice?). God chooses some babies to be saved and does not choose others. Those that God chooses will go to heaven if they die; the others will not.

Still other Christians hold a third view. These Christians believe that God offers salvation to all (young and old), but that not all will accept it. Many will resist God. This is true for children also, they say. These Christians believe that babies are able to believe with their spirit or heart even if their minds are unformed (Psalm 22:9–10; Matthew 18:5–6; Luke 1:15). But they do not think that all babies will believe. Just like adults, some resist God. Only those babies who actually believe will go to heaven if they die.

Still other Christians hold a fourth belief; namely, that by God's grace and power all babies (or at least all babies of Christian parents) automatically believe in Jesus and are already in the kingdom of God (Mark 10:14–15; 1 Corinthians 7:14). Therefore, they believe that all babies who die (or at least all babies of Christian parents) go to heaven.

Finally, some Christians believe that although babies have a sinful nature, they do not commit actual sin. They say that babies are in a "state of innocence." Because of this opinion, these Christians believe that all babies who die go to heaven automatically.

---

[1] The word translated **babies** in Luke 18:15 means "newborns."

Summary

Whatever we believe about this matter, our responsibility as parents is clear. Baptism is important for every person, of course. Whether we baptize or dedicate our children, we must place them in God's hands, and trust Him for their salvation. We must teach them about God and His word (Deuteronomy 4:9–10; 6:6–7; Psalm 78:5–6), and we must discipline them in a loving way (Ephesians 6:4; Colossians 3:21). **The promise is for you and your children and for all who are far off—for all whom the Lord our God will call** (Acts 2:39).

CHRISTIAN MARRIAGE

Main Verses

Genesis 1:26–28; 2:23–24 Man and woman before their fall.
Song of Songs Chapters 1–8 The ideal of married love.
Matthew 5:31–32; 19:3–9 Jesus' teaching on marriage and divorce.
1 Corinthians 7:1–17 Paul's teaching on marriage and divorce.
Ephesians 5:21–33 Mutual submission in marriage.
1 Peter 3:1–7 Mutual honor and respect in marriage.

God's Plan for Marriage

God created us as male and female; both male and female were created in the image of God (Genesis 1:26). God Himself instituted marriage for three reasons. The first reason was for fellowship. God saw that it was **not good for the man to be alone**, and so He made a helper for the man (Genesis 2:18). The second reason God instituted marriage was so that families could be established by having children. God told the man and woman to be **fruitful and increase in number** (Genesis 1:28). A third reason for marriage was for sexual satisfaction. **For this reason a man will leave his father and mother and be united to his wife, and they will become one flesh. The man and his wife were both naked, and they felt no shame** (Genesis 2:24–25; Proverbs 5:15–21; Song of Songs Chapters 1–8). Both Adam (the first man) and Eve (the first woman) shared in dominion over all the earth (Genesis 1:26–28).

But through sin Adam and Eve fell from God's original plan. Their sin immediately resulted in shame and separation between them (Genesis 3:7), accusation (Genesis 3:12), and the rule of husband over wife (Genesis 3:16). In addition, nature was no longer under their dominion but was now their enemy (Genesis 3:17–19). It did not take long for other evils to appear, among them murder (Genesis 4:8), polygamy (Genesis 4:19), and revenge (Genesis 4:23). Divorce became common as well. The LAW of MOSES included statutes that were intended to limit the abuses of polygamy (Exodus 21:10; Deuteronomy 21:15–17) and divorce (Deuteronomy 24:1–4), but God never wanted either polygamy or divorce. From the beginning, His ideal for mankind was that a man should remain married to one woman for life (Matthew 19:4–9).

Christian Marriage

Marriage for Christians has a special significance, because it is related to the spiritual union between Christ and His church (Ephesians 5:32). When Jesus walked on the earth, He blessed marriage at the time of His first miracle (John 2:1–11). Jesus also announced the beginning of the kingdom of God. Therefore, we should expect a new relationship between husbands and wives. Paul said that there is **neither Jew nor Greek, slave nor free, male nor female, for you are all one in Christ Jesus** (Galatians 3:28). Does this mean that the husband and wife are also equal in their marriage?

All Christians agree that husbands and wives are equal in sexual relations. Paul clearly stated that they both should fulfill their marital duty to each other (1 Corinthians 7:3). He wrote that the **wife's body does not belong to her alone but also to her husband** (1 Corinthians 7:4). This was nothing new to the people of Paul's day; from the time of Adam and Eve to Paul's time the world had considered the wife to be the property of her husband. But Paul didn't stop with only that statement. In the same verse he went on to say that, in the same way, the **husband's body does not belong to him alone but also to his wife**. This teaching was totally new to Paul's first-century readers. Further, Paul taught that husbands and wives should never refuse to satisfy each other's sexual desires, **except by mutual consent and for a time** so that they might devote themselves to prayer (1 Corinthians 7:5). Some religions teach that the wife is like a "garden" in which the husband plants his seed. But in a Christian marriage the wife is a full partner in the relationship, not just a piece of property. Christian marriage is a partnership.

Are husband and wife equal in the other aspects of their relationship also? Christians give different answers to this question. There are two main opinions about the roles of husband and wife in a Christian marriage. The first opinion, which is held by most Christians, is that the wife is under the rule or leadership of her husband, whom she should obey. They point to Paul's statement that **the head of every man is Christ, and the head of the woman is man, and the head of Christ is God** (1 Corinthians 11:3). Paul goes on to say that woman was created **from man** and also **for man** (1 Corinthians 11:8–9), although in the Lord they need each other (1 Corinthians 11:11–12). These Christians believe that the word "head" means that the husband is to "rule" or "lead," and also to protect and preserve (Ephesians 5:25), feed and care for (Ephesians 5:29), and generally to be responsible for his wife. They point out that fathers are given the responsibility for their children (Ephesians 6:4; 1 Timothy 3:4–5). These Christians also point to Paul's command to wives to submit to their husbands **as to the Lord** and **in everything,** for **the husband is the head of the wife as Christ is the head of the church, his body** (Ephesians 5:22–24). At the same time, husbands are commanded to love their wives, **just as Christ loved the church and gave himself up for her** (Ephesians 5:25); they are to love their wives just as they love **their own bodies** (Ephesians 5:28). The Apostle Peter also commanded wives to submit to their husbands, and he gave the example of Sarah **who obeyed Abraham** (1 Peter 3:1–6).

But submission in marriage was never meant to be one-way. The section from Ephesians begins with a command to all believers: **Submit to one another out of reverence for Christ** (Ephesians 5:21). Although Christ is equal with God, He submitted Himself to the Father (Philippians 2:6–8). Similarly, these Christians think that the husband's "headship" is a headship among equals. Although husbands and wives are equal in their nature as humans, each has a different role to play, and thus they submit to each other in a different way. The wife submits to the husband as the leader or ruler in the home, just as we all submit to Christ; the husband submits to the wife by denying himself and giving himself up for her, just as Christ did for the church.

The second main opinion concerning the roles of husband and wife in a Christian marriage is that their roles are not actually different at all. Christians who hold this opinion point out that although children and slaves are commanded to "obey" (Ephesians 6:1,5), wives are never told to "obey" their husbands. Wives are commanded to "submit" to their husbands, just as everyone is commanded to submit to each other (Ephesians 5:21). Therefore, husbands also should submit to their wives. Peter reversed the usual custom of his time by telling the husbands to treat their wives **with respect**, instead of the other way around (1 Peter 3:7). Many Christian scholars believe that the Greek word translated "head" does not mean "ruler." They say that it was never used in the New Testament to mean "ruler," but rather it was used to mean "source of life" or "origin" (Ephesians 1:22; 4:15; Colossians 1:18; 2:10,19). Thus, according the view of these Christians, in 1 Corinthians 11:3 Paul means that Christ is the "source of life" of every man, that woman came from man, and Christ came from God. This meaning fits very well with 1 Corinthians 11:8,11–12. These Christians believe that God originally intended husband and wife to be equal. Although the sin of Adam and Eve in the Garden of Eden brought a curse on the woman (Genesis 3:1–6,16), Christ has broken that curse, and Christian marriage should reflect that fact. If man and woman in marriage are indeed **one flesh** (Genesis 2:24), they should not be divided into "one who rules" and "one who obeys."

Whichever of these two opinions one believes, the Bible makes it clear that both husband and wife are to commit themselves to their spouse. In fact, Jesus quoted approvingly the Old Testament statement that a man should **leave his father and mother and be united to his wife** (Mark 10:7). This doesn't necessarily mean that a man has to leave his parent's house, but it does mean that in his heart a man must "leave" his parents. A man must place his commitment to his wife above his commitment to his parents—and above his commitment to his children also! In marriage the man and woman are no longer two but become **one flesh** (Mark 10:8). In some cultures, the spouse is actually called one's "other half."

God, of course, must be placed higher than any other human. In fact, the closer a husband and wife come to God, the closer they will come to each other. In Ecclesiastes 4:9–12, it is stated that two people are better than one, and that a **cord of three strands is not quickly broken**. A Christian husband and wife, along with the third cord, God, make a powerful combination.

Divorce and Remarriage

Promises given by Christians in the marriage ceremony are given before God Himself, as well as before the church as a group. Marriage is a lifelong commitment. The Bible teaches that God hates divorce (Malachi 2:14–16). Divorce was common in Old Testament times, and God desired to stop "easy" divorce that had no good reason. He also desired to provide legal protection for the wife who had been discarded by her husband. The law of Moses required that a man have a proper reason for divorcing his wife, namely uncleanness, and that he give his wife a proper certificate of divorce (Deuteronomy 24:1–4). By the time of Jesus, some PHARISEES taught that a man could divorce his wife for any reason at all (Matthew 19:3). Jesus answered that it was wrong for anyone to break the marriage relationship that God had made. He said, "**Therefore what God has joined together, let man not separate**" (Matthew 19:6). Jesus said that God never wanted divorce, but the law of Moses had allowed it because the Jews' **hearts were hard** (Matthew 19:8). All Christians believe that it is wrong to break up a marriage.

But then Jesus said further that "**anyone who divorces his wife, except for marital unfaithfulness, and marries another woman commits adultery**" (Matthew 19:9). Elsewhere Jesus had said that "**anyone who divorces his wife, except for marital unfaithfulness, causes her to become an adulteress, and anyone who marries the divorced woman commits adultery**" (Matthew 5:32). What does

Jesus mean in these last two statements? There are three main views among Christians.

First, many Christians believe that divorce is never allowable, and therefore that remarriage is always wrong while the first spouse is still alive (Romans 7:2–3). They note that the words of Jesus in Mark 10:11–12 do not include the phrase **except for marital unfaithfulness**. These Christians believe that those who remarry are committing adultery because they are still married in God's eyes to their previous spouse. They believe that divorcing one's wife causes her to either commit actual adultery or to get married again, which in their view is equal to adultery (Matthew 5:32). These Christians also point to Paul's words in Romans 7:3, where a woman who marries another while her husband is still alive **is called an adulteress**. Paul also said that those who divorce their spouses **must remain unmarried or else be reconciled** to each other (1 Corinthians 7:11). Therefore, according to this interpretation, a person who is divorced is never allowed to get married again while the first spouse is still alive.

Many other Christians have a second view: namely, that divorce is allowable in some circumstances when the marriage is already broken. For example, if one's spouse has already committed adultery, a divorce does not "cause" adultery to take place. Some Christians consider desertion (for example, when a husband leaves his wife without a formal divorce) or other unusual circumstances (such as physical cruelty) to be the equivalent of adultery. Some of these Christians further believe that in cases where an unbelieving spouse wants to get a divorce, the Christian spouse should follow Paul's advice to let the unbelieving partner go (1 Corinthians 7:15). Regarding remarriage, some of these Christians think that a believer who divorces his or her spouse for any reason (even for a reason they allow) must not get married again as long as the first spouse is alive (1 Corinthians 7:11). Others believe that the innocent believer is free to marry again at once. These Christians point to Paul's words that the **believing man or woman is not bound in such circumstances** (1 Corinthians 7:15).

Still other Christians hold a third view: namely, that breaking a marriage is always wrong, but that remarriage to another spouse is allowable regardless of the reason for the first divorce. They believe Jesus meant that anyone who divorces his wife without due cause just to marry another is committing adultery, whether it is legal according to the law of Moses or not (Matthew 19:9). But these Christians argue that when Jesus said in Matthew 5:32 that "**anyone who divorces his wife . . . causes her to become an adulteress**", He could not mean that she becomes an adulteress simply because of the divorce. And Jesus could not mean that every innocent woman who is divorced (when she herself has not committed adultery) will later either remarry or without remarriage commit actual adultery. Some women will neither remarry nor commit adultery. Rather, Jesus meant that if a man divorces his wife when she has not committed adultery, he will make her "look like" an adulteress; others will believe she was divorced for "marital unfaithfulness". If she marries again, her new husband will "look like" an adulterer. This interpretation fits well with Paul's words in Romans 7:3 that a woman who marries while her first husband is still living **is called an adulteress**; Paul does not say that she is, in fact, an adulteress.

Christians who hold this third view think that believers should not divorce their spouses, but that they should allow an unbelieving spouse to divorce them if that unbelieving spouse wants to do so (1 Cor-inthians 7:10–16). Since the word for "unmarried" in 1 Corinthians 7:8–9 is different from the word for "virgin" in 1 Corinthians 7:25, these Christians believe that in verses 8–9 Paul was writing about "previously married" people, whether divorced or widowed. If this is so, then he was allowing them to remarry if they could not control their sexual desires. Therefore, following this interpretation, this group of Christians do not examine the particular reason for the previous (wrong) divorce. They allow everyone to remarry if they have repented of their part in the breakup of their previous marriage.

The issue of divorce and remarriage is complex. One must prayerfully study all the relevant verses before coming to a conclusion on this subject. It is also important to consult with one's pastor or the elders of one's church before making any plans to divorce or remarry. Different churches will have differing policies on this matter.

Polygamy

Although many of the Old Testament characters had more than one wife, this may have been the result of Adam and Eve's sin in the Garden of Eden. In marriage, the two become "one flesh"; the addition of a third person does not fit God's original model. Whatever was allowed previously, the New Testament is very clear that Christians should not have more than one wife at a time (1 Corinthians 7:2). All Christians agree with this. Yet if a man had two or more wives before he became a believer, he should not abandon any of them, but care for them all (Exodus 21:10). However, Paul did not want a man who already had two or more wives at one time to be chosen as a leader in the church[1] (1 Timothy 3:2,12; Titus 1:6).

---

[1] A person who remarries after a spouse has died remains eligible for church leadership. According to the Bible, both men and women are free to remarry after the death of a spouse.

It is clear that sexual relations with anyone except one's own spouse are strictly forbidden for all Christians, whether the other person is married, unmarried, or is only a prostitute (1 Corinthians 6:15). **Marriage should be honored by all, and the marriage bed kept pure, for God will judge the adulterer and all the sexually immoral** (Hebrews 13:4).

HEALING AND DELIVERANCE

Main Verses

Matthew 8:16–17 Healing and deliverance in Jesus' ministry.
Matthew 12:43–45 Teaching about evil spirits.
Mark 5:1–17 Jesus frees a demon-possessed man.
Mark 9:14–29 Jesus casts out a demon from a boy with seizures.
Mark 16:16–18 Healing and deliverance are signs of believers.
1 Corinthians 12:9–10 Gifts of healing, miracles, and distinguishing between spirits.
James 5:14–16 Anointing with oil and praying for the sick by the elders.

Divine Healing of Diseases

There are many promises of healing from diseases in the Bible. The JEWS in the Old Testament were given promises of healing (Psalm 103:1–5), as well as protection from disease (Exodus 15:26). The Bible identifies SATAN as the source of sickness (Luke 13:16; Acts 10:38). Jesus said that one of the reasons He was anointed with the HOLY SPIRIT and power was in order to heal (Luke 4:17–18; 5:17). The Bible says that Jesus healed **all the sick** (Matthew 8:16), and that He healed **every disease and sickness** (Matthew 4:23). Jesus' disciples also were given this power to heal (Matthew 10:1,8; Mark 6:7,13; Luke 10:9). Jesus included healing as one of the signs of those who believe (Mark 16:18), and we see healing all through the book of Acts. James expected the church to pray for the sick and see them become healed (James 5:14–16). Among the gifts of the Holy Spirit are the gifts of healing and of miracles (1 Corinthians 12:9–10,28). Many healings occurred in the early church during the time of the APOSTLES and for several centuries afterward.

Many Christians believe that God still heals today, just as He did in the past. They point to Hebrews 13:8, where the writer says that **Jesus Christ is the same yesterday and today and forever**; and they point to Mark 1:40–41 to show that Jesus was always willing to heal. Many Christians around the world today claim to have been healed by divine power, and many others claim to have seen such healings. They point to the prophecies in the Old Testament that said the Savior would not only carry our sins on the CROSS but also our sicknesses (Numbers 21:8–9; Isaiah 53:4–5). The section from Isaiah Chapter 53 actually says in the Hebrew[1] that He **took up our infirmities and carried our diseases**, and it is quoted that way in Matthew 8:17. If Jesus took both our sins and our sicknesses on the cross, we should expect that God would continue to heal today just as He is continuing to forgive sins. These Christians believe that Paul's **thorn in the flesh** was not a physical illness, but an actual **messenger of Satan** (2 Corinthians 12:7). Many believe that the gifts of the Holy Spirit are still available to Christians today, and included among them are the **gifts of healing** and **miraculous power** (1 Corinthians 12:9–10). Some of these Christians believe that we should expect all our diseases to be healed by God. Others believe that healing is available for most diseases, but that we should not expect every one of them to be healed.

Other Christians believe that God no longer heals by supernatural means today, but only uses doctors and medicines to heal people. Most Christians throughout church history have not seen someone healed by supernatural means. Thus they believe that this divine healing power was given only to the Christians of the first few centuries of the church's existence. These Christians point to Paul himself who left behind a sick friend (2 Timothy 4:20), and they interpret Paul's **thorn in the flesh** to be a physical illness (2 Corinthians 12:7), possibly an eye disease (Galatians 4:15). They interpret Matthew 8:16–17 to mean that Jesus took our infirmities while He was on earth healing people, but that He only took our sins on the cross. They believe that Jesus did not die on the cross for both our sins and our sicknesses, but only for our sins.

A third view is that the truth lies somewhere between these two main views. Those who think this believe that both views are partly true. For a related topic, see General Article: Holy Spirit Baptism.

Praying for Healing

In the Bible people were healed in many different ways. Jesus said that we must "ask" in order to receive (Matthew 7:7; James 4:2). Jesus told many that their FAITH had healed them (Matthew 8:10–13; Mark 10:52), and the apostles did likewise (Acts 3:16). Others were healed through their "obedience" (2 Kings 5:1–14; Luke 17:14; John 9:7). Many paralytics were healed through a "word of command" given by Jesus or one of the apostles (Mark 2:10–11; John 5:8; Acts 3:6; 14:10). Jesus told His disciples to "claim His promises" (Mark 11:22–24; John 14:13–14). Many illnesses were healed by "anointing with oil" (Mark 6:13), and James advised the elders of the church to

---

[1] The Old Testament was written originally in the Hebrew language.

anoint the sick person with oil to bring about healing (James 5:14–16). Many were healed by the "laying on of hands" with prayer (Mark 6:5–6; Luke 4:40; Acts 28:8), and Jesus said that those who believe would lay hands on the sick and they would recover (Mark 16:16; Hebrews 6:1–2). Some unusual healings occurred by the "touch" of Jesus' clothes (Luke 6:19; 8:43–46), Peter's shadow (Acts 5:15), and Paul's handkerchieves and aprons (Acts 19:12). At least once, "repeated prayer" by Jesus was necessary (Mark 8:22–25).

However, one should not refuse modern medicine or other scientific treatment. God can heal directly, but often He uses some "means" to bring healing. He has used touch, oil, and even mud (John 9:6–7). In the same way, medicine should also be viewed as a means of healing. Paul advised Timothy to use wine as a medicine for his **stomach** and his **frequent illnesses** (1 Timothy 5:23). Paul called Luke, the doctor who accompanied him on his missionary journeys, **our dear friend Luke, the doctor** (Colossians 4:14). Therefore, we should not seek healing only from God directly, or only from "means" such as medicine and doctors; rather we should seek healing both directly from God and also from medicine (2 Kings 20:5–7), and then thank Him for whatever way He chooses to heal us.

Many reasons are given to explain why some people are not healed. The main reason for an unanswered prayer is unbelief, whether it be our own unbelief (Mark 9:23–24), or the unbelief of those trying to heal us (Matthew 17:19–20), or the unbelief of others around us (Mark 6:5–6). There may be unconfessed sin (John 5:14; James 5:16), such as unforgiveness (Mark 11:24–25), disobedience (2 Kings 5:1,8–14), or a wrong relationship with one's spouse (1 Peter 3:7). Partaking of the LORD'S SUPPER in an improper manner or without confession of sin can also result in illness (1 Corinthians 11:27–30). Some do not even ask for healing (James 4:2), either because they don't know or don't believe that it is available. If we misuse our bodies or refuse other means of healing which God provides, we may be "testing" God, which is forbidden (Matthew 4:6–7).

Sometimes it may not be the right time for healing. For example, Jesus did not go immediately to heal a sick friend, but later raised him from the dead (John 11:6,43–44). In that way Jesus was able to do a greater miracle. To demonstrate His own power, God may wait many years before healing someone and then use a special person or a special means to perform the healing (Mark 9:29; John 5:5–9; 9:3). Or God may give an individual only a certain length of time to live. In the Old Testament, God gave Hezekiah an additional fifteen years of life and no more (2 Kings 20:5–7).

Of course, the diagnosis may also be wrong; we may be thinking a person has a physical illness when, in fact, he has a problem with an evil spirit or DEMON.

Deliverance from Demons

As with physical illness, there are many promises in the Bible of deliverance from Satan and his demons or evil spirits. Jesus said that one of the reasons He was anointed with the Holy Spirit and power was **to release the oppressed** (Luke 4:18). Everywhere He went, He drove out demons from those who were oppressed (Matthew 4:24; Mark 1:34; 3:11). Jesus gave this authority to drive out **all demons** to His original twelve disciples and later to seventy-two others (Luke 9:1; 10:1,17–19). Jesus included the casting out of demons as one of the activities of those who believe (Mark 16:17), and we see this throughout the book of Acts (Acts 5:16; 8:7; 16:18; 19:11–12). Among the gifts of the Holy Spirit is the gift of **distinguishing between spirits** (1 Corinthians 12:10).

Demons are not the spirits of dead persons that have come back to oppress people on earth. The Bible teaches clearly that the spirits of dead men and women go to heaven to be with Christ (Philippians 1:23), or to hell to await the final JUDGMENT (Hebrews 9:27; Revelation 20:5,13). Demons are evil or unclean spirits (Matthew 10:1; 12:43), who are the servants of Satan (Matthew 12:26–27; Mark 3:22–26). Satan and his spirits were created by God, but later rebelled against God (Isaiah 14:12–15; Ezekiel 28:13–17). Demons are very numerous and are found everywhere in the world (Mark 5:9; Ephesians 6:12). They can enter and control both men and animals; indeed, they do not like to remain outside a body (Matthew 12:43–45; Mark 5:2,12–13). They recognize Jesus Christ as the Son of God (Mark 1:23–24,34; Acts 19:15), and in that sense they "believe" in Christ (James 2:19); but they know their own final fate will be "torment" in the **Abyss** (Matthew 8:29; Luke 8:31). Paul said that sacrifices offered to idols are, in fact, offered to demons (1 Corinthians 10:19–21).

Sometimes a person is actually "possessed" by an evil spirit, meaning that his own personality is suppressed by the personality of the evil spirit who is "ruling" that person's mind and body (Mark 5:15–16). But many times the person is not completely "ruled," but only "attacked" or "oppressed" in mind and body by the evil spirit (Matthew 9:32; 12:22; Mark 9:17–29; Luke 6:18).

All Christians know that believers cannot be possessed completely by an evil spirit, since believers are ruled and owned by God Himself (1 Corinthians 6:19–20). However, many Christians think that believers can be "oppressed" or "attacked" by evil spirits within them. They point to Paul's **messenger of Satan** that tormented his **flesh** (2 Corinthians 12:7), and to Paul's warning to believers not to be **participants with demons** by eating food sacrificed to idols (1 Corinthians 10:20–22). They point to the many people who had physical illnesses possibly caused by demons and who were brought to Jesus for deliverance (Mark 3:10–11; Luke 6:18–19). They believe that not all of them were totally ruled by the evil spirit, but that some were only oppressed by an evil spirit within. Christians can be influenced by evil spirits, even to the point of believing their lies and teaching (1 Timothy 4:1–3); and Paul warns us that our constant fight is not against **flesh and blood** but with these evil spirits (Ephesians 6:12). We must **test the spirits to see whether they are from God** (1 John 4:1–3).

Other Christians, however, think that believers can never have an evil spirit within them. They say that the Holy Spirit and an evil spirit cannot exist inside a believer at the same time (1 Corinthians 6:19). Some of these Christians believe that a true Christian can never be attacked by an evil spirit at all. Others think that an evil spirit can attack or influence a believer from the outside, but cannot enter inside that believer's body.

The matter is important, because it determines how we pray for others. If a believer can have a demon, he will need to have the demon cast out of his body to obtain full freedom from certain illnesses and emotional problems, or to obtain victory over certain sins. We must remember, however, that most sins are the result of our own sinful nature, and not the result of a demon or of Satan (Galatians 5:19–21).

Praying for Deliverance

Whether or not a Christian can have a demon, we at least need to know how to deliver other non-Christian people from Satan and his evil spirits. All Christians need the **full armor of God**, the parts of which are listed in Ephesians 6:10–17: truth, righteousness, peace, faith, salvation, and God's word. Prior to deliverance, preparation in prayer is very important (Mark 9:28–29; Ephesians 6:18). Some Christians believe that Mark 9:29 should be translated "by prayer and fasting" and not "by prayer" alone, and that a special dedicated time of prayer is essential for a deliverance ministry to be successful. If possible, prayer for deliverance should be done in a group rather than alone. All those who undertake a deliverance ministry should be mature spiritual Christians (see Acts 19:13–16).

There must be a time of consideration with the afflicted person beforehand. If the person is not a Christian or shows no interest in becoming a Christian (which would leave him without the Holy Spirit's power) or cannot be followed afterward, we should be very cautious about praying for such a person's deliverance. A short quick prayer may leave the person worse off than he or she was before (Matthew 12:43–45). Some think that a person should not be delivered if any existing idols are not taken out of his home or destroyed (Acts 19:19). Otherwise, the evil spirit can easily return.

Many physical illnesses may have a demonic component. But many mental or physical illnesses may seem as if they were demonic in origin, but are not. For example, seizures can seem like demonic activity, but usually they are caused by a physical illness in the brain. An important help is the gift of being able to distinguish spirits, a gift which comes from the Holy Spirit and enables one to identify the demon oppressing or possessing an individual (1 Corinthians 12:10).

The actual prayer should begin with a request for protection for those taking part in the deliverance, all of whom must be believers (Acts 19:13–16). Then Satan and his forces should be bound (Matthew 16:19; 18:18), and the afflicted person should renounce any sin that may be involved. Prayer for healing is usually a "request" to God for healing (and may be silent prayer in the heart); but deliverance is a "command" given to the demon in the name and authority of Jesus Christ (Luke 10:17; Acts 16:18; 19:13–16). However, there is no need for shouting loudly; the demon cannot be scared out of a person. The demon is commanded to leave the person without harming him or anyone else and to go to Jesus Christ Himself for judgment (Jude 9). The name of Jesus is very powerful and will usually cause immediate deliverance, so that the person will know he is free.

This prayer should be immediately followed by a prayer that the delivered person might be filled with God's love and His Holy Spirit (Matthew 12:43–45). Of course, the delivered person should become a child of God if he is not already. He should also be taught to resist Satan and to avoid the sin that may have allowed the demon to enter his life (James 4:7; 1 John 1:9). The main reasons that may block full deliverance are unbelief (Matthew 17:16–20), rejection of Christ, failure to renounce any associated sin, such as unforgiveness, and failure to distinguish or identify the spirit (that is, trying to deliver a person who does not have an evil spirit).

Summary

Both healing and deliverance demonstrate God's love to us, and His concern not only for our spirits but also for our minds and bodies. God is ready to heal our diseases and weaknesses, and to deliver us from bondage. God desires that we **enjoy good health** and that **all may go well** with us (3 John 2).

RESISTING EVIL—HOW MUCH SHOULD WE DO?

Main Verses

Exodus 20:13 **You shall not murder.**
Exodus 21:12–17; 22:18–20 Death penalty given for certain sins.
Joshua 8:1–8 God authorized destruction by war.
1 Samuel 15:2–3 God authorized punishment by war.
Matthew 5:38–48 **Do not resist an evil person. If someone strikes you on the right cheek, turn to him the other also . . . . Love your enemies.**
Luke 6:30 **Give to everyone who asks you, and if anyone takes what belongs to you, do not demand it back.**
Romans 13:1–7 Government is established by God to punish evil.
1 Peter 2:13–14 Authorities are instituted by God to punish wrongdoers.

The Questions

Jesus Christ taught us and showed us that God is love. Jesus did not abolish the Old Testament LAW (Matthew 5:17). However, compared to what the law said, Jesus' teachings were deeper and more spiritual. The law dealt with people's outward behavior, but Jesus looked at what people thought in their hearts. He took many points of the law and made them harder by demanding love in addition to justice.

For example, the law condemned murder, but Jesus condemned anger and hate in one's heart (Matthew 5:21–22). The law condemned adultery, but Jesus condemned lust in one's heart (Matthew 5:27–28). The law commanded us to love our neighbor, but Jesus commanded us to love our enemies (Matthew 5:43–47). The law forbade excessive personal revenge, but Jesus forbade revenge altogether. He said, "**Do not resist an evil person. If someone strikes you on the right cheek, turn to him the other also. And if someone wants to sue you and take your tunic, let him have your cloak as well**" (Matthew 5:39–40). Jesus also said, "**Give to everyone who asks you, and if anyone takes what belongs to**

you, do not demand it back" (Luke 6:30). He added, "**So in everything, do to others what you would have them do to you**" (Matthew 7:12; Luke 6:31).

Many questions arise about resisting evil. Are we never to resist evil? May we never use force to oppose those who are doing wrong? Paul and Peter said that government authorities are ordained by God to punish wrongdoers, and that they do not **bear the sword for nothing** (Romans 13:1–7; 1 Peter 2:13–14). Are societies and governments also commanded never to use violence or harm any person? If so, can a Christian be a member of the police and use a gun or club to fight criminals? Can a Christian be a judge in the courts and give sentences of physical punishment or even the death penalty? Can a Christian be a member of the armed forces and fight in war?

The First View: No One Should Ever Resist Evil

Many Christians believe that no one under any circumstances should use force to resist those doing evil. Jesus asked us to follow Him (Mark 8:34–35) and gave us His example of humble servanthood (Mark 10:42–45). We are commanded to follow Christ in His suffering (1 Peter 2:19–24). Paul says we are not to take revenge, but overcome evil with good (Romans 12:17–21; 1 Thessalonians 5:15). Peter says the same, telling us to return cursing with blessing (1 Peter 3:8–9). These Christians believe that the law was fulfilled in Christ (Matthew 5:17), whose moral way of love is more difficult, but higher. Since Jesus changed the Old Testament law to a "law of love" (Romans 13:10), what was allowed in the Old Testament by God cannot be used as the standard for Christians today.

Therefore, these Christians do not think that believers can be soldiers in the army to fight and kill other human beings. They point out that the source of war is sin (James 4:1–4), and that **all who draw the sword will die by the sword** (Matthew 26:52). They note that the early wars in the Old Testament were mostly fought by God Himself, with very little help from the ISRAELITES (Exodus 14:13–14, 24–28; Joshua 5:13–15; 6:1–5; Judges 4:14–15; 7:2–7,22). And later wars not authorized by God were condemned by the prophets, who warned the Israelites to depend on God, not on armies (Isaiah 31:1–3; Zechariah 4:6). Even in the Old Testament, God's highest standard was clearly for man to be peaceful. For example, DAVID'S request to build the temple of God was denied him because his hands had been bloodied in war (1 Chronicles 28:3).

Consistent with this view of war, most of these Christians believe that the death penalty is wrong also. In addition to verses about not resisting evil (Matthew 5:39), these Christians point to Jesus' refusal to stone the woman caught in the act of adultery (John 8:1–11). Therefore, many of these Christians think that a Christian should not be a judge or member of the government, since then he would have to "bear the sword" to punish wrongdoers and would have to decide when to give the death penalty and when to go to war. They believe that a Christian cannot be a member of the police either, since a policeman may have to use physical violence or even kill a criminal to protect society. These believers point out that we are citizens of heaven, not of earth (Philippians 3:20), and that we are called to a life of peace (Hebrews 12:14). Although these Christians refuse to be a part of government themselves, they do submit to their country's government. For example, they pay taxes, and they pray for government authorities (Mark 12:13–17; Romans 13:1–7; 1 Timothy 2:1–2; 1 Peter 2:13–17).

The Second View: Only Those in Authority Should Resist Evil

Many other Christians interpret these sayings of Jesus differently. These Christians believe that Jesus' words must be followed by every individual believer in his personal life, but that Jesus was not talking about governments or about policemen and other officials doing their public duty. If we as indiviual believers are hurt by a "brother" or an "adversary," Jesus tells us to get rid of our anger and "be reconciled" to our brother and "settle matters" with our adversary (Matthew 5:22–26). If we as individuals are slapped by someone, we should not fight back or seek revenge, but rather we should show him our love by "turning the other cheek" (Matthew 5:38–41). As individuals we should be ready to give or lend to whoever asks (Matthew 5:42), even if they are our enemies (Luke 6:35). According to this second view, these sayings of Jesus refer to private individuals only.

These Christians say further that Jesus was speaking to private individuals in an unarmed nation. He would have been thinking of the daily arguments of village life. Jesus' hearers would not have applied His words to the police or army. According to this viewpoint, these authorities must resist evil. Further, these Christians say, if the authorities do wrong, it is good to resist them as well. There are three examples of resisting authorities in the New Testament. First, Jesus Himself showed anger and resisted evil physically when he cleared the temple with a whip and overturned the money tables (John 2:13–16). Second, Jesus protested an illegal slap on the cheek during His own court case (John 18:19–23). And Paul resisted evil to his own person by appealing to a higher court (Acts 25:11). Because of these examples, these Christians believe that we also should resist evil in this way.

Regarding war, this group of Christians recognize the sinfulness of war, but they note that Paul approves of the government's use of the "sword" to punish wrongdoers (Romans 13:4). John the Baptist was asked by soldiers what they must do to show true repentance, and he told them to be content with their pay; he did not tell them to leave the army (Luke 3:14). These Christians distinguish between those things, on the one hand, that are allowed by God in the Old Testament law but which Jesus said we should no longer do, such as divorce (Matthew 5:31) and oaths (Matthew 5:33); and on the other hand those things which God specifically ordered in the Old Testament, which they believe Jesus did not deny, such as the judicial death penalty or war in a just cause (Numbers 31:1–7; Joshua Chapters 6–8; Judges 4:14–16; 7:2–22; 1 Samuel 15:2–3). John's vision presents Jesus at the end time as a warrior leader coming to destroy completely those who fight with God (Revelation 19:11–19). Therefore, although these Christians recognize that most wars are unjust and wrong, they believe certain wars are necessary and "just." Most of these Christians believe that the death penalty is still allowed as well. Even in the New Testament, God used Peter to pronounce death on two people trying to tell a falsehood to God (Acts 5:1–10). They believe that war or the death penalty is not God's perfect will, but that God still requires it to prevent certain injustices or to show the seriousness of certain sins.

Regarding participation in government, these Christians point to Paul's instructions to submit to the government and to its laws and taxes (Romans 13:1–7). Even though the Roman emperor at the time was a vicious persecutor of Christians, Paul said that the authorities are **established by God**, and that they are **God's servants** (Romans 13:1,4,6). Tax collectors do not have to leave their jobs, but must collect fair taxes (Luke 3:12–13; Romans 13:6–7). These Christians believe that it is good for believers to be members of the government or police in order to encourage the government and police to follow God's way of justice, and to show mercy when appropriate. They say that Christians should be a "light" in government (Matthew 5:14–16). Although as individuals they should not "fight back" to get revenge or protect their own interests, as members of the police or government they should help to see that wrongdoers are punished and the interests of others are protected.

The Third View: Evil May Be Resisted by Private Individuals Also

A third group of Christians believe that any person can resist an evil person, with violence if necessary. These Christians believe that when Jesus gave these teachings about resisting evil, He did not intend that they be applied in every situation. These Christians say that there are obvious exceptions, which Jesus' hearers would have understood without being told. For example, if a drunkard tries to murder an innocent victim, he should be resisted in any way possible. They further point out that it is not good for children to be allowed to slap or insult their parents, or when they grab one sweet to be given a second sweet also. These Christians believe that there are many examples like these in which God wants all of us to resist evil.

These Christians also believe that individuals can resist major criminal violence, even if it is one's own interests that are being threatened. They believe that some sayings of Jesus are hyperbolic statements designed to make the teaching more vivid and emphatic, but are not meant to be taken literally, as in Matthew 5:29–30. They note that the typical teacher of Jesus' time used such hyperboles frequently. They agree that Christians should not fight or quarrel with others, even when challenged (Matthew 5:39). But, they say, if someone is trying to do permanent damage to us or is trying to kill us, we are allowed to fight back to save ourselves. They agree that Christians should do good to their enemies and be merciful by giving to others anything they truly need (Matthew 5:43–44; Luke 6:30–36). But they do not believe that we must give all of our money or property away if someone who is not in need asks for it or tries to steal it.

These Christians accept all the arguments of the second view (mentioned above) about participation in the police, the army, and the government. They believe that such participation is not only acceptable, but may also be God's will as well.

Some Christians may decide that some ideas from all of these three main views are correct. Each Christian should come to a decision about these questions only after thorough Bible study, meditation, and prayer, and with the help of the Holy Spirit. Through all of church history, mature spiritual Christians have differed on these questions. The Bible does not give definite answers to these questions. Whatever view we hold ourselves, we should not condemn another for holding a different view, nor should we fight over these issues.

Persecution—Our Response

Related to the question of resisting evil is the question of persecution of believers. Persecution is the suffering inflicted on us by other people because of our good actions or because of our faith in Jesus Christ (Matthew 5:10–11; Luke 6:22; 1 Peter 2:20). The New Testament teaches that all Christians will be persecuted in some way (Mark 13:9; Luke 21:12; 2 Timothy 3:12). Jesus also taught us how to respond to persecution as Christians. He told us not to be afraid (Matthew 10:26), but to rejoice (Matthew 5:10–12). Paul said that he delighted in persecution, because then he could experience God's GRACE, which was always **sufficient** to enable him to bear anything (2 Corinthians 12:7–10). However, Jesus also told us to **be as shrewd as snakes** and to be **on** [our] **guard** (Matthew 10:16–17).

Regarding the persecutor, we are instructed to **bless and . . . not curse** those who persecute us (Romans 12:14), and to **love . . . and pray** for them (Matthew 5:44). We also will be brought before government officials in courts and prisons, but we are not to **worry beforehand about what to say**, because Jesus through the Holy Spirit will teach us at the time what to say (Mark 13:9–11; Luke 21:12–19).

Jesus did not tell us to fight when we are attacked for our faith in Him. Just before His own arrest Jesus said to His disciples to buy swords (Luke 22:35–38), but He did not allow them to use their swords to defend Him (Luke 22:51). Rather, He warned them that those who take the sword will die by it (Matthew 26:52). Most Christians think that believers who are being persecuted because of their faith in Jesus should never defend themselves by violent means.

Summary

Whatever we think about some of these difficult sayings of Jesus, all Christians agree that we should live in peace as much as we are able (Hebrews 12:14). We all look forward to the future day when the Lord's kingdom is established on earth, when men **will beat their swords into plowshares and their spears into pruning hooks. Nation will not take up sword against nation, nor will they train for war anymore** (Isaiah 2:4; Micah 4:3). Meanwhile, **if it is possible, as far as it depends on you, live at peace with everyone** (Romans 12:18).

THE SECOND COMING OF JESUS CHRIST

Main Verses

Ezekiel Chapters 37–47 Israel's restoration, invasion, and new temple.
Daniel Chapters 7–12 Daniel's visions of the future.
Matthew Chapter 24 Signs of the end of the age.
Mark Chapter 13 Signs of the end of the age.
Luke 17:20–37; 21:5–36 The Coming of the Kingdom of God.
1 Corinthians 15:12–58 The resurrection of the body.
1 Thessalonians 4:13–18 The Coming of the Lord.
2 Thessalonians 2:1–10 The **man of lawlessness** before the Lord comes.
2 Peter 3:3–13 Destruction by fire on the day of the Lord.
1 John 2:18; 4:1–3 The antichrist and the spirit of antichrist.
Revelation Chapters 6–22 Visions of God's wrath, man's tribulation, the work of antichrist, and Christ's victorious reign.

The Second Coming of Christ in Scripture

All Christians believe that Jesus Christ will "come again to judge the living and the dead" (see Matthew 25:31–46; Revelation 20:11–15; General Articles: Introduction). Jesus not only predicted His own death and resurrection (Matthew 16:21; Mark 8:31–32; 9:9–10; 10:33–34), but He also predicted His second coming (Matthew 16:27; 25:31; Mark 8:38; 13:26). After His resurrection from death, Jesus remained on earth for forty days, encouraging the disciples (Acts 1:3). While witnessing His ascension to heaven, the disciples were told that Jesus would return **in the same way** as He had left (see Luke 24:51; Acts 1:9–11). From the beginning, the apostles taught believers to **wait** and **hope** for Christ's **second** coming (Acts 3:19–21; Titus 2:13; Hebrews 9:28).

Jesus promised to go and **prepare a place** for us in heaven, and to **come back and take** us to live with Him there (John 14:2–3). Jesus also promised His followers that He would **raise them up at the last day** (John 6:39–40,54). Paul said that **in Christ all will be made**

alive. But each in his own turn: Christ, the firstfruits; then, when he comes, those who belong to him. Then the end will come (1 Corinthians 15:22–24). Paul described this resurrection of our bodies as our final **adoption as sons,** when we will be **glorified** at the completion of our salvation (see Romans 8:18–25,30; Philippians 3:20–21; General Article: Way of Salvation).

This resurrection will be a sudden event. In 1 Thessalonians 4:13–17, Paul wrote that **God will bring with Jesus** the spirits of those believers who have already died. **For the Lord himself will come down from heaven, with a loud command, with the voice of the archangel and with the trumpet call of God, and the dead in Christ will rise first. After that, we who are still alive and are left will be caught up together with them in the clouds to meet the Lord in the air.** The dead will be given new bodies that cannot die, and those who are alive will have their old bodies **changed** to new ones; this will happen **in a flash, in the twinkling of an eye, at the last trumpet** (1 Corinthians 15:51–53). Jesus also mentioned a **trumpet call** from the clouds, when He will send His angels to gather the **elect** from all over the earth (Matthew 24:30–31; Mark 13:26–27). Jesus warned that of two people sleeping in one bed (or working in a field or grinding grain together) one will be taken and the other left (Matthew 24:40–41; Luke 17:34–35). Many refer to these events as the "rapture" of the church.

But the second coming is also important as a time when God will bring justice and peace to the earth. The Old Testament records many prophecies about Jesus Christ as the Messiah. Some prophecies predicted His death for the sins and sorrows of the people (Psalm 22:1–31; Isaiah 53:1–12; Daniel 9:25–26); these were fulfilled almost two thousand years ago when Jesus was crucified and rose again. Other prophecies predicted that the Messiah would establish a righteous kingdom for God's chosen people, the Jews (Isaiah 2:1–4; 11:1–16; Jeremiah 23:3–8; Ezekiel 37:15–28); these were not fulfilled during Jesus' life on earth.

Some passages of the Bible speak of the second coming as very near or **soon** (Hebrews 10:25; James 5:9; 1 John 2:18; Revelation 22:7,12,20), but that **no one** will know the exact day or hour (Matthew 24:36,44; Mark 13:32–35). Jesus said His coming in judgment will be like **lightning** in the sky, and that all nations will see His **sign . . . appear in the sky** and they will **mourn** (Matthew 24:27,30; Luke 17:24; Revelation 1:7). Jesus compared His return to a **thief** breaking into a house or to a **master** returning to his house and servants without warning (Matthew 24:42–51; Mark 13:34–37; Revelation 3:3; 16:15). Paul and Peter gave similar warnings (1 Thessalonians 5:1–4; 2 Peter 3:10).

However, the Bible also teaches that there will be certain signs beforehand, so that we may know when Jesus' coming is **near** (Mark 13:28–29). Jesus said that "**this gospel of the kingdom will be preached in the whole world as a testimony to all nations, and then the end will come**" (Matthew 24:14; Mark 13:10). In the **last days**, evil men will go from **bad to worse**, many will reject the faith, and men will **scoff** at the second coming (Matthew 24:9–14; 2 Timothy 3:1–7,13; 2 Peter 3:3–10; Jude 17–19). Jesus also predicted that there will be wars, earthquakes, famines, and disease epidemics on earth, as well as signs in the sun, moon, and stars (Mark 13:24–28; Luke 21:10–11,25–26; Revelation Chapters 6,8,9,16). This period of trouble is called the **great tribulation** (Daniel 12:1; Mark 13:19–20; Revelation 7:14).

Jesus also warned of **false Christs and false prophets** who will perform **signs and miracles to deceive** men (Mark 13:6,21–23). John wrote not only that many antichrists had already come, but also that a particular **antichrist is coming** (1 John 2:18–22; 4:1–3). Paul reassured the Thessalonians that the day of the Lord had not come already by pointing out that the **man of lawlessness** had not yet been revealed; this man will do **counterfeit miracles, signs and wonders**, and set **himself up in God's temple, proclaiming himself to be God** (2 Thessalonians 2:1–10; Revelation 13:14–15). This idol in the temple may be the **abomination that causes desolation**, which Jesus predicted[1] (Daniel 9:26–27; 12:11; Matthew 24:15; Mark 13:14).

Revelation Chapters 6–16 present many symbolic visions of great tribulations and calamities, ending with the return of Jesus to set up a righteous kingdom. Chapters 13–19 tell of a political ruler (pictured as a **beast** from the sea) and a **false prophet** who will do the evil works described for the antichrist (Daniel 7:24–25; 9:26–27; 11:36–45; 12:1–13; Mark 13:14,22; 2 Thessalonians 2:1–10; 1 John 2:18). This ruler will gather the armies of the earth to Armageddon, where he will be defeated by the returning Christ (Revelation 16:16; 17:14; 19:11–21). Ezekiel Chapters 38–39 and 2 Thessalonians 2:8 also seem to describe this battle.

Revelation 20:1–7 describes a period of a **thousand years** in which Satan is bound in the **Abyss**, unable to deceive the nations. This period is called the "millennium," from the Latin word for "one thousand." The souls of those who had been killed for refusing to worship the image of the beast during his terrible rule are raised to life. **The rest of the dead did not come to life until the thousand**

---

[1] Jesus also prophesied that the temple would be demolished and the city surrounded by armies (Luke 21:6,20–24); in A.D. 70 Jerusalem and its temple were destroyed by the Roman army. Some scholars believe that the **abomination** that Jesus prophesied was the unsuccessful attempt by the Roman emperor Caligula (37–41 A.D.) to set up his statue in the Jewish temple for worship. Others believe that this part of Jesus' prophecy will be fulfilled only in the last days.

years were ended. Those who are raised will reign with Christ for a thousand years. After this thousand-year period, Satan is released and again deceives the nations, gathering them for war against God and His people. Fire falls **from heaven** and destroys them. Satan is thrown into hell, and a final judgment of the dead takes place. **If anyone's name was not found written in the book of life, he was thrown into the lake of fire** (Revelation 20:7–15).

Three Main Views About the Second Coming

In spite of many passages in the Bible on the second coming of Christ, much remains unclear. No single passage of Scripture presents the complete order of events during the last days. Because of this, three main views about the second coming have been proposed. These three views have different beliefs about the timing of Jesus' second coming in relation to the thousand-year period of Revelation Chapter 20.

The first view says that there will be "no actual thousand-year kingdom on earth"; rather, the vision is symbolic of the present reign of Christ in heaven with believers who have died. The Christians who hold this first view believe that the number "thousand" symbolizes completeness and represents the entire time between Jesus' first coming and His second coming. They believe that the binding of the **dragon . . . or Satan** (Revelation 20:2) is symbolic of the spiritual overthrow of Satan at Christ's first coming as well as the restraining power of the Holy Spirit (Luke 10:18; 2 Thessalonians 2:7; 1 John 3:8). These Christians emphasize that the **souls** (Revelation 20:4) of deceased believers are with Christ now (2 Corinthians 5:6–8; Philippians 1:23–24; 1 Thessalonians 4:14; 2 Peter 1:13–14), and that the **kingdom of God** has already begun (Matthew 11:12; 12:28; Colossians 1:13) but is not a visible kingdom of this world (Luke 17:20–21; John 18:36–37; Romans 14:17). These Christians believe that Daniel's **seventy 'sevens'** prophecy (Daniel 9:24–27) was completely fulfilled in the events that followed Jesus' death and resurrection—the establishment of the church, the attempt by the Roman emperor to place his statue in the Jewish temple, and the destruction of Jerusalem and its temple which ended the Jewish sacrifices. Those who hold this view believe that the **first resurrection** (Revelation 20:5) is a spiritual resurrection only, pointing out that, for us who believe, God has already **made us alive with Christ . . . raised us up . . . and seated us with him in the heavenly realms** (Ephesians 2:4–6; 5:14; Colossians 3:1).

According to this first view, the "second resurrection" will be the resurrection of the body, and will take place when Christ returns to earth. These Christians believe that there is only one bodily resurrection—for both believers and unbelievers at the same time—and only one final judgment (Daniel 12:2; Matthew 25:31–46; John 5:28–29; Revelation 20:11–15). Believers will meet Christ coming in the air (1 Thessalonians 4:17), but immediately return with Him to earth for the final overthrow of Satan and his followers at one final battle (Revelation 19:11–21; 20:7–10). They believe that the prophecies in the Old Testament of a future earthly kingdom for the Jews have been transferred fully to the Christian church. (Compare Joel 2:28–32 with Acts 2:14–21, Zechariah 9:9–13 with Matthew 21:1–9, and Malachi 4:1–6 with Matthew 11:11–14; 17:10–13; Romans 4:16; Galatians 4:22–31.) Therefore, they believe these prophecies are either symbolically fulfilled in the present church age, or will be fulfilled only in the final **new heaven and new earth** of Revelation Chapters 21–22.

The second view concerning Christ's second coming is that Jesus' return will occur "after an actual long period of peace and prosperity on the earth," in which most of the world will turn to God and Christ in faith. This long period may not be exactly one thousand years long. Those who hold this second view agree with the first view that the kingdom of God has already begun at Christ's first coming, but these Christians believe that the earth will gradually see more and more of Christ's kingdom rule through the church (Matthew 28:18; Ephesians 1:19–23). The **gospel of the kingdom** (Matthew 24:14) will eventually win most people to faith in Christ, bringing a thousand years (or a very long period) of peace and spiritual blessings through the church (Joel 2:28–32; Acts 2:17–21). They point to many prophecies which indicate that in the last days the nations of the earth will cease warring against each other and seek knowledge about God (Isaiah 2:1–4; Micah 4:1–5; Zechariah 8:20–23). These Christians believe that many other prophecies are symbolic of this long period, when Jesus will rule His kingdom through the church before His actual return from heaven (Psalms 2; 72; Isaiah 11:6–10; Ezekiel 37:15–28; Zechariah 9:9–10). This second view agrees with the first view that the return of Christ, the bodily resurrection, and the final judgment will all take place in a single event just before the beginning of the **new heaven and new earth** described in Revelation Chapters 21–22.

The third main view of Christ's second coming is that Jesus will return to earth "before the thousand-year earthly kingdom begins," and that all believers will be resurrected to reign with Him during this period. Christians holding this third view agree that the prophets spoke in symbols, but they emphasize that all the events symbolically described will actually occur. Therefore, most of them believe that the Old Testament promises to the Jews will actually be fulfilled in the future thousand-year kingdom (Isaiah 11:1–16; 65:18–25; Jeremiah 23:5–8; Ezekiel 37:15–28; Zechariah 14:9–21).

In Romans 11:25–29, Paul pointed to Old Testament promises to show that eventually the Jews would turn to the Gospel. Furthermore, these Christians believe that all time periods given in prophecy are actual times, not symbolic only. They believe that Revelation Chapters 6–19 describe an actual future tribulation, which will take place right before the return of Christ for His thousand-year reign (Daniel 12:1; Mark 13:24–27; Luke 21:10–11,25–27). They believe that Daniel's **seventy "sevens"** (Daniel 9:24–27) stand for 490 years of actual history. The first 69 "sevens" (or 483 years) were to begin from the date of the **decree to restore and rebuild Jerusalem**, which was in 445 B.C. (Nehemiah 2:1–9), and continue **until the Anointed One, the ruler, comes**, meaning Jesus, the Messiah.[2] This Anointed One was to be **cut off** (fulfilled by Jesus' death on the cross), and Jerusalem and its temple were to be destroyed (fulfilled in 70 A.D. by the Roman army). These Christians believe that the events of Daniel's seventieth "seven," or final seven years, were not fulfilled during the first century after Christ, but will only be fulfilled in a final seven year period of tribulation immediately before Christ returns to set up His kingdom.

This third view identifies Daniel's **king** or **ruler who will come** (Daniel 7:24–25; 9:26–27; 11:36) with Paul's **man of lawlessness** (2 Thessalonians 2:1–10) and with either the **beast** or the **false prophet** of Revelation Chapters 13–19. This ruler will break his **covenant** with Israel in the middle of the seven-year tribulation, setting up his image for worship (Daniel 9:27; 12:11; Mark 13:14; 2 Thessalonians 2:4; Revelation 13:14–15) in the new Jewish temple (Ezekiel Chapters 40–47). During this tribulation many of the Jews, as well as many from all the nations of the earth, will turn to Jesus in faith (Romans 11:25–31; Revelation 7:4,9,14), but will suffer persecution and death for their refusal to worship the image of the beast (Revelation 6:9–11; 14:3; 15:2–4; 20:4). At the end of the great tribulation, the armies of the beast will be destroyed at Armageddon by the triumphant return of Jesus Christ (Zechariah 14:1–9; Revelation 19:11–21). These Christians believe that Matthew 25:31–46 describes the judgment of the living nations before the thousand-year earthly kingdom begins, and that both resurrections in Revelation 20:1–12 are actual resurrections of the body—the first, a resurrection of deceased believers before the thousand-year period; and the second, a resurrection afterward of the unbelieving

[2] Many scholars believe that each of these 483 years was only 360 days long (each month thirty days), since the comparable three-and-a-half-year (or forty-two-month) period in Daniel and in Revelation is said to be 1260 days long (Daniel 7:25; 12:7–11; Revelation 11:2–3; 12:6,14). Thus the 483 years of Daniel's 69 "sevens" actually do end at the historical time of Jesus' ministry and death in about 30 A.D..

dead for final judgment. Then the old heaven and earth will be destroyed **by fire**, and a **new heaven and new earth** created (2 Peter 3:10–13; Revelation 21:1).

Those who hold this third main view do not agree among themselves as to when believers will be resurrected (or their bodies changed) to meet the Lord in the air. Most believe that Jesus' second coming involves two visits to earth. The first is a brief, sudden return **in the clouds** before the tribulation period begins in order to raise all those who have believed in Jesus prior to that time (1 Thessalonians 4:17), followed by an immediate return to heaven for the **wedding supper of the Lamb** (Matthew 25:1–13; Revelation 19:9). This first visit will come unexpectedly, as a **thief** in the night (Matthew 24:42–51; 1 Thessalonians 5:1–4; Revelation 3:3). The second visit is Jesus' actual return to earth with His resurrected believers to defeat the beast and begin His earthly kingdom. Jesus promised in John 14:2–3 to return from heaven to **take** us with Him. These Christians note the sudden separation between those **taken** and those **left** (Matthew 24:40–41). Paul said that **God did not appoint us to suffer wrath** (1 Thessalonians 5:9). Jesus told us to pray for **escape** from **all that is about to happen** (Luke 21:36). These Christians point out that Revelation 20:4–6 only describes the resurrection of those who were **beheaded** for refusing to worship the beast. These Christians believe that all true believers will be resurrected and taken to heaven before the tribulation begins, and that the resurrection of Revelation 20:4–6 only involves those who had become believers and died during the seven-year tribulation. The unbelieving dead will be raised just before the final judgment.

However, others who hold the third main view (that Jesus will return before the thousand-year period) believe that the church will suffer on earth during the seven-year tribulation. They agree that believers who are alive at the second coming will be caught up to meet Christ coming with deceased believers; but since they believe this takes place at the end of the seven-year tribulation period, they say that Jesus will immediately continue on to earth to defeat the beast at Armageddon and set up His kingdom. They point out that the sudden **trumpet** call and gathering of resurrected believers is connected in Matthew 24:15–31 with the visible return of Christ in power and glory after a time of terrible persecution, and that the prophecy in Luke 17:26–37 that one person will suddenly be taken and one be left is connected with sudden destruction. Jesus never actually taught that He would come twice. Therefore, they believe that the return of Christ will be a single event, as in the first and second main views; but unlike those views, they say the second coming will occur before an actual thousand-year reign of Christ on earth. These Christians believe that there are only two resurrections:

first, a resurrection of all believers at the return of Christ, after the tribulation and before the thousand-year kingdom begins; and second, a resurrection of the unbelieving dead just before the final judgment.

Summary

Whatever view we hold, we should not argue and fight about this issue. We all believe in the return of Jesus Christ to raise us up for eternal life with Him. The exact details are not important for our salvation. The second coming should encourage us in our personal lives and in our public service. We are warned to be ready to meet Him by not letting the **lamps** of our faith and witness go out (Matthew 25:1–13). We are warned to **be alert** as regards our behavior, to be **self-controlled**, living **holy and godly lives**, not allowing our hearts to be **weighed down with . . . the anxieties of life** (Luke 21:34–36; 1 Thessalonians 5:4–11; 2 Peter 3:11–14). We are to **stand firm** and to **watch**, so as not to be caught **sleeping** or lording it over others, but to be found faithfully doing the **work of the Lord** that He has given us to do (Matthew 24:45–51; 25:14–30; Mark 13:35–37; 1 Corinthians 3:11–15; 15:58; 2 Corinthians 5:10). That work may be evangelism (Matthew 24:14; Mark 13:10), or service ministries (Matthew 25:31–46). Our personal repentance, personal behavior, and personal witness may actually **speed** His return (Mark 13:10; Acts 3:19–21; 2 Peter 3:11–12). **For the grace of God . . . teaches us . . . to live self-controlled, upright and godly lives in this present age, while we wait for the blessed hope—the glorious appearing of our great God and Savior, Jesus Christ** (Titus 2:11–13). **Amen. Come, Lord Jesus** (Revelation 22:20).

THE PURPOSE OF THE CHURCH

Just before He ascended into heaven, Jesus spoke these final words to His disciples: "... **you will receive power when the Holy Spirit comes on you; and you will be my witnesses in Jerusalem, and in all Judea and Samaria, and to the ends of the earth**" (Acts 1:8). We Christians are to be **witnesses** of Jesus Christ. The purpose of the CHURCH is to be a witness to Jesus Christ in the world. This is the church's primary purpose; all other functions of the church are secondary to it.

What does it mean to be a witness to Jesus Christ? It means to reach out to the world by word and deed to draw men and women to Him. It means to be a light in the world. Jesus said: "... **let your light shine before men, that they may see your good deeds and praise your Father in heaven**" (Matthew 5:16). Let your light shine. That means we are to be Christ's ambassadors in the world. Paul wrote: **We are therefore Christ's ambassadors** (2 Corinthians 5:20). And our work as **ambassadors** is to reconcile men and women to God.

Finally, to be a witness of Jesus Christ means to go into all the world and make disciples. Jesus said to His disciples: "... **go and make disciples of all nations, baptizing them in the name of the Father and of the Son and of the Holy Spirit, and teaching them to obey everything I have commanded you**" (Matthew 28:19–20).

What is the motive for our being witnesses? It is love. The second greatest commandment says: **Love your neighbor as yourself** (Mark 12:31). We believers have found the bread of life; if we love our neighbor, we will want to show him where he can find it too.

The reason Jesus calls us to Himself and makes us into His church is so that we might go and bear fruit. Jesus said: "**You did not choose me, but I chose you and appointed you to go and bear fruit—fruit that will last**" (John 15:16). In this context, **fruit** primarily means new disciples. Jesus said, "**As the Father has sent me, I am sending you**" (John 20:21). Why was Jesus sent? He was sent into the world so that **whoever believes in him shall not perish but have eternal life** (John 3:16). Think of it! We are being sent into the world in the same way and for the same purpose that the Father sent Jesus! Today we, the church, have been appointed to continue the work of Jesus upon this earth, to be a light showing men and women the way to heaven and to eternal life.

Thus we see that the overriding purpose of the church is to reach out—just as light "reaches out" into the darkness. Sadly, many churches, once they have been established, become preoccupied with their own internal affairs. They become like clubs or private societies. The members think only about the blessings they hope to receive from the church, and they stop thinking about the blessings they should be giving to others through the church. The church was never meant to be merely a safe haven for Christians. The church was meant primarily to prepare and send out witnesses—that is, ambassadors, fruit bearers, disciple makers, missionaries.

The church of Jesus Christ is a witnessing church, a missionary church. How did the church start in Europe? It started because someone named Paul went to Philippi in Macedonia (Greece) and planted a church there (Acts 16:9–15,40). How did the church start in India? It started because Christians traveled to India to preach the GOSPEL. Many say that the first missionary to India was the Apostle Thomas himself. How did the church start in China? In Korea? In Africa? Same reason: witnesses went to those places and preached the Gospel.

Of course, not every member of the church is called to go to a distant place and preach; in fact, only a few are called to do this. But every Christian is called to be a witness wherever he or she lives and works (Acts 1:8). And every church member needs to keep in mind that the main purpose of the church is to be a witness, not only in the local area but also to the ends of the earth.

The church is like a body (1 Corinthians 12:27). The heart's main job is to pump blood; the lung's main job is to breathe; the ear's main job is to hear; the legs' main job is to walk. But the overall purpose of each organ is to help the body live and work. And so it is with each member of the church.

If any church is not witnessing, not reaching out, it is a dying church. Indeed, the spiritual health of any church is best measured not by the number of Christians it attracts, but rather by the number of missionaries (witnesses) it sends out.

Some people say that missions outreach is only one of several equally important functions of the church. They describe the church as a four-legged stool, with the four legs being worship, fellowship, teaching, and missions outreach. But that is an inadequate representation of the church of Christ. The missions outreach is the light that should be sitting on top of the stool! A stool only needs three legs—worship, fellowship, and teaching. Worship, fellowship, and teaching are not ends in themselves; they are means to an end. They are the means of supporting the stool—of supporting the missions outreach of the church.

So, again, we must state that missions (witness, evangelism) is the primary purpose of the church of Christ. In other words, missions isn't just one of several programs of the church; it is the one all-embracing program of the church.

When we keep this truth in mind, the ministry of the church and of each believer will remain in proper balance. Often as Christians we get caught up in secondary causes, and we lose sight of our overall direction and purpose. These secondary causes (social justice, protection of the environment, better health, better education, economic development, etc.) are all very good and important concerns, and Christians must be involved in them. But these concerns are secondary to the primary concern of leading men and women to Jesus Christ and to SALVATION. Giving a person a few years of improved life on this earth is a very small gift compared with leading that person into eternal life in heaven. We always need to keep our eye on the ultimate goal of all ministry: to reconcile people to God and to bring them into His kingdom (see 2 Corinthians 5:18–20 and comment).

Jesus kept His eye on the goal. He preached, taught, healed, and performed miracles, but the goal of all these activities was one: to reconcile men to God. His healings and other miraculous works were not ends in themselves; they were signs demonstrating that He was God's Son, and that therefore people should listen to His words. He didn't want to become known as a miracle worker; He instructed almost everyone He healed not to tell anyone about it. He didn't want to take people's eyes off their spiritual need. When the people tried to persuade Him to stay in their village and keep on healing them, Jesus refused to stay, saying, "**I must preach the good news of the kingdom of God to the other towns also, because that is why I was sent**" (Luke 4:43). Jesus' main work was to bring men and women into the kingdom of God; and if that was His main work, it is also ours—both as individuals and as a church.

There is a final thing to say about the purpose or mission of the church: when that mission has been fulfilled, Jesus will come again and the world will end. Jesus said: "**And this gospel of the kingdom will be preached in the whole world as a testimony to all nations, and then the end will come**" (Matthew 24:14).

Jesus is waiting for us to proclaim the Gospel to every tribe and cultural group. There are many thousands of these distinct cultural groups in the world. In Matthew 24:14 and 28:19, these groups are called **nations.**[1] It is estimated that there are approximately 10,000[2] of these groups which still have no permanent indigenous witness

[1] The Greek word **nations** in Matthew 28:19 does not mean countries in a political sense, but rather groups of people with a similar language and culture.

[2] This figure is currently under debate. The figure used depends on how one defines such groups and on how finely they are subdivided.

among them. The supreme task of every Christian is to help spread the Gospel of Christ to these remaining unreached cultural groups, and to help establish a witnessing, self-reproducing church within each group. Until this is accomplished, the purpose of the church will not be fulfilled, and Christ will not return.

How big is the task? Because of the growth of world population, there are today more non-Christians in the world than ever before in history. On the other hand, there are also many more Christians available to accomplish the task than ever before. The task can be done. In 100 A.D., there was one witnessing Christian for every 360 non-Christians. In 1950, there was one witnessing Christian for every twenty non-Christians. Today there is one witnessing Christian for every seven non-Christians. By the year 2000, the ratio of witnessing Christians to non-Christians will be only four to one. The task can indeed be done!

There are 2 billion people on earth who have not yet had the chance to hear the Gospel in a relevant way. The purpose of the church of Christ is to reach these people. Some Christians are called to be senders of missionaries—that is, to pray for them and to support and encourage them. Others are called to go themselves. God needs both senders and goers. But regardless of whether one goes abroad or stays at home, every Christian must be a witness. Jesus demands the same degree of commitment and consecration from each one of us, wherever we are called to serve.

REVIVAL

Most people, when they first come to Christ, are filled with great joy, freedom, and love. They feel close to Jesus. Their hearts burn with a desire to serve Him. But then, as time passes, their initial zeal grows less and less, and often fades almost completely away. Why? What has happened? How can we bring back that first experience of coming to Jesus?

There is no greater problem in our Christian lives than the loss of zeal, the loss of our love for Jesus. Jesus wrote these frightening words to the ancient church at Ephesus: **Yet I hold this against you: You have forsaken your first love. Remember the height from which you have fallen! Repent and do the things you did at first. If you do not repent, I will come to you and remove your lampstand from its place** (Revelation 2:4–5).

Satan is furious whenever anyone leaves his kingdom of darkness and through faith in Christ enters the kingdom of God. Therefore, from the moment a person becomes a Christian, Satan attacks that new believer with every weapon he has. Satan's main goal is to take away the believer's love for Jesus. Satan knows that he cannot snatch a true believer out of Jesus' hand (John 10:28). But he can make that believer ineffective; he can make him loveless and lifeless. And he all too frequently succeeds.

Thus in our Christian lives, we often need to be spiritually revived. Not only individuals need to be revived, but churches also need to be revived. We need to be constantly examining ourselves. Do we love Jesus more than anything else in the world? (Mark 12:30). Do we seek the kingdom of God first of all? (Matthew 6:33). Are we in complete love and fellowship with every Christian brother and sister? (1 John 1:7; 4:20). Are we experiencing the fruit of the Holy Spirit in our lives daily? (Galatians 5:22–23). Is there spiritual power in our lives? In our church? (Luke 24:49; Acts 1:8). If the answer to any of these questions is no, then we need to be revived.

One of the main reasons we study the word of God is to experience renewal and revival. That is one of the main reasons this commentary has been written. As you study and use this commentary, let your prayer be that the words of God might spring to life in your heart with new meaning and new power. As you study and use this commentary, pray for revival in your own heart and in your own local church.

Let us look now at this matter of revival. First of all, what is revival? Revival is the restoring of our first love for Christ. Revival is walking in the light with Jesus and letting Him live His life in us. Revival is being restored to spiritual health after a period of decline. Revival is admitting our sins and calling out to Jesus for forgiveness and cleansing. Revival is giving Jesus control of every area of our lives.

Revival is a time of deep stirring in our lives. However, revival does not mean working oneself into an emotional frenzy. It is a time of prayer, of meditation, of sober self-evaluation; it is a time of drawing close to Jesus. Revival is a time when our hypocrisy and self-deception is exposed. Revival is a time when strife, criticism, and bitterness in the church is revealed and repented of. Revival is a time when our lives are changed so much that others are affected and drawn to Christ. Above all, revival is a time when the Holy Spirit comes to us in power, working in us both individually and as a church.

How does revival begin? Almost invariably revival begins with the awareness and confession of our sins. Sin is the reason that we need revival in the first place. The devil's main method of attack is to tempt us to sin. When we sin, we become separated from God. We grieve God's Holy Spirit within us. We lose our fellowship with Jesus; we lose our joy, our peace, our power. If there was no sin in us, there would be no need for revival. Thus revival begins with the acknowledgement and confession of our sins.

We don't like to think of ourselves as sinners. We minimize our sins. Often we don't even recognize them. We are like the rich young man who told Jesus he had kept all the commandments since he was a boy (Mark 10:17–21). He was sure he had no sin!

But even if we don't see our sin, God does. Sin is not just breaking a commandment. Sin is anything in our lives which is not in agreement with God's will as revealed in the Bible. This means that sin includes wrong attitudes: self-love, pride, envy, covetousness, resentment, anxiousness, faithlessness. Sin is not only doing what is wrong; it is failing to do what is right (James 4:17). It is failing to love God with all our heart, soul, mind, and strength (Mark 12:30). It is failing to love our neighbor as ourself (Mark 12:31). It is failing to stand firm in faith to the end (Mark 13:13). It is failing to share the Gospel when we have opportunity (1 Peter 3:15). It is failing to help our brother in need (Matthew 25:41–45). Who among us can say we have no sin? (1 John 1:8).

The first step in revival, then, is to confess our sins. Let us remember the price Jesus paid to cleanse us from sin. Let us ask the

Holy Spirit to reveal to us our hidden sins. Here follows a sample list of questions we should ask ourselves, in order to detect those areas of our lives which are not fully surrendered to the lordship of Jesus:

Do I love anything more than God: my family, my work, my pleasures, myself? (Matthew 6:33; Mark 12:30).

Have I been complaining or murmuring against God about any situation in my life? (1 Corinthians 10:10; Philippians 2:14; 1 Thessalonians 5:18).

Do I love praise from other men? Do I desire to be commended for the good I do? Do I love to be the center of attention? (Matthew 6:1–5; John 12:43).

Am I impatient with others? Am I critical of others? Am I touchy or sensitive when others criticize me? Do I have a spirit of resentment toward anyone? Is there any bitterness in me? (Hebrews 12:15).

Am I stubborn and unyielding? Am I headstrong and argumentative? Am I always sure I'm right? Am I harsh or sarcastic? (Philippians 2:3; Ephesians 5:21).

Do I fear what men will say? Do I shrink from duty? Do I hide the talents God has given to me? (Matthew 25:24–28).

Am I jealous of anyone? Am I secretly happy when someone else fails? Am I secretly unhappy when someone else succeeds? (1 Corinthians 13:4–6).

Is there anything about which I have not been completely honest? Is there some truth I am concealing? Do I try to cover up my faults? Do I try to give a better impression of myself than is really true? Do I exaggerate? (Matthew 23:27–28; James 5:16).

Am I discouraged or depressed? Have I stopped fully trusting God? Has my faith become weak? (Romans 1:17; 14:23; Hebrews 11:6).

Has my spiritual life become dry and formal? Have I lost my concern for those who do not know Christ? Have I become spiritually weak? Have I become lukewarm? Have I turned back from the life of a disciple? (Mark 8:34; Revelation 2:4–5; 3:15–16).

Have I become conformed to the world? Have I begun to think as unbelievers think? Have I begun to love the world and its pleasures? (Romans 12:2; 1 John 2:15–17).

If the answer to any of these questions is yes, then we need to acknowledge and confess that sin to God. If we do, we open up the way for God to revive us. If we do not, we shall become progressively weaker and farther removed from God.

The second step in revival is to repent of all the sins the Holy Spirit has revealed to us. REPENTANCE means to sorrow deeply for our sins, and then to turn from them completely. When we do this,

God will forgive us and cleanse us (1 John 1:9). If we do not experience this forgiveness and cleansing, there is only one explanation: We have not fully turned from our sin.

The third step in revival is to make right any wrong we have done to others (Matthew 5:23–24; Luke 19:8). We may need to apologize to someone. We may need to restore someone's possessions we have taken. We may need to restore someone's reputation that we have slandered. Above all, we may need to forgive someone, for to harbor bitterness or resentment against anyone is a great sin (Matthew 6:12,14–15).

The fourth step in revival is to rededicate our lives to Christ. We must surrender every part of our lives to Him; we must hold nothing back. We must commit ourselves to obey everything He asks us to do (John 14:15). We are not our own; we belong to Him (1 Corinthians 6:19–20).

The fifth step in revival is to claim what God has promised to those who turn to him with a humble and repentant heart. We must open our hearts to the filling of God's Holy Spirit. God has commanded us to be filled with the Spirit (Ephesians 5:18). Therefore, we must desire this filling. We must present ourselves to God to be filled (Romans 12:1). We must ask to be filled (Matthew 7:7–8,11; Luke 11:13).

The sixth and final step in revival is to live in submission to the Holy Spirit. No one can be filled with the Spirit who is not controlled by the Spirit. Paul wrote: **So I say, live by the Spirit, and you will not gratify the desires of the sinful nature** (Galatians 5:16). This is the key to living a Christlike life. This is the key to spiritual victory. To live a life of victory means that Christ Himself lives His life in us and through us (Galatians 2:20). This, then, is our goal: to be conformed to the likeness of Christ (Romans 8:29). There is no higher goal.

These, then, are the steps that we must take to prepare for revival. But remember, the reviving work itself is done totally by the Holy Spirit, in His way and in His time. Having done all that we can do, we must then look expectantly to Him.

> **If my people, who are called by my name, will humble themselves and pray and seek my face and turn from their wicked ways, then will I hear from heaven and will forgive their sin and will heal their land** (2 Chronicles 7:14).

O God, revive us!

SUMMARY OF THE OLD TESTAMENT

The New Testament writers expected their readers to have some knowledge of the Old Testament. They refer frequently to the Old Testament Scriptures and to the history of the Jewish people recorded there (see Acts Chapter 7; Hebrews Chapter 11). This article briefly presents a summary of the Old Testament, emphasizing the events and persons that are mentioned in the New Testament. It also notes the main New Testament references that relate to that event or person. The names of the books of the Old Testament are printed in bold type.

The book of **Genesis** starts at the beginning. God created the heavens and the earth (Genesis 1:1–25; John 1:1–3). God made the world in six days, and on the sixth day He created the first man and woman, Adam and Eve (Genesis 1:26–31). On the seventh day God rested from His work. This was the beginning of the Sabbath rest, which later God commanded mankind to observe (Genesis 2:1–3; Hebrews 4:1–11).

Adam and Eve were placed in the Garden of Eden and given only one command: they were not to eat from the tree of the knowledge of good and evil. But SATAN came in the form of a serpent and deceived Eve, and tempted her to eat the forbidden fruit. She ate, and then Adam ate also. Thus sin and death first entered the world (Genesis 3:1–19; Romans 5:12–19). This is called the "fall of man." Then the oldest son of Adam and Eve, Cain, murdered his brother Abel because of jealousy, which was the first shedding of human blood (Genesis 4:1–12; Hebrews 11:4; 1 John 3:12). After that, Adam and Eve had another son named Seth (Genesis 5:3).

One of the descendants of Seth was Enoch, who never died but was taken directly to heaven (Genesis 5:21–24; Hebrews 11:5). After Enoch's time, men became very corrupt before God, and so He decided to destroy the world in a flood. He instructed a righteous man named Noah to build a large boat to hold his family and at least one pair of every type of animal; all those on the boat were saved from the flood, whereas every other living creature perished (Genesis 6:1–22; 7:11–24; 1 Peter 3:18–20).

Abraham, was a descendant of Noah's son Shem, and was born in Ur, located in present-day Iraq. God called Abraham to move from Ur to the land of Canaan (modern Israel), a land which God promised to give to Abraham's descendants. God also promised to make a great nation from Abraham's descendants and to bless all the peoples of the world through him (Genesis 12:1–7). This blessing was fulfilled in the coming of Jesus Christ, a direct descendant of Abraham (Matthew 1:1; Romans 4:16–18; Galatians 3:6–9,14,29).

Abraham obeyed God and left his home country. One time after a battle, Abraham gave a tenth of his winnings to Melchizedek, a priest of God (Genesis 14:17–20; Hebrews 5:6,10). This is the first mention of the tithe, that is, the giving of one tenth of one's income and produce.

God had promised to give Abraham and Sarah a son; but when the answer was slow in coming, Sarah gave Abraham her servant Hagar, and she bore him a son, who was named Ishmael (Genesis 16:1–4,15). But God had promised Abraham a legitimate son by Sarah, his wife, so Abraham continued to place his hope in God. Finally, Sarah did bear a son when she was ninety and Abraham was one hundred years old! They named the child Isaac, and he founded the Jewish race. It is commonly believed that Ishmael founded the Arab race. The Arabs remain enemies of the Jews to this very day (Genesis 17:15–22; 21:1–5; Galatians 4:21–31).

God made a COVENANT with Abraham, the sign of which was CIRCUMCISION, the cutting away of the skin at the tip of the penis. From then on, all male descendants of Abraham (through Isaac) were circumcised at eight days of age, as a sign that they were part of the people of God (Genesis 17:1–14). Circumcision was a requirement for the Jews, but Paul insisted that other peoples did not need to follow this requirement (Romans 2:25–29; 4:9–12; Galatians 5:2–6; Colossians 2:11–12).

Abraham's nephew Lot lived in the extremely sinful cities of Sodom and Gomorrah. God sent three angels to Abraham to warn him of the coming judgment and destruction of those cities (Genesis 18:1–2,20–21). Lot escaped with the help of the angels (Genesis 19:15–29; Matthew 10:15; Luke 17:28–30).

A few years later God tested Abraham by asking him to sacrifice his only son Isaac, and Abraham was obedient. At the moment he was about to kill Isaac, God stopped him and provided a ram for the sacrifice instead (Genesis 22:1–18; Hebrews 11:17–19). In the same way, God sent Jesus Christ to die as a sacrifice in our place (Hebrews 10:10).

Isaac married Rebecca, and she bore twins, Esau and Jacob. Esau was older, but Jacob stole Esau's birthright and his blessing (Genesis 25:19–34; 27:1–40). Jacob escaped from Esau's anger, and on his way to another place he met the Lord in a dream. God promised Jacob what He had promised Abraham: namely, that through his descendants all the people of the world would be blessed (Genesis 28:10–17). As we saw above, this promise was fulfilled in Jesus Christ.

Jacob married two sisters, Leah and Rachel. They and their servants bore Jacob twelve sons, who founded the twelve tribes of ISRAEL (Acts 7:8): Reuben, Simeon, Levi (whose tribe became the priestly tribe), Judah (from whom Jesus was descended), Issachar, Zebulun, Dan, Naphtali, Gad, Asher, Joseph, and Benjamin (Genesis 35:23–26; Revelation 7:3–8). The family came back to Canaan, and on the way God gave Jacob a new name, Israel. Thus the Jewish people came to be called Israelites (Genesis 32:22–32).

Joseph was Jacob's favorite son. Because of their jealousy, Joseph's brothers sold him as a slave to some traders who then took him to Egypt (Genesis 37:12–36). However, God was with Joseph and worked things out for good by making him a high government official (Genesis 39:1–5; 41:41–57). At the time of a famine, Joseph's family came to him to buy food, but they didn't recognize him until he revealed himself to them (Genesis 42:1–8; 45:1–11). The family then moved to Egypt and settled there. Jacob (Israel) adopted Joseph's two sons, Ephraim and Manesseh, as his own (Genesis 48:1,5; Acts 7:9–16).

The book of **Job** was probably written about the time of Abraham. It deals with the sufferings of a man named Job, and his steadfast faith in spite of all his troubles.

The Israelites stayed in Egypt for about four hundred years, and their population grew. The Egyptians became afraid of them and made them their slaves. The oppression of the Israelites in Egypt was very great, and finally God raised up MOSES to be their deliverer. The book of **Exodus** records the story of the Israelites' deliverance and their journey to Mount Sinai. This took place in approximately 1400 B.C. Moses and his older brother Aaron repeatedly asked Pharaoh, the ruler of Egypt, to let the Israelites go. Each time Pharaoh refused, God sent a plague upon the Egyptians. To protect the Israelites from the final plague, the killing of all the firstborn of Egypt, the "PASSOVER" was instituted. An unblemished lamb was sacrificed and eaten by each Israelite family, and the blood was sprinkled on the doorposts as a sign to the destroying angel to "pass over" that house (Exodus 12:1–23). Jesus is said to be our "Passover lamb," since it is by Jesus' blood that we are saved from death (1 Corinthians 5:7; 1 Peter 1:19; Revelation 5:6–10). Unleavened bread was eaten because there was not time to let the dough rise. When Pharaoh discovered his firstborn son was dead, he ordered the Israelites to leave that same day (Exodus

12:29–39). But as soon as the Israelites had gone, Pharaoh changed his mind and sent the Egyptian army after them (Exodus 14:5–14). The cloud of the Lord moved between the Egyptian army and the Israelites. God parted the water of the Red Sea, and the Israelites passed through on dry land (Exodus 14:15–22; 1 Corinthians 10:1–2). But when the Egyptians tried to follow, the water came together again and they were drowned (Exodus 14:23–31).

The Israelites traveled on to Mount Sinai, where God gave Moses directions for making the tabernacle, the tent of worship (Hebrews 9:1–10). God also gave Moses the LAW on Mount Sinai. The first five books of the Old Testament are called the books of the law. In these books, all the rules and regulations for the Jewish nation are found, especially in the book of **Leviticus**. All these laws had to be obeyed in order for the Jewish people to remain in a right relationship with God and to be blessed by God. These laws can be divided into different categories: 1) offerings and animal sacrifices, 2) regulations for priests and the temple, 3) purity and cleanliness, 4) festivals, and 5) social relationships.

We are no longer required to follow the Jewish law,[1] because it has been fulfilled in Jesus Christ (Matthew 5:17). God asked for animal sacrifices because **without the shedding of blood there is no forgiveness** of sin (Hebrews 9:22). However, the Old Testament sacrifices did not truly cleanse the people and did not change their hearts (Hebrews 9:9–10). Christ has become the final, perfect sacrifice, the One who can truly cleanse us and make us holy before God (Hebrews 9:14; 10:10). Therefore, Christ has fulfilled the laws relating to sacrifice and purity. The earthly temple has been destroyed. Jesus is our great high priest, serving in the true heavenly temple (Hebrews 8:1–2).

The Old Testament festivals (Leviticus Chapter 23) also have been fulfilled by Christ at His first coming, or they will be fulfilled at His second coming. The festival of Passover and Unleavened Bread (Leviticus 23:4–8) was fulfilled when Jesus became our Passover lamb by dying at Passover time to truly save us from death. (Jesus' last meal with His disciples, the first LORD'S SUPPER, was a Passover meal.) The festival of Firstfruits (Leviticus 23:9–14) was fulfilled when on that festival day Christ became the first to rise from the dead; He was the "firstfruits." Believers in Him will be resurrected later (1 Corinthians 15:22–23). The festival of PENTECOST, also called the Feast of Weeks (Leviticus 23:15–21), was fulfilled when the HOLY

[1] Christians are expected to obey the "moral" law of the Old Testament, in particular the ten commandments (Exodus 20:1–17). But Jesus summarized the moral law in the two great commandments to love God and to love one's neighbor (Mark 12:30–31). If we follow these two great commandments, we shall also be fulfilling the ten commandments (Matthew 22:40; Romans 13:9).

SPIRIT came on the day of Pentecost to empower the church (Acts 2:1–4). The Day of Atonement (Leviticus 16:1–34; 23:26–32) was fulfilled by Christ through His death on the CROSS and completed when He ascended to heaven and offered His shed blood in the heavenly temple for our cleansing (Hebrews 9:11–14,24–28). The two remaining festivals, Trumpets and Tabernacles (Leviticus 23:23–25,33–36), will be fulfilled at Jesus' second coming.

The laws of social relationships, such as the ten commandments (Exodus 20:1–17), were also required by God; but we know that no one can be considered righteous by observing the law, because no one can obey all of the law all the time (Galatians 2:15–16; James 2:10). The law was **put in charge** of us to **lead us** to faith in Christ (Galatians 3:24). As believers in Jesus Christ, we are no longer "under" the law (Romans 7:6; Galatians 3:13,25), but we are not to misuse our freedom by leading a life of sin (Galatians 5:13). A major teaching of the New Testament is that love for one another is the fulfillment of the law (Matthew 22:36–40; Romans 13:8–10; Galatians 5:14), and that those who truly love Jesus will do what He commands (John 14:15; 1 John 2:4–5).

In the book of **Numbers**, we read about the further travels of the Israelites in the Sinai desert. Many times they complained and rebelled against God and Moses. A man named Korah led one of these rebellions, and God destroyed him and his men (Numbers 16:1–40). At the end of the journey in the desert, twelve spies were sent out to look at the "promised land," the land of Canaan (Israel), which God had promised to give to Abraham's descendants, the Israelites. Ten of the spies reported that there were giants and strong cities, and that it would be impossible to conquer the land (Numbers 13:17–33; 1 Corinthians 10:1-11). The people were afraid because of the report of the spies. So God punished the people for their lack of faith by causing them to wander for forty years in the desert wilderness (Numbers 14:1–38). During the forty years they were fed daily with "manna" from heaven (Exodus 16:14–31; John 6:30–35). Twice they complained of thirst, and God provided water from a rock (Exodus 17:1–7; Numbers 20:1–11; 1 Corinthians 10:3–5). Once, when the people were being punished for grumbling by being bitten by poisonous snakes, God in His mercy told Moses how to help the people. Moses made a bronze snake and put it up on a pole. If those who were bitten by snakes looked at the bronze snake on the pole, they lived (Numbers 21:4–9). In the same way we too can obtain deliverance from sin and death by looking in faith at Jesus lifted up on the cross (John 3:14–15).

Toward the end of the forty years in the wilderness, the Israelites traveled to the land of Moab. When Balak, the king of Moab, heard about it, he was angry and afraid. So he tried to hire a local prophet named Balaam to curse the Israelites. Balaam begged God for permission to go, and finally obtained it; but God was very angry with Balaam. On the way, Balaam's donkey saw a fearsome angel of God and the donkey spoke to warn Balaam. So Balaam did not curse the Israelites, but blessed them instead. However, Balaam still tried to earn the money from Balak by telling him how to weaken the Israelites by seducing them to worship an idol named Baal (Numbers 22:21–35; 25:1–3; 2 Peter 2:15–16; Revelation 2:14).

Before the Israelites entered Canaan, the promised land, Moses spoke one last time to the people. This speech is recorded in the book of **Deuteronomy**. Moses reviewed the Israelites' history and the law, noting the blessings that would come if they followed the law, and the curses that would come if they did not (Deuteronomy 11:26–28). Then Moses died, and God buried him.

In the book of **Joshua**, we read how Joshua succeeded Moses as the leader of Israel. The Israelites conquered the city of Jericho, their first conquest, by means of God's plan and God's power. After they had marched around the city as the Lord had commanded, they blew their trumpets and shouted. The city walls fell down, and they marched in (Joshua 6:1–21). A harlot named Rahab had hidden two Israelite spies in the city earlier, and after the city fell she was rewarded by being spared (Joshua 2:1–21; 6:22–25; Hebrews 11:30–31). She became an ancestor of Jesus Christ (Matthew 1:5). Joshua conquered the rest of the land of Canaan, and divided it among the twelve tribes of Israel.

The book of **Judges** tells about the judges who governed the nation of Israel after Joshua died. God remained their king. However, the people did not live in obedience to God. Many times they turned away to the gods and idols of their neighbors and thus sinned against God. So God sold them into the hands of their oppressors. Each time, when they cried out to God to save them from their enemies, God in His mercy raised up a deliverer to free them (Judges 2:10–19). The most famous deliverers, or judges, were Gideon, Barak, and Samson (Hebrews 11:32).

The book of **Ruth** tells the story of DAVID'S great-grandmother, who was not an Israelite, but a Moabite woman who believed in the true God. She married an Israelite and became an ancestor of Jesus (Matthew 1:5).

1 Samuel tells the story of the last judge. Samuel's mother had dedicated her son to God and sent him to work in the temple as a child. There God spoke to Samuel and he became a prophet as well as a judge. When he became old, the people demanded to have a king, as the other nations around them had. Samuel warned them of the problems with earthly kings, but the people persisted, and so God finally agreed to give them a king (1 Samuel 8:6–22). A man named Saul was chosen by God, and at first he ruled well. However, he did not repent after sinning on several occasions, and so God in the end rejected him.

God told Samuel to anoint a young shepherd boy, David, to be the next king of Israel, and the Spirit of the Lord came upon him from that day onward. One time, an enemy giant named Goliath challenged the Israelites, but no one dared to fight him. Finally David volunteered, and knocked the giant down with a stone from a slingshot (1 Samuel 17:32–51). David afterward became a great soldier, and Saul became jealous. Saul attempted to kill David several times, but David always escaped. Although David had the opportunity to kill Saul on two occasions, he refused to harm the man whom God had anointed to be king—even if God had later rejected him.

2 Samuel and **1 Chronicles** both tell about how David became king after Saul died in battle. David reigned from 1010 to 970 B.C. Soon after becoming king, David recaptured the ark of the Lord that had been previously seized by the enemy Philistines, and brought it to Jerusalem, the Jewish capital, with great rejoicing (2 Samuel 6:12–15). David wanted to build a permanent temple for the Lord, but God told him to let his son build it. David won great victories in war and was blessed by God. God promised David that his throne would be established forever, and this promise was fulfilled in Jesus Christ, whose kingdom will never end. Jesus was descended from David (Matthew 1:1), and was called the "Root of David" and the "Lion of Judah" (Revelation 5:5). David was considered the ideal king by later prophets, but he did sin at times. However, he was different from Saul, because he always repented and renewed his relationship with God. He was also a musician and poet, and wrote many of the **Psalms**. Some of the Psalms prophesied about Jesus Christ and His death (Psalms 22, 69).

1 and **2 Kings** and **2 Chronicles** tell about the kingdom of Israel, beginning with the reign of David's son Solomon. God told Solomon to ask from Him whatever he wanted and He would give it. Many would have asked for riches or honor, but Solomon asked for an understanding heart, for wisdom (1 Kings 3:5–9). God gave him the wisdom he asked for, and also great riches and honor as well (Matthew 12:42; Luke 12:27). Solomon wrote three books of wisdom in the Bible: **Proverbs**, **Ecclesiastes**, and the **Song of Songs**. His great work was the building of the permanent temple, the house of the Lord, in Jerusalem.

After Solomon died, the kingdom of Israel was divided. The northern ten tribes split away and this new kingdom was called the kingdom of Israel. The remaining two tribes formed the kingdom of Judah in the south. The kingdom of Judah was ruled by descendants of David, beginning with Solomon's son, Rehoboam. The period of the divided kingdoms continued for 344 years. Some of the kings of Judah obeyed God and brought the people back from worshiping idols to the true God, but others did evil in God's sight and encouraged the worship of idols. None of the kings of the northern kingdom of Israel worshiped God. Their first king set up two golden calves, one at Bethel and the other at Dan, and the people (later called Samaritans) continued to worship those idols instead of worshiping the true God at the temple in Jerusalem. This was one of the reasons the Samaritans were despised by the Jews in Jesus' day (John 4:9,19–24). One notorious king of Israel was Ahab, who was married to a foreigner named Jezebel. They both hated Elijah (1 Kings Chapters 17–18), a powerful prophet of God at the time. Elijah and his successor, Elisha (2 Kings Chapters 2–8), performed many miracles, by which they showed that God was the true Lord (Luke 4:24–27). Elijah did not die, but was taken directly up into heaven (2 Kings 2:11; Mark 9:4–5).

Many other prophets spoke to the people of Israel and Judah during those years. The prophets also warned the people of coming judgment if they continued in rebellion and sin. The prophets predicted that the Jews of the two kingdoms would be exiled in a foreign land if they did not repent. Sometimes the people listened to the warnings and repented, but usually they did not. Finally it came true as the prophets had said. God did exile them to other lands. The people of Israel were taken to Assyria (modern Syria) in 722 B.C., and the people of Judah were taken to Babylon (modern Iraq) in 586 B.C. The prophets who wrote during the period of the divided kingdom are as follows (in chronological order): **Joel** (Acts 2:16–21), **Jonah** (Matthew 12:38–41), **Amos, Hosea, Isaiah** (who is quoted more often in the New Testament than any other prophet), **Micah, Nahum, Zephaniah, Habbakuk**, and **Jeremiah**, who also wrote **Lamentations**. Many of the prophets also prophesied about Jesus Christ, His birth, His death, and His second coming.

There were no historical writings during the period of the exile, but the prophets **Ezekiel** and **Daniel** wrote during this time. Possibly **Obadiah** also prophesied during this period. Toward the end of the exile, the kingdom of Persia (modern Iran) conquered Babylon.

In 538 B.C. Cyrus, king of Persia, made a proclamation saying that anyone who wished to could return to Jerusalem and rebuild the temple. We read about this in the historical book of **Ezra**. The first group returned under the leadership of Zerubbabel and began to rebuild the temple. There was opposition and the work stopped for a time. The people were encouraged by the prophets **Haggai** and **Zechariah**, and the temple was finally finished (Ezra 6:14–16). In

458 B.C. Ezra led the second group to Jerusalem. Ezra, a priest, taught the Jewish law again, and led some reforms that dealt with the sin of intermarriage with foreign women who enticed their Jewish husbands into worshiping false gods. During this same period the story of **Esther**, the Jewish queen of Persia, took place. She was used by God to save the Jewish people from a plot to destroy them.

Years later **Nehemiah**, the Persian king's cupbearer, returned with a third group of Israelites to organize the rebuilding of the walls around the city of Jerusalem (Nehemiah 6:15–16). The prophet **Malachi** spoke during this time also. After about 400 B.C., no more prophets spoke to Israel until John the Baptist came to announce the arrival of the Savior Jesus Christ.

A CHRONOLOGICAL CHART OF THE OLD TESTAMENT

1100 | 1000 | 900 | 800 | 700 | 600 | 500 B.C.

Creation – Abraham | Abraham – Joseph | 400 years Bondage in Egypt | The Judges | Divided Kingdom

40 years of wandering | The Promised Land | United Kingdom | 70 years of exile | Restoration

GENESIS
Creation
Flood
Covenant
ABRAHAM
Isaac
Jacob
Joseph
12 tribes
Reuben
Simeon
Levi
Judah
Dan
Naphtali
Gad
Asher
Issachar
Zebulun
Benjamin
Manasseh
Ephraim

JOB ?
A good man suffers

EXODUS
Egypt to Sinai

NUMBERS
Sinai to Jordan

DEUT.
Moses' final discourse

GOD SPEAKS THROUGH MOSES

LEVITICUS
The Law

JOSHUA
Entering the Promised Land
Conquering and Dividing

GOD LEADS THROUGH JOSHUA

JUDGES
Everyone does what is right in his own eyes

RUTH
One of Christ's ancestors

1 SAMUEL
King Saul
Saul/David conflict

2 SAMUEL
1 CHRON.
King David

1 KINGS
2 CHRON.
Solomon

PSALMS

PROVERBS
ECCLES.
SONG OF SOLOMON

2 KINGS
2 CHRON.
Israel
Judah

Israel
JONAH
AMOS
HOSEA

Judah
OBADIAH
JOEL
ISAIAH
MICAH
NAHUM
ZEPHANIAH
JEREMIAH
LAMENT.
HABAKKUK

EZEKIEL
DANIEL

EZRA
First and second returns
Temple built

NEHEMIAH
Third return
Walls built

ESTHER
She saves her people

HAGGAI
ZECHARIAH

MALACHI

KEY

(wavy lines)	Exact dates not known
(bracket)	Approximately 100 years
↓	From here on dates are verified
(light shading)	HISTORY
(dark shading)	POETRY
(medium shading)	PROPHECY

Rebecca Thorson, 1981

HOW WE GOT OUR BIBLE

The Old Testament

The Old Testament was written over a period of one thousand years, from approximately 1400 to 400 B.C. The first five books of the Old Testament, sometimes called the books of the law, or the Law of Moses, were written mainly by MOSES in about 1400 B.C. The last Old Testament book was written by the prophet Malachi in about 400 B.C.

The Old Testament Scriptures were carefully hand copied by Jewish scribes and thus passed on from generation to generation. Each time a scribe made a new copy of Scripture, he destroyed the old copy. For this reason the most ancient copies of the Old Testament are no longer in existence. Indeed, the earliest copy of the entire Old Testament that exists today was copied in the 10th century A.D.

However, in 1947 some very ancient leather scrolls were discovered in Israel by a shepherd boy. He found them in some caves eight miles south of the city of Jericho near the Dead Sea, and so they have become known as the Dead Sea scrolls. The scrolls contain sections from almost every book of the Old Testament. The Dead Sea scrolls were copied sometime during the 1st and 2nd centuries B.C. Except for tiny differences in spelling and style, they are exactly the same as the existing Old Testament copies from the 10th century. This proves that the Jewish scribes carried out their copying with great care and accuracy. Thus we can have full confidence that the more recent copies of the Old Testament (from which our modern Bibles are taken) are completely accurate copies of the original writings of the Old Testament authors. This is very important, because, as we shall see below, the original writers were inspired directly by God in a special way to write what God wanted them to write. Thus we can be assured that the copies of what they wrote have been faithfully and accurately passed down to us through the centuries.

Most of the Old Testament manuscripts were written in the Hebrew language, the ancient language of the Jews. However, in the time of Christ, Hebrew was not spoken by the ordinary people; it was used mainly by the Jewish priests and religious scholars. The common language of the Middle East in Christ's time was Aramaic, the language which Christ Himself spoke. Aramaic is related to Hebrew in much the same way that modern Indian languages are related to Sanskrit.

However, there was another major language in use during Christ's time, that is, the Greek language. Greek was spoken throughout the entire Mediterranean region and was known by most of the educated people. Because so few people understood Hebrew, the Old Testament was translated into Greek in about 200 B.C. When the New Testament writers quoted from the Old Testament Scriptures, they usually used this Greek translation rather than the original Hebrew.

The Old Testament contains thirty-nine books written by many different authors. For a discussion of the contents of these books, see General Article: Summary of Old Testament.

The New Testament

The New Testament was written in the Greek language, beginning about twenty years after Christ's death. Christ's last command to His disciples was that they should be His witnesses to the whole world (Acts 1:8). Therefore, starting on the day of PENTECOST, the disciples began to tell others about Christ's life and teachings. For the first twenty years after Christ's death, the disciples, or APOSTLES, taught mainly by word of mouth. But as the apostles got older, it became apparent that a written record of their teaching would be needed in order to insure its accurate transmission down through the future generations. Therefore, some of the apostles and their close associates began to write down an account of Christ's life. The Apostle Peter worked with Mark to write Mark's Gospel (see Mark: Introduction). The Apostle Matthew wrote the Gospel of Matthew, and the Apostle John wrote the Gospel of John. Luke, a close associate of the Apostle Paul, wrote the Gospel of Luke and the book of Acts, the story of the early church.

In addition to writing an account of Christ's life, it also became necessary for the apostles to write down a fuller explanation of the reason for Christ's coming to earth, and to correct some errors and false teaching that had begun to arise in the new churches. So they began to write letters to the new churches that they had established. The Apostle Paul wrote thirteen such letters, beginning with his letter to the Galatians written in about 50 A.D. (see Galatians: Introduction). Some scholars believe that the earliest New Testament book to be written was the letter of James, the brother of Jesus (see James: Introduction).

The last book of the New Testament to be written was Revelation, written by the Apostle John in about 90–95 A.D. Thus the entire New Testament was completed between 50 A.D. and 100 A.D.

Most of the original writings of the New Testament authors were written on a kind of paper made from a plant called papyrus.[1] This papyrus was not durable like our modern paper, and it did not last. As a result, the papyrus scrolls on which the New Testament authors actually wrote have been lost, and as is the case with the Old Testament, all that remains today are copies of the original writings.

For the first three centuries after Christ, the New Testament was carefully and accurately copied by scribes onto papyrus scrolls. In the early 1900s, some of these ancient papyrus copies of the New Testament were discovered in Egypt buried in sand. Still others were found preserved in protective containers. The oldest of these copies was made in 135 A.D., and contains part of John's Gospel. The next earliest scrolls were copied in about 200 A.D., and contain large parts of the New Testament. These ancient scrolls are now preserved in museums.

Another kind of "paper" that was used in Bible times was parchment, which was made from the specially treated skin of goats or sheep. Parchment was more expensive than papyrus. It is possible that a few of the New Testament books were first written on parchment, but if so, they have not been preserved. The oldest copy of the complete New Testament was made in the 4th century and was written on parchment. This oldest copy was found in the mid-1800's stored in a monastery near Mount Sinai in Egypt. In addition to this oldest copy, there are another 270 copies of the Greek New Testament still in existence that were written on parchment between the 4th and 9th centuries.

From the 9th century up to the 15th century, numerous additional copies of the Greek New Testament were made, over 2700 of which have been preserved to the present time. Then in 1456 A.D., the printing press was invented by a German named Johann Gutenburg, and the first book was printed—the Bible. After that, books didn't need to be copied by hand; they could be published quickly and cheaply and in large numbers by means of printing presses. Translations of the Bible into different languages could now be widely distributed to the common people. Today the Bible or parts of it have been translated into over 1200 different languages of the world. There is no other book in world history that has been translated into so many languages or read by so many people.

These hundreds and thousands of ancient manuscripts which

[1] Papyrus is a tall water plant native to Egypt. Thin slices of the stalk of this plant were laid together, and then another layer was crossed on top of the first layer. Papyrus was the main kind of "paper" in use up until the 3rd century A.D.

have been preserved to the present time prove that the Bible has been handed down to us from the original Greek manuscripts with great accuracy. Although we know that individual scribes made an occasional error in copying, when all the manuscripts are studied together it can be determined in almost every case what the original writers actually wrote. No other ancient book has so many early copies still in existence. This is why we can be confident that our modern Bibles are accurate translations of the words that God first gave to the original writers of the Bible.

There is another important reason why we can trust the accuracy of our Bibles today. That is because God has said that He will preserve His word to all generations (Psalm 119:89,152,160). We can have full confidence that God has not allowed His word to be lost or to be changed in any significant way.

The New Testament Canon

From the beginning there was general agreement about what books should be included in the New Testament canon.[2] By 200 A.D. the New Testament contained essentially the same books that we have in our present Bibles. However, there was disagreement over several books, and this disagreement persisted until the 4th century. In particular, some Christians questioned whether Hebrews, James, 2 Peter, 2 and 3 John, Jude, and Revelation should be included in the New Testament. In addition to that, there were other non-Biblical writings written by Christian leaders at the turn of the 1st century, which some people thought should be included in the canon but others thought should not be. By the end of the 4th century, however, all these disagreements had been resolved, and the worldwide church unanimously accepted the present New Testament canon and made it official. Since then, there has been no disagreement on any part of the New Testament canon.

The decision as to which books should be included in the New Testament was based on four factors. First, a book had to have been written either by an apostle or the close associate of an apostle. Second, the contents of the book had to be of high spirituality and to be in agreement with the teaching of the Old Testament and the apostles. Third, the book had to be accepted by the great majority of the churches. Fourth, the book had to be clearly inspired by God. In determining what books to include, the early church was guided by the Holy Spirit. It wasn't a matter of men deciding on their own what books they wanted in their Bible. Rather, it was a matter of

[2] The New Testament canon is the list of officially authorized Scriptures that has been accepted by all Christian churches.

men being shown by the Holy Spirit what books were indeed God's word.

Why Is the Bible Different from All Other Books?

The Bible is different from other books because the writers of the Bible were directly inspired in a special way by God Himself. God's Holy Spirit guided the writers of the Bible to write what God wanted them to write (see 2 Timothy 3:16; 2 Peter 1:21 and comments). The Bible is not only the words of men; it is the word of God Himself.

However, God used men to write His word. God didn't dictate each word. The writers of the Bible, under the guidance of the Holy Spirit, used their own minds to write. Their individual personalities and character can be seen through their writings. Just as Jesus Himself was both God and man together, so the Bible is both God's word and man's word together. It was written by men who knew God's mind in a special way. God revealed His mind to them, and they wrote according to what God revealed to them. It is true that other Christian writers have been inspired by the Holy Spirit in a general way and have written books pleasing to God; but they have not had the same special knowledge of God's mind that the Bible writers had. For this reason, then, the Bible is different from all other books: it is the only revealed and authoritative word of God.

Because the Bible is God's word, it is totally true. It is without error. Some have at times thought they found an error in the Bible, but later have discovered it was they who were in error, not the Bible. Time and again, historical and archeological discoveries have confirmed the truth of the Biblical writings. The Bible is historically and scientifically true in every regard.

However, it is not enough to read the Bible in the same way we would read a history or science book. It is not enough to read the Bible only with our minds. We must also read the Bible with our spirits, or else we will miss the deep spiritual truths of the Bible. When we read the Bible, we must humble ourselves and open our minds to receive God's truth. We must pray for spiritual understanding. When we do this in faith, then the Bible will come alive for us and will change our lives.

It is the Holy Spirit who makes the Bible "alive" and powerful in the heart of the reader (2 Corinthians 3:6). Those who have the Holy Spirit living within them know in their own experience that the Bible is the true and living word of God. From the Bible they can know with certainty who God is and who Christ is. They also know from the Bible what God has done. The Old Testament is the record of God's reaching out to men and of men's disobedience and sin.

The Old Testament shows clearly that men are sinners in need of a Savior. The New Testament reveals a God who loved men so much that He Himself came to earth in the likeness of a man, Jesus Christ, to suffer and die in order to save men from their sins and give them eternal life.

It is hoped that as the reader studies this commentary, he will let God speak to him through the Scriptures. It is not enough only to understand the Bible; we must also live by it.

THE COMMENTARY

Matthew

INTRODUCTION

This book is often called the GOSPEL according to Matthew. The Gospel is the good news that Jesus Christ came into the world and gave His own life to save sinful men, and that all who place FAITH in Him will receive forgiveness of sins and enter into the KINGDOM OF GOD. A summary of the Gospel is given in John 3:16: **For God so loved the world that he gave his one and only Son, that whoever believes in him shall not perish but have eternal life.**

Matthew, the writer of this Gospel, was originally a tax collector, who was called by Jesus to be one of His first twelve disciples (Matthew 10:3; Mark 3:18). Although Matthew's Gospel comes first in the New Testament, most Bible scholars believe that the first complete Gospel to be written was Mark's Gospel (see Mark: Introduction). However, many scholars think that Matthew wrote a rough description of the life of Jesus in the Aramaic[1] language before Mark's Gospel was written. Then after Mark's Gospel was published in 55–65 A.D., Matthew revised his Gospel and included much of Mark's Gospel in his own. Indeed, all but fifty-five verses of Mark's Gospel is included in Matthew's Gospel. According to these scholars, the final revision of Matthew's Gospel was written in the Greek[2], language, either by Matthew himself or someone associated with him.

[1] Aramaic was the most common language spoken in Israel in Jesus' time. It was the language spoken by Jesus Himself.

[2] The Greek language was spoken by most of the educated people living throughout the Middle East and southern Europe during New Testament times. The New Testament books were originally written in the Greek language. Most of the earliest New Testament manuscripts that still exist today are copies of those original manuscripts (see General Article: How We Got Our Bible).

Of the approximately 1050 verses in Matthew, 500 are also found in Mark. Another 250 are found in Luke's Gospel. Many Bible scholars believe that in addition to Mark's Gospel there was an early written collection of Christ's teachings that both Matthew and Luke knew about, and which they added to their Gospels.

Accordng to many scholars, the final edition of Matthew's Gospel was written in the city of Antioch[3] in northern Syria sometime between 70 and 80 A.D. It was written mainly for Jewish readers. In this Gospel, Matthew shows again and again how the PROPHECIES of the Old Testament, the Jewish Scriptures, were fulfilled in the birth and life of Jesus.

For the comments on those sections of Matthew that are also found in Mark, the reader is asked to refer to Mark's Gospel.

OUTLINE

A. The Birth and Childhood of Jesus Christ (1:1–2:23).
   1. The Genealogy of Jesus (1:1–17).
   2. The Birth of Jesus (1:18–25).
   3. The Visit of the Magi (2:1–12).
   4. The Escape to Egypt and the Return to Nazareth (2:13–23).

B. The Beginning of the Ministry of Jesus Christ (3:1–4:11).
   1. John the Baptist Prepares the Way (3:1–12).
   2. The Baptism of Jesus (3:13–17).
   3. The Temptation of Jesus (4:1–11).

C. The Ministry of Jesus Christ (4:12–25:46).
   1. Jesus Begins to Preach (4:12–17).
   2. The Calling of the First Disciples (4:18–25).
   3. The Sermon on the Mount (5:1–7:29).
   4. Ten Miracles (8:1–9:38).
   5. Jesus Sends Out the Twelve (10:1–42).
   6. Jesus' Answer to John the Baptist and Related Teachings (11:1–30).
   7. Opposition from the Pharisees (12:1–50).
   8. Parables of the Kingdom (13:1–58).
   9. Withdrawal of Jesus after John's Beheading (14:1–36).
   10. Conflict with the Pharisees (15:1–20).
   11. More Miracles (15:21–39).
   12. Further Teachings (16:1–28).
   13. The Transfiguration (17:1–23).
   14. In Capernaum (17:24–18:35).
   15. In Perea (19:1–20:16).

[3] Antioch was one of the leading cities of the Middle East in New Testament times.

16. In Judea (20:17–34).
17. In Jerusalem (21:1–22:46).
18. Jesus' Denunciation of the Pharisees (23:1–39).
19. Teachings on the End of the Age (24:1–25:46).

D. The Passion of Jesus Christ (26:1–27:66).
1. The Plot against Jesus (26:1–16).
2. The Lord's Supper (26:17–30).
3. In the Garden of Gethsemane (26:31–56).
4. The Arrest and Trial of Jesus (26:57–27:31).
5. The Death of Jesus (27:32–56).
6. The Burial of Jesus (27:57–66).

E. The Resurrection of Jesus Christ (28:1–20).
1. Discovery of the Empty Tomb (28:1–8).
2. Jesus Appears (28:9–10).
3. The Guard's Report (28:11–15).
4. The Great Commission (28:16–20).

CHAPTER 1

The Genealogy of Jesus (1:1–17)
(Luke 3:23–38)

1 Matthew, the APOSTLE who wrote this Gospel, was himself a JEW. One of Matthew's purposes in writing his Gospel was to show other Jews that Jesus was the **Christ,**[4] that is, the Messiah. He calls Christ the **son of** DAVID, because according to the prophecies written in the Old Testament, the Messiah was to be descended from King David, the greatest king of the Jews (2 Samuel 7:12–14; Psalm 89:3–4; 132:11; Mark 10:47–48). Therefore, Matthew outlines Christ's genealogy in verses 2–17 in order to prove that Christ was indeed descended from King David and also from **ABRAHAM**, the first Jew (Genesis 12:1–3).

The names in this genealogy are all mentioned in the Old Testament (Ruth 4:18–22; 1 Chronicles 2:1–15; 3:10–16). However, Matthew does not give the complete genealogy; there are three names missing between Abraham (verse 2) and David (verse 6). There are also three names missing between Joram and Uzziah in verse 8 (1 Chronicles 3:11–12).

2–17 When Matthew's genealogy of Christ is compared with the genealogy in Luke 3:23–38, two major differences can be seen. First, Luke's genealogy goes back before Abraham's time; it goes all the way back to Adam,[5] the very first man that God created on earth. Luke was not a Jew; his purpose was to show that Christ was not only the Messiah of the Jews, but also the Savior of the whole world, both Jews and GENTILES. For this reason, he started his genealogy with Adam.

Second, between David and Christ the genealogy in Luke is completely different from Matthew's genealogy. Only two names, Shealtiel and Zerubbabel (verse 12), are the same. The common explanation for this difference is that Matthew has given the legal genealogy of Joseph, who was Jesus' legal father according to marriage. But, because Joseph was not Jesus' natural father (the Holy Spirit was Jesus' real father), Luke has given the genealogy not of Joseph but of Mary, the mother of Jesus. This, of course, was different from Joseph's genealogy. But the interesting fact is that both Joseph and Mary were descended from King David.[6] Therefore, both Matthew and Luke prove by different means that Jesus was the **son of David**, the Messiah.[7]

The **exile to Babylon** (modern Iraq) mentioned in verses 11,17 refers to the defeat of Jerusalem and the surrounding province of Judea by the Babylonians in 587 B.C., at which time the Jews were made prisoners and taken into exile in Babylon (2 Kings 25:1–12). This brought the earthly kingdom of David and his descendants to an end.

The Birth of Jesus Christ (1:18–25)

18 Jesus had no human father. Other men mentioned in the Bible, such as Isaac and John the Baptist, were conceived by the supernatural power of God, but they all had human fathers (Genesis 18:10–14; Luke 1:5–7,11–13,18–19). But Mary, Jesus' mother, had never slept with a man before Jesus' birth; she was a virgin.

[4] In the Greek language, the word **Christ** means "anointed one." "Messiah" is the Jewish or Hebrew word for Christ.

[5] The word "Adam" means man.

[6] This is why there is no discrepancy between Matthew and Luke's genealogy during the period before David.

[7] Jewish genealogies were extremely complicated. Many adopted children were included in the genealogies, and thus the genealogies of different families became intermixed. Sometimes members of the same family married each other. (This is the reason that Shealtiel and Zerubbabel are mentioned in both Joseph's and Mary's genealogies.)

Jesus' father was the HOLY SPIRIT (see Luke 1:26–35 and comment).

19 In Joseph's mind, Mary had committed adultery. According to Jewish custom, anyone pledged to be married who was then unfaithful was considered to be an adulterer. Whenever an engagement was broken off, a formal divorce was necessary. Joseph planned to divorce Mary quietly in the presence of two witnesses. He was a merciful and righteous man, and did not want to shame Mary in public.

20 An ANGEL told Joseph in a dream that Mary had not committed adultery with another man, but that the father of her child was the Holy Spirit Himself.

21 The angel told Joseph to name the child Jesus, which is the Greek form of the name Joshua, which means "the Lord saves." Jesus is the Savior because He saves **his people from their sins**. He saves them from the punishment of sin, which is eternal death (see John 3:16–17; Romans 6:23 and comments). And He saves them from the power of sin through the working of the Holy Spirit (see Romans 8:1–2 and comment).

22–23 Matthew then quotes from Isaiah the PROPHET to show that Isaiah's prophecy was fulfilled by the birth of Jesus (Isaiah 7:14). Jesus is also called **Immanuel**, or "**God with us**," because in Jesus God came to earth and dwelt among men. And in Christ, God is with us always (Matthew 28:20).

24–25 Many Christians believe that Mary and Joseph had other children after Jesus. The brothers and sisters of Jesus mentioned in Mark 6:3 and John 7:3–5 are probably children of Mary. However, other Christians believe that Mary remained a virgin. They say that the brothers and sisters mentioned above were sons of Joseph by a previous marriage.

For a further description of Jesus' birth, see Luke 2:17 and comment.

CHAPTER 2

The Visit of the Magi (2:1–12)

1 **Bethlehem** was a small town in the province of **Judea** (southern Israel) about five miles from **Jerusalem**.[8] It was the town where King David had been born (1 Samuel 16:1). Although Joseph and Mary lived in the town of Nazareth in the northern province of Galilee, they had gone down to Bethlehem to register for the census, because they were descendants of King David (see Luke 2:4). This census took place during the reign of King Herod, a puppet ruler who had been given the title "King of the Jews" by the Roman Emperor. Herod's kingdom was part of the Roman Empire[9] and included the province of Judea and its capital Jerusalem (see Luke 1:5). Herod reigned from 40 B.C. to 4 A.D. Most modern scholars believe that Jesus was born in the last year of Herod's reign, that is, in 4 A.D.

2 At the time of Jesus' birth, some **Magi**, or astrologers, from the east saw a very bright and unusual star rising in the east. They interpreted this to be a sign that a great king had been born. These astrologers knew that the Jews were expecting a Messiah to come, so they traveled to Jerusalem, the Jewish capital, thinking that the Messiah had now been born. "**Where is the one who has been born king of the JEWS?**" they asked.

3 King Herod was not happy to hear

---

[8] In Jesus' time, **Jerusalem** was the capital of **Judea**, the southern province of the Jewish nation of Israel. Today Jerusalem is one of the major cities of modern Israel.

[9] The Roman Empire was the most powerful empire in the world during New Testament times. It had extended its authority over most of the countries surrounding the Mediterranean Sea. Its capital city was Rome, which is today the capital of the modern nation of Italy in southern Europe. For further discussion, see Word List: Roman Empire.

that there was now another "king of the Jews" besides himself. Matthew repeatedly reminds us that Christ was indeed born a king, who would inherit the kingdom of David. The Jews thought that this would be an earthly kingdom; however, Christ came to establish a spiritual kingdom.

4–6 According to the prophecy of Micah (Micah 5:2), this Christ, or Messiah, was to be born in Bethlehem[10] (John 7:42). Here in verse 6, through the prophet Micah, God says that Christ "**will be the shepherd of my people** ISRAEL" (see John 10:11; 1 Peter 5:4). **Israel** is the name of the Jewish nation.

7–8 Herod asked the astrologers to find out where Jesus had been born so he could **go and worship him**. Of course, he really intended to go and kill Him.

9–12 The amazing star led the astrologers right to the place where Jesus was. No doubt they were surprised to find the **king of the Jews** born in such humble circumstances (Luke 2:7).

The Escape to Egypt (2:13–23)

13–15 An angel told Joseph to take his wife and child and flee to EGYPT. As is recorded in the Old Testament book of Exodus, Egypt had once been a land of bondage and oppression for the Jews. Now it had become a place of safety for Jesus. Just as MOSES led the Jews out of bondage in Egypt 1400 years earlier, so Christ will lead His people out of bondage to sin. Just as Moses led the Jews to the land of Israel, which God had promised to them, so Jesus will lead His people into the kingdom of heaven. In verse 15, Matthew quotes the prophet Hosea: **Out of Egypt I called my son** (Hosea 11:1). In saying "son," Hosea was referring to the Jews, to the nation of Israel. In Exodus 4:22, Israel is called God's **firstborn son**. Matthew considers Jesus to be the representation of the nation of Israel, so he applies Hosea's words to Jesus Himself.

16–18 Herod had found out from the astrologers exactly when they had seen the star (verse 7). Therefore, when some months had passed and the astrologers had not returned as he had requested (verse 8), Herod gave orders that all male children near Bethlehem under two years of age should be killed (verse 16). In that way, he thought, Jesus would surely be among those who were killed.

Matthew then quotes from Jeremiah 31:15. Rachel was the wife of Jacob and the mother of Joseph and Benjamin, two of the twelve sons of Jacob. She was buried at **Ramah** near Bethlehem (Genesis 35:19). In this verse Jeremiah was describing the time when the Jews were taken into exile in Babylon and on the way passed by Rachel's tomb. Rachel is a symbol for all the mothers of Israel who were weeping at the loss of their sons. In the same way the mothers of Bethlehem mourned the loss of their sons killed by Herod. In the next two verses in Jeremiah, following the verse quoted here, the Lord said, "**Restrain your voice from weeping and your eyes from tears, for your work will be rewarded . . . there is hope for your future**" (Jeremiah 31:16–17). And indeed the exile of the Jews was followed by the reestablishment of a new and purer kingdom of Israel. In the same way, the death of the infants of Bethlehem was followed by the establishment of the kingdom of Christ. God brings great blessing out of suffering. There can be no resurrection without death; there can be no crown without a CROSS.

19–23 **After Herod died. . . .** How quickly God punished Herod. Herod thought to prolong his reign by killing Jesus. But, in fact, he quickly lost his reign and his life.

Again, angels guided Joseph by means of dreams (Matthew 1:20; 2:13). God will always give guidance to those who seek to do His will. Usually He guides by means of His word, the Bible, or through Christian family members and friends, such guidance being confirmed by the

---

[10] Matthew does not give an exact quotation from Micah's prophecy here. He is really making a comment on Micah 5:2.

Holy Spirit. But sometimes He guides directly through visions and dreams. Such direct guidance may be more common among those who cannot read.

An angel told Joseph to return to Nazareth, his own home town in the district of Galilee, which was not under the authority of Herod's son Archelaus. Matthew says this was to fulfill the prophecy: **He will be called a Nazarene** (verse 23). This prophecy is not written in the Old Testament. The Old Testament prophets prophesied that Jesus would have humble origins and be despised (Isaiah 53:1–3). People raised in a Galilean[11] town like Nazareth were despised by other Jews (see John 1:46). Therefore, to be called a "Nazarene" would fulfill prophecies such as Isaiah 53:3.

CHAPTER 3

John the Baptist Prepares the Way (3:1–12)

(Mark 1:2–8; Luke 3:3–4,16–17; John 1:23,26)

1–6 See Mark 1:2–6 and comment.

7 When John the Baptist began BAPTIZING people, many of the PHARISEES and SADDUCEES also came to be baptized. The Pharisees were a very strict party of the Jews; they prided themselves on following the Jewish law exactly. The Sadducees were the second main party of the Jews. Most of the Jewish chief priests were Sadducees. The Pharisees and Sadducees were leaders among the Jewish people. Yet John called them a **brood of vipers** when they came to be baptized. Why did he say that?

The reason is this: The Jewish leaders were hypocrites. They were religious outwardly, but not inwardly. They honored God with their lips, but not with their hearts (see Mark 7:6–7 and comment). They thought that by being baptized they could escape God's **wrath**, that is, God's judgment. But John knew they were not truly repentant. They did not really intend to turn from their sins. They were only being baptized to show others how religious they were.

The Pharisees and Sadducees were like a **brood of vipers** (Matthew 12:34; 23:33). They were crafty and deceitful. They were also poisonous. There is nothing so poisonous to the church as leaders who pretend to be religious outwardly but who inwardly are not (see Matthew 7:15 and comment).

8 John's baptism was a **baptism of repentance for the forgiveness of sins** (Mark 1:4). REPENTANCE means not only to feel sorry for sin but also to turn from sin. The Pharisees and Sadducees said, "We repent," but they continued sinning as before. John asked them, "Where is your repentance? Show me the proof of your repentance. **Produce fruit in keeping with repentance.**" Just as faith must be followed by works (James 2:17), so repentance must be followed by a turning from sin. Otherwise our repentance is false.

9 The Jewish leaders were proud. They despised non-Jews, that is, Gentiles. They thought to themselves: "We are the true descendants of Abraham, the first Jew. God has promised to bless us (Genesis 12:1–3). Therefore, we are better than other people; we have found favor with God."

But John warned them that being a descendant of Abraham according to the flesh was not important to God. Just as God created the first man out of the dust of the ground (Genesis 2:7), so God can create children of Abraham out of stones. What is important to God is that a man be a true Jew in his heart, not just in body.

---

[11] Jews from other parts of Israel looked down on Jews from Galilee. Galileans were generally less educated and cultured than other Jews.

Even though the Pharisees and Sadducees were descendants of Abraham according to the flesh, they were not true Jews in God's eyes, because they were not righteous in their hearts. A true "Jew" is one who does God's will and who puts his faith in God's only Son, Jesus Christ (see John 8:39; Romans 2:28–29; Galatians 3:6–9 and comments).

In the same way, those who are Christians only outwardly are not true Christians. A man is not born a Christian. A man is not a Christian simply because his father is a Christian. He is not a Christian simply because he is a member of some church. Rather, a man is a Christian only if he is a Christian inwardly; that is, a man must have true faith in Christ from his heart.

10 Then, using the example of a barren tree, John warned the Pharisees and Sadducees that God would reject them and punish them if they did not bear the good fruit of repentance and faith (see Matthew 7:17–20; John 15:1–2,5–6).

11 See Mark 1:7–8 and comment.

12 John the Baptist said, "**After me will come one who is more powerful than I,**" that is, Christ (verse 11). Christ will come not only as a Savior but also as a judge. He will come with a **winnowing fork**, which is a sign of judgment. He will separate the wheat from the chaff; that is, He will reward the truly righteous and will punish those who only appear righteous outwardly, the hypocrites. God looks at a person's heart, not at his outward appearance (1 Samuel 16:7).

The Baptism of Jesus (3:13–17)
(Mark 1:9–11; Luke 3:21–22)

13–17 See Mark 1:9–11 and comment.

CHAPTER 4

The Temptation of Jesus (4:1–11)
(Luke 4:1–13)

1 At the time of His baptism Jesus was about thirty years old (Luke 3:23). Immediately after the baptism He was **led by the Spirit** into the desert to be **tempted** by the devil, that is, SATAN.

In order for the sinless Christ to fully become man, it was necessary that He experience the temptations common to all men (see Hebrews 2:17–18; 4:14–15 and comments). God allows Satan to tempt and test each one of us in order that our faith might be strengthened and purified (see 1 Peter 1:6–7 and comment). In the New Testament two kinds of TEMPTATION are mentioned: first, the pain and trouble that comes from outside of us; and second, the inner desires that lead us into sin. In this verse, Matthew is talking mainly about this second kind of inner temptation. God never tempts us to sin. It is Satan who tempts us to sin, and he does so through our evil desires (see James 1:13–14 and comment). Jesus Himself had no evil desires; therefore, the Spirit had to lead Him into the desert to be tempted. To only be tempted is not a sin; the sin is to fall into temptation.[12] Jesus did not fall.

Jesus was tempted by the devil immediately after His baptism. This is also the experience of many Christians. When we escape from the devil's authority and through faith enter God's family, the devil is furious and attacks us and tries to draw us back under his authority. One of the main ways we have of resisting the devil's attack is by being fully assured that we are now the children of God. God had just spoken saying about Jesus: "**This is my Son**" (Matthew 3:17). The Spirit had descended upon Him (Matthew 3:16). He went into the wilderness **full of the Holy Spirit** (Luke 4:1). When we

---

[12] Here the expression "to fall into temptation" means "to succumb to temptation"; that is, it means to sin.

face temptation, let us remember that we are sons and daughters of God, and let us pray that we might be full of the Spirit so that we, like Jesus, might overcome Satan.

2 Before being tempted by the devil, Jesus fasted for forty days. This was a sign of the forty years the Jews were tested in the Sinai desert[13] after escaping from Egypt. (These years are described in the Old Testament books of Exodus and Numbers.) Just as the Jews, God's chosen people, were tempted (Deuteronomy 8:2), so Jesus also was tempted. However, Jesus did not fall into sin as the Jews did.

The three temptations described in this section correspond to the three temptations into which the first man and woman, Adam and Eve, fell (Genesis 3:1–6). The forbidden fruit that Adam and Eve ate was **good for food, pleasing to the eye**, and **desirable for gaining wisdom** (Genesis 3:6).

The three temptations mentioned here by Matthew also correspond to the three temptations mentioned in 1 John 2:16: the **cravings of sinful man**, the **lust of his eyes**, and the **boasting of what he has and does**.

3 The **tempter**, Satan, first tried to make Jesus doubt that He was God's Son. Satan said, "**If you are the Son of God**, then prove it. Do a miracle. You are hungry; you have not eaten in forty days. Turn these stones into bread."[14]

Jesus had the power to turn stones into bread. Satan was tempting Jesus to use His power for His own comfort and convenience. Why should Jesus suffer hunger and pain? He could have a life of ease. Yet Jesus came into the world to suffer for us and to give His life for us (see Mark 10:45 and comment). When Jesus was hanging on the cross, those mocking Him said, "**. . . save yourself! Come down from the cross, if you are the Son of God**" (Matthew 27:40). The temptation to come down from the cross was essentially the same as the temptation to turn stones into bread. Because Jesus overcame Satan in the wilderness, He was better prepared to overcome Satan on the cross.

This first temptation corresponds to the **cravings of sinful man** mentioned by John (1 John 2:16). The forbidden fruit eaten by Adam and Eve was **good for food** (Genesis 3:6).

4 Jesus overcame Satan by quoting God's word in Deuteronomy 8:3. This passage refers to the time when God fed the starving Jews in the desert with special food from heaven (called "manna") in order to show them that they must trust only in Him and live by His word (Exodus 16:1–8,13–16,31). Man cannot live a full spiritual life by eating only bread. Man needs spiritual food, namely, the word of God (see John 6:30–35,48–51).

To live by God's word means to obey God's word. It means to accept God's will for our lives. Let us not complain about the "food" God gives us. The Jews in the desert complained about the manna from heaven that they were given, and as a result they were punished by a plague (Numbers 11:4–6,31–34).

5–6 Then Satan took Jesus to the highest point of the temple in Jerusalem. "**If you are the Son of God . . . throw yourself down**," said Satan. Then Satan himself quoted from Psalm 91:11–12, in order to persuade Jesus to jump. But Satan did not use the verses from Psalms correctly. The promise given in Psalms is true: God's angels will protect us. But we cannot use this promise to demand protection from God in situations where we are not doing His will. It is very easy to misuse Scripture in this way. Quoting a verse of Scripture incompletely or out of

---

[13] The Sinai Desert lies between Egypt and Israel. After God freed the Jews (the nation of Israel) from bondage in Egypt, the Jews wandered for forty years in the desert before arriving in the land that God had prepared for them. Today that land is the modern nation of Israel.

[14] Bread is the main staple food of the Middle East.

context often gives a totally wrong meaning, and we must take care to avoid it.[15]

This second[16] temptation was the temptation for Jesus to show He was God's Son by doing miraculous signs and wonders. By doing miracles He could have gained the praise of everyone. In the eyes of the world, in the eyes of men, Jesus could have been like a king. This was a temptation for Jesus' mind. It corresponds to the **lust of** [man's] **eyes** in 1 John 2:16. The forbidden apple eaten by Adam and Eve was **pleasing to the eye** (Genesis 3:6).

But Jesus was not sent into the world to be an earthly king. He was not sent into the world to receive honor from men (Isaiah 53:3; Philippians 2:6–8). He was sent into the world to suffer and die for our sins. Therefore, it was necessary for Jesus to reject Satan's temptation.

7 Again, Jesus overcame Satan by quoting God's word in Deuteronomy 6:16. This passage refers to the time when the Jews in the desert demanded a sign of God's presence (Exodus 17:1–7). Jesus was not to tempt[17] or "test" God by demanding that God use a miraculous sign to prove that Jesus was the Messiah. In the same way, we should not put God to the test by demanding special signs (see Mark 8:11–12 and comment).

8–9 The third temptation of Jesus was the greatest. Satan promised to give Christ authority over all the kingdoms of the world. It was in Satan's power to do so. Satan is the **prince of this world** (John 12:31; 14:30). The **whole world is under the control of the evil one** (1 John 5:19). Therefore, Satan could have easily fulfilled this promise to Jesus, and Jesus could have been an earthly king of kings. He could have gained the entire world. There was only one condition: Jesus had to worship Satan instead of God.

The third temptation was the temptation to pride. This is the temptation to **boasting** (in some translations called the "pride of life") mentioned in 1 John 2:16. This corresponds to the desire to be **like God** (Genesis 3:5) and to gain wisdom (Genesis 3:6). Without any effort, without any suffering, Christ could have had all the wisdom and power and authority in the world. All men would have bowed at His feet. Yet Jesus rejected Satan's offer.

10 For the third time Christ overcame Satan by quoting God's word, this time from Deuteronomy 6:13. This verse refers to the time when the Jews made a golden calf to worship in place of God (Exodus 32:1–6). Men must worship God alone and nothing else (Exodus 20:3–6).

In these temptations Jesus demonstrated how the word of God can be used as a weapon to overcome Satan and to resist temptation. The word of God is the **sword of the Spirit** (Ephesians 6:17); it is part of the armor of a Christian. If we resist Satan, he will flee from us (see James 4:7 and comment). When the tempter comes, let us say, as Jesus did, **"Away from me, Satan!"**

11 **Then the devil left him**. But not forever. According to Luke 4:13, Satan left Jesus **until an opportune time**. We know that Satan tempted Christ again in the garden of Gethsemane and on the cross (Mark 14:32–35; 15:30–32). Satan even spoke through Jesus' chief disciple Peter in order to tempt Jesus to avoid the cross (Mark 8:31–33).

Jesus Begins to Preach (4:12–17) (Mark 1:14–15)

12 See Mark 1:14 and comment.

13–16 Jesus began His public ministry in **Capernaum**, a town on the north side of **the lake**, that is, the Sea of Galilee.

---

[15] A well-known example of quoting Scripture incorrectly is found in Psalm 14:1, where the following words are written: **There is no God**. However, the full sentence reads: **The fool says in his heart, "There is no God."** Thus the partial quotation gives a meaning that is opposite to the true meaning of the verse.

[16] In Luke's account of Jesus' temptations, the second and third temptations are reversed (see Luke 4:5–12).

[17] To tempt or test God in this context means to put Him to the test, or to test Him out in a demanding way in order to gain something from Him.

The home of Jesus' first two disciples, Simon and Andrew, was in Capernaum (Mark 1:21,29).

Matthew quotes from Isaiah 9:1–2 to show that the Old Testament prophecies about the Messiah were fulfilled by Christ. In Isaiah's time, the **area of Zebulum and Naphtali** in the northern part of Israel was under the control of the kingdom of Assyria.[18] Isaiah prophesied about the deliverance of the people of that area from bondage: **the people living in darkness have seen a great light . . . a light has dawned** (verse 16). That light was Christ. Christ's ministry began in **Galilee** in the north of Israel, just as Isaiah's prophecy had foretold (verse 15).

17 See Mark 1:15 and comment.

The Calling of the First Disciples (4:18–22)

(Mark 1:16–20)

18–22 See Mark 1:16–20 and comment.

Jesus Heals the Sick (4:23–25)

23–25 Jesus carried out a complete ministry, **teaching . . . preaching . . . and healing** (verse 23). He taught in the Jewish **synagogues.**[19] Christ preached the **good news of the kingdom** (see Mark 1:14–15 and comment). He healed **every disease and sickness**; there was no disease He could not cure. He healed not only people's bodies, but He also healed their souls. Sin is the sickness of the soul. Jesus came to free men and women from bondage to sin. He came to forgive sins. He came to give us abundant life, both physically and spiritually (John 10:10).

Crowds came to Jesus from all over Israel, even from the **Decapolis**[20] and from the **region across the Jordan.**[21]

CHAPTER 5

The Beatitudes (5:1–12)

(Luke 6:20–23)

1–2 Here begins the greatest sermon ever preached, Jesus' Sermon on the Mount, which Matthew records in Chapters 5–7. Here Jesus sets forth how we ought to live. He spoke on this occasion mainly to His twelve disciples, but others listened also and were amazed at His teaching (Matthew 7:28).

3 **Blessed are the poor in spirit**. This is Jesus' first recorded teaching, and it is perhaps His most important teaching of all. Because without being **poor in spirit,** no one can enter the KINGDOM OF HEAVEN. The world teaches that in order to be blessed, one must be powerful, rich, self-sufficient. But this is a great mistake (see Luke 6:24 and comment). Jesus teaches that to be truly blessed one must first become **poor** (Luke 6:20). In order to be rich in things of the Spirit, one must become poor in things of the flesh.

To be "poor in spirit" means to empty oneself. Before we can be filled with God's blessings, we must first be emptied. Every man is by nature filled with selfishness and pride. This is called our "old man" or **old self** (Romans 6:6). Jesus first condemns our old sinful self, and then He saves those who are poor in

---

18 In Old Testament times, Assyria was a powerful kingdom located to the north of Israel.

19 The **synagogue** was the Jewish house of worship.

20 The **Decapolis** was a league of ten cities mainly to the east of Galilee.

21 The **Jordan** was an important river flowing south from the Sea of Galilee. It forms part of the eastern boundary of present-day Israel.

spirit. Therefore, to be poor in spirit also means that we confess we are worthy of condemnation. It means that we confess that we are **dead in . . . transgressions and sins** (Ephesians 2:1).

Therefore, right from the beginning we must understand that it is impossible to live the Christian life and to follow the teaching of Jesus by our own strength. We are unworthy; we are condemned; we are dead. If we think we are worthy, if we think that we can follow Christ by our own strength, then we are not being **poor in spirit**.

Anyone who is not poor in spirit has not met God. If we truly know God, we will become poor in spirit. God is so great, so powerful, so holy, so good, that once we know Him we will consider ourselves poor and wretched by comparison.

To be poor in spirit does not mean to be shy or fearful. To be poor in spirit is not a natural quality; it is a spiritual quality. Indeed, all these beatitudes mentioned in verses 3–10 represent spiritual qualities. To be poor in spirit means to be inwardly humble. Many people say with their lips: "I am weak, I can do nothing," but in their hearts they don't believe it. They only say it as an excuse for doing nothing for God. They only pretend to be humble.

God accepts only those who truly humble themselves before Him. God said: **"I live in a high and holy place, but also with him who is contrite and lowly in spirit, to revive the spirit of the lowly and to revive the heart of the contrite"** (Isaiah 57:15). **God opposes the proud but gives grace to the humble** (Proverbs 3:34; 1 Peter 5:5).

Peter, Jesus' chief disciple, was by nature a bold and confident man. But when He first recognized who Jesus was, he fell on his knees and exclaimed, **"Go away from me, Lord; I am a sinful man!"** (Luke 5:8). The great Apostle Paul was also a man who was poor in spirit (see 1 Corinthians 2:1–5; 2 Corinthians 3:5; 4:7; Philippians 3:7–9). And finally Jesus Himself, even though He was God, became poor in spirit for our sakes (see Philippians 2:5–8 and comment).

Therefore, let us remember that in God's sight we have nothing to boast about. We cannot boast of our caste, our name, our education, our skill, our wealth. All these things are worthless and vain. We can bring nothing to God. We can only come to God as empty earthen vessels. As we come to Him, let us pray that in His mercy He might fill us with spiritual blessings. **Humble yourselves, therefore, under God's mighty hand, that he may lift you up in due time** (1 Peter 5:6).

4 **Blessed are those who mourn**. The word "blessed" means "happy." So Jesus is saying: "Happy are those who mourn."

Jesus' teaching is the opposite of the world's teaching. The world says, "Don't mourn. Escape from sorrow. Seek happiness." But Jesus says: "In order to be truly happy, one must first mourn."

What does Jesus mean when He says that we must mourn? His meaning is this: we must mourn for our sins. He is talking about spiritual sorrow, not worldly sorrow. Before we can receive the joy of SALVATION, we must first mourn for our sin. Such mourning leads to REPENTANCE. **Godly sorrow brings repentance that leads to salvation and leaves no regret, but worldly sorrow brings death** (2 Corinthians 7:10).

How often do we mourn for our sin? We usually do not mourn; instead, we call our sins "mistakes." But God calls them sins. Until we begin to look at our sins in the same way God looks at them, we will not truly repent.

Those who mourn **will be comforted**. When we repent of our sins, Christ will comfort us. We look at ourselves and mourn. We look at Christ and find hope and peace and joy. Without sorrow there can be no joy. Without true repentance, there can be no salvation.

5 **Blessed are the meek**. Again, this is the opposite of the world's teaching. The world says: "If you want to **inherit the earth**, get money, get power, get fame. Be strong, be proud. Put yourself forward." But Jesus says the opposite: "Be meek." Only the meek will inherit the earth.

Worldly men cannot understand the teaching of Christ. They cannot understand Christians. Our principles are completely different from the principles of the world. It is not possible for those who belong to the world to be of one mind with those who belong to Christ.

The first beatitude, being **poor in spirit,** means to be humble before God. This third beatitude, meekness, means to be humble before men. That is even more difficult. When God calls us sinners, we can accept it. But if our neighbor calls us a sinner, that is more difficult to accept.

Jesus gave us an example of meekness. He said, "**. . . learn from me, for I am gentle and humble in heart**" (Matthew 11:29). This meekness or gentleness is not a natural quality; it is a spiritual quality. It can come only from the HOLY SPIRIT. It is a fruit of the Holy Spirit (Galatians 5:23). Only when we are born anew of the Spirit and receive a new spiritual nature can we possess true meekness (see John 3:3,5 and comment).

Some people think that to be meek means to be weak. But this is not true. A truly meek person is spiritually strong in the Lord.

How can a person become **meek**? First he must become poor in spirit (verse 3). Then he must mourn for his unworthiness and sin (verse 4). Then he must place his FAITH in Jesus. When a person does that, the Holy Spirit will enter him and make him new (see 2 Corinthians 5:17). The Holy Spirit will give him a spirit of meekness.

There are five signs of meekness. First, a meek person does not seek his own rights, his own advantage. Second, a meek person does not become offended and hurt when another person wrongs him. A meek person doesn't care about his honor. He doesn't try to defend himself, to make excuses, to hide his sins. Third, a meek person never tries to take revenge (see Romans 12:19; 1 Peter 2:19–23 and comments). Fourth, a meek person is always willing to learn. And fifth, a meek person does not try to have his own way. He does not seek his own will. He submits to the will of God and to the will of others (Ephesians 5:21). He gives his life and all that he has to God; he keeps nothing for himself.

And when a person gives up everything to God, what does he get? The **earth**! Blessed are the meek, **for they will inherit the earth**. This is what Paul meant when he said he was **sorrowful, yet always rejoicing; poor, yet making many rich; having nothing, and yet possessing everything** (2 Corinthians 6:10). If we are children of God, then we are heirs—**heirs of God and co-heirs with Christ** (Romans 8:17).

What earth shall we inherit? The new earth in the kingdom of heaven (Revelation 21:1–4). This present earth and all the proud people who oppose God's will shall pass away (1 John 2:17). Only the meek will be left to inherit the new earth in the kingdom of heaven (Psalm 37:10–11). **For whoever exalts himself will be humbled, and whoever humbles himself will be exalted** (Matthew 23:12).

6 Blessed are those who hunger and thirst for RIGHTEOUSNESS. Men of the world hunger for pleasure and happiness, but they are not satisfied. If a man seeks for happiness he will not find it. But if a man seeks first for righteousness, he will find both righteousness and true happiness. He will be filled. He will be fully satisfied.

Men hunger for happiness but remain unhappy. Why? Because of sin. In order to become free from unhappiness, one must become free from sin. That is, one must become RIGHTEOUS.

Many Christians, even, do not understand this teaching. Such Christians seek for joy, peace, spiritual power, and other blessings; they hunger and thirst for these things. But Jesus said, "Hunger for righteousness first of all, and then all these other things shall be given" (see Matthew 6:33).

To be righteous means to be holy, to be near God, to be like Christ, to be filled with the Holy Spirit. In order to be righteous we must be free of sin, because sin separates us from God and blocks the work of the Holy Spirit in our lives (see Ephesians 4:30 and comment).

Blessed are those who **hunger and thirst** for righteousness. A person who hasn't eaten for three days hungers for food. Our hunger for righteousness must be like that. If we hunger a little, God will give us a little. If we hunger much, God will give us much. If we come to God hungry, He has promised to fill us. Jesus said, "**. . . whoever comes to me I will never drive away.**" (John 6:37). As soon as we come to Jesus hungering for righteousness, He will give it. And to give us righteousness is essentially the same thing as to give us salvation. We become righteous in God's eyes through faith in Christ (see Romans 5:1; Galatians 2:15–16 and comments). We are no longer under condemnation (see Romans 8:1; General Article: Way of Salvation).

We must keep on hungering for righteousness. As we continue to hunger, God will continue to fill us. We shall become more and more holy; we shall manifest more and more of the fruits of the Holy Spirit (Galatians 5:22–23). **From the fullness of His grace we have all received one blessing after another** (John 1:16). Christ's desire is that we be **filled to the measure of the fullness of God** (Ephesians 3:19).

A question arises here: How righteous must we be in order to be justified by God, to be saved? The answer is: We must be 100 percent righteous. Jesus said, "**Be perfect, therefore, as your heavenly father is perfect**" (verse 48). People say two opposite things about salvation. Some say it is easy to obtain salvation; others say it is impossible. Both statements are true! It is impossible to obtain salvation by our own righteousness, by our own effort. But it is easy to obtain salvation, because through faith in Christ we receive Christ's own righteousness. And because of His righteousness, because of His sacrifice for our sins, we obtain salvation (see Mark 10:45 and comment). There is only one thing we must do to obtain the righteousness of Christ: We must **hunger** for it.

Let us do nothing that will reduce our hunger for righteousness. Let us not partake in worldly pleasures that distract our minds and hearts from seeking God. If we eat sweets before a meal, what happens to our appetite? It is decreased. Sweets are not evil in themselves, but if they decrease our appetite for real food, they do us harm. Worldly "sweets" are the same; they reduce our hunger for God and for righteousness (see Luke 6:25 and comment). Rather, we must increase our appetite for righteousness by reading God's word, by fellowship with other believers, and by prayer. We must continually pray for righteousness. Because without righteousness we cannot stand before God. Without righteousness, we cannot be saved.

7 Blessed are the merciful. These eight beatitudes do not describe what we should do; rather they describe what we should be. First we must "be"; then we can "do." First we must be Christians; then we can act like Christians. We are Christians by God's GRACE; it is a gift of God. Having become Christians, having become sons of God, we receive through the Holy Spirit the power to lead a Christian life and to obey Jesus' commands. Without having Christ's Holy Spirit within us, we could never follow these teachings. In the same way, through the working of the Holy Spirit within us, we must first be **merciful** in our hearts; then we shall be able to show mercy in our actions. Mercy, or kindness, is a fruit of the Holy Spirit (Galatians 5:22). Without the Holy Spirit we cannot be truly merciful.

True mercy always manifests itself in acts of mercy. Acts of mercy are the proof of our mercy, just as obedience to Christ is the proof of our faith (see James 2:17 and comment). If we do not show mercy, we are not merciful. To be merciful and to show mercy must always go together. To be a Christian and to act like a Christian must always go together. Those who do not act like Christians outwardly cannot be true Christians inwardly.[22] And those who are not true Christians inwardly will not be able to act like Christians outwardly.[23] What we are and what we do cannot be separated.

To show mercy does not mean that we

---

[22] However, from time to time true Christians do fall into sin, and at those times their outward actions can be very wrong. But the true Christian will immediately repent of his sin and be cleansed (1 John 1:9).

[23] The lives of some non-believers can appear righteous from a distance; but when one observes them from close up, the fruits of the Spirit cannot be seen in their lives.

ignore someone's sin. That is worldly mercy. God never ignores sin. He cannot tolerate even the smallest sin—the kind of sin we like to call a "mistake." He punishes every sin, and the punishment is the death sentence.

This is why Christ, when He took our sins upon Himself, had to die. This is how great God's mercy is toward us, that in order to save us He gave His own Son to die in our place.

Blessed are the merciful, **for they will be shown mercy**. If we show mercy to others, God will show mercy to us. If we do not show mercy to others, God will not show mercy to us (see Matthew 6:14–15).

First, God shows mercy to man. Not one of us could have been saved without God's mercy. While we were still sinners, God forgave us and saved us (Romans 5:8). While we were still unmerciful, God showed us mercy. However, after we become Christians, we must begin showing mercy to others. We received forgiveness from God even though we did not deserve forgiveness. In the same way, we must forgive others even though they do not deserve it. If we do not show mercy to others, God will take away His mercy from us (see Matthew 18:23–35). And, some say, if God takes away His mercy, He takes away our salvation. For if God stops forgiving us, how shall we be saved? (See General Article: Can We Lose Our Salvation?)

The greatest example of mercy is Jesus Himself. In order to show mercy to us, He died for us. He even forgave the men who crucified Him (Luke 23:34). In the same way, Stephen, the first Christian to be killed because of his faith, forgave his killers (Acts 7:60). When our neighbor sins against us, let us remember the example of Jesus and Stephen.

If we do not forgive others, God's Holy Spirit is not in us. And if the Holy Spirit is not in us, we do not belong to Christ (Romans 8:9). If we want to remain in God's mercy, we must continue to be merciful to others, that is to forgive them. On the day of judgment, when we must all stand before God, we shall surely need mercy. And on that day, if we have shown mercy to others, God will show mercy to us.

8 **Blessed are the pure in heart**. In God's sight our heart is most important. **Man looks at the outward appearance, but the Lord looks at the heart** (1 Samuel 16:7). He looks to see if our hearts are **pure**.

First, to be pure in heart means to have a single mind. We must not be **double-minded** (Psalm 86:11; James 1:7–8).

Second, to be pure in heart means to be holy, without sin, without love of self. The person who is pure in heart loves God with all his heart, soul, mind, and strength. This is the greatest commandment (see Mark 12:30 and comment).

Only those who are pure in heart, that is, who are holy, will see God (Hebrews 12:14). In order to enter the kingdom of God (kingdom of heaven), we must be holy. But to be holy, we need God's help. King David wrote in Psalm 51:10: **Create in me a pure heart, O God**. Only by God's Holy Spirit living in us can our hearts be made pure.

If we come to God, poor in spirit (verse 3) and hungering for righteousness (verse 6), He will purify our hearts. If we draw near to God, He will draw near to us (James 4:8). He will prepare our hearts so that we might be able to enter His presence. God will carry to completion the work He has begun in us (see Philippians 1:6 and comment). The main work of salvation is done by God, but we must do our part (see Philippians 2:12–13 and comment). James tells us: **Wash your hands, you sinners, and purify your hearts, you double-minded** (James 4:8). We must flee from sin; we must resist the devil (James 4:7). We must put to death the works of our sinful nature (see Romans 6:12; 8:13; Colossians 3:5 and comments). These things we ourselves must do; this is our part in our salvation.

9 **Blessed are the peacemakers**. The **peacemakers** mentioned here are those who make PEACE between man and God. Many people call themselves "peacemakers," such as presidents, kings, prime ministers. They talk about peace; they make peace treaties. But in the world there is no peace. There is no peace because of man's sin. Worldly peacemakers try to make peace by covering over sin, by trying to make arrangements with evil men. But the true spiritual peacemakers try to remove the injustice, the pain, the sin that is in the world. They help men find peace with God. This is true peace.

To be a peacemaker, we must first find peace with God ourselves. We can only find peace through faith in Christ (Romans 5:1). To find true peace we must be like those described in these beatitudes: we must be poor in spirit, meek, hungry for righteousness, merciful, pure in heart (verses 3–8). All of these beatitudes go together. We cannot have one quality without the others.

How do we make peace? We make peace by loving our neighbor as ourselves (see Mark 12:31 and comment). Love is the main weapon of the peacemaker. Paul wrote: **If your enemy is hungry, feed him** (Romans 12:20). Jesus said: **"Love your enemies and pray for those who persecute you, that you may be sons of your Father in heaven"**, (verses 44–45). Blessed are the peacemakers, **for they will be called sons of God** (see John 1:12; Galatians 3:26; 4:7 and comments).

The greatest peacemaker was Jesus (Ephesians 2:17; Colossians 1:19–20). He said to His disciples, **"Peace be with you! As the Father has sent me, I am sending you"** (John 20:21). Jesus has sent us to be peacemakers. We are ambassadors for Christ (see 2 Corinthians 5:20 and comment).

However, we must not forget another truth. On another occasion Jesus said, **"I did not come to bring peace, but a sword"** (Matthew 10:34). Jesus not only came to reconcile men with God. He also came to separate the good from the evil. He will be the judge on the day of judgment (Matthew 25:31–32; John 5:22; 2 Corinthians 5:10). Jesus brings peace to those who turn to God in faith; but He brings the sword of judgment to those who refuse to obey and worship God.

Christ came to earth as a peacemaker. Yet He suffered and was killed by His enemies. In the same way, we too, even though we are peacemakers, will suffer opposition and persecution from the enemies of Christ (2 Timothy 3:12). Jesus said, **"If they persecuted me, they will persecute you also"** (John 15:20). We cannot make peace with those that oppose Christ.

10 **Blessed are those who are persecuted** (see 1 Peter 3:14; 4:14). Like the poor in spirit in verse 3, **theirs is the kingdom of heaven.**

Men are persecuted for many reasons, such as sin, foolishness, bad habits. But only those persecuted **because of righteousness** are blessed.

Sometimes we bring trouble on ourselves unnecessarily. We think we are righteous, but in fact we are suffering because of our mistakes or lack of knowledge. Let us be certain that what we are doing will bring honor to God. Only if we suffer for bringing honor to God will we be blessed.

According to the New Testament, we must suffer persecution (2 Timothy 3:12). If we do not suffer some kind of persecution, we are probably not living for God's glory. If we love God, the world will hate us (John 15:18–19). Worldly men[24] will always oppose righteous men. Righteous men, that is, those who have received Christ's righteousness, are like lights in the darkness. Worldly men hate the light, because the light exposes their evil deeds (John 3:20).

Many worldly men are called "righteous," "honorable," "excellent" by other worldly men. But this is worldly talk. Such men are not persecuted by the world; they belong to the world. They receive honor from the world. They have their reward (see Luke 6:26 and comment). The truly righteous person is not of the world; he is a citizen of the kingdom of heaven. Therefore, worldly men persecute him.

11–12 When He had finished describing the eight beatitudes, Jesus turned to His disciples and said, **"Blessed are you . . .". "Blessed are you when people insult you, persecute you and falsely say all kinds of evil against**

---

[24] Worldly men are those who love the things of the world more than they love God.

you because of me." If we suffer because of Christ, we will be blessed.

Therefore, let each follower of Christ be prepared to suffer insults, slander, and persecution. And when it comes, what must the believer do? **Rejoice and be glad** (see Acts 5:40–41). We shall be counted with the prophets of the Old Testament, who also suffered persecution (2 Chronicles 36:15–16). We shall have the honor of sharing in the sufferings of Christ (Philippians 3:10).

What do we usually do when someone wrongs us? We get angry. We oppose that person. We seek revenge. But Jesus says we are not to do that.

Therefore, we hide our anger inside. We remain inwardly bitter and angry. But Jesus says that is also wrong.

Since anger is wrong, we try to hide our anger even from ourselves. As a result, we become depressed, hurt, discouraged. But that is not right either. When someone wrongs us or persecutes us because of Christ, there is only one thing Jesus tells us to do: rejoice. **Rejoice and be glad.**

No one naturally rejoices when trouble comes to him. Only one who has the Holy Spirit within him can rejoice in persecution. Joy is a fruit of the Holy Spirit (Galatians 5:22). God allows persecution to come upon us to test whether we are being led by the Holy Spirit, to test our faith (1 Peter 1:6–7). If we respond to persecution with anger or depression, then we know that we are not filled with the Holy Spirit.

When an orange or grape or some other fruit is squeezed, juice comes out. When we are "squeezed" by persecution, what kind of juice flows out from us? The bitter juice of anger? Or the sweet juice of joy, which comes from the Holy Spirit within us?

Why rejoice? **Because great is your reward in heaven** (verse 12). How great is our reward? It is so great that it cannot be measured. Our reward is the **kingdom of heaven** itself (verse 10). Our reward is to live in that kingdom, to see God (verse 8), to be sons of God (verse 9). Paul wrote: **I consider that our present sufferings are not worth comparing with the glory that will be revealed in us** (Romans 8:18). **For our light and momentary troubles are achieving for us an eternal glory that far outweighs them all** (2 Corinthians 4:17).

God is a loving heavenly Father, and all who believe in Christ are His children. God wants to reward us. He wants us to share His glory. God is not obliged to reward us; rather, He chooses to do so according to His own will. He rewards us because of His love for us.

We are God's children. It is our duty to obey our Father. It is our duty to be people such as are described in these eight beatitudes. If we, through the Holy Spirit, possess these eight qualities described in verses 3–10, then we shall be truly blessed.

Salt and Light (5:13–16)
(Mark 14:21; Luke 14:33)

13 Christians are the **salt of the earth.** Salt purifies. Salt preserves. Salt prevents decay. If you put salt on meat, it can be kept for months without refrigeration and it will not spoil.

The world is like meat. It is decaying. There is evil in the world. Men disobey God. They become spiritually decayed, like bad meat. Again and again the Jewish nation disobeyed God, and God sent prophets to call the Jews to repentance. The prophets were like salt. The people that heeded their words were purified and cleansed. We Christians are called to be salt, like the prophets of the Old Testament.[25]

Salt has another quality: it is very salty. A tiny amount of salt has a big effect. A little pinch of salt can make a large amount of water salty. Salt makes a difference. Salt is effective. We Christians

---

[25] The Old Testament prophets didn't only predict the future. They also spoke God's words to the Jewish people. They acted as God's mouthpiece; through them God gave His commands and warnings to the people. Thus, in the Bible the word "prophet" means much more than just a "teller of the future."

must be like salt; we must make a difference in the world. We must change the "taste" of the world, just as salt changes the taste of water. And from the eight beatitudes listed in verses 3–10, we can see what the "taste" of a Christian should be.

We must ask ourselves: "Do we taste like salt? Do we taste different from the world around us?" If we lose our taste, we are worthless. We are false Christians. According to Luke 14:35, savorless salt isn't even good for manure.[26] It is good for nothing. So it is with savorless Christians, that is, Christians who do not have the Holy Spirit. If a Christian does not have the Holy Spirit, there is no way he can become "tasty," or "salty" (see Mark 9:50 and comment). Our taste comes from the Holy Spirit.

Many people talk about progress. All countries want progress. But what kind of "progress" is needed? Christian progress. More than roads and factories and conveniences, people need God. They need peace, love, forgiveness, salvation. In other words, they need spiritual salt. Each Christian is like a grain of salt. It is only believers in Christ who can bring about true progress, spiritual progress. But we can only do so if we remain salty.

14–15 Christians are not only salt; they are also the **light of the world**. It is the Holy Spirit in us that gives light; the light is Christ's light, not our own. We are lights because Christ was light (see John 8:12).

The world is in darkness, the darkness of sin, ignorance, and separation from God. We, too, were once darkness, but now are light (Ephesians 5:8; Philippians 2:15).

We are lights to show men and women the way to God, the way to salvation. We shine forth our light by our witness, by our example, both in word and in deed. The eight qualities mentioned in verses 3–10 and the eight fruits of the Spirit (Galatians 5:22–23) are like lights.

Our behavior must be different from the behavior of other people, just as light is different from darkness. And others must be able to see our light. Our church must be like a **city on a hill** (verse 14).

Only if people follow our light (the light of Christ) will they find salvation. They can only escape from darkness by following our light. God sent Christ into the world to save men and women (John 3:17). And as God sent Christ, so Christ sends us (John 17:18; 20:21). Therefore, let us not hide our light. Just as saltless salt is useless, so is light useless that is hid under a bowl. A Christian whose light does not shine is a useless Christian. He is like a fruit tree that bears no fruit (John 15:5–6). No taste. No light. No fruit. Such a person cannot be a true Christian.

Let us constantly ask ourselves: "Is my light shining? Is there oil in my lamp—the oil of the Holy Spirit?" Without the Holy Spirit, our light cannot shine. Oil gets used up. We need to keep adding oil to our lamps every day. We need to remain **filled with the Spirit** (Ephesians 5:18).

16 How can others know if we have the Holy Spirit? They can see our **good deeds**. Our light is manifest by good deeds. But our light must glorify God, not ourselves. The purpose of our light, of our good deeds, is not to gain praise for ourselves, but to gain praise for God. Remember, the light is not our own. The light is God's Holy Spirit within us. In everything we must give Him all the glory.

The Fulfillment of the Law (5:17–20)

17 Jesus did not come to abolish **the Law and the Prophets**—that is, the

[26] In New Testament times, salt was used as fertilizer throughout much of the Middle East.

teachings of the Old Testament.[27] He came **to fulfill them**. He came to fulfill both the law and the writings of the prophets.

How did Jesus fulfill the law? By obeying it fully. The Jews did not accept Jesus. They accused Him of breaking the Jewish law. But their charge was false. It was they who broke the law; they followed it outwardly, but not in their hearts. Jesus showed that the law must be followed not only in outward action, but also in inward attitude.

How did Jesus fulfill the words of the Old Testament prophets? In this way: all their prophecies about the Messiah, the Savior, were fulfilled in His own life. The prophets prophesied that Jesus would die for men's sins. He would take the punishment for their sins (see Isaiah 53:5–6; Mark 10:45 and comment). Christ would make His life a **guilt offering** (Leviticus 5:14–16; Isaiah 53:10); that is, He would lay down His life for us in order to take away our guilt. All this came true when Jesus died on the cross. Christ offered Himself as the final sacrifice for sin; no other sacrifice is needed. Through His death all who believe in Him will escape punishment and receive salvation. In this way Christ is the fulfillment of the prophecies and promises of the Old Testament.

18 Nothing will disappear from the law **until everything is accomplished**—that is, until everything written in the Old Testament about Jesus is accomplished. Before Jesus' death and resurrection, the entire law was in effect. But after Jesus died and rose from the dead, part of the law became unnecessary. That part didn't "disappear"; it merely ceased to be in effect. The part of the law no longer in effect is the "ceremonial" part of the law. The Jewish law included many regulations about sacrifices and the removal of guilt, and about purifying oneself from sin. These rules are no longer necessary, because Christ has now come and removed our sin and guilt (see Colossians 2:13–14; Hebrews 8:12–13 and comments).

19 Do Christians have to obey any of the law? Yes, they do. They must obey the main commandments of the law, the so-called "moral law." These main commandments that make up the moral law have not been canceled; we must obey them.

Back in the time of Moses, God made a COVENANT with the Jews in which He said to them that if they obeyed His law He would protect them and be their God (Exodus 19:5–6). God wrote His law on two tablets of stone (Exodus 31:18). But when God sent Christ into the world, He made a **new covenant**[28] with men. God said: **"I will put my laws in their minds and write them on their hearts"** (Jeremiah 31:31–33; Hebrews 8:8–10). **"I will forgive their wickedness and will remember their sins no more"** (Jeremiah 31:34; Hebrews 8:12).

Now, through the Holy Spirit, God gives us help in obeying His commandments. We are not free of the "moral law." Christ did not come to **abolish** the law; He came to give us the power to obey it.

The "moral law" is that part of the Jewish law that deals with our daily behavior. The moral law includes such commands as the ten commandments (Exodus 20:1–17), and the commandments to love God and to love our neighbor (Deuteronomy 6:4–5; Leviticus 19:18; Mark 12:29–31). Indeed, the two great commandments to love God and neighbor are the summation of the entire

---

[27] The first five books of the Old Testament are called the **Law**. The law was given to the Jewish people by God. It consisted of ten main commandments (Exodus 20:1–17) and then many other rules. The Jews believed that by following the law they could find salvation. For further discussion, see Word List: Law.

The remainder of the Old Testament consists of the history of the Jewish people and the writings of the Jewish prophets. The entire Old Testament, therefore, is often called the **Law and the Prophets**.

[28] "New covenant" is the real meaning of the words "New Testament." The New Testament describes the **new covenant** that God has made with man through Jesus Christ.

law (Matthew 22:40; Galatians 5:14). The Apostle Paul wrote that **love is the fulfillment of the law** (Romans 13:10). If we obey the two great commandments fully, we have obeyed the entire law.

Therefore, in this verse 19, when Matthew writes the words "command" or "commandment," we must understand that he is talking about the "moral law," not the "ceremonial law." We must obey all the commands of the moral law, both great and small, and we must teach others to do likewise.

20 The **Pharisees and teachers of the law** were the most religious of the Jews. The Pharisees were the strictest Jewish sect, and the teachers of the law knew the most about all the rules that had to be obeyed. How could anyone be more righteous than the Pharisees and the teachers of the law?

Jesus' meaning was this: Outwardly these Jewish leaders appeared righteous, but inwardly they were not. They obeyed the law outwardly so that men would praise them (Luke 16:14–15). They followed the little rules, but neglected the important ones (see Matthew 23:23–24; Luke 11:42). They forgot that God doesn't look on man's outer appearance but on his heart. The hearts of the Pharisees and Jewish teachers were far from God; their hearts were cold. They had no love, mercy, humility. They were deceiving others; they were hypocrites.

They were also deceiving themselves. They were putting confidence in their own righteousness. They said to themselves: "We are good and holy. We are not like other men" (see Luke 18:9–14). They thought, "God will accept us." But in thinking this they were making a great mistake. In God's sight their "righteousness" was false.

That is why Jesus taught that unless our righteousness exceeds that of the Pharisees and teachers of the law, we will not enter the kingdom of heaven; that is, we will not gain salvation. No one can ever enter heaven by his or her own righteousness. We are not saved by man's righteousness; we are saved only by Christ's righteousness. We are not saved by our own effort and work; we are saved only by Christ's work, that is, His sacrifice for us. We are not saved because we are worthy. We are saved only by God's grace (see Galatians 2:15–16; Ephesians 2:8–9 and comments).

Because we have received such grace from God, we must live lives pleasing to God. If we have received the Holy Spirit, we will manifest the fruit of the Spirit in our lives (Matthew 5:3–10; Galatians 5:22–23). If we do not manifest the Spirit's fruit, the Spirit is not in us. And if the Spirit is not in us, we are not of Christ (Romans 8:9). We are not true Christians. We are not saved.

Let every person examine himself.

Murder (5:21–26)
(Luke 12:57–59)

21 In the remainder of Chapter 5, Jesus gives six examples of the teaching of the Jewish leaders. Then following each example, Jesus gives His own teaching. The Jews' teaching concerned man's outward behavior. Jesus' teaching concerned man's heart. He taught that we must not only follow the law literally; we must also follow the spirit of the law, that is, the inner meaning of the law.

The law said, "**You shall not murder**" (Exodus 20:13). Its outward meaning is: "You shall not kill the body."

22 Jesus showed that there was a deeper meaning in that command. He said, "Do not desire to kill." That is, we must not hate another person, we must not desire to harm or hurt another person. In God's sight that is like killing him. We must not despise and condemn and insult another person. That is the same as killing his honor, his reputation.

Raca was an Aramaic word meaning "silly" or "dumb." The **Sanhedrin** was the main Jewish governing body. It also was like a court. Someone who insulted another person could be brought before the Sanhedrin.

According to Jesus' teaching, to say "**You fool**" was even worse. To say "You fool" to someone is to have complete contempt for that person. A person who does this is in danger of going to hell.

This teaching does not mean that we must never correct or rebuke anyone.

Those in authority, such as parents, teachers, and pastors, must correct and discipline those under them. If our brother sins against us, we must tell him (Matthew 18:15). But we must never despise or hate a person. If someone does something foolish, we can call his work foolish, but we must not call him a fool.

Men do foolish things. It is foolish to disobey God. It is foolish to reject Christ. It is foolish to love this world. It was foolish for the Pharisees and teachers of the law to trust in their own righteousness. In Matthew Chapter 23, Jesus severely rebuked them for doing so. Yet at the same time, He loved them. He had come to die for them. He told them the truth in love (Ephesians 4:15). Paul wrote: **Brothers, if someone is caught in a sin, you who are spiritual should restore him gently** (Galatians 6:1). When we rebuke another person, our purpose must be to restore that person, and we must do it in love, not in anger. We must be angry with the sin, but not with the sinner. Paul said, **In your anger do not sin** (Ephesians 4:26). We must be angry with sin because God is angry with sin (Romans 1:18). But we must not get angry with the sinner. If we do, we ourselves will be sinning; we too will be **subject to** JUDGMENT, God's final judgment.

23–24 Not only must we not murder, not only must we not be angry with our brother or despise him, but we also must not let any personal disagreement or misunderstanding remain between us. We must remove the bad spirit between us and replace it with the spirit of love and forgiveness. We must do this before offering our **gift at the alter.**[29]

Jesus' meaning is this: Before we come to God to worship and pray and offer gifts, we must confess and remove sinful feelings against our brother. If we have wronged our brother in any way, we must first make that right. If we have an unforgiving spirit toward our brother, we must first forgive him (see Mark 11:25). Only then will God accept our offerings and hear our prayers. In Psalm 66:18 it is written: **If I had cherished sin in my heart, the Lord would not have listened.** To treat our brother without love, or even to think unloving thoughts, is a sin. Before we come to worship, pray, and offer gifts to God, we must first remove the sin in our hearts (see 1 Samuel 15:22; Hosea 6:6; Mark 12:33 and comment).

25–26 The **judge** in verse 25 is God. God demands that we pay up to the **last penny**; that is, He demands that we obey every command. And one of His main commands is to love our neighbor and even to love our enemy (verse 44). Let us examine our hearts. Is there anyone we do not love?

At any time we could die, and then we will have to stand before the great Judge. What will we say to Him? "I have believed; I have worshiped and offered sacrifices; I have given money; I have done much work for the church." But then what will the Judge say to us? He will say: "How is your heart? Is your heart pure? Why is there anger in your heart? Why have you not loved your brother? Why have you not forgiven him? You may not enter my kingdom." Jesus said, "**Not everyone who says to me, 'Lord, Lord,' will enter the kingdom of heaven, but only he who does the will of my Father who is in heaven**" (Matthew 7:21).

Adultery (5:27–30)
(Matthew 18:8–9; Mark 9:43–48)

27–28 Like the command not to murder (verse 21), the command not to commit adultery is one of the ten commandments of the Old Testament (Exodus 20:14). But Jesus taught that the desire to commit murder or adultery is as bad as actually doing it. He taught that sin begins in the heart (see Matthew 15:19). Many people obey most of the ten commandments outwardly, but in their hearts they have sinful desires. For example, many people can say, "I have

[29] Notice that it's not a question of who is at fault or mostly at fault. If you are aware that another person is grieved by you or feels negative toward you, Jesus says you must **go and be reconciled to your brother** (verse 24).

obeyed the first nine commandments"; but they cannot say, "I have obeyed the tenth commandment: **You shall not covet**." (Exodus 20:17). To "covet" means to desire something unlawful. It means to desire to sin. To "covet" your neighbor's wife is the same as to desire to commit adultery with her. Sin is not only outward action; it is also unlawful and selfish desire.

All men are sinners (Romans 3:10). Men's hearts are filled with evil desires. **The heart is deceitful above all things and beyond cure** (Jeremiah 17:9). All men deserve the death sentence because of sin. We cannot save ourselves. That is why Jesus had to die for us. In order to save us, it was necessary for an innocent and sinless man to take our punishment. God cannot stand sin. He is completely holy (1 John 1:5). He must punish sin; therefore, He punished Jesus in our place. It was because of our sin that Jesus came to earth.

Therefore, when we preach the Gospel we must begin with man's sin and with man's condemnation because of sin. This is how the preaching in the New Testament began—"**Repent**" (see Mark 1:4,15; Acts 2:38). No one can be saved unless he first realizes that he is a sinner who needs salvation. We must confess the sin in our heart. We must confess not only big sins, but little sins as well. We must confess not only sinful actions, but also sinful thoughts and desires. And when we have confessed and repented, God will forgive and cleanse us (see 1 John 1:9 and comment). He will give us a new mind and a new heart through the Holy Spirit.

This teaching is not only for non-Christians; it is also for Christians. We continually need to confess our sins and to renew our minds (Romans 12:2). Satan is continually trying to lead us into sin. He is trying to quench the Holy Spirit in us (1 Thessalonians 5:19). He is trying to make our hearts lukewarm, cold. We must continually remain filled with the Holy Spirit (Ephesians 5:18). The Spirit will show us our hidden sins, and give us a repentant and humble mind. Only when we have repented of our sins and been cleansed will the Holy Spirit be able to fully work in our lives.

29–30 Outward sins like adultery are only the outward signs of a "diseased" or sinful heart. The disease is in our heart.

Sin is like an infection, or a cancer. To cure an infection, the doctor must drain out the pus, that is, the sin. To cure a cancer, the doctor must cut it out. In the same way, we must "cut out" the sin in our life.

How? First we must confess and repent. Then we must flee from sin (2 Timothy 2:22). We must give up all things that lead us into temptation to sin. We must stay away from any activity or any person that stirs up sinful desires in our hearts. We must resist the first beginnings of sinful desire. Even though something is in itself good and lawful, if it leads us into temptation we must give it up. For example, to earn money is good. But if we begin to love money more than God, then money is leading us into sin (1 Timothy 6:10). If we begin to love anything more than God or Jesus,[30] we are sinning. And if we continue to sin in this way, we shall not enter into heaven. This is why Jesus said, "**What good is it for a man to gain the whole world, yet forfeit his soul?**" (Mark 8:36). If we love anything more than Jesus, we are not worthy of Him (see Matthew 10:37).

If there is anything in our life that we love more than Jesus—parents, children, money, our "right eye," our "right hand"—let us give it up. The Apostle Paul said, **. . . if by the Spirit you put to death the misdeeds of the body, you will live** (Romans 8:13). By the help of the Holy Spirit, we must "put to death" our sinful deeds and desires. Then we shall be able to enter the kingdom of heaven.

In verse 29, the **right eye** represents the medium or means by which evil desires enter our mind. In verse 30, the **right hand** represents any member of our body by which a sin is carried out (see Mark 9:43–48 and comment). If our eye or hand is leading us into sin, it would be much

---

[30] God and Jesus are one (see John 10:30).

better to give up our eye or hand than to lose our soul.

Divorce (5:31–32)

(Mark 10:11–12; Luke 16:18)

31 See Mark 10:3–4; 1 Corinthians 7:10–11 and comments.
32 See Mark 10:11–12 and comment.

Oaths (5:33–37)

33 According to the Old Testament law, anyone who made an oath was obliged to keep it (Numbers 30:2; Deuteronomy 23:21).
34–35 However, the Jews of Jesus' time considered that any oath which didn't mention God's name did not need to be kept. Therefore, in order to avoid having to fulfill their oaths, the Jews didn't use God's name in their oaths. Rather they swore **by heaven**, or **by the earth**, or **by Jerusalem**. But in doing this, they were deceiving themselves. Because all these things—heaven, earth, and Jerusalem—belong to God. Heaven is God's throne, and the earth is His footstool (Isaiah 66:1; Acts 7:49). To swear by these things was the same as swearing by God Himself.

Jesus taught that we shouldn't swear at all. It is unnecessary. All oaths must be kept, no matter what name we swear by. So there is no need for swearing.
36 The Jews sometimes swore "by their head." But that also was vain. There is no point in swearing by anything belonging to man. Man has no final power to guarantee an oath. He can't even change the color of his hair.
37 When we say "Yes," let us mean "yes." When we say "No," let us mean "no." There is no need to swear. We must obey the ninth commandment: **You shall not give false testimony** (Exodus 20:16). People often swear in order to hide the fact that they are lying. If we are telling the truth, there is no need to add any oath. Oaths are tricks of the **evil one**, that is, the devil (see James 5:12 and comment).

Jesus didn't mean that we should not swear in court. When Jesus Himself was on trial, the high priest asked Him **under oath** if He was the Christ, and Jesus answered him (Matthew 26:63–64). But in this section, Jesus is talking about personal relationships, not official proceedings. In our personal dealings we must not make oaths.

An Eye for an Eye (5:38–42)

(Luke 6:29–30)

38 **Eye for eye, and tooth for tooth** was an Old Testament rule that prohibited taking excessive revenge (Exodus 21:23–25; Leviticus 24:19–20; Deuteronomy 19:21). But the rule was written only for judges and government officials. The purpose of the rule was to prevent a judge from giving a punishment that was greater than the crime.
39 The Jewish leaders in Jesus' time gave a wrong meaning to this rule. They taught that the rule allowed ordinary Jews to take revenge for personal injuries. But Jesus said, "Do not take personal revenge. **Do not resist an evil person**."

We must understand Jesus' meaning. It is necessary for judges and police officers to resist evil persons. It is necessary for administrators of an organization to punish an employee who breaks a rule. It is necessary for teachers to discipline their students. We all must accept the punishment and discipline of those in authority (see Romans 13:1–5; 1 Peter 2:13–14 and comments).

In this section, Jesus is only dealing with personal matters. If we are personally wronged by another person, we must not take our own revenge on that person. Rather, following Jesus' example, we must forgive him (Luke 23:34).

Do not resist an evil person. The meaning of this saying is very deep. It means that we must love our enemy (verse 44), we must be merciful and meek. We must not defend ourselves. We must not seek our own advantage.

No matter what kind of personal wrong we receive, we must never take revenge. Instead, we must be prepared to accept further wrong. If someone strikes us, we must let him strike us a second time. If someone insults us, we are not to defend ourselves; rather, we should suffer it quietly (1 Peter 2:19–21). God will defend us; He will avenge us (Proverbs 24:29; Romans 12:19). We can trust Him to judge righteously (1 Peter 2:23).

However, Jesus does not say that we must "turn our other cheek" in every situation. If a drunken man strikes us, we may defend ourselves. When an officer struck Jesus at His trial, Jesus didn't turn His other cheek (John 18:19–23). Jesus opposed the officer. The officer was dishonoring God. The trial was illegal. Jesus was not trying to defend His own honor; He was defending God's honor. We must always defend God's honor in appropriate ways; we must always oppose those who oppose God. But let us make sure it is really God's honor that we are defending, and not our own.

40 Here Jesus gives a second example. According to Jewish law, if a man could not pay a debt, he had to give his inner garment in place of the money he owed. But he did not have to give his outer cloak (Exodus 22:26–27). But Jesus taught, "Give more than is necessary. Give more than the law requires. Do not try to keep things for yourself, even if the law says you can."

41 In Jesus' time, Israel and most of the countries around the Mediterranean Sea were under the control of the Roman Empire. Israel was a colony. According to Roman law, a Roman soldier could demand a resident of a colony to carry his baggage as far as one mile. Then the soldier was supposed to find another man to carry his things for the next mile.

Jesus taught that if a Roman soldier forced someone to go one mile, that man should happily go with the soldier an extra mile. We must be willing to do more than our duty. Worldly men do only their duty. Christians must be ready to do more, so that our light might shine among men.

42 **Give to the one who asks you**. What does Jesus mean here? Must we always give what people ask for? No (see Acts 3:6). We must not give liquor to a drunk person. We must not give matches to a small child. We must not give to a beggar who is able to work (2 Thessalonians 3:10–12).

Jesus' meaning is this: We must always give to those whose need is greater than ours. Our money, our property is not our own; it is God's. We are only stewards of our possessions. We must never say, "This is my house. These are my clothes." That is wrong; these things belong to God. He is merely giving us the use of them. And so, when we meet someone in need, we must give what we have to him (see 1 John 3:17–18).

In this section, Jesus is not giving us new laws to follow; He is teaching us to be new people. He is telling us to be different from worldly men. He is teaching us to be unselfish, to live for others more than for ourselves. He is teaching us to deny ourselves. He said, "**If anyone would come after me, he must deny himself**" (see Mark 8:34 and comment).

How can we deny ourselves? First, we need the help of the Holy Spirit. No worldly person can ever deny himself; only a person who has the Holy Spirit can do that.

Then we must recognize the selfishness in our lives. Almost everything natural man does is motivated by selfishness—that is, by self-interest, or self-love. What we do, we do for ourselves. Whenever we feel hurt, it is usually because of selfishness. When we get angry, it is usually because of selfishness. Man's selfish nature is the cause of all the sin and unhappiness in the world. Because of selfishness, man is separated from God. Christ came to deliver us from selfishness and reconcile us to God. Christ **died for all, that those who live should no longer live for themselves but for him who died for them** (2 Corinthians 5:15).

The man born again by Christ's Holy Spirit does not live for himself; he lives for Christ. Such a man happily "turns the other cheek," gives up his outer garment, and walks two miles, four miles, ten miles. Such a man gives freely to those in need, and does not think of himself.

To what extent do we live according to these teachings of Christ? Let each person examine himself.

Love for Enemies (5:43–48)
(Luke 6:27–28,32–36)

43 The Jewish leaders said: "**Love your neighbor but hate your enemy.**" They taught that only other Jews should be considered "neighbors." They did not consider non-Jews to be neighbors; instead, they despised non-Jews.

Jesus taught that anyone in need is our "neighbor" (Luke 10:29–37). That means that all people are our neighbors, because all people are in need in some way, either spiritually or materially. Therefore, when Jesus said, "Love your neighbor," He was teaching that we must love all people.

But here a question arises. In the Old Testament much is written about punishing the enemies of Israel. (One example is found in 1 Samuel 15:1–3.) Even Jesus showed great anger towards the Pharisees in Matthew Chapter 23, especially in verse 33. He drove people out of the temple who were changing money and selling animals to be sacrificed (Mark 11:15–16; John 2:13–15). How can Jesus teach us to love our enemies when the Bible talks so much about opposing our enemies?

44 The answer is this: We must love our personal enemies, that is, those who have wronged us personally. But we must oppose and rebuke God's enemies. God will sometimes use us to punish His enemies. But even though we must oppose such an enemy of God for God's sake, we must continue to love that enemy personally. We must hate the sin and love the sinner.

45 Jesus said that we must be **sons** of our Father in heaven. Not only that, He also said that we should be like our heavenly Father (verse 48). God shows love to His enemies; therefore, we should do likewise. God gives sun and rain to both the wicked and the righteous. God sent Jesus to die for sinners. **While we were still sinners, Christ died for us** (Romans 5:8). God did not love us according to our worth or according to our behavior. He loved us fully even though we were His enemies. In the same way, we also must love other men.

Why did God show such love to sinful men—to His enemies? Because **God is love** (1 John 4:16). God is the source of all true spiritual love (see 1 John 4:7–9). **For God so loved the world that He gave His one and only Son, that whoever believes in him shall not perish but have eternal life** (John 3:16).

How can we show this love to our enemies? Jesus gave the answer in Luke 6:27–28. He said: "**. . . do good to those who hate you, bless those that curse you, pray for those who mistreat you.**" If we do this, how great will our witness be! How bright will be our light! In what other religion is such teaching found? (see 1 Peter 3:9).

Is it possible to obey such commands? Yes, by the help of the Holy Spirit within us. The first Christian martyr, Stephen, prayed for those who were killing him (Acts 7:59–60). We, too, must love in this way, or else we will be disobeying Christ's command. But remember, Jesus never gives a command without also giving us the help and strength to fulfill it. He will give us His love through the Holy Spirit (Romans 5:5). If we do not obey, it is our fault.

46–47 In these verses Jesus teaches that if we do not love our enemies, there will be no difference between us and worldly men. We need to ask ourselves: "Are we different from non-believers? Are we different from worldly men?" Think: most men do not commit adultery, do not murder. Most men do their duty, help their neighbor, give to the poor, loan to their friends. Jesus asks us: "How are you different from that?"

We can be different only if we follow Jesus' teaching. The world says, "Do not do evil work"; Jesus says, "Do not have evil thoughts." The world says, "Do not murder"; Jesus says, "Do not be angry." The world says, "Do not take excessive revenge"; Jesus says, "Take no revenge at all." The world says, "Love your friends"; Jesus says, "Love your enemies." Jesus asks us today: "**. . . what are you doing more than others?**"

48 Finally Jesus gives us the most difficult command of all: "**Be perfect, therefore, as your heavenly Father is perfect.**" In the corresponding verse in Luke, Jesus says: "**Be merciful, just as your Father is merciful**" (Luke 6:36).

God is our Father. Because we are His children we must act like His children. We must be different from others; we must be light in the darkness. We must be the salt of the world. God is not the Father of all men; He is the Father only of those who believe in Jesus (John 1:12). He is the Creator of all men, but He is only a Father to those who follow Jesus. And because we are His children, we must be perfect as He is perfect.

How is this possible? How can we love as God loves, and be merciful as God is merciful? It is possible because God has poured out His love upon us through His Holy Spirit (see Romans 5:5). Through the Holy Spirit all things are possible. Paul said: **I can do everything through him who gives me strength** (Philippians 4:13). Paul also said: **And my God will meet all your needs according to his glorious riches in Christ Jesus** (Philippians 4:19). God will especially meet all our spiritual needs. Whatever we lack, He is ready to give (Matthew 7:7,11).

On the day of judgment, God will ask each one of us: "Why did you not love your enemies as I loved you at first? Why did you not forgive your debtors, as I forgave you? Why did you not do more than your duty? Why did you not do more than worldly men?" On that day, what answer will we give?

Friends, let us not be ashamed on that day. Let us seek, through the Holy Spirit, to be like Jesus. Let us hunger for God's righteousness. **Be perfect, therefore, as your heavenly Father is perfect.** Though in this life we can never be as perfect as our heavenly Father, to be so must always be our foremost goal.

CHAPTER 6

Giving to the Needy (6:1–4)

1 Jesus taught: "**Be careful not to do your 'acts of righteousness' before men, to be seen by them.**" Whatever work we do, God always looks mainly at our motive and reason for doing it. In God's sight, the reason why we have done a work is more important than the work itself. If we do good works to gain praise for ourselves, God is not pleased. That is selfish. God is only pleased when we do things for His glory. The main teaching here is that God looks mainly at our motives, at our heart, and not on our outward works. God wants us first to be inwardly righteous in our hearts. Only those good works that arise from a righteous heart are pleasing to God.

In Matthew 5:16, Jesus said: "... **let your light shine before men, that they may see your good deeds....**" This statement at first glance seems to be opposite from the teaching given in this section. But in Matthew 5:16, the main point is that men must see our good deeds **and praise** [our] **Father in heaven.** The motive for our good deeds must be to win praise for God. Whenever we do any good work, we must always ask ourselves, "Why am I doing this?" Is it because of pride? Is it to win for myself the praise of men?" If so, then the praise of men will be the only reward we get; we shall get no eternal reward from God.

The Jewish leaders made such a big mistake: they thought they could gain salvation by righteous acts. But their inward lives did not match their outward lives. They were men **having a form of godliness but denying its power** (2 Timothy 3:5). God is never fooled. He knows our hearts. What worldly men consider good, God considers **detestable** (Luke 16:15). The Jewish leaders were worldly. Worldly men seek praise only from men. Spiritual men seek praise only from God.

When we look at our own hearts, sometimes it is not easy to determine why we do things. We often fool ourselves. We think we are doing something for God, but in fact we are doing it for ourselves. Remember what the prophet Jeremiah said about the human heart: **The heart is deceitful above all**

things . . . who can understand it? (Jeremiah 17:9). We must continually pray that the Holy Spirit will show us what is in our hearts, that He will show us what our real motives are.

2 If we seek praise from men, that is the only reward we shall get. We shall lose our heavenly reward from God. The praises of men will pass away; only the reward that comes from God will last. **What good is it for a man to gain the whole world, yet forfeit his soul?** (Mark 8:36).

3–4 Therefore, when we do our good works, we must do them quietly, in secret. We must not tell others. We must not even tell ourselves! We must **not let** [our] **left hand know what** [our] **right hand is doing** (verse 3). This is a parable. The left hand sees the right hand giving money or other help to the needy. The left hand says, "Ah, what a good person I am. Look at how much I am giving." The left hand represents our pride. It also represents our selfish nature. The left hand says, "You don't need to give so much. To appear righteous, you only have to give a little." The left hand is always calculating what our right hand (the spiritual part of us) should give. Let that not be. Let us give without calculation, freely, for God's sake. Just as God gave to us without calculation, let us give to others without calculating. God will calculate what we give from our hearts, and reward us accordingly (Luke 14:13–14; Colossians 3:23–24).

Prayer (6:5–15)

(Luke 11:2–4)

5 Many of the Jewish leaders prayed in public places so that men would see them praying and call them righteous. Such men may indeed receive the praise of other men, but they will receive nothing from God, either in this life or the next.

6 Jesus taught, "**When you pray, go into your room . . . close the door.**" This means that we must put all our attention on God, and not on ourselves. We must shut out worldly thoughts when we speak to God. This does not mean that we must pray only privately and alone. It is also good and necessary to pray together with other believers. But whether together or alone, we all must look only to God at times of prayer, and not pray **to be seen by men** (verse 5).

7 There is a second mistake people make when they pray. They think that they must pray in a special way in order to receive an answer from God. They think they must use special words, or pray for a long time or in a special place. But this is not necessary. God answers our prayers according to our faith, not according to what words we use or how we pray.[31]

8 We must remember that God is a loving heavenly father. He knows all our needs before we ask; but He wants us to ask. He wants us to depend on Him, just as children depend on their earthly fathers. God is eager to give us what we need (see Matthew 7:11 and comment). And He is able to give us **immeasurably more than all we ask or imagine** (Ephesians 3:20). This is the God we meet when we go into our rooms to pray. He wants to give us unlimited spiritual blessings. All we have to do is ask in faith.

9 The disciples asked Jesus to teach them to pray (Luke 11:1). So He gave them the "Lord's prayer" as an example of a proper prayer.

Our Father in heaven. We must address our prayer to our **Father**, and not to any idol, spirit, angel, or saint. To all believers, God is a loving Father who wants the greatest good for all His children. At the same time, God is also the all-powerful Creator in heaven. He knows everything about us (Hebrews 4:13), and He will be our judge. He has the power to bless man with unlimited blessings (Ephesians 1:3), and He has the power to send man to hell for all eternity.

---

[31] Sometimes the Holy Spirit will lead us to pray a long time for a special reason. Jesus prayed all night before He chose His twelve disciples (Luke 6:12–13). But in most situations this is not necessary.

Therefore, we must come to such a God **with reverence and awe** (Hebrews 12:28–29). We need to come with thanksgiving for His blessings. We need to begin every prayer with praise for His greatness and glory (Psalm 34:1–3). This is what the phrase "**hallowed be your name**" means: "May God be praised; to God be the glory." How often, when we pray, we think only of our own needs, and nothing of the greatness of God.

10 . . . **your kingdom come**. When Christ came, God's kingdom came to earth. And God's kingdom is present in everyone who believes in Christ (Luke 17:20–21). This is why Christ preached: "**The kingdom of God is near**" (see Mark 1:14–15 and comment).

But in another way, the kingdom of God has not yet fully come. Satan still rules in this world. He is the **prince of this world** (John 12:31; 16:11). Most men still are prisoners in Satan's kingdom, the kingdom of darkness. Therefore, we need to pray that God will come into the lives of more people, that more and more people might be delivered from Satan's kingdom and brought into the kingdom of God.

But not only that, we need to pray that God's kingdom will fully come, that is, that Christ will come again quickly and destroy Satan. **Come, Lord Jesus** (Revelation 22:20). Because when Jesus comes again, then God's kingdom will be fully established both in heaven and on earth.

. . . **your will be done**. Wherever the kingdom of God is, there His will is being fulfilled. We need to pray constantly that God's will might be fulfilled in our lives each day.

11 After praising God, then we may bring to Him our petitions. In verses 11–13, all our needs are mentioned: for our body, bread (verse 11); for our soul, forgiveness (verse 12); and for our spirits, deliverance from the evil one (verse 13).

Give us today our daily bread. This means: Give us day by day all the things we need for our bodies—food, clothing, houses, health. (It does not mean unnecessary luxuries or conveniences.) Every day we are completely dependent upon God. We could not live one day without His sustaining power. He can stop the rainfall, and there would be no food. Or He could allow hail and wind to destroy our crops. Our lives are in His hands. Even atheists cannot live one day without God!

God cares for our needs. The great God who created the heavens and the earth cares about our daily bread. In His eyes the nations are accounted as **dust** (Isaiah 40:15). Yet He knows when each of us is hungry. He cares when each sparrow falls (see Matthew 10:29–31). Let us cast all our cares upon Him, for He cares for us (1 Peter 5:7).

12 **Forgive us our debts**. According to Luke 11:4, Jesus also said, "**Forgive us our sins**." The original word that Matthew wrote here was "debts." In Jesus' thought, a sin was a debt owed to God. According to the original Greek[32] text of Luke 11:4, Jesus said: "**Forgive us our sins, for we also forgive everyone who** [is indebted to] **us**." Those who are "indebted" to us are those who have sinned against us. Therefore, we must understand that in the Lord's prayer, "debt" and "sin" have the same meaning.

Forgive us our debts, **as we also have forgiven our debtors**. In the same way we forgive our debtors, so God will forgive us. Jesus is not talking here about the first time God forgave us when we believed and received salvation. Here Jesus is talking about our daily lives as Christians. At first, God forgave us freely all the sins we had committed before we believed. Because of His grace and mercy, He forgave us. But after we become Christians, we still sin from time to time and need God's forgiveness (1 John 1:9). He will forgive us **as we also** forgive others. If we stop forgiving others, God will stop forgiving us (see Matthew 6:14–15; 18:23–35). We are like pipes. God's forgiveness is like water flowing through us. To not forgive others is like shutting off one end of our pipe. If no forgiveness flows out to others, God's forgiveness

[32] The New Testament was originally written in the Greek language.

cannot flow into us (see Mark 11:25–26 and comment).

13 **And lead us not into TEMPTATION.** In this verse, to be "led into temptation" means to be defeated by Satan, to fall into sin, to become separated from God. The word "temptation," as used in this verse, does not mean the kind of "test" that God allows to come upon all Christians in order to test their faith (1 Peter 1:6–7). These ordinary kinds of tests which strengthen our faith are sent to us for our benefit; when they come upon us, we should rejoice and be thankful (James 1:2).

In this verse, however, the word "temptation" has a different meaning. Jesus is teaching us here to pray that we might not fall into that final temptation, that is, the temptation to turn away from God. "**. . . deliver us from the evil one**" must be our constant prayer. The devil is a **roaring lion looking for someone to devour** (1 Peter 5:8). And in the last days before Jesus comes again, Christians will suffer the severest trials. Many will fall away. In that day Christians will need to pray this prayer more than ever before.

The Lord's prayer ends as it began—praising God. Many Greek manuscripts here include the words: "for yours is the kingdom and the power and the glory forever. Amen." The word "amen" means "so be it." It expresses our faith that God will accept and answer our prayer.

14–15 See verse 12 and comment.

Fasting (6:16–18)

16–18 Just as the Jews performed righteous acts and prayed in order to be praised by men, so also did they fast for the same reason. They put ashes on their faces so that others could tell they were fasting. Their purpose was to gain honor for themselves, not for God. The praise of men will be their only reward; they will gain no reward from God.

When you fast. . . . This means that Jesus approved of fasting, as long as it was done for the right reasons. Christians fast in order to humble themselves before God, to bring their bodies under control, and to receive additional guidance and power from the Holy Spirit.

The prophet Isaiah said that the "fasting" that is most pleasing to God is humility and works of love (Isaiah 58:1–7). Without humility and works of love, fasting is only an empty show.

Treasures in Heaven (6:19–24)
(Luke 11:34–36; 12:33–34; 16:13)

19 Just as we should not seek honor and praise in this world, so we should not seek to store up **treasures**. "Treasure" means not only money, but all kinds of property and possessions. To "store up" treasure means to keep it for oneself, to love it. To have possessions is not wrong. What is wrong is to love our possessions, and to use them for ourselves (see 1 Timothy 6:10). It is also wrong to seek for more possessions than we need.

But in these verses Jesus is not only talking about possessions. He is talking about all the things that we value in this world, such as education, security for the future, and even our children. He is also talking about our honor; that is a kind of "treasure." All these things are worldly treasures. And Jesus says, "Do not store them up. Do not love them.[33] Do not put your hope in them." If we put our hope in the things of this world, we shall have no hope in the next world. If we store up treasure in this world, we shall have none in the next. And the treasure of this world will soon perish; it does not last. Moth and rust destroy it. Flowers wither. Men get old and their beauty fades. And there are thieves, too. Illness is like a thief; it steals our health. There are floods and earthquakes. Wind and hail "steal" our crops. Death steals our life. Everything on earth—even earth itself—passes away. Jesus said, "**Do not work for food that spoils, but for food that endures to**

[33] We must love our children, but we must love them for their own sakes and not for our sakes. We must not love our children because of the benefit we hope to receive from them. That is a selfish "love." It is really a form of self-love.

eternal life, which the Son of Man will give you" (John 6:27).

20 But store up for yourselves treasures in heaven. Jesus' meaning is this: every good work we do for God in this world will be counted or "stored up" as treasure in heaven. When we do good on earth, we are laying a foundation for ourselves in heaven (see 1 Timothy 6:17–19).

This does not mean that we are saved by good works. We are saved only by grace through faith (see Ephesians 2:8). But good works are the external evidence of faith. True faith always produces good works, just as a good tree produces good fruit. Whether we have true faith or not can be shown by our good works (see James 2:14–24 and comment).

Those who do good works because of their faith in Christ will receive their **inheritance**, the **kingdom** prepared for them (see Matthew 25:34–40). A rich young man once came to Jesus asking, "**Good teacher . . . what must I do to inherit eternal life?**" (Mark 10:17). He was seeking treasure in heaven. Jesus told him, "**Go, sell everything you have and give to the poor, and you will have treasure in heaven**" (Mark 10:21). But the young man did not take Jesus' advice. He had stored up his treasure on earth and he loved it. He didn't want to give it up, even to obtain eternal life. Truly, he had obtained his reward on earth and lost his reward in heaven (Mark 10:22–23).

Man is only a traveler on this earth, a foreigner. Our true home is in heaven. We are only servants and ambassadors of God. Everything we have with us on this earth belongs to God; it is not ours. And on the day of judgment we will have to give an account to God concerning how we have used our possessions. We will have to give account not only concerning how we have used our money, but also concerning how we have used our skills, our gifts, our education. All these are from God; they belong to Him. If we store up these things selfishly for ourselves, we shall surely lose our reward in heaven (see Mark 8:36; Luke 12:16–21). Jesus said, "**Sell your possessions and give to the poor**" (Luke 12:33). We must keep for ourselves no more than we need, and we must calculate our needs according to the needs of the **poor** around us.

21 There are two reasons why it is foolish to store up treasure on earth. The first is that it will perish. The second is that it becomes our master. To the extent that we love our treasure, to that extent it will control us. We become slaves of our treasure. Satan uses earthly treasure to entrap us, to turn us from God. When we store up treasure in heaven, we give our heart to God. When we store up treasure on earth, we give our heart to Satan. **For where your treasure is, there your heart will be also.**

Let us heed this teaching. Let us not say, "This teaching does not apply to me. I am poor." The main question we must ask ourselves is this: "What do I desire? What am I seeking?" The poor seek for riches too! Jesus asks: "What is in your heart? What is your goal? Who is your master; whom do you serve?" Let us turn from the treasure of this world and turn our eyes toward God. And when we do, we shall begin to store up treasure in heaven that will last forever.

22 The eye is the lamp of the body. The **eye** here means the "eye" of the heart or mind, that is, our "spiritual eye." With our bodily eye we see worldly things; with our spiritual eye we can see spiritual things. With our spiritual eye we can recognize good and evil, worldly treasure and heavenly treaure.

If our spiritual eyes are **good**, that is, sound and healthy, our **whole body will be full of light**, God's light.

23 God's Spirit comes into our lives through our spiritual eyes. If our spiritual eyes are shut or blind, God's light cannot shine within our soul, and we will remain in spiritual darkness. The only source of spiritual light is God. If that light **is darkness**, we are in darkness indeed! Jesus said, "**See to it, then, that the light within you is not darkness**" (see Luke 11:35–36).

How are our spiritual eyes? Are they clear, sound? Do we see Jesus? Jesus is the light of the world (John 1:9; 8:12). Do we see that light?

24 No one can serve two masters. The two masters are **God and Money**. "Money" here means any kind of worldly treasure: land, house, animals, family, education, job, authority, fame. In place of the word "money" we could substitute the word "self."

Every person must choose which master he will serve. In the same way, everyone must choose which kingdom he will live in: the kingdom of God or the kingdom of darkness. No one can be a citizen of both kingdoms at the same time. Just as there are only two masters and only two kingdoms, there also are only two roads a person can walk on: a narrow road leading to eternal life, and a wide road leading to eternal punishment (see Matthew 7:13–14 and comment).

Many people are deceived by Satan. They think that they can serve God and "Money" together. They want to store up treasure on earth and treasure in heaven at the same time. But it never works. Jesus said, "**Love the Lord your God with all your heart and with all your soul and with all your mind and with all your strength**" (Mark 12:30). The important word here is the word "all." Not half, not 90 percent, but all.

Jesus told the rich young man, "**Go, sell everything you have**" (Mark 10:21). He said this because the young man loved his possessions. The Apostle John wrote: **Do not love the world or anything in the world. If anyone loves the world, the love of the Father is not in him** (1 John 2:15). Either we love the world, or we love the Father; we cannot love both. We must choose.

Why do men keep laying up treasure on earth? They know it will perish. And even if the treasure doesn't perish quickly, men perish. And when they perish, they cannot take their treasure with them. Even their education, their fame, will be of no use in heaven. Why do men keep seeking worldly treasure and thereby lose their heavenly treasure?

The reason is sin. Sin enters man's heart, and from sin arises selfishness. And from selfishness comes all the other sins, such as pride, greed, lust.

Sin does three things. First, it makes us its slaves. Second, it makes us spiritually blind. We can't see we are slaves. We can't see the true light, which is Jesus. We can't find the narrow path to heaven. Third, sin destroys us. The punishment for sin is eternal death.

This is why Jesus taught men to turn from sin, to put away worldly treasure. There is no greater mistake a man can make than to store up treasure on earth.

Do Not Worry (6:25–34)
(Luke 12:22–32)

25 **Therefore ... do not worry about your life**. This does not mean that we should not look ahead and plan. It does not mean that we can stop working and expect God to feed us. God feeds the birds (verse 26), but they have to look for their food. God will feed men too, but men must plant and plow and water. If a man doesn't work, he won't eat (2 Thessalonians 3:10).

Jesus teaches here only that we must not worry. Paul wrote the same thing: **Do not be anxious about anything, but in everything, by prayer and petition, with thanksgiving, present your requests to God** (Philippians 4:6).

Why do we not need to worry? Because it is unnecessary. If God gives us life, will He not give us little things like food and clothes? Having one day given us a body, will He the next day let it die of hunger? Certainly not. If God can give big gifts like life, He will certainly give the small gifts too. God doesn't promise to give us more than we need, but we can rely on Him to provide our necessities.

26 The same is true for birds. God gave them bodies. Will He not also provide food for them? And if He provides food for birds, will He not provide food for us, who are more valuable than birds? (Matthew 10:31).

The same thing applies to spiritual gifts also. If God gave us the greatest gift of all, His own Son Jesus, He surely will give us all other blessings, both spiritual and physical (see Romans 8:32 and comment).

27 To worry is not only unnecessary, it is also pointless. By worrying we cannot **add a single hour to [our] life,**

or a "single cubit to our height."[34] According to Luke 12:26, Jesus also said, **"Since you cannot do this very little thing, why do you worry about the rest?"** Jesus' meaning is that worry accomplishes nothing.

28–30 Just as God feeds the birds (verse 26), so He clothes the flowers. If He clothes the flowers, who are not His children, surely He will clothe us who are His children. Even King Solomon, David's son, the richest king of the Jews, was never dressed as beautifully as a lily.

Then Jesus said: "... **will** [God] **not much more clothe you, O you of little faith?"** (verse 30). Worry is a sign of **little faith**. Jesus didn't say "no faith"; He was talking mainly to His disciples, to believers. But many believers have little faith. They have enough faith to be saved, but they do not have enough faith to stop worrying. They believe in Jesus, but they don't believe everything He says.

Jesus said, "God will give you food and clothing." Do we believe it? He said, "**Come to me ... and I will give you rest**" (Matthew 11:28). Do we believe it? He said, "**... whoever drinks the water I give him will never thirst**" (John 4:14). Do we believe it? Do we have this kind of living water in us? We need to confess that we are men of **little faith**.

"Little faith" has another meaning, too. It means to be discouraged by our circumstances. Our circumstances can become like a master. Our circumstances can weaken and even destroy our faith. No matter what our circumstances are, we need to continue hoping, rejoicing, believing. Because all of our circumstances are in God's control. And God is our loving Father. He will not let anything happen to us that is not for our good (see Romans 8:28 and comment). Therefore, why should we worry? If we truly believe in a loving God, we will not worry (see Romans 8:35,37). But even Jesus' disciples in the beginning had but little faith (see Mark 4:37–40). Every Christian needs to grow in faith. It is a process that lasts our entire life.

31–32 Jesus said: "Do not worry about food and drink and clothes. **For the pagans run after all these things**". Here in this context, the word "pagan" means not only Gentiles, or non-Jews, but also all those who do not believe in the one true God.[35] God is not a loving Father for unbelievers. They do not rely on God. Therefore, they worry about food and clothing. They seek these things first, instead of God.

Many believers, however, are just like unbelieving "pagans." They, too, worry about food, clothes, and other necessities. They worry about the future. They think mostly about worldly things. Such Christians indeed have little faith.

How can we increase our faith? First, we must remember who we are. We are God's children. God always does what is best for His children. Second, we must remember who God is. God is our Father, and His love, His power, and His wisdom are without limit. Not a sparrow falls to the ground without God knowing it. He knows the number of hairs on our heads (Matthew 10:29–30). If He knows that, He surely knows all our needs (verse 32).

33 Jesus said, "Do not be like unbelievers, who seek only the things of this world. Put your confidence in God. "... **seek first his kingdom and his righteousness, and all these things will be given to you as well.**"

In Hebrews 11:6, it is written: ... **without faith it is impossible to please God, because anyone who comes to him must believe that he exists and that he rewards those who earnestly seek him.** God Himself said through the prophet Jeremiah: "**You will seek me and find me when you seek me with all your heart**" (Jeremiah 29:13). How earnestly do we

---

[34] In place of the words **a single hour to his life**, some versions of the Bible say, "a single cubit to his height." The Greek text of this verse can be translated either way. However, it fits better with the context to say, **add a single hour to his life**. People worry more about the length of their life than they do about their height.

[35] In Jesus' time, only Jews and those Gentiles who followed the Jewish religion believed in the one true God.

seek God? Do we seek Him above all else? Do we think about our treasure in heaven? Paul wrote: **Set your mind on things above, not on earthly things** (Colossians 3:2).

We must seek not only God's kingdom, but also His **righteousness**, that is, we must seek to be like Christ. We must **hunger and thirst for righteousness** (Matthew 5:6). As we do this, we shall be filled. Our faith will grow. When we stop seeking God and His righteousness, our faith decreases and our worry increases. To increase our faith we must come close to God, pray to Him, read His word. James wrote: **Come near to God and He will come near to you** (James 4:8). God is ready to give us everything we need, if we believe and draw near to Him. He says, "Seek me first, **and all these things will be given to you as well.**" Not only that, God has given us His kingdom. Jesus said to His disciples: **"Do not be afraid, little flock, for your Father has been pleased to give you the kingdom"** (Luke 12:32). When we seek God first, He gives us food, drink, clothes; He gives us His righteousness; He gives us every spiritual blessing in Christ (Ephesians 1:3). And finally, He gives us His kingdom! Jesus said: **"Come, you who are blessed by my Father; take your inheritance, the kingdom prepared for you since the creation of the world"** (Matthew 25:34). Friends, let us not lose so great a blessing!

34 **Therefore, do not worry about tomorrow**. God has promised to supply everything we need, if we seek Him first. Paul wrote: **And my God will meet all your needs according to his glorious riches in Christ Jesus** (Philippians 4:19).

Here Jesus teaches that we must live one day at a time. We must not worry about the mistakes of yesterday; they are passed. We must not worry about tomorrow; it hasn't come yet. **Tomorrow will worry about itself. Each day has enough trouble of its own**. Only today we must think about. We must obey God today; we must walk with God today; we must trust Him today. Jesus prayed: **"Give us today our daily bread"** (verse 11). We don't need to pray for tomorrow's bread. God gives us what we need day by day.

Let us understand Jesus. Yes, we must think about tomorrow. We must plan. We must plant today, so that we can harvest tomorrow. But we must not **worry** about tomorrow.

Worry is from the devil. It is one of his weapons. By means of worry Satan tries to weaken and destroy our faith. How can we overcome worry, then? By resisting Satan. James wrote: **Resist the devil, and he will flee from you** (James 4:7). We must continually tell the devil: **"Away from me, Satan!"** (Matthew 4:10).

Together with resisting the devil, we must put our confidence in God. Peter wrote: **Cast all your anxiety on him because he cares for you** (1 Peter 5:7). Let us believe this verse. Let us apply our faith, and our worry will end.

God never fails to fulfill His promises. David wrote: **I was young and now I am old, yet I have never seen the righteous forsaken or their children begging bread** (Psalm 37:25). Trust in the love and faithfulness of God. Love Him with all your heart, soul, mind, and strength. Seek Him above all else, **and all these things will be given to you as well**. The incalculable riches of God are ours in Christ, not only in this life, but for all eternity.

CHAPTER 7

Judging Others (7:1–6)
(Luke 6:37–38,41–42)

1 **Do not judge** others. In order to understand this verse, we must distinguish between two kinds of judgment: one is the judgment of a man's work and behavior, and the other is the judgment of the man himself. Here Jesus is talking about the judgment of man himself.

We must not judge any man's character, his motives, his thoughts, his inner life, his soul. Only God can judge in this way. Paul wrote: **Who are you to judge someone else's servant? To his own master he stands or falls** (Romans 14:4).

In Luke 18:11, Jesus gave the example of a Pharisee who judged in the wrong way. The Pharisee said, "**God, I thank you that I am not like all other men—robbers, evildoers, adulterers—or even like this tax collector**." In saying this the Pharisee was judging the tax collector standing beside him. He was saying, "I am good; you are no good."

This condemning, despising attitude toward others is wrong. This kind of judgment we must never do. People like that Pharisee are always looking for others' faults. They are always trying to "put down" others. They are happy when someone else stumbles and falls into sin. They like to hear bad things about others (see Romans 14:10,13). Such a judging attitude is the opposite of love (see 1 Corinthians 13:4,6–7).

However, there is a second kind of judgment which is correct and necessary. This is the judgment of other men's outward actions. We must not judge the sinner, but we must judge his sin. We must judge other men's work and words. Jesus said, "**Watch out for false prophets**" (verse 15). Therefore, we must be able to recognize false prophets and false teachers. We must compare their teaching to the teaching of the Bible. Jesus said, "**Do not give dogs what is sacred**" (verse 6). "Dogs" are those who oppose God; they disobey God. We must be able to recognize God's enemies. Jesus said that we will be able to recognize them **by their fruit** (verses 16,20). Therefore, we must judge their fruit.

Those in authority also must make judgments about men's actions. Judges must make judgments in court. Leaders in the church must DISCIPLINE those under them (see 1 Corinthians 5:1,3–4). But even though those in authority must make judgments concerning man's behavior, they cannot know all about the person they are judging and disciplining. Only God can give an absolutely true and final judgment about man, because only God knows everything.

2 **Do not judge, or you too will be judged**. If we judge others in the wrong way, God will judge us. If we condemn others, God will condemn us. If we forgive others, God will forgive us (Luke 6:37). God forgave us while we were sinners. If we do not forgive others, it means we have not received God's forgiveness. We do not know what forgiveness is. We are condemned (see Matthew 6:14–15).

From this, we see that God will treat us as we treat others. In the same way we judge others, God will judge us. God will show us as much mercy as we show to others. As much as we give to others, God will give to us. In Luke 6:38, Jesus says: "**Give, and it will be given to you. A good measure, pressed down, shaken together and running over, will be poured into your lap**." This refers to a container of flour; God will pack the container full. God will not be stingy. He is completely fair. Whatever we give, He will give back in full measure, and even more (see Mark 4:24 and comment).

On the final day of judgment, **we will all stand before God's judgment seat** (Romans 14:10). Even those who have been saved must be judged for their works (see 1 Corinthians 5:10 and comment). We shall be judged for every careless word we speak (see Matthew 12:36–37). Therefore, let us heed the teaching of these verses. Let us not condemn others; rather, let us show mercy. Because on the day of judgment we will need much mercy from God.

3 In verses 3–5, Jesus gives us another reason why we must not judge: namely, we are not worthy to judge; we cannot see clearly enough to judge.

When we see another person making a mistake or sinning, how quick we are to accuse and criticize! "Oho, such a thing!" we say. We suppose that it is our duty to point out the faults of others. But when we do this we are hypocrites, says Jesus. We seek to get rid of the **speck of sawdust**, the tiny sin, from our brother's heart, but we don't care about removing the **plank**, the big sin, from our own heart.

4 It is because of our own sin that we cannot see clearly to remove the **speck** from another's eye, that is, to remove his sin. Our own sin makes us spiritually blind; it is like having a **plank** in our eye. When we try to remove our brother's fault, we are like a blind eye doctor trying to remove a cataract. On one occasion, the Jews caught a woman committing adultery and they wanted to stone her according to the Jewish law (John 8:1–11). Jesus said to them: **"If any one of you is without sin, let him be the first to throw a stone at her"** (John 8:7). These Jews, because of their own sin, were unworthy to judge the woman.

5 **You hypocrite**. "Hypocrite" is a strong word. Hypocrites are those who appear righteous outwardly, but inwardly are evil. They are people who say one thing, but in their hearts they believe the opposite. Their speech is slippery. They show concern for their brother's sin, but secretly they are happy he has sinned. They try to remove their brother's tiny sin, but make no effort to remove their own sin, which is big and obvious to others, like a **plank** sticking out of their eye.

You hypocrite, first take the plank out of your own eye. Our "plank" is our hypocrisy. It is our judging and condemning spirit. It is our pride and self-righteousness. Whatever sin our brother has committed, our judging and condemning spirit is a greater sin. Think about that.

Instead of judging others, let us judge ourselves (see 1 Corinthians 11:31). Let us remove the "plank" from our own eye. It is not easy to remove the plank. It is humiliating; it is painful. But we must do it.

Having removed the plank from our eye we will be more humble, more sympathetic toward others. When we start judging ourselves, we stop judging others. Not only that, we shall be able to see clearly. We will be able to see our brother as God sees him. We will look at him with love and mercy. Yes, we will still see the "speck" in his eye. We will want to help him remove it (see Galatians 6:1 and comment). But our judging and condemning spirit will be gone.

6 The Jews considered dogs and pigs to be unclean. They would never think of giving meat offered at the temple to a dog. And to share spiritual blessings with unspiritual Gentiles would, in their mind, be like feeding pearls to pigs. What would happen if pigs were given pearls to eat? The pigs would spit out the pearls and trample on them, and then turn and attack those who gave them.

Therefore, we must understand that the **dogs** and **pigs** mentioned here are hard-hearted unbelievers who deliberately and continually oppose God. They are those who cannot accept the words, the "pearls," of God. To such men there is no use telling spiritual things (see Luke 23:9; Acts 13:44–46; 18:5–6).

However, we must be very careful who we call "dogs" and "pigs." Most men are not dogs and pigs. Such men are very few. But even though they are enemies of God, we must love them (Matthew 5:44). Even though we may not speak with them, we must pray for them and show mercy to them (see Romans 12:14,17,19–21). Such men are slaves of Satan. They are without hope, without light. May God help us to love them.

Ask, Seek, Knock (7:7–12)
(Luke 6:31; 11:9–13)

7-8 The Christian life is a journey. Jesus never told us that the journey would be easy. But here in these verses He says that there is One who will give us everything we need for that journey, who will show us the way, who will open doors, and who at the end will open the door into heaven and eternal life. And all we have to do is to **ask**, **seek**, and **knock** (verse 7).

Jesus did not say that if we ask we will get what we want. Many times we ask and do not receive (see James 4:3). We are disappointed with God. But then, at the right time, God gives us something better. God knows much better than we do what is needed for our journey.

Ask and it will be given to you. What are we to ask for? We are to ask for help to be a Christian, to follow Christ. It is for this that the promises of these verses are given. Everything we need to follow Christ is available, and it will be given—if we ask in faith (see Mark 11:24 and comment).

Therefore, if our Christian life is weak, it is not God's fault; it is our own fault. We have no excuse. God has promised to help us on our journey. All we have to do is to ask, seek, and knock, and our Christian life will not be weak.

In the original Greek text, the words **ask, seek,** and **knock** really mean "keep on asking," "keep on seeking," "keep on knocking." We must keep on asking until we receive (see Luke 18:1–8). As much as we ask in faith, that much we shall receive.

What do we need, above all, to follow Christ? The Holy Spirit. We need Christ's presence, Christ's Spirit[36] within us. Jesus said, "**. . . apart from me you can do nothing**" (John 15:5). We do not travel on our journey alone. One of the last things Jesus said to His disciples was this: "**And surely I will be with you always, to the very end of the age**" (Matthew 28:20).

9–11 God gives **good gifts** to all men: life, sun, rain, food. But besides that, He gives special spiritual gifts to His own children, that is, believers in Christ.

The Bible clearly teaches that not all men are God's children; only believers in Christ are God's children. All men are born as children of Satan; they are born into the kingdom of darkness. By nature all men are evil. In the beginning, every one of us was an enemy of God, a sinner (Romans 3:10). But now, through faith in Christ, we who were once God's enemies have become God's children (John 1:12). For us, then, God is now a loving heavenly Father. And when we come to Him and ask, we shall receive.

We shall receive **good gifts** (verse 11). If evil earthly fathers give "good gifts" to their children, certainly our heavenly Father will give much better gifts to His children. God's gifts will always be good for us. Perhaps from time to time He will give us various trials, but it will always be for our good (see Romans 5:3–4 and comment). Whatever God gives His children will, in the end, be for their good (see Romans 8:28 and comment).

What is the greatest gift that God wants to give us? The Holy Spirit. In the corresponding verse in Luke's Gospel, instead of **good gifts** Luke has written **Holy Spirit** (Luke 11:13). All spiritual gifts are included in the gift of the Holy Spirit. If we have received the Holy Spirit, we have received everything we need for our Christian life, such as the fruit of the Spirit (see Galatians 5:22–23), the fellowship of the Spirit, the power of the Spirit.

Let us ask for the highest gift, the Holy Spirit. Let us seek for the highest things—to know God, to know Jesus. Let us knock, and we shall enter into the joyful and glorious life of Christ. With Him we shall be a sharer in all the spiritual riches of heaven—in this life and the next.

12 **In everything, do to others what you would have them do to you**. Many Christians call this the "golden rule," because among Jesus' teachings this rule is so important. This rule is, in fact, connected with the second great commandment: **Love your neighbor as yourself** (Mark 12:31). This "golden rule" tells us how we should love our neighbor. It is easy to say, "Love your neighbor"; but we must ask, "How should I love him?" This golden rule gives the answer. Like the second great commandment, it also **sums up the Law and the Prophets**[37] (see Galatians 5:14 and comment).

This golden rule does not say that parents must stop punishing their children, for example. It does not mean that judges and other authorities must stop punishing criminals. The golden rule refers only to personal relationships with our neighbor.

Think: if everyone would follow this rule, there would be no arguments, no

---

[36] God, Christ, and the Holy Spirit are one (see General Article: Holy Spirit). The Holy Spirit is God's Spirit; therefore, the Holy Spirit is also Christ's Spirit.

[37] The **Law and the Prophets** is another name for the Old Testament. The first five books of the Old Testament are called "the Law." For further discussion, see footnote to comment on Matthew 5:17.

wars, no strikes, no divorce. There would be no need for kings, judges, police, armies. There would be no problems in the world.

In that case, then, why don't men obey this golden rule? Because of sin. Because man loves himself more than his neighbor. Man's root sin is self-love, or selfishness. Self love is the cause of all the strife and trouble in the world.

Our Christian life starts when our self-love begins to die. Our "old man," our old selfish self, must die (Romans 6:6). But not only must we die; we must be born again by the Holy Spirit (John 3:5). Without receiving the Holy Spirit, without receiving new spiritual life, we cannot follow Christ. Without the love of God, which is poured into our hearts by the Holy Spirit (Romans 5:5), we cannot follow this golden rule.

The Narrow and Wide Gates (7:13–14)

13-14 Almost all who read or hear Jesus' Sermon on the Mount given here in Matthew Chapters 5–7 agree that it is an excellent sermon, excellent teaching; they agree that Jesus is a good teacher. But Jesus doesn't want to hear that. Jesus does not want praise. He wants people to obey Him; He wants them to heed His teaching.

Therefore, Jesus says to us: "Okay, you have heard my teaching. Now what are you going to do about it? Heed it, or not heed it? Go through the **narrow gate**, or go through the **wide gate**? There are only two gates. You must choose."

Let us imagine that we are walking along a path and we come to two gates. There are only two; we must go through one or the other. One of the gates is wide, and the road leading on from it is easy, level. Many people are walking along that road. We think, "Surely so many people cannot be mistaken; they must be on the right road."

The second gate is narrow. The road leading on from it is also narrow, steep, rocky. Very few people are walking on this road. But Jesus says, "If you want to follow me, you must pass through this small gate and walk on this narrow road."

To follow Jesus it is necessary to leave the crowd. We must leave the world. Even if all our friends and relatives are walking through the wide gate, we must separate from them. We must stand alone; we must be different. We must turn from the customs of the world. How difficult it is to leave family and friends to follow Christ! (see Matthew 10:35–37). But that is the first step if we are to pass through the narrow gate: we must leave the crowd, the world. We must remember that each of us one day must face God alone. God will judge us one by one. And if on that day we want to enter heaven, we must leave the crowd today and enter in at the narrow gate.

In one way, the Christian life is easy. Jesus said: "**Come to me, all you who are weary and burdened, and I will give you rest . . . my yoke is easy and my burden is light**" (Matthew 11:28–30). The people walking along the wide road are carrying heavy burdens of sins, worries, fears. Those walking on the narrow road do not carry those burdens: Jesus carries them.

However, those on the narrow road must carry one thing: a cross. In order to pass through the narrow gate we must deny ourselves and take up our cross (see Mark 8:34 and comment). We must leave our old self, our "old man," outside the gate. We must leave our property, our rights, our honor, outside the gate. Our **old self** must be crucified (Romans 6:6). The only thing we can take with us through that gate is a cross. Paul wrote: **I have been crucified with Christ and I no longer live, but Christ lives in me** (Galatians 2:20). And he wrote: **May I never boast except in the cross of our Lord Jesus Christ, through which the world has been crucified to me, and I to the world** (Galatians 6:14).

The narrow road is difficult. On the way we will meet all kinds of trouble and persecution (2 Timothy 3:12). Satan will put many obstacles and temptations in our way. There will be few conveniences (Matthew 8:19–20). And the road will not get easier. For every stage in our lives, Satan has new temptations to give us.

Therefore, why walk on such a road? Because that narrow road **leads to life,** ETERNAL LIFE (verse 14). The broad road **leads to destruction** (Jeremiah 21:8).

Friends, there are only two roads. If you are not walking on the narrow road, then you must be walking on the broad one.

What is the purpose of a road? It leads to some destination. Think of the people walking on the broad road. For them the journey is easy, pleasant. Some are dancing, singing. Some are storing up treasures. Some are getting land and houses. And then they will come to the end of the road. What is that? Death. Where will their singing and dancing be then? What good will their possessions be to them then (see Mark 8:36; Luke 12:16–20)?

Let each man think of where his road is leading. Only the narrow road leads to life eternal. Yes, in this life the road is difficult, but remember the destination! (Romans 18:18; 2 Corinthians 4:17).

Jesus says to everyone: "**Enter through the narrow gate.**" It is not enough to listen to Jesus' wonderful teaching. We must obey it. We must enter the gate. When Jesus first called His disciples, He said: "**Follow me**" (Mark 1:17; 2:14). Jesus gives each of us a choice: to follow, or not to follow. We must choose. Let us not wait. Let us not delay. Jesus may not call to us again.

A Tree and Its Fruit (7:15–20)
(Luke 6:43–44)

15 **Watch out for false prophets**. These **false prophets** are false teachers, false Christians, who try to stop people from passing through the narrow gate. They say: "This is not the way; we'll show you a wider gate and an easier way."

Why are they so dangerous? Because they seem on the outside to be good. Their teaching sounds good. But they lead men to destruction. That's why Jesus calls them **ferocious wolves** (see Acts 20:29–31).

16 We can recognize false prophets by their fruit, that is, by their teaching and by their work. They talk about God, about Jesus, about love and joy, but they do not talk about the narrow gate. They teach only the easy things, the pleasant things about the Christian religion. But they never teach about the holiness of God, about His wrath against sin.

The false prophets say to sinful man: "Don't worry; all is well. God will forgive you." But they don't preach about repentance, about turning from sin, about denying oneself. Jeremiah spoke of such false prophets in his time: "**They dress the wound of my people as though it were not serious. 'Peace, peace,' they say, when there is no peace**" (Jeremiah 6:13–14). And men like to listen to such prophets, because they say things that men like to hear (2 Timothy 4:3–4).

17–18 Some false prophets are easy to recognize. They are like **thornbushes** and **thistles** (verse 16). But other false prophets are hard to recognize. They are like fig trees with beautiful leaves, but they bear bad fruit, or no fruit.

According to the tree, so will be its fruit. According to what we are, so ultimately will our actions be. If we are of the world, our fruit will also be of the world. If we are of the Spirit, our fruit will also be of the Spirit. In Luke 6:45, Jesus said: "**The good man brings good things out of the good stored up in his heart, and the evil man brings evil things out of the evil stored up in his heart. For out of the overflow of his heart his mouth speaks.**" As are our hearts, so will we speak (see Matthew 12:33–35 and comment).

Sometimes a bad tree seems to give good fruit. We are fooled. A person may say, "I am a Christian; I believe." For some time he may act like a Christian. But in the end he falls away. Peter says that such people are like pigs who have been washed, but then return to the mud (see 2 Peter 2:20–22). We can wash a pig on the outside, but if his inward nature is not changed, it will soon go back into the mud. False Christians are like that.

19 A tree that bears no fruit or bad fruit will be cut down. A person who says, "I believe," but bears no fruit of the Holy Spirit will also be "cut down" and rejected by God (John 15:6).

20 Jesus said: "**I chose you . . . to go**

and bear fruit—fruit that will last" (John 15:16). The fruit we must bear is described in Matthew 5:3–10. The same fruit is also described in other words in Galatians 5:22–23. These fruits are the fruits of the Holy Spirit.[38] They are the signs of a true Christian. People will know us by our fruit.

Words and Works (7:21-23)

21 People deceive themselves in two ways. Some suppose: "If I believe—if I say 'Lord, Lord'—then I am saved. Then I can do anything I want. I can commit all kinds of sins; I don't have to obey Christ."

Others deceive themselves in the opposite way. They suppose that if they do great works, they will be saved. They suppose that if their outward behavior is okay, they will be accepted by God (verses 22–23).

But Jesus teaches in this section that those who only say "Lord, Lord," but do not obey Him, are going to hell. And those who only do good works but do not have true faith are also going to hell. To obtain salvation both faith and good works are necessary (James 2:24).

To do true good works means to obey Christ. Good works are the proof of our faith. Faith must always give rise to good works, or it is not true faith. Therefore, we can never separate faith and works. Faith without works is dead (see James 2:14–17 and comment). And works without faith are vain. Without faith **it is impossible to please God** (Hebrews 11:6). Without faith natural man cannot obey God's will. Without believing in Christ and being born again, no one can follow the teachings of Jesus. Only when we have received Christ's Holy Spirit through faith can we begin to obey these teachings.

In this verse Jesus speaks of those who call Jesus "Lord," but don't do what He says (see 1 John 2:4). They claim to know Christ, but they forget that demons also know Him (Mark 1:23–24; James 2:19). The faith of such people is false faith; it will not save them.

Such people may believe Jesus' teaching, but there is no change in their lives. Some people even pray fervently. They don't say "Lord" once; they say it twice: **"Lord, Lord."** They speak and pray with fervor and great emotion. But, without obedience, such fervor and emotion is of the flesh and not of the Holy Spirit. Only those in whom the Holy Spirit dwells and who live in obedience to Christ will enter the kingdom of heaven. If **anyone does not have the Spirit of Christ, he does not belong to Christ** (Romans 8:9). And **no one can say, "Jesus is Lord," except by the Holy Spirit** (1 Corinthians 12:3).

22–23 In these verses Jesus talks about those who do great works but who do not have true faith nor the fruit of the Holy Spirit. It is possible even to prophesy and drive out demons and to perform miracles in Christ's name without having true faith. But such people will not enter the kingdom of heaven.

Paul the great apostle knew this truth. He knew that even though he preached the Gospel and did miracles, if he did not control his body and keep living in faith and obedience, he himself would be **disqualified for the prize** (1 Corinthians 9:25–27).

Paul also wrote: **If I speak in the tongues of men and of angels, but have not love, I am only a resounding gong or a clanging cymbal. If I have the gift of prophecy . . . but have not love, I am nothing** (1 Corinthians 13:1–3). Without the love that comes from the Holy Spirit, without the love that comes from true faith, Paul's great works meant nothing.

How can people do great works, prophesy, and cast out demons without the Holy Spirit? Where do they get their power to do such works? The answer is: from Satan. Satan is powerful; he controls all the kingdoms of the world (Matthew 4:8–9). Not only is he powerful, but he is also a deceiver (2 Corinthians 11:14). Through Satan, many false prophets perform signs and miracles in order to deceive Christians (Mark 13:22). Above all, these false prophets deceive

[38] In John 15:16, the word "fruit" also means new believers. Bearing fruit also means bringing others to Christ through our witness.

themselves. They say, "Look at the works I have done." But Christ says to them, "I **never knew you**" (verse 23).

How can we distinguish between works that are from Satan and works that are from the Holy Spirit? The answer is this: The works of the Holy Spirit always bring glory to Christ; the works of Satan always bring glory to Satan and to those who do his work.

Jesus said to His disciples: "**. . . do not rejoice that the spirits submit to you, but rejoice that your names are written in heaven**" (Luke 10:20). In other words, Jesus is saying: "Do not put confidence in the works that you do; only if your name is written in heaven will you be saved."

There is no more important question we can ask than this: Is my name written in heaven? Is Christ living in me? Is the Holy Spirit living within me? Because if the answer to these questions is "No," then on the day of judgment Jesus will say to us: "**I never knew you. Away from me, you evildoers!** All your works were for your own glory, not for mine."

Think of the day of judgment. Each one of us will stand before Jesus on that day. What will Jesus say to us? Will He say: "**Come . . . take your inheritance, the kingdom prepared for you since the creation of the world**"? (Matthew 25:34). Or will He say: "**I never knew you. Away from me, you evildoers**"?

The Wise and Foolish Builders (7:24–29)

(Luke 6:46–49)

24-27 In this parable, Jesus talks about a **wise man** and a **foolish man**, that is, a true Christian and a false Christian. Both men think that they are true Christians; both think that they are building their houses on the rock. But the second man is fooling himself.

These two men built the same kind of house. Their houses looked the same. There was only one difference: one had a foundation and the other didn't. According to Luke 6:48–49, the first man **dug down deep and laid the foundation on rock**. The second man built his house **on the ground without a foundation**.

From this parable we can learn an important truth: the difference between a true Christian and a false Christian cannot easily be seen. False Christians are like the false prophets of verse 15, who wear sheep's clothing but really are wolves. When you look at them, they seem just like sheep, that is, true Christians.

What is the most important thing about a house? Its foundation. No matter how excellent a house looks, if there is no foundation, the house has been built in vain. Men need foundations also; and for men there is only one sure foundation: Jesus Christ (1 Corinthians 3:11). All else is sand.

The false Christian who built his house on sand supposed: "I am safe. I am a Christian. My house will not fall." Satan desires to give men false security in this way. Judas, the disciple who betrayed Christ, surely supposed at first that he was a true disciple. But from the beginning he was a servant of Satan.

Let each of us examine himself. What kind of house are we building? If our greatest desire is to get security, comfort, peace, then we are building our house on the sand. If our greatest desire is to know Christ and to be like Him, then we are building our house on the rock.

The false Christian seeks his own good first of all. He does not seek first God's kingdom and His righteousness (Matthew 6:33). He lives to please himself. He seeks God's blessings, but he doesn't seek God. He loves God's blessings, but he doesn't love God. He never becomes a true Christian, because he does not put Christ first, he does not make Christ the Lord of his life, he does not make Christ the foundation of his life. His house is built on sand.

The true Christian is the one who knows Christ and obeys Him. He hears the words of Christ and **puts them into practice** (verse 24). To know Christ is to love Christ. To love Christ is to obey Christ. Jesus said, "**Whoever has my commands and obeys them, he is the one who loves me**" (John 14:21). He is the one who builds his house upon the rock (see Luke 11:28; John 13:17).

How can we distinguish between these two houses? Usually we cannot tell them apart until the **rain, streams,** and **winds** come upon them. Only then will the house built on sand fall down.

It is the same with men. Only when trials and troubles come can we tell who are the true Christians. God allows trials and temptations to come upon us in order to test our faith, our foundation (1 Peter 1:6–7). Jesus asks each one of us: "When trials come, will your faith remain firm?"

There are three kinds of trials: the **rain,** the **streams,** and the **winds** (verse 27). The **rain** stands for various kinds of trouble such as persecution, loss of property, loss of health, and finally, death. These are the trials that come from outside us. The **streams** stand for worldly desires, worldly pride (see 1 John 2:15). These are the temptations that arise within us. By these two kinds of temptations, outer and inner, Satan tries to overcome us. First Satan tries to make us love the world. Then, if we refuse, he persecutes us.

The **winds** stand for Satan himself. If the first two kinds of trials fail, Satan attacks us directly with doubt and fear and despair. These are the **flaming arrows** Paul mentions in Ephesians 6:16. Satan is an evil wind.

Jesus told about these three kinds of trial in the parable of the sower (Mark 4:3–8). Some seed (the word of God) was taken away by birds, that is, by Satan (Mark 4:15). Other seed sprouted, but was scorched by the sun, that is, by outer **trouble** and **persecution** (Mark 4:16–17). Other seed sprouted but was choked by thorns, that is, by inner **worries** and **desires** (Mark 4:18–19).

God will test each Christian's foundation. When the **rain, streams,** and **winds** come, will our house stand?

28–29 When Jesus had finished the Sermon on the Mount, the people were **amazed**. They were amazed at Jesus' teaching. They were also amazed at Jesus Himself (Mark 1:22).

There have been many great teachers in the world. Their teaching has been wise and deep. There have been great prophets. There have been founders of religions like Buddha and Mohammed. But all these teachers have been men. Jesus is different; He is God. And therefore, He speaks with the authority of God. That is why the crowds were **amazed**.

In the sight of those who listened, Jesus appeared to be just an ordinary man. He was a carpenter's son. His speech was ordinary. But there was something unusual about Him. He was not like other Jewish teachers of the law. He spoke with the wisdom and authority of God. We, too, are amazed.

But to be amazed is not enough. It is not enough to say, "This is wonderful teaching." It is not enough to say, "**Lord, Lord**" (verse 21). We must obey this teaching. Jesus said that the wise man is he "**who hears these words of mine and puts them into practice**" (verse 24).

Let each person ask: "Is my house built on rock, or is it built on sand?"

CHAPTER 8

The Man With Leprosy (8:1–4)
(Mark 1:40–45; Luke 5:12–16)

1–4 See Mark 1:40–45 and comment.

The Faith of the Centurion (8:5–13)
(Luke 7:1–10)

5–6 As Jesus entered Capernaum, a city on the north shore of the Sea of Galilee, a centurion in the Roman army came to Jesus to ask Him to heal his servant. According to the corresponding passage in Luke 7:3–5, the centurion first sent some elders of the Jews to Jesus. The centurion, being a Roman Gentile, was afraid to come to Jesus, who was a Jew.[39] These Jewish elders told Jesus that this

---

[39] In Bible times, the Jews despised Gentiles, that is, all non-Jews. Supposing that Jesus was like all other Jews, the centurion was afraid to go to Jesus directly.

centurion was a worthy Gentile. "He **loves our nation and has built our synagogue**," they said to Jesus (Luke 7:5).

7–9 As Jesus was going with the elders, some friends of the centurion also came with a further message for Jesus, which is recorded in Luke 7:6–8. Then the centurion himself came to Jesus and repeated the message himself.[40]

The centurion said to Jesus, "You don't need to come yourself to my house. I am not worthy. I am a Gentile sinner. **But just say the word, and my servant will be healed**" (verse 8). The centurion recognized that Jesus had authority. The centurion himself knew about authority. Just as he had authority over the soldiers under him, so he knew that Jesus would have the authority to heal.

10 Jesus was amazed at the centurion's **faith**.[41] The centurion not only believed that Jesus could heal, but that He could heal at a distance. Jesus had not yet found such faith in **Israel**,[42] that is, among the Jews.

11–12 This centurion was a forerunner of those Gentiles who would later believe in Jesus and receive salvation. Jesus said that **many will come from the east and the west**—that is, the Gentiles—and will be welcome in the kingdom of heaven (verse 11). Jesus described the kingdom of heaven as a **feast**. Abraham, Isaac, and Jacob, the first three ancestors of the Jews, would also be there. But the Jews of Jesus' time would not be invited, even though they were **subjects of the kingdom**—that is, sons of Abraham according to the flesh. They would lose their place at the feast, because they had rejected Jesus, the Messiah. They **will be thrown outside, into the darkness**, that is, into hell (see Luke 13:28–29). Only those who believe will be invited to the feast. Only those who believe in Christ are the true **subjects of the kingdom**, the true sons of Abraham (see Galatians 3:7–8,29 and comment).

13 Then Jesus healed the servant from afar. He did not even lay hands on him.

Jesus Heals Many (8:14–17)
(Mark 1:29–34; Luke 4:38–41)

14–17 See Mark 1:29–34 and comment.

The Cost of Following Jesus (8:18–22)
(Luke 9:57–62)

18–20 There are many who are at first willing to follow Jesus, but who do not realize that it means walking on the "narrow road" (Matthew 7:14). The person who follows Jesus must be ready to **deny himself** (see Mark 8:34 and comment). He must also count the cost of being a disciple of Jesus (see Luke 14:26–32 and comment). To be a disciple one must **give up everything he has** (Luke 14:33). The disciple possibly may not even have a place to lay his head, much less a home to live in. The cost of following Jesus is very high.

21–22 One of Jesus' disciples then asked permission to go and bury his father. Perhaps the father was not yet dead, and the disciple wanted to return home in order to receive his inheritance.

Jesus said, "**. . . let the dead bury their own dead**." In other words, let the spiritually dead take care of the things of this world. Those who are spiritually

---

[40] Notice that in this account of the healing of the centurion's servant, Matthew does not mention the Jewish elders and friends coming to Jesus, and Luke doesn't mention that the centurion himself came to Jesus. By joining the two accounts, the full story can be obtained. We must remember that as each of the Gospel writers wrote down their account of Jesus' life, they did not include every possible detail; one writer would include one detail, and another writer, another (see John 20:30; 21:25).

[41] This centurion had deep faith in Jesus' power. He now needed to take one more step of faith and believe that Jesus was the Son of God, the Savior.

[42] In the Bible, the word **Israel** is most commonly used as a name for the Jewish people. Thus, in this verse, "Israel" means the Jewish people. For further discussion, see Word List: Israel.

alive, who have been called to be disciples, must first do the work of the kingdom of God. The work of the kingdom of God is urgent. Nothing else can come before it (see Matthew 10:37–38).

Jesus does not teach here that disciples don't have to honor their parents. Usually it is possible to follow Jesus and also fulfill our responsibility to our family. But when we cannot do both, we must put Jesus above our family.

Then, according to Luke 9:61–62, a third man came to Jesus and said, "**I will follow you, Lord; but first let me go back and say good-bye to my family.**" Jesus knew the man's heart. He knew that the man was still greatly attached to his family. The man wanted to follow Jesus, but not with all his heart. Jesus said to him, "**No one who puts his hand to the plow and looks back is fit for service in the kingdom of God.**"

Like a farmer plowing his field, a follower of Jesus must look only ahead. He must have a single goal. He must never seek to return to his old life. Lot's wife looked back and was turned to a pillar of salt (Genesis 19:15–17,23–26). The Jews, after escaping from Egypt, grumbled against God and desired to go back to Egypt; and so, because of their grumbling and looking back, God destroyed them (Numbers 14:1–4,26–29).

Jesus Calms the Storm (8:23–27)
(Mark 4:35–41; Luke 8:22–25)

23–27 See Mark 4:35–41 and comment.

The Healing of Two Demon-possessed Men (8:28–34)
(Mark 5:1–20; Luke 8:26–39)

28–34 See Mark 5:1–20 and comment.

CHAPTER 9

Jesus Heals a Paralytic (9:1–8)
(Mark 2:1–12; Luke 5:17–26)

1–8 See Mark 2:1–12 and comment.

The Calling of Matthew (9:9–13)
(Mark 2:13–17; Luke 5:27–32)

9–13 See Mark 2:13–17 and comment.

Jesus Questioned About Fasting (9:14–17)
(Mark 2:18–22; Luke 5:33–39)

14–17 See Mark 2:18–22 and comment.

A Dead Girl and a Sick Woman (9:18–26)
(Mark 5:21–43; Luke 8:40–56)

18–26 See Mark 5:21–43 and comment.

Jesus Heals Two Blind Men (9:27–31)

27 Two blind men heard that Jesus had come and cried out: "**Have mercy on us, Son of David!**" (see Mark 10:47–48 and comment).

28 Before Jesus healed them, He made sure they had faith. Man's faith is necessary for Jesus' power to become manifest in men's lives. Without faith on our part, Jesus can do no mighty works (see Mark 6:4–6 and comment).

29–31 As always, Jesus healed their eyes completely. "**According to your faith will it be done to you**" (see Mark 5:34; 10:52 and comments). Then He commanded the men to tell no one (see Mark 1:44–45; 5:43; 7:36 and comments).

According to your faith. . . . If we believe that Jesus is a healer, He will heal us. If we believe He is the Savior, He will save us. Let us enlarge our faith!

Jesus Heals a Demon-possessed Man (9:32–34)
(Matthew 12:22–24; Mark 3:22; Luke 11:14–15)

32–34 See Matthew 12:22–24; Mark 3:22 and comments.

The Workers Are Few (9:35–38)
(Luke 10:2)

35 See Matthew 4:23; Mark 1:14–15 and comments.

36 Jesus was motivated throughout His ministry by compassion. He gave His life because of His compassion for mankind. Even when He had traveled and preached all day, He didn't turn the people away. They were like lost sheep and He was their shepherd (see Mark 6:34 and comment).

37 Jesus, looking over the crowd, said to His disciples, "**The harvest is plentiful.**" This was not a harvest of rice or corn, but a harvest of men. Men are like a field of grain, waiting to be harvested (John 4:35–36). But **the workers are few.**

38 The harvest is God's, but He has entrusted it to us. He has given us complete responsibility for His harvest. Jesus said, "**Ask the Lord of the harvest, therefore, to send out workers.**" He could send out more workers without our prayers, but He has told us to pray that more be sent.

What happens if there are not enough workers at harvest time? Part of the harvest will be lost. And if the harvest is lost, it will be because we didn't ask for enough workers.

Do we really care about God's harvest? Do we really care for the souls of the men and women around us? If we care, we will pray for workers. But before God answers our prayer, He will ask us a question: "Are you working yourself? Or are you only praying for me to send someone else to work in the harvest?" Then God will say to us: "First, go into the field yourself and begin to work. And when I see you working with all your heart and strength, then I will answer your prayer and send others to help you."

Many Christians have prayed that God would send people to work in the harvest, and then God has surprised them and said: "Okay, I'll send you."

Let us be like the prophet Isaiah. He heard God say, "**Whom shall I send?**" And Isaiah answered, "**Here am I. Send me**" (Isaiah 6:8).

CHAPTER 10

The Twelve Disciples (10:1–4)
(Mark 3:13–19; Luke 6:12–16)

1-4 See Mark 3:13–19 and comment.

Jesus Sends Out the Twelve (10:5–15)
(Mark 6:7–13; Luke 9:1–6; 10:4–12)

5–6 Do not go among the GENTILES or enter any town of the Samaritans.[43] It was God's plan that Jesus and His twelve disciples should preach the Gospel first to **Israel**, that is, to the Jewish people (Matthew 15:24; Romans 1:16). The Jews were to be given the opportunity first of all to hear the Gospel and to believe in Christ and receive salvation. Then, the Jews themselves were to be the means of extending this blessing to all the other peoples of the earth (Genesis 12:3). But most of the Jews rejected Christ, and so in the end Christ sent His disciples out to proclaim the Gospel to **all nations**

---

[43] The **Samaritans** lived in Samaria, which was a region of Israel that lay between the provinces of Judea and Galilee. They were half-Jews, who had long ago intermarried with foreign women. Thus they were despised by all true Jews (see John 4:8–9 and comment).

(Matthew 28:19).

The Jews themselves had become like **lost sheep** (Matthew 9:36), because of the false teaching of their own leaders.

7 See Mark 1:14–15 and comment.

8 Jesus gave these first disciples His power to heal and cast out demons. He even gave them power to **raise the dead**. They had freely received the mercy and grace of God; now they had to share those blessings with others. If we try to keep God's gifts for ourselves, He will take them away. Because He forgave us, we must forgive others (Matthew 6:14–15). Because He loved us, we must love others (1 John 4:11).

This healing work of Jesus and His disciples was a sign of the love and power of God. It was one of the signs that the kingdom of heaven had indeed begun. As Jesus did, so did His disciples (see John 14:12). As the Father had sent Jesus, so Jesus sent them (John 17:18). And it is the same also with Jesus' followers today.

9–15 See Mark 6:7–13 and comment.

Persecution To Be Expected (10:16–25)

(Mark 13:9–13; Luke 10:3; 12:11–12; 21:12–19)

16 When Jesus' disciples went out to preach, they were, in the world's eyes, defenseless like sheep. They carried no weapons; they did not even have money (verse 9). Therefore, they needed to be **shrewd as snakes**, that is, wary and wise. At the same time they had to remain **innocent as doves**, that is, pure and obedient, in order to receive God's protection. God protects those who do His will.

17–20 See Mark 13:9–11 and comment.

21–22 See Mark 13:12–13 and comment.

23 Followers of Jesus must be ready to suffer persecution, but they must not look for trouble unnecessarily. Jesus taught His disciples that if persecution came to them in one village, they must flee and go to another village. They may flee from danger, but not from Christ's service.

Jesus then said that the disciples will **not finish going through the cities of Israel before the Son of Man**[44] **comes**, that is, before Jesus' RESURRECTION. After Jesus rose from the dead, He came to His disciples and told them that now they must go **to all nations**, not only to Israel (Matthew 28:18–20).

24–25 A student is not greater than his teacher. Therefore, if his teacher is persecuted, the student shall not escape persecution (see John 15:20 and comment). The same is true of a master and his servant. If a master or the head of a house is called **Beelzebub**[45]—that is, the devil, so shall the members of his household also be called devils (see Mark 3:22 and comment). So it will be with all Jesus' followers. As He suffered abuse and persecution, so His followers will suffer in the same way (1 Peter 2:20–21).

No Need to Fear (10:26–33)

(Luke 12:2–9)

26 Jesus told His disciples not to fear; they were doing God's work. No one can prevent the preaching of the Gospel. Through the disciples, the teaching of Christ and the way of salvation was being made known to all men (see Mark 4:22 and comment).

27 The main work of the disciples was to preach openly what they had heard from Christ. All Christians must be witnesses. We must not hide Christ's light **under a bowl** (Matthew 5:15).

28 Let the disciples fear no man. Let them not even fear Satan. Let them fear God alone. Men and evil spirits can only destroy the body. But God alone can destroy a soul. Only God can give eternal life, and only He can take it away. Man's soul is destroyed when it is cast into hell, because there it is separated from God.

---

[44] Jesus called Himself the **Son of Man** (see Mark 2:10 and comment).

[45] The Jews used to call Satan **Beelzebub**.

Believers in Christ need fear no man, nor any kind of persecution, because nothing can separate the believer from God (see Romans 8:35,38–39).

29–31 God has the power to destroy man's soul and every other kind of power as well. But God isn't only an all-powerful Creator; He is also our loving Father. He cares for every bird, even though their value is small. He knows how many hairs we have on our heads. He cares for every detail of our lives. And if He cares so much for these small things like birds and the hairs of our head, He will surely care for us who are His children.

32–33 According to Jesus' teaching in these verses, we must understand that in God's sight there can be no such thing as a "secret believer." He who follows Christ secretly is no Christian.[46] We must **acknowledge** Jesus **before men**. Otherwise, on the day of judgment Jesus will say to God, "I do not know this person." To be saved we must confess Christ with our mouth (see Romans 10:9–10 and comment).

Jesus is our advocate before God (1 John 2:1). He is our intercessor (see Romans 8:34; Hebrews 7:25 and comments). If He speaks in our favor, God will accept us and save us. If Jesus does not acknowledge us, neither will God. To the extent that we speak on Jesus' behalf before men, to that extent Jesus will speak on our behalf before God and His angels (see Luke 12:8–9; Revelation 3:5). But if we are afraid or ashamed to confess we are followers of Christ, Christ will not acknowledge us on the day of judgment (see Mark 8:38 and comment).

Being Worthy of Christ (10:34–42)
(Mark 8:34–35; 9:41; Luke 9:23–24; 12:51–53; 14:26–27)

34 Jesus was a peacemaker. But He did not come primarily to make peace between men; He came primarily to make peace between man and God.

But not all men believe Jesus. Not all men make peace with God; that is, not all men repent and receive forgiveness from God. Those that do not repent and do not believe always oppose those who do. Those that remain in Satan's kingdom always oppose those who enter the kingdom of God. There can be no peace between the kingdom of Satan and the kingdom of God. That is why Jesus said, **"I did not come to bring peace, but a sword,"** or **"division,"** as Luke says (Luke 12:51). Jesus has divided those who believe from those who don't believe. Jesus said to His disciples: **"I have chosen you out of the world. That is why the world hates you"** (John 15:19). As a sword divides things into two, so Jesus' word divides believers from non-believers (Hebrews 4:12).

35–36 Jesus here quotes from Micah 7:6 to show that even within one's own family, non-believers will oppose believers in Jesus (see Matthew 10:21–22; Mark 13:12–13 and comments).

37 Many believers in Jesus have to face the opposition of their non-believing family members. Jesus says, "You must love me more than your father and mother. If you don't, you are not worthy to be my disciple."

To follow Jesus, we must often give up worldly advantage. We may suffer loss of our property, our inheritance, our job. Such disadvantages will fall upon our children also. But we must put love for Jesus above our love for our children. Jesus said this in an even stronger way in Luke 14:26: **"If anyone comes to me and does not hate his father and mother, his wife and children, his brothers and sisters—yes, even his own life—he cannot be my disciple."** When Jesus uses the word "hate" here, He means that we must be ready to leave even our

---

[46] It is possible for one to become a true believer, but for some time to keep it hidden. At the beginning of one's Christian life, one's faith may be weak. But sooner or later, every Christian must become ready to confess his faith openly—or else he will show that his faith was never real to begin with. Joseph of Arimathea and Nicodemus are good examples of so-called "secret believers" (see Mark 15:42–47: John 3:1–2 and comments). But, in time, they too came forward and identified themselves as followers of Jesus.

parents and wife and children for His sake. Not only that, to be a disciple we must "hate" our own life (see John 12:25 and comment). That is, we must deny ourselves. Jesus said, "**If anyone would come after me, he must deny himself**" (Mark 8:34). To "come after" Jesus means to be His disciple. All Christians are called to be disciples. Jesus said, "... **anyone who does not carry his cross and follow me cannot be my disciple**" (Luke 14:27). A person who does not carry his cross is not **worthy** to be a disciple (verse 38).

38–39 See Mark 8:34–35 and comment.

40 Just as those who persecute Jesus also persecute His disciples, so will those who accept Jesus also accept His disciples. Whatever happens to the teacher happens also to the student (see Mark 9:37; Luke 10:16; John 15:20).

41 In this verse, to receive a **prophet** or a **righteous man** means to receive one of Christ's disciples. Those who receive Jesus' disciples will receive a great reward. They will share in the blessings of the disciples. People share in the blessings of whomever they accept and believe. We who have received Christ also receive the blessings of Christ. When we welcome a disciple, we welcome Christ Himself. When we welcome Christ, we welcome God. The smallest act of service rendered to a disciple of Christ will be counted as a service to Christ Himself (see Matthew 10:42; 25:40).

42 See Mark 9:41 and comment.

CHAPTER 11

Jesus and John the Baptist (11:1–19)

(Luke 7:18–28,31–35)

1–3 John the Baptist had been put into prison by King Herod (see Mark 1:14; 6:17–20). While in prison John could learn only a little about Jesus' activities. John had recognized Jesus when he baptized Him (John 1:32–34). John supposed, as other Jews did, that the Messiah[47] would free the Jews from the political control of the Romans and local rulers like Herod. But now John had been cast into prison, and so he began to wonder if Jesus really was the Messiah. Why had Jesus not brought about John's release? Therefore, John sent two of his disciples to Jesus to ask if He was the Messiah or not (Luke 7:18–20).

4 Jesus knew that John had not received a true report of His activities. That is why John had begun to doubt.

5 Therefore, Jesus told John's disciples to inform John about what He was doing. By His works of healing and preaching and raising the dead, Jesus was fulfilling the Old Testament prophecies. Isaiah prophesied that in the days of the Messiah **the eyes of the blind** [will] **be opened and the ears of the deaf unstopped. Then will the lame leap like a deer, and the tongue of the dumb shout for joy** (Isaiah 35:5–6). And good news will be preached to the **poor**[48] (Isaiah 61:1)—that is, the **poor in spirit** (Matthew 5:3). Notice that Jesus did not have "five-year plans" and complicated budgets. He did not have teams of advisors and evaluators. John's disciples asked for proof that Jesus was the Messiah. And Jesus answered, "Look about you. My program is simple. Hear the preaching; see the healing. That is proof."

6 Therefore, Jesus was in effect saying to John's disciples: "Let John not doubt that I am the Messiah. Let John not fall away through discouragement and unbelief." The faith of even the greatest saints is mixed with some doubt and disbelief.

7 After John's disciples left, Jesus

---

[47] "Messiah" is the Hebrew word for Christ; it means "anointed one."

[48] In Isaiah 61:1, the word **poor** can also be translated "afflicted" or "humble."

taught the crowd about John. John was not a **reed swayed by the wind**; that is, he did not follow the opinions of the world and of evil men. He stood straight and firm for the truth. He did not waver under abuse and persecution.

8 John did not seek an easy life. He denied himself (see Mark 1:6).

9–10 John was a true prophet—**more than a prophet**—because he came to prepare the way for the Messiah. Here Jesus quotes from Malachi 3:1 (see Mark 1:2–3 and comment).

11 John was greater than all the Old Testament prophets. Up until the coming of Christ there had never been a greater man than John. Yet John belonged to the old covenant; he was the last of the Jewish prophets. He did not see Jesus' resurrection; he did not receive the Holy Spirit in the same way that Jesus' disciples did (John 20:22). Although John announced the arrival of the kingdom of heaven (see Matthew 3:1–2), he was not a part of it during his lifetime. Thus in heaven even the least believer in Christ will have a greater position than John.

12 Then Jesus said, "**From the days of John the Baptist until now, the kingdom of heaven has been forcefully advancing, and forceful men lay hold of it.**"[49] That is, since John's time, men have been eagerly trying to receive the blessings of the Messiah, Christ. They are forcefully striving to enter the kingdom of heaven. In Luke 16:16, Christ gave a similar teaching. He said: "**Since that** (John's) **time, the good news of the kingdom of God is being preached, and everyone is forcing his way into it.**"

Thus Jesus gave John great praise; John's ministry was successful. Many Jews heeded John and repented. Tax collectors and other sinners repented. All kinds of people began to enter the kingdom of heaven. Indeed, the kingdom of heaven had come into the world "forcefully."

13 All the **Prophets and the Law**[50] prophesied about the coming of Christ and the establishment of His kingdom. John was the last prophet of the old covenant (verse 11). When Christ came, the Old Testament prophecies were fulfilled and came to an end (Hebrews 1:1).

14–15 John was the **Elijah** about whom Malachi prophesied (Malachi 4:5). The first Elijah was one of the greatest of the Old Testament prophets. Because Elijah was not buried but was carried into heaven, the Jews believed that he would come again (2 Kings 2:11). John was not an incarnation of Elijah (John 1:21); but he fulfilled the work of Elijah as prophesied by Malachi (Luke 1:17). Jesus' meaning was: "Anyone with spiritual understanding would understand that John was indeed the prophet that Malachi spoke about" (see Matthew 17:10–13).

Malachi's prophecy about John the Baptist, the "second Elijah," is the last prophecy of the Old Testament. Thus John, in a way, served as a link between the Old and New Testaments. John announced the beginning of a new age, a new kingdom, a new covenant (see Hebrews 8:8,13 and comment).

16–17 The Jews of Jesus' time—that is, **this generation**—were given the chance to enter the kingdom of God. Both John the Baptist and Jesus preached that the **kingdom of heaven is near** (Matthew 3:1–2; Mark 1:14–15). But most of the Jews were like children playing a game called "weddings and funerals." The game went like this: one group of children **played the flute**, and the others were supposed to **dance**. But the Jews didn't "dance." The second group of children then **sang a dirge**, and the others were supposed to **mourn**, that is, cry out as people did at funerals. But the Jews also refused to "mourn." The Jews were like fickle children who refused to play each other's game.

---

[49] In place of the words **has been forcefully advancing,** some versions of the Bible say, "has suffered violence." The Greek text can be translated either way.

[50] Here the **Law** means the first five books of the Old Testament. The **Prophets and the Law** together refer to the entire Old Testament.

18 In the same way, John came **neither eating nor drinking**. He came singing a "dirge," like the children playing the "funeral" game. But many of the Jews rejected John's word, saying, "**He has a demon**." Those who reject God's word commonly abuse the preacher who speaks it.

19 Jesus the Son of Man came **eating and drinking**. He came playing the "flute," like the children playing the "wedding" game. But the Jews didn't accept Him either. They said, "**Here is a glutton and a drunkard**", when, in fact, He had come to save gluttons and drunkards and **tax collectors and "sinners"** (Mark 2:15–16,18). Even the holiest of men suffer slander and abuse. Very often people speak evil even of a man's highest virtues and greatest work.

Thus most of the Jews were like the fickle and foolish children who couldn't agree about what game to play. No matter in what form God spoke to them—by a "dirge" or by a "flute"—they rejected His word.

But wisdom is proved right by her actions. Jesus and John were despised by many, but their actions proved them to be right. Everyone who believed in Jesus received salvation, new life. This was proof that the teachings of John and Jesus were true.

According to Luke 7:35, Jesus also said, "**. . . wisdom is proved right by all her children**." Here the word **children** means "actions." Good actions are the "children" of wisdom.

Woe on Unrepentant Cities (11:20–24)

(Luke 10:13–15)

20–21 Jesus had performed many miracles in Korazin and Bethsaida.[51] Jesus fed five thousand men near Bethsaida (Mark 6:44–45). But the people of those Jewish cities did not repent of their sins and turn to Christ. Tyre and Sidon were two great Gentile cities on the coast of the Mediterranean Sea north of Israel (in modern Lebanon). In Jesus' time they were known for their wealth and their wickedness. But, said Jesus, if He had performed such miracles in Tyre and Sidon, the people of those cities would have repented **in sackcloth and ashes**.[52]

22 Therefore, the guilt of Korazin and Bethsaida was much greater, because even though they had witnessed Jesus' miracles they had still rejected Him and refused to repent. **From everyone who has been given much, much will be demanded** (Luke 12:48).

23–24 **And you, Capernaum, will you be lifted up to the skies**? Capernaum, located on the north shore of the Sea of Galilee, was Jesus' **own town** (Matthew 9:1; Mark 2:1). It was a proud city. Its people exalted themselves. But Jesus said that they will be cast down. Because they rejected Christ, they will receive a greater punishment than the people of Sodom (Genesis 19:1–29; Matthew 10:14–15). Sodom was destroyed by God because of its wickedness; Capernaum will receive an even worse punishment on the final day of judgment.

Rest For the Weary (11:25–30)

(Luke 10:21–22)

25-26 Jesus was happy because even though God had hidden the meaning of Jesus' words and miracles from the **wise and learned**, yet He had revealed their meaning to **little children**, that is, to those who have faith (see Mark 10:15). Jesus was not happy that the **wise and learned** were spiritually ignorant; He was happy that the **little children** were spiritually wise.

The **wise and learned** are those who suppose they can understand spiritual things by their own human understanding. But this is impossible (see 1 Corinthians 2:14). The **world through its**

---

[51] Korazin was a city three miles north of the Sea of Galilee. Bethsaida was nearby. Nothing is known about the miracles Jesus performed at Korazin. From this we can understand that Jesus did many things that are not written in the four Gospels (John 21:25).

[52] In Bible times, to wear sackcloth and to apply ashes to the face was a sign of repentance.

wisdom did not know him (1 Corinthians 1:21). The **little children** are those who are humble, who are dependent on the Holy Spirit, whose minds are open. Only such people can receive the things of God (see 1 Corinthians 2:7–10,12). **God opposes the proud but gives grace to the humble** (James 4:6). This is the Father's **good pleasure** (verse 26).

27 **"All things have been committed to me by my Father,"** said Jesus. **All things** means all the power and wisdom and authority of the Father (Matthew 28:18). God gave Christ the Spirit **without limit** (John 3:34). **The Father loves the Son and has placed everything in his hands** (John 3:35). Jesus said, **"All that belongs to the Father is mine"** (John 16:15).

Only the Father has complete knowledge of Jesus. In the same way, only Jesus has full knowledge of the Father, because He and the Father are **one** (John 10:30). And Jesus has given this knowledge to those **to whom the Son chooses to reveal him**. We did not choose Jesus; He chose us (John 15:16). Everything Jesus received from the Father He has revealed to those who believe in Him (John 15:15).

No one can truly know God unless Jesus reveals Him. **No one has ever seen God, but God the only Son, who is at the Father's side, has made him known** (John 1:18). People from every race and nation are continually seeking God, but only those who believe in Jesus can ever truly know God. Only Jesus has revealed the true nature of God (see Colossians 2:9 and comment). God has been fully revealed in Jesus Christ. When we know Jesus, we will know God. Those who reject Jesus seek God in vain.

28 Jesus promises **rest** to all the weary and burdened who repent and come to Him. He takes away their burden of sin. His **rest** is spiritual. It is inner peace. It is freedom from fear and anxiety. It is **rest for your souls** (verse 29). It is a rest that will last forever (see Hebrews 4:9–10).

Worldly men seek rest and peace in religious rituals and good works, but they do not find it. In order to find true rest and peace, it is necessary to come to the one true giver of peace, Jesus; true rest and peace cannot be found anywhere else (see John 14:27 and comment).

The rest that Jesus gives is not a cessation of activity. It is filled with joy and praise. It is filled with love and fellowship. It is filled with the presence of God Himself.

29 **Take my yoke upon you**. The Jews lived under the **yoke** of the law. This yoke was a heavy burden (Matthew 23:4). They were obliged to obey hundreds of regulations. If they broke even one, it counted as if they had broken the whole law (James 2:10). Not even the Jews could bear the demands of the law (Acts 15:10).

Jesus freed men from the yoke of the law, but He gave them another yoke. His "yoke" was also a yoke of obedience, but it was obedience not to a law, but to Jesus Himself. To obey Jesus is not a burden, because He is our friend, our shepherd, our Savior. Those who love Jesus desire to keep His commands (John 14:15).

Jesus is **gentle and humble**. He is not impatient with us when we are slow to learn. He is not harsh with us when we stumble. **A bruised reed he will not break, and a smoldering wick he will not snuff out** (Isaiah 42:3; Matthew 12:20). Who would not want to learn from such a teacher?

30 Jesus' yoke is **easy**. This does not mean that Jesus' followers will have an easy life. The path of the Christian is narrow and difficult (Matthew 7:13–14). But the Christian's yoke is easy, his burden is light. We do not have to labor under the yoke of the law (see Romans 8:2). We do not have to carry a burden of sin and sorrow and worry. Jesus helps us, strengthens us. And He gives us joy as we follow Him (John 15:11).

CHAPTER 12

Lord of the Sabbath (12:1–8)
(Mark 2:23–28; Luke 6:1–5)

1–8 See Mark 2:23–28 and comment.

A Man Healed on the Sabbath (12:9–14)
(Mark 3:1–6; Luke 6:6–11)

9–14 See Mark 3:1–6 and comment.

God's Chosen Servant (12:15–21)

15–16 See Mark 3:7–12 and comment.
17 Jesus told those He healed not to tell who He was (verse 16). Here Matthew quotes from Isaiah 42:1–4 to explain why Jesus wanted to keep His identity secret.
18 God, speaking through the prophet Isaiah, says about Christ: "**Here is my servant whom I have chosen**." Christ was called not only a Son, but also a **servant**. God put His Spirit on Him (Mark 1:10–11; John 3:34). Christ **will proclaim justice to the nations**—that is, to all nations, both Jews and Gentiles. Christ came to establish God's justice and righteousness on earth.
19 But Christ **will not quarrel or cry out**. He did not come as an earthly king to defeat His enemies. He did not seek arguments. He did not seek to establish His kingdom by force. Christ came quietly, without show. His kingdom was not visible; it was within men (see Luke 17:20–21 and comment). Christ came to establish God's rule in men's hearts.

However, the Jews believed their Messiah would be like an earthly king. Therefore, Jesus did not want everyone to know He was the Messiah. Otherwise, the people would have tried to make Him a king. They would have prevented Him from being crucified. They would have prevented Him from giving His life as a ransom for many (Mark 10:45). Thus God's plan for man's salvation would have been blocked (see Mark 1:34; 3:12; 5:43 and comments).

20–21 Jesus came not with force but with gentleness (Matthew 11:29). **A bruised reed he will not break**. A person bruised and weakened by sin, discouragement, and failure Christ will strengthen and restore. If such a person comes to Christ, He will not break or reject him. Jesus said: "**. . . whoever comes to me I will never drive away**" (John 6:37).

A **smoldering wick he will not snuff out**. A person whose faith is weak Christ will not condemn.

In the end Christ will prevail completely over Satan. Christ will **lead justice to victory**. He will raise up the downtrodden, He will **release the oppressed** (Luke 4:18). He will bring salvation to all who turn to God and believe. All **nations will put their hope** in Christ (verse 21).

Jesus and Beelzebub (12:22–32)
(Mark 3:20–30; Luke 11:14–23; 12:10)

22–32 See Mark 3:20–30 and comment.

A Tree and Its Fruit (12:33–37)
(Matthew 7:16–18; Luke 6:43–45)

33–35 As a man's heart is, so will be his actions and his words. Jesus called the Pharisees **vipers**, because there was poison in their hearts. Because their hearts were poisonous, their words were poisonous too, even though they at first sounded sweet. An evil heart produces evil and false words, just as a bad tree produces bad fruit. A tree is recognized by its fruit (see Matthew 7:16–18; James 3:10–12 and comments).
36 Here Jesus gives a very stern warning: On the day of judgment we will have to give an account of every **careless word** we have ever uttered.

We do not think enough about the day of judgment. God remembers everything we do, whether big or small, good or evil[53] (see Matthew 25:31–46). He even remembers every **careless word**. And we shall receive our eternal reward according to what we have done in this life (see 2 Corinthians 5:10 and comment).

A man's heart is revealed by his careless words. These are the words men say without thinking; they just come out. Evil men and hypocrites can, with practice, speak eloquently and pray fervently. They can say all the right things if they make an effort. But their careless words will reveal their true inner thoughts (see James 3:10–12). If there is evil in our heart, it will sooner or later be manifest by our words (verse 34).

37 Our careless words so accurately reveal what is in our hearts that Jesus says we will be judged by our words; we will be either acquitted or condemned by our words. When God judges us, He looks at our heart. These careless words issue from our heart. A good heart will always produce good words, and an evil heart will produce evil words. Therefore, by our words God is able to judge our hearts.

How can we control our **careless words**? We can control them by making our heart right. If our heart is right, then our careless words will be right also.

The Sign of Jonah (12:38–45)
(Mark 8:11–12; Luke 11:24–26,29–32)

38–39 See Mark 8:11–12 and comment.

40 When the Jewish leaders asked Jesus to show them a sign proving that He was the Messiah, Jesus said that only the **sign of the prophet Jonah** would be given to them (verse 39). Jonah was an Old Testament prophet. God sent him to the wicked city of Nineveh to tell the people there to repent. But Jonah disobeyed God and took a ship to another city instead. But a terrible storm came up at sea, and Jonah was forced to confess that he had been disobedient to God. The ship's sailors, supposing the storm to be a curse from God upon Jonah, threw Jonah overboard in order to save the ship. A **huge fish** swallowed Jonah, and Jonah remained in the belly of the fish for three days (Jonah 1:1–17). In the same way, Christ would remain three days in the **heart of the earth**[54] after He was killed. Therefore, the **sign of the prophet Jonah** means that Christ would die and after three days rise from the dead. This would be the sign to the Jews that Christ was truly the Messiah.

41 God caused the huge fish to vomit up Jonah (Jonah 2:10). Then God again commanded Jonah to go to Nineveh, and this time Jonah obeyed. The people listened to Jonah's preaching and repented and believed God. Therefore, God spared them the punishment He had planned for them (Jonah 3:1–10).

Thus, at the last judgment, the men of Nineveh will be saved. They will be counted righteous by God, because they repented and believed. It can be said that the men of Nineveh, by their example, by their righteousness, will in a way bring to light the unrighteousness of the Jews; they will **condemn** the Jews of Jesus' day. The men of Nineveh repented at the preaching of Jonah. Now the Messiah Himself had come, **one greater than Jonah**, and still the Jews refused to repent. Therefore, their guilt will be counted very great. This is why Jesus called the Jews of His day a **wicked and adulterous generation** (verse 39). They were **wicked** because of their evil hearts, and they were **adulterous** because they had betrayed God, their true husband, and had gone with the world.

42 The **Queen of the South** will also judge **this generation**, that is, the Jews of Jesus' time. This queen is the Queen of

---

[53] In Jeremiah 31:34 and Hebrews 8:12, God says: "I **will remember their sins no more**." This means that on the day of judgment, those who believe in Christ will not receive condemnation (Romans 8:1). When God judges believers, He will not take into account their sins. It will be as if their sins had been erased, forgotten. But for believers there will be another kind of "judgment," in which God will reward them for everything they have done on this earth. When God judges what our reward should be, He will examine every work we have ever done and every word we have ever spoken.

[54] The **heart of the earth** here means the abode of the dead, or Hades.

"Sheba" (part of Arabia), who came to listen to King **Solomon's**[55] **wisdom**. She sought the truth from Solomon (1 Kings 10:1–13). But from Christ, who is greater than Solomon, the Jews did not seek the truth. Therefore, the Queen of the South also will condemn those Jews at the last judgment.

43 When an evil spirit is driven out of one person it seeks for someone else to enter (see Mark 5:8–12). If there is no one to enter, the spirit goes to an **arid place** where it waits until it finds a new person to enter.

44–45 However, the evil spirit may return to the same person from whom it was driven out. If that person is **unoccupied** and **swept clean** (verse 44), then the evil spirit will re-enter that person. Perhaps other evil spirits will also enter.

The meaning of this teaching is as follows. When a man comes to Jesus and repents of his sin, Jesus forgives him. Jesus cleanses him. He casts out his sin. Just as Jesus cast out evil spirits, so He casts out our spirit of selfishness and pride when we repent. However, many people came to Jesus and to John the Baptist and repented of their sins, but then quickly fell away. Why? Because they did not receive the Holy Spirit. The spirit of sin had left them, but the Holy Spirit had not come in. Their "houses" had been left **unoccupied** and **swept clean**. They had not brought forth the **fruits in keeping with repentance** (Matthew 3:8). Their faith had not grown. And so the old spirit of sin and selfishness came back in.

And the final condition of that man is worse than the first. Such people have tasted the blessing of Christ, but in the end reject Him. Such people cannot be brought back to repentance again (see Hebrews 6:4–6; 2 Peter 2:20 and comments).

Jesus' Mother and Brothers (12:46–50)
(Mark 3:31–35; Luke 8:19–21)

46–50 See Mark 3:31–35 and comment.

CHAPTER 13

The Parable of the Sower (13:1–23)
(Mark 4:1–20; Luke 8:4–15)

1–23 See Mark 4:1–20 and comment.

The Parable of the Weeds (13:24–30)

24–30 This is the first of five parables in this chapter about the kingdom of heaven. In the parable of the weeds, the kingdom of heaven is **like a man who sowed good seed in his field** (verse 24). But an enemy sowed weeds in the same field, and the wheat and the weeds grew up together (verses 25–26). The servants of the man wanted to pull up the weeds at once, but their master told them to wait until the harvest, lest the wheat also be destroyed (verses 29–30). The meaning of the parable is given in verses 36–43.

The Parables of the Mustard Seed and the Yeast (13:31–35)
(Mark 4:30–34; Luke 13:20–21)

31–32 See Mark 4:30–32 and comment.

33 The kingdom of heaven is like **yeast**. Its influence spreads throughout the whole world like yeast spreads through dough. The kingdom of heaven changes the world. It is like salt. It is like light in the darkness.

34–35 When Jesus spoke to the crowds, He spoke in **parables**. Usually

---

[55] **Solomon** was the son of King David. He was known for his wisdom. He wrote most of the Old Testament book of Proverbs.

the crowds did not understand the meaning of the parables, and sometimes Jesus' own disciples didn't either (verse 36). The purpose of the parables was not to give simple examples that ordinary people could easily understand. Rather, the parables were revelations of **things hidden**, which only those with spiritual insight could understand[56] (see Mark 4:10–12,33–34 and comment).

The Parable of the Weeds Explained (13:36–43)

36–39 The meaning of the parable of the weeds is this: Christ sows good seed in the world. The good seed are believers. But at the same time, Christ's enemy, Satan, also sows evil seed, the weeds. The kind of weed mentioned in this parable looks like wheat. Therefore, when the wheat and the weeds begin to grow, it is difficult to tell them apart.

In the same way, among believers in the church there are also "weeds," that is, false believers. These are the **sons of the evil one** (verse 38), that is, servants of Satan. They say, "I believe." They in some ways act like other Christians. They receive the same blessings of rain and sunshine as the good seed (Matthew 5:45). But, in fact, they are weeds.

In this parable, the servants ask their master, "**Do you want us to go and pull** [the weeds] **up?**" (verse 28). Many of us are like those servants. We are quick to judge, quick to condemn. We want to get rid of the weeds at once.

But Christ says: "**No . . . because while you are pulling the weeds, you may root up the wheat** (verse 29). You cannot be certain which are the weeds. **Let both grow together until the harvest**" (verse 30).

40–43 Christ teaches in this parable that until the last judgment, there will be evil in the world. Only then will Satan be finally overcome. Only then will the weeds be pulled up and burned. It is not for us to pull up the weeds, that is, to judge and condemn others. That work is only for the Son of Man and His angels (verse 41).

There will also be weeds in the church. Just as among the twelve disciples there was one, Judas, who betrayed Christ, so in the church there are weeds, false Christians, wolves in sheep's clothing (Matthew 7:15). We must beware of them. We must examine their teaching. We must rebuke wrongdoing and discipline brothers who fall into error (see 1 Corinthians 5:1–5 and comment). But we must not judge them (see Matthew 7:1; 1 Corinthians 4:5 and comments).

There are two great dangers that every church confronts. One is weeds. The weeds make the church weak. They weaken the faith of other Christians. They bring dishonor on the church.

But the second danger is equally great. It comes from zealous Christians who are quick to pull up weeds. They desire to purify the church and this is good. But they also have a judging spirit, and this is wrong. Yes, they pull up many weeds. They expose false Christians. But at the same time, they judge true Christians. They split the church. And in the end they do more harm than if they had left the weeds alone. This is the deepest meaning of the parable of the weeds.

Only God, the Son of Man, can truly judge. At the right time, He will separate the wheat and the weeds. There will be a **new heaven and a new earth . . . the new Jerusalem** (Revelation 21:1–2). **Nothing impure will ever enter it** (Revelation 21:27). At that time the weeds will be removed and destroyed. And then Christ **will send his angels and gather his elect** (Mark 13:26–27). **Then the righteous will shine like the sun** (verse 43). Those who are lights in this world will shine even more brightly in the next (Matthew 5:14).

Three Other Parables of the Kingdom of Heaven (13:44–52)

44 The kingdom of heaven is **like**

---

[56] It is not only parables that we need special spiritual insight to understand; we need help to understand the deeper meaning of the entire Bible. The Holy Spirit gives us this help. Whenever we study the Bible, we must pray that the Holy Spirit will give us spiritual understanding.

treasure hidden in a field. The treasure is so valuable that a wise man will sell **all** he has in order to obtain it. To obtain the kingdom of heaven means to obtain salvation, eternal life with God in heaven.

45–46 In this parable of the pearls, Jesus teaches that the kingdom of heaven is more valuable than anything else a man can obtain. There are many kinds of religion in the world, but only one leads to heaven. There are many teachers in the world, but only one—namely, Jesus—leads to the full truth. There are many blessings in the world, but only Jesus leads a man to the highest blessing of all—salvation, eternal life. Jesus said, "**I am the way and the truth and the life. No one comes to the Father except through me**" (John 14:6). There are many pearls in the world, but only from Jesus can we receive this pearl **of great value**, the greatest pearl of all. Indeed, the pearl is Christ Himself. The wise man will sell everything he has, he will give up whatever is necessary, in order to obtain this pearl (see Philippians 3:7–8 and comment).

47–50 The parable of the net gives the same teaching as the parable of the weeds (verses 37–43). Christ and His disciples cast out the net into the sea (the world), and both good and bad fish are caught. As long as the net is in the sea, the fisherman cannot tell what is in it. Only in the final judgment **at the end of the age** (verse 49) when the net is dragged to shore, will the bad fish be taken out and thrown away.

51–52 The disciples at first did not understand all of the parables (verse 36). But soon they were able to understand them. They were learning to become teachers themselves. All twelve disciples were Jews, and thus each was, in a way, a **teacher of the law**, the Jewish law, or the Old Testament. But now they were becoming **instructed about the kingdom of heaven** (verse 52). Thus they possessed **old** treasure, the law, and **new treasures**, that is, the Gospel of Christ.

A Prophet Without Honor (13:53–58)

(Mark 6:1–6)

53–58 See Mark 6:1–6 and comment.

CHAPTER 14

John the Baptist Beheaded (14:1–12)

(Mark 6:14–29; Luke 9:7–9)

1–12 See Mark 6:14–29 and comment.

Jesus Feeds the Five Thousand (14:13–21)

(Mark 6:30–44; Luke 9:10–17; John 6:1–15)

13–21 See Mark 6:30–44 and comment.

Jesus Walks on the Water (14:22–36)

(Mark 6:45–56; John 6:16–24)

22–36 See Mark 6:45–56 and comment.

CHAPTER 15

Clean and Unclean (15:1–20)
(Mark 7:1–23)

1–20 See Mark 7:1–23 and comment.

The Faith of the Canaanite Woman (15:21–28)
(Mark 7:24–30)

21–28 See Mark 7:24–30 and comment.

Jesus Heals Many (15:29–31)
(Mark 7:31–37)

29–31 See Mark 7:31–37 and comment.

Jesus Feeds the Four Thousand (15:32–39)
(Mark 8:1–10)

32–39 See Mark 8:1–10 and comment.

CHAPTER 16

The Demand for a Sign (16:1–4)
(Mark 8:11–13; Luke 12:54–56)

1–4 See Mark 8:11–13 and comment.

The Yeast of the Pharisees and Sadducees (16:5–12)
(Mark 8:14–21)

5–12 See Mark 8:14–21 and comment.

Peter's Confession of Christ (16:13–20)
(Mark 8:27–30; Luke 9:18–21)

13–20 See Mark 8:27–30 and comment.

Jesus Predicts His Death (16:21–23)
(Mark 8:31–33; Luke 9:22)

21–23 See Mark 8:31–33 and comment.

Denying Self (16:24–28)
(Mark 8:34–38; Luke 9:23–26)

24–28 See Mark 8:34–38; 9:1 and comments.

CHAPTER 17

The Transfiguration (17:1–13)
(Mark 9:2–13; Luke 9:27–36)

1–13 See Mark 9:2–13 and comment.

The Healing of an Epileptic Boy (17:14–23)
(Mark 9:14–32; 11:22–23; Luke 9:37–45)

14–19 See Mark 9:14–29 and comment.

20 See Mark 11:22–23 and comment.

21–23 See Mark 9:29–32 and comment.[57]

[57] Not all ancient manuscripts of Matthew contain verse 21. A similar verse is found in Mark 9:29.

The Temple Tax (17:24–27)

24 All Jews over twenty were required to pay a two-drachma[58] temple tax (Exodus 30:11–14). In Jesus' time there was no two-drachma coin, so two men would join together and pay four drachmas between them (verse 27). The temple was an enormous complex of buildings in Jerusalem, which was costly to maintain. It was the center of the Jewish religion; Jews came to the temple from all areas to worship God and to offer sacrifices. Therefore, by taxing all these Jews, the Jewish priests were able to pay for the maintenance of the temple.

25–26 Peter told the tax collectors that Jesus would pay the temple tax. In Peter's mind, Jesus and His disciples were required to pay the tax, just like all other Jews.

But Jesus told Peter that it was not necessary for **the sons** to pay the tax (verse 26). By **sons,** Jesus means the true sons of God—that is, those who believe in Christ. Ordinary earthly kings did not collect tribute from their own children. Therefore, the Jewish leaders should not demand taxes from God's true sons—Jesus and His followers.

For believers in Christ, worship in the temple was no longer necessary. Before Christ's time it was necessary to offer sacrifices for sin in the temple. But Christ Himself was the final sacrifice for sin (see Hebrews 7:27 and comment). Therefore, sacrifices were no longer necessary after Christ came. The old Jewish temple was no longer necessary. **One greater than the temple** had come, that is, Jesus (Matthew 12:6). Indeed, the believers, the "new Israel," had themselves become the new spiritual temple (see 1 Corinthians 3:16–17; Ephesians 2:21–22 and comments). Therefore, Jesus told Peter, "It is not necessary for us to pay the tax."

27 However, Jesus told Peter to pay the tax anyway, "**so that we may not offend them.**" Even though they did not have to pay the tax, Jesus and Peter paid it so that they might not give unnecessary offense to the Jews, and thereby turn some of them away from Jesus (see 1 Corinthians 8:9 and comment). God provided the needed four-drachma coin in a miraculous way—it was in the mouth of a fish!

CHAPTER 18

The Greatest in the Kingdom of Heaven (18:1–5)
(Mark 9:36–37; 10:15)

1–4 See Mark 9:33–35; 10:14–15 and comments.

5 See Matthew 10:40; Mark 9:36–37 and comments.

Teaching on Sin (18:6–9)
(Mark 9:42–50; Luke 17:1–2)

6–9 See Mark 9:42–50 and comment.

The Parable of the Lost Sheep (18:10–14)
(Luke 15:3–7)

10 Jesus taught that we must cherish and respect **these little ones**, that is, new and weak Christians (verses 5–6). We must love them in the same way He loves them (John 13:34). God places great value on the least of His children, and so should we.

Every Christian has a guardian angel in heaven (see Psalm 91:11; Acts 12:15). These **angels** stand before God's throne (Revelation 5:11). They **always see the**

---

[58] The drachma was a Greek coin. Four drachmas equaled one "shekel," a small Jewish coin. In place of the words **two-drachma tax**, some translations of the Bible say "half-shekel tax."

face of my Father in heaven. If we mistreat one of Christ's **little ones**, or if we cause anyone of them to sin (verse 6), God will immediately know about it. Through their guardian angels God will protect His little ones. When we oppose a little child of Jesus, we oppose his angel also.

11 See Luke 19:10 and comment.[59]

12–14 God cares for each Christian. But He especially cares for the young and weak Christian who goes astray. We too should care for such Christians, and make every effort to bring them back. We must encourage such lost brothers and sisters to repent and turn back to Christ, their great Shepherd. God is happier about one of His children who comes back than about ninety-nine others who never went astray. God is **not willing that any of these little ones should be lost.**

This teaching applies not only to Christians who have strayed but to all men. According to Luke 15:7, **there is more rejoicing in heaven over one sinner who repents than over ninety-nine righteous persons who do not need to repent.** That is, there is more joy in heaven over each new person that believes in Christ than there is over ninety-nine persons who already believe. Our God is a God who is always seeking the lost and rejoicing when each one is saved (see Luke 15:8–10; 19:10 and comments).

A Brother Who Sins Against You (18:15–20)

15 Jesus here teaches us what to do if a fellow believer sins against us. We must speak to him about it face to face. We must speak to our brother in love and humility. If we do this, we shall almost always be able to achieve reconciliation with our brother.

There are three things we must not do when our brother sins against us. First, we must not go to him in anger. We shall not win our brother over with anger. Second, we must not hold bitterness in our hearts. We must speak openly with our brother and tell about the hurt we have received. Third, we must not initially speak negatively or critically about our brother to any other person. This kind of negative and critical talk about others is one of the commonest sins found in the church. Jesus says: "... **show him his fault, just between the two of you.**"

When we go to our brother in this way, we often find out that our brother has not really sinned against us—we only thought he had. Not only that, perhaps he will tell us about a sin that we have committed against him!

16 If our Christian brother has truly sinned against us and does not make the injury right, then there are two courses of action we can take. First, if our brother's sin is small or if it is only a sin against us personally, we can simply forgive him (even if he doesn't repent) and forget the matter. Love may prompt us to overlook his sin. **Love covers over a multitude of sins** (1 Peter 4:8).

However, if our brother's sin affects others or if it appears necessary to oppose his sin actively,[60] we must take two or three elders in the church and go again to our brother. Our purpose is still to bring about a reconciliation, not to accuse our brother. If, however, it later becomes necessary to accuse our brother before the church (verse 17), then the testimony of these elders will be necessary. No accusation can be made in the church without two or three witnesses present to confirm the accusation (Deuteronomy 19:15; 2 Corinthians 13:1).

17 If our brother still does not repent and he persists in his sin against us, then, Jesus says, **tell it to the church**. We must

---

[59] Not all ancient manuscripts of Matthew contain verse 11. A similar verse is found in Luke 19:10.

[60] For example, if our brother knowingly and blatantly persists in sinning against us, or if we see that from his sin harm is going to come either to himself or to the church, then we must take the steps outlined in verses 15–17 to oppose his sin.

not go to a civil magistrate about disputes between believers (see 1 Corinthians 6:1–6 and comment). The CHURCH that is meant here is the local church. "Church" can mean the entire committee of elders or it can mean the entire congregation. The witnesses must also give their testimony before the church.

If the brother still does not repent, he should be expelled from the church, and members of the church should have nothing further to do with him. If a man does not abide by the judgments and laws of the church, he doesn't deserve to be a member. Nevertheless, the purpose of this severe punishment is not to destroy the soul of the offending brother, but rather to bring him back to repentance (see 1 Corinthians 5:4–5 and comment).

A brother who refuses to repent and persists in his sin should be treated as a **pagan or a tax collector**. Pagans and tax collectors were considered by the Jews to be sinners who were not in God's family. Unrepentant believers should be treated like that.

A question arises here: Must we forgive such a hard and unrepentant brother? If he repents we certainly must forgive him (see Luke 17:3–4). But even if he does not repent, we must still forgive him (verses 21–22).

If we are able to fully and freely forgive our brother and to forget his offense, then we can drop the matter. If his sin is only against us, then it is not necessary to accuse him before others (1 Corinthians 6:7). But if we are led by the Holy Spirit to confront our brother, then Jesus has shown us in these three verses exactly how we must go about it.

18 The church or its board of elders has the final authority to render judgment in such matters. Their ruling will be **bound in heaven**; that is, it will be approved by God. Likewise, if they forgive, or **loose** the offending brother, God will also forgive him. God has given the church and its leaders the full authority to act in His name (see Matthew 16:19; John 20:23).

19–20 These two verses follow in the same context from verse 18. In order for the church to **bind** and **loose**, its members must be in agreement. The Holy Spirit must guide the members of the church to make the right decision. And He will guide everyone in the same way. If there is disagreement among church members, then it is very hard to determine what is God's will. If there is not full agreement, the church should not take action against a brother. But if there is agreement on a course of action, then that action will be according to God's will and it will have God's authority behind it.

These verses, however, are not written only about rendering judgments against a brother. These verses are also written about any kind of prayer or request. When two or three gather together in Jesus' name, Jesus is present with them (verse 20). His Holy Spirit is in them. And when they agree in their prayer, they can be sure that the Holy Spirit has guided them and that they are praying according to God's will.[61]

For truly united prayer to exist, our minds must be "one" (verse 19). The prayer must be for something specific about which we are in agreement. The second thing necessary for united prayer is that it must be **in [Jesus'] name** (verse 20), that is, for Jesus' sake. If we pray together with one mind and in Jesus' name, **it will be done** for us. If God does not grant our request, it will often be because we have not prayed in a united way.

Individual prayer is, of course, very important (Matthew 6:6). But group prayer is equally important. Both kinds of prayer are necessary. Group prayer is especially effective when we are requesting guidance and help from God. Since the same Holy Spirit is working in all believers, when we pray together the Holy Spirit can more fully manifest His power.

If two of you on earth agree about anything you ask for, it will be done for you. What an amazing promise! Do we

[61] Their prayer must not be contrary to God's will as revealed in the Bible; the Holy Spirit never guides in any way that opposes what is written in the Scriptures.

believe it? When husbands and wives pray together, do they believe it? When we gather in prayer meetings, do we believe this promise? All we have to do is to agree with one another and pray in Jesus' name, and God has promised to give us what we ask.

Therefore, when we gather together, let us not pray only for small things. Let us be bold to pray for great things, to make great requests to God. All the power of God is in our hands through united prayer! We must pray for God's kingdom to come (Matthew 6:10). We must pray for laborers for the harvest (Matthew 9:38). We must pray for the Holy Spirit (Luke 11:13). We must pray that the love and power of the Holy Spirit will fill our church and fill our lives. We must pray that Jesus Christ will be glorified by His church, by us.

The Parable of the Unmerciful Servant (18:21–35)

21–22 According to Luke 17:4, Jesus earlier had said: "**If** [your brother] **sins against you seven times in a day, and seven times comes back to you and says, 'I repent,' forgive him.**" This was a new teaching for the disciples. Perhaps Peter had not been present when Jesus said those words, and so had doubts about Jesus' meaning. So Peter came to Jesus and asked how many times he had to forgive his brother. **"Up to seven times?" Peter was looking for an easy rule to follow.**

And Jesus answered, "**I tell you, not seven times, but seventy-seven times.**"[62] Jesus didn't mean that we should forgive our brother only seventy-seven (or 490) times and then stop. Jesus' meaning was this: No matter how many times our brother sins against us or how great his sins are, we must keep on forgiving him—even more than seventy-seven (or 490) times. And in these verses Jesus doesn't even say that our brother has to repent in order to obtain our forgiveness. As we have been freely forgiven by God, so we must freely and unconditionally forgive others, whether they repent or not (see Matthew 6:12,14–15; Mark 11:25–26 and comments).

Sometimes we must forgive our brother for several different sins. Sometimes we must keep on forgiving him for one sin committed over and over. But sometimes we must forgive him over and over for one sin committed just once. Perhaps we have forgiven our brother for a particular sin on one day, but the next day an unforgiving spirit comes upon us. If so, we must forgive him for that sin again—and again and again. Maybe we will have to forgive our brother seventy-seven times for that one sin!

23 Then Jesus told this parable to illustrate His teaching about forgiveness. In the Old Testament, the rule was an **eye for an eye** (Matthew 5:38). But in the kingdom of heaven, the rule is: "Forgive your brother and you will be forgiven." The **king** in this parable is God, and His **servants** represent believers.

24 The first servant owed the king **ten thousand talents**, that is, several million dollars.

25 When he could not pay what he owed, the king ordered that he and his family be sold as slaves.

26–27 But when the servant begged for more time, the king had pity and forgave him. He forgave him his entire debt.

28–31 But then the first servant went to another fellow servant who owed him a **hundred denarii**, that is, a few dollars. And the first servant showed the second man no mercy. He would not forgive his debt, nor even give him more time to pay it back.

32–35 When the king heard about this, he withdrew his forgiveness from that wicked unmerciful servant and put him in prison until he paid what he owed. **And this is how my heavenly Father will**

[62] In place of the words **seventy-seven times**, some versions of the Bible say "seven times seventy." The original Greek text can be translated either way. The point of the teaching is the same in either case.

treat each of you unless you forgive your brother from your heart (verse 35).

God keeps an account of the debts (the sins) of all men. The debt we owe God because of our sin is like the debt of the first servant—very large. We can never pay it back no matter how many good works we do. But God in His mercy forgives us completely. How can we, then, who have received such great forgiveness, not show mercy to others? Let us, therefore, forgive our brother, not just in words but **from** [our] **heart**.

This parable teaches that if we do not forgive our brother, God will withdraw the mercy He has shown to us. Some Christians say that anyone who does not show mercy to others has himself never received the mercy of God; that is, he was never a true Christian to begin with (Luke 7:41–43,47). But others believe that having received mercy and forgiveness from God, it is possible to lose it by refusing to forgive others (see General Article: Can We Lose Our Salvation?).

CHAPTER 19

Divorce (19:1–12)
(Mark 10:1–12)

1–9 See Mark 10:1–12 and comment.

10 Jesus, in teaching about marriage, had just said, "... **what God has joined together, let man not separate**" (verse 6). In other words, except for marital unfaithfulness, a man may not divorce his wife and marry another (verse 9). God's plan and desire is this: Once a man and woman are married they should remain married. Men are not like animals (see 1 Corinthians 7:10–11 and comment).

The disciples knew that problems often arise between husband and wife. If divorce is not allowed, then it would be better not to marry, they thought. "Better no marriage than an unhappy marriage" was a Jewish saying (Proverbs 21:9,19).

11 But Jesus answered that the teaching "**it is better not to marry**" (verse 10) is not meant for most people. Only those whom God especially calls to remain unmarried **can accept this teaching**; that is, **only those to whom it has been given** should remain unmarried (see 1 Corinthians 7:7–9 and comment).

Most people are called to be married. Indeed, the Jews considered marriage a duty (Genesis 2:24). To marry was a command of God to be obeyed (Jeremiah 29:6). The fact that the yoke of marriage cannot easily be thrown off is not sufficient reason for us to avoid marriage.

12 Jesus then mentioned three kinds of people who are free from the duty to marry. First are those who are **eunuchs** from birth. A few people are born with some bodily defect that makes it impossible for them to have sexual intercourse. Second are those who have been made eunuchs by other men. In Jesus' time, one cruel type of torture was to destroy or damage a man's sexual organs. Third are those who have been called by God to remain single **because of the kingdom of heaven**. They have been called to give all their attention to serving Christ. The Apostle Paul was such a person (see 1 Corinthians 7:32–35).

Therefore, Jesus concludes: "**The one who can accept this** (teaching not to marry) **should accept it**."

The Little Children and Jesus (19:13–15)
(Mark 10:13–16; Luke 18:15–17)

13–15 See Mark 10:13–16 and comment.

The Rich Young Man (19:16–30)
(Mark 10:17–31; Luke 18:18–30)

16–30 See Mark 10:17–31 and comment.

CHAPTER 20

The Parable of the Workers in the Vineyard (20:1–16)

1–2 Here, as in the parables of Matthew Chapter 13, Jesus describes what the kingdom of heaven is like. In this parable the **landowner** is God. In the parable, the landowner called some workers in the morning to work in his vineyard. In Jesus' time, farm workers worked twelve hours a day, from 6 A.M. to 6 P.M. The landowner **agreed to pay them a denarius for the day.**[63] That was a fair wage, and the workers were happy.

3–7 At the **third, sixth, ninth,** and **eleventh hour** (that is, at 9 A.M., 12 noon, 3 P.M., and 5 P.M.), the landowner found other workers who were unemployed. He sent them into his vineyard saying, "**I will pay you whatever is right**" (verse 4).

8–10 When **evening** came (6 P.M.), the landowner paid all the workers the same amount, **a denarius**, no matter how long they had worked.

We must understand two things in this parable. First, the **denarius** represents salvation. All who are chosen by God receive the same salvation equally, no matter how long they have served God—no matter how long they have been Christians.[64] The criminal on the cross beside Jesus believed only in the last minutes of his life, but he received the same salvation as any other believer in Christ (see Luke 23:39–43).

The second thing we must understand from these verses is that God is fair. He agreed to pay those who worked twelve hours **a denarius**, and He kept His agreement. But He was generous with those who worked less. He paid them more than they deserved. To be generous is never unfair. God can be generous with whom He chooses. God gives His grace to whom He chooses (see Romans 9:18–21 and comment).

Our salvation is always of grace. It does not depend on how many "hours" we work. We cannot earn our salvation; it is a gift of God (see Ephesians 2:8–9 and comment).

11–12 When those who had worked twelve hours found out that those who worked less got the same wage they did, they **began to grumble**. Why? Not because of any injustice, but because of their own envy.

Do we not often experience this same kind of envy? Someone gets a promotion or a higher salary, and what do we do? We grumble. We grumble because we are envious. We claim to grumble because of "injustice," but we are mistaken. It is because of envy. It is because we covet our neighbor's good fortune (Exodus 20:17).

Another example of this envy is found in the older brother in the parable of the lost son (see Luke 15:25–32). The older brother in that parable was like the workers who worked twelve hours. He had not been treated unfairly. His father told him, "**My son . . . everything I have is yours**" (Luke 15:31). Yet the older brother was angry. Why? Because he was envious of his younger brother.

13–15 Then the landowner said to one of them who had worked all day, "**I am not being unfair to you** (verse 13). If I want to be generous with those who worked less, that is my right. Are **you envious because I am generous?**" (verse 15).

Let us never grumble against God. When we grumble against our human masters, we grumble against God, because God put those human masters over us. If a human master is truly unjust, we can cry out to God (see James 5:4). But we may not grumble because of envy.

God has made an agreement with all

[63] The **denarius** was a Roman coin in common use during New Testament times.

[64] In heaven all believers receive the same salvation, the same eternal life. But they do receive different **rewards** according to their work on earth (see Matthew 16:27; 2 Corinthians 5:10 and comments).

believers. God agrees to give us a "wage," namely, eternal life;[65] and we agree to serve Him. Therefore, if along the way our work becomes hard or our situation becomes difficult, we have nothing to complain about. God will keep His end of the bargain; we must keep ours.

16 **So the last will be first, and the first will be last.** The last workers were paid first (verses 8–9). Sometimes those who believe in Christ late in life are given more grace and more fruitfulness than those who have been Christians most of their lives.

Those that work hard and try to make themselves first will often end up last. Those who rely on the grace of God will be first; those who rely on their own works will be last. Those who are grateful will be first; those who grumble and are envious will be last (see Mark 10:31 and comment).

Jesus Again Predicts His Death (20:17–19)
(Mark 10:32–34; Luke 18:31–34)

17–19 See Mark 10:32–34 and comment.

A Mother's Request (20:20–28)
(Mark 10:35–45; Luke 22:24–27)

20–28 See Mark 10:35–45 and comment.

Two Blind Men Receive Sight (20:29–34)
(Mark 10:46–52; Luke 18:35–43)

29–34 See Mark 10:46–52 and comment.

CHAPTER 21

The Triumphal Entry (21:1–11)
(Mark 11:1–11; Luke 19:28–40; John 12:12–16)

1–11 See Mark 11:1–11 and comment.

Jesus at the Temple (21:12–17)
(Mark 11:15–19; Luke 19:45–48)

12–17 See Mark 11:15–19 and comment.

The Fig Tree Withers (21:18–22)
(Mark 11:12–14,20–24)

18–19 See Mark 11:12–14 and comment.

20–22 See Mark 11:20–24 and comment.

The Authority of Jesus Questioned (21:23–27)
(Mark 11:27–33; Luke 20:1–8)

23–27 See Mark 11:27–33 and comment.

The Parable of the Two Sons (21:28–32)

28–29 Jesus told this parable to the Jewish leaders who prided themselves that they followed the law. The first son represents the **tax collectors and the prostitutes** (verse 31). They considered themselves unrighteous. They said to Jesus, as Peter had, "**Go away from me, Lord; I am a sinful man!**" (Luke 5:8). Such people give no promise of being religious. They say "No" to Jesus; but then they repent and turn to God (see Luke 18:13–14). And God will consider repentant sinners righteous, because in the end they do His will.

30–31 The second son represents the Jewish leaders. They said, "We are righteous, we are obedient. We will certainly obey God." But then they did not. God said through John the Baptist, "**Repent.**" But they did not repent. They did not believe in Christ. They did not love God;

---

[65] Eternal life is not like a real wage, because eternal life is always a gift. We never earn our eternal life.

they loved themselves. Thus, in the end, they did not obey God.

Jesus told the Jewish leaders that the repentant sinners like tax collectors and prostitutes would enter the kingdom of God before they would (see Luke 18:9–14). The **last will be first** (see Matthew 20:16 and comment).

Notice in the parable that neither son's behavior is good. The first son was wrong in speech; the second wrong in action. We can understand from the parable that God considers action to be more important than promises (see Matthew 7:21).

32 Then Jesus told the Jewish leaders in what way they had disobeyed God. John came to show them the **way of righteousness**, that is, how they should behave. But they did not believe John. They did not obey John; that is, they did not repent and do the works of repentance (Matthew 3:8). But the Gentiles, the sinners, believed John (see Luke 7:29–30).

Not only that, the Jewish leaders saw many people going after John and repenting. But still they refused to believe. Their condemnation will be great. And our condemnation will be great also, if we do not repent and turn to Christ and do God's will.

The Parable of the Tenants (21:33–46)

(Mark 12:1–12; Luke 20:9–19)

33–46 See Mark 12:1–12 and comment.

CHAPTER 22

The Parable of the Wedding Banquet (22:1–14)

1–2 Jesus often compared the kingdom of heaven to a great banquet (Matthew 8:11; Luke 14:15). In this parable the **king** represents God, and the **son** represents Christ.

3–5 The king had invited many guests, that is, the Jews. But most Jews did not believe that Christ was the Messiah, the Son of God. Therefore, they refused to come to a banquet in His honor. The king, with great patience, sent his servants two times to call the guests, but still they refused to come.

6 Not only did they refuse to come, but they also mistreated the **servants** who invited them. The servants represent Christ's disciples, whom the Jews persecuted.

7 The king, therefore, destroyed those **murderers** and **burned their city**. This was a prophecy of the destruction of Jerusalem, which was fulfilled forty years after Jesus' death. In 70 A.D. the Roman army came and destroyed Jerusalem and all the Jews living in it.

8–9 Because most of the Jews rejected God's invitation to Christ's banquet, God then invited the Gentiles (see Matthew 8:11–12; 21:43; Luke 14:15–24 and comments).

10 The servants went and called all kinds of people to the banquet, **both good and bad**. They invited **tax collectors** and **prostitutes** (see Matthew 21:31–32), outcasts and sinners. They gathered **all the people they could find**. There were **wheat** and **weeds** together (Matthew 13:29–30, 40–41). There were **good fish** and **bad** in the same net (Matthew 13:47–49).

11–13 One guest had no **wedding clothes**. The wedding clothes represent righteousness, that is, the righteousness of Christ, which we put on by faith. All who come to the banquet must be clothed in Christ's righteousness (Romans 13:14; Galatians 3:26–27; Philippians 3:8–9 and comments).

The one guest without proper wedding clothes represents all those who have not truly believed in Christ and put on His righteousness. They are the **bad** guests mentioned in verse 10, the "weeds," the "bad fish." Even though they have come to the king's house with all the other guests, they may not sit down to eat. They will be thrown out.

14 **For many are invited**, or called, **but few are chosen**. The Gospel of Christ is preached to all men, and many hear Christ's call. They come at first. They say Christ's Gospel is pleasing. They may agree with it. But in their hearts they do not fully give their lives to Christ. They come to Christ's wedding banquet to partake of all the tasty food—the blessings of Christ—but they are not prepared to stay and be servants of Christ. They are not **chosen**. Christ's servants must be chosen (see John 15:16).

Paying Taxes to Caesar (22:15–22)

(Mark 12:13–17; Luke 20:20–26)

15–22 See Mark 12:13–17 and comment.

Marriage at the Resurrection (22:23–33)

(Mark 12:18–27; Luke 20:27–40)

23–33 See Mark 12:18–27 and comment.

The Greatest Commandment (22:34–40)

(Mark 12:28–34)

34–40 See Mark 12:28–34 and comment.

Whose Son Is the Christ? (22:41–46)

(Mark 12:35–37; Luke 20:41–44)

41–46 See Mark 12:35–37 and comment.

CHAPTER 23

The Sins of the Jewish Leaders (23:1–12)

(Luke 11:46; 14:11)

1–2 In this chapter Jesus speaks in opposition to the **teachers of the law and the Pharisees**, the leaders of the Jewish people. But we must understand that this chapter is written about all religious leaders who act improperly, who misuse their authority. In this chapter Jesus describes the bad behavior of the Jewish leaders. Their main sin was hypocrisy. They tried to appear righteous outwardly, but inwardly they were unrighteous. All religious leaders are in constant danger of falling into this sin.

The teachers of the law and the Pharisees sit in Moses' seat. Moses, the great Jewish leader of the Old Testament, received the Jewish law from God and gave it to the Jews. The **teachers** and the **Pharisees** were experts in this law. They had now taken Moses' place in teaching the law to the people.

3 Therefore, Jesus says: "... **you must obey them.**" As long as they teach the true law as it is written in the Old Testament, then their teaching is correct and must be heeded. We must not condemn good teaching just because it is given by bad teachers. Nor can we disobey good laws just because they are executed by bad magistrates.

But Jesus warns: "Do not follow their example. Do as they say, but not as they do, **for they do not practice what they preach.**" They demand that others do things they won't do themselves.

4 The teachers of the law and the Pharisees added many unnecessary rules to the main Jewish law. These rules were a heavy load put on men's shoulders. The Jewish leaders did not **lift a finger** to help men carry that load. They gave no encouragement. They didn't set an example. Instead of helping men live better and more joyful lives, the Jewish leaders oppressed and discouraged men by giving them even more rules. These were rules and traditions of men, not of God (see Mark 7:8 and comment).

Compared with the heavy load placed on men by the Jewish leaders, the load

Jesus placed on men was very **light** (see Matthew 11:28,30).

5 Everything the Jewish leaders did was done in order to receive praise from men (see Matthew 6:1–2 and comment).

They made **their phylacteries wide**. A "phylactery" was a little leather box in which verses of Scripture were kept. These boxes were worn on the forehead and on the arm. The Jewish leaders wore large phylacteries so that people would think they were religious. Wearing a phylactery was not wrong in itself. But wearing it to receive praise was wrong. God always looks at the reason we do things.

In the same way, the Jewish leaders made the **tassles on their garments long** (Numbers 15:37–39). By this they hoped to show people that they were more religious than other men.

6 **They love the place of honor . . . and the most important seats**. It is not wrong to sit in "important seats." (Someone must sit in them!) But it is wrong to love sitting in them. It is not wrong to be honored; it is wrong to love honor (see Mark 12:38–39 and comment).

7 The Jewish leaders loved praise. They loved to be called "**Rabbi**," which means "great one." They especially loved to receive honor in public where all could see them honored.

They considered themselves great teachers, but they had not learned the first lesson taught in the school of Christ, namely, to be humble.

8 Jesus here warns His disciples that they must not seek such honor from men. They have only one **Master**, one **Rabbi**, that is, Jesus Himself. Compared with Jesus, all other Christians are equal, brothers and sisters in the family of God.

9 In the same way, Christians must not call any other man **father**, that is, "spiritual father." Only God is our spiritual Father. When we became Christians, we were born anew of the Spirit of God. We did not receive our new life from any man, only from God.

10 The disciples are not to be called **teacher**, or "master." They must not seek honor, as if their teaching came from themselves. They only teach what Christ and the Holy Spirit teach them. The one true teacher is Christ, the Messiah.

11 Instead of seeking to be great among men, the disciples are to be the servants of men (see Mark 10:43–44 and comment). The one who is most submissive and most servant-like will stand highest in the favor of God.

12 The teaching of Jesus is the opposite of the teaching of the world. Men of the world seek to exalt themselves. Jesus says that in the end they will be humbled, put down. But those who repent of their sin and humble themselves on earth will be exalted in heaven (see Matthew 5:5; 18:1–4; Mark 9:35; 1 Peter 5:5–6 and comments).

Woes On the Jewish Leaders (23:13–39)

(Mark 12:40; Luke 11:42–43,49–51; 13:34–35)

13 Now Jesus brings a number of charges or "woes" against the Jewish leaders. The first is that they **shut the kingdom of heaven in men's faces**. They prevented men from entering heaven because of their false teaching. They taught that man is saved by obeying the law, but that is false. No man is saved by obeying the law (see Galatians 15–16 and comment). Man is saved only by grace through faith (Ephesians 2:8).

The Jewish leaders themselves refused to repent and believe. They refused to accept Christ, who is the **way** to heaven (John 14:6). And not only that, they prevented others from believing in Him and finding salvation (see Luke 11:52). The people saw that their leaders did not believe, and so they followed their example.

14 See Mark 12:40 and comment.[66]

15 The Jews did attempt to win converts to the Jewish religion. Occasionally they traveled to foreign countries to do so. Some Gentiles became Jews as a

---

[66] Not all ancient manuscripts of Matthew contain verse 14. A similar verse is found in Mark 12:40.

result. But they became Jews just like the teachers of the law and the Pharisees, who were their teachers. They became Jews only outwardly (see Romans 2:28–29 and comment). They, too, refused to accept Christ. Thus they received no benefit from becoming Jews. They became sons **of hell**, that is, they became worthy of eternal punishment. The hypocritical Jewish leaders were also sons of hell; but their converts, who were not even Jews according to the flesh, were doubly sons of hell.

16–20 The Jewish leaders used to swear an oath whenever they made an agreement or promise (see Matthew 5:33 and comment). But they tried to invent ways to avoid having to keep their oaths. They said, "If we swear by the temple, the oath is not binding. Only if we swear by the gold of the temple do we have to keep our oath" (verse 16). They also said that swearing by the altar meant nothing. Only if they swore by the gift on the altar would they have to keep their oath (verse 18).

But their teaching was totally false. The temple was greater than the gold of the temple. The altar was greater than the gift on the altar. How could they say that swearing by the temple and altar meant nothing? The gold of the temple was included in the temple; the gift on the altar was included in the altar. Therefore, there was no difference between swearing by the temple and swearing by the gold, or between swearing by the altar and swearing by the gift. Whatever they swore by, they had to keep their oath.

But the Jewish leaders were hypocrites. They never intended to keep their oaths. There were only inventing excuses for not keeping their word.

21–22 When we swear by anything that belongs to God, we swear by God Himself. If we swear by the gold, we swear by His temple. If we swear by the temple, we swear by the **one who dwells in it**—God (verse 21). If we swear by heaven, we swear by God's throne, and by **the one who sits on it**—God (verse 22). Whatever we swear by, we swear by God, because He made everything.

But Jesus' main teaching is this: Do not swear at all. If a man is honest and sincere, he does not need to swear. Swearing oaths is a sign of dishonesty (see Matthew 5:34–37 and comment).

23 The Jews always tithed; that is, they set aside one tenth of all their crops and animals and offered them to the Lord (Leviticus 27:30). This was good and necessary. All Christians, under ordinary circumstances, ought to give at least one tenth of their income to the Lord. After all, even the Pharisees did that much.

However, there are more important laws than the law of tithing (Micah 6:8). The Jewish leaders tithed, it is true, but they neglected the most important matters of the law—**justice, mercy and faithfulness**. They neglected the **love of God** (Luke 11:42). True obedience to God means to obey God in these great matters; such things as tithes and sacrifices are less important (1 Samuel 15:22). **"For I desire mercy, not sacrifice,"** God said through the prophet Hosea (Hosea 6:6).

24 Here Jesus quotes a Jewish parable. To keep the small laws and disobey the important laws was like fussily picking a small object (like a **gnat**) out of one's tea, but ignoring a large object (like a cockroach—or a **camel**!) and swallowing it down with the tea.

25 The Jewish leaders observed many rules concerning the cleaning of cups and dishes (Mark 7:4). Jesus said that the teachers of the law and the Pharisees were like cups washed on the outside but not on the inside. The Jews obeyed the law outwardly so that men would praise them; but they did not keep the law in their hearts. They were **full of greed and self-indulgence**.

How useless it is to wash the outside of a cup while leaving the inside dirty! If the inside is dirty, whatever is in the cup will be dirty too, and thus unfit to drink (see Luke 11:40–41 and comment).

26 Jesus told the Jewish leaders that they should first clean their hearts, the **inside of the cup and dish**. Jesus said, **"What comes out of a man is what makes him 'unclean'"** (see Mark 7:20 and comment). If one's heart is clean, that is, if one's inner motives are pure, then one's outward behavior will also be pure.

If the heart is unclean, washing the outside will do no good. God looks at the heart (1 Samuel 16:7).

Blind Pharisee! That man is truly blind who does not see the sin in his own heart.

27–28 The Jewish leaders were like tombs that had been whitewashed on the outside. Outwardly they appeared to be spiritually alive and well, but inwardly they were spiritually dead, corrupt.

29 The Jews of Jesus' time honored the Old Testament prophets. They built large tombs for them like martyrs' memorials. Yet they refused to honor Christ and His disciples. It is much easier to honor a dead prophet than to heed a living one.

30 The Jews admitted that their ancestors had killed the prophets. When the Old Testament prophets came to denounce Israel's sins and turn the people to God, most of the Jews of that time rejected them and killed them (Hebrews 11:32–38). But the Jews of Jesus' time said, "We wouldn't have done that if we had been alive then." But even as they said that, they were planning to murder Christ, the Messiah, of whom all the Old Testament prophets bore witness.

31–32 As their ancestors had done before them, so also did the Jews of Jesus' time. They were no better than their forefathers. The Jews caused Jesus to be put to death (see Acts 7:51–52). And they persecuted and killed His followers (see Acts 7:58–60; 8:1). Therefore, Jesus said to them in an ironical way: "Okay, I know you are planning to kill me. Go ahead; do it. **Fill up . . . the measure of the sin of your forefathers!**". Their forefathers had killed the Old Testament prophets. But there was still some killing left to do. There was still some guilt to add to their forefathers' guilt, because the Messiah and His followers had not yet been killed. Only when the Jews had killed Christ and His disciples, would the measure of the sin of their forefathers be "filled up." The evil work of their forefathers would then be complete.

33 How will such evildoers escape God's wrath? **You snakes! You brood of vipers!** The Jewish leaders were deceitful and poisonous, like snakes and vipers. Christ was usually meek and gentle, but when He was opposing hypocrites and false teachers His rebukes could be severe (see Mark 11:15–17).

34 Then Jesus again said ironically: "**Therefore**—so you can finish filling up your father's guilt—**I am sending you prophets and wise men and teachers.**" These **prophets and wise men and teachers** were Jesus' disciples. Jesus knew that the Jews would persecute them, just as they would persecute Him (see Mark 8:31; 13:13; Acts 14:19; 17:13).

35–36 Then Jesus warned the Jews that the final punishment for killing all the prophets was going to fall upon the Jews of His generation. They would be held responsible not only for the murders they carried out themselves but also for the murders carried out by their forefathers. **All this will come upon this generation** (see Luke 11:50–51). The punishment was the destruction of Jerusalem and all its inhabitants, which occurred in 70 A.D.

The Jews of Jesus' generation would receive the punishment for all the murders of righteous men in the Old Testament from **Abel** to **Zechariah, son of Berakiah**[67] (verse 35). Abel was the son of the first man and woman, and he was killed by his own brother (Genesis 4:1–8). Zechariah was the prophet whose murder is mentioned in 2 Chronicles 24:20–21. In the Jewish version of the Old Testament, 2 Chronicles is the last book. Therefore, the expression "from Abel to Zechariah" signifies all of the Old Testament prophets.

37 Jesus came to seek and save the lost sheep of Israel (Matthew 15:24). He was Himself a Jew. He loved the Jews. Even when He rebuked the Jewish leaders, He loved them. He wept over

[67] The father of the Zechariah mentioned in this verse was Jehoiada (2 Chronicles 24:20). Berakiah was the father of another Zechariah (Zechariah 1:1). It is not known if this second Zechariah was killed or not. Therefore, there is some uncertainty as to which Zechariah Matthew means here.

the city of Jerusalem (Luke 19:41). He longed to protect the Jews from the coming tribulation, from God's wrath. But they would not accept His protection. They would not accept Him as Savior and Messiah.

38 Therefore, the Jews were left alone without protection. Jesus said to them, "**Your house is left to you desolate**. That is, your great temple will be destroyed, together with your entire city."

39 So the Jews killed the only one who could have saved them. But they will see Him again at the end of the world when He comes to call His elect (Mark 13:26–27). At that time all men will recognize Him. They will call out: "**Blessed is he who comes in the name of the Lord**" (Psalm 118:26). But those who have rejected Him in this world will call out in fear, because at that time Christ will come not as Savior but as judge. Those who have rejected Christ will not enter His kingdom; rather, they will remain forever in hell.

CHAPTER 24

Signs of the End of the Age (24:1–14)

(Mark 13:1–13; Luke 21:5–19)

1–14 See Mark 13:1–13 and comment.

The Great Tribulation (24:15–28)

(Mark 13:14–23; Luke 21:20–24)

15–28 See Mark 13:14–23 and comment.

The End of the World (24:29–31)

(Mark 13:24–27; Luke 21:25–28)

29–31 See Mark 13:24–27 and comment.

The End of Jerusalem (24:32–35)

(Mark 13:28–31; Luke 21:29–33)

32–35 See Mark 13:28–31 and comment.

The Day and Hour Unknown (24:36–44)

(Mark 13:32,35; Luke 12:39–40; 17:26–27,34–35)

36 No one knows **that day or hour** when Christ will come again—not even Christ Himself. Therefore, to try to predict when He will return is a vain exercise (see Mark 13:32 and comment).

37–39 In ancient times man's wickedness was great, and God was displeased. Therefore, He determined to destroy all men and all living creatures by sending a great flood upon the earth. One man, **Noah**, was righteous and found favor with God. Therefore, God told Noah to build a great boat, so that he and his family might be spared.

All other men at that time were enjoying the pleasures of the world. They did not fear the judgment of God. They probably laughed at Noah for building a boat. They didn't believe that a flood would come. They were not ready. And they all perished (Genesis 6:5–22; 7:6–12,17–24).

The **coming of the Son of Man**—that is, the coming of Christ at the end of the world—will be like that flood. It will come without warning. And all who are not counted righteous in God's sight will receive eternal punishment in hell.[68]

40–41 When the Son of Man comes there will be judgment on the earth. His angels will gather the chosen (Mark 13:27). Those who are not chosen—the unrighteous, those without faith—will be

---

[68] When a person dies, for him the world has, in effect, come to an end. After death, there is no longer any chance to repent and become righteous in God's sight. Those who have died will be judged at the end of the world according to how they have behaved while they were alive.

destroyed (see Matthew 13:40–42,47–50 and comment).

The two men in the field (verse 40) appear the same outwardly. But one will be taken to heaven (1 Thessalonians 4:16–17), and the other will be left to perish in hell. And it will be the same with the two women grinding (verse 41).

42 We cannot tell the day Christ will come; therefore, for that very reason, we must remain always ready for His coming (see Mark 13:33–37 and comment).

43–44 Christ will come like a thief in the night—that is, when He is not expected. A burglar never announces at what time he is going to rob a house! Therefore, we must remain alert all night (see 1 Thessalonians 5:2–6). Let us constantly remain obedient and pure in our Lord's eyes. Let us not leave one sin unconfessed. Then when He comes, we shall be ready (see Revelation 3:3).

Therefore, **to keep watch** (verse 42) and **to be ready** (verse 44) means to look always for the Lord, to meditate on Him, to desire His company, to remain obedient to His will, and to immediately repent of any known sin. Only if we do these things will we be ready for His coming.

Two Kinds of Servant (24:45–51) (Luke 12:42–46)

45 In this parable about Christ's second coming, the **master** is Christ, and the **faithful and wise servant** is any disciple to whom Christ has given some responsibility in the church. Especially, the parable is a warning for church leaders, who have been given the work of feeding those in the church with spiritual food.

46–47 Let all of Christ's servants remain busy at the task Christ has given them. If they are faithful in fulfilling a small responsibility, Christ will give them responsibility for much more (Matthew 25:20–21). Indeed, in heaven they will be put in charge of **all** Christ's possessions.

48–51 But if any disciple misuses the authority Christ has given him, or does not fulfill his responsibility, Christ will return on a day which that disciple does not expect. And He will punish that disciple, that servant. That servant will be driven out of God's household and sent to hell, **where there will be weeping and gnashing of teeth** (see Matthew 25:28–30; Luke 21:34–36).

CHAPTER 25

The Parable of the Ten Virgins (25:1–13)

1 This is a parable of Christ's second coming and of the final judgment. In this parable, the **bridegroom** is Christ, and the **ten virgins** represent the church waiting for Christ's return.

According to Jewish marriage custom in Jesus' time, the bridegroom came to the bride's house to fetch her. At that time there was a banquet. The bridesmaids would go out to welcome the bridegroom on his arrival. If he came at night, they would need lamps.

2–5 There are two kinds of people in the church: the **wise** and the **foolish** (see Matthew 7:24–27). The foolish have no **oil** in their lamps, that is, no Holy Spirit. They are not prepared to meet Christ. They have not truly known Christ and have not been born again of the Spirit (John 3:5). They are, in fact, false Christians (see Matthew 13:40–42,47–50). Only by the Holy Spirit will our lamps burn; only by the oil of the Holy Spirit can we be lights in the world (Matthew 5:14).

6–8 When the bridegroom arrived, the foolish virgins realized that they had no oil. So they asked the wise virgins to give them some of theirs.

9 But the wise virgins refused to give the foolish virgins any oil. From this we must learn an important spiritual lesson. The Holy Spirit comes directly from God. Grace and salvation come directly from God. We cannot borrow them from other men. Each of us must stand alone before the judgment seat of Christ. On that day we will not be able to call upon our friends for help. It will be too late then to get oil for our lamp.

10 The foolish virgins went to the shop to get oil. Perhaps the shops were not open; it was the middle of the night. While they were away, the bridegroom came. The wise virgins went in with him. **And the door was shut**.

11–13 The foolish virgins had lost their chance. They had not been ready. Christ did not know them (see Luke 13:24–27). There was a time when, if they had knocked, the door would have opened (Matthew 7:7). But now that time was gone forever.

Therefore keep watch (see Matthew 24:42–44; Mark 13:35 and comments). Let us be sure there is oil in our lamps (see Luke 12:35–38).

The Parable of the Talents (25:14–30)
(Luke 19:11–27)

14–18 **Again, it** (the second coming of Christ) **will be like a man going on a journey**. The **man** is Christ. Christ entrusts His followers with different gifts, or **talents**.[69] These gifts are both natural and spiritual. They may be natural abilities; or they may be the gifts of the Holy Spirit (1 Corinthians 12:7–11); or they may be fruits of the Holy Spirit (Galatians 5:22–23). The Holy Spirit Himself is a gift. Everything we have is a gift from God. We can boast of nothing that is our own. Indeed, the only thing we can call our own is our sin.

The parable's meaning is this: Christ gives different gifts to different people according to their ability. He gives to some more, and to others less. But whatever gifts He gives, He wants us to use them. If He gives us land, He wants us to diligently raise crops. If He gives us the chance to study, He wants us to study hard. If He gives us the gift of teaching, or of leadership, then we must teach and lead diligently and wisely. If He gives us wealth, we must use it in His service. Christ does not expect everyone to return the same amount to Him (Mark 4:20). But He does expect that we return to Him all that we can. Especially, He expects from us our love, our faith, our obedience.

In the parable, one servant received only a small gift, just one talent. He was ashamed. He was lazy. He did not use the gift the master had given him. He buried the money in the ground (verse 18).

Although they are not mentioned in this parable, there are many people who receive two or five talents in this life and bury all of them in the ground. Their guilt will be even greater than the guilt of the man with only one talent.

19–23 The servants who had used their gifts well were rewarded. Because they had been faithful with a **few things** on earth, the master put them in charge of **many things** in heaven (see Matthew 24:45–47).

24–25 However, the servant with the one talent had despised his gift. He thought his gift was so small that he could never please his master. He thought his master would demand more from him than he could ever earn with his gift. He even accused his master of being unjust—"**harvesting where you have not sown**". His accusation was untrue. God is always just. But wicked men always try to blame God for their own wickedness.

The wicked servant tried to defend himself. He said, "**I . . . hid your talent**. I put it in a safe place. Here, take what is yours. I have not made it more, but neither have I made it less." He hoped thereby to escape punishment for his laziness.

26–27 The master replied, "You say that you knew I was a **hard man**? Then why didn't you at least put the money in a bank, so that I might have gained interest? You have cheated me. You have not rightly used what I gave you."

28–29 The wicked and lazy servant in the end did not preserve his talent; he lost it. If we do not use our spiritual and material blessings in God's service, they will be taken away from us. If we grieve the Holy Spirit, He will depart from us.

---

[69] A talent was a weight or measure of money. One talent was worth more than a thousand dollars.

To the extent we use God's gifts in His service, to that extent He will give us more. Paul wrote to Timothy: **Do not neglect your gift** (1 Timothy 4:14). But if we hide His gifts, or use them selfishly for ourselves, He will take them back (see Matthew 13:12; Mark 4:24–25 and comments).

30 The punishment for a servant who misuses a gift of God is very severe. When we do not use God's gift in His service, we cheat God, we oppose God. Therefore, He will oppose us. Many people say to themselves, "I can do so little for God," and they use that as an excuse for doing nothing. Such people are like the wicked and lazy servant of this parable.

The parable of the ten minas[70] recorded in Luke 19:11–27 is very similar to this parable of the talents. There are two main differences between these two parables. First, in Luke's parable, there are ten servants instead of three, and all ten get the same gift—that is, ten minas. However, they get different rewards according to how faithfully they used their gifts. The servant who earned ten additional minas was very faithful. The servant who earned five additional minas was less faithful. The servant who hid his mina was unfaithful. Each of the servants received a reward according to his faithfulness. Therefore, the meaning of Luke's parable is the same as that of Matthew's parable: namely, that we all must use the gifts of God as diligently as we can, and that God will reward each of us according to our work and faithfulness (Matthew 16:27; 2 Corinthians 5:10).

The second difference in Luke's parable of the minas is that the master **went to a distant country to have himself appointed king** (Luke 19:12). But his subjects **sent a delegation after him to say, 'We don't want this man to be our king'** (Luke 19:14). Then at the end of the parable, the king had those enemies put to death (Luke 19:27).

These extra details about the king do not change the meaning of the parable. However, they do describe a historic occurrence. Archelaus, the son of King Herod (see Matthew 2:1,22) went to the Roman emperor after his father's death to confirm his succession to his father's throne. But a delegation of Jews went after him and appealed to the emperor asking that Archelaus not be made king over them. As a result, the emperor reduced Archelaus' authority. Later, Archelaus persecuted the Jews who had opposed him.

Let us not be among those who oppose the true king, Christ, the King of kings. If we reject His gifts, if we refuse to serve Him, we shall bring upon ourselves eternal condemnation.

The Sheep and the Goats (25:31–46)

31 In this section Jesus gives us a description of what the final judgment will be like. He Himself will come in glory to judge (Mark 13:26; John 5:22). Christ **will sit on his throne**, which is the throne of judgment (Revelation 20:11).

32–33 Christ will judge all the **nations**. On that day every man of every nation will acknowledge that Christ is Lord (Philippians 2:10–11). And Christ will **separate the people one from another**. Judgment is the act of separation. Christ will be like a shepherd who separates sheep and goats (Ezekiel 34:17). He will put the **sheep**, that is, the **righteous** (verse 37), on His right hand, and the **goats**, the unrighteous, on His left.

34 Then Christ will invite the righteous to receive their inheritance, prepared for them **since the creation of the world**. The righteous have been chosen from before the beginning of the world (see Ephesians 1:4). God knew from the beginning who would live righteously; that is, He knew who would repent and believe in Christ.

Man has the freedom to choose between right and wrong. Man has the freedom to go through the **narrow gate** or the **wide gate** (see Matthew 7:13–14). It is each man's choice. If a man chooses to

---

[70] A mina was worth three month's wages.

disobey God and walk through the wide gate, it is his own fault. He cannot blame God (see Romans 9:19–21).

Even though people are free to choose, yet God knows beforehand how each one will choose. God's knowledge is without limit. He knows everything. **The Lord knows those who are his** (2 Timothy 2:19). Their names are written in the **book of life** (Revelation 3:5; 21:27). And He has prepared a **kingdom** for each one (see Luke 12:32).

There is no more important question anyone can ask than this: "On the day of judgment, will I be standing on the King's right hand, or on His left?"

35–36 On what basis, by what means, will Christ separate men? For what reason will He call some to be on His right hand, and others to be on His left? The answer is this: Those who during their life on earth performed acts of love to Jesus will be placed on His right hand. They will be counted righteous (Hebrews 6:10).

37–39 But the righteous at first will not understand. They don't remember that they had done anything for Jesus Himself. They don't consider their simple acts of love to be worthy of special credit. They do not consider themselves worthy of honor. They are humble.

40 Then Jesus will answer: "**What you did for one of the least of these brothers of mine, you did for me.** All those acts of love and mercy you showed to others, you showed also to me."

Jesus is a loving shepherd. He came to earth to seek the lost. He loves all men. He loves them like brothers. He can put Himself in man's place. He feels our infirmities (Hebrews 4:15; 5:2). That is why when we show love to another person, it is as if we were showing love to Christ. Christ is not here on earth in the flesh. But we all have the chance to serve Him by serving others[71] (see Proverbs 19:17; Matthew 10:42; Mark 9:41).

It is important to remember one thing here: It is not because the righteous have performed acts of love that they are saved. They are saved only through faith. But these acts of love are signs of true faith. When Christ sees us perform these acts of love, He knows our faith is true. First comes faith; then, second, comes the fruit of faith, which is works of love (see Ephesians 2:8–9; James 2:14–17 and comments). **The only thing that counts is faith expressing itself through love** (Galatians 5:6).

41–45 Then the King will send those on His left hand to eternal punishment, **the eternal fire prepared for the devil and his angels** (see Revelation 20:10). Those on His left hand are the ones who did not perform acts of love to Christ. They had thought they were serving Christ. Perhaps they went to church. Perhaps they gave tithes. They took pride in their "religious" works. But they did these works only to win praise for themselves. They did not truly love their neighbor. They did not realize that when they refused to help their neighbor in need, they were also, in fact, refusing to help Christ. **If anyone says, "I love God," yet hates his brother, he is a liar. For anyone who does not love his brother, whom he has seen, cannot love God, whom he has not seen** (1 John 4:20).

46 **Then they will go away to eternal punishment**. The last judgment is final. There is no appeal. God judges fairly, but His judgment remains forever. Let every man and woman think about the judgment of God. On that day, will God say to us: "**Come . . . take your inheritance**" (verse 34)? Or will He say: "**Depart from me . . . into the eternal fire**" (verse 41)?

There is another thing to think about also. For what kind of sins did those on the King's left hand receive eternal punishment? Murder? Adultery? Theft? Big sins? No. Their sin was neglecting to do good. Many people wouldn't call that a sin at all. Many people suppose that sin means only doing something bad. But Jesus teaches us here that sin is also

---

71 Usually in the New Testament, only Christians are called **brothers** of Christ. Only Christians are sons of God. But according to the context of this verse, Christ here calls all men "brothers." We are to show love to all men, not only to Christians (Matthew 5:44; Mark 12:31).

omitting to do something good when we have opportunity. Such sins are called "sins of omission." These are things we ought to have done but did not. Such was the sin of the ten virgins: they did not bring oil for their lamps (verse 3). Such was the sin of the wicked servant: he did not use his one talent (verse 27). It is mainly for sins like these that people will be punished on the day of judgment.

How many opportunities have we missed to do good this past month? This past week? This very day? How many times could we have fed someone, clothed someone, visited someone, cared for someone, but didn't? Oh God, forgive us. We have not done what we ought to have done. We have not loved as we ought to have loved. Oh Father, have mercy upon us!

Now, is it not clear why we can never be saved by our righteous works? Only by the grace and mercy of God, and through faith in the Savior Jesus Christ, can we be saved from eternal punishment.

CHAPTER 26

The Plot Against Jesus (26:1–5)
(Mark 14:1–2; Luke 22:1–2)

1–5 See Mark 14:1–2 and comment.

Jesus Anointed at Bethany (26:6–13)
(Mark 14:3–9; John 12:1–8)

6–13 See Mark 14:3–9 and comment.

Judas Agrees to Betray Jesus (26:14–16)
(Mark 14:10–11; Luke 22:3–6)

14–16 See Mark 14:10–11 and comment.

The Lord's Supper (26:17–30)
(Mark 14:12–26; Luke 22:7–23)

17–30 See Mark 14:12–26 and comment.

Jesus Predicts Peter's Denial (26:31–35)
(Mark 14:27–31; Luke 22:33–34; John 13:37–38)

31–35 See Mark 14:27–31 and comment.

Gethsemane (26:36–46)
(Mark 14:32–42; Luke 22:39–46)

36–46 See Mark 14:32–42 and comment.

Jesus Arrested (26:47–56)
(Mark 14:43–52; Luke 22:47–53; John 18:1–11)

47–56 See Mark 43–52 and comment.

Before the Sanhedrin (26:57–68)
(Mark 14:53–65; Luke 22:63–71)

57–68 See Mark 14:53–65 and comment.

Peter Disowns Jesus (26:69–75)
(Mark 14:66–72; Luke 22:54–62; John 18:15–18,25–27)

69–75 See Mark 14:66–72 and comment.

CHAPTER 27

Judas Hangs Himself (27:1–10)

1–2 See Mark 15:1 and comment.

3 When Judas, the disciple who had betrayed Christ (Mark 14:10–11), **saw that Jesus was condemned** and led away as a criminal, **he was seized with remorse**. Judas had perhaps supposed that at the last minute Jesus would overcome His captors and escape, and then he would have the thirty silver coins and no harm would have been done. But now Judas saw Jesus being led away to die, and he was filled with remorse.

This remorse, however, was not true repentance, but rather the regret that comes from an unclean conscience. Judas thought he could clear his conscience by returning the money the chief priests had given him for betraying Jesus (Matthew 26:15).

4–5 But returning the money did nothing for Judas' conscience. Without true repentance a man cannot be cleansed. Judas felt bad. The Jews despised him. (No one respects a traitor.) Jesus' followers despised him. He despised himself. He had no friends. He knew he had sinned. He even confessed his sin to the priests and elders (verse 4). But this was not enough. Many hardened criminals can say, "I have sinned," without repenting. To repent is to humble oneself before God and cry out for mercy, and to turn utterly from that sin. To confess one's sin is only the first step in repentance (see 1 John 1:9 and comment).

The chief priests and elders didn't care about Judas' unclean conscience. They shared in his sin, but they felt no remorse. Nor did they try to comfort Judas. They left him to his own terror and despair. Partners in sin never make loyal friends in the end.

Judas, in despair and hating his own life, went and hanged himself. As he was dying, or shortly after he was dead, **he fell headlong** and **his body burst open** (see Acts 1:18 and comment).

6 The chief priests had been happy to take the money from the temple treasury to pay Judas. But they were not happy to put the money back into the treasury. It was **blood money**, they said—that is, money used to arrest and execute someone, namely Jesus.

7–8 The priests took the money that Judas returned and bought a field with it known as the **potter's field**. They bought it for use as a burial ground for Gentiles who happened to die in Jerusalem. Because it was a burial ground, it became known as the **Field of Blood**. It was also called a "field of blood" because Judas killed himself there (see Acts 1:18–19).

According to Acts 1:18, Judas bought the field. But he "bought" it only in a legal sense. It was the priests who bought the field; but because they refused to accept Judas' money as belonging to the treasury, they bought it in Judas' name. Legally, then, it was Judas' field. Therefore, it can be said that he bought it.

9–10 Matthew mentions two prophecies in these verses: one from Zechariah, and the second from Jeremiah. In the Old Testament, these two prophecies are not connected historically.

According to Zechariah 11:12–13, the people of Israel paid Zechariah **thirty pieces of silver** for his service as a prophet. But the Lord told him to return the money to the **potter**.[72] So Zechariah threw the thirty pieces of silver **into the house of the Lord to the potter** (Zechariah 11:13). In the same way, Judas threw the thirty silver coins he had gotten into the temple (verse 5). And then the money was used to buy the **potter's field**.

According to Jeremiah 32:8–9, Jeremiah bought a field with **seventeen shekels of silver**. In the same way, the priests bought the potter's field for thirty silver coins.

Matthew joins these two prophecies together to show how everything that

[72] The word **potter** in Zechariah 11:13 can also be translated "treasury."

happened in Jesus' life was a fulfillment of what was written in the Old Testament.

Thirty silver coins was the value the leaders of Israel placed on Christ—**the price set on him by the people of Israel** (verse 9). That was all the Son of God was worth to them—just the value of a potter's field!

Jesus Before Pilate (27:11–31)
(Mark 15:2–20; Luke 23:1–3,18–25; John 19:1–3)

11–31 See Mark 15:2–20 and comment.

The Crucifixion (27:32–44)
(Mark 15:21–32; Luke 23:26–43; John 19:17–24)

32–44 See Mark 15:21–32 and comment.

The Death of Jesus (27:45–56)
(Mark 15:33–41; Luke 23:44–49; John 19:28–30)

45–56 See Mark 15:33–41 and comment.

The Burial of Jesus (27:57–61)
(Mark 15:42–47; Luke 23:50–56; John 19:38–42)

57–61 See Mark 15:42–47 and comment.

The Guard at the Tomb (27:62–66)

62 **The next day, the one after Preparation Day,**[73] was the Sabbath, Saturday. The last supper occurred on Thursday. The crucifixion and burial of Jesus occurred on Friday, the day of preparation. Then, the **next day**, Saturday, the Jewish leaders went to Pilate to ask for an extra guard of Roman soldiers.

63–64 They remembered that Jesus had said He would rise again (Mark 8:31; 9:31; 10:34). They considered that Jesus was a **deceiver** (verse 63). They supposed, therefore, that His disciples were deceivers also, and that they would come and steal Jesus' body from the tomb and then say, "Look, He has risen!" If that happened, all the people would believe that Jesus was the Messiah after all, and they would follow His disciples. The Jewish leaders would be disgraced. Therefore, the leaders wanted to make sure that Jesus' disciples did not steal His body from the tomb.

In the end, it wasn't Jesus and His disciples who were the deceivers. It was the Jewish leaders themselves who were deceivers. When the tomb was found to be empty on Sunday morning, they began to spread the rumor that the disciples had stolen the body (Matthew 28:12–13).

65–66 But Matthew in these verses proves that rumor to be false. The Jews had probably already placed their own temple guard at the tomb. Pilate's words "**Take a guard**" can also be translated, "You have a guard." In addition to the temple guard, Pilate apparently gave them an extra guard of Roman soldiers (verse 66). Therefore, there was no way the disciples could have broken into the tomb to steal the body.

These same guards would the next day bear witness that Christ had indeed risen. The Jewish leaders had called the guards to keep the tomb shut. Next day the Jews would have to pay them to keep their mouths shut! (see Matthew 28:11–15).

---

[73] Preparation Day was the day before the Sabbath; that is, it was the preparation for the Sabbath (Saturday). **Preparation Day**, therefore, was always on a Friday (see Mark 14:12 and comment).

CHAPTER 28

The Resurrection (28:1–8)
(Mark 16:1–8; Luke 24:1–8; John 20:1)

1–8 See Mark 16:1–8 and comment.

Jesus Appears to the Women (28:9–10)

9–10 The first people to whom Jesus appeared after His resurrection were Mary Magdalene and Mary the mother of James, the same women who had watched Jesus on the cross (see Mark 15:40 and comment). He appeared to them **suddenly**. Imagine their surprise and joy! Here was Jesus Himself. He was not dead: He had overcome death!

Jesus instructed the women to go and tell the disciples to go to Galilee, where He would meet them. Thus the promise Jesus made to His disciples at the last supper would soon be fulfilled (see Mark 14:28). The women did as they were commanded and went at once and told the disciples (see John 20:10–18 and comment).

The Guards' Report (28:11–15)

11 The soldiers sent to guard the tomb saw the angel of the Lord roll back the stone from the mouth of the tomb (verses 2–3). Then they trembled and **became like dead men**—that is, they fainted (verse 4). When they came to their senses they went and reported to the chief priests what had happened.

12–13 The Jewish priests and elders decided to pay the soldiers to tell a lie, the lie that Jesus' disciples stole the body while the soldiers slept (see Matthew 27:63–64 and comment). It was a poor lie: if they were asleep, how could they have told what had happened?

14 To sleep on duty was a great crime for a guard to commit. Guards who neglected their duty in this way could receive the death sentence (Acts 12:19). If the Roman soldiers guarding the tomb said that they had been sleeping, they would be in great danger from Pilate. This explains why the soldiers went first to the Jewish chief priests. The Jewish leaders promised to defend them if Pilate should hear of the matter. It was a false promise; the Jews could have done very little to protect Roman soldiers.

15 However, because of the money they were offered, the soldiers were willing to take the risk of being punished. So they went about and spread the rumor that they had fallen asleep, and that Jesus' disciples had come and stolen the body. Many people believed that story. They still believed it at the time Matthew wrote his Gospel.

The Great Commission (28:16–20)

16 When the disciples learned from the women that Jesus had risen, they did not immediately go to Galilee. First, Peter and John went to the tomb to see if the women's report was true (Luke 24:9–12; John 20:1–3). But even though they found the tomb empty as the women had said, the disciples continued to remain in hiding in Jerusalem for fear of the Jews (John 20:10,19). There Jesus appeared to them at least twice (Luke 24:36; John 20:19,26). Only after that did the eleven disciples depart for the mountain in Galilee where Jesus had told them to go.

17 When the eleven disciples saw Him, they worshiped Him. **But some doubted**. These doubters were probably other disciples and followers of Jesus who had not yet seen Christ since His death and resurrection. Paul wrote that Jesus **appeared to more than five hundred of the brothers at the same time** (1 Corinthians 15:6). Some of these five hundred may have **doubted** initially. Like the disciples themselves at first, they may have thought they were seeing a ghost (Luke 24:37).

18 **Then Jesus came to them**, and He said one of the most amazing things ever spoken: **"All authority in heaven and on earth has been given to me."** No ordinary man could ever have said that.

Only God's own Son could make such a statement.

The devil had once offered Jesus **all the kingdoms of the world** (Matthew 4:8–9). But now, having been obedient to His Father, Jesus had received not only authority over all the earth but also over the heavens as well, authority over the entire universe (see Ephesians 1:20–22; Philippians 2:9–11 and comments).

In the beginning, before He came to earth, all the authority in heaven and earth belonged to Jesus. But even though He was **in very nature God** ... [He] **made himself nothing, taking the very nature of a servant, being made in human likeness** (Philippians 2:6–7). In other words, Jesus gave up His authority temporarily while He was here on earth. Now, after His resurrection, He received it back again.

19 **Therefore**—that is, because Jesus has all authority—He told His followers to **make disciples of all nations.**[74] Because Jesus is Lord of the universe, we must go and establish His rule in every corner of the earth. He is the Lord **of all nations**; therefore, we must go to all nations.

Jesus told us to go and **make disciples.** He told us not only to teach and preach, but to make disciples. In fact, in verses 18–20, the main verb in the original Greek text is the verb **make.** The other verbs—**baptizing** and **teaching**—are auxiliary verbs. From this we can understand that the most important element in this "Great Commission" is the making of disciples. We must confirm individual believers in the faith. We must help them grow into mature Christians. In this way we shall be able to build up the church, so that it will be strong and faithful to its Lord.

We must baptize new disciples **in the name of the Father and of the Son and of the Holy Spirit**. The Father, Son, and Holy Spirit are one God, not three gods. God is triune. He has three forms or modes of existence. He is the Almighty Creator, maker of heaven and earth. He is the Son, Jesus, the one true incarnation of God, who came to earth to save us from our sins and to show us the way to salvation. And third, He is the Holy Spirit, who lives in the hearts of believers and gives them new life, eternal spiritual life that will never end. This is the Triune God whom we worship. And to be baptized in His name means to belong to Him. When we are baptized in His name, we say to the world: "I am God's. I am Christ's" (see 2 Corinthians 13:14).

Jesus in the beginning preached and healed mainly among the Jews (see Matthew 10:5–6; 15:24 and comments). Now having risen from the dead and obtained authority over all the universe, He told His disciples to go to all nations. At first, however, they continued to work mainly among the Jews. The disciples themselves were Jews. It took them time to realize that Christ's church really was to be established among all nations, all peoples. God had to send Peter a special vision before he would agree to preach in a Gentile's house (Acts 10:9–20). But step by step, they spread the Gospel of Christ into all the world. Jesus told them, "... **you will be my witnesses in Jerusalem, and in all Judea and Samaria, and to the ends of the earth**" (Acts 1:8). And so it came to pass (see Mark 16:15–18 and comment).

20 What is the main job of a disciple? To obey. Jesus said to His followers, "Make disciples, **teaching them to obey everything I have commanded you.**" A disciple who does not obey is no disciple at all.

This "Great Commission" was given not only to the eleven disciples but to every follower of Jesus right down to the present time. Jesus told those first eleven disciples to teach all the new disciples they made **to obey everything I have commanded you**—and that, of course, includes the Great Commission itself. Every Christian must obey Jesus' command to make disciples of all nations. The reason there are so many non-Christians

---

[74] The Greek word for **nation** that Matthew uses means any group of people of similar culture and outlook. Such groups today are called "people groups." Within any country, there can be many of these "nations," or "people groups."

in the world today is because so many Christians have failed to obey this last great command of our Lord (see General Article: Purpose of the Church).

Finally, after giving His disciples their last assignment, Jesus gave them a promise: **"I will be with you always."** Earlier Jesus had said to His disciples: **"I will not leave you as orphans; I will come to you. . . . Because I live, you also will live. On that day you will realize that I am in my Father, and you are in me, and I am in you"** (John 14:18–20). Jesus is not only **with** us; He is also **in** us. His Holy Spirit lives in us (John 14:17). His Holy Spirit gives us the power to be His disciples, to be His witnesses (see Acts 1:8 and comment). If Jesus is in us, His authority is also in us. Friends, all the power and authority in the universe is ours in Christ! As we go out into the world, Christ goes with us also; we shall never be alone. **"Surely I will be with you always, to the very end of the age."**

Mark

INTRODUCTION

Mark was a close associate of the Apostle Peter, the leader among Jesus' twelve disciples. Peter called Mark "**my son**" in 1 Peter 5:13. Mark was the cousin of Barnabas, and a colleague of the Apostle Paul (Acts 12:25; Colossians 4:10; 2 Timothy 4:11).

Although Mark was not one of the original twelve disciples, he was able to learn a great deal about the life of Jesus directly from Peter. Mark based his GOSPEL, in large part on the information Peter gave him. Most Bible scholars believe that Mark wrote his Gospel in ROME, the capital of the ROMAN EMPIRE. Just as Matthew wrote his Gospel mainly for Jewish readers, so Mark wrote his Gospel mainly for Romans. Among the four Gospels, Mark's Gospel was written first. It was written between 55 A.D. and 65 A.D., that is, about thirty years after Jesus' death. Both Matthew and Luke included material written by Mark in their own Gospels. Indeed, almost all of Mark's Gospel is included in Matthew's Gospel.

OUTLINE

A. The Preparation for Christ's Ministry (1:1–13).
   1. John the Baptist (1:1–8).
   2. The Baptism and Temptation of Jesus (1:9–13).
B. Christ's Ministry in Galilee (1:14–10:52).
   1. The Call of the First Disciples (1:14–20).
   2. Early Ministry in Capernaum (1:21–45).
   3. The Beginnings of Opposition (2:1–3:12).
   4. The Appointment of the Twelve Disciples (3:13–19).
   5. Charges Against Jesus (3:20–35).

6. Parables (4:1–34).
7. Mighty Works (4:35–5:43).
8. Further Miracles and Teaching in Galilee and Beyond (6:1–8:26).
9. Messiahship and Suffering and Related Discussions (8:27–9:50).
10. Further Teachings on the Way to Jerusalem (10:1–52).

C. Christ's Ministry in Jerusalem (11:1–13:37).
1. The Triumphal Entry (11:1–26).
2. Final Controversies with the Jewish Leaders (11:27–12:44).
3. The Prophetic Discourse (13:1–37).

D. Christ's Passion and Resurrection (14:1–16:20).
1. Jesus Anointed and Betrayed (14:1–11).
2. The Lord's Supper (14:12–31).
3. The Arrest and Trial of Jesus (14:32–15:20).
4. The Death of Jesus (15:21–47).
5. The Resurrection of Jesus (16:1–20).

CHAPTER 1

John the Baptist Prepares the Way (1:1–8)

(Matthew 3:1–6,11; Luke 3:3–4,16; John 1:23,26)

1 In this very first verse of his Gospel, Mark introduces Jesus Christ as the **Son of God** (see Mark 1:11; 3:11; 9:7; 13:32; 14:60–61). The most important thing we must understand about Jesus is that He was not only a man but He was also God. He was God's own Son (see General Article: Jesus Christ). He had no human father, but was born **through the Holy Spirit** (Matthew 1:18,20–21).

2–3 Mark here quotes from **Isaiah the prophet**[1] (Isaiah 40:3), and also from the prophet Malachi (Malachi 3:1). These Old Testament prophets prophesied about John the Baptist, who came before Christ to announce His coming. Here, through the prophet, God says to Christ: "**I will send my messenger** (John the Baptist) **ahead of you.**" John came to prepare people's hearts to receive Jesus, and he did this by preaching that they should repent of their sins (verse 4).

Luke in his Gospel quotes not only Isaiah 40:3 but also Isaiah 40:4–5 (see Luke 3:5–6). Isaiah prophesied that one would come to make **straight paths** for the Lord, Christ. **Every valley shall be filled in, every mountain and hill made low. The crooked roads shall become straight** (Luke 3:5). This means that in order for the people to receive the salvation which Christ will bring, the **valleys**—that is, whatever is spiritually lacking (such as faith)—must be filled up. Obstructions in the way like a **mountain** or **hill**—that is, pride or self-confidence—must be **made low**. Those walking on **crooked roads** must return to **straight paths** (Luke 3:4). Only then will **all mankind** see **God's** SALVATION (Luke 3:6). Salvation will be given not only to the JEWS but also to non-Jews. Salvation will be given to all men and women who have prepared their hearts by repenting and by turning to Christ in faith.

The birth of John the Baptist is described in Luke 1:5–17,57–60,80.

4 **And so John came . . . preaching a** BAPTISM **of** REPENTANCE. In order to receive Jesus as Savior, a man must first realize he is a sinner and then repent of his sin. The man who does not consider himself a sinner in God's sight will think, "I have no need of a savior." But every man is a sinner (Romans 3:9–10), and every man needs a savior. Therefore, John called all men to repent—that is, to confess and turn from their sins. His message was: "**Repent, for the kingdom of heaven is near**" (Matthew 3:2). This was the same message that Jesus Himself preached (verse 15). Those who repented John then baptized with water, which was a sign that their sins were washed away, that they were now forgiven and cleansed from sin (see General Article: Water Baptism).

5 The people of the province of Judea[2] and the city of **Jerusalem**[3] came to John to be baptized. John baptized them in the **Jordan River**, probably by immersion. The **Jordan River** is the major river of Israel; it forms part of the eastern boundary of modern Israel. The area on either side of the Jordan River is desert wasteland. It was here that John lived, preached, and baptized.

6 John was a prophet of God, who announced the coming of the Savior Christ. As a prophet, he gave up worldly

---

[1] The prophets of the Old Testament were not merely "tellers of the future." They spoke the words of God Himself. They were God's spokesmen. Through the prophets, God admonished and taught the people. For further discussion, see Word List: Prophecy, Prophet.

[2] Judea is the southern province of the country of Israel. During New Testament times Judea was a province of the Roman Empire.

[3] In New Testament times **Jerusalem** was the capital of the province of Judea. Today it is one of the leading cities of the modern nation of Israel.

comfort and pleasure (Matthew 11:7–9). He led a life of poverty. Like other Old Testament prophets, he wore very rough clothing (2 Kings 1:8) and ate locusts, which only the poorest people ate.

7 John was the greatest and most powerful of all the Jewish prophets (Matthew 11:11). Yet he was not worthy to untie the thongs of the One coming after him—Jesus. According to Jewish custom, even the lowliest slave did not have to untie his master's sandals; it was too demeaning a task for even a slave to perform. But here the greatest man born of woman was not worthy to do this lowly task for Jesus, because Jesus was not just a man—He was God Himself.

8 John only baptized with water. But Jesus baptized with the **HOLY SPIRIT** (Isaiah 44:3: Ezekiel 36:24–27; Joel 2:28–32). The Holy Spirit is God's own Spirit, which enters a person when he or she believes in Christ. Or we can equally well say that the Holy Spirit is Christ's Spirit; it is saying the same thing. Because the one true God is a "triune" God. That is, He has three forms, or persons:[4] God the Father, Christ the Son, and the Holy Spirit. These three are one God.

Therefore, when a man accepts Jesus, Jesus comes into that man's life in the form of the Holy Spirit (Revelation 3:20). In this way a man is born anew (see John 3:5 and comment). Through the Holy Spirit he becomes a **new creation** (see 2 Corinthians 5:17 and comment). And through the Holy Spirit he is anointed and empowered for ministry (see Acts 1:4–5 and comment). This is, broadly speaking, what it means to be baptized with the Holy Spirit (see General Article: Holy Spirit Baptism).

Therefore, John's baptism with water was a temporary outward cleansing of sins. Water washes only the surface. But Jesus' baptism with the Holy Spirit is a permanent inward cleansing, a changing of the heart and the creating of new spiritual life within. The purpose of John's baptism with water was to prepare men to receive the greater baptism of the Holy Spirit.

In the corresponding passage in Matthew 3:11, Matthew writes that Jesus will not only baptize with the Holy Spirit, but He will also baptize **with fire**. Fire, like water, is also a sign of cleansing, of burning away the chaff, the impurities, the burning away of our old sinful nature (Matthew 3:10,12; 1 Peter 1:7). Fire is a sign of God's presence (see Acts 2:2–3 and comment). Fire is also a sign of JUDGMENT. Those who accept Christ will be saved on the day of judgment. Those who do not accept Christ will be condemned (see John 3:16–18,36 and comment).

The Baptism and Temptation of Jesus (1:9–13)

(Matthew 3:13–17; Luke 3:21–22)

9 Jesus was raised in **Nazareth**, a town in **Galilee**, the northern province of Israel. He came with all the other Jews to be baptized.

Jesus Himself had no sin (Hebrews 4:14–15). Therefore, He did not need to be baptized for His own sake. Rather, He was baptized for our sake. Jesus, the Son of God, humbled Himself. He took our sins upon Himself. He came and received the death penalty for sin in our place. He was **numbered with the transgressors** (Isaiah 53:12). According to Matthew 3:13–15, Jesus was baptized **to fulfill all righteousness**. It was God's righteous will that Jesus come to earth in the form of a man, take man's sins upon Himself, and suffer the punishment for sin in man's place. Therefore, because Jesus came to take man's sins upon Himself, it was necessary for Him to be baptized like other men.

According to Matthew 3:14, John at first

[4] When speaking of the triune God—Father, Son and Holy Spirit—the term "mode of existence" is more accurate than "form" or "person." For simplicity, however, the word "form" is generally used in this commentary.

[5] Even though John knew Jesus was different from the other men coming to be baptized, he did not know at first that, in fact, Jesus was the Savior, the Lord Christ, whose way he was preparing. Only after the Holy Spirit descended on Jesus did John fully know who Jesus was (see John 1:32–34).

did not want to baptize Jesus. He somehow knew that Jesus was sinless, that He was different from all the other sinful men who were coming to be baptized. Compared with Jesus, John felt like a sinner who needed baptism himself.[5]

10–11 As Jesus was coming out of the water after being baptized, the Holy Spirit descended upon Him (Isaiah 11:2; 42:1; 61:1). The Spirit descended **in bodily form like a dove** (Luke 3:22). Then God spoke from heaven saying to Jesus: "**You are my son, whom I love; with you I am well pleased**" (see verse 1 and comment). In this way God manifested to John and to all men that Jesus was indeed the Christ, the Savior, the Son of God (Psalm 2:7).

Jesus did not suddenly become God's Son and receive the Holy Spirit only at the time of His baptism. He had always been God's Son from before the beginning of the world (John 1:1–3). The Holy Spirit had always been with Jesus; the Holy Spirit was Jesus' own Spirit (Genesis 1:1–2). But at His baptism Jesus was made manifest as the Son of God publicly before men.

Therefore, in the beginning of his Gospel, Mark has made clear that the Jesus about whom he is writing is no ordinary man, but is the sinless Son of the living God, who has come to baptize men and women with the Holy Spirit and to save them from their sins.

12–13 Immediately after His baptism, Jesus was sent into the desert, where He was **tempted by SATAN**. Jesus came to earth to defeat and destroy Satan. Thus, right in the beginning of His earthly ministry, Jesus struggled with Satan and overcame him. Satan attempted to turn Jesus from obedience to God's will by tempting Him, but Jesus remained firm. In this Jesus has set an example for us. He suffered every TEMPTATION we suffer (Hebrews 2:18: 4:15). Every Christian who determines to follow Jesus must be ready to face similar temptations from Satan. And as Jesus was victorious over temptation, so He gives us the strength to be victorious also.

For a full description of the temptations of Jesus, see Matthew 4:1–11 and comment.

The Calling of the First Disciples (1:14–20)

(Matthew 4:12,17–22)

14-15 After John was put in prison,[6] Jesus returned to Galilee and began to preach. His preaching was simple: "**The time has come. The kingdom of God[7] is near**" (see 2 Corinthians 6:2). The kingdom of God is God's presence, power, and rule in men's hearts and in society. In a way, Christ was Himself God's kingdom which had come to earth. Through Him the power of evil was broken and men began experiencing joy and peace and healing. Christ was the embodiment of God's kingdom. When men and women accept Jesus, they become citizens of the kingdom of God. Jesus came to establish a new nation of believers, whose ruler is God (see Mark 9:1; John 3:3 and comments).

Therefore, Jesus says to us, "**Repent and believe the good news**" (verse 15). The first step always is to repent (Acts 2:38; 17:30). Repentance is not only feeling sorry for our sins; it is also turning from our sins. To truly repent of a sin means that we cease committing that sin. Otherwise our repentance is false.

When we have repented, we are ready for the second step: to **believe** in the Savior Jesus Christ. To "believe," that is, to have FAITH in Christ means not only

---

[5] Even though John knew Jesus was different from the other men coming to be baptized, he did not know at first that, in fact, Jesus was the Savior, the Lord Christ, whose way he was preparing. Only after the Holy Spirit descended on Jesus did John fully know who Jesus was (see John 1:32–34).

[6] The imprisonment of John is described in Mark 6:17–20.

[7] In Matthew 4:17, instead of the words **kingdom of God**, Jesus uses the words **kingdom of heaven**. The meaning is the same; it is the same kingdom. For further discussion, see Word List: Kingdom of God.

that we accept Him as Lord of our lives but that we also obey Him. If we say we believe in Jesus but do not obey Him, we are liars (see Matthew 7:21; James 2:14,17,20–24; 1 John 2:4 and comments).

The **good news** is this: Jesus has come into the world to save sinners and to give all who believe in Him eternal life (see John 3:16 and comment). This, in short, is the Gospel of Christ.

Thus Jesus gives everyone a choice: to be a citizen of the kingdom of God or to be a citizen of the kingdom of Satan; to believe and receive eternal life, or to disbelieve and receive eternal punishment. In this life there are only two choices (see Matthew 7:13–14 and comment).

16–20 Mark here describes how Jesus chose His first four disciples. First He met **Simon**[8] and his brother **Andrew** fishing in the **Sea of Galilee.**[9]

Jesus said, **"Come, follow me." At once** they left their work and followed Him (verse 18). In the same way, He called **James** and **John** (not John the Baptist); they, too, immediately arose, left their family, their boat, their work, and followed Him[10] (see Luke 5:1-11 and comment). Like Abraham, they didn't know where they were going (Hebrews 11:8); but they knew who they were going with.

Earlier, Simon and Andrew had met Jesus and believed in Him (see John 1:35–42). Now Jesus was calling them to be His close disciples. He was telling them to leave everything and follow Him. In the same way, Jesus also calls us to be His disciples. He says to us only this: **"Come, follow me."** Like Peter and Andrew, James and John, let us, too, rise and without a word of argument follow Jesus.

Jesus said to Simon (Peter) and Andrew, **"I will make you fishers of men"** (verse 17). Jesus took their natural abilities (as fishermen) and transformed them into something useful for the kingdom of God. In the same way, Jesus takes us and our natural gifts and abilities and transforms us into useful disciples fit for the work He has appointed us to do.

Finally, we can see that these disciples were ordinary men—fishermen. They were poor men. They had to work hard and endure hardship. They were uneducated. They were from Galilee, the most backward province of Israel. Yet Jesus chose these men to help establish His kingdom.

Jesus Drives Out an Evil Spirit (1:21–28)
(Luke 4:31–37)

21–22 Jesus and His four new disciples then went to **Capernaum**, Peter's home town, near the Sea of Galilee. On the **Sabbath**—that is, Saturday—they went to the Jewish **synagogue,**[11] where the Jews met each week. There Jesus was invited to teach the people. The people were amazed because He did not teach like the **teachers of the law.**[12] These teachers of the law were scholars who knew all about the Jewish LAW, the Jewish scriptures (the Old Testament), and other writings. These teachers taught not by their own authority but only with an authority derived from other writers. But Jesus taught by His own authority, which

---

[8] **Simon** was also called Peter (his Greek name) and Cephas (his Aramaic name). Simon was Peter's Jewish name (see John 1:42). Aramaic was the common language of Israel in the time of Jesus.

[9] The **Sea of Galilee** is a small sea about eight miles in diameter, located in northern Israel.

[10] These first disciples gave up their jobs and worldly security in order to follow Jesus. Today there are many so-called "disciples" who follow Jesus in order to gain jobs and worldly security. Let this not be!

[11] The **synagogue** is the Jewish house of worship. The Jews meet for worship every **Sabbath**—that is, Saturday.

[12] In place of the words **teachers of the law**, many versions of the Bible say "scribes." The meaning is the same.

came directly from God (see Matthew 7:28–29 and comment).

23–28 One of the Jews in the synagogue was **possessed by an** EVIL SPIRIT. This evil spirit, or demon, immediately recognized who Jesus was. Though the others in the synagogue had read the prophecies about Jesus in the Old Testament week after week, none of them recognized Jesus; only the evil spirit recognized Him. The evil spirit knew that Jesus had already overcome Satan during Jesus' time of temptation in the desert (verse 13). He knew that Jesus had also come to destroy all of the evil spirits working under Satan. By saying Jesus' name, the evil spirit hoped to prevent Jesus from exercising authority over him[13] (verse 24).

But Jesus, with only a word, drove out the evil spirit, and the man was at once completely healed. Jesus' power was in His word. The people were amazed. They had never seen anyone exercise authority over evil spirits like this.

We must remember that demon possession is not a form of mental disease. Demons, or evil spirits, are servants of the chief demon, Satan. They are workers of evil. When they come into a man, they make him a prisoner or slave of Satan. Only through the power of Jesus can these demons be overcome and the man be given freedom.

Jesus Heals Many (1:29–39)
(Matthew 8:14–17; Luke 4:38–44)

29–31 Jesus then went to Simon and Andrew's house, where He healed Simon's mother-in-law. She was healed so quickly and completely that she was able at once to get up and serve Jesus and the four disciples.

32–34 Jesus is known as the "Great Physician." According to Matthew 8:16, on this occasion He **healed all the sick**. He didn't use medicine. His "treatment" was always successful; the sick were healed immediately and completely. Matthew says that this was to fulfill what was spoken by the prophet Isaiah: **"He took up our infirmities and carried our diseases"** (Isaiah 53:4; Matthew 8:17).

The people brought the sick to Jesus **after sunset**, because it was against the Jewish law to move the sick on the Sabbath day. According to the law, no work of any kind could be done on the Sabbath.

Jesus also cast out DEMONS from all who were demon-possessed. Again, only the demons knew who He was. Other people thought He was only a wonder-worker. But Jesus forbade the demons to say who He was (verse 34). Except for the disciples, He did not want others to know He was the Christ. Otherwise, all the people would try to make Him an earthly king. They would not understand that He had come to earth to suffer and die for their sins (see Mark 10:45 and comment).

35–39 Even though Jesus was the Son of God, He still needed to be alone and to pray and receive strength from God. Therefore, before dawn Jesus went away to a solitary place to pray. The disciples couldn't understand why He had left suddenly and for no apparent reason, because there were still sick people coming to be healed. But Jesus told them that He hadn't come to earth only to heal the sick. He had come mainly to preach that men should repent and believe the Gospel (verses 14–15). But when crowds of sick people gathered, it was difficult to preach. Therefore, He and His disciples left Capernaum and traveled to other towns throughout Galilee.

A Man With Leprosy (1:40–45)
(Matthew 8:1–4; Luke 5:12–16)

40–42 A man with leprosy came to Jesus and **begged him on his knees** to heal him: **"If you are willing, you can make me clean."** The man had faith in Jesus' power, but he also submitted himself to Jesus' will. So we, too, must pray with complete faith in Jesus and with earnestness. But at the same time we

[13] In Jesus' time, people thought that by speaking another person's name one could gain some power over that person.

must also pray for Christ's will to be done.

Christ was willing to heal the man. **"Be clean!"** He said. He healed the man's leprosy by His word alone.

43–44 After Jesus healed the man with leprosy, He told him to go to the priest and offer sacrifices according to the commandment of **Moses,**[14] that is, according to the Jewish law (Leviticus 14:1–20). Only the Jewish priests were qualified to determine if a leprosy victim had been cleansed or not. Therefore, Jesus wanted this man whom He'd healed to be a witness, a **testimony**, to the priests and other Jews of the healing power that He possessed. Man is not healed and saved by following the law. Only through the power of Christ can man be healed and saved. Only through Christ's power can the requirements of the law be fulfilled (see Romans 8:1–4 and comment).

45 In verse 44, Jesus had commanded the man with leprosy not to tell anyone about his healing (see verse 34 and comment). But the man, not obeying, announced the news everywhere, with the result that more and more people sought Jesus for healing. Therefore, Jesus could no longer go into the cities because of the crowds of sick people. Instead He preached in the countryside.

CHAPTER 2

Jesus Heals a Paralytic (2:1–12)
(Matthew 9:1–8: Luke 5:17–26)

1–4 After preaching in the countryside for several days, Jesus came back to the home of Peter and Andrew (Mark 1:29). While He was teaching there, four men brought a paralyzed man. They carried him up the outer stairs to the flat roof, and removing some of the tiles (Luke 5:19), they lowered the patient on his bed into the room where Jesus was.

5 Then Jesus said a surprising thing to the paralyzed man: **"Son, your sins are forgiven."**

Why did Jesus say that? Because He knew that the man's main problem was not his paralysis but his sin. His main problem wasn't physical, it was spiritual. It is possible that the man's paralysis had come because of his sin.[15] If this was so, then before Jesus could cure the man's body He first had to cure his soul.

All men become ill; all fall into sin. Sin is always a greater problem than physical illness. Jesus can cure both a man's body and his soul. Here He first forgave the man's sins. That was the big job. Then, to give proof that the man's sins were indeed forgiven, Jesus healed his body also (verse 10).

To heal a man's bodily illness without cleansing his soul or spirit from sin is like applying a bandage to a thorn wound without removing the thorn. Jesus came into the world mainly to cleanse and save men from sin. In addition, in order to demonstrate His compassion and power, Jesus also healed men's bodies. God's desire is that man might be fully healed in body, soul, and spirit.

6–7 In these verses we see the beginning of opposition to Jesus. No matter how good or merciful a man's work is, there are always some who will find fault with it. Some **teachers of the law** (see Mark 1:22) heard Jesus forgive the sins of

---

[14] Moses was the great leader of the Jews who received the Jewish law from God and delivered it to the people. That is why the Jewish law is often called the "law of Moses." For further discussion, see Word List: Moses.

[15] Some illnesses come directly as a result of sin. For example, syphilis, gonorrhea, and most cases of AIDS are the result of fornication or sodomy. Some kinds of liver disease are brought on by the excessive drinking of alcoholic beverages. Other illnesses, too, can result from sin. But not all illnesses and accidents are the direct result of sin; indeed, most are not (see Luke 13:1–5; John 9:2).

the paralyzed man. In their eyes Jesus was guilty of blasphemy, because they knew that only God had the authority to forgive sins. In their opinion, Jesus was taking for Himself authority that belonged only to God. In doing this He was insulting God; He was taking God's honor as His own. He was boastfully saying: "I can do what God does!"

The teachers of the law were correct in one way: it is true that only God can forgive sins. But what they didn't realize was that Jesus Himself was God!

8–12 Jesus knew the thoughts of these teachers of the law. He saw that they doubted He had the authority to forgive sins. They thought: "Anyone can say, 'Your sins are forgiven.' That's easy to say. But to heal someone is not easy." Therefore, Jesus said in effect, "All right, to prove that I have the authority to forgive sins, I will heal this man. I will do what is more difficult in your eyes, so that you will know I am not speaking empty words." Thereupon He told the paralyzed man to take up his mat and walk. And immediately, by the power of Jesus' word, the man was cured and walked out.

Therefore, let us understand that this miracle was not only an act of mercy; it was also a sign for us that Jesus did indeed have the full nature and authority of God. It was a sign that the kingdom of God had indeed come among men.

Here in verse 10, Jesus calls Himself the **Son of Man**. This was the name Jesus usually gave Himself. It means that even though he was fully God (see Colossians 2:9 and comment), He was also fully human, having been born of a woman, Mary (see Philippians 2:5–8 and comment). This is why Jesus called Himself the **Son of Man** (see Daniel 7:13–14; John 1:51 and comment).

The Calling of Levi (2:13–17)
(Matthew 9:9–13; Luke 5:27–32)

13–14 **Levi** is the same man as the Matthew mentioned in Matthew 9:9.[16] Although a Jew, he was a tax collector in the government of King Herod, the ruler of Galilee.[17] The tax collectors were hated and despised by everyone, because they levied more tax than was legal and kept the excess for themselves. Thus they became rich. That Jesus should choose such an evildoer as a tax collector to be one of His disciples was an amazing thing (see Luke 19:2–7 and comment).

Yet we see here the grace and wisdom of Jesus: grace to call such a sinner, and the wisdom to call a man who could speak both Greek and Aramaic.[18] And what did Levi do when he was called? He immediately left his riches and followed Jesus. He gave up everything but his pen and writing paper. Later this same Levi—that is, Matthew—would write the first Gospel in the New Testament, the Gospel of Matthew.

Notice here that Levi didn't choose Jesus; Jesus first chose him. In the same way, Christ first chooses us; only then do we rise and follow Him (John 15:16).

15 To celebrate the new joy and freedom and salvation that he had received from Jesus, Levi gave a feast at his house, and invited his old friends and colleagues to meet Jesus. He wanted them to have the opportunity to find salvation also. The blessings of Christ are to be shared, not kept for ourselves. If we do not share our new life with others, it will quickly dry up.

16–17 Some of the teachers of the

---

[16] Just as Jesus gave Simon the name "Peter," so some scholars think that Jesus gave Levi the name "Matthew," which means "gift of God."

[17] Although all of Israel had fallen under the control of the Roman Empire, the Roman emperor allowed local kings and rulers to exercise limited authority over different parts of the empire. Thus Herod had been given authority over the province of Galilee.

[18] Greek was the language spoken by most of the educated people of the Roman Empire during New Testament times; it was the language in which the New Testament was originally written.
Aramaic was the main language of the common people in the Middle East during that same period.

law who were **Pharisees**[19] disapproved of Jesus eating with such sinners as tax collectors. Again we see how quick men are to speak evil of acts that are good. But Jesus answered: **"I have not come to call the righteous, but sinners"** (verse 17). The **righteous** are those, like the Pharisees, who consider themselves righteous. In their mind, they have no need of a savior. They do not listen to Jesus. Only those who acknowledge that they are sinners can hear Jesus' call. And only those who repent can be spiritually healed.

Jesus is not only a doctor of man's body; He is the doctor of man's soul. And the chief sickness of the soul is sin. There is no other doctor besides Jesus who can heal the soul from sin.

According to Matthew 9:13, Jesus reminded the Pharisees of what God had said through the prophet Hosea: **"I desire mercy, not sacrifice"** (Hosea 6:6). The Pharisees thought they could please God by carrying out proper sacrifices and by obeying the Jewish law, but Jesus says that it is **mercy** that God is pleased with. Instead of avoiding and condemning sinners, as the Pharisees did, Jesus reached out and called them and forgave them and loved them.

Jesus Questioned About Fasting (2:18–22)

(Matthew 9:14–17; Luke 5:33–39)

18–19 According to the Jewish law, the Jews only had to fast once a year, on the Day of ATONEMENT (Leviticus 23:27–29). But the Pharisees used to observe many other fasts in order to appear righteous in men's eyes. On one such fast day, the Pharisees and John the Baptist's disciples were fasting, but Jesus and His disciples were not. Some Jews attempted to accuse Jesus' disciples of not following Jewish traditions. But Jesus said, "Why should my disciples fast? While I am here it is like a wedding feast. No one fasts while the bridegroom is present; that is a time for eating and rejoicing."

For John the Baptist's disciples, however, it was suitable to fast, because John had been thrown into prison (Mark 1:14). But it was not suitable for Jesus' disciples to fast, because He was still present with them. **There is a time for everything, and a season for every activity under heaven . . . a time to weep and a time to laugh, a time to mourn and a time to dance** (Ecclesiastes 3:1,4).

20 Then Jesus said that one day the **bridegroom will be taken from them.** He meant that one day He would be killed. Then would be the time for His disciples to mourn and fast.

21 To make Jesus' disciples follow the old Jewish traditions[20] was as unsuitable as sewing a patch of new material on old clothing. The new material will shrink and tear away from the old material and the hole will become bigger. The new spiritual life of a Christian does not mix easily with the old traditions of the world.

22 In the same way, new wine must not be poured into old, hard wineskins.[21] The new wine will expand and burst the old skins, and both wine and skin will be lost. New wine needs new wineskins that will stretch. Similarly, for new spiritual life new behavior is needed. Fasting was done by the Jews mainly in times of sorrow and or out of fear of judgment. But Christ has brought joy and salvation; therefore, fasting because of sorrow or fear is no longer suitable.

Nevertheless, Jesus does not teach that we should never fast (Matthew 6:16–18). It is good to fast during special times of prayer, especially when important decisions need to be made (Acts 13:2–3; 14:23). Jesus fasted forty days while He was being tempted (Matthew 4:2).

---

[19] The Pharisees were the strictest sect of the Jews. They could be called, in a sense, "high-caste" Jews; they refused to associate with other lower people lest they be made impure. They thought that Jesus was defiling Himself by associating with "sinners." For further discussion, see Word List: Pharisee.

[20] Many of these traditions were man-made (see Mark 7:1–8 and comment).

[21] In Bible times, wine was kept in bags made from skins.

Christians fast not because of any law or desire to appear righteous, but because they desire through fasting to better worship God and to more clearly understand His will. But let us not think that by fasting we will be reckoned more righteous than those who do not fast. Righteousness comes from the heart, not from following outward customs.

Luke in his Gospel adds another saying to this section: **And no one after drinking old wine wants the new, for he says, "The old is better"** (Luke 5:39). The Pharisees and other Jews who rejected Christ liked the old wine of the Jewish religion. They did not want to try the new wine of the Christian life.

But anyone who actually tastes the new wine of Christ will not want to turn back to the old.

Lord of the Sabbath (2:23–28)
(Matthew 12:1–8; Luke 6:1–5)

23–24 According to Jewish law, it was legal to pluck a neighbor's harvest by hand (Deuteronomy 23:25), but it was not lawful to do so on the Sabbath. The Pharisees called it "reaping," which was forbidden on the Sabbath (Exodus 34:21). According to the Jews, no work of any kind could be done on the **Sabbath**,[22] and the Jews considered "picking" heads of grain to be a kind of work. Therefore, they accused Jesus' disciples of breaking the Sabbath law because, being hungry, they were picking grain.

25–27 But Jesus reminded the Jews of their own King DAVID, who also disobeyed one of the Jewish laws. He was hungry and so ate some special bread that only the priests were allowed to eat[23] (1 Samuel 21:1–6). Jesus' meaning was this: God made the Sabbath law for man's benefit, not to add a burden (Exodus 20:8–11; 23:12). If a man was hungry, he had a right to eat on the Sabbath. Therefore, the disciples had a right to pick grain on the Sabbath to satisfy their hunger. **The Sabbath was made for man, not man for the Sabbath** (verse 27). The Sabbath was meant by God to be a day of rest and joy, not of hunger! The rules of the Pharisees were too strict. They had turned the Sabbath into a day of oppression (see John 5:10 and comment).

28 The **Son of Man**—that is, Jesus (verse 10)—has final authority over the Sabbath. He can decide what can and cannot be done on the Sabbath. Jesus taught that works of necessity (such as satisfying hunger) and works of mercy (Mark 3:1–5) are legal on the Sabbath.

According to Matthew 12:5–7, on this same occasion Jesus also gave the example of the priests who had to work at their priestly duties in the temple on the Sabbath. They, like King David, also "broke" the Sabbath law, but they were not considered guilty. But now someone greater than King David had come, that is, Christ. Not only that, but "**one greater than the temple is here**," said Jesus (Matthew 12:6). When Jesus came, all of the temple rules and sacrifices became unnecessary. Jesus was the true temple. The Jews thought that God's presence was in the temple, but in fact, God's presence was fully in Jesus. If priests serving in the temple could "break" the Sabbath law, then surely these disciples serving Christ could break it too, because Christ was **greater than the temple**.

Then in Matthew 12:7, Jesus again reminds the Pharisees of God's words: "**I desire mercy, not sacrifice**" (Hosea 6:6; Matthew 9:13). In God's sight, it is more important to show mercy on the Sabbath than to follow all the customs and sacrifices of the Jews. If the Jews had

---

[22] The **Sabbath** is the seventh day of the week. God created the universe in six days, and then rested on the seventh day (Genesis 2:1–3). Therefore, God set apart the seventh day of the week as a special day of rest (Exodus 20:8–11). The Jews observe the Sabbath on Saturday, and Christians observe it on Sunday. Nowhere in the Bible does it actually say which day of the week the "seventh day" is.

[23] According to 1 Samuel 21:1–6, Ahimelech was the high priest who gave David the holy bread. Abiathar was Ahimelech's son (1 Samuel 22:20). It is not certain why Mark mentions Abiathar here.

remembered these words of God, they would not have accused Jesus' disciples of breaking the Sabbath law.

CHAPTER 3

The Man With the Shriveled Hand (3:1–12)

(Matthew 12:9–16; Luke 6:6–11, 17–19)

1–3 On another Sabbath day, Jesus encountered a man with a shriveled hand. According to Jewish tradition,[24] it was lawful only to save life on the Sabbath. All other works of healing had to wait until the next day. Therefore, the Jews waited to see what Jesus would do. According to the Jewish law, it was a serious crime to break the Sabbath law; the punishment for doing so was death (Exodus 31:14–17).

4 The Jews perverted the purpose and meaning of the Sabbath. If a sheep fell into a pit, they would have pulled it out on the Sabbath (Matthew 12:11–12). Why, then, would they not show mercy to a man on the Sabbath? A man is of much more value than a sheep!

God established the Sabbath for man's benefit. Therefore, men should do good on the Sabbath. They should help their neighbor in need. Jesus was ready to do good to the man with the shriveled hand on the Sabbath. But on that same Sabbath day, the Jews were plotting to kill Him (verse 6). "Which work is suitable on the Sabbath " Jesus asked them. "Your work, or mine?" The Jews could not answer (see John 5:8–10 and comment).

5–6 Jesus healed the man's hand. He had put the Pharisees and other Jews to shame by exposing their hypocrisy and lack of love. In their minds, He had broken the Sabbath law. They could no longer endure this healer and teacher from Nazareth. He had blasphemed against God (Mark 2:5–7). He ate with tax collectors and sinners (Mark 2:15–16). Not only that, He was becoming famous; all the people were following after Him. The Pharisees were afraid they would lose their own prestige and authority in the eyes of the people. Therefore, they joined with the **Herodians**[25] and plotted to kill Him (see John 5:16–17).

7–12 Jesus and His disciples **withdrew . . . to the lake**, that is, the Sea of Galilee (Mark 1:16). Jesus did not stay in the place where men plotted to kill Him. He did not look for danger unnecessarily. He still had much preaching to do; His time to die had not yet come.

The crowds came from all over Israel and from **Tyre and Sidon** in southern Lebanon[26] to hear Jesus and to be healed. The people pushed forward in order to touch even the edge of His cloak and thereby be healed (Mark 6:56). They pushed forward so vigorously that Jesus had to have a small boat ready so that He could escape from the press of people. Perhaps He also preached from the boat to people standing on the shore (see Mark 4:1).

Those possessed with demons fell down before Jesus. As is mentioned also in Mark 1:24–25,34, the demons recognized Jesus but He forbade them to tell who He was. Jesus did not seek to have His name spread about. He was not looking for fame or the praise of men. His only purpose was to preach the good news and to show men and women the way to salvation (see Matthew 4:23–25; 12:17–19; Mark 1:34; 5:43 and comments).

---

[24] See footnote to comment on Mark 2:21.

[25] The **Herodians** were followers of King Herod of Galilee. They also were afraid of Jesus' fame. They feared He would cause an uprising against Herod.

[26] **Tyre** and **Sidon** are important cities of Lebanon, located on the coast of the Mediterranean Sea. Lebanon is a small nation just north of Israel.

The Appointing of the Twelve Apostles (3:13–19)
(Matthew 10:1–4; Luke 6:12–16)

13 According to Luke 6:12, Jesus spent all night in prayer before choosing the remainder of His disciples. These were the men who would establish His church after His death. These were the men who would do even greater works than He had done (John 14:12). From now on, Jesus' main work would be to teach and train these twelve disciples. Jesus couldn't preach to the whole world Himself, but twelve men could. And these twelve men would each train other men. Thus the number of disciples would be multiplied. It is in this way that the church has grown and has now been established in nearly every country of the world.

Jesus **called to him those he wanted**. The choice and the call were His. But **they came to him**. They answered, "Yes, I will come." They obeyed Christ's call.

14–15 Jesus called His twelve disciples APOSTLES—that is, men who were "sent" or "driven" by Jesus' Spirit, the Holy Spirit. He called them **to be with him**, to learn by His example, to share in His ministry. He gave them His authority to preach in His name, **to heal every disease and every sickness** (Matthew 10:1), and to drive out demons in His name. Demons are Satan's evil spirits, Satan's soldiers. Thus, one of the main responsibilities of the twelve new apostles was to fight and overcome the power of Satan and his demons.

16–19 Simon (Peter), James, John, Andrew, and Matthew (Levi) have already been mentioned in Mark 1:16,19; 2:14. The first meeting of **Philip** with Jesus is described in John 1:43. **Bartholomew** may be the same as **Nathanael** mentioned in John 1:45–50. **James son of Alphaeus** may be the brother of Levi, who is also called the **son of Alphaeus** in Mark 2:14. **Thaddaeus** is the same as **Judas son of James** mentioned in Luke 6:16 and Acts 1:13. **Judas Iscariot**, that is, the "man of Kerioth," was the only one who was not from Galilee. He was the one who later betrayed Jesus.

Jesus and Beelzebub (3:20–30)
(Matthew 12:22–32; Luke 11:14–23; 12:10)

20–21 When Jesus' family heard of His activities, they thought He was **out of his mind**, because He never allowed proper time to eat and sleep. He was always preaching and healing. Therefore, they came to **take charge of him** (see verses 31–34).

22 According to Matthew 12:22–23, Jesus at that same time cured a demon-possessed man, whom the demon had rendered blind and dumb. The people were amazed and said, **"Could this be the Son of David?"**—that is, the Messiah.[27] But the Pharisees denied that Christ was the "Son of David" whom the Jews had been waiting for. They said that His power came not from God but from Satan. They accused Jesus Himself of being demon-possessed (John 10:19–20). They said that He was possessed by **Beelzebub**, that is, by Satan. They said that He cast out demon's by Satan's power. (Another similar incident is described in Matthew 9:32–34.)

Notice that the teachers of the law and the Pharisees couldn't deny Jesus' power; it was evident to all. So they tried to discredit His power by saying it came from Satan.

23–26 But Jesus showed that this was impossible. Why would the **prince of demons**—that is, Satan—cast out his own demons? If he did that, his **kingdom**, or his **house**, would be divided against itself and, as a result, would quickly be destroyed. But Satan's kingdom is not yet destroyed. Satan and his demons are still working hard and with great power. Therefore, it cannot be by Satan's power that Jesus cast out demons.

According to Matthew 12:27–28 and Luke 11:19–20, Jesus at this time

---

[27] "Messiah" is a name for Christ. It is the Hebrew word meaning "anointed by God." "Christ" is the Greek word meaning the same thing. God had promised the Jews that one of King David's descendants would be the Savior, the Messiah (2 Samuel 7:12–14; Jeremiah 23:5). Thus the Messiah was often referred to as the **Son of David**.

reminded the Pharisees that their own **sons**—that is, their disciples—also cast out demons using God's name. Why, then, when Jesus did the same thing, did the Pharisees say that He was doing it by Satan's power? The accusation of the Pharisees was false. Demons can only be driven out by the **finger of God** (Luke 11:20), that is, by the Spirit of God. The casting out of demons was a sign that the kingdom of God had indeed come to earth (see Mark 1:15) and that the final battle against the kingdom of Satan had begun.

27 To free the demon-possessed—that is, those under bondage to Satan—Christ had to enter the **strong man's house** (Satan's house) and bind Satan. Each time Christ drove out a demon, he first bound Satan. Yet Christ did not completely defeat Satan while He was here on earth. Only at the end of the world will Satan finally be completely destroyed (Revelation 20:10).

In another way, not only the demon-possessed, but all unbelieving men are in bondage to Satan. This world is Satan's kingdom. Whenever a person hears the call of Jesus and believes in Him, he is set free from Satan's kingdom and enters the kingdom of God.

Both Matthew and Luke here add a saying of Jesus: **"He who is not with me is against me, and he who does not gather with me scatters"**[28] (Matthew 12:30; Luke 11:23). In the warfare with Satan and his evil spirits, one cannot remain neutral. Men are either on Satan's side or on Christ's side; there is no middle ground. Those who do not take Christ's side are automatically on Satan's side. They may think that they haven't taken a side, but, in fact, they are serving Satan. There are only two kingdoms: God's kingdom (that is, Christ's kingdom) and Satan's kingdom. Every person is in one kingdom or the other.

He . . . who does not gather with me scatters (Matthew 12:30). Christ came to gather a harvest of men. If we do not help in this, we are, in fact, hindering. It is not enough that we merely do no harm; we must do good.

28–30 The Pharisees had said that Jesus was working by the power of Satan. But, in fact, Jesus was working by the power of God's Spirit, the Holy Spirit. Thus the Pharisees were calling the Holy Spirit "Satan"! This is why Jesus gave this warning about blaspheming the Holy Spirit. Jesus says here that **all the sins and blasphemies of men**, even words spoken **against the Son of Man** (Matthew 12:32) will be forgiven, if one repents. Only one sin cannot be forgiven, that is, **blasphemy against the Spirit** (Matthew 12:31).

What is **blasphemy against the Spirit**? It is persistent rejection of God's Spirit. God calls us through His Spirit. When we reject and abuse His Spirit, God has no other way of calling us further. We cut ourselves off from the mercy and forgiveness of God. Man can only know God through the Holy Spirit. Man can only repent and receive forgiveness through the work of the Holy Spirit in his life. The Holy Spirit is like a bridge between us and God. If we destroy the bridge, our hope of salvation, our hope of entering the kingdom of God, will be lost.

Some Christians worry and ask, "Have I committed this unforgivable sin of blasphemy against the Holy Spirit? Have I lost my salvation?" But they do not need to fear. Anyone who worries about this has certainly not committed this sin.[29]

The person who has blasphemed the Holy Spirit doesn't worry about it. He doesn't care about God. His heart is

---

[28] In Mark 9:40, Jesus gave the opposite teaching. He said: "**He that is not against us is for us.**" By this, Jesus means that in small differences between believers, we must not count each other as enemies. But here in Matthew and Luke, Jesus means that in the big conflict between Christ and Satan, those who are not on Christ's side are indeed enemies (see Mark 9:40 and comment). Thus there is no contradiction between these two teachings; they deal with different issues.

[29] There are two other ways to describe this unforgivable sin. First, it is any sin we refuse to confess. Second, it is the denial that we have sinned (see 1 John 1:8–10).

hardened. He refuses to repent. He knowingly lives in opposition to God.

Therefore, when we fall into sin, let us be quick to repent. Let us keep our hearts open to God. Because if we deliberately keep turning from God, in the end He will turn from us. Let that situation never happen.

Jesus' Mother and Brothers (3:31–35)

(Matthew 12:46–50; Luke 8:19–21)

31–32 Then Jesus' family arrived where He was teaching (see verse 21). Mark mentions here Jesus' **brothers.** Some Christians think that these were not true brothers of Jesus. They believe that Mary had no other children besides Jesus. But according to an ordinary understanding of these verses, Mark is talking here about Jesus' younger brothers, sons of Mary and Joseph. However, only Jesus was born by the Holy Spirit (see Matthew 1:18,24–25; Mark 6:3; Luke 2:7).

33–35 When Jesus heard that His family had arrived, He asked, "**Who are my mother and my brothers?**" (verse 33). By this He did not mean to dishonor His own family. He was simply teaching that while our fleshly family is very important, our spiritual family is even more important. Those who believe in Christ and obey God's will are of one spiritual family, children of God, brothers and sisters of Christ and of each other. This spiritual family will last for all eternity. We must be closer to our believing brothers and sisters than to our own unbelieving fleshly family. We must always put Christ and His church above our own father and mother, brothers and sisters (see Matthew 10:37).

CHAPTER 4

The Parable of the Sower (4:1–20)

(Matthew 13:1–23; Luke 8:4–15)

1–2 Jesus taught many things by **parables**. A parable is a simple saying or story which illustrates a spiritual truth. Those with spiritual understanding could understand the parables, but those without spiritual understanding could not.

3–9 The parable of the sower is about preaching the word of God. The word is like seed that falls on different kinds of soil. In this parable four kinds of soil are mentioned. The different kinds of soil represent different kinds of people. The question we must each ask ourselves as we study this parable is: "Of these four kinds of soil, which kind of soil am I? That is, what kind of heart do I have?" Jesus gives the meaning of the parable in verses 14–20.

10–11 After Jesus had finished telling the parable of the sower and the crowd had gone, the twelve disciples and some other believers gathered around Jesus and asked Him about the parable. Jesus said to them, "**The secret of the kingdom of God has been given to you**"—that is, to those who have open hearts, to those who seek God. But to those **on the outside**—that is, those whose hearts are hard and proud, those who do not seek God—to them the secret of the kingdom of God is not given. They cannot receive it. The **secret of the kingdom of God** is God's plan of salvation in Jesus Christ. Only those with humble, repentant, believing hearts can understand and receive this salvation.

12 Verse 12 is a very difficult verse to understand. Jesus taught in parables **so that** those with open believing hearts would better understand, but those with hard unbelieving hearts—that is, **those on the outside**—would not understand.[30]

---

[30] Jesus did not try to keep people from understanding. That was not the reason He taught in parables. Jesus taught in parables **so that** the prophecy of Isaiah 6:9–10 would be fulfilled that **they may be ever seeing but never perceiving, and ever hearing but never understanding**. The words "so that" refer to the fulfilling of Isaiah's prophecy, not to the reason for teaching in parables (see Matthew 13:14–15).

A parable reveals truth to the believing heart, but hides it from the unbelieving heart. By teaching in parables, Jesus could discern those with open, humble hearts and those with hard, proud hearts. Those with hard, proud hearts see with their eyes, but do not understand what they see. They see Jesus, but do not understand who He is. They hear God's word with their ears, but do not understand it. Such people in their hearts have already turned from God. They have already denied God. God has called to them from before, but they have rejected Him. These people who persist in unbelief have lost the chance for forgiveness. Because they have repeatedly rejected and disobeyed God, God has let them go (see Romans 1:24–26,28 and comment).

Therefore, the spiritual eyes and hearts of such people are closed. They cannot understand Jesus' parables, **otherwise they might turn and be forgiven**. If they had been able to understand the parables, they might then have repented and obtained forgiveness and salvation through Christ.

God Himself does not close people's spiritual eyes. God does not hide spiritual truth from people. He wants all men to understand; He wants all men to be saved (1 Timothy 2:3–4). But men themselves close their eyes and turn from God. They reject God's grace. This is why in Matthew 13:12 Jesus says: **"Whoever has will be given more, and he will have an abundance. Whoever does not have, even what he has will be taken from him"** (see Mark 4:25 and comment). This is an important spiritual truth. He who continues to reject God's word (he who **does not have**) will soon lose all ability to understand it. But he who has received God's word (he who **has**) will receive even more spiritual understanding (see Matthew 25:29 and comment).

In Matthew 13:14–15, Jesus quotes the full prophecy from Isaiah 6:9–10, which Mark mentions only in part here in verse 12. In Matthew 13:15, the people's guilt is clearly shown: **For this people's heart has become calloused; they hardly hear with their ears, and they have closed their eyes. Otherwise they might see with their eyes, hear with their ears, understand with their hearts and turn, and I would heal them** (see John 12:39–40).

Then in Matthew 13:16–17, Jesus says to His disciples, **"But blessed are your eyes because they see, and your ears because they hear."** The disciples were blessed because they had seen and heard Jesus Himself. Jesus said, **"For I tell you the truth, many prophets and righteous men longed to see what you see but did not see it, and to hear what you hear but did not hear it"** (Matthew 13:17). The prophets and righteous men of the Old Testament looked forward to the coming of the Messiah, Christ, but did not live to see it.

13–14 In verses 13–20, Jesus privately gives the meaning of the parable of the sower to His followers. **The farmer sows the word**. Jesus is the **farmer**.[31] The word of God is like a seed. When it is planted in people's hearts, new spiritual life springs up. Without this new spiritual life, a person cannot be a true Christian (see 1 Peter 1:23).

15 The different kinds of soil stand for different kinds of people. Some people are like the hard soil of a **path**. The seed falls on the path but does not sprout. Such people hear the word but it does not enter their hard hearts. And immediately Satan, like a bird, comes and snatches the word away. These are people like the Pharisees and the teachers of the law; they are like the people who hear Jesus' parables but do not understand them (verse 12). These are the people who hear a sermon with unprepared hearts, and who afterward do not meditate and pray about what they have heard. Jesus said, **"Consider carefully what you hear"** (verse 24). Let us not remain like hard soil. Let us plow up the ground to receive the seed, and let us cover over the seed afterward with meditation and prayer.

16–17 The **rocky places** have shallow soil; the rock is just below the surface.

[31] Every preacher of the Gospel is a **farmer**, or a "seed-sower." Every Christian, through his own witness, is also a "seed-sower."

At first the seed sprouts. This kind of person **at once** receives the word **with joy**. Such a person receives any new idea eagerly. Or perhaps by receiving the word of God he just hopes to gain some benefit. Some people become Christians in order to get a job or a scholarship. Some want to find easy salvation—cheap grace. And they do believe at first. But their faith is not strong. The roots of their faith do not go deep because of the rock. Therefore, as soon as the sun shines, that is, as soon as any **trouble or persecution** comes, the new plant—their new faith—dies, and they **quickly fall away**. They wanted God's blessing, but they were not willing to pay the price. They did not realize that persecution comes to all those who seek to follow Christ (see 2 Timothy 3:12 and comment). Or perhaps they did not get the material benefit they had hoped for, so they become disappointed and bitter. There are many who endure for a short time, but do not endure to the end. Such people will not be saved (see Mark 13:13 and comment).

Trials and hardships confirm the faith of some Christians, but shake the faith of others. We need the sun to grow; but the same sun will kill us if we have no root. Trials test our faith (James 1:2–3; 1 Peter 1:6–7). Trials separate true Christians from false Christians (see Matthew 7:24–27 and comment).

18–19 The soil with the **thorns** is very good soil. It is not hard; it is not rocky. It is deep and fertile. The seed that falls in this soil sprouts and grows well. This soil represents people who receive God's word, believe it deeply and begin their Christian lives well (Galatians 5:7). But in that good soil are also thorns, that is, selfishness, the **worries of this life, the deceitfulness of wealth and the desires for other things**. These grow faster than the word of God and soon choke the spiritual life of the Christian. The Christian's spiritual life perhaps doesn't die, but it becomes **unfruitful**. And what does God do with unfruitful branches? He cuts them off and throws them into the fire (John 15:2,6). How many Christians have started well, but then have fallen because of these worries and desires! Are any among us like this thorny soil?

20 But the farmer does not sow in vain. True, in some places no fruit comes from God's word; however, in other places it does. God says: "**. . . so is my word that goes out from my mouth: It will not return to me empty, but will accomplish what I desire and achieve the purpose for which I sent it**" (Isaiah 55:11). Whenever we preach God's word, there will be a harvest from part of the soil. The good soil is soil that bears fruit. Jesus does not say that there are no rocks and no thorns in the good soil. What He does say is that this soil bears fruit. Some of us will bear more fruit than others, but let us all bear fruit according to the grace God gives us. And with God's help, let us remove as many rocks and thorns from our soil as we can.

What fruit must we bear? First, we must bear the fruit of the Holy Spirit (see Galatians 5:22–23). True, this is the Spirit's fruit and not our fruit, but even so, we must still prepare the soil for it to grow in, and we must water it. Second, we too must sow seed, and thus produce new Christians. New Christians are also fruit. According to the fruit we produce, we bring glory to God (John 15:8).

In summary, we must understand from this parable that man's heart is like soil. In this soil are rocks and thorns. These thorns—that is, greed, evil desires, anger, slander, jealousy—grow very quickly. Therefore, in order for our new spiritual life to grow, it is necessary that our "soil" be kept in good condition. It must be kept watered with Bible study and prayer and fellowship, and the thorns must be removed as soon as they appear. Otherwise the new spiritual life in us will die.

A Lamp on a Stand (4:21–25)

(Matthew 5:15; 7:2; 10:26; 13:12; 25:29; Luke 6:38; 8:16–18; 11:33; 12:2; 19:26)

21–23 **Do you bring in a lamp to put it under a bowl or a bed?** The lamp here is Christ, or His word (John 8:12). Christ's coming was at first to some extent concealed. He forbade demons to say who He was (Mark 3:11–12). He spoke in parables, which not everyone could understand. But in the end, Christ will be fully **disclosed**, fully manifest (see Matthew 10:26–27). Not everyone accepts Christ now, but one day all will acknowledge Him as Lord (see Philippians 2:9–11). On that day His light will be set on its stand.

24–25 **Consider carefully what you hear**. Consider and believe. **With the measure you use**—that is, according to the faith you exercise—**it will be measured to you**. As much as you believe, that much will you receive—new life, joy, power—**and even more**, eternal life in heaven.

Whoever has—that is, whoever has faith—**will be given more** (verse 25). He will be given more understanding (Matthew 13:12), more joy and power, more faith, more life. But **whoever does not have** faith, even that which he has will be taken away. He is like the soil of the path where the seed was sown but couldn't sprout, and the devil snatched the seed away.

If we do not use our gift of faith and the other gifts God has given us, we shall lose them (Matthew 25:24–30). If we do not exercise our legs, we will soon be unable to walk. As it is with our bodies, so it is with our spiritual lives. Therefore, let us use our ears (verse 23) and **consider carefully** what we hear!

The Parable of the Growing Seed (4:26–29)

26–29 In this parable, Jesus compares the kingdom of God to a harvest. A man, that is, Jesus, **scatters seed**. Then the seed sprouts and grows by itself—by God's power. No man can say, "I produced the harvest." Man's part is to sow, to water, and to reap. God gives the growth (see 1 Corinthians 3:6–7).

The Parable of the Mustard Seed (4:30–34)

(Matthew 13:31–32; Luke 13:18–19)

30–32 The kingdom of God in the beginning was like a tiny mustard seed. When Jesus started preaching, only a few heard and believed. Most people rejected Him. They mocked Him and killed Him. His disciples fled. But look what happened. By the power of the Holy Spirit, from that tiny seed a mighty church has grown up, and it has spread to every country in the world. Such is the kingdom of God.

33–34 In this way, Jesus taught the people in parables, **as much as they could understand** (verse 33). People can't understand spiritual things all at once. They need first to hear a simple illustration or parable. Then, as they open their hearts, they slowly begin to understand more (see Matthew 13:34–35 and comment).

Christ, however, explained everything to His twelve disciples and other followers. They had opened their hearts and were ready to learn more. Jesus' most important work was to train these disciples to become teachers, to become **fishers of men** (Mark 1:17).

Jesus Calms the Storm (4:35–41)

(Matthew 8:23–27; Luke 8:22–25)

35–36 Jesus had taught the crowds all day from the boat. He was certainly tired. So His disciples took Him, **just as he was**—that is, still in the boat—across the Sea of Galilee to the other side.

37–38 In the middle of the sea a furious squall came up. Such wind often occurs on the Sea of Galilee. The boat was tossed to and fro, and waves poured into it. The boat began to sink. Though some of the disciples were experienced fishermen, they were afraid.

But Jesus was asleep. The disciples were a little upset with Him. **"Teacher, don't you care if we drown?"** they asked, waking Him up.

39 Jesus, the Son of God, had complete control over all the power of nature. Mark has described, so far, His power over sickness and over demons. Now we see His complete authority over the forces of nature. At His word the wind stopped.

40–41 Then Jesus rebuked His disciples because of their lack of faith: **"Do**

you still have no faith?" And they asked among themselves, **"Who is this?"** Even the disciples did not have a full understanding of who Jesus was. They were learning step by step.

In Matthew's description of this event, Jesus rebukes His disciples first and then calms the storm. Both Matthew and Mark's accounts are true. Jesus rebuked His disciples both before and after calming the storm. We must remember as we compare the four Gospels that each writer did not always write a complete account of these events. When we study the four Gospels together, we can obtain a fuller description of what happened.

CHAPTER 5

The Healing of a Demon-possessed Man (5:1–20)

(Matthew 8:28–34; Luke 8:26–39)

1 Jesus and His disciples again went across the **lake**—that is, the Sea of Galilee—to the **region of the Gerasenes.**[32] Matthew, in his account of this event, mentions two demon-possessed men (Matthew 8:28), but Mark writes only about one of them (see Mark 4:40–41 and comment).

2–8 Here again the demon recognized Jesus (see Mark 1:23–24). **"What do you want with me?"** the demon said (verse 7). In some Bible versions, this is translated: "What do you have to do with me." The demon certainly did not want to have anything to do with Jesus! The demon begged Jesus not to torture him; that is, the demon begged Jesus not to drive him out of the man.

Let us remember that it is not enough only to recognize Jesus; the demons also know and confess that Jesus is the Son of God. Not only must we know Him; we must also love and obey Him (see James 2:18–19 and comment).

9–10 The demon's name was **Legion**, which is a Latin[33] word meaning a troop of six thousand men. The man had not one demon, but many demons! The demon begged Jesus not to send him and his fellow demons **out of the area.** According to Luke's account of this event, the demons asked not to be sent **into the Abyss** (Luke 8:31). The "abyss" was the place where evil spirits were imprisoned (Revelation 9:1–2; 20:2–3). The demons knew that Jesus would punish them; therefore, they asked that their punishment not be severe. The worst punishment demons can receive is to be sent to the **Abyss**, where there are no bodies for them to live in.

11–12 Because demons cannot easily live outside a living body, they asked to be allowed to enter a herd of pigs that was nearby.

13 When the demons entered the pigs, the pigs became wild and rushed down a steep bank and into the lake. The owner of the pigs suffered great loss. But two things are clear from this event. First, one man is more valuable in the sight of God than many pigs. A herd of two thousand pigs was lost, but at the same time a demon-possessed man was made completely well. Second, from this event we can see Jesus' great power. He not only had the power to heal; He also had the power to destroy.

14–15 When the people of the town came to see what had happened and saw Jesus, together with the demon-possessed man sitting in his right mind, they were afraid. They had come into the presence of God and experienced His awesome

---

[32] The name **Gerasenes** is not certain. Some manuscripts have "Gadarenes" (see Matthew 8:28). Gerasa was a town thirty miles from the eastern shore of the Sea of Galilee. The town of Gadara was six miles away from the shore.

[33] Latin was the main language of the Roman Empire. Today Latin is no longer spoken as an ordinary language.

power. Unbelieving men are always afraid when they come into God's presence.

16–17 The townspeople then began to ask Jesus to leave. They didn't want to have any more of their animals destroyed. They put more value on pigs than they did on Jesus, the Son of God.

18–20 Jesus at once proceeded to leave that region. Jesus does not stay where He is not wanted.

The man who had been healed wanted to go with Jesus, but Jesus sent him home to witness to his family and neighbors **in the Decapolis**[34] (verse 20). Most Christians are not called to leave their homes and travel to far places. Most Christians are called to serve Jesus and witness to Him in their own towns. The first place we should witness to Christ is in our own homes.

A Dead Girl and a Sick Woman (5:21–43)

(Matthew 9:18–26; Luke 8:40–56)

21–24 After healing the demon-possessed man, Jesus left that place as the villagers had asked (verse 17), and crossed back over the lake. Jesus did not stay in a place where He was not welcome. A **synagogue ruler**, that is, a Jewish elder, named Jairus came to Jesus and asked Him to come at once to heal his daughter. "**My little daughter is dying,**" he said.[35]

25–29 On the way to Jairus' house, a woman who had been bleeding for twelve years followed Jesus in the crowd. Any woman with such a disease was considered unclean by the Jews (Leviticus 15:25). Therefore, she **came up behind him** (verse 27). "Just by touching His clothes, I will be healed," she thought (see Mark 6:56; Acts 5:15; 19:12). And as she touched His cloak, she was healed at once. For twelve years doctors had tried to heal her, but could not; she had paid them all the money she had. Now, after touching Jesus' clothes, she was completely healed. The healing power wasn't in Jesus' clothes; it was in Him. Mark writes: **At once Jesus realized that power had gone out from him** (verse 30). The woman was healed not by the contact with Jesus' clothes, as if by magic; rather, she was healed by Jesus' power working through her faith (verse 34). Many people crowd around Jesus but receive no blessing or benefit. Only those who accept Jesus as Lord and put their faith in Him in a personal way can be healed and saved.

30–31 The disciples were amazed when Jesus asked who had touched Him. The whole crowd of people were pressing against Him and touching Him.

32–34 But Jesus kept looking for the person who had touched Him. He wanted the woman to come forward, so that she and others would understand that it was by His power and her faith in Him that she had been cured. Faith alone, without Jesus, is blind faith. On the other hand, without our faith Jesus cannot help us. Both Jesus' power and our faith working together are necessary for us to be healed and saved.

35–36 The woman with the bleeding had caused a delay. In the meantime, Jairus' daughter had died. But Jesus said to Jairus: "**. . . just believe.**[36] You came to me in faith; don't stop believing now. Continue to believe."

37–39 At Jairus' house there was a great commotion going on. Just as singers are hired for a wedding, so in Jesus' time mourners were hired when someone in the family died or was about to die. A rich man like Jairus could afford to hire many mourners. These mourners had probably been called before Jairus had gone to find Jesus.

But Jesus said to them, "**The child is not dead but asleep**". Jesus had already

---

[34] **Decapolis** means "ten cities." Therefore, the healed man witnessed to Christ in the ten cities that were located near his home on the east side of the Sea of Galilee.

[35] According to Matthew 9:18, Jairus tells Jesus, "**My daughter has just died.**" In Jairus' mind, she was as good as dead. Only Jesus could give her life again.

[36] In the Greek text, the meaning of these words is: "continue to believe."

saved the child from death. The child had indeed died (Luke 8:53). Luke, in his account of this event, says that her **spirit returned** (Luke 8:55); this means that she had been dead.

40 But the mourners laughed when Jesus said that the girl was not dead. They were false mourners—one moment crying, the next moment laughing. They didn't want the child to live; if she lived there would be no more need for mourners. They would be out of a job. They would get no more pay.

41–42 After the mourners had been put out, Jesus raised the girl to life. Jesus had power over demons, over sickness, even over the wind (Mark 4:39). Now we see that He had power also over death. Those who die are still in the hands of Jesus. Jesus' voice can reach them. For believers, death is like sleep (1 Thessalonians 4:13–14). And perhaps from this story we can understand how Jesus cares for the little children and babies who die before they have a chance to believe.

Peter surely learned from watching Jesus at this time. Later he, too, raised a woman, Tabitha, from the dead (Acts 9:36–43). Jesus said: "**. . . anyone who has faith in me will do what I have been doing. He will do even greater things than these**" (John 14:12).

43 Jesus gave strict orders not to let anyone know about His raising this girl from the dead.[37] In the first place, there was no point in telling the unbelieving crowd of mourners outside the house, because they would only mock and say the child had never been dead to begin with. Secondly, He did not want to become famous as a miracle worker, or else people wouldn't concentrate on His preaching. His main purpose was to teach people about the kingdom of God and to show them the way of salvation (see Matthew 12:17–19; Mark 1:34 and comments).

There was a third reason why Jesus did not want news of this miracle to spread everywhere. If it did, people would begin to think He was the Messiah, and would try to make Him their king (see Mark 8:30 and comment). But He had not come to be an earthly king; He had come to suffer and die. His kingdom was a spiritual kingdom.

CHAPTER 6

A Prophet Without Honor (6:1–6)
(Matthew 13:53–58)

1 Jesus then went to **his home town**, Nazareth, and its neighboring villages.[38] The people there had rejected Him once before (Luke 4:16,28–30), but now He wanted to give them a second chance.

2–3 At first the people of Nazareth were amazed at Jesus' teaching. He taught with authority (Matthew 7:28–29). They were amazed at His **wisdom** and at His **miracles**. Jesus was not like other teachers they had heard.

But then what happened? The people realized that Jesus was from their own village. They remembered Him as a boy. He was one of them. And they became jealous and angry; they **took offense at him**. "Who is he to teach us?" they scoffed. "He is only the carpenter's son."

4 This kind of rejection is a very common thing. If someone from our own village becomes famous and then comes

---

[37] Jesus usually gave this command after performing a miracle (Mark 1:43–44; 3:12; 7:36). He told the demon-possessed man to tell his family about how he had been cured, but He didn't say he should tell everyone (Mark 5:19).

[38] Many Bible scholars believe that this visit to Nazareth is not the same as the visit described in Luke 4:16–30. They say that the visit mentioned by Luke occurred a year earlier. But for the opposite view, see Luke 4:16–17 and comment.

back and begins to teach us, we don't like it. We reject his teaching because of jealousy. We do not show honor to him. Yet if he goes elsewhere, he will receive honor.

5–6 Jesus **could not do any miracles there**. Jesus has all power. Nevertheless, He will not do any great work among people who do not believe. He taught His disciples that if any village rejected them, they should go elsewhere (verse 11). In the same way, Christ will not work in the heart of one who does not believe. If we want to experience the power of Christ in our community and in our individual lives, we must believe.

Jesus Sends Out the Twelve (6:7–13)

(Matthew 10:9–15; Luke 9:1–6)

7 Mark here describes the first time that Jesus sent the twelve disciples out on their own. From this experience the disciples learned that even when Jesus was not with them, they had His authority and power over evil spirits and every kind of sickness (Matthew 10:1,8; Luke 9:1). Mark here says that Jesus sent them out **two by two**. Whenever possible, it is good for preachers and Christian workers to travel in pairs (Luke 10:1; Acts 13:2–3; 15:40).

8–9 The disciples also learned that God would provide all their needs. Jesus told them to take no **bread**,[39] no **bag**,[40] and no **money** (see Matthew 10:9–10). Those whom they preached to and healed should give them their food and lodging. According to Matthew 10:10, Jesus said that the **worker is worth his keep** (see 1 Corinthians 9:14; 1 Timothy 5:18).

According to Mark's account, the disciples were allowed to take a **staff** (verse 8) and **sandals** (verse 9). But according to Matthew 10:10, Jesus ordered His disciples not to take staff and sandals. Most Bible scholars think that Jesus gave different instructions for different kinds of journey. Sandals and staff would be necessary for long, rocky, mountainous trails. Jesus' meaning was that the disciples should take only what was necessary. They were to depend on God for everything else.

10 When the disciples entered a town, they first were to find someone **worthy** (Matthew 10:11); that is, they were to find someone upright and God-fearing who would accept their message and give them hospitality. When they found such a person, they were to stay at his home until they left that town. They were not to move from one house to another looking for more convenient accommodations, or else their first host might be offended. According to Matthew 10:12–13, they were to give the **deserving** home their **greeting**; that is, they were to pronounce the benediction of peace upon that home.[41] They were to bring the peace of God into that home. But if the home was not deserving, they were to take back the blessing they had spoken. On such a house God's peace would not rest (see Luke 10:5–7).

11 Any home or town that did not accept the disciples' message and did not offer them hospitality was "unworthy" or "undeserving." The disciples were to **shake the dust** of such a home or town off their feet. This was a sign of judgment against that unworthy place (Acts 13:51). According to Matthew 10:15, such a town will receive greater punishment than did the cities of Sodom and Gomorrah, which God destroyed with burning sulphur (Genesis 19:1–29). The people of Sodom and Gomorrah had mistreated two angels sent by God. But the towns that rejected Christ's disciples rejected Christ Himself, God's Son. Therefore, their punishment will be greater (see Luke 10:8–12).

Today also, when we travel from place to place preaching God's word, the same is true for us as it was for those first disciples. Those who reject our word

---

[39] Bread is the main food of the Middle Eastern countries. In this context, it means any kind of food.

[40] The **bag** may be a begging bag, or it may be a bag for carrying provisions.

[41] The usual Jewish greeting was: "Peace be unto you."

reject Christ. They lose the opportunity to be saved. But those who accept our word are accepted by Christ and brought into His family and receive salvation.

12–13 The disciples went out, and as Christ had done, so they did also. They preached that **people should repent** (see Mark 1:15 and comment). And they healed the sick and drove out demons (Luke 9:6). Mark says that they **anointed many sick with oil and healed them**. Anointing the sick with oil was a custom in Jesus' time. It was considered to be a type of medical treatment (see Luke 10:34; James 5:14 and comments).

Many people ask: Why do Christ's disciples not have this kind of power today to heal the sick and to drive out demons? Many Bible scholars give the answer that in New Testament times there was a special need for miracles in order to prove to people that Jesus was indeed the Savior, the Son of God, and that the kingdom of God had indeed come among men. Also, the many miracles performed by the first apostles played an important role in the establishing of the church. These Bible scholars say that in modern times there is not such a great need for miracles. However, other Christians point out that there are many miracles happening in different countries of the world today. They say that Christ is ready to give His servants today the same power He gave His first disciples (John 14:12). Both of these answers can be true. But we should remember one thing: The most important miracle is the conversion and spiritual rebirth of sinful men. Leading men and women to Christ is the greatest work that God gives us to do.

John the Baptist Beheaded (6:14–29)

(Matthew 14:1–12; Luke 9:7–9)

14–15 King Herod heard about **this,** that is, about Jesus' fame. This King Herod was the son of King Herod the Great mentioned in Matthew Chapter 2. Herod had been given authority by the Roman Emperor to rule over Galilee. Therefore, Herod was worried about this Jesus, because as a result of all the miracles Jesus was doing in Galilee, He was becoming more famous than Herod himself.

In New Testament times, people believed that the spirit of a dead person had greater power than the person himself had when he was alive. Therefore, some people supposed that the miracle-working Jesus must be John the Baptist risen from the dead. John had done no miracles during his lifetime (John 10:41); therefore, these people supposed that John had come back to life and was now doing miracles.

Other people thought Jesus was the great Old Testament prophet Elijah. Many Jews believed that Elijah would come again (Malachi 4:5). Still others thought Jesus was one of the other Old Testament prophets.

16 But Herod had a special reason for supposing Jesus was, in fact, John the Baptist—because he had killed John. He was afraid that John's spirit had come back to punish him. A guilty conscience leads to many kinds of unnecessary fears. **The wicked man flees though no one pursues** (Proverbs 28:1).

17–18 In verses 17–29, Mark describes how John was killed. Herod had taken his brother's wife Herodias and married her, while his brother was still living. John had spoken against this act of adultery. Therefore, Herodias had become angry with John and sought for an opportunity to kill him. People are either benefited by the reproofs of God's ministers or provoked by them. John, like most of God's servants, suffered for doing good.

19–20 However, Herod was afraid to put John to death. He feared John, **knowing him to be a righteous and holy man**. Herod also feared the anger of the people, **because they considered him a prophet** (Matthew 14:5). Therefore, Herod protected John from the plots of his wife Herodias.

Mark says that Herod **liked to listen** to John. But though he listened, Herod never believed in John's message; he never repented of his sins. He rejected the word of God given through John. Herod was a hearer of the word, but not a doer of it (see James 1:23). But hearing is not enough. In the end, Herod killed the greatest prophet of them all (verse 27).

21–29 Mark here gives a description of the death of John the Baptist.

Jesus Feeds the Five Thousand (6:30–44)

(Matthew 14:13–21; Luke 9:10–17; John 6:1–15)

30–34 The twelve disciples (that is, apostles) returned from their preaching journey and reported to Jesus all that had happened. Then, because they were tired, they crossed the sea by boat, hoping to find a solitary place.[42] But the crowds saw them leave and ran around by the shore, and were waiting for them when they landed on the opposite side.

But Jesus did not say, "I am tired." He did not send the crowd away. The people were **like sheep without a shepherd** (verse 34), and Jesus, being a **good shepherd** (John 10:11), had compassion on them and **began teaching them many things** (see Matthew 9:36). He also **healed their sick** (Matthew 14:14).

35–37 The disciples began to worry about how all the people gathered there were going to find food in such a remote place. The disciples were always worrying about such things. They said to Jesus, "**Send the people away**". But Jesus did not want to send the people away. He had a plan: He was going to use His disciples to feed the crowd. So Jesus said, "**You give them something to eat.**"

The disciples protested that it would take two hundred denarii—eight months' wages—to buy enough food for that many people (2 Kings 4:42–44).

38 Then Jesus asked how much food they had with them. When they had found out, they said, "Five loaves and two fish." The five loaves and two fish, in fact, belonged to a small boy whom Andrew had found in the crowd (John 6:8–9). So they gave the loaves and the fish to Jesus. That was the boy's supper—hardly enough to feed one adult, let alone thousands.

39–44 Then Jesus performed one of His greatest miracles. Taking the five loaves and two fish, He divided them among the crowd. There were five thousand men there, and besides the men, there were women and children as well (Matthew 14:21). **They all ate and were satisfied** (verse 42).

Out of those loaves and fish, Jesus, the living God, created enough food to feed the entire crowd. With God nothing is impossible (Mark 10:27). But Jesus first took what the little boy had given to the disciples. In the same way, Jesus also asks us to give Him what we have. We may not have much. We may say, "I am poor; our church is poor." But Jesus says: "Give me what you have." And when we obey Him, when we are ready to share what little we have, He will take what we give Him and use it to do mighty works. Let us, therefore, not look at our own resources and say, "We can never feed all those people." Rather, let us look at Jesus and His power. He is able to feed them. And when Jesus feeds people, they are **satisfied**.

Just as Jesus gave the crowd physical food, so He also gives people spiritual food. He offers us **living water** (John 4:10), and when we have drunk it we shall never thirst again (John 4:13–14). He offers us the **bread of life**, and when we have eaten it we shall never hunger again (John 6:35). If Jesus could feed over five thousand people with five loaves and two fish, He can certainly feed, both bodily and spiritually, everyone who comes to Him in faith. Jesus is not only the creator of all life (John 1:3); He is also the sustainer of all life, both physical and spiritual.

The feeding of the five thousand is not only a tremendous miracle; it is also an illustration of how the kingdom of God grows. It is a parable of missions. We

---

[42] In Matthew 14:13, a second reason is mentioned why Jesus wanted to find a solitary place. Jesus had just learned that Herod had heard about Him and thought that He was John the Baptist (Mark 6:16). Therefore, Herod would certainly try to capture Jesus and perhaps kill Him. But Jesus still had much work to do. His time to die had not yet come. Therefore, He withdrew to the other side of the Sea of Galilee outside Herod's jurisdiction.

need to ask the question: At what point did the loaves and fish begin to multiply? They began to multiply as they left the disciples' hands. As the disciples began to give, they kept on having more and more to give.

Some Christians are like the little boy—they are providers. Other Christians are like the disciples—they are distributors. And out in the world are the hungry multitudes, waiting to be fed the bread of life.

Jesus, the Son of God, with whom is all authority in heaven and on earth, has chosen us to help Him feed the multitudes. He could do it by Himself, but He has chosen not to. He has chosen, instead, to use us. And as we give to Him our resources, our time, our skills, ourselves, He will use us to reach the hungry multitudes, and in the process He will enrich us beyond all imagining.

Jesus Walks on the Water (6:45–56)
(Matthew 14:22–36; John 6:16–24)

45 According to John's Gospel, when Jesus had finished feeding the five thousand, the people said among themselves, **"Surely this is the Prophet who is to come into the world"** (Deuteronomy 18:15; John 6:14). John says that the people wanted to make Jesus their king by force. But Jesus didn't let them. He dismissed the people and withdrew by Himself to pray (John 6:15).

When Jesus saw that the people were about to try to make Him their king, He **immediately** sent His disciples away by boat to Bethsaida.[43] Jesus' disciples also wanted Him to be a king. They didn't understand yet that instead of becoming a king, Jesus must suffer and die. If He became an earthly king, He would have no chance to suffer and be killed, and thus God's plan for man's salvation would have been blocked. Therefore, Jesus didn't want His disciples to remain in that place and listen to the crowd talk about making Him a king. So He immediately sent them away from there.

Satan had promised to make Jesus the ruler of many nations if Jesus would agree to worship him (Matthew 4:8–9). Again the temptation had come. Again Christ resisted the temptation. He was not to be an earthly king, but rather a suffering servant (Isaiah 53:3,11). His kingdom was not of this world (John 18:36).

46–47 Therefore, after sending away His disciples, Jesus then dismissed the crowd, and **went into the hills to pray**. His disciples, meanwhile, were in a boat trying to row toward Bethsaida. But the wind was blowing against them, and they were blown off course toward the middle of the lake.

48–50 At the **fourth watch of the night**—about 3 A.M.—Jesus came to them walking on the water. He was **about to pass by them** (verse 48). He wanted to test their faith. The disciples were terrified because they thought they were seeing a ghost. But Jesus told them not to be afraid. **"It is I."**

Then, according to Matthew 14:28–31, Peter said: **"Lord, if it's you . . . tell me to come to you on the water"** (Matthew 14:28). Peter was testing Jesus to see if He was real or only a ghost. Jesus said, **"Come."** So Peter, at first full of courage, stepped onto the water and walked toward Jesus. But then his faith failed him. He took his eyes off Jesus, and began to look at the wind and the waves. Peter forgot that Jesus was Lord of the wind and waves (Mark 4:39–41). And he began to sink. But Jesus held on to him and brought him into the boat. Then Jesus said to him, **"You of little faith . . . why did you doubt?"** (Matthew 14:31).

We, likewise, whenever we take our eyes off Jesus and begin to look at our troubles, will surely sink. If we have faith in Jesus and in His promises, we shall not be afraid of wind and waves.

According to Matthew 14:30, after Peter had looked at the waves and begun

[43] According to Luke's Gospel, Jesus fed the five thousand near a place called Bethsaida (Luke 9:10). Here, according to Mark, He sends them **on ahead of him to Bethsaida**; or as other versions translate it, He sent them "to the other side to Bethsaida." Therefore, some Bible scholars believe that there may have been two different towns called Bethsaida.

to be afraid, he again turned his eyes to Jesus and cried out, **"Lord, save me!"** We, too, when troubles come upon us and we feel like we are sinking, can call out to Jesus, and He will hold out His hand and keep us from sinking. Peter did not try to save himself; neither should we.

51–52 The disciples were amazed. They had seen Jesus feed the multitude. They had just seen Him walk on water. Earlier, they had seen Him still the storm (Mark 4:39–41). But even having seen all this, they still did not understand who Jesus really was. When they saw Him on the water, they said, **"It's a ghost"** (Matthew 14:26); but they should have said: "It's the Lord." If they had known that Jesus was God, they would not have been amazed at these miracles. They would not have been terrified. They didn't know who Jesus was because **their hearts were hardened** (verse 52). They did not fully believe in Jesus. They were still men of **little faith**.

Nevertheless, Matthew writes that after Peter and Jesus got into the boat and the wind died down, the disciples worshiped Jesus and said, **"Truly you are the Son of God"** (Matthew 14:33). Finally they had begun to be aware of who Jesus was.

53–56 Here Mark gives a final description of Jesus' healing ministry in Galilee (see Matthew 15:29–31). And **all who touched him were healed** (verse 56). Even those who touched the edge of His cloak were healed (see Mark 5:27–29).

According to John 6:22–24, the morning after the feeding of the five thousand, the crowd looked for Jesus. They had seen the disciples leave in the boat without Jesus, so they supposed that Jesus was still nearby. They still wanted to make Him a king.

But finally, when they could not find Jesus anywhere, they got into some boats that had come from the city of Tiberias,[44] and went across the lake in search of Him.

CHAPTER 7

Clean and Unclean (7:1–23)
(Matthew 15:1–20)

1–4 The Jews had many religious **traditions** which they followed. Many of these were oral traditions; that is, they were the traditions **of the elders**, the traditions of men (verse 3). They were not written in the Old Testament,[45] which is the word of God. One such tradition was the washing of hands before eating. The Jews didn't wash to clean the dirt from their hands. The washing was only a sign that their hands were ritually "clean." They believed that if they ate with **unclean hands**, their food would be made "unclean." For the same reason, the Jews also ritually washed their **cups, pitchers and kettles** (verse 4).

Not only that, when the Jews went to the crowded bazaars they often accidentally touched non-Jews—that is, Gentiles—and thus became "unclean." Therefore, they had to ritually bathe before they ate. There were hundreds of such rules.

5 The Pharisees and teachers of the law accused Jesus' disciples of not obeying the traditions of the elders, because they did not ritually wash their hands before they ate.

6–8 But Jesus knew the hypocrisy of the Pharisees and the teachers of the law. They cleaned the outside of their bodies, but their hearts remained unclean, that is, proud and unloving. They repeated eloquent prayers with their lips, but they did not worship and honor God from their hearts. They were indeed hypocrites

---

[44] Tiberias is a large town on the west shore of the Sea of Galilee. In Jesus' time, it was King Herod's capital.

[45] The Old Testament is the Jewish Scripture.

(see Matthew 6:5; 23:25–28). In verses 6–7 Jesus quotes from Isaiah 29:13.

What the Jews had done was to make the traditions of the elders equal to the commands of God written in the Old Testament. The traditions of the elders were only the teachings of men, not God.[46] Many of these traditions opposed the commands of God. In following these traditions, the Jews were disobeying some of God's commands. Jesus said to them, "**You have let go of the commands of God and are holding on to the traditions of men.**"

9–13 In these verses, Jesus gives an example of how the Jews broke God's law by observing one of their traditions. One of the written commands of God given through **Moses**[47] says: **Honor your father and your mother** (Exodus 20:12). According to this command, a son had to help provide for his parents in their old age. But the Jews also had an oral tradition, according to which they used to vow to give a gift to God. Perhaps they would set aside some property or money as a gift devoted to God, called a **Corban.**[48] They wouldn't actually have to give up the property or money during their lifetime; it could be turned over to God after their death. In this way, they got to keep their property and money for their own use, and avoided having to use it to support their aged parents. In other words, the Jews used this tradition of promising a gift to God as an excuse for not helping their parents. If someone's elderly father or mother needed help from their son, the son would say: "No, I can't help you. I have vowed to give my money to God." In this way, by following their tradition, they disobeyed God's command to honor their parents. The Jews should have remembered that breaking this command was a serious crime in God's eyes: **Anyone who curses his father or mother must be put to death** (Exodus 21:17).

From this we can learn an important principle: We must not use one part of God's word to avoid obeying another part. We must not use one verse of the Bible to contradict another verse. God does not contradict Himself. We must obey the whole teaching of the Bible, not just one part of it that we happen to like. To give offerings to God is good. But in giving offerings to God, we must not break God's command to honor our father and mother.

14–16 The Jews worried about eating with "unclean" hands. They feared that eating with unclean hands would make their food unclean, and that eating unclean food would, in turn, make them unclean. But Jesus taught that it is not what goes in but **what comes out of a man** that makes him unclean—that is, his evil thoughts and desires, words and actions (see verses 20–23). If our thoughts, desires, and actions are unclean, our hearts will be unclean also. It is these things which make us truly unclean.

According to Matthew 15:12–14, the disciples came to Jesus and told Him that the Pharisees were offended when they heard His teaching about inward defilement. Jesus answered: "**Every plant that my heavenly Father has not planted will be pulled up by the roots**" (Matthew 15:13). The Pharisees were like plants that God had not planted. They soon would be **pulled up**. Indeed, forty years later Jerusalem was destroyed by the Romans, and the Jews were either killed or scattered.

Like the Pharisees in Jesus' time, there are always those in the church who are not planted by God. While Jesus is sowing good seed, the devil is busy sowing bad seed (see Matthew 13:24–26). We can distinguish the good seed from the bad seed by its fruit (Matthew 7:20).

---

[46] In the beginning, the first traditions did not contradict the Jewish law. They gave guidance about many little things that were not mentioned in the law. However, some of the traditions added later on did contradict the law.

[47] **Moses** was the great Jewish leader who led the Jews out of bondage in Egypt. He also received the ten commandments from God. The Jewish law is often called the "law of Moses" because it is written in the first five books of the Old Testament, which Moses wrote.

[48] **Corban** is a Hebrew word meaning "gift devoted to God."

But God will pull up the weeds—the fruit of the bad seed—and destroy them at a time of His choosing (Matthew 13:27–30).

Then, according to Matthew's account, Jesus told His disciples to leave the Pharisees alone. "**Leave them,**" He said; "**they are blind guides. If a blind man leads a blind man, both will fall into a pit**" (Matthew 15:14). The Jews were spiritually blind, and their leaders were also blind. As a result, they lost the road and strayed from God's word, and disaster soon overtook them. Those who deceive others and lead them astray will not escape punishment themselves.

17–19 The disciples were slow to understand Jesus' teaching, because Jesus was overturning everything they had been taught as Jews from their youth up. Now Jesus was teaching that they did not have to ritually clean their hands and cups. But not only that, Jesus also **declared all foods "clean"** (see Romans 14:14). This was amazing to the disciples. The Jews were very strict about what they ate. Some things were considered clean, some unclean (see Leviticus 11:1–47; Acts 10:9–16). Now Jesus was saying that these laws were no longer necessary. Food couldn't make a man clean or unclean. Food went into the stomach and came out in the stool. It didn't go into the heart! No man can clean his heart by outward rules and rituals.

20–23 In these verses Jesus gives some examples of things coming out of a man's heart that make him unclean (see Romans 1:28–31; Galatians 5:19–21). All these sins arise first as evil desires in man's heart (James 1:14–15).

The Faith of a Syrophoenician Woman (7:24–30)

(Matthew 15:21–28)

24 Jesus needed a day of rest. He went to the area of Tyre and Sidon (Mark 3:8) and entered a certain house hoping to rest.

25–27 However, a woman whose daughter was demon-possessed immediately found out Jesus was there and came to ask Him to heal her daughter. The woman was a **Greek,**[49] born in **Syrian Pheonicia**, that is, modern Syria.[50] The people from that place were first called "Canaanites" (Matthew 15:22). These people were Gentiles, that is, non-Jews.

According to Matthew 15:23–24, Jesus at first did not answer her. God does not always answer our petitions at once. Then He said, "**I was sent only to the lost sheep of Israel**"—that is, to the Jews.

Jesus was sent by His Father to bring salvation to the Jews. In the beginning, God had chosen ABRAHAM to become the father of a special nation, Israel—the Jewish people (Genesis 12:2; 17:3–7). Later, in Moses' time, God told the Jews: "**. . . if you obey me fully and keep my covenant, then out of all the nations you will be my treasured possession . . . you will be for me a kingdom of priests and a holy nation**" (Exodus 19:5–6). Many times through the Old Testament prophets, God promised that a Savior would come who would save His people, Israel (Matthew 1:21; Luke 1:68–70). That Savior was Jesus, who Himself was a Jew, descended from Abraham and David (Matthew 1:1; 15:22). Christ, therefore, was sent first to the Jewish people. His work in the beginning was only among the Jews.

But in this important story, we see a non-Jewish woman ask Jesus to heal her daughter. Jesus at first told her that God had sent Him only to the Jews, not to the Gentiles. He said this to test her faith. He said to her, "**First let the children** (the Jews) **eat all they want . . . for it is not right to take the children's bread and toss it to the dogs** (the Gentiles)."[51] Jesus' meaning was this: In any house, the

---

[49] Greece is an important country of southern Europe. In Jesus' time it was part of the Roman Empire.

[50] Syria is a Middle Eastern country which lies to the east of Lebanon and Israel.

[51] The Jews despised the Gentiles and considered them sinful and unclean. However, here Jesus does not use the word "dog" to insult the Gentile woman, but rather to illustrate His reason for not healing her daughter.

children are fed first, and afterward the animals. That is, first the Jews should have a chance to hear the Gospel of salvation. Only afterward would the Gospel be preached to the Gentiles.

God never said that He would bless only the Jews. In the beginning, God had said to Abraham, "... **all peoples on earth will be blessed through you**" (Genesis 12:3). And this has indeed come to pass: through Abraham's descendant, Christ, all nations of the earth have been blessed (see Ephesians 2:11–13,17–19 and comment). Christ is not only a light **for glory to . . . Israel**; He is also a **light for revelation to the Gentiles** (Luke 2:32).

28 The woman replied, "But we Gentile 'dogs' are happy to **eat the children's crumbs** that fall from the table." The woman was clever. The dogs eat the crumbs even while the children are eating; they don't have to wait until later. If Jesus gave her only a "crumb," that would be enough to heal her daughter. This woman had more faith in Jesus than even His own disciples had! She understood who Jesus was. Even crumbs from Jesus are the bread of life.

29–30 Jesus answered her: "**Woman, you have great faith!**" (Matthew 15:28). And Jesus healed her daughter immediately. He didn't even go to the house where the daughter was, but healed her from a distance. This was Christ's first work among the Gentiles. The Jews were rejecting Christ and opposing Him; but this Gentile woman had shown true faith. **And without faith it is impossible to please God** (Hebrews 11:6).

The Healing of a Deaf and Dumb Man (7:31–37)

31–37 Jesus then returned to the **region of the Decapolis**—the ten cities—where he had first healed the man possessed by many demons (Mark 5:20). There he healed a man who **was deaf and could hardly talk**. In addition to using His word to heal the man, Jesus also used His own saliva (see Mark 8:23; John 9:6). Jesus then ordered the man not to tell anyone (see Mark 5:43 and comment), but he did not obey.

People learn to speak mainly by hearing themselves and others speak. Therefore, those who are born deaf usually cannot speak properly. But if their ears are opened, they can then learn to speak. It is the same with spiritual things. When our ears are **opened** to hear God's voice, then our tongue shall be **loosened** to praise Him and to witness to Him.

According to Matthew 15:29–31, on this same occasion Jesus healed many others who were **lame, blind, crippled,** and **dumb. The people were amazed when they saw the dumb speaking, the crippled made well, the lame walking and the blind seeing** (Matthew 15:31). Truly the prophecy of Isaiah had been fulfilled by Jesus: **Then will the eyes of the blind be opened and the ears of the deaf unstopped. Then will the lame leap like a deer, and the tongue of the dumb shout for joy** (Isaiah 35:5–6).

CHAPTER 8

Jesus Feeds the Four Thousand (8:1–10)

(Matthew 15:32–39)

1–10 Here Mark describes a second occasion when Jesus fed a multitude. As on the first occasion, Jesus fed the people because He had compassion on them (Mark 6:34). This time there were four thousand men, seven loaves, and seven baskets[52] of fragments gathered after everyone had eaten (see Mark 6:32–44 and comment).

---

[52] It is interesting that the seven baskets used on this occasion were different from the twelve baskets mentioned in Mark 6:43. A different Greek word for "basket" is used in this section. The baskets used here were a larger type of basket; thus fewer were needed.

After Jesus had fed the multitude, He went to **Dalmanutha**. According to Matthew 15:39, He went to **Magadan**. It is not known where either of these two places were located. Or perhaps Matthew and Mark were referring to one place with two different names.

This crowd had been with Jesus for three days with nothing to eat (verse 2). They had come to hear God's words. They had come to receive spiritual food for their spirits, and God gave them food for their bodies as well.

Here we can see a very important principle. If we seek first of all God's word and His righteousness, He will take care of all our bodily needs (see Matthew 6:31–33 and comment). But if we come to Christ only to receive some bodily or material benefit—food, a scholarship, a job—then we shall receive nothing from God. Indeed, if one insincerely comes to a church meeting or Bible study only in order to get some material benefit, his guilt will increase in God's sight. Because, as that person's knowledge of God increases, so will his responsibility to obey God also increase—together with his guilt for not doing so (see Luke 12:47–48).

The Pharisees Ask For a Sign (8:11–13)

(Matthew 16:1–4; Luke 12:54–56)

11–13 The Pharisees, in order to **test** Jesus, asked Him to show them a **sign**. They were not seeking a sign to find out if Jesus was the Savior, the Messiah. They had already decided that He was not. They were not sincere in their request for a sign. They only wanted to prove that Jesus was not the Messiah.

The **sign** they sought was some kind of absolute proof that Jesus was the Son of God, the Messiah. They wanted a **sign from heaven**. They had seen Christ's miracles, but they did not consider these sufficient proof that He was God's Son. In fact, the Jews had said that Jesus did His miracles by the power of Satan! (see Mark 3:22). Therefore, the **sign** that the Pharisees demanded was a special proof that Jesus' power came from God, not from Satan.

Jesus answered the Pharisees: "**. . . no sign will be given it** (this generation)." According to Matthew 16:4, Jesus said that no sign would be given **except the sign of Jonah**. Jonah was a prophet who was swallowed by a **great fish** and spent three days in its stomach (Jonah 1:17). In the same way, Christ would be killed and spend three days in the earth and then rise from the dead. That would be the sign that He was truly the Son of God (see Matthew 12:38–41 and comment). Yet, in the end, the Jews did not even accept that sign. They said after Christ's resurrection that His **disciples came during the night and stole him away** (Matthew 28:12–13).

Jesus did not want to give a sign—that is, complete proof—that He was the Son of God, because if He did so there would no longer be any room for faith. Faith can only exist when the object of our faith is something beyond our finite knowledge. Jesus wanted to find out who had faith and who did not. If He had given an absolute sign, everyone would have followed Him. But He wanted for followers only those who had faith. To demand a sign is the same as not to believe. Jesus did not want to show a sign to unbelievers.

According to Matthew 16:2–3, Jesus reminded the Pharisees that by looking at the sky, they could predict what the weather would be. A red sky in the evening was a sign of fair weather. A red sky in the morning was a sign of bad weather. If the Pharisees could interpret these signs of the coming weather, why couldn't they interpret the spiritual signs of the coming of the kingdom of God? (see Luke 12:54–56). For those with open believing hearts, Christ had already shown more than enough "signs" that He was the Son of God. But the Pharisees wouldn't believe no matter what signs Jesus showed them (John 10:24–25).

The Yeast of the Pharisees and Herod (8:14–21)

(Matthew 16:5–12)

14–16 Here Mark describes the slowness of the disciples to understand Jesus' teaching. Whenever Jesus tried to teach them some spiritual truth, they thought He was talking about ordinary worldly matters.

Jesus wanted to warn them about the **yeast**—that is, the evil and hypocrisy—of the Pharisees and of King Herod (Luke 12:1) and of the Sadducees[53] (Matthew 16:6). "Yeast" is usually used as an illustration of evil in the New Testament (see 1 Corinthians 5:6–8 and comment). A little evil can spread like yeast through the whole church. A little false teaching can destroy the faith of new Christians (Galatians 5:7–9).

But the disciples didn't at first realize that Jesus was speaking of spiritual "yeast"—the evil yeast of hypocrisy and false teaching (Matthew 16:12). They thought He was chiding them for having forgotten to bring enough bread (verse 14).

17–21 Jesus said to His disciples, "How can you be talking about not having enough bread? Have you not just seen me feed five thousand men with five little loaves and four thousand men with seven loaves? How can you think there is not enough bread? Don't you realize who I am? I am the Lord and Creator of the universe. Do you suppose that I can't create more bread out of your one loaf? **Do you still not see or understand? Are your hearts hardened?**" The disciples had **eyes** and **ears** (verse 18), but they could not yet discern spiritual things (see 1 Corinthians 2:12–14).[54]

The Healing of a Blind Man at Bethsaida (8:22–26)

22–26 Jesus then healed a blind man (see John 9:1–7). First He healed the man's eyes only partly. Then a second time He put His hands on his eyes, and his sight was fully restored.

Spiritually, the disciples were like this blind man. At first they could not see and understand spiritual things. Then they began to see in part. To the blind man, people looked **like trees walking around** (verse 24). To the disciples, Christ looked only like a miracle worker, a healer, a teacher, a prophet. They could not yet see that He was more than all these, that He was the Messiah, the Son of God.

Peter's Confession of Christ (8:27–30)

(Matthew 16:13–20; Luke 9:18–21)

27 As they were journeying to Caesarea Philippi, an important city in northern Israel, Jesus asked His disciples, "**Who do people say I am?**" Who is Jesus? For every man and woman on earth, there is no more important question than this.

28–29 Some people thought that Jesus was John the Baptist risen from the dead (Mark 6:14). Others thought He was an Old Testament prophet like Elijah or Jeremiah (Matthew 16:14; Mark 6:15).

But Jesus knew what others thought. He wanted to know what His disciples thought. "**Who do you say I am?**"

Peter answered: "**You are the Christ.**"[55] According to Matthew 16:16, Peter gave a fuller answer: "**You are the Christ, the Son of the living God.**" At last, the disciples' eyes were opened!

Then, according to Matthew 16:17–19, Jesus pronounced upon Peter a great blessing.[56] He said to Peter: "**Blessed are you, Simon son of Jonah,**[57] **for this**

---

[53] According to Matthew 16:6,11–12, Jesus also mentioned on this occasion the evil and hypocrisy of the Sadducees. The Sadducees were another Jewish sect like the Pharisees (see Mark 12:18; Acts 23:6–8 and comments).

[54] Mark uses two different Greek words for "basket" in verses 19–20. For further discussion, see footnote to comment on verses 1–10.

[55] **Christ** is the Greek word meaning "anointed one." "Messiah" is the Hebrew word meaning the same thing.

[56] Mark wrote his Gospel mainly according to what Peter told him about the life of Christ (see Mark: Introduction). However, out of humility, Peter did not mention to Mark the blessing he received on this occasion; this is described only in Matthew 16:17–19.

[57] In place of **son of Jonah**, some translations of the Bible say "Bar-Jona," which means the same thing (see John 1:42).

was not revealed to you by man, but by my Father in heaven." Faith is a gift of God. It is always God who reveals to us who Christ is.

Then Jesus said to Peter: "**. . . you are Peter, and on this rock I will build my** CHURCH" (Matthew 16:18). In the Greek language the name Peter means "rock." Jesus' meaning was that Peter and the other apostles would be the foundation for Christ's church (Ephesians 2:19–20). The **gates of Hades** (Isaiah 38:10)—that is, the power of death—would not be able to overcome this church (Matthew 16:18). The gates of Hades are like the gates of a fortress. They keep the spirits of the dead shut up inside, and they keep Christ from coming in to rescue them. These gates will not be able to stand against Christ and His church. Christ, by His victory over death, has destroyed Satan's stronghold and set the captives free (Isaiah 61:1; Luke 4:18; 1 Peter 3:18–20 and comments).

Then, according to Matthew's account, Jesus said to His disciples: "**I will give you the keys of the kingdom of heaven; whatever you bind on earth will be bound in heaven, and whatever you loose on earth will be loosed in heaven**" (Matthew 16:19). In saying this, Jesus gave the apostles the authority to establish His church and to be its leaders. Jesus did not say this only to Peter, but to all the apostles (see Matthew 18:18). The **keys of the kingdom of heaven** gave the apostles the authority to preach the message of salvation and to bring into the church all those who would believe and be saved. Christ, **who holds the key of David** (Isaiah 22:22; Revelation 3:7), gave His own key to His apostles. They received from Him the authority to **bind** and to **loose** in Christ's name.[58] This means that they had the authority to determine true doctrine, to punish false teachers and unrepentant sinners, and to exercise complete authority in the church.

This didn't mean that everything the apostles did after that was right, or that they never sinned again. Peter later denied Jesus (Mark 14:66–72). In Galatia, Peter again fell into grave error, and was rebuked by the Apostle Paul (Galatians 2:11–14). But insofar as the apostles acted in accordance with the will of Christ, they acted with His full authority, and what they decided on earth, Christ confirmed in heaven.

30 Then Jesus told His disciples to tell no one that He was the Christ, the Messiah (see Mark 5:43; 7:36).

We must understand why Jesus said this. All the Jews were expecting a victorious Messiah (Isaiah 11:1–5), who would come and be their king, free them from bondage to the Romans, and re-establish the kingdom of Israel (see John 6:14–15). But the Jews forgot that the Messiah must also suffer and die (Isaiah 53:1–12; Luke 24:26). The Jews thought that the Messiah was coming to establish an earthly kingdom; but instead, He came to establish a spiritual kingdom, a kingdom that would last forever (Isaiah 9:7; Daniel 7:13–14; Luke 1:33; Revelation 11:15). Christ didn't come to give men political liberation; He came to give them salvation and eternal life.

Therefore, if the disciples immediately began to tell everyone that Jesus was the Christ, the Messiah, then the people would surely have tried to make Him their king. He would not have been given the chance to suffer and die on the cross. His purpose in coming to earth to die for the sins of all men would not have been fulfilled (see Mark 10:45 and comment). Without His death men could not obtain salvation. Therefore, it was necessary to keep secret the fact that Jesus was the Messiah until after He had died and risen again (Mark 9:9).

Jesus Predicts His Death (8:31–33)
(Matthew 16:21–23; Luke 9:22)

31–32 Peter had just confessed that Jesus was the Christ, the Messiah, the Son of the living God (verse 29). But he still did not fully understand what Christ came to earth to do. He thought like the others Jews thought, namely, that Christ had come to be an earthly king. There-

[58] To **bind** and **loose** means to set up rules of conduct for daily life.

fore, when Jesus told him that the **Son of Man must suffer many things and be rejected . . . and that he must be killed,** Peter could not accept it. He rebuked Jesus for saying such a thing.

Jesus also said that **after three days** the Son of Man would **rise again**. Jesus knew not only that He would die, but also that He would rise from the dead on the third day. The disciples didn't understand this at all.

33 Through Peter's lips, Jesus heard the voice of Satan again trying to tempt Him (see Matthew 4:8–10 and comment). He heard Satan telling Him, "You don't have to suffer and die. I will make you a king if you worship me." Therefore, Jesus turned to Peter and said, **"Out of my sight, Satan!"**

Sometimes our best friends, our most faithful colleagues, try to dissuade us from doing God's will. Their intention is good: they desire to spare us trouble and pain. But we must not listen to them; we must do God's will instead (see Acts 21:10–14).

Peter was not thinking God's thoughts, but man's thoughts. God said through the prophet Isaiah: **"For my thoughts are not your thoughts, neither are your ways my ways. . . . As the heavens are higher than the earth, so are my ways higher than your ways and my thoughts than your thoughts"** (Isaiah 55:8–9). Peter's mind was on earthly things, not heavenly things (Colossians 3:2). He was opposing God's plan and purpose. Jesus told him: **"You are a stumbling block to me; you do not have in mind the things of God, but the things of men"** (Matthew 16:23).

True Discipleship (8:34–38)
(Matthew 16:24–27; Luke 9:23–26)

34 Jesus had just told the disciples a difficult saying—namely, that He would have to suffer and die. Now He tells them an even more difficult thing: they, too, will have to suffer, and perhaps even die. **If anyone would come after me, he must deny himself and take up his cross and follow me** (see Matthew 10:38; Luke 14:27).

If **anyone** would come after me—that means all Christians. All Christians are called to be disciples. Let us never suppose that there are two kinds of Christians: one kind that follows Jesus and suffers with Him, and a second kind that can lead an easy life. There is only one kind of true Christian; that is, a disciple.

If anyone would come after me, **let him deny himself**. Many people say, "I want to follow Christ," but in the end they do not follow Him. Why not? Because Christ says: "You must **deny** yourself." That means that to follow Christ a person must give up his own desires and live only according to Christ's desire. We must deny our own pleasure, our own advantage, our own comfort. Before we became Christians we lived completely for ourselves. But after we become Christians, we must live completely for God. This is why many people at first come to Christ, but afterward turn away. In their minds, it is too difficult to follow Christ.

If anyone would come after me, **he must . . . take up his CROSS**. This is the first time Mark mentions the **cross**. The cross was the Roman method of carrying out the death sentence. Criminals were suspended alive on an upright post, and their hands were nailed or tied to a crossbar. Then the criminal slowly died an agonizing death. Not only were criminals put to death in this way, but they were also made to carry their own cross to the place of execution. Therefore, when Jesus told His followers that they must **take up** [their] **cross**, in their minds that could mean only one thing: namely, they must be ready to suffer and die for Him. Suffering and persecution will come to all who follow Christ (see John 15:19; 2 Timothy 3:12 and comments). There can be no crown without the cross.

It is because Jesus died on a cross that the cross has become the main symbol of the Christian church. The cross is a sign of Jesus' death for our sins.

Finally Jesus says: "**. . . and follow me.**" We must turn around. We must stop going our own way and start going Jesus' way. Jesus' way was the way of suffering, the way of the cross. That is to be our way, too.

Christians do not follow after an idea

or a philosophy or a political party. They do not even follow a religion. They follow a person—Jesus Christ.

35 Then Jesus said an amazing thing: "**For whoever wants to save his life will lose it, but whoever loses his life for me and for the gospel will save it.**" Whoever denies Christ in order to save his **life** (his life in this world, his pleasures, his pride, his honor and reputation, his possessions, his physical life) will lose his life (his true life, spiritual life, eternal life). But **whoever loses his life** for Christ (that is, his life in this world, his pride, honor, possessions, physical life itself) will save his life; he will obtain true spiritual life, eternal life. To **lose** one's life for Christ and the Gospel means to **deny** one's self and **take up** [one's] **cross** and follow Jesus (verse 34).

Worldly life and spiritual life are opposed to each other (Galatians 5:17). To the extent we seek worldly blessings, to that extent we shall lose spiritual blessings. To the extent we give up worldly advantage for Christ's sake, to that extent we shall gain spiritual advantage. Usually, however, once we have given up worldly advantage for Christ, Christ will bless us in worldly things also (see Matthew 6:33; Mark 10:29–31 and comments). The abundant life that Jesus promised to His followers (John 10:10) begins here in this world. Eternal life begins the moment we believe. Jesus only says to us: "Do not seek these worldly blessings; seek only me, and I will bless you now and forever" (see John 12:25; 1 John 2:15–17 and comments). And let us not fool ourselves: We cannot seek after Christ and worldly blessings at the same time; we must choose (see Matthew 6:24 and comment).

36 What would be the advantage in gaining the whole world if, as a result, one were to lose his **life**,[59] that is, his soul? In other words, what good is the world to us if we lose our eternal soul? Life in this world is very short. Why give up eternal life with God in order to gain a few years of pleasure in this life?

37 There is nothing in this world more valuable than our soul. There is nothing in this world greater than eternal life. Jesus said, ". . . **what can a man give in exchange for his soul?**" The answer is: nothing. One soul is worth more than the whole world. If our soul is lost, the loss can never be made up.

Then, according to Matthew 16:27, Jesus said, "**For the Son of Man is going to come in his Father's glory with his angels, and then he will reward each person according to what he has done**" (see Mark 13:26–27 and comment). Christ will come again as judge at the end of the world (John 5:22). And He will reward us for whatever we have done for Him (see 2 Corinthians 5:10 and comment). For whatever loss we have suffered for His sake in this world, He will repay us abundantly in heaven.

38 If we are ashamed of Christ here on earth, He will be ashamed of us when He comes again at the end of the world. If we deny Christ before men, He will deny us before the Father in heaven (see Matthew 10:32–33 and comment). We must never be ashamed that we are Christians. We must not hide it because of fear. Christ does not want secret followers.

---

[59] The Greek word for **soul** that Mark uses here and in verse 37 is the same word that he used in verse 35, where it is translated **life**. The same Greek word can mean both "soul" and "life." In verses 36 and 37, the meaning is **soul**. In verse 35, Jesus is talking mainly about **life** in this world; in verses 36–37, He is talking mainly about man's eternal **soul**.

CHAPTER 9

The Transfiguration (9:1–13)
(Matthew 16:28; 17:1–13;
Luke 9:27–36)

1 Jesus said, "... **some who are standing here will not taste death before they see the kingdom of God come with power.**" The **kingdom of God** in this verse means Jesus Himself (see Mark 1:14 and comment). According to Matthew 16:28, Jesus said, "... **some who are standing here will not taste death before they see the Son of Man** (Christ) **coming in his kingdom.**" Therefore, by comparing these corresponding verses in Matthew and Mark, we can understand that the "kingdom of God coming with power" is the same as the "Son of Man coming in his kingdom." Christ not only has brought the kingdom of God to earth; He is Himself the kingdom of God. When Christ lives in us, the kingdom of God lives in us also (Luke 17:20–21). And when Jesus comes again, then the kingdom of God will be established forever both in heaven and on earth.

What did Jesus mean when He said, "... **before they see the kingdom of God come with power**"? To what event does the expression "kingdom of God coming with power" refer to? There are two possible answers. Some Bible scholars say that the expression means Jesus' transfiguration, which is described by Mark, Matthew, and Luke immediately after Jesus made this statement. The transfiguration was indeed a manifestation of the kingdom of God—of the **Son of Man coming in his kingdom**.

But other scholars believe that the expression means the resurrection of Christ, His ascent into heaven, and the coming of the Holy Spirit (Acts 2:1–4). Through the Holy Spirit, Christ established the kingdom of God in the hearts of believers. In the person of the Holy Spirit, the kingdom of God has indeed come with power.

In other verses in the New Testament, such as Matthew 25:31 and Mark 8:38; 13:26, the "coming of the Son of Man" means the second coming of Christ at the end of the world. However, this cannot be the meaning in this verse, because Jesus says here that some **will not taste death** before the kingdom of God comes with power. Since the end of the world has not yet come, and since all the people who heard Jesus speak these words have died, Jesus cannot have been talking about His second coming in this verse or in Matthew 16:28.

2–3 Six days later Peter, James, and John[60] saw Jesus changed into a glorified form. Having confessed that Jesus was truly the Christ (Mark 8:29), now Jesus confirmed the disciples' faith by appearing to three of them as the glorified Son of God.

4 **Moses** and **Elijah** (see Mark 6:15) also appeared with Jesus **in glorious splendor** (Luke 9:31). According to Luke's account, they talked with Jesus about His coming **departure**—that is, about His coming death, resurrection, and ascension into heaven (Luke 9:31).

From this we clearly see that the saints of God who have left this earth do not die; they only sleep (1 Thessalonians 4:13–14). Christ easily awakens them. Just as the disciples recognized Moses and Elijah, so shall we recognize each other in heaven.

5–6 Peter said, "**Rabbi, it is good for us to be here.**" Peter thought that he should make three shelters for Moses, Elijah, and Jesus to stay in. He thought that Moses and Elijah would remain on the mountain with Jesus. The three disciples didn't really understand what was happening.

7–8 The transfiguration was a sign that Christ was the Son of God. This was further confirmed by God Himself speak-

[60] Peter, James, and John would later see Christ in trouble and distress (Mark 14:33). But now they saw Him in glory.

ing from a cloud: "**This is my Son, whom I love. Listen to him!**" (see Matthew 17:5; Mark 1:11; 2 Peter 1:17–18). From now on, let the disciples have no doubt who Jesus is. And let them listen to Him! Peter especially had not been ready to listen to Jesus before (Mark 8:32). Those who want to know the mind of God must listen to Christ.

At the sound of God's voice, the three disciples fell on their faces in fear. But Jesus said to them, "**Get up. . . . Don't be afraid**" (Matthew 17:6–7).

9 See Mark 8:30 and comment.

10 The disciples didn't know what Jesus meant when He talked about "rising from the dead" in verse 9. They still didn't understand that the Son of God first had to suffer and die and only then would He rise from the dead (see Luke 24:25–27,45–46).

11 Having seen Elijah on the mountain with Jesus, the disciples recalled that in the Old Testament the prophet Malachi wrote that Elijah would come to earth again before the coming of the Messiah (Malachi 4:5). If Jesus was the Messiah, why hadn't Elijah come, the disciples wanted to know. The Jews believed that Elijah would come to anoint the Messiah as king of Israel.

12 Jesus answered the three disciples: "Yes, Elijah must come before the Messiah and restore **all things**." "All things" are restored through repentance and forgiveness. This is the meaning of the next verse of Malachi's prophecy (Malachi 4:6).

But Jesus knew His disciples did not understand why He had to **suffer much and be rejected**. They had forgotten Isaiah's prophecy about the Messiah (Isaiah 53:1–12). In their minds was this question: If Elijah was going to restore all things, why should the Messiah still have to suffer?

13 Then Jesus gave the answer: Elijah had already come again in the form of John the Baptist[61] (Matthew 11:13–14; 17:13). The teachers of the law had said that Elijah must come again, and they were correct in this. But when he did come, they didn't recognize him (Matthew 17:11–12). They could repeat scripture, but they could not recognize the signs of the kingdom of God (Matthew 16:3).

The Old Testament Elijah had been rejected (1 Kings 19:1–3,9–10). So also had John the Baptist been rejected, and finally killed. In the same way, Jesus' calling would be fulfilled through suffering and death. The road to glory is always through suffering.

The Healing of a Boy With an Evil Spirit (9:14–32)

(Matthew 17:14–23; Luke 9:37–45)

14–18 Here we see the tremendous contrast between the top of the mountain of transfiguration and the valley below. Down at the foot of the mountain we see the devil's attack on a poor child, the father's anguish, the impotence of nine disciples who had earlier been given power to cast out demons (Mark 3:14–15; 6:7) but this time could not. And finally, the teachers of the law, the religious authorities, were there arguing. They weren't healing the child; they were only criticizing and talking. What an exact picture of our world!

19 Jesus rebuked His disciples for their lack of faith. It was because of lack of faith that they could not cast out the demon (Matthew 17:20). Jesus asked: "**How long shall I put up with you?** How long must I endure your faithlessness?" In saying this, Jesus was not only rebuking the disciples; He was also rebuking the father of the demon-possessed boy and the teachers of the law for their lack of faith. "**O unbelieving generation.**"

20–22 The father said to Jesus, "**But if you can do anything, take pity on us and help us.**"

The father asked Jesus the wrong question: ". . . **if you can do anything.**" Jesus can do everything! His power is infinite.

23 "'**If you can**'," said Jesus. "I can

---

[61] John the Baptist was not a reincarnation of Elijah. He merely fulfilled Malachi's prophecy concerning Elijah.

indeed heal your son. But the question is: Can you believe? **Everything is possible for him who believes.**"

The boy's healing did not depend on Jesus' power. His power is always sufficient; it is without limit. Rather, the boy's healing depended on the father's faith in Jesus. Without faith on the father's part, Jesus' power in this case would not work. With the father's faith, Jesus' power could do anything.

24 Then the father said, "**I do believe**. But my faith is not sufficient; **help me overcome my unbelief**."

This is the plea of every Christian. We all have some faith, but it is mixed with unbelief, with doubt. We must continually ask Jesus to increase our faith, so that our doubt and unbelief might be overcome. It is mainly because of unbelief that we receive so little from Christ and that our work for Christ is so weak and ineffective.

25–29 After Jesus had healed the demon-possessed boy, the disciples asked Him, "**Why couldn't we drive it out?**" One reason they already knew: lack of faith.[62] But Jesus gave them two other reasons: They hadn't prayed enough, and they hadn't fasted[63] (see Matthew 17:21; Mark 9:29). Prayer is the means of receiving power. We must combine prayer with faith. Without faith, our prayers are ineffective; without prayer, our faith is ineffective. For effective praying, faith is necessary; and to obtain faith, prayer is necessary. The more we pray, the more will be our faith. The more we believe, the more effective our prayers will be. In Matthew 9:29, Jesus says: "**According to your faith will it be done to you.**" Praying in faith is like turning on the switch of an engine: if we do not turn it on, the engine will not run.

In some situations it is necessary to fast in order to receive our request from God. Many Christians have experienced greater results from prayer—more power, more blessing, more guidance—when they have fasted.

To fast does not mean merely to go without eating for a period. Fasting is a demonstration of our desire to control our bodily appetites and put aside all worldly thoughts and desires in order to gain some spiritual benefit. Fasting is a sign of our readiness to offer ourselves fully to God so that His will might be accomplished. It is a sign that we are willing to give up even legitimate things such as food in order to better concentrate on serving Him. When, by fasting, we show God that we are serious about offering ourselves to Him, then He will respond to our prayers by giving us a greater measure of power and wisdom and spiritual blessing.

30–32 Here Mark records the second time Jesus predicted His death and resurrection (see Mark 8:31 and comment). Jesus knew exactly what was going to happen to Him. He knew that God was going to deliver Him into the hands of evil men, and that after three days God would raise Him up (see Acts 2:22–24). But the disciples still could not understand Jesus' meaning.

Who Is the Greatest? (9:33–41)
(Luke 9:46–50)

33–34 The disciples began to discuss among themselves which of them was greatest. When Jesus asked them what they were talking about they were embarrassed, because they had been discussing who among them would be the leader if Jesus died. But Jesus knew what they had been discussing, and He knew that it was because of pride that they were arguing about who was greatest among themselves. The disciples were

---

[62] According to Matthew 17:20, Jesus told the disciples that if they had **faith as small as a mustard seed**, they could move mountains (see Mark 11:22–23 and comment). A small seed of true faith will grow into strong, effective faith, by which impossible things can be accomplished.

[63] In verse 29, instead of the single word **prayer**, some ancient manuscripts have the words "prayer and fasting." In the corresponding verse in Matthew 17:21, the words "prayer and fasting" are also present.

eager to reign in Christ's kingdom, but, as events would soon prove, they were not so eager to labor and suffer for Him.

35 Then Jesus gave them another very important teaching: If anyone wants to be a leader, he must become a servant (see Mark 10:43–44). The first shall be last, and the last shall be first (Mark 10:31). No one should ever seek to be first. God will appoint leaders from among those who have put themselves last. **For whoever exalts himself will be humbled, and whoever humbles himself will be exalted** (Matthew 23:12). **Therefore, whoever humbles himself like this child is the greatest in the kingdom of heaven** (Matthew 18:4).

Again we see that the teaching of Christ is the opposite of the teaching of the world. Worldly men[64] seek to be first; spiritual men seek to be last. Those who are last in the eyes of the world are often first in the eyes of God. That which is **highly valued** among men is **detestable** to God (Luke 16:15). The world is the opposite of the kingdom of God. The world is opposed to God; the flesh is opposed to the Spirit (Galatians 5:17).

Those who seek worldly gain will suffer spiritual loss; those who suffer worldly loss for Christ's sake will receive spiritual gain (see Mark 8:35 and comment).

36–37 Having said that those who want to be first must be servants, Jesus took a little child into His arms as an example of what He was talking about. In the Aramaic language, which was the language Jesus spoke, the word for "servant" and "child" is the same. Thus Jesus here was saying that to be a servant (or a disciple), one must become like a child. A small child is innocent. A small child does not try to make himself great. Rather, he tries to please others (see Matthew 18:1–5 and comment).

Then Jesus said that whoever receives a child—that is, a disciple—in His name receives Him. And whoever receives Jesus receives God, who sent Him (see Matthew 10:40; John 12:44–45; 13:20 and comments). Those who make themselves like children, like humble servants, Jesus will make His representatives. Thus those who receive Jesus' representatives receive Jesus; those who reject His representatives reject both Jesus and God (Luke 10:16). It is a great honor to be the representative, the ambassador of Christ, the Son of God; but only the humble and childlike will obtain that honor.

38 Here Mark describes a mistake made by the disciples, a mistake Christians have been making ever since Jesus' time. The disciples thought that only their group, their party, were true followers of Jesus. When they saw someone who was not one of their group, they tried to stop him from driving out demons in Jesus' name. "Only we are true disciples," they thought. "Only we have the authority to work in Jesus' name." From this kind of attitude have come divisions and controversy in the church. If someone is doing good work in Jesus' name, we must not oppose him, or else we will find ourselves opposing Jesus Himself.

39–40 **"Do not stop him,"** Jesus said to His disciples. "Such a man is on my side; **for whoever is not against us is for us.**"

We must consider that all who do not oppose Jesus are on His side. No one can remain neutral in the great conflict between Satan and Christ. Therefore, those who do not oppose Jesus must be for Him. Others may have different ways of serving Jesus. They may be of another group, another denomination, but if they work in His name we must accept them as brothers and fellow servants of Christ[65] (see Matthew 12:30; Mark 3:27 and comment).

41 All who serve Christ will receive

---

[64] "Worldly men" are those men who love the world and the things in it more than they love God.

[65] To work **in [Jesus'] name** means to work for Jesus' sake. It means to work in a way that brings honor to Jesus. It means to work for Him sincerely, from the heart. There are false Christians who say they are working in Jesus' name, but their work does not glorify Jesus. Such people are not on Jesus' side.

a reward for what they have done (Matthew 16:27; 2 Corinthians 5:10). Christ will not forget even the smallest work done in His name—even giving a disciple a cup of water (Matthew 10:42). Christ will reward us not according to the size of the gift but according to the love with which we give it (see Mark 12:42–44).

Causing to Sin (9:42–50)
(Matthew 18:6–9; Luke 17:1–2)

42 To cause a brother to stumble—that is, **to sin**—is a very great sin in God's sight. One **of these little ones** means any humble, childlike servant of Christ. Perhaps the disciples had caused the man driving out demons (verse 38) to stumble, **to sin**. Perhaps they had discouraged him and driven him away from Jesus. Let us remember this warning and take great care that we do nothing that in any way might cause our brother to stumble, to sin (see Romans 14:13,21). Whenever we discourage our brother or lead him into any kind of temptation, we are causing him to sin. The man who continues causing his brother to stumble in this way would be better off being drowned in the sea, because on the day of judgment God is going to punish him for the evil he has done.

43 **If your hand causes you to sin, cut it off.** Jesus did not mean that we should take a knife and actually cut off our hand. The hand is only an instrument of sin. We need to cut the sin out of our heart. If we desire to steal, it is not our hand that is evil, but our heart. We must do whatever is necessary to remove that sin, that evil desire, from our heart. Just as a surgeon cuts off a diseased hand or foot in order to save the patient's life, so must we cut away the sin from our lives in order to save our souls. We must be ready to part with what is dearest to us if it leads us to sin.

Removing sin from our heart may be very painful—like cutting off a hand, or a foot (verse 45). But we must do it if we would **enter life**—that is, life with God in heaven. We cannot take sin with us into the kingdom of God (see Matthew 5:29–30; Romans 8:13; 13:14; Colossians 3:5–6; Revelation 21:27 and comments).

44–48 Here the same teaching is repeated using the foot and eye as examples of sinful members. If our **foot** causes us to flee from Christ, to walk on the wrong road, then we must "**cut it off.**" If our eye causes us to lust after a woman, to commit adultery, we must "**pluck it out**" (see Matthew 5:29–30). That is, we must do whatever is necessary to remove that sin from our lives.

Jesus clearly taught that hell was a very bad place. It is a place of eternal torment, or fire, of **weeping and gnashing of teeth** (Matthew 13:40–42).

In verse 48 Jesus quotes from Isaiah 66:12. Their **worm does not die**. The destruction, the decay of those sent to hell goes on forever.

It is our chief enemy Satan who is the author of our destruction, and his main instrument is sin. Therefore, we can also say that our chief enemy is sin. Unrepented sin separates us forever from God and heaven.

Since sin is the enemy that condemns us to hell, we must not let it remain in our lives. If it enters and remains in us, it will destroy us. We must not let even the tiniest sin remain in our lives. Even the tiniest hole in the bottom of a boat will eventually allow the boat to fill with water and sink. In the same way, if we let even a tiny sin into our lives, it will grow and eventually destroy us.

49 **Everyone will be salted with fire.** "Fire" in this verse means persecution. Our faith is tested by **fire** (1 Peter 1:6–7). To be **salted** means to be made effective. Thus it is through persecution that disciples are made effective, made strong for Christ.

50 Salt is essential for life. There is salt in our blood, in our bodies. Faith is like salt in the world. We must remain "salty"—that is, faithful and obedient. Otherwise we will be worthless, tasteless (see Matthew 5:13 and comment).

It is the Holy Spirit who makes us salty. If the Holy Spirit goes out of our lives, how will we be salty again? We must keep the salt of the Holy Spirit in our lives.

If the Holy Spirit is in us, we shall be of one spirit and one mind. Instead of trying to be greater than others (verse 34), we should **be at peace with each other**.

CHAPTER 10

Divorce (10:1–12)
(Matthew 19:1–9)

1–2 The Pharisees again tried to test Jesus by asking Him a difficult question. Their aim was not to learn the truth, but to make Jesus say something by which they could condemn Him. By asking a question about divorce, they hoped to stir up Herod's anger against Jesus, so that he might do to Jesus what he had done to John the Baptist (Mark 6:16–17). They asked, **"Is it lawful for a man to divorce his wife?"**

3–4 Very often Jesus answered such questions by asking another question. He asked the Pharisees what the law of Moses (the Jewish law) said about divorce.

The law said that if a man wanted to divorce his wife, he should write out a certificate of divorce (Deuteronomy 24:1–4). This was written in order to protect the rights of the woman, not to justify divorce. The certificate of divorce gave the woman certain legal rights, such as the right to marry again.

5 Moses wrote the divorce law because men were putting away their wives without good cause. They were separating what God had joined together (verse 9). Men's hearts had become hardened against both God and their wives.

According to Matthew's account, Jesus said, **"Moses permitted you to divorce your wives because your hearts were hard. But it was not this way from the beginning"** (Matthew 19:8).

6–8 Jesus then described how God made men and women (Genesis 1:27), and intended that they should leave their parents and join together as husband and wife and become **one flesh** (Genesis 2:24). A man and his wife are closer together than parents and their children. If it is wrong for parents to desert their children, it is even more wrong for a husband to desert his wife.

9 Therefore, God's intention was that husband and wife should never be divorced. Marriage was established by God; therefore, He is never pleased when a marriage is broken up.

10–12 Then Jesus gave a new teaching. According to the Jewish law, only a woman committed adultery. A husband could go off with another woman and it was not considered adultery. Thus the law did not treat men and women equally.

But according to Jesus' teaching, a man is also guilty of adultery if he goes off with another woman. In marriage, husband and wife have equal responsibilities and equal rights. Even if the husband or wife fills out a certificate of divorce before marrying someone else, it is still adultery in God's sight. God's law is much higher than man's law.

According to Matthew 5:32 and Luke 16:18, Jesus also taught that if any man, even a single man, married a divorced woman, he committed adultery. The same rule would apply to a single woman who marries a divorced man.[66]

Jesus taught that divorce was suitable only if one partner had already committed adultery (Matthew 5:32; 19:9). If one partner commits adultery, then the innocent partner is free to marry again (see 1 Corinthians 7:10–11 and comment).

After Jesus' death, as more and more people began believing in Him, the question arose as to what to do if a husband or wife became a Christian but their partner did not. The Apostle Paul discusses this matter in his first letter to the Corinthians (see 1 Corinthians 7:12–16 and comment).

The Little Children and Jesus (10:13–16)
(Matthew 19:13–15; Luke 18:15–17)

13 The disciples often misused their authority (Mark 9:38). Here they tried to

[66] However, it is all right to marry a divorced person if that person's former spouse is living in adultery with someone else. For further discussion of the subject of divorce and remarriage, see General Article: Christian Marriage.

prevent little children from coming to Jesus.

14 But Jesus rebuked the disciples: "**Let the little children come to me.**" Then Jesus said, "... **for the kingdom of God belongs to such as these.**" The kingdom of God belongs to those having the qualities of little children. Little children are straightforward, without hypocrisy. Little children do not strive for honor or power (see Mark 9:36–37 and comment). Little children are innocent, humble, trusting. These are qualities that are needed if we are to be sharers in the kingdom of God.

We can see from this verse God's great love and care for small children. The Bible does not say what happens to small children who die, but we cannot believe that they are separated from God's love (see General Article: Children and the Kingdom of God).

15 Jesus not only loves children; He taught that unless we become like children we cannot enter the kingdom of God (see Matthew 18:3). ... **anyone who will not receive the kingdom of God like a little child will never enter it**. How does a little child receive something? He holds out his hands. He asks. A little child is helpless. He cannot earn anything. He cannot pay money for what he wants. He cannot say, "I have worked hard; I deserve to receive a reward." The child just trusts that what he needs will be given to him. Whatever he asks for he asks in faith; he doesn't doubt.

This is how we must enter the kingdom of God. We do not deserve to enter. We cannot earn our entrance. We cannot buy a ticket into heaven. We must receive the kingdom of God by faith like a little child. There is no other way.

16 Jesus **took the children in his arms.** Let us follow Jesus' example. Let us take care never to despise or mistreat children. Rather, let us remember how much Jesus loves them.

The Rich Young Man (10:17–31)
(Matthew 19:16–30; Luke 18:18–30)

17 A man ran up to Jesus and asked, "... **what must I do to inherit** ETERNAL LIFE?" What he was asking was: "How can I be saved? "This is the main question deep in the heart of every person. This man was rich (verse 22), and he was young (Matthew 19:22). According to Luke 18:18, he was also a **ruler**. He had everything the world could offer; but he still was looking for eternal life in heaven.

18 Although the young man was seeking eternal life, he was thinking in worldly ways. He called Jesus **Good teacher** (verse 17), supposing Him to be only a human teacher. He thought he himself was **good**; that is, he believed that he had followed the law exactly from his youth up (verse 20). He thought that to obtain eternal life one had to be "good," and he was asking Jesus if he needed to do any further "good" work in order to be saved.

Therefore, Jesus told him that no man can be **good** by his own work. Only God is good. In God's sight, all man's righteousness is like **filthy rags** (Isaiah 64:6). Paul wrote: **I know that nothing good lives in me** (Romans 7:18). No man can be good enough by his own effort to merit salvation.

19–20 Jesus then reminded the young man of some of the ten commandments (Exodus 20:12–16). He also mentioned the second great command: **Love your neighbor as yourself** (Matthew 19:19; Mark 12:31; Romans 13:9–10; Galatians 5:14). The young man assured Jesus that as far as he knew he had obeyed all of these commandments from his youth. Like Paul, he was **faultless** as far as legalistic righteousness was concerned (Philippians 3:6). Yet the young man still had no confidence he was saved. If one could indeed obey the law perfectly in every respect, he would obtain eternal life[67] But there is only one problem: no one has ever been able to obey the law perfectly (James 2:10–11). Neither had

[67] According to Matthew 19:17, Jesus, in order to test the young man, said to him, "**If you want to enter life, obey the commandments.**" Jesus was, in effect, saying, "If you can obey them perfectly, you will inherit eternal life."

this young man obeyed the law perfectly. He had broken the first of the ten commandments: **You shall have no other gods before me** (Exodus 20:3). He had made his possessions his god. He had also broken the greatest commandment of all: **Love the Lord your God with all your heart and with all your soul and with all your mind and with all your strength** (Deuteronomy 6:5; Mark 12:30). Yes, he had loved God to some extent, but he had not given to God all his love. He loved his possessions more than God. Because of this, even though he may have followed all the other commandments, he was not worthy to receive eternal life.

21 **Jesus looked at him and loved him**. Then Jesus said, "**One thing you lack.**" What did the young man lack? Love for God, love for neighbor (Mark 12:30–31). How could that young man show his love for God? By giving up that which he loved most, his possessions. Those who give up their earthly possessions for God will receive eternal treasure in heaven (see Matthew 6:19–21; Luke 12:33 and comments).

Jesus did not say that if the young man sold all his possessions he would automatically receive eternal life. Paul wrote: **If I give all I possess to the poor . . . but have not love, I gain nothing** (1 Corinthians 13:3). Rather, Jesus was showing the man what it meant to follow the law perfectly. The law teaches us what we must do, but it does not give us the power to do it. The law leads us to Christ (Galatians 3:24), but it cannot save us. It is only by faith in Christ that we can be saved, not by works of the law (see Galatians 2:15–16 and comment).

In telling the young man to sell his possessions, Jesus wasn't giving the man a new law to follow. Jesus does not tell everyone to sell their possessions. But he knew that love of possessions was preventing this young man from giving his life to God. Whenever we love anything more than God, we must give it up, we must "sell it." We **cannot serve both God and Money** (see Matthew 6:24 and comment).

22 Jesus said to the young man: "**Go, sell everything you have. . . . Then come, follow me.**"

At this the man's face fell. To be a disciple of Jesus was too hard. The cost was too great. The young man had come to Jesus seeking eternal life. Jesus said to him, "**. . . follow me,** and I will lead you to eternal life." But the young man went away sad. He loved his possessions more than Jesus. He had hoped he could have eternal life and keep his possessions too. But Jesus told him, "You must choose. You cannot have both."

It is not only love of possessions that keeps us from following Jesus. It can be love of family, love of friends, love of work, love of fame (see Matthew 10:37–38). Jesus asks each one of us: "**. . . do you truly love me more than these?**" (John 21:15). Paul wrote to the Philippians: **I consider everything a loss compared to the surpassing greatness of knowing Christ Jesus my Lord, for whose sake I have lost all things. I consider them** (all these things) **rubbish, that I may gain Christ and be found in him, not having a righteousness of my own that comes from the law, but that which is through faith in Christ** (Philippians 3:8–9).

23–25 Jesus then told His disciples that it was extremely difficult for a rich man to enter the kingdom of God. Jesus wasn't talking only about those rich in money, but about all those who value worldly things above God.

Poor men can also love their few possessions just as much as the rich love theirs. But in the world's eyes, the rich man has more to lose by following Christ. Therefore, it is usually harder for a rich man to enter the kingdom of heaven. The rich are usually less willing to put aside their possessions for Christ's sake.

26–27 The disciples understood Jesus' deeper meaning. Jesus was saying that it is impossible to enter the kingdom of God by one's own effort. No man can save himself; it is impossible. But God can save us; with Him all things are possible. Salvation is a gift of God (Ephesians 2:8).

28 Then Peter began to compare himself and the other disciples with the rich young man. "**We have left everything to follow you.**" Then, according to Matthew 19:27, Peter asked, "**What then will there be for us?**" It is not wrong for us to inquire what we shall gain by following Christ. Christ calls us to our profit, not to our loss.

According to Matthew 19:28, Jesus first answered Peter by saying that **at the renewal of all things**—that is, at the end of the world when Christ comes again—the twelve disciples will **sit on twelve thrones, judging the twelve tribes of Israel**. They will in some way share in Christ's rule and in His work of judgment in God's kingdom. They will receive great honor. In this world they would be abased; in the next world they will be exalted.

29–30 Then Jesus gave a promise to all who leave home, family, and fields for His sake. They will lose nothing. Instead, they will gain. First, they will gain eternal life (verse 30). They will gain Christ, and with Christ they will gain **all things** (Romans 8:32; Ephesians 1:3). Christ promised that whatever they give up, they will receive a hundred times as much, not only in heaven but on earth as well.

When Christ said we shall receive **homes, brothers, sisters, mothers, children and fields,** He was talking about the church. When we become Christians, we become members of a great family, which collectively possesses many homes and many fields. But as members of that family, we shall also suffer persecution (2 Timothy 3:12). **Now if we are children, then we are heirs—heirs of God and co-heirs with Christ, if indeed we share in his sufferings** (Romans 8:17).

31 The disciples wanted to be **first,** or "great" (see Mark 9:34; 10:37). They thought that because they had followed Christ and had given up everything for Him, they should be **first**. But Jesus taught: "Don't seek to be first." We must never try to bargain with God. We must never think: "I have done this for God; now He must reward me." God does not reward men according to men's opinions. Those who think they deserve to be **first** will usually end up **last**. Those who put themselves last will often end up first (Matthew 20:16; Luke 13:30). God will raise up the humble and put down the proud (see James 4:6,10; 1 Peter 5:6). Let each believer seek only Christ, and follow after Him. Then God Himself will put each man in the place prepared for him (see verse 40).

Jesus Again Predicts His Death (10:32–34)

(Matthew 20:17–19; Luke 18:31–34)

32 Jesus and His disciples had begun their final journey to Jerusalem, where Jesus would be put to death. The disciples were **astonished** at His teaching, at His miracles, and at His transfiguration.

Besides the disciples, many others also followed Jesus. They were **afraid**. Perhaps they had a premonition that something terrible was going to happen in Jerusalem.

33–34 For the third time Jesus predicted His death (see Mark 8:31; 9:31 and comments). This time Jesus said that the chief priests and teachers of the law would **condemn him to death,** and that they would hand Him over to the **Gentiles,**[68] that is, the Romans. The Gentiles would then kill Him. According to Matthew 20:19, Jesus said that He would be **crucified**, which was the Roman method of executing criminals.

All this came to pass exactly as Jesus said (Mark 14:64; 15:1,19–20). But even having heard this three times, the disciples did not understand what Jesus was talking about (Luke 18:34).

The Request of James and John (10:35–45)

(Matthew 20:20–28; Luke 22:24–27)

35–37 After Jesus had finished talking about His death and resurrection, James and John (Mark 1:19–20) asked Jesus to give them the highest places in His kingdom—on His right hand and on His left. According to Matthew 20:20–21, James and John's mother also made the

---

[68] In the Bible, the **Gentiles** usually refer to any non-Jewish people. But here in this verse, Mark is specifically referring to the Roman Gentiles who crucified Christ. For further discussion, see Word List: Gentile.

same request on their behalf. They were probably thinking of Jesus' earthly kingdom. They were jealous of Peter and desired to get ahead of him. Even after Jesus had taught them that they must never seek to be first (Mark 9:34; 10:31), His disciples continued to struggle with each other for the highest place.

38 Jesus asked James and John: "**Can you drink the cup I drink?**" "To drink the cup" was a Jewish saying which meant "to suffer." The cup was a "cup" of suffering (see Mark 14:36).

"**Can you . . . be baptized with the baptism I am baptized with?**" asked Jesus. Here **baptism** means "death" (see Romans 6:3–4). Jesus was called not only to suffer but also to die. Were James and John ready to suffer and die with Christ? Those who desire to be glorified with Christ must first suffer with Him (Romans 8:17).

39 In answer to Jesus' question about whether they could drink His cup and be baptized with His baptism (death), James and John confidently replied: "**We can.**" And Jesus said to them: "And indeed you will." James and John didn't realize what they were saying. But Jesus knew that later on both of them would indeed suffer for Him (see Acts 12:2; Revelation 1:9). They weren't ready to suffer then, but later they would be filled with the Holy Spirit and receive the strength to suffer all things for Christ's sake.

40 Even if James and John suffered and died for Christ, it was not Christ's place to appoint them to sit on His right and left. God Himself will give each person his proper place in the kingdom of heaven, and He will show no favoritism (Acts 10:34; Romans 2:6,11; 1 Peter 1:17). God will give us a place in heaven according to our faith and according to our love for Him.

41 The other ten disciples were indignant with James and John for asking to be put ahead of them in Christ's kingdom. But they were no better than James and John: they wanted the highest places also! They were not happy to be last. How quickly we become indignant at the sin of others, not because it is sin, but because our own selfish interests are affected!

42–44 Jesus then once more reminded His disciples that they were not to be like men of the world (see Mark 9:35; 10:31 and comments). In the world men strive to be first, to gain power and authority for their own advantage. Once they have gained authority, they **lord it over** other men, they put others down. But the disciples of Christ must not be like that. If they want to be leaders, they must become servants. Among Christians, to be a true leader means to be a servant of others. It is not wrong to desire to be a leader in the church (1 Timothy 3:1). But it is wrong to desire to be a leader in order to benefit oneself or to lord it over others (1 Peter 5:2–3). We must desire to be leaders only in order to serve others.

45 This is one of the most important verses in Mark's Gospel, because here for the first time Jesus explains to His disciples why He has come to earth. The **Son of Man**—that is, the Son of God—the greatest leader the world has ever seen, came not **to be served, but to serve**. He came as a servant, not as a master (see Philippians 2:6–8 and comment).

But Jesus did not come only to serve; He came to give His life for us. He came to suffer and die for us. Service is good, but it is not enough. We need more than service; we need salvation. We need salvation from the penalty of sin, which is eternal death (see Romans 6:23). Therefore, Jesus came to take upon Himself the punishment for our sin, which otherwise would have come upon us. He died in our place. He became a **guilt offering** for us (see Leviticus 5:17–19; Isaiah 53:10; Hebrews 9:28 and comment). He gave His life **as a ransom for many**; that is, He gave His own life in exchange for our lives (see 1 Timothy 2:5–6). We were once slaves of sin and Satan; Jesus bought us—He bought our freedom. And the price He paid was His own blood. Paul wrote the Corinthians: **You are not your own; you were bought at a price** (1 Corinthians 6:19–20). Christ poured out His own blood to purchase our salvation (Mark 14:24).

The prophet Isaiah, in the great fifty-third chapter of his book of prophecy, fully described the life and work of the coming Savior, Jesus Christ: He **was pierced for our transgressions, he was crushed for our iniquities; the punishment that brought us peace was upon him, and by his wounds we are healed . . . the Lord has laid on him the iniquity of us all . . . my righteous servant will justify many, and he will bear their iniquities . . . he poured out his life unto death** (Isaiah 53:5–6,11–12).

The two most important things that anyone can know in this world are that Jesus is the **Son of God** (Mark 1:1), and that He came **to give his life as a ransom for many**. He is the Savior of all who believe in Him (Romans 10:9). **Salvation is found in no one else, for there is no other name under heaven given to men by which we must be saved** (Acts 4:12).

Blind Bartimaeus Receives His Sight (10:46–52)

(Matthew 20:29–34; Luke 18:35–43)

46 On their journey to Jerusalem, Jesus and His disciples came to the city of **Jericho**,[69] eighteen miles northeast of Jerusalem.

According to Matthew 20:30, Jesus healed two blind men on this occasion, but Mark mentions only one of them, Bartimaeus.

47–48 When Bartimaeus heard that Jesus had come, he called out: "**Jesus, Son of David.**" Jeremiah had prophesied that the Messiah would be descended from King David, the great king of the Jews (Jeremiah 23:5). And indeed Jeremiah's prophecy was fulfilled (Matthew 1:1,6,20–21; Romans 1:2–3). Bartimaeus, although he was blind, recognized Jesus to be the Messiah. And even though the crowd rebuked him, he persisted in his request (see Luke 18:1–8).

49–51 Jesus asked Bartimaeus, "**What do you want me to do for you?**" Bartimaeus was a beggar (Luke 18:35). Jesus asked the question so that the crowd would know that Bartimaeus was not asking for money but for his sight. To us, also, Jesus asks: "**What do you want me to do for you?**" He wants us to say exactly what we want. **Ask and it shall be given to you** (Matthew 7:7).

52 Bartimaeus was healed because of his faith. "**. . . your faith has healed you**" (see Mark 5:34 and comment).

CHAPTER 11

The Triumphal Entry (11:1–11)

(Matthew 21:1–11; Luke 19:28–40; John 12:12–16)

1 Up until this point, the events of Jesus' life that Mark has described have taken place over a period of three years. Now Mark begins the account of the final week before Jesus' death.

Jesus and His disciples arrived in **Bethphage** and **Bethany**, two small villages near the Mount of Olives, a large hill just outside Jerusalem.

2–3 The prophet Zechariah had prophesied that the Messiah would enter Jerusalem **riding on a donkey, on a colt, the foal of a donkey**[70] (Zechariah 9:9; Matthew 21:5). Jesus knew that a colt would be ready for Him and sent two of His disciples to fetch it. According to Matthew 21:2,7, the disciples brought back both the colt and its mother, but

---

[69] The city of Jericho is also mentioned in Joshua 6:1–21.

[70] Instead of the words **on a donkey, on a colt**, the original Hebrew text says, "on a donkey and on a colt." This gives the idea that Jesus rode on two animals. But the "and" in this verse is a Hebrew idiom, and means "that is." Thus the prophecy of Zechariah is only talking about Jesus riding on one animal.

Jesus rode on the colt, on which no one had ever ridden before.

4–7 The disciples brought the donkey and its colt to Jesus, and spread their cloaks on the animals (Matthew 21:7). Jesus then sat on the cloaks, and rode on the colt into Jerusalem.

8–10 **Many people spread their cloaks on the road.** Some of the people had followed Jesus from Galilee; others were disciples of Jesus who lived in Jerusalem. They spread their cloaks on the road as a sign of their subjection to Christ (2 Kings 9:13). Others spread palm branches before Him as a sign of joy and victory.

The people shouted, "**Hosanna!**[71] **Blessed is he who comes in the name of the Lord!**" (Psalm 118:25–26). According to Luke 19:39–40, there was so great a tumult that some of the Pharisees in the crowd told Jesus to rebuke His disciples for creating such a disturbance. But Jesus answered them, "**. . . if they keep quiet, the stones will cry out**" (Luke 19:40). Jesus entered Jerusalem openly as the Messiah, the Son of God. It was impossible that there should be silence during such a great event!

According to John 12:16, Jesus' disciples did not at first understand the significance of His riding into Jerusalem on the colt of a donkey. Only after Jesus was **glorified**—that is, raised from the dead—did they understand that in this way the prophecy of Zechariah had been fulfilled (see Luke 24:25–27,45; John 12:12–16). Only after Jesus' death and resurrection did the Holy Spirit guide them into all truth (John 16:13).

The Messiah did not ride into Jerusalem on a great horse at the head of a grand army like an earthly king. He had come as one **righteous and having salvation, gentle and riding on a donkey** (Zechariah 9:9). He had come to **proclaim peace to the nations** (Zechariah 9:10).

11 During this last week in Jerusalem, Jesus returned each evening to Bethany and spent the night there.

Jesus Clears the Temple (11:12–19)
(Matthew 21:12–19; Luke 19:45–48)

12–14 On the way into Jerusalem the next morning, Jesus saw a fig tree on which there was no fruit. He **found nothing but leaves, because it was not the season for figs.** Then Jesus cursed the fig tree, and according to Matthew 21:19, the fig tree immediately withered (see verses 20–21).

Why did Jesus do this? It wasn't the tree's fault there was no fruit: it was not the season for figs. Jesus cursed the fig tree in order to give an illustration of what was about to happen to ISRAEL, the Jewish nation. He did this as a warning to the Jews. The Old Testament prophets had often compared Israel with a fig tree (Jeremiah 8:13; 29:17; Micah 7:1–2). From a distance, Israel looked good—covered with "leaves." But when one looked closely, there was no "fruit" of righteousness to be seen. From henceforth, no one would ever **eat fruit**—that is, obtain blessing—from Israel again. Israel should have been a light, a blessing, for the nations of the world. Instead, it had become spiritually dead, without spiritual fruit. It had become like a barren fig tree. And just as Christ caused the fig tree to wither, so forty years later God's judgment fell on Jerusalem, the capital of Israel. In 70 A.D. it was totally destroyed by the Roman army.

Many who call themselves Christians are also like this barren fig tree. Where there are leaves, there ought to be fruit. If our religion is only outward, our spiritual life—like that fig tree—will soon wither and die. A religion that does not bear fruit is a dead religion.

15–16 For all Jews there was one great temple, which was in Jerusalem. Around the main temple building there was an outer compound called the courtyard of the Gentiles, where Gentiles could come to pray. In this courtyard the Jewish temple authorities had set up small booths where pilgrims coming to the temple could buy doves to sacrifice and where money could be changed. (The

---

[71] **Hosanna** is a Hebrew word meaning "save." It was used as an expression of praise, like "Hallelujah."

temple tax could only be paid with special coins.) But those operating the booths were cheating the people and taking large profits for themselves. Therefore, Jesus drove them out and overturned their tables and benches.[72]

17 Then Jesus, quoting from Isaiah 56:7, taught the people that the temple should be a **house of prayer for all nations**; but instead, the Jews had turned it into a **den of robbers** (Jeremiah 7:11). Like the fig tree, the temple was an illustration of the Jewish nation. On the outside it was splendid; on the inside it was a "den of robbers."

18–19 Naturally, the Jewish leaders were furious at what Jesus had done. Jesus had embarrassed them and exposed their greed and hypocrisy. Therefore, they **began looking for a way to kill him**. They couldn't seize Him openly, because they feared the people. Most of the people respected Jesus, and considered Him to be a great prophet (Matthew 21:10–11). Indeed, many thought that He was the Messiah.

According to Matthew 21:14–16, after Jesus had driven out the money changers, He began to heal the blind and the lame who had come to the temple. Even children shouted in the temple area: "**Hosanna to the Son of David**."[73] The chief priests and teachers of the law didn't want to believe that Jesus was the Messiah; they were already jealous of His fame. They were offended that even children should be calling Him the **Son of David**, that is, the Messiah. But Jesus answered them that this was the fulfillment of one of the prophecies concerning the Messiah: **From the lips of children and infants you have ordained praise**[74] (Psalm 8:2; Matthew 21:16).

The Withered Fig Tree (11:20–26) (Matthew 21:20–22)

20–21 On the next morning Jesus and the disciples again saw the fig tree that had withered the day before.[75] Peter was amazed that at the word of Jesus the tree had **withered from the roots**.

22–24 Jesus then used the fig tree to teach a further important lesson to the disciples. That is, if one has faith, whatever he asks will be done (verse 24). If one has faith, he can say to a fig tree, "Wither," and it will wither. If one has faith, he can say to a mountain, "**Go, throw yourself into the sea**,"[76] and it will happen. Jesus' meaning is that God can do anything, if we pray in faith. Truly, **all things are possible with God** (Mark 10:27).

Jesus does not mean here that we can pray for anything we want and God will do it. Certain conditions must be fulfilled in order for our requests to be granted. First of all, we must pray in faith. Without faith, prayer accomplishes nothing. Second, we must pray **according to** [God's] **will** (1 John 5:14–15). God will not do anything that contradicts His purpose. Third, we must pray in Jesus' name—that is, for Jesus' sake, not for our sake (John 14:13–14; 16:23). Fourth, we must remain in Christ and His words must remain in us (John 15:7). To be "IN CHRIST" means that we are in His love, that we are under His authority, that we are obedient to His will (1 John 3:22). In short, it means that Christ is the Lord of our life. It means that His Spirit, the Holy Spirit, is in us, directing us. Indeed, the Holy Spirit not only teaches us what to pray for, but He gives us the faith to pray

---

[72] Here Mark describes the second time Jesus cleared the temple in Jerusalem. According to John 2:12–17, Jesus also came to the temple in the beginning of His public ministry and drove out the money changers and dove sellers.

[73] **Son of David** was one of the names of the Messiah, or Christ. For further discussion, see footnote to comment on Mark 3:22.

[74] In some versions of the Bible, the word **praise** in Psalm 8:2 is translated "strength."

[75] In his Gospel, Matthew joins together the two parts of the account of the fig tree into one section and places it after his description of Jesus in the temple (Matthew 21:18–22).

[76] Telling a mountain to throw itself into the sea was a Jewish proverbial saying used to describe any impossible request.

for it. Thus, when we are "in Christ" in this way, then **all** that we ask in faith on Christ's behalf He will do.

From this we understand that praying in faith to God is not some kind of magic formula, or ritual, or merely words. To pray in faith in the right way releases the infinite power of the living God. When we pray, God listens, God acts.

We must remember one other thing: God always answers our prayer of faith, but He may not answer it in the way we expect. We may pray for one thing, but God in His wisdom will give us something better. God desires to enrich and bless our lives even more than we desire it. We can trust Him to answer our prayers in the best way.

Jesus says in verse 24: "**. . . whatever you ask for in prayer, believe that you have received it, and it will be yours.**" God will certainly fulfill our request; He has promised to do so. And what God promises, He will always do. King David's son, Solomon, said in praise of God: "**Praise be to the Lord, the God of Israel, who with his hands has fulfilled what he promised with his mouth to my father David**" (2 Chronicles 6:4).

However, even though we have the assurance that God has answered our request, we sometimes do not experience the answer immediately. Sometimes God waits for a while before showing us the answer. He knows the best time for fulfilling our prayer. He knows when we are ready to receive His answer. Therefore, until we receive the answer, we must continue praying for it in faith. Elijah had to pray for rain seven times, and only then did rain come (1 Kings 18:41–45). We may have the assurance that our request has been granted, but we must continue in prayer until we actually receive the answer in our experience—in our hand. Both faith and patience (persistence) are necessary to receive the answer to our prayer (see Luke 18:1–8; Hebrews 6:12 and comments).

If the answer to our prayer is slow in coming, it may be that there is something in our own life that is keeping our prayer from being fulfilled. We must always be examining ourselves. Are we walking in God's will? Is there a brother whom we have not forgiven? (verse 25). Do we have an unconfessed sin hidden in our hearts? (Psalm 66:18). Are we really crying out day and night? (Luke 18:7). Are we seeking Christ Himself—or only His blessings? Let us examine ourselves. Let us seek only Christ and His will. Believe on Him completely, and **whatever you ask for in prayer . . . will be yours**.

25–26 Here Jesus gives a fifth condition for effective prayer: we must not be harboring any resentment or bitterness against anyone. If there is anyone whom we have not forgiven, God will not hear our prayer. To refuse to forgive someone is to disobey God. David wrote: **If I had cherished sin in my heart, the Lord would not have listened** (Psalm 66:18).

If we refuse to forgive someone, not only will God not listen to our prayer, but He will also refuse to forgive us (see Matthew 6:14–15). God forgives us **as we also have forgiven our debtors** (Matthew 6:12). It is true that when we first come to God and believe in Christ, God forgives us freely (Ephesians 4:32; Colossians 3:13). But after that, if we continue to live in disobedience to God, if we refuse to forgive someone else, then God will withdraw His forgiveness from us and will refuse to hear our prayers.

From these verses[77] we can understand a further truth. To forgive is one of the chief proofs of love. If we want God to answer our prayers, we must not only forgive others, we must love them. In these verses, Jesus is saying to us: "First go and forgive and love your neighbor, and then God will hear your prayer." In order to come to God in prayer, we must love Him. But if we do not love our neighbor whom we can see, we certainly cannot love God, whom we cannot see (see 1 John 4:20–21).

During times of prayer, we are tempted

[77] Not all ancient manuscripts of Mark contain verse 26. A similar verse is found in Matthew 6:15.

to feel that we are more than usually righteous. But God does not look at our lives only during times of prayer. God looks to see what our lives are like all day long. Does our loving and forgiving spirit toward our neighbor last all day long? Do we continue walking in faith all day long? This is what God is looking to see. God will hear our prayers according to our daylong behavior.

The Authority of Jesus Questioned (11:27–33)

(Matthew 21:23–27; Luke 20:1–8)

27–28 The Jewish leaders asked Jesus who gave Him authority to teach and to heal, and to drive the money changers and dove sellers out of the temple. They asked Him this to trap Him. If He said, "Some man gave me authority," the people would lose respect for Him. If He said, "God gave me the authority," then the Jewish leaders could accuse Jesus of "blasphemy"—that is, of claiming to have the authority of God. Because in the Jews' sight, to claim to have God's authority was the same as claiming to be like God.[78] And for a man to claim to be like God—for a man to presume to stand in the place of God—was a great insult to God. According to the Jewish law, any man who insulted God in this way was to be given the death sentence (Leviticus 24:16). Therefore, whatever answer Jesus gave to their question about His authority, the Jewish leaders would be able to use it against Him.

29–30 It was a common custom among the Jews to answer one question by asking another (see Mark 10:3). Therefore, Jesus asked the Jewish leaders to first tell Him where John the Baptist got his authority—from God or from man? If they said John's authority was from God, then they would have to acknowledge that Jesus' authority came from God also.

31–32 Just as they had tried to trap Jesus, so Jesus trapped them. Almost all the people at that time believed that John the Baptist was a great prophet, whose authority came from God. Therefore, if the Jewish leaders answered that John's authority was only from man, the crowds would mock and abuse them.

However, the Jewish leaders did not want to admit that John's authority was from God. John had told them to repent and prepare for the coming of the Messiah (Mark 1:4,7–8). He had told them that Jesus was the Messiah (John 1:29–34). If they answered that John's authority was from God, Jesus would say, **"Then why didn't you believe him?"** (verse 31).

33 Therefore, the Jewish leaders answered, "**We don't know** where John's authority came from." Of course, they knew; only they refused to say. Therefore, Jesus refused to say where His authority came from.

CHAPTER 12

The Parable of the Tenants (12:1–12)

(Matthew 21:33–46; Luke 20:9–19)

1 **A man planted a vineyard.** In this parable the **man** stands for God. The **vineyard** stands for the Jewish nation, Israel (Isaiah 5:1–7).

The man dug a pit for a winepress. In Jesus' time, the commonest reason for planting a vineyard was to produce wine. The grapes were put in the press and then stepped upon. The juice ran down a trough and was collected.

2–6 These verses describe the history of Israel. God sent His servants, the Old

---

[78] The Old Testament prophets spoke with God's authority, of course, and they were not considered blasphemers. But the Jewish leaders did not consider Jesus to be a prophet. Thus, in their eyes, for Jesus to claim God's authority was indeed blasphemy.

Testament prophets, to Israel one by one to look for the fruits of repentance and righteousness. Last of all, He sent His own Son, Jesus. The **tenants** were the Jews, who repeatedly rejected and killed God's prophets.

7 The tenants mistakenly supposed that the master was dead, and that the son had come to take his inheritance. If they killed the son, then, by Jewish law, the vineyard would be theirs.

8 Here the parable becomes a prophecy. When Jesus, God's Son, came to the Jewish nation, the Jews rejected Him and caused Him to be killed.

9 This verse is also a prophecy which was fulfilled in 70 A.D., when the Romans destroyed Jerusalem. After killing the tenants, the owner, God, will **give the vineyard to others**—that is, to the Gentiles. And indeed, this came to pass. When the Jews rejected Jesus and His apostles, the Gospel of salvation was given to the Gentiles.

10–11 Then Jesus quoted Psalm 118:22–23 to show that even though the **builders** of the Jewish temple—that is, the leaders of the Jewish nation—rejected Him, He would become the **capstone** of a new "temple," the church, the new Israel (see Acts 4:11; Ephesians 2:19–20; 1 Peter 2:4–7 and comments).

Then, according to Matthew 21:43–44, Jesus said to the Jewish leaders: "**Therefore I tell you that the kingdom of God will be taken away from you and given to a people who will produce its fruit.**" The kingdom of God has been taken from the unbelieving Jews and given to the believing Gentiles. The kingdom of God belongs not to the descendants of Abraham according to the flesh, but to the true spiritual descendants of Abraham by faith (see Galatians 3:6–9 and comment).

Then in Matthew 21:44, Jesus said, "**He who falls on this stone will be broken to pieces, but he on whom it falls will be crushed**" (Luke 20:18). The Jews had cast the "stone" (Christ) aside. But then they stumbled upon it because of their unbelief (Isaiah 8:14–15; Romans 9:32–33; 1 Peter 2:8). Not only that, the "stone" also fell upon them and they were crushed. That is, this same Jesus whom they had rejected later "fell upon them" in judgment.

The Gentiles have now been given the vineyard, that is, the kingdom of God. The Gentiles have now received the blessing of salvation, which the Jews rejected. We are now the "tenants" of the vineyard. What kind of tenants are we? Do we reject God's servants who come to us? Do we give to God what we owe Him? Do we give Him the fruits of righteousness He asks for?

12 The Jewish leaders understood that Jesus **had spoken the parable against them**. They were the **tenants** in the parable. Therefore, they were even more angry with Jesus, and continued to look for a secret way to arrest Him (see Mark 11:18 and comment).

Paying Taxes to Caesar (12:13–17)
(Matthew 22:15–22; Luke 20:20–26)

13 Later the Jewish leaders sent some **Pharisees** and **Herodians**[79] to try and trap Jesus. Luke calls them **spies** (Luke 20:20). According to Luke 20:20, these spies wanted to trap Jesus into saying something against Caesar, the Roman Emperor, **so that they might hand him over to the power and authority of the governor**—that is, the Roman governor, Pontius Pilate.

In Jesus' time, Israel was under the authority of the Roman Empire,[80] and the chief ruler of Israel was the Roman governor. The Jewish leaders hoped to accuse Jesus of being a revolutionary, of trying to lead a revolt against Rome. If they could make this accusation against Him, then the Romans would have Him

---

[79] The **Herodians** are mentioned in Mark 3:6 and comment.

[80] The Roman Empire was established in 27 B.C., and lasted for four hundred years. Its capital was Rome, which today is the capital of the modern country of Italy. The Roman Empire included most of the nations of southern Europe, the Middle East, and northern Africa. For further discussion, see Word List: Roman Empire.

arrested and executed. This was the way the Jewish leaders hoped to get rid of Jesus.

14 Therefore, the Pharisees and Herodians, after flattering Jesus, asked Him, **"Is it right to pay taxes to Caesar**[81] **or not?"** If Jesus answered that it was not right, then they could accuse Him before the governor of disobeying Roman law. However, if Jesus answered that it was right to pay taxes to Caesar, then the ordinary Jews would be angry with Him and turn against Him. The reason the common people would be angry with Him was that they hated the Romans, and they especially hated to pay taxes to the Roman emperor. Thus, no matter what answer Jesus gave, He would bring trouble upon Himself (see Mark 11:28 and comment).

15–17 Then Jesus asked to see a **denarius**, a Roman coin with Caesar's image on it. Then He gave the perfect answer: **"Give to Caesar what is Caesar's and to God what is God's."**

It is right for people to pay taxes. Although the Jews had lost their independence, Caesar had given them many other benefits, such as roads, peace, security. The Jews needed to pay for these benefits. There is usually no conflict in our duty to the government and our duty to God. Only when the government forces us to disobey God's law must we oppose the government in that particular matter (see Acts 4:18–20; 5:29; Romans 13:1–7 and comments).

In Jesus' time, anything that had a man's stamp or inscription on it belonged to that man. A Roman coin had Caesar's inscription on it—Caesar's image—and therefore, it belonged to Caesar.

In the same way, it can be said that man has God's stamp on him. Man is made in God's image (Genesis 1:27). Therefore, man belongs to God. Our taxes belong to Caesar, but we ourselves belong to God. Therefore, we must give taxes to "Caesar," and ourselves to God.

Marriage at the Resurrection (12:18–27)

(Matthew 22:23–33; Luke 20:27–40)

18–23 Then the SADDUCEES came to Jesus and asked Him a long question. The Sadducees were a party of the Jews who did not believe in life after death or in the RESURRECTION of the body (see Acts 23:6–8 and comment). The Sadducees knew that Jesus taught that there was a resurrection, so they asked a question in order to embarrass Him. They made up a story of one woman who married seven brothers one after another.[82] Then they asked, **"At the resurrection whose wife will she be?"** (verse 23). The meaning of their question was this: If the seven brothers were all resurrected in heaven, then she would be married to all seven. But according to the Jewish law, a woman could have only one husband. Thus, Jesus' teaching about the resurrection contradicted the Jewish Scriptures. Therefore, in the Sadducees' opinion, the resurrection of the body was impossible.

24 But Jesus showed that the Sadducees were wrong on two counts. First, by denying the resurrection they were denying the **power of God**. The resurrection of the body is a proof of the power of God. Second, they didn't **know the Scriptures**. There is no need for marriage in heaven. Marriage is necessary in this world to produce children, so that the human race doesn't die out. But in heaven there is no death (Revelation 21:4); therefore, there is no need for births, and hence no need for marriage.

25 In heaven men **will be like** ANGELS, that is, they will live forever. According to Luke 20:35–36, Jesus said at this point: "**. . . those who are considered worthy of taking part in that age** (the next life) **and in the resurrection from the dead . . . are God's children, since they are children of the resurrection.**" All who believe in Christ become God's children, and partake in the resurrection

---

[81] **Caesar** means "emperor." All Roman emperors were called "Caesar."

[82] According to the Jewish law, if a man died leaving no heir, a younger unmarried brother was required to marry his widow so that he would not remain without descendants (Deuteronomy 25:5–10).

from the dead[83] (see Romans 8:16,23; 1 Corinthians 15:20–22,42–49; Galatians 3:26; 4:7 and comments).

26–27 The Sadducees believed mainly in the first five books of the Old Testament, which were written by Moses. In Exodus 3:6, Moses quotes God as saying: **"I am . . . the God of Abraham, the God of Isaac, the God of Jacob."** Abraham, the father of the Jews, and Isaac his son and Jacob his grandson had all died when Moses wrote this. Yet God says that He continues to be their God; "I **am** their God," He says. Therefore, they all must still be alive, because God is a God of the living, not of the dead. Thus even the first five books of the Old Testament teach that there is life after death, which the Sadducees denied.

The Greatest Commandment (12:28–34)

(Matthew 22:34–40)

28–30 The Jews considered themselves righteous. They were careful to obey the commandments written in the Jewish law. The Jews considered the ten commandments very important (Exodus 20:1–17), and also the laws concerning sacrifices and offerings. If a Jew obeyed the ten commandments and performed all the proper sacrifices and offerings, he could be called "righteous."

But here in verse 30, one of the most important verses in the entire Bible, Jesus teaches that there is a higher law, a greater law: to love God. More than sacrifices and offerings, God wants our love.

In fact, the Jews knew about this law. It is written in Deuteronomy 6:4–5, and devout Jews repeated it out loud twice a day. But they didn't consider it the highest law, a law from which all other laws were derived (Matthew 22:40).

Love the Lord your God. How much of our love does God want? All of it. Four times the word "all" is repeated here. We are to give God **all** our love; that means we are not to keep back any love for ourselves.

We are to love God with our whole life—**heart, soul, mind, strength**. We are to give our lives in love to God. God doesn't want animal sacrifices; He wants human sacrifices! He wants us to give ourselves as **living sacrifices** to Him (see Romans 12:1 and comment).

If we say we have given our life to God, how can we then keep back other things for ourselves? How can we say, "This is my house, my radio, my job, my honor, my future? If we belong to God, then all these things belong to Him too.

A question arises here: How can we show our love for God? It is easy to say, "I love God," but what does that really mean? To love God means to obey God. If we do not obey God, we do not love Him. Obedience is the proof and demonstration of our love (John 14:15,21,23–24). However, our obedience must not be like that of the Pharisees and teachers of the law. They obeyed God not because they loved God, but to show other men how religious they were (see Matthew 5:20).

31 Then Jesus gave a second command: **"Love your neighbor as yourself"** (Leviticus 19:18). Our love for God must be demonstrated in our love for other people. The last six of the ten commandments are concerned with loving our neighbor (Exodus 20:12–17). The first four are concerned with loving God (Exodus 20:3–4,7–8). Therefore, Jesus said in Matthew 22:40, **"All the Law and the Prophets[84] hang on these two commandments"** (see Romans 13:8–10; Galatians 5:14 and comments).

How must we love our neighbor? As we love ourselves. What we would want for ourselves, we must want for our neighbor. Jesus did not say: "Love yourself and your neighbor equally." He said: "Love your neighbor as if he were

---

[83] In these verses in Luke, Jesus is talking about the resurrection of believers in heaven. There will also be a resurrection of unbelievers on the day of judgment (see John 5:28–29 and comment).

[84] The Old Testament is often called the **Law and the Prophets**. The first five books of the Old Testament are called the "Law."

yourself." The natural worldly man loves himself first of all. That is how we should love our neighbor—first of all, after God.

The Christian must love his neighbor more than himself. In fact, the Christian should no longer love himself at all.[85] The Christian is called to deny himself (Mark 8:34), and to give **all** his love to God and his neighbor. We must love each other as Jesus loved us (see John 13:34; 15:12–13). Jesus loved us so much that He gave His life for us (1 John 3:16).

Love your **neighbor** as yourself. Who is our neighbor? The Jews considered only other Jews to be their neighbors. But Jesus taught that all men are our neighbors, especially those in any kind of need (see Luke 10:25–37).

These two great commandments to love God and to love our neighbor are, in essence, one command. To love God and to love other men must always go together. We do not truly love God if we do not love our neighbor. **If anyone says, "I love God," yet hates his brother, he is a liar** (see 1 John 4:20–21 and comment).

Then again, many people make the opposite error: they try to show love to others without loving God. This is a humanitarian "love," and it does not last. All true love flows out of our love for God and our faith in Him. John wrote that **love comes from God** (1 John 4:7). Paul wrote: **God has poured out His love into our hearts by the Holy Spirit, whom He has given us** (Romans 5:5). When we truly love our neighbor, it is not with our own selfish human love that we love him, but with God's love given to us through the Holy Spirit which dwells within us. We are like pipes or channels through which God's love can flow to other people. May our constant prayer be that we might remain open channels and that nothing might block the flow of God's love through us. Water cannot flow into a pipe that is blocked at one end. In the same way, if love does not flow out from us, God's love cannot flow in.

32–34 The teacher of the law who had asked Jesus, "Which is the greatest commandment?" understood Jesus' answer. He spoke correctly when he said that to love God was **more important than all burnt offerings and sacrifices**. God Himself spoke through the prophet Hosea saying: **"I desire mercy,[86] not sacrifice, and acknowledgment of God rather than burnt offerings"** (Hosea 6:6). And in the book of 1 Samuel, Samuel says: **"Does the Lord delight in burnt offerings and sacrifices as much as in obeying the voice of the Lord? To obey is better than sacrifice, and to heed is better than the fat of rams"** (1 Samuel 15:22).

Then Jesus, seeing that the teacher of the law had answered wisely, said to him, **"You are not far from the kingdom of God."**

Whose Son Is the Christ? (12:35–40)

(Matthew 22:41–46; Luke 20:41–47)

35 The Jews believed that the Christ, the Messiah, would be descended from King David. Therefore, they called the Messiah the **son of David** (Mark 10:47–48). In the Jews' mind, the Messiah would be another earthly king like David and would establish an earthly kingdom like the old Israel of David's time.

36 But Jesus wanted to show that the Messiah was more than just David's son. He was also David's Lord at the same time. To show this, Jesus quoted Psalm 110:1, which David himself wrote: **The Lord** (God) **said to my Lord** (the Messiah): **"Sit at my right hand. . . ."** From this we can understand that David was calling the Messiah "Lord."

37 Jesus asked, "If David called the Messiah 'Lord,' how can the Messiah also be David's son?" The truth is that the Messiah, Christ, was both David's son and also David's Lord. Christ the "Son of Man" was David's son; Christ the "Son of

---

[85] This does not mean that believers should despise themselves. To cease loving self does not mean we must have a poor self-image. We are members of God's family; we are made in His image. Our worth is derived from Him.

[86] In place of the word **mercy** in this verse, some versions of the Bible say "steadfast love."

God" was David's Lord. As Lord, Christ came to establish not an earthly kingdom but a spiritual kingdom that would never end (Daniel 7:13–14).

38–39 Then Jesus gave a warning concerning the teachers of the law. They held high positions and were respected by the people. But because of that, they had become proud. Religious leaders are supposed to seek God's glory, but often they seek mainly their own glory. The greatest temptation of any leader is pride, whether he be a Christian or not (see Matthew 23:5–7).

40 They devour widows' houses. Teachers of the law were not supposed to demand payment for their religious services. If people wanted to give them something, it was to be given freely.

However, the teachers of the law expected to be paid. They made people feel they ought to give them something. They lived off the poor people, such as widows. The poor respected and trusted them, and therefore felt obliged to give to them.

These teachers of the law made **lengthy prayers**, so that people would think they were religious and thus praise and respect them all the more (see Matthew 6:5–6 and comment). By such a show of piety they gained the confidence of people and thus could "devour" their houses more easily. "Men who pray so long surely will not cheat us," people supposed. Yet the teachers of the law were really wolves in sheep's clothing (see Matthew 7:15 and comment). Such men will receive their "reward" only in this life; in the next life they shall receive severe punishment for their greed and hypocrisy.[87]

The Widow's Offering (12:41–44)
(Luke 21:1–4)

41–44 When we give a gift to God, we think about how much we give. But God thinks about how much we don't give! That is, He thinks about how much we have remaining. A rich man may give thousands of dollars, but that is nothing to God. God doesn't need our money. In God's eyes, the poor widow had given more than all the rich people put together. After she gave, she had nothing left. She gave all to God. Even though it was only a **fraction of a penny**, it was worth more to God than all the money given by the rich (see 2 Corinthians 8:12).

The essence of giving is sacrifice. When we give to God, we should go without something we want or need. We should not be content to give only what we can afford. We need to give more than we can afford (2 Corinthians 8:1–3). If we do this, God will reward us. As much as we give sacrificially to others, God will give to us (see 2 Corinthians 9:6–9 and comment). **One man gives freely, yet gains even more; another withholds unduly, but comes to poverty. A generous man will prosper; he who refreshes others will himself be refreshed** (Proverbs 11:24–25).

CHAPTER 13

Signs of the End of the Age (13:1–13)
(Matthew 10:17–22; 24:1–14; Luke 21:5–19)

1 The Jewish temple in Jerusalem was one of the biggest and most magnificent buildings in the ancient world. Around it were many colonnades and courtyards and smaller buildings. The temple area filled one sixth of the city of Jerusalem. Its front was covered with gold. Some of its stones were thirty feet long and twelve feet wide.

---

[87] Any priest or religious teacher who grows rich at the expense of those whom he is serving is a false priest and a false teacher.

Therefore, it was not surprising that one of Jesus' disciples exclaimed: **"What massive stones! What magnificent buildings!"**

2 It surely seemed as if the temple could never be destroyed. Yet Jesus told His disciples that every one of those stones would be thrown down (see Luke 19:41–44 and comment). And forty years later, when the Romans destroyed Jerusalem in 70 A.D., they destroyed the temple, too. And since that time, the temple has never been rebuilt.

3–4 Peter, James, John, and Andrew (Mark 1:16–20) were amazed at Jesus' statement that the temple would be destroyed. **"Tell us, when will these things happen?"** they asked. According to Matthew 24:3, the disciples also asked, **". . . and what will be the sign of your coming and of the end of the age?"** The disciples asked both of these questions together, because they supposed that the destruction of Jerusalem and the end of the world would come at the same time. But Jesus answered their question in two parts. To understand this chapter, we must not confuse the two parts of Jesus' answer. In verses 5–23,28–31 (Matthew 24:4–28,32–35; Luke 21:8–24,29–33), Jesus answers the disciples' question about the destruction of Jerusalem. In verses 24–27,32–37 (Matthew 24:29–31,36–44; Luke 21:25–28,34–36), Jesus answers their question about the end of the world and His second coming. We must also keep in mind that although Jesus knew when the destruction of Jerusalem would come (verse 30), He did not know when the end of the world would come (verse 32). Only God Himself knows that.

But we can understand from this chapter that the signs that preceded the destruction of Jerusalem are similar to the signs that will precede the end of the world. In other words, the destruction of Jerusalem is a foretaste of the events that will occur at the end of the world. Therefore, even those parts of this chapter that refer to the destruction of Jerusalem can also serve as a warning to us about what will happen at the end of the world.[88]

5 The disciples wanted to know **when** these things would happen. But Jesus tells them something more important: **"Watch"** (verses 5,37). **"Be on guard"** (verses 9,33). If the disciples remained always ready and on guard, then it would not be so necessary for them to know the exact time at which these events would take place. This is Jesus' word for us today also. Let us not always be asking, "When?" "Where?" Rather, let us remain always ready and watchful.

"Watch out that no one deceives you," Jesus said. Deceivers are much more dangerous to the church than persecutors. Satan's main weapon against Christians is not persecution but deception (see verse 22 and comment). **"Many will come in my name . . . and will deceive many"** (verse 6). Many have been seduced into following new Christs and new Gospels, and have thereby lost their faith in the true Christ.

6–8 In these verses, Jesus prophesied that three kinds of events would occur before the fall of Jerusalem. First, many would appear saying, **"I am he**; I am the Christ" (Matthew 24:4). The disciples must not believe these false Christs (verses 21–22). Many of these false Christs did appear before the fall of Jerusalem (see Acts 5:36–37).

Second, Jesus said that there would be **wars and rumors of wars** between nations. Indeed, in 62–66 A.D., only a few years before Jerusalem was destroyed, there were many wars throughout the Roman Empire and many rumors of revolts against the emperor.

Third, Jesus said that there would be **earthquakes in various places, and famines**. Indeed, there were famines in various parts of the Roman Empire before the destruction of Jerusalem (Acts 11:28). According to Roman historians, there

---

[88] It should be mentioned that this entire chapter is difficult to understand. Bible scholars have different opinions about the meaning of certain verses. This commentary attempts to present the most common interpretations.

were also several earthquakes in different parts of the Empire during that time.

According to Luke 21:11, Jesus also said that there would be **great signs from heaven** before the destruction of Jerusalem. According to both Roman and Jewish historians, these signs did take place. For example, according to the Jewish historian Josephus, a comet appeared over Jerusalem for many nights with a tail shaped like a sword.

Yet all these things were only the **beginning of birth pains** (verse 8). These events that occurred before the destruction of Jerusalem were only the beginning of the events that will ultimately lead to the end of the world. We know that in the past 1900 years, even greater wars have occurred, and even greater earthquakes and famines. False Christs even today are rising up in different parts of the world. Jesus' prophecy not only was fulfilled before the fall of Jerusalem, but it is also continuing to be fulfilled right up to this present time, as we await His coming again at the end of the world.

9 The prophecies mentioned in this verse were fulfilled in the lives of Jesus' twelve disciples and in the life of Paul. The persecution of Jesus' followers is described in detail in the book of Acts.

10 **And the GOSPEL must first be preached to all nations**. According to the corresponding verse in Matthew, the Gospel must be **preached in the whole world as a testimony to all nations, and then the end will come** (Matthew 24:14)—that is, the **end** of the world. Many Christians believe that as soon as **all nations**[89] have heard the Gospel, Christ will come again and the world will end.

According to Revelation 14:6–7, just before the end an angel will proclaim the Gospel one last time **to every nation, tribe, language and people**. Regardless of how we understand this verse, the duty of every Christian is clear. Jesus' last command to His disciples was this: **"Therefore go and make disciples of all nations, baptizing them in the name of the Father and of the Son and of the Holy Spirit, and teaching them to obey everything I have commanded you. And surely I will be with you always, to the very end of the age"** (Matthew 28:19–20).

Jesus' disciples suffered because they preached the **gospel of the kingdom** (Matthew 24:14)—that is, the Gospel of the kingdom of God. The preachers of this Gospel must always be prepared to suffer.

11 As we preach and **make disciples of all nations**, Jesus is with us. That is, His Holy Spirit is with us and in us. When difficult situations arise, His Holy Spirit will give us the words we are to speak. The **Holy Spirit will teach you at that time what you should say** (Luke 12:12). Many Christians who have been arrested because of their witness for Christ can testify that the Holy Spirit has indeed given them the words to speak (see Matthew 10:19–20; Luke 21:14–15).

12 In the last days, families will be split apart because of Christ. Those in a family who do not believe in Christ will oppose those who do (Matthew 10:35–36). Fathers will disown their sons. Members of the same family will have each other put to death. Because of persecution, **many will turn away from the faith and will betray and hate each other. . . . Because of the increase of wickedness, the love of most will grow cold** (Matthew 24:10–12). All these things came to pass before the destruction of

---

[89] It is not certain whether **all nations** means every single small tribe in the world, or whether it means "people throughout the world" in a general sense (see Romans 1:5,8; 10:17–18; Colossians 1:6,23).

Some Bible scholars believe that by saying **all nations**, Jesus meant all known nations at the time of the Roman Empire. If this is so, then the prophecy of Matthew 24:14 was fulfilled before the destruction of Jerusalem. In this case, the word **end** in Matthew 24:14 would refer to the "end" of Jerusalem, not the end of the world.

However, it's possible that Jesus' prophecy in Matthew refers both to the destruction of Jerusalem and to the end of the world, in which case it can be interpreted on two levels. On one level, the prophecy was partially fulfilled at the destruction of Jerusalem; on another level, the prophecy will be completely fulfilled at the end of the world.

Jerusalem. And these same things will happen again before the end of the world. Indeed, these things are happening even today in many parts of the world.

13 **All men will hate you because of me**. We either belong to this world or we belong to the kingdom of God. If we belong to the kingdom of God, the world will hate us (see John 15:18–19). We cannot follow the world and Christ at the same time.

But **he who stands firm until the end will be saved**. Here the words **until the end** do not mean "to the end of the world." They mean to "stand firm unto death," to stand firm completely, to stand firm no matter what persecution comes upon us. To "stand firm" means to stand firm in faith. Those who stand firm in the faith will be saved. Those who do not stand firm will not be saved.

Many Christians interpret this verse to mean that if we deliberately abandon our faith we will lose our salvation. Others believe that if a person abandons his faith, he was never a true Christian to begin with.[90] But, whatever we think about the above question, the clear teaching of the Bible to every Christian is this: **Stand firm**. Stand firm **to the end** (see 1 Corinthians 16:13; Galatians 5:1; Ephesians 6:14–15; Philippians 4:1; Colossians 1:22–23; Hebrews 10:35–36; James 5:8; 1 Peter 5:9). Let us not be like the seed planted on rocky soil that withered and died as soon as the sun came out. Those that endure for a while and then fall away have believed in vain (see Mark 4:16–17 and comment).

According to Luke 21:18, on this same occasion Jesus said to His disciples, ". . . **not a hair of your head will perish**." Jesus did not mean that His followers would not die. In fact, all of Jesus' disciples except John were violently put to death, and countless other Christians have been put to death since. Jesus meant that in the next life in heaven, our resurrected bodies will be perfect, without even a hair missing. Men may kill our bodies in this world, but God will preserve our spiritual bodies in the next (see Matthew 10:28–31).

The Abomination that Causes Desolation (13:14–23)
(Matthew 24:15–28; Luke 21:20–24)

14 The **abomination that causes desolation**[91] mentioned by Jesus in this verse was the desecration of the Jewish temple in Jerusalem by the Roman army in 70 A.D. (see Luke 21:20). According to some historians, the Jewish Zealots fighting against Rome also occupied the temple for a short time and committed acts of sacrilege inside it.

The main warning, however, that Jesus wanted to give His followers was that when they saw the army of Rome approaching, they should flee from Jerusalem. Let **those in Judea**[92] **flee to the mountains**. Sometimes God calls us to stand and face danger. But at other times He tells us to flee. In each circumstance Christians must seek God's will. It is all right to flee from danger, but not from duty.

15–16 These Christians were to flee from Jerusalem without delay. If they were on the top of their house, they were to run down the outside stairs and flee to the hills. There would be no time to gather together their possessions.

17–18 Those times would be especially difficult for pregnant women and mothers with young children. They could not flee quickly, and the Romans would catch them and kill them (Luke 23:28–29).

Let the Christians also pray that this terrible time would not occur in winter. In winter it rains in Israel, and the rivers swell. Thus people's flight would be blocked. (Indeed, many people fleeing from the Romans were blocked by the

[90] For further discussion of this subject, see General Article: Can We Lose Our Salvation?

[91] The name **abomination that causes desolation** comes from Daniel 9:27; 11:31; 12:11. Its meaning in the Old Testament is any idol or evil person by which the Jewish temple was desecrated.

[92] Judea is the southern province of Israel, in which Jerusalem is located.

swollen Jordan River.) According to Matthew 24:20, they should also pray that the day of flight would not fall on the Sabbath. The many Sabbath laws would make flight difficult. For example, according to the Jewish law one could only travel three miles on the Sabbath! (Acts 1:12).

19 The destruction of Jerusalem was a time of distress more severe than any in the history of the world. The slaughter of the Jews by the Romans is fully described by the Jewish historian, Josephus. The Romans committed unbelievable atrocities, and those Jews that escaped the sword died of famine and pestilence, or were made slaves (Luke 21:24). Over a million Jews were killed. Not a single Jew remained alive in the city. Jesus said in Luke 21:24, **"Jerusalem will be trampled on by the Gentiles until the times of the Gentiles are fulfilled."**[93] This was God's judgment on the unbelieving Jewish nation which had rejected and put to death His own Son Jesus (see Luke 21:22–24).

20 Most of the Christians in Jerusalem fled in 68 A.D., two years before the Romans came. But others fled just before the Roman army arrived. Some of these almost starved in the countryside, because the Roman soldiers destroyed crops and fields and took all available food for themselves. But God **cut short those days,** so that all the **elect**—that is, all believers—were able to survive.

21–23 Again Jesus repeated His warning about false Christs. Before and during the invasion of Jerusalem by the Roman army, certain Jews rose up claiming to be the Messiah and calling on people to fight the Romans. Here Jesus warns that the fleeing Christians must not follow such false Christs. They should continue their flight (see verses 5–6).

Although the context of these verses relates to the destruction of Jerusalem, we can understand that false Christs will continue to rise up until the end of the world. Especially as the end of the world draws near, powerful men and evil forces sent by Satan will rise up and oppose Christ and His followers (see 2 Thessalonians 2:1–10; 1 John 2:18; 4:1–3; Revelation 13:1–8,11–17 and comments). These false Christs will even perform **signs and miracles.**[94] But we must not be deceived. We will be able to recognize the false Christs because they will not bring glory to Jesus; they will deny that He is the true Son of God (see 1 John 4:1–3 and comment).

Jesus said that false Christs and false prophets will try **to deceive the elect—if that were possible**. It is not possible to deceive those who are **elect**. In fact, the elect are the very people who will remain undeceived to the end. Only God knows who the "elect" are and who are not. Those who heed the warning to remain on guard (verses 9,23) and who remain faithful to the end (verse 13) will prove to be the **elect**. Therefore, Jesus says to all: **". . . be on your guard."**

According to Matthew 24:26–27, Jesus also added here that if a person claiming to be the Messiah appeared in one special place, such as **in the desert** or **in the inner rooms,** then it would be certain that he was a false Messiah. Because the true Messiah, Jesus, will appear to all men at once like lightning flashing across the sky.

Then Jesus said, **"Wherever there is a**

---

[93] The **times of the Gentiles** is the period during which the Gentiles dominated Jerusalem. That period started in 70 A.D. and lasted until 1948, when the modern nation of Israel was established. The Jews regained full control of all Jerusalem in 1966. This is one reason that many Christians today believe that the last days of the world have drawn near.

[94] Some Bible scholars believe that false Christs and false prophets never perform true supernatural miracles, but only magical tricks that appear to be miraculous. They say that only through the power of Christ can the laws of nature be set aside. However, others believe that Satan and his servants also can perform true miracles. For example, the Egyptian sorcerers caused their wooden staffs to become real snakes (Exodus 7:10–12). The important point, however, is that we cannot distinguish miracles performed by Satan and his servants from those performed by Christians by looking at the miracles alone. We must look to see if the miracle brings glory to Christ; that is the test.

carcass, there the vultures[95] **will gather"** (Matthew 24:28). The **carcass** was the Jewish nation, and the **vultures** (or eagles) were the Romans.[96] Such was the destruction of Jerusalem and Judea.

The End of the World (13:24–27)
(Matthew 24:29–31; Luke 21:25–28)

24–25 After talking about the destruction of Jerusalem, Jesus then began to describe the end of the world, which would occur in the days **following that distress**. According to Matthew 24:29, Jesus said that the end of the world would occur **immediately after the distress of those days**, that is, immediately after the fall of Jerusalem. This is difficult to understand. Over 1900 years have passed since the fall of Jerusalem, and the end of the world has not yet come. But in God's eyes, 1900 years is like a moment (2 Peter 3:8). We must also remember that Jesus Himself said that He did not know when the end of the world would come (verse 32).

To describe what the end of the world would be like, Jesus quoted from Isaiah 13:10 and 34:4. According to Luke 21:25–26, Jesus at this point also said: **"There will be signs in the sun, moon and stars. On the earth, nations will be in anguish and perplexity at the roaring and tossing of the sea. Men will faint from terror, apprehensive of what is coming on the world, for the heavenly bodies will be shaken"** (see 2 Peter 3:10).

26–27 **At that time men will see the Son of Man coming in clouds with great power and glory.** The Old Testament prophet Daniel saw a vision of this event and wrote about it: **In my vision at night I looked, and there before me was one like a son of man, coming with the clouds of heaven** (Daniel 7:13).

In all of history since the creation of the world, there are only two events whose significance will last forever. These two events are greater and more important than all the other events in history put together. Every other event, every king, every war, every empire will be forgotten. Only two things will be remembered. First, the coming of Jesus Christ into the world the first time. Second, the coming again of Jesus Christ, the Son of Man, **on the clouds of the sky, with power and great glory** (Matthew 24:30). At the time of His second coming, Jesus will **gather his elect**—that is, those who have believed—**from the ends of the earth to the ends of the heavens** (verse 27). He will gather us into His eternal kingdom where we shall live together with Him forever (1 Thessalonians 4:16–18).

When Christ comes again, all other men will **faint from terror** (Luke 21:26). **At that time . . . all the nations of the earth will mourn** (Matthew 24:30). Those who have rejected Christ as Savior will have to face Him as their judge (John 5:22). But those who have believed in Jesus will have no fear. For Jesus said, **"When these things begin to take place, stand up and lift up your heads, because your REDEMPTION is drawing near"** (Luke 21:28).

The Destruction of Jerusalem (13:28–31)
(Matthew 24:32–35; Luke 21:29–33)

28–29 In verses 5–23, Jesus described many events that would occur just before the destruction of Jerusalem. These were like signs that the end was near. Just as the new leaves on a fig tree are a sign that summer has come, so the events described in verses 5–23 were signs that Jerusalem was about to be destroyed.

30 Jesus prophesied that **all these things**—that is, the above mentioned signs together with the destruction of Jerusalem—would occur within the lifetime of His own generation. This prophecy was fulfilled in 70 A.D.

31 **My words will never pass away.** Jesus' words, His prophecies, His teachings are absolutely certain. They are more certain and permanent than the earth and

---

[95] In place of the word **vultures**, some translations of the Bible say "eagles."

[96] The sign or standard of the Roman army was an eagle.

sky. When we see great trees and great mountains, we think: "These things are certain; they will last." When we look at the sun and moon and stars, we think: "These things will last forever." But they will one day pass away. The only things that will last are Jesus and His words. Remember, Jesus Himself is the **Word** of God, who in the beginning was **with God, and . . . was God** (John 1:1), and whose **kingdom will never end.**

The Day and Hour Unknown (13:32–37)

32 **No one knows about that day or hour**; that is, no one except the Father knows when Christ will come again. Not even Christ Himself knows. Therefore we must be always ready. Jesus could come today, tomorrow. Will He find us sleeping? (verse 36). Will He find us faithful?

Many Christians spend time trying to predict when Christ will come again. This is folly. They'd be better off spending their time doing the work Christ has given them to do instead of wondering when He is going to come again.

33–37 Christ is like a **man going away** (verse 34). Christ went away into heaven and left **his house**, that is, His church, in our hands. He has given each of us a special **assigned task**. But not only that, He has also given all of us the task of praying, watching, and witnessing. He will come back to earth **like a thief**, that is, when no one expects Him (see Matthew 24:42–44; Luke 12:35–38; 1 Thessalonians 5:1–2). What will He find us doing? Let us not say to ourselves: "He will not come soon. I have time to get ready. I'll sleep a little longer. I'll witness to that person another time. I'll do that good deed some other day. I'll give up that sin tomorrow." Let us not make such a terrible mistake. Jesus can come any time, and if He does not find us ready and doing His will, He will throw us out (see Matthew 24:45–51; Luke 21:34–36).

To **keep watch** (verse 35) means to remain in Christ's will at all times. We need to live each day as if Christ was going to return tomorrow. We need to test ourselves by asking ourselves this question: If an angel from heaven were to tell us today that Christ was going to come next week, or next month, would we live our lives any differently? If the answer is "Yes," then we are not watching, we are not ready. **"What I say to you, I say to everyone: 'Watch!'"**

CHAPTER 14

Jesus Anointed at Bethany (14:1–11) (Matthew 26:1–16; Luke 22:1–6; John 12:1–8)

1–2 Jesus had been in Jerusalem for some days before the **Passover**[97] festival. The Passover was celebrated each year in commemoration of the Jews' deliverance from EGYPT. On the day following the Passover, the Feast of Unleavened Bread began, and it lasted for one week (Exodus 12:15–20; Deuteronomy 16:1–8). Sometimes the Passover was called the **first day of the Feast of Unleavened Bread** (verse 12), although it was, in fact, a separate day.

---

[97] On the Jews' last night of bondage in Egypt, God killed all of the firstborn of Egypt, both men and animals. Moses had instructed the Jews to sacrifice a lamb and sprinkle its blood on the doorframes of their houses. By means of this sign, the **destroyer**—that is, the destroying angel—was able to identify the houses of the Jews and thus bypass or "pass over" their houses and spare their firstborn. When Pharaoh, the king of Egypt, saw the terrible calamity that God had brought upon his land on account of the Jews, he decided to let the Jews go free that very night (Exodus 12:1–14,21–36). The word **Passover**, therefore, means the "passing over" or the sparing of the firstborn in the Jewish homes. It also signifies the deliverance of the Jews from bondage in Egypt.

According to Matthew 26:3, the chief priests and teachers of the law met at the palace of the Jewish high priest, Caiaphas; and according to John 11:47–53, Caiaphas was the chief instigator of the plot against Jesus.

During the Passover and the Feast of Unleavened Bread, Jerusalem's usual population of 50,000 swelled to 250,000, because of all the Jewish pilgrims coming to celebrate the festivals. The Jewish leaders were afraid to seize Jesus during that time, because many of these pilgrims supported Jesus and would surely have created a great disturbance in the city if they heard that Jesus had been arrested.

3 The anointing of Jesus described here in verses 3–9 is probably the same as the anointing described in John 12:1–8. It took place six days before the Passover (John 12:1) and one day before Jesus' triumphal entry into Jerusalem[98] (Mark 11:1–11; John 12:12). The woman who anointed Jesus was Mary, the sister of Martha and Lazarus (John 11:1–2; 12:2–3).

The perfume was extremely valuable. It probably had been kept in the family from generation to generation, the way people keep gold. It was financial security for the family, and according to verse 5, it was worth three hundred denarii, that is, a year's wages. Nevertheless, the woman poured it all out on Jesus' head and feet and then wiped His feet with her hair (John 12:3). This was the greatest possible demonstration of love and respect anyone could give to another person.

In Jesus' mind, what Mary did was extremely important (verse 9). She gave to Him something of great value. Perhaps that perfume was all the savings she had (Mark 12:43–44). This is what Jesus wants from each of us. He doesn't want just a tithe—that is, ten percent; He wants us to offer all that we have to Him.

After the alabaster jar was broken, **the house was filled with the fragrance of the perfume** (John 12:3). As long as the perfume was kept in the jar, there was no fragrance. The perfume was benefiting no one. But once the jar was broken and the perfume was poured out on Jesus, then its fragrance filled the house.

For us, this story of the anointing of Jesus is like a parable. God has given each of us a "jar of perfume"; that is, He has given to each of us gifts and skills and possessions. If we keep these for ourselves, they do not benefit anyone. In the end, they do not even benefit us, because we cannot take them with us when we die. Only when we pour out all our gifts, skills, and possessions at Jesus' feet can He take them and use them for God's glory and for the benefit of others.

We are like jars. Only when we are broken can the spirit within us flow out. Only when our selfishnesss and pride is broken, can our lives truly glorify God.

4–5 **Some of those present**, however, rebuked the woman for wasting the perfume. One of these was Judas Iscariot, who was about to betray Jesus (see John 12:4–6).

When we pour out our gifts, skills, and possessions for Jesus, people will also say that we are wasting our lives. What we do for Jesus the world considers wasted. But, in fact, nothing is ever wasted on Jesus.

Let us also learn from this story never to criticize the expressions and works of love done by others. How quick the disciples were to criticize this woman! And how great was their error!

6–7 Some of those present thought that the ointment should have been sold and given to the poor. Except for Judas (John 12:6), the others perhaps sincerely cared about the poor.

But Jesus answered, "You can help the poor any time. There will always be poor people to help. But I will be here only a short time." To love Jesus is our highest duty; it is the greatest commandment (Mark 12:30). To love the poor, that is, our neighbor, is our second duty (Mark 12:31).

8–9 **She did what she could . . . to prepare for my burial**. Except for

---

[98] Mark writes about Jesus' anointing after his description of Jesus' entry into Jerusalem, but, in fact, the anointing came beforehand. Mark does not tell us on what day the anointing took place; we learn that from John's Gospel.

executed criminals, the Jews always anointed a corpse with ointment. But Jesus knew that He would be executed as a criminal, and that therefore His body would not be properly anointed. This woman had anointed Him **beforehand**. She herself did not realize what she had done, but Jesus knew. And Jesus promised that wherever the Gospel is preached, what she did will also be told. And that promise has, of course, come true.

10–11 Judas' offer to betray Jesus delighted the Jewish leaders, because now they would not have to wait until the end of the Feast of Unleavened Bread (verse 2) to seize Jesus. They offered Judas **thirty silver coins**[99] if he would give Jesus into their hands (Matthew 26:14–15). Now with Judas' help, it would be easy for the Jews to put Jesus to death.

Why did Judas betray Jesus? Surely Judas had never given his heart to Jesus. He was a **thief** (John 12:6). He followed Jesus in the hope that he would be an important official in an earthly kingdom which he expected the Messiah to establish. But when Judas finally realized that Jesus would have no earthly kingdom, and that this woman in Bethany had, in fact, anointed Him for burial, he saw that there was no further advantage in following Jesus. So, greedy for money, Judas betrayed Him for thirty coins. **Satan entered into him** (John 13:27).

It was written in the Old Testament that one of Jesus' own disciples would betray Him (Psalm 41:9; John 13:18). And Jesus knew beforehand that it would be Judas (Matthew 26:21–25; John 13:21–26). Yet Judas betrayed Jesus of his own free will. He didn't have to let Satan enter him. He could have remained faithful. But Jesus, because He was God, knew in advance what Judas would do.

Let us learn from Judas' sin. Those who have tasted the blessings of Christ and then turn away will receive the greatest punishment. For them there is no hope of repentance, no hope of salvation (see Hebrews 6:4–6 and comment).

The Lord's Supper (14:12–26)
(Matthew 26:17–30; Luke 22:7–23)

12 The Passover was also called the **first day of the Feast of Unleavened Bread** (see verse 1 and comment). Therefore, Matthew, Mark, and Luke say that the Lord's last supper took place on the Passover,[100] the day **when it was**

---

[99] According to Exodus 21:32, **thirty shekels of silver** was the value of a slave.

[100] Some Bible scholars say that, according to John 18:28 and 19:14,31,42, Jesus' death took place on the Passover day. If this is so, then the last supper had to have taken place on the day before the Passover, not on the Passover, as Matthew, Mark, and Luke have written.

Why does John seem not to agree with Matthew, Mark, and Luke? On this question, Bible scholars have different opinions. Some say that among the Jews at that time there were two different calendars in use, and that Jesus and His disciples followed one calendar and the Jewish leaders followed another. According to this explanation, John wrote according to the calendar used by the Jewish leaders, while Matthew, Mark, and Luke wrote according to the other calendar.

A second explanation is that the word **Passover** used in John 18:28 does not mean the actual Passover day, but is a general word meaning "any meal" during the week of the Feast of Unleavened Bread (the Passover week). The scholars who hold this opinion also say that the expression **day of Preparation** mentioned in John 19:14,31,42 does not mean the day before the Passover but rather the "Friday" of Passover week, which happened to fall on Passover day that year. (The **day of Preparation** is a Jewish term meaning the day before the Sabbath; thus it always falls on Friday.)

If either of these two explanations are correct, then there is no disagreement between John and the other three Gospel writers. (There are other explanations also.) It is the opinion of this commentary that the second explanation above is most likely the correct one. We believe that all four Gospel writers agree that the Lord's last supper occurred on Thursday evening, which was the beginning of Passover day that year. (The Jews reckoned the day to begin at 6 P.M.) As Matthew, Mark, and Luke clearly state, this was the main Passover meal (Matthew 26:17–19; Mark 14:12; Luke 22:7–8). Then He was crucified the next day on Friday, the "day of Preparation" (see John 18:28 and comment).

customary to sacrifice the Passover lamb (see Matthew 27:62 and comment).

13–16 Jesus sent **two of his disciples**, Peter and John (Luke 22:8), to prepare for the Passover meal. Jesus had made a secret arrangement beforehand, so that He could eat the Passover meal with His disciples without being disturbed by His enemies. Peter and John were to find a man **carrying a jar of water** (verse 13). Since only women carried water in Jesus' time, the disciples would be able to recognize him easily. According to Matthew, they were to say to the man, **"The Teacher says: my appointed time is near. I am going to celebrate the Passover with my disciples at your house"** (Matthew 26:18). By this the man would know that Peter and John were Jesus' disciples.

17–20 While they were eating the last supper, Jesus told His disciples that one of them would betray Him. They all in amazement said, "**Surely not I?**" Jesus answered, "It is the **one who dips bread into the bowl with me**" (see John 13:22–26 and comment).

Jesus knew His disciples better than they knew themselves. In the same way, He knows us better than we know ourselves.

21 Then Jesus said, "**The Son of Man will go just as it is written about him.**" He was referring to the prophecy written in Psalm 41:9, which says that the Messiah will be betrayed (see John 13:18). "**But woe to that man who betrays the Son of Man.**" Judas, though appointed to be the instrument of Jesus' betrayal, was completely responsible for his actions. And he paid the full penalty.

According to Matthew 26:25, Judas then said to Jesus, "**Surely not I.**" And Jesus said to him, "**Yes, it is you.**"[101] Then, according to John 13:26, Jesus dipped a piece of bread in the dish of sauce and gave it to Judas. And when Judas took the bread, he went out (see John 13:27–30).

22 While Jesus and His remaining eleven disciples were eating, Jesus took bread and said, "**Take it; this is my body.**" According to Luke 22:19, Jesus said, "**This is my body given for you; do this in remembrance of me**" (see 1 Corinthians 11:23–24). With these words Jesus established the first part of the sacrament of the LORD'S SUPPER.

This is my body. The bread represents Jesus' body. It is a sign of Jesus' presence. Every time we celebrate the Lord's supper we know that just as the bread is present with us, so is Jesus present with us. Jesus said, "**I am the bread of life**" (John 6:35). Just as our bodily life is sustained by bread,[102] so our spiritual life is sustained by Jesus (see General Article: Lord's Supper).

This is my body given for you (Luke 22:19). Jesus **broke** the bread and gave it to His disciples. His body was **broken**. Jesus gave His body, His life, for us. He came **to give his life as a ransom for many** (see Mark 10:45 and comment).

Then He said to His disciples, "**Take it,**" or according to Matthew, "**Take and eat**" (Matthew 26:26). Jesus' life is a gift for us, but we must "take it." Just as we appropriate food by eating it, so by faith we must appropriate Jesus' sacrifice for us. We must take and symbolically eat His body. To "take and eat" Jesus' body is to believe in Him. It is to receive His life, to receive eternal life (John 6:56–58).

But to "eat" Jesus' body also means to share in His death; it means to die with Him. We too must be **broken**. We too must die (see Romans 6:3–8 and comment). Jesus said: "**I tell you the truth, unless a kernel of wheat falls to the ground and dies, it remains only a single seed. But if it dies, it produces many seeds** (John 12:24). Jesus spoke this not only about Himself, but also about us.

23–24 Then Jesus took the cup and said, "**This is my blood of the COVENANT which is poured out for many.**" Matthew

---

[101] In place of the words, **Yes, it is you**, some versions of the Bible say, "You yourself have said it," which is a literal translation of the Greek. The expression "You yourself have said it" is a Jewish idiom meaning, "Yes, it is you."

[102] Bread is the main food of Middle Eastern countries. In the New Testament, the word "bread" is often used to mean any kind of food.

adds the words, "**. . . for the forgiveness of sins**" (Matthew 26:28). According to Luke 22:20, Jesus also said, "**This cup is the new covenant in my blood, which is poured out for you**" (see 1 Corinthians 11:25–26 and comment).

The old **covenant** was a promise given to the Jewish people by God that He would bless and protect their nation, Israel, provided that they obeyed His law. It was necessary to ratify a covenant with blood (Exodus 24:6–8). Even today in parts of the Middle East, people still ratify important agreements with blood.

The Jews did not keep their part of the covenant. They disobeyed God's law again and again. They rejected God's warnings sent through the Old Testament prophets. As a result, the Jews lost the blessing of God.

But God in His mercy determined to make a **new covenant** with Israel, about which the prophet Jeremiah prophesied (Jeremiah 31:31–34). According to this new covenant, God promised forgiveness and salvation to all who believed. Jesus came to fulfill that covenant and to ratify it with His own blood. This is the **blood of the covenant**, Jesus' own blood, **poured out for many**—that is, for all who believe. And as with the bread, when we partake of the cup at the Lord's supper, we in a way partake again in Jesus' suffering and death. And we remember anew how He poured out His life for us so that we might receive forgiveness for sins and eternal life.

The blood of the old covenant was poured out only for the Jews. But the blood of the new covenant is poured out for **many**—for the whole world. Jesus is the **atoning sacrifice for our sins, and not only for ours but also for the sins of the whole world** (1 John 2:2).

25–26 Finally Jesus told His disciples that this would be the last time He would drink wine until His kingdom was completely established at the end of the world.[103] According to Luke 22:16, Jesus also said at this point that He would not eat the Passover feast again **until it finds fulfillment in the kingdom of God**. The Passover feast symbolized Israel's deliverance from Egypt. The **fulfillment** of the Passover will be the salvation of a "new Israel" of believers and the establishment of Christ's eternal kingdom in heaven.

Jesus Predicts Peter's Denial (14:27–31)

(Matthew 26:31–35; Luke 22:33–34; John 14:37–38)

27 Jesus told His disciples that they would all **fall away**. The prophecy of Zechariah 13:7 had to be fulfilled. God would smite the **shepherd**, Jesus. The **sheep**, that is, the disciples, would be scattered (John 16:32).

28 But even though the faith of all would be shaken when Jesus died, their faith would be restored when they saw Him risen from the dead. They would meet Him again in Galilee (see Mark 16:6–7). Even though they forsook Jesus, He would not forsake them.

29–31 Peter had a big mouth, but little faith. He was proud (see 1 Corinthians 10:12 and comment). However, not just Peter but all the other disciples also insisted that they would stand firm. Yet everyone of them fled when Jesus was arrested (verse 50).

Jesus went to His death all alone, except for God. None of His disciples remained faithful to Him. All deserted Him.[104]

Gethsemane (14:32–42)

(Matthew 26:36–46; Luke 22:39–46)

32-33 Telling His other eight disciples, "**Sit here while I pray,**" Jesus took His chief disciples, Peter, James, and John

[103] Jesus did not mean that people will eat and drink ordinary food in the kingdom of heaven. Our "food" there will be spiritual food.

[104] However, Jesus was not totally deserted. Some of the women who had followed Him came and watched His crucifixion from a distance (Mark 15:40–41). The Apostle John was also there (John 19:25–27).

(Mark 5:37; 9:2), to a separate place in the garden of **Gethsemane**. Then He began to be **deeply distressed and troubled**. This was not because He was afraid of death or pain, but because He was about to be separated from God for a period. He was about to receive God's full wrath against sinful mankind. He was about to take on Himself the punishment for our sins, so that we who believe in Him might be saved from the wrath of God and receive salvation (see Mark 10:45 and comment).

34 **My soul is overwhelmed with sorrow**. Here we can see that Jesus was indeed not only God but also fully human. He desired the support and comfort of His three closest disciples in His sorrow. He said to them, "**Stay here and keep watch with me**" (Matthew 26:38).

35–36 Jesus Himself experienced every temptation known to man (Hebrews 4:15). But He experienced much more. We can never know the agony He endured. He was the sinless man who stood in our place and received the punishment for our sin, which was death and separation from God (Romans 6:23). Christ was a **sin offering** for us (Romans 8:3). The sinless Son of God was **made . . . to be sin for us** (2 Corinthians 5:21). Christ tasted death for everyone (Hebrews 2:9), **so that by his death he might destroy him who holds the power of death—that is, the devil** (Hebrews 2:14). Christ, by His death, has made possible the salvation of all who come to Him in faith (Romans 5:8–10).

At first Jesus asked that the **hour**—that is, His death and separation from God—**might pass from Him**. He asked God if there wasn't another way to save men—surely God could find another way if He chose to. "**Abba,**[105] **Father,**" He said, "**everything is possible for you.**"

Jesus prayed, "**Take this cup from me.**" The **cup** was the "cup" of God's wrath (Isaiah 51:17; Mark 10:38). It was Christ's own desire that He not die on the cross. Even though Christ was God's Son, His own human desire was different from God's desire. Therefore, He prayed to God that He might be spared. But having prayed that, He submitted to God's will: "**Yet not what I will, but what you will.**" By submitting to God's will, Jesus gained victory over Satan; He overcame the temptation to avoid death. In this, Jesus has given us an example to follow, that we also in all things might seek to do God's will and not our own.

37–38 While Christ was praying, the disciples had fallen asleep. They should have been watching with Him, praying for Him and for themselves, so that Satan would not come upon them unawares. Many years later Peter, in his first letter, warned Christians that Satan was like a **roaring lion** looking for someone to devour; therefore, they must remain **self-controlled and alert** (1 Peter 5:8). But in the garden of Gethsemane Peter fell asleep and soon fell prey to Satan (see verses 66–72). Not only Peter, but all the other disciples likewise **deserted** [Jesus] **and fled** (verse 50).

Today Jesus continues to say to every believer: "**Watch and pray so that you will not fall into temptation**" (see Matthew 6:13). How often we are spiritually asleep, even though our bodies are awake! How many times each day do we pray? How often do we think of Jesus? In order to overcome Satan, we must watch and pray. Our human spirits are willing to watch with Jesus, but our bodies are weak (verse 38). Even Peter, James, and John—fishermen who had passed many sleepless nights in their boats on the Sea of Galilee—could not stay awake with Jesus. They had said they would die for Jesus (verse 31); but when the time of testing came, they could not even watch with Jesus for one hour. The saying is true that it is easier to die for Jesus than it is to live for him!

39–40 Two more times Jesus went apart to pray. **An angel from heaven appeared to him and stengthened him** (Luke 22:43). His **anguish** was so great that His sweat fell in great drops, **like drops of blood** (Luke 22:44).

41–42 Each time Jesus came back, He found the disciples sleeping. Then He

---

[105] **Abba** was an Aramaic word which meant "father" (Romans 8:15; Galatians 4:6).

saw that Judas and a great crowd sent from the Jewish leaders had arrived to seize Him. **"Rise! Let us go!"** He said to His disciples. He did not mean that they should flee, but that they should go and meet their enemies.

Jesus Arrested (14:43–52)
(Matthew 26:47–56; Luke 22:47–53; John 18:1–11)

43 As soon as Judas and the crowd appeared, **Jesus, knowing all that was going to happen to him, went out and asked them, "Who is it you want?"** (John 18:4). When they answered, **"Jesus of Nazareth,"** He said, **"I am he."** And when He had said that, **they drew back and fell to the ground** (John 18:5–6). In some way, the crowd knew that Jesus was not an ordinary man. When He said, **"I am he,"** they were filled with dread.

Then, according to John 18:8–9, Jesus told the crowd to let His disciples go free. The crowd obeyed. In this way, the words of Jesus in John 6:39 and 7:12 were fulfilled.

44–47 Then Jesus' own disciple Judas betrayed Him with a kiss. The crowd seized Jesus. And then Peter woke up! He suddenly realized what was happening. He sprang into action. But what did he do? Something stupid. He cut off the ear of the servant of the high priest (John 18:10). Peter, the chief disciple, was either asleep and doing nothing for God; or he was awake and doing something opposed to God. Peter still could not understand that it was God's plan that Jesus should suffer and die.

Then Jesus rebuked Peter and healed the man's severed ear (Luke 22:51). Then He told Peter that **all who draw the sword will die by the sword** (Matthew 26:52). That is, violence always leads to violence. If at that time the disciples had tried to fight the crowd, they would all have been killed. Jesus does not teach here that in every situation it is wrong to draw the sword; Jesus was only talking about the situation at that moment. We know that there have been many instances when those who have drawn the sword have not died.[106]

Then Jesus reminded Peter that if God had wanted to rescue Him, He could have at once sent **twelve legions of angels** (Matthew 26:53–54). But that was not God's plan. God didn't need Peter's help to accomplish His purpose. And it is good for us to remember that He doesn't need our help either. None of us is indispensable. Whether we serve Him or not, He is able to fulfill His purpose. However, it is also true that He has chosen to fulfill many of His purposes through weak and failing human beings like Peter—and us.

48–49 **But the Scriptures must be fulfilled**. According to the prophecy of Isaiah 53:12, Jesus **was numbered with the transgressors**. Therefore, the crowd had come at night with swords and clubs, as if Jesus had been an outlaw leading a rebellion.

50 When the disciples finally saw there was no hope, they all deserted Jesus and fled (see verse 27). This short verse is one of the saddest verses in the New Testament. But at the same time, it is one of the greatest proofs that Jesus rose from the dead. If Jesus had not risen from the dead, no one would ever have heard from these disciples again. Christianity would have ended right at this verse!

51–52 One young man fled naked, leaving his garment in the hands of the crowd. Many Bible scholars believe that this young man was Mark himself, the writer of this Gospel. They also believe that Mark was the son of the owner of the house where Jesus ate His last supper (verse 14).

Before the Sanhedrin (14:53–65)
(Matthew 26:57–68; Luke 22:63–71)

53 According to John's Gospel, the crowd included soldiers and officers of the Jews (John 18:3,12). They brought Jesus first to Annas, the father-in-law of the high priest (see John 18:13–14,19–24).

---

[106] For further discussion of this subject, see General Article: Resisting Evil.

Then they brought Him to the high priest, Caiaphas (Matthew 26:57).

54 Peter followed **at a distance**. He followed not out of loyalty to Jesus, but out of curiosity. According to Matthew 26:58, he entered the courtyard of Caiaphas and **sat down with the guards to see the outcome**.

55–56 The Jewish leaders met at Caiaphas' house in the middle of the night. Then, at daybreak, the **whole Sanhedrin**—that is, the **council of the elders of the people** (Luke 22:66)—met together. This council consisted of seventy members and was the governing body of the Jews. It held authority over all religious matters that concerned the Jewish nation.

The Sanhedrin tried to find two witnesses who agreed in their charge against Christ. According to Jewish law, a man had to be accused by at least two witnesses before he could be judged guilty (Deuteronomy 17:6; 19:15). But two witnesses who agreed could not be found; the charges of the witnesses conflicted with each other. Therefore, they could not be accepted as evidence against Jesus.

57–59 Then some witnesses falsely accused Jesus of having said, "**I will destroy this man-made temple and in three days will build another.**" They were misquoting Jesus. Jesus had said, "**Destroy this temple, and I will raise it again in three days**" (John 2:19). But Jesus had not been talking about the temple in Jerusalem; He had been talking about the "temple" of His body (John 2:21–22).

To threaten to destroy the temple was a very serious crime in the Jews' eyes (see Acts 6:12–14). But even though the charge was serious, the witnesses did not agree about exactly what Jesus had said (verse 59).

60–61 The high priest then began to question Jesus, but Jesus at first remained silent. He did not defend Himself against the charges (Mark 15:3–5; 1 Peter 2:23). He **was led like a lamb to the slaughter, and as a sheep before her shearers is silent, so he did not open his mouth** (Isaiah 53:7).

Unable to find an accusation that two witnesses agreed on, the high priest decided to ask Jesus outright if He was the Messiah, the Christ, the **Son of the Blessed One**—that is, the Son of God.

62 Jesus answered, "**I am.**" According to Matthew 26:64, Jesus said, "**Yes, it is as you say.**" Some versions of the Bible translate this: "You have said so," which is a literal translation of a Jewish expression meaning "Yes."[107]

Here Jesus for the first time publicly acknowledged that He was the Messiah. But He was not the kind of Messiah that the high priest supposed. He was not just a miracle worker who could tear down a building and build it up in three days. He was the true Messiah, sent from God to save Israel from her sins. And though He was now a prisoner, the high priest and other Jewish leaders would one day see Him **sitting at the right hand of the Mighty One** (God) **and coming on the clouds of heaven** (see Daniel 7:13; Mark 13:26).

Notice in this verse that Jesus identified Himself both as the Son of God and as the Son of Man (see Mark 1:1; 2:10 and comments). He is indeed both fully God and fully man together. He is God come to earth in the form of a man. He is the one true incarnation of the living God (see General Article: Jesus Christ).

63–64 For a man to claim to be God—or the Son of God—was a crime worthy of death according to Jewish law (see John 5:18 and comment). Jesus had confessed to the high priest that He was the **Son of the Blessed One**—that is, the Son of God, the Messiah, **Christ**. For Jesus even to claim to be the Messiah was an offense to the Jewish leaders. It was clear to them that this man could not be the Messiah. They expected that the Messiah would appear as a mighty king, not a humble prisoner! Jesus was obviously lying. He was a blasphemer. Therefore, the Jews condemned Him to death. No other evidence was necessary. Jesus had condemned Himself!

---

[107] The same expression is found in Matthew 26:25 (see Mark 14:21 and comment).

The high priest tore his clothes. Among the Jews, tearing one's clothes was a sign of the sorrow and anger one felt on hearing someone blaspheme God (Acts 14:14).

The Jewish leaders themselves could not carry out the death sentence. Only the Roman governor could authorize someone to be executed. Therefore, the Jews determined to hand Jesus over to Pontius Pilate, the Roman governor at that time (Mark 15:1).

65 Then the Jewish officials and the soldiers began to abuse Jesus. They blindfolded Him, hit Him, and then said to Him, "**Prophesy to us, Christ.** Tell us: **Who hit you?**" (Matthew 26:67–68).

Peter Disowns Jesus (14:66–72)
(Matthew 26:69–75; Luke 22:54–62; John 18:15–18,25–27)

66 According to John 18:15–16, another disciple had come with Peter to the house of the high priest. This other disciple, because he was acquainted with the high priest, was able to obtain permission for Peter to come into the courtyard.

67–69 The first servant girl who recognized Peter also told others, "**This fellow is one of them**" (verse 69). Then a second servant girl also said that Peter had been with Jesus (Matthew 26:71).

70 Then others recognized Peter's accent. Peter was from the northern province of Galilee, and the people of Galilee spoke with a distinct accent. One man, a relative of the man whose ear Peter had cut off, also accused Peter of having been with Jesus (John 18:26).

71 For the third time, Peter denied that he knew Jesus. **He began to call down curses on himself**. That is, he said, "If I am lying, may I be cursed."

72 Then the rooster crowed twice. **The Lord turned and looked straight at Peter** (Luke 22:61). Then Peter remembered what Jesus had said (verse 30). **And he went outside and wept bitterly** (Luke 22:62).

It was said by an ancient writer that for the rest of his life, whenever Peter heard a rooster crow, he wept, because he remembered the night he denied his Lord. After that night, Peter never denied his Lord again.

CHAPTER 15

Jesus Before Pilate (15:1–20)
(Matthew 27:1–2,11–31; Luke 23:1–3,18–25; John 19:1–3)

1 **Very early in the morning** the Jewish leaders **reached a decision**. During the night they had condemned Jesus to death for blaspheming God (Mark 14:64). But they themselves had no authority to carry out the death penalty. Israel was a colony of the Roman Empire, and only the Roman governor Pontius **Pilate**[108] could execute criminals. However, the charge of blasphemy against God meant nothing to the Romans. That was purely a Jewish religious matter. Pilate would not agree to execute a man for that reason. Therefore, the Jewish leaders had to bring a charge against Jesus that in Pilate's eyes would justify the death penalty. The Sanhedrin **reached a decision** to charge Jesus with making Himself the "king of the Jews." The Jewish leaders would say that Jesus was trying to set up an independent kingdom. To the Romans this would be treason; surely, Pilate would agree to execute Jesus on that charge. The Jewish leaders also falsely charged Jesus with

---

[108] Pontius Pilate was governor of the province of Judea from 26–36 A.D. Usually he resided at Caesarea, but during Passover each year he came to Jerusalem to ensure that there was no rioting among the Jews, because during Passover week Jewish nationalistic feelings ran high.

opposing the payment of taxes to Caesar (see Luke 23:1–2).

2 Therefore, when Pilate had heard the charge against Jesus, he asked Him, "**Are you the king of the Jews?**" Jesus answered, "**Yes, it is as you say.**"[109] But Jesus was not the kind of king Pilate imagined. Jesus' kingdom was not of this world (John 18:36).

3–5 Then the Jews made many more accusations, but Jesus did not answer them (see Mark 14:61 and comment).

For a more complete description of Jesus' trial before Pilate, see John 18:28–40 and comment.

According to Luke's Gospel, Pilate found no basis for the charges against Jesus. King Herod of Galilee was also in Jerusalem at that time, and because Jesus was a Galilean, Pilate sent Him to Herod to get Herod's opinion on the matter. But Herod also found nothing that Jesus had done to deserve the death penalty, and so he sent Jesus back to Pilate (see Luke 23:4–16 and comment).

6–8 Each year at the Passover festival the Roman governor used to release a Jewish prisoner. This was done as a gesture to please the Jews. The Jews could choose whichever person they wanted to be freed. This year the crowd asked Pilate **to do for them what he usually did**, that is, to release a prisoner.

9–11 Pilate, having found no guilt in Jesus, wanted to release Him (Luke 23:20). Pilate knew that it was because of envy at Jesus' popularity that the Jewish leaders wanted Him to be killed (verse 10). However, Pilate thought the crowd of ordinary Jews would be pleased to have Jesus released. He thought that by letting the common people choose which prisoner should be released he could keep them happy and at the same time avoid condemning an innocent man to death. Thus Pilate would be able to satisfy the people and keep a clear conscience as well.

But, to Pilate's surprise, the people didn't choose Jesus. Only a few days before, they had been shouting "Hosanna" as Jesus entered Jerusalem (Mark 11:9–10). Now they turned against Jesus. Why? Because **the chief priests stirred up the crowd to have Pilate release Barabbas instead** (verse 11). Barabbas was a convicted murderer and insurrectionist. How deeply the people were under the influence of their chief priests! How fickle the people were! One moment they had considered Jesus to be the Messiah; the next moment they considered Him worse than a murderer (see Acts 14:11,19; 2 Corinthians 6:8).

According to Matthew 27:19–21, on that same day Pilate's wife had a dream about Jesus and sent Pilate a message saying, "**Don't have anything to do with that innocent man.**" By this means, God sent Pilate a special warning. God in His mercy is always sending men warnings to keep them from sinning; and it is man's responsibility to heed such warnings. But Pilate didn't heed the warning. He gave in to the wishes of the people. He was more interested in pleasing men than in pleasing God.

12–14 Pilate was in a dilemma. He did not want to release Barabbas, because he was an insurrectionist and a murderer. And he didn't want to condemn Jesus to death, because He had committed no crime worthy of death. According to Luke 23:22, three times Pilate appealed to the people to reconsider and allow him to release Jesus. To appease them, Pilate offered to **have him punished** and then release Him. **But they shouted all the louder, "Crucify him!"**[110] (verse 14).

According to Matthew 27:24–25, **Pilate saw that he was getting nowhere**. An uproar was starting. If he released Jesus, surely a greater uproar would occur. And if such an uproar came to the attention of the emperor in Rome, Pilate would lose

---

[109] In place of the words, **Yes, it is as you say**, some versions of the Bible say, "You have said so," which is a literal translation of the Greek text. The expression, "You have said so," is a Jewish idiom meaning "Yes" (see Matthew 26:25,64; Mark 14:62 and comment).

[110] The Roman method of executing condemned criminals was to hang them on a cross (see Mark 8:34 and comment). It was a shameful and painful method of execution. For further discussion, see Word List: Cross.

his job for failing to keep order. Therefore, he decided to send Jesus to be crucified. But first **he took water and washed his hands in front of the crowd** (Matthew 27:24). This was a Jewish custom which signified the removing of guilt (Deuteronomy 21:6–7).

"I am innocent of this man's blood," said Pilate.[111] And all the people answered, **"Let his blood be on us and on our children!"** (Matthew 27:24–25). And indeed they paid for Christ's death with their own blood forty years later when the Romans came and destroyed Jerusalem and massacred all the Jews in the city.

15 In Jesus' time, those condemned to die on the cross were first flogged. The flogging was done with whips made of leather with pieces of metal or bone attached to the end. Many people died from the flogging alone. According to John 19:1–4, Pilate hoped that by flogging Jesus the crowd would be satisfied, and stop insisting that He be crucified. However, it did not work. The crowd cried louder than ever for Jesus' death.

16–20 Pilate handed Jesus over to the Roman soldiers to be crucified. The soldiers first spent some time mocking and beating Jesus. During that time, according to John's Gospel, Pilate made one final attempt to persuade the crowd to let Jesus go free. But he was unsuccessful (see John 19:1–16 and comment).

The Crucifixion (15:21–32)
(Matthew 27:32–44; Luke 23:26–43; John 19:17–24)

21 Criminals sentenced to death had to carry their own cross to the execution site. Jesus at first carried His cross (John 19:17). But because of the flogging He had been given, He was too weak to continue, and a man from **Cyrene**[112] called **Simon**[113] was forced to carry it for Him.

According to Luke 23:27–31, many people followed Jesus on His way to the site of execution. The women in the crowd mourned and wept for Him. But Jesus said to them, **"Daughters of Jerusalem, do not weep for me; weep for yourselves and for your children"** (Luke 23:28). Then Jesus prophesied about the destruction of Jerusalem by the Roman army. In those days, He said, those without children would be fortunate, because they would not have to see their children suffer. Also they would be able to flee more easily. As Hosea prophesied, the suffering inflicted by the Romans would be so great that people would ask the mountains and hills to fall on them and thus end their suffering (Hosea 10:8; Luke 23:30).

Then according to Luke's account, Jesus said, **"For if men do these things when the tree is green, what will happen when it is dry?"** (Luke 23:31). That is, if the Romans are crucifying Jesus, who is innocent, what will they do to the Jews of Jerusalem, who are guilty of Jesus' death?

22–24 Golgotha, the **Place of the Skull**, was a small hill outside Jerusalem shaped like a skull. The women offered Jesus **wine mixed with myrrh.**[114] Myrrh was an opiate, and it was the Jewish custom to give this to criminals about to be executed (Proverbs 31:6–7). But Jesus refused to drink this, because He had

---

[111] In God's sight, of course, Pilate was not innocent. He was a sharer in the Jews' crime. He could have released Christ, but he chose not to in order to save his own position. But he tried to shift the blame for killing Jesus onto the Jews. He said, **"I am innocent. . . . It is your responsibility"** (Matthew 27:24). However, it is not possible to transfer guilt in this way. Those who consent to the sins of others share in those same sins.

[112] **Cyrene** was a region of northern Africa where modern Libya is now located.

[113] Simon's son Rufus may be the same Rufus mentioned in Romans 16:13, who was a member of the church at Rome.

[114] According to Matthew 27:34, others gave Jesus wine mixed with **gall** to drink. Gall is very bitter. It is possible that the soldiers did this in order to mock Jesus. Later one of the soldiers gave Jesus **wine vinegar** to drink (verse 36), a cheap wine commonly drunk by soldiers (Matthew 27:48; Luke 23:36).

determined to endure the full suffering of the cross without the help of any drug.

It was customary for the Roman soldiers to divide up the clothes of executed criminals. According to John 19:23–24, the four soldiers who crucified Jesus divided His clothes into four shares, one for each soldier. However, Jesus' undergarment was one piece of cloth without a seam. So instead of tearing it into four parts, the soldiers cast lots for it. In this way, the prophecy of Psalm 22:18 was fulfilled.

25 Jesus was crucified about the **third hour**, that is, 9 A.M. According to John 19:14, Jesus was still before Pilate at the **sixth hour**, or 12 noon. Some Bible scholars believe that John was calculating the "sixth hour" from midnight, according to the Roman custom, while Mark was calculating the "third hour" from sunrise, the Jewish custom. If this explanation is correct, Jesus left Pilate at 6 A.M. and was crucified at 9 A.M.[115]

26 The Romans used to post the charge against the criminal on the cross over the criminal's head. Jesus' complete inscription read: "This is Jesus of Nazareth, King of the Jews" (Matthew 27:37; Luke 23:38; John 19:19). In the Romans' eyes, Jesus' guilt was that He tried to make Himself a king. By writing this inscription, the Romans were giving warning to the Jews that anyone else who rose up against Rome would also receive the same punishment. According to John 19:20–22, the Jews were upset by this inscription; it mocked the Jewish nation. They tried to get Pilate to change the inscription, but Pilate refused.

After Jesus was placed on the cross, according to Luke 23:34, Jesus' first words were: "**Father, forgive them, for they do not know what they are doing.**" Jesus here has given us the supreme example of how we should forgive our enemies (see Luke 6:27; Acts 7:60).

27–28 Two robbers were also crucified with Jesus. These robbers had committed some crime against the Roman government; otherwise, they would not have received the death penalty. Their presence with Jesus was a fulfillment of the prophecy in Isaiah 53:12, which says that He **was numbered with the transgressors.**[116]

29–31 The Romans and Jews mocked Jesus. They said, "He claimed He could build the temple in three days (Mark 14:57–58); why, then, can He not come down from the cross? **He saved others . . . but he can't save himself.**" They thought that Jesus was unable to come down from the cross. But, in fact, He could have come down. However, in order to save us from our sins, it was necessary for Him to die, just as He had three times previously told His disciples (Mark 8:31; 9:31; 10:33–34).

32 "**Let this Christ . . . come down now from the cross, that we may see and believe,**" said the chief priests and teachers of the law. These Jewish leaders had earlier asked Christ for a sign, but He had refused to give them one (see Mark 8:11–12 and comment). Those whose hearts are hard will not believe even if they see a sign. Jesus rose from the dead, which was a greater miracle than coming down from the cross; but the Jews still did not believe that He was the Messiah (see Luke 16:19–31 and comment).

The two robbers being crucified on either side of Jesus also insulted Him. But, according to Luke 23:39–43, one of the robbers repented and rebuked his fellow robber. He said, "We are being punished justly, but this man Jesus has done nothing wrong." Then the repentant robber said to Jesus, "**Remember me when you come into your kingdom**" (Luke 23:42). And Jesus replied: "**Today you will be with me in Paradise**" (Luke 23:43).

There are two things to learn from this. First, even though a man believes only at the very end of his life, he will be saved. Second, as soon as believers die, their

---

[115] There are other explanations for the difference between Mark and John. It is not certain which explanation is correct.

[116] Not all ancient manuscripts of Mark contain verse 28. A similar verse is found in Luke 22:37.

spirits go to **Paradise**. Paradise is a place of happiness in heaven where our spirits go to await the resurrection of our bodies (see 2 Corinthians 12:2–4; Revelation 2:7 and comments).

The Death of Jesus (15:33–41)
(Matthew 27:45–56; Luke 23:44–49; John 19:28–30)

33 A **darkness came over the whole land** from 12 noon to 3 P.M. This was not an ordinary solar eclipse,[117] because the Passover festival always fell during the full moon. According to Luke, **the sun stopped shining** (Luke 23:45). Some great and special event occurred in the heavens during the last three hours of Jesus' life on earth. The darkness was a sign of God's curse upon sinful mankind; it was a sign that God had withdrawn His presence from men. Because, of all the terrible acts of men throughout history, the most terrible of all was the crucifying of Jesus, the Son of God. In the entire history of the world, there has been no time as dark and evil as those three hours.

34 Then, just before He died, Jesus called out, **"My God, my God, why have you forsaken me?"** This is a quotation from Psalm 22:1.

Why did Jesus say that? Because the darkness that fell on the whole land fell on Jesus also. He also, in full measure, experienced separation from God. He experienced God's full wrath, God's full curse upon sinful men. He knew that **cursed is everyone who is hung on a tree**, that is, on a cross (see Deuteronomy 21:23; Galatians 3:13 and comment). During the time Jesus hung on the cross, God indeed did forsake Him. Our sin was laid on Jesus; He was made **to be sin for us** (2 Corinthians 5:21). But God cannot look upon sin; therefore, God withdrew His face from Jesus. In the garden of Gethsemane, an angel had come to strengthen Jesus (Luke 22:43). But on the cross, there was no one to comfort and strengthen Him. This was the price that Jesus paid to redeem us, to deliver us from God's wrath. This is what it meant for Him to **give his life as a ransom for many** (see Mark 10:45 and comment).

35–36 The people standing nearby heard Jesus say, "**Eloi, Eloi,**" and mistakenly thought He was calling the prophet Elijah.

According to John 19:28–30, Jesus said He was thirsty, so He was given a drink. When He had received the drink from the soldier, he said, **"It is finished."** His work was finished. He had accomplished what His Father had sent Him into the world to do (see John 17:4).

37 At this time, according to Luke 23:46, Jesus also said, **"Father, into your hands I commit my spirit."** And after saying this, Jesus gave a **loud cry** and **breathed his last**.

38 The **curtain of the temple** mentioned in this verse was the curtain at the entrance to the innermost room of the Jewish temple, the "Most Holy Place," where only the high priest was allowed to enter. The Jews considered that God's presence dwelled in that room (see Hebrews 9:1–5 and comment). Once a year the high priest entered the Most Holy Place to offer a sacrifice for his own sins and for the sins of the people (see Hebrews 9:7 and comment). At the moment of Jesus' death, this **curtain** at the entrance of the Most Holy Place was **torn in two from top to bottom**, that is, it was destroyed. This meant that no longer would the high priest have to enter the Most Holy Place to offer sacrifices for the sins of the people. Jesus was the final sacrifice for sin; no other sacrifice would ever be necessary.

Because of Jesus' sacrifice, God has now forgiven the sins of believers and has declared them righteous. Not only that, because believers have been declared righteous by God, they can now enter directly into His presence (see Hebrews 4:16; 1 Peter 3:18). No longer is there a **curtain** keeping us from drawing near to God. **Therefore, brothers, since we have confidence to enter the Most Holy Place by the blood of Jesus, by a new and**

---

[117] Ordinary solar eclipses occur when the moon comes between the earth and sun; but during the full moon this is impossible.

living way opened for us through the curtain, that is, his body . . . let us draw near to God with a sincere heart in full assurance of faith (Hebrews 10:19–22).

Many of the Jewish priests learned about the tearing of the curtain. Perhaps it is for this reason that later a **large number of priests became obedient to the faith** (Acts 6:7).

According to Matthew 27:51–53, there was also an earthquake at the time of Jesus' death. Tombs broke open, and the **bodies of many holy people who had died were raised to life**. And **after Jesus' resurrection** they came into Jerusalem and appeared to many people. This was a sign of the resurrection of all believers that will occur at the end of the world. This was like an "advance" of what will happen to us when Jesus comes again. Jesus was the **firstfruits of those who have fallen asleep** (see 1 Corinthians 15:20–23 and comment). He was the **firstborn from among the dead** (Colossians 1:18). Thus at the time of Jesus' death and resurrection, some of the Old Testament saints also rose. Then, when Jesus comes again, the rest of us shall rise also.

From this we can see that the faithful saints of the Old Testament who never knew Christ will in the end be brought to life. Christ, through His death, conquered death indeed! (1 Corinthians 15:54,57). And by His death He destroyed **him who holds the power of death—that is, the devil** (Hebrews 2:14).

39 The centurion and the soldiers who crucified Jesus (Matthew 27:54) were amazed as they watched Him die. Only a short time before they had been mocking Jesus. They had driven the nails through Jesus' hands as they placed Him on the cross. But then they saw the earth darken. They felt the earthquake. They heard the words of Jesus from the cross. They heard His final cry. Jesus did not die like other men they had seen. The centurion said, "**Surely this was a righteous man**" (Luke 23:47). "**Surely this man was the Son of God.**"

40–41 The women who had come with Jesus from Galilee were more faithful and devoted than Jesus' disciples were.[118] They witnessed Jesus' death, and they later reported to the disciples what they had seen and heard.

Mary Magdalene had been healed by Jesus of seven demons (Luke 8:2). **Salome** was the wife of Zebedee and the mother of the disciples James and John (Matthew 27:56). Some Bible scholars believe that the second **Mary** mentioned here was Mary the mother of Jesus, but this is not certain.

The Burial of Jesus (15:42–47)
(Matthew 27:57–61; Luke 23:50–56; John 19:38–42)

42–43 On the **Preparation Day** of Passover week, that is, the Friday before the Sabbath, Joseph of Arimathea went to Pilate and asked for Jesus' body.[119] Joseph was a member of the **Council**, the Sanhedrin. He was a disciple of Jesus, but he only believed secretly, because he feared the Jews (John 19:38). He was a **good and upright man** who had not agreed with the decision of the Jewish leaders to condemn Christ (Luke 23:50–51).

44–46 Pilate agreed to Joseph's request. Joseph took the body and laid it in a new tomb, which he had just recently prepared for himself (Matthew 27:60; Luke 23:53). Then he sealed the entrance of the tomb with a **very large** stone (Mark 16:4).

Just as Jesus had no place to lay His head while He was alive (Luke 9:58), so He had no tomb in which to lay His body when He was dead. He was laid in another man's tomb.

47 Two of the women who had come with Jesus from Galilee, Mary and Mary

---

[118] Among the disciples only John is recorded as being present at the cross (John 19:26).

[119] Usually the Romans did not allow crucified criminals to be buried; they left their bodies hanging on the cross for the birds to eat. (They did this as a warning to others.) But according to Jewish law, it was necessary to bury the body of a person on the day he died (Deuteronomy 21:22–23). This is the reason Joseph asked Pilate for permission to bury Jesus' body.

Magdalene (verse 40) saw where Jesus was buried. Then they went home and prepared spices and perfumes with which to embalm the body (Luke 23:56).

According to John 19:39–42, Nicodemus[120] accompanied Joseph when he went to Pilate, and then helped him bury Jesus' body. They wrapped the body with spices according to the Jewish custom. The women wanted to add additional spices as a token of their love and devotion to Jesus.

CHAPTER 16

The Resurrection (16:1–8)
(Matthew 28:1–8; Luke 24:1–8; John 20:1)

1 **When the Sabbath was over**, that is, at 6 P.M. on Saturday,[121] the same women who had watched Jesus on the cross (Mark 15:40) bought and prepared spices and aromatic oils with which to further anoint Jesus' body (see Luke 23:56).

2–4 When the women got to the tomb, they found the great stone rolled away. According to Matthew 28:2–4, there had been an earthquake, and an angel had come from heaven and rolled away the stone. The guards who had been appointed to guard the tomb (Matthew 27:62–66) **were so afraid of him that they shook and became as dead men** (Matthew 28:4).

5 The angel, who appeared in the form of a **young man**, was sitting on the stone at the right side of the entrance to the tomb. The women were alarmed because his **appearance was like lightning** (Matthew 28:3). According to Luke 24:4, there was also a second angel present, who is not mentioned by Matthew and Mark.

6–7 The angels said to the women, **"Why do you look for the living among the dead?"** (Luke 24:5). **"He has risen. . . . He is going ahead of you into Galilee . . . just as he told you"** (see Mark 14:28; Luke 24:6–7).

8 The women fled from the tomb. At first, **they said nothing to anyone**. But then, they obeyed the order of the angel (verse 7) and ran to tell the disciples (Matthew 28:8).

He has risen! Since the creation of the world, there has never been another event as important as the rising of Christ from the dead. If Christ had not risen from the dead, there would be no Christian religion, no Christians. There would be no salvation for man (1 Corinthians 15:17–19). The whole course of history would have been totally different. Because, by rising from the dead, Jesus gave final and absolute proof that He was indeed God's own Son. God Himself came to earth and overcame the last enemy, death (2 Timothy 1:10), and showed men and women the way to heaven.

Some atheists try to say that Christ never rose, that it is only a myth invented by Jesus' disciples. However, they are wrong. Jesus' resurrection is a fact of history. How do we know this?

First of all, the tomb was empty. No one denies this. If Jesus did not rise from the dead, where did His body go? Roman soldiers were guarding the tomb. Some Jews to this day say that Jesus' disciples stole the body; but that would have been impossible with Roman guards at the entrance. Besides, the disciples had deserted Jesus and were hiding in fear of the Jews (John 20:19). Furthermore, the Jews and Romans surely made a careful search for Jesus' body. The Jews especially wanted some means of disproving Jesus' resurrection (Matthew 27:64); what better way than to find His body! But it was nowhere to be found.

---

[120] Nicodemus is mentioned also in John 3:1–5.

[121] The Jews considered that the Sabbath began at 6 P.M. on Friday and ended at 6 P.M. on Saturday.

The second reason we know that Jesus rose from the dead is that after His resurrection He appeared to many people. He **appeared to more than five hundred of the brothers at the same time** (1 Corinthians 15:6), and many of these were still alive at the time Paul wrote his letter to the Corinthians about twenty five years later. These were all witnesses to Christ's resurrection.

The third reason we know that Christ rose from the dead is because of the amazing change that took place in the lives of those eleven frightened, faithless disciples. One moment they were fleeing, hiding. But when they had seen the risen Jesus, they became totally new men, filled with joy and empowered with His Holy Spirit (John 20:22; Acts 2:4). There is no other way to explain the extraordinary change that took place in the lives of those disciples. Only the risen Christ could have brought about such a change.

But not only did a change take place in those eleven disciples. Changes began to occur in other people too. The Apostle Paul met the risen Jesus on the road to Damascus, and his life was totally changed (see Acts 9:1–9,17–20). Millions upon millions of other Christians down through history have known the risen Christ, and His Holy Spirit has filled their lives. We know that Christ has risen, because He lives within our hearts.

What is the meaning of Christ's resurrection? It is this: Christ overcame death. He is able to save us from death. He is the Son of the living God. And He lives today in the heart of every believer. "**I will be with you always to the very end of the age**" (Matthew 28:20). Therefore, let us obey His command and go **into all the world and preach the good news to all creation** (verse 15).

Jesus Appears to His Followers (16:9–20)

9–11 See Matthew 28:9–10; Luke 24:9–12; John 20:1-18 and comments.[122]

12–13 See Luke 24:13–35 and comment.

14 See Luke 24:36–44; John 20:19–31 and comments.

15 Jesus commanded His disciples: "**Go into all the world and preach the good news.**" He also told them to **make disciples of all nations** (see Matthew 28:16–20 and comment). Not all Christians are called to be preachers, and not all are called to go as foreign missionaries **into all the world**. But all Christians are called to take some part in fulfilling the great commission, if not as "goers," then as "senders" through their gifts and prayers. And, of course, all Christians are called to be witnesses to their own families and neighbors.

16 Man is saved through faith (see Galatians 2:15–16; Ephesians 2:8 and comments). It is also necessary to be baptized in order to demonstrate publicly that we have believed (see General Article: Water Baptism). The Apostle Peter said: "**Repent and be baptized, every one of you**" (Acts 2:38). If we say we believe but refuse to be baptized, we are being disobedient, and therefore our faith is false. Faith without obedience is not true faith (see James 2:17 and comment).

What happens if a person believes in Christ and intends to be baptized, but dies before he gets the opportunity to be baptized? Such a person is still saved. But it is important to receive baptism as soon as possible after believing in Christ. To delay deliberately is to disobey.

17–18 Christ promised that those who believe will receive power to **drive out demons** (see Acts 5:14–16; 6:8; 14:3), and to **speak in new tongues** (see Acts 2:4; 10:44–46; 19:6 and comments). They will **pick up snakes** (see Acts 28:3–5). Indeed, throughout the New Testament we read that the preaching of the Gospel was frequently accompanied by signs and miraculous works (verse 20). These were performed through the power of the Holy Spirit (see 1 Corinthians 12:7–11 and comment).

19–20 After the resurrection, Jesus remained on earth for forty days (Acts 1:3). Then He ascended into heaven (see Luke

[122] Not all ancient manuscripts of Mark contain verses 9–20.

24:50–53), and sat at the right hand of God (see Acts 2:32–33; Ephesians 1:20–22 and comments). And at the end of the world this **same Jesus will come back** in the same way that He went (Acts 1:9–11). He will come **in clouds with great power and glory** (Mark 13:26). Until that day, let each of us remain faithful and busy doing the work the Lord has assigned to us. And as we do so, the Lord—the risen Christ—will be with us, **to the very end of the age** (Matthew 28:20).

Luke

INTRODUCTION

Luke was a doctor (Colossians 4:14) and a close companion of the Apostle Paul. In addition to this Gospel, Luke also wrote the book of Acts (see Luke 1:1–4; Acts 1:1–2). Luke accompanied Paul during parts of Paul's second and third missionary journeys to Greece and Turkey (see Acts 16:10; 20:6), and on Paul's final voyage to Rome (Acts 27:1–2). Luke also remained with Paul during Paul's imprisonment in Rome (2 Timothy 4:11).

Thus Luke not only wrote about the beginnings of the Christian religion; he took part in it as well.

Whereas Matthew was a JEW who wrote his Gospel mainly for Jewish readers, Luke was a Greek[1], that is, a Gentile.[2] Therefore, Luke has written his Gospel in a way that Gentiles would easily understand.

While writing his own Gospel, Luke had with him a copy of Mark's Gospel. Therefore, Luke has repeated in his Gospel many of the verses that Mark wrote. (In this commentary the reader will be asked to refer to Mark's Gospel for comments on those verses.)

Luke also used other material to write his history of Jesus' life. Some of this material is also included in Matthew's Gospel. Some material, however, is found only in Luke.

Luke was, above all, a historian. He was very careful both in his Gospel and in the book of Acts to give accurate historical details. Luke's accuracy has been completely confirmed by other historical writings of that period and by numerous archeological findings. The

[1] A Greek is an inhabitant of Greece, an important country of southern Europe. Greek is also the language in which the New Testament was originally written.

[2] In the Bible, all people who are not Jews are called Gentiles. Thus the Greeks also are Gentiles.

story of Jesus Christ recorded in the New Testament is not something made up by man's imagination; it is totally true and historical.

It is not certain when Luke wrote his Gospel. Many Bible scholars believe it was written between 65 and 70 A.D. Others suggest it was written some time later than that.

OUTLINE

A. The Announcement of the Savior (1:1–2:52).
   1. The Announcement to Zechariah (1:1–25).
   2. The Announcement to Mary (1:26–56).
   3. The Birth of John (1:57–80).
   4. The Birth of Jesus (2:1–20).
   5. The Presentation in the Temple (2:21–38).
   6. The Childhood of Jesus (2:39–52).
B. The Appearance of Jesus Christ (3:1–4:13).
   1. John the Baptist and the Baptism of Jesus (3:1–22).
   2. The Genealogy of Jesus (3:23–38).
   3. The Temptation of Jesus (4:1–13).
C. The Ministry of Jesus Christ (4:14–9:62).
   1. The Definition of Jesus' Ministry (4:14–44).
   2. The Proofs of Jesus' Power (5:1–6:11).
   3. The Choice of the Apostles (6:12–19).
   4. Major Teachings (6:20–49).
   5. Further Miracles and Teachings (7:1–9:17).
   6. The Climax of Jesus' Ministry (9:18–62).
D. The Road to the Cross (10:1–18:30).
   1. The Ministry of the Seventy (10:1–24).
   2. Popular Teaching (10:25–13:21).
   3. The Beginning of Public Debate (13:22–16:31).
   4. Instruction of the Disciples (17:1–18:30).
E. The Suffering of Jesus Christ (18:31–23:56).
   1. The Road to Jerusalem (18:31–19:27).
   2. The Entry into Jerusalem (19:28–44).
   3. The Teaching in Jerusalem (19:45–21:4).
   4. Teachings on the End of the Age (21:5–38).
   5. The Lord's Supper (22:1–38).
   6. The Arrest and Trial of Jesus (22:39–23:25).
   7. The Death of Jesus (23:26–49).
   8. The Burial of Jesus (23:50–56).
F. The Resurrection of Jesus Christ (24:1–53).
   1. The Empty Tomb (24:1–12).
   2. The Walk to Emmaus (24:13–35).
   3. Jesus' Appearance to the Disciples (24:36–43).
   4. The Last Commission (24:44–49).
   5. The Ascension of Jesus (24:50–53).

CHAPTER 1

Introduction (1:1–4)

1–2 For some years after Jesus' death, the account of His life spread by word of mouth. It was told by **eye-witnesses,** those who had seen and heard Jesus, and by **servants of the word,** that is, His disciples.

Then some people began to write down the accounts of these eyewitnesses. For example, Peter, Jesus' chief disciple, told what he knew to Mark, who then wrote Mark's Gospel (see Mark: Introduction). But everything that was written was directly based on the testimony of those who had seen and heard Jesus with their own eyes and ears (see 1 John 1:1).

3–4 Luke obtained these written accounts and also talked with many people who had known Jesus. From all this information he wrote a history of the life of Christ, which is the Gospel of Luke.

He addressed his history to a man called **Theophilus** (Acts 1:1). It is not known who Theophilus was. Some believe that he was an official of the ROMAN EMPIRE who was sympathetic toward this new religion, Christianity.

Theophilus had learned some things about Christ and this new religion, but his knowledge was not complete. Perhaps he had heard some bad things about Christ. The Jews called Christ an imposter and blasphemer. The Romans called Him an agitator, a troublemaker.

Therefore, Luke wanted to give Theophilus a true history of Jesus, an **orderly account,** so that Theophilus might **know the certainty** of the things he had heard. But Luke, according to God's plan, did not write only for Theophilus; he wrote also for us. We too can know the certainty of the Gospel of Christ. Our faith is not based on myths, but on history.

But to **know with certainty** is not enough. We must also believe in our hearts **that Jesus is the Christ, the Son of God;** for it is only by believing in Jesus that we can receive **life in his name** (John 20:31).

The Birth of John the Baptist Foretold (1:5–25)

5–7 In the time of King **Herod**[3] there was a Jewish priest named **Zechariah.** (This Zechariah is different from the Old Testament prophet Zechariah, and he is also different from the other prophet Zechariah mentioned in Matthew 23:35.) He was a priest of the division of Abijah. The Jewish priests were divided into twenty-four divisions, and Abijah's was one of these (1 Chronicles 24:10).

Zechariah's wife **Elizabeth** was also the daughter of a priest, and a descendant of **Aaron.**[4] They had had no children, because Elizabeth was barren. The Jews believed that if a woman was barren it was because of some sin; but according to Luke, both Zechariah and his wife were **upright in the sight of God** (verse 6). They had prayed to God that they might have a child (verse 13), but God had not yet granted their request.

8–10 Each of the twenty-four priestly divisions had the duty of serving in the Jewish temple in Jerusalem for two weeks each year. Twice a day incense was burned in an inner room of the temple called the **Holy Place** (Hebrews 9:2). Since there were many priests in each division, the one selected to burn incense was chosen by lot each day (verse 9). While the priest was burning the incense inside the Holy Place, the people who had come to worship waited outside (verse 10). Then after burning the incense, the priest would come out and bless the people.

On this particular day Zechariah had been chosen to burn the incense.

---

[3] King **Herod** is mentioned in Matthew 2:1 and comment.

[4] **Aaron** was the brother of Moses, the great leader who led the Jews out of Egypt. All Jewish priests were descended from Aaron.

11–13 While Zechariah was inside the Holy Place, an ANGEL appeared to him and told him that he and his wife Elizabeth would have a son. They were to name their son John, which means, "God is gracious."

14–15 The angel said that John would be **great in the sight of the Lord.** John the Baptist was indeed great. Jesus said that in his time John was the greatest man born of woman (Matthew 11:11). The angel also said that John would be **filled with the HOLY SPIRIT.** In the Old Testament, God's Holy Spirit came upon men of God for short periods to help them accomplish some special task. But in John's case, the Holy Spirit filled him **even from birth** (verse 15), and remained with him always.

16 The angel said that John would **bring back to the Lord** many of the people of **Israel** (the Jewish nation). That is, John would turn many Jews back to God by preaching a **baptism of** REPENTANCE **for the forgiveness of sins** (Mark 1:4). And indeed, one of John's main works was to exhort the Jews to repent of their sins and turn back to God.

17 **And he will go on before the Lord.** John's other main work was to prepare the Jews to receive the **Lord,** Christ, their Messiah,[5] their Savior—that is, **to make ready a people prepared for the Lord.**

The angel said that John would do this **in the spirit and power of Elijah.** Elijah was a great Old Testament prophet, who the people expected would one day return to earth (see Malachi 4:5; Matthew 11:13–15 and comment).

John would **turn the hearts of the fathers to their children.** The **children** were the present Jewish generation and the **fathers** were their ancestors. By leading the present generation of Jews to repent, John would, in a sense, be satisfying their righteous ancestors. Luke also means that reconciliation would take place within the families of the present generation. When children repent, parents turn to them with forgiveness.

John would turn the **disobedient to the wisdom of the righteous;** that is, he would cause the present rebellious generation of Jews to turn from sin and begin again to fear and obey God. To fear God is the beginning of wisdom (Proverbs 1:7).

18–20 Zechariah doubted what the angel told him. "How can I believe you?" he asked. The angel said, **"I am Gabriel. I stand in the presence of God.** Therefore, what I speak is true."

Gabriel is the chief messenger of God; he is one of the greatest of God's angels (Daniel 8:15–16; 9:20–23). Angels stand in the presence of God (Matthew 18:10; Revelation 5:11) and carry out His bidding (Hebrews 1:14). To disbelieve an angel is to disbelieve God.

"**How can I be sure of this?**" Zechariah asked (verse 18). He wanted a sign. So the angel gave him a "sign"; he caused him to be deaf and dumb as a punishment for his unbelief.

21–25 When Zechariah came out of the Holy Place after burning incense, he could not speak and bless the people as was customarily done. Then, after his period of service in the temple was finished, he returned home and his wife became pregnant. **"The Lord has . . . taken away my disgrace,"** she said (verse 25). For a woman, to fail to bear children was considered by the Jews to be a **disgrace** (Genesis 30:22–23).

The Birth of Jesus Foretold (1:26–38)

26–28 **In the sixth month** of Elizabeth's pregnancy, the angel Gabriel was sent by God to a young virgin named **Mary,** who lived in the town of **Nazareth.** She was engaged to be married. At that time she had not slept with any man.

29–32 The angel told Mary that she would give birth to a son, and that he should be named **Jesus,** which means "savior." This son would be called the **Son of the Most High**—that is, the Son of

[5] "Messiah" is a Hebrew word meaning "one anointed by God." Messiah is another name for "Christ" (see John 1:41; 4:25).

God. He would inherit the **throne of his father DAVID**, the great king of the Jews (see Matthew 1:1 and comment). From this we know that Mary, Jesus' mother, was descended from David. Joseph, the man Mary was engaged to marry, was also a descendant of David (see verse 27).

33 The angel also said that Jesus would **reign over the house of Jacob forever**. The **house of Jacob** is Israel, the Jewish nation.[6]

Jesus Christ will rule over a new spiritual Israel, that is, His church. His kingdom will be a spiritual kingdom; therefore, it will last forever (2 Samuel 7:12–13; Psalm 89:3–4).

34 Mary asked, **"How will this be?"** She didn't ask, "How will I know this?" as Zechariah had asked. His question arose from unbelief. Her question arose from a desire to know the way in which God would perform this great miracle.

35 Then the angel told Mary that her son would not be born by a human father, but by God's own Spirit. Jesus would truly be the **Son of God** (see Matthew 1:18 and comment).

When Joseph found out about Mary's pregnancy, he decided to divorce her (Matthew 1:19). But an angel spoke to him also and told him not to divorce Mary, because she was pregnant not by a another man but by the Holy Spirit (see Matthew 1:20–21,24–25 and comment).

36–38 Then the angel told Mary about Elizabeth's pregnancy. Elizabeth was a relative of Mary on the side of Mary's mother. Let Mary not doubt. If God could give an old barren woman like Elizabeth a child, He could also give a virgin a child (Genesis 18:10–14; Mark 10:27).

Mary Visits Elizabeth (1:39–45)

39–40 When Mary heard about Elizabeth's pregnancy, she went to visit her at her home in Judah (the province of Judea) south of Jerusalem.

41–44 When Elizabeth saw Mary, the Holy Spirit filled her and she knew at once that Mary would be the mother of the Messiah, the Savior. She called Mary the **mother of my Lord** (verse 43). As a sign that what the angel had told Mary was indeed true, Elizabeth's baby **leaped in her womb**.

45 Then Elizabeth blessed Mary for believing God would fulfill His word to her.

Mary's Song (1:46–56)

46–49 When Mary heard Elizabeth's words, she began to praise God for choosing her, an ordinary village woman, to be the mother of the Messiah, the Christ, the Son of God (see 1 Corinthians 1:26–29 and comment). No woman has ever received a greater honor. She called God her **Savior**, because through His Son in her womb, He would save all who believe in Him (1 Timothy 2:3).

50–56 Then Mary praised God for His mercy to His **servant Israel**, that is, the Jewish nation (verses 54–55). In particular, she praised Him for His mercy in fulfilling, through her son Jesus, the promise He had given to **ABRAHAM and his descendants** (Genesis 17:7; 22:17). Abraham was the father of the Jewish nation.

God always shows mercy to those that fear Him (verse 50). He casts down the proud and exalts the humble (verses 51–52). **God opposes the proud but gives grace to the humble** (Proverbs 3:34; James 4:6). He helps the poor, but turns the rich away empty (verse 53). And now, through Mary, God was going to show His greatest mercy, His greatest love to the world, by sending His own Son into the world to save men (see John 3:16 and comment). How can Mary not praise such a God? How can we, too, not praise Him?

The Birth of John the Baptist (1:57–66)

57–60 All Jewish male babies were CIRCUMCISED on the eighth day of life

---

[6] **Jacob** was the grandson of Abraham, the first Jew. Jacob's other name was Israel. He had twelve sons, from which the twelve tribes of Israel are descended.

(Genesis 17:12; Leviticus 12:3). Usually Jewish children were named at birth by the father, but Zechariah was still deaf and dumb from the time he had seen the angel Gabriel (verse 20). Then Elizabeth, in obedience to the command of the angel (verse 13), said, **"He is to be called John."**[7]

61–63 Then Zechariah confirmed that the child's name was John.

64–66 As soon as he had written, **"His name is John,"** Zechariah received again his power to speak. The friends and neighbors who had come for the circumcision ceremony were filled with fear and amazement. They knew that God had given John some special work to do because of the amazing circumstances of his birth.

Zechariah's Song (1:67–80)

67 Then Zechariah was **filled with the Holy Spirit and prophesied**. Whenever the Old Testament prophets prophesied, they did so by the power of the Holy Spirit. God's Holy Spirit, that is, God Himself, spoke through the prophets' mouths and through their writings (see 2 Peter 1:19–21 and comment).

After Christ's death and resurrection, the Holy Spirit came upon the disciples and remained with them. Jesus said to them, "[The Holy Spirit] **lives with you and will be in you**" (John 14:17). For Christians, the Spirit doesn't come only at special times. The Holy Spirit lives in every believer constantly (see 1 Corinthians 6:19).

68–69 Zechariah knew that his son was appointed **to make ready a people** (the Jews) **prepared for the Lord** (verse 17). He knew that that Lord was now in Mary's womb. Therefore, he praised God, "**because he has come and has redeemed his people**" (verse 68). God had sent the Messiah, the Redeemer, to earth. Zechariah called him a **horn**[8] **of** SALVATION (verse 69), a Savior, descended from the house of David. The Savior came to redeem His people; that is, He came to pay the price for their sins and thus reconcile them to God.

70 God had said through His prophets in the Old Testament that He would send such a Savior. Now these prophecies had been fulfilled.

71 The Jews believed that the Messiah, the Savior, would deliver them from their enemies. In Jesus' time, Israel had fallen under the control of the Roman Empire. They had lost their freedom. They were a persecuted people. Therefore, they looked to the Messiah to save them from their enemies, the Romans.

72 God raised up a "horn of salvation" **to show mercy** to the Jews and **to remember his holy** COVENANT. This covenant was the agreement made between God and the Jews. God said that if the Jews obeyed His law, He would be their God and would protect and guide them (Exodus 19:5–6).

73–75 God also raised up a "horn of salvation," that is, a Savior, to fulfill the oath He made to Abraham, the first Jew, two thousand years before the time of Christ. Because Abraham was obedient to God, God promised to bless his descendants (Genesis 22:15–18), and **to rescue** [them] **from the hand of** [their] **enemies** (verse 74). He promised to give them a land (Genesis 15:18), in which they could live in safety **without fear**, and serve God **in holiness and righteousness** (verse 75).

76 At this point Zechariah's song changes from a song of praise to a song of prophecy. Zechariah prophesied that his son would be a PROPHET **of the Most High**—that is, a prophet of God (Matthew 11:9)—and that he would **prepare the way** for the Lord, Christ (see Mark 1:2–3; Luke 1:17 and comment).

77 John was to give his people, the Jews, the **knowledge of salvation**, the salvation of their souls, spiritual salvation. Most of the Jews thought only about worldly "salvation," that is, deliverance from their worldly enemies. But John

---

[7] Though Zechariah could not speak, he no doubt had related to Elizabeth in writing the words that the angel had spoken to him.

[8] The horn is a sign of strength.

came to tell them that what they really needed was deliverance, or salvation, from their spiritual enemies—their sins (see Matthew 1:21 and comment). This salvation would only come to them if they confessed their sins and received forgiveness. That is why John came preaching repentance and baptizing people, so that they might be cleansed of their sins (see Mark 1:4 and comment).

78 Man's salvation is possible because of the **tender mercy** of God, who sent His Son Jesus, the **rising sun,** from heaven to save His people, Israel.

79 Here Zechariah says that Jesus will be a shining light in the darkness guiding men **into the path of PEACE,** that is, peace with God (see Matthew 4:16; John 1:4; 8:12; Romans 5:1 and comments). And John the Baptist will be the one who announces the coming of Jesus, the Savior (John 1:6–9).

All these things that Zechariah prophesied came to pass exactly as he had foretold.

80 John the Baptist grew up in the desert. He remained there until he began his public ministry. He didn't need the education of schools; he received his education directly from God.

CHAPTER 2

The Birth of Jesus (2:1–20)

1 **Caesar**[9] **Augustus** was the emperor of the Roman Empire from 31 B.C. to 14 A.D. The capital of the Roman Empire was Rome (now the capital of modern Italy). In New Testament times, the Romans had conquered almost all of the countries around the Mediterranean Sea. Their authority had even reached to France and England. Thus the Roman Empire extended across almost all of Europe, North Africa, and the Middle East. Among the conquered countries were Israel and Syria.

Augustus had recently reorganized the administration of these conquered countries and provinces, and he had ordered that a new census be taken.

2 This census began in about 4 B.C., which is the date of Jesus' birth (see Matthew 2:1 and comment). The census was completed while Quirinius was governor of Syria, which was in 6–9 A.D.[10]

3–4 According to the emperor's decree, everyone had to register for the census in his own town. Joseph, Mary's betrothed husband, was a descendant of David (Matthew 1:20; Luke 1:27). David had been born in **Bethlehem** a thousand years previously. So all David's descendants were required to register in Bethlehem, which was a small town six miles south of Jerusalem.

In this way, the prophecy of Micah that the Messiah would be born in Bethlehem was fulfilled (Micah 5:2; Matthew 2:4–6).

5–7 At the time they went to Bethlehem, Joseph had not yet slept with Mary, his betrothed wife (Matthew 1:24–25). Luke says that **Mary was pledged to be married** (verse 5). That is, she was legally married, but was still living as if only pledged to be married.

After arriving in Bethlehem, Mary gave birth to Jesus. Because there was no room in the inn, Mary and the baby stayed in a manger. Such was the humble birth of the Son of God!

8–12 The announcement of Jesus' birth was given first to ordinary humble people—shepherds. **"I bring you good news of great joy,"** the angels said to them (verse 10). That **good news** was the Gospel of Christ, the good news of

---

[9] **Caesar** means emperor.

[10] There is much historical evidence that Quirinius was governor of Syria at the time of Jesus' birth also. Syria is northeast of Israel. In Jesus' time, Judea (the southern province of Israel, whose capital is Jerusalem) was part of Syria.

salvation. The good news was for **all the people**—that is, initially, for all the people of Israel, the Jews. But it was also good news for the Gentiles, the non-Jews (verses 30–32). Salvation is for all people—both Jews and Gentiles—who receive the good news and believe in Christ (John 3:16).

In this way the prophecy of Isaiah was fulfilled: **For to us a child is born, to us a son is given, and the government will be upon his shoulders. And he will be called Wonderful Counselor, Mighty God, Everlasting Father, Prince of Peace. Of the increase of his government and peace there will be no end** (Isaiah 9:6–7).

13–15 A **great company of the heavenly host**—that is, other angels—appeared to the shepherds, praising God. As soon as the angels had left, the shepherds, filled with amazement and excitement, went to find the Savior.

16–20 The shepherds found Jesus just where the angels had said. The shepherds told everyone about how the angels had appeared to them and had told them about the birth of the Savior, the Messiah. **And Mary treasured up all these things and pondered them in her heart** (verse 19). And surely, years later, Mary told some of **these things** to Jesus' followers. Perhaps Mary even told Luke himself, and Luke then used what she said to write this chapter of his Gospel.

Jesus Presented in the Temple (2:21–38)

21 When Christ was eight days old he was circumcised and given the name Jesus, as commanded by the angel Gabriel (Luke 1:31). Though He was the Son of God, He submitted to the Jewish law, so that He might fulfill the law perfectly, and thus **fulfill all righteousness** (Matthew 3:15; 5:17; Galatians 4:4).

22–24 Forty days after Jesus's birth, Mary and Joseph went to **Jerusalem**.[11] They went for two reasons. First, they went to the temple to **present** Jesus to the Lord (verse 22). According to the **Law of the Lord** (the Jewish law), all firstborn offspring, both human and animal, were considered to be consecrated to God (verse 23). The firstborn of "clean" animals were sacrificed, that is, offered to God. The firstborn of humans were not sacrificed; instead, they had to be redeemed by a payment of money when they were a month old (Exodus 13:2,12–13; Numbers 18:15–16).

The second reason Mary and Joseph went to Jerusalem was to offer the sacrifice of purification (verse 24). According to Jewish law, a mother and her male offspring were considered "unclean" for a period of forty days after the child's birth. At that time a sacrifice had to be offered in order for the mother and child to be purified. For poor people, the sacrifice to be offered was a **pair of doves or two young pigeons** (Leviticus 12:1–8).

25 Luke describes another sign that Jesus was indeed the Savior, the Messiah of Israel. He mentions a man called Simeon, who had been waiting for the **consolation**, that is, the salvation of Israel. In other words, he had been waiting to see the **Lord's Christ**, that is, God's Christ,[12] the Messiah, who was coming to save His people.

26–28 The Holy Spirit had told Simeon that he would get to see Christ before he died. Therefore, when Mary and Joseph brought Jesus into the temple, Simeon, led by the Holy Spirit, recognized the baby Jesus at once and took Him in his arms.

29–32 Then Simeon praised God. He could now die in peace, because he had seen the salvation that God had promised, the salvation not only of Israel, but of the **Gentiles** also—the salvation of the entire world (Isaiah 49:6; 52:10; Psalm 98:2–3).

33 Even though the angel had told

---

[11] **Jerusalem** was the capital of Judea, the southern province of Israel. Jerusalem was the main city of the Jews. The Jewish temple was located there.

[12] **Christ** means "anointed one" in the Greek language. "Messiah" means the same thing in the Hebrew language.

Mary and Joseph that their son Jesus was the Savior, the Son of God, they were still amazed at Simeon's words. Their son would be the Savior not only of Israel, but of the whole world!

34 After blessing Mary, Joseph, and their child, Simeon said, "**This child is destined to cause the falling and rising of many in Israel**." Those who believe in Christ and accept the salvation He brings will "rise." Those who reject Him will "fall," that is, be condemned (see John 3:18,36). Christ is the cornerstone upon which the church, the "new Israel," will rise (see Ephesians 2:19–21; 1 Peter 2:6 and comments). But that same stone, if rejected, will become a stone by which men fall (see Matthew 21:44; 1 Peter 2:7–8 and comment).

Simeon also said that Jesus would be a **sign that will be spoken against**. Jesus is a **sign** of judgment. He came the first time to save men, but He will come a second time to judge them (see Matthew 24:30; Mark 13:26; 14:61–62; John 5:22–23 and comments). Jesus came with a sword to separate the righteous from the unrighteous (Matthew 10:34). Jesus is a "sign" which says: "All those who do not place their faith in me and follow me are doomed. **No one comes to the Father except through me**" (John 14:6).

Nevertheless, most of the Jews, the very people Christ came first to save, rejected Him and spoke against Him and, in the end, killed Him. The Jews, the chosen and blessed people of God, lost their blessing, lost their inheritance; they fell. And the blessing passed to the Gentiles who believed and accepted Christ (Matthew 21:43).

35 The coming of Christ into the world would cause the **thoughts of many hearts** to be revealed. It would then be manifest who had faith and who hadn't, who were the true servants of God and who were not. It is not outward righteousness that God looks at; it is our attitude toward Christ that is most important. Only those who receive Christ's righteousness through faith will in the end be considered righteous by God (see Galatians 2:15–16 and comment).

Then Simeon prophesied that Mary's soul would be pierced by a **sword**. The "sword" was the murder of her own son. She would watch the leaders of her own nation kill her firstborn son on the CROSS.

36–38 After Simeon had spoken, Anna, a prophetess, also spoke about the child Jesus. She was of the **tribe of Asher**.[13] She spoke **to all who were looking forward to the redemption of Jerusalem**. Many among the Jews of Jerusalem were indeed waiting for the Messiah, the Savior, to come and bring redemption for Israel. Yet when He did come, most of them did not recognize Him. They did not believe that the Son of God would be born in a manger, the son of a poor carpenter and a village woman.

The Childhood of Jesus (2:39–52)

39 Luke here says that the family of Jesus returned to their own town of Nazareth in the province of Galilee, in northern Israel. But before they returned, they were visited by astrologers from the East, as described in Matthew 2:1–12. Then, in fear of the wicked King Herod, the family fled to Egypt (see Matthew 2:13–23). Only after Herod died did Joseph and Mary return to Nazareth with Jesus.

40 Nothing else is known about Jesus' early childhood except what is written in verses 40–52. Even though Jesus was the Son of God, He had taken on Himself the form of a man, and was born of a woman. Therefore, like other men, Jesus had to grow and become strong. But from the beginning, He was filled with the wisdom and the grace of His heavenly Father.

41 Jerusalem was the capital of the Jewish nation. It was also the location of the great Jewish temple, the center of worship for all Jews (see Mark 13:1 and comment). Every year thousands of Jews traveled to Jerusalem to celebrate the

[13] **Asher** was one of the twelve sons of Jacob, the grandson of Abraham. The twelve tribes of Israel are descended from Jacob's twelve sons.

Feast of the Passover (see Mark 14:1 and comment). So each year Joseph and Mary also traveled to Jerusalem for this purpose.

42–45 When Jesus was twelve, Joseph and Mary went with Jesus to Jerusalem for the Passover as usual, but when it came time to return home, Jesus did not go with His parents. There were hundreds of Jews who were returning together to Nazareth, and Joseph and Mary assumed that Jesus was in the group but walking with relatives and friends instead of with His parents. But after walking a day, Joseph and Mary discovered that Jesus was not with the group at all. So Joseph and Mary returned to Jerusalem.

46–48 After three days they found Jesus in the temple talking with the teachers of the law. Those who heard Jesus were amazed at His understanding (verse 47). But His parents rebuked Him for giving them such anxiety.

49–50 But Jesus replied, "You should have known where to find me. I have things to do **in my Father's house**"—that is, in the temple.

From this we know that Jesus, even in childhood, knew that He was God's Son, the Messiah. But His parents still didn't fully understand why their twelve-year-old son had to stay behind in the temple for three days.

51–52 Jesus' parents insisted that He return home with them, and Luke says that He **was obedient to them**. And Jesus **grew in wisdom and stature**.

After this, little is known about Jesus until He came to be baptized by John the Baptist about eighteen years later. From Mark 6:3, it seems that Jesus learned to be a carpenter like His father Joseph (Matthew 13:55).

CHAPTER 3

John the Baptist Prepares the Way (3:1–20)

(Matthew 3:1–3,7–12;
Mark 1:3–4,7–8)

1 **Tiberius Caesar** was emperor of the Roman Empire in 14–37 A.D. Therefore, the **fifteenth year** of his reign was about 28 A.D.; in that year John began his public ministry.

Pontius Pilate was the Roman governor of Judea, 26–36 A.D. He later caused Jesus to be executed. **Herod** was the son of the King Herod who ruled at the time of Jesus' birth (Matthew 2:1). Here Herod is called the **tetrarch of Galilee**, that is, ruler over the district of Galilee.[14] He later beheaded John the Baptist (Mark 6:16–17).

2 At the time John appeared, **Caiaphas** was the Jewish high priest. **Annas**, Caiaphas' father-in-law, had been high priest before him, but had been deposed by the Romans. Nevertheless, the people still considered him a high priest and he continued to have great influence (John 18:12–13; Acts 4:6).

3–6 See Mark 1:3–4 and comment.

7–9 See Matthew 3:7–10 and comment.

10 John's preaching was a new thing for the Jews. He said that men must repent and then be baptized. The Jews baptized Gentiles who wanted to follow the Jewish religion, but they didn't think baptism was necessary for themselves. They considered themselves to be righteous because they were God's chosen people, descendants of Abraham. Gentiles needed baptism, the Jews said, because Gentiles were "sinners" (Galatians 2:15). But Jews, they thought, had no need to be purified in this way.[15]

---

[14] The Roman emperor allowed local rulers like Herod and Philip to administer small sections of the Roman Empire.

[15] The Jews atoned for sin by offering sacrifices.

Nevertheless, many Jews accepted John's preaching and came to be baptized. They feared God, and thought that by baptism they could protect themselves from God's judgment. But John knew that many of the Jews weren't sincere. Especially he knew that the Pharisees and Sadducees among them were not sincere (see Matthew 3:7 and comment). They considered baptism only an outward ceremony like the other Jewish customs. But John told them that they must truly repent, and that to truly repent they must do the works of repentance (verse 8).

Therefore, here in verse 10, the Jews ask John, "What are these works of repentance?"

11 John answered that they should do the works of love. They should love their neighbor (Mark 12:31). They should do to him as they would want him to do to them (Matthew 7:12). They should share their goods with those in need (James 2:14–16).

12–13 The tax collectors[16] also asked what work they should do. Most of the tax collectors cheated the people, and as a result, the people hated them and considered them great sinners.

John didn't tell them to stop collecting taxes. Collecting taxes was not a sin (see Mark 12:17). But he told them they must be honest.

14 John gave the same kind of advice to the soldiers. These soldiers were Jewish soldiers in the service of Herod, the tetrarch of Galilee. Notice the three things John said to them: First, **"don't extort money"**; second, **"don't accuse people falsely"**; and third, **"be content with your pay"**—that is, "do not complain or seek extra advantages for yourself." John's words apply not only to soldiers, but to all of us.

15 Many of the Jews began to think that John was the Messiah Himself. But he quickly told them that he was not (John 1:19–20). **". . . one more powerful than I will come,"** said John (verse 16).

16 See Mark 1:7–8 and comment.

17–18 See Matthew 3:12 and comment.

19–20 See Mark 6:17-18 and comment.

The Baptism of Jesus (3:21–22)
(Matthew 3:13–17; Mark 1:9–11)

21–22 See Mark 1:9–11 and comment.

The Genealogy of Jesus (3:23–38)
(Matthew 1:1–17)

23–38 See Matthew 1:1–17 and comment.

CHAPTER 4

The Temptation of Jesus (4:1–13)
(Matthew 4:1–17)

1–13 See Matthew 4:1–17 and comment.

Jesus Rejected at Nazareth (4:14–30)

14–15 When Jesus was baptized, the Holy Spirit descended on Him (Luke 3:22). He was filled with the Holy Spirit (verse 1). Having been filled with the Spirit, Jesus was prepared to face the temptations given to Him by SATAN (verses 3–13). Then, when He had resisted Satan and gained victory over him, Jesus returned to Galilee **in the power of the Spirit** (verse 14).

When we resist Satan—when we turn from sin and sinful desires—the power of the Holy Spirit is fully released in our lives. But if in one point we give in to Satan, we forfeit that power.

---

[16] Tax collectors are discussed in Mark 2:14 and comment.

Jesus did His mighty works through the power of the Holy Spirit. He told His disciples to wait for the Holy Spirit to come upon them and give them power (see Luke 24:49; Acts 1:8 and comments). Only after that could they be effective witnesses for Him. Without the power of the Holy Spirit, a follower of Christ cannot work effectively for God. Without the Spirit, our preaching and teaching is without power. This is why, when Jesus taught the people, they were amazed and spread the news about Him **through the whole countryside** (see Matthew 7:28–29 and comment).

16–17 Many Bible scholars believe that the visit to Nazareth described here in verses 16–30 is the same visit described in Matthew 13:53–58 and Mark 6:1–6.[17] They say that Luke placed this story near the beginning of his Gospel because it explains so clearly the purpose of Jesus' ministry (verses 18–19). According to verse 23, Jesus first went to other cities, such as Capernaum, before going to Nazareth.

The Jews held their religious services in the synagogue in each village. The services took place each Saturday, the **Sabbath day**. It was the custom during the service to read from a scroll[18] of the Old Testament. Often visitors to the synagogue were invited to read the lesson or to give a comment on it (Acts 13:14–15,42; 17:1–4).

18–19 The scroll of Isaiah the prophet was handed to Jesus to read. He read from Isaiah 61:1–2, in which Isaiah prophesies about the Messiah. Thus, when Jesus read it, He was truly speaking about Himself.

The Spirit of the Lord is on me (verse 18). Jesus was filled and empowered by the Holy Spirit (verses 1,14). He had been given the Spirit **without limit** (John 3:34).

. . . because he has anointed me to preach good news to the poor. Jesus was the "anointed one," that is, the Messiah, the Christ (see Luke 2:25). The **poor** here are not only the poor in possessions, but also the **poor in spirit** (see Matthew 5:3). It is the poor in spirit who gladly receive the **good news** of salvation.

He has sent me to proclaim freedom for the prisoners. These are not only actual prisoners in jail, but they are also spiritual prisoners of sin, of Satan. Christ came to set them free; that is, He came to forgive their sins (Mark 2:5,10–12).

Christ was sent to bring **sight for the blind**. He not only opens men's bodily eyes, but He opens their spiritual eyes as well.

He was sent **to release the oppressed**.[19] People were oppressed by their rulers the Romans, by their own hypocritical religious leaders, and by the rich and powerful. But they were also oppressed by fears and doubts and sinful lusts. Christ offered them release, peace, joy.

Finally, Jesus was sent **to proclaim the year of the Lord's favor**—that is, the coming of the Messiah, the consolation of Israel (Luke 2:25).

20 Everyone in the synagogue was amazed at the way Jesus read these words. The people had heard these words from Isaiah read to them many times before, but they had never heard them read like this! It was as if the prophet Isaiah himself were speaking—no, more than that—the Messiah Himself!

21 After He had finished reading from the book of Isaiah, Jesus said to the people, "**Today this scripture is fulfilled in your hearing**. The Messiah has come! The Gospel is being preached, prisoners are being set free, the blind are receiving their sight. The day of the Messiah has dawned."

22 At first, the people spoke well of Jesus (verse 15). But then someone recognized Him! "Why, He is only the carpenter's son," they began to say (see Mark 6:1–3; John 6:42 and comments).

23 Jesus saw that the people of Nazareth, His own home town, were filled with an attitude of unbelief. They

---

[17] See comment on Mark 6:1 and footnote to comment.

[18] In New Testament times, books were written on long strips of paper or parchment, which were rolled up into a scroll (see Hebrews 10:7).

[19] Jesus added these words from Isaiah 58:6.

couldn't believe that a carpenter's son from their own town could be anyone important. Perhaps they were jealous. But mainly, they refused to believe.

Jesus knew their hearts. They wanted Him to perform a miracle before their eyes to prove that He was the Messiah. "Let Him heal someone in His own town," they said. They had heard that He had done miracles elsewhere; let Him do one in Nazareth.

24 But Jesus knew they wouldn't believe even if He performed a miracle in their presence. Indeed, He did heal a few people. But because of the people's unbelief, He could do no other great works in Nazareth (see Matthew 13:58; Mark 6:6 and comment).

25–26 Then Jesus said something that angered the people. He reminded them that the prophet Elijah encountered unbelief in Israel during a time of drought; therefore, he went to live with a Gentile, a widow in Zarephath, north of Israel (1 Kings 17:7–16).

27 In the same way, the Jews did not believe in the prophet Elisha. So he withheld his blessing from Israel, and healed a Gentile with leprosy instead (2 Kings 5:1–15).

Jesus' meaning was this: If the Jews reject Him as they did Elijah and Elisha, He too will reject them and turn to the Gentiles (see Matthew 21:43). Indeed, Christ often found more faith among the Gentiles than among the Jews (Matthew 8:8–10).

28–30 The people of Nazareth could stand Jesus' words no longer. They tried to kill Him by throwing Him off a cliff located near the edge of the town. But He miraculously escaped from them (John 8:59; 10:39). It was not God's time for Him to die.

Jesus Drives Out an Evil Spirit (4:31–37)

(Mark 1:21–28)

31–37 See Mark 1:21–28 and comment.

Jesus Heals Many (4:38–44)

(Matthew 8:14–17; Mark 1:29–39)

38–44 See Mark 1:29–39 and comment.

CHAPTER 5

The Calling of the First Disciples (5:1–11)

(Matthew 4:18–22; Mark 1:16–20)

1–3 In these verses Luke describes how Jesus called His first four disciples. Mark's description is a shorter version (see Mark 1:16–20).

Jesus came to the **Lake of Gennesaret**, that is, the Sea of Galilee. At first, Jesus preached to the crowd from Simon's (Peter's) boat. Peter and the others with him were doubtless amazed at His teaching like everyone else was.

4–5 Therefore, when Jesus gave Peter an unusual and seemingly futile command, Peter was ready to obey. Jesus said, "**. . . let down the nets**." But Peter knew that they couldn't catch anything. He and his colleagues had been fishing all night and had caught nothing. And Jesus wasn't even a fisherman; He was a carpenter!

Many are the pastors and preachers who labor long and hard and "catch" nothing. But Christ continues to say: "Let down your nets." One day there will be fish.

6–7 Then Jesus performed a miracle. When they pulled in their nets, they were so full of fish that it began to break.

8 Then Peter realized that Jesus had power over nature; He had God's power. He was the Lord. And Peter felt his own unworthiness and sinfulness in the presence of such a man as Jesus (Isaiah 6:5).

"**Go away,**" Peter said to Jesus. "I am not worthy to remain in your presence. **I am a sinful man.**"

Peter was no more sinful than other men. Compared with Jesus, who was without sin, we are all sinful men who are not worthy to come into His presence. If there is anyone who does not feel this unworthiness, this sinfulness, then that person has not known Jesus.

9–11 See Mark 1:17–20 and comment.

The Man With Leprosy (5:12–16)
(Matthew 8:1–4; Mark 1:40–45)

12–16 See Mark 1:40–45 and comment.

Jesus Heals a Paralytic (5:17–26)
(Matthew 9:1–8; Mark 2:1–12)

17–26 See Mark 2:1–12 and comment.

The Calling of Levi (5:27–32)
(Matthew 9:9–13; Mark 2:13–17)

27–32 See Mark 2:13–17 and comment.

Jesus Questioned About Fasting (5:33–39)
(Matthew 9:14–17; Mark 2:18–22)

33–39 See Mark 2:18–22 and comment.

CHAPTER 6

Lord of the Sabbath (6:1–5)
(Matthew 12:1–8; Mark 2:23–28)

1–5 See Mark 2:23–28 and comment.

The Man With a Shriveled Hand (6:6–11)
(Matthew 12:9–14; Mark 3:1–6)

6–11 See Mark 3:1–6 and comment.

The Twelve Apostles (6:12–16)
(Matthew 10:14; Mark 3:13–19)

12–16 See Mark 3:13–19 and comment.

Jesus Heals Many (6:17–19)
(Matthew 12:15–16; Mark 3:7–12)

17–19 See Mark 3:7–12 and comment.

Blessings and Woes (6:20–26)
(Matthew 5:1–12)

20 See Matthew 5:3 and comment.
21 See Matthew 5:4,6 and comment.
22–23 See Matthew 5:10-12 and comment.
24 In verses 24–26, Jesus mentions the opposite of the blessings written above in verses 20–22.

If it is a blessing to be poor (verse 20), then it cannot be a blessing to be rich. Yes, those who store up riches for themselves have a temporary blessing in this life, but it will not last. The comfort they receive from their wealth will end with their death, and that is all the comfort they will ever receive (see Mark 10:25; Luke 12:16–21; 16:19–26 and comments).

We must understand Jesus' teaching. It is not a sin to be rich; but it is a sin to love riches and to keep them for ourselves. If we do not use our possessions for God's service, they will turn into a curse (see James 5:15 and comment). Therefore, let us be rich in generosity and in good deeds (see 1 Timothy 6:17–19 and comment).

25 Those who **hunger** for righteousness will be satisfied (verse 21). Those who consider themselves **well fed**, that is, righteous, will soon find no food on their plate. Those whose stomachs are full do not hunger. Those who are satisfied with themselves and with the things of this life will not hunger for the things of the next life. And when the next life comes, they will be hungry indeed! Only Jesus can give the food that will last for all eternity (see John 6:35,48–51 and comment).

Those who mourn and weep for their sins will be comforted (verse 21). Those who **laugh now**, that is, those who do not care about their sins, will surely mourn and weep when they stand before God on the day of judgment.

26 **Woe to you when all men speak well of you.** What an amazing teaching! All of us desire that men speak well of us. Yet here Jesus says that if they do, we shall not be blessed.

Why? Because men of the world do not speak well of those who truly belong to Christ, who truly belong to the kingdom of heaven. Darkness hates the light (John 3:19–20). The world—that is, worldly men—hated Christ. Therefore, the world will also hate His disciples (see John 15:18–19 and comment).

Therefore, if the world speaks well of us, then we should worry lest we are not truly following in Christ's steps.[20] We must examine ourselves. The world follows after and praises false prophets. Worldly men praise those who do not condemn their sin, who do not call on them to repent. Worldly men praise those who live like they do. Let us beware of the praise of the world!

Love for Enemies (6:27–36)
(Matthew 5:38–48; 7:12)

27–28 See Matthew 5:43–44 and comment.

29–30 See Matthew 5:38–42 and comment.

31 See Matthew 7:12 and comment.

32–35 See Matthew 5:44–47 and comment.

36 See Matthew 5:48 and comment.

Judging Others (6:37–42)
(Matthew 6:14; 7:1–5)

37–38 See Matthew 6:14; 7:1–2 and comments.

39 See Matthew 15:14; Mark 7:14–16 and comment.

40 See Matthew 10:24–25; John 13:13–16 and comments.

41–42 See Matthew 7:3–5 and comment.

A Tree and Its Fruit (6:43–45)
(Matthew 7:16–18; 12:33–35)

43–45 See Matthew 7:16–18; 12:33–35 and comments.

The Wise and Foolish Builders (6:46–49)
(Matthew 7:24–27)

46–49 See Matthew 7:24–27 and comment.

CHAPTER 7

The Faith of the Centurion (7:1–10)
(Matthew 8:5–13)

1–10 See Matthew 8:5–13 and comment.

Jesus Raises a Widow's Son (7:11–17)

11–17 Jesus and His disciples met a widow whose only son had just died. Jesus had special compassion on the woman, because this son was her only means of support and comfort (verse 13). Therefore, He raised the dead boy to life and restored him to his mother.

The people recognized that Jesus was a great prophet. He was like the Old Testament prophets Elijah and Elisha, who also had raised the dead (1 Kings 17:17–24; 2 Kings 4:18–37). This was not

---

[20] Notice in this verse that Jesus is talking about **all men** speaking well of us. When that happens, we should worry! Men of the world with hardened hearts should not be speaking well of us; if they are, it can only mean that we have become too much like them.

There is another sense, however, in which ordinary non-believers should speak well of Christians. They should be able to see Christ in us. They should be drawn to Christ by our good behavior (see Acts 5:12–14; 1 Timothy 3:7).

the only dead person Jesus raised. He raised His friend Lazarus, who had been dead four days (John 11:38–44). He also raised others, for He said to John's disciples, "**Go back and report to John what you hear and see . . . the dead are raised**" (Matthew 11:4–5).

Many Jews considered Jesus a great prophet because of His mighty works, such as raising the dead (Matthew 21:11; Luke 24:19; John 6:14). But it was only after He was Himself raised from the dead that people began to realize that He was much more than a prophet—He was the Messiah Himself, the Son of God.

Jesus and John the Baptist (7:18–35)

(Matthew 11:1–11,16–19)

18–28 See Matthew 11:1–11 and comment.
29–30 See Matthew 21:32 and comment.
31–35 See Matthew 11:16–19 and comment.

Jesus Anointed by a Sinful Woman (7:36–50)

36–38 The anointing Luke describes in this section is similar to the anointing described in Mark 14:1–9. But the events are not the same. The woman described here was a **sinner**, that is, a prostitute, and the anointing took place in the house of Simon, a PHARISEE (see Mark 14:1–9 and comment).
39 When Simon the Pharisee saw the sinful woman touch Jesus, he decided that Jesus could not be a true prophet. A true prophet would surely have known that the woman was a sinner, and thus would never have let her touch him. The Jews, especially the Pharisees, believed that they would contaminate themselves if they associated with sinners (see Mark 2:15–17 and comment).
40 But Jesus knew the woman was a sinner, and he also knew Simon's thoughts. Therefore, He told Simon a parable.
41–43 In this parable Jesus taught that a man will love and thank God according to the mercy God has shown him. The greater the sins God forgives, the greater will be the sinner's love for God. Sin is like a debt. If a man knows his sins are great, he will be more grateful for forgiveness. If a man considers his sins to be small, he will be less grateful for forgiveness. Notice that a man's gratitude depends not on how sinful he actually is, but on how sinful he thinks he is. Notice also that whether our sins are great or small, we cannot pay back our debt to God by our own righteousness. **Neither of them had the money to pay him back** (verse 42). Only by God's mercy can our debts be forgiven.

It is best that a man considers his sins to be very great, because that is how God considers them.
44–47 Then Jesus turned to Simon the Pharisee and contrasted him with the sinful woman he despised. The Pharisees did not consider themselves to be sinful. Therefore, God's mercy and forgiveness meant nothing to them. In their own minds they had no reason to be grateful to God, to love God. They loved God only with their lips.

But Jesus said to Simon, "This sinful woman loves me from the depths of her heart. She has shown her love for me. Therefore, this is proof that her sins have been forgiven. Her love is the proof that she is washed from sin and accepted by God. But you, Simon, have not shown me love. Your sins, therefore, have evidently not been forgiven. Otherwise, you would have loved me as this woman has loved me."

God first loved us and forgave us. That is why we love Him (see 1 John 4:10). No one can truly love God until he first recognizes his own sinfulness and receives forgiveness through faith in Christ.
48–49 Then Jesus said to the woman, "**Your sins are forgiven**." Jesus said this so that the other guests could hear. The woman already had been forgiven; now Jesus was just confirming this so that others might also know it (see Mark 2:5–11).
50 Then Jesus said to the woman, "**Your faith has saved you**." It wasn't the

woman's love for Jesus that saved her; it was her FAITH. Because she had faith that Jesus was her Savior and could forgive her sins, she received salvation.

It is only through faith that we can receive the forgiveness, the healing, the salvation that God in His GRACE offers to sinful man (see Mark 5:34; 10:52 and comments).

CHAPTER 8

Jesus Preaches the Good News (8:1–3)

1 Jesus was an itinerant evangelist. He didn't stay in one city. He wasn't the pastor of a church. He traveled from village to village, preaching the **good news of the KINGDOM OF GOD** (see Mark 1:14–15 and comment). His twelve disciples went with Him so that He could train them to take over His work when He was gone. In addition to His twelve main disciples, there were others also who followed Jesus (Luke 10:1).

2–3 Together with His disciples, many women went with Jesus. These women helped serve Jesus and His disciples on their journeys. Many of these women had been cured by Jesus of evil spirits and other diseases. They showed their gratitude by leaving their own homes and helping to support Him and His disciples wherever they went (see Mark 15:40–41 and comment). One of them, Mary Magdalene, was later the first to see Jesus risen from the dead (Mark 16:9). Joanna went with Mary Magdalene to tell the disciples of Jesus' resurrection (Luke 24:10).

The Parable of the Sower (8:4–15)
(Matthew 13:1–23; Mark 4:1–20)

4–15 See Mark 4:1–20 and comment.

A Lamp on a Stand (8:16–18)
(Matthew 5:15; 10:26; 13:12; Mark 4:21–25)

16–18 See Matthew 5:15; Mark 4:21–25 and comments.

Jesus' Mother and Brothers (8:19–21)
(Matthew 12:46–50; Mark 3:31–35)

19–21 See Mark 3:31–35 and comment.

Jesus Calms the Storm (8:22–25)
(Matthew 8:23–27; Mark 4:35–41)

22–25 See Mark 4:35–41 and comment.

The Healing of a Demon-possessed Man (8:26–39)
(Matthew 8:28–34; Mark 5:1–20)

26–39 See Mark 5:1–20 and comment.

A Dead Girl and a Sick Woman (8:40–56)
(Matthew 9:18–26; Mark 5:21–43)

40–56 See Mark 5:21–43 and comment.

CHAPTER 9

Jesus Sends Out the Twelve (9:1–6)
(Matthew 10:9–15; Mark 6:7–13)

1–6 See Mark 6:7–13 and comment.

Herod Is Perplexed (9:7–9)
(Matthew 14:1–2; Mark 6:14–16)

7–9 See Mark 6:14–16 and comment.

Jesus Feeds the Five Thousand (9:10–17)
(Matthew 14:13–21; Mark 6:30–44; John 6:1–15)

10–17 See Mark 6:30–44 and comment.

Peter's Confession of Christ (9:18–22)
(Matthew 16:13–21; Mark 8:27–31)

18–21 See Mark 8:27–30 and comment.
22 See Mark 8:31 and comment.

Teaching on Self-denial (9:23–27)
(Matthew 16:24–26; Mark 8:34–38; 9:1)

23–26 See Mark 8:34–38 and comment.
27 See Mark 9:1 and comment.

The Transfiguration (9:28–36)
(Matthew 17:1–13; Mark 9:2–13)

28–36 See Mark 9:2–13 and comment.

A Boy With an Evil Spirit (9:37–45)
(Matthew 17:14–23; Mark 9:14–32)

37–45 See Mark 9:14–32 and comment.

Who Will Be the Greatest? (9:46–50)
(Mark 9:33–40)

46–50 See Mark 9:33–40 and comment.

Samaritan Opposition (9:51–56)

51 Jesus knew that He must suffer and die at the hands of the Jewish leaders in Jerusalem (Mark 8:31). Therefore, when the time of His death drew near, He and His disciples went from Galilee in the north of Israel to Jerusalem, the capital.
52 On the way, the road went through the region of Samaria. The Samaritans were Jews who had intermarried with foreign women. They were half-Jews; therefore, ordinary Jews despised them (see Matthew 10:5; John 4:4-9; Acts 8:4-5).
53 The Samaritans also hated the Jews. When they learned that Jesus and His disciples were going to Jerusalem, the Jewish capital, they offered them no hospitality.
54 James and John, two of Jesus' disciples (Mark 3:17), wanted to punish the Samaritans (see Mark 6:11). Taking the example of the prophet Elijah (2 Kings 1:9–12), they suggested destroying them by calling **fire down from heaven.**
55 But Jesus rebuked James and John. They should have called for grace from heaven, not fire. Their suggestion did not arise from the Spirit of Christ. Their suggestion came from a spirit of revenge and anger, not a spirit of love and forgiveness. According to some ancient manuscripts of Luke, Jesus told them at this point: "You do not know what kind of spirit you are of, for the Son of Man did not come to destroy men's lives, but to save them."
56 Nevertheless, Jesus and His disciples did not go to that Samaritan village, but went by another way.

The Cost of Following Jesus (9:57–62)
(Matthew 8:18–22)

57–62 See Matthew 8:18–22 and comment.

CHAPTER 10

Jesus Sends Out the Seventy-two (10:1–20)
(Matthew 9:37–38; 10:9–15; 11:20–24; Mark 6:7–13)

1 In addition to His twelve main disciples, many others followed Jesus and became disciples also. Jesus had already sent His twelve disciples out to preach and heal (see Mark 6:7; Luke 9:1–2 and comment). Now in this section, Luke describes how Jesus sent out seventy-two[21] other disciples, giving them similar instructions.

2 See Matthew 9:37–38 and comment.

3 See Matthew 10:16 and comment.

4 See Matthew 10:9–10; Mark 6:8–9 and comment.

5–12 See Matthew 10:11–15; Mark 6:10–11 and comment.

13–15 See Matthew 11:20–24 and comment.

16 See Matthew 10:40 and comment.

17 When the seventy-two disciples returned from their journey, they reported to Jesus what they had done. Just as the first twelve disciples had performed mighty works, so these seventy-two disciples also performed similar works (see Mark 6:12–13 and comment). The works they did were done in Jesus' name and by His power. Demons submitted to the disciples because Christ had given the disciples His own authority (verse 19).

18 Then Jesus told His disciples why the demons had submitted to them. The reason was because Satan's power had been overcome (John 12:31). Christ had already defeated Satan in the wilderness during His time of temptation (Matthew 4:10–11). While the disciples had been away, Jesus had seen a vision of Satan falling from heaven (Revelation 12:9). Now, not only was Christ victorious over Satan, but His disciples were also.

19 Jesus had given His disciples His own authority. That authority was very great, because all **authority in heaven and on earth** belonged to Jesus (Matthew 28:18). And that same authority is given to all who believe in Jesus and do His will.

Snakes and scorpions represent all kinds of evil. Jesus told His disciples that having received His authority they would be protected from all spiritual harm that Satan would try to inflict on them.[22] They would **overcome all the power of the enemy** (see Mark 16:17–18). Satan could attack their bodies, but he would not be able to harm their souls (Matthew 10:28).

20 Then Jesus said to His disciples: "... **do not rejoice that the spirits submit to you**. That is not the most important thing. The most important thing is to have faith, to belong to me, to have an inheritance in the kingdom of heaven. That is what you must rejoice in; **rejoice that your names are written in heaven**." Power to become children of God is more important than power to do miracles (John 1:12).

Many people who are not Christians do mighty works. There are some who do mighty works in Jesus' name, yet they will not enter heaven. Only those who truly believe in Jesus and love and obey Him have their names written in heaven (see Matthew 7:21–23 and comment).

Jesus Praises the Father (10:21–24)
(Matthew 11:25–27; 13:16–17)

21–24 See Matthew 11:25–27 and comment.

23–24 See Matthew 13:16–17; Mark 4:12 and comment.

The Parable of the Good Samaritan (10:25–37)

25 An **expert in the law** asked Jesus, "... **what must I do to inherit** ETERNAL

[21] Some ancient manuscripts say "seventy," instead of seventy-two.

[22] At certain times, according to God's purposes, Christians are protected from physical harm also (see Acts 12:5–11; 28:3–6).

LIFE?" He did not ask sincerely; he was only trying to test Jesus.

26 The expert in the law should have known the answer to his question, because it is written in the Jewish law itself. **Keep my decrees and laws, for the man who obeys them will live by them** (Leviticus 18:5; Galatians 3:12). That is, the man who obeys all of God's law perfectly all the time shall inherit eternal life. Therefore, instead of answering the man's question directly, Jesus asked a question of His own: **"What is written in the Law?"**[23]

27 The expert in the law answered Jesus' question correctly. He summed up the entire law by quoting the two greatest commandments (see Matthew 22:40; Mark 12:30–31 and comment).

28 Then Jesus said, **"Do this and you will live**; that is, obey these two commandments perfectly and you will live."

Jesus did not mean that a man can be saved by obeying the law, because man is saved by faith alone (see Galatians 2:15–16 and comment). The reason that man cannot be saved by the law is that no man (except Christ) has ever been able to obey the law perfectly (see Galatians 3:10; James 2:10 and comments). Who can ever perfectly obey the two great commandments all the time? No one. Only when we believe in Christ and His love is poured out into our hearts (Romans 5:5) can we begin to obey these two commandments. Without faith, there can be no true love. Only by faith **expressing itself through love** (Galatians 5:6) can a person inherit eternal life.

29 The expert in the law was not happy with Jesus' answer. He knew he had not loved God as he ought. He knew he had not loved all men. For example, he had not loved Gentiles. Most Jews did not consider Gentiles to be their "neighbor." They claimed that the second commandment about loving one's neighbor did not include loving Gentiles. The expert in the law hoped that Jesus would agree that Gentiles were not "neighbors"; then he would not feel so guilty for not having loved them. He was trying to **justify himself**. He preferred to show how good he was, rather than to learn how bad he was.

Then Jesus, through this parable of the Good Samaritan, told the expert in the law that all men—both Jew and Gentile—were his neighbors, and that he must therefore love all men, not just his friends (Matthew 5:44). In the parable it was the non-Jew, the Samaritan,[24] who was obedient to the law, not the two proud unmerciful Jews. It was this Samaritan who was closer to the kingdom of heaven than the Jewish priest and Levite (verses 31–32).

30 **Jericho** was a city eighteen miles east of Jerusalem and 3300 feet lower in altitude. The road between Jericho and Jerusalem was steep and rocky. The area was a hide-out of robbers, and people were often robbed along the way. The parable may have been based on a true occurrence.

31–32 The **priest** and the **Levite**[25] were considered the most righteous of the Jews. Yet they were too busy to show love to their fellow Jew who had been beaten by robbers. Perhaps they had important work to do in the temple and could give no time to help their neighbor.

33–35 But a Samaritan stopped. Even though the Samaritans were not full Jews, and even though the Jews and the Samaritans usually hated each other, this Samaritan showed mercy on the Jew who had been robbed.

He didn't only show sympathy. He took complete care of the injured man. He treated his wounds. He took him to an inn. He paid all his expenses. This is what it means to love your neighbor. Therefore,

---

[23] Here the **Law** means the first five books of the Old Testament.

[24] Samaritans are mentioned in Luke 9:52 and comment.

[25] The Levites were descended from Levi, one of the twelve sons of Jacob. They had responsibility for the services of the Jewish temple. The priests, on the other hand, were descended from Aaron, the brother of Moses, a great grandson of Levi. Only those descended from Aaron could be priests.

let us not love with words or tongue but with actions and in truth (1 John 3:18).

36–37 The expert in the law had asked, "**And who is my neighbor?**" (verse 29). The answer: All men are our neighbors, especially those who are in need.

But the parable asks another question: Am I a neighbor? Do I behave like a neighbor? It is more essential to ask ourselves that question than to ask who our neighbor is. The despised "unclean" Samaritan was the true neighbor, and therefore he was the one who would inherit eternal life.

Jesus said to the expert in the law, "**Go and do likewise**. As that Samaritan did for the injured Jew, so you go and do likewise for anyone who needs your help—even for a Samaritan."

At the Home of Martha and Mary (10:38–42)

38–39 **Martha** and **Mary** lived in Bethany, near Jerusalem (John 11:1–2). When Jesus came to their home, Martha busied herself preparing the meal. But Mary, instead of helping her sister, remained with Jesus listening to His words. This is the same Mary who on another occasion anointed Jesus with precious ointment (Mark 14:3; John 12:1–3).

40 **Martha was distracted**. She desired to prepare a good meal for the Lord, but she was anxious about it. She complained about her sister. She rebuked Christ. "**Don't you care?**" she said to Him. "I have all this work and my sister doesn't help me."

41–42 Then Jesus gently told Martha that she should not be anxious. She should not rebuke her sister. "**Mary has chosen what is better.**" Mary had chosen to listen to the words of life. By listening to Jesus, by desiring to be with Him, she was showing Him honor. She was also receiving the blessing of His fellowship, which Martha, because of her anxiety and complaining spirit, could not enjoy.

In preparing the meal Martha was doing a good thing. She also was showing love to Jesus through her service (1 John 3:18). But she was wrong to worry and fret. It is not wrong to be busy in serving; it is wrong, however, to be **distracted** in serving. She was also wrong to complain about her sister. The Apostle Paul writes: **Do everything without complaining or arguing** (Philippians 2:14).

Notice that Jesus does not tell Martha to sit down and listen. Neither does He tell Mary to get up and help her sister. Both sisters were doing what was pleasing to the Lord; one was serving, one was listening. Both things are necessary and good. Some Christians spend more time in service and different kinds of work, while other Christians spend more time in prayer and meditation and worship. Let them not criticize each other. Let everything they do be done out of love for Christ, and Christ will be pleased.

In our individual Christian lives, there should be some balance between the time we spend in service and the time we spend in prayer and worship. If we do not pray and worship, our service becomes dry and powerless. On the other hand, if we do no works of service, our religion becomes dead (James 2:17). Let each of us seek God's guidance concerning how much time we should spend in service and how much time we should spend in prayer and worship.

However, let us not forget what Jesus said to Martha: "**. . . only one thing is needed**" (verse 42). That thing is spiritual fellowship with Christ. **If a man remains in me and I in him, he will bear much fruit; apart from me you can do nothing** (John 15:5). Mary knew this; she had chosen **what is better**. Fellowship with Christ will not end with our death, but our service will. Mary's fellowship with Christ **will not be taken away from her**. Nothing **will be able to separate us from the love of God that is in Christ Jesus** (Romans 8:38–39).

It was not what Martha and Mary were actually doing that was important to Christ; it was their attitudes. Martha had the wrong attitude, and Mary, the right one. If Martha had had the right attitude, she could have enjoyed fellowship with Christ in the midst of her duties. On the other hand, Mary could have been sitting at Jesus' feet for the wrong reason—such as laziness. It is not what we do that is most important; it is why we do it. Martha was rebuked for her worldly anxiety, not for her serving. Mary was commended for her love for Jesus, not for her sitting. Let us all remember that there is **only one thing needed** no matter what we are doing: fellowship with Christ. That can never be taken away from us.

CHAPTER 11

Jesus' Teaching on Prayer (11:1–4)
(Matthew 6:9–13)

1–4 See Matthew 6:9–13 and comment.

Persistent Prayer (11:5–8)

5–8 Jesus here tells a parable about how men should pray. They should pray with **persistence** (verse 8).

In the parable, the friend at first refuses the request of the first man. Yet in the end he gives the bread because of the first man's persistence. Men grant us our requests because they are displeased with our persistence. However, God gives us our requests because He is pleased with our persistence.

According to this parable, we must go to God as to a friend. We must go to Him with the expectation that He will grant our request. We must go to Him **with confidence** (Hebrews 4:16).

Notice that the first man is not making a request for himself, but for another man, a guest, who has suddenly come. The request is not a selfish request. God is more ready to hear us when we request things for the sake of others or for the sake of Christ. God greatly desires to give us blessings; but even more, He desires to bless others through us, through our prayers.

Is there someone you are praying for? Is there someone you want to bring to Christ? Do you have a neighbor who is in need of spiritual bread? Ask. Ask even at midnight. Ask with persistence and confidence. If a human friend will rise at midnight and give you bread, how much more will God rise and give you what you request! (see Matthew 7:11; Luke 11:13 and comment). God may not answer immediately, but He surely will answer if we continue to pray.

Let us ask ourselves: Are we willing to get up at midnight for a friend in need? If we are willing, God will also be willing to answer our request.

Ask, Seek, Knock (11:9–13)
(Matthew 7:7–11)

9–13 See Matthew 7:7–11 and comment.

Jesus and Beelzebub (11:14–28)
(Matthew 12:22–30,43–45; Mark 3:20–27)

14–23 See Mark 3:20–27 and comment.
24–26 See Matthew 12:43–45 and comment.
27–28 A woman, having heard Jesus' teaching, cried out, "**Blessed is the mother who gave you birth**." She wished that she could have had a son like Jesus.

But Jesus answers that she does not need to be His mother in order to be blessed. Anyone who obeys God's word will also be blessed, just as Jesus' own mother was blessed (see Mark 3:33–35 and comment).

The Sign of Jonah (11:29–32)
(Matthew 12:38–45; Mark 8:11–12)

29–32 See Matthew 12:38–45; Mark 8:11–12 and comments.

The Lamp of the Body (11:33–36)
(Matthew 5:15; 6:22–23; Mark 4:21; Luke 8:16)

33 See Matthew 5:15; Mark 4:21 and comments.
34–36 See Matthew 6:22–23 and comment.

Six Woes (11:37–54)
(Matthew 23:4,23–26,29–31,34–38)

37–38 See Mark 7:1–5 and comment.
39 See Matthew 23:25–26 and comment.
40 Men are like cups. God made not only the outside of the cup, but the inside also. He made both the outside of the body and the inside, the heart. What use is it to keep the outside clean if the inside remains dirty? It is as if we offered a cup to God which was clean outside, but inside was full of filth.
41 The inside of the cup is our heart, our love. It can also mean our possessions. Christ tells us to give our love to the poor, to share our possessions with them. Then we shall be truly clean. If the inside of our cup is clean—that is, if our heart is generous, if our possessions are shared with the poor—then our whole life, together with our possessions, will be holy in God's sight (see Titus 1:15).
42 See Matthew 23:23–24 and comment.
43 See Mark 12:38–39 and comment.
44 The Jews believed that to touch a grave made one unclean (Numbers 19:16). Therefore, the Jews whitewashed graves so that they could be easily seen. Otherwise a Jew might walk over a grave without knowing it and thereby become unclean.

The Pharisees had become like **unmarked**, or unwhitewashed graves. Men, without knowing it, were becoming impure through the false teaching and bad example of the Pharisees.
45 The **experts in the law** felt insulted, because they too taught the same things the Pharisees taught. Thus, in verse 46, Jesus begins to rebuke the experts in the law.
46 See Matthew 23:4 and comment.
47–48 The Jews of Jesus' time built tombs for the prophets whom their ancestors had killed. They pretended to give honor to the prophets but, in fact, in their hearts they were just like their fathers. In a way, by building tombs for the murdered prophets, they showed their approval of what their fathers had done (see Matthew 23:29–32 and comment).
49–51 See Matthew 23:34–36 and comment.
52 The experts of the law had **taken away the key of knowledge**—that is, the knowledge of Christ, the knowledge of salvation. The key to salvation is faith in Christ. The experts in the law falsely taught that man is saved by works alone. They denied that Christ was the Messiah, the Savior of the world. Thus, by their false teaching, they hid the true key to salvation from men. They refused to believe in Christ themselves and, what was worse, they prevented others from believing in Him too (see Matthew 23:13 and comment).
53–54 Naturally, the Pharisees and experts in the law were angry at what Jesus had said. Therefore, they tried **to catch him in something he might say**, so that they could bring charges against Him. Their desire was to kill Him (see Mark 3;6; 11:18; 12:12–13 and comments).

CHAPTER 12

Warnings and Encouragements (12:1–12)
(Matthew 10:19–20,26–33; 12:31–32; Mark 3:28–29; 4:22; 13:11)

1 See Mark 8:15 and comment.
2–3 See Matthew 10:26–27; Mark 4:22 and comments.
4–9 See Matthew 10:28–33 and comment.
10 See Mark 3:28–29 and comment.
11–12 See Mark 13:11 and comment.

The Parable of the Rich Fool (12:13–21)

13 Some of the common people regarded Jesus as a great teacher and prophet. Therefore, one of them asked Jesus to settle a dispute with his brother over their inheritance. The man wanted his share of the inheritance, but his brother would not give it.

14 Jesus refused the man's request. Jesus was not an ordinary judge sitting in a court. He had not come to earth to settle disputes like this. He was a judge of spiritual matters. Man should not come to Christ thinking to gain some worldly benefit for himself. Christ's kingdom is not of this world[26] (John 18:36).

15 Furthermore, Jesus knew the man's heart. He had asked for his share of the inheritance because he coveted possessions. He was greedy. To "covet" doesn't only mean to desire someone else's property. It also means to desire to possess more than we have. To covet means to love something. And the New Testament teaches that we should love nothing that belongs to this world (see Matthew 6:19–21; 1 John 2:15).

"A **man's life does not consist in the abundance of his possessions,**" said Jesus. Possessions will never give us eternal life. Possessions will not even give us joy and peace in this life. They give anxiety instead. In fact, the more possessions we store up for ourselves, the more we will become spiritually poor. We will rely on our possessions instead of on God. We will soon stop trusting God altogether. And when that happens, we will lose our soul (see Matthew 6:24; Mark 8:35–37; 10:21–25; 1 Timothy 6:6–10 and comments).

16–21 Then Jesus told this parable of a man who stored up riches for himself. The man thought he was secure. But God came to him and said, "**This very night your life will be demanded from you**. This night you will die. What, then, will be the benefit of all your wealth?" (Job 27:8).

We come into the world naked, and naked we shall leave (Job 1:21). We shall not get to take our worldly wealth with us when we die (1 Timothy 6:7). The man who does not store up eternal treasure in heaven is a fool indeed. Why take the risk of losing our eternal inheritance just to get some earthly treasure that will last only a few years?

Do Not Worry (12:22–34)
(Matthew 6:19–21,25–33)

22–32 See Matthew 6:25–33 and comment.

33–34 See Matthew 6:19–21 and comment.

Watchfulness (12:35–48)
(Matthew 24:43–51)

35–37 Jesus here gives a short parable about His second coming that is similar to the parable of the ten virgins in Matthew's Gospel (see Matthew 25:1–13 and comment). Instead of a bridegroom and virgins, this parable is about a master and his servants, but the teaching is the same. In this parable the master will not only commend his servants for their watchfulness; he will, in fact, serve them as if they were the master and he the servant. Christ said, "**. . . the Son of Man did not come to be served, but to serve**" (Mark 10:45). If we watch, and are ready to open the door of our hearts to Christ, then He will serve us spiritual food and drink and every spiritual blessing (John 4:13; 6:27,51; Ephesians 1:3; Revelation 3:20).

38 Therefore, watch and remain ready. Jesus may come at any time (see Mark 13:35–37 and comment).

39–40 See Matthew 24:43–44 and comment.

41 Peter asked Jesus if He was telling this parable only for the disciples or for unbelievers also.

Jesus didn't answer Peter's question directly. Instead, He told a second parable (verses 42–46). But the next parable was also about servants and their master. Therefore, it was about disciples, especially those who were to be leaders in the church. This, then, served as the answer

---

[26] Jesus is not indifferent to the injustice and inequality found in this world. He will one day judge those who cheat their brother or exploit the poor. However, Jesus' primary reason for coming to earth was not to redress grievances or right wrongs. His primary reason for coming was to show men the way to the kingdom of heaven.

to Peter's question: The first parable about watchfulness (the one Peter asked about) was for believers—disciples—not for unbelievers.

42–46 See Matthew 24:45–51 and comment.

47–48 In these verses Jesus teaches an important spiritual truth: those who sin in ignorance will receive a small punishment, but those who commit the same sin knowingly will receive a great punishment. In fact, according to the Old Testament law, there was no forgiveness for sins committed knowingly (Numbers 15:27–31).

From this we can understand that in hell there are different degrees of punishment. Those who have heard the Gospel of Christ but have deliberately rejected it will receive the greater punishment (see verse 49 and comment). Those who have never heard the Gospel will receive a lesser punishment.[27]

In the same way, there will be different rewards in heaven. Those who have served Christ well and faithfully will receive a greater reward. Those who have not used Christ's gifts well and faithfully will receive a lesser reward (see Matthew 16:27; 2 Corinthians 5:10).

Then Jesus said, "**From everyone who has been given much, much will be demanded**" (verse 48). God will judge and reward each of us according to what spiritual knowledge and gifts we have been given. In the parable of the talents, one man was given five talents; therefore, he was expected to earn five talents more (Matthew 25:19–21). But the man to whom only two talents had been given was only expected to earn two talents more (Matthew 25:22–23). Notice that both these men received the same reward. They received the same reward because according to the talents each had been given they each had done the same thing—they each had doubled their talents.

In the parable of the ten minas, Jesus taught this same truth, but in a different way (see Luke 19:11–26). In the parable of the minas, the gifts were the same. All the men received one mina. But each man then used his mina differently; some used it better than others. One made ten minas more (Luke 19:16). Another made five minas more (Luke 19:18). These men then received different rewards (Luke 19:17,19). All of the men had received **much**, but not all gave back **much**. Those who did not give back **much** received a lesser reward.

Friends, let us not misuse our gifts. Let us not waste what God has given us. He has given us spiritual gifts and He has given us earthly gifts—health, education, wealth. Let us take care that we use all these gifts in His service to the fullest extent we can.

From these verses there is another thing we can learn. Those who are Christians cannot live in the manner of non-Christians; they must live better lives. Those who have been given the Holy Spirit cannot live like those who do not have the Holy Spirit; they must live better, that is, more holy lives. Those who have been given much of the Spirit must lead better lives than those who have been given but little of the Spirit. Those who are mature Christians must live better lives than those who are new, immature Christians. That which is a small sin for a new Christian may be a big sin for an older Christian. Those who have been given responsibility will be judged with greater severity than those who have not (see James 3:1). **From everyone who has been given much, much will be demanded; and from the one who has been entrusted with much, much more will be asked.**

Not Peace But Division (12:49–59)
(Matthew 5:23–26; 10:34–36; 16:1–4; Mark 8:11–13)

49 **I have come to bring fire on the earth.** Jesus' coming divides people into

[27] Even a person who has never heard of Christ will still be punished in the next life, because all men have sinned against God in some way. All men know to some extent what God's will is. Therefore, all men are without excuse (see Romans 1:18–20; 3:10–12 and comments).

two groups: those who reject Him and those who accept Him. For those who reject Him, the **fire** is the fire of judgment. It is, in a sense, the fire of hell. But for those who accept Christ, the **fire** is the fire of purification, of strengthening (see 1 Peter 1:6–7). It is the fire of the Holy Spirit (see Matthew 3:11; Mark 1:8 and comment).

Christ said, "**How I wish it were already kindled.**" He wished that His Gospel would spread like "fire." He wished His work of salvation would spread quickly all over the world. When a fire is kindled, it spreads by itself. The fire had to be kindled before Christ died; otherwise, it might go out. The fire was soon kindled in the hearts of His disciples, and it has been burning in the hearts of each generation of disciples ever since.

50 Christ had a **baptism** to undergo. Here "baptism" means suffering and death (see Mark 10:38 and comment). Before the fire of the Holy Spirit could come, Christ first had to suffer and die. He longed that this "baptism" might be finished quickly.

51–53 See Matthew 10:34–36 and comment.

54–56 See Mark 8:11–13 and comment.

57–59 See Matthew 5:23–26 and comment.

CHAPTER 13

Repent or Perish (13:1–9)

1 In Luke 12:49–59, Jesus had been teaching the people about the signs of the end of the world. In this section, Jesus urges men and women to repent before it is too late.

Some time earlier some Jews from Galilee had been sacrificing at the temple in Jerusalem, and Pilate, the Roman governor of Judea, had ordered them to be killed. He had **mixed** their blood with their sacrifices. It is not known why Pilate did this. Pilate was known to be a very cruel man.

2–3 This incident was reported to Jesus. Most Jews in Jesus' time supposed that if such a calamity befell a person it meant that he was very sinful and that the calamity was a punishment from God. But Jesus said that this was not so.[28] These Galileans were no worse sinners that any other Jews. Indeed, the calamity that fell on those Galileans was a warning to all other Jews that if they did not repent, the same kind of destruction would fall on them. (We know now that the Jews did not repent, and that forty years later all those living in Jerusalem were killed by the Roman army.)

4–5 Then Jesus Himself gave the example of another catastrophe that killed eighteen people: a tower fell on them. But those eighteen people were no more guilty in God's sight than all the other unbelieving Jews in Jerusalem. Those other Jews, too, would be destroyed.

6–7 But God was giving the Jewish nation more time to repent. He was delaying the destruction that was about to fall on them. To show this, Jesus told a parable about a man who planted a fig tree. The man represents God, and the fig tree represents the Jewish nation.[29] Like the barren fig tree in the parable, the Jewish nation had not borne any fruit of repentance and righteousness.

Therefore, the man said to the gardener, "**Cut it down**" (see Matthew

---

[28] It is also true that sometimes calamities come on people because they have sinned. But often, calamities are not caused by sin. Calamities fall on men for different reasons. For some examples of these reasons, see John 9:1–3; James 1:2-3; 1 Peter 1:6–7; 4:12–13 and comments. We cannot judge a man's sins by the suffering that comes upon him.

[29] The fig tree was often used as a sign of the Jewish nation (Hosea 9:10; Joel 1:7; Mark 11:12–14,21).

3:10; 7:19). The tree was not only doing no good; it was doing harm. It was preventing other things from growing, because it was using up the soil.

It is the same with men as it is with trees. Men who do not do good usually do harm by their bad example. Men either do good—or they do harm.

8–9 But the gardener said to the man, "Give the tree more time. Give it one more year." Some Bible scholars think that the gardener represents Christ; in which case, Christ was asking the Father to delay the punishment of the Jewish nation in order to give them time to repent.

In the same way, God is today showing mercy to men. He is giving all men and women more time to repent. But He will not delay forever (see 2 Peter 3:3–4,9–10 and comment). Our warning to all men today is the same as it was in Jesus' time: Repent—there is not much time left. When Christ comes again, it will then be too late.

We too, like the gardener, can pray to God that men might have more time to repent. We are not commanded to pray that Christ come quickly—only that He come (Revelation 22:20).

But notice what the gardener must do in the meantime. He must cultivate and fertilize the barren tree. That is, we must not only pray that men might have more time to repent, but we must at the same time share with them the Gospel of Christ and actively encourage them to repent.

A Crippled Woman Healed on the Sabbath (13:10–17)

10–14 This story of Jesus healing the crippled woman on the Sabbath is similar to His healing of the man with the withered hand (see Mark 3:1–3 and comment). This woman was a **daughter of Abraham** (verse 16), that is, a Jew, and she had been crippled by a spirit for eighteen years. Satan had caused her deformity.[30]

15–17 When the Jews objected to His healing the woman on the Sabbath, Jesus called them **hypocrites**. If a sheep fell into a pit on the Sabbath, they would pull it out. Are sheep and other animals more valuable than humans? (see Matthew 12:11–12; Mark 3:4–6; Luke 14:1–6 and comments). If it is okay to untie or loose animals on the Sabbath so that they might drink, then surely it is also okay on the Sabbath to loose a sick person from Satan's bonds.

The Parables of the Mustard Seed and the Yeast (13:18–21)
(Matthew 13:31–33; Mark 4:30–32)

18–19 See Mark 4:30–32 and comment.

20–21 See Matthew 13:33 and comment.

The Narrow Door (13:22–30)

22–23 Although many people believed that Jesus was a prophet and a miracle worker, not many believed that He was the Savior, the Messiah. Most people did not repent and believe in Him. Someone, having noticed that only a few people followed Him, asked, "**Lord, are only a few people going to be saved?**"[31]

24 Jesus didn't answer the question directly. Instead He said, "**Make every effort to enter through the narrow door, because many . . . will try to enter and will not be able to**. Don't ask how many are going to be saved. Ask only if you yourself are going to be saved. Before you worry about others, make sure that you yourself have entered through the **narrow door** to heaven" (see Matthew 7:13–14 and comment).

25 Jesus' meaning is this: To get to heaven we must all go through the "narrow door." It is not easy to go

---

[30] It can be said that all illness is caused by Satan. Ever since Adam and Eve sinned in the Garden of Eden, mankind has been under the curse of death and sickness. This is Satan's work (Genesis 3:1–6,17–19).

[31] The Jews thought that all Jews would be saved, but Jesus taught that only those who believed in Him would be saved.

through. We must make **every effort** to go through. And we must not delay. Once the door is shut, it will be too late to enter. We must go through the door while it is still open. Because the time will come when Jesus will return and shut the door. Then we will have lost our chance (see Matthew 25:6–13 and comment).

Until Jesus comes again, there is still opportunity for all men to enter the narrow door. It is open to all who repent and believe. . . . **knock and the door shall be opened to you** (Matthew 7:7). Only do not delay. Make every effort to enter while there is still time.

When Jesus comes again in power and glory, many will at that time try to get through the door. They will realize that He is indeed the Savior, the Son of God. But it will be too late. He will answer: "**I don't know you.**"

26–27 People at that time will say to Jesus, "**We ate and drank with you**. We went to church. We heard your word. We called out to you, '**Lord, Lord**' " (see Matthew 7:21–23 and comment). At that time the Jews of Jesus' time will also say: "We are Jews just like you. We are Abraham's descendants. We are God's chosen people. Surely we have a place in the kingdom of heaven." But Jesus will say to all of them, "You did not truly believe in me. **I don't know you**."

28–30 Then Jesus said to the Jews who were standing around listening, "You will weep on that day. Because you did not believe, people **from the east and west and north and south**—that is, the Gentiles—will be given your place in the **kingdom of God** (see Matthew 8:11–12 and comment). You thought you were **first**; but in the end you will be **last**. You thought you were saved; but in the end you will be lost" (see Mark 10:31 and comment).

Jesus' Sorrow for Jerusalem (13:31–35)

31 While Jesus was still in Galilee, some Pharisees warned Him to leave the district, because King Herod, the ruler of Galilee, wanted to kill Him.

32 But Jesus despised Herod. Herod had murdered John the Baptist. He had power and he was crafty, like a **fox**. But he had no power to stop Jesus. Jesus had His work to do before He died. "**Today and tomorrow**—that is, in the time remaining—I will work, **and on the third day I will reach my goal**." Jesus' goal was to die and to be resurrected. It was through His death that His goal of saving men from their sins would be completed (see Mark 10:45 and comment).

33 No threat stopped Jesus from doing God's will. He knew He must be killed, but it would not be in Galilee by Herod. Prophets were killed in Jerusalem. It was only the Sanhedrin in Jerusalem that could condemn prophets to death. And Jerusalem was not under Herod's jurisdiction.

34–35 See Matthew 23:37–39 and comment.

CHAPTER 14

Jesus Heals a Man on the Sabbath (14:1–6)

1 Wherever Jesus went, He was **carefully watched**. His enemies among the Pharisees were hoping He would do something for which they could condemn Him to death. To heal a person on the Sabbath was considered by the Jews to be a violation of the Jewish law (see Mark 3:1–3 and comment).

2 While eating at the house of a prominent Pharisee on the Sabbath, a man with dropsy was brought to Jesus. The Pharisees watched to see what Jesus would do.

3 But Jesus first asked the Pharisees and experts in the law, "**Is it lawful to heal on the Sabbath or not?**" If they answered "Yes," they would have no charge to make against Jesus. If they said "No," the people would be angry with them, because of their lack of compassion for the sick man. So they **remained silent**.

4–6 Jesus healed the man with dropsy. The Jews considered it lawful to pull an animal out of a well on the Sabbath. Therefore, surely it was right in God's eyes to deliver a man from his misery on the Sabbath (see Matthew 12:10–12; Mark 3:4–6; Luke 13:15–17 and comments).

Teaching on Humility (14:7–14)

7 While Jesus was at the Pharisee's house, other guests arrived. As they came in, they chose the best seats to sit on (see Mark 12:38–39). Seeing their pride and desire to be exalted before men, Jesus told them a parable.

8–10 The parable is about being invited to a wedding feast. At wedding feasts, some seats are reserved for important people; other seats are for less important people. Usually the most important guest arrives last. If an unimportant guest were to sit down in an important guest's seat, the host of the feast would have to ask that person to move to a less honored seat. What an embarrassment! It is better to take a lower seat first (Proverbs 25:6–7).

Jesus does not mean we should show false humility. Some people deliberately choose a lower seat, knowing that they will be asked to move to a higher seat. They pretend to be humble, but they really seek to be honored. Such people put on the appearance of humility, but really they are proud.

The parable also has a spiritual meaning. God has prepared a "wedding feast" and given each guest an assigned seat. When we come before Him, let us not claim a good seat. He knows our hearts. He knows which seat we are worthy to sit in. Let us humble ourselves before Him and take the lowest seat. Because God will humble those who try to exalt themselves (verse 11).

11 See Matthew 23:12; 1 Peter 5:5–6 and comments.

12 As Jesus sat at the house of the prominent Pharisee (verse 1), He saw that the host had invited only his rich friends and relatives. It was costly to feed all those guests, but the host would suffer no loss in the end, because all those guests would later on invite him to their homes, and he would be **repaid**.

Jesus said to the Pharisee, "**. . . do not invite your friends, your brothers or relatives, or your rich neighbors**." Jesus' meaning was this: Do not invite only such guests; invite also those who cannot pay you back.

13–14 Jesus knew that the Pharisee had invited only those guests who could pay him back in some way. His purpose in inviting people was to gain some favor or advantage. But Jesus said to him, "If you want to receive the blessing of God, invite those who cannot repay you. If you do, God Himself will repay you **at the resurrection of the righteous**,[32] that is, in heaven."

Jesus' meaning is this: If we do things only to be paid back or rewarded in this life, we will have received our reward; we shall receive no reward from God in heaven (see Matthew 6:1–4 and comment). It is much better to receive a reward from God than from man. The rewards of this earth end, but the rewards from God last forever.

Every good work we do is recorded in heaven. We shall be rewarded for it (Matthew 16:27). When we invite those who are **poor, crippled, lame and blind**, we are inviting Christ Himself (Matthew 25:40). And He will not leave us unrewarded.

It is necessary to mention two further things. First, it is not wrong to invite rich friends and neighbors. The rich also need salvation; they need love. But we must invite them because of our love for them, not for what we can gain from them.

---

[32] All the dead, whether righteous or unrighteous, will be resurrected at the end of the world and receive a new body (see John 5:28–29; Acts 24:15; Romans 8:23 and comments). The resurrection of the righteous will be in heaven. For further discussion, see Word List: Resurrection.

Second, we must not invite poor people only because we hope to get a reward in heaven. That is selfish. We must invite them because we love them. We must remember how Christ invited us, called us, forgave us, loved us; and we must do likewise to the least of these His brothers. **Dear friends, since God so loved us, we ought also to love one another** (1 John 4:11).

The Parable of the Great Banquet (14:15–24)

15 The Jews often compared the kingdom of God with a great and joyful banquet (Matthew 22:1–2). After Jesus had finished speaking about whom one should invite to dinner (verses 12–13), one of those listening said spontaneously, "Blessed is the man who is invited to God's feast." His meaning was: We Jews are blessed because it is only we who will be invited to that feast.

16–17 To answer the man, Jesus told another parable. He told it in order to show the Jews that they were about to lose their places at God's banquet (see Matthew 22:1–14 and comment).

A certain man . . . invited many guests. The **man** is God, and the **guests** are the Jews. God had first invited the Jews through the prophets of the Old Testament. Then He called them a final time. He sent His **servant**, Christ, to tell the Jews that the banquet was now ready to begin.

18–20 But all the invited guests said they could not come. They all gave different reasons. The reasons were true, not false. But they were not good reasons. In each case, the guests could have come if they had wanted to. But instead, they put other things before God's invitation.

21–23 Therefore, since the Jews would not come to the banquet, since they would not listen to the final call of the servant, Christ, God invited the Gentiles in their place (see Matthew 21:43). He invited them "**so that my house will be full**" (verse 23). None are excluded from God's banquet except those who refuse to come.

24 Then Jesus said to the Jews who were listening to the parable, "**I tell you, not one of those men who were invited will get a taste of my banquet.**" The banquet was Jesus' banquet. It was in His honor. It was His wedding banquet (see Revelation 19:7–9 and comment). But the Jews had lost their chance to taste it.

The Jew who had first said, "**Blessed is the man who will eat at the feast in the kingdom of God**" (verse 15) was right. But he was at that very moment refusing the invitation. He was losing the chance to eat at that feast because he was rejecting Jesus.

Although Jesus first told this parable to the Jews at the Pharisee's house, we must remember that this parable is written for us also. It is written for everyone, Jew or Gentile, who has been invited by Christ to His banquet. All who hear Christ's words are invited. Christ is saying to us today: "Come to my banquet." What is our answer? Are we also, like the Jews, putting other things first? If we are, we too will lose our chance to eat at the banquet. Friends, let us leave our worldly concerns. Let us leave our fields, our oxen, our wives (see Matthew 10:37; Mark 10:29–31 and comments). We can take care of them another day. Christ calls us now. What will our answer be?

No man can enter heaven unless God invites him. But man can refuse the invitation. No man can save himself; but man can condemn himself. Christ does not at first reject us; it is we who reject Christ. Jesus said, "**. . . whoever comes to me I will never drive away**" (John 6:37). **Whoever believes in the Son has eternal life, but whoever rejects the Son will not see life, for God's wrath remains on him** (John 3:36).

As God sent Christ into the world to invite men and women to His banquet, so Christ sends us into the world to invite still others to His banquet (John 17:18). When was the last time we invited someone to Christ's banquet?

The Cost of Being a Disciple (14:25–35)

(Matthew 5:13; 10:37; 16:24; Mark 8:34; 9:50)

25–26 See Matthew 10:37; John 12:25 and comments.

27 See Mark 8:34 and comment.

28–30 Jesus has invited us to His banquet. He has called us to follow Him. But He also gives us a warning. He reminds us that it is not easy to be a disciple. Many people quickly say to Jesus, "I will follow you," but they don't know what they are saying (see Matthew 8:19–20; Luke 9:57–58 and comment). They have not taken account of the difficulty and hardship of following Christ.

Jesus here gives two examples to show that we must first count the cost of being a disciple before jumping up to follow Jesus. The first example is of a man building a tower. Before he begins, he must make sure he can pay for it. Because if he begins the job, he must complete it. Otherwise, he will be ridiculed. In the same way, once we start following Jesus, there is no stopping; there is no turning back (see Matthew 8:21–22; Luke 9:61–62 and comment).

31–32 The second example is of a king about to go to war. Before he attacks, he must count his own soldiers and the enemy's soldiers. If he doesn't have enough soldiers to win the battle, he had better not attack!

So it is with Christ's disciples. When we follow Christ, we are entering into battle against sin, against temptation, against Satan. Let us not go into battle with too few soldiers! Also, let us be ready to endure the hardships of battle; otherwise, we shall be defeated.

33 To be a disciple of Christ, we must not only count the cost; we must also pay it. We must be prepared happily to give everything up for Christ's sake: wealth, comfort, family, even life itself. Otherwise, we cannot be Christ's disciples (see Matthew 10:37; Mark 8:34; Luke 14:26–27).

34–35 See Matthew 5:13; Mark 9:50 and comments.

CHAPTER 15

The Parable of the Lost Sheep (15:1–7)

(Matthew 18:12–14)

1 As Jesus traveled and taught, He brought hope and forgiveness to many who had gone astray, who had fallen into bondage to sin. "Repent, be baptized, and believe in me, and you will be saved," He said to them (see Acts 2:38 and comment). And thus many **tax collectors and "sinners"** gathered to hear Him wherever He went (see Mark 2:15 and comment).

2 But the Pharisees and teachers of the law murmured against Jesus, because He associated with such sinners (see Mark 2:16–17 and comment). Therefore, Jesus told them three parables to show why He welcomed sinners to come to Him: the parable of the lost sheep (verses 3–7), the parable of the lost coin (verses 8–10), and the parable of the lost son (verses 11–32).

3–7 See Matthew 18:12–14 and comment.

The Parable of the Lost Coin (15:8–10)

8–10 This parable gives the same teaching as the parable of the lost sheep (verses 3–7). It applies to both believers who have lost the way and to nonbelievers who have not yet found the way.

These two parables teach that God is a loving Father who seeks those who are lost. No other religion in the world teaches about a God who seeks men. God sent His own Son Christ to earth to seek us (Luke 19:10). Christ was like a shepherd, who gave His life to find the lost sheep (John 10:11). God shed the blood of His own Son in order to find us and save us (Mark 10:45; 14:24; Ephesians 2:13). We were **bought at a price**, the price of Christ's blood (1 Corinthians 6:20). If God was willing to pay that high a price, think how valuable each man and woman must be in His sight! This is why there is such rejoicing in heaven over each sinner who repents (verse 7).

The Parable of the Lost Son (15:11–32)

11–16 Jesus then told a third parable about a younger son who took his inheritance and went and spent it in **wild living** in a foreign country. The son thought to himself, "Now I will be free; I will do what I please. No longer will I have to obey my father."

Here we see man's basic sin against God: disobedience and rebellion. Man wants to do what he pleases, and so he leaves God. He goes to a **distant country** and spends his life in sin.

But what happened to that younger son? All the blessing, all the inheritance his father had given him was wasted, lost. He thought he was gaining his freedom, but instead he lost it. He became a slave to sin. Life with his father was free and happy compared to living with pigs!

17 Then the younger son **came to his senses**. He realized how unhappy his situation was and how foolish he had been. This realization of our bad state is the first step leading to repentance.

18–19 Then the son confessed his sin: "**I have sinned against heaven**." Then he determined to turn from his sin, and return to his father. The son's repentance was now complete: he realized his sin, he confessed his sin, and he turned from his sin. True repentance must include these three things.

True repentance also includes humility. The son said, "**I am no longer worthy to be called your son**; I will be a hired servant" (verse 19).

Notice that the son prepared exactly what he would say to his father. If we have sinned against God or another man and desire to repent of that sin, it is well to prepare what we shall say. Let us not make excuses. Let us not try to hide our sin. Let us honestly confess our guilt. Only then will we receive forgiveness (see Psalm 32:5; 1 John 1:9 and comment). We cannot demand forgiveness; forgiveness comes from the grace and mercy of the one against whom we have sinned.

Notice that the son confessed, "**I have sinned against heaven and against you**." Whenever we sin against another person, we also sin against God. All sins are, in fact, against God.

20 The father had been waiting and watching for his lost son. He had never given up hope. He had never stopped loving his son, even though his son had stopped loving him. And while the son was **still a long way off, his father saw him, and was filled with compassion for him.**

21–24 Before the son could even finish his prepared confession of sin, his father had forgiven him and reinstated him to full sonship. The son didn't deserve to be called his son; but the father did not treat his son according to what he deserved, but according to love and grace. This is how God treats all who truly repent.

Just as the shepherd rejoiced when he found the lost sheep (verse 6), so the father rejoiced when he had found his lost son. For his son was dead, and was now alive again (Ephesians 2:1).

See from this parable the love and mercy of God to all who come to Him with repentant hearts. He will not rebuke and punish us. He will accept us as if we had never sinned. He will remember our sins no more (Isaiah 1:18; 43:25).

25–30 When the older brother heard that his younger brother was being honored, **he became angry** (verse 28). He was jealous. He said to his father, "... **you never even gave me a young goat ...** [but] **you kill the fattened calf for him**" (verses 29–30).

The older son was like the Pharisees. The Pharisees were angry with Jesus because He welcomed sinners to associate with Him. They were angry when He said that repentant sinners would take part in the heavenly banquet. The Jews considered themselves to be the rightful heirs; why should these sinners, these Gentiles, share in their inheritance.

Like the Pharisees, the older brother considered himself righteous. "**All these years I've ... never disobeyed your orders,**" he said. But now he was refusing to forgive and to love his brother. He was angry with his father. His heart was cold. It was now he who was the sinner, who was far from God.

From this we must understand that

envy is a great sin in God's eyes (Romans 13:13; 1 Corinthians 3:3; 2 Corinthians 12:20; Galatians 5:21; James 3:14–16). He who envies his brother is unhappy with his brother's good fortune. He who envies does not love his brother. Love does not envy (1 Corinthians 13:4). Thus, when we envy our brother, we are sinning against him.

31–32 The father loved his older son also. He reminded the older son that "**everything I have is yours**." The older son had lost nothing because of his brother's return. The father's love was great enough for both sons. God's grace is great enough for everyone. If others share with us in the warmth and light of the sunshine, we do not thereby get less warmth and light. God's grace is infinite. God's inheritance is infinite. We have no reason to be envious.

The father also explained to the older son why he was celebrating. It was not to give the younger son special honor above the older son. It was to express joy that the younger son had returned.

Notice again the father's patience and kindness toward his older son. The father tried to reason with him. So likewise should all in authority try to reason gently with those under them. It is better to lead by gentle persuasion than by force (see Ephesians 6:4,9 and comment).

From this parable, we see the difference between Christianity and all other religions. Christianity is a religion of grace, mercy, and love. We do not earn our forgiveness. God forgives us freely and completely. All we must do is to repent and receive the forgiveness of Christ through faith.

All other religions are represented by the older brother. The older brother says: "Sinners should not be freely forgiven. They must first earn forgiveness. They must deserve it."

But this is false teaching. No one deserves to receive anything from God. None of us can say that we have obeyed God in everything. We all need to cast ourselves on God's mercy. Everyone of us is a "lost son"—even the older brother!

CHAPTER 16

The Parable of the Shrewd Manager (16:1–9)

1–7 Jesus in this parable describes a dishonest manager who is about to lose his job. Because the manager had been accused of **wasting** his master's possessions, the master had determined to remove him from his position (verse 2).

Before the manager was fired, however, he did a shrewd thing. He called his master's debtors in and lessened their debts. He thought to himself, "Because I have done them this favor, they will then help me when I have lost my job." In this way, the manager cheated his master in order to benefit himself.

8 **The master commended the dishonest manager because he had acted shrewdly**. The master didn't commend him for his dishonesty, but for his shrewdness.

One meaning of the parable is this: Men should act wisely and shrewdly—but not dishonestly. People **of the light**, that is, Christians, often are not wise and shrewd in their dealings with others. They sometimes do not make friends quickly. They sometimes offend people unnecessarily. They do not make suitable preparation for their future. They fall easily into error. Let them be "shrewd," says Christ. Jesus said that we should be **as shrewd as snakes**; but He also said that we should be **as innocent as doves** (see Matthew 10:16 and comment).

The parable can also mean that Christians should be as wise and shrewd in getting spiritual benefit as the worldly man is in getting worldly benefit.

9 Then Jesus gave still another meaning of the parable. While we are in the world, we should use our position and wealth in a way that will gain us God's friendship. The dishonest manager used his position to gain worldly friends. We should be "shrewd" in gaining God's friendship. Because soon we will lose our position and wealth in this life. Therefore, we will need **friends** in heaven (God and His angels) who will **welcome** us into their **eternal dwellings**.

Some Bible scholars think that Jesus also meant that we should share our wealth with the poor here on earth. Then when the poor we have shared with go to heaven, they will be our **friends** there and testify before God in our favor. This also can be a meaning of the parable.[33]

The Proper Use of Wealth (16:10–18)

(Matthew 6:24; 19:9; Mark 10:11–12)

10 In this section Jesus gives us some principles concerning the use of our worldly wealth.

All worldly wealth belongs to God, and men are only stewards of it. The way a man uses a small amount of wealth will show how he will use a large amount. (The man who steals one dollar will steal a thousand if he gets the chance.) The man who is faithful with a few things will be put in charge of many things (Matthew 25:21).

11 God watches us. If we use our worldly gifts and riches wisely and honestly, He will give us spiritual gifts and riches too. If we misuse our gifts in this life, we shall receive nothing in the next life (see Mark 8:36 and comment).

12 If we are not honest in using the property of our master, to whom we must give account, we will not be entrusted with property of our own—that is, our own spiritual inheritance in heaven, which has been stored up for all those who remain faithful to God. If a man uses another's property irresponsibly, he will use his own property irresponsibly too. Therefore, God will withhold that man's inheritance.

13 See Matthew 6:24 and comment.

14 The Pharisees did not like Jesus' teaching about money, because they loved to store up money for themselves. The Pharisees were rich, and they considered their worldly riches to be a reward for being Jews. Jesus was poor; therefore, the Pharisees **sneered** at Him. In the Pharisees' mind, Jesus' poverty was proof that He was not a good Jew.

15 But Jesus, knowing this, rebuked the Pharisees. They tried to **justify** themselves in the eyes of men; that is, they tried to appear religious before men. But their hearts were filled with the love of money. Men respected the Pharisees for their wealth and outward piety, but God detests what men respect. God looks at the heart, and God did not like the greed He saw in the hearts of the Pharisees (1 Samuel 16:7).

It is a great mistake to place importance on the opinions of men. What men highly value is often detested by God, who sees all things as they really are. At the same time, those things which men despise, God often approves of (see 1 Corinthians 1:26–29 and comment).

16 When John the Baptist came, the Old Testament (or old covenant) between God and Israel ended, and the New Testament (or new covenant) began (see Hebrews 8:7–13 and comment). Until the time of John, only the **Law and the Prophets**, that is, the Old Testament, was proclaimed. But after John a new teaching began to be proclaimed—**the good news of the kingdom of God**, that is, the Gospel of Christ. Christ proclaimed that man is saved not by following any law but rather by God's grace through faith (see Ephesians 2:8–9 and comment).

As ordinary Jews and other people like sinners and tax collectors heard about this salvation by grace, they came to Jesus in great numbers. They wanted forgiveness and new life. They wanted to enter the kingdom of God. They, in a way, were **forcing** [their] **way into it** (see Matthew 11:12–13). And the Pharisees were not happy about this.

17 Therefore, the Pharisees and other Jewish leaders began to accuse Jesus and His disciples of breaking the old Jewish law (Mark 2:23–24; 3:1–5; 7:5). They said, "These Christians don't follow any

---

[33] The parables of Jesus can sometimes have more than one true meaning.

rules." But Jesus denied that. He did not reject or nullify the moral law of the Old Testament (see Matthew 5:17–19 and comment).

18 See Mark 10:11–12 and comment.

The Rich Man and Lazarus (16:19–31)

19–21 Here Jesus gives His most frightening warning to the rich Jewish leaders. And this warning is for all who live in comfort and ignore the poor at their door.

Jesus described two men, a rich Jew and a beggar. One lived in happiness and contentment, and the other lived in misery. One was praised by men; the other was despised by men. Only the dogs cared for Lazarus the beggar.

The rich man thought he was a religious man, a good Jew. Jesus doesn't say that he was a wicked man, or that he did evil. He was a good man in the world's eyes. He perhaps was a Pharisee, a leader of the people. He was respected by all.

22–24 However, what man respects, God detests (verse 15). God opposes the proud and exalts the humble (1 Peter 5:5). Therefore, when Lazarus died, the angels carried his spirit to heaven, **to Abraham's side**. But the rich man was cast into **hell**.[34]

The rich man was not cast into hell because he was rich. He was cast into hell because he loved his riches (1 Timothy 6:10). He did not use his riches to help the poor; he was unmerciful (see Matthew 25:41–46 and comment).

When the rich man reached hell, his mind was suddenly opened. At that moment he realized what a terrible mistake he had made. He had lived for his money, for his pride, for himself, instead of for God. That was his mistake.

The rich man asked for mercy from Abraham. He had shown no mercy while on earth; now in hell he asked for mercy. He called Abraham his father, because Abraham is the father of all Jews. He asked only that his tongue might be cooled with a drop of water.[35]

25–26 But there was no relief possible for the rich man. Between heaven and hell a **great chasm has been fixed**. No one can pass from one side to the other. The judgment of God is final. If a man does not care for God and for his neighbor in this life, God will not care for him in the next life, and he will be sent to hell for all eternity. The judgment of God cannot be overturned after it has been made. The rich man had received his consolation on earth, and now it was no more (Luke 6:24).

Therefore, friends, while there is still time before you die, make peace with God. Repent of your sins, and turn to Jesus. Because after death you will never have another chance.

Repent today. Don't wait until tomorrow. Because you may die tonight (see Luke 12:20). And if you do, you will spend eternity in hell.

Think how long eternity is. Men go to jail for one year, five years, twenty years, and they think that's a very long time. But eternity in hell is not like that. It never ends.

Let no one say, "I am not rich; therefore, this parable does not apply to me." Because it applies to anyone—rich or poor—who seeks possessions for himself, who does not help his neighbor, who is not **rich toward God** (Luke 12:21). Therefore, let each person ask himself: "What am I seeking? What kind of treasure am I storing up—spiritual treasure or earthly treasure? Am I serving God or am I, in fact, serving my possessions? Who is my master—God or money?" The

---

[34] In place of the word **hell**, some translations of the Bible say "Hades." "Hades" is the place where the spirits of the unsaved dead go to await the final judgment.

[35] We must remember that this is a parable. Therefore, it does not give a complete teaching about life after death. For example, the spirits of the dead do not have bodies, fingers, and tongues. Only after the general resurrection of the dead at the end of the world will the dead receive new bodies. The rich man's request that his tongue might be cooled is only meant to signify the torment he was experiencing.

poor man also makes money his "god." This parable is for everyone.

27–28 When the rich man saw that there was no hope, no means of finding relief, he thought of his family still living, his five brothers. He begged Abraham to let Lazarus go and warn them. He said, "Tell them what condition I am in. Tell them what hell is like, so that they might repent and not have to come to this terrible place."

29 Abraham replied, "They don't need any new warning. **They have Moses and the Prophets.**[36] Let them read and obey the Old Testament. If they don't believe the Old Testament, they are not going to believe Lazarus" (see John 5:46–47).

30 But the rich man said, "If someone comes from the dead, they will believe and repent."

31 But Abraham said, "If they have not believed already, they will not believe **even if someone rises from the dead.**" And it was true. Even though Christ rose from the dead, most of the Jews refused to believe. They said His body had been stolen!

This parable does not teach that all rich men go to hell and all poor men go to heaven. Some rich people get to heaven and many poor people do not. There is only one key to heaven for both rich and poor, and that key is faith. If the rich man had repented and believed, he would have had mercy on the poor man. He would have used his wealth to help his neighbor. And he would have gone to heaven.

In the same way, the beggar might not have gone to heaven. He might have been angry with God, bitter. He might have refused to believe. If so, he would have gone to hell.

Therefore, for both rich and poor, there is only one road to heaven. It is a **narrow** road, and **only a few find it** (Matthew 7:14). It is the road of repentance and faith in Christ.

CHAPTER 17

Sin, Faith, Duty (17:1–10)

(Matthew 17:20; 18:6–7,15,21–22; Mark 9:42)

1–2 See Mark 9:42 and comment.

3–4 See Matthew 18:15,21–22 and comment.

5–6 See Matthew 17:20; Mark 9:24–29 and comment.

7–8 Here Jesus teaches about the relationship between master and servant. A worldly master sends his servant out to plow or look after the animals. When the servant returns at the end of the day, he must prepare the master's meal. The master does not serve the servant. Even though the servant has worked all day and is tired, he must still keep on serving his master.

9 The master does not have to say "Thankyou" to the servant. The master doesn't owe the servant anything, because the servant is only doing his duty. The servant is obligated to serve his master constantly, and therefore, he doesn't deserve any special thanks or gratitude. A master never thanks a servant for obeying an order.

10 In the same way, we are Christ's servants. We are God's possession, God's slaves (see Romans 1:1 and comment). In Jesus' time, a slave had no rights. His master bought him. The slave had to do whatever his master ordered. So, too, we have been bought by Christ. He bought us with His own blood (see 1 Corinthians 6:20; 1 Peter 1:18–19 and comments).

Therefore, all day long throughout our

---

[36] Here the word **Moses** refers to the first five books of the Old Testament, which were written by Moses. Therefore, the expression, **Moses and the Prophets**, means the entire Old Testament. The Old Testament is also sometimes called the "Law and the Prophets" (verse 16).

whole lives we must do whatever Christ says. And when we have done **everything** we have been told to do, then we must say: "**We are unworthy servants; we have only done our duty.**"

What a deep teaching! Even if we obey Christ in **everything**, we ourselves are still **unworthy**. There is nothing we ourselves can do to make us "worthy" in God's sight. We can never be worthy of God's thanks. We can never be worthy to receive God's grace, God's salvation—even if we have done everything God has told us to do. If God gives us any blessing, it is never because we are worthy of it; it is only because of His mercy and grace.

One more question remains: Is there anyone among us who has done **everything** that God has told us to do? No, not one. Therefore, even if after doing **everything** one is still called **unworthy**, we who have not done everything must be less than unworthy. God, have mercy upon us!

Ten Healed of Leprosy (17:11–19)

11 On the way to Jerusalem (Luke 9:51; 13:22), Jesus traveled between Galilee and Samaria. He had not been welcome in Samaria (Luke 9:52), so He was now journeying around Samaria.[37]

12–13 On the way Jesus met ten men who had leprosy. According to Jewish law, **they stood at a distance**. A person with leprosy couldn't come near people; he was required to shout "**Unclean! Unclean!**" whenever anyone came too near[38] (Leviticus 13:45–46). These ten men had heard of Jesus, and so they cried out for mercy.

14 Jesus healed them from a distance. He only said, "**Go, show yourselves to the priests**" (see Mark 1:44 and comment). And as they went to the priests, they were healed. They had great faith, for they obeyed Christ's command even before they saw that they were healed. They did their part—to obey; and Jesus did His part.

15–18 Nine of the ten men with leprosy were Jews, and they did not return to thank Jesus. Only the **foreigner**, the Samaritan, gave praise and thanks to Christ.

19 Jesus said to the Samaritan, ". . . **your faith has made you well**" (see Mark 5:34 and comment). Jesus not only meant that his body had been made well, but that his spirit had been made well also. He had received salvation.

The other nine men with leprosy received bodily healing only. If we do not come to God and thank Him for the blessings we have received in this life, we shall receive no blessings in the life to come.

The Coming of the Kingdom of God (17:20–37)

(Matthew 16:25; 24:17–18,26–28, 37–41; Mark 8:35; 13:15–16,21,23)

20–21 The Jewish leaders were always seeking to know when the kingdom of God would come. They expected that the Messiah would come like a powerful earthly king, overthrow the Romans, and establish the nation of Israel once more. Then, of course, they supposed that they themselves would be the main officials in this new Jewish kingdom.

Therefore, thinking that Jesus was some kind of prophet, they asked Him when the kingdom of God would come.

He answered, "**The kingdom of God does not come visibly.**" People want to be able to say, "Ah, there it is over there." But the kingdom of God is something spiritual; it is not a kingdom of this world. The kingdom of God is really the rule of God in men's hearts (see Matthew 12:19 and comment).

Not only that, the kingdom of God has already come. Jesus brought the kingdom with Him. When men accept Christ, they enter the kingdom of God and the king-

---

[37] To do this, Jesus had to travel down the east side of the Jordan River, because Samaria lay on the direct route between Galilee and Jerusalem. At the city of Jericho, He crossed back to the west side of the Jordan River (Luke 19:1).

[38] Leprosy is a communicable disease. In Jesus' day, there was no medicine for leprosy, as there is now.

dom of God enters them. **"The kingdom of God is within you,"**[39] said Jesus.

The Pharisees wanted to know when the kingdom of God would come. But if their spiritual eyes had been open, they would have known that it had already come.

22 In verses 20–21, Jesus talked to the Pharisees about the coming of the kingdom of God—that is, about His first coming. Now in verse 22, Jesus begins to talk to His disciples about His second coming, **the days of the Son of Man,**[40] which will occur at the end of the world.

Jesus said, **"The time is coming when you will long to see one of the days of the Son of Man."** Jesus' meaning was as follows. After Jesus' death and ascension to heaven, the disciples would experience severe persecution. Indeed, most of the disciples would be killed. In those dark days, they would long to see Jesus come again in power and glory (Mark 13:26). "But," said Jesus, "**you will not see it**. I will not return before you die."

23–24 See Matthew 24:26–27; Mark 13:21 and comment.

25 Here Jesus again tells His disciples that He Himself must suffer and die before He can come again in glory (see Mark 8:31 and comment).

26–27 Here Jesus describes how He, the **Son of Man,** will come. He will come unexpectedly. He will come as a judge. And just as men were destroyed by the flood in the days of Noah, so also at Christ's second coming evil men will be condemned and destroyed (see Matthew 24:37–39 and comment).

28–29 The coming of the Son of Man will also be like the fire and sulfur that came suddenly down from heaven and destroyed the wicked city of Sodom in the days of Lot, Abraham's nephew. The people were not expecting God's judgment. They were eating and drinking and making merry. They believed they were secure. But as soon as God had rescued Lot and his daughters, He destroyed the city and all the people in it (see Genesis 19:1–29; Matthew 11:23–24).

30–31 See Mark 13:15-16 and comment.

32 **Remember Lot's wife!** Lot's wife at first escaped from Sodom before it was destroyed. But she looked back. She did not want to leave the wicked city. She did not want to give it up. Her heart was in the city and not with God. So she was turned into a **pillar of salt** (Genesis 19:16–17,26).

Remember Lot's wife! Let us who have escaped from "Sodom" take heed, and not turn back to our old life. For if we do, we too, like Lot's wife, will be turned spiritually into "pillars of salt."

33 See Mark 8:35 and comment.

34–36 See Matthew 24:40–41 and comment.[41]

37 See Matthew 24:28; Mark 13:23 and comment.

CHAPTER 18

The Parable of the Persistent Widow (18:1–8)

1–5 Here Jesus tells a parable about a widow who appealed to an unjust judge for justice. The judge **neither feared God nor cared about men** (verse 2). He was an evil judge, who treated men without justice or mercy. He was waiting for the widow to pay him a bribe; but the widow

---

[39] In the Greek language, which was the language Luke used, the word **within** in this verse can also mean "among." Both meanings are true. The kingdom of God is "among" us, because Jesus through His Spirit is among us. The kingdom of God is also "within" us, because Jesus's Spirit is within us.

Jesus didn't mean that the kingdom of God was "within" the unbelieving Pharisees. He was saying in a general way that the kingdom of God is within anyone who believes. However, it was true that the kingdom of God was "among" the Pharisees, because Jesus was present among them at that time.

[40] Jesus usually referred to Himself as the **Son of Man** (see Mark 2:10 and comment).

[41] Not all ancient manuscripts of Luke contain verse 36. The same verse is found in Matthew 24:40.

was too poor. Her only means of gaining justice was to be persistent. In the end, by her persistence alone, she obtained justice.

Jesus told this parable so that we might follow the widow's example, and be persistent in prayer and not become discouraged and give up (verse 1).

6–8 Then Jesus compared the unjust judge with God. If a wicked and unjust judge would grant justice to the widow, how much more will a merciful and just God grant justice to **his chosen ones**[42] who cry out to Him? Let us not doubt. **He will see that they get justice, and quickly**.

From this parable we can learn two main things. First, like the unjust judge, God may not answer our appeal immediately. He wants each of us to experience some kind of injustice and persecution in order that our faith might be tested (see Romans 5:3–4; James 1:2–4; 1 Peter 1:6–7 and comments). He also wants us to share in the suffering of Christ in this life, so that we might share in His glory in the next life (see Romans 8:17; 1 Peter 4:12–13 and comments). Therefore, we must understand that if God lets us suffer injustice for some period, it is for our good (see Romans 8:28 and comment).

Therefore, why does Jesus say that God will see that His chosen ones get justice, **and quickly**? God's time and our time are not the same. A thousand years is like a day to God (2 Peter 3:8). Here the word **quickly** means "at the right time." God will not delay unnecessarily.

The second thing to learn from this parable is that we must persist in prayer. God wants us to continue in prayer, even though the answer does not come immediately. He wants us to be **persistent** (see Luke 11:5–8 and comment).

Why does God want us to be persistent? The answer is: to show our faith. Especially we must persist in prayer during times of persecution. That is when our faith is being tested. Jesus said, "**. . . he who stands firm to the end will be saved**" (Mark 13:13). We must continue to cry out to God with faith, never doubting that in the end He will grant us justice. He may not grant it in this life, but He will certainly grant it in the next.

But this teaching is not only for times of persecution. We must persist in prayer at other times also. Is there a friend or relative for whom you are praying? Do you see no answer? Continue to pray.

Are you troubled by some sin or bad habit in your life, over which you cannot obtain victory? Continue to pray. Do not give up. And God, in the end, at the right time, will answer your prayer.

However, when the Son of Man comes, will he find faith on earth? (verse 8). Will He find men persisting in prayer, even though they are being persecuted and killed? In the last days before Christ comes again, trouble and distress will come upon all men. **At that time many will turn away from the faith** (Matthew 24:10). Will Christ find any that have remained faithful?

The Pharisee and the Tax Collector (18:9–14)

9 Then Jesus told a parable to **some who were confident in their own righteousness and looked down on everybody else**. In Jesus' time, most of the Jews—especially the Pharisees—were like that: they trusted in their own RIGHTEOUSNESS and considered themselves better than everyone else. But this parable, as with all of Jesus' parables, is not spoken to Jews only, but to everyone. Are there those among us who are saying to God: "I am worthy; I am righteous"? If so, this parable is for them.

10–12 The parable is about two men. One was a Pharisee, a strict Jew, who believed in God and obeyed the law as he understood it. Like the rich man of Luke 16:19, the Pharisee in this parable was an upright man. He was not evil. He not only obeyed the Jewish law; he did even more than the law demanded. According to the law, a man had to fast only once a year; this man, however, fasted twice a week. According to the law, a man had to give a tenth of only certain

[42] The **chosen ones** are those who are chosen by God, that is, believers in Christ.

kinds of income; this man gave a tenth of all his income (verse 12).

Therefore, what was this Pharisee's sin? His sin was that he considered himself righteous. He did not consider that he needed God's forgiveness and mercy. He considered that he was worthy to receive God's salvation because of his good works. In God's eyes, this was a sinful attitude. This Pharisee was proud.

Not only that, this Pharisee in his heart was not truly righteous. He despised other men. He didn't love them. He judged them (Matthew 7:1–2). In doing this he disobeyed God (see Matthew 23:23 and comment).

The Pharisee **went up to the temple to pray**. There are many who can be seen praying in temples and churches today who shall not be seen in the kingdom of heaven!

13 But the attitude of the second man, the **tax collector**, was totally different (see Mark 2:14 and comment). He knew that he was a sinner. He knew that he deserved only punishment from God for his sins. He was **poor in spirit**; he **mourned** for his sins (see Matthew 5:3–4 and comment). The only thing that he dared to ask for from God was mercy.

14 The tax collector went home **justified before God**. The Pharisee, however, was not justified in God's sight. The tax collector was forgiven and cleansed of his sin and was accepted by God. The Pharisee, on the other hand, was condemned by God because of his pride and lack of love.

From this important parable we learn that to be accepted and justified by God we must first humble ourselves and repent of our sins and beg God's mercy. David wrote: A **humble and contrite heart, O God, you will not despise** (Psalm 51:17). Only when we have humbled ourselves before God will He then come to us and lift us up and clothe our nakedness with the righteousness of Christ.

But those who exalt themselves, like this Pharisee, God will humble. Such people will not be admitted into the kingdom of heaven. **For everyone who exalts himself will be humbled, and he who humbles himself will be exalted** (see Matthew 23:12 and comment).

The Little Children and Jesus (18:15–17)

(Matthew 19:13–15; Mark 10:13–16)

15–17 See Mark 10:13–16 and comment.

The Rich Ruler (18:18–30)

(Matthew 19:16–30; Mark 10:17–31)

18–30 See Mark 10:17–31 and comment.

Jesus Again Predicts His Death (18:31–34)

(Matthew 20:17–19; Mark 10:32–34)

31–34 See Mark 10:32–34 and comment.

A Blind Beggar Receives His Sight (18:35–43)

(Matthew 20:29–34; Mark 10:46–52)

35–43 See Mark 10:46–52 and comment.

CHAPTER 19

Zacchaeus the Tax Collector (19:1–10)

1 Having journeyed down the east side of the Jordan River, Jesus crossed the river at the city of Jericho, sixteen miles east of Jerusalem (Luke 10:30; 17:11)

2–4 A chief tax collector, **Zacchaeus,** heard that Jesus had come. Jesus had become known as a **friend of tax collectors and "sinners"** (Matthew

11:19), and Zacchaeus was curious to see Him.

Zacchaeus was **wealthy**. The Romans gave the work of collecting taxes in each Roman province to the man who paid the most to get the job. The tax collector received no salary from the Romans; instead, he collected as much money as he could from the people. After paying the Romans the proper amount, he could then keep the excess he had dishonestly collected. Thus almost all tax collectors cheated the people and got rich. As a result, everyone hated them (see Mark 2:13–14 and comment).

5–6 Even though Zacchaeus was an evil and greedy man, Jesus called to him. He told Zacchaeus that He would be staying at his house that day.

Zacchaeus **welcomed him gladly**. When Zacchaeus saw the honor that Jesus had given him, his heart softened. He saw that Jesus was ready to forgive his sins. So he gladly brought Jesus to his house.

7 But others watching grumbled against Jesus. They said, "No proper Jew, especially a teacher or prophet, would ever stay at the house of a sinner like a tax collector" (see Mark 2:15–17; Luke 15:1–2 and comments).

8 When they reached his house, Zacchaeus fully repented of the evil he had done. He confessed that he had cheated people, and he promised Jesus that he would turn from his old sinful ways. "**Here and now I give half my possessions to the poor**," he promised Jesus. He also promised to pay back to everyone he had cheated **four times the amount**.[43]

Many dishonest people are forced to be honest by the law, and they receive no credit from God for that. But Zacchaeus became honest by his own choice. Thus Jesus knew that he had truly repented.

That day a complete change took place in Zacchaeus' life. The change took place because Jesus had come into his house and into his heart. Whenever we welcome Jesus into our life, we can never be the same again. We become a **new creation** (see 2 Corinthians 5:17 and comment).

9–10 When Jesus heard Zacchaeus' words of repentance, He said, "**Today salvation has come to this house**." Zacchaeus had been **lost** in sin and unbelief. Now he was saved.

This is the reason Jesus came to earth. This is the reason He went to a tax collector's house. Why should Zacchaeus not be given a chance to repent? He was a Jew, a **son of Abraham** according to the flesh, just like any other Jew. Now he would be a true "son of Abraham" according to faith (Galatians 3:7).

It was lost sinners like Zacchaeus whom Jesus came to save (see Matthew 18:12; Mark 2:17). If this Jesus has truly saved us and is living in us, then we will want to tell the good news of salvation to other lost sinners also.

The Parable of the Ten Minas (19:11–27)
(Matthew 25:14–30)

11–25 See Matthew 25:14–28 and comment.

26 See Matthew 25:29; Mark 4:25 and comments.

27 See Matthew 25:30 and comment.

The Triumphal Entry (19:28–40)
(Matthew 21:1–11; Mark 11:1–11)

28–40 See Mark 11:1–11 and comment.

Jesus Mourns For Jerusalem (19:41–44)

41–42 Jesus entered Jerusalem from the Mount of Olives (verse 37). From the Mount of Olives He could see the whole city laid out before Him. He knew that the Jewish leaders had rejected Him. He knew that the people of Jerusalem would soon cry out for His death (Mark 15:12–15). And He also knew that a great disaster would soon come upon the city and its people because they had killed the Son of God.

---

[43] According to Jewish law, the person who takes someone else's goods must pay back double the amount (Exodus 22:9).

Therefore, He **wept** over the city (verse 41). He said, **"If you . . . had only known on this day what would bring you peace."** If only the people of Jerusalem had repented and welcomed Christ,[44] the city would have been spared. There would have been **peace** for the people of **Jerusalem.**[45] "But now peace is **hidden from your eyes,**" said Jesus. Their chance to repent was lost. Their hearts were hardened, their eyes were shut. They **did not recognize the time of God's coming** (verse 44)—that is, the coming of God's Son Jesus (see Matthew 23:37–39 and comment).

43–44 Then Jesus prophesied that, instead of peace, a sword would come to Jerusalem. Enemy armies would surround the city and destroy it completely and kill all the inhabitants (Jeremiah 6:6; Luke 21:6,20–24). This prophecy was fulfilled forty years later, in 70 A.D., when the Roman army came and utterly destroyed Jerusalem.

God is a loving God. He calls people and cities and nations to repent. He has great patience. God **wants all men to be saved and to come to a knowledge of the truth** (1 Timothy 2:4). He does not want **anyone to perish, but everyone to come to repentance** (2 Peter 3:9). But in the end, if men do not repent, He will come as a judge and destroy them.

God spared the great city of Nineveh, because its people repented (Jonah 3:3–10). But He did not spare Sodom. He promised Abraham that if He found ten righteous people in Sodom He would spare it; but He could not find ten people who would repent, and so He destroyed the city (Genesis 18:20–33). **God cannot be mocked**; what we sow, we shall reap (Galatians 6:7–8). If we do not repent, we shall be destroyed. The **time of God's coming** is now. **I tell you, now is the time of God's favor, now is the day of salvation** (2 Corinthians 6:2). Tomorrow may be too late.

Jesus at the Temple (19:45–48)
(Matthew 21:12–19; Mark 11:15–19)

45–48 See Mark 11:15–19 and comment.

CHAPTER 20

The Authority of Jesus Questioned (20:1–8)
(Matthew 21:23–27; Mark 11:27–33)

1–8 See Mark 11:27–33 and comment.

The Parable of the Tenants (20:9–19)
(Matthew 21:33–46; Mark 12:1–12)

9–19 See Mark 12:1–12 and comment.

Paying Taxes to Caesar (20:20–26)
(Matthew 22:15–22; Mark 12:13–17)

20–26 See Mark 12:13–17 and comment.

The Resurrection and Marriage (20:27–40)
(Matthew 22:23–33; Mark 12:18–27)

27–40 See Mark 12:18–27 and comment.

Whose Son Is the Christ? (20:41–47)
(Matthew 22:41–46; Mark 12:35–40)

41–47 See Mark 12:35–40 and comment.

---

[44] Those who welcomed Christ during His triumphal entry into Jerusalem were mostly His own followers (verse 37).

[45] The word **Jerusalem** means "city of peace."

CHAPTER 21

The Widow's Offering (21:1–4)
(Mark 12:41–44)

1–4 See Mark 12:41–44 and comment.

Signs of the End of the Age (21:5–19)
(Matthew 10:17–22; 24:1–14; Mark 13:1–13)

5–19 See Mark 13:1–13 and comment.

The Destruction of Jerusalem (21:20–24)
(Matthew 24:15–28; Mark 13:14–23)

20–24 See Mark 13:14–23 and comment.

The End of the World (21:25–28)
(Matthew 24:29–31; Mark 13:24–27)

25–28 See Mark 13:24–27 and comment.

The End of Jerusalem (21:29–33)
(Matthew 24:32–35; Mark 13:28–31)

29–33 See Mark 13:28–31 and comment.

Warning To Be Watchful (21:34–38)

34 Jesus has given in this chapter a description of the signs preceding the end of the world, at which time Jesus will come again. Here in this section, He warns us to be watchful. We cannot know when exactly He will come again, but we must remain ready for Him (see Mark 13:32–33 and comment).

Therefore, Jesus warns us: "**Be careful,**" lest our hearts be **weighed down with dissipation, drunkenness and the anxieties of life**. Christ's second coming will be like that of a master who returns unexpectedly from a trip. What will He find His servants doing? Therefore, let us be awake and not sleeping; let us be working diligently at the job Jesus has given us. He will return at any time (see Matthew 24:48–51; Mark 13:34–37; 1 Thessalonians 5:4–8 and comments).

It is not important to know when Jesus is coming. In fact, it is not our place to know (Acts 1:7). It is only important that we be ready at all times. If we remain always ready and watching, that day cannot come on us **like a trap**.

35 That day of Christ's return in judgment will come upon all men—believers and non-believers, Jews and Gentiles.

36 There will be terrible persecution in those days, and many will fall away (Matthew 24:10–12). We must pray that we shall escape the temptation to fall back, to leave the faith, to deny Christ. For only **he who stands firm to the end will be saved** (Mark 13:13). Only those whose faith remains firm will be able to **stand before the Son of Man** on the day of judgment (see Hebrews 10:35–39 and comment).

37–38 During that final week in Jerusalem, Jesus taught each day in the temple. And each evening He left the city and spent the night in the town of Bethany, located on the **Mount of Olives** just outside Jerusalem (Mark 11:1,11).

CHAPTER 22

Judas Agrees to Betray Jesus (22:1–6)
(Matthew 26:1–5,14–16; Mark 14:1–2,10–11)

1–2 See Mark 14:1–2 and comment.
3–6 See Mark 14:10–11 and comment.

The Lord's Supper (22:7–23)
(Matthew 26:17–30; Mark 14:12–26)

7–23 See Mark 14:12–26 and comment.

Teaching About Who Is Greatest (22:24–27)

(Matthew 20:25–28; Mark 10:42–45)

24–27 See Mark 10:42–45 and comment.

Jesus and His Disciples (22:28–38)

28–30 In verses 24–27, Jesus rebuked His disciples for seeking to be greatest. Now He gives them some praise. Up to that time they all had stood by Him in His trials. Therefore, Jesus said to them, "**I confer on you a kingdom**"—that is, rule or authority—"**just as my Father conferred one on me**" (verse 29). They will **eat and drink at** [Jesus'] **table**; that is, they will share in the joy of the kingdom of heaven. As the Father gave Christ all authority in heaven and earth (Matthew 28:18), so Christ will share His authority with His disciples. They will share in the work of judging the **twelve tribes of Israel**[46] (see Matthew 19:28 and comment). Some Bible scholars believe that this means that they will have leadership in heaven over the "new Israel," that is, the church.

As the disciples honored Christ in this life, so He will honor them in the next (see Matthew 25:21). But they must not seek honor for themselves; Christ Himself will honor them.

31 Then Jesus turned to Simon Peter and said, "**Simon, Simon, Satan has asked to sift you**[47] **as wheat**." Just as Satan asked that he might test Job (Job 1:6–12; 2:3–10), so he now asks that he might test the disciples. Satan hoped that the disciples would all blow away like the chaff. And indeed, the disciples did all run away when Jesus was arrested (Mark 14:50). It seemed like Satan had won.

32 But then Jesus prayed for Simon Peter himself, because he was the leader of the disciples. He prayed especially that Peter's faith would not fail. Jesus knew that Peter would deny Him (verses 33–34), but it would be only for a short time. Then Peter would have to return and strengthen and lead the other disciples. And we can be certain that it was because of Christ's prayers that Peter did return. If Christ is praying for us, our faith will stand (see Romans 8:34–37).

33–34 See Mark 14:27–31 and comment.

35–36 When the disciples first were sent out, they carried no **purse, bag or sandals** (see Mark 6:8–10). At that time people gave them hospitality wherever they went, so that they lacked nothing.

But now the situation was completely different. Jesus was about to be killed. The disciples would now be persecuted. Instead of receiving hospitality they would have to flee from town to town. Therefore, they would need purse and bag.

Not only that, Jesus said that they would need a **sword** also. Jesus did not mean a steel sword for fighting, but a spiritual sword. The disciples would need the **sword of the Spirit**, which is God's word (Ephesians 6:17). They must be always ready for spiritual battle. Their spiritual weapons would be far more important than their ordinary clothes.

37 Then Jesus again predicted His suffering. As Isaiah had prophesied, Christ would be **numbered with the transgressors** (Isaiah 53:12). And so would His disciples be likewise. Therefore, they must be spiritually armed.

38 The disciples failed to understand Jesus' meaning. They still thought Jesus was going to overcome His enemies with ordinary weapons. They should have known better. Jesus' way was the way of love, not violence. Later, when Peter raised his sword, Jesus rebuked him (Luke 22:49–51; John 18:10–11).

The disciples then showed Jesus two swords that they had with them. Jesus was discouraged that they hadn't understood what kind of sword he had been talking about. He said, "**That is enough**,"[48]

---

[46] The **twelve tribes of Israel** are descended from the twelve sons of Jacob, Abraham's grandson. Therefore, the "twelve tribes of Israel" make up the entire nation of Israel.

[47] In the Greek text of this verse, the **you** is pleural.

[48] **That is enough** is a Jewish saying which means "the matter is finished."

meaning, "Enough said; the matter is finished."

Gethsemane (22:39–46)
(Matthew 26:36–46; Mark 14:32–42)

39–46 See Mark 14:32–42 and comment.

Jesus Arrested (22:47–53)
(Matthew 26:47–56; Mark 14:43–52; John 18:1–11)

47–53 See Mark 14:43–52 and comment.

Peter Disowns Jesus (22:54–62)
(Matthew 26:69–75; Mark 14:66–72; John 18:15–18,25–27)

54–62 See Mark 14:66–72 and comment.

Jesus Before the Chief Priests (22:63–71)
(Matthew 26:57–68; Mark 14:53–65)

63–71 See Mark 14:53–65 and comment.

CHAPTER 23

Jesus Before Pilate (23:1–5)
(Matthew 27:1–2,11–14; Mark 15:1–2)

1–3 See Mark 15:1–2 and comment.

4–5 **Pilate**, the Roman governor, found **no basis for a charge** against Jesus. He considered the charge of the Jewish leaders to be only a local Jewish matter (see John 18:33–38 and comment). Furthermore, Roman officials like Pilate did not judge in religious disputes that arose among the people of their provinces (see Acts 18:12–16). But the Jewish leaders persisted. They had cleverly decided not to accuse Jesus of blasphemy, which Pilate would surely have considered a religious matter. Instead, they said, **"He stirs up the people"** (verse 5). In other words, they accused Jesus of inciting a rebellion against the Roman emperor, Caesar. They said that Jesus was trying to make Himself a king (verse 2). Such a charge, they figured, would be sure to alarm Pilate, and force him to take some severe action against Jesus.

Jesus Before Herod (23:6–16)

6–7 When Pilate heard that Jesus had begun His preaching in Galilee (verse 5), he asked if Jesus was a Galilean. When he found out that He was, Pilate at once sent Jesus to the puppet ruler, King **Herod**,[49] who had jurisdiction over the province of Galilee.

8 Herod had heard much about the great works that Jesus had performed. He hoped to be able to see Jesus perform a miracle. But Herod wasn't interested in finding out who Jesus really was. He only wanted to be entertained.

9 But Jesus would do nothing for Herod. He would not even speak to him. For the poorest and lowest of men Jesus did miracles, but not for proud and unbelieving kings.

10 The Jewish leaders had also gone with Jesus to Herod so that they could further accuse him. They hoped that Herod would agree to passing the death sentence on Jesus.

11–12 Herod became angry when Jesus refused to speak to him. So he and his soldiers mocked Jesus. Because of Jesus' silence, Herod was unable to render a verdict, and so he sent Jesus back to Pilate.

13–16 Again Pilate said to the Jews that Jesus had done nothing worthy of death (verses 14–15). But in order to mollify the Jews, Pilate agreed to **punish**

---

[49] This is the same **Herod** who had earlier put John the Baptist to death, and who afterwards began to think that Jesus was John the Baptist risen from the dead (see Mark 6:14–16).

Jesus by scourging Him. By doing this, Pilate hoped that the Jews would drop their demands for Jesus' death (see Mark 15:3–5).

Jesus and Barabbas (23:17–25)
(Matthew 27:15–26; Mark 15:6–15)

17–25 See Mark 15:6–15 and comment.

The Crucifixion (23:26–43)
(Matthew 27:32–44; Mark 15:21–32; John 19:17–24)

26–38 See Mark 15:21–31 and comment.

39–43 See Mark 15:32 and comment.

The Death of Jesus (23:44–49)
(Matthew 27:45–56; Mark 15:33–41; John 19:28–30)

44–49 See Mark 15:33–41 and comment.

The Burial of Jesus (23:50–56)
(Matthew 27:57–61; Mark 15:42–47; John 19:38–42)

50–56 See Mark 15:42–47 and comment.

CHAPTER 24

The Resurrection (24:1–8)
(Matthew 28:1–8; Mark 16:1–8; John 20:1)

1–8 See Mark 16:1–8 and comment.

Peter Sees the Empty Tomb (24:9–12)

9–11 After discovering that the tomb was empty and after seeing the two angels, the first thing the women did was to run and tell Jesus' eleven[50] disciples that His body was gone (John 20:2). At first the disciples didn't believe what the women said.

12 But then Peter decided to go and see the tomb for himself. He took John with him (see John 20:3–8). They saw the strips of linen that Jesus' body had been bound with. But there was no body. Peter was confused. He couldn't understand what had happened. He still did not understand that Jesus must rise from the dead (John 20:9). Then the two disciples returned to their homes (John 20:10).

Meanwhile, the women had followed Peter and John back to the tomb. After the two disciples had gone home, Jesus Himself appeared to the women (see Matthew 28:9–10; John 20:11–18 and comments). Then, according to Jesus' command, they ran for the second time to tell the disciples this new news: Jesus was alive! They had seen Him!

However, according to Mark 16:11, the disciples again did not believe the women's story—except for John.[51] It was only after the Lord appeared to Peter himself (1 Corinthians 15:5), that the other disciples began to believe that Jesus was truly risen and alive,[52] (see verses 33–34).

---

[50] Judas Iscariot was no longer among the disciples, so they numbered eleven.

[51] John had believed when he first saw the empty tomb (John 20:8).

[52] The writers of the four Gospels each give part of the account of Jesus' appearances after His resurrection. Imagine any four men who have witnessed some great event. They each will describe that event from their own viewpoint. One will mention one thing, another will mention another. When the four accounts are put together, one can then obtain a full description of that event. The four Gospels are like that. Everything that each Gospel writer has written is true, but each writer has not included every detail in his own Gospel. Therefore, in order to obtain a full description of Jesus' life and, in particular, of the events following His resurrection, we must study the four Gospel accounts together.

Even when we do this, however, there will still be many details about Jesus' life that we shall never know, because they have not been written (see John 21:25).

On the Road to Emmaus (24:13–35)

13–14 On that same Sunday on which Jesus rose from the dead, two of His followers were going to their homes in the village of **Emmaus**. They had come to Jerusalem for the Feast of Unleavened Bread (see Mark 14:1), and were now returning home. They had heard about all that had happened to Jesus and were talking about it as they walked along.

15–16 Then a third man joined them. It was the man Jesus. But because His body was now changed into an eternal spiritual body, they could not recognize Him at first. He appeared to them as a normal man, but they could not tell it was Jesus (see John 20:14). Their spiritual eyes were not open. They did not believe yet that Jesus had really risen from the dead.

17 Jesus asked them what they were talking about on the road. He knew the answer, but He wanted them to say it. Jesus many times taught His disciples by asking them questions.

18 One of the disciples, **Cleopas**,[53] said to Jesus, "Do you not know what we are talking about? Haven't you heard what has taken place in Jerusalem these past three days?"

19 Jesus asked, **"What things?"** Then they told Him about their leader Jesus, who was a **prophet, powerful in word and deed before God and all the people**.

Those who do not believe that Christ is risen from the dead regard Him as no more than a "**prophet, powerful in word and deed**" (see Matthew 21:11; Luke 7:16). To them He is only a great man, a wise man, a good man. But to those who have met the risen living Christ and have welcomed Him into their hearts by faith, He is the Savior, the **Lord of lords and King of kings** (1 Timothy 6:15; Revelation 17:14), the Son of God. He is God Himself.

20–21 The two disciples then told about their disappointment that Jesus had died. They had hoped He would be the Messiah, the king of Israel, but now all their hopes were crushed. This Jesus had now been dead three days. All Jews believed that the Messiah would lead Israel to victory over its enemies. They did not believe in a Messiah who would be killed on a cross!

22–24 "But today we heard an amazing thing," the two disciples said. "This morning the tomb where Jesus' body was laid was found empty." And they described to Jesus what had been reported by the women and by Peter and John (see verse 12).

However, an empty tomb was not proof that Jesus was alive. None of the disciples had yet seen Jesus Himself. All they knew was that His body was missing.

25–27 Then Jesus began to teach the two disciples what had been written about Himself in **Moses and all the Prophets**, that is, the Old Testament. According to many prophecies in the Old Testament, the Messiah would have to suffer and die (Psalm 22:1–31; 69:1–36; Isaiah 52:13–15; 53:1–12). Only after suffering would the Messiah, Christ, **enter his glory**. Only after suffering would He establish His kingdom, a spiritual kingdom that would last forever. The Jews knew about the "suffering servant" described in the Old Testament, but they did not think that he would be the same as the Messiah. They thought that the suffering servant and the Messiah would be two different people. It was Jesus Himself that taught that the suffering servant was, in fact, the Messiah. Jesus had taught His disciples over and over that He must suffer and die, but they had not been able to accept it (Mark 8:31–32; 9:31–32; Luke 18:31–34).

The two disciples listened eagerly. Their hearts **burned within them** as Jesus spoke (verse 32).

28–29 They invited Jesus to their home. If they had not invited Him in, He would have passed on, and they would never have known who had walked with them on the road to Emmaus.

Let us ask ourselves: "How many times has Jesus spoken to us along the road and

---

[53] **Cleopas** may be the same man as the Clopas mentioned in John 19:25, but with a slightly different spelling of his name.

we have not invited Him in?" (Revelation 3:20).

30–32 After they had reached the house and were ready to eat, Jesus **took bread, gave thanks, broke it and began to give it to them**. These disciples had seen Him do this many times before His death (Mark 6:41; 8:6; 14:22). And suddenly their spiritual eyes were opened, and they recognized Jesus! And at that moment, He disappeared from their sight.

33–35 Even though it was now dark, the two disciples hurried back to Jerusalem to tell the other disciples about their meeting with Jesus. By that time, Jesus had appeared to Peter also. Some of the disciples were now beginning to believe that Jesus was indeed alive, risen from the dead. But others still didn't believe (see Mark 16:13). And even when Jesus Himself appeared a few minutes later to all of the disciples at once, they still doubted and thought that they were seeing a ghost (verses 37–38).

Jesus Appears to the Disciples (24:36–43)

(John 20:19–20)

36–40 While the two disciples from Emmaus were still talking with the other disciples, Jesus Himself appeared before them all. Jesus passed miraculously through the locked door of the room where they were gathered (see John 20:19–20 and comment). The disciples thought they were seeing a ghost, a spirit without a body. But then Jesus showed them the nail wounds in His hands and feet.[54] He told them to reach out and touch His body, so that they might know that it was real (1 John 1:1). Jesus was not a ghost. He had a body of flesh and bones. He had a resurrected body, a glorified heavenly body (see 1 Corinthians 15:35–37 and comment).

41–43 The disciples were so filled with amazement and joy that they didn't know what to think. It was all like a dream. They still couldn't believe it was really true.

Jesus, knowing the weakness of their faith, asked for something to eat, and then ate it before them. After that, their doubt ended. They knew then that He was truly alive.

A week later, Jesus again appeared to the disciples in Jerusalem (see John 20:24–29). Then He appeared to His disciples in Galilee (Matthew 28:16). After that, He appeared to **five hundred of the brothers** at one time (1 Corinthians 15:6). Then He appeared to James, His own brother (1 Corinthians 15:7). All these appearances took place during the forty days Jesus was on earth between His resurrection and His ascension into heaven (Acts 1:3).

Final Teaching (24:44–49)

44 During the next forty days, Jesus gave His disciples many teachings. Luke mentions only a few of them in this section.

Jesus wanted His disciples to understand the Scriptures. He wanted them to know that what was written in the Old Testament about Himself had now been fulfilled. He had told all these things to two of His disciples on the road to Emmaus (see verses 25–27 and comment). Now He began to teach these things to all of the disciples.

45–46 He told them again what He had told them many times before: namely, that the **Christ will suffer and rise from the dead on the third day** (see Mark 8:31; 9:31; 1 Corinthians 15:3–4). He **opened their minds so they could understand the Scriptures** (verse 45). Only when our minds are opened by the Holy Spirit can we fully understand the Bible and the preaching of God's word.

47 Jesus also taught His disciples from the Old Testament that **repentance and forgiveness of sins** will be preached to all nations, not only to the Jews but to the Gentiles as well (Isaiah 2:2–3; 49:6; 51:4–6; Matthew 28:19; Romans 15:9–12). Repentance and forgiveness of sins are the first two steps in man's salvation. Without repentance there can be no

---

[54] The Romans usually hung criminals on the cross by driving great nails through their hands and feet.

forgiveness. Without forgiveness, there can be no salvation (see General Article: Way of Salvation).

48 Then Jesus said, "**You are witnesses to these things**." The disciples themselves had seen **these things**; now they were to go out into the whole world and proclaim these things to others. (see Acts 1:8 and comment).

49 Then Jesus said, "**I am going to send you what my Father has promised**"—that is, the Holy Spirit (see John 15:16–17,26). Then Jesus told them to stay in Jerusalem[55] until the Holy Spirit should come upon them and give them the power they would need to be His witnesses (see Acts 1:4–5,8; 2:1–4 and comments). Without the Holy Spirit they would not be able to accomplish anything for Christ (John 15:5). Indeed, without the Holy Spirit, the disciples could never have established Christ's church.

The Ascension of Jesus (24:50–53)

50–51 Forty days after His resurrection from the dead, Jesus went with His disciples to Bethany, just outside Jerusalem (Mark 11:1,11). After blessing them, He ascended into heaven **before their very eyes** (Acts 1:9). As they stood looking into heaven, two angels came and said to them, "**This same Jesus, who has been taken from you into heaven, will come back in the same way you have seen him go into heaven**" (Acts 1:10–11).

52–53 Then the disciples were filled with joy. No longer was there any doubt in their minds that Jesus was the Lord, the Messiah, the Son of God. Then they returned to Jerusalem to wait for the coming of the Holy Spirit. During that time, they stayed continually in the temple praying and praising God. The Holy Spirit comes to those who spend much time in praise and prayer.

[55] Jesus gave this command to the disciples after they had returned to Jerusalem from Galilee.

John

INTRODUCTION

The Gospel of John was written by the Apostle John, the son of Zebedee (Mark 1:19). Most Bible scholars believe it was written sometime between 70 and 90 A.D., but the exact date is not known (see John 5:2 and comment). John was known as Jesus' "beloved disciple" (John 13:23; 21:20). Of Jesus' original twelve disciples, John was the closest to Jesus in spiritual fellowship. John knew Jesus' mind better than anyone else. Thus in this Gospel, John has written for us some of Jesus' deepest thoughts and sayings.

John lived to be a very old man. He lived for many years in Ephesus, where this Gospel is said to have been written. The three New Testament letters of John were also written by this same Apostle John, the son of Zebedee. At the end of his life, John was banished to the island of Patmos in the Mediterranean Sea, where he received a revelation of Christ. John's description of this revelation is written in the last book of the New Testament, the book of Revelation.

John's Gospel is quite different from the Gospels of Matthew, Mark, and Luke. In John's Gospel we see in more depth the mind and spirit of Christ. John has explained in great detail Christ's nature. He has recorded Jesus' teaching about Himself: **I am the bread of life** (John 6:35); **I am the light of the world** (John 8:12); **I am the good shepherd** (John 10:11); **I am the gate** (John 10:9), **the true vine** (John 15:1), **the way and the truth and the life** (John 14:6).

John has recorded Jesus' deepest conversations with His disciples, especially the long conversation during Jesus' last supper, which is recorded in Chapters 14–17.

From John's Gospel we also learn most fully about the Holy Spirit. We learn that without Christ's Spirit dwelling in us, we can do nothing (John 15:5). John shows us that the work of Christ can continue only through the empowering of the Holy Spirit in the lives of believers.

Thus, when we join the first three Gospels together with John's Gospel, we obtain a complete picture of Jesus' life and work. But above all, as we study this Gospel, let us remember John's purpose in writing it: namely, **that you may believe that Jesus is the Christ, the Son of God, and that by believing you may have life in his name** (John 20:31).

OUTLINE

A. Prologue (1:1–18).
   1. The Word (1:1–5).
   2. The Testimony of John the Baptist (1:6–18).

B. The Ministry of Jesus Christ in the World (1:19–12:50).
   1. The Testimony of John the Baptist (1:19–34).
   2. The Calling of the First Disciples (1:35–51).
   3. The Wedding at Cana (2:1–11).
   4. The First Visit to Jerusalem and Judea (2:12–3:36).
   5. The Mission to Samaria (4:1–42).
   6. Miracles and Teachings (4:43–6:71).
   7. Jesus at the Feast of Tabernacles (7:1–53).
   8. The Self-disclosure of Jesus (8:1–59).
   9. The Healing of the Man Born Blind (9:1–41).
   10. Jesus the Good Shepherd (10:1–42).
   11. The Raising of Lazarus (11:1–57).
   12. Jesus in Bethany and Jerusalem (12:1–50).

C. The Ministry of Jesus Christ to His Disciples (13:1–17:26).
   1. The Foot Washing (13:1–17).
   2. The Announcement of the Betrayal (13:18–30).
   3. The Discourse in the Upper Room (13:31–16:33).
   4. The Great Prayer (17:1–26).

D. The Suffering and Resurrection of Jesus Christ (18:1–21:25).
   1. The Betrayal of Jesus (18:1–14).
   2. Jesus on Trial before the Jews (18:15–27).
   3. Jesus on Trial before Pilate (18:28–19:16).
   4. The Death of Jesus (19:17–42).
   5. Discovery of the Empty Tomb (20:1–10).
   6. The Resurrection Appearances of Jesus (20:11–21:25).

CHAPTER 1

The Word Became Flesh (1:1–5)

1–2 **In the beginning was the Word.** The **Word** is Christ. John writes: **The Word became flesh and lived for a while among us** (verse 14). What John is saying right in the beginning of his Gospel is that Jesus Christ was no ordinary man. He was the "Word" of God, who had been with God from before the creation of the world.

The **Word**, that is, Christ, existed **in the beginning.** Before the world was formed, Christ existed (John 17:5). The first verse in the Bible says: **In the beginning God created the heavens and the earth** (Genesis 1:1). But Christ was with God before the **beginning.** God has no beginning; He has always existed. And God has always had His Word with Him. God has never been without His Word.

The Word was **with God.** This means that, in one way, there is a difference between God and the Word; they are distinct, just as a father and his son are distinct. But then John says that **the Word was God** (verse 1). Christ was not only **with** God; He **was** God. Christ is not only God's Son; He is God Himself. Christ is God in the form of a man. He is the one true incarnation of the living God, who came to earth 2000 years ago. God was in Christ, and Christ was in God. Jesus said to His disciples: "**Anyone who has seen me has seen the Father**" (John 14:9). "**I am in the Father, and . . . the Father is in me**" (John 14:11). "**I and the Father are one**" (John 10:30).

3 **Through him** (Christ) **all things were made.** God's word is not like man's word. When God speaks, God acts. Man often speaks but does nothing. But when God speaks, something happens. God's word has power. God said, "**Let there be light,**" and light came into being (Genesis 1:3). And this word of power was with Jesus. Jesus said to a man with leprosy, "**Be clean!**" and immediately the man became clean (Mark 1:41). When Jesus spoke, demons came out of people (Mark 1:25). By His word the wind was stilled (Mark 4:39) and the dead were raised (Luke 7:14–15; John 11:43–44). And here in verse 3, John says something even more amazing: Through Christ **all things were made.** When God created the heavens and earth, He did it through His word, that is, through Christ. Everything that has been created has been created through Christ. The APOSTLE Paul writes that **all things were created by him and for him** (Colossians 1:15–17). Christ is God's powerful word. God **has spoken to us by his Son** (see Hebrews 1:1–3 and comment).

4 Therefore, John says: **In him was life.** God created life through Christ. He created not only physical life, but also spiritual, eternal life. John has written: **God has given us eternal life, and this life is in his Son** (1 John 5:11). Jesus said: "**I have come that they might have life, and have it to the full**" (John 10:10). "**I am the resurrection and the life**" (John 11:25). "**I am the way and the truth and the life**" (John 14:6).

With **life** there is always **light.** In fact, life is dependent on light. God created light first; only after that did He create life (Genesis 1:3,11). When we receive life through Christ, we also receive His light. His light is the light of conscience and reason that is in every human being. It is also spiritual light (John 12:46). In the darkness, we can see nothing. But in the light, we can see. Above all, through Christ's light, we can see and understand God. Jesus said: "**I am the light of the world. Whoever follows me will never walk in darkness, but will have the light of life**" (John 8:12).

5 Just as a tiny candle overcomes the darkness of a room, so Christ's light overcomes the darkness of the world. Darkness can never overcome light.

Thus the light of Christ shines in the darkness of sin and unbelief, but the

darkness has not understood[1] **it.** Darkness does not understand God or Christ. Men whose minds are darkened and blinded by sin and unbelief cannot see God's light. They refuse to see it, because they prefer to live in darkness (see John 3:19–21 and comment).

The Testimony of John the Baptist (1:6–18)

6–8 Here John describes the coming of **John** the Baptist. John the Baptist was **sent from God**. His birth was miraculous (see Luke 1:5–25,57–66). He was sent with a specific purpose: namely, **to testify concerning that light**, that is, the light of Christ. John came to prepare men's hearts to receive that light (see Mark 1:2–4 and comment). John witnessed to Christ **so that through him** (John) **all men might believe** (in Christ). "All men" means both JEWS and GENTILES. Christ brings salvation to every man and woman who believes in Him.

9 **The true light . . . was coming into the world.** John the Baptist gave witness to that light. He told people that Christ, the Messiah,[2] was about to appear (see Mark 1:7–8 and comment).

The **true light**, Christ, **gives light to every man**. We must understand John's meaning here. God, through Christ, gives some light to all men. God **causes his sun to rise on the evil and the good, and sends rain on the righteous and the unrighteous** (Matthew 5:45). The Apostle Paul said: "God **has not left himself without testimony.** He has given **rain . . . crops . . . food . . . joy**" (Acts 14:17). Paul has also written: **For since the creation of the world God's invisible qualities—his eternal power and divine nature—have been clearly seen, being understood from what has been made** (Romans 1:20).

Therefore, creation itself and all God's natural blessings give witness to God. They give some light, some understanding, to all men.

But most men do not receive the full light. The Word, Christ, can give full light only to those who believe. Those who do not believe remain in spiritual darkness. They deny the light. They reject Christ. **Whoever rejects Christ will not see life** (John 3:36). That's why John the Baptist came into the world, so that **through him** (John) **all might believe** (verse 7). That is why the Apostle John wrote this Gospel, **that you may believe that Jesus is the Christ, the Son of God, and that by believing you may have life in His name** (John 20:31). Whether we believe or not is up to us.

10 When Jesus came into the world, **the world**[3] **did not recognize him**; that is, the men of the world did not recognize Him. Most men did not believe Jesus was the Messiah. Instead, they considered Him to be a criminal, a blasphemer, and they killed Him.

11 **He came to that which was his own.** Christ came to the world which He Himself had created (verse 3). He came to His own nation, Israel,[4] to His own people. He was not a stranger. He was a Jew coming to Jews. Nevertheless, they **did not receive him**. They rejected Him. The people of His own village tried to throw Him off a cliff (Luke 4:28–30). Finally, the Jewish leaders caused Him to be put to death.

12 Yet a few did **receive** Him; that is, they put FAITH in Christ. They **believed in his name.**[5] And to these believers, Christ

---

[1] In place of the word **understood**, many translations of the Bible say "overcome." The Greek word can have both meanings. Whichever meaning is used, the statement is equally true.

[2] For the meaning of the word "Messiah," see footnote to comment on John 1:41.

[3] In the New Testament, the word **world** is often used to mean "unbelieving men," that is, men who reject God's grace and truth.

[4] Israel is the name of the Jewish nation.

[5] To believe in Jesus' name is the same as to believe in Jesus. The name "Jesus" represents Jesus Himself.

gave the **right to become children of God**.

All men are created by God, but not all men are His **children**. To receive the right to be a child of God, we must believe in His Son Jesus. We must receive Jesus into our hearts through faith (see Galatians 3:26 and comment). This is what it means to "receive" Jesus. When we receive God's Son Jesus, God receives us, and we become members of God's family. **How great is the love the Father has lavished on us, that we should be called the children of God!** (1 John 3:1).

13 The **children of God** are not born **of natural descent**;[6] they are born spiritually. They are **born of God**. To be a Christian, to be a member of God's family, one must be born again (see John 3:3,5 and comment). It is not by our own power or desire that we become children of God; it is only by God's grace. He first chooses us (John 15:16). Human children are born according to the will of a husband and his wife. God's children are born according to His will.

When we accept Christ as our Lord and Savior, we are born into God's family. When we are born into His family, we become His children. When we become His children, we become heirs (Romans 8:16–17; Galatians 4:7).

In order to receive an inheritance, we first must be children. In order to be children, we first must be born. In order to be born into God's family, we first must accept Christ as our Lord and Savior. We do not become children by our own effort or by good works. Even if a servant works in someone's house faithfully for many years, that servant will never become a son; he will always remain a servant. We are children of God not by works, but by birth—spiritual birth.

14 In this verse, we read that Jesus Christ is the true incarnation of God. **The Word became flesh and lived for a while among us**. God in Christ became a man. He was fully and in every way a man like us, except that He never sinned (Hebrews 4:15). But at the same time, He was fully God. The **Word was God** (verse 1). In order to understand who Christ is, we must always remember that He is both God and man (see General Article: Jesus Christ).

One of the men with whom Jesus lived was the Apostle John, who was very close to Jesus and knew Him well. John writes here: **We have seen his glory**. John isn't writing someone else's opinion. He is writing about what he himself has seen (1 John 1:1–3).

John saw Christ's **glory**, His sinlessness, His love, His light, His truth, His grace, His humility, His power. All of these qualities are included in Christ's glory. Such was God's **one and only Son**. We believers also are God's sons, but we are not like Jesus. There can be no other son like Jesus, who was born not of a human father but by God's own Holy Spirit[7] (see Matthew 1:18,20–23; Luke 1:29–35 and comments).

Jesus was **full of grace and truth**. Grace is God's great mercy and love toward men (see Ephesians 1:2 and comment). God's grace was manifested most clearly when He sent His only Son Jesus to earth to die for our sins (see Mark 10:45 and comment). All of God's blessings to men come because of His grace (verse 16). Our salvation comes from God's grace (see Ephesians 2:8 and comment). And this grace is IN CHRIST. God **has blessed us with every spiritual blessing in Christ** (Ephesians 1:3).

But God has revealed in Christ more than just His **grace**. In Christ He has also revealed His **truth**. God is true. In God there is no falsehood or error. God's judgments are true. He separates good from evil, righteousness from unrighteousness. Because He is true, He will punish all those who oppose His truth and His righteousness. God's truth has

---

[6] In place of the words **of natural descent**, some versions of the Bible say "of blood" or "of bloods," which is a literal translation of the original Greek text. The meaning is the same.

[7] Jesus is called God's **Son** because He was born by God's Holy Spirit and a human mother. However, Jesus did not become God's Son only when He became a human baby. Jesus has always been God's Son (see John 1:1–2; Hebrews 1:2).

been manifested fully in Christ. Christ is God's true Word. Jesus said, "**I am the . . . truth**" (John 14:6).

Therefore, when we see Christ, **full of grace and truth,** we see God (John 14:9). God was perfectly revealed in Christ. However, those who do not believe in Christ cannot fully know God. They remain in spiritual darkness.

15 John the Baptist **testifies** concerning Christ. Even today, John's testimony continues through the words of the New Testament: "**I have seen and I testify that this is the Son of God**" (verse 34). John the Baptist had said, "**After me will come one more powerful than I**" (Mark 1:7). John came a few months before Jesus, and his work began before Jesus' work. But John the Baptist knew he was only sent to prepare the way for someone greater (see John 3:30). In this verse John the Baptist says, "**Christ has surpassed me because he was before me.**" Christ was greater than John because Christ was with God before the world was made. John was an ordinary man. Christ is the eternal Son of God.

16 Christ was **full of grace** (verse 14); and from the **fullness of his grace** all believers have received **one blessing after another.**[8] Christ is the source of all our blessings. Christ's **fullness** is without limit, because **God was pleased to have all his fullness dwell in him** (Colossians 1:19). In Christ **all the fullness of the Deity lives in bodily form** (Colossians 2:9).

17 God gave Israel some blessings in the Old Testament. God gave the Jews His **law.**[9] He first gave the law to MOSES on the top of Mount Sinai, and then Moses gave it to the people (Exodus 24:15–18; 31:18). But the law could not save men; rather, it condemned them, because they could not obey it perfectly (see Galatians 2:15–16 and comment). The law was righteous and true, but it did not give men eternal life.

But **grace and truth came through Jesus Christ.** In Christ not only God's truth but also His grace is given to man. Through Christ, man is free from the condemnation of the law (see Romans 8:1–4 and comment). God by His grace has sent Christ to save us from punishment and to give us eternal life (John 3:16).

Notice in this verse that the Apostle John uses Jesus' full name: **Jesus Christ. Jesus** was His human name. **Christ**[10] was His divine name.

18 **No one has ever seen God.** Moses himself never fully saw God. "You **cannot see my face,**" God said to Moses, "**for no one may see me and live**" (Exodus 33:19–20). All over the world men seek after God, and through the teachings of various religions they receive a partial understanding of Him. But their knowledge of God is never adequate. Only Christ, who came from God and is God, fully knows the Father and has seen Him. And only Christ, therefore, can make God fully known to men.

Christ is here called **God the only son.**[11] Christ is not only God's Son; He is also God Himself. All true knowledge of God comes from Christ.

Christ and John the Baptist (1:19–28)

19 When John the Baptist began to preach, many people came out to hear him and be BAPTIZED (see Mark 1:4–5 and

---

[8] In place of the words **one blessing after another**, some translations of the Bible say "grace upon grace." In this context, "grace" means "blessing."

[9] Here the word **law** has two meanings. It means the ten commandments written on tablets of stone, which Moses brought down from Mount Sinai. It also means the first five books of the Old Testament, which were later written by Moses. For further discussion, see Word List: Law.

[10] **Christ** is the Greek word meaning "anointed one," that is, one chosen and empowered by God. "Messiah" is the equivalent word in the Hebrew language.

[11] In place of the words **only Son**, some translations of the Bible say "only begotten." The meaning is the same.

comment). When the Jewish leaders heard about John, they wanted to find out about this new prophet. Therefore, they sent **priests and Levites**[12] from **Jerusalem**[13] to inquire who John was.

20 John knew that the Jewish leaders thought that he himself might be the Christ. All the Jews were expecting the Christ, the Messiah, to come and deliver them from bondage to the ROMAN EMPIRE and to reestablish the independent kingdom of Israel. But John immediately told them that he was not the Christ.

21 Then the Jewish leaders asked John the Baptist if he was **Elijah**. Elijah was one of the greatest prophets of the Old Testament. He did not die in an ordinary way, but was carried up to heaven in a chariot (2 Kings 2:11). The prophet Malachi prophesied that Elijah would return before the **great and dreadful day of the Lord** (Malachi 4:5). The Jews interpreted this prophecy to mean that Elijah himself would return before the Messiah came. But John told them that he was not the Elijah of the Old Testament.[14]

Then the Jewish leaders asked John if he was the **Prophet**. Moses had prophesied that a prophet like himself would rise up from among the Jews (Deuteronomy 18:15). This prophet was thought by the Jews to be different from Elijah and the Messiah.

Again John the Baptist denied that he was this prophet.

22–23 Finally, the priests and Levites asked John, "**Who are you?**" And John answered in the words of the prophet Isaiah that he was the **voice of one calling in the desert** (Isaiah 40:3). He was appointed to announce the coming of the real Messiah, Jesus Christ (see Mark 1:2–3 and comment).

24–25 Some of the Jews questioning John were **PHARISEES**, the strictest sect of the Jews. They wanted to know from where John the Baptist got his authority to **baptize**. It was a common practice for the Jews to baptize Gentiles who wanted to become followers of the Jewish religion, but nobody baptized Jews. "We don't need to be baptized," the Jews thought. "We are not sinners like the Gentiles."[15] Therefore, they wanted to know who was this John who was baptizing Jews.

26–27 John did not answer their question directly. He said, "**I baptize with water**. My baptism is an ordinary baptism. But there is one here in the crowd who will **baptize you with the Holy Spirit**?" (see Mark 1:7–8 and comment).

John's meaning was this: The Jewish leaders shouldn't question John's authority. He was only the announcer of One who had much greater authority.

28 The **Jordan** River where John baptized formed the eastern border of Israel; it was about eighteen miles from Jerusalem. The **Bethany** mentioned here is not the same Bethany where Mary and Martha lived, which was much closer to Jerusalem (John 11:1).

---

[12] The **priests** were descended from the first chief priest, Aaron, the brother of Moses. The **Levites** were descended from Levi, one of the twelves sons of Jacob, Abraham's grandson. Aaron himself was also descended from Levi. The Levites were in charge of services in the Jewish temple.

[13] In New Testament times, **Jerusalem** was the capital of the Jewish nation and the center of Jewish religious life. Today it is one of the chief cities of modern Israel.

[14] In Matthew 11:13–14 and 17:12–13, Jesus said that John the Baptist was the Elijah about whom Malachi prophesied. Jesus' meaning was that John had come in Elijah's place, **in the spirit and power of Elijah** (Luke 1:17). John the Baptist was like Elijah in a spiritual sense. Although John wasn't himself Elijah, he was the fulfillment of Malachi's prophecy.

[15] The Jews considered Gentiles to be "sinners" because they did not follow the Jewish law.

Jesus the Lamb of God (1:29–34)

29 The day after the Jewish leaders' questioning of John the Baptist, John saw Jesus coming[16] and said to the crowd, **"Look! the Lamb of God, who takes away the sin of the world."** All Jews knew what the term "Lamb of God" meant; it was a sacrifice offered to God. Every morning and evening a lamb was sacrificed to God in the Jewish temple in Jerusalem (Exodus 29:38–46). In the greatest Jewish festival, the Passover, a lamb was sacrificed in memory of the time God delivered the Jews out of bondage in Egypt (Exodus 12:1–30). Indeed, both the Apostles John and Paul considered Jesus to be the **Passover Lamb** (see John 19:36; 1 Corinthians 5:7 and comments).

The Jews sacrificed animals to God in order to atone for their sins. The animal served as a PROPITIATION for sin. Through animal sacrifices, the people's guilt was removed and they received forgiveness from God (Leviticus 5:5; 6:14–19). The punishment that would have fallen on the sinful person fell on the sacrificed animal instead. Therefore, it could be said that the sacrificed animal "took away" the person's sin.

In the same way, Christ was sacrificed to "take away" the **sin of the world**, that is, the sins of all who believe in Him (see 1 John 2:2 and comment). He was the **lamb** led to the slaughter about which the prophet Isaiah prophesied (Isaiah 53:7; Acts 8:32). He was a **guilt offering** (Isaiah 53:10). And by His sacrifice, believers are cleansed from their sins once and for all (see Hebrews 9:13–15,28; 10:10 and comments).

John knew that Jesus was not only the Christ, the Messiah, but that He was also the Lamb of God, through whom all the sins of the world could be washed away. Christ's sacrifice was great enough for all men to be cleansed by it. It was great enough, because Christ was God's own Son. Christ came as Savior to bring men salvation. But He came not as a worldly king to save men by force; He came as a "lamb" to save men by His death. **Worthy is the Lamb who was slain. . . . To him who sits on the throne and to the Lamb be praise and honor and glory and power, forever and ever!** (Revelation 5:6,12–13).

30–31 Before Jesus came to be baptized, He and John the Baptist had not met. **"I myself did not know him,"** John said (verse 31). But as soon as John saw Jesus, John knew that there was something unusual about Him. John had some awareness that Jesus was the Messiah, because according to Matthew 3:14, John said to Jesus, **"I need to be baptized by you, and do you come to me?"**

The entire purpose of John the Baptist's work was to prepare Israel, the Jewish nation, to receive their Messiah Jesus Christ. John had come so that Christ **might be revealed to ISRAEL.**

32–34 Although John recognized Jesus before he baptized Him, only after the baptism did John fully learn that Jesus was God's own Son. He learned this when he saw the Holy Spirit descend on Jesus in the form of a dove (see Mark 1:9–11; Luke 3:21–22 and comment). God had told John that the person on whom the Spirit descended would be the One who would baptize with the Holy Spirit (see Mark 1:8 and comment). Thus John could now say with complete certainty: **"I have seen and I testify that this is the Son of God"** (verse 34).

Step by step, the other disciples also came to understand who Jesus was (verses 41,49). But the greatest moment came when Peter, the chief disciple, confessed to Jesus: **"You are the Christ, the Son of the living God"** (see Matthew 16:16; Mark 8:29 and comment).

Jesus' First Disciples (1:35–42)

35–39 Next day John the Baptist pointed Jesus out to two of his own disciples. So the two disciples went with Jesus and spent the day with Him. It was the **tenth hour** when they went with

---

[16] John had already baptized Jesus some weeks earlier. After Jesus was baptized, He first went into the desert to be tempted by the devil (Matthew 4:1–11). The events of this section took place after Jesus returned from the desert.

Jesus, that is, about 4 P.M. Therefore, they probably spent the night with Jesus.

40–41 One of these two disciples of John the Baptist was **Andrew**, who afterward became one of Jesus' twelve disciples. The next day Andrew went and told his brother **Peter** that he had found the **Messiah**,[17] that is, the Christ (see verse 17 and comment).

42 Peter's ordinary Jewish name was **Simon**. When Jesus saw him, Jesus gave him a new name, **Cephas**, which in the Aramaic[18] language means "rock." In the Greek[19] language, the word for rock is "Peter."

In New Testament times, the meaning of a man's name was very important. The name was a sign of a man's character and authority. But why did Jesus name Peter a "rock"? In the Gospels, Peter certainly never acted like a rock. A rock is stable and strong. Peter was unstable and his faith was weak. But in the end God turned Peter into a "rock" through the power of the Holy Spirit. Afterward, Jesus made Peter His chief disciple. He told Peter that he was to be the "rock" on which His church would be built (see Matthew 16:17–18; Mark 8:29 and comment).

The meeting of Jesus with Peter and Andrew described in this section occurred some time before Jesus actually called them to leave everything and become His disciples (see Mark 1:16–18 and comment). Even though they recognized that Jesus was the Messiah, the Christ, they did not have a good understanding of what the Messiah was supposed to do. Like most other Jews, they thought that the Messiah would act like an earthly king and reestablish the earthly kingdom of Israel. They did not understand that, in fact, Jesus had come as the **Lamb of God** to suffer and die. They didn't realize that He had come to establish a spiritual kingdom that was not of this world.

Andrew **brought Simon to Jesus**. It has been said that the greatest service ever done for Christ's church was done when Andrew brought Simon to Jesus. Think of it! On that day, Andrew brought to Jesus the "rock" on which Jesus would build His church.

Andrew is mentioned three times in the Gospel of John, and each time we see him bringing someone to Jesus (John 6:8; 12:22). Let us ask ourselves: When was the last time we brought someone to meet Jesus?

Jesus Calls Philip and Nathanael (1:43–51)

43–44 Jesus' home was in Nazareth, in the province of Galilee in northern Israel. He had come down from **Galilee** to the southern part of Israel to be baptized. Now He decided to return to Galilee.

He then found **Philip** (Mark 3:18). Philip was an ordinary man. In the other places where Philip is mentioned by John, he does not appear to have been a very effective disciple (see John 6:5–7; 12:21–22; 14:8–9). But he followed Jesus when he was called; and later, through the power of the Holy Spirit, Philip became a great apostle (see Acts 8:4–8,26–40).

Philip, Peter, and Andrew were all from the town of **Bethsaida** in Galilee. Peter and Andrew also had a home in Capernaum (Mark 1:21,29). Jesus did many great works in both Bethsaida and

---

[17] **Messiah** is the Hebrew word meaning "anointed one." In the Greek language, "Christ" is the equivalent word meaning the same thing. Thus the names "Messiah" and "Christ" have the same meaning. In the New Testament the name **Messiah** is found only in this verse and in John 4:25.

[18] Aramaic was the language spoken by Jesus and by most other inhabitants of the Middle East in New Testament times.

[19] John wrote his Gospel in the Greek language. Most of the other books of the New Testament were also originally written in Greek. Greek was the language of the people of Greece, an important country of southern Europe. In New Testament times, the Greek language was commonly used by educated people in the Middle East.

Capernaum, but in the end very few of the residents of those towns believed in Him (Matthew 11:21,23).

45 Philip found **Nathanael**. Many Bible scholars believe that Nathanael is the same as Bartholomew, who also was one of Jesus' twelve disciples (Mark 3:18). They say that Bartholomew's second name was "Nathanael."

Philip told Nathanael that this Jesus of Nazareth was the one **Moses** wrote about in the **Law**.[20] He was the Messiah about whom the Old Testament **PROPHETS** prophesied.

Philip then called Jesus the **son of Joseph**. He didn't mean that Joseph was Jesus' real natural father, but that he was Jesus' legal father. Jesus' real Father was the Holy Spirit (Matthew 1:18,24–25).

46 Nathanael couldn't believe that the Messiah would come from such an insignificant town as **Nazareth**. Nazareth was not famous for anything; it was an ordinary little town in Galilee. The people of Nazareth, in fact, are most remembered today for trying to throw Jesus off a cliff! (Luke 4:28–29).

47 Even though Jesus had never met Nathanael, Jesus through His divine knowledge already knew everything about Nathanael. He knew that Nathanael was not a hypocrite like most of the Jewish leaders, but was a devout and sincere **Israelite**, that is, a true Jew (see Romans 2:28–29 and comment).

48–49 Nathanael was amazed that Jesus knew about him. He was even more amazed that Jesus knew he had been sitting under a fig tree before Philip had called him. Then Nathanael believed and confessed that Christ was indeed the Son of God. He also called Him the **King of Israel**, because he thought that the Messiah would be an earthly king (see Mark 15:32; John 12:13). In fact, Jesus is much greater than any earthly king; He is the King of kings. He is the true spiritual king of Israel, and His kingdom will have no end.

50–51 Jesus told Nathanael that he would see much greater things. Nathanael would **see heaven open, and the angels of God ascending and descending on the Son of Man**. That is, there would now be continuous communication between heaven and earth. Jesus had come down from heaven to show men the way to the Father. Heaven was now opened. And Jesus Himself was the road between earth and heaven (John 14:6).

Notice that Jesus called Himself the **Son of Man**. Jesus was both Son of God and Son of Man. He was completely God and completely man (see Mark 2:10 and comment). He was the **Son of Man** to whom was given **authority, glory and sovereign power. . . . His dominion is an everlasting dominion that will not pass away, and his kingdom is one that will never be destroyed** (Daniel 7:13–14).

In Chapter 1, the Apostle John has called Jesus many names: the **Word** (verse 1), the **light of men** (verse 4), the **true light** (verse 9), the **one and only Son** (verse 14), **Jesus Christ** (verse 17), the **Lord** (verse 23), the **Lamb of God** (verse 29), the **Messiah** (verse 41), the **Son of God** (verse 49). These are names that other people called Jesus. But Jesus called Himself simply the **Son of Man.**[21] It was because Jesus came to earth and became a "son of man," born of a woman, that He was able to open the door of heaven and show men the way to eternal life.

This, then, is the "good news," the GOSPEL of Christ: God came to earth in the form of the man Jesus, and took upon Himself the punishment for our sins by offering Himself as a sacrifice in our place. And to all who believe in Him, He promises to give eternal life.

[20] Here the **Law** means the first five books of the Old Testament, which were written by Moses. Messianic passages include Genesis 3:15; 49:10; Deuteronomy 18:15.

[21] To the Jews, however, the title **Son of Man** was not a simple name; it referred to the **son of man** mentioned by the prophet Daniel, whose kingdom would last forever (see Daniel 7:13; Mark 13:26–27 and comment).

CHAPTER 2

Jesus Changes Water to Wine (2:1–11)

1–2 Three days after the meeting between Jesus and Nathanael (John 1:47–51), Jesus and His new disciples[22] arrived in Galilee. There they received an invitation to a wedding in a small town called **Cana**, which was the home of Nathanael (John 21:2).

3 In the middle of the wedding feast the wine ran out. This was a great embarrassment to the bridegroom, who was responsible for the feast. Jesus' mother Mary knew that her son was the Messiah, the Son of God (Luke 1:30–32). Therefore, she supposed that He could perform a miracle and produce some more wine.

4 But Jesus told His mother that it was not suitable for her to make such requests of Him. He now must follow His heavenly Father's instructions, not His mother's. He had left His home, and now there was a new relationship between Himself and her.

Furthermore, Jesus' **time had not yet come**. That means that it was not yet time for Jesus to reveal Himself as the Messiah publicly. He knew that if He did so, the people would try to make Him a king, and God's plan for Him to suffer and die would be thwarted (see Mark 6:45 and comment). Also Jesus didn't want to be known just as a traveling miracle worker. He wanted people to concentrate on His teaching (see Mark 5:43 and comment).

5 However, Mary was sure that Jesus would do something to help the bridegroom. Therefore, she told the servants: "If Jesus gives you any instructions, just carry them out."

6–8 Jesus then told the servants to fill six big jars with water. Each jar could hold twenty to thirty gallons. Such jars were used by the Jews to store water for cleansing their hands before eating and for washing various cups and pitchers (Mark 7:1–4).

9–10 When the servants drew off the water, they found it had turned to wine.[23] The **master of the banquet**—that is, the chief steward—was amazed. He didn't know that a miracle had taken place. He was amazed because the bridegroom had saved the best wine for last! When Jesus turned the water into wine, He turned it into the best wine!

Notice in the story how man's need becomes an opportunity for God's power to work. When we are in despair, with no human solution in sight, that is when God delights to do His greatest works.

11 This was the first miracle Jesus performed. John calls it a **sign**. Jesus' miracles were signs that He was indeed the Son of God. These signs revealed Jesus' **glory**. John describes such miracles so that we might believe that Jesus is truly the Christ (see John 20:31).

After this miracle at the wedding in Cana, **his disciples put their faith in him**. That is, the disciples began to have real faith in Jesus. Before, only Nathanael had believed (John 1:49). Now the others believed also.

John does not say that anyone else believed, such as the servants, who knew that Jesus had turned the water to wine (verse 9). Even miracles will not produce faith in those whose minds are closed. Jesus' glory was manifest to some, but not to others. If we are to believe that Jesus is the Christ, the Son of God, we must come to Him with humble and open minds.

Jesus Clears the Temple (2:12–25)

12 From Cana, Jesus went to **Capernaum**, on the north side of the Sea of Galilee, where Peter and Andrew had a

[22] Together with Peter, Andrew, Philip, and Nathanael, there were also the sons of Zebedee, James and John (see Mark 1:19–20). John, the son of Zebedee, was the writer of this Gospel.

[23] John does not say whether all the water in the jars had become wine, or if only the water drawn off was turned to wine. Whichever it was, it was an extraordinary miracle.

house (Mark 1:21,29). Jesus' mother and **brothers** were with Him. Many Bible scholars believe that these brothers were sons of Joseph and Mary. One of these brothers was James, who later became the leader of the Jerusalem church and wrote the New Testament letter called "James" (see Mark 3:31–32; 6:3; John 7:3–5 and comments).

13 Each year most devout Jews went to Jerusalem to celebrate the PASSOVER festival (see Luke 2:41). In this first year after His baptism, Jesus also, with His disciples, went to Jerusalem for the Passover.

14–16 When Jesus arrived in the temple in Jerusalem, He saw merchants in the temple courtyard selling animals to be sacrificed. Those who had come to worship were exchanging their money with the money changers in order to obtain the special currency used in the temple. (Everyone had to pay the temple tax with special temple coins.) Jesus was upset that merchants should be doing business and making profits within the temple court, and so He drove them out.

Two years later, on His final trip to Jerusalem, Jesus cleansed the temple a second time (see Mark 11:15–17 and comment).

Jesus called the temple **my Father's house** (verse 16). God was Jesus' Father in a special way. We believers become God's children by ADOPTION (Ephesians 1:5). But Jesus was God's child by birth (Matthew 1:18).

17 For Jesus' disciples, the cleansing of the temple was another sign that Jesus was truly the Messiah. Only the Messiah would dare to drive out all the merchants and their animals. This was a fulfillment of prophecy, for in Psalm 69:9 the Messiah says, "**. . . zeal for your house consumes me.**" The Psalmist is saying that the Messiah will be anxious and eager to protect the honor of God's temple. Jesus was concerned for God's honor. To turn God's temple into a marketplace was to dishonor God. God's house was for worship and prayer, not for making money (Mark 11:17).

18 The Jews also understood that by cleansing the temple, Jesus was claiming to be the Messiah. Therefore, they asked Him to show them a **sign**, a miracle, to prove that He had the authority to do such a thing. The Jews were always seeking signs. Without a miraculous sign, they would not believe that Jesus was the Christ, the Messiah (see Mark 8:11–13; 1 Corinthians 1:22 and comments). Without a sign, they would consider Him to be only a troublemaker and lawbreaker!

19 Jesus said, "All right, I'll give you a sign. Let this temple be destroyed, **and I will raise it again in three days**."

20 Of course, the Jews did not understand Jesus' meaning. Already it had taken forty-six years to build the temple, and the temple was still not completed. (The temple was finally completed in 64 A.D.) How could Jesus build such a great temple in just three days, when hundreds of workmen hadn't been able to finish it in forty-six years?

Later the Jews used this statement of Jesus to accuse Him of opposing the law of Moses and the Jewish religion (Mark 14:57–59). The Jews claimed that Jesus said He would destroy the **temple**; but, in fact, it was they themselves who in the end destroyed the "temple"—that is, Jesus' body—by causing Him to be put to death. They had asked for a sign of His authority, and the "sign" He gave them was to **raise** from the dead the body they had destroyed.

21 Here John gives Jesus' meaning. Jesus was not talking about the Jewish temple in Jerusalem; He was talking about His own body. When He said, "**I will raise it again in three days**," He meant: "Three days after my death, my body will be resurrected."

The only sign that Jesus agreed to give to the Jews was the sign of His resurrection (see Matthew 12:39–40 and comment). His resurrection would be the final proof that He was the Messiah, the Son of God.

John says here that the **temple** was Jesus' **body**. God dwelled in the Jewish temple; God also dwelled in Jesus' body (Colossians 2:9). But now the church is also Jesus' body (see Ephesians 1:22–23; Colossians 1:18 and comments). John is saying that the old Jewish temple with its sacrifices would disappear, and that a new spiritual temple, or body—that is, the church—would be raised up. God does not live only in temples built by human hands (see Acts 7:48–49; 17:24 and comments); He lives also in the heart of every believer.

22 Even Jesus' own disciples did not understand His saying at the time. Only after the resurrection did they remember what He had said about rebuilding the temple in three days. They remembered that He had also taught them that He would be killed and be raised after three days (Mark 8:31; 9:31). Only after they saw Him risen from the dead did they fully understand and believe what the Scriptures had said about Jesus and what Jesus had said about Himself (John 12:16). Jesus told His disciples, "**. . . the Holy Spirit . . . will teach you all things and will remind you of everything I have said to you**" (John 14:26). For the disciples, this promise was fulfilled; and it continues to be fulfilled today in the life of every true believer.

23–24 Many people **believed** in Jesus because of His miracles (see John 6:2). But their faith was not deep. They regarded Him as a wonderworker, a great leader—even, perhaps, a king. But they had no spiritual understanding that He was, in fact, the Son of God.

These people "believed" Christ one day, but the next day they were ready to condemn Him to death. Their faith was not true faith. Their faith was only in miracles. Such people believe one day and forget the next.

Therefore, when Jesus saw the crowds praising Him and following Him, He did not **entrust himself to them** (verse 24). That is, He did not rely on their support. He did not seek to be their leader. He did not seek their approval and praise. He knew that they praised Him mainly with their lips. He knew that their faith was shallow.

Today, also, many people follow after Jesus who have no real faith. They may profess faith in hope of receiving some benefit or assistance—a scholarship, a job, some food, money. Some come to Christ because they have been healed, but their faith is often weak. They look mainly for what they can get from Christ, not for what they can give to Him. Such people quickly turn away when the benefits they are seeking come to an end.

It is true that everyone who comes to Christ comes, at first, for some selfish reason—that is, because of some need. But after meeting Christ and believing in Him, we must then renounce selfishness and follow Him, not for our own sakes, but for His sake.

25 Jesus **did not need man's testimony about man**. That is, He did not need anyone to tell Him what the human heart was like. Because of His supernatural knowledge, He knew every man's heart. . . . **for you alone know the hearts of all men** (1 Kings 8:39). Therefore, because Christ knows everything about us, He is perfectly suited to be the doctor of our souls (John 4:29). He is also—for the same reason—perfectly suited to be our judge! (John 5:22).

CHAPTER 3

Being Born Again of the Spirit (3:1–15)

1 **Nicodemus** was a Pharisee, and also a **ruler of the Jews**; that is, he was a member of the main Jewish religious committee called the SANHEDRIN. This Sanhedrin, made up of seventy members, exercised authority in all Jewish religious matters. The Roman governor held authority in all civil matters, but the Romans allowed the Jews to take charge of their own religious affairs—as long as they did not oppose the Roman government.

2 Nicodemus was a properly educated Jew. He was himself a teacher (verse 10). He went to Jesus **at night** because he didn't want anyone else to know he had gone to talk with Jesus, who in the Jews' eyes was not a legitimate teacher. But

Nicodemus had seen Jesus' miracles. He knew that Jesus was a special teacher or **Rabbi** (Jewish religious teacher) who had **come from God**, and he wanted to learn more from Him.

Unlike the other Pharisees, Nicodemus was not opposed to Jesus. He didn't try to trap Jesus in His conversation, as other Jewish leaders did (Matthew 22:15). Later, he took Jesus' side before the Sanhedrin (John 7:50–52). And after Jesus' death, when all the other disciples had fled, Nicodemus helped bury Jesus' body (John 19:39). Although in the beginning Nicodemus was a timid and fearful follower of Jesus, in the end he proved more faithful than Jesus' twelve disciples.

3 As a Pharisee, Nicodemus believed that if a man carefully followed the Jewish law and the traditions of the elders, he would obtain salvation. That is, Nicodemus believed, like all Jews, that salvation came by works of the law. Jesus knew that Nicodemus was sincerely seeking to obey God and to enter the kingdom of heaven.[24] Therefore, Jesus immediately told Nicodemus what he wanted to know; namely, that a man can enter the kingdom of heaven only by being born again.

In this one statement Jesus told Nicodemus that he could never be saved by doing the works of the law. Man in his nature is so sinful that God will never accept him into heaven, unless he is made completely new. What Nicodemus needed was not a new law, but a new heart. He needed a new spiritual power that would change his inward nature and make him acceptable before God. "You must be **born again** from above," said Jesus. **". . . no one can see[25] the kingdom of God unless he is born again."[26]** Man cannot enter heaven by his own effort; he can enter heaven only by receiving a new life through faith in Christ (see Galatians 2:15–16; Ephesians 2:8–9 and comments).

The **kingdom of God** means the reign of God both in heaven and on earth. When a person believes in Christ and gives his or her life to God, that person enters the "kingdom of God." In other words, as soon as we place true faith in Christ, we are **born again** into the kingdom of God. The kingdom of God is a spiritual kingdom. Therefore, even when our bodies die, our spirits continue to live on in His kingdom. The person who has been "born again" never dies. To enter the kingdom of God is the same as to receive **eternal life** (verse 15). This eternal life begins as soon as we believe in Jesus, and it never ends (see 1 Peter 1:23 and comment).

4 "How can a man be born again?" asked Nicodemus. No one can enter his mother's womb again. Therefore, since bodily rebirth is not possible, how then can one get a new heart and a new nature? It seemed impossible to Nicodemus.

5 Jesus then repeated what He said in verse 3 (see verse 3 and comment). This time He added that to enter the kingdom of God one must be born **of water and the Spirit**.

The **water** is a sign of purification and baptism. Baptism is a sign of the washing away of our sin. In order for a man's sin to be washed away, he must first repent. That is why both John the Baptist and Jesus preached a **baptism of REPENTANCE for the forgiveness of sins** (see Mark 1:4,14–15 and comment).

Therefore, in order to be born again, one must first repent and receive forgiveness for his sins; that is, he must have his sins washed away. The sign of this is baptism with water (see General Article: Water Baptism).

Baptism with water also means the dying of our old sinful self. Unless our old self dies, we cannot receive a new self (see John 12:24; Romans 6:3–7; Galatians 2:20 and comments).

---

[24] The "kingdom of heaven" is the same as the **kingdom of God** (see Matthew 4:17; Mark 1:14–15 and comment). For further discussion, see Word List: Kingdom of God.

[25] To **see** the kingdom of God is the same as to "enter" it. We cannot "see" it unless we enter it.

[26] In place of the word **again**, some ancient manuscripts of John say "from above." The meaning is the same.

Thus, to be born again, we must first be washed, baptized, purified. Our old sinful self must die. Then we shall be ready for the second step: to be reborn **of the Spirit**.

The **Spirit**, is God's HOLY SPIRIT (see John 14:16 and comment). It is God Himself. When a person repents and believes in Christ, God enters that person and gives him new spiritual life. That person is then born again **of the Spirit**. This new spiritual life is true life, eternal life, life in the kingdom of God. Just as physical life is impossible without being born of a woman, so spiritual life is impossible without being born of the Spirit.

Only when we are born again of the Spirit can our lives be acceptable to God. Only through the power of the Holy Spirit in our lives can we obey God's commands and lead a life pleasing to Him (Ezekiel 36:25–27).

Imagine what Nicodemus thought when he heard Jesus say these words. Nicodemus was a mature and upright man, a leader of the people, a teacher. He was a strict Jew, and considered himself righteous. He honored God. But Jesus told him, "You cannot enter the kingdom of God the way you are. You are still controlled by your sinful nature. You need to repent, to be cleansed, to die. And then you must be completely reborn spiritually through the power of God's Holy Spirit. You must be completely changed—just like being born from your mother's womb a second time."

Jesus says the same thing to every man and woman today. No one is ever a Christian from birth. No one is a Christian just because his parents and grandparents were Christians. Every man or woman must be born again spiritually. And that is the greatest and most amazing thing that can ever happen in any person's life.

There is one final question: How can we be born again in this way? There is only one answer: through faith. Just as we were not physically born through our own efforts, so we cannot be spiritually reborn through our own efforts. Only through faith in Christ can we be spiritually reborn. For this reason Christ came to earth and died in order to wash us from our sins and give us new life through the Holy Spirit (see John 1:4 and comment). He came to give us eternal life. He came to save the world (verse 17). Therefore, whoever believes in Him is not condemned (verse 18), but has eternal life (verse 36).

Jesus is the Savior of the world. He is the Lord. He is God Himself. Let us come to Him in faith, that we might be cleansed of our sins and receive new life from above. In this way we shall be able to enter the kingdom of God.

6–7 When we are born from our mothers, we are born as **flesh**. We cannot become spiritual unless we are born again of the Spirit. Our nature is determined by that which gives us birth. We are born as citizens of a sinful world. In order to become citizens of the kingdom of God, our sinful self must die and we must be born again spiritually. . . . **flesh and blood cannot inherit the kingdom of God** (1 Corinthians 15:50). Let not Nicodemus be **surprised** at this.

8 The person born of the Spirit is like the **wind**. We can hear the wind, but we cannot tell where it has come from or where it is going. In the same way, natural worldly men[27] can see and hear a person who has been born of the Spirit, but they cannot understand from where his spiritual life and power have come. They cannot understand what motivates a person born of the Spirit. And they cannot understand what is the goal and destination of a person born of the Spirit.

9–10 Nicodemus still didn't fully understand what Jesus was saying. Jesus asked him, "How can you not understand these things? You claim to know about God. You should know that you cannot come to God by your own strength."

---

[27] "Natural" or "worldly" people are those who have never been born again of the Holy Spirit. They love the world and the things of the world rather than God.

11 "You speak only of what you think about God," said Jesus to Nicodemus, "but **we**[28] **speak of what we know**. We have seen and experienced these spiritual things. We don't merely have opinions about these things; we have certain knowledge" (see John 1:18; 8:26).

Nevertheless, even though Jesus spoke of what He knew, most of the Jews did not believe His teaching.

12 Jesus had spoken to Nicodemus of **earthly things**, such as **birth, flesh, wind**. If Nicodemus couldn't understand these **earthly** illustrations, how would he ever be able to understand **heavenly things**, that is, pure spiritual teaching?

13 Only Jesus could speak about heavenly things, because only He had come from heaven to earth (Proverbs 30:4). Only He had true knowledge of the things of heaven.

When men are spiritually born again through faith, they enter the kingdom of God, that is, the kingdom of heaven. But they do not enter heaven itself. We must understand that there is a difference between "heaven" and the "kingdom of heaven." We enter the kingdom of heaven as soon as we believe in Christ. We enter heaven itself only after we die. Therefore, when Jesus said, "**No one has ever gone into heaven**," He was talking about living men. Jesus was the only living man who had ever been in heaven.

14 According to Numbers 21:4–9, God sent poisonous snakes among the Jews, because they had been grumbling against Him. Then the Jews repented. Therefore, God told Moses to make a snake from bronze and put it on a pole so that all the people could see it. Those who looked at the bronze snake were not harmed by the poisonous snakes.

Therefore, just as Moses lifted up the bronze snake, so the **Son of Man** (Christ) **must be lifted up**. This has two meanings. First, Jesus had to be **lifted up** on the CROSS. That is, Jesus had to die (John 12:32–33). Second, Jesus had to be **lifted up** into heaven. That is, He had to be raised from the dead and exalted at God's right hand (Ephesians 1:20–21; Philippians 2:9–11). Thus, through His death, resurrection, and ascension, Jesus has gained complete victory over death and over Satan. Therefore, He is able to give ETERNAL LIFE to all who believe in Him (see Hebrews 2:14–15).

Notice that for Christ to be lifted up to heaven, He first had to be lifted up on the cross. In order to be glorified in heaven, Jesus first had to die on earth. And as it was for Jesus, so it is with each believer. For each of us, the road to heaven goes by way of the cross (see Mark 8:34–35).

15 The purpose of Jesus' death was that we might have life, eternal life. **While we were still sinners, Christ died for us** (Romans 5:8). He came **to give his life as a ransom for many** (see Mark 10:45 and comment). Christ died that we might live.

To whom does Christ give life? To all who believe in Him. To "believe" has a very deep meaning. It means to believe fully, deeply. It means to depend totally on Christ, to trust in Him and not on oneself. Above all, to "believe" means to obey Christ and to love Him. If our faith does not result in obedience to Christ, it is a false faith (see Matthew 7:21; Galatians 5:6; James 2:14–17 and comments).

What kind of life does Christ give? He gives **eternal life**. Eternal life is not just a life that lasts forever. It is life with God. It is a life of joy, peace, righteousness. It is life without tears, sorrow, or pain (see Revelation 21:1–4). It is the reward, the heavenly inheritance for all those who believe in Jesus. It is our salvation.

---

[28] Jesus says **we**, not "I." Some Bible scholars believe that He means Himself and His disciples. Other scholars believe that He means Himself, the Father, and the Holy Spirit—the triune God. Both meanings are possible.

God's Love for the World (3:16–21)

16 In this verse John gives us the entire Gospel of Christ in brief.[29] Everything begins with the love of God for the world. **God is love** (1 John 4:8). God loves the whole world. He doesn't love only Jews (as the Jews thought), but He loves everyone—high caste and low caste, rich and poor, black and white. And He loves us so much that He gave up His only Son to save us (see 1 John 4:9–10 and comment).

Christ is a gift, the highest gift. God gave us what was most dear to Him. God does not want **anyone to perish** (2 Peter 3:9). Therefore, in order to give everyone the opportunity to be saved, He gave us His Son.

But only by faith can man receive this salvation, that is, eternal life (see verse 15 and comment). If a man believes in Jesus, he will not **perish**; he will receive **eternal life**. If a man does not believe, he will perish. To "perish" means to be separated from God, to suffer forever in hell, where there is **weeping and gnashing of teeth** (Matthew 8:12; 25:30,41).

There are only two roads for men: one leads to **life**, and the other leads to **destruction** (Matthew 7:13–14). Thus there are only two ends for men: one is to receive **eternal life**, the other is to **perish**. Christ came to show us the right road, the road that leads to eternal life. Christ is **the way and the truth and the life** (John 14:6). Not to believe in Christ is to choose destruction.

17 Jesus did not come into the world to condemn the world, but to save the world (Luke 19:10). His purpose in coming was to save us. If He had not come, all men would have been condemned. Now there is **no condemnation** for those who believe in Jesus Christ (see Romans 8:1 and comment).

But we must understand another truth. When Christ came into the world, some people believed and some did not. Those who believed were saved; those who did not believe were condemned. And the same is true today.

Therefore, when Jesus came into the world, some people were condemned because they refused to believe His words. They brought condemnation upon themselves (see verse 18). Jesus' coming separated believers from unbelievers.

Although Christ's main purpose was to save men and women, He also through His word brings judgment on those who refuse to believe (John 12:47–48). The sun shines in order to give light; but at the same time, it also creates shadows. Just as the sun causes shadows to appear, so the light of Christ reveals unbelief and sin, and condemns it (verses 19–20).

Christ is man's Savior (1 John 4:14). But it is also true that He will be man's judge on the day of judgment. God has **entrusted all judgment to the Son** (John 5:22,27). If we do not accept Christ as our Savior today, we will have to accept Him as our judge tomorrow.

18 Here again, John emphasizes the importance of faith (see verse 15). We are judged according to our faith. Those who believe are not condemned, but those who do not believe are condemned. John is talking about those who continue in unbelief until their death. Such people are already condemned.

19–20 **Light**—that is, Christ—**has come into the world** (see John 1:4–5,9). But men did not want the light, because it exposed their evil deeds (Ephesians 5:13). Rather, men loved the darkness—that is, evil. In this, they condemned themselves.

What is the main reason people refuse to believe in Christ? In these verses John has given us the answer. They do not believe because they do not want to give up their evil and selfish ways. They love darkness, because in the darkness their evil remains hidden—though not from God!

This is why faith is so important to God. When we believe, it means we truly want to leave the darkness and come into

---

[29] It is not certain whether verses 16–21 are spoken by Christ to Nicodemus, or whether they are statements of John, the writer of this Gospel. No punctuation marks were used in the original Greek manuscripts, so it is not known where the quotation marks should be placed. It does not matter; the truth is the same.

the light of Christ. Thus, in God's eyes, unbelief is the same as unrighteousness. Likewise, faith is the same as righteousness. We are justifed—declared RIGHTEOUS—by faith (see Romans 5:1; Galatians 2:15–16 and comments).

21 **. . . whoever lives by the truth comes into the light**. To live **by the truth** means to repent of one's sins and to open one's heart to receive Christ. It means to turn from darkness and to hate evil. Such men do not need to fear the light.

Those who come **into the light** are born again of the Spirit (verse 5). Their new life and new heart is from God. They cannot say, "These are my good works." All good works are done **through God**. Man can claim no credit for his good works (see Ephesians 2:8–9). All our righteousness comes from the Holy Spirit, who lives within us who believe.

John the Baptist's Testimony About Jesus (3:22–36)

22 After the Passover festival (John 2:13) and the conversation with Nicodemus, Jesus went out into the **Judean countryside**—into the surrounding district of Judea.[30] He and His disciples began to baptize also, calling on people to repent and turn to God (Mark 1:15). The actual baptizing was done by Jesus' disciples under Jesus' direction (John 4:2).

23–24 John was also baptizing nearby. John had not yet been put in prison (Mark 6:17–29). From this we can understand that the Galilean ministry of Jesus mentioned in Mark 1:14 had not yet begun. According to this, Jesus had not yet finally called Peter, Andrew, John, and James (Mark 1:16–20). Only after He returned to Galilee (John 4:43) did He finally call those four disciples.

25 Some of John the Baptist's disciples began to argue with a certain Jew about the Jewish purification laws. Perhaps the Jew was one of Jesus' disciples. Perhaps he had said it was not necessary to follow the purification laws (Mark 7:1–2,5).

26 During the argument over purifying, John's disciples learned that people in increasing numbers were going to Jesus to be baptized. More people were now going to Him than to John. John's disciples felt badly about this. It seemed to them as if **everyone** was now going to Jesus. They were envious.

27 John admonished his disciples not to complain about Jesus' success. Each man is appointed by God for a certain task. Each man is given different gifts to enable him to fulfill that task. **A man can receive only what is given him from heaven**. John was appointed only to prepare the way for Christ. Therefore, it was according to God's will that people should now begin to turn to Jesus.

Let us never envy others who have received from God a greater appointment or greater gifts. Envy is one of the most common and also one of the most harmful sins found among Christians. Envy is a great cause of strife within the church. Let each of us be thankful for the gifts God has given us, and let us use them diligently in His service (1 Corinthians 4:7).

28 John the Baptist himself had said, **"I am not the Christ"** (John 1:20). John had never tried to exalt himself. When people tried to give him more honor than he deserved, he did not accept it. How many of us do likewise? Let us strive to follow John's example. John's sole aim was to lead men and women to Jesus, not to himself. Let that be our sole aim also.

29 John was only the **friend** of the bridegroom. The **bridegroom** is Christ. The **bride** is the church, that is, all believers (Ephesians 5:23,31–32; Revelation 19:7–8). The bride belongs to the bridegroom, not to the friend of the bridegroom.

Instead, the friend rejoices in the bridegroom's happiness. In the same way, John rejoiced that people were coming to Jesus.

30 As the morning light increases,

---

[30] Judea is a southern province of Israel. In New Testament times, Jerusalem was its capital city.

the light of the morning star decreases. John the Baptist was like the morning star, sent to announce the coming dawn of Christ.

John knew his place. His entire goal was to magnify Jesus. That is the purpose of all disciples of Christ. Our work is to show forth the light of Christ among men, not our own light. We must remain nothing, in order that Christ might be all.

If church leaders would concentrate only on exalting Christ, they would soon stop trying to exalt themselves above each other. Let every church leader continually say to himself, as John did: **"I must become less."** Paul gave us the rule: **Honor one another above yourselves** (Romans 12:10). And, of course, we must honor Christ **above all** (verse 31).

31 The **one who comes from above**—that is, Christ—**is above all.**[31] John the Baptist was **from the earth.** Only Jesus came from heaven (John 3:13; 8:23). Therefore, Jesus was greater than John—indeed, greater than all men. He is **above all.**

32 Jesus testified to what He had seen and heard in heaven. His testimony, then, was absolutely sure and true (see verse 11 and comment). The prophets of the Old Testament saw and heard things in visions and dreams. But Christ received the things of God directly from God Himself.

Nevertheless, **no one** accepted Jesus' testimony. That is, worldly men did not accept Jesus' testimony. They refused to believe. They rejected the light. Natural worldly men cannot accept Jesus. They cannot understand heavenly things. Only when a man's heart is humble and open to the Holy Spirit can he accept the testimony and teaching of Jesus.

33 Whenever we "certify" someone's testimony, we are agreeing that that person's testimony is fully true and trustworthy; that is what certifying means. The man who has opened his heart to Christ and has accepted His testimony has also **certified** that God is truthful. Christ is God's **Word** (John 1:1). If Christ is true, then God also is true. But if a man rejects Christ, he also rejects God. The man who does not accept the testimony of Christ calls God a liar (1 John 5:9–10).

34 Jesus **speaks the words of God.** Jesus has come from above. He knows the Father's mind completely. He has God's Spirit **without limit**, that is, in full measure. We believers receive the Holy Spirit according to measure. . . . **to each one of us grace has been given as Christ apportioned it** (Ephesians 4:7). But to Christ unlimited grace was given. Christ was given the Spirit in full measure. He was filled with all the fullness of God. **For God was pleased to have all his fullness dwell in him** (Colossians 1:19).

35 We can trust Christ completely, because God the Father **has placed everything in his hands** (see John 13:3). The Father has given Christ the Spirit **without limit** (verse 34). Jesus said, "**All things have been committed to me by my Father**" (Matthew 11:27). "**All authority in heaven and on earth has been given to me**" (Matthew 28:18).

Men can come to Christ as they would come to God. All of God's spiritual blessings are available to us in Christ (Ephesians 1:3). As God has given His Holy Spirit to Christ,[32] so Christ gives the Spirit to those who believe in Him. And when Jesus gives us His Spirit, He also gives us His knowledge (John 15:15), His **authority** (John 17:2), His **joy** (John 17:13) and His **glory** (John 17:22).

36 Above all, Jesus gives us **eternal life.** This is the sum of all His spiritual blessings. To believe in Jesus is to have eternal life. Jesus said, "**Now this is eternal life: that they may know you, the only true God, and Jesus Christ, whom you have sent**" (John 17:3).

---

[31] It is not certain whether verses 31–36 are spoken by John the Baptist, or whether they are comments by the Apostle John, the writer of this Gospel. For further discussion, see footnote to comment on John 3:16.

[32] God's Holy Spirit is also Christ's Spirit; they are the same. There is only one Spirit (Ephesians 4:4).

When we believe in Christ, we are reborn from "above" (from heaven) and receive new spiritual life. This life begins as soon as we believe and it never ends. Our bodies will die, but our spirits will never die.

But there is a greater gift even than eternal life. And that gift is Christ Himself. All gifts are included in Christ. When we receive Christ as our Savior and Lord, we receive all the riches of heaven. **He who has the Son has life** (1 John 5:12). He who has the Son has everything (see Romans 8:32 and comment).

But we must never forget what happens to the man who **rejects**[33] Christ. **He will not see life, for God's wrath remains on him** (see verses 16–17 and comment). He **stands condemned already because he has not believed in the name of God's one and only Son** (verse 18).

We Christians talk much about God's love, but we must not neglect to talk about God's wrath. God is opposed to all who oppose Him. To refuse to believe in Christ is to oppose God. It is to disobey God. Man must either believe and be saved, or not believe and be condemned. Man must choose one of these two; there is no other choice.

CHAPTER 4

Jesus Talks With a Samaritan Woman (4:1–26)

1–3 Just as the Pharisees had taken a close interest in John the Baptist, so they now began to watch Jesus. They were not happy that these men were so popular with the people. If everyone followed after John and Jesus, the Pharisees would lose their own power and influence over the people (see Mark 3:6 and comment).

Therefore, in order to avoid a conflict with the Pharisees, Jesus left Judea and returned to Galilee. He did not want to stir up the anger of the Pharisees and other Jewish leaders at that time. He had much teaching and preaching to do. His time to suffer and die at their hands had not yet come.

4–5 To reach Galilee, Jesus had to go through the district of **Samaria,** which lay between Judea and Galilee. Jesus stopped near a plot of land that Jacob, Abraham's grandson, had given to his son Joseph[34] (Genesis 33:19: 48:22).

Jesus later told His disciples not to **go among the Gentiles or enter any town of the Samaritans** (see Matthew 10:5 and comment). But this time on His way to Galilee He stopped in a Samaritan village for two days and brought the people of that village great blessing (verses 40–41).

6 Jacob was especially revered by the Samaritans. He had discovered a well at that place, and thus it was called Jacob's well.

Jesus was tired. He was a man such as we are. At the **sixth hour,** that is, noon, He reached the well and sat down on the edge of it.

7 Then a woman came to the well, and Jesus asked her to give Him a drink. His purpose was to satisfy her spiritual need, but He began by asking her to satisfy His physical need. Many Christians have found that when they themselves are in some physical need, others are usually more willing to listen to their spiritual witness.

8–9 Jesus' request to the Samaritan woman for a drink was unusual for two

---

[33] In place of the word "reject," some ancient manuscripts of John say "disobey." But the meaning is the same. When we reject Christ, we are disobeying Him. We are refusing to leave our sin and come to the light. To not believe is to disobey God. It is to be unrighteous. This is why, without faith, no one can ever be reckoned righteous in God's sight. . . . **without faith it is impossible to please God** (Hebrews 11:6).

[34] Joseph was the eleventh of Jacob's twelve sons.

reasons. First, a Jewish man, especially a teacher, never talked alone with any woman if he could help it. Second, this woman was a Samaritan. The Jews and the Samaritans hated each other. Many years earlier the Samaritans had been ordinary Jews. Then they were conquered by the Assyrians. The Assyrians brought many foreigners into Samaria to settle there, and the Samaritans had intermarried with them and had begun to worship their gods (2 Kings 17:22–33). Thus the Samaritans became half-Jews. Although in Jesus' time they had begun again to worship the one true God, they still refused to worship at the Jewish temple in Jerusalem. They had built their own temple on the top of a nearby mountain in Samaria (see verse 20), but the Jews had later burned it down. Thus there was great hostility between the two nations. This is why John says in verse 9: **Jews do not associate with Samaritans**.

10 Jesus did not want to talk about the differences between Jews and Samaritans. He wanted to tell the woman about the **gift of God**, that is, the gift of new life that He could give her, which Jesus called **living water**. We can also understand the **gift of God** to mean Christ Himself.

In Jesus' time, any water that flowed was called "living water." It was considered the best water to use to purify one's hands and drinking cups. But here Jesus gives the term "living water" a much deeper meaning. "Living water" is new spiritual life, which comes from the Holy Spirit (John 3:5). It not only flows into a person; it also flows out of him (John 7:38–39). The Holy Spirit is a spring of water that never dries up[35] (verse 14).

If the woman had known who Jesus was, she would instead have asked Him for water! Only Jesus can give the gift of **living water** (Revelation 21:6).

11–12 Like others (John 2:20; 3:4), the woman did not understand Jesus' spiritual meaning. She thought He was talking about ordinary drinking water. "Can you give us better water than our ancestor Jacob did, who made this well?"

13–14 Then Jesus explained to the woman that the water He could give was different from ordinary water. Those who drink Jesus' water never thirst again. Jesus' water continuously "wells up" in a person. It continuously gives life, **eternal life**.

Jesus did not mean that, once a person believes in Him, that person will no longer thirst for spiritual things. We must continously hunger and thirst for righteousness (Matthew 5:6). We must hunger for God's fellowship, His blessings, His grace. But when we do so, we are immediately filled. We never remain thirsty. As much as we thirst for God's grace, He fills us. His living water never runs dry.

15 The woman still misunderstood what kind of water Jesus was talking about. She thought, "If I drink His water, I'll never need to come and get more water from this well. I'll never have to drink again."

16 Jesus knew the woman's deep spiritual need. He knew that she was living in sin with a man who was not her legal husband. She had not understood about His spiritual water. Therefore, He changed the subject, and confronted her with her sin. "**Go, call your husband**," He said to her. In saying this, His purpose was to awaken her consciousness of her sin.

17–18 The woman didn't want to talk about her husband or her previous husbands. So she lied. "**I have no husband**," she said. She meant: "I am not living with any man."

But even though the woman had tried to deceive Jesus, her answer, in fact, was in one way true. She was living with a man who was not her legal husband. According to the Jewish law, if a woman's first husband was still living, any other man she lived with was not considered to be her husband. In other words, this Samaritan woman was living in adultery (Mark 10:12).

We can never deceive God. Because Jesus had God's knowledge, He knew all

[35] In the Old Testament, God Himself is called a **spring of living water** (Jeremiah 2:13; 17:13).

about this woman. She could not deceive Him.

19 The woman was amazed by Jesus' knowledge of her past life. She at once realized that He was some kind of prophet.

The Samaritans believed only in the first five books of the Old Testament. The only prophet they recognized, therefore, was the prophet that Moses spoke about in the book of Deuteronomy. Moses said that God would **raise up** a prophet (Deuteronomy 18:15), and the Samaritans thought that this prophet would be the Messiah.

Thus when the woman called Jesus a "prophet," she, in fact, was suggesting that He might be the Messiah Himself (see verse 25).

20 But again the woman tried to change the subject. She knew the Jews believed that God must be worshipped in Jerusalem according to 2 Chronicles 6:6; 7:12 and Psalm 78:68. But since these passages were not in the first five books of the Old Testament, the Samaritans did not accept them. The Samaritans worshiped only on Mount Gerizim in Samaria, where "**our fathers**"—that is, Abraham and Jacob—worshipped (Genesis 12:7; 33:20; Deuteronomy 11:29).

Since Jesus was a prophet, the woman supposed that He could tell her who was right, the Samaritans or the Jews.

21 Jesus told the woman that the time was coming when men would worship neither in Jerusalem nor on Mount Gerizim. In forty years Jerusalem would be destroyed by the Romans. Men would then realize that God does not live in a temple made with hands (Acts 7:48–49; 17:24). Neither does He live only on one mountain top. God can be worshiped anywhere, because **God is spirit** (verse 24).

22 The Samaritans did not know what they worshipped (Acts 17:23). They did not have a full knowledge of God, because they rejected most of the Old Testament. But the Jews had a much greater understanding of God, because they believed in the complete Old Testament Scriptures. Not only that, but SALVATION—that is, the means of obtaining salvation—was **from the Jews**. Jesus' meaning was this: The means of obtaining salvation was the Messiah, the Christ—and Christ was a Jew.

23 "Even now," said Jesus, "the time has come when men can worship the true God, who is spirit." Those who are **true worshippers** understand that **God is spirit** (verse 24). God cannot be worshipped outwardly, or by special rituals in special places. God can only be worshiped **in spirit and truth**. This means that man must worship God with his **spirit**.[36] And he must worship God in **truth**, that is, truly, sincerely, from his heart and spirit.

God seeks men who will worship Him spiritually from their hearts. Men worship stones and idols in one way. But God must be worshipped in another way. He must be worshipped **in spirit and truth**.

24 **God is spirit**. God's essential nature is spirit. He is a life-giving spirit. God is not stone; He is not flesh; He is not earth; He is not air. He is spirit. Therefore, He must be worshipped spiritually. Only with our spirits can we truly worship God.

25 The woman couldn't understand the spiritual things Jesus was telling her. She said that when the **Messiah**[37] came, He would explain everything. Perhaps she wondered if Jesus Himself was the Messiah.

26 "**I . . . am he**," Jesus said to the woman. "I myself am the Messiah."

Jesus did not often reveal to Jews that He was the Messiah, because they would try to make Him a king (see Mark 5:43; 8:30 and comments). But among the Samaritans, He did not try to hide His identity.

---

[36] Every person has his or her own spirit. A person's spirit (together with the soul) is not destroyed by the death of the body.

[37] **Messiah** is the Hebrew word for Christ, or "anointed one." For further discussion, see footnote to comment on John 1:41.

Jesus Talks With His Disciples (4:27–42)

27 The disciples had earlier gone to town to buy food (verse 8). They were surprised to see Jesus talking with a woman. In the Jews' eyes, it wasn't proper for a Rabbi (teacher) to converse with a woman. But they were embarrassed to ask Jesus why He was talking with her.
28–30 The woman now began to think that Jesus was the Messiah. His knowledge of her own life had amazed her. Even though Jesus had only spoken about her five "husbands," she knew that He could have told her **everything** that she had ever done.

The woman could not keep these things to herself. She went and told the people of her town. Christ had made Himself known to her. Now she went to make Him known to others. The blessings we receive are to be shared. If we put a light under a bushel, it will go out (Matthew 5:15).
31–33 After the woman had gone to call the people of her town to see Christ, the disciples suggested that Jesus eat some of the food they had purchased in the town. But He told them that He had food they didn't know about. They did not understand that He was talking about spiritual food (see Matthew 4:4).
34 Jesus' **food** was to do God's will. Jesus desired to do God's will as much as a hungry man desires to eat. Jesus received satisfaction from obeying God. As He obeyed God, He received spiritual strength and nourishment. So it is with everyone who obeys God.

God had sent Jesus to save the world, **to save sinners** (1 Timothy 1:15). To do that, Jesus had to die (see Mark 10:45 and comment). Jesus not only had to do God's will each moment, but He had to **finish** His work. He could not be fully satisfied until He had finished it. Jesus finished God's work when He died on the cross.
35 When a farmer sows, he must wait a few months for the harvest. But the disciples of Christ are not like farmers. Those who sow spiritual seed do not have to wait four months to reap. They can at once begin to call men into God's kingdom.

Jesus' work was reaping. It was the disciples' work too (see Mark 1:17). Perhaps, even as Jesus talked, the people from the Samaritan woman's town were coming toward Him. They were the **harvest**! The seed had been sown in the mind of the woman, and now already the harvest had come!

Jesus' main meaning was this. Harvest time is a busy time. It is also a short time. If the crop is not quickly harvested, it will be lost. Therefore, Christ's disciples must work quickly and diligently. The task of harvesting is urgent (see Matthew 9:37–38 and comment).
36 For the disciples of Christ, sowing and reaping go together. The disciple sows the word (see Mark 4:14). But he also reaps; that is, he calls people to believe and to enter God's kingdom. The Samaritans were coming toward them. Christ had sown; now He was about to reap. He was already drawing **his wages**.

The reaper will receive a wage, a reward. We each will be rewarded according to our work (Matthew 16:27). But not only will the reaper be benefited; others also will benefit from his work. The souls he "harvests" will receive eternal life. Thus the work of the reaper lasts for eternity.
37 Among farmers, usually the one who sows reaps his own crop. But with spiritual sowing and reaping, usually one man sows and another man reaps. Since spiritual sowing and reaping go on together, the sower and reaper will **be glad together** (verse 36).
38 Then Jesus reminded His disciples that others had worked before them, especially John the Baptist and his followers. These earlier workers had prepared the ground and planted the seed. They had done the hard work, but had not seen the harvest. Now Jesus and His disciples were about to reap the **benefits of their labor**.

Jesus here gives a principle that is true in all Christian work. We must not try to take credit for the success of any spiritual work. Usually someone else has gone ahead of us and prepared the ground. But that is not all. It is God alone who makes the seed grow. Paul wrote to the Corinthians: **I planted the seed, Apollos**

watered it, but God made it grow. So neither he who plants nor he who waters is anything, but only God, who makes things grow (1 Corinthians 3:6–7).

39–41 Here we can see how a small work of Christ led to a great work. Jesus began by teaching one woman. He ended by teaching an entire town. Let none of us despise a small work; it will often lead to a greater one.

The Samaritan woman's testimony caused many of the townspeople to believe. See how much fruit resulted from the testimony of an ordinary sinful woman! In the same way, our own testimony concerning what Christ has done in our life is very effective. Therefore, let us not be hesitant to share our testimony with others.

42 However, even though men and women may believe in Christ through the testimony of others—such as parents, preachers, and friends—their faith becomes strong only when they themselves have met Christ. We can witness to others, but they must themselves invite Christ into their lives. It's not enough to learn about Christ with our minds; we must meet Jesus with our spirits if we are to have true faith.

This is what happened to the people of that Samaritan town. When they heard Christ's words for themselves, their hearts and spirits were opened, and they then knew that He was the Messiah, the **Savior of the world** (see 1 John 4:14). He was the Savior not only of the Jews, but of the Samaritans also.

Jesus Heals the Official's Son (4:43–54)

43–44 From Samaria, Jesus then went to Galilee, which was where he had been brought up (Luke 2:39–40). He knew that **a prophet has no honor in his own country** (see Mark 6:4 and comment). He went to Galilee knowing that He would be rejected (Mark 6:1–6; Luke 4:28–30).

45 At first, however, the Galileans welcomed Jesus. Many of them had gone to Jerusalem for the Passover festival, and had seen the **miraculous signs** Jesus had done there (John 2:23). But most of them didn't really believe that Jesus was the Messiah, the Christ (see John 2:23–24 and comment).

46–47 In Cana, a royal official asked Jesus to heal his son. This incident is similar to the healing described in Matthew 8:5–13; but the healing described here is a different event.

48 Jesus knew that the official did not have true faith. He had come to Jesus only because he had heard about the miracles Jesus had performed. Jesus told him and those standing around, "You only believe when you see a miracle. That's not real faith" (see John 2:18 and comment).

However, belief in miracles is often a first step to real faith. Christ did not reject people who believed in His miracles. His miracles were **signs** that He was indeed the Messiah (see John 14:11 and comment).

49–50 Jesus then healed the official's son right then and there. The healing was instant and complete. Jesus didn't even go to the village where the child was. Jesus was in Cana and the child was in Capernaum, sixteen miles away (see Matthew 8:13).

The father believed Jesus' word and started for home. He believed without having seen any sign or miracle. He had accepted the rebuke Jesus gave him in verse 48.

51–53 On the journey home, the official learned that his son had been healed at the exact hour that Jesus had said, "**Your son will live**" (verse 50). As a result, the official and his family placed complete faith in Christ; that is, they became Christians. The miracle had produced true faith.

The sickness of the child had in the end brought great blessing upon his parent's house. To those who love and believe God, God will bring good out of all their afflictions (see Romans 8:28 and comment).

54 This was the second miracle Jesus did in Galilee. The first miracle was turning the water into wine (John 2:11). Both times Jesus had just returned from a trip to Judea, where He had done other miracles which John has not recorded (see John 2:23: 4:45).

CHAPTER 5

The Healing at the Pool (5:1–15)

1–2 In verse 2, John describes a pool called, in the **Aramaic**[38] (or Hebrew) language, **Bethesda**. He writes that **there is in Jerusalem . . . a pool**. Because John has used the present tense here, some Bible scholars believe that this Gospel was written before the destruction of Jerusalem in 70 A.D. If the Gospel had been written after 70 A.D., John would have written that there "was" a pool.

3–4 Many people in Jesus' time believed that the water of this pool had healing power. It was said that an angel stirred up the water in the pool from time to time, and as soon as the water was stirred, the sick people waiting near the pool would rush to get into the water. John doesn't explain how the angel stirred up the water, but it was believed that the one who could get into the water first after it had been stirred would be healed.[39]

5–6 Jesus learned that there was a man unable to walk, who had been lying by the pool for thirty-eight years. Jesus asked him, "**Do you want to get well?**" Notice that the man did not go to Jesus; Jesus went to him. The man did not know Jesus was a healer.

7 The man explained to Jesus why he had not been healed: he could not get into the water in time. All his thoughts were on the supposed power of the water, not on the power of Jesus.

8–9 Jesus healed the man instantly and completely (see Mark 2:11). Jesus healed him even though the man himself had no faith. The man had not asked to be healed. He didn't even know Jesus.

This miracle took place on the **Sabbath**, that is, Saturday. According to the Jewish law, one was not supposed to do any kind of "work" on the Sabbath (Exodus 20:8–11).

10 The **Jews**—that is, the Jewish leaders—rebuked the man for disobeying this Sabbath law. According to the law, it was illegal even to carry a bed or **mat** on the Sabbath! That was considered "work"[40] (Jeremiah 17:21–22).

The Pharisees and the teachers of the law had added many kinds of regulations concerning what was "work" and what was not "work." Many of these regulations were not written in the Old Testament. The rules forbidding work were made in order to keep the Sabbath day holy; it was supposed to be a day set aside for worship and prayer and rest. But the Jewish leaders had added so many little rules that the original meaning of the Sabbath had been lost. Because of all these rules, it was no longer possible to do any healing or other good works on the Sabbath.

But Jesus' teaching was that it was always lawful to "do good" on the Sabbath (see Mark 2:23–28; 3:1–5; Luke 13:10–17 and comments).

11–13 The man who was healed put the "blame" on Jesus for breaking the Sabbath law. He said to the Jewish leaders, "He (Jesus) told me to pick up my mat and walk."

Then the Jews looked for Jesus but could not find Him. He had disappeared into the crowd that had gathered there. The crowd had gathered because of the miracle that had taken place.

14 Some time later, Jesus met the

[38] The **Aramaic** language was the language most commonly spoken by the people of the Middle East in New Testament times. In this verse, instead of **Aramaic** language, some translations of the Bible say "Hebrew" language. Hebrew is closely related to Aramaic; it is the language of the Jews. Even so, most of the Jews of Jesus' day spoke Aramaic, rather than Hebrew.

[39] Not all ancient manuscripts of John contain verse 4.

[40] It was legal, however, to carry a bed if there was someone lying on it. That was not considered "work."

healed man again. He said to him, "**Stop sinning or something worse may happen to you.**" From this we can understand that this man's illness had come about because of some sin.[41] Jesus told him that if he continued to sin, something worse would happen to him. That is, he would be condemned at the last judgment and receive eternal punishment.

15 The healed man was very ungrateful to Jesus. Even though he knew that the Jewish leaders were hostile to Jesus, he went and told them that it was Jesus who had healed him.

Life Through the Son (5:16–30)

16 When the Jewish leaders found out it was Jesus who had healed on the Sabbath, they began to **persecute** Him. The Jews were zealous for the **form of godliness**, but they denied the **power** of godliness (2 Timothy 3:5).

17 Jesus reminded the Jews that God is always working. Yes, He created the world in six days and rested on the seventh day (Genesis 2:2–3). But it is also true that God is continuously **working**. If He stopped "working" one minute, the universe and all life would end. For **he himself gives all men life and breath and everything else** (Acts 17:25). Since God is "working" seven days a week, so must Christ be **working** seven days a week. For just as God created the heavens and the earth through Christ (John 1:3), so God sustains the heavens and the earth through Christ (Colossians 1:17). Since the works of Jesus are the same as the works of God, the works of Jesus must take place continuously—even on the Sabbath.

18 Jesus had called God **my Father** (verse 17). This made the Jews more angry than anything else. They knew Jesus was claiming that God was His Father in a special way—that is, that He and God had the same nature. They knew that Jesus was making Himself equal with God. In the Jews' mind this was a terrible blasphemy against God. The Jews believed in the one true God,[42] a God infinitely greater than any human being. Thus, for any person to claim to be God or to be like God was an insult to this one true God. According to the Jewish law, the punishment for such blasphemy against God was death (Leviticus 24:16). Therefore, the Jewish leaders **tried all the harder to kill him** (see Mark 3:6; John 10:33).

But in verses 19–30, Jesus showed the Jews that He was indeed equal with God. Their charges of blasphemy were false.

19 In everything Jesus was dependent on His Father, God, and was obedient to Him. The **Son can do nothing by himself**. At the same time, Jesus had all the authority and power of His Father. . . . **whatever the Father does the Son does also** (see Matthew 11:25; John 13:3; 14:10).

20 **For the Father loves the Son**; that is, He continuously loves Him. The unity and closeness between God and Jesus comes from God's love for Jesus. That is why God shows Jesus **all he does** (see John 3:35).

Jesus told the Jews that He would do still **greater things** than they had already seen, because God **will show him** (Jesus) **even greater things than these**. These **greater things** are Jesus' work of giving life (verse 21) and judging (verse 22).

21 The Old Testament teaches that God **makes alive . . . and raises up** the dead (1 Samuel 2:6). But here Jesus says that He also **gives life. . . . whatever the Father does the Son does also** (verse 19).

The life that Jesus gives is new spiritual life. All men, before they believe, are spiritually **dead in** [their] **transgressions and sins** (see Ephesians 2:1 and comment). But Christ has the power to bring them to life. The life that Jesus gives is eternal life. It begins as soon as a man

---

[41] Some illnesses occur because of sin (see Mark 2:5 and comment). But other illnesses occur that are not caused by sin (see John 9:1–3 and comment).

[42] In Old Testament times, out of all the peoples of the world, the Jews were the only people who believed in the one true living God. The people of other nations believed in many different gods. This was the main difference between the Jews and all other people.

believes in Christ, and it lasts forever (see John 1:4; 3:15,36 and comments). And Jesus gives this life **to whom he is pleased to give it**. We can't demand this life; we can't earn it. We don't deserve it. We receive it only through the love and grace of the Father and the Son.

22 The authority to judge belongs to God. But He has turned over this authority to Christ. Therefore, on the day of JUDGMENT, which will come at the end of the world, it is Christ Himself who will be our judge (Acts 17:31; 2 Corinthians 5:10).

23 God has given Christ the authority to judge so that **all may honor the Son just as they honor the Father**. Christ must receive the same honor as God receives. In the Jews' eyes, to say such a thing was blasphemy (see verse 18). But, in fact, they were blind. They didn't realize that Christ was indeed equal with God. Therefore, they refused to honor Christ. They said, "We honor only God." But Jesus told them, "**He who does not honor the Son does not honor the Father**." It's the same among men: whenever we dishonor a man's son, we dishonor the man himself.

Here is a deep and important truth. Many people say, "I believe in God. Why is it necessary to believe in Christ also?" It's necessary because only when we believe in Christ can we truly believe in God. He who does not know Christ cannot fully know God. He who does not honor Christ does not honor God (see Luke 10:16; John 12:44–45; 14:9; 15:23).

24 Jesus here repeats what is written in John 3:15,36. Here He adds that man must not only believe in Christ, but must also believe **him** (God) **who sent** Christ. Christ and God cannot be separated: they are **one** (John 10:30).

Faith in Christ comes from the recognition that Christ is sent from God, that He is one with God. His words are God's words (John 3:34). Hearing Christ's **word**—that is, the Gospel—leads to faith in God Himself (Romans 10:14; 1 Peter 1:21). Christ's purpose is to **bring** [us] **to God** (1 Peter 3:18).

The person who has eternal life has crossed over from death to life. For man there are only two possible states: life or death. A man is either spiritually alive, or he is spiritually dead. He is either in the kingdom of Satan, or he is in the kingdom of God. Only through faith in Christ and God can a person pass from Satan's kingdom into God's kingdom.

25 The **dead**—that is, the spiritually dead—**will hear the voice of the Son of God**. Among those who live in darkness—in **transgressions and sins** (Ephesians 2:1)—there will be some in this life who hear Christ's voice and believe. Those who hear and believe **will live** (see verse 21 and comment). Jesus said, "The **time is coming and has now come** when this will begin to happen—the dead will begin to live."

26 Just as the Father is the source of all life, so the Son (Christ) is also the source of life, both physical life and spiritual life. God has given His own life to Christ (see John 1:4; 3:35; 1 John 5:11). This is why death could not conquer Christ. Because of God's life within Him, Christ Himself rose from the dead. And because of God's life within Him, Christ is also able to give life to those who are dead in sin (verse 25).

27 Because Jesus is the Messiah, the **Son of Man**, God has given Him the authority to judge (see Matthew 28:18; John 5:22; 17:2 and comments). Being the **Son of Man**, Jesus knows men's hearts; therefore, He is qualified to judge (see John 2:24–25). Being the **Son of Man**, Jesus has the **authority, glory and sovereign power** to execute judgment on all men (Daniel 7:13–14).

28–29 In these verses Jesus is not speaking of this present life; He is speaking of the last judgment, which will occur at the end of the world. He is speaking not only in a spiritual sense, but also in a physical sense. All who are dead and buried will be raised at the end of the world. There will be a resurrection of the bodies of all men, both good men and evil (see Acts 24:15 and comment). The righteous will receive new bodies in heaven. The unrighteous will receive new bodies in hell.

All the dead will rise from their graves at the voice of the Son of God. At that time the Son will judge men according to their works (2 Corinthians 5:10). Those who have done good will obtain eternal life in heaven; those who have done evil will receive eternal punishment in hell.

We must remember two truths. First, salvation comes only by faith, not by works (Ephesians 2:8–9). But, second, we are rewarded or condemned according to our works (see Matthew 16:27 and comment). Works are the proof our faith.

In one sense, our judgment is taking place on earth right now. Because what we do in this life will determine how Christ judges us on that final day of judgment.

30 When Christ judges, His judgment is not independent of God's judgment. Christ does nothing by Himself (verse 19). "**I judge only as I hear,**" said Jesus. Christ's will is the same as God's will. For that reason, Christ's judgment is always just and true (John 6:38; 8:16).

As it is for Christ, so it is for us. When we remain in God's will, our life is righteous. But when we follow our own will and seek to please ourselves, our life becomes unrighteous. In everything let us pray as Christ prayed: "**Yet not what I will, but what you will**" (Mark 14:36).

Testimonies About Jesus (5:31–47)

31 If Jesus alone had testified about Himself, His testimony would not have been **valid;**[43] that is, it would not have been legally acceptable. According to the Bible, everything must be determined on the testimony of two or three witnesses (Deuteronomy 19:15; Matthew 18:16; 2 Corinthians 13:1). Therefore, Christ alone cannot give a valid testimony about Himself; another witness is necessary.

32 But He has another witness, and that witness is God Himself (John 8:17–18). God had spoken from heaven: "**You are my Son**" (Mark 1:11; 9:7).

33–35 After saying that God was His main witness, Jesus here mentions the witness of John the Baptist. The Jews had gone to John (John 1:19). Some of the Jews had been attracted by John's preaching. John **testified to the truth** (verse 33). He was a **lamp** showing the way of salvation. If the Jews had believed John fully, they would also have believed Jesus and found salvation.

The Jews couldn't accept God's witness directly (verses 37–38). But they could have believed John, who gave the same true witness. Jesus did not need John's witness to prove He was the Messiah. Jesus does not accept **human testimony** (verse 34). God's witness is sufficient. Jesus only mentions John the Baptist to remind the Jews that John had indeed shown them the way of salvation.

36 Jesus' greatest witness was God (verse 32). But the Jews did not accept God's witness. Therefore, Jesus mentions still another "witness"—that is, His **work**. The Jews could see Christ's **work**. Christ's work is the same as God's work (verse 19). Therefore, Christ's work **testifies** or proves that Christ is **sent** from God (see Matthew 11:2–5). Surely the Jews should have accepted the witness of Christ's works (John 14:11). And surely today men should also.

37–38 Here Jesus again says: "**And the Father . . . has himself testified concerning me**". God had Himself spoken from heaven (verse 32). He had testified through the prophets, through the Old Testament, through John the Baptist. But the Jews had not heard His voice or accepted His word. They had refused to believe God's testimony. Because of unbelief, God's word did not dwell in them. They heard God's word with their ears, but they did not accept it in their hearts.

The meaning of these verses is this: Only when we believe in Christ can we then accept the witness of God. God has come to earth in the form of Christ. If man rejects Christ, he rejects God (verse 23). And if he rejects God, he rejects God's witness.

39–40 The Jews prided themselves on their knowledge of the **Scriptures**, that is, the Old Testament. Yet they didn't believe the testimony of the Scriptures. The Old Testament spoke clearly of Christ; but when Christ actually came, the Jews rejected Him (John 1:11).

---

[43] His testimony would be true, but it could not be legally regarded as true.

The Jews made a terrible mistake. They supposed that by following the Jewish law written in the Old Testament they would possess eternal life. But they were wrong. Eternal life comes only through faith in Christ (John 3:15). When they rejected Christ, they rejected life (John 3:36).

Notice that Jesus says: "**You refuse to come to me**." It is not because of ignorance or poor understanding that men don't come to Jesus. The reason is because they **refuse** to come. They love darkness. They do not want to give up their sin (John 3:19–20). Ignorance is no excuse for not believing in Christ.

41 Jesus did not accept **praise from men**. That is, He did not seek the honor and praise of men. He did not try to please men in order to receive their praise. He desired only to please God. Whether men praised Him or not, He did not care.

42 Jesus didn't want the praise of the Jews, because they did not truly love God. God's love was not in them (see John 2:24 and comment).

43 Jesus said to the Jews, "**. . . if someone comes in his own name, you will accept him**." The Jews loved to receive honor from men. They gave honor to others, hoping they would be honored in return. They readily accepted others, hoping they would be accepted in return.

Those who come **in** [their] **own name** are false prophets. They are of the world. They speak the thoughts of the world. Therefore, the Jews accepted them. But the One who came in God's name, that is, Jesus, they couldn't accept. They couldn't accept Him because He came from a different world.

44 Because the Jews only thought about the praise of men, they had no desire **to obtain the praise that comes only from God**. They preferred to receive temporary honor from one another rather than lasting honor from God Himself.

Those who love God seek to honor God. Those who do not love God—such as these Jews (verse 42)—seek only their own honor. It is impossible to seek one's own honor and God's honor at the same time (see Matthew 6:24 and comment).

45 On the day of judgment, Christ will not have to accuse the Jews, because Moses will accuse them. The writings of Moses will accuse them.[44]

The Jews set their hope on Moses, their ancient leader. Moses gave them the Jewish law. They thought that by obeying the law they would gain salvation (verse 39). But they didn't understand the law. No one could follow the law perfectly. Instead, the law showed them their sin (see Romans 7:7–11 and comment). The law condemned them (see Romans 8:1–2 and comment). The law, above all, showed them that they needed a Savior. And Moses prophesied that, indeed, a Savior would come (Deuteronomy 18:15; John 1:45).

46–47 Therefore, the Jews didn't really believe Moses, because when the Savior about whom Moses had written came, they rejected Him. That is why Moses will be the Jews' accuser.

If the Jews didn't believe Moses, whom they respected, how would they believe Christ, whom they hated?

CHAPTER 6

Jesus Feeds the Five Thousand (6:1–15)

(Matthew 14:13–21; Mark 6:30–44; Luke 9:10–17

1–15 See Mark 6:30–44 and comment.

Jesus Walks on the Water (6:16–24)

(Matthew 14:22–36; Mark 6:45–56)

16–24 See Mark 6:45–56 and comment.

---

[44] The writings of Moses are the first five books of the Old Testament. These five books are also called the Law.

Jesus the Bread of Life (6:25–59)

25 After miraculously feeding five thousand men (verses 1–15), Jesus crossed the Sea of Galilee walking on the water (verses 16–24). The crowd who had been fed with the five loaves and two fish came by land the next day to look for Him.

26 But when the crowd found Jesus, He rebuked them. They were only seeking more bread, more healing. The miracles Jesus had performed had not led the people to believe in Him; they had only led to a desire for more miracles. In the people's minds, Jesus' miracles were not a sign that He was the Son of God; they were merely a means of obtaining bodily necessities—such as more food.

27 Jesus said to them, "**Do not work for food that spoils**." Instead, they should **work** for spiritual "food," which only Jesus can give. Such "food" lasts forever, and it gives life that lasts forever. To "work for spiritual food" means to pray, to study the Bible, and to obey Christ. Yet, even though one must **work** for it, it is always a gift. Christ, the **Son of Man**, gives this spiritual food to whom He pleases (John 5:21). Man can never earn it, nor can he by his own effort make himself worthy to receive it.

"Food that spoils" represents not only ordinary food for eating, but also all worldly things, such as wealth, honor, and pleasure (see Matthew 6:19–20 and comment).

The food that the Son of Man gives is true food indeed, because God has placed His **seal** on the Son. In New Testament times, important people placed their seal on their letters. The seal proved that the letter was indeed written by the owner of the seal and not by someone else. So God's "seal" proves that Jesus has come from God. Jesus is not only the Son of Man (John 1:51); He is also the Son of God.

28–29 The people supposed that they must do some kind of good work in order to earn this spiritual food. But Jesus told them that only one "work" was necessary: **to believe**[45] **in the one he** (God) **has sent** (verse 29).

In one way, **to believe**—to have faith—is a kind of "work." In another way, faith is a gift of God (see John 6:44; Romans 12:3 and comments). Faith is first of all a gift; but having received the gift, we must then use it.

30 Again the Jews sought for a sign (see Mark 8:11; John 2:18 and comments). Jesus had just fed five thousand people, but they wanted a greater sign. They wanted to be continuously filled with bread.

31 Then they suggested a sign He could give them: Let Him send **manna** from heaven, as God did in Moses' time. When the Jews had escaped from Egypt and were in the Sinai desert, God sent them a kind of "bread" from heaven each day for forty years to satisfy their hunger (Exodus 16:1–4,14–15,31; Psalm 78:24).

The Jews in New Testament times believed that the Messiah, when He came, would also send "manna" from heaven. They believed that that would be one of the signs of the Messiah. Therefore, if Jesus claimed to be the Messiah, let Him perform that sign. Then they would believe in Him.

Even today, people ask for signs. They say, "If you give me proof that Jesus is the Son of God, I will believe." But such people are only testing God (Matthew 4:7). Their demand for sure proof is only an excuse for not believing. They will not believe no matter what "proof" they are given (see Luke 16:27–31 and comment).

32 Jesus told the people that Moses didn't give the manna; God gave it. Furthermore, manna was not **true bread from heaven**. Manna was earthly bread that fell from the sky. The true bread[46] from heaven is spiritual "bread," the **bread of God** (verse 33).

33 This "bread of God" **comes down from heaven and gives life to the world**.

---

[45] In the Greek text, the words **to believe** mean "to continue to believe."

[46] Bread is the main food of the Middle East. Therefore, in the context of this chapter, **bread** means "food."

The bread Jesus gives is spiritual bread, and it gives men spiritual life, eternal life.

34 Like the Samaritan woman (John 4:15), the people did not understand Jesus' spiritual meaning.

35 Then Jesus said "I am that bread. I am the life-giving bread" (John 1:4; 3:36; 1 John 5:11–12). He who comes to Jesus and eats this bread **will never go hungry** (see John 4:14 and comment).

Then Jesus added, "**He who believes in me will never go thirsty.**" We must understand that the **bread of life** is the same as the **living water** mentioned in John 4:10–11. We must also understand that to "eat" this bread and to "drink" this water means to believe in Jesus. It means to receive Jesus into our life. Just as we take food and drink into our stomachs, so we take Christ into our hearts through faith.

Jesus says here: "**He who comes to me will never go hungry.**" To **come** to Jesus is the same as to believe in Jesus.[47] Jesus says to all men: "**Come to me**" (Matthew 11:28).

36 Even though the Jews saw Jesus and saw His miracles with their own eyes, they did not believe. At first they had asked for bread from heaven (verse 34). They thought that it would be tasty and pleasing. They came to Christ only to receive His blessing. But when they found out that the bread was Christ Himself, they despised the "bread," and turned away from Christ.

37 Jesus said, "**All** (men) **that the Father gives me will come to me.**" Most of the Jews did not believe, because the Father had not "given them" to Christ. God had not given them the gift of faith. If God does not first "draw" a man, that man cannot come to Christ (verse 44). Men don't first decide to believe; first God calls them (John 15:16).

A difficult question arises here: Why is it a sin not to believe? If faith is a gift of God, how can it be a sin not to receive it?

The answer is this. God gives faith only to those whose hearts are open and humble. Thus, if we have not received the gift of faith, it is because we have hardened our hearts against God. Yes, faith is a gift. But to receive it, we must first repent of our sin and turn toward God. Then God will give us faith (see Romans 9:14–21 and comment; General Article: Salvation—God's Choice or Man's Choice?).

Christ will never turn away those who come to Him in faith. No matter how unworthy we are, He will accept us. We do not have to be perfect and pure in order to come to Christ; He will receive us just as we are. But we must come to Him. That is our part.

On the one hand, we cannot come to Christ unless God draws us. But, on the other hand, God cannot draw us if we refuse to come.

38–39 Christ came to do God's will (John 5:30). God's will is that Christ lose **none of all that he has given** to Christ (verse 39)—that is, none of all the people that God has given to Christ, which means all true Christians (John 10:28–29). Christ fulfilled God's will in this regard (and in all other regards) while He was here on earth (John 17:12).

It was God's will not only that Christ lose no one, but also that Christ **raise them** (believers) **up at the last day**—that is, give them salvation, eternal life. The **last day** is the day of judgment at the end of the world, when all men shall either be raised to heaven or sent to hell (John 5:28–29).

40 Here Jesus repeats the thought of verse 39. Jesus gives new spiritual life to all who believe in Him. Surely those to whom He has given spiritual life on earth He will also raise to eternal life in heaven **on the last day**.

. . . everyone who looks to the Son and believes in him shall have eternal life. We must look to the Son with the eye of faith. The Christian's faith is not blind faith. We behold Jesus,[48] and then we believe.

41–42 The Jews took offense at Jesus' sayings. They grumbled, "How

---

[47] Jesus uses different words and different illustrations to explain the same spiritual truth.

[48] In order to "behold Jesus," one must listen to the Gospel and read the Bible with an open and humble heart.

can He say He came down from heaven, when He is only the son of Joseph and Mary? He is from earth, just as we are" (see Mark 6:2–3 and comment).

43–44 **No one can come to me unless the Father . . . draws him**. Here Jesus repeats the idea of verse 37. Let no one think he can come to Christ only by his own thought or desire. He must first be drawn by God (see verses 37,65 and comment).

45 Jesus here repeats the same truth in different words. God "draws" men by teaching them. Everyone who is **taught** by God and **learns** from Him comes to Christ. If our minds are not enlightened by God's Spirit, we cannot come to Christ (see verse 65 and comment). Notice it is God who does the teaching; but it is we who must do the learning!

Jesus quotes from the **Prophets**, that is, that part of the Old Testament which contains the writings of the prophets. He quotes from Isaiah 54:13.

46 God teaches men. But He does not have to teach the Son, Jesus, because Jesus has seen God and has come from God (see John 1:18 and comment). Jesus has received the things of God; therefore, Jesus is fully able to teach those things to men. No man has ever seen God Himself; therefore, what we learn from God we learn mainly through Christ. We can be sure that whatever teaching we learn from Christ is a teaching that has come from God.

47 The only thing necessary to receive eternal life is to believe in Jesus (see John 3:15,36 and comment).

48–50 Here Jesus again says that He is the life-giving bread, which is much better than manna. In the Jews' opinion, manna was the best of all foods. But the Old Testament Jews ate manna and eventually died. But those who eat the "bread of life,"—that is, those who believe in Jesus—will never die. That is, their souls[49] will never die. They have eternal life.

51 Jesus is the **living bread**. Not only does Jesus Himself have God's eternal life within Him (John 5:26), but whoever "eats" Jesus will also receive eternal life. "**If anyone eats of this bread, he will live forever**." Even though a person's body will die, his soul will not die.

Here Jesus gives a new teaching. He says: "**This bread is my flesh, which I will give for the life of the world**." That is, Jesus will give His **flesh**, His body, to save men and women. He will give His life as a sacrifice that we might live. Here Jesus is talking about His death on the cross (see Mark 10:45; John 3:14–16 and comments).

52 The Jews argued among themselves concerning Jesus' statement. They couldn't understand His meaning. "How are we to eat His flesh," they wondered.

53 To answer them, Jesus repeated even more clearly that in order to obtain eternal life a man must eat His (Jesus') flesh and drink His blood. That is, in order to be saved, a man must receive Christ into his heart by faith (see verse 35 and comment). Just as our bodies cannot live without food and drink, so our souls cannot live without Christ.[50]

To drink blood was an extremely offensive thought to the Jews. According to the Old Testament, the Jews were forbidden to drink any kind of blood (Genesis 9:4).

54 Jesus here repeats the thought of verses 47 and 53.

55 The Jews worked for **food that spoils** (verse 27), but Jesus gives the **food that endures to eternal life**—that is, His flesh and blood. That is **real food** and **real drink**.

Let us remember here that it is not only

---

[49] A man's soul includes his mind, emotions, and desires. The soul of a man determines his character and personality. The soul is one's real self. The soul of a Christian, together with his spirit, is not destroyed by death.

[50] Some Christians believe that the words **eat** [Christ's] **flesh** and **drink his blood** mean only to "believe in Christ." But other Christians believe that, in addition, these words also refer to the Lord's Supper. This second group of Christians is not saying that we receive eternal life simply from partaking in the Lord's Supper. Rather they say that partaking in the Lord's Supper is one of the means by which we, through faith, receive spiritual blessing. For further discussion, see General Article: Lord's Supper.

Jews that work for food that spoils. All these sayings of Jesus are not just for the Jews; they are also for us.

56 When we have, in a spiritual way, eaten Christ's flesh and drunk His blood, He remains in us spiritually.[51] His life, His Holy Spirit, dwells within us. And we spiritually become part of Christ. We become part of His body (1 Corinthians 12:27). Jesus later said to His disciples: **"Remain in me, and I will remain in you. . . . If a man remain in me and I in him, he will bear much fruit; apart from me you can do nothing"** (John 15:4–5). Whoever abides in Christ abides also in God (1 John 4:15).

Here we see a very important truth about the Christian life: Believers are united with Christ. We must remain in Christ. That is, we must remain in His love, in His strength, in His peace and joy. We must remain in obedience to Him. We must remain in His kingdom. And Christ, for His part, will remain in us. That is, His life, His "living water," His "bread of life," His Holy Spirit—all these will remain in us. And our entire life will be in Christ, through Christ, and for Christ.

58 See verses 49–50 and comment.

59 All these things Jesus taught in the synagogue at Capernaum (verses 17,24).

Many Disciples Desert Jesus (6:60–71)

60 Besides the twelve main disciples (Mark 3:13–19), Jesus had many other disciples also. These had to some extent believed Jesus' words, but their faith was very weak and shallow. It was some of these disciples who began to say, **"This is a hard teaching."** They meant: "This teaching about eating Jesus' flesh is hard for us to accept."

61 At first, it had been the Jews that grumbled about Jesus' teaching (verse 41). Now Jesus' own followers had begun to grumble. Jesus knew their thoughts. He knows the thoughts of each of us. We must be careful not only about what we say; we must also be careful about what we think!

The disciples were not grumbling because they couldn't understand Jesus. They were grumbling because Jesus was demanding that they become united with Him. Jesus was demanding that they follow Him with their whole heart. They were not prepared to do that.

62 Jesus answered them, **"What if you see the Son of Man ascend to where he was before!"** Jesus' meaning is this. If the disciples find it difficult to accept Jesus' teachings now, it will be even more difficult for them when He ascends **to where he was before**, that is, heaven. Because, before He can ascend to heaven, He must first be killed. His disciples will be scattered. They will be persecuted by the Jews. And when Jesus ascends to heaven, they will in one way be alone. He will be gone from them. True, He will be with them in the form of the Holy Spirit, but if they can't receive Jesus' spiritual teachings now, how will they be able to receive the Holy Spirit's teachings then?

63 The **Spirit**—that is, the Holy Spirit—**gives life**. When men "eat" Jesus' **flesh**, it is not flesh they are eating; it is the Holy Spirit. **Flesh counts for nothing.**

Jesus is trying to teach us to understand the spiritual meaning of His words. His **words . . . are spirit**. Just as **God is spirit** (John 4:24), so Jesus' words **are spirit**. His words come from God (John 7:16; 12:49–50). They are not the fleshly words of a man. Jesus' words can be understood only by our spirits, with the help of God's Holy Spirit (see 1 Corinthians 2:12–14 and comment).

The words of Jesus are also **life**; that is, His words give life (see John 5:24). Just as God's word created the heavens and the earth and gave life to all creatures (John 1:1–4), so Jesus' words continue to give spiritual life to all who heed them.

64 Jesus knew from the beginning who would remain faithful to Him and who would fall away. He knows that also about each one of us.

---

[51] Some Christians also believe that when we eat the bread and drink the wine of the Lord's Supper we, through faith, receive or experience the presence of Christ in a special way.

Even though the disciples had heard Jesus' words, most of them understood the words only in a fleshly sense. They had followed Jesus because of the miracles they could see, but they didn't really believe in Christ in a deep spiritual way. Now, as soon as Jesus' teaching became difficult, they fell away (see Mark 4:5–6,16–17).

65 Then Jesus reminded them that no one can follow Him unless God first draws him: "**. . . no one can come to me unless the Father has enabled him**" (see verses 37,44 and comment). If God does not Himself first draw a man out of darkness and sin, he can never come to God. A sinner will never turn to God by his own desire; he always wants to remain in his sin (John 3:19). Therefore, when anyone comes to God and Jesus, it is always the result of God's grace. The **Father has enabled him** to come.

Therefore, Jesus knew that some of His disciples would fall away, because they had not been truly "drawn" by God. Their faith was not real. Even among Jesus' own special twelve disciples, one would in the end betray Him (see verses 70–71).

66 Therefore, just as Jesus said, many of His disciples turned away. They had thought that the Messiah would be like an earthly king. Perhaps they had thought they would get some worldly advantage by following Jesus. Now they saw that being a disciple of Jesus was different than they had expected. Therefore, they left Him.

67–69 Then Jesus turned to His twelve disciples. Would they also leave?

But Peter, acting as spokesman for the twelve disciples, answered Jesus: "Where would we go? **You have the words of eternal life**" (verse 68). He had understood what Jesus said in verse 63. To have the **words of eternal life** is the same as having the power to give eternal life. If Jesus had the the power to give eternal life, why should the twelve disciples go elsewhere?

Then Peter said, "**We believe and know you are the Holy One of God**"—that is, the Messiah (see Mark 8:29 and comment). The twelve disciples (except for Judas) truly believed. Yes, later, they too would fall away for a short time (Mark 14:50); but their faith never totally left them.

70–71 Then Jesus told His disciples that one of them would betray Him. But He didn't say who it would be. John tells us that it would be **Judas, the son of Simon Iscariot** (see Mark 14:10–11,17–20,44–46).

Jesus called Judas a **devil,** because he became a servant of the devil, Satan. **Satan entered into him** (see John 13:2,27).

CHAPTER 7

Jesus Goes to the Feast of Tabernacles (7:1–13)

1 The Jewish leaders in Jerusalem and the surrounding province of Judea were plotting to kill Jesus (John 5:16,18). Therefore, Jesus stayed and preached in Galilee. He stayed in Galilee not because He was afraid of the Jewish leaders, but because the time appointed by God for Him to die had not yet come.

2 The **Feast of Tabernacles** was a Jewish celebration held each year to show thanks to God for the harvest (Leviticus 23:33–34; Deuteronomy 16:13–15).

3 Jesus' brothers advised Jesus to go to the province of **Judea** (or to Jerusalem, the capital of Judea) so that His **disciples** might see His miracles—that is, His disciples who lived in Judea. Many of these Judean disciples had already forsaken Jesus (John 6:66).

4 Jesus' brothers thought that He wanted **to become a public figure.** Jesus was performing miracles like the Messiah was expected to do. But why perform them up in the northern hill district of Galilee? That was like performing miracles **in secret**. Instead, the brothers said, Jesus should go to the capital city of Jerusalem and show Himself **to the world.**[52]

5 Jesus' brothers didn't understand the work of the Messiah. They did not understand Jesus' plan. They thought Jesus was trying to make Himself a king (see Mark 5:43; 6:44–45; 8:30 and comments). They didn't understand, because they didn't believe. They were His brothers in flesh, but not in spirit. Only those who believe Christ can understand Him. Only those who believe in Christ are His true brothers (see Mark 3:31–35 and comment).

6 Jesus told His brothers to go to the feast themselves. It was not the right time for Him to go. All "times" for Jesus were fixed by God. But He said to His brothers, "**For you any time is right**." They did not walk according to God's will; therefore, all times were the same for them. They had no special time for going to Jerusalem; they could go whenever they pleased. So let them go to the feast when all the other Jews were going.

7 Jesus said to His brothers, "**The world cannot hate you**." The world cannot hate them because they **belong to the world**, and the world loves its own (see John 15:18–19 and comment).

But unbelieving men of the world hate Jesus, because Jesus exposes their sin. That is why the Jewish leaders opposed Jesus so strongly.

8–9 Jesus said, "**I am not yet**[53] **going up**[54] **to this feast**." He meant that He would not go up to the feast with His brothers as they requested. He would go later, at the right time for Him.

Jesus wanted to go to the feast in order to teach the people. For that, it was better to go near the end of the festival; then the crowds would be greatest.

10 Some days later, Jesus also went up to Jerusalem. He went **in secret**, that is, not with a big crowd but privately. Perhaps only He and His closest disciples went. He did not want to attract attention, lest the Jewish leaders discover Him on the way and arrest Him before He could get to Jerusalem.

11 The **Jews**—that is, the Jewish leaders and Jesus' enemies among the Jews—watched for Jesus. They were looking for an opportunity to arrest Him (verse 32).

12–13 The **crowds** also were talking about Jesus quietly. The crowds were also Jews, but they were the common people. They didn't know what to think about Jesus. Some said one thing and some said another (verses 42–43). But **for fear of the Jews**—that is, the Jewish leaders—the crowds did not talk openly; they were **whispering** (verse 12).

Jesus Teaches at the Feast (7:14–24)

14–15 Halfway[55] through the feast, Jesus began to teach the people in the courts of the temple. The **Jews**, that is, the Jewish leaders, were amazed at Jesus' knowledge of the Scriptures. They were Pharisees and teachers of the law. They had been properly trained. But this fellow Jesus knew more than they did! (see Matthew 7:28–29; Mark 6:2–3 and comments).

16 Jesus' knowledge came from God. When people hear Jesus' teaching, they are hearing God.

17 The Jewish leaders questioned Jesus' authority; they questioned the truth of His teaching. But then Jesus questioned their ability to hear the truth.

---

[52] The **Feast of Tabernacles** was one of three Jewish festivals held each year for which many Jews traveled to Jerusalem (Deuteronomy 16:16). Therefore, at that time Jews from all over the **world** would be in Jerusalem to celebrate the feast. That's why Jesus' brothers suggested that at that time Jesus could show Himself **to the world**.

[53] Some ancient manuscripts of John do not have the word **yet**.

[54] Jerusalem is higher in elevation than Galilee. Therefore, to go from Galilee to Jerusalem it is necessary to climb **up**.

[55] The Feast of Tabernacles lasted for a week.

Those who choose to do God's will do not doubt that Jesus' teaching is true. But these Jewish leaders did not choose to do God's will; therefore, they were unable to tell whether Jesus' teaching was true or not.

Here Jesus gives us a very important truth. Whoever **chooses to do God's will** will know if Jesus' teaching comes from God. If we determine to do God's will, God will reveal His will to us. He will open our spiritual eyes. We will know that Jesus' teaching is true.

Many people say, "How can I know God's will? How can I know if Jesus' teaching is true?" The answer is: First choose to do God's will, whatever it might be, and then you will find out what His will is.

Many people say, "If I knew that Jesus' teaching was true, I would follow Him. If I knew for sure what God's will was, I would obey it." But such people are deceiving themselves. They are not sure what God's will is because they have not agreed in their hearts to obey God. They are using their uncertainty about God's will as an excuse for not obeying God. God says: "First agree to obey me; then I will show you what my will is for you."[56] Christ says: "First have faith in me; then you will fully understand that my teaching is true and comes from God."

18 Jesus said that there was another way to tell if His teaching was from God. The man who tries to gain honor for himself speaks **on his own**. But the man who **works for the honor of** [God] is a **man of truth**. Therefore, Jesus' teaching was the **truth** and was from God, because He worked only for the honor of God.

When we listen to a man's teaching, let us ask ourselves: Does his teaching bring honor to God? Does it bring honor to Christ? If it does, then that man's teaching is true and can be trusted.[57] But if a man tries only to exalt himself, then his teaching cannot be trusted. It will usually be at least partly false.

19 Jesus added that there is **nothing false**[58] in the man who works for God's honor (verse 18). But in the Jewish leaders there was much falsehood, much unrighteousness. Jesus said to them, "**Not one of you keeps the law**. You all disobey the law in something" (James 2:10). They were falsely accusing Jesus of breaking the law (John 5:18); but they were the ones breaking the law by trying to kill Him (Exodus 20:13).

It is a very common observation that those who are themselves guilty of an offense are the quickest to accuse others of that same offense! (see Romans 2:1 and comment).

20 The crowd who heard Jesus didn't know anything about the plot of the Jewish leaders to kill Jesus. Some of them thought that Jesus must be **demon-possessed** (see Mark 3:22).

21 Then Jesus mentioned the man He had healed at the pool of Bethesda on the Sabbath (John 5:2–9). Everyone had been amazed by that miracle. Yet the Jews had opposed Him because He had healed the man on the Sabbath (John 5:16).

22–23 But the Jews **circumcised**[59] male children on the Sabbath according to God's command (Genesis 17:9–12). So why can't Jesus heal a man on the Sabbath? God not only commanded the Jews to circumcise their male children,

---

[56] God has already shown to all men what His general will is: it has been clearly written throughout the Bible.

[57] For a man's teaching to be true, it must also agree with what is written in the Bible.

[58] In place of the words **nothing false**, some translations of the Bible say "no unrighteousness." The meaning is essentially the same.

[59] Circumcision is the cutting away of the excess skin of the penis. According to Genesis 17:12, it had to be performed on the eighth day of a child's life, even if that day fell on the Sabbath. For further discussion, see Word List: Circumcision.

Jesus said, "**Moses gave you circumcision**" (verse 22). He said that because the command to circumcise is mentioned in the book of Genesis, which Moses wrote. But the command didn't come through Moses himself. It was given directly by God to Abraham. God Himself told Abraham that all of his descendants must be circumcised (Genesis 17:10).

but He also commanded them to do good to their neighbor (Leviticus 19:18). To circumcise and to show mercy were both commands of God written in the law. Therefore, both commands should be obeyed on the Sabbath, not just the command to circumcise.

Furthermore, the command to circumcise involved just one small part of the body. But the command to love one's neighbor and to show him mercy involved his whole body. Jesus healed people's whole bodies, and He also healed their souls as well. If it was right on the Sabbath to perform the ceremony of circumcision, which involved only one part of the body, it surely was right on the Sabbath to heal the whole body (see Mark 3:1–5; Luke 13:10–16; 14:1–6; John 5:10 and comments).

24 Then Jesus rebuked the Jews for observing the law only outwardly. They cared only that they appeared righteous in the sight of other men. They neglected the more important commandments of the law, such as showing mercy (see Matthew 23:23,28 and comment). They made judgments only according to outward appearance, and not according to man's heart. Therefore, their judgments were not **right**. Their judgments were not in accordance with God's judgments, because God looks not **at the outward appearance, but . . . at the heart** (1 Samuel 16:7).

Is Jesus the Christ? (7:25–44)

25–26 Some of the crowd knew the Jewish leaders had been trying to kill Jesus. Therefore, when they saw Jesus teaching openly in the temple, they thought that perhaps the Jewish leaders had changed their minds about Jesus. Otherwise, they would have arrested Him. Perhaps the leaders had decided that Jesus was the Christ, the Messiah, after all.

27 But some said, "No, it's not possible that Jesus is the Christ. When the true Christ (Messiah) comes, **no one will know where he is from.**[60] But we know this Jesus is the son of Joseph and Mary from Nazareth; therefore, he cannot be the Christ."

28–29 Jesus said to the people, "Yes, you know my name and my town. But you do not know who my real Father is. You do not know where I really come from. I come from God. **I am not here on my own**. I have come to do my Father's will (John 6:38). You do not know God, **but I know him, because I am from him**" (see John 6:46). The Jews didn't know where Jesus was from because they didn't know God.

30 The Jewish leaders then tried to seize Jesus, but they could not (see verse 44). John does not explain how they were prevented from seizing Jesus; he only gives the reason why they were prevented: it was not yet Jesus' time to die. **His time had not yet come**. Wicked men cannot change God's plan.

31 But some of the crowd believed in Jesus because of the miraculous signs that He performed (see John 2:23–24 and comment). Such faith based on signs is usually weak, but it can be the beginning of real faith. Christ does not reject such faith. It is better to believe because of signs than not to believe at all!

32 When the Pharisees heard that many in the crowd believed in Jesus, they were even more upset. The more people respected Jesus, the less they would respect the Pharisees and other Jewish leaders. The Pharisees joined with the **chief priests**[61] and sent officers (the temple police) to arrest Jesus.

33 Jesus was not worried about the plot to arrest Him. He knew about it. "**I am with you only a short time,**" He said to the Jews. "Nothing you can do will change that time. I am in God's hands. I will soon go to Him."

34 Jesus said to them, "When I go, **you will look for me, but you will not**

---

[60] It was believed that the Messiah would be born in Bethlehem (see Matthew 2:3–6; John 7:41–42). But it was not known who His parents would be.

[61] At any one time there was only one Jewish "high priest." But under him, there were a number of **chief priests**. Then under the chief priests there were the ordinary priests.

find me." Those who seek to persecute Jesus will not have the opportunity to persecute Him after He is gone. Neither will they be able to enter into heaven themselves. The door will be shut to the enemies of Jesus (see John 8:21).

35–36 The Jews, as usual, did not understand Jesus' meaning. They did not understand that He was talking about His death and His ascension to heaven. They thought He meant that He would go to the **Greeks**[62]—that is, to other Gentile countries, where many Jews also lived.

37 On the last day of the feast, Jesus stood up and gave an extraordinary invitation to the crowd of people: "**If anyone is thirsty, let him come to me and drink.**" Jesus has **living water** to give to whoever comes to Him (see John 4:10,14; 1 Corinthians 10:4 and comments).

But to receive that "living water," we must first thirst for it (see Matthew 5:6 and comment). If we do not seek God, we shall not find Him (Jeremiah 29:13; Matthew 7:7–8). If we are not thirsty for righteousness and for spiritual life, we shall not be filled.

38 To **drink** from Christ means to believe in Christ and to receive new spiritual life from Him. Here Jesus teaches from the Old Testament that when we have received this **living water**, it will then flow out from us to others (Isaiah 58:11; Zechariah 14:8). We are like pipes. Whatever "water" flows in, that much will flow out. The more we come to Christ to drink, the more blessings we will have to give to others. But if we do not let Christ's blessings flow out from us to others, no more blessings will be able to flow into our lives. He who gives blessings to others will receive more blessings himself (Proverbs 11:24–25).

The world around us is spiritually like a desert. It is dry, without spiritual life. For life to arise in the desert water is needed, and that water must come from Christ's disciples, from Christ's church. Drops of water are not enough. Little trickles of water are not enough. The world needs **streams**—rivers—**of living water** (Isaiah 44:3; Joel 3:18).

39 Here Jesus tells us that the **living water** is the Holy Spirit. When we come to Christ in faith, He gives us the Holy Spirit. The Holy Spirit is both God's Spirit and Christ's Spirit. We cannot see God the Father and Jesus the Son with our bodily eyes; but we can know them and have fellowship with them, because they are present with us in the form of the Holy Spirit. God the Father, God the Son, and God the Holy Spirit are all one God. They are three forms (or modes of existence) of one God.

When we believe in Christ, then God and Christ together give us **living water**, that is, the Holy Spirit (see John 14:16,26; 15:26; 16:13 and comments). But when Jesus was on earth, the Holy Spirit had not yet been fully given. The Old Testament prophets had from time to time received God's Spirit for a special work, but the Holy Spirit had not dwelled permanently in them. Only after Christ was **glorified**—that is, killed and then raised from the dead—was the Holy Spirit given to men and women as a permanent gift (see John 16:7; 20:22 and comments). And only after Christ ascended into heaven did the Holy Spirit fill the lives of the apostles and give them the power to be witnesses for Christ (see Acts 1:8–9; 2:1–4 and comments).

All believers are totally dependent on the Holy Spirit. Everything we do for Christ we do through the power of the Holy Spirit. We cannot live the Christian life even for one hour without the enabling of the Holy Spirit. Just as our bodies need water constantly, so our souls need the Holy Spirit constantly.

40 After the people had heard Jesus speak, some thought He must be the prophet that Moses wrote about in Deuteronomy 18:15 (see John 1:21; 6:14).

---

[62] The **Greeks** lived not only in the country of Greece, but they, like the Jews, had spread to all the other countries around the Mediterranean Sea. The Greeks, being non-Jews, were also called Gentiles. In fact, in many verses in the New Testament (including verse 35), the word **Greeks** is used to mean all Gentiles, not just Greek Gentiles.

41–42 Some people among the crowd thought that Jesus was the **Christ**, the Messiah—that is, the "anointed one."[63] But others disagreed. According to the Old Testament, the Messiah was supposed to be descended from David and come from Bethlehem, where King David was born (2 Samuel 7:12–14; Psalm 89:3–4; Micah 5:2). But the crowd didn't realize that, in fact, Jesus was a descendant of David and had been born in Bethlehem (see Matthew 1:1; 2:1–6; Luke 2:4–7,11 and comments). They thought He had been born in Galilee! The very passages from the Old Testament which the people were using to try to prove that Jesus was not the Messiah were, in fact, passages which proved that He was the Messiah!

43 **The people were divided because of Jesus**. In every age people are divided about Jesus (see Matthew 10:34; Luke 12:51). Some believe He is the Messiah, and some believe He is not. Each person must decide: Who is Jesus?

But there can only be two main opinions about Christ. Either He is the Messiah, the Son of God, like He said He was (Mark 14:62; John 4:26). Or He is a liar, or badly deluded, or demon-possessed. One must accept all of Christ's teachings—or none of them.

Could a liar or lunatic have taught the way Christ taught? The answer is no. Therefore, what Jesus said about Himself must be true: He must be the Son of God, the Savior of the world (see John 10:19–21).

But it is not enough to say, "**He is the Christ**" (verse 41). That is only the first step. A person must then believe in his heart and obey (see Matthew 7:21 and comment).

44 Then Jesus' enemies among the Jews wanted to capture Him, but God again prevented them. Jesus' life was in God's hands and under God's control (see verse 30 and comment).

Unbelief of the Jewish Leaders (7:45–53)

45 The temple guards had been waiting for the right chance to arrest Jesus (verse 32). They didn't want to seize Jesus violently in front of the crowd. They knew that many in the crowd believed in Him (verse 31). If they seized Jesus openly, there could be a riot. And if there was a riot, the Roman governor would be angry, because his job was to keep the peace.

46 But while the temple guards were waiting for the chance to seize Jesus, they listened to His words. And because of His words, they could not arrest Him. "**No one ever spoke the way this man does**," they said.

47–49 The Jewish leaders rebuked the guards. "Has He deceived you also?" they asked sarcastically. They pointed out to the guards that none of the important Jews were following Jesus. Only the ignorant crowd followed Him. The crowd didn't have a good knowledge of the Old Testament law. They didn't keep the law. They were sinners. "**. . . this mob that knows nothing of the law—there is a curse upon them**," said the Jewish leaders (verse 49). They said this because in the Old Testament it is written: **Cursed is the man who does not uphold the words of this law by carrying them out** (Deuteronomy 27:26).

The Jewish leaders were arrogant. They despised the common people. But the common people, in fact, followed the meaning and spirit of the law better than most of the Jewish leaders did.

50–51 However, there were some Jewish leaders that secretly believed in Christ (John 12:42–43). One of them was **Nicodemus**, a Pharisee, and a member of the ruling council of the Jews (see John 3:1; 19:39).

Nicodemus told his fellow leaders that according to Jewish law, a man should

[63] The meaning of both **Christ** and Messiah is the "anointed one." Christ was "anointed" by God to be the Savior of the world (see John 1:41; 4:25).

not be condemned until he had first had a fair trial. The Jewish leaders had condemned the crowd for not heeding the law. Now they weren't heeding the law themselves. They called Christ a lawbreaker, but in the effort to punish Him, they had become lawbreakers themselves.

52–53 The other Jewish leaders mocked Nicodemus. "**Are you from Galilee, too?**" they asked him. That is: "Are you one of His followers, too?"

Then the Jews said that no prophet had ever come from Galilee. But in this they were wrong. The prophet Jonah had come from Galilee (2 Kings 14:25), and perhaps other prophets had come from there also. God can raise up prophets from anywhere.

CHAPTER 8

The Woman Caught in Adultery (8:1–11)

1 After Jesus had finished teaching in the temple, He went to the Mount of Olives near Jerusalem for the night. This was His usual custom when He was in Jerusalem (Luke 21:37).[64]

2–6 The next day, the Jewish leaders brought before Jesus a woman who had been caught in the act of adultery. According to the Jewish law, **Moses commanded**[65] that both the man and the woman caught in adultery were to be executed (Leviticus 20:10; Deuteronomy 22:22–23). So the Jewish leaders asked Jesus what should be done to the woman. They asked this in order to trap Him (see Mark 12:13–17 and comment). If Jesus said to stone her, He would appear unmerciful. Also the Roman authorities would oppose Him, because it was against Roman law for the Jews to execute anyone. But if Jesus said not to stone her, He would be disobeying the Jewish law, and thus the Jews would be able to accuse Him of breaking the law. So whatever He answered, Jesus would be contradicting one law or another, thereby bringing discredit upon Himself.

Jesus didn't answer at once. He bent down and **started to write on the ground with his finger**. It is not known what He wrote.

7–8 Jesus did not fall into their trap. Jesus said, in effect: "Let her be stoned; she has sinned. But those who throw the stones must be **without sin** themselves."[66]

Jesus meant that their motives, their purpose, in stoning the woman should be completely pure. No judge is without sin, yet he must still judge. But he must judge with pure motives. He must judge justly and according to law. These Jewish leaders were accusing this woman for evil reasons. It is even possible that the woman had been unlawfully seized. If the Jews stoned the woman illegally, they too could be punished for murder.

9–10 All the woman's accusers left. The older ones left first, because they understood Jesus' meaning the quickest. But every one knew in his heart that he was unworthy to cast a stone at the woman.

There is a great lesson in this story for all of us. How quick we are to pick up "stones" to throw at our brother or sister! Such stones are things like evil talk, slander, false witness, murmuring. Let us look first to ourselves, and we shall see that we are not worthy to throw "stones" at anyone but ourselves (see Matthew 7:1–5; Romans 2:1; 2 Corinthians 11:31 and comments).

11 Jesus did not condemn the woman. But He condemned her sin.

---

[64] Not all ancient manuscripts of John contain verses 1–11.

[65] Moses received the law from God and transmitted it to the Jewish people.

[66] According to the Jewish law, the witness to a crime was supposed to throw the first stone (see Deuteronomy 17:7; Acts 7:57–58 and comment).

"**Go now and leave your life of sin**." We must not think from this story that Jesus ignores our sin. Jesus never ignores sin. On the final day of judgment we will not receive mercy; on that day we will be judged according to our works. But in this life, if a person truly repents, he has the chance to obtain mercy and forgiveness.

Notice that according to what is written, Jesus did not forgive the woman of her sin. That is because she had not yet repented. She had not yet asked for forgiveness. To receive forgiveness, one must repent.

The Light of the World (8:12–20)

12 Jesus said to the people:[67] "**I am the light of the world**" (see John 9:5; 12:46). Jesus' light is God's light. **God is light** (1 John 1:5). Light is a sign of righteousness and truth and knowledge. It is also a sign of life. **In him** (in Jesus) **was life, and that life was the light of men** (see John 1:4 and comment). Jesus fills a man's entire life with light. Jesus **gives light to every man** (John 1:9), just as the sun gives light to every man. Some men are blind and cannot see the sun. Some men close their eyes and refuse to see the sun. But the sun is there. It shines whether men see it or not. So it is with Christ.

Whoever follows me . . . will have the light of life. Only those who believe in Jesus and follow Him can receive His light. Only those who follow Jesus are delivered from the **darkness** of the world. Here "darkness" is a sign of sin, of spiritual ignorance, of spiritual death. Those who follow Christ will **never walk in darkness**. They are like men walking on a path at night carrying a bright lantern before them.

Those who follow Jesus also become lights themselves (see Matthew 5:14 and comment). But their light is not their own light; it is the light of Jesus shining in their lives. Jesus is the source of all light coming into the world (see John 1:9 and comment).

13 The Pharisees did not accept Jesus' testimony about Himself. In a court, the judge does not fully trust a man's testimony about himself, because a man usually says only what is good about himself and does not speak the full truth. Therefore, according to the Old Testament, in order to establish the truth of someone's testimony, at least two witnesses are necessary (Deuteronomy 19:15; John 8:17). But Jesus was only one witness. Therefore, in the opinion of the Jews, Jesus' witness could not be considered **valid**[68] or reliable (see John 5:31 and comment).

The Pharisees refused to see Jesus' light. They said, "Where is your other witness? We don't believe you." But light does not need a witness. It gives its own witness by shining. The man who says, "There is no light," does not condemn the light—he condemns himself! He is blind!

14 Jesus said, "**My testimony is valid**. It does not stand alone. God is my **other witness**" (verse 18). Further, Jesus said that He was qualified to testify about Himself. He knew who He was. He knew He came from God, and He knew He would return to God. But the Pharisees did not know who Jesus was. How, therefore, could they oppose Jesus' testimony?

15 The Pharisees only judged **by human standards**. They only knew about what they could see with their eyes and hear with their ears; they knew nothing of spiritual things.

Jesus did not judge in the way the

[67] It is not certain when the discussion recorded in verses 12–59 took place. Some Bible scholars believe it follows the discussion described in John 7:37–44, and thus took place on the last day of the Feast of Tabernacles (John 7:2). Others believe it took place after the feast was over, at which time most of the Jews who had come to celebrate the feast would have gone back to their own homes (John 7:53).

[68] In place of the word **valid**, some translations of the Bible say "true." The meaning is the same. According to Jewish law, the testimony of only one witness could not legally be considered "true." It might, in fact, be true, but it could not be accepted in court as true. Two witnesses were necessary to establish the truth.

Pharisees judged. He did not come to earth to judge; that was not His main purpose in coming. While Jesus was on earth, He did not make Himself a judge of men (Luke 12:13–14; John 8:11).

16 But in another way, Jesus was a judge (see John 3:17 and comment). He is our judge now. And He will be our judge at the end of the world (John 5:22,27). And if Jesus judges us, we can be sure that His decisions are right, because Jesus is not **alone**. He judges only according to what He hears from God (see John 5:30 and comment). He does not judge according to **human standards**.

In the eyes of the Pharisees, Jesus seemed alone in the world. But God was with Him. Jesus did nothing on His own (see John 5:19; 8:29).

17–18 If the testimony of two men is valid according to the Old Testament law, then certainly the testimony of God and His Son must be valid (see John 8:13–14 and comment).

19 Jesus had just told the Pharisees that the **Father** was His witness (verse 18). The Pharisees then asked mockingly, "**Where is your father?**" They meant Jesus' human father.

But Jesus' answer was about His heavenly Father, whom the Pharisees did not know. Jesus told them, "**If you knew me, you would know my Father also.**" A man who does not know Christ cannot have a full and true knowledge of God (see John 1:18 and comment).

20 See John 7:30,44 and comment.

Warning of the Coming Judgment (8:21–30)

21 Jesus here repeats the thought of John 7:33–34. But He adds here: "**. . . you will die in your sin.**" The Jewish leaders who oppose Jesus will not be able to go with Jesus to heaven, because they refuse to repent of their sins.

The Jews will look for Jesus after He dies. Some will look for His body, so that they might prove He did not rise from the dead (see Matthew 27:64; 28:12–13). Others will realize after His death who Jesus really was (verse 28), but then it will be too late; their hearts will be hardened. They had been given the opportunity to repent and follow Jesus, but they had refused to do so. And when He dies, that opportunity will be gone forever. They will look for Him in vain[69] (see John 7:33–34 and comment). Therefore, let them repent and follow Jesus, while there was yet time (see verse 24).

22 The Jewish leaders realized that Jesus was talking about His death. But even though they themselves were plotting to kill Him (John 5:18), they thought He was talking about killing Himself!

23 The Jews were **from below**, that is, from the world. Jesus was **from above**, that is, from heaven (see John 3:31 and comment).

24 Jesus said that only by believing in Him could the Jews escape from this world of sin and darkness and enter into the kingdom of heaven. They must believe that Jesus is who He said He was—that is, the Son of God, the Messiah. Otherwise, they would indeed **die in [their] sins**; that is, they would die without repenting and without receiving forgiveness. To die "in one's sins" is to spend eternity in hell.

It is not enough for us only to believe that Jesus is a great man, a great teacher, a great prophet. We must believe that He is God's Son, the Savior of the world. If we do not believe that He is our Lord and Savior, He cannot save us.

Jesus says to everyone: "**. . . if you do not believe that I am the one I claim to be**[70] (that is, the Son of God), **you will indeed die in your sins.**"

---

[69] Some Jews, of course, did repent after Jesus' death; but Jesus is not referring to them here. He is speaking here of the Jews, especially the leaders, whose hearts were becoming more and more hardened. Those whose hearts become totally hardened no longer have the capacity to repent. Notice in verse 30, however, that many (with unhardened hearts) did repent and put their faith in Him.

[70] In place of the words **I am the one I claim to be**, some translations of the Bible say, "I am he." The meaning is the same: Unless we believe that Jesus is the Son of God, we shall **die in [our] sins**.

25 When Jesus told the Jews that they must believe that "**I am the one I claim to be**," they didn't understand Him. They asked, "**Who are you?**"

Jesus answered, "**Just what I have been claiming all along**. That is, I am what I have said I am. I am the **bread of life** (John 6:35). I am the **light of the world** (verse 12). I am the Messiah" (John 4:25–26).

26 In this verse Jesus returns to the subject of judgment, which He had mentioned earlier in verse 24. He had already twice told the Jews that they would die in their sins. Now He tells them He has much more concerning which He will judge them. They may question His judgment and His authority. But God has sent Him into the world, and the words He speaks are true because they have come from God Himself (see John 5:30; 8:16 and comments).

27–30 When the Jewish leaders **have lifted up the Son of Man**—that is, when they have lifted Jesus up on the cross to kill Him—then they will know who He is. Because He will rise from the dead. And on the day of judgment, they will all have to stand before His judgment seat (2 Corinthians 5:10).

In the second part of verse 28 and in verse 29, Jesus repeats the thoughts of John 5:30; 8:16,26.

Further Discussion With the Jews (8:31–47)

31 Many ordinary Jews did put their faith in Jesus (verse 30). To these Jesus said, "**If you hold to my teaching, you will be my disciples.**" Jesus knew that their faith was weak. He taught them that true faith means to "**hold to my teaching**"—that is, to heed it, to obey it. They must continue in His teaching (see Matthew 7:21; Mark 4:16–17; 13:13; Luke 9:62; John 15:7; 2 John 9 and comments). Only if they do this will they be true disciples.

32 The person who "holds" to Christ's teaching will know the truth. Christ's teachings are true. . . . **grace and truth came through Jesus Christ** (John 1:17). But not only that, the man who holds to Christ's teaching will be set **free**. The truth of Christ will set him free from the bondage of ignorance and sin. God sent Jesus into the world **to proclaim freedom for the prisoners** (Luke 4:18). To be **free** from sin means to be saved.

Most people are not aware that spiritually they are in bondage. The Jews supposed that they were "free" (verse 33). But, in fact, they were in bondage to sin. They were in bondage to their law. They were condemned to death by their law. It was only the truth of Jesus that could set them free (see Romans 8:1–2; Galatians 5:1 and comments).

33 Along with the Jews who believed, there were other Jews present who had not put their faith in Jesus. Some of these Jews said, "**We are Abraham's**[71] **descendants.**" It is very common for unrighteous children to boast of the righteousness of their parents. They rely on their family name, but at the same time they bring dishonor upon it. The unbelieving Jews were like that.

The Jews were **Abraham's descendants** according to the flesh. "We are sons of Abraham, not slaves," the Jews insisted. "**We have never been slaves of anyone.**" But they were wrong in two ways. First, even at that very time they were, in a worldly sense, the slaves of the Romans. And second, in a spiritual sense, they were slaves of sin.

34 They were slaves of sin because they lived in sin. Jesus told them: ". . . **everyone who sins**[72] **is a slave to sin.**" The slave of sin cannot free himself from sin. He has no power in himself to stop sinning. He needs a power greater than his own (see Romans 6:16; 2 Peter 2:19 and comments).

35 The Jews supposed that they were sons of Abraham and had the rights of

---

[71] **Abraham** was the first Jew, the ancestor of all the Jews.

[72] In the Greek text, the word **sins** means "continues to sin." Jesus is not talking here about a person who sins from time to time and who then genuinely repents of his sin (see 1 John 3:6 and comment).

sons. But the Jews were not true sons of Abraham spiritually (Romans 2:28–29). They were like slaves instead.

Jesus says here: "A **slave has no permanent place in the family, but a son belongs to it forever**." A son remains a son. We ourselves are sons of God through faith in Christ (see John 1:12; Galatians 4:4–7 and comments). But Jesus is here talking in particular about Himself. He is the one and only Son of God. He is a son forever (1 Chronicles 17:13–14).

36 Because Jesus is the eternal Son and heir of God, He has the power and authority to set us free (see Galatians 5:1). We cannot free ourselves from slavery to sin. But He can free us. He not only frees us from the power of sin, but He also frees us from the punishment for sin. He freed us from the punishment for sin once and for all when He took our punishment upon Himself on the cross (see Mark 10:45 and comment).

37 Jesus acknowledged that the Jews were Abraham's fleshly descendants. But they didn't act as Abraham would have acted (verses 39–40). They were trying to kill Jesus. They were trying to kill Jesus because they had **no room** for His word. That is, they refused to "make room" for His word—they refused to accept His teaching. To reject Jesus' word is the same as to reject Jesus.

38 Then Jesus told the Jews, "I do what I have heard from my Father, but **you do what you have heard from your father**." Jesus meant that their father was the **devil** (verse 44).

39–40 The Jews said that Abraham was their father. But Jesus said that they were not true descendants of Abraham, because they didn't act as Abraham did. Abraham was righteous. But these Jews were unrighteous. They were trying to kill Jesus (see Matthew 3:9 and comment).

41 Again, Jesus said that the Jews were doing the things that their own father the devil did (see verse 44).

Then the Jews said, "**We are not illegitimate children**." This statement can have two meanings. First, the Jews may have been thinking that Jesus Himself was illegitimate. They may have heard about Mary's becoming pregnant before she was married (Matthew 1:18). Thus they could have been saying: "We are not illegitimate like you are."

Or second, they may simply have been saying, "We have remained faithful to God." In the Old Testament, Jews who forsook God were called adulterers, whose children would then have been "illegitimate." The Jews' meaning would then be: "We are not like that."

42–43 The Jews said, "**The only Father we have is God himself**" (verse 41). But Jesus denied that. God was not their Father. If God was their Father, they would have loved Christ, because Christ was God's Son. Only those who love Christ can call God their Father.

44 But these Jews were trying to murder Christ. Therefore, their father was the **devil**, SATAN, who **was a murderer from the beginning**. Satan caused Cain to murder his brother Abel, the first murder in history (Genesis 4:4–8; 1 John 3:12). But more than that, Satan caused sin to enter mankind, and because of that, all men are condemned to death because of him (see Romans 5:12 and comment). Thus Satan can, in a spiritual sense, be called the "murderer" of all men.

Not only is Satan a murderer; he is also a **liar**. (Notice that if we let just one sin—like murder—master us, there will always be other sins—like lying—that join it!) All lies come from Satan, even the smallest falsehood. He is the **father of lies**—and the father of liars. Just as there is no falsehood in God, so there is no truth in Satan. Satan's main method of attacking men is by deceiving them (Genesis 3:4–5). He calls good evil, and evil good. He calls truth falsehood, and falsehood truth. He makes men slaves, but says they are free!

45 The Jews couldn't believe Jesus, because they believed the lies of Satan instead. Jesus spoke the truth, but they believed only lies. Satan had closed their minds and hardened their hearts. The truth of Christ was speaking, but they could not hear it. The light of Christ was shining, but they could not see it. Such is Satan's effect upon men.

46 Jesus said to the Jews, "Show me a sin that I have committed." What other man would ever dare to say that? Only

Jesus could have said it, because only Jesus was without sin (Hebrews 4:15; 1 John 3:5).

If the Jews could prove that Jesus was a sinner, then let them not believe His words. But if He was indeed without sin, if He was telling them the truth, then let them believe Him.

But, in fact, the Jews could not prove that Jesus was guilty of any sin. Yet they still didn't believe Him. It wasn't because of any sin of Jesus that the Jews refused to believe in Him; it was because of their own sin (John 3:19–20).

47 Those who **belong to God** hear God. Those who do not belong to God can't hear God; they can't understand God (see John 8:23; 1 Corinthians 2:12,14; 1 John 4:6). Those who belong to God are those who have been reborn by the Holy Spirit. They can understand spiritual things. To teach spiritual things to unrepentant people is like trying to describe color to a man born blind or music to a man born deaf. It is in vain.

The Claims of Jesus About Himself (8:48–59)

48 The only answer the Jews could give Jesus was to abuse Him. They called Him a **Samaritan**, which in the Jews' mind was a great insult. The Samaritans said that the Jews weren't the only sons of Abraham; the Samaritans considered themselves sons of Abraham too (see John 4:8–9 and comment).

The Jews also called Jesus **demon-possessed** (see Mark 3:22,30; John 7:20; 8:52). It is easier to call a man names than to answer his arguments.

49 Jesus was not demon-possessed, because He honored God. Demon-possessed men never honor God; they are under the control of Satan.

Jesus honored God, but He was dishonored by men. God has promised that He Himself will honor those who honor Him, but He has never promised that they would be honored by other men.

50 Jesus did not care if men insulted Him. He was not seeking glory for Himself. But **there is one who seeks glory**, and that is God. He will in the end glorify the Son Christ, because when Christ is glorified, God also is glorified (see John 17:1).

God is also the **judge**. But God will turn the work of judgment over to Christ, so that all men will honor Christ (John 5:22–23). In this way, God will obtain glory, both for Himself and for His Son. And, through Christ, He will bring judgment on all those who dishonor Christ (verse 49).

Jesus did not have to fight back against the Jews. He did not have to defend His honor. **Instead, he entrusted himself to him who judges justly** (see 1 Peter 2:23–24 and comment).

51 But the person who keeps Christ's word (see verse 31) will **never see death**; that is, his soul will never die. He will be saved from eternal punishment. Eternal punishment means to be separated from God in hell; it means to be dead spiritually. It means the opposite of eternal life (see John 3:15 and comment).

52–53 The Jews were offended when Jesus said that whoever kept His word would not see death. **"Who do you think you are?"** they asked contemptuously. "Everyone dies. Abraham died, the prophets died, all the great people of history have died. Are you greater than they are? Can you prevent death in others when these great men couldn't even prevent death in themselves?"

The Jews were wrong in their thinking in two ways. First, Abraham and the prophets were not dead. Their souls were alive (see Mark 12:26–27 and comment). Their second mistake was this. The Old Testament clearly taught that one greater than Abraham and the prophets would come, and that person would be the Messiah. Therefore, when Christ showed them that He was greater than Abraham (verse 58), they should have concluded that He was the Messiah. Instead, they concluded that He was demon-possessed!

54 To the question, **"Who do you think you are?"** Jesus replied: "I don't need to answer that question. God will answer it. I don't need to glorify myself (verse 50). **My Father** will glorify me. He is your God, but He is **my Father**." The Jews could not claim to be God's children, because they had rejected Christ, God's one true Son. Only those who accept Christ are given the right to be children of God and to call God their "Father" (John 1:12).

55 But the Jews could not even rightly call Him "God," because they did not know Him. Only Christ and those who believe in Christ truly know God (John 1:18; 7:28–29; 8:19).

56 Then Jesus said, "**Your father Abraham rejoiced at the thought of seeing my day;**[73] **he saw it and was glad.**" My **day** means the time of Christ's coming to earth. God had promised Abraham that in him **shall all the families of the earth be blessed** (Genesis 12:3). This promise was fulfilled in Christ. It is through Christ that all the people of the world have been blessed. Abraham **saw it** (Christ's day) through the eye of faith, **and was glad**.

57 The Jews thought Jesus was saying that Abraham had actually seen Him with his own eyes. They asked Him mockingly, "Were you alive when Abraham was alive nearly two thousand years ago? You're not even **fifty years old**."[74]

58 But Jesus' claim was even greater than they had supposed. He answered that He was alive not only during Abraham's lifetime—He was alive before Abraham even existed! Jesus has always been alive. He has been with God from the beginning (John 1:1–2). "**Before Abraham was born, I am,**" said Jesus. Only God can use the words "**I am.**" In fact, "I Am" is the name God gave Himself. And He told the Jews to call Him by that name (Exodus 3:14). "I Am" means: "I have always been and always will be. I have no beginning and no end."

Therefore, when Jesus spoke the words **I am**, He was saying, "**I am** God."

59 The Jews immediately understood that Jesus had said, "I am God." It was blasphemy for any man to call himself God (see John 5:18 and comment). So they at once picked up stones in order to stone Him to death, because according to the Jewish law, the punishment for blasphemy was death[75] (Leviticus 24:16).

But Jesus disappeared from their sight. God hid Him, because it was not yet His time to die (see John 7:30).

CHAPTER 9

Jesus Heals a Man Born Blind (9:1–12)

1 Jesus healed many blind people, but this was the only recorded time He healed a man **blind from birth**. Jesus could heal any illness, even longstanding illnesses that ordinary doctors can't cure (see Mark 5:25–29; John 5:5–9).

2 The Jews, and Jesus' disciples also, thought that an illness such as blindness was a punishment for some sin. But how could a man born blind have sinned before he was even born? Therefore, the disciples thought that his parents must have been the ones who had sinned. In the Old Testament, it is written that God punishes children for the sins of their parents up to the third and fourth generations[76] (Exodus 20:5).

3 But Jesus told His disciples that both ideas were wrong. The man's blindness had happened **so that the**

---

[73] In place of the words **rejoiced at the thought of seeing my day**, some translations of the Bible say, "rejoiced to see my day." The meaning in the Greek language is the same.

[74] Jesus was at that time about thirty-two or thirty-three years old (Luke 3:23).

[75] To put someone to death without a proper trial was against the Jewish law. However, the Jews were so eager to kill Jesus that they didn't want to wait to hold a trial.

[76] Nowadays doctors know about many diseases which are transmitted from parents to children before the children are even born.

work of God might be displayed in his life. Very often God allows trials and catastrophes to come upon men, because at those times He has an opportunity to show men His power and His glory (see John 11:4; Romans 8:28 and comments). If this man had not been blind, he might not have had the chance to know Christ and to believe in Him.

When trouble comes to another person, let us never think to ourselves, "He must have sinned." In the first place, we all have sinned and deserve punishment. Secondly, we cannot know why trouble comes to a particular person at a particular time. It is not our place to know. Only God knows. But from this verse we can understand that sin is not the only reason why trouble comes on people (see Luke 13:2–5; Acts 28:4 and comments).

4 After Jesus had answered His disciples' question, He said to them, "**While it is day**—that is, while there is opportunity—**we must do the work of him** (God) **who sent me**." This man was born blind so that God's work might be displayed. Therefore, God's work on that occasion was to restore sight to the blind man.

There is an urgency about God's work. Opportunities come and then quickly go. The opportunity to do a good work for God may come today, but not tomorrow. A good work delayed is often a good work never done.

Night is coming, when no one can work. Here "night" means bodily death. Bodily death comes to every man. Then we shall no longer be able to work. We shall be judged according to what we did while we were alive, while it was **day** (2 Corinthians 5:10). Therefore, let us never put off what God has given us to do.

5 See John 1:4; 8:12 and comments.

6–7 Jesus used different methods to cure people (see Mark 8:22–25). Usually he only spoke a word and people were healed.

The name of the pool of Siloam means "**Sent**." That is appropriate, because Jesus Himself was sent from God.

8–12 The healing of the blind man aroused much discussion and amazement among his neighbors. When they asked him how he had been healed, he said, "**The man they call Jesus made some mud and put it on my eyes**" (verse 11). In the blind man's mind, Jesus was only a man, perhaps a very skillful doctor. He didn't even know where He lived.

The Pharisees Investigate the Healing (9:13–34)

13–15 The blind man's neighbors brought him to a group of Pharisees. It is possible that these Pharisees were a committee from the Jewish Sanhedrin appointed to investigate the healing of the blind man, which had taken place on the Sabbath (see verse 16 and comment).

16 The Pharisees were divided among themselves about Christ (see John 7:43 and comment). Some said that because He did not obey the Sabbath law, He could not be from God. Others said that only a man from God could do such a miracle[77] (see verses 31–33). But the party in favor of Jesus must have been small, because they are not mentioned again.

The charge that Jesus did not obey the Sabbath law was false. True, He didn't obey it according to the traditions of the Jewish leaders. But He did obey it according to the command of God (see Mark 3:1–5; Luke 13:10–17; John 5:8–10 and comments).

17 Since the Pharisees couldn't agree among themselves, they asked the blind man himself what he thought. He ought to have some idea, because he was the one who was healed.

"**He is a prophet**," the man said. The blind man had no doubt now. Jesus must be more than just a man (verse 11). He was a prophet. A prophet was the highest thing the man could think of.

18–19 The Pharisees did not want to

---

[77] It is also true that Satan has the power to perform miracles, and he gives that power to evil men. But such miracles never bring glory to Christ or to God. They bring glory only to Satan and to those who serve him (see Mark 13:22 and comment).

accept the blind man's opinion. They were trying to prove that Jesus was a sinner, a lawbreaker. So they decided that this blind man was lying, and that he had never been blind at all! To prove this, they called the blind man's parents. The Pharisees hoped that his parents would testify that their son had not been born blind.

20–21 The parents, however, said that he had indeed been born blind. But they didn't want to say anything about how he had been healed. They weren't there when it happened. Let the Pharisees ask their son directly.

22–23 The parents were afraid to say anything good about Jesus. They knew that all those who were calling Jesus the Messiah were being expelled from the Jewish synagogues. They were losing their rights as Jews. The parents feared that if they acknowledged that Jesus had healed their son, they themselves might be expelled from their synagogue (see Luke 6:22; John 12:42).

A question arises here: Why did the Pharisees oppose Jesus and His followers so much? Why did they refuse to believe that He was the Messiah? There are two main reasons. First, Jesus' teaching opposed the teaching of the Pharisees and other Jewish leaders. They followed the Jewish law outwardly; but Jesus said the law must be followed inwardly from the heart. Jesus showed that the Jewish leaders were hypocrites, and this made them angry (see Matthew 23:1–32).

The second main reason the Jewish leaders opposed Jesus was that Jesus had not come in the way the Jews expected their Messiah to come. Jesus came humbly. He taught that His followers must endure persecution in this world. The Jewish leaders thought that the Messiah would come as a victorious king. They didn't want anyone like Jesus to be their Messiah!

24 After they talked with the blind man's parents, the Pharisees called the man a second time. They couldn't let the matter drop. "**Give glory to God**," they said to him. This can have two meanings. First, it can mean: "Give glory to God by telling the truth" (Joshua 7:19). Second, it can mean: "Give the glory for this healing to God, not to Christ." Both these meanings are possible.

The Pharisees tried to persuade the blind man that Jesus should get no credit for his healing. "**We know this man** (Jesus) **is a sinner**," they said.

25 The blind man didn't care what the Pharisees thought. He didn't care if Christ was a sinner or not. That wasn't his concern. He only knew one thing, and all the Pharisees put together weren't going to change his mind. "**One thing I know. I was blind but now I see**."

This is the testimony of every true Christian: "Once I was spiritually blind, but now I see. Once I was dead in sin, but now I am alive in Christ. Once I was in bondage, but now I am free." The Christian has no doubt. He has experienced these things for himself.

26 The Pharisees repeated the same question to the man. They hoped that by mistake he might contradict something he had said before. Then they could accuse him of lying.

27 When the Pharisees kept asking the same questions, the blind man became irritated. He said to them: "Why do you ask the same thing again? **Do you want to become his disciples, too?**" He knew they didn't; he was only mocking them.

Notice that the blind man said "too." That meant that he now considered himself a disciple of Jesus.

28–29 Then the Pharisees scoffed at the blind man. They said that they were disciples of the great Moses. They obeyed the law which God had given to Moses. God Himself spoke to Moses many times.

But as for **this fellow** called Jesus, who was He? "**We don't even know where he comes from**." The Pharisees thought that by saying this they could show that Jesus was a "nobody," that He could not be the Messiah. But, in fact, they were showing the opposite. Everyone believed that when the Messiah came, no one would know where He came from (see John 7:27 and comment). Thus the Pharisees were unwittingly giving evidence that Jesus was indeed the Messiah.

30 The blind man was amazed at the spiritual blindness of the Pharisees. They should have known where Jesus was from. Any man who could heal in this way had to be from God (verse 33). How could the Pharisees not know that?

31 The blind man agreed that God did not listen to the prayers of sinners—that is, those who continue in sin and do not repent (Psalm 66:18; Proverbs 15:29). He listens only to the **godly man who does his will**. In saying this, the blind man spoke the truth.

32 This is the very reason that Jesus had to be a **godly man**, not a **sinner**. In order for Jesus to have healed the blind man, God must have been listening to Jesus. And God had obviously answered Jesus' prayer. In all of the Old Testament, in all of history, there had never been an instance of the opening of the eyes of a person born blind. No "sinner" could have done such a miracle.

33 Therefore, Jesus had to have come from God. Otherwise, He could have done **nothing**.

34 The Pharisees became even more angry, because this uneducated blind beggar was lecturing them! They insulted him, saying, "**You were steeped in sin at birth**." That is, "You were born in sin. Your blindness was caused by sin in the beginning." It was nothing to them that he was no longer blind! Then they expelled him from the synagogue.

Spiritual Blindness (9:35–41)

35–36 Jesus heard that the Pharisees had expelled the blind man from the synagogue, so He went to find him. The blind man had not yet seen Jesus with his own eyes. But perhaps he recognized Jesus' voice. He was ready to believe, but he was not yet sure exactly who he was supposed to believe in. Jesus asked him, "**Do you believe in the Son of Man?**"[78] And the man replied, "**Who is he?**"

37 "I am he," said Jesus (see John 4:26). Those who seek to know who Jesus is often find Him nearer at hand than they imagined!

38 Now the blind man fully realized who Jesus was. First he had thought He was a man (verse 11). Then he had thought He was a prophet (verse 17). Now he knew that Jesus was more than a prophet; He was the Son of God, the Messiah, the Christ. The man's faith was complete. "**Lord, I believe**" (see John 20:28).

39 Then Jesus said, "**For judgment I have come into this world**." Judgment was not Jesus' main reason for coming (see John 3:17; 12:47 and comments). However, when Jesus came to save men, He also brought **judgment** with Him at the same time. Jesus brings both salvation and judgment: whoever believes in Him receives salvation; whoever does not believe is condemned and receives judgment (see John 3:18 and comment).

When Jesus comes, He brings our sins into the light, His light. Our inner thoughts and motives are revealed. In His light, all men stand condemned. Only through faith in Him can our condemnation be removed (see Romans 8:1 and comment).

Jesus came **so that the blind will see**. Here Jesus is talking mainly about those who are spiritually blind. Like the blind man of this story, who was blind from birth, all men are spiritually blind from birth. Jesus came that all men might have the chance to receive spiritual sight.

At the same time, He came so that **those who see will become blind** (see Mark 4:10–12 and comment). Jesus' meaning is this: He came so that those, like the Pharisees, who claim to have spiritual sight will be shown to be spiritually blind. The Pharisees by their words and actions proved themselves to be blind. Those who receive Jesus receive spiritual sight. Those who reject Jesus remain spiritually blind.

40 The Pharisees who were listening asked, "Are you saying that we are blind?" They did not think they were blind. They considered themselves the guides and leaders of the people.

---

[78] For a discussion of the meaning of the term **Son of Man**, see Mark 2:10; John 1:51 and comments.

In place of the words **Son of Man**, some ancient manuscripts of John say "Son of God."

41 Jesus answered, "No, I am not saying you are completely blind. If you were completely blind, you would have an excuse for your sin (John 15:22). **You would not be guilty of sin.** But **you claim you can see.** And indeed you do have some spiritual sight. You have enough spiritual knowledge to have believed in me, but instead you refused to believe. Therefore, **your guilt remains.**"

The Pharisees had a little spiritual knowledge, but they boasted that they had much. They were proud. Those who think they don't have anything to learn will learn nothing. The Pharisees knew that the Messiah would come; but when Jesus came and stood before them, they didn't recognize Him. To recognize Jesus, the first thing we must do is to acknowledge our own spiritual weakness and blindness (see Matthew 5:3 and comment). Only then will Jesus give us full spiritual sight.

CHAPTER 10

The Shepherd and His Flock (10:1–21)

1 As soon as Jesus had finished telling the Pharisees about their blindness (John 9:39–41), He began to teach about the good shepherd. According to the Old Testament, the Jewish leaders were supposed to be **watchmen** and **shepherds** of Israel. But they had failed to do their duty. They had become **blind**; they lacked **understanding** (Isaiah 56:9–11). They had become false shepherds. They had become like thieves and robbers, who do not enter the sheep pen through the **gate**.

2–3 The true shepherd (Christ) always goes through the gate. He comes openly, in truth. He calls His sheep and they recognize Him.[79]

4–6 The sheep will only follow the shepherd whose voice they recognize. They do not recognize the voice of a false shepherd.

In the Old Testament, God Himself was the shepherd of Israel (Psalm 23:1; Ezekiel 34:15–16). But now He has appointed Jesus to be our shepherd, and He has also appointed under-shepherds—that is, pastors and teachers—for the church (see Acts 20:28–31). The Apostle Peter was Jesus' chief "under-shepherd" (see John 21:15–17). And in his first letter, Peter has written to us how true under-shepherds must behave (see 1 Peter 5:1–4 and comment).

7 Jesus is the **gate for the sheep**. He is the **gate** by which the sheep enter the sheep pen and find safety. In the same way, Jesus is the "gate"—the **way**—by which believers enter heaven and find eternal life (John 14:6).

8 **"All who ever came before me were thieves and robbers,"** said Jesus.[80] This means that all those who come in the morning before light are not true shepherds. The true shepherd comes at dawn to graze his sheep; anyone who comes before that is a thief.

The thief doesn't go in through the gate. Anyone who desires to be a true shepherd must go through the gate, which is Christ. If we want to save others, we must first be saved ourselves.

9 **I am the gate**. No one can enter heaven unless he enters by way of Christ (John 14:6). That is, no one can be **saved** apart from Christ (Acts 4:12). There is only one **gate**.

10 The false shepherd, the thief,

[79] In the Middle East, the sheep of several different shepherds used to be kept in the same sheep pen. Each shepherd had a special call for his own sheep, which his sheep could recognize.

[80] Jesus cannot mean here the Old Testament prophets. He would not have called them **thieves and robbers**. But perhaps He means the false priests and leaders of Israel who acted like thieves and robbers (Jeremiah 23:1–4; Ezekiel 34:1–10,15–16).

comes to do harm. He is like a wolf in sheep's clothing (Matthew 7:15; Acts 20:29).

But the true shepherd Jesus comes to the sheep—to believers—that they might have **life, and have it to the full**. The false shepherd brings death; the true shepherd brings **life**. This life is **eternal life** (verse 28). It begins when one believes, and it never ends (see John 3:15; 8:51 and comments). The life that Jesus gives is spiritual life, life filled with all the fullness of God (Ephesians 3:19). It is a life of joy, of peace, of power; and it lasts forever.

11 **I am the good shepherd**. The good shepherd loves the flock. In Bible times, even good shepherds did not usually lay down their own lives for their sheep. But the one Good Shepherd, Jesus, did lay down His life (Mark 10:45). He laid it down of His own accord (verse 18).

12–13 The true shepherd is the owner of the sheep. He cares much more for the sheep than a **hired hand**. The hired hand runs away when the wolf comes, and the flock is scattered and destroyed.

In every generation there are some among the leaders of the church who are only "hired hands." They do not put their flock first. They do not put the welfare of Christ's church first. They run when trouble comes. To them, being a church leader is a means of making a living. Let each of us examine our hearts. Are we serving Christ for love—or are we serving Christ for money? (see Matthew 6:24; 1 Timothy 6:3–5,9–11; 1 Peter 5:2 and comments).

14 The **good shepherd** knows his sheep, and the sheep know their shepherd (verse 4). **The Lord knows those who are his** (2 Timothy 2:19); and believers **know whom** [they] **have believed** (2 Timothy 1:12).

15 The relationship between the sheep and their shepherd is intimate, like the relationship between God and Christ. Jesus knows and loves His sheep, and He is ready to lay down His life for them.

16 Jesus also had **other sheep** that were **not of this sheep pen**. These were Gentile (non-Jewish) believers. Already God had chosen people from among the Gentiles who would believe in Christ. But they had not yet been called; they had not yet been brought to faith. They needed to be brought into the sheep pen, the church. These Gentiles would listen to Christ's voice, and come to Him. Then there would be **one flock**, one church, which would include all believers, both Jews and Gentiles.

The job of calling the Gentiles into the church Jesus gave to His disciples—to us. In every generation God has set aside sheep for Christ. But we must call them in.

. . . **there shall be one flock**. Christ does not have many flocks; He has only one. Let us never be a cause of division in Christ's flock.

17–18 God loved Christ because Christ was completely obedient to Him. It was God's will and purpose that Christ lay down His life for the sheep. And Christ obeyed.

But Christ took His life up again. According to the command of the Father, Jesus laid down His life in order **to take it up again**. There could be no resurrection without death. In order to conquer death and release us from the death penalty, Jesus had to die Himself.

Jesus laid down His life, and then took it up again. Christ raised Himself from the dead, and God also raised Him. Christ and God always work together. Everything they do is done by both of them (see verse 30).

19–21 Again the people were divided about Jesus (see John 7:20,43; 8:48–49; 9:16 and comments).

Some said, "**He is demon-possessed and raving mad**" (verse 20). Demon possession and madness are two different things. But often a demon-possessed person will appear mad.

Jesus in the Temple in Jerusalem (10:22–30)

22–24 Some time later came the **Feast of Dedication**.[81] As Jesus was

[81] The **Feast of Dedication** was held in Jerusalem each year to commemorate the rededication of the Jewish temple in 165 B.C., after it had been desecrated by a foreign king.

walking in a section of the temple called **Solomon's Colonnade** (Acts 3:11; 5:12), the Jews asked Jesus to tell them openly if He was the Christ or not. Some perhaps were ready to believe. Others may have merely been trying to trap Him in His speech. If He said He was the Christ (the Messiah), the Romans would arrest Him for making Himself a king. If He said He was not the Messiah, then the people would stop following Him. Thus whatever answer Jesus gave, it would be to the advantage of His enemies.

25 Jesus answered, "**I did tell you**. I have told you who I am." Jesus had told the Samaritan woman who He was (John 4:26). He also had told the blind man who He was (John 9:35–37), at which time some of the Jews probably overheard Him. He also had told the Jews, "... **before Abraham was born, I am**" (see John 8:58 and comment). He called Himself the **Son**, which means the "Son of God," the Messiah. In all these ways Jesus had said who He was. But the Jews did not believe. They did not even believe Jesus' miracles, which they could easily see. The miracles were signs proving that Jesus was the Christ. The miracles testified that Jesus had been sent from the Father (see John 5:36). But the Jews, for the most part, were spiritually blind.

26 The Jews didn't believe, because they were not Jesus' sheep. They didn't know Jesus. They couldn't recognize His voice. They had not been chosen by God to receive the gift of faith (see John 6:37,44; 8:47 and comments).

If the Jews were not Jesus' sheep, whose sheep were they? They were Satan's sheep. There are only two flocks: Christ's and Satan's. Every one needs to ask himself: Whose flock do I belong to? If we belong to Christ's flock, we will hear His voice.

27 Jesus knows His sheep, and His sheep know Him (see verse 15 and comment). That is, the sheep have full faith in their shepherd.

28 Jesus gives **eternal life** to His sheep. He gives it not only in the future, but He gives it now (John 3:15–16; 8:51). He gives His sheep complete protection. This does not mean that He will save us from all trouble and calamity in this life. Rather, it means that He will preserve our souls and spirits, no matter what earthly troubles come upon us.

Jesus said, "... **no one can snatch them out of my hand**." The strong hand of the Great Shepherd holds us. The devil tries to pull us away, but Christ's hold is stronger (see 1 John 4:4 and comment). Our salvation does not depend on our weak hold on Christ; it depends on His strong hold on us.

There is only one way we can lose Christ's protection: We ourselves can jump out of His hand. That is, we can knowingly continue in sin; we can separate ourselves from God; we can decide to stop believing. Some say that anyone who leaves the faith never had true faith to begin with. They never were in Christ's hand. And it's possible that they are right in saying this. But other New Testament verses seem to say that even those who have once truly believed can later turn away from Christ (see Hebrews 6:4–6; 10:26–29 and comments; General Article: Can We Lose Our Salvation?).

29 Here Jesus repeats the thought of verse 28. No evil power can snatch us from Christ's hand, because God gave us to Christ (John 6:37), and God is stronger than all evil powers. It is His will that none of His sheep be lost (see John 6:39).

30 Then Jesus gave His final answer to the question the Jews had asked. The Jews had asked, "Are you the Christ?" (verse 24). But Christ told them He was not only the Messiah—He was God Himself! (see John 1:1 and comment). The true Messiah is God. "**I and the Father are one**."

This great statement is the foundation for all the teachings Christ has given in this Gospel and the other three Gospels. The Jews didn't believe, because they saw only the man Jesus—a poor and humble man, a carpenter's son from the hills of Galilee. But this Jesus was not only a man; He was God Himself, God's true and only incarnation.

When we look at Jesus, let us not make the mistake of the unbelieving Jews who could only see a man, but could not see God. Let us pray that we might not be spiritually blind like the Jews, and thus lose the chance to receive eternal life.

The Hostility of the Jews (10:31–42)

31 The Jews immediately understood from what Jesus said in verse 30 that He was claiming to be God (verse 33). Such a claim, in their eyes, was **blasphemy** (see Mark 14:64; John 5:18; 8:59 and comments).

32 Jesus did not run away when the Jews picked up stones. He only said, "What are you stoning me for? I have done nothing but the work of God. For which of the miracles I've done do you seek to stone me?"

33 "We don't stone you for any miracle you've done," the Jews said. "We stone you only **because you, a mere man, claim to be God**."

The Jews were right about what Jesus claimed. He did claim to be God. What the Jews did not consider was that His claim was indeed true.

34 Jesus then quoted from Psalm 82:6: "**I have said you are gods**."[82] In this verse, God is calling the judges of Israel "gods," because they had been given a high office by God Himself.

35–36 Therefore, if mere men are called "gods" in the Old Testament, why is it wrong for Jesus to call Himself the **Son of God**? If men can be called god in the Bible, surely the true Son of God, **whom the Father set apart for his very own**, can be called a "god." Jesus was not claiming to be anything except what He, in fact, was!

Notice in verse 35 that Jesus says, "**The Scripture cannot be broken**." Every word of Scripture is true. The verse Jesus quoted was not a very important verse; nevertheless, each word of it was completely true. We must not throw out or change the meaning of any verse of the Bible.[83]

37–38 Jesus told the Jews to examine His works. Were they the works of God? If so, then the Jews should believe that God is in Jesus and that Jesus is in God (see John 10:30; 17:21). The works show this to be true. No man could have done such works if he were not of God (see John 9:32–33).

39 But the Jews wouldn't listen. They again tried to seize Jesus, but could not (see John 7:30,44).

40–42 Jesus then left Jerusalem and went to the east side of the **Jordan** River, where John the Baptist had first baptized people (see John 1:28). John's testimony concerning Christ was still remembered. His influence still remained among the people. When the people themselves saw Jesus, they could see that John's testimony was indeed true. Yet John was only a witness. He himself did no miracles. His work was only to prepare the people to meet Christ. And when they met Him, they believed in Him (verse 42).

---

[82] Jesus said that He was quoting from the **Law**. Usually the "Law" means the first five books of the Old Testament. But sometimes the entire Old Testament was also called the "Law."

[83] We must remember that in a few verses it is not fully certain what was originally written. The reason for this is that the original manuscripts and earliest copies of the New Testament have been destroyed or lost. Only later copies exist today. Thus, when these later copies are compared, some minor differences can be seen in the way a few verses are written. However, none of the differences affect the meaning of any important Christian teaching. Furthermore, the number of verses involved is very small. For further discussion, see General Article: How We Got Our Bible.

CHAPTER 11

The Death of Lazarus (11:1–16)

1 Lazarus was the brother of **Mary** and **Martha,** who are mentioned in Luke 10:38–42. They lived in **Bethany,** which was less than two miles from Jerusalem.[84]

2 Mary was the one who later anointed Jesus with expensive perfume (see Mark 14:3–9; John 12:1–8).

3 When Lazarus became sick (verse 1), his sisters sent messengers to Jesus, who was staying on the other side of the Jordan River, about sixteen miles away (John 10:40). The messengers told Jesus: "The **one you love** is sick." Jesus knew Lazarus and his sisters well, and had great love for them (verse 5).

4 Jesus said, "**This sickness will not end in death**—that is, Lazarus will survive in the end." The purpose of Lazarus' sickness was to bring glory to God and to God's Son, Jesus (see John 9:3).

Even while Jesus was saying this, He knew that Lazarus had already died (verse 14). Lazarus had died just after the messengers had been sent.

5–6 Because He knew that Lazarus was already dead, Jesus did not go immediately. He waited for two days. He knew that He was going to raise Lazarus from the dead, and whether He did it two days later or four days later didn't make that much difference. He waited until it was the right time for Him to go.

7–8 Bethany was located near Jerusalem in the province of **Judea,** where the Jews had several times tried to kill Jesus (John 8:59; 10:31,39). His disciples knew it was very dangerous to return to Judea.

9 Jesus said, "**Are there not twelve hours of daylight?**"[85] In New Testament times, no one had watches. Daylight was considered to be twelve hours long. (In winter months the "twelve hours" would be shorter.) Therefore, Jesus is saying here that there are only twelve hours of daylight in which a man can work and walk without stumbling. In those twelve hours he can easily see **by this world's light**, that is, the sun. Therefore, a man must work while he has opportunity (see John 9:4 and comment).

A man's life is like twelve hours of daylight. A man must finish his work before he dies. Even though there was danger in Judea, Jesus had work there that had to be done while He was still on earth—while there was still light. There were still "one or two hours of daylight" left in His life, and the Jews could not kill Him until His work was done.

10 At night it is difficult for a man to walk, because **he has no light**. This has a spiritual meaning. While Christ is with us, there is spiritual light. But when we walk without Christ, there is no light in us, in our souls. The man who does not have the light of Christ in his soul will surely stumble (see John 8:12; 12:35 and comments).

11 Jesus then told His disciples that Lazarus had **fallen asleep**. He meant that Lazarus had died. Often in the Bible, to fall **asleep** means "to die" (Acts 7:60; 1 Corinthians 15:20; 1 Thessalonians 4:13–15).

For believers in Christ, death is like sleep. Christians never completely die. Soon they will awake again in heaven.

12–13 The disciples, who did not

[84] This story of raising Lazarus from the dead is not mentioned in Matthew, Mark, and Luke. The first three Gospel writers do not describe the miracles Jesus did in Jerusalem; they describe miracles that were done mainly in Galilee. John, on the other hand, describes mostly the miracles Jesus did in Jerusalem and Judea.

Matthew, Mark, and Luke do describe the raising of Jairus' daughter from the dead (Matthew 9:18–26; Mark 5:21–43; Luke 8:40–56). Also Luke describes the raising of the son of the widow of Nain from the dead (Luke 7:11–15).

[85] In place of the words **twelve hours of daylight**, some translations of the Bible say, "twelve hours in a day." The first translation, however, gives the true meaning.

know Lazarus was dead, thought that Jesus only meant that Lazarus had fallen asleep in an ordinary way. In that case he would recover, they thought.

14–15 Jesus told His disciples plainly that Lazarus was actually dead. He knew this by supernatural means; no one had told Him. Then He said, "**. . . for your sake I am glad I was not there, so that you may believe**." If Jesus had been there, He would have healed Lazarus before he died. That would have been a lesser miracle. But to raise a dead man—especially one who had been dead for four days (verse 17)—was a very great miracle. Such a miracle would increase and strengthen the faith of the disciples (see Luke 17:5).

16 Thomas, called **Didymus**,[86] one of the twelve disciples (Mark 3:18), urged his fellow disciples to accompany Jesus to Judea, **that we might die with him**. Thomas was ready to die for Jesus, and so were the others. But in the end, when Jesus was arrested, they all deserted Him and fled (Mark 14:50). The disciples' faith was weak.

Jesus Comforts the Sisters (11:17–37)

17 Lazarus had been dead for four days when Jesus arrived at his house. It had taken the messengers one day to reach Jesus. Jesus had waited two days. Then it had taken Jesus one day to reach Bethany.

18–20 Many Jewish friends of the family had come to comfort Mary and Martha. However, as soon as she heard Jesus was coming, Martha left Mary and their Jewish friends and went out to meet Jesus.

21 Martha didn't rebuke Jesus for being late. She only said that if He had been there before Lazarus died, He could have healed him. Perhaps Martha had not heard that Jesus was able to heal people even from a distance (see Matthew 8:5–13; Mark 7:24–30).

22 Then Martha expressed her faith that God would give Jesus anything He asked for. Perhaps she was suggesting to Jesus that He could raise her brother from the dead. But later, when Jesus actually went to raise Lazarus, Martha didn't think it would be possible (verse 39). Like the disciples, Martha had some faith. But when her faith was really tested, it failed.

23–24 Jesus then told Martha that Lazarus would **rise again**. Martha thought He meant that Lazarus would rise at the end of the world, **at the last day**, when there would be a resurrection of all bodies (see John 5:28–29; Acts 24:15).

25 But Jesus was not talking only about the end of the world. He was bringing to Martha and Lazarus the power to rise from the dead even in this life.

I am the resurrection and the life. Jesus gives us a resurrection for our bodies, and eternal life for our souls. Jesus not only gives life; He is life. **In him was life** (John 1:4; 5:26). That life is eternal life, spiritual life. To receive such spiritual life one must first die, and then be resurrected, or reborn. Death to the old sinful life comes first; then **resurrection**; then **life** (see John 3:3; 12:24; Romans 6:3–5 and comments).

To show that He had the power to give new spiritual life, Jesus gave Lazarus new physical life. To show that He could raise men from spiritual death into spiritual life, Jesus raised Lazarus from physical death to physical life.[87]

Then Jesus told Martha that everyone who believes in Him **will live, even though he dies**. The believer's body dies, but his soul and spirit does not. Physical death is only a gateway to eternal life. The believer need have no fear of death. Death cannot harm our soul.

26 Whoever is spiritually alive and believes in Christ will never die (see John

---

[86] The word **Thomas** means "twin" in the Hebrew language. **Didymus** means "twin" in the Greek language.

[87] In the same way, to prove that He had the spiritual authority to forgive sins, Jesus restored a paralyzed man to complete health (see Mark 2:3–12 and comment).

3:15; 8:51 and comments). This is not just some idea or theory. This is a truth we need to believe and act on. Eternal life comes only through faith. "**Do you believe this?**" Jesus asked Martha.

27 Martha believed. Especially she believed in Christ; she believed that He was indeed the Messiah, the Son of God, the Savior of the world. To believe less than this about Christ is not adequate; it will not save us.

28–32 Then Mary went out to meet Jesus. She repeated to Jesus the same words that Martha had said to Him earlier (verse 21).

33 When Jesus saw the sorrow of Mary and her Jewish friends, He Himself was **deeply moved in spirit**, that is, in His human spirit, in His heart. He was **troubled**. It is not certain why Jesus was moved and troubled. He was about to raise Lazarus from the dead; therefore, He had no reason to feel sorrow on His own account. Some believe that He was angry at the unbelief of the Jews who were with Mary. Others say He was troubled because He knew that after raising Lazarus, the Jewish leaders would quickly arrest Him and put Him to death. Perhaps, however, He was troubled simply by seeing the sorrow which Mary and Martha had had to endure for four days.

34–37 **Jesus wept** (verse 35). Jesus was a man like us and could experience sorrow. The Jews did not understand why He wept. They thought He wept because Lazarus had died and He couldn't do anything about it. The Jews asked each other, "Why couldn't Jesus have kept Lazarus from dying? What happened to His power? He healed the blind man (John 9:6–7). Why couldn't He help Lazarus?"

Jesus Raises Lazarus From the Dead (11:38–44)

38–39 When Martha saw that Jesus was about to raise Lazarus, her faith faltered. "Don't you know that Lazarus has been dead for four days?" she said to Jesus.

40 Jesus gently rebuked Martha for her lack of faith. She believed that He was the Son of God (verse 27), and that God would give Him whatever He asked (verse 22). Jesus had told her that she would see the glory of God, as He had also told His disciples (verse 4). Let her faith not waver!

Notice that, in order for Martha to see God's glory, faith was necessary. Those without faith would simply see a miracle—a man rising from the dead. Those with faith, on the other hand, would see the significance of the miracle—that is, the **glory of God**.

41 Jesus knew that God would answer His request and raise Lazarus. Therefore, He first thanked God for hearing His request. Even before He received the answer to His prayer, Jesus knew that He had obtained it (see 1 John 5:14–15).

42 Jesus thanked God out loud, so that the people standing around could hear. He wanted them to know that it was by God's power that He was raising Lazarus. The people needed to know that Jesus did not work on His own (see John 5:19). He had been sent by God to do the works of God.

Ordinary wonderworkers always try to glorify themselves. Jesus, however, always gave the glory to God.

43–44 Then Jesus called to Lazarus, and he came out of the tomb. He was wrapped with **strips of linen**. It was the Jews' custom to wrap the bodies of the dead before burial (John 19:40). Lazarus' legs were wrapped separately; thus he was able to walk. It must have been an extraordinary sight! How could one not believe in Jesus after seeing such a miracle?

The Plot to Kill Jesus (11:45–57)

45 Among the Jews who had come to console Mary and Martha,[88] many

[88] John mentions only the **Jews who had come to visit Mary**. Perhaps Mary had a softer heart and, therefore, needed greater consolation; but we must understand that the Jews came to console both sisters.

believed in Christ because of Lazarus' resurrection.

46 But others among them did not believe. Instead, they reported to Jesus' enemies, the Pharisees, what Jesus had done.

47 The Pharisees and chief Jewish priests joined together and called a meeting of the **Sanhedrin.**[89] **"What are we accomplishing?"** they asked each other. Some of them had been trying to arrest Jesus, but had been unsuccessful (John 7:30; 10:39). Some even had tried to kill Him (John 8:59; 10:31). But Jesus was continuing to do miracles, and more and more people were believing in Him. "We must do something to stop Him," they said.

When men's hearts are hardened, even miracles will not change their minds.

48 The Jewish leaders especially feared that if many people began to believe that Jesus was the Messiah, they would try to make Him their king. Then the **Romans**[90] would consider this to be a revolt against their authority, and would surely take away the Jews' **place** (their temple) and their **nation**. That is, the Romans would take complete control over the temple and all Jewish affairs, and the Jews would lose their religious freedom. The Jewish leaders would also lose their own position and authority.

49–50 **Caiaphas** was high priest **that year.**[91] He said to the Sanhedrin, "It is better that Jesus die, than to have our whole nation perish. It is better to kill one innocent man than to lose our nation. If we do not destroy Jesus, the Romans will destroy us."

That is why Caiaphas said that Jesus should **die for the people** (verse 50). By Jesus' death, he thought, the Jews would be saved from the Romans.

Caiaphas was speaking from a worldly point of view. But his words also had a spiritual meaning, which Caiaphas did not intend. In a spiritual sense, Jesus did **die for the people**. He died to save the people spiritually, to give them eternal life. Thus Caiaphas, without realizing it, was actually prophesying that by Jesus' death many people would be saved—a prophecy which was soon fulfilled, and is still being fulfilled!

51 Caiaphas did not speak these words on his own; he was really speaking God's words. Because he was the high priest at that time, God spoke through him. But Caiaphas, of course, didn't realize that he was making a prophecy for God.

52 John adds here that Jesus not only died for the **Jewish nation** (verse 51), but also for the **scattered children of God**, that is, the Gentiles. These were the **other sheep** that Jesus was going to bring into His flock (see John 10:16 and comment).

While Jesus was on earth, He did not preach much among the Gentiles. He concentrated on preaching to the Jews and on training His disciples. But after His death, His disciples went out and preached to the whole world (Acts 1:8). In this way, through His disciples, Jesus has now brought people from all over the world into the church. He died not just for the Jews, but for the whole world.

53 From then on, all the Jewish leaders plotted together to take Jesus' life. The Sanhedrin made an official decision to put Jesus to death. They thought that by killing Jesus their nation would be saved. But how wrong they were! Instead, because they killed Jesus, their nation was utterly destroyed. Only forty years later, the Roman army destroyed not only the Jewish temple

---

[89] The **Sanhedrin** was the ruling council of the Jews, It exercised final authority over all Jewish religious matters. For further discussion, see John 3:1 and comment; Word List: Sanhedrin.

[90] The **Romans** exercised full political authority over their colonies, such as Israel. But they usually gave religious freedom to the local people of each colony. However, if the Romans thought that the Jews were revolting, they would take away their religious freedom also.

[91] **Caiaphas** was high priest in 18–36 A.D. When John says he was high priest **that year,** he means that he was high priest in **that** important **year,** when Jesus died and rose again. Caiaphas is also mentioned in Matthew 26:3.

but also the entire city of Jerusalem and all its inhabitants. The Jews, in the end, lost both their **place** and their **nation** (verse 48). They lost not only their nation on earth; they also lost their salvation in heaven.

54 Jesus' appointed time to die was to be during the Passover festival (verse 55). Before that time Jesus stayed away from the Jews. He spent that time with His disciples.

55–56 As the time of the **Passover**[92] festival approached, many Jewish pilgrims went up to Jerusalem a few days early to purify themselves, as was the custom. These pilgrims **kept looking for Jesus.**[93] They wondered if Jesus would come to the festival. They knew that the Jewish leaders wanted to kill Jesus (verse 57). "Will He come anyway?" they asked.

57 The Jewish leaders had ordered the people to tell them if anyone found out where Jesus was. Anyone who knew but did not report it would be guilty of disobeying the leaders. Thus, if Jesus came to Jerusalem, He would not be able to remain hidden, because many people out of fear would surely report His whereabouts.

CHAPTER 12

Jesus Anointed at Bethany (12:1–11)

(Matthew 26:6–13; Mark 14:3–9)

1–8 See Mark 14:3–9 and comment.

9 Six days before the Passover festival, Jesus again came to Bethany, where Lazarus' home was (verse 1). When the crowds in Jerusalem heard about it, they came out to see Jesus. They also came to see Lazarus, whom Jesus had miraculously raised from the dead.

10–11 Many of the crowds were going over to Jesus because of Lazarus. Therefore, the Jewish leaders decided to kill Lazarus, too. As long as Lazarus was alive, he was visible proof of Jesus' power; if he was killed, the people would soon forget about him.

Caiaphas the high priest had said **one man** must die for the people (John 11:50). Now the Jews said two people had to die: Jesus and Lazarus. Thus does evil grow!

The Triumphal Entry (12:12–19)

(Matthew 21:1–11; Mark 11:1–11; Luke 19:28–40)

12–16 See Mark 11:1–11 and comment.

17–19 The people continued to come out to see Jesus because He had raised Lazarus from the dead. The Jewish leaders were becoming even more anxious. It seemed to them that the **whole world** was going after Jesus (see John 11:47–48 and comment). Because of the increased number of Jesus' admirers, it was going to be more difficult than ever to kill Jesus.

Jesus Predicts His Death (12:20–36)

20 At that time some **Greeks**[94] had come to Jerusalem to worship. Even though these Greeks were Gentiles, they

---

[92] For further discussion of the **Passover,** see Mark 14:1 and comment; Word List: Passover.

[93] Jesus' enemies among the Jews were also looking for Him in order to arrest Him.

[94] These **Greeks** were probably not from the country of Greece, but were Greek-speaking people from various cities in the Middle East (see John 7:35 and comment).

were followers of the Jewish religion. But they had not become true Jews,[95] because they had not been circumcised.

21–22 These Greeks came to Philip, one of Jesus' twelve disciples (John 1:43–44), and asked to see Jesus. They had heard about Him and now wanted to meet Him. Philip was not sure what to do, so he told Andrew, Peter's brother (John 1:40).

23 When Jesus heard that some Greek Gentiles were looking for Him, He knew that this was a sign that the hour had come for Him to be **glorified,** that is, killed on the cross[96] (see John 17:1). Now the Gentiles had begun to turn to Him. Now His witness would begin to spread outside Israel through the preaching of His disciples. Now it would be seen that He was the Savior not just of the Jews but of the whole world. Now His own work on earth had come to an end. The **hour**, the time for Him to die, had come.

24 Then Jesus gave the reason why it was the right time for Him to die. It was God's plan that only after Jesus' death would the Holy Spirit be sent to live in the disciples (John 14:16–17; 16:7). Through the power of the Holy Spirit the disciples would then spread the Gospel all over the world. They would do greater things than Jesus had done (see John 14:12 and comment).

Then Jesus gave an agricultural illustration to show why His death was necessary. Any seed that is sown must in a way "die" before it can "come to life" again (1 Corinthians 15:36). Jesus was like a **kernel of wheat**. By dying, He produced **many seeds**— that is, the twelve disciples.[97] And from the twelve disciples, many other seeds have sprung up and are still springing up today in ever increasing numbers.

25 Although Jesus was comparing Himself, in particular, with a **kernel of wheat** (verse 24), the comparison is also true for all Jesus' followers. By dying, we too produce the most fruit for Christ. This doesn't mean that we all have to physically die in order to produce fruit; only some Christians are called to be martyrs. But we all must "die" to ourselves. Our old sinful self must die, otherwise we shall not be able to bear fruit for Christ (see Mark 8:34–35; Romans 6:2–6; Galatians 5:24 and comments).

Jesus said that the man who **hates his life in this world**[98] will gain eternal life. Jesus didn't mean we must actually "hate" ourselves. Rather He was saying that our love for Him must be so great that, in comparison, our love for ourselves will seem like hate (see Luke 14:26 and comment). Indeed, we cannot love our old sinful self and Christ at the same time (Matthew 6:24).

26 **Whoever serves me must follow me**. The Greeks sought Jesus (verses 20–21). But to seek Jesus is not enough. Seeking Jesus is only the first step. We must then believe in Him, and then serve Him. If we love Jesus and want to serve Him, we must follow Him. Where Jesus goes, we must go. That means we must be ready to suffer and die with Him.

The man who follows Jesus may lose his **life in this world**. He may lose his possessions. He may lose his honor in men's eyes. But in exchange, he will get to live with Jesus forever. That is, he will receive eternal life in heaven. He will also receive honor from God. God honors those who honor Christ (John 5:23)— because those who honor Christ honor God.

27 Then Jesus said to those around Him, "**Now my heart is troubled.**" He

---

[95] If they had been true Jews, John would not have called them **Greeks**. The Jews commonly called the Gentiles "Greeks."

[96] For Jesus, to die meant to be **glorified**. He knew that three days after His death He would rise in glory from the dead. Therefore, He often talked about His death and resurrection together, as if they were a single event, by which He would be **glorified**.

[97] After Jesus' death, the twelve disciples were called "apostles."

[98] Here the word **life** means not only our body, but also all the pleasures and conveniences and honors of life **in this world**.

was troubled because He was about to die. He was a man, and men don't ordinarily like to die. But Jesus wasn't troubled only about dying; He was troubled because He was about to take on Himself the punishment for the sins of all men (see Mark 14:32–34 and comment). He was about to be **made . . . sin** for the sake of men (2 Corinthians 5:21). He was about to be forsaken both by His disciples and by God (Mark 14:50; 15:34).

Jesus in His mind wondered for a moment if it would be possible to avoid such an **hour**, that is, such a death. He asked Himself: "Should I pray, '**Father, save me from this hour**'?" But immediately He thought, "No, such a prayer would be against the Father's will. It was to die that I came into the world. It was to take men's punishment that I have come to this **hour** of death" (see Mark 14:35–36 and comment).

28 Then Jesus said, "**Father, glorify your name.**" That is, "Let your name be glorified through my death" (see John 17:1,4).

Then God said from heaven, "**I have glorified it, and will glorify it again.**" God had glorified Jesus by speaking at His baptism (Mark 1:9–11) and at His transfiguration (Mark 9:2–7). He had glorified Jesus by giving Him the Holy Spirit **without limit** (John 3:34). By glorifying Jesus in this way, God had also glorified His own name. And now God was about to glorify His name once again through Jesus' death and resurrection.

29 The people heard the sound of the voice from heaven, but not all of them understood it (see Acts 22:6–9). To some it was like thunder; to others it was like an angel speaking.

30 The voice was for the people's benefit, so that they might know that Jesus had come from God. In particular, it was an encouragement to the believers among the crowd. From the voice they could understand that Jesus' life was in God's hands.

31 Jesus said, "**Now is the time for judgment on this world.**" That is, the men of this world will in a sense be condemned by Jesus' cross. Men condemned themselves by hanging Jesus on the cross (see John 3:18–19). Thus the cross of Christ is a sign of judgment on the world.

The cross is not only a sign of judgment; it is also a sign of Satan's downfall. On the cross, Jesus achieved final victory over Satan. It seemed like Satan had won, but in fact, he had lost.

Satan is called the **prince of this world**, because he rules over the hearts of unbelieving men (see John 14:30; 16:11). But Jesus never fell into Satan's temptations (Matthew 4:1–11). Satan, to the end, tried to tempt Jesus to flee from the cross, but Jesus did not listen (verse 27). Satan knew that, through Jesus' death, many people would be delivered from his control. Therefore, he did not want Jesus to die on the cross.

Therefore, Jesus says: "**. . . now the prince of this world will be driven out.** He will be cast into outer darkness (Matthew 22:13; 25:30). Through my death on the cross, Satan's power over believers will be broken; and at the end of the world he will be utterly destroyed" (Revelation 20:10).

32 **But I, when I am lifted up from the earth, will draw all men to myself.** That is, when Jesus is lifted up on the cross and then is lifted up into heaven (Acts 1:9), He will draw men into the kingdom of heaven (see John 6:44 and comment). He will begin to free men from bondage to Satan.

Jesus says here: "**I . . . will draw all men to myself.**" That means He will draw **all** believers to Himself. And He will draw believers from **all** nations, not just from Israel (see John 3:14–15 and comment).

33 John here explains that in the above verses, Jesus has been talking about His death on the cross and about His resurrection and ascension into heaven.

34 The crowd understood that Jesus was talking about His death. They had supposed from reading the **Law**, that is, the Old Testament (John 10:34), that the Messiah would never die (Isaiah 9:7; Daniel 7:14). Now Jesus had said that He, the Son of Man, must be lifted up on the cross. The crowd was confused. Many of them thought that Jesus was the Messiah; but the Messiah wasn't supposed to die. Yet Jesus had said that the **Son of Man** must die. Therefore, the crowd asked, "**Who is this Son of Man?** Is He the same as the Messiah?"

The crowd had understood only part of the Old Testament. It was true that the Christ, the Messiah, would never die. But the Old Testament also taught that Christ in His bodily form would pour out His life **unto death** (Isaiah 53:12). To understand fully who Christ is, one must read all of Scripture, not just part of it.

35 Jesus did not answer their question directly. But He did say that they were **going to have light just a little while longer**. The **light** was Christ Himself. Let the people listen to Him and believe in Him while they had opportunity.

Every man receives some spiritual light from God. If he rejects that light and turns from it, he will soon fall into spiritual darkness. The light will be withdrawn from him. Therefore, each man must walk while he has the light. He must walk according to the light he has received. Today, perhaps, a man's heart is soft, his mind open. Tomorrow his heart may be hard and his mind closed. Today, perhaps, a man is ready to believe; but tomorrow it may be too late, and he will have lost the chance to receive salvation. **. . . now is the time of God's favor, now is the day of salvation** (2 Corinthians 6:2).

The Jews in Jesus' day had received a great light—Christ Himself. But they rejected the light, and from then on they walked in darkness. They lost their nation, and they lost their souls (see John 1:4–5; 8:12 and comments).

36 In verse 35, Jesus said, "While you have the light, **walk** in it." Here in verse 36, He says, "While you have the light, put your **trust** in it." To **walk** in the light is the same as to believe in the light. The **light** is Christ. It is not enough only to see the light; we must believe in it. Moths see light and come to it. But when we see the light, we must believe in it. That is, when we see Jesus, we must believe in Him and follow Him.

When we believe in Christ, we become **sons of light** (see Ephesians 5:8; 1 Thessalonians 5:5). That is, we become sons of God (John 1:12). **God is light** (1 John 1:5). Sons receive the character and qualities of their father. Thus, when we believe in Christ, we receive the character and qualities of God Himself.

After He finished speaking, Jesus **hid himself**. He knew that He was going to die at the hands of men. But He would not die before the appointed time.

The Jews Continue in Their Unbelief (12:37–50)

37–38 Jesus, a Jew, had come to be the Messiah of Israel. Yet the Jews themselves rejected Him. How could this be? John says this happened in order that the prophecies of the Old Testament might be fulfilled. Isaiah the prophet wrote: **Who has believed our message?** No one. **To whom has the arm of the Lord** (that is, Christ's mighty works) **been revealed?** (Isaiah 53:1). Christ did mighty works, but the Jews did not see the **arm of the Lord** in them. Christ was **revealed**, but they did not recognize Him.

39–40 John then says that the Jews could not believe because God had **blinded their eyes and deadened their hearts**. But God didn't blind them at first. They first chose to reject God's prophets. They chose to turn from God to sin. It was only as a result of their sin and disobedience that God gave them up to hardness of heart and unbelief. After that, they could not believe. The person who says to God, "I will not believe," soon finds that he is unable to believe (see Romans 1:24,26,28 and comment).

John here quotes from Isaiah 6:10. This same passage is quoted by Matthew, Mark, and Luke in slightly different forms, but the meaning is the same (see Matthew 13:14–15; Mark 4:12; Acts 28:26–27 and comments).

God knew that the Jews would reject Jesus. He knows everything that will happen in the future. He knows who will accept Christ and who will reject Him. But even though God knows in advance what each man will do, each man is still free to do as he chooses. If a man rejects Christ, he does so by his own choice. He is responsible. He cannot blame God (see

Romans 9:14–21 and comment; General Article: Salvation—God's Choice or Man's Choice?).

41 When Isaiah wrote this prophecy, he was writing about the glory of the Messiah. In a spiritual way, he saw in the future the glory of Christ and knew that the Jews would reject that glory.

42–43 But many Jews, including some of the Jewish leaders, did not reject Christ's glory. The Pharisees had thought that no Jewish leader had believed in Christ (John 7:48). But John here says that many believed in Him secretly. Only two of them are mentioned in the New Testament: Nicodemus and Joseph of Arimathea (John 3:1; 19:38–39). It is doubtful whether the other Jewish leaders had real faith, because John says that they **would not confess their faith**. The person who refuses to confess Christ because he fears what men will think usually does not have true faith (see Matthew 10:32–33 and comment).

Then in verse 43, John gives the reason why these leaders did not confess their faith: namely, **they loved praise from men more than praise from God**. They knew that if they believed in Christ and served Him they would receive honor and praise from God (verse 26). Nevertheless, they preferred the praise of men more than praise from God (see John 5:44). They didn't want to take the risk of being put out of the synagogue, because, for a Jew, to be put out of the synagogue was a very great disgrace (see John 9:22).

44 These words of Jesus recorded by John in verses 44–50 are His last words to the public. In these verses Jesus gives a final call for men and women to believe.

Throughout John's Gospel, Jesus has talked about His unity with God. He who honors Jesus honors God (John 5:23). He who has seen Jesus has seen God (John 14:9). He who hates Jesus hates God (John 15:23). He who accepts Jesus accepts God (Matthew 10:40; Mark 9:37; John 13:20). And here Jesus says that he who puts his faith in Him puts his faith in God also.

45 Here Jesus repeats the idea of verse 44. When we look at Jesus through the eyes of faith, we do not see only a man; we see God Himself.

46 See John 8:12 and comment.

47 Those who hear Jesus' teaching and reject it will be judged. Jesus Himself does not judge men in this life. He did not come into the world to judge but to save (see John 3:17–18 and comment).

48 However, **in the last day**, that is, at the end of the world, Jesus will be our judge (see John 5:22,27). But even then Jesus Himself will not have to judge the person who rejects His word. Jesus' own word will judge him. And on the **last day** the "judge" (Jesus' word) will say to that person: "The word of salvation came to you, but you rejected it. You may not enter heaven."

Here a question arises: What will happen to the person who has never heard God's word in his lifetime? That person will not be judged according to God's word. Instead, he will be judged according to the spiritual light and knowledge he has received from God (see Luke 12:47–48; Romans 1:18–20 and comments).

49 Jesus' word is a fitting "judge," because it is, in fact, God's word. All that Jesus spoke was exactly as the Father commanded. When a person is judged by Jesus' word, it is the same as being judged by God Himself (see John 5:30; 8:16 and comments).

50 Jesus spoke according to God's command (verse 49). God's command is not harsh. It is the promise of eternal life to all who believe and obey it. Moses at the end of his life said to the Jews: **I have set before you life and death. . . . Now choose life, so that you and your children may live** (Deuteronomy 30:19). Today Jesus says the same thing to every man and woman.

CHAPTER 13

Jesus Washes His Disciples' Feet (1–17)

1 In Chapters 13–17, John describes the final meal Jesus had with His disciples and the teaching He gave them during and after the meal. This meal was the Passover feast, which is described in Mark 14:12–26.

In this first verse of Chapter 13, John tells us that Jesus knew His time to die had come, and that He would soon return to the Father, from whom He had first come (verse 3). He had loved **his own who were in the world**, that is, His disciples. Now He was going to show by His death the **full extent of his love**;[99] that is, He was going to show them that He loved them fully—without limit.

2 Judas had already made an agreement with the Jewish leaders to betray Jesus. Therefore, he was looking for an opportunity to hand Jesus over to them (Mark 14:10–11).

3 Although Jesus was about to be betrayed and killed, He knew that God had put all things under His power (see John 3:35; 17:2 and comments). He was God's Son. He had come from God and was going back to God (John 16:28). He had God's full authority. Yet He was about to perform the work of a slave: He was about to wash His disciples' feet.

4–5 Luke has written that at the last supper Jesus' disciples had been arguing about which of them was going to be greatest (Luke 22:24). So Jesus showed them by example that they should not seek to be masters, but rather they should seek to be servants. He told them, "**I am among you as one who serves**" (Luke 22:27).

Then, to show them that He had **not come to be served but to serve** (Mark 10:45), He washed their feet. He took the **very nature of a servant** (see Philippians 2:5–7 and comment).

According to Jewish custom, even the lowliest slave didn't have to untie his master's sandals. Thus Jesus was doing the lowest kind of service for His disciples.

6–7 Peter did not really understand the reason why Jesus was washing the disciples' feet. Jesus told him that he would understand better **later**, that is, after He had explained the reason (verses 14–15). The word **later** can also mean "after Jesus' death and resurrection." For at that time the Holy Spirit would teach the disciples **all things** and guide them **into all truth** (John 14:26; 16:13). Then the disciples would understand the full meaning of all Jesus' actions and teachings.

8 As Jesus was about to wash Peter's feet, Peter refused. Peter felt it was wrong that His master and teacher should act like his slave. Rather, Peter would have happily washed Jesus' feet.

But Jesus said to Peter, "**Unless I wash you, you have no part with me.**" Jesus' washing of His disciples' feet was a sign of His washing them from sin. Only those who have been forgiven and cleansed from sin can have a **part** with Jesus—can have a part in His kingdom.

9 Peter at once changed his mind. He didn't want to be shut out of Christ's kingdom. So he asked Jesus to wash his hands and head too!

10 Jesus then told Peter that only his feet needed washing. Peter had already **had a bath**. Jesus meant that Peter had already been baptized and had his sins washed away. His **whole body** was clean; that is, his inner heart and mind and spirit were clean. Once a man is cleansed of his sins through faith in Christ, he doesn't need to be cleansed of those same sins again (see John 15:3).

In the Middle East in Bible times, if a man was invited to his neighbor's house to eat, he first took a bath at home. Then

---

[99] In place of the words **he now showed them the full extent of his love**, some translations of the Bible say, "He loved them to the last," which is a literal translation of the original Greek text. The meaning is the same.

as he walked to his neighbor's house, his feet would become dirty. And so before supper, his neighbor would provide water so that he could wash his feet.

It is the same with Christians. We have all had a spiritual "bath." But as we walk through the world, we fall into temptation, we sin, we become tired and discouraged. In other words, our feet become dirty. Therefore, we regularly need to "wash our feet" by confessing our sins daily (see 1 John 1:9 and comment). Not only must we wash our own feet; we also must follow Jesus' example and wash each other's feet (verse 14). We ourselves cannot purify our brother; only Christ can do that. But we can admonish one another, and encourage and refresh one another. This is the meaning of foot-washing.

There is a further thing to remember: We must be willing to let a brother wash our feet. Let us not refuse, as Peter did. We must be willing to humbly accept service, as well as give it.

11 Then Jesus said to His disciples, "You are all clean except for one of you" (verse 10). He was speaking about Judas. He knew that Judas was going to betray Him. But Jesus did not tell the disciples at that time; He only said, "One of you is not **clean**."

12 After washing all His disciples' feet—Judas' feet also—Jesus explained the meaning of what He had done.

13–15 Like all good teachers, Jesus taught not only by word but also by example. By the example of washing their feet, He taught His disciples that they should in love and humility serve each other, and help and encourage each other. Each one should consider his brother better than himself (see Philippians 2:3).

In Jesus' time, a humble man was despised. He was considered weak. But Jesus taught that the humble man is, in fact, the strong man spiritually. He may be despised by men, but he is honored by God.

Some Christians understand these words of Jesus to mean that we should actually wash each other's feet in a literal manner. They hold foot-washing ceremonies from time to time. They do it as a witness that they are ready to offer any kind of humble service to their brother.

16 If their master humbled Himself, the disciples should do likewise. They are not higher or better than Christ. Let them not say, "I won't do such a menial task." If Christ did it, they can do it. Just as the disciples should expect to be persecuted like their master, so should they expect to humble themselves like their master. . . . **no servant is greater than his master** (see Matthew 10:24; John 15:20). As the master does, so must the servant do also.

The disciples were messengers, sent out by their master. To be appointed a **messenger** of the Son of God was a great honor. But it would also lead to humiliation in the sight of men.

17 Knowing God's will is not enough. Only those who do God's will will be blessed (see Luke 11:28; James 1:22; 4:17). For example, we all know that it is right to be humble. But how often do we actually humble ourselves?

Jesus Predicts His Betrayal (13:18–30)

18 Jesus had told His disciples that not everyone of them was **clean** (verse 10). He knew about each one of them. He had chosen them, knowing beforehand that Judas would betray Him. It was prophesied in Psalm 41:9 that one **who shares my bread**—that is, a close colleague of Jesus—would be the betrayer. He would "lift up his heel" against Jesus, in the same way a horse lifts up its heel before it kicks.

A question arises: If Jesus knew from the beginning that Judas was going to betray Him, how could Judas be considered guilty This same issue also arose concerning the Jews who did not believe in Jesus (see John 12:37–40 and comment). Even though Jesus knew that Judas would betray Him, Judas, like the unbelieving Jews, was nonetheless held guilty. He was responsible for his behavior. Judas was like the Pharaoh of Egypt whose heart was hardened so that God's glory and power might be manifested (see Romans 9:14–21 and comment).

19 Jesus warned His disciples several

times that one of them would betray Him. If He had not told them in advance, their faith would have been completely shattered when they saw Judas, one of their own fellow disciples, come with soldiers to arrest Jesus. Having been warned, the disciples at least would know that it had all been according to God's plan from the beginning (see John 14:29 and comment).

20 See Matthew 10:40; Mark 9:37; John 12:44–45 and comments.

21 Jesus was **troubled in mind** by the knowledge that one of His own disciples was going to betray Him. Again He told His disciples about His betrayal. Up to then He had only told them that a close colleague would be the betrayer (verse 18). Now He said that it would be one of the Twelve.

22 When they heard this, the disciples were amazed. Surely none of them would betray Jesus deliberately! They supposed that He meant that one of them would betray Him by accident, without realizing it. "**Surely not I?**" each one asked (Mark 14:18–19).

23–26 The **disciple whom Jesus loved** was John, the writer of this Gospel (John 21:20,24). Jesus had a special love for John. Of all the disciples, John had the closest relationship to Jesus. Therefore, Peter told John to ask Jesus which of the disciples would be the betrayer.

Jesus told John that He would dip a piece of bread in a dish of sauce and give it to the disciple who would betray Him. Then Jesus dipped the bread and gave it to Judas (see Mark 14:20–21).

27–28 Jesus did not want to tell everyone who the betrayer was. That is why He told John by means of a sign—by dipping the bread. But even John didn't fully understand the sign. He understood that Judas was to be the betrayer, but he didn't realize that Judas was going to betray Jesus that very night! Otherwise, he surely would have tried to stop Judas.

29–30 Therefore, when Judas went out, John and the other disciples simply thought that Judas had some business to do for Jesus. He was the treasurer of the group of disciples (John 12:6).

Judas went out into the darkness. For Judas, spiritual night had fallen indeed!

Jesus Predicts Peter's Denial (13:31–38)

31 After Judas had gone out, Jesus began to give His disciples some of the most important teaching He had yet given them, which teaching John now relates for us beginning with verse 31 and going on to the end of Chapter 17.

Judas had gone out to call the Jewish leaders to arrest Jesus. Thus Jesus' death was about to occur. Therefore, Jesus said, "**Now is the Son of Man glorified.**" Jesus was **glorified** through His death. His glorification, therefore, had now begun.

God was also glorified **in him**—that is, by Jesus' death—because Jesus died according to God's will. Jesus glorified God by following God's will in complete obedience.

32 God received glory from Christ. Therefore, God would give glory to Christ. **God will glorify the Son in himself**. The words **in himself** can mean "in God," or "in heaven." They can also mean "in Christ." That is, God will give Christ a glory of His own. Whichever the meaning is, Jesus was talking about His resurrection. The resurrection would be the sign that God had indeed glorified His Son. This was going to happen **at once**. There would be no more delay. Jesus' hour had come.

33 Jesus then told His disciples that He was soon to die. They could not come with Him, because it was not yet their time to die. "**Where I am going, you cannot come,**" He said to them. They would come later, but not right then (see verse 36).

Jesus had said this same thing to the unbelieving Jews. However, He had also told the Jews, "**You will look for me, but you will not find me.**" He did not say that to His disciples. Those who do not believe in Jesus in this life will not find Jesus in the next life. They will not live with Jesus in heaven (see John 7:33–34; 8:21 and comments).

34–35 Then Jesus gave the disciples a **new command. Love one another**. It is often called the third great commandment. The second great commandment says: **Love your neighbor as yourself** (see Mark 12:31 and comment). This third commandment says: Love your Christian brother as Jesus loved you.

Christians must have a special love for each other, a brotherly love. This love must be fervent (1 Peter 1:22). It must be visible to others, because it is by this love that others will know that we are Jesus' disciples. This love will be the proof that we are His disciples. Men won't know we are disciples by our great works; they will know it only by our love (see 1 Corinthians 13:1–3).

As I have loved you, so you must love one another. How did Jesus love us? He gave His life for us (see John 15:12–13). To this extent, then, we must love our brother. This is the meaning of true Christian fellowship. But unless one has accepted Christ as Lord, one can have no part in this fellowship.

When other people see our love for each other, they will be attracted to our fellowship. They will want to become part of our fellowship. When they see our love, they will understand how great Jesus' love was for them. That is why we must love each other as Jesus loved us. By loving each other in this way, our love will then be a testimony to Jesus' love (see 1 John 3:23; 4:7,11–12,21 and comments).

36 Peter was still thinking about Jesus' words, **"Where I am going, you cannot come"** (verse 33). He asked Jesus, **"Where are you going?"** But Jesus only answered that Peter could not follow right then.

37 Peter sensed that Jesus was talking about His death. So Peter told Jesus that he would go anywhere with Jesus. He was even ready to die with Jesus.

38 Peter was promising more than he could fulfill. He wasn't ready to die for Jesus. He was about to deny Jesus (see Mark 14:27–31,66–72 and comment). Instead, it was Jesus who was about to die for Peter.

Peter was proud. He had confidence in his own strength. He should have been more humble. Those who think they are strong in themselves will soon find out that they are really weak (see 1 Corinthians 10:12).

CHAPTER 14

Jesus the Way to the Father (14:1–14)

1 The disciples' hearts were certainly troubled, and they were soon to become even more troubled. Jesus had just said that He was going away (John 13:33). He had said one of them would betray Him (John 13:21). He had said that Peter, His chief disciple, would deny Him three times (John 13:38) That meant that terrible trouble was surely coming! They had left all for Jesus. Now they were about to be left alone. Perhaps they too would be arrested, tortured, killed. Certainly the disciples were troubled! But in spite of all this, Jesus still said to them: **"Do not let your hearts be troubled."** His meaning was: "Stop being troubled; stop being anxious."

What is the way to remove trouble and anxiety from our hearts? By believing, trusting. And so Jesus said: **"You trust in God;**[100] **trust also in me."** All Jews trusted in God; the disciples, being Jews, trusted in God too. But here Jesus adds: **". . . trust also in me."** Trusting in God and trusting in Christ go together. If a person truly trusts in one, he will also trust in the other.

It was no small thing Jesus was asking His disciples to do. He was about to be hung on a cross like a criminal. It was one thing to trust in the mighty God of Israel. But, in the disciples' mind, it was another thing to trust in this man who had just

---

[100] In the Greek language, the words **You trust in God** (a statement) can also be translated, "Trust in God" (a command).

washed their feet like a slave, and who was about to be killed like a criminal. Nevertheless, Jesus said to them, "... **trust also in me**. It is the same as trusting in God."

2 **In my Father's house are many rooms**. The **Father's house** is heaven. The **many rooms** are the resting places of believers. There is space in heaven for every believer. That is why the disciples do not need to be troubled. If they only believe, they will have a sure place in heaven. Jesus told them that He was going now to His Father's house to prepare their rooms.

Christian, are you troubled? Or afraid? Are you being afflicted with persecution or calamity? If so, then remember this: Jesus has gone to prepare your place in heaven. Trust in Him.

3 Then Jesus promised His disciples, "**I will come back and take you to be with me**." He was referring to His second coming at the end of the world (see Mark 13:26–27; 1 Thessalonians 4:16–18 and comments).

Jesus didn't say exactly what His **Father's house** was like. He only said that we will be with Him. If we are with our Lord, we don't need to think about anything else. A small child doesn't care about what his house is like; all he cares about is that his parents are there.

4 Then Jesus said to His disciples, "**You know the way to the place where I am going**." He had shown them the **way**. The **way** was His teaching and example. If they followed His teaching and example, they would get to heaven.

5 But the disciples were confused. What did Jesus mean when He said that He was going to His **Father's house**? He had just told them that **where I am going, you cannot come** (John 13:33). Therefore, how can they know the way? "**We don't know where you are going**," Thomas said.

Notice that Thomas was an honest man. When he had doubt in his mind, he spoke about it openly (John 20:24–25). In the end, his doubt was replaced with faith (John 20:27–28).

6 When the disciples said that they didn't know the way, Jesus told them, "**I am the way**." Jesus not only shows men the way to heaven; He is Himself the way. He is the way, because He is the means by which we enter heaven. It is through His sacrifice, His death, that our sins are forgiven and we are counted righteous in God's sight (see Mark 10:45 and comment). Jesus' righteousness, which we receive through faith, is our passport to heaven.

I am ... the truth. Jesus not only teaches the truth; He is Himself the truth. He is totally trustworthy. His Gospel is true. When we believe in the truth of Jesus, when we accept His teaching, we receive salvation. We are set free from ignorance and sin (see John 8:31–32).

I am ... the life. Jesus not only gives life; He is Himself life. **In him was life** (see John 1:4; 5:26 and comments). To know Jesus is to have eternal life (John 17:3).

Showing the **way**, teaching the **truth**, and giving **life** are all different parts of Jesus' great work of saving men. Only Jesus can save men. Only Jesus is the Savior of the world. Only by faith in Jesus can we come to the Father and dwell in His **house** (verse 2).

Think on these words. Jesus was about to be hung helpless on the cross, yet He said: "**I am the way**." He was about to be condemned by the lies of men, yet He said: "**I am ... the truth**." His own corpse was soon to be placed in a tomb, yet He said: "**I am ... the life**."

Men of this world believe in many different kinds of gods and incarnations. But there is only one, Jesus Christ, who can say: "**I am the way and the truth and the life**." Only He can give men salvation, eternal life. There is no other way to heaven besides Christ. Other religions and other religious leaders may point men to heaven, but only Christ can lead them there.

A question arises here: What happens to the person who has never heard of Christ Will he never be able to "come to the Father"—that is, get to heaven? The Bible indicates that he will not. All men are sinners (Romans 3:10–12); they all are deserving of God's wrath (see Romans 1:18–20 and comment). On the other hand, God judges men according to their knowledge. Thus the Bible indicates that the person who has never heard of Christ will be judged less severely than the one who has heard of Christ but then rejected Him (see Luke 12:47–48 and comment). God is the final judge. He will show mercy to whom He wants to show mercy (Romans 9:15). It is not for us to judge. It is for us, however, to show all men the one sure way to heaven—namely, Jesus Christ.[101]

7 The disciples still did not know Jesus fully. They would not know Him fully until after the resurrection. They would not have been so confused at that time if they had truly known who Jesus was. They would have known where He was going. They would have known the Father. "**If you really knew me, you would know my Father as well.**" Those who know Jesus, know the Father. To see the one is to see the other (see John 8:19; 12:44–45 and comments).

8 Philip still didn't understand. According to the Old Testament, no one had ever seen God face to face. Now Jesus had just said, "You **have seen him**" (verse 7). Therefore, Philip answered, "Let us see the Father, and we'll believe." In Philip's mind, Jesus was only a man. He still didn't understand that Jesus was actually God Himself.

9 Jesus gently rebuked Philip. "Do you still not know who I am?" He asked Philip. Philip had known from the first day he met Jesus that Jesus was the Messiah (John 1:45). But he had never really seen God in Jesus.

Then Jesus said, "**Anyone who has seen me has seen the Father.**" Jesus was the revelation of the Father. Those who look at Christ without faith see only a man. Those who look at Christ with faith see God.

Even for us today, Jesus remains the revelation of God, even though He is no longer present with us in bodily form. Through the reading of the New Testament, together with the help of the Holy Spirit, we too can see Jesus; and when we see Jesus, we also see God (John 12:44–45).

10 Philip should have known that Jesus was **in the Father, and that the Father** [was in Jesus]. Even ordinary Jews who saw Jesus' works should have known that (John 10:37–38). Philip should have known that the Father was **living** in Jesus, because the works and the words of Jesus clearly came from the Father (John 7:16). Jesus had said, "**The Son can do nothing by himself**" (John 5:19).

When we see Jesus' works and hear His words, we are really seeing God's works and hearing God's words. From this we can know that God is in Jesus and Jesus is in God—or, in other words, that Jesus and God are **one** (see John 10:30).

11 Then Jesus told His disciples, "**Believe me**. Believe not only in me, but also believe what I say." The faith of a Christian has two parts. First, we must believe in Jesus Himself personally. Second, we must believe that what He has said is true. Faith in Jesus without faith also in the truth of His words is nothing but blind faith.

But Jesus knew that the disciples' faith was weak. So He said, "Even if you can't believe my words now, at least believe the **miracles** I have done. My miracles will show you who I am" (see John 5:36; 10:25). Faith based on miracles is weak faith, but it is better than no faith. Jesus never despised weak faith; after all, most Christians start out with weak faith in the beginning. But faith must be strengthened, or it will not endure when trials come.

We must remember that the devil and his servants can also do miracles (Mark 13:22–23). We must look not only at Jesus' miracles, but also at His character, at His inner qualities. We must look at His motives. False Christs and false prophets do miracles to bring glory to themselves. Christ performed His miracles to bring glory to God. Christ's miracles are signs that point men to God.

12 Then Jesus gave His disciples a great promise: They would do greater works than He had done. Indeed, the

---

[101] For further discussion of what happens to little children who die before they hear about Jesus, see General Article: Children and the Kingdom of God.

apostles did perform many great miracles, just as Christ did. Many of them are described in the book of Acts. Peter even raised a woman from the dead (Acts 9:36–42). But when Jesus said that His disciples would do **greater things,** He meant mainly that they would bring more people to God than He had brought. These greater works would be converting works. On the day of Pentecost, about three thousand people believed through the preaching of the apostles (Acts 2:41). That was more people than had believed during Jesus' entire three years of public ministry.

Jesus told the disciples that they would do **greater things** because He was **going to the Father**. The disciples needed the Holy Spirit in order to do these greater works, but the Holy Spirit could not come to them until after Jesus had died and gone to the Father (John 16:7). That is why Jesus said, "Because I am going to the Father, you will do these greater things."

Today also, Jesus' disciples, through the power of the Holy Spirit, are continuing to do **greater things** than Jesus did. Jesus' promise is for us too!

13 In order to do mighty works, the disciples would need to pray. In order to receive the power of the Holy Spirit, we need to pray for it. We need to pray for it in the name of the risen Christ, with whom is all authority and dominion in heaven and on earth. Jesus said, "**I will do whatever you ask in my name**." "Whatever" we ask in Jesus' name He will do! There are no limits to the power of prayer.

We usually ask Jesus for such small things. But He can do anything. He can do more than all we can ask or imagine (Ephesians 3:20–21). Let us not set limits on Christ by our small prayers!

To pray in Jesus' name means to pray in His stead, to pray as His representatives on earth. We are Christ's **ambassadors** (2 Corinthians 5:20). When we pray in His name, we pray with His authority. We pray for His sake. We pray according to His will. When we pray in this way, Jesus will do **whatever** we ask (see Matthew 7:7–8; Mark 11:22–24; John 15:7,16 and comments).

Notice here that Jesus Himself answers our prayers. God answers them; Jesus answers them. God and Jesus do everything together; there is no difference. It does not matter whether we pray to Jesus or to God; they both hear and answer together.

Jesus answers prayer **so that the Son may bring glory to the Father**. Everything Jesus did on earth was to bring glory to the Father. Everything He does through us is also to bring glory to the Father. Therefore, the purpose of our prayers and requests must be to glorify God. If what we ask for is not going to glorify God, Jesus will not do it.

Let us examine ourselves. Can we say as Jesus did, "I don't seek my own glory"? (John 8:50). For what do we pray? For God's benefit, or for our own? And in between our prayer times what do we live for? For God's glory, or for our own? God doesn't only hear our prayers—He looks at our whole life. If we do not live our lives for His glory, He will not believe us when pray for His glory. **So whether you eat or drink or whatever you do, do it all for the glory of God** (1 Corinthians 10:31).

But we ask: Who can live all day solely for God's glory? We can't do it, we say. True, in our own strength we cannot. But we have no excuse, because the power of the Holy Spirit has been promised to us. But we must pray for it. Through the Holy Spirit's power, we shall be able to lead lives to the glory of God.

Jesus Promises the Holy Spirit (14:15–31)

15 Just as the proof of faith is obedience, so the proof of love is also obedience. It is easy to say to Jesus, "I love you," but we must then prove it by our actions. Love without obedience is a false love. True Christians obey Christ not because they are obliged to, but because they want to. They obey Him because they love Him. If a man does not obey Christ, that means he does not love Christ (verse 24). **This is love for God: to obey his commands** (1 John 5:3).

16 If we love and obey Christ, He

will send us **another Counselor,** that is, the Holy Spirit (verse 26). Christ will send the Holy Spirit only to those who love and obey Him. If we are not experiencing the power of the Holy Spirit in our lives, it is because in some area of our life, we are not obeying Christ.

Who is this **Counselor**? Who is this Holy Spirit? The Holy Spirit is the Spirit of God and of Christ. God and Christ are in heaven, but the Spirit is with us here on earth. The Holy Spirit is **in** us (verse 17). All of our spiritual knowledge, our spiritual strength, our spiritual joy, peace, and love come from the Spirit (see Galatians 5:22–23). Our new birth, our new spiritual life, comes from the Holy Spirit (see John 3:5 and comment). God has three forms or modes of existence: the Father, the Son, and the Holy Spirit. These are all one God. But the form of God that touches and enters our lives here on earth is the Holy Spirit. God the Father is invisible. God the Son has returned to heaven. But God the Holy Spirit is with us who believe. Jesus said that the Holy Spirit would be with us **forever**.

After His death Jesus sent the Holy Spirit to take His place, so that the disciples would not be left alone. Therefore, the Holy Spirit was sent to do the same things that Christ Himself did on earth. When we think of the Holy Spirit, we must think of Him as being Christ's presence with us. What Christ did, the Holy Spirit is still doing. The work of the Holy Spirit is to continue the work of Christ on earth.

Christ was with the disciples; so is the Holy Spirit with us (verse 16). Christ was their teacher; so is the Holy Spirit our teacher (verse 26). Christ bore witness to Himself; so does the Holy Spirit bear witness to Christ (John 15:26). Christ strengthened, admonished, encouraged His disciples; so the Holy Spirit strengthens, admonishes, and encourages us. Everything Christ did for His disciples, the Holy Spirit will do for us. This is why Jesus called the Holy Spirit **another Counselor**. Jesus was the "first Counselor"; now the Holy Spirit has come in His place.

17 The Holy Spirit is the **Spirit of truth** (John 15:26). Christ is the **truth** (verse 6); therefore, His Spirit must be the Spirit of truth. The Spirit guides believers **into all truth** (John 16:13).

The **world,** that is, the world of unbelieving men, cannot accept the Spirit (see 1 Corinthians 2:14). Those who do not accept Christ cannot accept His Spirit. But to those who believe in Him, Jesus has sent His Spirit. And the Spirit lives not only **with** the believer, but also **in** the believer.

18 **"I will not leave you as orphans; I will come to you,"** said Jesus to His disciples. This can have two meanings. First, it can mean that Jesus would come again to His disciples in the form of the Holy Spirit. Second, it can mean that He would appear to them after His resurrection in bodily form. Both meanings are true.

19 **Before long, the world will not see me anymore**. The next day Christ was going to die. After that, He would not appear again to unbelieving men of the **world**. But He would appear to His disciples. **But you will see me** (see John 20:19,26). Jesus rose from the dead and appeared to those who had believed in Him (see 1 Corinthians 15:3–8). He conquered death. Even though His earthly body had been killed, nevertheless, He continued to live. Because He conquered death, so will we, His disciples, conquer death. Because of His resurrection, we too will live forever. **Death has been swallowed up in victory** (1 Corinthians 15:54).

20 **On that day,** that is, on the day of Jesus' resurrection, the disciples would realize the spiritual nature of Christ. On that day, Jesus **breathed on them and said, "Receive the Holy Spirit"** (John 20:22). As soon as they received the Holy Spirit, they fully realized that Jesus was indeed **in** [His] **Father**. They also realized that they were now in Jesus, and Jesus, through the Holy Spirit, was now in them.

21 In the first part of this verse, the thought of verse 15 is repeated.

Then Jesus said that the one who loves Him will be loved by both Him and His Father. Jesus does not mean that God loves us because we love Him. That is not so. Rather, we love God because He loves us. God loved us first (see 1 John 4:10,19). God loved us while we were still sinners (Romans 5:8).

However, after we have received God's love, we must love Him in return. Through the Holy Spirit, God's love flows into us (Romans 5:5), and that same love can then flow out from us both to God and to other men. The more our love flows out to God and to others, the more His love will flow into us. Love gives birth to love.

Not only will God love the believer who loves Him, but Christ also will love that believer. And Christ will show Himself to the believer through the Holy Spirit. Jesus says: "**I will . . . show myself** to the one who loves me."

22 **Judas**,[102] one of the twelve disciples (but not Judas Iscariot), was still thinking that Jesus was going to show Himself to the whole world in the form of a victorious Messiah. Now it seemed that Jesus was going to show Himself only to His followers. "Why is that?" Judas wanted to know.

23 Jesus didn't answer Judas directly. He simply repeated what He had already said in verse 21. That is, Jesus would manifest Himself to those who love Him. Not only that, but He and the Father would make their home with those who love Him. Think of it! The almighty God in the form of the Holy Spirit lives in each believer (verse 17).

24 Love for Jesus and obedience to His teaching must always go together (see verse 15). If there is no love, there will be no obedience. To disobey Christ's words is to disobey God, because the words that Christ speaks are really the words of God (John 7:16; 12:49).

25–26 The **Counselor, the Holy Spirit** (verse 16), is sent to us by the Father in the name of the Son. The Holy Spirit comes from both the Father and the Son together (see John 15:26).

There were many teachings of Jesus that the disciples could not fully understand while Jesus was with them on earth. But after His death, the Holy Spirit not only reminded the disciples of Jesus' words and actions, but He also taught them the meaning of those words and actions.

The Holy Spirit does the same for us today. Even though we now have the New Testament in written form,[103] we still need the help of the Holy Spirit to fully understand it and to apply it to our daily lives. The Holy Spirit is still today the chief guide and teacher of the church. But remember, the guidance of the Holy Spirit will never contradict or oppose the teaching of the Bible in any way. If anyone receives any teaching that is contrary to the teaching of the Bible, let him know that that teaching is not from the Holy Spirit.

27 One of the greatest gifts Jesus left with His disciples was PEACE. This was not the kind of peace that the world gives. The world's peace depends on outward circumstances. It is a false peace. It doesn't last. The world's peace lasts only as long as there is no trouble or sorrow or fighting. As soon as any kind of trial comes, immediately the world's peace vanishes.

But Christ's **peace** is spiritual peace. First, it is peace with God (see Romans 5:1 and comment). Second, it is an inner peace in our hearts and minds. Even though outer trials come, Christ's peace remains in us. Third, Christ's peace is one of the fruits of the Holy Spirit (Galatians 5:22–23). As long as the Holy Spirit is in us, the fruits of the Spirit will also be in us.

---

[102] **Judas** is mentioned in Luke 6:16 and Acts 1:13. Some Bible scholars believe that Judas is the same as Thaddaeus, who is mentioned in Mark 3:18.

[103] The only Scriptures the disciples had were the Old Testament writings. Most of the New Testament wasn't written until twenty to forty years after Jesus' death.

It is important for us to remember that it was because of the promise given in this very verse that the disciples were later able to write the New Testament Scriptures. The New Testament (and the Old Testament also) was written entirely with the help and inspiration of the Holy Spirit (see 2 Timothy 3:16; 2 Peter 1:20–21 and comments).

Therefore, Jesus said to His disciples, "You do not need to be troubled or afraid (verse 1). Wherever you go, whatever happens, you will have my peace" (see John 16:33; Philippians 4:7).

28 The disciples were upset and sad, because Jesus had said that He was about to leave them. But they were only thinking of themselves and their own fear and disappointment. If they had truly loved Jesus, they would have rejoiced that Jesus was going to heaven to be with His Father. His Father was about to glorify Jesus and honor Him. The disciples should have been rejoicing!

Jesus said to the disciples, "You should be glad that I am going to the Father, because **the Father is greater than I**. Therefore, He is able to glorify me. He is able to raise me from the dead and set me at His right hand in heaven!" (Ephesians 1:20–22).

A question arises here. We have said many times that God and Christ are equal; they are one. And that is true. Yet here Jesus says, "**. . . the Father is greater that I**." What did He mean?

His meaning is this. When Jesus came to earth, He gave up some of His glory, which He had had with God from the beginning. He had been equal with God, but when He came to earth He voluntarily gave up that equality for a time, and took the form of a man (see Philippians 2:6–8). Therefore, while Jesus was on earth, the Father was **greater** than He was. Then, through the resurrection, the Father gave Jesus back the glory that He had had from the beginning of creation (see John 17:5).

29 Jesus told these things to His disciples in advance, so that when His death came, their faith would not be destroyed (see John 13:19 and comment). Indeed, when they saw the things spoken of by Jesus come true, their faith was actually strengthened.

30 The **prince of this world** (John 12:31), that is, Satan, was about to come in the form of Judas and the soldiers. Even at that moment they were preparing to arrest Jesus. But though Satan was able to cause Jesus' arrest, he had **no hold** on Jesus. Satan "holds" men through the sin in their lives. But Jesus had no sin, and therefore Satan had no way to gain victory over Jesus. Yes, for three days Satan put Jesus in a tomb. But longer than that, Satan could not **hold** Him.

31 Jesus of His own choice allowed wicked men to kill Him and put Him in a tomb. This was to show the world that He loved the Father and obeyed Him (see John 10:18). This is why Jesus said: "**He** (Satan) **has no hold on me, but the world must learn that I love the Father** (verse 30). God's will is that I should die and then be raised again. Therefore, I will let Satan kill my body and hold it in a tomb for three days, that the world may see that I have obeyed my Father's will" (see John 10:17–18).

Then Jesus said, "**Come now, let us leave**. Let us go, then, and meet Satan." Jesus probably didn't mean that they should get up immediately and leave the room. He meant that they should do so as soon as He had finished speaking with them.[104]

CHAPTER 15

The Vine and the Branches (15:1–17)

1 **I am the true vine and my Father** (God) **is the gardener**. In order to show what the Christian life is like, Jesus here gives the illustration of a vine and its branches. In the Old Testament, Israel was called a vine. But it became a barren and corrupt vine (Psalm 80:8–16; Isaiah 5:1–7; Jeremiah 2:21). God's **true vine** is Jesus Himself.

---

[104] Some Bible scholars, however, believe that Jesus and His disciples did get up at this point and leave the room. These scholars believe that Jesus gave the teachings of Chapters 15–17 on the way to the garden of Gethsemane.

2 Christians are the branches (verse 5). Just as a branch cannot live unless the sap of the vine flows into it, so a Christian cannot live unless Christ's Holy Spirit flows into him. Without Christ's Spirit, we soon die spiritually. If we do not bear fruit, it is a sign that Christ's Spirit is not in us. Such a **branch** God cuts away. A fruitless branch is useless to God (see Matthew 3:10).

However, the fruitful branch God **trims clean,**[105] or cleanses, that it might bear more fruit. God cuts away the bad twigs—that is, our bad habits and sins. To be pruned or trimmed clean can be very painful. Often God leads Christians through difficult experiences in order to "trim them clean" (see James 1:2–4 and comment). Especially, He leads us through humbling experiences to remove our pride. Just as a branch bears more fruit after it has been trimmed clean or cleansed, so it is with us.

Only Christians who have been cleansed from sin, from pride, can bear good fruit for God. The fruit that God looks for is of two kinds. First, He looks for the fruits of the Holy Spirit (Galatians 5:22–23), which correspond to the qualities manifested in Christ's life (see Matthew 5:3–10). Second, God looks for another type of "fruit," namely, new believers who have come to Christ through our witness. New Christians are also "fruit" pleasing to God.

3 Jesus assured His disciples that, except for Judas Iscariot, they were all **clean** (see John 13:10 and comment). The disciples were living branches ready to bear fruit. Yes, they would need additional periodic trimming, but they had already been cleansed of sin through faith in Christ's **word**, Christ's teaching.

4 **Remain in me, and I will remain in you.** To **remain** in Christ means to love Him, to obey Him, to pray to Him, to worship Him. In other words, to remain in Christ means to remain joined to Him spiritually, just as a branch is joined to a vine. If we remain joined to Christ in this way, we will be like living branches. And just as the sap of the vine flows into the branches and gives them life, so will Christ's Spirit flow into us and give us spiritual life.

In order to bear fruit, we must remain in Christ. If we do not remain in Christ, we shall not bear fruit. Not only that, we shall wither and die (verse 6).

5 This verse repeats the thought of verse 4. This teaching about the vine and its branches is like Paul's teaching about the body and its members (1 Corinthians 12:27). Here we are like branches in Christ's vine. In Paul's illustration, we are like members of Christ's body. The teaching is the same. We must remain joined to Christ, or we shall die.

Jesus said, "**. . . apart from me you can do nothing**." We can do no spiritual work apart from Christ. We can do nothing pleasing to God apart from Christ. But in Christ, joined to Him, we can do everything. Paul said: **I can do everything through him who gives me strength** (Philippians 4:13). But let us remember that whatever fruit we bear, it is not our fruit; it is Christ's fruit. It is the vine that produces the fruit, not the branches. The branches only bear the vine's fruit.

6 Let us never forget what happens to branches that become separated from the vine. They die and are thrown into the fire. Let us allow nothing to disrupt our union with Christ.

There is only one thing that can separate us from Christ: sin. Sin is like a disease that eats at the base of the branch. We will surely lose our union with Christ if any known sin remains in our life for which we have not repented.

7 If we remain in Christ, He will remain in us. If He remains in us, His **words** will remain in us also. We cannot separate Christ and His teaching. But Christ's words only remain in those who obey His words.

For us today, Christ's **words** are the Scriptures, especially the New Testament. The **words** of the Scriptures must remain in us. Thus, we can say that in our Christian lives two main things are

---

105 In place of the words **trims clean,** some translations of the Bible say "cleanses," which is a literal translation of the Greek text. The meaning is the same.

necessary: first, Christ through the Holy Spirit must remain in us; and second, Christ's **words,** that is the words of the Bible, must remain in our hearts.

If we are in Christ, and He is in us, we can ask anything and He will do it. In John 14:13, Jesus taught that if we ask anything **in** [His] **name,** He will do it. These two statements are really the same. Anyone who abides in Christ will surely pray in Christ's name. Not only that, if we abide in Christ and keep Christ's words in our heart, we shall always pray according to Christ's will. Whatever we ask for, God will be pleased to give us. That is why those who remain in Christ will receive whatever they ask for (see John 14:13 and comment).

In the Christian life, we always find two things appearing together: promises and conditions. If we fulfill the condition, God will fulfill His promise. God has never given a promise without also stating a condition along with the promise.

What are some of these promises and their corresponding conditions? One example is: If a man has faith, God will fulfill his request (Mark 11:24). The condition is that the man must have faith; the promise is that the request will be fulfilled. A second example: If a man forgives others, God will forgive him (Matthew 6:14). A third example: If a man draws near to God, God will draw near to him (James 4:8). And a fourth example is found in this verse 7: **If you remain in me and my words remain in you, ask whatever you wish, and it will be given you.**

Let us ask ourselves: Do we always receive what we ask for from God? Often—perhaps usually—we do not. Why? Because we have not fulfilled the condition.

When God doesn't grant our request, what do we usually say? We say: "It wasn't God's will to grant it." But that's not the real reason our request wasn't granted. When we say it wasn't God's will, we are in a sense blaming God for not fulfilling our wishes. When we are not successful in prayer, let us not blame God! Rather let us blame ourselves. There is only one reason for our prayers not being successful: namely, we have not prayed in the right way (see James 4:3). We have not fulfilled the conditions.

We have another habit that is generally not suitable. After we have finished our prayer, we often say to God, "Please grant our request—if it is your will." When we add these words, "if it is your will," we are admitting that we have prayed without really knowing what God's will is. Such requests are usually not granted. This verse teaches us an important truth: If we remain in Christ and His words remain in us, then we shall know what God's will is, and our prayers will then be in accordance with His will. And when our prayer is in accordance with His will, then He will grant our request.

How can we find out what God's will is? For the most part we can find out God's will simply by reading the Bible. There is a saying: When I pray, I talk to God; when I read the Bible (which is God's word) He talks to me. True prayer is not just talking to God—it's also listening to God. Prayer is like a conversation, in which we both talk and listen. First, having read God's word, we understand His will; then, according to His will, we make our requests.

When Christ is in us, His **words** will be in us also. But this statement is also true in reverse: When Christ's words are in us, then Christ Himself will be in us. Because Christ and His words are, in a sense, the same. Christ is God's living Word (see John 1:1–2,14). Therefore, Christ's words come not only from the Bible but also directly from Christ Himself, who lives within us in the form of the Holy Spirit. Thus, from these two sources of Christ's words, the Bible and the Holy Spirit, we can gain a sure understanding of what God's will is.

How, then, can we learn from Christ's **words** what God's will is? First, we can learn what God's "general will" is by accepting Christ's words, by accepting the Bible and studying it, by letting His words become "written" in our hearts (Hebrews 8:10). Second, we learn what God's "particular will" is (that is, His will in specific circumstances) through the leading of the Holy Spirit. We encounter many circumstances in life about which the Bible does not give us specific instructions. For example, the Bible doesn't specifically tell us who we should marry, what kind of work we should do, or what subjects we should study in school. To determine what God's will is in these matters, the guidance of the Holy Spirit is necessary.

But before we can learn what God's "particular will" is in any specific circumstance, a third thing is necessary: namely, we must be willing to do anything God asks—no matter what. If we are not willing to obey what God says—whatever it might be—then He will not reveal His will to us. Our own selfish desires will prevent us from knowing what His will is. We shall be drawn to our own will instead of to God's will. When this happens, we shall not learn what God's particular will is for that specific circumstance.

Therefore, in summary, if God does not grant a prayer request of ours, it is because we have failed to learn what His will is in that matter. His will has not entered our heart; we have not committed ourselves to do His will. In other words, we have not fulfilled the condition necessary for obtaining our request. Because of our own weakness, disobedience, and sin, our prayer request has not been granted.

Who among us has experienced the full meaning of this verse? Jesus is the vine, and we are the branches. And as a vine and its branches grow, so likewise must we grow in the Christian life. Our life in Christ must grow ever fuller, ever deeper.

Remain in me (verse 4). Now we can understand the full meaning of these words: namely, that our spirits must be the same as Christ's Spirit, that our mind and our will must be the same as Christ's mind and will. We must live not for ourselves, but for Christ. We are not our own; we are Christ's! And for those who remain in Christ in this way, the promise of this verse will be fulfilled: **. . . ask whatever you wish, and it will be given you**.

8 What brings God glory? Our **fruit** brings Him glory. Just as God was glorified in Christ (John 13:31), so God will also be glorified in us, that is, by our fruit (see Matthew 5:16; John 15:2). By our fruit—especially by our love—men will know that we are Christ's disciples (John 13:35).

9 **Now remain in my love**. To remain in Christ's love is the same as to remain in Christ (see verse 4). Let us not forget how much Christ loves us. He loves us as much as God loved Him. When we remain in Christ's love, we remain in God's love also.

10 To remain in Christ's love, we must love Him. To love Him, we must obey Him (see John 14:15 and comment). As long as we continue to obey Christ, we shall remain in His love, and He and the Father will abide in us (see John 14:21).

11 Jesus told these things to the disciples so that His **joy** might be in them—that is, so that they might experience the joy that He Himself always experienced. This joy was a spiritual joy, an inner joy. And like the peace that Jesus promised to give them (John 14:27), this joy would remain with them even during trials and persecution. Such joy is the fruit of the Holy Spirit (Galatians 5:22). Thus it is experienced by everyone in whom the Holy Spirit dwells.

All men of the world seek joy and happiness above all things. But they seek in vain. Only when a man seeks Christ will he find true joy.

12 Here Jesus repeats the **new command** that He gave to His disciples in John 13:34: **Love each other as I have loved you**.

13 Then Jesus told His disciples that the greatest love they could ever show to each other was to lay down their lives for each other. That is how Jesus loved them, and He proved it by laying down His life on the cross for them. There could be no greater love than that.

Jesus commands us, also, to love each other as He has loved us. That means that we, too, must be ready to lay down our lives for each other—not only for Christ, but for our brother also! This is one reason why Jesus' disciples must hate their own lives in this world (see John 12:25 and comment). The person who loves his own life will never be willing to give it up for Christ and for others.

We should remember that Jesus gave

up His life not only for His friends, but also for His enemies (see Romans 5:6,8). He commands us to love our enemies (Matthew 5:44). It is true that He has not directly commanded us to lay down our lives for our enemies. However, true love does not ask, "Who is my friend and who is my enemy?" Love always gives, without calculation. Jesus gave everything for all men. His disciples should be happy to do likewise.

14 Jesus called His disciples **friends,** and He calls us **friends** today. But in order to be a "friend" of Jesus, one must obey His commands.

15 Jesus called His disciples **friends,** because He made known to them everything He Himself learned from His Father. He had even more to tell them, but they could not have borne it then (John 16:12). He would tell them later through the Holy Spirit (John 16:13).

The disciples were no longer servants. A servant receives only orders from his master. The master does not have to give the servant a reason for an order. But Jesus treats us as friends. He takes us into His confidence. Through the Holy Spirit, He reveals to us everything we need to know.[106]

16 Men do not first choose to follow Jesus. Rather, Jesus chooses men to follow Him. First Jesus calls. Then men are free to follow or not to follow. But no man can follow Christ unless he has first been called (see John 5:37,44 and comment).

Jesus not only chose His disciples, but He also gave them an appointment. The appointment was to **go,** that is, to be witnesses. And their work was to **bear fruit.** Jesus told them, "**I chose you . . . to go and bear fruit.**" Jesus' disciples were like branches. The work of a branch is to bear fruit. In the context of this verse, to "bear fruit" means primarily to bring others to faith in Christ (see verse 2 and comment).

Every Christian has been appointed to **go and bear fruit**. We may not be called to go far away. But we are all called **to go**. We are called to go at least to our own family and to our neighbors. Let no Christian think that he does not have to go and bear fruit. Just as every Christian is a disciple, so is every Christian a missionary.

The work God gives every Christian to do is a lasting work. If we are truly doing God's work, that work will last. If we are bearing God's fruit, that fruit will last. Let us each be certain that it is God's work we are doing—God's fruit we are bearing—and not our own. If we are truly doing His work according to His will, God will give us whatever we ask for in Jesus' name. If we do what God says, He will do what we say! (see John 14:13; 15:7 and comments).

How many times we have prayed for grace and strength to bear fruit, but nothing seems to happen. Our request is not granted. And we ask: "Why has no answer come?" The reason is this: We have reversed the command given by Jesus in this verse. That is, we have first asked for grace and strength, so that we can go out and bear fruit with ease. But here Jesus says: "**. . . go and bear fruit. Then** God will grant your request for grace and stength." Only after God sees our willingness to obey will He give us the grace and strength we need to bear fruit for Him.

Here we can see an important truth: There is only one way we can bring glory to God and share in that glory ourselves, and that way is the way of obedience. Only when we are obedient will we receive the Holy Spirit (John 14:15–16). Only when we are obedient will Jesus be manifested in our lives (John 14:21). Only when we are obedient will God come and live in us (John 14:23). Only through obedience can we remain in Christ's love (John 15:10). Only through obedience can we obtain Christ's friendship (John 15:14). And only when we are obedient will we obtain the answer to our prayers. All of these great blessings come to us only when we obey Jesus.

There is one further thing that should

[106] Most religious leaders treat their disciples as servants. But our leader, Jesus, does not treat us that way. Instead, He has made Himself our servant. For example, what other leader has ever washed his disciples' feet? (John 13:5).

be mentioned concerning this verse. There are three little words here—**in my name**. In the comment on John 14:13, it was said that the expression "in Christ's name" means "in Christ's stead." When we pray, we must pray in Christ's stead.

The following illustration shows us this truth clearly. Jesus is like a merchant who went away on a long trip. Before leaving, the merchant put his business into the hands of his servant. The merchant gave the servant full authority to manage his business during his absence. The merchant even gave the servant the authority to use his (the merchant's) name.

Now a servant under such circumstances does nothing by his own authority. He does nothing in his own name. If he were to try to get his master's money out of the bank in his own name, his master would certainly punish him. Why did the merchant trust his servant? Because his servant was obedient and trustworthy. It's because the servant was obedient and trustworthy that the merchant was able to give him complete authority over his business—including even the right to use his name.

In the same way, when Jesus left this earth and went to heaven, He put all his work, His "business," into our hands. He gave us full authority to use His name, so that we might be able to draw from His "bank account" all the riches and blessings of heaven. Servant of Christ! Learn to use His name properly! Let His name rule in your life. Concentrate on the work He has given you. Jesus says to us: "I have appointed you to go and bear fruit. I have appointed you to be my witnesses to the ends of the earth (Acts 1:8). I have appointed you to be streams of living water (John 7:38). I have appointed you to pour out upon a parched and suffering world all the riches and blessings of heaven."

What have we done about our appointment? What are we doing about it now? From now on, let us stop asking for blessings for ourselves, such as joy, peace, and comfort. Rather, let there be only this thought in our minds: "I am not my own; I am His. I am His servant. My life has only one meaning and purpose, and that is to do His will." And when we have made the doing of His will the sole desire of our lives, then He will come to us and lift us up, and say to us: "**I no longer call you servants. . . . Instead, I have called you friends**" (verse 15).

Servants of Christ! Take your appointment, and in obedience **go and bear fruit** to His glory.

17 See John 13:34 and comment.

The World Hates the Disciples (15:18–27)

18 **If the world[107] hates you, keep in mind that it hated me first.** Jesus' meaning is this: "The world will indeed hate you, because it first hated me." Let the disciples not be surprised. If the world hated Jesus, it will certainly hate His followers (see Matthew 10:24–25).

Notice that Jesus' disciples are to be known by their love. Men of the world are known by their hatred.

19 The world hates the followers of Jesus because they are not of the world. They have been called out of the world to enter Christ's kingdom. Even in this life, Christians have left the kingdom of darkness and have become citizens of the kingdom of God. That is why Satan, the **prince of this world** (John 14:30), is so angry. Christians have left his kingdom. He hates them. And all those under Satan's rule, that is, all who are of the world, also hate Christians. There will always be hostility between Christians and the world (Satan's kingdom). Just as there can be no reconciliation between good and evil, truth and falsehood, light and darkness, so there can be no reconciliation between Christians and the world.

20 Servants usually receive the same treatment from others that their master receives. Those who persecuted Jesus will persecute His disciples also, because the disciples will do the same things Jesus did. They will be lights in the darkness.

---

[107] In this context, the word **world** means "unbelieving men of the world." It can also mean "worldly men," that is, men who love the things of the world more than they love God.

Men of the world hate the light, because the light exposes their evil deeds (see John 3:19–20 and comment). That is why the world persecuted Christ, and that is why the world will persecute Christ's disciples.

In the same way, those who obeyed Jesus' teaching will obey the disciples' teaching also. But those who obey the disciples will be fewer in number than those who persecute them. So it has been with Jesus' disciples in every generation (see Matthew 10:24–25; John 13:16 and comments).

All faithful Christians will suffer persecution (2 Timothy 3:12). Jesus sends us out as sheep among wolves (Matthew 10:16). But let us remember that those who share in Christ's sufferings will also share in His glory (see Matthew 5:10–12; Romans 8:17; 1 Peter 4:13–14).

21 Jesus said to His disciples: "**They will treat you this way because of my name**, that is, because of me." The world treats Jesus' disciples badly because the world does not know God. And the world does not know God because it does not recognize and accept Jesus, who is the revelation of God.

22 If Jesus had not come to earth, the Jews would not have been guilty of the sin of rejecting God's Son. Jesus did not mean that the Jews would have been totally guiltless and without sin if He had not come. Even the best Jews were sinners, just like all other men (Romans 3:9–10). He only meant that they would not have been guilty of rejecting the true revelation of God. When the Jews rejected Christ, they rejected God; this was their greatest sin. If Christ had not come, they would not have fallen into that sin. Christ's coming into the world resulted in the condemnation of all those who rejected Him (see John 3:18 and comment).

23 **He who hates me hates my Father as well**. The followers of other religions say: "I believe in God, but not in Christ." But it is not possible to fully believe in the true God without believing in Christ. He who rejects Christ rejects God also (see John 12:44–45 and comment). And to reject Christ is the same as to "hate" Him. Therefore, he who rejects Christ hates both Christ and God.

Some people say: "I accept Christ, but I don't accept His lordship over my life." This also is impossible. Those who do not accept the lordship of Christ do not truly accept Christ. Men must accept Christ as their Lord and Savior—as the Son of God; otherwise they are, in effect, rejecting Him.

24 This verse adds to the thought of verse 22. The Jews not only rejected Christ's teaching; they also rejected His works, His **miracles**. To refuse to believe in Christ was bad enough, but to refuse to believe His miracles was even worse. It showed an even greater hardness of heart on the part of the Jews. In spite of the great works of God that Jesus performed, the Jews continued to hate Him. And because they hated Jesus, they hated the Father too (verse 23).

Jesus' miracles gave testimony that He had been sent from God (John 5:36; 10:25). When the Jews rejected Christ's miracles, they rejected God Himself, because the miracles had been done by God's power. Thus the Jews were without excuse. God in His mercy had given them signs; the signs were the miracles themselves. They had seen these miracles. They had seen Christ. And in seeing Christ, they had seen the Father (John 12:45). But they rejected both Christ and the Father. Their guilt was indeed great (see Matthew 11:20–24 and comment).

25 The **Law**, that is, the Old Testament, prophesied that the Jews would reject Christ. Here Jesus quotes from Psalms 35:19 and 69:4.

26 Then Jesus again mentioned the **Counselor**, the Holy Spirit (see John 14:16–17,26 and comment). Earlier He had said that God would send the Spirit. This time Jesus said that He Himself would send the Spirit. It's saying the same thing: Jesus and God always act together.

The Holy Spirit testifies about Jesus. When people hear and believe the Gospel of Christ, it is because the Holy Spirit has testified about Jesus in their hearts. Man's testimony alone is never enough; in order for anyone to believe in Christ, the testimony of the Holy Spirit is essential. Christians do not "convert" other people;

people are converted only by the Holy Spirit.

27 However, the disciples' testimony was also essential. They had been with Jesus from the beginning. They were eyewitnesses.

In the same way, the testimony of Christians today is also necessary. The Holy Spirit has no audible voice. We are the voice of the Holy Spirit. We must testify to other people about Christ, or they will never hear (see Romans 10:14). Our testimony reaches their ears; the Holy Spirit then carries it to their hearts.

CHAPTER 16

The Work of the Holy Spirit (16:1–15)

1 At their last meal together, Jesus gave these teachings to His disciples (Chapters 14–16) so that they would **not go astray**—that is, so that their faith would not fail. Great persecution was about to fall on them. If they had not been warned in advance about the world's hatred and about the troubles that were coming, they might have given up their faith in Christ (verse 4).

2 Jesus told His disciples that they would be especially persecuted by the Jewish religious leaders. They would be expelled from their synagogues. Perhaps they would be expelled from their jobs, from their homes. Such has happened to many Christians in every generation. Some religious leaders have been so blind and perverted that they have even killed innocent Christians and thought that in so doing they were serving God (see Acts 8:1–3; 26:9–11). Indeed, it is said that except for the Apostle John, all the remaining eleven of Jesus' disciples were killed because of their faith. Down through history, Christians have been persecuted not only by Jews but by men of other religions as well. But worst of all, there have been times when some Christians have actually persecuted other Christians! Such is the great power of Satan to deceive even believers, and to lead them to oppose their brothers.

3 Men oppose true Christians because they do not know the one true God, who has been revealed by Jesus Christ (see John 15:21 and comment). Usually men's ignorance of God is their own fault. God has given them signs through Christ, but they have refused to learn from them. This was true of the Jews. It is also true of unbelieving men in every generation.

4 When Jesus was with His disciples, He did not speak so much about the great trials that would fall upon them. It was not necessary, because most of the persecution fell on Jesus, not on the disciples. But now, Jesus was about to leave them, and then all the hatred of the world would fall on them. Therefore, it was necessary to prepare them for that time.

5 Jesus had told His disciples that He was going away, but they hadn't really asked where He was going. True, Peter had asked once (John 13:36). But Peter had not been thinking about Jesus' destination; he had only been thinking about going with Jesus wherever He went. He had thought that Jesus was going to some other city or country.

6 The disciples were filled with grief, because Jesus had told them He was leaving them. But they still did not fully realize that He was talking about His death.

7 Jesus told them that His going away would be to their advantage, not to their disadvantage. Because only after He left would the **Counselor**, the Holy Spirit, come to them (John 14:16). Jesus Himself could be in only one place at a time. But the Holy Spirit could be everywhere at once!

The disciples didn't understand at the time what Jesus was talking about, but later they understood. Indeed, it proved true that it was better to have the Holy Spirit inside them than to have Jesus with them. Before Jesus' death they were weak and wavering and fearful men. After Jesus' death the Holy Spirit came upon them and transformed them into powerful, steady, and courageous men. That is why Jesus said that it was to their advantage that He go away.

8 Jesus had already explained some things about the Holy Spirit (see John 14:16–17,26; 15:26). Here He says that the Holy Spirit will reveal the guilt of worldly men in regard to **sin and righteousness and judgment**.

9 First, in regard to **sin**, the Holy Spirit shows men that they are sinners, because they have refused to believe in Christ. Man's basic sin is that he makes himself the master of his own life. This is self-centeredness, or selfishness. Everything natural man does is ultimately for himself. Because of this selfishness, man refuses to accept any other master besides himself—such as God, or Christ. Jesus says: "You must serve me." Man says: "No, I will only serve myself. I don't believe in you." The Holy Spirit comes to **convict** men for this attitude of selfishness and unbelief. Because only when the Holy Spirit convicts a man's conscience can that man fully realize his selfishness and turn to God in repentance.

10 Second, in regard to RIGHTEOUSNESS, the Holy Spirit shows men that Christ is righteous. The world called Jesus a "sinner" (John 9:24). But Jesus was shown to be righteous, because He rose from the dead and went to His Father in heaven.

Furthermore, the Holy Spirit shows men that they have no **righteousness** of their own. Only Christ is righteous. And only through Christ's death on the cross can men be cleansed of their sin and made righteous in God's sight (see Mark 10:45 and comment). The Holy Spirit shows men that they can never be righteous by their own efforts. Only the Holy Spirit can show this to a man; he would never believe it otherwise.

11 Third, in regard to **judgment**, the Holy Spirit shows men that judgment has already fallen upon Satan, the **prince of this world**. Jesus defeated Satan on the cross (see John 12:31 and comment). Satan has been **condemned**, and in the end he will be destroyed.

12 Although Jesus did not hide anything from His disciples (John 15:15), He could not explain everything to them before He died. They were not ready to hear it. They could not have understood it or accepted it. They would need the help of the Holy Spirit to understand the deeper lessons they had yet to learn.

13 Therefore, Jesus told them that the Holy Spirit would come and teach them what was left for them to learn. The Holy Spirit would **guide them into all truth**. The Spirit would tell them **what is yet to come**; that is, the Spirit would prepare them for the future. The Spirit would prepare them for the great work of establishing Christ's church throughout the world. The Spirit would also prepare them to face suffering and death. All these things the Holy Spirit did for those first disciples, and the Spirit has been doing the same things for every true Christian ever since.

The Holy Spirit helped the disciples do one other thing: He helped them write the New Testament. The **Spirit of truth**, the Holy Spirit, guided their minds and pens as they wrote. Everything written in our Bible is, in fact, written by God's Holy Spirit. Therefore, we can rely on the Bible completely; every word of it is true. It is indeed God's word.

The Holy Spirit does not speak **on his own**. He speaks **only what he hears** from God. The Holy Spirit is God's Spirit; therefore, He speaks God's words.

14 The Holy Spirit always glorifies Christ. Whatever kind of work the Holy Spirit does, or whatever kind of guidance the Holy Spirit gives, it will always be for Christ's glory.

This is an important way to test whether or not we are really being led by the Spirit in any particular endeavor: Will what we are doing bring glory to Christ? If so, then we can be sure it is the Holy Spirit who is leading us. However, if what we are doing does not bring glory to Christ, then it is not from the Holy Spirit.

15 The Spirit does for us what Jesus would have done if He had remained on earth. Jesus said, **"He will bring glory to me by taking from what is mine"** (verse 14). The Holy Spirit takes Christ's righteousness, His authority, His power, and

His glory and makes it known to us. All these belong to both Christ and God together. Whatever belongs to God belongs also to Christ. And all these things will be made known to us through the Holy Spirit. We shall not only know of Christ's righteousness, power, and glory; we shall share in them!

The Disciples' Grief Will Turn to Joy (16:16–33)

16 Jesus then said something that confused His disciples: "**In a little while you will see me no more, and then after a little while you will see me.**" He meant by this that soon He was going to die, and then after three days He was going to rise again from the dead. He had told them this many times, but they had never understood it (Mark 8:31: 9:31–32; 10:32–34).

17–18 Why were the disciples so confused? They were confused because they still thought, like other Jews, that Jesus was going to establish an earthly kingdom. If that were true, why was He going away? And if it was not true, why should He return? To the disciples it didn't make any sense.

19 When Jesus saw them so perplexed, He began to explain to them His meaning, using the example of a woman in childbirth.

20 He told His disciples that they would weep and mourn for a time. They would weep and mourn because of His death. At the same time the world, that is, the unbelieving men of the world, would rejoice that Jesus was dead.

But then Jesus said, "**Your grief will turn to joy.**" Jesus' death would bring them grief. His resurrection would bring them joy.

21 The grief of the disciples would be like the pain of woman in childbirth. The pain of childbirth is soon over, and is replaced by the joy of having a new child.

22 In the same way, the disciples would grieve for three days. Then Jesus would rise from the dead and come to them. He would breathe on them the Holy Spirit (John 20:22). And the Holy Spirit would remain with them forever (John 14:16), and give them a joy that the world could never take away (see John 15:11; Galatians 5:22).

23 **In that day**—that is, after Jesus rises from the dead—the disciples will not have to ask Jesus any more questions about where He is going. They will understand. Anything else they need to know will be taught them by the Holy Spirit, not by Jesus Himself (verse 13).

Furthermore, from that time on, the disciples will pray mainly to the Father.[108] But they must pray in Jesus' name. If they do, the Father will give them whatever they request (see John 14:13–14 and comment). And this promise was not only for those first disciples; it is for every believer.

24 Up until then the disciples had not really asked God for anything using Jesus' name. They had either asked Jesus directly, or they had prayed to God directly. Now, let them ask God for everything in Jesus' name. Above all, let them ask that the Holy Spirit might fill them. Then their joy will be complete (John 15:11).

25 Up until then, Jesus had not spoken clearly to the disciples about heavenly things. It was a mystery to them. But after His resurrection, Jesus told them everything much more clearly, and they then were able to understand (see Luke 24:27,45–46).

26 After Jesus' resurrection and ascension, the disciples would begin to ask the Father for things directly. While Jesus was with them on earth, He often prayed to the Father on behalf of the disciples. Now they would be on their own; they would not need Jesus in person to pray for them. Through the Holy Spirit, they would be able to come directly to God.

Because of the coming of the Holy Spirit, all Christians can now make their requests directly to God. But we must make all our requests in Jesus' name.

---

[108] Most Christians do not make any distinction between praying to God and praying to Jesus. It is the same thing.

Only because of our faith in Jesus are we worthy to come into God's presence. Only when we pray in Jesus' name and for His sake will God hear our prayers.

Jesus says here that He will no longer ask the Father on behalf of His disciples. He means that He will no longer do so while He is in bodily form here on earth. But we know from other New Testament verses that Jesus is now in heaven interceding for all believers before the throne of God (see Romans 8:34; Hebrews 7:25 and comments). This means that Jesus' death—Jesus' sacrifice—is interceding for us. Jesus' presence before the Father is the proof that He has died for our sins and that we are now no longer guilty of sin. Jesus does not need to ask God to save us; He has already gained our salvation for us by dying on the cross. Jesus does not need to ask God to bless us; He has already blessed us by sending us the Holy Spirit. Jesus' work on earth is finished. All we need to do now is to ask God directly in Jesus' name, and God will grant our request for the sake of His Son Jesus.

27 Therefore, Christ no longer needs to pray for His disciples. The disciples can pray to God directly because God loves them. His love for them is especially great because they have loved and believed in His Son. God loves all men (John 3:16), but He especially loves His own children, that is, those who have believed in Jesus (see John 14:21 and comment).

28 Then Jesus told His disciples clearly that He had come from the Father in heaven, and that He was now about to return to His Father. This was the answer to the question the disciples had been asking each other in verses 17–18. But they hadn't yet asked Jesus Himself. Nevertheless, Jesus knew what was in their minds (verse 19) and gave them the answer that they were looking for.

29–30 Because Jesus had answered their question before they even asked it, they realized that He had supernatural knowledge; He knew what was in their minds. That is why they said: "**Now we see that you know all things and that you do not even need to have anyone ask you questions**. You can give the answer before we even ask."

Because of Jesus' knowledge of their thoughts, they believed even more strongly that He had indeed come from God.

31 "**You believe at last!**" said Jesus. Some versions of the Bible translate Jesus' words: "Do you now believe?" The disciples thought they believed, but Jesus knew how weak their faith was.

32 The disciples had just confessed their faith in Jesus, but within several hours they would all flee to their homes (Mark 14:27,50).

Before we say with certainty, "I have strong faith," let us humbly remember those eleven disciples. They were sure they had strong faith too, but they didn't.

33 Jesus told His disciples about His going away and about the trials that were soon to come upon them, so that they would have **peace** in Him. He said, "**I have told you these things so that in me you may have peace**." He told them not to look for peace in the world; their peace would come only from Him (see John 14:27 and comment).

Our peace is in Jesus. Our trouble is in the world. But the trouble of the world cannot destroy our peace, because Jesus has gained victory over the world—that is, over the rule and power of Satan.

I have overcome the world. What an amazing statement! Jesus knew that evil men of the world were coming to arrest Him that very night. The next day they would crucify Him. Yet the "world" could not overcome Him. Instead, He overcame the world. The cross was not a sign of defeat; it was a sign of victory over Satan.

Therefore, when trouble comes upon us, let us take heart. Through the power of the Holy Spirit within us, we too can gain victory over Satan, over fear, doubt, sin. **In all these things we are more than conquerors through him who loved us** (Romans 8:37).

CHAPTER 17

Jesus Prays For Himself (17:1–5)

1 Jesus prayed: "**Father, the time has come**; that is, the time of my death has come. **Glorify your Son, that your Son may glorify you.**" God glorified Jesus by letting Him be crucified and then raising Him from the dead. Jesus glorified God through His death and through His victory over Satan on the cross (see John 12:31; 13:31 and comments). Whatever brings glory to Christ also brings glory to God. Christ prayed that He might be glorified only in order to bring glory to God.

In this Jesus has given us an example. Whatever we pray for, it must be for God's glory, not our own. If we pray for health, let it be for God's glory. If we pray for wealth, it must be for God's glory. We can ask God for anything if it is for His glory, and He will give it.[109]

2 God had already glorified Christ by giving Him **authority over all people** (see Matthew 28:18; John 3:35; 5:27 and comments). This authority was given so that Jesus might give eternal life to all that God had given Him (see John 3:15; 6:37–40 and comments).

3 Eternal life is to know God and to know Christ. We have all had the experience of knowing a person, from whom we have received great blessing and inspiration. It could be our wife, husband, parent, teacher, friend. Our life has been changed—it has become richer or more joyful—because of that person.

To know God is like that, but much more. To know God is to receive His life. To know God is to enter into eternal life.

Jesus didn't say that eternal life was knowing any god. He said that eternal life was to know the **only true God**, and to know His only Son, **Jesus Christ**. One cannot truly know God without knowing Jesus Christ.

4 Jesus fully completed all the work that God had given Him to do on earth. But the main work God gave Christ to do was to die on the cross in order to save men and women. Knowing that He would be crucified the next day, Jesus could pray as if that work had already been completed. It was that "work," that is, His death on the cross, which brought the greatest glory to God (verse 1).

5 Jesus then prayed that God would restore to Him the glory which He had from before the world began. Jesus here clearly states that He was with God in the beginning (see John 1:1 and comment). God answered this prayer when He carried Christ into heaven forty days after His resurrection (Acts 1:9).

Jesus Prays for His Disciples (17:6–19)

6 Jesus prayed: "**I have revealed you**[110] **to those you gave me out of the world**"—that is, to the disciples. Jesus had made God known to His disciples.[111] These disciples had been chosen by God in the beginning (Ephesians 1:4). They belonged to God. God gave them to Jesus (see John 6:37). God took them **out of the world**—that is, out of Satan's hands—and put them into Jesus' hands.

7 The disciples had at last realized

---

[109] God doesn't only hear prayers for His glory. Many times Christians in pain or suffering or fear simply cry out to God for mercy and relief, and God certainly listens to them and often grants their requests. But God may not grant their request; He may have a special and eternal purpose in allowing a person to suffer. However, a prayer for His glory He is always ready to answer positively.

[110] In place of the word **you**, some translations of the Bible say "your name," which is a literal translation of the original Greek text. The meaning is the same; to reveal God's name is the same as to reveal God Himself.

[111] Jesus was mainly referring here to His eleven close disciples, who were soon to become apostles. But He could also mean all those who had truly believed in Him up to that time.

that Jesus had come from God (John 16:30), and that all the words Jesus had spoken and the works He had performed were really God's words and God's works.

8 Jesus had passed on God's words to His disciples, and they had **accepted** them. As a result, they now **knew** with certainty that Jesus had come from God, and they **believed** that He had been sent by God to be the Messiah, the Savior of the world.

In this verse we can see three steps to becoming a Christian. First, a person must "accept" the words of God and Christ with an open and repentant mind. Second, he must then "know" who Jesus is; he must recognize Jesus as the Son of God. And third, he must "believe" in Jesus and follow Him. The faith of a true Christian is not a blind faith. We know **with certainty** whom we have believed (see 2 Timothy 1:12).

9 Jesus said, "**I am not praying for the world**." He was only praying for **them**—that is, for His disciples—and for all others who would believe their message (verse 20).

This does not mean that Jesus didn't love this world. He was sent to be the Savior of the world (John 3:16), and now His disciples were to spread the Gospel of salvation to all people. But Jesus could not pray for the **world** in the same way He prayed for His disciples. The "world," that is, unbelieving mankind, was opposed to God. Jesus' prayer for the men of the world was that they might believe (verse 21), that they might come out of the world. God wants all men to be saved (1 Timothy 2:4). But for those who refuse to accept salvation through Christ, there is no other hope, no other means of salvation. Therefore, Jesus did not pray for those who had refused to accept God's mercy and forgiveness, who had refused to accept God's salvation through His Son. Such men have condemned themselves[112] (John 3:18).

10 Jesus said, "**All I have is yours** (God's)." All men can truthfully say that to God. Everything we have has come from God and ultimately belongs to Him. But then Jesus said, "**. . . and all you have is mine**." No ordinary man can say that! Only the Son of God can say that (John 3:35).

Jesus said that glory had come to Him from His disciples. In saying this, He was thinking of the future. He knew what great works the disciples would do in His name. Yet even while they were still weak and ineffective, He talked about the glory they brought Him. Jesus had more faith in in His disciples than they had in Him!

11 The disciples were to remain in the world. Therefore, Jesus prayed that God would **protect them**, that is, protect them from evil. Jesus did not ask that they be protected from trouble—only from evil. That is His prayer for us also.

. . . protect them by the power of your name.[113] The **name** was the name God had given to His Son—"**the name you gave me**"—which was "Jesus." God had given Jesus all power and authority. To pray in Jesus' name is the same as to pray in God's name.

How important this prayer of Jesus has been, not only for those first disciples, but for every believer who has come since! This prayer has placed us under God's protection.

Jesus prayed for God's protection over the disciples **so that they** [might] **be one**. Jesus knew that Satan would attack the disciples after He had gone. Satan's main method of destroying them would be to divide them. Jesus had Himself taught that **if a house is divided against itself, that house cannot stand** (Mark 3:25). That is why Jesus gave His disciples the "new command" that they should love one another (John 13:34). Only in this

---

[112] Jesus, because He is God, knows who will not accept Him. But we believers do not have that knowledge. Therefore, we must continue to pray for all men, in accordance with Paul's instructions in 1 Timothy 2:1.

[113] In place of the words **protect them by the power of your name**, some translations of the Bible say, "Keep them in your name." The first translation gives the meaning of the Greek text more clearly.

way could they overcome Satan and remain united. Their unity among themselves must be like the unity of the Father and the Son. This unity is based on the love between Father and Son. All true unity among believers must be based on this divine love, which is given to us through the Holy Spirit (Romans 5:5).

12 Jesus had protected His disciples from evil while He was with them. He kept them safe **by that name**—that is, by God's power and authority which God had given to Jesus. Only Judas Iscariot was lost, so that the **Scripture** (Old Testament prophecy) might be fulfilled (see John 13:18 and comment).

Let us never forget the frightening example of Judas. He was counted among the twelve, but he did not belong to Christ. Likewise, in every church there are those who are counted members, but who do not belong to Christ.

13 See John 5:11 and comment.

14 Jesus had given His disciples God's **word**, that is, God's entire teaching. The disciples were not of this world, because they had been called out of the world. That is why the world hated them. The same is true for all who have ever followed Jesus (see John 15:18–19 and comment).

15 The place of Jesus' disciples was in the world. They were to establish Christ's church in the world (see verse 18). They were to be in the world, but not of it. Jesus' main concern was that they be protected from the **evil one**, that is, Satan, the ruler of the world (see Matthew 6:13; John 12:31; 1 John 5:19).

16 See verse 14 and comment.

17 **Sanctify them by the truth**. To "sanctify" means to "set apart," to "make holy." This is done by God's **truth**, that is, by God's word. . . . **your word is truth**. All believers are sanctified by God's word; that is, they are set apart for a holy purpose. We can also say that all believers are sanctified by faith in Christ. Christ is God's Word; He is **full of grace and truth** (John 1:1,14).

Only when we are sanctified are we fit to serve God in this world. But to be sanctified, we must obey God's word, God's truth. God's word by itself does not sanctify us; we must obey it.

18 Jesus sends us into the world just as God sent Jesus into the world. We have been given an opportunity by Christ to be His witnesses. Just as Christ came to be a witness for God, so we are called to be witnesses for Christ (Acts 1:8).

19 **For them** (the disciples) **I sanctify myself**. Jesus sanctified Himself through His death on the cross. He died **for them**, His disciples. By His death, the disciples were made holy in God's sight. Jesus took their sins upon Himself, and they became clean.

In the same way, through faith in Jesus and through His death for us, we too are sanctified and made fit for God's service.

Jesus Prays for All Believers (17:20–26)

20 Here we see that Jesus was not praying for His eleven disciples alone, but also for all who have ever believed (and will yet believe) in the Gospel of Christ. Now in this third part of Jesus' final prayer, He prays especially for us.

21 What does He pray for us above all? He prays that we might be **one**. All believers are to be one in mind and heart. We are to be one in love. We are to be one in Christ and in God, just as God and Christ are one in each other (John 10:30). This oneness is a spiritual oneness. It is a unity brought about by the Holy Spirit (see Ephesians 4:3–4 and comment).

Next, Jesus prays that we might remain in Him and in God (see John 15:4–5,8). Only when we are united with God and Christ can we be united with each other. When we remain in God and in Christ we will bear fruit. People will see that we are continuing Christ's work. Then, because of the fruit we are bearing in Christ's name, people will believe that God indeed did send Christ into the world. The two fruits that are easiest for the world to see are our unity and our love. If Christ's followers demonstrate these fruits, then the world will surely know that Christ was sent from God.

22 Christ gave His disciples His own glory, which He had received from His Father. This glory is spiritual life and love. It is the glory of sanctification. Jesus gave them His glory, **that they** [might] **be one**, even as He and the Father were one (see verse 11 and comment).

23 This verse repeats the thought of verse 21. Our unity with each other comes from our unity with God and Christ. We are in them. They are in us. They are in each other. We are branches of the same vine. When the world sees our unity, it will **know**[114] that God sent Christ, and that God loves us, even as He loves Christ (see John 15:9). The world will know that our unity is not based on human love, but on divine love.

Think of that! God loves us as much as He loves His own Son Jesus. And He has made us sons also, because we have believed in Jesus (see John 1:12 and comment).

But let us ask ourselves something. Does the world see unity among Christians? Does the world see love among Christians? How successful the devil has been in dividing us! May God forgive us for not having preserved the unity of His church.

24 Jesus had already told His disciples that He would come back to get them (John 14:3). Here He expresses this same intention to God. He wanted His disciples to see His glory, the glory that He had from the beginning (see verse 5).

25 The world does not know God, but Christ knows Him (John 8:55). Christ came from God to reveal God to men (see Matthew 11:27; John 1:18 and comments). He revealed God especially to His closest disciples. Therefore, He could say to God, "**They know that you have sent me.**"

26 Jesus said, "**I have made you**[115] **known to them, and will continue to make you known.**" Jesus continued to make God known to the disciples through the Holy Spirit. And He is still doing so today. Jesus makes God known to us through the Holy Spirit, so that God's love might be in us and so that Jesus Himself might be in us. Through the Holy Spirit we know God, we know His love (Romans 5:5), and we have Jesus living in us. All this is the work of the Holy Spirit. And the Holy Spirit is continuing to do this work in the life of every believer today.

CHAPTER 18

Jesus Arrested (18:1–14)

(Matthew 26:47–56; Mark 14:43–52; Luke 22:47–53)

1–11 See Mark 14:43–52 and comment.

12–13 Jesus was arrested by a detachment of Roman soldiers and some Jewish officials. There was also a crowd with them, which had been sent by the Jewish leaders (Mark 14:43). After His arrest, Jesus was taken first for informal questioning by Annas, who was a former high priest. Annas was the father-in-law of Caiaphas, who was the high priest at that time.

14 See John 11:49–52 and comment.

Jesus Before Annas and Peter's Denial (18:15–27)

(Matthew 26:69–75; Mark 14:66–72; Luke 22:54–62)

15–18 See Mark 14:66–68 and comment.

19 Among the Gospel writers, only John describes the questioning of Jesus by Annas. In verse 19 John calls Annas the **high priest**. He had been the high priest previously and had been deposed by the Romans. According to Jewish law, however, the high priest received his office for life. Therefore, many Jews still called Annas the "high priest."

The Jewish leaders first brought Jesus

---

[114] In this verse, the meaning of to **know** is to "be convinced" or to "believe strongly."

[115] In place of **you**, some translations of the Bible say "your name." The meaning is the same; to make God's name known is the same as to make God known (see verse 6 and comment).

to Annas, because according to Jewish law, it was not legal to question and condemn a person on the same day. In order to pass sentence on someone, it was necessary to wait until the following day after questioning him. Therefore, because the Jews didn't want to wait an extra day, they brought Jesus to Annas that same night for questioning. Thus the next morning they could legally take Him before the Sanhedrin and sentence Him (see verse 24).

John reports that Annas questioned Jesus. This was itself illegal. According to Jewish law, the judge or chief court official could not directly question the defendant. Witnesses were supposed to be called to testify, some who would testify for the defendant and others who would testify against him.

20–21 Because Annas was proceeding illegally, Jesus did not answer his question directly. Instead, He said that all of His teaching had been done in public places. Many had heard Him. Therefore, let those who had heard be called as witnesses. "**I said nothing in secret.**[116] **Why question me? Ask those who heard me,**" Jesus said.

22 Then an official, angered by Jesus' words, struck Him.

23 Jesus told the official that if he didn't like what He had said, he should have testified against it. Hitting a defendant was highly illegal.

24 Annas saw that there was no advantage to be gained in continuing to question Jesus, so he sent Him to Caiaphas, the regular high priest at that time. It is probable that both these meetings with Annas and Caiaphas took place in different buildings of the Jewish temple. The second meeting was a formal meeting of the Jewish Sanhedrin, over which Caiaphas, being the high priest, presided. This meeting is described in Mark 14:53–65.

25–27 See Mark 14:69–72 and comment.

Jesus Before Pilate (18:28–40)

28 After the Sanhedrin had condemned Jesus to death for blasphemy (see Mark 14:63–64 and comment), Jesus was led away to the **palace** of the Roman governor, whose name was **Pilate** (see Mark 15:1 and comment).

Since it was the week of the Passover festival, the Jews did not want to enter Pilate's palace, because he was a Gentile. If a Jew went into a Gentile's house, he became unclean for seven days and could not take part in any religious festival during that time. Therefore, if the Jews had gone inside Pilate's palace, they would not have been able to **eat the Passover**; that is, they would not have been able to eat any of the main Passover meals during Passover week (see Mark 14:12 and comment).

Notice that the Jews thought it was more important to avoid ceremonial uncleanness than it was to avoid causing the murder of an innocent man! They kept their bodies clean, but their hearts were unclean! (see Matthew 23:28).

29 Since the Jewish leaders would not go into Pilate's palace, Pilate came out to them. He wanted to keep the Jews happy; he wanted to keep peace in the province over which he was governor. He asked the Jews what the charge against Jesus was.

30 The Jews had condemned Jesus for blasphemy (Mark 14:64). But that charge didn't mean anything to Pilate. That was a local Jewish religious matter. The Romans usually did not involve themselves in the religious affairs of their provinces. They only cared about political and military matters, and about keeping the peace (see Acts 18:12–16).

Therefore, the Jews did not at first answer Pilate directly. They could not prove any charge against Jesus that would make Jesus worthy of the death sentence according to Roman law. Yet their chief desire was to get Pilate to

---

[116] Jesus had taught His disciples privately from time to time. But in this verse Jesus' meaning is that everything He had said to His disciples in private He had also said to others in public. He had kept nothing **secret** from the people.

sentence Jesus to death. So they said to Pilate, "You don't need to ask what the charges are. You can be sure Jesus is guilty. We would not have brought Him to you otherwise. Just accept our judgment." At the Jews' request, Pilate's soldiers had helped arrest Jesus (verse 12); now the Jews wanted Pilate to render a judgment according to their wishes also.

31 But Pilate knew that the charge against Jesus involved a religious matter, so at first he refused to pass judgment on the case.

But the Jews wanted Jesus executed, and according to Roman law, only the Roman officials had authority to execute criminals.[117]

32 The Jews had an additional purpose in bringing Jesus to Pilate. They wanted Jesus to be killed by crucifixion (the Roman method of executing people), and not by stoning (the Jewish method). In the Old Testament it is written: . . . **anyone who is hung on a tree is under God's curse** (Deuteronomy 21:23). This referred to hanging the bodies of condemned criminals on a tree after they had been executed in order to let everyone see their terrible fate and be warned by it. The Jews wanted to kill Jesus by hanging Him on a cross, so that He might be utterly disgraced in the eyes of the Jewish people. But only the Romans could crucify criminals, and that was another reason why the Jews had brought Jesus to Pilate.

John tells us of yet another reason—God's reason—why Jesus was to be crucified. It fulfilled the prophecy that Jesus Himself gave concerning the kind of death He was to die (see Matthew 20:19; John 12:32 and comments).

Therefore, at this point the Jews told Pilate the "special charge" they had decided to bring against Jesus: namely, the charge that Jesus had tried to make Himself the king of the Jews. Pilate would have to look into such a charge, because it was a crime against the Roman emperor for any man to set himself up as another king (see Mark 15:1; John 19:12 and comments). In the Romans' eyes there could be only one king, and that was the Roman emperor. The Romans considered anyone who tried to make himself a king to be an insurrectionist and an enemy of the emperor.

33 When Pilate heard this charge, he took Jesus aside and asked Him, "Is this charge true? **Are you the king of the Jews?**" (see Mark 15:2). Jesus certainly didn't look like someone trying to make himself a king! Pilate must have thought the charge was absurd.

34 Jesus asked Pilate if this idea about His being a king was his own idea or whether the idea had been put in his mind by the Jewish leaders. If it was Pilate's idea, Pilate would be thinking of a political king. Jesus was not that kind of king. But if the charge was the idea of the Jews, then they would be thinking of a religious "king," the Messiah. And Jesus was indeed the Messiah. Therefore, Jesus couldn't give a simple "yes" or "no" answer to Pilate's question: "**Are you the king of the Jews?**" Because the answer depended on what kind of king Pilate was asking about.

35 Pilate answered Jesus, "**Do you think I am a Jew?** Why would I think up something like this? This idea came from your own leaders."

Pilate wondered what Jesus had done to get the Jewish leaders so angry at Him. He had to make sure Jesus had not broken a Roman law. "**What is it you have done?**" he asked.

36 Jesus said, "**My kingdom is not of this world.**" He admitted that He was a "king," but not the kind of king Pilate thought. If He had been an earthly king, He would have fought the Romans by force, in the manner of earthly kings. But His kingdom was a spiritual kingdom, not an earthly kingdom. He did not need to fight with earthly weapons. Jesus' kingdom was the kingdom of God (see Mark 1:15 and comment).

How silly it was for Pilate to suppose that He was the earthly king of the Jews.

[117] The Jews did from time to time stone people for breaking the Jewish law (see Acts 7:57–60). But according to Roman law, it was illegal for them to do so.

Would the Jews be trying to arrest and kill their own king? Of course, not.

37 Pilate then said, **"You are a king, then!"**[118] Jesus answered, **"You are right in saying I am a king."**[119] Jesus was indeed a king, the king of a greater kingdom than the Roman Empire!

Indeed, Jesus had been sent by God into the world to testify about this kingdom. The kingdom of God is the true kingdom; it is the only kingdom that will last forever. This is the **truth** that Jesus came to testify about. Those who are **of the truth**—that is, those who are on the side of truth—listen to Jesus and believe Him (see 1 John 4:6).

38 **"What is truth?** How can a man know the truth?" Pilate wanted to know. One man says one thing; another man says another. Who can say what the "truth" is?

Jesus could say what the truth was! Jesus Himself was the **truth** (John 14:6). He was full of **grace and truth** (John 1:14). And He spoke the word of God, which is the truth (John 17:17). Unbelieving man says: "I cannot accept God's word, because I cannot know the truth." Jesus says: "Believe in me. **Then you will know the truth**" (John 8:32).

Pilate didn't think he could learn the truth from questioning Jesus, so he ended the interview. But he had decided that Jesus was innocent of wrongdoing. "I **find no basis for a charge against him**," he said to the crowd of Jews outside his palace.

39–40 Then he suggested that he release Jesus. At each Passover festival it was the custom that the Roman governor release one Jewish prisoner as a sign of friendship toward the Jews. But the crowd, under the influence of the chief priests (Mark 15:11), demanded that another prisoner, Barabbas, be released instead. John tells us that Barabbas **had taken part in a rebellion.**[120] Barabbas had led a revolt against the Romans. He was probably popular among the Jewish people. Let Barabbas be released, and let Pilate crucify Jesus! The Jews preferred an outlaw to the Son of God! (see Mark 15:6–14 and comment).

Think of how false and hypocritical the Jews were. They demanded the release of a man who had committed the very crime that they had falsely accused Jesus of—the crime of rising up against the Roman emperor!

CHAPTER 19

Jesus Sentenced to be Crucified (19:1–16)

1–3 A fuller description of the flogging of Jesus and the mocking of the soldiers is given in Mark's Gospel (see Mark 15:15–19 and comment).

4–5 Here in verses 4–15, John describes the final attempt by Pilate to free Jesus. This is not mentioned by the other three Gospel writers.

Pilate brought Jesus out before the crowd after His flogging. The soldiers had dressed Him up like a king. Pilate

---

118 It is not certain whether Pilate's words, **"You are a king, then,"** form a statement or a question. In some translations of the Bible, these words are written as a question. In the original Greek manuscripts of the New Testament, there are no punctuation marks, so it is impossible to tell whether John intended this to be a question or not. The sense seems clearer, however, if the words are taken as a statement.

119 In place of the words, **You are right in saying I am a king,** some versions of the Bible say, "You say I am a king," which is a literal translation of the original Greek text. The meaning is the same. However, the first translation gives the true meaning more clearly. When the Jews of Jesus' time said, "You say I am a king," they actually meant, "Yes, I am a king" (see Mark 15:2 and comment).

120 In place of the words **Barabbas had taken part in a rebellion,** some translations of the Bible say, "Barabbas was a robber," which means he was an "outlaw."

hoped that the crowd would see that this pathetic man could not possibly be any kind of king.

6 But Pilate's plan did not work. The **chief priests and their officials** cried out, "**Crucify! Crucify!**" It was mainly the Jewish leaders who demanded Jesus' death. The crowd of ordinary Jews followed the direction of their leaders (Mark 15:11).

Pilate was displeased with the Jews. "**You take him and crucify him,**" he said to them. Pilate knew that the Jews could not crucify criminals. His meaning was: "I will have nothing to do with this man. If you insist that He be crucified, you'll have to do it yourselves. But if you do, of course, you'll be breaking the Roman law."

7 The Jews then told Pilate that Jesus had claimed to be the Son of God. According to the Jewish law, a man who claimed to be equal to God had to be executed (see Leviticus 24:16; John 5:18 and comment).

8–9 Pilate was superstitious. When he heard that Jesus had claimed to be God's Son, he became afraid. The Romans had many different gods, and they believed that their gods often came to earth disguised as men and had children by earthly women. Pilate feared that if he were to unknowingly put to death a "son" of some Roman god, that god would surely take revenge on him. Also Pilate's wife had had a dream about Jesus, and she had warned her husband not to have anything to do with Him (Matthew 27:19).

Therefore, Pilate again took Jesus inside and asked Him, "**Where do you come from?** Do you come from earth or from heaven?" But Jesus didn't answer. It is not known why Jesus remained silent at this point. He had refused to answer some of Pilate's earlier questions (see Mark 15:3–5). Perhaps He knew that Pilate would not believe His answer. Also, Jesus had already answered that question before (John 18:36–37). There was no use answering it again.

10 Pilate became angry. He was the chief official in the whole province. If he asked a question, he expected an answer. He demanded respect from people. He surely expected Jesus to respect him. After all, Pilate held the power of life and death over Jesus. "**Don't you realize I have power either to free you or crucify you?**" Pilate asked.

11 Jesus told Pilate that any power he possessed had been given to him **from above,** that is, by God. All authority belongs to God (Romans 13:1). From this, we can take comfort. When we fall into persecution, let us remember that those who persecute us can do no more to us than God allows.

Furthermore, Pilate was not the only one responsible in this matter. If he crucified Jesus, the guilt would not fall entirely on Pilate. Indeed, most of the guilt would fall on Caiaphas, the high priest, who had handed Jesus over to Pilate (John 18:28).

12 Pilate again tried to convince the Jews that Jesus should be released. Pilate had the authority to release Jesus, but he did not want to oppose the wishes of the Jewish leaders. He wanted peace in his province of Judea. He wanted to keep the Jewish leaders happy.

But the Jews would not listen to Pilate. They again raised their charge that Jesus was trying to make Himself a king. There was only one true king in the Roman Empire, they said, and that was **Caesar,**[121] the Roman emperor. Therefore, Jesus was opposing Caesar.

Then the Jews told Pilate, "If you do not crucify this Jesus, **you are no friend of Caesar**. If you let Him go free, you will be opposing Caesar."

13 Pilate was even more afraid. He knew the Jews could send bad reports about him to the emperor. If the emperor learned that Pilate had protected a traitor and insurrectionist, the emperor would surely punish him. Therefore, for the sake of his own safety, Pilate decided to crucify Jesus.

14 It was the **day of Preparation of Passover Week,** which means it was the day of preparation for the Sabbath

---

[121] All Roman emperors were called **Caesar**. "Caesar" is the Roman word for emperor.

(Saturday) of Passover week. That is, it was Friday (see Mark 14:12 and comment).

John says it was about the **sixth hour,** which by Jewish reckoning was 12 noon. However, Mark writes that Jesus was crucified at 9 A.M. Many Bible scholars believe that here John has reckoned the time by the Roman method, according to which the "sixth hour" would be 6 A.M. (see Mark 15:25 and comment).

15–16 After Pilate had passed judgment that Jesus should be crucified, he asked the Jews, **"Shall I crucify your king?"** He was mocking them.

Then the chief priests said, **"We have no king but Caesar."** They were complete hypocrites. They hated Caesar. They said this only to please Pilate. But in saying this they betrayed God, because according to the Old Testament, God Himself was their only King (Judges 8:23; 1 Samuel 8:7).

Thus in the end the Jewish leaders got their wish. Pilate handed Jesus over **to them**—that is, to the Roman soldiers—to be crucified.

The Crucifixion (19:17–27)
(Matthew 27:32–44; Mark 15:21–32; Luke 23:26–43)

17–24 See Mark 15:21–32 and comment.

25 Four women were standing watching while Jesus was crucified. One was Jesus' **mother** Mary. Think of Mary's sorrow to see her son dying on the cross. The prophecy of Simeon had indeed come true: **And a sword will pierce your own soul too** (Luke 2:35).

The second woman at the cross was the **sister** of Jesus' mother. Some Bible scholars believe that this sister was Salome (Mark 15:40), who was the mother of James and John,[122] the sons of Zebedee (Matthew 27:56). If this is so, then John was related to Jesus.

The third woman at the cross was another **Mary,** the wife of **Clopas.** Some think that this Clopas is the same as the Cleopas mentioned in Luke 24:18.

The fourth woman at the cross was **Mary of Magdala,** called Mary Magdalene by the other Gospel writers (see Mark 15:40,47; Luke 8:2; John 20:1,11).

26 Even as He was dying, Jesus thought of His mother. She was standing there with the **disciple whom he loved**—that is, John, the writer of this Gospel. So He told His mother, **"Dear woman, here is your son;** that is, from now on John is going to be like your own son and care for you." From this, we can surmise that Jesus' father Joseph had died sometime before; otherwise, he would have been the one responsible for Jesus' mother. Jesus didn't place His mother in the care of His own brothers (Mary's other sons), because they were not yet believers (John 7:5). Only after Jesus' resurrection and ascension did His brothers come to believe in Him (Acts 1:14).

27 Then Jesus said to John, **"Here is your mother."** In this way Jesus placed His mother in John's care. And from then on John took responsibility for her, as if he were her own son.

The Death of Jesus (19:28–37)

28–30 See Mark 15:36–37 and comment.

31 Jesus died on the **day of Preparation,** that is, Friday (see verse 14). According to Jewish law, an executed criminal's body could not be left hanging on a tree or cross overnight. To do so was considered to be "defiling" the land (Deuteronomy 21:22–23). It was especially important to observe this law in Jesus' case, because the next day was the Sabbath of Passover week. Therefore, the Jews asked permission[123] to break the legs of Jesus and the two robbers who had been crucified with Him, so that they

---

[122] This John was the Apostle John, the "beloved disciple" (verse 26), who wrote this Gospel.

[123] The Romans used to let the bodies of crucified criminals hang on the cross for days, to serve as a warning to others not to break the Roman law. Therefore, it was necessary for the Jews to ask permission to take the bodies down.

would all die quickly, thus making it possible to bury the bodies before sunset.[124]

32–33 However, the soldiers found that Jesus was already dead, so it was not necessary to break his legs.

34 One of the soldiers pierced Jesus' side with a spear. Perhaps he wanted to make sure Jesus was really dead. Blood and water came out of the wound. It is possible that the soldier pierced Jesus' stomach; this would explain why **blood and water** came out together.

35 **The man who saw it** is the Apostle John, the writer of this Gospel. He tells this story to show that Jesus had a real human body and that He really died. He also testifies to these things **so that you also may believe** (see John 20:31). And **his testimony is true** (see John 21:24).

36 The fact that Jesus had no bones broken was a fulfillment of Old Testament prophecy. According to Exodus 12:46 and Numbers 9:12, no bone was to be broken in the animal sacrificed at the Passover feast. John considered Jesus to be the true Passover sacrifice (see John 1:29; 1 Corinthians 5:7 and comments); therefore, it was fitting that none of His bones were broken. Thus the soldiers, by not breaking Jesus' legs, fulfilled the prophecy of Psalm 34:20, in which it is written: **. . . he protects all his bones, not one of them will be broken**.

37 The piercing of Jesus' side also fulfilled the prophecy of Zechariah: **They will look on me, the one they have pierced** (Zechariah 12:10).

The Burial of Jesus (19:38–42)

(Matthew 27:57–61; Mark 15:42–47; Luke 23:50–56)

38–40 See Mark 15:42–47 and comment.

CHAPTER 20

The Empty Tomb (20:1–10)

1 On the **first day of the week**, that is, Sunday, Mary of Magdala left her dwelling before dawn. According to Mark 16:2, she and two other women reached the tomb just after sunrise. She found the stone rolled away from the entrance of the tomb (see Mark 16:1–8 and comment).

2 After the events described in Mark 16:1–8 had taken place, Mary of Magdala ran to Peter and the **other disciple, the one Jesus loved**—that is, John—and told them that Jesus' body had been taken away. The thought that Jesus had risen from the dead didn't enter her mind (see Luke 24:9–11).

3–7 When Peter and John heard Mary's report, they at once ran to the tomb. Notice the small details that John remembers here. Surely this was the most important day in his life. Indeed, it was the most important day in the history of the world!

Notice also that the burial clothes were laid neatly (verse 7). If the body had been stolen, the clothes would have been taken away with the body, or they would have been scattered about. But Jesus' body had not been stolen. He had risen!

8 After Peter had entered the tomb, John went in also. John saw it was empty and **believed**. He believed that Jesus had indeed risen from the dead. Jesus had told them He would rise from the dead after three days (Mark 8:31; 9:31; 10:34). And here, on the third day, it had come to pass just as Jesus had said.

But Peter at first did not believe. He

---

[124] The Jewish "day" began at sunset. Therefore, the Sabbath actually began at 6 P.M. Friday evening. For this reason, it was necessary to remove the bodies and bury them before 6 P.M. on that same Friday, the day they were crucified.

went away, wondering to himself what had happened (Luke 24:12).

9–10 That Jesus would rise from the dead was also prophesied in the Old Testament, but Peter and John had not yet fully understood those prophecies. John's belief in Jesus' resurrection came first from his own eyes, not from the Old Testament. Prophecies of Jesus' resurrection are found in Psalm 16:10, Isaiah 53:10–12, Hosea 6:2, and Jonah 1:17.

Jesus Appears to Mary of Magdala (20:11–18)

11 When Peter and John ran to see the tomb, the women followed after them. After the two disciples had gone home (verse 10), Mary remained standing by the tomb.

12–13 She saw two angels. Mary and the other women had earlier seen the angels when they had first come to the tomb (see Mark 16:5; Luke 24:4). Then Mary saw the two angels again. They asked her why she was crying.

14–15 After she answered them, she saw a man standing there, whom she supposed to be the gardener.[125] But it was Jesus. There was something different about His resurrection body; as a result, she did not recognize Him at first (see Luke 24:15–16). She thought that perhaps this "gardener" had carried Jesus' body away.

16 Then Jesus called her name, and at once she recognized Him (see Luke 24:30–31). Jesus' sheep know His voice (John 10:4).

Mary had been hoping only to find Jesus' dead body; instead, she found His living body!

17 Mary probably fell on her knees and clasped Jesus' feet (Matthew 28:9). Jesus said to her, "**Do not hold on to me**." He meant: "Do not keep on holding me."

Jesus told Mary, "**Do not hold on to me, for I have not yet returned to the Father**." Jesus' meaning here is not certain. Some Bible scholars believe He meant that Mary didn't need to cling to Him, because He was not ascending to heaven immediately. She would have other opportunities to see Him before He left the earth. Other Bible scholars believe Jesus was trying to tell Mary that things had now changed; He was not like He used to be. One could not hold on to His body as before. Lazarus had also been raised from the dead, but he had received his old earthly body back. He would die again (John 11:43–44; 12:2). But Jesus had received a completely new body, a spiritual body, which would never die.

Then Jesus told Mary to tell His disciples that He was going to return to His Father; that is, He was going to ascend into heaven. He was going to prepare a place for them (John 14:2). Notice here that Jesus calls God **my Father and your Father . . . my God and your God**. God was Jesus' Father in a special way. Jesus was God's Son by nature from the beginning. We are God's adopted children by grace, not by nature.

According to Matthew 28:10, Jesus also told Mary and the other women with her to tell His disciples to go to Galilee, where He would meet them. In both Matthew 28:10 and in this verse, Jesus calls His disciples **brothers**. He had called them his **friends** before the resurrection (John 15:14). Now they have become His brothers. And all of us who believe are also counted as Jesus' brothers. Jesus was the firstborn among many brothers (Romans 8:29).

18 According to Matthew 28:9–10, not only Mary but also the other women with her saw Jesus at this time. Mary met Him first (Mark 16:9). Then, perhaps, she went at once and called the other women. Or perhaps Jesus appeared to the other women a short while later. Whatever happened, the women went a second time to tell the disciples the new news: They had actually seen the risen Lord! (see Matthew 28:9–10: Luke 24:12 and comments).

Jesus Appears to His Disciples (20:19–31)

19 On the evening of that same resurrection day, Jesus' disciples had

[125] The tomb was in a garden (John 19:41).

gathered together in a house. It was the greatest, most joyful, most victorious day in the history of the world—but where were the disciples? They were hiding in fear! They had locked the doors of the house **for fear of the Jews**. The Jewish leaders had learned that Jesus' body was gone, and had accused the disciples of having stolen it (Matthew 28:11–13). They would surely be searching for the disciples.

Suddenly, in a miraculous way, Jesus **came and stood among them**. The doors had not been opened. John does not say how Jesus entered the room where the disciples were, but it was not through an open door. He said, "**Peace be with you!**" This was a common Jewish greeting, but His words had a deeper meaning. For by "peace" He meant the spiritual peace He had promised them earlier (see John 14:27 and comment).

Jesus did not rebuke His disciples for having deserted Him. He greeted them as His friends and brothers. The disciples had failed Jesus, but He had not failed them. He came to them and gave them His peace. By His death on the cross He had brought peace between them and God (see Romans 5:1 and comment).

20 At first the disciples were **startled and frightened**, because they thought they were seeing a **ghost** (Luke 24:37). But as soon as they saw Jesus' wounds and realized it was really He, they rejoiced. Their sorrow turned to joy (John 16:20–22).

Luke has also described this first appearance of Jesus before all of His disciples together (see Luke 24:36–40 and comment). Only Thomas was absent (verse 24).

21 Jesus then said, "**As the Father has sent me, I am sending you.**" It was at this time that Jesus appointed them to be apostles, which means "men who are sent." But Jesus said this not only to His first disciples; He says it also to His disciples in every generation: "**I am sending you.**" Our work of spreading the Gospel and showing God's love to men is a continuation of Jesus' work here on earth. As God appointed Jesus to preach the Gospel and do good works, so God has appointed us to do the same (see Matthew 28:19–20; John 17:18 and comments; General Article: Purpose of the Church).

22 Then Jesus breathed on His disciples and gave them the Holy Spirit, which He had promised them earlier (see John 14:16 and comment). In order to do the work He was sending them to do, they would need the Holy Spirit. Christ never gives us a task to do without also giving us the means by which to do it. But more than that, the giving of the Holy Spirit was the most important event in the lives of the disciples. Because it was then that they were born again of the Spirit (see John 3:3,5 and comment). This is when they received true and full faith. This is when they received spiritual life. No man can be a true Christian without having received the Holy Spirit of Christ.

. . . if anyone does not have the Spirit of Christ, he does not belong to Christ (Romans 8:9)

On the day of Pentecost, ten days after Christ's ascension, the disciples were **filled with the Holy Spirit** (see Acts 2:1–4 and comment). The disciples had already received the Holy Spirit on this resurrection Sunday; but on the day of Pentecost, they were to be **filled** with the Holy Spirit and receive the gifts and the power of the Spirit.

Therefore, Christians must not only have the Holy Spirit in them; they must also pray that they might be filled with the Spirit. All of us must manifest the fruits of the Holy Spirit in our lives (see Galatians 5:22–23 and comment). But God wants to give us the gifts and power of the Holy Spirit as well (see 1 Corinthians 12:7–11 and comment). Being **filled with the Holy Spirit** means not only having His fruits but also having His power.

Jesus **breathed on them**. In Ezekiel 37:1–10, the prophet Ezekiel describes a valley filled with bones. The Lord told Ezekiel to prophesy to those dead bones. And as Ezekiel spoke the word of God to the bones, they joined together and were covered with flesh and skin. They became men. But they were still dead. . . . **there was no breath in them** (Ezekiel 37:8). Then the breath of God entered those dead men, and **they came to life and**

stood up on their feet—a vast army (Ezekiel 37:10).

We, too, have had the breath of God, the Holy Spirit, breathed into us. We too—all Christians—have become a **vast army**. We are not just spectators; we are not just church members. We are an **army**. And our general, our king, is Christ.

23 After giving His disciples the Holy Spirit, Jesus then gave them the authority to proclaim the forgiveness of sins. This is a difficult verse to understand. No man can himself forgive the sins of anyone; only God and Christ can forgive sins. But Christians are ambassadors for Christ (2 Corinthians 5:20). Through the guidance of the Holy Spirit, we can tell a person that his sins are forgiven because of Christ's death on the cross. If someone believes in Jesus and repents of his sins, we can say to that person with the full authority of Jesus: "Your sins are forgiven."

However, if someone does not repent and does not believe, then we can inform that person that his sins **are not forgiven**; they are retained.[126] This authority Jesus has given to the whole church, especially to the leaders of the church (see Matthew 16:19; 18:18–19 and comments).

24–25 **Thomas**, called Didymus (John 11:16), was not present that first night when Jesus appeared to the disciples. He said he would not believe that Jesus had risen until he had seen and touched Jesus' wounds.

Thomas has been called "doubting Thomas." But we must remember that, except for John (verse 8), the other disciples didn't believe either until they had seen Jesus. All of them doubted at first (Mark 16:11; Luke 24:10–12).

26–27 One week later, Jesus appeared again to the disciples in the same house and in the same way as before (verse 19). Thomas was there this time. Jesus said to him, "Touch me, touch my wounds. Put away your doubts, and believe." Jesus knew what Thomas had said earlier (verse 25). Jesus knows every doubting thought we think.

28 John doesn't say that Thomas actually touched Jesus' wounds. But Thomas saw Jesus; he heard Jesus' voice. And that was enough. He said, "**My Lord and my God!**" None of the disciples had ever called Jesus "God" before. Thomas had been the last of the disciples to believe. But he was the first to realize that Jesus was more than the Lord, more than the Messiah; He was almighty God Himself!

29 Jesus did not rebuke Thomas for being slow to believe. But He looked toward the future when He would no longer be on earth. Soon men would not be able to see Him and hear Him as Thomas had. They would have to believe without seeing. They would have to believe the testimony of others. But when they believed, they would be **blessed** indeed (see 1 Peter 1:8).

30–31 John did not write everything Jesus did, nor did the other Gospel writers (see John 21:25). But John had one main purpose in writing his Gospel: namely, **that you may believe that Jesus is the Christ, the Son of God**. It is not enough just to believe. We must believe in something. We must believe in Jesus, our Lord and our God.

Why must we believe? We must believe so that we will have life, eternal life, in His name. No faith, no life. Man can receive eternal life only through faith in Christ (see John 3:15,18,36 and comment).

[126] In place of the words **they are not forgiven**, some translations of the Bible say, "They are retained." The meaning is the same.

CHAPTER 21

Jesus and the Miraculous Catch of Fish (21:1–14)

1 After Jesus appeared to His disciples the second time (John 21:26), He went to Galilee, where He had told His disciples to meet Him (Matthew 28:10,16).

The **Sea of Tiberias** was the Roman name for the Sea of Galilee (John 6:1). Tiberius was one of the Roman emperors during Jesus' lifetime; he reigned from 14 to 37 A.D. When John wrote his Gospel, the name of the Sea of Galilee had been changed to the "Sea of Tiberias" in honor of this emperor.

2 Peter, Thomas (John 11:16; 20:24–28), Nathanael (John 1:45), and the sons of Zebedee (Mark 1:19–20), and two other disciples whose names are not mentioned were all together near the Sea of Galilee. They were waiting for the Lord to appear, as He had said He would.

3 While they were waiting, the disciples went out on the sea to fish. But after fishing all night, they had caught nothing.

4 Jesus then appeared on the shore. But, like Mary of Magdala, they at first did not recognize Him (see John 20:14 and comment).

5 Jesus asked the disciples, **"Friends, haven't you any fish?"** He meant: "Have you caught any fish?" Jesus knew that they hadn't caught any fish, but He wanted the disciples to say so themselves. When we have confessed our own lack of ability and power to Christ, then He will supply our needs.

6 When the disciples said "No," He told them to lower their net on the other side of the boat. They caught so many fish that they couldn't pull the net up to the boat.

Many a disciple has fished all night on the wrong side of the boat and caught nothing. It is Jesus who must tell us where to cast our nets. It is Jesus who must draw the fish into the net (see Luke 5:4–6).

7 When John, **the disciple whom Jesus loved** (John 13:23), saw the miracle that had taken place, he knew at once who the man on the shore was. **"It is the Lord!"**

As soon as Peter heard that, he jumped into the water. Peter was always quick to act (Matthew 14:28–29; John 18:10). John doesn't say, but it seems that Peter went to the shore to meet Jesus. Peter wrapped his **outer garment** around himself, for he had stripped for work and was wearing only his undergarments.

8–9 The other disciples towed the net full of fish toward the shore. On the shore they saw some fish being cooked on a fire.

10 Evidently, there was not enough fish for all the disciples to eat their fill, so Jesus told them to bring some of their recently caught fish.

11 When they finally dragged the net onto the shore, they counted 153 large fish!

12 Even though the disciples now knew that the man on the shore was Jesus, there was something different about Him. They wanted to ask, "Is it really you, Lord?" But they didn't dare. We never like to ask someone we know, "Who are you?"

13–14 This was the third time Jesus appeared to His disciples as a group (John 20:19,26). Before that, He had appeared to Mary of Magdala (John 20:14), to some women (Matthew 28:8–9), and to Peter (Luke 24:33–34).

Jesus Reinstates Peter (21:15–25)

15 When they had finished eating, Jesus asked Peter, **"Simon son of John,[127] do you truly love me more than these?"** "These" means "these other disciples." Jesus was asking Peter, "Do you love me more than **these** other

[127] Peter's father's name is mentioned also in John 1:42. Nothing else is known about this John.

disciples love me?"[128] Peter had earlier told Jesus, "**Even if all fall away, I will not**" (Mark 14:29). Yet Peter himself had fallen away; he had denied Jesus (Mark 14:66–72). Therefore, Jesus was now asking Peter, "Do you really love me more than these other disciples do? You haven't shown it by your actions."

Peter did not try to prove how much he loved Jesus. He knew he had failed. He knew that his love was weak. He knew that he didn't love Jesus more than these other disciples did. They had not denied their Lord. But in his heart Peter did love Jesus, and Jesus knew Peter's heart. Therefore, Peter only said, "**Lord . . . you know that I love you**."

Then Jesus said to him, "Okay, if you love me, do this: **Feed my lambs**. From now on, prove your love by obeying me. I am the **good shepherd**; I came to lay down my life for the lambs (John 10:11). Therefore, I am entrusting my lambs to you. Feed them. Care for them. Set for them an example (1 Peter 5:2–3). Die for them."

16–17 Two more times Jesus asked Peter, "Do you love me?" Peter was **hurt** when Jesus asked the third time. Perhaps it brought to his mind the three times he had denied Jesus. Because Peter had denied Jesus three times, he now had to tell Jesus three times that he loved Him. And each time Peter answered, Jesus told him to be a shepherd to the flock. In doing this, Jesus restored to Peter his authority as a leader in the church. The other disciples might not have accepted Peter because of his sin of denying Jesus. But Jesus here appointed Peter three times to be a shepherd in His church. Peter had been forgiven; Peter had been reinstated.

Notice that Jesus only asked Peter about his love. To be a shepherd, there is only one thing necessary; love for Jesus. Without love for Jesus, no man can love the flock. And without love for the flock, no man can be a shepherd. Those who do not love Jesus do not truly love men.

What Jesus told Peter, He tells to every disciple: "**Feed my sheep**" (verse 17). We are called not only to be fishers of men (Mark 1:17); we are called also to be feeders of the flock. True, we are not all called to be leaders. But we all have opportunities to "feed" our brothers and sisters with words of encouragement and life, and we must do so.

18 Jesus then told Peter, "Later, **when you are old you will stretch out your hands**." Jesus meant that Peter would stretch out his hands on a cross, just as Jesus had done. Then he would be led to a place of crucifixion—a place "**where you do not want to go**." It was the Roman custom to first tie a criminal's outstretched arms to the cross and then make him carry the cross to the site of execution.

19 John explains that Jesus, by saying this, was prophesying the **kind of death by which Peter would glorify God**. Jesus, by His death on the cross, glorified God (see John 12:23; 17:1). In the same way, through obedience, suffering, and death, Peter would also glorify God. So, also, should it be the concern of each one of us to be sure that, however we die, our death will bring glory to God. God will be glorified if we remain patient, faithful, and loving to the end.

According to the writings of early church historians, Peter did indeed die on a cross. It is said that he asked the Roman soldiers if he could be crucified hanging upside down, because he did not feel worthy to be crucified upright in the same way His Lord was crucified.

Finally Jesus said to Peter, "**Follow me**."[129] Jesus had said these same words to Peter three years earlier by the shore of that same Sea of Galilee where they were now standing (Mark 1:16–17). But Peter had not followed well. Now Jesus was giving him another chance. Peter would never deny his Lord again.

---

128 Some Bible scholars, however, believe that Jesus' meaning is this: "Do you love me more than you love **these** disciples?" This meaning is also possible according to the Greek text, but it's less likely to be what Jesus meant.

129 In the Greek, this means "keep on following me."

Follow me. Those words have come down to us through the generations. Jesus is still saying to us today: **"Follow me."** When Jesus called men while He was here on earth, He did not usually say, "Receive me," or "Believe in me." He said, "Follow me." To receive Jesus, to believe in Him, means to follow Him. So often we think that all we have to do to be Christians is to receive Jesus and His blessings and to be a member of His church. But the Christian life means more than that. It means to follow Jesus. It means to get up and go where He went. And where did Jesus go? To a cross. And, if we are truly His disciples, that is where we too will go (see Mark 8:34 and comment).

20–21 Then Peter saw John, the disciple whom Jesus loved (John 13:23–25). Peter asked Jesus, **"Lord, what about him?"** That is, "What will happen to this man (John)?" Peter was curious about John's future. Perhaps he remembered how John and his brother James had once asked to be placed in seats of honor in Jesus' kingdom (Mark 10:35–37). Perhaps Peter wondered if John would receive greater honor than he would. Was John going to be a martyr?

22 But Jesus rebuked Peter for asking about John. "It's not your business what happens to John," Jesus said. "If I want him to die as a martyr, he will die as a martyr. **If I want him to remain alive until I return**, he will remain alive until I return; **what is that to you?** You have only one thing to think about: **You must follow me.**"

23 Apparently some other disciples heard Jesus say to Peter, **"If I want him to remain alive until I return, what is that to you?"** They thought Jesus meant that John was not going to die. But Jesus had not said that.

Nevertheless, the rumor spread that John would not die before Jesus returned. It was important for John to correct this false rumor, because if John died before Jesus returned, many people's faith in Jesus' word would be shaken. Therefore, John here clearly states that Jesus never said that John would be alive when He returned.

24 John never mentions his own name in this Gospel. He needs no credentials. He knew that what he wrote was true, because he had seen these things with his own eyes and heard them with his own ears (see John 19:35; 1 John 1:1).

25 John wrote only a small part of what Jesus said and did (John 20:30). Even when we join together what is written in the four Gospels, we only know a small part of Jesus' life. "If everything had been written, **I suppose even the whole world would not have room for the books that would be written**," says John. This was a Jewish way of saying that there would be many, many books!

Acts

INTRODUCTION

The book of Acts[1] is the second part of the history written by Luke; the first part was the Gospel of Luke. In his Gospel, Luke has written mainly about the work of Jesus Christ. In the book of Acts, however, Luke has written mainly about the work of Jesus' disciples (apostles) and the Apostle Paul.

Many Bible scholars believe that Acts was written between 60 and 65 A.D. At that time the Apostle Paul was under house arrest in ROME, waiting for his trial to take place. Many important Romans were wondering about this new religion, Christianity, which Paul had been talking about. Therefore, Luke decided to write a proper two-part history about the beginnings of Christianity, about who Jesus Christ was, and about how this new religion had spread from Jerusalem all the way to the great city of Rome, the capital of the Roman Empire. After Luke had written his history, he sent both parts of it (Luke and Acts) to a Roman official whom Luke calls **most excellent Theophilus** (Luke 1:1–4; Acts 1:1). Nothing else is known about this Theophilus.

The Apostle Paul calls Luke "our **dear friend, Luke, the doctor**" (Colossians 4:14). Luke was from Antioch, an important city in the Middle Eastern country of Syria. It is possible that Luke met Paul while Paul was living in Antioch. Luke later accompanied Paul on part of Paul's second missionary journey and again on Paul's final voyage to Rome (Acts 27:1; 28:16). Luke knew Paul well; he was, therefore, well qualified to write an account of Paul's life.

Although the book of Acts has been called the "Acts of the

[1] The book of Acts is often called the "Acts of the Apostles." The apostles were the early leaders of the church, most of whom had known or at least seen Jesus, and whom Jesus had appointed to preach the Gospel and establish His church. These apostles included Jesus' original twelve disciples (except for Judas Iscariot), Paul, James, and several others. Through the power of the Holy Spirit, these apostles did many great works.

Apostles," it can just as appropriately be called the "Acts of the Holy Spirit"; because everything the apostles did, they did through the power and guidance of the Holy Spirit. The book of Acts, therefore, is not written only about the acts of men; it is written also about the acts of God's Holy Spirit, who lived within those men.

OUTLINE

A. The Beginnings of the Church (1:1–2:47).
   1. The Post-resurrection Ministry and Ascension of Jesus (1:1–11).
   2. The Choice of Matthias (1:12–26).
   3. The Coming of the Holy Spirit (2:1–41).
   4. Life in the Early Church (2:42–47).

B. The Church in Jerusalem (3:1–5:42).
   1. A Miracle and a Sermon (3:1–26).
   2. First Opposition from the Jewish Leaders (4:1–37).
   3. The Death of Ananias and Sapphira (5:1–16).
   4. Second Opposition of the Jewish Leaders (5:17–42).

C. The Extension of the Church throughout Israel (6:1–12:25).
   1. The Appointment of the Seven (6:1–7).
   2. The Ministry and Death of Stephen (6:8–7:60).
   3. The Gospel in Samaria (8:1–25).
   4. The Conversion of the Ethiopian Eunuch (8:26–40).
   5. The Conversion of Saul (9:1–31).
   6. Peter's Ministry in Israel and the First Gentile Converts (9:32–11:18).
   7. The Establishment of a Gentile Church at Antioch (11:19–30).
   8. Persecution by Herod (12:1–25).

D. The Extension of the Church in Turkey and Greece (13:1–21:16).
   1. Paul's First Missionary Journey (13:1–14:28).
   2. The Council of Jerusalem (15:1–35).
   3. Paul's Second Missionary Journey (15:36–18:23).
   4. Paul's Third Missionary Journey (18:24–21:16).

E. The Extension of the Church to Rome (21:17–28:31).
   1. The Rejection of the Gospel in Jerusalem (21:17–26:32).
   2. The Reception of the Gospel in Rome (27:1–28:31).

CHAPTER 1

Introduction (1:1–5)

1–2 In his **former book** (Luke's Gospel), which Luke sent to **Theophilus,** Luke wrote about **all that Jesus began to do and to teach until the day he was taken up to heaven** (see Luke 1:1–4; 24:51). But after Jesus went into heaven, He did not stop working and teaching. In His place He sent His own Spirit, the Holy Spirit, to live within His disciples (John 20:22). In this way, Jesus continued to work and teach through His Spirit dwelling within the disciples. Through Christ's Holy Spirit the disciples received the power to be Christ's witnesses in the world (verse 8). They were no longer merely "disciples"; they were now APOSTLES, that is, men inspired and sent by the Holy Spirit. No longer were they men filled with fear, hiding and fleeing from their enemies; they were now new men, filled with Christ's Spirit, bold and fearless. As we study the book of Acts, let us remember that just as God worked through these apostles in New Testament times, so He wants also to work through us today. Just as God filled the apostles with His Holy Spirit, so also He wants to fill each one of us today.

3 When Jesus was arrested, the disciples lost all hope (Mark 14:50). Peter, the chief disciple, denied Jesus three times (Mark 14:66–72). In their minds, their leader's life and work had come to an end. This new Christian religion was finished before it even began! These disciples had left everything to follow Jesus (Mark 10:28); now all was lost!

But then the disciples saw the risen Jesus. He was not dead after all! He had risen from the dead! And over a period of forty days following His resurrection, Jesus appeared at various times to His eleven disciples and to many other believers as well (1 Corinthians 15:3–7). The disciples' hope returned. Their faith that Jesus was indeed the Son of God returned. This is why the resurrection of Christ was such an important and central subject in the preaching of the apostles—because it was the resurrection, above all, that proved the GOSPEL of Christ to be true.

Before He died and also after He rose again, Jesus taught His followers a great deal about the KINGDOM OF GOD (Mark 1:14–15). The Jews thought that the "kingdom of God" would be some kind of earthly kingdom. But the true kingdom of God is a spiritual kingdom, which began while Jesus was here on earth. The kingdom of God was manifested in the hearts of men (Luke 17:21). And the kingdom of God is present today in the hearts of all those who believe in Jesus. And when Jesus comes again, this present world—the kingdom of darkness—will come to an end, and the kingdom of God will be fully manifest. Then **at the name of Jesus every knee** [will] **bow, in heaven and on earth and under the earth, and every tongue confess that Jesus Christ is Lord, to the glory of God the Father** (Philippians 2:10–11).

4 After Jesus rose from the dead, He told His disciples to wait in **Jerusalem.**[2] Before they began to preach, before they could be Christ's witnesses, there was something they needed. They needed the **gift** promised by the Father (Luke 24:49). That **gift** was the Holy Spirit (John 14:16,26). In one way they had already received the Holy Spirit (John 20:22). But now they needed the special anointing of the Spirit, that is, the power and authority of the Spirit. They needed to be **baptized with the HOLY SPIRIT** (verse 5). This "baptism" would occur some days later on the day of Pentecost (Acts 2:1–4). For this reason Jesus commanded the

---

[2] **Jerusalem** is one of the main cities of the modern Middle Eastern nation of Israel. In New Testament times it was the capital of Judea, the southern province of Israel. Jerusalem was the center of Jewish religious life; the Jewish temple was located there. Jesus was crucified near Jerusalem.

disciples: **"Do not leave Jerusalem, but wait for the gift my Father promised"**—namely, the baptism, the empowering, of the Holy Spirit.

Today we too need to wait for the **gift** of the Holy Spirit promised by the Father. We must not try to do things for God in our own strength. When Jesus was on earth with His disciples He said to them: **". . . apart from me you can do nothing"** (John 15:5). In the same way, after Jesus left the earth, these disciples (apostles) could do nothing apart from the Holy Spirit.

Let us remember that all true believers in Jesus have received the Holy Spirit. Whatever strength we need for fulfilling God's will is available to us through the Spirit. Let us never say: "I don't have the strength or means to do God's will." Instead, let us just get up and do it. Let us say with the Apostle Paul: **I can do everything through him** (Jesus) **who gives me strength** (Philippians 4:13). For Jesus has promised us: **"I will be with you always, to the very end of the age"** (Matthew 28:20).

5 John the Baptist had said to those who came to him for BAPTISM: **"I baptize you with water, but he** (Christ) **will baptize you with the Holy Spirit"** (Mark 1:8). Here in this verse Jesus says to His disciples: **". . . in a few days you will be baptized with the Holy Spirit."** This was the gift they must wait for. The baptism of the Spirit is the filling, the empowering, the anointing of the Spirit for doing the work of Christ (see 1 Corinthians 12:13 and comment; General Article: Holy Spirit).

Jesus Taken Up Into Heaven (1:6–11)

6–7 Because Jesus' disciples were JEWS, they were hoping that Jesus would still reestablish the independent kingdom of ISRAEL—that is, that He would **restore the kingdom to Israel** (verse 6). Israel was the name of the Jewish nation. In Jesus' time, Israel had fallen under the control of the ROMAN EMPIRE. The Jews had lost their independence. Therefore, whenever Jesus preached, **"The kingdom of God is near"** (Mark 1:15), His disciples thought that He was talking about an earthly kingdom of the Jews. Jesus had told His disciples, **"I confer on you a kingdom . . . so that you may . . . sit on thrones"** (Luke 22:29–30). Here the disciples were hoping that they would get to sit on those thrones right away!

But Jesus did not come to establish such an earthly kingdom. He came to establish a spiritual kingdom. And that kingdom will be fully established when Jesus comes to earth again (Mark 13:26). When that day will be no one knows (Mark 13:32).

8 Then Jesus told His disciples that the kind of power and authority they would receive was not earthly or political. Rather it would be much better than that: it would be the power and authority of the Holy Spirit. This was the **gift** promised by the Father that the disciples must wait for (verses 4–5).

Then Jesus said an amazing thing to His disciples: **"You will be my witnesses . . . to the ends of the earth."** These uneducated, humble, ordinary men would now be the **witnesses**—the representatives and **ambassadors**—of the Son of God! (2 Corinthians 5:20). Along with that, they would also suffer for Christ, and in the end all (except John) would be killed because of Him.

Jesus said that the disciples were to witness in Jerusalem. They were also to be His witnesses **in all Judea and Samaria.**[3] And they were to preach the message of Christ to the **ends of the earth**. And their message was that the kingdom of God had come near, that Jesus Christ had come into the world to save men and women from the punishment for their sin and to reconcile them with God (2 Corinthians 5:18–19).

Not all Christians are called to be preachers. But all Christians are called to be witnesses. The Holy Spirit has been sent to us so that we might be witnesses

---

[3] **Judea** was the southernmost province of Israel, and **Samaria** was the province just north of it. North of Samaria was the province of Galilee.

for Christ. However, there are many Christians today who say, "I have received the Holy Spirit," but who do not witness. This is impossible. A person filled with the Holy Spirit will always witness for Christ. If a person does not witness, it must be said that he is not filled with the Spirit.

9 After His resurrection, Christ appeared a number of times to different groups of believers. Then after forty days he ascended into heaven (see Luke 24:50–51).

10–11 The disciples saw Jesus rise into heaven with their own eyes. Then **two men dressed in white**—that is, two angels—appeared to the disciples. These angels said to the disciples, "It is not necessary for you to be looking toward heaven for Jesus. He has gone to heaven to be with His Father. Don't stand here gazing into the sky. You have much work to do. At the appointed time, Jesus will return to earth the same way He has departed" (Mark 14:61–62).

The two angels called the disciples "men of **Galilee**." Galilee is Israel's northernmost province. Jesus and His disciples first came from Galilee.

Matthias Chosen to Replace Judas (1:12–26)

12 The place from which Jesus ascended into heaven was called the **Mount of Olives**. That mountain was a **Sabbath day's walk** from Jerusalem; that is, it was about three quarters of a mile from Jerusalem. According to the Jewish LAW, the Jews were not supposed to walk more than three quarters of a mile on the **Sabbath**[4] (Saturday).

13 Here Luke gives us the names of Jesus' disciples—except for Judas Iscariot, who betrayed Jesus. When this list of disciples is compared with the list of disciples given in Mark 3:16–19, it can be seen that one name is different. Here, in place of Thaddaeus, **Judas son of James** is written. However, it is the same man; he had two different names.

14 While Jesus' disciples were waiting for the gift of the Holy Spirit, they all **joined together constantly in prayer.** It is mainly through prayer that we obtain the power of the Holy Spirit (Luke 11:13). The disciples **joined together** in prayer. If we want our individual requests to be granted, we need to join together and agree with one another about what to pray for (see Matthew 18:19). Where there is no unity of mind among believers, there the power of the Spirit will not be manifest.

With the disciples were Jesus' mother Mary, some other women, and Jesus' own younger brothers, who were sons of Mary and Joseph. Jesus' best-known brother was James, who later wrote the New Testament letter called "James." The other three brothers were Joses, Judas, and Simon (Mark 6:3). Before Jesus' resurrection, His brothers did not believe in Him (John 7:5). But now they had accepted Him as the Son of God. James himself saw Jesus after He had risen from the dead (1 Corinthians 15:7); later he went on to become the main leader of the church in Jerusalem (Galatians 1:19; 2:9).

15 In addition to Jesus' main disciples, there were in Jerusalem at that time about one hundred and twenty other believers. Perhaps among them were the seventy-two believers whom Jesus sent out ahead of Him to announce the coming of the kingdom of God (Luke 10:1–11).

From this we can understand that during His time on earth Jesus didn't lead great numbers of people to believe in Himself. Jesus' main goal while on earth was to train and spiritually equip a small number of disciples. To these disciples, then, Jesus gave the work of preaching the Gospel and establishing His church all over the world.

16–17 Peter, it seems, was the main leader of this group of believers. Here Peter refers to a prophecy of **DAVID**, the great king of the Jews. David had

[4] The **Sabbath** (Saturday) was the Jewish day of rest, set apart for the worship of God. According to the Jewish law, a Jew was not supposed to do any kind of work on the Sabbath (Exodus 20:8–11). To walk more than three quarters of a mile was considered "work."

prophesied in the Old Testament that one of Jesus' close friends would betray Him (see Psalm 41:9; John 13:18; 17:12).

18–19 In these verses, Luke describes what happened to Judas after he betrayed Jesus. According to Matthew 27:3–8, Judas gave back the money he had received from the Jewish elders and chief priests for betraying Jesus into their hands; then the chief priests, not Judas, went out and bought a field with the money. But because it was really Judas' money, they bought the field in Judas' name. But Judas never received any benefit from that field. Because of remorse for what he had done, Judas hanged himself, and his body swelled up and burst open.

Judas had known that the Jewish leaders were trying to kill Jesus. Perhaps he feared they would try to kill the disciples also. So he thought to himself: "If I cooperate with these Jewish leaders and deliver Jesus into their hands, I will be able to save my own life." But his plan didn't work; in the end he lost his life (see Mark 8:35).

20 Here Peter quotes from Psalm 69:25. Judas' **place**, that is, his field, became deserted. No one wanted it. So it was used as a burial place for foreigners who happened to die in Jerusalem (Matthew 27:7).

Next Peter quotes from Psalm 109:8 to show that they must now select another disciple to take Judas' place. Jesus had chosen twelve main disciples to judge the twelve tribes of Israel[5] (Matthew 19:28); therefore, it was not right that only eleven disciples should remain.

21–22 To qualify for taking Judas' place among the twelve disciples, one needed to have been with Jesus from the beginning of His ministry and to have seen Him after He rose from the dead.

23–24 First the disciples chose two men who were equally qualified to be the twelfth disciple. Then they asked the Lord to show them which of the two He had chosen. Then they drew lots. They trusted that the lot would fall to the man of God's choice, because they knew that God controlled the casting of lots (Proverbs 16:33).

This is the only place in the New Testament where the casting of lots is mentioned as a means of finding out God's will. Most Christians believe that ever since the Holy Spirit came upon the disciples on the day of Pentecost (Acts 2:1–4), it has not been necessary to cast lots to learn what God's will is. The reason, they say, is because the Holy Spirit is now available to all believers, and He is fully able to show them what God's will is in specific circumstances.

CHAPTER 2

The Holy Spirit Comes at Pentecost (2:1–13)

1 The day of Pentecost fell fifty days after Jesus' resurrection. In the Greek[6] language, Pentecost means "fiftieth." According to the Old Testament, the day of Pentecost came on the fiftieth day following the Sunday after the Jewish PASSOVER festival (Leviticus 23:15), which for Christians is the fiftieth day after Easter. The Jews celebrate the **Feast of Weeks** on the day of Pentecost (Exodus 34:22; Deuteronomy 16:9–10). The Jews observe the day of Pentecost for a second reason: they believe that on that day God gave them the Jewish law. Therefore, it was very suitable that on that day God

---

[5] The twelve tribes of Israel were descended from the twelve sons of Jacob, who was the grandson of Abraham, the father of the Jews.

[6] The New Testament was originally written in the Greek language. In New Testament times, Greek was commonly spoken by educated people in the Middle East. For further discussion, see footnotes to comment on Acts 2:4.

should give the disciples the baptism of the Holy Spirit for the first time.

2–3 In the entire history of mankind there have been three events that have been more important than any other: the birth of Jesus, the death and resurrection of Jesus, and the coming of the Holy Spirit in full power on that first day of Pentecost after Jesus' resurrection. No other event in history can compare in importance with these three events. In these verses Luke gives us a description of the third of these three great events.

Jesus' disciples had gathered in a house in Jerusalem.[7] Then all of a sudden they heard a **sound like the blowing of a violent wind** (see John 3:8), and they saw **what seemed to be tongues of fire**. John the Baptist had said that Jesus would baptize **with the Holy Spirit and with fire** (Matthew 3:11). Fire is a sign of God's presence. God appeared before the great Jewish leader Moses **in flames of fire from within a bush** (Exodus 3:2). When the Jews fled from bondage in EGYPT, God went before them **in a pillar of fire** to show them the way (Exodus 13:21–22). And when believers today experience the presence and power of the Holy Spirit, they often say that it's like a fire burning in their hearts. May that fire never go out!

4 Whatever exactly the disciples heard and saw, the important thing is this: **All of them were filled with the Holy Spirit**. From that day on their lives were changed. From that day on they had the power of the risen Christ in their lives. Their fears and doubts were gone. From that day on when they spoke, they spoke with the power and authority of the Holy Spirit. When they healed, they healed through the power of the Holy Spirit. From then on their lives remained fully dependent upon the Holy Spirit and under His control.

Let us remember that today we too can receive that power. That power was not just for those first disciples; it is for all believers. Let it be our constant prayer for ourselves and for each other that we may all remain filled with the Holy Spirit and that His fire will continue burning brightly in our hearts.

The filling of the Holy Spirit does not just take place once. This filling is a continual experience; it is constantly being renewed (see Acts 4:31). From time to time in a believer's life the filling of the Spirit can occur in new and special ways. But it was on that first day of Pentecost that the Holy Spirit first came in power upon believers. And the Holy Spirit has been filling the lives of believers ever since.

Some Christians believe that the "filling" of the Spirit and the "baptism" of the Spirit are two different things. But according to the book of Acts, the event on the day of Pentecost is called both a "baptism" (Acts 1:5) and a "filling" (verse 4). Therefore, from these two verses we cannot see any clear difference between the "baptism" and the "filling" of the Holy Spirit (see 1 Corinthians 12:13 and comment; General Article: Holy Spirit Baptism).

How can we tell if a person is filled with the Holy Spirit? First, we will be able to see the fruit of the Spirit in his life, such as **love, joy, peace** (Galatians 5:22–23). Second, we will be able to see the gifts of the Spirit manifested in his life, such as the gifts of **healing**, of **prophecy**, of speaking in **different kinds of tongues** (see 1 Corinthians 12:7–11). One of these gifts, the gift of speaking in **different kinds of tongues**, was manifested by the disciples on the day of Pentecost.

Usually when the gift of "tongues" is manifested, the language spoken is a spiritual language, not an earthly language. To understand this spiritual language, another gift of the Spirit is needed, the gift of **interpretation of**

---

[7] Some Bible scholars believe that only Jesus' twelve main disciples were present in that house on the day of Pentecost, because in verse 7 it says: "**Are not all these men who are speaking Galileans?**" But among the one hundred and twenty other believers in Jerusalem at that time (Acts 1:15) there were many from Galilee. Therefore, most scholars believe that in addition to Jesus' twelve main disciples there were also other followers of Jesus present in that house when the Holy Spirit came, and that all of them received the baptism of the Spirit.

tongues (see 1 Corinthians 12:10; 14:2,13, 27–28). However, on the day of Pentecost these disciples spoke in the ordinary earthly languages of other countries, which the men of those countries could understand naturally[8] (verse 6).

Christ had commanded His disciples to **go and make disciples of all nations** (Matthew 28:19). Now, through the Holy Spirit's gift of speaking in other languages, the disciples were able to speak to men of different nations in their own languages. However, in New Testament times, the use of this gift in spreading the Gospel was usually not necessary, because most of the people living in the Middle East spoke either Greek[9] or Aramaic,[10] both of which languages the disciples themselves could speak.

Some Christians believe that the ability to speak in other languages is the main sign of the baptism of the Holy Spirit (see Acts 10:44–46; 19:6). These Christians say that whoever does not speak in other tongues has not received the baptism of the Spirit. But most Christians do not agree with this opinion; rather, they believe that the gifts and workings of the Holy Spirit are of many kinds and that the ability to speak in other languages is just one of many manifestations of the Holy Spirit.

It is important to remember one other thing: False spirits and false prophets can also speak in other tongues. Followers of other religions have also spoken in tongues. Therefore, it is always necessary to test what is being said in tongues by understanding its meaning. Simply speaking in some other tongue or making strange noises is not necessarily a sign of the Holy Spirit. The main thing is to understand what is being said. If what is said agrees with Scripture and glorifies Christ, then it is of the Holy Spirit. If what is spoken does not agree with Scripture or if it dishonors Christ, then it most certainly is not of the Holy Spirit (see John 16:13–14; 1 Corinthians 12:3; 1 John 4:1–3 and comments).

5–6 In New Testament times, there were Jews scattered about living in many different nations. Many of these Jews used to come each year to Jerusalem to celebrate the main Jewish religious festivals. One of these festivals was the **Feast of Weeks**, that is, the day of Pentecost (Exodus 34:22; Deuteronomy 16:9–10). Therefore, when Jesus' disciples got up and began speaking in other languages, many of these Jewish pilgrims from other countries heard the commotion and gathered around to see what was happening. To their amazement, they heard these uneducated men from the province of Galilee speaking in their own languages. Perhaps one disciple spoke in one language, and another disciple spoke in another language. Perhaps they spoke in turn, or perhaps they spoke all at once. But however they spoke, the listeners were astounded. "**Are not all these men who are speaking Galileans?**" they asked (verse 7). By the power of the Holy Spirit these disciples were speaking foreign languages they had never spoken or learned before, and they were speaking them perfectly!

7–12 In these verses Luke mentions the different countries and provinces from which these foreign Jewish pilgrims had come. Most of the places were at that

---

[8] When the New Testament writers mention "other languages" (or tongues), they mean either spiritual languages or earthly languages that the speaker has never learned. The point is that those who speak in other languages or tongues have been given a supernatural gift which enables them to speak in that language—whether that language is "spiritual" or "earthly."

[9] Greek was the language spoken by the people of Greece, an important country of southern Europe located on the northern shore of the Mediterranean Sea. However, Greek was commonly spoken by the educated people of most of the other Mediterranean countries as well.

[10] In Christ's time, most of the common people living in the Middle East spoke the Aramaic language. Christ also spoke Aramaic. Today, however, Aramaic is spoken by only a few people in the Middle East.

time provinces of the Roman Empire.[11]

13 Some of the people listening thought that the disciples were drunk. **"They have had too much wine,"** they said. Probably the people who thought this could not understand any of the languages the disciples were speaking; therefore, it seemed to them as if the disciples were just babbling nonsense (see 1 Corinthians 14:23).

Peter Addresses the Crowd (2:14–36)

14–15 After the disciples had finished speaking in tongues, Peter, their chief spokesman, stood up and spoke to the people. He said first of all that the disciples were not drunk, because it was then only **nine in the morning.**[12] Men don't usually drink wine that early!

16–21 Then, in order to explain to the Jews the significance of what they had been hearing, Peter quoted from the Old Testament prophet Joel (Joel 2:28–32).

The term **last days** (verse 17) means the period between Christ's first coming to earth and his second coming at the end of the world; that is, it means this present time. Through the prophet Joel, God said: **"I will pour out my Spirit on all people** (that is, on all believers in Christ), on Jewish and Gentile believers, on their **sons and daughters**, and on all believing **servants, both men and women"** (verse 18).

Joel also wrote that along with the coming of the Holy Spirit there would be other signs as well, such as prophecies, **visions**, and **dreams** (verse 17). One kind of prophecy is the speaking in tongues followed by its interpretation (see 1 Corinthians 14:5). There would be natural signs also: **wonders in the heaven above and signs on the earth below** (verse 19). Joel wrote: **The sun will be turned to darkness** (verse 20). On the day that Christ died, **darkness came over the whole land** from noon until 3 P.M. (Mark 15:33). In such darkness the moon (there was a full moon on the day Christ died) would appear red like **blood**.

But in verses 19 and 20, God, through the prophet Joel, is talking especially about the end of the world and about that **great and glorious day of the Lord**, when Christ will come again to judge all men. That day will be a day of judgment, to be sure; but before then, these **last days**—that is, these present days—are days of salvation for **everyone who calls on the name of the Lord** (verse 21).

22 Almost everyone in Israel knew about the great signs and miracles that **Jesus of Nazareth**[13] had performed during His three years of public ministry (Mark 1:28; Luke 7:14–17).

23 "Nevertheless," Peter said to the Jews, **"you . . . put him to death by nailing him to the cross."**[14] The Jewish leaders had seized Jesus and handed Him over to the Roman governor Pilate to be sentenced to death[15] (see Mark 15:1,9–15). The Jews put Jesus to death **with the help of wicked men**—that is, the Romans, whom the Jews considered to be wicked, or unrighteous, because they did not worship the one true God and did not follow His law.

---

[11] In New Testament times, most of the countries of Europe, northern Africa, and the Middle East had fallen under the control of the Roman Empire. The capital of the Roman Empire was Rome, which is today the capital of the modern European nation of Italy.

[12] In place of the words **nine in the morning**, some versions of the Bible say, "the third hour." According to Jewish custom, the time was reckoned from sunrise, that is, approximately 6 A.M.

[13] **Nazareth** was the town in the province of Galilee where Jesus grew up.

[14] According to Roman custom, the usual method of executing criminals was to nail them to a **cross**. For further discussion, see Word List: Cross.

[15] Because Israel in New Testament times was a province under the control of the Roman Empire, the leaders of Israel (the Jewish leaders) were not allowed to carry out the death penalty themselves. Only the Roman officials could legally put a man to death.

However, Jesus did not suffer and die simply by chance; He died according to **God's set purpose and foreknowledge**. God's purpose was that Jesus should suffer and die for mankind (see Luke 24:25–26,46 and comment). But even though God had determined beforehand that Jesus should die, those who killed Jesus were still fully guilty of His death.

24 Wicked men sentenced Christ to death. But in the end God overturned their judgment by raising Christ from the dead.

25–28 Peter then quoted from Psalm 16:8–11, a Psalm written by David. The main section that Peter wanted to quote comes in verse 27: . . . **you will not abandon me to the grave, nor will you let your Holy One see decay** (see Acts 13:35–37). David was not writing about himself in this Psalm, but was making a prophecy about Christ. In fact, in the Psalm Christ Himself is talking. Here we can see the mind of Christ. He says in the Psalm: "**. . . my heart is glad and my tongue rejoices** (verse 26); **you** (God) **will fill me with joy in your presence**" (verse 28). Indeed, Jesus' suffering did turn to joy; and His shame turned to glory (see Hebrews 12:2).

29–30 Then Peter pointed out that David couldn't have been talking about himself in this Psalm, because later on David did die; that is, he was abandoned **to the grave** and his body saw **decay** (verse 27). Instead, as David wrote this Psalm, he was thinking of a descendant who would not remain in the grave and whose body would not see decay, a descendant whom God had promised to place on David's throne (Psalm 132:11). That descendant was Christ (see Luke 1:30–33).

31–32 God did not abandon Christ **to the grave**, nor did He let Him **see decay**. This has to mean, then, that God raised Him from the dead. In saying this, Peter was trying to show the Jews that their own Scriptures[16] prophesied about the RESURRECTION **of the Christ**[17] (verse 31). But not only did the Old Testament testify of Christ's resurrection; Peter and the other disciples had seen the risen Christ with their own eyes! This Old Testament prophecy had indeed come true!

33 God not only raised Christ to life, but He also exalted Him to His right hand (Luke 22:69). God had given His Holy Spirit to Christ, and now Christ had poured this same Spirit out upon His disciples.

However, let us remember that we are talking here about just one God—Father, Son, and Holy Spirit—always acting together.

34–35 When God raised Jesus to sit at His right hand, the prophecy of Psalm 110:1, which Peter quotes here, was fulfilled. **The Lord** (God) **said to my Lord** (Christ): **"Sit at my right hand . . .** " (verse 34). Here again, David is talking about Christ in this Psalm (see Mark 12:35–36).

36 Finally, we come to the main point of Peter's sermon: "**Therefore let all Israel be assured of this: God has made this Jesus . . . both Lord and Christ**."

Peter has quoted the prophecies of Joel and David to prove that Jesus was not only the **Christ** but also the **Lord**, that is, God. The Jews gave the name "Lord" only to God. Now in this verse, Peter gives the name "Lord" to Jesus also. Above all, it is Jesus' resurrection from the dead that gives the final proof that He is both **Lord and Christ** (see Romans 1:4).

Jesus Christ is not only the greatest teacher; He is not only the greatest prophet; He is not only the greatest incarnation. He is God Himself. **Jesus is Lord** (see Romans 10:9; Philippians 2:11).

---

[16] The Jewish Scriptures are contained in the Old Testament.

[17] The word **Christ** is a Greek word meaning "anointed one." In Hebrew, the Jewish language, the word for "anointed one" is "Messiah." Thus "Christ" and "Messiah" have the same meaning.

Three Thousand Are Baptized (2:37–41)

37 Peter's words **cut** the people **to the heart**. Why? Because Peter had spoken God's word in the power of the Holy Spirit. The word of God is like a sword (Ephesians 6:17), which **penetrates even to dividing soul and spirit, joints and marrow; it judges the thoughts and attitudes of the heart** (Hebrews 4:12). When we speak God's word by the power of the Holy Spirit, then our listeners also will be cut to the heart by our words. Therefore, let us never dare to preach God's word without first asking Him for the power of His Spirit.

38 Then those who had been listening to Peter's sermon asked the disciples, "**Brothers, what shall we do?**" (verse 37). Peter answered: "**Repent and be baptized . . . in the name of Jesus Christ.**" That was all! That was all these men needed to do—men who only a short while before had murdered the Son of God!

But let us examine what Peter says here. **Repent**. To repent means to confess your sins and to turn from them. Many people feel sorry about their sins, but they don't stop committing them. This kind of sorrow is not repentance. To repent of a sin always means to leave that sin.

The second thing Peter says must be done is to be **baptized** in Jesus' name. But baptism doesn't only mean to be immersed in water or to have water sprinkled on one's head. In order to be truly baptized, one must put FAITH in Jesus Christ.[18]

Peter says that we are to be baptized **in the name of Jesus Christ**. When we receive baptism, we tell the world: "Now I stand with Jesus; I will follow Him; I will take up my cross and suffer for His sake" (Mark 8:34). If we are not ready to do this, then we are not ready to be baptized.[19] Because if we are not ready to take up our cross and follow Jesus, we haven't really put faith in Him. Baptism is an outward demonstration of our inner faith. Without faith in our hearts, baptism has no meaning.[20]

After telling the people to repent and be baptized, Peter then said two other things to them. First, after repenting and being baptized, they would receive forgiveness of their sins. Baptism is a sign that our sins have been washed away and that we are now cleansed and pure in God's sight (see Mark 1:4 and comment). Then, after becoming Christians, we must continue to repent each time we sin, and God each time will forgive us and cleanse us afresh (see 1 John 1:9 and comment).

The second thing that Peter said after telling the people to repent and be baptized was that they would **receive the gift of the Holy Spirit**. Peter did not say "gifts" of the Holy Spirit, such as the gift of healing or the gift of prophecy. Rather, he said **gift** of the Holy Spirit—that is, the Holy Spirit Himself. As soon as one becomes a Christian, one receives the Holy Spirit. Without the Holy Spirit, one cannot be a true Christian (Romans 8:9; 1 Corinthians 6:19).

Many Christians say that some time after having put faith in Christ and having received the Holy Spirit the first time, they then have experienced a new filling of the Spirit. These Christians call this new experience of the Spirit a "second blessing," or the "baptism" of the Spirit.[21] They are filled with the Spirit

---

[18] In many churches, Christian parents have their children baptized at a very young age before they are able to have true faith of their own. However, when such children get older, they must believe in Christ for themselves, or their baptism will have no meaning.

[19] Infant baptism is not under discussion here; that is a separate subject (see General Article: Water Baptism).

[20] For further discussion of the significance of baptism, see General Article: Water Baptism.

[21] These Christians believe that the "baptism" of the Holy Spirit is something different from the ordinary receiving of the Spirit that all Christians experience when they first believe. They say that the "baptism" of the Spirit is a special experience that not all Christians have, but one that all Christians should desire and ask God for. For further discussion, see General Article: Holy Spirit Baptism.

in a new and deeper way, and they receive a new power and zeal for serving Christ. But other Christians say that they have experienced this kind of power and zeal from the moment they became Christians. Surely the Holy Spirit can work in different ways in different people's lives. Whatever way we describe the Spirit's work or whatever name we give it, it is the Spirit that is doing the work in each person's life. It is not necessary to compare our own experiences of the Spirit with the experiences of others. Rather, let us be grateful to God for whatever blessings of the Spirit He has given us, and let us daily pray that He might fill us with His Spirit more and more (see 1 Corinthians 12:13 and comment; General Article: Holy Spirit).

39 Even though Peter was himself a Jew speaking to a crowd made up mainly of Jews, he told them that the **promise** (of the Holy Spirit) was not only for Jews, but was also **for all who are far off**—that is, the Gentiles (see Ephesians 2:11–13). The promise of the Holy Spirit is for everyone **whom the Lord our God will call**. God has chosen us, called us, from before the creation of the world (Ephesians 1:4). God knows beforehand who will believe in Christ and who will not. Whoever believes in Christ **will be saved** (verse 21), and will receive the **promise** of the Holy Spirit.

40–41 Peter called his generation a **corrupt generation**, because the men of that generation had crucified Christ, the Son of God. But we must also understand that every generation of men is "corrupt," because most people in every generation refuse to believe in Christ. They too, like Peter's generation, stand condemned.

On that day of Pentecost, about three thousand men accepted Peter's message; that is, they believed in Christ and were baptized. It is not enough to only hear the word; we must also accept it and obey it. Here, on this one day, more people came to believe in Christ than had believed during Christ's entire three years of public ministry (see John 14:12). Truly the Holy Spirit had come upon these disciples with power. From now on they would not simply be disciples—they would be apostles.

The Fellowship of the Believers (2:42–47)

42 In this section Luke gives us a description of the first Christian church. The believers **devoted themselves** to four main things. First, they devoted themselves to the **apostles' teaching.** Those believers didn't have the New Testament, as we do; they had only the Old Testament. Therefore, it was necessary for them to devote themselves to the apostles' teaching, because it was through that teaching that they would learn about Christ and about how to follow Him. And, of course, that same teaching of the apostles later was written down and became the New Testament. Thus, in the same way those early Christians devoted themselves to the teaching of the apostles, so we today should devote ourselves to the study of the New Testament.

The second thing those early believers devoted themselves to was the **fellowship**.

The third thing they devoted themselves to was the **breaking of bread**, that is, the LORD'S SUPPER (see Luke 22:19; 1 Corinthians 11:23–25).

And fourth, they devoted themselves to **prayer**.

When we compare our own church today with that first church, what do we see?

43 The Holy Spirit never ceased working through those apostles. They continued to perform **many wonders and miraculous signs** (see Acts 3:6–7).

44–45 Those first believers turned over all their possessions to the apostles for use by the church as a whole. They didn't keep anything back for themselves.[22] They didn't say of anything, "This is my

[22] They probably did not turn their houses over to the apostles, because in verse 46 Luke says that **they broke bread in their homes**. However, they surely made their homes available to meet any need. They considered that their homes, along with all their other possessions, belonged not to themselves but to God.

own." Instead, they were constantly thinking about the needs of others (see Acts 4:32–35).

Nowadays most Christians don't sell their possessions; they don't have **everything in common** (verse 44). Perhaps it is not necessary for us to do exactly as that first church did in this regard. There is no command saying that we must do as they did.[23] However, there are two things that we must do: one, we must regard all of our possessions, including our own bodies, as belonging to God (Romans 12:1; 1 Corinthians 6:19–20); and two, we must love our neighbors as ourselves (Mark 12:31). If we do these two things, then in God's sight we will be doing as those first Christians did.

46–47 Those first believers did everything together. They broke bread in each other's homes; that is, they celebrated the Lord's supper together, one time in one home, another time in another home. Together with the Lord's supper, they also ate an ordinary meal.

What a godly, joyful, and caring community that first church was! When other people saw the lives of those first believers, they came to join their fellowship. **And the Lord added to their number daily those who were being saved.**

CHAPTER 3

Peter Heals the Crippled Beggar (3:1–10)

1 The apostles continued going to the Jewish temple in Jerusalem to worship. Even though they had put their faith in Christ, they still followed the Jewish religion. Christ and His disciples were Jews. The Christian religion arose out of Judaism. Therefore, it was not necessary for them to stop observing their old religion. Christianity includes Judaism, just as the Christian Scriptures include the Old Testament.

One day **at three in the afternoon,**[24] Peter and John went up to the Jewish temple to pray.

2–5 There they met a man **crippled from birth**. The limbs of any person crippled from birth are always badly shrunken and deformed; so this man's legs would certainly have been very deformed. No medicine or operation could ever restore such a deformity.

The crippled man hoped to get a little money from Peter and John; that was all he was looking for. He held out his hand toward them.

6–7 But Peter and John had no money to give him. They were poor too! They had originally been fishermen, and they had left all in order to follow Jesus. But what they had with them was far better than money. What they had was the power of the Lord Jesus Christ.[25] Peter said to the crippled man, **"In the name of Jesus Christ of Nazareth, walk"**. And then, through the power of the Holy Spirit living within Peter, Jesus healed that man. Notice that the healing was instant and complete.

8–10 What joy! The crippled man had asked for a few pennies. Now he was walking and jumping and praising God!

---

[23] It is not a sin to have possessions; it is a sin to love possessions (see Matthew 6:24; 1 John 2:15 and comments).

[24] In place of the words **at three in the afternoon**, some versions of the Bible say, "at the ninth hour," which is a literal translation of the Greek text.

[25] There are many preachers today who have with them plenty of "silver and gold," but who do not have the power of Christ!

He had never walked in his life before that day.

The people who had seen the miracle were astounded. They had seen this man sitting at one of the temple gates[26] for years. "What has happened? How has it happened?" the people wondered. The prophecy of Isaiah about the coming age of the Messiah (Christ) had come to pass: **Then will the lame leap like a deer** (Isaiah 35:6).

Is there anyone among us who is lame, weak, cast down? Is there anyone without hope, without peace, without purpose? Let that person lift his or her eyes to Jesus and believe. Because Jesus has the complete power and authority to heal, to give strength, to give life—eternal life.

Peter Speaks to the Onlookers (3:11–26)

11 Peter, John, and the newly healed man moved to another part of the temple called **Solomon's Colonnade**. There again a crowd quickly gathered around them.

12 Peter told the crowd, "Don't stare at us in such amazement. We ourselves haven't made this man able to walk. We are ordinary men like yourselves. No, the One who healed this man is the Lord Jesus Christ Himself."

Peter had just performed a great miracle, but he himself refused to accept any credit or praise for it. He gave the entire praise to Christ. Likewise, in everything we do let us follow Peter's example. We can do nothing apart from Christ (John 15:5); therefore, whatever good work we do, we must give Him all the credit. We can take credit only for our sins!

13 Here Peter says that, through this miracle, God **has glorified his servant Jesus**. The miracle was a sign that God was indeed bringing glory to Jesus.

Peter here calls God the **God of Abraham, Isaac and Jacob**. ABRAHAM, Isaac, and Jacob were the three main ancestors of the Jewish people. Abraham was first, then Abraham's son Isaac, and then Isaac's son Jacob. From these three men all Jews are descended.

Even though Jesus was the Son of God, the Jews **handed him over to be killed**. They handed Jesus over to the Roman governor Pilate, because according to Roman law only the Roman governor could condemn a criminal to death. After examining Jesus, Pilate found that He was not guilty of any crime and wanted to release Him, but the Jews refused to accept Pilate's judgment and demanded that He be killed (see Mark 15:1,12–15; Acts 2:23 and comments).

14 The Jews rejected the **Holy and Righteous One**, that is, Christ. Christ was totally pure and without sin (Hebrews 4:15). Because the Jews rejected amd murdered One who was completely holy and righteous, their guilt was even greater.

During the Jewish Passover festival, it was the custom for the Roman governor to release one Jewish prisoner as a gesture of good will. Pilate wanted to release Jesus, but the Jews demanded that Pilate release a murderer named Barabbas instead (see Mark 15:6–11).

15 Peter here calls Jesus the **author of life**. While He was on earth, Jesus raised the dead to life (Luke 7:14–15; John 11:21–25,38–44). But more than that, He gives eternal life to all who believe in Him (John 3:16). Nevertheless, the Jews had caused Him to be put to death. They spared the murderer Barabbas, a taker of life, and killed Jesus, the giver of life! But in the end, **God raised him from the dead**. And Peter says, **"We are witnesses of this"** (see Acts 2:24,32).

16 Peter says that the crippled man was healed by **faith in the name of Jesus**. Having faith in Jesus' name is the same as having faith in Jesus. From Jesus' name we can tell who Jesus is. He is **both Lord and Christ** (see Acts 2:36 and comment).

Here Peter says: **"It is Jesus' name . . . that has given this complete healing to** [the crippled man]." We can understand

[26] There were nine gates leading into the inner part of the Jewish temple. One of them was called **Beautiful**.

here that the expression **Jesus' name** means Jesus Himself.

For the crippled man to be healed, two things were necessary: first, Jesus' power; and second, man's faith—either Peter's faith or the crippled man's faith. For any spiritual work to be accomplished, these two things—Jesus' power and man's faith—are always necessary.

17 The Jews had killed Jesus **in ignorance**. God is always ready to forgive those who sin in ignorance (see Luke 23:34; 1 Timothy 1:13). It is suitable that Peter here shows the Jews a little mercy, because it was only a few weeks earlier that he himself had knowingly denied His Lord three times (Mark 14:66–72).

18 However, it was not by accident that Christ suffered and died. The Old Testament prophets, especially Isaiah, had written that Christ must suffer (Isaiah 53:3–12).

19 In this verse we see the unlimited grace and mercy of God. These Jews had just put to death God's only Son. But now if they repent and turn to God, He will forgive them and wipe away their sins (see Acts 2:38 and comment). They had just taken Christ's life, but God is ready to give them life—if they repent.

20–21 If the Jews repent, Christ will come to them and **restore everything**[27] (verse 21). Christ had been **appointed** for the Jews; that is, He had been appointed to be their Savior. Jesus said: **"I was sent only to the lost sheep of Israel"** (Matthew 15:24). Some Jews did accept Christ; but most did not.

Peter says that Jesus must remain in heaven until the time appointed by God for Him to return again to earth. Then He will truly **restore everything**. Then He will fully establish the kingdom of God. Indeed, He will redeem all creation (Romans 8:19–21).

22–23 Peter here quotes from the words of the great Jewish leader **Moses** in Deuteronomy 18:15,19. Here Moses talks about a **"prophet like me"**—that is, Christ—to whom the Jews must listen (see Hebrews 3:3,5–6). Whoever does not listen to Christ will suffer punishment from God.

24 Not counting Moses, **Samuel** was the first of the regular Old Testament prophets. All of the prophets **foretold these days**—that is, the days of Christ.

25 The Old Testament prophets spoke about Christ's coming. In addition, God had made a COVENANT with Abraham, the father of the Jews, at which time God promised Abraham: **"Through your offspring all peoples on earth will be blessed"** (Genesis 22:18; 26:4). That **offspring** was Christ. In Christ all the nations of the earth—both Jews and Gentiles—will be blessed. Peter says to the Jews: "**. . . you are heirs of . . . the covenant**." If the Gentiles can receive the promise of the covenant, surely the Jews, the original **heirs**, should be able to receive it also.

26 Because the Jews were the original heirs of the prophets and of the covenant, God sent Christ first to them. The opportunity to obtain salvation was given first to the Jews (see Matthew 10:5–6; Luke 24:47; Acts 13:45–46; Romans 1:16). Therefore, Peter exhorts the Jews to repent and to turn from their **wicked ways**, so that they do not lose the chance for salvation that has come to them through God's Son, Jesus Christ.

---

[27] The Jews believed that one day a Messiah (Christ) would come and **restore everything**—in particular, their nation Israel. In New Testament times, Israel had lost its independence and had fallen under the control of the Roman Empire.

CHAPTER 4

Peter and John Before the Sanhedrin (4:1–22)

1–2 The Jewish priests and the **Sadducees**[28] were very unhappy about the commotion that Peter and John were stirring up among the people because of the healing of the crippled man. Worse than that, the Jewish leaders had just caused Jesus to be put to death as a criminal, and now here were His disciples telling everyone that Jesus had risen from the dead!

3–4 So the priests and Sadducees seized Peter and John. But because it was then evening there was not sufficient time left that day for them to be brought before the SANHEDRIN (verse 15), the highest Jewish assembly. Therefore, they put Peter and John into prison for the night.

But the Jewish leaders were too late to stop the effects of the apostles' preaching. On that very day many had believed in Jesus after seeing the healing of the crippled man and hearing Peter's sermon. Now the **number of men**[29] who believed had reached five thousand. Whenever trouble and persecution come upon Christians, their numbers usually grow more rapidly. Therefore, let us rejoice whenever we have the chance to suffer for Christ's sake (Matthew 5:11–12; James 1:2; 1 Peter 4:12–14 and comments).

5–6 **Annas** was the former high priest; his son-in-law **Caiaphas** was the present high priest. Together with other Jewish **elders and teachers of the law,** these men had made the decision to condemn Jesus to death (Mark 15:1; John 18:13–14,24). They had thought that after Jesus' death this new religion would quickly die out. What a mistake they made! Now this new religion had begun to spread out of control!

7 The Jewish rulers, elders, and teachers were worried about the healing of the crippled man. Everybody in Jerusalem was talking about it. So they asked Peter and John, "**By what power or what name did you do this?**"

8–10 Then Peter, the humble, uneducated fisherman from Galilee, stood up before all these leaders and chief men of the Jewish nation. How could he speak to such a group? He was **filled with the Holy Spirit** (verse 8). Jesus Himself had said to His disciples: "**. . . when they arrest you, do not worry about what to say or how to say it. At that time you will be given what to say, for it will not be you speaking, but the Spirit of your Father speaking through you**" (Matthew 10:19–20).

Peter answered their question with great boldness, saying: "**. . . know this, you and everyone else in Israel: It is by the name of Jesus Christ of Nazareth . . . that this man stands before you completely healed** (verse 10). This is the Jesus whom you crucified, but whom God three days later raised from the dead. It is through the power of the risen Christ that this man has been healed" (see Acts 3:16 and comment).

Again Peter took no credit for the healing of the crippled man; he gave all the glory to Christ.

11 Here Peter quotes from Psalm 118:22. The **stone . . . which has become the capstone** is Christ, whom the **builders** (the Jewish leaders) **rejected** (see 1 Peter 2:4,6–8).

12 Not only are men's bodies healed of physical sickness by the name of Jesus; even more important, their souls are saved from spiritual sickness—that is, sin. If the Jewish leaders persist in rejecting Jesus, says Peter, they will find out that they have rejected the only way to heaven. "**. . . for there is no other name under heaven given to men by which we**

[28] The **Sadducees** were a sect of the Jews who did not believe in the resurrection of the dead. Most of the Jewish chief priests were Sadducees. For further discussion, see Word List: Sadducee.

[29] In counting groups of people, the Jews usually counted only the men. Besides the five thousand men, there were also many women who believed.

must be saved." SALVATION is found in no one else.

Some people ask: Why do Christians preach Christ? Why can't Christians leave other people alone to practice their own religions? This verse gives the answer. Only through faith in Christ can a man or woman be saved (see John 14:6 and comment). And Christians are commanded to share this news with others (see Matthew 28:19; Romans 10:13–15; 1 Peter 3:15 and comments).

13 The Jewish leaders were amazed at Peter's answer, and **they took note that these men had been with Jesus**. People had been amazed at Jesus' teaching too (see Matthew 7:28–29; John 7:15). And if we remain in Jesus, and His words remain in us, people will be amazed at our teaching also; they will look at us and take note that we, too, have been **with Jesus**.

14 Peter spoke with great boldness and authority before the Sanhedrin. But not only that, the crippled man who had been healed was standing there also. The presence of the healed man gave proof that Peter's words were true. Peter had said that the crippled man had been healed by faith in the name of Jesus (Acts 3:16), and the Jewish leaders couldn't say anything against it.

15–17 The Jewish leaders were in a dilemma. The apostles had done a great miracle, and thousands of people had begun to follow after them. All the people were praising God and acclaiming the apostles because of this miracle they had done. Besides that, Peter and John had committed no crime. If the Jewish leaders punished the apostles in any way, the people would turn against their leaders. Therefore, the leaders were afraid to take any action against the apostles.

On the other hand, the Jewish leaders didn't want to let the apostles keep on preaching in Jesus' name. If still more people began believing in Jesus, the Jewish leaders would gradually lose their own authority and influence over the people. Their great fear was that the people would turn from them and start following this new religion.

In the end, the leaders decided merely to threaten the apostles and command them to stop preaching in Jesus' name.

18–20 Peter and John did not accept the command of the Jewish leaders. Jesus had given them the opposite command: "**. . . go and make disciples of all nations . . . teaching them to obey everything I have commanded you**" (Matthew 28:19–20). Therefore, Peter and John said to the leaders, "We cannot obey you; we must obey God rather than men" (see Acts 5:29).

In other verses in the New Testament, we are commanded to obey those in authority over us (see Romans 13:1–2; 1 Peter 2:13–14 and comments). However, if those in authority oppose something that God Himself has commanded, then we must not obey them in that matter. We must always obey God over man.

In many countries of the world Christians are forbidden to speak openly about Christ. Who will these Christians obey—God or man? Let them think about the example of Peter and John.

21–22 Even though Peter and John had defied them, the Jewish leaders didn't have the courage to take any action against them except to threaten them once more. After that, they let Peter and John go. The apostles were popular with the people, and the Jewish leaders feared the people. They didn't want to oppose men who had done such an amazing thing as to heal a person crippled for **over forty years**.

However, the thing the Jewish leaders feared most was this preaching that Jesus had risen from the dead. If they could have proved that Jesus did not rise from the dead, then this new religion would have quickly died out. But they were unable to prove that Jesus did not rise; they couldn't find His body.[30] No matter how hard they searched, they couldn't find it. And now this Jesus, who was supposed to be dead, had caused this crippled man to be healed.[31] This crippled

---

[30] They couldn't find Jesus' corpse, because there was no corpse. Jesus had risen!

[31] Jesus Himself, through the Holy Spirit, worked with His apostles to heal the crippled man (Mark 16:20). The actual healer was the Holy Spirit.

man, who was now walking and jumping around, was clear proof that Jesus was indeed alive and working through His apostles. This thought upset the Jewish leaders more than anything.

The Believers' Prayer (4:23–31)

23–24 When the believers heard Peter and John's report, they at once raised their voices in prayer.

25–26 The believers then repeated the words in Psalm 2:1–2. David had prophesied that the **nations**, the **peoples**, the **kings**, and the **rulers** would **gather together against the Lord and against his Anointed One**[32] (Christ). Now this prophecy of David had indeed come true.

27 In this verse, as the believers are praying, they interpret the Psalm they have just quoted. The raging **nations** (verse 25) are the Romans. The **peoples** who **plot in vain** (verse 25) are the **people of Israel**. **Herod** was one of the local **kings** (verse 26) appointed by the Romans to rule over small parts of the Roman Empire.[33] **Pontius Pilate**, the Roman governor in Jerusalem, was one of the **rulers** referred to in the Psalm (verse 26). These were the **kings** and **rulers** who took their stand against the Lord's **Anointed One**.

Notice that the believers here call Jesus "God's **holy servant**" (see Acts 3:26). The Greek word for **servant** that is used here can also mean "son." Jesus was both God's servant and God's Son. He was an obedient **servant** who suffered unto death (Isaiah 42:1; 52:13–14; 53:11–12). And He was God's only Son (Psalm 2:7; Mark 1:11), who was appointed and **anointed** to be the Messiah (Christ), the Savior of the world.

28 The enemies of Christ thought that they had killed Him by their own decision and power. But, in fact, they had merely fulfilled God's own plan and purpose. God had decided long before that His Son Christ must suffer and die (Acts 2:23; 3:17–18). Christ was appointed to be man's Savior; and in order to save men from their sins, it was necessary for Him to take the punishment for their sins, which was death (see Mark 10:45 and comment).

Notice how God is able to use men's evil actions to bring about great good. Men oppose God, but He overcomes their evil with good (Romans 12:21). Evil men murdered the innocent Christ; but by means of that murder God made Christ a sacrifice for the forgiveness of sins—that is, He made Christ our Savior.

29–30 Then the believers prayed for **boldness**. They prayed that in spite of the threats of the Jewish leaders the apostles might have **great boldness** to continue preaching God's word. They also asked God to continue working through the apostles **to heal and perform miraculous signs and wonders**.

31 After they had finished praying the Holy Spirit again came upon them in power. An earthquake struck the room where they had gathered. **And they were all filled with the Holy Spirit**. From this we can understand that believers are not just filled with the Spirit once at the beginning of their Christian lives; they can be filled with the Spirit many times (see verse 8). In fact, we need to keep on being filled with the Spirit over and over again (see Ephesians 5:18 and comment). When we are filled with the Spirit, then we shall speak the word of God **boldly**.

The Believers Share Their Possessions (4:32–37)

32–35 Let us look again at this first Christian church. All the believers were **one in heart and mind**. They **shared everything they had** (verse 32); that is, they let others use their possessions as if they were commonly owned by everyone (see Acts 2:44–45 and comment). **With**

---

[32] The Greek word for **Anointed One** is "Christ." In the Hebrew (Jewish) and Aramaic languages the word for **Anointed One** is "Messiah."

[33] Throughout the Roman Empire there were a number of these "puppet rulers," who had been given limited authority by the Romans to rule over their local area. King **Herod** was the ruler of the province of Galilee (see Luke 23:6–7; Acts 12:1 and comments).

great power the apostles continued to testify . . . and much grace was upon them all (verse 33). **There were no needy persons among them** (verse 34), because everyone's possessions were **distributed to anyone as he had need** (verse 35).

These things are written to be an example for us today, so that our churches also might be like that first church in Jerusalem. If our church today is not like that first church, then we need to pray urgently that it will soon become so (see Acts 2:42–47).

36–37 Luke here gives us the example of **Barnabas**, who sold a field and handed the money over to the church. That same Barnabas later became a famous preacher and a close colleague of the Apostle Paul (see Acts 9:26–27; 11:25–26; 13:2–3).

CHAPTER 5

Ananias and Sapphira (5:1–11)

1–2 What was Ananias and Sapphira's sin? They turned over part of the money from the sale of their land, saying it was the whole price. Their sin was to lie. They had a right to keep back as much of the money as they wanted; there was nothing wrong in that. They were not obligated to give any of it. What they did wrong was to lie about it. **SATAN** the liar had filled their hearts (verse 3).

3–4 How did Peter know that Ananias had lied? He knew through the Holy Spirit. The Holy Spirit had given Peter a **message of knowledge** (1 Corinthians 12:8).

Ananias didn't have to give Peter any of the money; he didn't have to sell the land in the first place. Then, why did Ananias lie about the money he kept back for himself? Because he wanted to show Peter and the others that he was more generous and devoted than he really was. He wanted to appear like a very good Christian who was willing to sacrifice everything for Christ. But it wasn't only men he had tried to deceive; he had tried to deceive the Holy Spirit of God.

Let each of us examine ourselves. Have we from time to time tried to appear better or more worthy than we really are? Have we ever tried to take the praise for some good work that we didn't do? Or have we tried to avoid the blame for some bad work that we did do? If the answer to any of these questions is yes, then we have behaved like Ananias. We have tried to deceive the Holy Spirit.

5–6 Ananias' guilt had been revealed. He was filled with fear. Perhaps his heart stopped because of fear. Whatever happened, it wasn't Peter who killed him. God's judgment fell on him. Ananias had lied to the Holy Spirit; therefore, the Holy Spirit punished him.

7–11 Sapphira also lied to Peter. Peter gave her an opportunity to tell the truth, but she lied. She and her husband had conspired **to test the Spirit of the Lord** (verse 9). That is, they had knowingly sinned, thinking that God wouldn't see or wouldn't care. How wrong they were!

Peter knew through the Holy Spirit that Sapphira would die just like her husband. He said to her, "The men who buried your husband are here, **and they will carry you out also**". And immediately she fell dead at Peter's feet.

Were Ananias and Sapphira true believers? Only God knows. Perhaps God destroyed their **sinful nature** so that their spirits might **be saved on the day of the Lord** (see 1 Corinthians 5:5 and comment). We do not know. But one thing we do know is this: to deliberately sin against God is an extremely dangerous thing (see Hebrews 10:26–27 and comment). That is why the **whole church** was seized with **fear** (verse 11). The other believers began to ask themselves: "Have I tried to deceive God in this way? Will God judge me in this way also?" If anyone has any doubt on this matter, let him remember the words of the Apostle Paul: **The Lord knows those who are his. . . . Everyone who confesses the name of the Lord must turn away from wickedness** (2 Timothy 2:19).

The Apostles Heal Many (5:12–16)

12–14 The believers continued meeting in the part of the temple called Solomon's Colonnade (Acts 3:11). **No one else dared join them** (verse 13)—that is, no one who was not a true believer dared join them—because everyone had heard what had happened to Ananias and Sapphira. Therefore, only those with true faith joined the believers. **Nevertheless, more and more men and women believed in the Lord and were added to their number.**

15–16 The Holy Spirit continued performing signs and wonders through the apostles. From this verse we can understand that some people were healed simply by having Peter's shadow fall on them (see Acts 19:11–12). The apostles were doing the same things that Jesus did while He was here on earth (see Mark 1:32–34; 5:27–29).

The Apostles Persecuted (5:17–32)

17–18 When Peter and John healed the man who had been crippled for over forty years (Acts 3:1–7), many people at that time began to follow this new Christian religion. But now every day the apostles were healing many who were sick, and so more people than ever were following after the apostles. Therefore, the high priest and the other Jewish leaders were **filled with jealousy** (verse 17), and put the apostles in jail.

19–20 God then sent an ANGEL to open the doors of the jail (see Acts 12:5–10). The angel didn't say to the apostles, "Now, run home and hide." Instead, the angel said, "Go back to the temple and keep on teaching. Tell the people the **full message of this new life**"—that is, the full message of salvation.[34]

21–26 The next day the high priest called together the **Sanhedrin**, that is, the **full assembly of the elders** of the Jews (Acts 4:5). They all thought that the apostles were still in jail. But when they sent officers to the jail to bring the apostles before the Sanhedrin, the apostles weren't there! They had gone. The angel who rescued them had even shut all the doors again! (verse 23). Perhaps when the angel freed the apostles, he had caused the guards to fall into a deep sleep.

27–28 The high priest accused the apostles not only of continuing to preach about Christ, but also of trying to blame the Jewish leaders for His death. The Jews thus had a double reason for being upset with the apostles.

29–32 Again Peter and the other apostles spoke boldly before the Sanhedrin. Indeed, Peter preached Christ right there in the assembly to the Jewish leaders themselves. The apostles called the Jewish leaders "murderers of Christ" right to their faces! "**. . . you had** [Christ] **killed by hanging him on a tree**[35] (cross)," said Peter (verse 30). "But then," says Peter in verse 31, "God raised Christ up and **exalted him to his own right hand**" (see Acts 2:23,32–33; 4:10; Ephesians 1:20–21).

"**We are witnesses of these things,**" said Peter. "We cannot keep silent; we are commanded to tell these things to others. **We must obey God rather than men!**" (verse 29).

The apostles had already said this to the Jewish leaders once before (Acts 4:18–20). Not only were the apostles witnesses of these things, but the Holy Spirit Himself was also giving witness through the believers. When they spoke, the Holy Spirit was also speaking; because every believer—that is, everyone who obeys

---

[34] In the Aramaic language (which was Peter's language), the word used in this verse for **life** can also mean "salvation" (see Acts 13:26).

[35] According to Jewish law, the bodies of executed criminals were hung on a tree so that all could see their disgrace (Deuteronomy 21:22–23). Therefore, to be crucified—which was like being hung on a "tree"—was a very great disgrace in Jewish eyes.

God—has been given the Holy Spirit (verse 32).

God exalted [Christ] **. . . as Prince and Savior** (verse 31). The word **Prince** used in this verse means "Lord." If we do not accept Christ as our **Prince** or Lord, He cannot be our **Savior**. Jesus is both our Lord and our Savior (Acts 2:36). If we want Him to save us, we must be ready to obey Him.

God exalted Christ **that he might give repentance and forgiveness of sins to Israel**. Christ gives us a new heart; He gives us GRACE to repent. But we ourselves must do the repenting. Without repentance, there can be no forgiveness of sin.

Gamaliel's Advice (5:33–42)

33–34 The Jewish leaders, especially the chief priests and Sadducees, wanted to sentence the apostles to death. But they couldn't do so without getting the agreement of those members of the Sanhedrin who were Pharisees.[36] **Gamaliel** was a leader of the Pharisees; furthermore, as a teacher of the law, he was highly respected by all Jews.

35–37 Gamaliel gave the examples of two people, **Theudas** (verse 36) and **Judas the Galilean** (verse 37), who some time earlier had led revolts against the Roman Empire. These two men had been killed and their followers had scattered and disappeared. Gamaliel was suggesting that perhaps, with their leader Jesus dead, these apostles, too, would soon scatter and disappear.

38–39 Therefore, Gamaliel advised the Jewish leaders to let the apostles go. If their preaching was not from God, it would come to nothing. But if it was from God, then to oppose the apostles' preaching would be to oppose God Himself. Besides, if this new religion was truly from God, it would be impossible to stamp out anyway! Such was Gamaliel's wise advice.

40 The Jewish leaders heeded Gamaliel's advice. They gave the apostles a small punishment, a flogging, and then let them go. The leaders also ordered the apostles one last time **not to speak in the name of Jesus**. But even as they gave the order, the leaders knew that the apostles would not obey it.

41–42 When we suffer **for the Name**—that is, for Jesus' sake—then we are truly His disciples, His friends, His brothers. This was the apostles' experience, and that is why they left the Sanhedrin **rejoicing**. If God appoints us to suffer disgrace for Christ's sake, then we, too, should rejoice. To receive dishonor from the world for Christ's sake is to receive honor from God (see Hebrews 11:24,26). The apostles rejoiced because they had been **counted worthy** to share in Christ's sufferings. There is no greater honor than to suffer dishonor for Christ's sake.

Jesus had warned His disciples that they would be called to suffer for His sake. He had told them: "**You will be handed over to the local councils and flogged in the synagogues**" (Mark 13:9). His words had now come true. Jesus had also said to them: "'**No servant is greater than his master.' If they persecuted me, they will persecute you also**" (John 15:20).

But Jesus also promised that those who suffer for Him would be abundantly rewarded. "**Blessed are you when people insult you, persecute you and falsely say all kinds of evil against you because of me. Rejoice and be glad, because great is your reward in heaven**" (Matthew 5:11–12). And Christians have been holding on to that promise ever since (see Romans 8:18; 2 Corinthians 4:16–17 and comments).

---

[36] The Pharisees were a party of the Jews. The Apostle Paul, before he became a Christian, had been a very strict Pharisee, and the Gamaliel mentioned here had been his teacher (Acts 22:3). For further discussion, see Word List: Pharisee.

CHAPTER 6

The Choosing of the Seven (6:1–7)

1 In this section, all the believers are called **disciples** (verses 1–2,7). The original twelve disciples had now become "apostles."

There is a very important truth to be seen here. All Christians are **disciples**. There are not two kinds of Christians—one kind who are ordinary believers and another kind who are specially chosen to be "disciples." That is a false idea; we are all called to be **disciples**. Some people think that for most Christians the road of life is supposed to be relatively easy, and that only for a few so-called "disciples" is the road supposed to be hard. But that is not so. Every Christian is called to pass through the **narrow gate** and to walk on the **narrow road** of discipleship (see Matthew 7:13–14 and comment). Every Christian is called to take up his cross and follow Jesus (see Mark 8:34; Luke 14:26–27 and comment).

Among the believers a disagreement arose between the **Grecian Jews** and the **Aramaic-speaking community**. While Jesus was on earth there had been only Aramaic-speaking Jews among His followers. At that time the Gentiles and Greek-speaking Jews from other countries had not yet begun to believe in Christ. In New Testament times there were two main groups of Jews: first, those who spoke Hebrew or Aramaic[37] and lived in Israel; and second, those who spoke Greek[38] and lived in other countries of the Roman Empire.

In Jesus' time, some Greek-speaking Jews also lived in Jerusalem, and after Jesus' resurrection some of them believed in Him. Among them were some widows. After some time, these Greek-speaking Jewish believers began to complain that their widows were not getting their fair share of the food that the apostles were distributing each day to the needy in the church. Recall that many of the believers had sold their possessions and turned the money over to the apostles to be distributed to those in need, among whom were always widows (Acts 4:34–35). It's possible that the apostles were so busy with other duties that they didn't have time to see that the food was distributed to everyone equally.

Notice how quickly complaining and division arose in that first Christian church! And the very first dispute was basically over a money matter—how the money of the church was to be spent and the goods distributed. Even though the number of disciples was rapidly increasing, Satan was there trying to bring division, discontent, and envy.

2–4 In the church different Christians have different tasks. The apostles had been especially appointed to preach and teach the word and to pray. Therefore, they appointed seven other men to distribute the food. Later on, those in the churches who performed such works of service became known as **deacons** (1 Timothy 3:8–10).

The apostles said that the seven men chosen for this work must be **full of the Spirit and wisdom**. Likewise, in our churches today we must select as pastors, elders, and deacons only those who are **full of the Spirit and wisdom**.

The apostles here have given us a good example to follow. If any leader becomes so busy that he can't fulfill all his obligations and duties satisfactorily, then he should delegate some of his duties to some other worthy person in the church. However, there are many leaders who prefer to keep all the authority for

---

[37] Hebrew and Aramaic are separate, though closely related, languages. Hebrew was the special language of the Jews, while Aramaic was the common language of most of the Middle Eastern people (including Jews).

[38] Greek was the language most commonly spoken by educated people throughout the Roman Empire—except in Italy, where Latin was spoken. (Latin was the official language of the Roman government.)

themselves and not share it with others. This is not right. For example, it is best if pastors and preachers do not take responsibility for the financial affairs of the church. It is better if they devote their time to **prayer and the ministry of the word** (verse 4).

5–6 The seven men chosen here all have Greek names; therefore, we can conclude that they were all Greek-speaking Jews. The first one mentioned here, **Stephen**, is the subject of verses 8–15 and all of Acts Chapter 7. The second, **Philip**, appears at length in Acts Chapter 8. Nothing is known about the other five.

Notice that all the disciples—that is, all the church members—first chose the seven men. Then, after that, the apostles laid hands on them and commissioned them for their work. To commission people by the laying on of hands was a Jewish custom (Numbers 27:22–23). The custom soon became common among Christians. Some Christians believe that for a person to obtain the full blessing of the Holy Spirit it is necessary to have a pastor or elder lay hands on him (see Acts 8:17; 9:17; 19:6). However, that does not seem to be the case in this passage, because these seven men were **full of the Spirit** before anyone laid hands on them (verse 3).

7 A growing church is a living church. A non-growing church is a dead church. That first church was certainly alive! Even many of the Jewish priests believed in Christ and came and joined the church.

Stephen Seized (6:8–15)

8–10 Stephen was a man **full of faith and of the Holy Spirit** (verse 5). For this reason, he was also **full of God's grace and power** (verse 8). Anyone who is filled with faith and with the Spirit inwardly will manifest God's **grace and power** outwardly.

There were many Jewish synagogues in Jerusalem. One of them was called the **Synagogue of the Freedmen**. The Jews of that synagogue began to oppose Stephen. But they couldn't stand up against his **wisdom or the Spirit by which he spoke** (verse 10); therefore, they began to accuse him falsely behind his back.

11 They **secretly persuaded** some men to bear false witness against Stephen. Perhaps they paid these men some money for doing this. Their false accusation was this: that Stephen had blasphemed **against Moses** (that is, against the Jewish law which Moses received from God) **and against God**. This same accusation of blasphemy had earlier been brought against Jesus Himself (Mark 14:61–64).

12–14 The Jews seized Stephen and brought him before the Sanhedrin. Then they called the false witnesses. These witnesses falsely accused Stephen of **speaking against the holy place** (the Jewish temple in Jerusalem) **and against the law** (verse 13). Jesus had spoken about the destruction of the "temple" of His body (John 2:19–21), and Stephen had evidently repeated Jesus' words. But just as Jesus' own words had been twisted by false witnesses, so Stephen's words were twisted by these false witnesses in the same way.[39] In Jesus' case, the witnesses had accused Jesus of saying: **"I will destroy this man-made temple"** (see Mark 14:57–58). Here these false witnesses accuse Stephen of using these same words.

Jesus had once said about Himself: **". . . one greater than the temple is here"** (Matthew 12:6). Stephen well understood Jesus' meaning: Now that the Messiah had come, the Jewish temple and all the Jewish sacrifices and ceremonial traditions were no longer necessary (see Hebrews 7:18–19; 8:7,13 and comments). Stephen no doubt had said this to the Jews, and this is what had made them so angry with him.

---

[39] False witnesses don't usually speak complete lies. Usually they take the truth and then twist it. In this way they are able to persuade many people that what they say is the truth. Satan is very clever! Let us remember, however, that a truth that is twisted is the same as a lie. To deliberately twist the truth is just as bad in God's sight as to speak an outright lie.

CHAPTER 7

Stephen's Speech—The Jewish Ancestors (7:1–16)

1 **"Are these charges true?"** the high priest asked Stephen. "Have you spoken these things against our temple and against the Jewish law?"

In replying, Stephen didn't speak in his own defense. Rather, he spoke in defense of the Gospel of Christ—that is, in defense of this new Christian religion that was being opposed by the Jews.

In his speech Stephen seeks to show that it was never God's intention to live among men in only one country and in only one temple. God's true people, that is, those who truly believe in Jesus Christ, can be of any race or of any country. To show this, Stephen in this chapter gives a brief history of the Jewish people beginning with Abraham, the first Jew, and continuing right up to the time of Christ. In his speech, Stephen shows from the Jews' own Scriptures (the Old Testament) that this new Christian religion is now God's true religion.

2–3 **Abraham** was the first Jew. At first Abraham lived in **Mesopotamia,** which was also called the **land of the Chaldeans** (verse 4), and is now the modern Middle Eastern nation of Iraq. While Abraham was living there, God spoke to him, saying: **"Leave your country . . . and go to the land I will show you"**. So Abraham left his country and went to the place where God led him. In doing this, Abraham has given an example of obedience for all of us to follow (see Hebrews 11:8 and comment).

4 Abraham first went to a city called **Haran,** which lay to the north of present-day Israel in what is now modern Turkey. After Abraham had been in Haran for some years, God spoke to him again saying: **"Leave your country . . . and go to the land I will show you"** (Genesis 12:1). So Abraham left Haran and journeyed to the **land of Canaan** (Genesis 12:4–5)—that is, Israel—**"this land where you are now living,"** says Stephen to the Jews.

5 Canaan (Israel) was the land that God had promised to give to Abraham and his descendants (Genesis 17:8). But Abraham himself never took possession of the land—**not even a foot of ground.** Abraham's true inheritance was in heaven (see Hebrews 11:9–10).

When God promised to give the land of Canaan to Abraham and his descendants, Abraham was an old man and had no children. Nevertheless, Abraham believed God's promise.

6–7 God said to Abraham, **"Your descendants will be strangers in a country** (Egypt) **not their own"**. God also told Abraham that after his descendants (the Jews) had been enslaved in EGYPT for four hundred years, He would punish Egypt and lead the Jews back to the promised land of Canaan (Genesis 15:13–16; Exodus 12:29–36).

Abraham's descendants (the Jews) remained for four hundred years in Egypt, as God had said. During that long period, God's promise to give them the land of Canaan remained unfulfilled. God does not always fulfill His promises immediately; we must learn to wait patiently (2 Peter 3:8–9).

8 Then God gave Abraham the **covenant of CIRCUMCISION.** Circumcision is the cutting away of the extra skin at the end of the penis. God commanded Abraham and all his descendants to be circumcised; this was to be the outward sign of being a Jew (Genesis 17:10–13). Circumcision was the sign of the **covenant** that God made with Abraham. And this was the covenant God made with Abraham: **"I will make you into a great nation . . . and all peoples on earth will be blessed through you"** (Genesis 12:2–3).

When Abraham was one hundred years old he became the father of **Isaac** (Genesis 21:2–5). Then Isaac became the father of **Jacob** (Genesis 25:26). Then Jacob had twelve sons, who became the

patriarchs of the twelve tribes of Israel, the Jewish nation (Genesis 35:23–26).

9 Here in verses 9–15, Stephen explains how the Jews first came to Egypt. **Joseph** was the eleventh son of Jacob. Jacob loved Joseph more than his other sons; therefore, Joseph's older brothers became jealous of him, and sold him as a slave to some merchants traveling to Egypt (Genesis 37:3–4,25–28,36).

Just as Joseph's brothers had been jealous of Joseph, so had the present Jews been jealous of Jesus. Evil men are always jealous of good men.

10 God gave Joseph **wisdom and enabled him to gain the goodwill of Pharaoh king of Egypt.**[40] In particular, God gave Joseph the ability to interpret dreams. Joseph interpreted one of Pharaoh's dreams, and Pharaoh was so impressed with Joseph's **wisdom** that he made Joseph **ruler over Egypt** (Genesis 41:15–43).

11 According to Joseph's interpretation, Pharaoh's dream indicated that a severe famine was coming to Egypt and Canaan (Israel), which would last for seven years. This came true, just as Joseph had said. When the famine came, Joseph's father and brothers living in Israel began to suffer from lack of food. But in Egypt, Joseph had wisely stored up much grain in advance, and no one went hungry (Genesis 41:54–57).

12 Hearing that there was plenty of food in Egypt, Jacob sent his sons there to get grain. The sons did not recognize their younger brother Joseph, whom they had earlier sold into slavery. He was now the ruler of Egypt under Pharaoh! (Genesis 42:1–3,6–8).

13–14 When Joseph's brothers came a second time to Egypt to get grain, Joseph revealed to them who he was. Then Joseph sent for his father Jacob and his entire family to come and live in Egypt (Genesis 43:1–2; 45:1–10).

15–16 Jacob and eventually all of his twelve sons died in Egypt. But later their bones were carried to Israel to be buried (Genesis 50:4–9; Joshua 24:32).

Stephen's Speech—Moses (7:17–43)

17 As the ancestors of the Jews moved from one country to another, God never forgot the covenant He had made with Abraham. God always fulfills His promises at the right time.

God had promised Abraham that his descendants would take possession of the land of Canaan (Israel). When the time came for the promise to be fulfilled, the **number of our people in Egypt**—that is, the Jews—had greatly increased.

18–19 A new king was ruling Egypt at that time. This new Pharaoh thought that the Jews had become too numerous, so he ordered all the newborn male children of the Jews to be thrown into the river (Exodus 1:7–9,22).

If such terrible persecution had not come upon the Jews, they would never have agreed to leave Egypt and go to the land that God had promised them. In order to fulfill His purposes, God allowed the necessary amount of persecution to come upon His people at the appointed time.

20–22 Moses was born just at this time. For three months, Moses' Jewish mother and father refused to obey the order of the new Pharaoh to throw the child into the river. Instead, they hid the child in their home, because they saw that **he was no ordinary child** (verse 20). They were not afraid of the king's edict (see Hebrews 11:23). Finally, when they could no longer hide Moses at home, they placed him by the river where the Pharaoh's daughter came to bathe. They hoped that she might find him and care for him because of his beauty. And indeed she did find Moses, and she took him home and made him her son (Exodus 2:1–10). Thus, as happened with Joseph in a previous generation, Moses also became powerful in the land of Egypt.

23–29 For forty years no one except

[40] Most of the kings of Egypt were called **Pharaoh,** just as the Roman emperors were called "Caesar."

Pharaoh's daughter knew that Moses was really an Israelite, that is, a Jew. For all that time he had remained separate from his **fellow Israelites**. But finally one day he decided to meet some of them (verse 23).

Moses saw an Egyptian mistreating one of the Jews; becoming angry, Moses killed the Egyptian. Moses knew somehow that he had been appointed by God to deliver the Jews from persecution. But his fellow Jews did not accept him (Exodus 2:11–14).

Not only that, the news quickly spread that Moses was a Jew, and that he had killed an Egyptian. Therefore, Moses fled from Egypt and went to **Midian**, located on the eastern edge of the Sinai desert (Exodus 2:15). Just as Joseph had been forced by his brothers to leave his own country and go to a foreign land, so Moses now had to leave Egypt and become a foreigner in another land, Midian.

30–34 Moses lived in Midian for forty years. By the end of that time, he had reached the age of eighty. It took God that long to prepare Moses for the work to which He had called him! At the end of the forty years, an angel of God[41] appeared to Moses **in the flames of a burning bush** (verse 30).

God told Moses that the place where he was standing was **holy ground** (verse 33). The Jews believed that there was only one "holy ground," and that was the site of their temple in Jerusalem. Stephen's point was that in whatever place God is present, that place is "holy." God appeared to Abraham in Mesopotamia (verse 2). Now God had appeared to Moses in the Sinai desert.

Speaking from the burning bush, God told Moses to go back to Egypt. It was God's plan that Moses should free the Jews from bondage (Exodus 3:1–10).

35 Here Stephen begins to compare Moses with Christ, though without mentioning Christ by name. The Jews at first rejected Moses. Nevertheless, God sent that same Moses to them to be their **ruler and deliverer**. Similarly, the Jews rejected Christ, whom God had sent to be their Lord and Savior.

36 Moses returned to Egypt and delivered the Jews by means of **wonders and miraculous signs**. The story of the Jews' escape from Egypt is told in Exodus Chapters 8–12.

As soon as the Jews left Egypt, Pharaoh and his army began to chase after them. With the Egyptian army close behind them, the Jews came to the shore of the **Red Sea**. Then, through Moses, God separated the water of the Sea to the right and to the left, so that the Jews could cross on dry land. Thus the Jews crossed to the other side in safety. But when the Egyptian army tried to cross after them, God allowed the water of the Red Sea to fall back over them, and they were all drowned (Exodus 14:5–28).

After that, Moses led the Jews for forty years in the desert of the Sinai peninsula, which lies between Egypt and Israel.

37 Here Stephen quotes Moses' words to the **Israelites** (Jews): **"The Lord your God will raise up for you a prophet like me from among your own people"** (Deuteronomy 18:15). Peter had already told the Jews earlier that Christ was the very prophet about whom Moses had spoken (Acts 3:22–23).

Now we can understand why Stephen has said all these things about Moses to the Jewish leaders of the Sanhedrin: because Christ was that prophet who Moses said would be **like** himself. Just as the Jews at first rejected Moses and then afterward in the Sinai desert repeatedly disobeyed him, so now the present-day Jews had rejected and disobeyed Christ. Jesus Himself said to the Jews: **"If you believed Moses, you would believe me, for he wrote about me"** (John 5:46–47). Stephen is, in effect, saying here: Let the Jews of the Sanhedrin recognize Christ! Christ is the very **prophet** Moses spoke of. Let the Jews know that this same Christ has been chosen and anointed by God to be their Savior and to deliver them from bondage

---

[41] In the Old Testament, when God appeared to people, He usually appeared to them in the form of an angel.

to sin, just as Moses delivered their ancestors from bondage in Egypt.

38 Moses was **in the assembly in the** (Sinai) **desert**. There in the desert were God's people, His "church." An **angel** was also with them—that is, God Himself was with them in the form of an angel (see verses 30–34 and comment). God had said to the Jews: "**My Presence will go with you**" (Exodus 33:14). The **angel**, therefore, was God's **Presence**. Through the angel, God spoke with Moses on Mount Sinai and gave him the law which God Himself had written on stone tablets—which Stephen here calls God's **living words** (Exodus 24:12; 31:18; 32:15–16).

39–41 Moses remained on the top of Mount Sinai for forty days in order to receive God's law. While Moses was on the mountain, the Jews got impatient and turned away from God. They built an image of a calf out of gold and began to worship it (Exodus 32:1–6).

42–43 Because the Jews deliberately disobeyed God and made an idol to worship in place of God, God **gave them over to the worship of the heavenly bodies**.[44] These disobedient Jews didn't just worship idols made with their own hands; they also began to worship stars and planets. Here Stephen quotes from the prophecy of Amos in Amos 5:25–27. In this prophecy, God says to the Jews: "Instead of worshiping me, you have worshiped the idols **Moloch** and **Rephan**. Because you have done this, **I will send you into exile beyond Babylon**" (verse 43). And indeed, God later did punish the Jews by driving them out of Israel and sending them as prisoners into exile in **Babylon**.[45]

Stephen's Speech—God's House (7:44–53)

44 In the Sinai desert, God's **tabernacle of Testimony** was with the Jews. The **Testimony** was God's testimony—that is, the two stone tablets on which God had written His law (see Exodus 31:18; Revelation 15:5–6 and comment).

God had told Moses exactly how to make the tabernacle (Exodus 25:8–9). While they were in the desert, the Jews did not have a big permanent temple like the one that was later built in Jerusalem. Their **tabernacle** was only a tent, and wherever the Jews went, they took the tent with them.

45 For forty years the Jews wandered in the Sinai desert. At the end of that time, a new leader, Joshua, led them into Israel, the land that God in the beginning had promised to give to Abraham's descendants.

At that time a number of Gentile tribes were living in Israel, and with God's help the Jews drove them out. Finally, in King David's time, after many battles, the Jews took possession of the entire land.

The Jews took the **tabernacle** into Israel with them, and for many years, up **until the time of David** when the main Jewish temple was built, the Jews worshiped God in that tabernacle.

46 King David desired to build a proper temple for God (2 Samuel 7:1–2). But God, through the prophet Nathan, told David He didn't need to dwell in a big temple. For all the years He had been with the Jews thus far, He had been dwelling in a tabernacle made out of a tent. Why should He now need a big temple? (2 Samuel 7:5–7).

Then God said to David: "**I will raise up your offspring** (Christ) **to succeed you, who will come from your own body, and I will establish his kingdom. He is the one who will build a house for my Name, and I will establish the throne of his kingdom forever. I will be his father, and he will be my son**" (2 Samuel 7:12–14).

47 In the end, David didn't build the Jewish temple; his son Solomon did. It was Solomon who built the great temple in Jerusalem, where the Jews worshiped right up to New Testament times. In one

---

[42] Whenever men deliberately sin against God, God then "gives them over" to the committing of even worse sins (see Romans 1:24,26,28).

[43] Ancient **Babylon** was located where the modern country of Iraq is today.

way, Solomon's building of the temple was a fulfillment of God's promise to David that one of his "offspring" would **build a house for my Name** (2 Samuel 7:13). But in another way, the promise was only fulfilled when Christ came, because it was He who built the true "house" of God. Christ was the true **offspring** of David. Christ's **throne** is a spiritual "throne" that will last forever (Luke 1:30–33). The **house** that Christ built is a spiritual "house." God's true house or temple is not a building; it is people—believers. Believers make up the true spiritual temple of God. This is the temple in which God dwells. The dwelling place of God is in the hearts of all those who believe in Christ. And the **chief cornerstone** of God's spiritual temple is Christ Himself (see Ephesians 2:19–22 and comment).

48–50 After Solomon had finished building the temple, he said: "**But will God really dwell on earth? The heavens, even the highest heaven, cannot contain you. How much less this temple I have built!**" (1 Kings 8:27). Stephen says here that the **Most High** (God) **does not live in houses made by men** (verse 48). Stephen then quotes from Isaiah 66:1–2, where the prophet Isaiah says the same thing. Therefore, these Old Testament prophets—including Solomon himself, the builder of the temple—have all said that God does not need a temple to live in. Let the Jews of the Sanhedrin not accuse Stephen of speaking against the temple; the Jews' own Scriptures (the Old Testament) have spoken against it! The Old Testament teaches that the true temple of God consists of His faithful and obedient people.

51 Here Stephen begins to openly oppose the Jews of the Sanhedrin. These Jews had accused Stephen of speaking in opposition to God. Now Stephen accuses the Jews themselves of resisting God, of resisting God's Holy Spirit, through whom the Old Testament prophets spoke. They are just like their ancestors, who repeatedly disobeyed Moses and the other Old Testament prophets. They are Jews who have been circumcised outwardly, but whose **hearts and ears** have never been "circumcised." That is, Stephen says, they are just like uncircumcised Gentiles who neither love nor obey God! (see Romans 2:28–29 and comment).

52 Throughout Old Testament times, God sent many prophets to the rebellious and disobedient Jews to warn them and to lead them to repentance. But the Jews always rejected and persecuted God's prophets (Matthew 23:29–31). Many of these prophets prophesied about the coming of Christ, and the Jews killed them. But worst of all, these same Jews, who were now accusing Stephen, had betrayed and murdered the **Righteous One**, Christ Himself (see Acts 2:23; 3:13–15).

53 Stephen says to the Jews: "**. . . you who have received the law . . . have not obeyed it**, because you have **betrayed and murdered** Christ. The Jews thought they were righteous because they had received the **law**. But, in fact, they disobeyed their own law. They had disobeyed Moses and the prophets. Now they had disobeyed Christ also.

Stephen says that the law **was put into effect through angels**. When God gave the law to Moses on top of Mount Sinai, there were many of God's angels present (see Deuteronomy 33:2; Galatians 3:19; Hebrews 2:2).

The Stoning of Stephen (7:54–60)

54–56 On one side were the Jewish leaders, gnashing their teeth at Stephen. On the other side was Christ, standing at the right hand of God. A few years earlier, Jesus Himself had stood before this same Sanhedrin. At that time the high priest had asked Jesus, "**Are you the Christ, the Son of the Blessed One?**" And Jesus had replied: "**I am. . . . And you will see the Son of Man sitting at the right hand of the Mighty One and coming on the clouds of heaven**" (Mark 14:61–62). Now Stephen says to the Jews of the Sanhedrin: "**Look . . . I see heaven open and the Son of Man standing at the right hand of God**" (verse 56).

Jesus is at God's right hand. We don't need a temple. We don't need to observe a lot of religious rituals. We have Jesus Christ, the Lord of heaven, standing at God's right hand interceding for us.

Because Christ has gone before us into heaven, we who believe in Him can now come directly into the presence of God (see Hebrews 7:24–26; 8:1–2).

57–58 All the Jews present determined at once to condemn Stephen to death. They were so angry that they didn't even wait to get permission from the Roman governor. In fact, Stephen hadn't said anything worthy of the death penalty. Nevertheless, they considered that he had committed blasphemy against God (Leviticus 24:13–16). Therefore, they rushed with him to the place for stoning criminals and began to stone him.

The Jews executed criminals by stoning them to death. The person to be executed was placed in a deep pit, and then heavy stones were thrown down upon him. Those who had testified against the person were required to throw the first stones (Deuteronomy 17:7). In Stephen's case, all the Jews of the Sanhedrin were witnesses against him; therefore, they were all entitled to throw the first stone. They all took off their outer clothing, so that they could more easily throw the stones. They laid their clothing **at the feet of a young man named Saul** (verse 58). This Saul later became the Apostle Paul. Paul never forgot how he had given approval to Stephen's death (Acts 22:20).

59–60 Even as he was dying, Stephen followed the example of His Lord. While He was on the cross, Jesus had prayed for those who were crucifying him: **"Father, forgive them, for they do not know what they are doing"** (Luke 23:34). In the same way, Stephen prayed: **"Lord, do not hold this sin against them"** (verse 60).

Even in the midst of intense suffering, Stephen didn't look at his persecutors; he looked to God. When trouble comes upon us, what do we see? Do we see our enemies, our bad circumstances? Or, like Stephen, do we see God?

Stephen was the first Christian to be killed for the sake of Christ; he was the first Christian martyr. And ever since, Stephen has been an example of strong faith and steadfastness for countless believers down through the centuries. We also, when great trouble or persecution comes upon us, can, like Stephen, lift our eyes to heaven and see Christ our Savior. And when we see Christ standing at the right hand of God, then we will have no need to fear. **If God is for us, who can be against us?** (Romans 8:31). **Who is he that condemns? Christ Jesus, who died—more than that, who was raised to life—is at the right hand of God and is also interceding for us. Who shall separate us from the love of Christ?** (see Romans 8:34–38 and comment).

CHAPTER 8

The Church Persecuted and Scattered (8:1–8)

1–2 After killing Stephen, the Jewish leaders grew bolder and decided to seize the other Christians also. Therefore, most of the believers left Jerusalem and scattered throughout **Judea** and **Samaria**, the two southern provinces of Israel. They did as Jesus had said: **"When you are persecuted in one place, flee to another"** (Matthew 10:23).

Jesus had also said to His disciples: "... **you will be my witnesses in Jerusalem, and in all Judea and Samaria, and to the ends of the earth"** (Acts 1:8). Now, by means of this persecution and the scattering of the believers, God caused the Gospel to be spread throughout Judea and Samaria (see verse 4).

3 The fiercest persecutor of the Christians was a Jew named Saul (who later became the Apostle Paul). Saul had heard Stephen's speech before the Sanhedrin. After hearing Stephen, Saul realized that this new Christian religion was irreconcilably opposed to many of the Jewish traditions. Saul saw that if this new religion continued to spread, the power and influence of the Jewish leaders would be undermined. Therefore, Saul decided that this new religion must be stamped out. He could no longer agree with his old teacher Gamaliel, who had advised that the Christians should be left alone (Acts 5:38–39). So Saul **began to destroy the church**. He seized both men and women and threw them into prison.

4–5 **Philip** was one of the seven ministers, or deacons, who had been appointed by the apostles to distribute food to the poorer members of the church (Acts 6:3–5). When the persecution came, Philip left Jerusalem and went northward to the province of Samaria. The Jews despised the Samaritans, because they were not pure Jews. Originally the Samaritans had been Jews, but then foreigners had invaded Samaria and had married the local Samaritan women. Thus the Samaritans in New Testament times were only half-Jews. As a result, there was much ill feeling between the Jews and Samaritans. Nevertheless, Philip, himself a Jew, went to Samaria and began to preach. This was the first time that any of the disciples had preached the Gospel to those who were not true Jews.

6–8 In these verses we again see how the Holy Spirit worked through those first Christian leaders (Acts 6:8). Philip, too, performed miraculous signs. Just as Christ had done, Philip also cast out EVIL SPIRITS (verse 7) and healed those who were crippled and paralyzed. For this reason, **all paid close attention to what he said** (verse 6).

Simon the Sorcerer (8:9–25)

9–11 In every age there have been men like **Simon**, who lead people astray by sorcery. Simon deceived people into thinking that he possessed some kind of **divine power** (verse 10). He **boasted that he was someone great**. Such false teachers and prophets are usually motivated by pride. Worst of all, many people believe these false teachers and become their followers.

12–13 The power that Philip had was greater than Simon's power. Therefore, the people believed Philip's word and were baptized.

Simon himself recognized that Philip's power was greater than his own. Therefore, he also believed. Simon hoped that by believing he, too, could get some of Philip's power for himself. We cannot be sure to what extent Simon's faith was real; however, it certainly was not a deep faith. Simon believed only because he saw the **great signs and miracles** that Philip performed. Jesus Himself did not have much confidence in faith that was based mainly on miracles (see John 2:23–24). Faith must be deeper than that.

14 When news of Philip's work in Samaria reached the apostles in Jerusalem, Peter and John went to Samaria to see for themselves what was happening. This is the same John who earlier had wanted to destroy a Samaritan village by calling **fire down from heaven** (Luke 9:51–56).

15–16 Peter and John found that the Samaritans had indeed believed and been baptized, but that the **Holy Spirit had not yet come upon any of them** (verse 16)—that is, the Spirit had not come upon them with power as He had come upon the disciples on the day of Pentecost (see Acts 2:1–4).

The New Testament teaches that everyone who believes in Christ and is baptized also receives the Holy Spirit (see Romans 5:5; 8:9; 1 Corinthians 6:19; 12:13; Ephesians 1:13). Therefore, when these Samaritans believed, they surely received the Holy Spirit. The Spirit had begun to dwell within them. But the Samaritans had not experienced the power of the Holy Spirit, such as was manifested on the day of Pentecost. They had not yet received the filling of the Spirit, or the "second blessing," as it is called by some (see Acts 2:4; 1 Corinthians 12:13 and comments; General Article: Holy Spirit Baptism).

17 When Peter and John laid their hands on these new Samaritan believers, **they received the Holy Spirit**—that is, the Spirit came upon them with power and with visible manifestations. Something happened that others standing there could see or hear, because according to verse 18, Simon **saw that the Spirit was given**. It is very possible that these Samaritans began to speak in tongues, just as the disciples had done on the day of Pentecost.

Some Christians believe that before anyone can receive the filling or anointing of the Holy Spirit, it is necessary that a specially appointed church leader lay hands on him (see Acts 19:1–7). But usually in the New Testament when people receive the Spirit, no mention is made of the laying on of hands (Acts 2:38,41; 8:38–39; 10:44–48; 16:30–33). If the laying on of hands were necessary, surely somewhere in the New Testament God would have clearly said so. The laying on of hands was a Jewish custom, which was used for granting special blessings or for appointing someone to a special task (see Acts 6:6 and comment). The custom was simply carried over into the new Christian church, and it has been commonly practiced ever since (Acts 13:3; 1 Timothy 5:22; Hebrews 6:2).

18–19 Simon saw that Peter and John's power was even greater than Philip's. Simon supposed that Peter and John could give other people the Holy Spirit just by laying hands on them. Simon wanted this power too, and he was prepared to pay money for it!

20–23 Simon's heart was not right. He was thinking only about his own glory and fame. He didn't realize that the power of the Spirit cannot be bought with money. Man cannot control the Holy Spirit for his own benefit. Simon was seeking only his own advantage. He wasn't thinking of using the Holy Spirit's power to serve and glorify God. Simon's heart was **full of bitterness** (verse 23)—that is, full of jealousy—because Peter, John, and Philip had more power than he had. Simon had fallen **captive to sin,** because he sought only his own glory, not God's.

What did Simon need to do? Peter told him what he must do: "**Repent of this wickedness and pray to the Lord**" (verse 22). Peter did not say: "Repent of this mistake." Rather, he said, "Repent of this **wickedness.**" We should never call our sin merely a "mistake"; in God's sight it is wickedness.

Then Peter said, "**Perhaps** [the Lord] **will forgive you for having such a thought in your heart**". Peter wasn't sure whether Simon would be forgiven or not, because he wasn't sure whether Simon would truly repent. Only if Simon truly repented would he be forgiven. All who truly repent of their sin are forgiven (1 John 1:9).

24–25 When Simon heard Peter's words, he was filled with fear. Simon had seen Peter's great power, and now he feared that the words of such a powerful man might indeed come true. So he asked Peter to pray for him, that God's judgment might not fall on him.

Whether Simon truly repented or not no one knows. He is not mentioned anywhere else in the New Testament.

After proclaiming God's word in that place, Peter and John returned to Jerusalem, preaching in the villages as they went.

Philip and the Ethiopian (8:26–40)

26 Some time later an **angel of the Lord** told Philip to go to the road running south from Jerusalem to Gaza. (Gaza was a city southwest of Jerusalem.) Notice how God led Philip. In this verse, an **angel** of the Lord spoke to him. In verse 29, the Holy **Spirit** spoke to him. Some think that the angel's voice was, in fact, the voice of the Holy Spirit. But regardless of whose voice He used, God spoke to Philip, and Philip immediately did what God commanded.

27 On the road to Gaza Philip met a **eunuch,**[44] who was an **official in charge of all the treasury** of the queen of the **Ethiopians.**[45]

28 Although the eunuch was not a true Jew, he was probably a follower of the Jewish religion. He had just been worshiping at the Jewish temple in

---

[44] In ancient times, the chief officials of kings and queens were often eunuchs. It was thought that a castrated man, more than other men, could be trusted with affairs of state, because he was not likely to usurp power for himself. He was also not likely to trouble the women of the royal family.

[45] Ethiopia is a large African nation located to the south of Egypt.

Jerusalem, and now he was returning in his **chariot**[46] to his own country. As he was riding along, he was reading from the Old Testament book of the prophet Isaiah.

29–31 The eunuch did not fully understand what he was reading. Where could he find a better teacher than Philip to explain the meaning of Isaiah's prophecy! Because the verses in Isaiah that the eunuch was reading were written specifically about Jesus Christ.

32–33 The eunuch was reading from Isaiah 53:7–8.[47] In these verses, Isaiah is prophesying that Christ will be **led like a sheep to the slaughter**.

Most of the Old Testament prophets prophesied that Christ would come as a king, or as an "anointed one" (the Messiah), or as a Savior. But in Isaiah Chapter 53, Isaiah writes that the coming One (Christ) would come as a "suffering servant," who would sacrifice His life as an atonement for the sins of mankind. The Jews could not believe that the king or Savior they were waiting for was actually the same person as this "suffering servant" described by Isaiah. But Christ clearly said concerning Himself: "**. . . the Son of Man did not come to be served, but to serve, and to give his life as a ransom for many**" (Mark 10:45). Jesus also said: "**Why then is it written that the Son of Man must suffer much and be rejected?**" (Mark 9:12). Therefore, from Jesus' own words about Himself, we can understand that the prophecy of Isaiah quoted here is indeed written about Christ.

34–35 At the time of Philip's meeting with the eunuch, the New Testament had not yet been written. There was only the Old Testament. Thus, aside from the Old Testament prophecies, there was nothing else written about Christ. It was indeed amazing that this very passage the eunuch was reading, Isaiah Chapter 53, gives the clearest description of Christ found anywhere in the Old Testament. Therefore, when the eunuch asked Philip who the prophet was talking about, Philip was immediately able to answer: "Jesus Christ." **Then Philip began with that very passage of Scripture and told him the good news about Jesus** (verse 35).

36–38 When he had finished telling the eunuch about Jesus Christ, Philip baptized him.[48] The eunuch did not have to wait a long time. Philip did not say: "I can't baptize you now. You need more teaching. Come back another time." Philip did not say: "Before I can baptize you, I need proof that your faith is genuine." No, Philip didn't say these things. Rather, as soon as Philip had finished explaining the Gospel and the eunuch had believed, Philip baptized him. Nowhere in the New Testament does it say that a person must wait a long time and receive extensive teaching before he can be baptized. Nowhere is it written that a person must first prove that his faith is genuine before being baptized. These ideas do not come from the New Testament. If any person, after hearing the Gospel, believes in Jesus Christ and asks for baptism, he should be baptized at the first suitable occasion and not be made to wait. Only God knows whether a person has truly believed from his heart or not. We men cannot know for sure.

---

[46] A **chariot** is a horse-drawn, two-wheeled cart. It was used in ancient times by soldiers and government officials as a means of transportation.

[47] There are two main texts of the Old Testament: one in the Hebrew language, and the other in the Greek language. The Old Testament was written originally in Hebrew, the language of the Jews. Then, several hundred years before Christ, the Hebrew version was translated into Greek. There are a number of small differences between these Greek and Hebrew texts. Most modern translations of the Old Testament are based on the Hebrew text. But some of the New Testament writers, particularly Luke and the writer of Hebrews, used mainly the Greek text when they quoted from the Old Testament. Therefore, when the section of Isaiah quoted here in verses 32–33 is compared with the same passage in Isaiah 53:7–8, one will notice several differences, especially in the second verse.

[48] Not all ancient manuscripts of Acts contain verse 37.

Therefore, even though we cannot be absolutely sure of a person's faith, we must not refuse him if he asks for baptism; otherwise we will be disobeying the New Testament. Yes, it's possible that a few will be baptized who do not have true faith; but it is God's business to judge them, not ours.

Notice that although Philip was not an apostle, he had the authority to baptize (verse 12). From this we can understand that deacons and elders of the church also have the authority to baptize.

39 The **Spirit of the Lord suddenly took Philip away,** and Philip disappeared from the eunuch's sight (2 Kings 2:16; Ezekiel 3:14; 8:3).

40 God's Spirit brought Philip to Azotus, a city north of Gaza on the Mediterranean coast. After that, Philip traveled farther northward to the city of **Caesarea,** preaching the Gospel as he went. It seems as if he decided to settle in Caesarea, because the next time Philip is mentioned in the book of Acts, he is living in Caesarea with four grown daughters, who were prophetesses (Acts 21:8–9).

CHAPTER 9

Saul's Conversion (9:1–9)

1–2 **Saul**[49] (who later changed his name to Paul) was not content to persecute Christians only in Jerusalem (see Acts 8:1,3). He pursued them wherever they fled. One place the believers fled to was **Damascus,** the capital of Syria. Some Christians had gone to the Jewish synagogues there. (Up until that time, all Christians were converted Jews; thus they still went to the Jewish synagogues to worship.) The Jewish high priest in Jerusalem had authority over these synagogues in Damascus, so Paul obtained a letter from the high priest authorizing him to seize the Christians there and bring them back to Jerusalem (Acts 22:4–5; 26:9–11).

In verse 2 the Christian religion is called **the Way.** It was the name usually used by the first Christians (Acts 19:9,23; 22:4; 24:14). The **Way** was a suitable name, because the Christian religion is, in fact, the way to salvation, to eternal life. Christ Himself is our true **way** (John 14:6).

3 At about noon, as Saul drew near Damascus, a light brighter than the sun flashed around him (Acts 22:6; 26:13).

4 Then Saul heard a voice. Those who were with him heard the sound, but they could not understand the words (Acts 22:7,9; 26:14). The voice was Jesus' voice. Jesus Himself was speaking personally to Saul. **"Saul, Saul, why do you persecute me?"** Jesus asked. Saul had thought that he was persecuting only men, but now he learned it was, in fact, the Lord Himself whom he had been persecuting.

5–6 Saul recognized that it was the **Lord** who was speaking to him. The light was so great and frightening that Saul knew at once that he was in the presence of God. Jesus, **the light of the world,** had appeared to him (John 8:12).

But even though he knew that the light was the "Lord," Saul up until then had not known that the Lord was actually the risen Christ. Therefore, Saul asked, **"Who are you, Lord?"** And the Lord answered, **"I am Jesus"** (verse 5).

Then, according to Acts 22:10, Saul asked Jesus, **"What shall I do, Lord?"** Here we see the first step in Saul's conversion. Now Saul was ready to do what the Lord wanted. He had given up his own desires and purposes. True conversion always means a change of a person's mind and will (see Romans 12:2).

After Saul asked the Lord what he should do, the Lord answered, **"Now get**

---

[49] **Saul** is a Hebrew name. Saul's Roman name was Paul.

up and go into the city" (Acts 22:8,10; 26:15).

According to Acts 26:16–18, the Lord also said some other words to Saul. He said to Saul: "**I have appeared to you to appoint you as a servant and as a witness of what you have seen of me and what I will show you**" (Acts 26:16). It was here that Jesus first appointed Saul to be an apostle.

7 The men with Saul were also amazed. At first they all fell to the ground with Saul (Acts 26:14). Then, as Saul still lay on the ground, they got up and **stood there speechless**.

It is written here that these men heard the sound from heaven. In Acts 22:9, it is written that **they did not understand the voice**. That is, they heard the voice, but couldn't make out the words that were spoken. It is not mentioned whether any of Saul's companions were converted. They saw the light and heard the voice, but God's Spirit did not enter their hearts. Man is not converted by outward signs alone; only when God's grace and God's Spirit enter into a man is he converted.

8–9 The great light blinded Saul (Acts 22:11). And he remained blind for three days, during which time he stayed in Damascus without either eating or drinking.

Saul and Ananias (9:10–19)

10–11 **Ananias** was a Christian of Damascus, who was a **devout observer of the law and highly respected by all Jews living there** (Acts 22:12). Ananias saw a vision in which the Lord told him to go to the place where Saul was staying.

12 The Lord told Ananias that Saul also had received a vision in which a man named Ananias came and laid hands on him. Therefore, Ananias had no need to fear Saul. Saul would recognize and accept him.

13–14 Even though the Lord had assured Ananias that Saul would receive him, Ananias was still skeptical. "Don't you know that this man is our enemy?" Ananias said to the Lord. "**And he has come here . . . to arrest all who call on your name**"—that is, all who believe in Christ.

15 But the Lord said to Ananias, "**Go!** Don't argue with me. Saul is **my chosen instrument to carry my name before the Gentiles and their kings and before the people of Israel.**"

Here the Lord announces His intention to appoint Saul as His apostle to the Gentiles (Acts 22:21). Before this time, Christ's Gospel had been preached only among the Jews and Samaritans. Christ here tells Ananias that from now on His Gospel must be preached to all people, Jew and Gentile alike.

Saul was appointed to carry Christ's name before **kings** (Acts 26:2) and the **people of Israel**, that is, the Jews. Saul (Paul) didn't preach only to the Gentiles. Whatever city he went to, he would first go to the local Jewish synagogue and preach to the Jews there. After that, he would preach to the Gentiles.

16 Saul was not only appointed to carry Christ's name before Jews and Gentiles; he was also appointed to suffer for Christ. Saul had inflicted great suffering upon the Christians; now it would be his turn to suffer (see 2 Corinthians 6:4–5; 11:23–28).

17 After Ananias laid hands on Saul, Saul's sight was restored. Not only Saul's sight but his entire life was made new by the Holy Spirit.

Then Ananias told Saul what he had heard from the Lord in his vision: namely, that Saul was to be Christ's **chosen instrument** to preach the Gospel to all men, both Jew and Gentile (Acts 22:12–16).

Christ Himself had said the same thing to Saul on the road to Damascus (Acts 26:15–18). Therefore, having heard the same thing twice—first from Christ and now again from Ananias—Saul knew with certainty that Christ had indeed appointed him to be His apostle (1 Corinthians 15:7–9). It was not Ananias who appointed him; it was the risen Lord Himself, whom Saul had now seen face to face on the Damascus road.

18–19 When Ananias placed his hands on Saul, immediately **something like scales fell from Saul's eyes**, and he received his sight. Then Saul was baptized. Although the Bible doesn't tell us, we can suppose that it was Ananias who baptized Saul.

What an amazing thing Saul's conversion was! Indeed, it has proven to be one of the most significant events in all of world history. How could such a fierce enemy of Christ so quickly become one of His apostles? Saul was a mature and learned man. He wasn't crazy. But suddenly his life was turned totally around. Within three days, Jesus' greatest enemy had become His greatest apostle! How can we explain it? It can only be explained by saying that Saul did, in fact, meet the living and glorified Christ on that road to Damascus. There is no other possible explanation. Saul's conversion is proof that Jesus Christ did indeed rise from the dead—and is alive today.

Is there anyone who thinks he is too evil, too sinful, to become a follower of Christ? Let him remember Saul! Jesus can change anyone—even the worst sinner on earth.

Saul in Damascus and Jerusalem (9:20–31)

20 According to Galatians 1:17, Saul went **immediately into Arabia** after his conversion, and only later returned again to Damascus. Here in the book of Acts, Luke does not mention Saul's trip to Arabia. As soon as Saul returned to Damascus, he at once **began to preach in the synagogues that Jesus is the Son of God**. Saul's heart had been converted; now his behavior had been converted too. Instead of persecuting Christians, he was now taking their side.

21–22 People were astonished at the change in Saul. Saul especially baffled the Jews of Damascus, because he set about proving to them that Jesus was the Christ—the Messiah—by quoting prophecies from their own Scriptures, the Old Testament. Not only that, Saul, himself a Jew, could say, "I have seen the risen Christ with my own eyes."

23–25 Just as the Jews of Jerusalem had become angry with Stephen and the other disciples, so in the same way did the Jews in Damascus quickly become angry with Saul. That was natural, because in their eyes, Saul had betrayed them. From that time on, wherever Saul went, most of the Jews became his enemies and bitterly opposed him.

Surrounding the city of Damascus there was a great wall, with gates for passing in and out of the city. Saul's Jewish enemies in Damascus tried to prevent him from escaping by setting a watch at each of these gates. But Saul's friends lowered him in a basket from an opening in the wall, and he escaped (see 2 Corinthians 11:32–33).

26 Three years after his conversion, Saul returned to Jerusalem (Galatians 1:18). No one welcomed him! The Jews, of course, were now his enemies. But the Christians didn't accept him either at first. They naturally doubted whether Saul had truly become a Christian.

Many new Christians have had an experience similar to Paul's. They have found themselves rejected by their old friends, and yet they are not accepted by their new brothers and sisters in Christ. Let this not be! We must wholeheartedly accept a newly baptized believer no matter how evil his previous life has been. Even if afterward he betrays our trust, that is God's concern, not ours. It is much better to let an enemy into our fellowship than to keep a true believer out. After all, even Jesus had His Judas.

27 But Saul found a friend in **Barnabas**. The name Barnabas means **Son of Encouragement** (Acts 4:36–37). Barnabas did indeed encourage Saul. He introduced Saul to the apostles, in particular to Peter and James, the Lord's brother (Galatians 1:18–19). In addition, Barnabas testified to the genuineness of Paul's conversion.

28–30 Saul stayed in Jerusalem with Peter and James for two weeks. Saul spoke boldly with the Jews in Jerusalem, especially with the Jews of Greek descent. But the Jews became angry and sought to kill him. At that time the Lord again appeared to Saul in a vision and told him to leave Jerusalem at once (Acts 22:17–21). Therefore, the apostles took Saul to Caesarea on the coast of the Mediterranean Sea. From there, Saul went by boat to **Tarsus** in present-day Turkey, the city where Saul was born (Acts 22:3). There Saul remained for some years.

Saul's (Paul's) story resumes in Acts 11:25 and continues to the end of the book.

31 In this verse, Luke talks about the CHURCH **throughout Judea, Galilee and Samaria.**[50] In one way, there are many local churches in different places; but in another way, all these local churches make up one universal church, that is, Christ's church. This is why Luke speaks here of the **church** in the singular.

Following the conversion of their main enemy Saul and his subsequent departure from Jerusalem, the Christians enjoyed a period of relative peace. During this period, through the working of the Holy Spirit, the church grew and prospered. If the church can prosper in persecution, it certainly ought to be able to prosper in peace! Even Christians need times of peace; if persecution is continuous, they become weary.

Notice here that Luke says the church grew both in strength and **in numbers**. Both kinds of growth are necessary; a church that grows only in numbers only grows fat.

Aeneas and Dorcas (9:32–43)

32–35 At that time Peter went to visit some of the churches located in Judea and Samaria. These churches had been established by the disciples who had fled from Jerusalem during the persecution following Stephen's death (Acts 8:1). One of the churches Peter visited was located in **Lydda**, a city north of Jerusalem. There Peter healed a man named **Aeneas**, and as a result, all who lived in Lydda and the surrounding plain of **Sharon** turned to the Lord.

Aeneas was healed instantly and completely. "**Jesus Christ heals you**," Peter said to Aeneas (verse 34). Not tomorrow, but today! "**Get up and take care of your mat**," said Peter. Aeneas had now no need to lie in bed; it was time to make his bed! Immediately Aeneas got up. When Jesus heals us, we must get up and not keep lying in bed.

36–38 While Peter was still in Lydda, a Christian woman named **Tabitha** got sick and died in the nearby city of **Joppa**. Joppa was on the Mediterranean coast about ten miles from Lydda. When the Joppa Christians heard that Peter was in Lydda, they sent for him to come and raise up Tabitha. Even though Tabitha was already dead, they still sent for Peter. It was too late to call a doctor, but not too late to call Peter!

39 When Peter arrived, the widows of Joppa showed him the clothes that Tabitha had made for them. They were grateful. Let these widows be an example for us. How often we fail to show gratitude for the help we have received! Instead of proclaiming what others have done for us, we hide it. Let this not be.

40–43 Just as Jesus raised up Jairus' daughter (Mark 5:22–24,35–43), so Peter raised up Tabitha. As a result, many people believed; they had seen the power of the risen Christ at work in His apostle Peter.

Whenever the apostles healed people or performed other miracles, we must understand that it was really Jesus Christ through His Holy Spirit who was doing the work. Today also, whenever Christians do the work of Christ, it is the Holy Spirit living in them who does the work. Christians are only the instruments. When we do any good work, others must be able to say: "That is Christ's work." For any work that we do, the credit goes not to us but to God and to Jesus Christ (see Matthew 5:16 and comment).

In Joppa Peter stayed at the house of a **tanner named Simon** (verse 43). While there, Peter received a very important vision, which is described in detail in Acts Chapter 10.

---

[50] **Judea, Galilee and Samaria** were the three provinces of Israel in New Testament times.

CHAPTER 10

Cornelius Calls for Peter (10:1–8)

1 **Caesarea** was a large city on the coast of the Mediterranean Sea about thirty miles north of Joppa (see Acts 8:40). In Caesarea lived a Gentile named **Cornelius**, who was a **centurion**[51] in the Roman army.
2 Cornelius and his family were **God-fearing**. Though they were not Jews, they believed in the one true God of Israel. They worshiped God and tried to do His will according to the spiritual understanding they possessed. Cornelius prayed to God regularly. Therefore, God looked with favor upon Cornelius. In this way, through God's grace, Cornelius became the first Gentile (non-Jewish) Christian.
3–4 God always remembers our prayers and our good works—that is, our **gifts to the poor** (verse 4). We are not sanctified or saved because of our prayers and good works, but we will be rewarded according to them (see Romans 2:6; 2 Corinthians 5;10 and comments).
5–6 Cornelius and his family were about to receive a great blessing, but first it was necessary to find a man called Peter.
7–8 With complete faith, Cornelius sent three men to the place described by the angel, where Peter was staying.

Peter's Vision (10:9–16)

9–10 Before a meeting between Cornelius and Peter could take place, Peter needed to receive a vision also. This was because Peter was a Jew, and Jews in New Testament times did not associate with Gentiles. According to Jewish tradition, Jews were not allowed to enter a Gentile's house and, especially, they were forbidden to eat with Gentiles. The difference between a Jew and a Gentile was as great as the difference between a high-caste Hindu and an untouchable.
11–13 The Jews were extremely strict about what they could eat and what they could not eat. According to Leviticus Chapter 11, there were "clean" animals which the Jews could lawfully eat, and there were "unclean" animals which they were forbidden to eat.[52]

In his vision, Peter saw **something like a large sheet**, in which were all kinds of animals, both clean and unclean. Then a voice said, **"Get up, Peter. Kill and eat"**.
14 Peter, being a Jew, was shocked. **"I have never eaten anything impure or unclean,"** he said.
15–16 God said to Peter: "There is nothing that is 'impure' or 'unclean.' From now on you are not to make a distinction between clean and unclean meat. That Old Testament rule is no longer valid. **Do not call anything impure that God has made clean"** (see Acts 11:5–10).

As Peter pondered the meaning of this vision, perhaps he recalled the words Jesus had spoken: **"Nothing outside a man can make him 'unclean' by going into him. Rather, it is what comes out of a man that makes him 'unclean'"** (Mark 7:15). Having written those words of Jesus, Mark then added: **In saying this, Jesus declared all foods "clean"** (Mark 7:19).

But Peter was soon to learn the real meaning of his vision. The real meaing was this: just as there was no "unclean" meat, so there were no "unclean" people. In God's sight, both Jews and Gentiles were equally "clean."

Peter at Cornelius' House (10:17–33)

17–20 When Peter's vision was finshed, the Holy Spirit told him that three men had come to see him. **"Do not hesitate to go with them, for I have sent them,"** the Spirit said (verse 20). If the

---

[51] A **centurion** in the Roman army was the commander of one hundred men.

[52] According to Jewish law, Jews were allowed to eat **any animal that has a split hoof completely divided and that chews the cud** (Leviticus 11:3).

Spirit had not said this, Peter certainly would have hesitated, because the men seeking him were Gentiles (see Acts 11:10–12).

21–23 Now Peter finally understood the meaning of the vision (see verse 28). A Gentile had called Peter to come to his house. Through the vision, God had prepared Peter to go.

Peter took some **brothers from Joppa** with him to Cornelius' house. These brothers were Jewish Christians. Peter knew that other Jewish believers would surely criticize him for going to the house of a Gentile. Therefore, Peter took these brothers with him as witnesses that Peter was indeed acting according to God's will.

24–26 When Peter arrived at Cornelius' house, Cornelius **fell at his feet in reverence** (verse 25). But Peter stopped him, and told him to get up. In other religions it is the custom to bow down at the feet of respected teachers or important officials. But it is not so among Christians. We show respect to men, but we show reverence only to Christ—to God.

For this reason, also, Christians must never take for themselves glory or honor that only Christ should receive. The spiritual treasures of Christ have been placed in **jars of clay**—that is, in our weak human bodies—so that all the glory will go to Christ and not to us (see 2 Corinthians 4:7 and comment).

27–29 In the vision, the Lord had shown Peter only clean and unclean animals. But He had said to Peter, "**Do not call anything impure that God has made clean**" (verse 15). Peter understood that the word **anything** meant not just meat but also men. No one was to be called **impure**—not even Gentiles.

30–33 Cornelius knew why the angel had told him to send for Peter. The angel had said to Cornelius, "**He** (Peter) **will bring you a message through which you and all your household will be saved**" (Acts 11:13–14). Now Cornelius and his entire household were ready to listen to Peter's words.

Peter's Sermon (10:34–43)

34–35 In these verses, Peter states one of the most important truths in the whole Bible: "**God does not show favoritism**" (see Romans 2:9–11).

God accepts equally all men **who fear him and do what is right** (verse 35). In the Old Testament, God gave men the ten commandments (Exodus 20:1–17). God accepted everyone—whether Jew or Gentile—who obeyed these commandments. The prophet Micah wrote: **He** (the Lord) **has showed you, O man, what is good. And what does the Lord require of you? To act justly and to love mercy and to walk humbly with your God** (Micah 6:8). Therefore, according to the Old Testament, God accepts not only upright Jews but upright Gentiles as well.

God accepts equally not only men of different races and nations, but also men of different castes and of different positions (see Ephesians 6:9). In God's sight, all men are of equal standing. And when we believe in Christ—whether we be Jew or Gentile, slave or free, man or woman—we become equal members of one family, the family of God (see Galatians 3:28 and comment).

Here an important truth must be added. Yes, God **accepts men from every nation who fear him and do what is right**. But this does not mean that such men will automatically receive salvation. In one way, they have done what is right and, therefore, God will accept them. But in another way, such "upright" men are still sinners and need a Savior (see Romans 3:9–12 and comment). Even though Cornelius appeared righteous in comparison with other men, he still needed a Savior. It was for this very reason that Peter had come, that Cornelius might be able to hear about Christ. Yes, Cornelius' work was good; but man is not saved by good works. Man is saved only by God's grace through faith (see Ephesians 2:8–9 and comment).

36 Then Peter told Cornelius and his household the good news about how men can have peace with God through Jesus Christ. God had sent this message first to the people of Israel—the Jews. "But now," said Peter, "God has given this message of peace through Christ to all people everywhere. Jesus Christ is **Lord of all**—both Jew and Gentile."

37–38 Then Peter reminded Cornelius of what he had already heard: namely, that in the beginning John the Baptist had come to prepare the people's hearts for the coming of Jesus the Messiah. Then John had baptized Jesus. At the time of His baptism, **God anointed Jesus of Nazareth with the Holy Spirit and with power** (verse 38). The Holy Spirit descended on Jesus **like a dove** (Mark 1:9–11).

39–40 Again and again the apostles said, "**We are witnesses**" (verse 39). The things Peter was telling Cornelius were not secondhand reports from other people. Peter had seen these things with his own eyes. He had seen Jesus die (Luke 23:49), and he had seen Him after He had risen from the dead (see Luke 24:34; Acts 2:32; 5:30 and comments).

41 Jesus didn't rise from the dead in the form of a ghost, or as the figment of someone's imagination. He rose in a bodily and fully visible form—even to the point of eating and drinking with His disciples after His resurrection (Luke 24:41–43).

42 Jesus Christ was appointed to be the judge of all men, both those living and those already dead (see Daniel 7:13–14; Acts 17:31). Jesus Himself said: "**. . . the Father . . . has entrusted all judgment to the Son**" (John 5:22,27).

43 Jesus was not only appointed to be man's judge; He was also appointed to be man's Savior. He was appointed not only to judge man's sin but also to save men from the punishment of sin. Peter said: "**. . . everyone who believes in him receives forgiveness of sins**" (see Luke 24:45–48).

Gentiles Receive the Holy Spirit (10:44–48)

44 Just as the Holy Spirit had come upon the disciples on the day of Pentecost, so, as Peter was speaking, did the Spirit come suddenly upon Cornelius and all his household (Acts 2:1–4; 11:15; 15:7–8). In Acts 2:38, Peter had said to the Jews: "**Repent and be baptized, every one of you, in the name of Jesus Christ so that your sins may be forgiven. And you will receive the gift of the Holy Spirit.**" But here, the Holy Spirit came upon Cornelius and his household first, before they even had a chance to be baptized. The Holy Spirit comes to men according to His own plans and purposes; we men must not try to set rules for Him.

45–46 Just as the disciples had spoken in tongues on the day of Pentecost, so these Gentiles began to speak in tongues when the Holy Spirit came upon them. If they had not spoken in tongues, it's possible that Peter and the **circumcised** (that is, Jewish) **believers** he had brought with him from Joppa would not have believed that the Holy Spirit had indeed come upon these Gentiles.

47–48 It is not actually written here that Cornelius and his family repented and believed in Jesus. But we can assume that they did. According to Acts 15:9, Peter later said that the Lord **purified their hearts by faith**.

After seeing the remarkable work that God had done in the lives of these Gentiles, Peter could see no reason why they should not immediately be baptized. If the Holy Spirit had not come upon them first, Peter would not have been prepared to baptize Gentiles. But now to refuse to baptize them would be to resist God (Acts 11;17). Baptism is the outward confirmation or sign of new spiritual life. If one has already received the life, why should he not also receive the sign of it?

The day that Peter came to Cornelius' house was an extremely important day in the history of the Christian religion. On that day the first Gentiles became Christians. From that day on, this new Christian religion was not only for Jews but for all people of every nation.

CHAPTER 11

Peter Explains His Actions (11:1–18)

1–3 God had just performed a great work among the Gentiles. The Gospel of Christ was now available to the whole world—to both Jews and Gentiles. All Christians should have rejoiced at this new development and praised God for it. But what happened? The **circumcised believers**—that is, Jewish Christians who had not given up their Jewish customs—began to criticize Peter. They accused Peter of having disregarded Jewish tradition; he had broken the man-made rule that Jews must not eat with Gentiles.

Whenever God does a great work in the church, there are always some Christians who are unhappy and complain. Often they are jealous because they didn't get to take part in the new work. Or they are unhappy because their ideas were not accepted or their plans not carried not. Or they are unhappy because they have not received as much honor and recognition as they think they ought to have received. But whatever the reason for their complaint, they are basically complaining against God, because He is the one behind the work. And to complain against God is a serious sin. Because of their complaining, God did not allow the ancient Jews to enter the promised land (Numbers 14:26–30). Brothers and sisters, let not this sin be found among us! When God does a work, let us with one mind rejoice and give Him our thanks and praise.

Not only did the Jewish Christians criticize Peter, but the non-Christian Jews began to oppose him as well. Before that time the Jews had shown respect for Peter and the other apostles because of the mighty works they had performed. But now the Jews began to persecute Peter and the other apostles also (see Acts 12:1–3).

4–14 In this section, Peter addresses the Jewish Christians and defends his actions. He here repeats everything that happened among the Gentiles, which Luke has described in the previous chapter (see Acts 10:9–33).

15 **"As I began to speak, the Holy Spirit came on them,"** said Peter. Peter's sermon is written in Acts 10:34–43. But Peter didn't get to complete his sermon, because in the middle of it the Holy Spirit suddenly came upon Cornelius and his household, and Peter could not continue (see Acts 10:44–46).

16 When Peter saw the Holy Spirit descend on the Gentiles, he remembered that Jesus had said, "**. . . you will be baptized with the Holy Spirit**" (Acts 1:5).

17 Peter realized that the same gift of the Holy Spirit that Jesus had promised His disciples had now been given to the Gentiles also. God Himself had given the gift. How was Peter going to oppose God? How could Peter refuse to baptize with water those whom God Himself had baptized with the Holy Spirit?

18 When the Jewish Christians heard Peter's explanation, their complaining stopped. And when their complaining stopped, their praising began.

When we complain against a brother, we usually don't know all the facts. Those Jewish Christians knew only that Peter had gone to the house of a Gentile. Why he went they did not know. Before we criticize our brother for doing something, let us first find out why he did what he did. If we do this, more often than not we will find there is nothing to criticize!

The Church in Antioch (11:19–30)

19 After Stephen's death, the disciples scattered throughout Israel (see Acts 8:1,4). Some disciples went even further to places like **Phoenicia** (modern Lebanon) and **Cyprus**, a large island in the eastern part of the Mediterranean Sea. Others went to **Antioch**, a large city of Syria located north of Phoenicia. At that time Antioch was the third largest city in the Western world.[53] Most of these

[53] The largest city was Rome, and the second largest was Alexandria in Egypt.

disciples preached only to Jews living in these places. They had not heard about the conversion of Cornelius and his family.

20 But the disciples who went to Antioch began to proclaim the Gospel also to the **Greeks**, that is, Gentiles. These disciples were mainly from Cyprus and **Cyrene**.[54]

21 Because the **Lord's hand**—that is, His power—was with the disciples, a **great number of people** believed and turned to the Lord. When the "Lord's hand" is with us, the church grows. We can assume that most of that **great number of people** who accepted the Lord in Antioch were Gentiles, because Antioch was predominantly a Gentile city.

22–24 At that time the church in Jerusalem was considered the "mother church" of all the churches scattered throughout the Middle East; accordingly, the apostles in Jerusalem watched over the affairs of these other churches. Therefore, when the apostles heard that many Gentiles in Antioch were turning to the Lord, they sent Barnabas, the **Son of Encouragement** (Acts 4:36–37), to find out about these new Gentile Christians.

Barnabas was a **good man, full of the Holy Spirit and faith** (verse 24). He encouraged the new Gentile believers, and through his encouragement (and also through the "Lord's hand"), still more people **were brought to the Lord**. Even though Barnabas was a Jew, he did not complain that the Gentiles were now receiving salvation. Instead, **he was glad** (verse 23).

25–26 Barnabas needed a colleague in Antioch to help in the work of preaching and teaching. He remembered Saul, and he went to Tarsus to find him (Acts 9:30). When Barnabas found Saul, he brought him to Antioch, and there they worked together for a year. And the church in Antioch grew.

The disciples were first called Christians at Antioch. From that time on, the believers stopped calling themselves "Jews," "Greeks," and "Gentiles." They took the name of Christ. To be a Christian means to belong to Christ. Let us use the name "Christian" openly and joyfully, without shame. Let us do nothing to dishonor that name.

27–28 At that time a prophet named **Agabus** (see Acts 21:10–11) came down from Jerusalem to Antioch and prophesied that a great famine would soon come. Luke, in a brief historical note here, tells us that that famine actually came during the reign of the Roman emperor, Claudius, 41–54 A.D. It is known from other history books also that there were famines throughout the Roman Empire during Claudius' reign.

29–30 During times of famine, Jerusalem and the surrounding province of Judea usually were affected more severely than other areas. On a number of occasions, Christians from other regions sent gifts to the believers in Judea. The first such collection was raised in Antioch during this period.

In Antioch Saul learned much about raising a collection. Here we see that the disciples gave **each according to his ability** (verse 29). This same rule Paul would later teach to other churches also (1 Corinthians 16:1–2; 2 Corinthians 9:6–11).

The Christians of Antioch sent their gift to Jerusalem by the hand of Barnabas and Saul. Some Bible scholars believe that this trip to Jerusalem was the same as the trip described in Galatians 2:1–10[55] (see Galatians 2:1 and comment). If this is so, then it was at this time that the leaders of the Jerusalem church agreed that Barnabas and Saul should work primarily among the Gentiles (Galatians 2:9). The apostles in Jerusalem asked only that Barnabas and Saul **continue to remember the poor**. Having just brought a gift from Antioch for the poor believers in Jerusalem and Judea, Saul (Paul) could say: "It was **the very thing I was eager to do**" (Galatians 2:10).

---

[54] **Cyrene** was an important city on the north coast of Africa west of Egypt in what is now modern Libya.

[55] Other Bible scholars, however, do not agree. These other scholars believe that the trip to Jerusalem mentioned in Galatians 2:1–10 is really a later trip which is described in Acts 15:1–29. It is not possible to say with certainty which of these two opinions is correct.

CHAPTER 12

Persecution Against the Christians Increases (12:1–5)

1 The **King Herod** mentioned here is the grandson of the Herod who reigned over Judea at the time of Christ's birth (Matthew 2:1; Luke 1:5). Herod was given the title "king" by the Roman emperor, and he ruled in the emperor's name. He had been given jurisdiction over Israel and part of Syria.

When Peter and the other apostles began to accept the new Gentile converts as brothers and sisters in Christ, the Jews living in Jerusalem and Judea began to raise an outcry against them. Wanting to preserve the peace, Herod looked for a way to pacify the Jews. He found the best way to keep the Jews happy was to arrest and execute the apostles, and so he set out to do this.

2 James, the son of Zebedee and the brother of John (Mark 1:19–20), was the first apostle to be killed. James experienced to the full what Jesus had said to him: "**You will drink the cup I drink and be baptized with the baptism I am baptized with**" (see Mark 10:35–40).

3–4 Seeing that the Jews were pleased by the killing of James, Herod next seized Peter with the intent to execute him also. But the **Feast of Unleavened Bread**[55]—that is, the Passover—fell just at that time, and Herod could not hold Peter's trial until after the feast. Therefore, Herod kept Peter in prison. To be sure Peter did not escape, Herod ordered that he be guarded around the clock **by four squads of four soldiers each** (verse 4).

5 The church prayed **earnestly** for Peter. If the church had not prayed, it is likely that Peter's life would have ended right then. God can work without our prayers, but usually He waits to hear our prayers before He acts.

Peter's Miraculous Escape from Prison (12:6–19)

6 The night before he was to be condemned to death, Peter slept soundly. Although he knew it would be his last night on earth, he was not afraid or anxious; he slept in peace. His right hand was chained to one soldier, and his left hand to another. Sentries guarded the door. The final moment had come. There was no way of escape. God often waits for such a moment before He acts. When there is no other hope, then God does His greatest work.

7–10 At the appointed time, God, through His angel, miraculously delivered Peter from jail. It was entirely God's work. The **chains fell from Peter's wrists** (verse 7), and the gate **opened for them by itself** (verse 10).

11 Peter thought he was seeing a vision; it was all like a dream. But then, when they were outside the jail, the angel suddenly disappeared, and Peter **came to himself**. It was no dream. He was free!

Why was James killed and Peter saved? We humans cannot easily understand the purposes of God. Did the church not pray for James? Or did God, through James' death, want to accomplish some great work—which we don't even know about? We cannot know the answers to such questions.

12 The first thing Peter had to do was to inform the other Christians that he had escaped. Peter went to the house of Mary, the mother of **Mark**,[56] where many of the believers had gathered to pray.

---

[55] The **Feast of Unleavened Bread** lasted for one week (Exodus 12:18). The actual Passover fell on the first day of that week, but the Jews commonly referred to the entire week as the "Passover."

[56] This is the **Mark** who wrote the second Gospel. He also witnessed Christ's arrest (Mark 14:51–52). He was a cousin of Barnabas, and accompanied Barnabas and Saul on part of their first missionary journey (Acts 12:25; 13:5,13; Colossians 4:10).

Though it was the middle of the night, Peter's friends were still awake praying.

13–16 When Rhoda heard Peter's voice outside, she became so excited that she forgot to open the door and let him in. She ran in to tell the others that Peter was outside, but they said to her, "**You're out of your mind**" (verse 15). When she persisted, they said it was only Peter's angel.

But Peter kept on knocking, and finally those inside went and opened the door. When they saw Peter they were astonished. There standing at the door was the very answer to their prayers, but they hadn't believed it!

17 Then they all began to rejoice and praise God, but Peter told them to be quiet. Perhaps at that moment the soldiers were searching for him, and they would surely be attracted to such a noisy gathering in the middle of the night.

Peter said to them, "**Tell James and the brothers about this**." By that time **James**, the brother of Jesus, had become the chief leader of the Jerusalem church. Then Peter went to another place to hide from Herod.

18–19 Under Roman law, if any prisoner escaped, the soldiers guarding him were given the same punishment the prisoner was to have received. Since Peter was to have received the death sentence, Herod ordered that all of Peter's guards be executed in his place. Perhaps Herod suspected that one or two of the guards had secretly helped Peter to escape.

Herod's Death (12:20–25)

20 **Tyre** and **Sidon** were large cities of Phoenicia (modern Lebanon) located on the Mediterranean coast. The residents of these cities received most of their food supplies from the province of Galilee, which was under the jurisdiction of Herod. For some reason Herod had become displeased with the people of Tyre and Sidon, and they were afraid that in anger he might cut off their food supply. So in an effort to make peace, they asked Blastus, one of Herod's servants, to arrange for them to meet with the king.

21–22 On the day of the audience, Herod delivered a speech to the people of Tyre and Sidon. In order to please and flatter Herod, the people began to call him a god. Because he did not give the praise to the true God, one of God's angels **struck him down** and he was eaten by worms. Some people believe that a large worm-filled cyst in Herod's liver ruptured.[57] Herod had exalted himself. Now God had made him food for worms!

24 Herod the oppressor and persecutor died, but the **word of God continued to increase and spread**. God raises up rulers and casts them down, but His word remains forever (see 1 Peter 1:24–25).

25 It was only after Herod's death that Barnabas and Saul actually left Antioch to take the collection to the believers in Jerusalem (Acts 11:29–30). When they returned to Antioch, they took with them **John** (also called Mark), Barnabas' cousin (Acts 12:12; Colossians 4:10).

CHAPTER 13

Barnabas and Saul in Cyprus (13:1–12)

1 In addition to Barnabas and Saul, three other leaders of the Antioch church are mentioned here: Simeon, Lucius, and Manaen. **Simeon called Niger**, some think, may have been the man who carried Jesus' cross (Mark 15:21).

---

[57] Such cysts are not uncommon in Middle Eastern countries.

Lucius of Cyrene[58] was among the first to preach to the Gentiles at Antioch (Acts 11:20). **Manaen** had been raised in the same household with **Herod**. This Herod is not the same as the Herod mentioned in Acts Chapter 12. The Herod referred to here is the son of the King Herod who was ruler of Judea at the time of Jesus' birth (Matthew 2:1; Luke 1:5). The Herod mentioned here ruled during most of Jesus' lifetime, that is, from 4 B.C.[59] to 39 A.D. This is the Herod who cut off the head of John the Baptist (Mark 6:14–28). This is the Herod who examined and mocked Jesus after His arrest (Luke 23:6–12). Here were two men, Manaen and Herod, brought up in the same household. How different they turned out to be!

Herod is here called a **tetrarch**, which means "ruler of a fourth part." The Roman emperors used to divide each province of the empire into four parts and then assign a local ruler to govern each part. It was in this way that Herod had obtained his title.

2–3 As these five leaders of the Antioch church were **worshiping the Lord**, the Holy Spirit spoke to them. The more Christians worship the Lord, the more the Holy Spirit will speak to them and guide them. There are many examples of this in the New Testament.

Luke also mentions that these men were **fasting**. Many Christians have testified that when they fast they are much better able to hear the voice of the Spirit and to receive His guidance.

The Holy Spirit said to the five men: "**Set apart for me Barnabas and Saul for the work to which I have called them**". God had already appointed Barnabas and Saul to preach among the Gentiles (Acts 9:15; Galatians 2:9). Now the time had come for them to begin preaching the Gospel in other cities also. Therefore, Simeon, Lucius, and Manaen placed their hands on Barnabas and Saul, and sent them on their way.

The three leaders laid their hands on Barnabas and Saul as a sign of their appointment as missionaries of the church and also as a sign of the fellowship and support of the congregation (see Acts 6:6 and comment). In this way, Barnabas and Saul were sent out by the church at Antioch. And when they returned from their journey, they gave the church a full report of all that they had done (Acts 14:26–27). This has been a common pattern for the sending out of missionaries ever since.

4 **Seleucia** was the port city of Antioch. From there Barnabas and Saul crossed the Mediterranean Sea to the island of **Cyprus**, which was Barnabas' birthplace (Acts 4:36).

5 **Salamis** was the main city on the east coast of Cyprus, and still is today. After arriving there, Barnabas and Saul went first to the local Jewish synagogue to preach. Wherever they went, it was their custom to go first to the Jewish synagogue in that place (verse 14). Mark, whose other name was John, also was with them (Acts 12:25).

6–8 **Paphos** was the main city on the west coast of Cyprus. Here lived the Roman **proconsul**, the chief governing official of the island. The proconsul at the time, Sergius Paulus, had an attendant named Bar-Jesus, or **Elymas** (which means **sorcerer**). Elymas immediately began to oppose Barnabas and Saul. He knew that he would lose his job as sorcerer if the proconsul believed their preaching.

9–11 From here on, Luke uses Saul's Roman name, **Paul**. Paul, **filled with Holy Spirit**, rebuked Elymas. And just as Paul had been struck blind on the road to Damascus, so also was Elymas struck blind at Paul's words. This sorcerer, who had tried to blind others from seeing the truth, now had become blind himself. And he **groped about, seeking someone to lead him by the hand** (verse 11). Where was his power now?

12 The proconsul was amazed by Paul's power and by his teaching, and

---

[58] **Cyrene** is a city of northern Africa (see Acts 11:20).

[59] Christ was actually born in 4 B.C. When the Western calendar was established, the year 1 A.D. was mistakenly placed four years later than Christ's true birth date.

as a result of what he saw and heard, he believed in the Lord.

Paul and Barnabas in Pisidian Antioch (13:13–41)

13 In the beginning Barnabas was the leader of this little group, but as time went on, it appears that Paul gradually assumed the leadership, perhaps partly as a result of his sucessful encounter with the sorcerer Elymas (verses 9–12). Up to this point Luke has always written "Barnabas and Saul." From now on he refers to them as "Paul and Barnabas" (verse 42) or, as in this verse, **Paul and his companions**. Did Barnabas complain that he had become less important than Paul? We don't see any mention of it in the Bible. Barnabas was a man full of grace. It takes much grace, having once been first, to then be second.

Paul, Barnabas, and John (that is, Mark) next sailed to Perga, a city in the district of Pamphylia located in the southern part of present-day Turkey. After arriving there, Mark left Paul and Barnabas and returned to Jerusalem. Luke doesn't say why Mark left, but whatever the reason was, Paul was not happy about it (see Acts 15:36–38 and comment).

14 Paul and Barnabas traveled on to another city called Antioch, located in the district of Pisidia, also in southern Turkey. Hence Luke refers to this city as **Pisidian Antioch** to distinguish it from the Antioch in Syria from which Paul and Barnabas had set out. Pisidian Antioch was a Roman colony. A number of the chief cities throughout the Roman Empire had been designated as Roman colonies, and Paul frequently preached in such colonies (see Acts 16:12). These city colonies were important political and commercial centers, and in Paul's mind, therefore, they were strategic locations from which the Gospel of Christ could spread rapidly throughout the Empire.

On the **Sabbath** (Saturday), Paul and Barnabas went to the synagogue in Pisidian Antioch, as was their custom after arriving in any new city.

15 In the synagogue service of Paul's day, it was customary to begin the service by reading a passage out loud from the **Law** (that is, the first five books of the Old Testament) and another passage from the **Prophets**. Then someone would get up and give a sermon. On this day, the synagogue rulers invited Paul and Barnabas to speak. Together with the reading and hearing of God's word, it is also necessary that someone clearly explain its meaning. This Paul was always ready and eager to do.

16 In every Jewish synagogue service, there were some who were true Jews, whom Paul here calls **Men of Israel**; and there were others who were Gentiles by birth but who followed the Jewish religion. This latter group Paul here addresses as **Gentiles who worship God**. In every place Paul went, it was mainly these Gentiles who accepted his message and believed in Christ. But the true Jews repeatedly rejected Paul's message and turned against him (verses 45,50).

17–19 Paul began his sermon by giving a short summary of Jewish history. In the beginning God, by His grace, chose Abraham, Isaac, and Jacob. By His **mighty power**[60] (verse 17) God brought the Jews out of bondage in Egypt. But in the desert those Jews, who so recently had been released from captivity by the mercy of God, began to grumble and complain against Him. Worse, they made idols to worship. Therefore, God punished that generation of Jews. But to the next generation He again showed mercy, for He led them into the promised land of **Canaan**—that is, Israel—and gave it to them as an inheritance (see Psalm 78:12–55; Acts 7:2–46). The **seven nations** (verse 19) that the Jews drove out of Canaan are mentioned in Deuteronomy 7:1–2.

20–21 At first the rulers of Israel were called **judges**. But eventually the Jews asked to have a king, as other

[60] In place of the words **mighty power**, some translations of the Bible say "uplifted arm." The meaning is the same.

nations had. So God appointed a man named **Saul** to be their first king. But Saul did not obey God, and so God became displeased with him (1 Samuel 13:13–14; 15:22–26,28).

22 Then God **made David their king,** a man **after his own heart** (1 Samuel 13:14). David was a man after God's own heart because, unlike Saul, he was obedient. God said: "**. . . he will do everything I want him to do.**" And God promised David that He would raise up one of his offspring and give him a throne that would last forever (see 2 Samuel 7:12–13; Psalm 89:20,28–29; Acts 7:46–47 and comment).

After many generations of kings, the kingdom originally established by David was split up and destroyed. The Jews were all sent into exile. God had said through the prophet Ezekiel: "**A ruin! A ruin! I will make it** (David's kingdom) **a ruin! It will not be restored until he comes to whom it rightfully belongs; to him I will give it**" (Ezekiel 21:27).

23 The One to whom David's kingdom **rightfully belongs** is Christ. In Christ, God fulfilled His promise to David to establish the throne of his offspring, a throne that would last forever. The prophet Jeremiah prophesied about the coming of a **righteous Branch** of David, who would save Israel (Jeremiah 23:5–6). Christ was that Savior, whom God promised to send. Christ was the Messiah that all Jews had been hoping and waiting for. This was Paul's good news for the Jews gathered in that synagogue in Pisidian Antioch. They should have received his news with joy! But they didn't.

24–25 First, John the Baptist had come to prepare **all the people of Israel** (the Jews) to repent and to accept Christ (Mark 1:2–3; Acts 10:37). But John himself was not the Christ. John wasn't even worthy to untie the thongs of Christ's sandals (Mark 1:7).

26 Paul kept both the Jews and Gentiles in mind as he spoke. Here he calls the Jews **children of Abraham,** and the Gentiles **God fearing Gentiles** (see verse 16). His message was the **message of salvation** for both Jews and Gentiles equally.

27–28 But the Jews in Jerusalem did not recognize the Savior when He finally came to them (Acts 3:17–18). Instead, they killed Him. But in killing Him they were, in fact, fulfilling the prophecies written in their own Scriptures, which they had heard read every Sabbath (Saturday) in their synagogues (Isaiah 53:3–12; Acts 2:23; 3:13 and comments).

29 After Christ was dead, **they took him down from the tree,** that is, from the cross (Deuteronomy 21:23; Acts 5:30; 10:39). Those who took Christ down from the cross were Joseph of Arimethea and Nicodemus, both of them Jews who had secretly sympathized with Jesus (see John 19:38–42). They then laid Jesus' body in a tomb. And Jesus' body remained in that tomb for three days.

30–31 **But God raised him from the dead.** This is the message of victory, victory over death. Without Christ's resurrection, there is no Gospel (Acts 2:24,32; 3:15; 4:10; 10:40–41).

32–33 The **good news,** the Gospel, in Paul's words is this: "**What God promised our fathers he has fulfilled for us, their children, by raising up Jesus.**"

First, God raised up Jesus to be His Son. Paul here quotes from Psalm 2:7, in which God says: "**You are my Son**" (see Mark 1:11).

34 Second, God raised up Jesus from the dead. Having first raised up Jesus to be His Son, God then allowed Him to be killed. Then, after three days, He raised Him up again. And God gave Jesus the blessing He had promised to David: namely, that Jesus' kingdom would have no end. Paul quotes that promise from Isaiah 55:3.

35 God also gave Jesus a body that would not decay but would last forever. Here Paul quotes from Psalm 16:10.

36–37 The promise of a body that would not decay wasn't made to David; it was made to Christ. For David died and his body decomposed. But Jesus died and rose again; His body never saw decay (see Acts 2:25–32 and comment).

38 In order for a person to be saved, his sins must first be forgiven. Without forgiveness of sins there can be no salvation. Forgiveness of sin is obtained through faith in Jesus Christ the Savior (Acts 2:38; 3:19–20; 10:43).

39 The **law of Moses**, that is, the Jewish law, provided forgiveness only for those sins done in ignorance. According to the Jewish law, there was no forgiveness possible for sins committed knowingly (Numbers 15:22–31). But through faith in Christ we are **justified**; that is, through faith we receive Christ's righteousness and become RIGHTEOUS in God's sight. All of our sins, whether done knowingly or unknowingly, are erased. The Jewish law could not justify anyone. The law could not purify anyone's heart or conscience. Through faith in Christ alone can a person be justified (see Galatians 2:15–16; Hebrews 7:27; 9:13–15 and comments).

40–41 Paul here quotes from Habakkuk 1:5. The prophet Habakkuk warned the Jews that if they did not obey God, God would destroy them. Through Habakkuk, God said to the Jews: "**I am going to do something in your days that you would never believe**" (verse 41). That is, God was going to give them a great punishment. But the Jews did not heed Habakkuk's warning. Instead, they scoffed. And an enemy nation overcame them, and they perished.

Now Jesus Christ had come. The **something** that God said He would do was not only the giving of a great punishment; the **something** was also the sending of Jesus. Jesus was God's great "work." But the Jews could not believe that Jesus was their Savior. They scoffed at Him. Thus Paul's warning to the Jews of his own day was this: "Do not scoff. Do not reject Christ. For if you do, an even worse fate will fall upon you than fell upon your fathers who scoffed in Habakkuk's time."

Paul and Barnabas Preach to the Gentiles (13:42–52)

42–43 Some of the Jews and many of the Gentile **converts to Judaism** accepted Paul's word. They asked to hear more. They had heard many sermons in the synagogue before, but never one like this!

44–45 On the next Sabbath, most of the Gentiles in the city came to hear Paul speak. As a result, the Jewish leaders became jealous of Paul's popularity. Furthermore, they feared that the Gentiles who had been following the Jewish religion would turn away and begin following Paul instead. Therefore, the Jews began to oppose Paul.

46 Paul and Barnabas said to the Jews, "**We had to speak the word of God to you first**." The Jews should have accepted Christ. If they had done so, they would have received ETERNAL LIFE. They would have been a **light for the Gentiles** (verse 47). That was what God wanted Israel to be—a light. But the Jews rejected God's word—that is, God's Son Jesus. "Therefore," Paul said to the Jews, "since you have rejected God's word, we must now preach it to the Gentiles."

47 Then Paul quoted from Isaiah 40:6. It was God's will that Israel should be a **light for the Gentiles**. It was His will that, through the Jews, salvation should be brought **to the ends of the earth**, that is, to the Gentiles. Therefore, no matter what the Jews of Pisidian Antioch thought, Paul and Barnabas were determined to preach to the Gentiles the good news of salvation in Christ, even **to the ends of the earth**.

48 The Jews didn't like Paul's message, but the Gentiles rejoiced in it, **and all who were appointed for eternal life believed**. Men are **appointed** for eternal life. God first chooses us. He calls us; He draws us (see John 6:44; Romans 9:16,18; Ephesians 1:4–5). We come to Christ by God's grace. But remember, we are also free to refuse God's grace.[61]

49–50 Whenever God begins to do a great work, Satan is always right there to oppose it. Wherever God opens up for us a door of opportunity for service, there we shall find opposition (see 1 Corinthians 16:8–9). And, sadly, Satan often uses **God-fearing women of high standing and leading men** to do his work.

But in spite of opposition, the **word of the Lord spread through the whole**

---

[61] For further discussion, see General Article: Salvation—God's Choice or Man's Choice?

region (verse 49). The new believers told their neighbors the good news of salvation in Christ. They did not hide their new faith. In the same way, if we ourselves have truly believed in Christ, then we will want to share with others the salvation we have received. Let us do so!

51–52 Paul and Barnabas **shook the dust from their feet in protest against them**; that is, they completely turned their backs on the hostile Jews (see Mark 6:11). Those who reject Christ's servants will themselves be rejected. The Jews of Pisidian Antioch had lost their chance to receive salvation. It was now time for Paul and Barnabas to move on to the next city, Iconium (Acts 14:1). But those Gentile **disciples** who had recently come to Christ **were filled with joy and with the Holy Spirit** (verse 52).

CHAPTER 14

Paul and Barnabas in Iconium (14:1–7)

1–2 The city of **Iconium** was situated about eighty miles west of Pisidian Antioch. The same thing happened in Iconium that had happened in Pisidian Antioch. First, Paul and Barnabas, through the power of the Holy Spirit, proclaimed the Gospel with such effectiveness that many people, both Jews and Gentiles, believed in Christ. But then the Jews of Iconium **who refused to believe** began to stir up opposition to the **brothers**, Paul and Barnabas.

3–4 In spite of opposition, Paul and Barnabas continued **speaking boldly for the Lord** (verse 3). For a **considerable time** they preached and taught the people; and the Lord performed miracles through them, which confirmed their message.

Gradually the city became divided into two groups: those who accepted the apostles' word, and those who did not.

In verses 4 and 14, both Paul and Barnabas together are called apostles. According to the New Testament, apostles are those who have received a special appointment to preach the Gospel and to establish churches (see 1 Corinthians 15:5,7; 1 Thessalonians 2:6).

5–7 Finally the opponents of Paul and Barnabas laid a plot to stone them. But the apostles learned about the plot and were able to escape to the nearby cities of **Lystra and Derbe**[62] (see Matthew 10:23). But once there, instead of hiding, they kept on preaching.

The cities mentioned so far—Pisidian Antioch, Iconium, Lystra and Derbe—were all located in Galatia, a province of the Roman Empire in the central part of present-day Turkey. The New Testament letter to the Galatians was written by Paul to the new churches in these cities, which had been established by Paul and Barnabas on this first missionary journey.

In Lystra and Derbe (14:8–20)

8–10 Just as Peter had healed the crippled beggar at the temple gate (Acts 3:1–10), so Paul healed a man of Lystra who had been crippled from birth. Paul saw that the man had **faith to be healed** (verse 9). Usually in the New Testament, one must have faith in order to be healed. True, even without faith on our part, God is able to heal us; but usually He waits for us to turn to Him in dependency and faith.

11 When the crowd saw how the crippled man was healed, they began to call Paul and Barnabas **gods**. But because they said this in their own language, Paul and Barnabas couldn't understand what they were saying at first.

12 In the religion of the Greeks there

---

[62] **Lystra** and **Derbe** were located in the district of Lycaonia, which was part of the province of Galatia. Like Pisidian Antioch, Lystra was also a Roman colony.

were many gods, the chief among them being **Zeus**. **Hermes**, another god, was the spokesman for the gods. Thus the crowd called Paul "Hermes," because he spoke more than Barnabas did.

13 Thinking Paul and Barnabas to be gods, the people tried to offer sacrifices to them. What mistaken thoughts men have! When Christ, the true God, came to earth, men didn't offer sacrifices to Him; instead, they turned Him—God—into a sacrifice by killing Him! Now these people of Lystra were trying to offer to ordinary men sacrifices that should have been offered only to God.

14 Finally Paul and Barnabas realized what the people were about to do. In horror, the apostles **tore their clothes.**[63] They refused to accept any honor or praise for themselves. Rather, they sought to give all honor to Christ. They hadn't forgotten what had happened to Herod! (see Acts 12:21–23).

15 "We are not gods!" cried Paul. "We are ordinary men who have been sent by the living God to bring you the good news of salvation. We have come to tell you to turn from worthless gods like Zeus and Hermes. There is only one true God, **who made heaven and earth and sea and everything in them**" (Exodus 20:11; Psalm 146:6).

In his preaching, Paul emphasized certain things when the listeners were Gentiles, and other things when the listeners were Jews. His approach was different for the two groups. The reason was that the Jews already knew the one true God. But the Gentiles did not. They worshiped many gods, such as Zeus and Hermes. Therefore, the first thing Paul had to tell the Gentiles was that they should turn to the one true God. The true God was a **living God**, not a dead idol.

16 Here Paul tells the Gentiles of Lystra that up until that time God had shown great patience toward the Gentiles. Paul says: "**In the past,** [God] **let all nations go their own way.**"

17 "But," says Paul, "even though God has not revealed Himself fully to the Gentiles, He **has not left himself without testimony.**" Even though the Gentiles did not have the Jewish law and the prophets (the Old Testament) to teach them about God, they could have learned about God simply by looking at the natural creation around them. They should have been able to recognize the true God. Because it was the true God who sent them rain and gave them crops—not Zeus and Hermes! Therefore, even though God had been patient with the Gentiles up till that time, they were still guilty because they had not recognized Him (see Romans 1:18–21 and comment).

Therefore, although in the past God **let all nations go their own way,** now the time had come when the Gentiles must repent and put their trust in Him (Acts 17:30). God would no longer overlook their guilt.

18 Even after saying these words, Paul and Barnabas **had difficulty** preventing the crowd from offering sacrifices to them.

19 Then Jews came from Pisidian Antioch and Iconium to oppose Paul. So great was their anger against him that they had walked one hundred miles from Antioch to oppose his teaching. These Jews **won the crowd over** and persuaded them to stone Paul. How fickle and double-minded men are! One moment the people were worshiping Paul; the next moment they were stoning him. One moment they were treating him like a god; the next moment like a dog!

Paul later wrote about that day's experience in two of his New Testament letters (see 2 Corinthians 11:25; Galatians 6:17).

20 After the stoning, the people left Paul for dead. But when the **disciples**, the new believers, gathered around him, Paul quickly recovered. Perhaps he had been temporarily knocked unconscious by a stone. Or perhaps God had miraculously brought him back from the dead. Whatever the case, as soon as Paul had gotten up, he went right back into the city. He had no fear of stones!

The next day Paul and Barnabas went

---

[63] The Jews customarily tore their clothes whenever they heard blasphemy against God (see Mark 14:63). To worship a man as if he was God was blasphemy, because it was making sinful man equal with God. This was an insult to God.

to the nearby city of Derbe and preached the good news there.

The Return to Antioch in Syria (14:21–28)

21–22 Paul and Barnabas made disciples in every city. When it came time for them to return home to Antioch in Syria, they traveled back by the same route they had come, and thus were able to visit all the newly made disciples. Even though Paul and Barnabas had recently been expelled from Pisidian Antioch, Iconium, and Lystra, they again entered those same cities in order to encourage the new disciples.

It is not enough to preach the Gospel in a place only once. It is necessary also to teach the new believers and to establish them in their faith. And this is what Paul and Barnabas did. They warned the new disciples that to enter the kingdom of God they would have to endure many hardships. If they wanted to be fellow heirs with Christ, they would have to suffer for Him (see Romans 8:17; 2 Timothy 2:12; 3:12 and comments).

23 Paul and Barnabas **appointed elders for them** (the new believers) **in each church**. These **elders** were themselves new believers! But in a recently established church there are often no older Christians to be leaders; everyone is a new Christian. Therefore, Paul and Barnabas had to trust that the Holy Spirit would guide and strengthen these new elders. And **with prayer and fasting,** Paul and Barnabas **committed them to the Lord**.

These "elders" were not chosen by the vote of the church members. They were **appointed** by the apostles. In the New Testament, this is the most frequently mentioned method of selecting leaders for the church (see Acts 6:3–6; Titus 1:5; General Article: Church Government).

24–26 The apostles returned to Perga (Acts 13:13), and then they went to the port city of Attalia. From there they sailed to Antioch.

27–28 Paul and Barnabas had been sent out by the Antioch church. They had been away for a year on their missionary journey. Now it was time for them to give a report of their activities to their home church. They reported not what they themselves had done; rather they reported **all that God had done through them** (verse 27). God can work without preachers, but preachers can't do anything for God unless God works through them. The Christians at Antioch had certainly been praying for their missionaries. The work of Paul and Barnabas was their work too. Without the prayers of the church, this first missionary journey would have been a failure.

CHAPTER 15

The Council at Jerusalem (15:1–5)

1 Some men came down from Judea[64] **to Antioch**; these men were mainly Jewish Christians from the church in Jerusalem. Although they had become Christians, they still believed that it was necessary to observe the Jewish law, that is, the law of **Moses**. These Jewish Christians had heard about the great number of Gentiles turning to Christ in Antioch and the surrounding districts, and they worried that these Gentiles would bring "impurity" into the church. The Jews considered the Gentiles to be impure and sinful. And to a certain extent the Jews were correct. Compared with the Jews, the Gentiles were definitely more impure in their outward behavior—especially in the matter of fornication. Therefore, these strict Jewish Christians wanted to find a way to protect the church from being contaminated by the new Gentile believers. The solution to the

---

[64] **Judea** is the southern province of Israel, in which the city of Jerusalem is located.

problem, they decided, was to require the Gentile Christians to obey the law of Moses. In this way, they thought, the Gentiles could be made "pure." So these Jewish Christians went to Antioch to teach the Gentile believers to obey the Jewish law.

But when the Jewish Christians got to Antioch, they added another teaching which was completely false. They began to teach that if the Gentiles did not become **circumcised, according to the custom taught by Moses**—that is, if they did not obey the Jewish law completely—they could not **be saved**. This teaching was false, because man is saved only by God's grace through faith, and not by any work of the law (see Galatians 2:15–16; Ephesians 2:8–9 and comments).

When the Jewish Christians first came to Antioch, Peter happened to be there also. Before they came, Peter had been having complete fellowship with the Gentile believers. But when the Jewish Christians from Jerusalem arrived, Peter, because of their teaching, stopped eating with the Gentile Christians. Even Barnabas soon fell into the same error along with Peter[65] (see Galatians 2:11–13). Paul immediately saw that because of this false teaching of the Jewish Christians, a great split was about to develop in the church. We know, however, that in the end Peter took Paul's concern seriously, because a little later at the Jerusalem council described below, Peter took Paul's side in the dispute that arose there (verses 7–11). Peter remembered how the Gentile Cornelius and his family had become Christians. It had not been necessary to circumcise them (Acts 10:44–48; 11:15–18).

These Jewish Christians from Jerusalem also carried their false teaching to the new Galatian churches established by Paul and Barnabas on their first missionary journey. It was mainly to counter this false teaching that Paul wrote his New Testament letter to the Galatians.

2 The Christians at Antioch, especially Paul and Barnabas, did not accept the teaching of the Jewish Christians from Jerusalem. The matter could not be settled between the two parties. Therefore, the church at Antioch sent Paul and Barnabas, together with some other believers, to discuss the matter with the apostles and elders in Jerusalem.

3–4 On the way to Jerusalem, Paul and Barnabas told the believers they met about how the Gentiles were turning to Christ.

5 The Jewish Christians who started the false teaching were mainly Pharisees, who were the strictest party among the Jews. (Paul himself was a Pharisee.) They insisted that the Gentile Christians **must be circumcised and required to obey the law of Moses**."[66]

Peter and James Give Their Opinions (15:6–21)

6–7 At the meeting, Peter got up and told the others about how God had commanded him to preach the Gospel to Cornelius and his family (Acts 10:19–20).

8–9 At that time Peter had learned that God **made no distinction** between Jews and Gentiles (Acts 10:34). Man is not made pure and righteous because of his work or his birth, but only because of his faith.

10 Peter said that they must not place on the "**disciples** (the Gentile Christians) **a yoke** (the Jewish law) **that neither we nor our fathers have been able to bear**."

The Jewish law was like a heavy yoke,

---

[65] Peter's other names were Cephas (his name in Aramaic) and Simon, which was his original Jewish name (see John 1:42).

[66] The command to be circumcised was given by God to Abraham four hundred years before God gave the Jewish law to Moses (Genesis 17:9–11). Paul knew that if he agreed that circumcision was necessary for salvation, then he'd have to agree that the whole Jewish law was also necessary for salvation—and that, he knew, was totally false (see Galatians 5:3). In principle, being circumcised and obeying the law were the same thing. Therefore, Paul rejected the idea that the Gentiles had to be circumcised.

because it contained hundreds of little rules that the Jews were required to obey. Except for the Pharisees, the Jews themselves found the law to be a heavy yoke. About the Pharisees Jesus had said, **"They tie up heavy loads and put them on men's shoulders"** (Matthew 23:4). But Peter had found that Jesus' load was light, not heavy (Matthew 11:28–30). Why should the Jewish Christians now make these new Gentile believers obey all these unnecessary rules, which the Jews themselves found such a burden to obey?

11 Then Peter said an important thing: The Jews themselves could not be saved by obeying these rules. The Jews, like the Gentiles, were saved only by grace through faith. **". . . it is through the grace of our Lord Jesus that we** (Jews) **are saved, just as they** (the Gentiles) **are,"** said Peter. Thus, if the Jews weren't saved by obeying the law, how were the Gentiles going to be saved by obeying it?

12 When Peter had finished speaking, Paul and Barnabas told the assembly how God was bringing the Gentiles to faith in Christ. This was further clear proof that God accepted the Gentiles just as much as He accepted the Jews.

13–15 James, the younger brother of Jesus, was the main leader of the Jerusalem church at that time. James said that what **Simon** (Peter) had said was in agreement with the prophecies of the Old Testament prophets.

16–18 Then James quoted from Amos 9:11–12. The prophet Amos wrote that God would rebuild **David's fallen tent** (verse 16). That is, God would restore David's true kingdom—which is the church of Christ. The **remnant of men** (verse 17) are the Jews who believe in Christ (see Romans 9:27; 11:5). Therefore, according to Amos' prophecy, God would establish Christ's kingdom, the church, so that both Jews and Gentiles **may seek the Lord** and find Him.

19 James made the judgment that it was not necessary for Gentile Christians to be circumcised or to obey the entire Jewish law.[67] **". . . we should not make it difficult for the Gentiles who are turning to God,"** James said. There is no other requirement for salvation except the one given by God: namely, faith in Jesus Christ. So let no man add any additional ones!

20 But James requested that the Gentile Christians observe three things: first, let them not eat meat offered to idols; second, let them abstain from any kind of sexual immorality (that is, any sexual conduct forbidden by Jewish Law); and third, let them not eat any meat from which the blood had not been properly drained (Genesis 9:4; Acts 15:29).

Why did James ask the Gentile Christians to observe these three things? The reason is this. It was extremely important that the Jewish and Gentile Christians remain in fellowship with each other. The things about the Gentiles which the Jews detested most were their tendency to sexual immorality and their eating of unclean meat. Therefore, so that the Jewish Christians might not be given unnecessary offense, let the Gentile believers not engage in these three practices. Let the Gentile believers refrain from these three things not by compulsion but freely, not to gain salvation but to show love for their Jewish brothers and sisters in the Lord (see Romans 14:15,19–21; 1 Corinthians 8:9–13 and comments).

21 Finally, James reminded the Jewish Christians that the Gentiles had many opportunities to learn about the Jewish law, because every Sabbath (Saturday) the law was read out loud in the Jewish synagogues. The law would not be forgotten. The Gentile Christians could be taught to respect the law. But for obtaining salvation the law was not necessary—neither for the Jew nor for the Gentile.

---

[67] It is necessary for all Christians to obey the ten commandments (Exodus 20:1–17). In this verse James is talking only about the rules pertaining to Jewish rituals, such as the offering of sacrifices, the eating and washing customs, etc. It is these rules which Christians do not have to follow (see Matthew 5:17–19 and comment).

The Council's Letter to Gentile Believers (15:22–35)

22 The leaders of the church in Jerusalem chose Judas and Silas to take a letter to the Gentile Christians of Antioch. **Silas**[68] (who was also called Silvanus, his Roman name) later became Paul's traveling companion (verse 40).

23–29 The Jerusalem apostles began their letter by clearly opposing the Jewish Christians that had initially gone down from Judea to Antioch. Because it was these Jewish Christians who had, by their false teaching, caused all the trouble in the first place. They had gone to Antioch without any authorization from the Jerusalem apostles.

Then, in their letter, the apostles repeated the things that James had said before the council (verse 20). Here in verse 29, they instruct the Gentile believers to abstain **from blood, from the meat of strangled animals**. That means that the Gentile Christians were not to eat the meat of any animal from which the blood had not been properly drained at the time it was killed. An animal that had been killed by strangling would not have had its blood drained, and thus should not be eaten.

Notice that in verse 28 the apostles write: **It seemed good to the Holy Spirit and to us**. The Holy Spirit was also present at that meeting. The Spirit had guided them. Let us remember that the Holy Spirit is present at all of our meetings. Whatever decision we come to, we need to be able to say: "This decision seems good to us and to the Holy Spirit."

30–35 The Gentile Christians at Antioch received the apostles' letter with gladness. The split that had threatened to come between the Jewish and Gentile Christians had been averted.

Disagreement Between Paul and Barnabas (15:36–41)

36 Paul proposed to Barnabas that they visit again the new churches which they had established in Cyprus and Galatia. It was essential that they do this. A pastor or preacher has a duty to follow up those who have heard and accepted God's word as the result of their preaching; they must at least appoint a representative to do this if they cannot do it themselves. Confirming new believers is just as important as converting unbelievers.

37–39 Paul was unhappy with Mark, because Mark had **deserted** Paul and Barnabas (verse 38) during their first missionary journey (Acts 13:13). The Bible does not give the reason why Mark deserted them.

However, Barnabas, who was Mark's cousin, wanted to take Mark with them. Paul would not agree, and so Paul and Barnabas decided not to travel together; from that time on, they each went their own way.

In one way, we are sad to read about this disagreement between Paul and Barnabas. We see their weakness. They are men like ourselves. Disagreements can arise even between good and godly men, and cause them to separate.

But, in another way, we can see a good side to this event. Paul and Mark were evidently not compatible with each other. It would have been unwise to force Mark to travel with Paul. We can guess that Mark's spiritual development might have been thwarted if he had remained under Paul's authority. But Barnabas believed that, in time, Mark would become a mature and effective disciple. Barnabas, more than Paul, would be able to help Mark grow spiritually. Thus we can see it was to Mark's benefit that he and Barnabas went off in one direction, while Paul and Silas went off in another.

We know that in the end Barnabas' assessment of Mark proved to be correct. Later on, Mark became an important colleague of Peter. He wrote the New Testament Gospel of Mark. And even Paul's opinion changed as time passed, because some years later Mark became one of Paul's closest colleagues (Colossians 4:10; 2 Timothy 4:11; Philemon 23).

---

[68] **Silas** (Silvanus) is also mentioned in 2 Corinthians 1:19; 1 Thessalonians 1:1; 1 Peter 5:12.

40–41 Another good thing resulted from the disagreement between Paul and Barnabas: instead of just one missionary team, there were now two. Barnabas and Mark went to Cyprus, where Barnabas was born (Acts 4:36). And Paul and Silas went to Syria and Cilicia, where Paul was born (Acts 21:39). Thus began Paul's second missionary journey.

CHAPTER 16

Timothy Joins Paul and Silas (16:1–5)

1–2 From Cilicia, Paul and Silas passed into the province of Galatia and visited the cities of Derbe, Lystra, and Iconium, where Paul and Barnabas had preached on their first missionary journey.

In Lystra, Paul met a young disciple named **Timothy**. Because the other Christians in Lystra spoke well of Timothy, Paul wanted to take Timothy along with him. Timothy's mother was a devout Jewish Christian named Eunice (2 Timothy 1:5).

3 Timothy was half Jew, half Gentile (verse 1). Since Timothy had been brought up as a Jew, Paul thought it would be better if he became a full Jew by being circumcised. As a full Jew, Timothy would be of much greater help to Paul when they went to Jewish synagogues to preach.

In many places in the New Testament, Paul has written that circumcision is not necessary for obtaining salvation (1 Corinthians 7:19; Galatians 5:2,6; 6:15). Paul did not tell Timothy to be circumcised so that he could be saved; Timothy was already saved through faith. Rather, Paul had Timothy circumcised in order that a greater number of Jews might be brought to faith in Christ. Paul wrote: **To the Jews I became like a Jew, to win the Jews. To those under the law, I became like one under the law (though I myself am not under the law), so as to win those under the law** (1 Corinthians 9:20). In everything he did, Paul had only one goal: namely, to win Jews and Gentiles to Christ.

4–5 Wherever Paul and Silas went, they told everyone about the decisions of the Jerusalem council (Acts 15:28–29).

Paul's Vision of the Man of Macedonia (16:6–10)

6–8 The **province of Asia** mentioned in verse 6 was a province located to the west of the provinces of Phrygia and Galatia. Today that area forms the western part of present-day Turkey. In Paul's time, the main city of the province of Asia was Ephesus. But on this journey, the Holy Spirit did not allow Paul to pass westward into the province of Asia. Instead, the Spirit led Paul and his companions northward toward the province of **Bithynia** (verse 7). When they came near Bithynia, the Holy Spirit again caused them to change their plans. They were directed by the Spirit to again head west instead of entering Bithynia. So, in obedience to the Spirit, they finally arrived at the port city of **Troas** on the coast of the Aegean Sea, which lies between Turkey and Greece.

9–10 While in Troas, Paul received a vision of a man saying to them: **"Come over to Macedonia and help us"** (verse 9). **Macedonia** was a northern province of Greece.[69] Its main cities were Philippi and Thessalonica. Luke writes in verse 10: **... we got ready at once to leave for Macedonia**. Luke says **we**, because at that point Luke himself joined Paul and traveled with him to Macedonia.

---

[69] Greece is an important southern European country on the Mediterranean Sea. To the east, it is separated from Turkey by the Aegean Sea; and to the west, it is separated from Italy by the Adriatic Sea. In New Testament times, Greece had fallen under the control of the Roman Empire. For further discussion, see comment on Acts 17:16.

In this verse we see one of the most important events in world history: namely, the carrying of the Gospel of Christ to Europe. Instead of going east, Paul and his companions went west. If Paul at that point had gone eastward into the countries of southern and central Asia, what a difference there would have been in world history! But God's plan was that the Gospel should spread first throughout the Roman Empire.

Lydia's Conversion in Philippi (16:11–15)

11–12 **Samothrace** is an island in the Aegean Sea. **Neapolis** was the port city connected with the city of Philippi. Here we see again Paul's custom of choosing a main center in which to preach the Gospel, for Philippi was an important Roman colony (see Acts 13:14 and comment).

13 There was no Jewish synagogue in Philippi at the time of Paul's arrival. According to Jewish law, there had to be at least ten Jewish men living in a place before a synagogue could be established there. Therefore, we can conclude that there were less than ten Jewish men living in Philippi when Paul arrived. However, there were a small number of people in Philippi who feared and worshiped the one true God, and they used to meet together outside the city gate near the bank of a river. On the first Sabbath (Saturday) after their arrival in Philippi, Paul and his companions went to that meeting place and spoke with the worshipers who had gathered there.

14 One of the worshipers, a woman named **Lydia**, heard Paul's message and put her faith in Christ. Thus she became the first European Christian. She was a seller of a purple dye used for dyeing cloth. This dye was produced in Thyatira, a city in the province of Asia (verse 6), from whence Lydia had come to Philippi to do business.

It is written here that the **Lord opened** [Lydia's] **heart to respond to God's message**. True religious conversion is always a work of God's grace. First, God opens our heart to **respond** to His word. But then we ourselves must open the door of our heart and let God in. That is our part. Jesus said: "**Here I am! I stand at the door and knock. If anyone hears my voice and opens the door, I will come in and eat with him, and he with me**" (Revelation 3:20).

15 As with Cornelius and his household, Lydia and her whole household believed and were baptized together. In New Testament times, it was a common thing for the members of a household to become Christians all at one time (see Acts 11:14; 16:31,33; 18;8). It is the responsibility of a husband and wife to see that all who live in their home have the opportunity to hear and to accept God's word—the Gospel of Christ.

Paul and Silas in Prison (16:16–40)

16 The second resident of Philippi mentioned in this chapter is a poor demon-possessed slave girl. Many people believed that she could predict the future, and they paid money to her masters to have their fortunes told. In this way the slave girl's masters made much money from her fortune-telling. But it was not the slave girl who was doing the fortune-telling; it was an evil **spirit** within her that did the talking.

17 This evil spirit recognized that Paul had been sent by God to show men the way of salvation. Evil spirits can always recognize Christ and His servants (see Mark 1:23–26).

18 For many days the slave girl followed Paul around raising a clamor. Finally Paul ordered the evil spirit to leave her, and the spirit immediately left her and she was free.

19 But the girl's ability to predict the future also left her, and she could no longer tell people's fortunes. Thus, when her masters realized that they had lost their income from her fortune-telling, they were furious.

20–21 The girl's masters accused Paul and Silas of "**advocating customs unlawful for us Romans to obey**", and to a large extent their accusation was true. By preaching the Gospel of Christ in a Roman colony like Philippi, Paul and his companions were, in fact, breaking the law of the Roman Empire. Because, according to Roman law, it was illegal for anyone to preach a strange or foreign religion among Roman citizens.

22–24 In New Testament times, the Jews used to punish criminals by whipping them. The Romans used to punish criminals by beating them with rods. Without even examining Paul and Silas, the magistrates of Philippi concluded on the basis of the crowd's uproar that they must be guilty of the accusation against them, and so they gave the order that they be beaten. After their beating, Paul and Silas were thrown into prison.

The jailer fastened Paul and Silas' feet in stocks. In Roman prisons such stocks were placed so that the prisoner's feet were spread widely apart; this resulted in intense discomfort for the prisoner.

In 2 Corinthians 11:25, Paul writes that three times he was **beaten with rods**. This beating in Philippi was one of those times.

25 Then what did these two apostles do? There they were—sitting in jail, just beaten with rods, their feet stretched apart in stocks. So what did they do? They began to sing hymns and praise God! The other prisoners in the jail surely must have been dumbfounded!

26 Then God, by means of an earthquake, caused the prison doors to open and the chains of the prisoners to come loose—not only the chains of Paul and Silas, but the chains of all the other prisoners as well. Such chains would have been securely attached to the walls and floor of the prison; nevertheless, God caused them to come apart.

27 The jailer awoke from the earthquake and ran to the jail. Seeing the doors of the jail wide open, he immediately assumed that all the prisoners had escaped. For a Roman jailer, there could be no greater disgrace. Fearing that he would receive the death penalty for allowing his prisoners to escape (Acts 12:18–19), the jailer at once decided that the best thing to do would be to kill himself.

28 Because of the darkness, the jailer could not see inside the prison. But Paul, from inside, could see the jailer drawing his sword to kill himself. "**We are all here!**" Paul shouted. The other prisoners hadn't even tried to escape. Perhaps Paul had ordered them to stay, and because they recognized that he was in some way sent from God, they had obeyed him. God had loosened their feet, but He had bound their hearts.

29–30 The jailer fell at Paul and Silas' feet trembling with fear. Perhaps earlier the jailor had heard that slave girl crying out: "**These men are servants of the Most High God, who are telling you the way to be saved**" (verse 17). These men possessed God's power. No jail was strong enough to hold them. "Such men can show me how to escape from God's wrath," thought the jailer. Having just barely been saved from killing himself, the jailer had now begun to think about his soul.

31–34 After they had spoken the word of the Lord to the jailer and his family, Paul and Silas baptized them. There was no reason to wait. Furthermore, Paul and Silas might be gone by tomorrow. Because they had believed, the jailer and his family were filled with joy. From this, we can assume that they were also filled with the Holy Spirit; one of the fruits of the Holy Spirit is joy (Galatians 5:22).

35-36 The magistrates of Philippi decided that the beating plus one night in jail was enough punishment for Paul and Silas, so the next morning they ordered that they be released.

37 Both Paul and Silas were Roman citizens.[70] According to Roman law, it was illegal to beat a Roman citizen. Thus, in causing Paul and Silas to be beaten, the magistrates had made a terrible mistake. They were filled with fear. If the news of what they had done spread, they would be severely punished.

It would seem that the previous day Paul and Silas had not told anyone they were Roman citizens. They were prepared to suffer for Christ's sake. They didn't

[70] For further discussion of the subject of Roman citizenship, see Acts 22:25 and comment.

want to give the appearance of being afraid. But now they demanded that the city magistrates apologize to them openly. By forcing them to do this, Paul and Silas hoped that the people would then have more respect for Christ's Gospel and for His servants. They also hoped that the people would have a higher regard for the new Philippian believers as well.

38–40 The magistrates had thrown Paul and Silas into jail publicly; let them now come and publicly let them out! Therefore, the magistrates came and apologized and released Paul and Silas, asking them to please leave their city. Before they left, however, Paul and Silas went to Lydia's house to encourage and comfort the new disciples who had gathered there to see them off.

We know from reading Paul's New Testament letter to the Philippians that the Philippian church grew rapidly and became strong. The Philippian believers continued to send gifts to Paul to support him in his travels (Philippians 4:10,14–16). And by their love and faithful Christian testimony, they continued to give Paul great joy.

CHAPTER 17

In Thessalonica (17:1–9)

1 **Thessalonica** was the capital of the province of Macedonia. Today the city is called Salonika, and it is still one of the chief cities of northern Greece. It was to the newly established church in this city that Paul wrote his New Testament letters, 1 and 2 Thessalonians (see 1 Thessalonians 2:1–2).

2–3 **Christ had to suffer and rise from the dead**. Here, in summary, we see Paul's Gospel. First, **Christ had to suffer** for our sins. He had to die in our place. Second, Christ had to **rise from the dead**. He ascended into heaven, and was seated at the right hand of God. The prophets of the Jewish **Scriptures** (the Old Testament) had prophesied that Christ would come. "**This Jesus . . . is the Christ**," said Paul (verse 3), the Christ (Messiah) for whom the Jews had been waiting (see Luke 24:25–27,45–46; 1 Corinthians 15:3–4).

4 Some Jews and many **God-fearing Greeks** (Greeks who worshiped the one true God) accepted Paul's message. Among these Greeks were Aristarchus and Secundus, who are mentioned in Acts 20:4.

5 Just as the Jews had done in Pisidian Antioch (Acts 13:50) and other cities, the Jews of Thessalonica vehemently opposed Paul and his companions. The **Jews were jealous**, because so many God-fearing Greeks were beginning to follow Paul's teaching instead of theirs.

6–7 Paul and Silas had been staying at the house of a new believer called **Jason**. Not finding Paul and Silas, the crowd seized Jason and some other **brothers** (new Christians), and dragged them before the officials of the city. They accused Jason of welcoming into his house these **men who have caused trouble all over the world** (verse 6). In one way this charge was true, because Paul and Silas were indeed turning Satan's kingdom upside down.

Paul and Silas were accused not only of preaching a foreign religion (see Acts 16:20–21), but they were also accused of proclaiming the existence of another king besides the Roman emperor **Caesar**.[71] To honor the name of any other king was a great crime against Caesar. Therefore, the crowd thought: "Surely these men must be enemies of the Roman Empire."

8–9 When the city officials could not find Paul and Silas, they made Jason and the other believers post a bond, which would guarantee that these

---

[71] All Roman emperors were called **Caesar**.

preachers would not come again into the city. If Paul and Silas did set foot in the city again, Jason and his friends would then have to forfeit their bond (see 1 Thessalonians 2:17–18).

Even though Paul and Silas had to hurriedly leave Thessalonica after only a few weeks, the new church they had established there grew in faith. By reading Paul's two New Testament letters to the Thessalonians, we can learn that the Thessalonian Christians, like the Philippian Christians, gave Paul much joy because of their faith and witness (see 1 Thessalonians 1:6–10).

In Berea (17:10–15)

10 **Berea** was a city about sixty miles west of Thessalonica. Christ had said to His disciples: **"When you are persecuted in one place, flee to another"** (Matthew 10:23). But Christians don't flee in order to hide; they flee in order to preach and witness in another place. By persecuting Christians the devil thinks he is stopping the Gospel, but in fact he is causing it to spread!

11–12 The Jews of Berea were open-minded, and they listened intently to this new preacher, Paul. And then they compared what Paul was saying with their own **Scriptures,** the Old Testament. We ought always to do as the Bereans did. Whenever we hear any new teaching, we must first make sure that it agrees with what is written in the Bible. If it does not, we must reject it as false.

13–15 The Thessalonian Jews were not content to persecute Paul and Silas only in their own city; they even came to Berea to persecute them. It is no wonder that Paul criticized the Jews so severely in his first letter to the Thessalonians (see 1 Thessalonians 2:14–16).

Paul again escaped from the Jews, and was brought by the **brothers** (the new disciples from Berea and Thessalonica) to **Athens,** one of the chief cities of Greece and the center of Greek culture and learning.

In Athens (17:16–21)

16 300–500 years before Christ's time, **Athens** was the greatest and most important city in the entire Western world. It was also the capital of the Greek Empire.[72] The Western world's most famous philosophers lived in Athens. The idea of democracy was first conceived in Athens; thus Athens is still called the birthplace of democracy.

Then in 146 B.C., the Romans conquered Athens and extended their authority over all of Greece. But they let Athens remain a free city. Indeed, the Romans admired Greek culture; thus in Paul's time, Athens still remained one of the main cultural and intellectual centers of the Roman Empire. In particular, many famous teachers and philosophers still came to Athens to teach and to debate (verse 21).

The Greeks worshiped many kinds of gods. In Athens there were temples and images of these gods everywhere. Paul was distressed to see this great city **full of idols**. The **sacrifices of pagans are offered to demons, not to God**, Paul wrote (1 Corinthians 10:20).

17 Paul had not planned to spend time in Athens. But, in order not to waste time while he was waiting for Silas and Timothy to join him, Paul began to preach the word of God to whoever would listen. Paul didn't speak only in Jewish synagogues; in accordance with Greek custom, he spoke also in the marketplace.

18 The **Epicurean** philosophers were followers of a famous philosopher named Epicurus, who was born about three hundred years before Christ. According to his philosophy, there was no meaning in life except to enjoy oneself and to remain at ease.

The **Stoic** philosophers held the opposite opinion. They believed that man should be strong and should be able to endure pain and hardship. They said that

[72] Today **Athens** is the capital of the modern nation of Greece.

man should not seek for pleasure, but rather should strive for self-control.

When they heard Paul's teaching, both groups of philosophers scoffed at him. They called him a **babbler**, which in the Greek language means one who goes around like a bird, picking up tiny bits of knowledge.

19–20 The **Areopagus** is actually the name of a large hill in the middle of Athens. The council of rulers and elders of the city used to meet on top of that hill. Later the council itself became known as the "Areopagus." The council had great authority over all that went on in the city. In Paul's time, the council used to question all new teachers that came to Athens. Thus Paul was brought before this council (the Areopagus) to explain his teaching.

21 One of the main reasons the Romans were able to conquer the Greeks was that the Greeks spent more time talking than they did fighting.

Paul's Speech Before the Areopagus (17:22–34)

22 Paul varied his preaching according to his audience. An excellent example of Paul's preaching to Jews and God-fearers (worshipers of the one true God) can be found in his sermon in the Jewish synagogue at Pisidian Antioch (Acts 13:16–41). In this section, on the other hand, we have the best example of Paul's preaching to the Greeks, most of whom worshiped the many false gods of the Greek religion. Therefore, Paul starts his speech by describing the **God who made the world and everything in it** (verse 24), and he ends his speech by saying that this is the God who **will judge the world with justice** (verse 31).

The residents of Athens were **very religious**. But neither religion in itself nor the rituals of religion are of any advantage to men. Millions of people follow a variety of religions; they may be **very religious**, but they are not saved. Only through faith in Christ can man be saved. Religion by itself saves no one.

In fact, the word **religious** that Paul uses here means "superstitious." These people of Athens offered sacrifices **to demons, not to God** (1 Corinthians 10:20). This is superstition, or so-called "blind faith." These men of Athens had the highest wisdom in the world, but they didn't know God. . . . **in the wisdom of God the world through its wisdom did not know him** (1 Corinthians 1:21).

23 Among the altars erected to these false gods, Paul found one on which was written the inscription: **To an Unknown God**. Apparently some of the Athenians suspected there might be a greater god than all the other gods which they worshiped, and so they had set up an altar to this unknown god. But they had no idea what this god was like. Therefore, Paul says here: "Now I will tell you about this 'unknown god.'"

Here we can see Paul's method of teaching and witnessing. The Greeks had some knowledge of religion. So Paul starts with what knowledge they had and then builds on it. Paul didn't show contempt for their religion; he didn't mock them. Paul even quotes one of the Greek poets to illustrate his point (verse 28). Because of this, the Greeks were more ready to listen to what Paul was saying. In this we should follow Paul's example.

24 Here Paul describes the "unknown god" of the Athenians. This God is the creator of all things. And because He created all things, He has lordship over all things. He is the **Lord of heaven and earth**. He **does not live in temples built by hands** (see Acts 7:48–50 and comment). He is a Spirit, and He must be worshiped **in spirit and in truth** (John 4:23).

25 This God doesn't need the sacrifices and offerings of the Athenians. He doesn't get hungry that we must feed Him! Rather it is we who are fed by Him. He gives us not only food but all other needed things as well. What have we to give Him? (Psalm 50:9–12; Isaiah 42:5). He gives us **life and breath**. We couldn't exist for one moment without God's life-giving power. Just as we can't live without breathing, so we can't live without God.

26 **From one man** (Adam) **he made every nation of men**. All men of every nation are descended from one man, Adam.[73] We men are all equal. In God's sight there is no difference between high caste and low caste, between slave and free. God loves equally the civilized Greeks and the uncivilized peoples around them, whom the Greeks despised. Men think that they themselves have established kingdoms and empires; but there is only one establisher of kingdoms and empires, and that is God. God has set the boundaries of every nation. He sets the time of all events. He determines the seasons and the movements of the earth and all heavenly bodies.

27 But in addition to all this, God also shows men His love, mercy, and power, in order that they might **seek him and perhaps reach out for him and find him**. Paul wrote to the Romans: **For since the creation of the world God's invisible qualities—his eternal power and divine nature—have been clearly seen, being understood from what has been made** (Romans 1:20)

Some of the Athenians were reaching out for this true God, whom they didn't know. Paul says that this God **is not far from each one of us**. Wherever we go, God is there with us. Whether we are in a temple or in the desert, whether we are in a palace or in a shack, God is there. **Where can I go from your Spirit? Where can I flee from your presence? If I go up to the heavens, you are there; if I make my bed in the depths, you are there. If I rise on the wings of dawn, if I settle on the far side of the sea, even there your hand will guide me, your right hand will hold me fast** (Psalm 139:7–10).

But even though we seek and find God in the things that He has created, we cannot fully know Him by these things alone. We cannot fully know God until we know Christ, because all of God's attributes have been manifested in His Son Jesus Christ, God's one true incarnation. **No one has ever seen God, but God the only Son, who is at the Father's side, has made him known** (John 1:18). Jesus said: "**Anyone who has seen me has seen the Father**" (John 14:9).

28 God is not far from anyone of us, because **in him we live and move and have our being**. This saying is a quotation from the poem of a Greek poet. Paul uses this quotation because he wants to show the Greeks that in their own literature there is already some reference to this true God. Another Greek poet had written concerning Zeus, the chief god of the Greeks (Acts 14:12): **We are his offspring**. So Paul uses that quotation also, in order to show the Greeks that they are the offspring, not of Zeus, but of the one true God.

Notice how Paul uses the words of pagan poets to teach the truth. By using expressions the Greeks were familiar with, Paul was able to explain to them more clearly the truth about God.

29 We are God's offspring. He created us. How can we think that an idol made by our own hands is worthy to receive worship? God alone is worthy to receive worship. What are idols? Can they speak? Can they hear? Can they create anything? Of course not! They can't even move one finger.

30 Through ignorance, such as idol worship, men dishonor God. But God has been patient with men. He has endured man's ignorance and the evil that has resulted from it. **In the past, he let all nations go their own way** (Acts 14:16). . . . **in his forbearance** [God] **had left the sins committed beforehand unpunished** (Romans 3:25). But now a new day has come. God may have overlooked our former ignorance and sin, but He will do so no longer. He Himself has come to earth to make Himself fully known to men. He has come in the form of Jesus Christ. If men now reject this revelation of God, they will certainly receive punishment. Therefore, God now **commands all people everywhere to repent**.

31 Therefore, let the people of Athens repent, because God **has set a day** when His judgment is going to fall upon them and upon the whole world

---

[73] Adam was the first man created by God (Genesis 1:27; 2:7). The name Adam means "man."

(Psalm 9:8; 96:13; Romans 2:5). God will judge the world **by the man he has appointed**—that is, Jesus Christ (see John 5:27; Acts 10:42; Romans 2:16). And we know that Jesus Christ is the appointed judge, because God has raised Him from the dead.

32 The Greeks did not believe in the resurrection of the body. They believed that man's soul was immortal, but not his body. They were convinced that the body died completely and turned to dust. Therefore, when the Athenians heard Paul mention the resurrection of Jesus, some of them **sneered** and mocked. Others said, "Let us hear more another time; we haven't been able to come to a conclusion on this subject yet." Many people today say the same thing. Many people lose the chance to receive eternal life, because they are not ready to accept God's word. They say, "I'll think about this later," but "later" never comes. These Athenians preferred seeking the truth to finding it. They preferred talking to believing. Let us not be like them!

33–34 Paul's preaching in Athens was not very successful. Only a few believed. Nothing is written in the New Testament about a church having been established in Athens. Nothing is written elsewhere about the two believers mentioned here in verse 34. The only thing we know about **Dionysius** is that he was a member of the Areopagus.[74]

CHAPTER 18

In Corinth (18:1–11)

1–3 Corinth was the main city of southern Greece (see 1 Corinthians: Introduction). When Paul first arrived in Corinth from Athens, he knew no one in the city. But he soon met a Jew named **Aquila** and his wife **Priscilla** (or Prisca). Aquila was a tentmaker, as was Paul. Wherever Paul went, he earned his own living by making tents (see Acts 20:34; 1 Thessalonians 2:9; 2 Thessalonians 3:7–8). In Paul's day, even highly educated Jews earned their living by some manual trade. For example, Jewish teachers did not demand payment for their teaching; they worked at some other job to make their living.

During the time Paul and Aquila lived in Corinth, Claudius was the Roman emperor. When the Christian Gospel was first preached in Rome,[75] the Jews living there had raised such a clamor in opposition to it that Claudius, angry at the disturbance, had expelled all the Jews from Rome. This was the reason that Aquila and Priscilla had left Rome and come to Corinth.[76]

4 As in other cities, Paul preached in the Jewish synagogue in Corinth. Paul proclaimed the Gospel both to the Jews and to those Greeks who feared the one true God.

5–6 When Silas and Timothy arrived in Corinth, they brought with them good news about the recently established church in Thessalonica. The Thessalonians had remained steadfast in their new faith (see 1 Thessalonians 3:6–10). It was after receiving this news that Paul wrote his first New Testament letter to the Thessalonians. Silas and Timothy also brought a gift for Paul from the recently established church at Philippi (see 2 Corinthians 11:9; Philippians 4:15).

As had happened in other cities (Acts 13:45,50; 14:2; 17:5), the Jews of Corinth also began to oppose Paul. Therefore,

---

[74] In place of the words **Dionysius, a member of the Areopagus**, some translations of the Bible say, "Dionysius the Areopagite." The meaning is the same.

[75] It is not known who first brought the Gospel to Rome.

[76] **Aquila** and **Priscilla** are also mentioned in Romans 16:3–4; 1 Corinthians 16:19; 2 Timothy 4:19.

Paul, as a sign of protest, **shook out his clothes** (verse 6), so that no dirt or dust from their synagogue would remain clinging to him. To shake out one's clothes in this way was a sign of extreme displeasure (Acts 13:51). Paul had announced to them the good news of salvation in Christ. By rejecting the Gospel, the Jews had brought upon themselves the judgment of God. Paul had fulfilled his obligation to tell the Jews about Christ. Now Paul would not be guilty of their destruction (see Acts 20:26–27; 1 Corinthians 9:16 and comments).

7 Therefore, Paul went next door and began to preach to the Gentiles. A God-fearing Greek named Titius Justus let Paul preach in his house. Many Bible scholars believe that this man's first name was Gaius, and that he is the same Gaius who is mentioned in Romans 16:23 and 1 Corinthians 1:14.

8 Paul was much more successful in Corinth that he had been in Athens. Here even the synagogue ruler **Crispus** believed in the Lord (1 Corinthians 1:14).

9–11 At this time Paul received a vision from the Lord, which gave him much support and strength. In the vision Jesus promised Paul that while he was in Corinth no one would harm him. The Jews would indeed oppose him (verse 12), but they wouldn't be able to **harm** him. God had chosen many people in Corinth, the Lord told Paul in the vision, and Paul was to be the means of bringing them to faith. So Paul spent the next year and a half in Corinth leading to Christ all those whom God had chosen.

Paul and Gallio (18:12–17)

12 **Gallio** was the Roman **proconsul** (chief official) of **Achaia,** the southern province of Greece.[77] Gallio's authority was great. He had the power to prevent Paul from preaching not only in Achaia but in every province of the Roman Empire. The order of the proconsul of one province was binding in every other province. If Gallio had ordered Paul to stop preaching in Achaia, Paul would then have been prohibited from preaching anywhere else in the Roman Empire.

13 The Jewish religion was one of the legal religions of the Roman Empire; Jews were permitted to have synagogues and to worship God according to the Jewish law. But the Jews charged that Paul was not preaching the Jewish religion but some new illegal religion, and that therefore he was opposing Roman law (see Acts 16:20–21 and comment).

14–16 When Gallio heard the Jews' charge against Paul, he immediately concluded that this was a dispute involving only the Jewish religion. Paul had not broken any Roman law. He was merely preaching a form of the Jewish religion which the Jews at Corinth didn't approve of. Therefore, Gallio refused to prohibit Paul from preaching. And because of this major decision of Gallio, the Christians were able for the next twelve years to legally preach and spread the Gospel of Christ all over the Roman Empire. At the end of that time, however, a new emperor, Nero, outlawed the Christian religion and began to cruelly persecute believers throughout the Empire.[78]

17 After Crispus believed in the Lord (verse 8), a man named **Sosthenes** took his place as ruler of the Jewish synagogue in Corinth. After Gallio had thrown Sosthenes and the other Jews out of the court, **they all** (that is, the Greeks) **turned on Sosthenes** and beat him. In New Testament times, most Gentiles (including the Greeks) harbored ill feelings against the Jews,[79] and they were always

---

[77] The capital of **Achaia** was Corinth.

[78] In 62 A.D. Nero married a woman who, though not a Jew by birth, was a follower of the Jewish religion. From that time on, Nero began to persecute the Christians. In 64 A.D. there was a great fire in Rome which destroyed much of the city, and Nero falsely accused the Christians of starting the fire. After that, Nero persecuted the Christians even more fiercely. Paul, Peter, and many other Christian leaders were put to death by Nero.

[79] The reason the Gentiles disliked the Jews was no doubt because the Jews despised the Gentiles and refused to associate with them.

ready to mistreat them whenever the opportunity arose. In this instance, Gallio had just insulted the Jews by expelling them from the court; now the Greeks added to the insult by beating up their leader Sosthenes.

Paul Returns to Antioch (18:18–23)

18 From time to time the Jews used to make a special **vow** to God. Paul perhaps made a vow of thanksgiving to God for protecting him during his time in Corinth. After such a vow was made, the person making the vow was not allowed to cut his hair until the period of the vow ended. Then on the last day of the vow, the person was to cut his hair and offer the hair to God (Numbers 6:1–21).

Cenchrea was the port city of Corinth (Romans 16:1). From there Paul, Aquila, and Priscilla sailed for Ephesus.

19–21 In Paul's time, **Ephesus** was one of the most important cities in the Middle East. It was a major commercial and cultural center. It was situated on the eastern coast of present-day Turkey. But even though Ephesus was a great city in New Testament times, today there is nothing left of it but ruins.

On this trip Paul spent only a few days teaching in the Jewish synagogue in Ephesus. "**I will come back if it is God's will**," Paul said, as he took his leave of the Jews there. But Aquila and Priscilla remained in Ephesus, and started a house fellowship in their home (1 Corinthians 16:19). In 54 A.D. the Roman emperor Claudius died, and following that, Aquila and Priscilla returned to Rome (Romans 16:3).

22 From Ephesus Paul sailed to Syria (Acts 8:40; 10:1). After he landed in Caesaria, he **went up** to Jerusalem to greet the church there. Some Bible scholars believe that Paul, in accordance with his vow, went to Jerusalem to celebrate the Passover, which was at that time. The word "Jerusalem" is not mentioned in this verse, but it can be understood from the context. Jerusalem was in the mountains; thus from Caesaria (on the coast) Paul **went up** to Jerusalem. Then from Jerusalem he **went down** again to Antioch.

23 The church at Antioch had sent Paul and Silas out on this second missionary journey (Acts 15:40); therefore, just as Paul and Barnabas had reported to the church after their first missionary journey, Paul also on this occasion reported to the church all that God had done through Silas and himself (Acts 14:26–27).

Then Paul again set out for Galatia and nearby Phrygia to strengthen and encourage the believers in the churches he and Barnabas had established on their first missionary journey. Thus began Paul's third missionary journey.

Apollos in Ephesus (18:24–28)

24 **Apollos** was a learned Jew from **Alexandria**.[80] He had a thorough knowledge of the **Scriptures**, that is, the Old Testament.

25 It is not known who first instructed Apollos **in the way of the Lord** (Christ). He knew much about Christ, and he preached the Gospel **with great fervor**.[81] But there was something missing in his teaching. He had learned only about John's baptism, which John had performed in order to prepare people to receive Jesus (Mark 1:2–4). He had not learned about the baptism in Jesus' name, of which Peter had spoken on the day of Pentecost (Acts 2:38). From this we can understand that Apollos had not received the Holy Spirit, because in the New Testament, baptism in Jesus' name usually takes place before one receives the Holy Spirit (see Acts 2:38; 8:15–17 and comments). Apollos had not heard the words that John the Baptist himself had

---

[80] **Alexandria**, situated on the Mediterranean coast, was the main city of Egypt in New Testament times. Today Alexandria is Egypt's second largest city (after Cairo).

[81] In place of the words **with great fervor**, some translations of the Bible say, "being fervent in spirit." The word "spirit" is used in the original Greek text, but it does not refer to the Holy Spirit but rather to Apollos' human spirit.

spoken: "**I baptize you with water, but he will baptize you with the Holy Spirit**" (Mark 1:8).

26 As soon as Aquila and Priscilla heard Apollos preach, they knew there was some lack in his understanding. But they did not point out Apollos' mistake in front of other people. They did not want to embarrass him. Instead, they invited Apollos to their home, and there in private they instructed him more fully in the faith. Even though Apollos was already a famous preacher, he humbly accepted the correction of this older brother and sister.

27–28 Paul had just left Corinth. There was now no apostle or other well-known Christian leader in Corinth. Therefore, the brothers in Ephesus encouraged Apollos to go to Corinth in order to give leadership to the church there. And so Apollos went to Corinth, and gave the church much help. Being a Jew like Paul, Apollos was able to argue effectively with the Jews from their own Scriptures, the Old Testament, that Jesus was the Christ, the Messiah.

Apollos went on to become a great Christian leader. He greatly benefited the church in Corinth. His influence there was so great that some members of the Corinthian church became his disciples and followed him (1 Corinthians 1:12; 3:4). Paul considered Apollos to be his fellow worker and fellow apostle (1 Corinthians 3:21–22; 4:6,9). In Corinth, Paul planted the seed, and Apollos watered it (1 Corinthians 3:6).

Let us learn from this story of Priscilla, Aquila, and Apollos. All of us have some lack or defect. Let us correct each other privately with humility and gentleness. And like Apollos, let us humbly accept such correction when it is given. Then we, too, will grow to be mature and effective servants of Jesus Christ.

CHAPTER 19

Paul in Ephesus (19:1–12)

1–2 After he had met with the disciples in Galatia and Phrygia (Acts 18:23), Paul then came to Ephesus. There he met **some disciples**[82] who had believed in Christ, but who had not yet received the Holy Spirit.

3 Paul's understanding was that being baptized and receiving the Holy Spirit always went together, or at least within a short time of each other. Sometimes the baptism came first (Acts 2:38; 8:15–17); sometimes the Holy Spirit came first (Acts 10:44,47–48). But, in whatever order it happened, to be a true Christian it was necessary both to be baptized and to receive the Holy Spirit.

Therefore, when Paul found out that these disciples had not received the Holy Spirit, he asked them, "**Then what baptism did you receive?**" They answered, "**John's baptism.**"

4–5 Then Paul taught them that John's baptism was given only to prepare men for the coming of Christ (Mark 1:2–4; Acts 18:25). Now, having believed in Jesus, they must be baptized in Jesus' name. Therefore, they were all baptized in Jesus' name. This is the only time in the New Testament where we read about someone having been baptized twice. The reason, of course, was because these disciples had not been baptized in Jesus' name the first time. Once someone has been baptized in Jesus' name—no matter by what method—he never needs to be baptized again (see General Article: Water Baptism).

6–7 This is the third place in the book of Acts where Luke explicitly states that believers spoke in tongues when they received the Holy Spirit[83] (see Acts

---

[82] Whenever Luke uses the word "disciple," he usually means a Christian disciple.

[83] In a fourth place, Acts 8:17–18, it is probable that believers spoke in tongues when they received the Holy Spirit, but it is not explicitly stated.

2:4; 10:44–46). From these examples we can understand that in the New Testament speaking in tongues was a common manifestation of being filled or "baptized" with the Holy Spirit. However, nowhere in the New Testament does it say that all people who are filled with the Spirit must be able to speak in tongues (see General Article: Holy Spirit Baptism).

The three times in the book of Acts where we read about believers speaking in tongues were all very important occasions. The first occasion was on the day of Pentecost, when the disciples received the filling of the Holy Spirit for the first time. The second occasion was on the day that the first Gentiles became Christians. And here, on this third occasion, Paul was in Ephesus, a new center for the spread of the Gospel, and twelve new disciples were needed (verse 7). And so God prepared and anointed these twelve men in a special way by pouring out His Spirit upon them.

These men **spoke in tongues and prophesied**. Speaking in tongues and prophesying are both gifts of the Holy Spirit (see 1 Corinthians 12:10: 14:5,13 and comments).

8–10 For three months Paul taught every Saturday in the Jewish synagogue in Ephesus. However, because of increasing opposition from the Jews, Paul and his disciples moved to the lecture hall of a teacher named Tyrannus, where Paul continued to teach for the next two years. In this way Paul got to preach not only on Saturdays but every day of the week. Furthermore, not only Jews but all the Gentiles of Ephesus could come and hear him as well.

It is likely that Tyrannus taught only in the mornings, since most people in Ephesus slept in the afternoon because of the heat. Thus Paul probably made tents in the mornings to earn his living; and then in the afternoons, instead of sleeping, he would go to Tyrannus' lecture hall and teach his disciples and any other people who came. Within two and half years all the people living in the province of Asia had heard the Gospel of Christ. Also during that time, the churches at Colosse and Laodicea were established by Paul's disciples (see Colossians 2:1; 4:13). Perhaps all seven of the churches mentioned in the second and third chapters of the book of Revelation were founded at this same time (Revelation 1:10–11).

11–12 **God** (by His Holy Spirit) **did extraordinary miracles through Paul**. Many people were healed simply by touching Paul's **handkerchiefs and aprons**[84] in faith (see Mark 5:27–29; 6:56; Acts 5:15). Even though Paul had stopped using these articles, there was still healing power associated with them.

The Sons of Sceva (19:13–22)

13–16 In New Testament times there were numerous sorcerers, many of whom were Jews. When they saw Paul driving out demons in Jesus' name, some of these sorcerers tried to imitate him (see Acts 8:9–13,18–19). Seven sons of a Jewish priest named Sceva once tried, following Paul's example, to drive an evil spirit out of a certain man. But the evil spirit did not recognize these seven brothers. And that demon-possessed man, through the power of the evil spirit within him, overcame those seven brothers and severely beat them.

Christ's name and power are indeed great. But only those whom Christ appoints have the authority to use His name and His power. Sorcerers and magicians have no authority to use Christ's name. Only true and obedient servants of Christ have the authority to act in His name.

17–18 When people saw that demons fled whenever Paul spoke Christ's name, they were filled with awe and fear. They realized that in opposing Christ they had, in fact, been serving Satan. They saw that no magic or demon could protect them from the power of Christ's

---

[84] Paul used to use these **handkerchiefs and aprons** during his work making tents. Such handkerchiefs were wrapped around one's forehead to soak up the sweat. The apron was worn to protect one's ordinary clothes.

name. Therefore, many people repented and believed in Christ.

19–20 The sorcerers and magicians in New Testament times used to recite various mantras, which consisted of strings of meaningless words written on **scrolls**. Great value was placed on such scrolls, because it was widely believed that by reading these mantras one could gain great power. But even some of the sorcerers repented and believed in Christ; they piled their scrolls together and burned them. The value of the scrolls burned that day came to **fifty thousand drachmas**[85]

21–22 Paul remained in Ephesus for two and a half years. His ministry there bore much fruit. During that period in Ephesus Paul faced many dangers, which Luke does not tell us about (see Acts 20:19; 1 Corinthians 15:30–32; 2 Corinthians 1:8–10). Also during his stay in Ephesus, Paul wrote the first and second New Testament letters to the Corinthians.

Paul decided to go to Jerusalem in order to take to the poor Christians there the collection that had been raised by the churches in **Macedonia and Achaia**[86] (see Romans 15:25–26; 1 Corinthians 16:3–5). After that Paul hoped to go to Spain by way of Rome (Romans 15:23–24). Spain was the westernmost region of the Roman Empire.

Timothy was also in Ephesus with Paul at that time, so Paul sent Timothy and Erastus on to Macedonia ahead of him. On a previous occasion Paul had sent Timothy from Ephesus to Corinth (1 Corinthians 4:17).

The Riot in Ephesus (19:23–41)

23 Toward the end of Paul's stay in Ephesus a great disturbance arose in connection with the **Way**—that is, the Christian religion (see Acts 9:2 and comment).

24 The Ephesians had built a huge temple in honor of the goddess **Artemis,** which measured 130 by 60 meters. Throughout the **province of Asia,**[87] people considered Artemis to be the greatest goddess of all. She was thought to be the mother of all other gods, and the mother of all men as well. Inside the temple was an image of Artemis, which actually was a meteorite that had fallen from the sky (verse 35). The surface of the meteorite was covered with bumps resembling breasts. Therefore, the Ephesians believed that this image of Artemis represented a many-breasted woman.

The silversmiths made little silver images of Artemis and sold them for a big profit. But when increasing numbers of people stopped worshiping Artemis and began turning to Christ, the sale of these images fell off and the income of the silversmiths dropped. Therefore, the silversmiths had two reasons for being angry with Paul: the first was religious, and the second was financial. Thus their opposition to Paul was doubly great.

25–27 The silversmiths made their living by making **man-made gods** (verse 26). But Paul was teaching everyone that these gods weren't gods at all; they were worthless. Naturally the silversmiths were angry at Paul!

28–29 The **theater** at Ephesus could seat twenty-five thousand people. The ruins of that theater still remain today. Public assemblies to settle legal matters were held regularly in the theater (verse 39).

Gaius and **Aristarchus** were from Macedonia. Aristarchus was a Thessalonian (Acts 20:4; 27:2; Colossians 4:21). **Gaius** could be the same person as the **Gaius from Derbe** mentioned in Acts 20:4; but it is not likely, because the city of Derbe was not in Macedonia but in Galatia. Gaius and Aristarchus, having been dragged into

[85] The **drachma** was a silver coin used in ancient Greece. One drachma was equivalent in value to one day's wage for an ordinary working man. Thus fifty thousand drachmas was a very large sum.

[86] **Macedonia** and **Achaia** were the northern and southern provinces of Greece respectively.

[87] The **province of Asia** was the westernmost province of what is now present-day Turkey. Ephesus was its chief city.

the theater, were probably the ones who later gave Luke a firsthand account of what happened.

30–31 Paul wanted to appear before the crowd. Paul never feared men. He was always ready to defend the Gospel of Christ at every opportunity. On this occasion, however, Paul's colleagues did not think it advisable for him to speak before such an angry mob. It was too great a risk. Christians may be called to lay down their lives, but they are never called to throw them away.

32–34 Although the crowd was angry mainly with Paul and the Christians, they were also mad at the Jews, who didn't worship Artemis either. Thus when the Jews saw this riot, they began to get worried. They forced **Alexander**,[88] one of their fellow Jews, to go forward and tell the crowd that the Jews had no connection with Christians and that therefore the people didn't need to blame the Jews for what the Christians were doing. But since Alexander was a Jew himself, no one listened to him.

35–37 Ephesus was a free city within the Roman Empire, and it had its own government. The chief official of the city was called the **city clerk** (verse 35). But even though Ephesus itself was a free city, the surrounding province of Asia was under the control of the Roman Empire, and the Roman governor of the province had his residence in Ephesus. If news of such a riot came to his ears, he would surely punish the people of Ephesus, and possibly take away their freedom. Therefore, the city clerk tried very hard to persuade the crowd to quiet down.

38–41 The city clerk reminded the people that if anyone had a complaint against someone else, the matter should be brought up in a court. Or if a dispute arose involving the laws of the city, that should be settled in one of the legal assemblies, which met regularly. But a riot like this was totally unsuitable, and must be ended at once.

CHAPTER 20

Through Macedonia and Greece (20:1–6)

1 Paul had sent Titus on ahead of him to Corinth in order to find out about the situation in the Corinthian church. After leaving Ephesus, therefore, Paul went first to Troas in hope of finding Titus (Acts 16:8). But not finding him there, Paul went on to Macedonia. There he finally met up with Titus, who gave him good news about the Corinthian church (see 2 Corinthians 2:12–13; 7:5–7).

2–3 Paul spent about a year traveling through Macedonia, during which time he reached as far as Illyricum, that is, modern Yugoslavia (Romans 15:19). After that, Paul arrived in **Greece**—that is, Achaia, the southern province of Greece. He remained for three months in Achaia—mainly in Corinth—where he wrote his New Testament letter to the Romans.

From Achaia, Paul planned to return by boat to **Syria**[89] (verse 3) and Jerusalem (Acts 19:21). But just as he was about to get on the boat, Paul heard that the Jews of Corinth were plotting to kill him; so in order to get away from them, he changed plans and decided to go by land back through Macedonia.

4–6 Paul's traveling companions, however, took the boat, and when they reached Troas they waited for Paul to

---

[88] A man named **Alexander** is mentioned in 1 Timothy 1:20 and 2 Timothy 4:14. It is not certain whether these are all the same man or whether they are different men.

[89] **Syria** was a province of the Roman Empire, in which the important New Testament cities of Damascus and Antioch were located (Acts 9:2–3; 11:19–26). Today Syria is a major Middle Eastern nation situated northeast of Israel.

catch up with them. Meanwhile, Paul went by foot to Philippi, where he met up again with Luke; they then together got on a boat going to Troas. (Notice that in verse 6 Luke writes: **we** sailed.) They left Philippi following the **Feast of Unleavened Bread** (Passover).

The brothers mentioned in verse 4 were, together with Paul, taking the collection raised by the Macedonian churches to the poor Christians in Jerusalem. These men were representatives of the various churches in Macedonia, Galatia, and Ephesus.[90] The representatives from Corinth (Achaia) are not mentioned here, but according to 2 Corinthians 8:6,18–24, we can understand that Titus and two other brothers were responsible for taking the Corinthian church's collection.

Eutychus Raised From the Dead at Troas (20:7–12)

7 Paul and his companions stayed in Troas for seven days. The last day of their stay was a Sunday, which is customarily called the **first day of the week**. The believers of Troas had gathered to **break bread**—that is, they had gathered to celebrate the Lord's supper. This is the first mention in the New Testament of Christians holding their weekly service on Sunday rather than on Saturday (as the Jews did).

8–10 As Paul was talking on and on, one of those present, a young man named **Eutychus**, fell asleep. Perhaps the smoke from the **many lamps** caused him to become sleepy. Whatever the reason, the young man fell out of the third story window and **was picked up dead** (verse 9). Luke, the author of the book of Acts, was himself a doctor, and so he was able to tell with certainty that Eutychus was dead. But Paul put his arms around the young man, and his life returned.

Let us heed what befell Eutychus and try not to fall asleep in church!

11–12 Then, after celebrating the Lord's supper and eating a meal together, Paul continued talking until daylight. Shortly thereafter, Paul's companions boarded a ship bound for Jerusalem.

Paul's Farewell to the Ephesian Elders (20:13–38)

13–14 All of Paul's traveling companions boarded the ship at Troas, but Paul did not. To reach the next port, the ship had to go around a peninsula of land jutting out into the sea. Since it was quicker going by foot, Paul decided to walk to the next port, **Assos**; thus he was able to spend an extra day in Troas, before leaving to meet the ship at Assos.

15–16 Ephesus was about thirty miles from Miletus. Because the ship had to stop at Miletus for several days, Paul sent word to the elders of the church at Ephesus to come to Miletus to meet him.

17 Paul was the spiritual father of the church at Ephesus. All the Ephesian elders had become Christians through the preaching and teaching of Paul. Paul himself had baptized most of them (see Acts 19:1–7). For this reason, all of the elders were eager for the opportunity to meet Paul, and they left whatever they were doing and came to Miletus to meet him. A thirty-mile walk was nothing to them!

In Acts 13:16–41, we are given an example of Paul's preaching among the Jews. In Acts 17:22–31, we are given an example of Paul's preaching among the Gentiles. Here in this section, verses 18–35, we have an example of Paul's preaching among Christians.

18–19 Paul reminds the Ephesian elders about his life and ministry among them during the time he lived in Ephesus. Paul had served among them **with great humility and with tears**. These two things, **humility** and **tears**, are necessary for the success of any

[90] Of those mentioned in verse 4, **Aristarchus** is also mentioned in Acts 19:29; 27:2 and Colossians 4:20; **Tychicus** is also mentioned in Ephesians 6:21–22 and Colossians 4:7–8; **Trophimus** is also mentioned in Acts 21:29 and 2 Timothy 4:20.

ministry. Paul's tears were tears of sorrow shed over the sins of his Christian brothers (verse 31). They were also tears shed because of the suffering he endured for Jesus' sake. In Ephesus Paul had experienced many trials. He had suffered because of the **plots of the Jews** (verse 19), and for other reasons as well (see 1 Corinthians 15:30–31; 2 Corinthians 1:8–10).

20–21 But even though he risked being persecuted, Paul had not hesitated to preach and teach openly whatever was beneficial to the believers at Ephesus. Paul didn't preach only the pleasant and reassuring aspects of the Gospel; he also preached about the cross of Christ. Even though the cross was a **stumbling block** to the Jews and **foolishness** to the Gentiles (1 Corinthians 1:23), Paul had fearlessly preached about the crucified Christ, both to the Jews and to the Greeks. Along with that, Paul told both Jews and Gentiles that they must repent and turn to God (Acts 17:30; 26:20). But it was not enough only to repent; Paul taught that men must also put faith in the Lord Jesus Christ.

Wherever he went, Paul by his own life set an example for new disciples to follow (1 Corinthians 11:1; Philippians 3:17; 4:9). This is why his preaching was so effective. Paul was not like the Pharisees of Jesus' time, who did not practice what they preached (Matthew 23:1–3). In many of his New Testament letters, Paul reminded his readers of his life and ministry among them (see 1 Corinthians 2:3–5; 2 Corinthians 6:4–10; 1 Thessalonians 2:1–12).

22–23 For Paul, going to Jerusalem was very dangerous. From the beginning, the Jews in Jerusalem had been trying to kill Paul (Acts 9:29). Nevertheless, in obedience to the leading of the Holy Spirit, Paul was determined to go to Jerusalem. For one thing, he felt under obligation to deliver to the Jerusalem church the collection that had been raised by the Gentile churches. Perhaps the Holy Spirit had given Paul still other reasons for going to Jerusalem, which are not mentioned in the New Testament.

While Paul was at Corinth, he had written to the Romans asking them to pray that he might be **rescued from the unbelievers in Judea** (Romans 15:31). And on his way to Jerusalem, Paul had heard repeated warnings from his brethren that he would surely face **prison and hardships** when he got there (verse 23). At every stop the Christians urged Paul to turn back and not go to Jerusalem (see Acts 21:4,10–14).

24 But Paul was not afraid of persecution or death. He was willing to give up his life for the sake of the Gospel of Christ (Acts 21:13; Philippians 2:17; Colossians 1:24). Paul had only one goal in life, and that was to **finish the race and complete the task** which the Lord Jesus had given him (see 2 Timothy 4:7–8). Paul had no care for either bodily life or bodily death. His only concern was that Christ be **exalted in** [his] **body, whether by life or by death** (Philippians 1:20).

25 Even if he was able to leave Jerusalem safely, Paul did not plan to return to Ephesus and the province of Asia. He had decided to go from Jerusalem to Rome,[91] and from there to Spain[92] (Acts 19:21; Romans 15:23–24,28). Therefore, no matter what happened to him in Jerusalem, Paul believed that he would never again see his Ephesian brothers.

26–27 If the people of Ephesus chose to condemn themselves by refusing to believe in Christ, Paul was not responsible, because in Ephesus he had faithfully proclaimed to all men the **whole will of God** (verse 27). Paul was **innocent of the blood of all men**; that is, he was not guilty of causing their eternal condemnation. He had warned them; he had shown them the way of salvation. By

---

[91] Rome was the capital of the Roman Empire, and was located in what is now the southern European nation of Italy. In New Testament times, Rome was the most important city in the Western world.

[92] Spain was the westernmost province of the Roman Empire; it is today an important country of western Europe.

rejecting Paul's message, they had brought condemnation upon themselves (see Acts 18:6).

28 **Keep watch over yourselves and all the flock**. The leaders of the church must first of all keep watch over themselves! Satan seeks to attack leaders more than others. If a leader falls to Satan's attack, great harm comes to the **flock**, that is, the church (see verse 30). Church leaders are appointed and equipped by the Holy Spirit to be **shepherds** of the flock. Therefore, they need to remain filled with the Holy Spirit. Let these Ephesian elders remember how the Holy Spirit had come upon them when Paul laid his hands on them (Acts 19:1–7).

In the New Testament, there is very little difference in meaning between the words **overseer**[93] (1 Timothy 3:1) and **elder** (Acts 14:23; 20:17). In New Testament times, overseers and elders had basically the same position in the church. They were also called **pastors** (Ephesians 4:11). In the New Testament, all these names are used more or less interchangeably[94] (see General Article: Church Government).

The leader of the church must "feed the flock" (see John 21:15–17; 1 Peter 5:1–4). He must follow the example of Christ, the greatest shepherd of the sheep (see John 10:11–15). Christ laid down His life for the sheep. He **bought** the church—that is, each believer—**with his own blood**. He died in order that we might live.

29 False teachers and false leaders are like **wolves** (Matthew 7:15). Not long after Paul's meeting with the Ephesian elders, such "wolves" did begin to come into the church (1 Timothy 4:1–2; 2 Peter 2:1–3; 1 John 2:18–19). Some time later, Paul wrote to Timothy: **. . . everyone in the province of Asia has deserted me** (2 Timothy 1:15), and that included the Christians in Ephesus! And finally, the Apostle John wrote to the church at Ephesus these words from Jesus Himself: **"Yet I hold this against you: You have forsaken your first love. Remember the height from which you have fallen! Repent and do the things you did at first. If you do not repent, I will come to you and remove your lampstand from its place"** (Revelation 2:4–5). And not many years later their "lampstand" was indeed removed: the church at Ephesus ceased to exist!

30 Even from among the leaders of the church, false prophets and false teachers rise up (1 Timothy 1:19–20; 2 Timothy 2:16–18; 3 John 9–10).

31 **So be on your guard!** (see 1 Corinthians 16:13; 1 Peter 5:8 and comments).

Paul says here: "**. . . for three years I never stopped warning each of you.**" According to Acts 19:8,10, Paul worked in Ephesus for two years and three months. Paul was in Ephesus from the end of 52 A.D. until the beginning of 55 A.D. Therefore, Paul here calls it "three years."

32 Paul commits the Ephesians to God and **to the word of his grace**. Paul will no longer be with them, but the word of Christ which Paul has taught them will remain with them (John 15:7). That word will **build** [them] **up**; it will cause them to progress in the Christian life. Even mature leaders need constantly to be strengthened and built up.

Today we have with us that same "word of God's grace." The leaders of the church at Ephesus had to keep that word in their memory. But we have that "word of grace" in written form: the New Testament. As long as we read it and obey it, that word will build us up, and give all of us **who are sanctified** an **inheritance** in heaven—that is, eternal life. Only the **sanctified** will receive an inheritance in heaven (see Hebrews 12:14; General Article: Way of Salvation).

33–35 Paul again offers his own life as an example for the Ephesians to follow. He labored to support himself with his

---

[93] In English, the word **overseer** is translated "bishop."

[94] Deacons, however, are different. Deacons are appointed to do many of the works of service in the church, such as taking care of the poor and the sick, and taking responsibility for the financial matters of the church (see Acts 6:2–4; 1 Timothy 3:8 and comments).

own hands. He did not covet anyone's **silver or gold or clothing** (see 2 Corinthians 11:9; 1 Thessalonians 2:9; 2 Thessalonians 3:7–9).

Jesus Himself said: "**It is more blessed to give than to receive**" (see Matthew 5:42; 2 Corinthians 9:6–11 and comments). This saying of Jesus is not recorded in any of the four Gospels. Jesus said many things which are not written in the Bible (see John 21:25).

Paul wrote many times in his letters about helping the weak (see Romans 15:1; Galatians 6:2). Paul even wrote concerning a converted thief: **He . . . must steal no longer, but must work, doing something useful with his own hands, that he may have something to share with those in need** (Ephesians 4:28).

36–38 Then, after praying with the Ephesian elders, Paul boarded the ship and sailed for Jerusalem.

CHAPTER 21

From Miletus to Tyre (21:1–6)

1–3 Paul and his companions set out across the eastern part of the Mediterranean Sea and headed for **Phoenicia** (modern Lebanon), which at that time was part of the Roman province of **Syria**. After passing by the southern coast of **Cyprus** (Acts 13:4), they arrived in **Tyre** (Acts 12:20), an important city of Phoenicia.

4 There was a church in Tyre; therefore, while the ship unloaded its cargo, Paul and his friends stayed with the disciples there. Some of these disciples had learned through the Holy Spirit that great trouble would come upon Paul in Jerusalem. Therefore, they advised Paul not to proceed on his journey (Acts 20:23). But because Paul had received guidance from the Spirit that he should go on to Jerusalem, he would not be deterred from going, no matter what the risk (Acts 20:22).

5–6 After the ship had been unloaded, Paul and his companions took leave of the disciples in Tyre, and sailed south until they reached **Ptolemais** (verse 7).

In Caesarea (21:7–16)

7–8 From Ptolemais, Paul's ship sailed to the city of **Caesarea** in northern Israel, where the first Gentiles had believed in Christ (Acts 10:1). Paul and his companions stayed at the home of Philip. Philip had come to Caesarea twenty years earlier (Acts 8:39–40). Philip was one of the seven original deacons of the Jerusalem church (Acts 6:3–5). His four daughters had become well-known for their prophesying. They lived to be very old, and for many years they gave much help to the church.

10–11 **Agabus** was a prophet from the Jerusalem church (Acts 11:27–28). He prophesied that the Jews of Jerusalem would seize Paul and **hand him over to the Gentiles**, that is, the Romans. But Agabus did not urge Paul to turn back from Jerusalem. He merely said what was going to happen when he got there.

Jesus had made a similar prophecy concerning Himself (Mark 10:32–33). He also had refused to turn back from fulfilling God's will.

12–14 But Paul's friends did not understand what God's will was. They were like Peter, who had tried to stop Jesus from going to Jerusalem (Mark 8:31–33). Paul asked them to stop weeping and pleading with him, lest they end up turning him from his resolve. Paul's main purpose in going to Jerusalem was to deliver to the church there the collection raised by the Gentile churches (Romans 15:25–28). Through this collection, Paul hoped that unity and reconciliation might be brought about between the Jewish and Gentile Christians.

15–16 **Mnason** was a Greek-speaking Jewish Christian, who had been among the first believers in Jerusalem.[95] Because he spoke Greek, he was well suited to be host for all of Paul's Greek-speaking traveling companions (Acts 20:4).

Paul's Arrival at Jerusalem (21:17–26)

17 The Christian **brothers** in Jerusalem welcomed Paul and his companions **warmly**. They were grateful for the collection that had been raised by the Gentile churches.

18–19 At that time Jesus' younger brother **James** was the chief leader of the Jerusalem church. Most of the other apostles had gone to other places to preach the Gospel.

Paul reported to the Jerusalem elders about the great numbers of Gentiles coming to Christ and the many churches that had been established in Asia and Greece (see Acts 14:27 and comment). With him were representatives sent from all these churches. They had come to give proof of the Gentiles' faith and love in the form of the collection which they had brought. Therefore, for all of these things the Jerusalem elders praised God (verse 20).

20–21 But there was also a problem. Jerusalem was a Jewish city, and most of the Christians there had originally been Jews. They still followed the Jewish law, that is, the law of **Moses** (verse 21). These Jewish Christians of Jerusalem had heard false rumors that Paul had been teaching Jewish converts that they should not follow the law of Moses or be circumcised. In their mind, it was all right to give such teaching to Gentile Christians, but not to Jewish Christians. In their eyes, to teach Jewish Christians that they did not need to follow the law of Moses was a grave offense. For this reason most of the Jewish Christians in Jerusalem had many doubts about Paul.

22–24 James and the elders of the Jerusalem church thought of a way to reassure the Jewish Christians about Paul and to bring about a reconciliation between them. James and the elders thought that if they could in some way show that Paul himself followed the Jewish law, the Jewish Christians would then be satisfied. By chance, at that very time there were four Jewish Christians who had made a Nazarite vow (see Acts 18:18 and comment). But during the period of the vow they had somehow become defiled, and now it was necessary for them to purify themselves (Matthew 6:5–6,9–12). If Paul were to go and purify himself along with them, and also pay their expenses, then everyone would know that Paul followed the law of Moses.

25 The elders of the Jerusalem church had no thought of reversing the decision they had made earlier: namely, that Gentile Christians were not required to follow the law of Moses. All that the elders had requested of the Gentile Christians was that they abstain from impure meat and **sexual immorality**,[96] so as not to give unnecessary offense to the Jewish believers (see Acts 15:19–20,28–29 and comment).

26 Paul agreed to the plan of the Jerusalem elders. Some people might criticize Paul for acting one way with Jews and another way with Gentiles; they might accuse him of being two-faced, or double-minded. But such criticism is not true. Paul had only one purpose, one goal, and that was to win both Jews and Gentiles to Christ by whatever means he could (see Acts 16:3; 1 Corinthians 9:20 and comments).

---

[95] Following Stephen's death, most of the Greek-speaking Jewish Christians had been driven out of Jerusalem as a result of the persecution stirred up by Paul (Acts 8:1–3). But Mnason had not left Jerusalem. He was willing to provide hospitality for Paul's Gentile companions. This would have been very difficult for an Aramaic-speaking Jewish Christian to do.

[96] By **sexual immorality**, Luke means sexual conduct forbidden by the Jewish law.

Paul Arrested (21:27–40)

27–29 Some Jews from Ephesus and the surrounding **province of Asia** had come to Jerusalem to celebrate PENTECOST (Acts 20:16). Previously the Jews of Ephesus had fiercely opposed Paul (Acts 20:19). A few days earlier, these Ephesian Jews had seen Paul together with Trophimus, a Gentile of Ephesus (Acts 20:4). Now having seen Paul enter the inner part of the Jewish temple to purify himself, these Jews assumed that Paul had taken the Gentile Trophimus inside the temple as well. Any Gentile passing into the inner courtyard of the temple was immediately sentenced to death. In the Jews' eyes it was a great crime for a Gentile to pass into the inner part of the temple, because the Jews believed that the temple would be defiled if a Gentile entered it.[97]

In this way Paul's enemies brought false charges against him. Even though Paul was completely innocent of the charge, it placed in jeopardy not only his name and reputation but also his very life. Let us take this as a reminder of the destructive power of any false charge, especially within the church.

30 Paul was seized by the Jews and dragged out of the inner courtyard. Then the temple officials closed the gate leading into the inner court, lest in the commotion the temple should somehow be defiled.

Just as the Ephesians had caused a riot when they thought their temple of Artemis was being dishonored (Acts 19:27–29), so the Jews in Jerusalem also caused a riot against Paul for the same reason.

31–32 The Jewish crowd tried to kill Paul. If some Roman soldiers had not arrived just then, Paul's life would surely have ended at that time. Just adjacent to the outer courtyard of the temple was a Roman fort, which was connected to the courtyard by a stairway. Therefore, as soon as the soldiers inside the fort heard the uproar, they were quickly able to get to Paul and save his life.

33–34 The commander of the soldiers supposed that Paul had committed some great crime, so he ordered him to be bound.

But the commander couldn't find out the cause of the uproar, because some people in the crowd said one thing and some said another.

35–36 As the soldiers were taking Paul toward the stairs leading up into the fort, the crowd renewed their efforts to seize him. The people cried, **"Away with him!"**—that is, "Let him be killed!" Twenty-seven years earlier, another crowd in that same city had shouted the very same thing in connection with another prisoner—named Jesus (John 19:15).

37–38 The commander mistakenly thought that Paul was an Egyptian who three years earlier had led a revolt against the Romans. When the Roman army attacked the Egyptian and his Jewish followers, the Egyptian had escaped but most of his men had been slaughtered by the Romans. Therefore, the surviving Jews were very angry with the Egyptian for running away and leaving them at the mercy of the Romans. The commander thought it was for this reason that the crowd was trying so hard to kill Paul.

---

[97] On the gate leading into the inner courtyard of the Jewish temple a warning was posted which said: "Any Gentile who enters through this gate will be put to death." This gate separated the inner court of the temple from the outer court (called the court of the Gentiles) where Gentiles were permitted to be. Paul wrote about this gate in his letter to the Ephesians, calling it a **dividing wall of hostility** between Jews and Gentiles (Ephesians 2:14–18). Christ has broken down that "dividing wall." Now both Jewish and Gentile believers are members of one family.

39–40 "I am not that Egyptian," Paul said to the commander. "**I am a Jew, from Tarsus in Cilicia**"[98]. Then, having obtained permission from the commander to speak in his defense, Paul addressed the crowd in their own **Aramaic** language.[99]

CHAPTER 22

Paul Speaks to the Crowd (22:1–21)

1–2 Because some of Paul's traveling companions were from Greece, the crowd assumed that Paul would speak to them in the Greek language. Therefore, when they heard Paul speaking in their own language, they suddenly became silent and listened intently.

3 Paul first reminded the crowd that he was a Jew just like they were, and that he had been brought up in their own city of Jerusalem. Paul had received his training from **Gamaliel,**[100] one of the greatest Jewish teachers. Like them, Paul was **zealous** for God.[101] In saying all this, Paul was trying to convince the crowd that he was as good a Jew as they were (see Galatians 1:13–14; Philippians 3:4–6 and comments). Let the crowd not think that Paul was an enemy of either the temple or the Jewish law.

4–5 Then Paul told the people how at first he had persecuted the **followers of this Way,** that is, Christians. Paul had not been content merely to seize the Christians and throw them in jail; he had persecuted them **to their death** (see Acts 26:9–10). The crowd was no doubt happy to hear that (see Acts 8:3; 9:1–2 and comments).

6–11 See Acts 9:3–9 and comment.

12–13 See Acts 9:10–19 and comment.

14–15 The words of Ananias written here are not mentioned in Acts Chapter 9. Here Paul is telling about his religious conversion in his own words. Paul wants to show the crowd that a Jew, a **devout observer of the law**—that is, Ananias (verse 12)—was the one who appointed him to be an apostle of Christ.

Ananias said to Paul, "**The God of our fathers has chosen you to know his will and to see the Righteous One** (Christ) **and to hear words from his mouth**". Paul had seen the risen Christ. He had seen His blinding glory. And he had heard His words from His own mouth: "**I am Jesus of Nazareth**" (verse 8). It was because Paul had seen and heard the Lord that his life was so radically changed. If Paul had not known Jesus with such certainty, he would never have been able to endure with joy all the suffering and hardship that came to him.

But let us not suppose that only apostles like Paul can know Christ in this way. We all, through the Holy Spirit, can know Christ with complete certainty.

Then Ananias said to Paul in verse 15: "**You will be his witness to all men**—both Jew and Gentile (see Luke 24:48; Acts 1:8). You will be a witness of **what you have seen and heard**" (see 1 John 1:1–3). In this way Paul received his appointment to be an apostle (see 1 Corinthians 9:1; 15:7–9 and comments).

16 Then Ananias baptized Paul in

---

[98] **Tarsus** was the main city of the Roman province of **Cilicia**. Tarsus was located in the southern part of what is now the modern country of Turkey (Acts 9:30).

[99] In New Testament times, **Aramaic** was the language spoken by most of the common people of Israel and the Middle East.

[100] **Gamaliel** is mentioned in Acts 5:33–39.

[101] The Jews were indeed "zealous," but their zeal was **not based on knowledge** (Romans 10:2). Therefore, Jesus could pray for them: "**Father, forgive them, for they do not know what they are doing**" (Luke 23:34).

the name of Jesus Christ, and Paul, through faith, was cleansed of his sins.

17–18 After Paul was converted, he spent some time in Damascus and Arabia (Acts 9:20–22; Galatians 1:17). Then he returned to Jerusalem (Acts 9:26–28; Galatians 1:18). While in Jerusalem, Paul had a vision of the **Lord speaking** to him (verse 18). The Lord said to Paul, "**Leave Jerusalem immediately**." The Lord knew that the Jews of Jerusalem would not accept Paul's testimony. The Jews considered Paul a traitor; they hated him and wanted to kill him (Acts 9:29).

19–20 But Paul started to argue with the Lord. He thought that because he had been such a zealous Jew and had so severely persecuted Christians like Stephen (Acts 7:57–58), that these Jerusalem Jews would surely listen to him. Paul imagined that the Jews would be so impressed with the story of his conversion that they themselves would be converted and accept Christ. And in a way Paul's thought was reasonable; on other occasions, no doubt, many Jews had been impressed by Paul's story. But this time Jesus knew that it was useless for Paul to remain in Jerusalem; He knew that the Jews there would not listen. Christ knows who will accept Him and who will not.

21 The Lord said to Paul, "**Go**." In Acts 9:30 it is written that when the brothers found out the Jews wanted to kill Paul, **they took him down to Caesarea and sent him off to Tarsus**. The Lord spoke, and the brothers brought Paul out of Jerusalem. By these two means, then, the Lord showed Paul that He wanted him to leave Jerusalem.

The Lord said to Paul, "**I will send you far away to the Gentiles**." Here Paul received from the Lord his special appointment to preach primarily among the Gentiles (see Galatians 2:8–9).

Paul the Roman Citizen (22:22–30)

22 The people had listened quietly to Paul up to that point, but as soon as he mentioned that he had been sent to the Gentiles, the crowd went wild. The reason they had gotten mad at Paul in the first place was that they thought he had brought a Gentile into the temple. So now, as soon as they heard the word "Gentile" mentioned, their anger was rekindled.

23–24 When the commander saw the great anger of the crowd, he brought Paul immediately into the fort. Since the commander couldn't understand the Aramaic language, he had not understood anything that Paul had said to the crowd. Therefore, in order to find out what crime Paul had committed and what he had done to get the people so angry, the commander decided to torture him by flogging.

In the Roman Empire, flogging was one of the most dreaded forms of torture. Small pieces of metal or bone were attached to the end of the whip, and these caused terrible wounds on the backs of the victims. Many people died from such flogging. Paul had already received five ordinary floggings from the Jews, and three times he had been beaten with rods by the Romans (Acts 16:22–23; 2 Corinthians 11:24–25). But up to that time Paul had not received a flogging with a metal-tipped whip.

25–26 According to Roman law, it was illegal to flog a Roman citizen. Even if a Roman citizen was found guilty in court, he usually did not receive this terrible punishment. Paul was well aware of this.

In New Testament times, it was a great advantage to be a Roman citizen. A man could either be born a citizen, or he could be awarded citizenship for some outstanding service rendered to the state. Paul had been born a Roman citizen (verse 28); therefore, we know that his father must have been a citizen also. It is not known how Paul's father received his citizenship; perhaps he had performed some valuable service for the Roman governor in Tarsus.

We can see from Paul's example that when trouble comes to us it is proper for us to use any reasonable and legal means to escape from that trouble. If we are innocent of some alleged wrongdoing, we need to say so; we need to defend ourselves. We should use all legal means to avoid punishment for crimes we did not commit. Christians in this world have the same legal rights as anyone else, and it is appropriate to claim those rights in a humble and respectful way. However, Christians must remember that they should not put their faith in any legal system but in God alone. Even if we do not obtain justice from men, we shall always obtain justice from God (see 1 Peter 2:19–23 and comment).

27–28 When the commander heard that Paul was a Roman citizen, he found it hard to believe. Paul's clothes were dirty and torn. He didn't look like a Roman citizen; he looked like an ordinary criminal!

In Paul's time it was possible to buy one's citizenship. Roman officials made extra money by selling citizenship papers. The commander himself had bought his citizenship and had paid a lot of money for it. Thinking that Paul must have bought his citizenship too, the commander wondered how such a tattered and dirty man could have gotten the money to pay for it! But Paul answered: **"I was born a citizen"**.

29 Like the Philippian magistrates in a similar situation (Acts 16:38), the commander became **alarmed**. He had almost committed a great crime himself! In fact, he had already committed a crime simply by ordering that Paul be **stretched . . . out** in preparation for flogging (verse 25).

30 In the commander's eyes, the anger of the crowd against Paul involved only a Jewish religious matter (see Acts 18:14–15). Since the Jewish Sanhedrin had authority to judge all cases involving the Jewish religion, the commander decided to call the Sanhedrin together and get their help in finding out what the charges against Paul were.

CHAPTER 23

Paul Before the Sanhedrin (23:1–11)

1 **"I have fulfilled my duty to God in all good conscience to this day."** How could Paul say such a thing? He had fiercely persecuted Christ's church. He had not only opposed God; he had been God's enemy! What was Paul's meaning?

Paul's meaning was this: He had sincerely believed that in all things he had been fulfilling his duty to God. He had opposed Christ and persecuted the church **in all good conscience** (see Acts 26:9). Even though Paul had, in fact, done great evil, his conscience had remained clear (see Acts 24:16 and comment).

But if this was so, how then could Paul have written Romans Chapter 7? **For I have the desire to do what is good, but I cannot carry it out. For what I do is not the good I want to do; no, the evil I do not want to do—this I keep on doing** (Romans 7:18–19). In Romans Chapter 7, Paul is describing his own inner spiritual conflict and his inclination to sin. Here before the Sanhedrin, however, Paul is talking not about his inner spiritual struggles but about his outward behavior. When Paul says here, **"I have fulfilled my duty to God,"** he means that he has fulfilled his duty to God outwardly. Paul wrote essentially the same thing to the Philippians, saying that as far as **legalistic righteousness** was concerned, he was **faultless** (Philippians 3:6).

Nevertheless, Paul put no confidence in his own righteousness; rather, he put his confidence in Christ's righteousness, which he had appropriated by faith (see Philippians 3:9 and comment). Even though our conscience may be clear, that in itself does not justify us in God's sight. Paul wrote to the Corinthians: **My conscience is clear, but that does not make me innocent. It is the Lord who judges me** (1 Corinthians 4:4). Very often, like Paul, we think we are doing good, but in fact we are doing evil. Our conscience is clear, but it has misled us. God will also judge us for the evil we have done in ignorance.

2 Paul had barely begun his speech

before the Sanhedrin; he was hoping to persuade them further that he was a good and faithful Jew. But when Ananias the high priest heard him say, "**I have fulfilled my duty to God in all good conscience**," he got so mad that he ordered Paul to be struck on the mouth.

We know from other history books that this **Ananias** was a corrupt and evil man. Ananias was high priest from 47 to 58 A.D.

3 To strike a man being questioned was against the rules of the Sanhedrin. It was highly illegal to strike or punish a man who had not yet been determined guilty.

Not knowing it was the high priest who had given the order to strike him, Paul turned to him and called him a **white-washed wall**. Such a wall looks new and strong on the outside, but inside it is weak and full of decay. Jesus called the Jewish leaders **white-washed tombs** (Matthew 23:27). These Jewish leaders appeared good outwardly, but inwardly they were evil and corrupt.

From this incident we can learn that there are times when we must speak out clearly against evil men (see Mark 13:11). But at other times it is better for us to remain silent (see Mark 14:60–61; 15:3–5; 1 Peter 2:23). The Holy Spirit will guide us as to when we should speak and when we should not.

4–5 If Paul had recognized the high priest, he would not have spoken against him in that way. In the Old Testament it is written: **Do not blaspheme God or curse the ruler of your people** (Exodus 22:28). Let us, likewise, remember that we are not to speak evil of our leaders—whether spiritual or secular. They have been appointed by God, and when we speak evil of them we are, in a sense, speaking evil of God (see Romans 13:1–2; 1 Peter 2:13–14,17 and comments).

6–8 The Jews were divided into two main parties, the **Sadducees** and the **Pharisees**. The Sadducees always tried to keep on good terms with the Roman authorities. Thus they always opposed any preacher like Paul who stirred up the people, because they were afraid that any disturbance might displease the Romans. Furthermore, the chief priests belonged to the Sadducee party; and if the priests allowed any disturbance to arise, the Romans would blame them and they would lose their positions. Thus the Sadducees of the Sanhedrin—especially the chief priests among them—were eager to condemn Paul, and thereby gain favor with the Roman governor.

The main difference between the Sadducees and Pharisees was that the Pharisees believed in the resurrection of the body and the Sadducees did not (Mark 12:18,24–27). Even before the time of Christ, the Pharisees believed in a bodily resurrection. The Pharisees hoped for eternal life. Therefore, those Pharisees who became Christians[102] believed that their hope had been fulfilled in Jesus Christ, the first man to rise from the dead (1 Corinthians 15:20).

Therefore, when Paul said that he was a Pharisee who believed in the **resurrection of the dead** (verse 6), the Pharisees of the Sanhedrin began to take his side. This led to a major dispute between the Pharisees and the Sadducees of the Sanhedrin. After that, the Sanhedrin couldn't come to any decision about Paul.

9 Paul had told the Sanhedrin that the risen Christ had spoken with him. The Pharisees of the Sanhedrin saw nothing wrong with that. They assumed Paul meant that an angel or a spirit had spoken with him; and since they themselves believed in angels and spirits (verse 8), they saw nothing unusual about Paul's statement.

---

[102] A Pharisee who became a Christian still remained a Pharisee, in the same way that a Jew who became a Christian still remained a Jew. For example, Paul was a Christian and yet remained both a Jew and a Pharisee. (This is possible only with the Jewish religion; it is not possible for a person to become a Christian and at the same time to remain a follower of any other religion—except for Judaism.) However, in 90 A.D. the Jewish leaders decided that those Jews who believed in Jesus could no longer attend the Jewish synagogues. Therefore, after 90 A.D., it became more and more difficult for Jewish Christians to have close contact or fellowship with other Jews.

10 The commander had hoped to find out from the Sanhedrin what crime Paul had committed, but he wasn't successful. In the end he found out nothing!

11 At certain times during Paul's life, Christ spoke to him in visions in order to encourage and instruct him (Acts 18:9; 22:17). Now again Jesus said to Paul in a vision: "**Take courage!** I have decided to send you to Rome."

Paul remained a prisoner in Israel for two more years after that, but he never worried or feared for his life. He knew that at the right time he would be going to Rome.

The Plot to Kill Paul (23:12–22)

12–15 It was common among the Jews to take an oath not to eat or drink until a certain task had been accomplished. According to Jewish custom, if the task proved impossible to carry out, the vow could be canceled.

Accordingly, about forty Jews joined together and vowed not to eat or drink until they had killed Paul. They told the **chief priests and elders** about their evil plot and requested their help in carrying it out. It seems that these Jewish leaders agreed to the plot; nothing is written that suggests they opposed it.

16–22 Except for this passage, nothing else is written about Paul's sister and her son. It is not said how this young man found out about the plot.

When the commander heard of the plot, he no longer dared to keep Paul under his authority. If Paul, a Roman citizen, should be killed, the commander would be blamed for failing to protect him.

Paul Transferred to Caesarea (23:23–35)

23–24 The commander decided to send Paul immediately to the Roman governor **Felix** under cover of night. He ordered 470 soldiers to accompany Paul, so that no one would be able to kill him on the way. The commander was taking no chances!

25–30 The commander, whose name was **Claudius Lysias**, wrote a letter to Governor Felix describing the facts about Paul. But on one point he did not write the truth. He wrote: **I came with my troops and rescued** [Paul], **for I had learned that he is a Roman citizen** (verse 27). This was not entirely true. The commander learned that Paul was a Roman citizen only after he had ordered him to be stretched out for flogging (Acts 22:24–25). The commander didn't write anything about that!

31–32 **Antipatris** was a town about thirty-five miles from Jerusalem. They traveled the entire distance in that one night. The foot soldiers surely walked quickly! By morning Paul was no longer in any danger from the Jews in Jerusalem, so only the seventy horsemen escorted Paul the remaining thirty miles to Caesarea, where the Roman governor lived.

33–35 Governor Felix, after reading the commander's letter, decided not to do anything about Paul until his accusers had come down from Jerusalem to make their charges against him in person. At that time he would hear Paul's case. Meanwhile, he ordered that Paul be kept securely in a palace which King Herod had originally built for himself (Acts 12:1,19).

CHAPTER 24

The Trial Before Felix (24:1–9)

1 When the Jewish leaders of the Sanhedrin came down to Caesarea to accuse Paul, they brought with them a lawyer named **Tertullus**.

2–4 Tertullus began his speech by praising Felix. That was the custom in New Testament times. But Felix was not worthy of such praise, because it is known from other history books that he was a cruel and despotic ruler.

5–6 Tertullus first charged that Paul was a **troublemaker** who was **stirring up riots among the Jews all over the world**. In New Testament times, the Jews were always bringing this charge against the Christians (Luke 23:1–2,5; Acts 16:20–21; 17:6–7). In fact, one of the main reasons Luke wrote his Gospel and also the book of Acts was to refute this very charge. One of Luke's purposes in writing was to show that the Christians had not committed any of the crimes they had been accused of. The Christians had not caused disturbances or revolted against the Roman government. Whenever they were brought into court, no one could prove they had been guilty of breaking any Roman law (Luke 23:4,13–15; Acts 18:14–15; 26:30–32).

Tertullus' second charge against Paul was that he was a **ringleader of the Nazarene sect** (verse 5). Jesus was called a "Nazarene," because He had been brought up in the town of Nazareth in Israel (Luke 4:16). This is the only place in the New Testament where Jesus' followers are called members of the "Nazarene sect."[103]

Tertullus' third charge against Paul was that he had **tried to desecrate the temple** (verse 6). The Jews knew there was no proof that Paul had actually desecrated the temple, so they didn't charge him with that. They only charged him with "trying" to desecrate it! Tertullus' point was that if the Jews had not first seized Paul, he would indeed have desecrated the temple. How hard it would be for Paul to disprove that charge! Tertullus was very clever. A crafty and skillful lawyer can make even an innocent man look guilty!

7–9 Then, in describing Paul's arrest, Tertullus twisted the truth. He said that the Jews had seized Paul "according to our law" (verse 6), but that the Roman commander Lysias had snatched Paul out of the Jews' hands "with the use of much force" (verse 7).[104] However, Tertullus' words were false. Rather, it was the Jews who "with the use of much force" almost succeeded in murdering Paul right in the courtyard of the temple, and only the arrival of the Roman soldiers saved his life! (Acts 21:30–32).

Paul's Defense (24:10–21)

10 Felix was the governor of Judea (the southern province of Israel) from 52 to 59 A.D. At the time of Paul's trial, Felix had already been governor for several years, and he knew a great deal about Jewish customs. Therefore, Paul was happy to make his defense before him.

11–13 Paul denied all the charges that Tertullus had brought against him. Notice that the charges of Tertullus were very vague. He didn't accuse Paul of any specific crime. He made only the loose and broad charges that Paul had "stirred up riots all over the world," and that he had "desecrated the temple." Such loose charges are easy to make. For example, it is easy to accuse someone of being a "troublemaker" or a "wrongdoer." Such accusations are nothing but slander.

But Paul's answer to the charges wasn't vague. He denied each of Tertullus' charges clearly and in detail. He said that he had not been arguing with anyone in the temple or stirring up a crowd anywhere in the city. He challenged his accusers to prove even one specific charge against him.

14 Having said what he did not do, Paul next stated to Felix what he did do. He worshiped the true God, and he followed the true **Way**, that is, Christ (John 14:6). He agreed with everything written in the **Law** and the **Prophets**, that is, the Old Testament. He was a true Jew, just as Christ Himself was a true Jew.

15 Not only that, like most Jews, Paul believed in the resurrection of the dead and in eternal life. The resurrection of the body, together with eternal life, was the chief hope of the Jews. Only the Sadducees refused to believe in the

---

[103] In the Hebrew and Arabic languages, the word for Christian is "Nazarene."

[104] Not all ancient manuscripts of Acts contain these quoted portions of verses 6 and 7.

resurrection and life after death (see Acts 23:6–8).

Paul says here that there will be a resurrection of **both the righteous and the wicked**. Jesus said: "A **time is coming when all who are in their graves will hear** [the Son of Man's] **voice and come out—those who have done good will rise to live, and those who have done evil will rise to be condemned**" (John 5:28–29). Everyone will be resurrected. The main question is this: Where will our resurrection take place—in the kingdom of God or in the kingdom of Satan?

16 For every Christian a clean conscience is essential. Our conscience becomes unclean when we sin knowingly and then refuse to repent (see Acts 23:1 and comment). God will not draw near us when we are in that situation. When we continue in sin we **grieve** the Holy Spirit (Ephesians 4:30) and **put out** [His] **fire** (1 Thessalonians 5:19). Our spiritual life dries up. Our faith becomes **shipwrecked** (see 1 Timothy 1:19). If anyone among us has an unclean conscience, let him repent without delay and receive forgiveness and cleansing (see 1 John 1:9 and comment).

17 Here Paul gives the main reason for his coming to Jerusalem this time: namely, to deliver to the Jerusalem church the collection raised by the Gentile churches (see Acts 19:21; 20:22; Romans 15:25–27).

18–19 Here again Paul states that he was presenting his offerings in the temple in a completely proper way. He was doing nothing contrary to Jewish custom. He was raising no commotion. Then suddenly some Jews from the province of Asia seized him (Acts 21:27–28). "These Jews from Asia should have come here and accused me in person," says Paul.

Here we can see an important principle. If it ever becomes necessary to accuse someone of wrongdoing, it must be done face to face. Those whose accusations are false or only half true always prefer to make their accusations behind a person's back. They don't dare accuse a person to his face, because if they do their falsehood will immediately be revealed. If we have something to say against someone but don't want to say it to his face, then we had better keep our mouth shut.

20 But those Jews from the province of Asia were not present. Therefore, Paul says: "Let the Jews of the Sanhedrin who are now here show what crime I have committed."

21 The only so-called "crime" the Sanhedrin had found Paul guilty of was the crime of being a Pharisee who believed in the resurrection of the dead. It was only because of the anger of the Sadducees[105] of the Sanhedrin that Paul had been brought to trial. In fact, these Sadducees had found no real crime that Paul had committed.

Paul and Felix (24:22–27)

22–23 It is not known whether or not Felix held a further hearing on Paul's case, or whether the commander Lysias ever came or not. But we do know that Felix, in hopes of getting a bribe from Paul and also in order to keep the Jews happy, kept Paul in prison for the next two years (verses 26–27).

24–25 Felix and his wife **Drusilla**[106] wanted to hear more about the Way—that is, the Christian faith—so they called for Paul to come and talk to them about it. But they were not really seeking God; rather, they only desired to be entertained by some new teaching. Therefore, when Paul began to talk about **righteousness, self-control and the judgment to come** (verse 25), Felix became uneasy and said, "Enough! Enough!" But it was these very three things—righteousness, self-control, and the judgment—that Felix and Drusilla most needed to hear about! Whenever God begins to show us our sin, we often, like Felix, become uneasy and say, **"That's enough for now**. I'll think about

---

[105] Most of the Jewish chief priests and elders were Sadducees. They did not believe in the resurrection (see Acts 23:6–8 and comment).

[106] **Drusilla** was the daughter of King Herod (Acts 12:1). She was already married to another man when Felix took her as his wife. Therefore, she was an adulteress.

it later." And when we say that to God, we are, in effect, losing an opportunity to repent and to receive forgiveness. Why was Felix afraid? Because he was an evil and greedy man. He didn't want to give up his sins; neither did he want to face the judgment of God.

It is not enough for us only to fear God's judgment; we must repent of our sins. Let us not say to God, as Felix said to Paul, "Enough for now; I'll think about it tomorrow." Because **now is the day of salvation** (2 Corinthians 6:2). Tomorrow may be too late!

26 Although Felix didn't care to talk with Paul any further about religion, he still continued to treat Paul reasonably well, because he hoped that some day Paul would pay him a bribe to gain his freedom.

27 Two years later, in 59 A.D., a civil war arose in Caesarea between the Jews and the Gentiles. At that time Felix's soldiers brutally attacked the Jews and killed many of them. Because of that incident, Felix was removed from his governorship and sent back to Rome. A new governor named **Festus** came to take his place.

Felix never released Paul. He was afraid that the Jews would complain to the Roman Emperor about his cruel conduct, so he **wanted to grant a favor** to them in order to gain their good will. Therefore, as a way to please the Jews, Felix kept Paul in prison.

Because Felix never completed Paul's trial, it was now necessary for the new governor, Festus, to reopen the case and make a judgment in the matter.

CHAPTER 25

The Trial Before Festus (25:1–12)

1–3 Shortly after **Festus**, the new governor, arrived in Caesarea, he went up to Jerusalem to meet the chief citizens of the province of Judea. The Jews there, seizing the opportunity, immediately began to accuse Paul before the new and inexperienced governor. Then they requested that Festus send Paul back to Jerusalem to stand trial. Their intention was to ambush and kill Paul on the road. Two years earlier a similar plot of the Jews had been unsuccessful (Acts 23:12–15). They hoped that, this time, their plot would succeed.

4–5 But even though Festus was new, he realized that he shouldn't put a Roman citizen into the hands of these angry Jews. Instead, he decided to hear Paul's case in Caesarea.

6–8 When the court was convened, the Jews again repeated their various charges against Paul. But they couldn't prove any of them. They could produce no witnesses. It is easy to make charges, but it is not so easy to prove them. If we have no proof, no witnesses, we have no business making accusations (see Matthew 18:15–16 and comment).

Again Paul denied all the charges against him. In particular, Paul denied that he had ever done anything wrong against **Caesar** (the Roman emperor). This was to refute one of the charges the Jews had brought against him—that of stirring up riots all over the Roman Empire (Acts 17:5–7; 24:5).

9 Festus wanted to gain the good will of the Jews in Judea, the province over which he was governor. The Jews had strongly opposed Felix, the previous governor, and Festus didn't want the Jews opposing him in the same way. Therefore, seeing a chance to make the Jews happy, Festus suggested to Paul that his trial be moved to Jerusalem in accordance with the Jews' request.

10–11 But Paul did not agree to the suggestion. Paul said, "**I am now standing before Caesar's court**. A Roman citizen should be tried before Caesar's court—not in Jerusalem." Paul called Festus' court "Caesar's court," because Festus was the official representative of Caesar in the province of Judea.

Paul knew that the Jews were looking

for an opportunity to kill him. Paul feared that, even if they didn't kill him, they would probably be successful in persuading this new governor Festus to pronounce him guilty. Therefore, for Paul to go to Jerusalem was very dangerous. If Festus was so willing to make the Jews happy by sending him to Jerusalem, Paul wondered what else Festus might do to him just to keep the Jews happy! Perhaps Festus might eventually hand him over to the Jews completely.

As a Roman citizen, Paul had the right to appeal directly to Caesar. Knowing that he was more likely to get a fair trial in Rome than in Jerusalem, Paul decided to appeal to the emperor, thus forcing Festus to move his trial to Rome.

At that time, 59 A.D., Nero[107] was the Roman emperor. In the beginning of his reign, Nero did not appear to be such an evil ruler. Therefore, it was reasonable to hope that he would judge Paul's case fairly. But after 62 A.D., Nero began to severely persecute the Christians throughout the empire.[108] He had them seized and fed to lions. For entertainment, Nero and his courtiers used to go and watch the lions devour the Christians in a large coliseum—a coliseum which still stands in Rome today. From other history books we know that Nero was the most cruel and wicked of all the Roman emperors. But when Paul made his appeal to Nero, he couldn't have known that.

12 Festus was surely happy that Paul had appealed to Caesar, because now he would no longer have to trouble himself with such a difficult case.

Festus Consults King Agrippa (25:13–27)

13 **King Agrippa** was the son of the King Herod mentioned in Acts Chapter 12. He was also the brother of Drusilla, the wife of Felix (Acts 24:24). The Roman emperor had given Agrippa a small kingdom[109] north of the province of Judea, and Agrippa ruled there under the emperor's authority.

Soon after the new Roman governor of Judea, Festus, had arrived at his residence in Caesarea, King Agrippa, along with his sister Bernice, went to Caesarea to welcome him.

14–21 Being a Jew himself, Agrippa knew much more about Jewish customs than Festus did. Therefore, Festus took the opportunity to discuss Paul's case with Agrippa.

In this section, Festus recounts to Agrippa all that had happened concerning Paul up until that time.

The Jews had spoken such evil things about Paul that Festus supposed he must be guilty of some great crime. But when Festus examined Paul's case, he could not find any crime that Paul had committed. So he concluded that Paul's case involved only a dispute over Jewish religious matters (see Acts 18:14–16).

22 When Agrippa heard what Festus had to say, he asked to see Paul himself. Agrippa had undoubtedly heard something about this "**dead man named Jesus whom Paul claimed was alive**" (verse 19). Now Agrippa wanted to hear more.

23 **The next day Agrippa and Bernice came with great pomp**. We can imagine the scene in that **audience room**. On one side was King Agrippa, Governor Festus, and the **high ranking officers** and **leading men**—all very important people. On the other side was a single Jewish prisoner bound with chains. Yet who in that audience room, we should ask, was most important in God's sight?

Today, Paul alone is famous. The only reason we remember Agrippa and Festus at all is because for a few short moments they were together with Paul; otherwise we wouldn't even recognize their names!

---

[107] All Roman emperors were called Caesar, but each also had his own personal name. Nero reigned from 54 to 68 A.D. The emperor before Nero was Claudius (Acts 11:28; 18:2).

[108] For further discussion of the persecution under Nero, see comment on Acts 18:14–16 and footnote to comment.

[109] Agrippa's kingdom included the southern part of present day Lebanon and also the province of Galilee, Israel's northernmost province.

God chose the weak things of the world to shame the strong. He chose the lowly things of this world and the despised things—and the things that are not—to nullify the things that are, so that no one may boast before him (1 Corinthians 1:27–29).

24–25 Here again we see that the Roman authorities could find no crime that Paul had committed (see Acts 26:30–32).

26–27 Festus had not been able to understand the charges brought against Paul by the Jews. He needed to send a report of those charges to Rome along with Paul, but he didn't know what to write. Therefore, Festus asked Agrippa to question Paul, so that he might **have something to write** to the emperor in Rome.

CHAPTER 26

Paul Before Agrippa (26:1–8)

1–3 Here in Chapter 26, Paul speaks in his defense before Agrippa in much the same way he spoke before the Jewish crowd in Acts 22:1–21.

In this chapter, Luke for the third time describes Paul's religious conversion. The reason Luke tells us the story three times is not hard to guess: of all the events in the history of Christianity following Christ's death and resurrection, there is no event more important than the conversion of the Apostle Paul (see Acts 9:1–19 and comment).

4–5 Everyone knew that, before his conversion, Paul had lived as a strict Pharisee (see Acts 22:3; Galatians 1:13–14). In regard to the Jewish law, Paul had lived faultlessly (see Philippians 3:4–6).

6 Here Paul again says that it is because of his hope **in what God has promised**—that is, the resurrection of the dead—that he is on trial (see Acts 23:6). God promised Abraham, the father of the Jews, that "**all peoples on earth will be blessed through you**" (Genesis 12:2–3). That promise was fulfilled by Christ, and especially by His resurrection. **God has given us eternal life, and this life is in his Son** (1 John 5:11).

7–8 Paul says that the resurrection of the dead, together with eternal life, is the main hope of the Jewish nation. From the beginning, the **twelve tribes**[110] of Israel had been looking forward to the fulfillment of this promise—the promise of a bodily resurrection and eternal life. Why is it so hard to believe that **God raises the dead?** Paul asks (verse 8). Only a few years earlier, God had raised Jesus from the dead. It is that same Jesus who is the fulfillment of the Jews' hope. Why should the Jews accuse Paul of having the same hope that they themselves have? He believed in the same promise they did (Acts 24:15). There was only one difference between Paul and these Jews: Paul knew that the promise had been fulfilled; the Jews didn't.

Paul's Conversion (26:9–23)

9–11 Before his conversion, Paul himself didn't believe that Jesus had risen from the dead. He considered the followers of Jesus to be enemies of the Jewish religion. In verse 10, Paul says: "**I put many of the SAINTS in prison, and when they were put to death, I cast my vote against them**" (see Acts 7:60; 8:3; 9:1; 22:4 and comments).

12–15 What is written in these verses has previously been mentioned in Acts Chapters 9 and 22 (see Acts 9:2–5; 22:5–8 and comments).

According to verse 14, Jesus said to Paul, "**It is hard for you to kick against the goads.**" The kind of **goad** or stick

---

[110] Abraham's grandson Jacob had twelve sons (Genesis 35:23–26). The **twelve tribes** of Israel are descended from those twelve sons.

referred to here was used to prick or beat animals. Here Jesus is speaking in a parable, according to which the goad is Paul's conscience. In his conscience Paul sensed that Christ's way was right, but he continued to oppose Him anyway. Paul was like an ox pulling a plow, who kicks its feet when the farmer hits it with the goad. Just as the ox kicks its feet in vain, so Paul had been "kicking his feet" against Christ in vain. It was time to stop opposing Christ and start following Him.

Paul asked, **"Who are you, Lord?"** (verse 15). Paul had assumed that Jesus had died and been buried. Now he hears Him speaking from heaven!

16–18 Then Jesus appointed Paul to be an apostle to the Gentiles (see Acts 9:15; 22:14–15 and comments).

Jesus first appointed Paul to be a **servant** (verse 16). Paul often called himself a **servant of Christ** (see Romans 1:1 and comment). After that, Jesus appointed Paul to be a **witness** (see Acts 1:8). From that time on, Paul was to devote his life to preaching the Gospel of Christ (see 1 Corinthians 9:16; Galatians 1:11–12; Ephesians 3:7–8).

According to Acts 9:16, Jesus said to Ananias, **"I will show** [Paul] **how much he must suffer for my name."** But here, in verse 17, Jesus also gives Paul a promise: **"I will rescue you from your own people** (the Jews) **and from the Gentiles."** And we know from reading the book of Acts how many times Jesus kept that promise to deliver Paul from his enemies! Often God allows trouble and persecution to come upon His servants, and then He reveals His power and glory by delivering them. Such was Paul's experience many times.

Jesus sent Paul especially to the Gentiles. Why? In order **to open their eyes and turn them from darkness to light, and from the power of Satan to God** (verse 18). Paul said to the Jews of Pisidian Antioch: **"For this is what the Lord has commanded us: 'I have made you a light for the Gentiles, that you may bring salvation to the ends of the earth'"** (Acts 13:47).

This appointment that Paul received from Jesus is the very same appointment that Jesus Himself received from God (see Isaiah 42:1,6–7; Acts 26:23). This was the chief work of all the apostles—to **bring salvation to the ends of the earth**. But this work is not just for a few special apostles; it is for every follower of Christ. Everyone who believes in Jesus is appointed to be a **light for the Gentiles**. Everyone who believes in Jesus is a witness for Him. Our work, in one way, is the same as His work—namely, to reconcile men with God (2 Corinthians 5:20), and bring them out of the kingdom of darkness into the kingdom of light. And when men through faith in Christ turn **from the power of Satan to God,** they will receive **forgiveness of sins** (verse 18). In addition, they will receive a **place among those who are sanctified;** that is, they will become sanctified citizens of the kingdom of heaven.

Paul was appointed to be an apostle primarily to Gentiles (Galatians 2:7–8). Through Paul's work, Christianity changed from a tiny Jewish sect into a religion reaching out to all people all over the world. Now not only Jews but Gentiles from every nation on earth have the chance to become citizens of the kingdom of God (see Ephesians 2:11–13,19; 3:6).

19 **"I was not disobedient to the vision from heaven."** Every believer in Christ has been given a **vision from heaven**. Like Paul, let each of us remain obedient to that vision.

20 As soon as Paul received his vision from heaven he began to preach, first in Damascus (Acts 9:19–20), and later in Jerusalem (Acts 9:28). His message was simple and clear: **". . . repent and turn to God."** Here we see the two parts of repentance: first, hating our sin; and second, turning from our sin. But that is not all; Paul told men to **prove their repentance by their deeds**. That is, men must show that their repentance is real by demonstrating a changed life (see Matthew 3:8). True repentance is not words but deeds. This applies to our faith also. We are saved through faith, but true faith is always manifested by good works (see Ephesians 2:9–10; James 2:14–17 and comments). True repentance and faith will always lead to a change in our speech, our behavior, even our thoughts.

21 The Jews opposed Paul because he preached among the Gentiles, whom the Jews despised. Because Paul had shown the way of salvation to the Gentiles, the Jews were jealous and wanted to kill him. The Jews didn't want to share the blessing of God with anyone else; as a result, they lost the blessing. Let us, as Christians, not make the same mistake!

22–23 Paul was not opposed to the Jews, nor to their Scriptures, the Old Testament (Acts 24:14). Paul taught nothing beyond what had already been written by the Old Testament **prophets** (Acts 3:18–21) and **Moses**[111] (Acts 3:22). Moses and the prophets themselves had prophesied that Christ must suffer and rise from the dead (see Luke 24:44–46; Acts 17:3). And it was also written in the Old Testament that Christ **would proclaim light to his own people and to the Gentiles** (Isaiah 42:6; 49:6). Jesus Himself said: **"I am the light of the world. Whoever follows me will never walk in darkness, but will have the light of life"** (John 8:12).

Paul's Discussion with Festus and Agrippa (26:24–32)

24 Festus couldn't understand why an educated man like Paul would give up his freedom and even his life for the sake of a dead man called Jesus. Paul surely must be **insane**, Festus thought.

25–27 But Paul was not insane. All these things concerning Jesus had been clearly foretold in the Old Testament. What had happened to Jesus during His lifetime was known by thousands of people. It was clear that this Jesus was the Savior described by the Old Testament prophets. King Agrippa believed the prophets; he would know that Paul was not insane. Let Festus ask him.

"King Agrippa, do you believe the prophets? I know you do," said Paul (verse 27).

28 Agrippa was in a dilemma as to how to answer. He didn't want to appear to take Paul's side, lest Festus think he was insane too. However, because he himself was a Jew, he couldn't deny what had been written by the prophets. Therefore, he didn't answer Paul's question about whether he believed the prophets. Instead, he jokingly said to Paul, "Are you trying to make me a Christian?"

29 Without joking, Paul said, in effect: "Yes." Paul's prayer was that not only Agrippa but everyone in that room might become a Christian just like himself—but without the chains. At that time, Paul's hands were bound with chains.

30–32 Everyone could see that Paul had committed no crime. He could have been set free. But because he had appealed to Caesar, Paul's case was no longer in Festus' hands. Having appealed to Caesar, now to Caesar he must go. Jesus had told Paul that he must testify about Him in Rome (Acts 23:11). Now Jesus' desire was about to be fulfilled.

CHAPTER 27

Paul Sails for Rome (27:1–12)

1–2 We know that Luke was with Paul on the voyage to **Italy**,[112] because Luke uses the word "we" throughout his account of the voyage: **We boarded a ship . . . we put out to sea** (verse 2). Thus Luke was a firsthand witness of all that happened. Also with them was **Aristarchus** (Acts 19:29; 20:4; Colossians

---

[111] Moses wrote the first five books of the Old Testament.

[112] **Italy** is an important country of southern Europe, and its capital is Rome. In New Testament times, Italy and its capital were the center of the Roman Empire.

4:10). There were also other prisoners on the ship who were being taken to Rome. The first ship they boarded was bound for the **province of Asia**.

3–5 After they reached the city of **Sidon** in Phoenicia (modern Lebanon), they sailed to **Myra**, a city on the south coast of Turkey.

6 Since that first ship was not going all the way to Rome, they boarded another ship at Myra, which had come from the famous Egyptian port of Alexandria and was on its way to Rome. This ship was loaded with grain (verse 38). In New Testament times, most of Rome's wheat and corn came from Egypt.

7–8 The wind was blowing against them, so it was difficult for the ship to go forward.[113] Finally they reached the harbor of **Fair Havens** on the southern coast of **Crete**, a large island south of Greece.

9–10 Because of the unfavorable wind, they had lost much time. It was very dangerous to sail on the Mediterranean Sea during the winter months. It was already mid-October. The **Fast** mentioned here (verse 9) is the Day of Atonement[114] (Exodus 30:10; Leviticus 23:27; Hebrews 9:7), which in that year (59 A.D.) fell during the first week of October.

Paul was an experienced traveler. He advised the centurion in charge of the voyage not to sail any further but to wait until winter was over. Paul predicted that if they sailed further at that time, there would be great damage to the ship, the cargo, and to the men as well.

11–12 Nevertheless, because the harbor of Fair Havens was small and unsuitable for spending the winter, the owner of the ship and the ship's pilot decided to sail on to **Phoenix**, a larger harbor lying farther to the west along the southern coast of Crete.

The Storm (27:13–26)

13–15 When they were only two hours from reaching Phoenix, a terrible storm from the northeast came upon them. The furious wind drove their ship away from land and toward the middle of the Mediterranean Sea.

16 They passed by the south side of a small island called Cauda. As they passed, the island blocked the wind for a brief time. During that short time, the sailors seized the chance to hoist up onto the main ship the small lifeboat that was being pulled along behind the ship by means of a rope. In fair weather it was customary for such small lifeboats to be pulled behind the main ship; but whenever a storm came up, the lifeboat would immediately be brought up onto the ship and made secure. However, this storm had come up so fast and so violently that the sailors had not had a chance earlier to make the lifeboat secure.

17 The sailors next passed strong ropes completely under the ship and tied them at the top to prevent the ship from being broken apart by the pounding of the huge waves. The sailors also took down the topmost sails, so that the wind would not be able to drive the ship so rapidly. Otherwise the ship would have been driven so far south that it would have run aground on the sandbars near the coast of present-day Libya (northern Africa).

18–19 The next day, to prevent the ship from sinking, the sailors began to throw the cargo overboard; the day after that they threw overboard the spare sails and other equipment.

---

[113] In New Testament times, all the large ships traveling on the Mediterranean Sea were sailing ships.

[114] The Day of Atonement was the one day of the year when the Jewish high priest offered a sacrifice of atonement for the sins of the people (Leviticus 16:1–34). For further discussion of atonement, see Word List: Atonement.

20 For fourteen days the ship was blown westward by the wind. The people in the ship, however, had no idea where they were, because during all that time the stars had been hidden by clouds.[115] The ship was probably beginning to leak. Surely they would all be lost.

21–22 Everyone on the ship had given up hope (verse 20). Because of the tossing to and fro of the ship, no one on board felt like eating; many no doubt were seasick. Perhaps the food had been soaked by sea water.

But during the period of deepest despair Paul stood up among them and said, "**I urge you to keep up your courage, because not one of you will be lost**".

23–26 An angel of God had appeared to Paul in the night. "You will reach Rome unharmed, because you must stand trial before Caesar," the angel said to Paul (see Acts 23:11). Not only would Paul be saved, but also, said the angel, "**God has graciously given you the lives of all who sail with you**". No person on board would be lost! But the ship itself would be destroyed; it would **run aground on some island** (verse 26).

There have been many times in history when God has shown special mercy to men because of the presence among them of one or more of God's servants (Genesis 18:22–32). Thus, because of Paul's presence on the ship, God spared the lives of everyone on board.

"**I have faith in God that it will happen just as he told me,**" Paul said (verse 25). With God, to speak and then to accomplish what He has spoken is one and the same thing. With us also, to believe and then to receive God's promise should be one and the same thing.

The Shipwreck (27:27–44)

27 In New Testament times, a large central portion of the Mediterranean Sea was called the **Adriatic Sea.**[116] One night, as the ship was reaching the western part of the sea, the sailors sensed that they were approaching land. They couldn't see the land, but they could probably hear the surf breaking against the shore. They measured how deep the water was by letting down a sound, and found that the water was only thirty meters deep. This proved that they were indeed near land.

28–29 It was still the middle of the night. The sailors feared that the ship would be dashed against the large rocks along the shore. Therefore, they let down four anchors to stop the ship from getting any closer to land. In the morning, they would be able to see the shore and find a safe place to beach the ship.

30–32 Then, fearing that the ship would not last through the night, the sailors began to lower the lifeboat with the intention of deserting the ship and escaping to shore. But Paul knew their intention. He told the soldiers guarding the prisoners, "Don't let the sailors desert the ship, or else **you cannot be saved**" (verse 31). The sailors would be needed in the morning to get the ship closer to shore. The ship was still so far from the shore that, with the lifeboat gone, no one else could have gotten to land. Therefore, to prevent the sailors from escaping, the soldiers cut the ropes holding the lifeboat and let it float away.

33–38 After everyone had eaten, the sailors, in order to lighten the ship further, threw overboard all the grain which the ship had been carrying (see verse 6 and comment). The lighter the ship, the higher in the water it would sit and the closer it could get to shore before running aground. This would make it easier for everyone to get to land safely.

39–41 When daylight came, the sailors saw a sandy beach without rocks and decided to try and run the ship aground there. But before the ship reached the beach, it ran into a sandbar

---

[115] In New Testament times, sailors determined their direction by looking at the position of the stars.

[116] Today the **Adriatic Sea** is only that northern extension of the Mediterranean Sea that lies between Italy and Yugoslavia. But in Paul's day, the Adriatic Sea was considered to extend well south of Italy.

that had not been visible.[117] With the front of the ship stuck fast in the sand, the waves very quickly broke up the back part of the ship.

42–44 According to Roman law, whenever a prisoner escaped, the soldier guarding him was given the prisoner's punishment (see Acts 12:19). Therefore, to prevent the prisoners from escaping, the soldiers decided to kill them all! But the centurion in charge of the soldiers wanted to spare Paul; he knew it was because of Paul that everyone's life had been saved. So he prevented the soldiers from killing any of the prisoners. In this way, just as the angel had said, everyone on the ship was spared and reached land safely.

CHAPTER 28

Ashore on Malta (28:1–10)

1–2 After everyone had reached shore, they learned that they had landed on **Malta**, a small island south of Italy. Although the people living there were not civilized, they showed great kindness to everyone who had been on the ship. If even uncivilized people know how to be hospitable, how much more should we who call ourselves Christians practice hospitality, especially to those in need.

3–4 Paul was a great man, but he was always ready to help in a small work—such as gathering sticks for the fire. But along with the sticks, Paul unknowingly picked up a poisonous snake. As Paul placed the sticks on the fire, the heat caused the snake to crawl out from the sticks and bite Paul on the hand. Seeing this, the inhabitants of the island concluded that Paul must be a murderer, because although he had escaped from the sea, the gods had found another way to punish him!

5–6 But Paul didn't suffer any harm (see Mark 16:18). Therefore, the islanders changed their minds and decided that Paul must be a god instead! How quickly men change their opinions! Paul had seen people change their minds like this before—particularly in Lystra, where men one moment were worshiping him as a god and the next moment were stoning him like a dog (Acts 14:11–19).

7–10 God had been with Paul at sea; now He was still with Paul on land. Because of Paul, everyone on the ship had survived. Now, because of Paul, everyone on Malta was being healed.

To show their gratitude for being healed, the people of Malta honored Paul and his companions **in many ways** (verse 10), that is, by giving many gifts. (Perhaps Luke also, himself a doctor, had helped in healing people.) Paul did not reject the gifts, but accepted them gratefully. Even though it is **more blessed to give than to receive** (Acts 20:35), there are many times when it is also good to graciously receive the gifts and help of others.

Arrival at Rome (28:11–16)

11 After spending three months in Malta, Paul and his companions boarded another ship from Alexandria which had wintered in Malta, and sailed toward Rome.

On the prow at the front of the ship was a carved wooden statue of the twin gods **Castor and Pollux**. In the time of the Roman Empire, sailors believed that these twin gods gave them special help at sea.

12–14 On the way to Rome the ship stopped at **Syracuse**, the main port of

---

[117] The place where Paul's ship ran aground was located in a small bay on the island of Malta. Today the bay is still called "Saint Paul's Bay." At the entrance of the bay the waves of the sea come in from two directions and, as a result, sand is piled up in the middle. It was in this sandbar that Paul's ship was stuck. In the Greek text, Luke calls this sandbar the "place of two seas," because the sandbar divides the bay in two.

Sicily, a large island situated just south of Italy. Then the ship sailed to **Rhegium**, a city on the southernmost tip of Italy. From there Paul and his companions sailed northward to **Puteoli**, which was a port near the present-day city of Naples. From there, in the company of the soldiers, they journeyed on foot to Rome.

15 Some Christians from Rome had walked forty miles south to meet Paul and his companions. How glad Paul was to see them! For many years Paul had wanted to visit the church in Rome. Three years earlier he had written to the Roman Christians to say that he was hoping soon to come to Rome and meet them (Romans 1:9–13; 15:23–24). Now finally he had arrived—not as a free man, but as a prisoner.

16 In Rome, even though he was a prisoner, Paul was allowed to live in his own rented house (verse 30). But there was always a soldier with him, and Paul was bound to the soldier by a chain (verse 20).

Paul Preaches at Rome Under Guard (28:17–31)

17–20 As he had done in every other city, so in Rome also Paul first sought out the Jews. He wasn't free to go to their synagogue, but he was free to invite them to his house.

Paul first assured the Jews in Rome that he had not committed any crime against the Jews in Jerusalem. Paul had appealed to Caesar not to oppose the Jews but only to establish his own innocence. He was a prisoner now **because of the hope of Israel** (verse 20)—that is, because of his belief in Jesus Christ. Because he preached Christ, the Jews had brought charges against him (Acts 26:6–7). Paul feared that the Jews in Rome had heard bad reports about him. Indeed, one of the main reasons he wanted to meet with them was to refute any false information they might have heard from the Jews in Jerusalem.

21–22 It turned out, however, that the Jews of Rome had heard nothing bad about Paul from their Jewish brethren in Jerusalem and Judea. However, they had heard bad reports about a new **sect** made up of followers of Christ (verse 22). Ten years earlier some Christian preachers had caused a great division and disturbance among the Jews in Rome and, as a result, the Roman emperor Claudius had expelled all the Jews from Rome (see Acts 18:2). Because of this, the Jews of Rome harbored ill feelings toward the Christians.

But these Jews had also heard some good things about the Christians, because the Roman Christians' **faith** [was] **being reported all over the world** (Romans 1:8). Therefore, the Jews wanted to hear from Paul more about this new Christian "sect."

23–24 Just as Paul had preached to Jews in other places (Acts 13:16–41), so he spoke to the Jews of Rome. He taught them from their own Scriptures, the **Law of Moses** and the **Prophets**, that Jesus Christ was the Savior, the Messiah of Israel. Some Jews believed, but most did not.

25–27 Then, as a warning to the non-believing Jews, Paul quoted from the prophecy of Isaiah written in Isaiah 6:9–10. Here Isaiah says, concerning the Jews, that they hear God's word but don't understand it, and they look at God's truth but don't really perceive it. The reason for this, says Isaiah, is that the Jews' hearts have become **calloused** (verse 27). They do not want to understand and perceive. Therefore, God has left them in their unbelief. Let the unbelieving Jews take heed! Those who reject God's light and God's word are blind and deaf indeed! (see Matthew 13:13–17; Mark 4:12; Romans 11:8 and comments).

28–29 Because most Jews rejected Christ, the Gospel of salvation was given to the Gentiles (Acts 13:46; 18:6). Christ **came to that which was his own** (the Jews), **but his own did not receive him** (John 1:11). Even up to the present time, the number of Jews who accept Christ remains very small.[118]

[118] Not all ancient manuscripts of Acts contain verse 29.

30–31 Paul arrived in Rome in 60 A.D. While in Rome, he wrote his New Testament letters to the Ephesians, to the Philippians, to the Colossians, and to Philemon. **Boldly and without hindrance** Paul preached for two years about the kingdom of God and about Jesus Christ. Paul preached to the **whole palace guard** (Philippians 1:12–14). He even preached in **Caesar's household** (Philippians 4:22).

On this victorious note, Luke brings his history to an end. What happened to Paul after that is not known. Some say he was set free for a time and then later put in prison again. Some say Paul was not set free. But according to all ancient historians, Paul was eventually put to death by the emperor Nero during the great persecution of Christians in 64–68 A.D.

Paul's work was finished. He had laid the foundation for the church of Christ throughout the whole Roman Empire. 250 years later the Roman emperor Constantine accepted Christ, and Christianity then became the main religion of the Roman Empire.

Such is the history of Christianity. It began with a carpenter from a small town in Israel. It spread initially through the work of twelve mostly uneducated apostles and, later, through the work of the Apostle Paul and his colleagues. It is this history which Luke has presented in his Gospel and in the book of Acts. But although the book of Acts is known as the "Acts of the Apostles," it could even more accurately be called the "Acts of the Holy Spirit." Because whatever the Apostles did, they did through the power of the Holy Spirit. And this same Holy Spirit is continuing to work throughout the world right up to this present day. The book of Acts is not finished.

Romans

INTRODUCTION

The writer of this letter to the Romans was the Apostle Paul. Paul (who was called Saul before his conversion) was not one of Jesus' first twelve disciples. It is probable that Paul never even met Jesus while He was here on earth. Paul was a very strict JEW (Philippians 3:4–6). When the Gospel of Christ began to spread, Paul fiercely persecuted the believers (Acts 8:3; 9:1–2; 22:3–5; 26:9–11). Then one day, as he was on his way to the city of Damascus,[1] Paul suddenly met the risen and living Lord Jesus Christ, and became a believer himself (Acts 9:3–9; 22:6–11; 26:12–18). It was then that Jesus appointed Paul to be an APOSTLE. Jesus sent Paul to preach the Gospel primarily among the GENTILES, that is, non-Jews. A complete description of Paul's life and work is found in Acts Chapter 9 and in Acts Chapters 13–28.

Paul went on three missionary journeys, during which he founded churches in Ephesus, Philippi, Thessalonica, Corinth, and many other cities throughout present-day Greece and Turkey. As he traveled, Paul wrote letters of encouragement and admonition to these new churches he had established. Paul also wrote letters to some churches he didn't found, such as the churches in Rome and Colosse. Paul also wrote personal letters to Timothy, Titus, and Philemon. All of these letters are included in the New Testament, and together they are extremely important in helping us understand Christ's teachings and in showing us how to live as Christians. Most of Paul's letters were actually written before the four Gospels of Matthew, Mark, Luke, and John were written. Therefore, Paul's letters make up the earliest writings in the New Testament.

Paul wrote this letter to the Roman Christians in about 55 A.D.,

---

[1] In Paul's day, Damascus was one of the leading cities of the Middle East. Today it is the capital of the modern nation of Syria.

while he was staying in the Greek city of Corinth. At that time, all the countries around the Mediterranean Sea had come under the control of the ROMAN EMPIRE, whose capital city was Rome. (Today Rome is still an important city; it is the capital of Italy, one of the major countries of Europe.) It is not known who first established the church (or churches) in Rome. However, by the time Paul wrote this letter there were many Christians in Rome, some of them Jewish believers and others of them Gentile believers.

Paul planned to make a fourth missionary journey to Rome, and then from there go on to Spain (Romans 15:23–24). But Paul never got to carry out this plan, because he was arrested in Jerusalem (the capital of the province of Judea in Israel), and was imprisoned in Israel for two years. When he finally got to go to Rome, it was as a prisoner, not as a free man. Paul remained in Rome under house arrest for two more years (Acts 28:30–31). After that time, there is no definite record of what happened to Paul. It is believed he was put to death by the Roman emperor Nero in about 67 A.D.

Paul's letter to the Romans is the most complete statement of the Gospel of Christ in the New Testament. The main theme of the letter is that all men are sinners, but that through faith in Christ man can be made righteous in God's sight and receive salvation and eternal life.

As with all the other writers of the Bible, Paul wrote his New Testament letters by the inspiration of the Holy Spirit. One could equally well say that the Holy Spirit is the author of all the books of the Bible; the human writers were merely the instruments of the Holy Spirit.[2] Therefore, as we read Paul's letters, let us remember that they (and all the books of the Bible) are works specially written and sent to us by God Himself. This letter of Paul to the Romans was written not only for the Romans; it was written also for us.

OUTLINE

A. The Prologue (1:1–17).
   1. Greetings (1–7).
   2. Thanksgiving and Prayer (1:8–15).
   3. The Power of the Gospel (1:16–17).

B. The Principles of the Gospel (1:18–5:21).
   1. Gentile Righteousness (1:18–32).
   2. Jewish Righteousness (2:1–3:20).
   3. God's Righteousness (3:21–31).
   4. Abraham's Righteousness (4:1–25).
   5. Believer's Righteousness (5:1–21).

---

[2] Though instruments, the writers actively cooperated with the Spirit; they were not passive. Their individual personalities flow through their writing.

C. Ethical Problems Raised by the Gospel (6:1–23).
   1. The Charge of Licence (6:1–14).
   2. The Charge of Lawlessness (6:15–23).

D. The Christian and the Law (7:1–8:39).
   1. The Law is Valid Only for this Lifetime (7:1–6).
   2. The Law and Sin (7:7–25).
   3. Liberation by the Spirit from the Law of Sin and Death (8:1–39).

E. The Problem of Jewish Rights and Privileges (9:1–11:36).
   1. The Absolute Sovereignty of God (9:1–29).
   2. Jewish Responsibility in History (9:30–10:21).
   3. The Merciful Purpose of God (11:1–36).

F. Christianity in Practice (12:1–15:13).
   1. Personal Ethics (12:1–21).
   2. Political Ethics (13:1–7).
   3. More Personal Ethics (13:8–14).
   4. The Strong and the Weak (14:1–15:13).

G. Epilogue (15:14–16:27).
   1. Paul's Reason for Writing (15:14–21).
   2. Plans for Future Journeys (15:22–33).
   3. Greetings to Friends in Rome (16:1–16).
   4. Final Admonition and Greeting (16:17–27).

CHAPTER 1

Greetings (1:1–7)

1 The word **apostle** is the title given to "one who is sent" by Christ especially to preach the GOSPEL and to plant churches. The title was first given to Jesus' original twelve disciples (Mark 3:13–19). Later on Paul[3] also, after meeting the risen Christ on the road to Damascus, was appointed by Christ to be an apostle (Acts 9:3–16; 26:15–18). Therefore, by calling himself an apostle right in the beginning of his letter, Paul is reminding the Romans (and all readers) that he is writing with the full authority of Christ. Paul was a true apostle appointed directly by Jesus Himself (see Galatians 1:1).

The **gospel of God** is the good news about Jesus Christ, God's Son, which Paul explains during the course of this letter to the Romans.

Paul here calls himself a **servant of Christ Jesus**. A **servant** does not live for himself, but for his master. This is how Paul lived his life, and it is the way all Christians should live theirs. In Paul's day a servant was bought by his master; his master owned him. The servant's life was not his own, but belonged to his master. In the same way, we believers have been bought by Jesus, and the price He paid for us was His own blood (see 1 Corinthians 6:19–20 and comment).

2 The Gospel, the good news of Jesus Christ, is foretold in the **Holy Scriptures**, that is, the Old Testament. (The New Testament, of course, was not yet completed when Paul wrote this letter.) The Old Testament prophets wrote many prophecies about the coming of the Savior Jesus Christ. That is why Paul says here that the Gospel of Christ was **promised beforehand** by God.

3–4 Who is Jesus Christ? There is no more important question a person can ask than this. Was He a man, or was He God? In these two verses Paul gives us the answer to this crucial question: Jesus was both fully man and fully God. As to His **human nature**, Jesus was descended from Israel's famous King DAVID (verse 3); as to His spiritual nature, Jesus was the **Son of God**, born directly of God's HOLY SPIRIT (verse 4). Jesus was born of a human mother, but His father was the Holy Spirit (see Matthew 1:18–21 and comment; General Article: Jesus Christ).

Christ gave proof that He was the Son of God by His RESURRECTION **from the dead**. No ordinary man can rise from the dead by himself. Paul knew with certainty that Christ had risen from the dead because he himself had met Him! (see Romans: Introduction).

5 Here Paul describes how he was appointed by Christ to be an apostle in order to **call people from among all the Gentiles**[4] **to the obedience that comes from faith**. To do this work Paul received **grace and apostleship**—that is, Christ's strength and authority. In the Bible the word **grace** usually means the free mercy of God shown to undeserving and sinful men (see verse 7). But here in this verse the word "grace" has a different meaning; here it means the strength given by God to do a special work (see Romans 15:15–16; Ephesians 3:7).

Notice that Paul's purpose is not only to bring people to faith, but also to call them to the **obedience that comes from faith**. Faith must always give rise to **obedience**, or it is not true faith (see James 2:17 and comment). It is not enough only to bring people to Christ; they must also be made into obedient disciples.

6–7 Paul writes this letter to **all in** ROME **who are loved by God** (verse 7)—

---

[3] Paul's original Hebrew name was Saul; after his conversion he used the Roman name Paul.

[4] In Paul's time, anyone who was not a Jew was called a "Gentile." The Gospel of Christ was preached first to the Jews; but now, through Paul and others, the Gospel was being brought to the **Gentiles** also.

that is, to all the Christians in Rome. God loves all men and women, but He especially loves those who have become His children through faith in Christ (see 1 Timothy 4:9–10 and comment).

All Christians are **called to be SAINTS**, that is, they are called to lead a holy life. True Christians are "holy" in God's eyes, not through their own merit but through faith in Christ, who died on the cross to take away their sins (see Philippians 1:1).

In the greetings of most of his letters, Paul expresses the wish that his readers might experience the "grace" and "peace" of God. **GRACE** is the freely given favor, love, and mercy of God, which we sinful men do not deserve and cannot earn. Through grace we then obtain **PEACE**, or reconciliation, with God and with each other. These two great gifts, grace and peace, are always given to us **from God our Father and from the Lord Jesus Christ**. The **Father** and **Jesus Christ** (and the Holy Spirit) always do all things together, because they are one God.

Paul here calls Jesus the **Lord Jesus Christ**. **Jesus** is a man's name, because Jesus was a man. **Christ** is the name of the Savior of the world, and it means "anointed one" (Psalm 2:2; Acts 4:26). Jesus' third name is **Lord**, which in the Greek[5] language means "God" (see James 1:1 and comment).

Paul's Longing to Visit Rome (1:8–15)

8 In Paul's time, Rome was the most important city in the Western world; it was the capital of the Roman Empire. Therefore, people from all over the world were constantly coming to Rome for one reason or another. Because of this, any news concerning the Roman Christians would naturally spread far and wide. Thus Paul could truthfully say that their faith was **being reported all over the world**. In the same way, the Gospel itself was spreading throughout the Roman Empire. In fact, the number of Christians was growing so rapidly that, in reaction, the Romans had begun to persecute them with increasing severity.[6]

Therefore, Paul is thankful because the Roman believers have stood firm in their faith in spite of such terrible persecution. Notice how Paul praises and values the Christians of Rome. Let us also, taking Paul's example, always consider all of our fellow Christians important and valuable, because so they are in the eyes of God. Therefore, instead of complaining about each other, let us, like Paul, gives thanks to God for each other.

9–10 At the time Paul wrote this letter, he had not yet been to Rome. But even though he had never met the Roman Christians, Paul cared for them and had been praying faithfully for them.

11–13 Paul wanted to go to Rome in order to impart to the Roman believers **some spiritual gift to make** [them] **strong** (verse 11). It is not enough only to preach; it is not enough only to plant churches. It is also necessary to **make** [the believers] **strong**. If they are not strong, how will they be able to withstand trouble and persecution? That's why Paul's work of establishing churches was usually so successful: his constant desire was to strengthen the believers wherever he went (see Acts 14:21–22).

Paul writes that he hopes to **have a harvest** among the Romans (verse 13); that is, he hopes to find in Rome many Christians who are being strengthened in their faith. Paul also hopes that new Romans converts will result from his visit.

14–15 Here Paul says he is **obligated** to both Greeks and non-Greeks and to both the wise and the foolish (verse 14). In what way was Paul obligated? He was

---

[5] The New Testament was originally written in the Greek language.

[6] Within a short time of Paul's death, a new law was put into effect requiring all people throughout the Empire to worship the Roman emperor as a god. When the Christians refused, they were put in prison and even given the death sentence. There is still standing in Rome today the ruins of a large stadium where, for entertainment, the emperor and many other Romans used to come and watch the Christians being killed and eaten by wild lions.

obligated to proclaim the Gospel of Christ to all people—especially to the Gentiles. Paul had been appointed to preach the Gospel and had received grace to do so; therefore, just as a debtor is obligated to return the money he owes, so Paul was obligated to fulfill his duty both to God and to those who had not yet heard the Gospel.

In the same way, we too are obligated to God because of the grace, mercy, and love He has shown to us who believe. To the extent we have been blessed by God, to that extent we are obligated to Him.

If we who have received salvation do not tell the good news of salvation to others, we will be like a man who borrows money but then refuses to pay it back. God is not pleased with such a man (Psalm 37:21). That is why Paul wrote elsewhere: **I am compelled to preach. Woe to me if I do not preach the gospel!** (1 Corinthians 9:16).

The **Greeks** were the residents of Greece, an important country of southeastern Europe located on the Mediterranean Sea between Italy and Turkey. In Paul's time, the Greeks were the most civilized and cultured people in the Western world—even more so than the Romans. Therefore, by the expression **Greeks and non-Greeks,**[7] Paul means "civilized people and uncivilized people."

In Rome there were many kinds of Christians: Jewish Christians, Gentile Christians, **Greeks, non-Greeks, wise,** and **foolish**. The Gospel of Christ is for all people—whether high or low, educated or uneducated, rich or poor; our outward condition makes no difference to God (see Galatians 3:28 and comment).

The Power of the Gospel (1:16–17)

16 The **gospel** is no ordinary news; it is the **power of God for . . .** SALVATION. The Gospel is contained in the Bible, which is God's word. The Bible, therefore, is no ordinary book; it is God's powerful word. The person who reads it and believes it will receive salvation together with the power to live eternally. And to live eternally one needs eternal power!

To receive this power we must believe in Christ. This power for salvation is given to **everyone who believes**—whether Greek or non-Greek, wise or foolish (verse 14). However, the Gospel was proclaimed first to the **Jew**. The Jews were God's specially chosen people; from the beginning they worshiped the one true God. In the Jewish Scriptures (the Old Testament) there were many prophecies written about the coming of Christ, the Savior. Therefore, when Jesus came, being Himself a Jew, He first preached the Gospel to His own nation, the Jews.

However, most of the Jews rejected Jesus; and in the end they had Him put to death on a cross.[8] Therefore, God appointed preachers like Paul to go and preach the Gospel to the Gentiles, that is, to all the other people in the world. That's why Paul says here that the Gospel was **first for the Jew, then for the Gentile**.

Paul was not ashamed to preach the Gospel. In Paul's time, to be a Christian was difficult. Christians were despised and persecuted. Christ Himself had been hung on a cross as a criminal. In the beginning, most Christians belonged to the poorer classes. Many were slaves; many others were in trouble of one kind or another. In the eyes of the world, to be a Christian was a shameful thing.

But Paul was not ashamed, nor were the Roman Christians ashamed—even under the most severe persecution. Why should they be ashamed? They had received the **power of God for . . . salvation**.

Are we ashamed of the Gospel of Christ? Are we afraid of what men will say and do to us? Do we hide our faith? Why should we? The Gospel is the power of God, the power to live eternally. But if we hide our faith and deny the Gospel, that power, that eternal life, will go out

---

[7] In place of the word **non-Greeks**, some translations of the Bible say "barbarians"—that is, uncivilized people.

[8] For further discussion as to why the Jews rejected Jesus, see John 9:22–23 and comment.

like a candle (see Matthew 10:32–33 and comment).

17 God's RIGHTEOUSNESS has been revealed in His Son Jesus. Jesus never sinned; He was in every way pure and righteous (Hebrews 4:15).

We too, **by** FAITH, can share in that righteousness. There is no righteousness naturally in us (Romans 3:10–12); but through faith we can obtain the righteousness of God (of Christ). If we do not obtain that righteousness, God, being righteous Himself, cannot accept us (see Hebrews 12:14 and comment). Without having obtained that righteousness through faith in Christ, we cannot be saved. That's why the Gospel is so important: It is the **power of God for the salvation of everyone who believes**; because when we believe it, we are considered righteous by God and are accepted into His kingdom.

The righteousness of God is not given to us only so that we might obtain salvation; it is also given that we might daily lead righteous lives here on earth. We must lead righteous lives **by faith**. That is, having become followers of Christ through faith, we must now live like Christ through faith. Faith is essential, not only at the beginning of our Christian lives but every day thereafter. To confirm this, Paul quotes from the Old Testament prophet Habakkuk: "**The righteous will live by faith**" (Habakkuk 2:4).

God's Wrath Against Mankind (1:18–32)

18 Just as the righteousness of God has been revealed in the Gospel of Christ, so also is God's wrath against all **godlessness and wickedness of men** revealed clearly to all men. The first and greatest sin of all is **godlessness**, that is, a refusal to acknowledge and worship the one true God. "Godlessness" is putting man in first place instead of God. It is trusting in man, in oneself, rather than in God. All the sin and unrighteousness of man springs from this one source: namely, godlessness—that is, the refusal to believe in God (see verses 29–31).

19–20 God's **invisible qualities—his eternal power and divine nature** have been clearly revealed through the things that He has created. All men can see these qualities of God. With their own eyes they can see the mountains, the stars. Who made all these things? Without God, how could all these things have been created? Only God could have done this (Psalm 19:1–4). Yet men **suppress the truth by their wickedness** (verse 18), and deny the existence of God. For this reason **men are without excuse** (verse 20).

21 For although they knew God, men rejected Him. All men, even though they deny God, have some natural knowledge that He exists. All men have the knowledge that if there is a creation, there has to be a creator. But that knowledge has been suppressed; men's hearts have been hardened and their understanding has been darkened (see Ephesians 4:17–18). Men prefer to deny God, because then they can do what they please.

22–23 Therefore, instead of worshiping God, men worship idols. Men worship the creation instead of the Creator. Some men even worship stones. Such is the wisdom of the world!

Yet men of the world consider themselves wise! They call the Gospel of Christ foolishness. Paul wrote to the Corinthians: **For the message of the cross** (that is, the Gospel of Christ) **is foolishness to those who are perishing, but to us who are being saved it is the power of God** (see 1 Corinthians 1:18–21 and comment).

24 Therefore, what did God do to these ungodly men? He **gave them over**. In other words, He left them alone; He let them remain in their sins (see Ephesians 4:19). God let them fulfill the **sinful desires of their hearts**.

Three times Paul writes: **God gave them over** (verses 24,26,28). From our own experience we know that small sins give rise to big sins, and that soon these turn into ever bigger and bigger sins. The more we sin, the farther we get from God. And when, through sin, we draw away from God, He draws away from us—that is, He "gives us over." If we confess our sins and draw near to God, He will draw near to us (James 4:8).

25 Idol worship is the chief sign of godlessness. To worship idols is to worship **created things rather than the Creator.** To worship an idol is to worship a false god, a demon (see 1 Corinthians 10:19–20). Idol worship is the number one sin against the true God. The first two of the ten great commandments in the Old Testament concern idol worship: **You shall have no other gods before me. . . . You shall not make yourself an idol** (Exodus 20:3–6).

One further thing: An idol is not only something made out of metal or stone or wood. An idol is anything we love more than God—whether it be money, possessions, fame, power, honor, or family. When we love these things more than we love God, then we are guilty of idol worship. These things—though good in themselves—have become for us idols.

26–27 Paul here talks about homosexuality. According to Paul's teaching, for women to lust for other women, and for men to lust for other men is a sin.[9] It is unnatural; it is against God's plan for men and women. And to satisfy such lust by committing unnatural acts with members of the same sex is even a worse sin. When men, in particular, commit **indecent acts** with other men, they are liable to get a number of serious, even fatal, diseases, such as AIDS. (Of course, promiscuous behavior between the sexes can result in such diseases as well.) Such diseases are the **due penalty for their perversion** (verse 27).

28 Notice that man's first sin is to worship and serve created things rather than God (verse 25). Since they do **not think it worthwhile to retain the knowledge of God,** God "gives them over," and they fall into various bodily sins (verses 26–27). Now, in verse 28, God "gives them over" to a **depraved mind.** The **mind** is the source of evil in a man. All of our evil thoughts and desires arise in our mind. Therefore, when any man's mind becomes **depraved,** then all of his thoughts and desires become depraved also. One can't get worse off than that!

God never causes a man to do evil. But when a man denies God and begins to worship idols, then God has to let him go. Man is free either to accept God or to reject Him; God has given man that freedom.[10] But once a man completely and deliberately rejects God, there is no way left for him to be reconciled with God; that man has taken himself out of the reach of God's grace and mercy.

29–31 Paul here gives some examples of various sins. It is easy to see such sins in other people, but it is not so easy to recognize them in ourselves. We don't like to see ourselves as being wicked or evil. But if we examine ourselves closely, we will likely find in ourselves some of these same sins: **greed**? **envy**? **deceit**? Are we **gossips**? **slanderers**? Are we **arrogant? boastful**? Are we full of **murder?** "No, no, not murder!" we say at once. But look again. Jesus taught that to get angry with our brother is like murdering him! (see Matthew 5:21–22 and comment). Do we not get angry with our brother from time to time? Or our sister?

Therefore, let us examine ourselves. These sinful works are not just in people whom we like to call "evil." These sins are in ourselves. And only the blood of Christ shed for us on the cross can cleanse us from these sins.

32 In Romans 6:23, Paul says: **For the wages of sin is death**. Sin, in one way, is a kind of work—a work that we do for Satan. And Satan pays us a wage for that work—and the wage is death. But even

---

[9] To have a natural attraction to a member of the same sex is not a sin. It is only when that attraction grows into a lust, an obsession, that it becomes a sin. Some people from an early age are attracted more to the same sex than to the opposite sex. There can be many reasons for this; it does not necessarily mean that the person is abnormal or sinful. It is only when such an attraction leads to lust and to unnatural acts that it becomes sinful.

[10] Some Christians believe that man does not have such freedom. They say it is only because of the grace of God that a man can come to God in the first place. This is true. But most believe that man has the freedom to reject that grace. This is a complicated subject; for further discussion, see General Article: Salvation—God's Choice or Man's Choice?

knowing that, men continue to sin. Take, as two small examples, the excessive drinking of alcohol and the smoking of cigarettes. Both of these activities do great harm to one's body, and can lead to fatal illnesses. But even knowing that, people continue to smoke and drink. They will certainly receive the "wages" of their sinful habits!

It is bad to commit these sins. But it is even worse to **approve of those** who commit them. The reason is this: it is possible for a man himself to fall into sin unknowingly; but when one "approves" of sin in others, it is always done knowingly. The man who does this is **depraved** indeed.

CHAPTER 2

God's Righteous Judgment (2:1–16)

1 Paul here gives a great warning to all men: do not judge others. How eager we are to judge others! We suppose that we ourselves are righteous, and that we are therefore qualified to judge. We see the sins and errors of others, but we do not see our own. **All a man's ways seem right to him, but the Lord weighs the heart** (Proverbs 21:2). We ought to be so busy concentrating on our own sins that we have no time left over to look at other people's sins!

We must confess to our shame that even among Christians this habit of judging one another is very common. Let us remember the words of Jesus: **"Do not judge, or you too will be judged"** (see Matthew 7:1–5; Romans 14:10 and comments).

Even though the warning in verse 1 is for all men, Paul is here speaking especially to his own people, the Jews. More than other races, the Jews had the habit of judging other people; they especially judged non-Jews, that is, Gentiles. The Jews were proud; they considered themselves righteous. Why was this?

To understand the answer to this question, it is necessary to look at the Jews' history. In the beginning, all men worshiped idols and lived in sin. God desired to establish a nation of people who would honor and obey Him. Therefore, about two thousand years before Christ's time, God called a man named Abraham (or Abram) to found a new nation, the Jewish nation (Genesis 12:1–3). God chose the Jews to be His own people. After that, God gave the Jews His law, the main part of which was the ten commandments (Exodus 20:1–17).

Then, because they had been especially chosen by God and had received His law, the Jews began to think that they must be more righteous than other people. Therefore, they began to despise all Gentiles (non-Jews). They considered the Gentiles to be godless and sinful.

But Paul here tells the Jews that, even though they are God's chosen people and have received His law, they do not obey God's law inwardly in their hearts. Instead, they obey it only outwardly. Their hearts are just as sinful as the hearts of the Gentiles. In a way, the Jews were more guilty of sin than the Gentiles, because the Jews knew exactly what God's commandments were. Nevertheless, they didn't recognize their own sin.

2 In this verse, the words **such things** refer to the various sins listed in Romans 1:29–31. God will render JUDGMENT against all those who do **such things**. God's judgment will be **based on truth**. He will judge fairly and without partiality. He will judge us not only according to our deeds but also according to what is in our hearts (Ecclesiastes 12:14; Revelation 2:23).

3 Those people (in particular, the Jews) who consider themselves righteous but continue to do these sins will not escape the judgment of God. Even though the Jews were God's chosen people, and even though they appeared outwardly more "righteous" than the Gentiles, they will still have to bear the full punishment for their sins.

4 The Jews thought that God would not count their sins, and that therefore they didn't need to repent. But they were mistaken. God had indeed shown great **kindness, tolerance**, and **patience** to the Jews, but they had been ungrateful; they had shown **contempt** for these blessings. They didn't realize that God had shown mercy to them, in order that they might repent of their sins. Whether for Jew or Gentile, the first step in coming to God is REPENTANCE. But if we remain proud and refuse to confess our sins, we shall certainly not find God.

What is repentance? First of all, it is recognizing and confessing our sin. Second, it is turning away from that sin. To only confess our sin is not enough; only when we have turned from that sin and given it up can we say we have fully repented (Proverbs 28:13).

When we truly repent, we change our desires and thoughts; we forsake evil and turn to God. Repentance is a change of mind and heart. Without repenting, no one can come to God.

Notice what kind of God our God is. He doesn't rebuke us; He doesn't despise us; He doesn't force us to do His will; He doesn't give us unnecessary trouble or hardship. Rather, out of **kindness**, He **leads [us] toward repentance**. Just as a loving human father calls his children, so God calls all men and women. He is extremely patient; He wants to give everyone the chance to repent (see 2 Peter 3:9). How can we not repent and come to such a loving God?

5 That God is our loving and merciful Father is completely true. But it is also equally true that God punishes men for their sin. His anger against sin is great and terrible (Hebrews 10:30–31; 12:29). If we do not repent, we will not obtain God's mercy, love, and forgiveness. Rather, we will obtain His wrath. The choice is ours.

6 God will judge all men on the **day of God's wrath, when his righteous judgment will be revealed** (verse 5). How will He judge us? Or by what measurement will He reward us? The answer is this: God will give to each man **according to what he has done** (see Psalm 62:12; Proverbs 24:12; Jeremiah 17:10; 32:19; 2 Corinthians 5:10; Revelation 22:12 and comments).

We must keep two truths in mind here. First, we are saved by faith. Second, we will be judged according to our works.

Only by faith in Christ can we obtain salvation (Ephesians 2:8–9). We cannot be saved by good works. No matter how many good works we do, we shall not be saved unless we have faith.

True faith in Christ, however, always results in good works. If our work and behavior is not good, then our "faith" is not true faith (see James 2:14–17 and comment). A man can do good works without having faith, but he can't have faith without doing good works. Good works are the visible proof of our faith, just as good fruit is the proof of a good tree (Matthew 7:17,20). Therefore, by looking at our works, God can tell if our faith is true or not. When God judges us according to our works, He is also judging our faith. But remember, it is only by faith, not by works, that we obtain salvation. Faith comes before works. After faith, then salvation; after salvation, then works.[11]

Many people do good works only to earn some religious merit or to receive some spiritual blessing. Such good works, then, arise out of selfishness. In contrast to these selfish "good works," the good works that arise out of faith are unselfish. The works that result from faith are always done for the glory of God and for the benefit of others.[12]

7 It is necessary to have **persistence in doing good**. Our good works must be continuous, because they arise out of a continuing faith.

---

[11] For further discussion of salvation, see General Article: Way of Salvation.

[12] However, the matter is not quite as simple as that, because people often do things for a mixture of reasons, partly selfish and partly unselfish. Only God fully knows the reasons for our actions, and He will judge our actions accordingly.

The **glory, honor,** and **immortality** that Paul says we should seek for are not earthly but heavenly. We must put our eyes on heavenly things (Colossians 3:1). God will give **glory, honor,** and **immortality** in heaven to all those who repent and believe in Christ.

8–9 The **wrath and anger** mentioned here (verse 8) signifies God's final judgment. God's judgment will be **first for the Jew, then for the Gentile.**[13] Because the Jews have been given the greatest favor and greatest knowledge, they will also be given the greatest punishment for their sins. We will be punished not only according to our evil deeds, but also according to our knowledge of God's will. We give little children less punishment because their knowledge of right and wrong is less. But for those whose knowledge is great, their punishment will also be great (see Luke 12:47–48 and comment).

10–11 The rewards of God will also be **first for the Jew, then for the Gentile.** The Jews will be first to receive their reward, because they are God's chosen people. But both Jew and Gentile will be rewarded or punished according to their works and according to their knowledge. God will judge both Jew and Gentile by the same principle. God does not play favorites (Colossians 3:25). The Jews thought that they would escape punishment. But they will not.

12 The LAW mentioned here is the Jewish law, that is, the law God gave to the Jews. This law is found in the first five books of the Old Testament, particularly in Exodus, Leviticus, Numbers, and Deuteronomy. When Paul talks here about those who sin **apart from the law,** he is referring to the Gentiles.

Both Jews and Gentiles will receive punishment for their sins. Gentiles, **who sin apart from the law,** will be punished according to the righteous judgment of God; the Jews, **who sin under the law,** will be punished according to the Jewish law. Indeed, the law will give the Jews no advantage. Rather, it will give them a disadvantage, because it is impossible to obey the law in every detail. Therefore, instead of protecting them, the law will actually condemn them (see Galatians 3:10; James 2:10 and comments).

Here a question arises: If the Gentiles have no law, how can they be punished? The answer is: They do have a law. It's not the Jewish law—it's a natural law. This goes back to Paul's discussion in Chapter 1, where he says that all men can see **God's invisible qualities—his eternal power and divine nature** (Romans 1:20). All men naturally know the difference between right and wrong. All men naturally can recognize sin. All men have a conscience. Therefore, we can say that for all men there is a natural law, which is **written on their hearts** (verse 15). It is according to this law that the Gentiles will be punished.

13 Paul tells the Jews that it is no advantage to only hear the law if they don't follow it (James 1:22). Only by following the law completely will one be **declared** RIGHTEOUS—that is, obtain salvation.

14–15 Many Gentiles, even though they don't know the Jewish law, **do by nature** what the law says (verse 14). They obey a "natural" law. For example, the Jewish law says: **You shall not murder** (Exodus 20:13). **You shall not steal** (Exodus 20:15). But the Gentiles also know that to murder and steal is wrong, even though they have never read the book of Exodus! The Jewish law says that a man must show mercy to his neighbor, he must respect his elders, he must help the sick. But the Gentiles also do all these things. Gentiles know the difference between right and wrong, because their **consciences** (verse 15) show them the difference. When they do evil, their consciences start **accusing** them; and when they do good, their consciences start **defending** them.

---

[13] In place of the word **Gentile,** some translations of the Bible say "Greek." In this context, the word "Greek" means "Gentile." The two words are often used interchangeably. The same situation occurs again in verse 10.

In fact, in important matters there is not much difference between the Jewish law and the natural law of the Gentiles.[14] The main difference is this: The Jewish law was written by God on two tablets of stone (Exodus 24:12), but the natural law of the Gentiles was **written on their hearts** (verse 15).

16 The **day when God will judge** is the day of the last judgment (see verse 5). God will judge men not only according to their outward works; He will also judge them according to their **secrets**, that is, their inner thoughts and motives. God knows every one of our "secrets." He sees everything.

God will judge **through Jesus Christ**. That is, all those who accept Christ will be saved, and all those who reject Christ will perish. In effect, Christ will be our judge (see John 5:22; Romans 14:10; 1 Corinthians 4:4; 2 Corinthians 5:10 and comments).

The Jews and the Law (2:17–29)

17–20 Here in this section, Paul sarcastically rebukes the Jews for their spiritual pride. His method is to ask a series of rhetorical questions.

The typical Jew would **brag about** [his] **relationship to God** (verse 17). He relied on himself. The Jew considered himself a **guide**, a **light**, an **instructor**. He considered others to be **blind**, to be **foolish**, to be **infants** (verses 19–20). The Jews had **in the law the embodiment of knowledge and truth** (verse 20), and this should have made them godly. But they had only the outward form of godliness (righteousness); they did not have true godliness. Paul described such people to Timothy as **having a form of godliness but denying its power** (2 Timothy 3:5).

21–23 Here Paul points out the faults of the Jews. Paul calls them hypocrites. What they teach others to do, they do not do themselves. On one side, they **brag about the law**; but on the other side, they keep **breaking the law** (verse 23). In Matthew Chapter 23, Jesus also called such Jews **hypocrites** (Matthew 23:13,25,27).

You who abhor idols, do you rob temples? Paul asks (verse 22). Yes, is the answer. Some Jews did break into Gentile temples and steal the idols (in order to sell them).

24 Paul here quotes from Isaiah 52:5. Just as a son's bad behavior brings dishonor upon his father, so did the Jews' bad behavior bring dishonor upon God . We Christians also must remember that whenever we sin we bring dishonor on God's name.

25 CIRCUMCISION is the cutting away of the excess skin at the tip of the penis. God had commanded that all Jewish male infants be circumcised on the eighth day of life. Circumcision was an outward bodily sign that a man was a Jew, a member of God's chosen nation (Genesis 17:9–14).

In actuality, there was no advantage to circumcision in itself. It was only an outward sign identifying a person as a Jew. If a Jew broke the law, he lost his special relationship with God, of which circumcision was the sign. Then, for that Jew, it would be as if he had never been circumcised. He would be, in effect, "uncircumcised" (1 Corinthians 7:19).

God does not look at the outer man; rather, He looks at the inner man, man's heart. The most important thing to God is that we obey Him from our heart. If our heart is right, our outward actions will be right also (Jeremiah 17:10).

26 Paul here asks another rhetorical question. **If those who are not circumcised** (that is, the Gentiles) were to follow the Jewish law, wouldn't they be regarded as though they were circumcised? The answer is yes. Paul's point is that a Gentile who follows the law will have the same standing with God as a Jew has.

27 Not only that, the **one who is not circumcised physically** (the Gentile) who

---

[14] Even in the matter of idol worship there is no basic difference between the Jewish law and "natural law." Idol worship is not part of any natural law. All mankind should be able to recognize the supreme Creator God and should worship Him (Romans 1:19–20).

obeys God's law will condemn the circumcised Jew who breaks the law.

28–29 Therefore, to be a Jew only outwardly is of no advantage; it has no meaning. A man is a true Jew only when he is a Jew inwardly in his heart.

By the same reasoning, true circumcision is not just a physical or outward thing; rather, true circumcision is an inward thing. True circumcision is a **circumcision of the heart, by the Spirit** (verse 29). True circumcision is a cutting away of the sin and evil in our hearts.[15]

Just as a **man is not a Jew if he is only one outwardly** (verse 28), so a man is not a Christian if he is only one outwardly. The Jews sought praise **from men**, who see only outward things (Matthew 23:5–7). It is much better to seek the praise that comes **from God**, who sees everything. That is the praise that counts!

CHAPTER 3

God's Faithfulness (3:1–8)

1–2 In Romans Chapter 2, Paul has talked about the guilt and unrighteousness of the Jews. Now in verses 1–8 of Chapter 3, Paul takes the Jews' side. Paul wants to present both sides—both the bad things about the Jews and the good things. Paul here acts the part of a defense lawyer defending the Jews in court. His method, as in Chapter 2, is to ask rhetorical questions.

Paul's first question is this: If Jews and Gentiles are going to be judged by the same standards, is there any advantage in being a Jew? Yes, says Paul. The advantage is that the Jews have received the **very words of God**, that is, the Old Testament. In this world they are the witnesses, the spokesmen, of God.

3 Paul has shown in Chapter 2 that many of the Jews have been unfaithful to God. Does that mean that God Himself has been unfaithful too? Certainly not! says Paul. Even though some Jews have been unfaithful, God has remained faithful to them. God still lovingly regards the Jews as His chosen people.

In what way were the Jews unfaithful? One of the main ways they were unfaithful is that they did not believe the promises and prophecies written in the Old Testament about the coming into the world of the Savior Jesus Christ. Even after Christ came, they rejected Him. However, the fact that the Jews didn't believe the promises about Christ doesn't thereby make the promises void. Just because a blind man can't see a light doesn't mean the light is not shining!

4 Even if every Jew was a liar, God would still remain true, and His word would remain true. God will be **proved right in** [His] **words**, and His judgment will **prevail** (Psalm 51:4).

When man's sin is revealed, God's righteousness, by contrast, can be seen even more clearly. Just as a candle seems brighter in the dark than in the daylight, so does God's righteousness appear brighter in the darkness of man's unrighteousness.

5 If man's unrighteousness **brings out God's righteousness more clearly**, why then should God be upset about man's unrighteousness? Someone could say (falsely) that God was being glorified by man's unrighteousness, and that therefore God would be **unjust** or unfair to punish man for it. **Certainly not!** says Paul (verse 6).

6 Even though God's righteousness appears more clearly when contrasted with man's sin, God still hates sin and will certainly punish it. And His judgement will be completely just.

---

[15] Some people regard the ceremony of baptism in the same way the Jews regarded circumcision; they mistakenly believe that simply being baptized makes them Christians. However, baptism is of no value unless it is accompanied by true inward faith (see General Article: Water Baptism).

7 The question Paul asks here is similar to the question in verse 5. If God's **truthfulness** (light) appears brighter when contrasted with man's **falsehood** (darkness), why should God condemn our falsehood? Because just as light overcomes and "condemns" darkness, so God's truth will condemn our falsehood.

8 In Paul's time, some people were actually saying: "It's okay to sin, because by sinning we are making God appear more holy and righteous." Such an idea is totally false. Paul says about such people: **Their condemnation is deserved**.

Some non-Christians were even falsely accusing the Christians of saying the same thing: namely, that is was okay to sin because it made God seem more righteous. For example, Christians were falsely accused of saying: "The more we sin, the greater will be God's mercy; therefore let us sin all the more so that God's mercy will be even greater." Or they were accused of saying: "Since we are saved by faith and not by works, it is no longer necessary to do any good works. No matter how much we sin, God will still forgive us and save us." All these accusations were, of course, false. Christians do not believe these things.

No One Is Righteous (3:9–20)

9 Here Paul repeats his point that the Jews aren't any better than the Gentiles, and the Gentiles aren't any better than the Jews. **Are we** (Jews) **any better?** Paul asks. **Not at all!** Paul answers. All men are by nature equally sinful. **Jews and Gentiles alike are all under sin. . . . There is no one righteous, not even one** (verse 10).

10–12 In this next section, Paul quotes from various Old Testament passages. Here in verses 10–12, Paul quotes from Psalm 14:1–3; 53:1–3; Ecclesiastes 7:20.

These quotations are hard sayings. How can God speak so critically and harshly of mankind? Mankind doesn't look at itself this way!

Nevertheless, these sayings are true. From these verses we can find out just how God does see mankind. When God created man in the beginning, He saw that what He had created was **very good** (Genesis 1:31). But then the first man and woman, Adam and Eve—the mother and father of all mankind—committed a very great sin (Genesis 3:1–6). After that, man's heart became wicked (Jeremiah 17:9). And from that time on, God was not happy with mankind.

When we look at the men and women around us, most of them seem to us like pretty decent people. They don't seem to be unrighteous. In what way, then, are all men by nature unrighteous?

All men are unrighteous because all men are basically selfish, or self-centered. Men naturally love themselves more than they love God. From childhood on, men put themselves first and seek first their own advantage. They may appear good on the outside, but in their hearts they do not heed God's will. Rather, they follow their own will. This putting of man's own will above God's will is, in God's sight, man's greatest and most basic sin[16] (see Romans 6:12 and comment).

To come to God, the first step a man must take is to recognize this, his most basic sin. If a man does not recognize his sinful state, he will see no need to come to God and ask for forgiveness. And if he doesn't ask for forgiveness, how will he receive it? And if he doesn't receive forgivness, how will he be saved? That's why, in verse 11, God says that **there is no one who understands**. There is no one who understands that all men are sinners. For this reason there is **no one who seeks God** to ask for forgiveness.

Let us learn to look at ourselves as God looks at us. Otherwise, we shall be deceived into thinking we are good when we are not. An ant may imagine

[16] We must remember here, however, that underlying the basic sin of self-centeredness is the root of all sin: unbelief (see Romans 1:18 and comment). The man who does not believe in God always ends up putting himself in God's place. Instead of being God-centered, he becomes self-centered. Instead of following God's will, he follows his own will. Thus unbelief inevitably leads to the sin of self-centeredness, which leads in turn to all other sins.

that it's an elephant, but it will still remain an ant! So it is with man; we are always imagining that we are better than we are. Our hearts are naturally deceitful (Jeremiah 17:9). One of Satan's chief tactics is to deceive us, to blind us to our own sin and wickedness.

13 The saying, **Their throats are open graves,** means that men speak words that deserve the death penalty (Psalm 5:9).

The expression **poison of vipers** means slander and abuse (Psalm 140:3).

14 Paul here quotes from Psalm 10:7. In verses 13–14, we see the importance of sins of the tongue in this overall picture of man's wickedness (see James 3:3–8).

15–17 These verses are quoted from Isaiah 59:7–8. The **way of peace** (verse 17) is the **way** of making **peace** with God. That way is to repent of one's sins and turn to God in obedience.

18 Paul here quotes from Psalm 36:1. The Psalmist says that man has **no fear of God**. Why should man fear God? Because God hates sin, and will punish man for it on the day of judgment. **The fear of the Lord is the beginning of knowledge** (Proverbs 1:7). The wise man acknowledges his sin and fears God.

19 The Jews, of course, were familiar with all these Old Testament passages that Paul quotes in verses 10–18. But they thought that they applied only to the Gentiles, and not to themselves! Here Paul tells the Jews that these verses apply to them also. **Whatever the law** (that is, the Old Testament) **says, it says to those who are under the law** (that is, the Jews). So when the **law** says, "**There is no one righteous**" (verse 10), that includes the Jews too. Therefore, **every mouth** will be **silenced**. No one will have anything to say in his own defense; there will be no excuses. On the day of judgment, every one will stand silent before God.

20 The Jews thought that by observing the law they would be declared righteous. But Paul says here that **no one will be declared righteous . . . by observing the law**. The reason is simple: No one can observe the law perfectly in every detail all the time. Only if one were to observe the law perfectly would he be declared righteous (see Galatians 3:11; James 2:10 and comments.)

Instead of declaring us righteous, the law, in fact, declares us guilty—both Jew and Gentile alike. But the law does one important thing for us: it makes us aware of our sin. It makes us aware of how far we have fallen from God's standard, of how far we have drawn apart from God. And for every man and woman, this awareness is the first step in turning to God.

Righteousness Through Faith (3:21–31)

21 Paul here repeats what he wrote in Romans 1:17, namely, that a new **righteousness** has been revealed, a righteousness that we can receive through faith in Jesus Christ (verse 22).

This righteousness is **apart from law**. That is, it is not based on the Jewish law; it is separate from the law. Paul has already shown in verse 20 that it is impossible to be declared righteous by observing the law. Therefore, if a person can't be declared righteous by observing the law, another way is needed; and that way is **through faith in Jesus Christ** (verse 22). This new righteousness, then, is Christ's righteousness, which we receive through faith in Him. Paul says here that the **Law and the Prophets**[17] (the Old Testament) **testify** to this new righteousness. This is not some new teaching that Paul has invented; it is taken right out of the Jewish Scriptures. The Old Testament pointed to the coming of Christ. It also pointed to a new day when the law—which had first been written on stone tablets—would be written on men's hearts (Jeremiah 31:31–33). When the law is written on

[17] Sometimes Paul refers to the Old Testament as the **law**, as in verse 19. But more commonly, the Old Testament is called the **Law and the Prophets**. The first five books of the Old Testament are known as the **Law**. Then much of the remainder of the Old Testament consists of the writings of prophets such as Isaiah and Jeremiah and many others; this part of the Old Testament, then, is called the **Prophets**.

men's hearts by faith, then they will be declared righteous in God's sight.

22 Before we can be saved, we must first be declared righteous by God (see Romans 1:17). No unrighteous person will ever be accepted by God or allowed into the kingdom of heaven. Therefore, this new righteousness, we can say, is a righteousness that gives salvation. And to obtain it, all we need to do is believe in Jesus; that's all. And this righteousness is for all people, not only Jews. **There is no difference**, says Paul, between Jew and Gentile; they can both equally receive this righteousness.

23 In this verse Paul repeats the truth written in verses 10–12. All men are unrighteous. All men have disobeyed God in matters large and small. Therefore, all men need this new righteousness.

All men **fall short of the glory of God.** We all are made in God's image (Genesis 1:27). Therefore, we all should reflect God's glory. But because of our unrighteousness, we do not. We are like a dirty mirror. Only one man has ever perfectly reflected God's glory—and that man is Jesus Christ (see John 1:14 and comment).

24 Here in this very important verse Paul gives us the essence of the Gospel of Christ. Men are **justified freely by** [God's] **grace**; this means that men are saved freely by God's grace (see Ephesians 2:8 and comment). At first men had no hope, no hope of being righteous, no sure hope of being saved.[18] But now, because of His great love and mercy, God has provided a means by which men can be saved: namely, faith in Jesus Christ.

Our salvation is given **freely**. We don't have to do all sorts of good works in order to be saved; we don't have to earn our salvation. Jesus Christ has "earned" our salvation for us; He has paid the price of our salvation. The price was His own life.

Paul says here that we are **justified . . . through the** REDEMPTION **that came by Christ Jesus**. Justification is one part of our salvation. When we are saved, it means we also have been justified. Being justified and being saved always go together; you can't have one without the other.

Both justification and salvation are free gifts of God, and both come through faith in Jesus Christ. Justification is the first stage of being saved; it opens the way for us to receive all the other blessings of salvation (see General Article: Way of Salvation).

25 How does Christ save us? Paul answers that question in this verse. **God presented him** (Christ) **as a sacrifice of** ATONEMENT, as a propitiation. A **sacrifice of atonement** is an act in which another person takes our punishment for sin. Once punishment has been given to someone else for our sins, then those sins are no longer counted against us; we are set right with God. Thus we can say that Jesus is our propitiation, or **sacrifice of atonement**. He took man's sins upon Himself and accepted the punishment for them. Our sins are "paid" for; God will no longer hold them against us.

What is the punishment that God gives for sin? It is death (Romans 6:23). Therefore, for Christ to take our punishment, He had to shed His **blood**; that is, He had to die. Thus it is **through faith in his blood** (or death) that Christ becomes our personal propitiation. We have to have faith that Christ has died to take away our sins; otherwise, His death, His **sacrifice of atonement**, will be of no benefit to us (see Mark 10:45; 1 John 2:2 and comments).

From all this we can see two things about God: first, His **justice** (or righteousness); and second, His love. Because God is just and righteous, He must punish sin. It was **to demonstrate his justice** that God punished Christ for our sins. But it was also because of His love for us that He punished Christ in our place. In punishing Christ, God was, in actuality, taking the punishment Himself. **For God so loved the world that he gave his one and only Son** (John 3:16).

---

[18] According to Hebrews 11:39–40, godly men and women who lived before Christ's time will be **made perfect** together with us who believe in Christ. Thus it would appear that God will honor their faith and save them. However, the Old Testament Jews did not have the sure hope of salvation that Christians have been given.

In order to appropriate the benefits of Christ's sacrificial death for us, we must do only one thing: believe in Him and in what He has done for us. Through faith in Christ, through faith in His death (blood), we are declared righteous and will escape condemnation on the day of judgment.

One phrase in this verse remains to be commented on: **in his forbearance he** (God) **had left the sins committed beforehand unpunished**. For hundreds of years God had shown the Jews great **forbearance** (patience). He had delayed punishing their sins. He wanted to give them the chance to repent and place their faith in Jesus. And still today, God continues to show **forbearance** to all men. He desires that all men obtain salvation (1 Timothy 2:4). Therefore let us encourage men and women to believe in Christ while there is yet opportunity!

26 Here Paul restates what he has said in verses 24–25. God sent Christ to be our propitiation in order **to demonstrate his justice** (by punishing sin). God did this for two reasons. First, He did it **so as to be just**. Second, He did it so as to be the **one who justifies those who have faith in Jesus**. In these two reasons we see again both God's justice (righteousness) and His love. We must never separate these two characteristics of God—righteousness and love; they always go together.

27 **On what principle**, or on what basis, does God justify man freely? Does He justify man on the principle **of observing the law**—that is, because of a man's good works? **No**, says Paul. No man is justified (declared righteous) by the works of the Jewish law (see Galatians 2:15–16 and comment). Thus there is no place for **boasting**. No on can say: "By my good works I have proved myself righteous and thus deserving of salvation." Rather, says Paul, it is by the principle **of faith** that man is justified and saved (see Ephesians 2:8–9 and comment).

28 Here Paul concludes the above discussion by saying that a man **is justified by faith apart from observing the** (Jewish) **law**.

29–30 Therefore, because man is justified apart from the Jewish law, the Gentiles have just as good a chance of being saved as the Jews. God is the God of both Jews and Gentiles, and He loves them both equally. God will justify the **circumcised** (the Jews) by faith, and He will also justify the **uncircumcised** (the Gentiles) by faith. **There is no difference** between Jew and Gentile (verse 22).

31 If faith is the only thing necessary for salvation, is Paul saying that the Jewish law is worthless? Not at all. Paul says he does not **nullify the law by this faith**, but rather he upholds the law. The law says: sin must be punished. Faith says: Christ bore that punishment. Therefore, faith does not oppose the law, or **nullify** the law; rather, faith upholds the law. Faith (or, we can say, Christ) fulfills the law. Because when the law could not save man, faith in Christ could (see Matthew 5:17 and comment). Christ Himself came and opened up for us the way of salvation. And through faith in Him we can enter into that salvation (see Romans 8:3–4 and comment).

CHAPTER 4

Abraham Justified by Faith (4:1–12)

1 **Abraham** (also called Abram) was the very first Jew. God called Abraham to be the father of a new nation (Genesis 12:1–5; 17:3–8). Abraham is thus the original ancestor of all the Jews (Matthew 1:1–2).

Abraham was born about two thousand years before Christ's time. He was born in the town of Ur, which was located in what is now modern Iraq. From there he moved with his father to the town of Haran in present-day Turkey (Genesis 11:31).

After that, in obedience to God's call (Genesis 12:1), Abraham moved to the land of Canaan (which would later become Israel), a land which God had specially prepared for Abraham and his descendants.

But there was one big problem: Abraham's wife Sarah (also called Sarai) was barren. God had promised Abraham: **"I will make you into a great nation"** (Genesis 12:2). But with Sarah unable to have children, how could God's promise be fulfilled? At the time God made this promise to Abraham, Sarah was already old and long past child-bearing age. Therefore, Abraham initially doubted God's word (Genesis 15:2–3). And so God told Abraham: **"Look up at the heavens and count the stars—if indeed you can count them. . . . So shall your offspring be"** (Genesis 15:5).

From that point on, Abraham didn't doubt God, but believed that He would indeed fulfill His promise to give him and his wife Sarah a son.

When Abraham was one hundred years old and Sarah was ninety, Sarah gave birth to a boy. Abraham named him Isaac (Genesis 21:1–5).

In verse 1, Paul calls Abraham **our forefather,**[19] because Paul, being a Jew, was also a descendant of Abraham. The Jews considered themselves the only legitimate descendants of Abraham.

2 According to the Old Testament, Abraham was considered to be righteous, or **justified**[20] (Genesis 15:6). How was he justified? The Jews mistakenly thought Abraham was **justified** (declared righteous by God) because he had been circumcised. God earlier had said to Abraham: **"You are to undergo circumcision, and it will be the sign of the covenant between me and you"** (Genesis 17:9–14). Thus the Jews thought that because Abraham obeyed God and was circumcised, he was therefore justified in God's sight. In addition, the Jews thought that if they, too, were properly circumcised and followed the Jewish law, they would then be justified just as Abraham was (see Romans 2:25 and comment).

When Paul uses the word **works** in this verse, he means the "work" of obeying the Jewish law. If Abraham had indeed been justified by his **works**—that is, his obedience—then he would have had something to **boast about**. He could have boasted: "Look at me; because of my good works God is honoring me."

But Paul says that is not so. Abraham was not justified because of his works, and therefore he didn't have anything to boast to God about.

Here it is well to mention again why being justified is so important. It is important because, without first being justified or declared righteous by God, a person cannot be saved (see Romans 3:24 and comment). If a person is not justified, he remains condemned because of his sin, and his punishment is eternal death. Therefore, everyone needs to ask the question: How can I be made righteous in God's sight? A righteous God will not accept an unrighteous man into His kingdom.

3 So how was Abraham justified or declared righteous? He was declared righteous not by his works but by his faith in God. By faith Abraham left his home and journeyed to the land of Canaan. By faith he accepted God's promise that he and Sarah would have a son—even though it was humanly impossible. Therefore, Abraham's faith **was credited to him as righteousness**. Paul here has quoted Genesis 15:6, a quotation he will repeat again in verses 9 and 22.

4 When a man works, his employer is obligated to pay him wages for his work. The worker has earned his wages. The employer owes the worker his wages.

5 But God is not like a human employer. God doesn't owe anyone anything. It is not because we have worked for God that He rewards us; rather, it is because of His mercy and grace in response to our faith that He rewards us.

One might even say that faith was a kind of "work." One could say that in

---

[19] Some translations of the Bible say, "our forefather according to the flesh."

[20] To be **justified** means to be declared righteous by God.

God's sight faith is the one essential "work" a man must do to be justified (see John 6:28–29 and comment). But it is misleading to speak of faith as a "work." After all, faith is also a free gift of God, which He gives to us out of His grace. Without God's grace, we can't even believe to begin with. Our salvation, from first to last, is brought about by God's grace. God is the initiator and finisher of our salvation (see General Article: Salvation—God's Choice or Man's Choice?).

Paul says here that God **justifies the wicked**. By this Paul means that God justifies all who have faith; because through faith in Christ, **wicked** (unrighteous) men become righteous in God's sight.

6–8 Paul here quotes from Psalm 32:1–3, written by **David**, the Jews' greatest king. In each of these verses 6–8, there is an action described: to "credit righteousness" (verse 6); to "forgive transgressions" and to "cover sins" (verse 7); to "not count sin" (verse 8). All of these expressions describe the same action: namely, the cleansing or removing of our past sins from God's sight so that we can stand innocent before God. When a man's sins are forgiven, that man is declared righteous by God; in other words, God **credits righteousness** to him. Such a man is blessed indeed.

Like righteousness, forgiveness (cleansing) is a gift from God. We are not forgiven because of our own work or effort, but because of God's free grace. There is only one thing we must do to obtain forgiveness, and that is to believe.

9 Is this **blessedness** (that is, the blessedness of righteousness and forgiveness) only for the **circumcised** (Jews)? The Jews thought "Yes," but Paul says "No." It's for the Gentiles too.

10 The Jews claimed that Abraham was declared righteous because he was circumcised. But Paul says that is not so, because well before Abraham was circumcised, he had already put his faith in God. Many years before he was circumcised, Abraham had believed God's promise that he would have a son and become the father of a great nation. It was because of that earlier faith in God that Abraham was declared righteous, not because of his circumcision. Circumcision was only the outward sign of Abraham's faith.

11 In Abraham's life, faith came before circumcision. Only after Abraham had faith, did God then give him the **sign of circumcision**. Paul calls this sign a **seal of the righteousness** [Abraham] **had by faith**.

Faith is the main thing; circumcision is only a **sign** (Genesis 17:11).

Abraham had faith **while he was still uncircumcised**, and it was this faith that made him acceptable in God's sight. Therefore, Paul says, Abraham is also the **father of all who believe but have not been circumcised**—that is, he is the spiritual "father" of all believing Gentiles.

12 In verse 11, Paul wrote that Abraham was the father of **all who believe**. Here in verse 12, Paul writes that Abraham is **also the father of the circumcised** (the Jews). Yes, Abraham is the father of the Jews according to the flesh. But those Jews who do not truly believe in God (and Christ) are not true spiritual Jews; they are not Abraham's true spiritual descendants. The true Jews are those **who walk in the footsteps of the faith that . . . Abraham had**. Likewise, true Christians are those who walk in the footsteps of Jesus Christ. It is not enough simply to say, "I believe." We must **walk in the footsteps of . . . faith**.

Abraham Received the Promise by Faith (4:13–25)

13–14 When Paul writes the word **law** in verse 13, he means "works of the law." In verse 14, the expresssion **those who live by the law** means "those who live by the works of the law."

The Jewish **law** was given by God to the Jews more than four hundred years after Abraham's time. Therefore, it couldn't have been by works of the law that Abraham received the promise that he would become **heir of the world** (verse 13), since the law hadn't even been given then.

In verse 14, Paul says: If we could become heirs through works of the law, then there would be no need for faith; faith would have **no value**. But the fact is that only through faith can we become **heirs**, that is, true spiritual heirs of Abraham (see Galatians 3:18 and comment).

In fact, it is completely impossible to become heirs through works of the law, because no one can fully obey the whole law all the time. If the promise could be received only by doing the works of the law, no one would ever receive the promise; the promise would then be **worthless** (verse 14).

15 The **law brings wrath**, that is, punishment. The law brings wrath because men can't obey it entirely and thus God must punish them. If there were no law, there would, of course, be no opportunity for disobedience and, hence, no punishment. But there is a law—and along with it, therefore, there must be punishment.

16 Therefore, the promise of being an **heir of the world** (verse 13) did not come to Abraham by the law, which leads only to wrath. Rather, the promise came **by faith** and **by grace**. And that promise of being heirs comes to us also by faith and by grace. Paul says here that the promise is **guaranteed to all Abraham's offspring**—not only to those **who are of the law** (that is, the Jews), but also to all those **who are of the faith of Abraham** (that is, those who have the same kind of faith Abraham had). Abraham is the **father of us all**—that is, **all** who have faith. All believers are Abraham's true spiritual heirs, not according to the flesh but according to faith. Only through faith can the promise of becoming an heir be **guaranteed** (see Galatians 3:29 and comment).

17 God made Abraham the **father of many nations** (Genesis 17:5)—not only of the Jewish nation, but also, in a spiritual sense, of the Gentile nations.

Paul here calls God the **God who gives life to the dead and calls things that are not as though they were.** Abraham and his wife were virtually **dead**, as far as their ability to have a child was concerned; they were very old. But from them God gave **life** in the form of a son; that is, from a situation of "death," God brought forth new life. God transformed **things that are not**—things that couldn't happen—into things that did happen! (Hebrews 11:11–12).

Also in Paul's mind here is the fact that two thousand years after God raised up Isaac from his "dead" parents, God also raised up His own Son Jesus Christ from the dead. But not only that; God raises us up too—we who were **dead in** [our] **transgressions and sins** (Ephesians 2:1,4–5).

18 Paul here quotes part of the promise God gave to Abraham in Genesis 15:5.

Against all hope, Abraham in hope believed. To have a son at the age of one hundred was surely a hopeless thing, an impossible thing. Nevertheless, Abraham **believed.**

19–21 Having trusted in God, Abraham gave God all the glory (verse 20). A believing man always gives God the glory, and God will always glorify the believing man.

Let us ourselves take Abraham's example. God has given to us also, as to Abraham, marvelous promises—promises of things such as salvation, the filling of the Holy Spirit, all the power and fullness of God Himself! Do we **waver through unbelief** regarding these promises? The root sin man commits against God is the sin of **unbelief** (see Romans 1:18 and comment). Unbelief dishonors God. Unbelief says: God can't fulfill the promises He has made. Unbelief is the root of all sin. This is why faith is so important and necessary in God's sight. This is why man is declared righteous by faith alone.

22 Paul here quotes again from Genesis 15:6 (see verse 3).

23–24 Here Paul says that, according to Abraham's example, God will also **credit righteousness** to us because of our faith. Having, like Abraham, been declared righteous, we too will becomes heirs, heirs not only of Abraham but also of the kingdom of God. And we shall not only be heirs of Abraham; we shall be fellow heirs with Christ Himself! (see Romans 8:17).

25 In Chapter 4, Paul has described two great blessings or gifts given by God: first forgiveness (verses 7–8); and second, righteousness, or **justification** (verses 3,6,9,11,22,24–25). These two blessings always go together. In fact, being forgiven and being declared righteous are two of the greatest blessings of all; they are two major parts of man's salvation. And Paul says that these two blessings, forgiveness and righteousness, are obtained not through works of the law but only through faith in Christ.

But here we want to ask a question: What exactly did Christ do for us? Why put faith in Him? Here in verse 25, Paul gives the answer. The reason for putting faith in Christ is this: It is through Him that we receive these two great blessings, forgiveness and righteousness (or justification).

First, it is Christ who **was delivered over to death** on the cross in order that we ourselves might not have to bear the punishment for our sins. He died in order that we might receive forgivness and cleansing from our sins and be able to stand guiltless before God. He did this by taking our sins upon Himself and by bearing our punishment (see Mark 10:45 and comment).

Second, Christ **was raised to life for our justification**. He rose from the dead in order that we might be declared righteous (justified) before God. And having been declared righteous, we receive salvation, acceptance into the kingdom of God, and eternal life. This, then, is the glorious work of our Lord and Savior Jesus Christ. This, then, is the amazing and joyful Gospel of Christ. Why should we hesitate to put faith in such a Savior!

CHAPTER 5

The Results of Faith (5:1–5)

1 In the first four chapters of Romans, Paul has showed us that man is **justified** (declared righteous) **through faith** alone. **Therefore,** Paul says here in verse 1, **since we have been justified through faith, we have peace with God.**[21]

Once having been justified, we are then in a state of **peace** or reconciliation with God. We no longer need to seek after peace, or make peace; we have it already. As soon as we believe, we are justified; and as soon as we are justified, we have peace with God. Right now, we can experience this peace with God.

Why is peace with God (or reconciliation with God) so important? Because from birth man is at enmity with God. Because of our sin, we cannot have peace with God. Jesus Christ came into the world and died to take away our sin. Thus, by His own death, he made peace between us and God; He removed that sin that stood between us and God. Therefore, through Christ alone can we find peace with God. Besides Jesus Christ, there is no other mediator between man and God.

2 Through Christ **we have gained access by faith into this grace**. An ordinary person can't just walk into a king's palace to meet the king; first he must obtain permission or authority to enter. And then one of the king's officials must bring that person into the king's presence. In the same way, Jesus Christ is the "official" who brings us into God's presence—that is, **into this grace**—where we experience God's **grace**. And God's grace includes His peace, His mercy, His

---

[21] In place of the words **we have peace with God**, some translations of the Bible say, "let us have peace with God." Some of the ancient manuscripts of Romans read one way, and some the other. Between the two, we cannot be absolutely certain which Paul wrote. However, looking at the meaning, the translation, **we have peace with God**, fits better with Paul's overall teaching.,

love, His joy. For Paul, the meaning of the word "grace" is broad and deep! Recall that in the beginning of Romans, and in most of his other letters as well, Paul prays that his readers might receive this **grace** of God, and along with it, God's **peace** (see Romans 1:7; 1 Corinthians 1:3; Ephesians 1:2).

An ordinary person can't come into the king's presence without permission, but the king's own children can. Through faith in Christ, we are now the children of God; therefore we can come into God's presence at any time (see Ephesians 2:18–19; 3:12; Hebrews 10:19–22 and comments).

Paul says **we now stand** in this grace; that is, we now stand in God's presence. An unrighteous, sinful man may not stand in God's presence, because such a man is not worthy. But now, through faith in Christ, we have been declared righteous and are therefore worthy to stand before God. We have obtained Christ's righteousness. It is not our own righteousness that makes us worthy, but Christ's.

Through God's grace, we also experience joy. We **rejoice**. What do we rejoice in? We rejoice **in the hope of the glory of God**; that is, we rejoice in the hope of sharing in God's glory. We all used to **fall short of the glory of God** (Romans 3:23), but now through Christ we have become partakers of God's glory (Romans 8:16–17).

3 To rejoice **in the glory of God** is easy; to rejoice **in our sufferings** is not easy! However, Christians rejoice in suffering and hardship, because they know that such suffering is ultimately for their own good (see Romans 8:28 and comment). Notice also that Paul says we rejoice **in** our sufferings, not in spite of them.

If suffering is supposed to be good for us, we naturally want to ask: What good does it do? The answer: Suffering **produces perseverance** (see James 1:2–4 and comment).

There are two kinds of suffering. One kind we bring on ourselves by our own foolishness and sin. This kind of suffering is hard to rejoice in! Nevertheless, we must remember that such suffering is really discipline from God, and we must accept it as such (see Hebrews 12:7,12; Revelation 3:19).

The second kind of suffering is that which we endure for righteousness' sake. In this kind of suffering we can rejoice greatly (see Matthew 5:10–12; 1 Peter 4:12–16 and comments). Let the suffering that comes to us henceforth come on account of righteousness, and not on account of sin!

4 Perseverance produces **character**; that is, perseverance makes our character stronger and more mature. Through perseverance in times of suffering, our faith is tested and made firm (see 1 Peter 1:6–7 and comment).

When our faith has been shown to be genuine by our perseverance, then we can have **hope**—hope in our salvation and eternal reward. Jesus said, "**. . . he who stands firm to the end will be saved**" (Mark 13:13). If in times of suffering we do not persevere to the end, many verses of Scripture suggest that we will be in danger of losing our salvation (see General Article: Can We Lose Our Salvation?).

Recall the parable that Jesus told about the sower. Some seed (God's word) **fell on rocky places** [and] **sprang up quickly. . . . But when the sun came up, the plants were scorched, and they withered because they had no root** (Mark 4:5–6). The **sun** in the parable represents suffering and persecution, and the new **plants**—that is, believers with shallow faith—cannot endure and so **wither** (see Mark 4:16–17; Luke 8:6,13 and comment). Therefore, Paul says here that when we endure suffering with **perseverance**, and our **character** develops strength and maturity (deep roots), then we can fully **hope** in the certainty of our salvation (see 2 Timothy 2:12; Hebrews 10:38–39; Revelation 3:11).

5 The hope that we place in God and in His promises **does not disappoint us**. Furthermore, God has already fulfilled our hope by giving us the **Holy Spirit**. The Holy Spirit is the advance, or guarantee, of the inheritance stored up for us in heaven (see Ephesians 1:13–14 and comment).

We know when we are filled with the

Holy Spirit, because God pours out **his love into our hearts by the Holy Spirit**. Through the Spirit, we experience the love of God and are filled with that love. And once we are filled, God's love will then overflow from us to others around us.

God's Love Revealed in Christ's Death (5:6–11)

6 First, God showed His great love for us by sending His Son Jesus to die for our sins (see John 3:16; 1 John 4:9–10 and comments). Even while we were still **powerless**—still **sinners** (verse 8), still **enemies** (verse 10)—Christ died for us. In using the word **powerless**, Paul means that we had no power to overcome sin, no power to obey the law.

7–8 We would never naturally think of giving our own lives for another person (except perhaps for our own spouse or child). Even if that other person was a **righteous man** (verse 7), we wouldn't give our own life for him. Well, perhaps if someone was a very **good man**, we might think about sacrificing ourselves for him. But for an evil or sinful man we would never think about giving our life. We wouldn't even want to help such a man, let alone die for him.

But see how amazing God's love is! See how much higher it is than man's love. Christ didn't die for **righteous** and **good** men only; He died also for evil and sinful men—His enemies.

Therefore, let us not be surprised that Christ commands us to love our enemies! (see Matthew 5:43–44 and comment).

9 We are justified by Christ's **blood**—that is, His sacrificial death (see Ephesians 1:7 and comment). Christ, through His own death, took upon Himself the punishment for our sins. We can say that our sins have been "washed away" by His blood. Having thus been cleansed of our sins, we are now **justified** (declared righteous) in God's sight. And having been justified, we will be saved from punishment—that is, **from God's wrath**.

10 Through Christ's death, we have been **reconciled** to God. If we have received such a great benefit from Christ's **death**, think how much more benefit we will receive from his resurrected **life**!

It is not enough to be reconciled to God just once; we must remain reconciled.[22] We need help to remain reconciled with God. We need strength to endure suffering and persecution, remembering that **he who stands firm to the end will be saved** (Mark 13:13). We need to grow in grace and faith. We need to **grow up into** [Christ] **who is the Head** (Ephesians 4:15). And in all this the risen living Christ will be with us, helping us.

11 There can be no deep and abiding joy in the heart of a person who is not reconciled to God. But as soon as we are reconciled to Him, our hearts are at once filled with His joy, and we can **rejoice in God**. Why should we not rejoice in a God who, through Christ, has done so much for us?

Death Through Adam, Life Through Christ (5:12–21)

12 **. . . sin entered the world through one man**. Who was that man? He was **Adam** (verse 14), the first man created by God.

After He had finished creating heaven and earth and everything in them, **God saw all that was made, and it was very good** (Genesis 1:31). But after that, the first man Adam sinned. Adam and his wife ate a fruit which God had commanded them not to eat (Genesis 2:15–17; 3:1–3). At that moment, sin entered mankind. And ever since Adam's time, all men have shared in Adam's sin. From our very first ancestor, we inherited a sinful nature. And since the punishment for sin is death, **in this way death came to all men**. That death is both physical and spiritual.

[22] Many Christians believe that there is a sense in which believers are reconciled to God once for all, and that once truly reconciled, they cannot become unreconciled. For further discussion of this subject, see General Article: Can We Lose Our Salvation?

Here a question arises. Paul says here that **all sinned.** But have tiny infants also sinned? No, we don't say they have sinned, but the seed of sin has been planted in them. And as the infant grows up, that seed will certainly sprout. Just as a puppy begins to bark without being taught, so a child begins to sin without being taught. To sin is in his nature.

What happens to a child who dies in infancy? Does he go to heaven or hell? The Bible does not give a specific answer to this question. Most people believe that since the child hasn't really sinned on purpose, he will go to heaven. We know that God has great love and concern for infants and small children. God will do what is right (see Matthew 18:10; Mark 10:14–15; General Article: Children and the Kingdom of God).

13 From Adam's time up to the time of MOSES (verse 14), the written **law**[23] did not exist. God gave the written law to Moses to pass on to the Jewish nation. (Moses was born about four hundred years after Abraham's time; before Moses' time, then, neither the Jews nor the Gentiles had a written law.)

Because the law did not exist before Moses' time, there was, of course, no such thing as disobedience to the law (Romans 4:15). Neither was there any punishment for disobeying the law. Sin is disobeying God's law. Where there is no law, **sin is not taken into account** in a legal sense.[24]

Take, for example, a child who does something wrong without realizing it. No one had ever told him it was wrong. So the child is not punished. But if the child is told it's wrong to do something and then goes ahead and does it anyway, his sin will be **taken into account**, and his parents will punish him.

14 Before Moses' time, even though the written law did not exist, **sin was in the world** (verse 13). Sin was in the world because it had originally entered Adam, who ate the fruit that God had told him not to eat; and from Adam sin had passed to all mankind. And along with sin came the punishment for sin, which is death. Some generations after Adam, God became so angry with sinful mankind that he sent a huge flood and destroyed all men living on the earth, except for Noah and his family (Genesis Chapters 6–7). In Abraham's time, God destroyed the cities of Sodom and Gomorrah because of the wickedness of the people living there (Genesis Chapter 19). Even those who didn't break a specific command of God died like everyone else, because death had entered mankind through Adam (see verse 12). Thus Paul says that **death reigned from the time of Adam to the time of Moses.**

Adam was a **pattern of the one to come**—that is, Christ. In what way was Adam a pattern of Christ? Adam was the head of the old human race; Christ is the Head of a new spiritual race. Being the very first man, Adam influenced all those who came after him; that is, just as Adam sinned, they too all sinned. They became sinners like he was. Christ, on the other hand, being the first man of the new spiritual race, the eldest among all the sons of God, influences all those who follow Him. They become righteous like Him.

15 **But the gift is not like the trespass.** Christ's work is not like Adam's work. From Adam came death; from Christ comes life. From Adam came sin; from Christ comes the **gift.** The **gift** mentioned here is the **gift of righteousness** (verse 17), which is given **by the grace of the one man, Jesus Christ.** Together with the gift of righteousness comes eternal life—salvation. And this gift will **overflow to the many**—that is, to all believers.

16 **The judgment followed one sin** (Adam's sin of eating the forbidden fruit). Thus from **one man's** (Adam's) sin came **judgment.** Then, **the gift followed many trespasses.** That is, after many other men had sinned, the **gift** of righteousness was given by the grace of Jesus Christ. From one man's sin came **condemnation** for all men; from one man's (Christ's) obedience

---

[23] Here the word **law** refers to the law which God wrote on stone tablets and gave to Moses.

[24] However, before Moses' time, there was a "natural law." Men broke this natural law and sinned against God, and God punished them for it (see verse 14 and comment).

came **justification** for all men who believe.

17 From Adam came the "reign of death"; from Christ came the "reign of life." From Adam, we have all received the inheritance of death; both our bodies and our spirits are under the power of death. We shall all die physically and, without Christ, we shall all die spiritually too.[25] But from Christ, we have received the inheritance of life, eternal life, not only on earth but in heaven also (see Romans 6:23; 1 Corinthians 15:21–22 and comments). This life has come to us through **God's abundant provision of grace** and through His provision of the **gift of righteousness**.

18 Here Paul repeats what he has written in verse 16. From **one trespass** came **condemnation for all men**. From **one act of righteousness** (Christ's act of giving His life for us) came **justification that brings life for all men** (see Romans 8:1–2).

19 Because of Adam's **disobedience**, many men were made **sinners**. Because of Christ's **obedience**, many men have been made **righteous** (see Philippians 2:8).

A question arises: How could one man, Adam, affect so many? How does Adam's sin pass from generation to generation? The answer is this: Adam is our bodily father, our common ancestor according to the flesh. Mankind is like a great tree, and Adam is the seed of that tree. As is the seed, so must be the tree.

Another question arises: How can one man, Christ, make many people righteous? By the same principle. As Adam was the seed of the old race, so Christ is the seed of a new spiritual race. From Christ have sprung up many who have been declared righteous by God. As is the seed of Christ, so will be those who believe in Him.

20 The **law** mentioned here is the written law given by God to Moses. After the law came, man's **sin increased**; because then men knew exactly what God's commandments were. To break a commandment knowingly is a much greater sin than to break one unknowingly. Before the law came men sinned, but they sinned without knowing what God's commands were; therefore, their guilt was less. This same principle applies to us also: if we sin knowingly, our sin will be considered greater by God (see Luke 12:47–48 and comment).

However, no matter how much sin has come from Adam, even more grace has come from Christ. As sin increases, so does grace increase.

21 Grace will always **reign** over sin. Grace reigns over sin as light reigns over darkness. Sin leads to **death**; grace leads to **eternal life through Jesus Christ**. Christ has completely overcome both sin and death (see Romans 8:1–2; 1 Corinthians 15:56 and comments).

In this verse, we see the three great steps in our salvation, the three great gifts of Christ: first, **grace**; second, through grace, **righteousness**; third, through righteousness, ETERNAL LIFE. In this way Christ has not only erased the harm brought about by Adam, but He has also done much more: He has made us sons and daughters of God, inheritors of all the riches of heaven.

CHAPTER 6

Dead to Sin, Alive in Christ (6:1–14)

1 In Romans 5:20, Paul wrote: **But where sin increased, grace increased all the more**. Paul's meaning is this: no matter how much our sins increase, no matter how great or how numerous they become, God's grace is always great

---

[25] There is a sense in which those without Christ are already spiritually "dead" (Ephesians 2:1). Becoming a Christian means to be "brought to life" spiritually by the Holy Spirit (see John 3:3,5 and comment). However, man is not completely dead spiritually until he actually dies; before that, there is always hope of life.

enough to forgive them.

However, some people might be tempted to say: "Well, then, let's sin all we want. Whatever we do, God is going to forgive us; we don't have to worry. The more we sin, the more grace we'll receive."

By no means! says Paul (verse 2). Such thinking couldn't be more wrong!

2 **We died to sin**. What does Paul mean by this? He means that when we believed in Christ, our old sinful self "died." First we were slaves of sin. Then we **died**. Any slave who dies is no longer under the control of his master; he is "free" (verse 7). So if we have been freed from our master, sin, why should we keep on living as if we were still slaves of sin? Through God's grace we have been freed from the power of sin; let us not live in it any longer!

3 When we believe in Christ, we are **baptized into his death**. When we receive baptism,[26] we go into the water and, in a spiritual sense, our sins are washed away and our old sinful self dies. After that, when we arise from the water, we are new creations in Christ with new spiritual life (2 Corinthians 5:17). Thus baptism, in a spiritual sense, is really the death of our old sinful self and the birth of a new spiritual self. Therefore, when we are **baptized into Christ Jesus**, our old self in a sense dies with Him. We are **baptized into his death**.

4 If we have died with Christ, we shall also rise with Him to **live a new life** (see Colossians 2:12). Just as Christ first had to die in order to rise from the dead, so also we must die to sin in order to rise to new life in Him. In order to **live a new life**, our old sinful self must first be put to death, it must be **put off** (Ephesians 4:22–24). Then, in place of the old self, we need a new mind and heart, a new spiritual self.

Therefore, to be **baptized into Christ** means to die with Christ, to be buried with Christ, and then to rise to new life with Christ.

5 To be **united with** [Christ] **in his death** means to die with Christ. To die is surely a painful and difficult experience. To give up one's old life is not easy. Yet Paul makes this promise: If we die with Christ, **we will certainly also be united with him in his resurrection**.

Many people acknowledge that Jesus is a great teacher, and they want to **live a new life** with Him. But they have no interest whatever in dying with Him!

We say easily, "I'm a Christian"; but we each need to ask ourselves: "Have I died with Christ?" Because if we have not died with Him—that is, if our "old sinful self" has not been put to death—we cannot receive new life in Him. And if we have not received new life in Him, how can we then say we are Christians?

6 **For we know that our old self was crucified with him**. Jesus Himself was **crucified**, that is, hung from a CROSS until He died. It was the Roman method of executing criminals, one of the cruelest forms of execution ever devised. Therefore, to say that **our old self was crucified** simply means that our old self was put to death.

What is the purpose of **our old self** being crucified, or put to death? Our old self is crucified **so that the body of sin might be rendered powerless**. Our **old self** is our old sinful self. The **body of sin** is man's body with all its pride and sinful desires. That **body of sin** was once our master; that is, we were once the slaves of our sinful desires. But when we die with Christ, that **old self** is hung on the cross,

[26] Baptism for a Christian is an extremely important event. It is the first public act a new Christian participates in, an act in which he testifies to the world that he now belongs to Jesus Christ. In the ceremony of baptism, water is applied to the believer, and by this means his sins are, in a spiritual sense, washed away.

Some Christians believe that baptism is only a sign or symbol of our cleansing from sin and our new life in Jesus. But other Christians, citing this verse, believe that God through the ceremony of baptism actually causes our "old sinful self" to be put to death spiritually, and at the same time causes our "new spiritual self" to come to life in Christ. For further discussion, see Word List: Baptism; General Article: Water Baptism.

and our **body of sin** [is] **rendered powerless.**

A question arises here: If, as Christians, our old sinful self has died, why then do we still sin? Some people answer that we keep on sinning because our "old self" isn't completely dead. It's still alive, though its power is mostly gone. These people say that since the old sinful self is weak, we ought not to be giving in to it! We ought to be able to overcome it.

Other people give a different answer as to why we continue to sin as Christians. They say that through Christ's death our "old self" did completely die. And now, as Christians, the Holy Spirit rules in our lives; the reign of our old sinful nature has ended. We are no longer under Satan's control; we have become free from sin. However, we must appropriate this new situation by faith. Christians continue to sin from time to time because they don't have complete faith that they are now free from sin! Because of their lack of faith the Holy Spirit cannot fully work in their lives. Thus these people say it's because of a lack of faith that we continue to sin after becoming Christians.

Whichever of these two answers is correct, we cannot deny the truth that Christians do sin from time to time. Therefore, Paul especially wants to remind us here that sin—that old **body of sin**—is no longer our master. Even though we may sin from time to time, we do not remain in sin. However, if one should knowingly continue in sin, then we would have to say that that person's "old self" had not died but was alive and more powerful than ever. Such a person does not truly know Christ (see 1 John 3:6,9 and comment).

To understand this important verse we must notice another thing. On the one hand Paul says that we have died with Christ (verses 3–5). On the other hand he says: **. . . count yourselves dead to sin** (verse 11), and **. . . do not let sin reign in your mortal body** (verse 12). On the one hand Paul tells us what our position in Christ actually is; on the other hand, he exhorts us to walk according to that position. In other words, he is giving us both the theoretical teaching and its practical application. Another example of this combined approach is found in verses 18–19. In verse 18, Paul writes that we **have been set free from sin**. Then in verse 19, he exhorts us not to offer our bodies as slaves of sin, but rather to offer them **in slavery to righteousness** (see Galatians 5:13).

Keeping the above discussion in mind, we can now see that Paul's main meaning is this: our **old self** (our old sinful self) has essentially died; nevertheless, it is still possible for us to serve it. "Don't do it!" Paul's exhorts us. "Put off that old sinful self! (see Ephesians 4:22). Do not fulfill the desires of that old **body of sin.**"[27]

7 **. . . anyone who has died has been freed from sin.** If a criminal dies, his punishment also ends. It's not possible to punish a dead man!

We were once criminals (sinners) in God's eyes. Now that our "old self" has died, we cannot be punished for the sins our "old self" committed. We are freed not only from sin itself, but also from the punishment for sin.

8 Here Paul repeats the thought of verse 5 (see 2 Timothy 2:11–12).

9 Having once died and been raised from the dead, Christ cannot die again. Similarly, if we have died and been raised with Christ, we too will not die again, but will live forever with Him.[28] Christ has conquered death, and through Him we have conquered it too (see John 5:24; 11:25–26 and comments).

10 Christ **died to sin once for all**; that is, He died for the sins of all men (see

---

[27] The crucifixion of our old self mentioned in this verse is a passive crucifixion. In Galatians 5:24, Paul speaks of an active crucifixion of our sinful nature, which we ourselves have to carry out. Our passive crucifixion is accomplished through faith in Christ. Our active crucifixion is accomplished by us, as we deny ourselves and submit to the Holy Spirit (see Mark 8:34; Romans 8:13; Galatians 5:24 and comments).

[28] Our earthly body will die, but the most important part of us—our soul and spirit—will never die.

Hebrews 9:26). Remember, Christ Himself never sinned. But He came into this sinful world and lived among sinful men. And He has taken men's sins and buried them together with Himself in death (see John 1:29). This, then, is what Paul means when he says that Christ **died to sin**.

Christ **died to sin**, but now He **lives to God** (see 1 Peter 3:18). In the same way, we too have died to sin and are **alive to God** (verse 11).

11 **In the same way, count yourselves . . .** To **count** means to think about something with great certainty. If we have truly believed in Christ, then we are certainly dead to sin and alive to God. This is certain; we can **count** on it. Therefore, let us act according to this knowledge; let us act like it was true! (see 1 Peter 2:24).

12 **Therefore**—since you are dead to sin—**do not let sin reign in your mortal body**. We need to ask ourselves: Who reigns in our bodies—sin or God? Under whose control are we? Who is our master, our ruler?

The word **sin** in this verse means all of man's sins taken together—such as, idolatry, murder, lying, stealing, pride, evil speech, evil desires and thoughts. But all of these different sins arise from one basic sin—that is, selfishness, or self centeredness.[29] Because of selfishness, we put ourselves first of all. Because of selfishness, we seek first of all to fulfill our own desires. These desires may be for things that are good in themselves—such as getting an education, or getting a job. God Himself usually wants us to have these things. But the sin lies in this: we put our own desires ahead of God's desires. We put our own desires in first place. We want what we ourselves want more than we want what God wants. That is selfishness. And from selfishness, or self-centeredness, all other sins arise.

Now to return to the question asked above: Who reigns in our bodies—sin or God? We can now restate the question by inserting the word "self in place of the word "sin": Who reigns in our bodies—self or God? It is the same question. Whose will do we obey—our own or God's? If the answer is "our own," then sin still reigns in our bodies.

How can we tell if a certain desire is our own desire or God's desire? For example, take the desire to study in school. One way to tell if this is God's will or only our own will is to ask the question: Who am I studying for—for myself or for God? We need to ask this same question for everything we are doing, and for everything we desire to do.

Many people think: "If I'm not doing anyone any harm, how can I be sinning? If I want to study or work, where's the sin in that? There's no sin at all." But such people are missing the point. Whenever we follow our own will without taking into consideration what God's will might be, we are sinning in God's sight. This is the basic sin we inherited from Adam: the putting of our own will above God's. Or we can say: man's main sin is to put himself in God's place. Man naturally seeks to fulfill his own desires, not God's. Such is our sinful nature. It is for this reason that, whatever we do, we Christians must always ask ourselves: Who am I doing this for—for myself or for God?

When a Christian dies to sin, his old sinful desires should die also. And in their place should come a new desire from the Holy Spirit—the desire to please and obey God. And from this new desire new behavior must arise as well.

13 Paul wrote in verse 12: **Therefore, do not let sin reign in your mortal body so that you obey its evil desires**. Here in verse 13, he says essentially the same thing: **Do not offer the parts of your body to sin, as instruments of wickedness**. Now God is the ruler of our life; therefore, all the parts of our bodies belong to Him. The parts of our body are to be used as **instruments of righteousness**. Therefore, we must offer our bodies to God completely and continuously (see Romans 12:1 and comment).

---

[29] Even though we can call self-centeredness man's most basic sin, the underlying cause of that sin is unbelief. Unbelief is the root of all sin (see Romans 4:19–21 and comment). For further discussion, see comment on Romans 3:10–12 and footnote to comment.

14 Paul implies in this verse that sin is the **master** of those **under law**—that is, those under the authority of the law.[30] Why should that be? The reason is this. The law says, "Obey," but it doesn't give man the power to obey. The law says, "Do this, do that," but man can't do all that the law says. Therefore, in effect, he ends up breaking the law—and that is sin. For those **under law**, there is no way to avoid sinning. Thus sin becomes their **master**. They cannot escape. And for this reason, those under the law are without forgiveness, without hope.[31]

But then Paul reminds us that we are not **under law**, we are **under grace**. That is, through God's mercy we have received forgiveness of sin. And not only that, we have also received new power for overcoming sin, so that we might live righteously in God's sight.

Perhaps someone is wondering why Paul, in these first six chapters of Romans, has talked so much about the Jewish law. Why should we Gentiles care about the Jewish law? The reason is that the Jewish law is only one example of many kinds of law that people follow. In every religion of the world there is some kind of law or set of rules and rituals that people are required to follow. And so the same problems that the Jews had in living under the Jewish law apply in a general way to the followers of all other religions also.

We must not think, however, that the Jewish law is just like the laws and rituals of other religions. That is not so. The Jewish law was given by God Himself; the laws of most other religions are man-made. Nevertheless, the Jews and the followers of other religions are similar in this respect: they both believe that obedience to law and ritual is the means of obtaining salvation and they place their hope in it. And this is their mistake. They remain **under law**. As long as men remain **under law**, they cannot be **under grace**; and if they are not **under grace**, they cannot be saved.

No man—whether he is a Jew or whether he is the follower of some other religion—can obtain salvation through the works of any law or ritual. Only by God's grace received through faith in Jesus Christ can man be saved (see Ephesians 2:8–9 and comment).

Slaves to Righteousness (6:15–23)

15 Since we who believe in Christ are no longer **under law** (verse 14), we will not be punished according to the law. Since we are now free of punishment, some might be tempted to say: "Let's sin! We can get away with it!" But Paul says to such a thought: **By no means!** (see verses 1–2 and comment).

16 When we sin, we become slaves to sin. When we obey God, we become "slaves" of God—or, as Paul says in verse 18, **slaves to righteousness** (see Matthew 6:24; John 8:34).

Who do we obey—sin or God? The one we obey will be the one whose slave we are. The proof of whose slave we are comes from seeing who we obey. If we say we are God's slaves but do not obey His commands, we are liars. The proof that we are Christians is demonstrated by our obedience to God (see 1 John 2:3–6 and comment).

Here a question arises. Paul has said that we are not **under law** (verse 14). But here Paul says that we must obey God. Isn't that like being "under law"? One moment Paul says that we are no longer under the authority of God's law; but the next moment he says that we must remain under the authority of God. What's the difference?

There is a big difference. To be **under law**—that is, under the authority of God's law—means to be under the punishment or condemnation of the law. Those under the authority of the law will be condemned by the law, because they can never fully obey the law.

To be under the authority of God Himself, however, is completely different.

[30] Those **under law** include the Jews and all other people who believe that salvation is earned by doing good works or by obeying some law or set of religious rules.

[31] Let us not think that the law is evil; it is men who are evil. They do not fully obey the law.

To be under the authority of God means to be **under grace** (verse 14). It means that through faith in Christ there is forgiveness of sin and deliverance from the punishment of the law. It means that when we stumble and fall, all we need to do is repent of our sin, and we will be cleansed and restored (see 1 John 1:9 and comment).

To be under the authority of God means another thing. It means to be under the authority of the Holy Spirit. And it is the Holy Spirit who gives us the desire to obey God's commands, and then, more important, gives us the power to obey them.

Thus we can see that being under God's authority is totally different from being under the law's authority. Under God, we receive both forgiveness of sin and the power to overcome sin. Under law, we receive no forgiveness and no power; only condemnation.

However, let us remember: we must remain under God's authority, we must obey His commands. Even though we are free from the condemnation of God's law, we are not free from God!

17–18 The Roman Christians had **wholeheartedly obeyed the form of teaching to which** [they] **were entrusted**; that is, they had obeyed the teachings of Paul and the other apostles. Because they obeyed, Paul tells them that they have been **set free from sin**.

But they have not been **set free** from God. Men are either **slaves to sin** (verse 17), or **slaves to righteousness** (verse 18)—that is, slaves of God. We are one or the other. And we cannot be both at the same time (Matthew 6:24). Therefore, since we have to be someone's slaves, it's much better to be slaves of God! He is loving and merciful. He is also all-powerful. And He gives all of His "slaves" a reward—eternal life! (verses 22–23).

The slaves of sin receive another kind of "reward"—namely, eternal death (verses 21,23).

Some people may be troubled by Paul's use of the word "slave." Paul uses the word "slave" only as an illustration. We are not only God's "slaves"; we are also His children and heirs.

In one way we are like slaves, because we are under God's authority. But in another way we are God's children, free members of His family.

19 When Paul calls the Roman Christians **weak in** [their] **natural selves**, he means that they are **weak** in understanding. In order to help them more easily understand his teaching, Paul has tried to put things **in human terms**; that is, he has used words from common everyday experience, such as the word "slave."

In the second part of this verse, Paul repeats the thought of verse 13.

20 We cannot be slaves of two masters at the same time. If we are the slave of one, that means we will be free from the other. Here Paul reminds the Romans that it was the same for them. When they were **slaves to sin**, they remained **free from the control of righteousness**.

21 We can choose which master we want to serve. We are free to choose. Let us, therefore, choose that master who gives the best reward!

Christians are free from slavery to sin; nevertheless, from time to time they act like slaves of sin. That is, Christians from time to time misuse their freedom to choose their own master. Sometimes they choose the wrong master—they choose to serve sin, or Satan. "Let that not be!" Paul exhorts us (see verse 6 and comment).

There is absolutely no advantage in being a slave to sin. Sin leads only to **death** (verse 23).

22 But there is great advantage in being a slave of God! First, it leads to **holiness**; and **without holiness no one will see the Lord** (Hebrews 12:14). Second, being a slave of God leads to **eternal life** (verse 23).

23 Men work and earn **wages**. When we sin, we earn sin's "wages." But eternal life (or salvation) is not something we earn by our own work or effort. That is a **gift** from God. Men don't "earn" gifts. Rather, gifts are freely given, according to the love and pleasure of the giver—that is, according to grace. Eternal life is a gift of God's grace. It is given to us **in Jesus Christ our Lord**. It was He who bought the gift for us; He paid for it with His own blood. Paul sums it up in his letter to the Ephesians: **For it is by grace you have been saved, through faith—and this not from yourselves, it is the gift of God** (Ephesians 2:8).

CHAPTER 7

An Illustration from Marriage (7:1–6)

1 The **law** which Paul refers to in this verse is the Jewish law, which God handed down to Moses about 1500 years before the time of Christ. This law contained many rules and commandments. The Jews believed that in order to be declared righteous by God, it was necessary for them to obey every one of these rules and commandments. For the Jews, the law was like a master. Just as—in the Jews' eyes—the husband was the "master" of the wife, so was the law the master of the Jews.

From verse 1, we can tell that many of the Roman Christians Paul was writing to were converted Jews, because he says here: **I am speaking to men who know the law**—that is, to Jews.

The law has no **authority** over a dead man; a dead man doesn't have to obey the law!

2–3 In these verses, Paul compares the law with a husband, and the Jews with a wife. His point is that the relationship between the law and the Jews is essentially the same as the relationship between a Jewish husband and his wife (see 1 Corinthians 7:39). According to Jewish tradition, as long as a husband lived his wife had to remain under his authority. But if the husband died, then his wife was freed from his authority and could marry another man. In the same way, whenever a person believes in Christ, the religion or the religious law that he or she had previously followed becomes as if "dead," and that person is then "free" to follow Christ. That person no longer remains under the authority of his former religion and its law.

4 **So . . . you also died to the law.** Paul doesn't say that the law itself died; he says, **you** died **to** the law. Paul means that, as far as we are concerned, the law is as if it were dead. Therefore, we are free to "marry another"—namely, Christ. We are free from our first husband (the law), and thus can marry a second husband (Christ).

We died to the law **through the body of Christ**—that is, through the death of Christ's body on the cross. We have been united in Christ's death, so that we might be united with Him in new life (Romans 6:4–5).

One of the main purposes of marriage is to **bear fruit**, that is, to bear children. When we are "married" to Christ, then we will **bear fruit to God**: new believers will be born through our witness, and the fruit of the Holy Spirit will appear in our lives—such as love, joy, peace (see Galatians 5:22–23).

5 For when we were controlled by the sinful nature,[32] we were, in a sense, "married" to the law; as a result, **we bore fruit for death**. The **fruit for death** is sin. Instead of doing good works for God, we did sinful works which led to death.

The Greek word which Paul uses for **sinful nature** literally means "flesh." The word "flesh" can have two meanings: first, "body" (eyes, arms, legs, etc); and second, "sinful nature" (sinful desires and sinful will).

Here in this verse, Paul uses the Greek word "flesh" to mean **sinful nature**. The

---

[32] In place of the words **controlled by the sinful nature**, some translations of the Bible say, "living in the flesh." The meaning is the same. In many verses in Romans where Paul uses the Greek word for "flesh," he means "sinful nature," not body. For further discussion, see Word List: Flesh.

body itself is not sinful; only our old nature is sinful. Where does sin arise? Sin does not arise from our eyes, hands, and feet; rather it arises from the sinful desires in our heart and mind.[33] Then, after sin has arisen in our heart and mind, our bodies (eyes, hands, feet) come under sin's control, and we begin to do the works of sin. Thus the word "flesh" is used in this verse to mean a "body under the sin's control." This meaning is most clearly expressed by the term **sinful nature**.[34]

Paul mentions here **sinful passions aroused by the law**. How can sinful passions be aroused by the law? Is the law sinful? Certainly not! However, **where there is no law there is no transgression** (Romans 4:15). Because the law exists, sinful passions also exist.

For example, a small child may take something belonging to someone else. The child doesn't realize this is called "stealing." He sees something, he likes it, and so he takes it. Afterwards, his mother and father say to the child: "You must not do this. This is called stealing; it is a sin." Now the child knows; he has received the "law." If he again takes something belonging to someone else, that will be counted against him as a sin.

But in spite of the warning of his parents, in spite of the "law," the child still desires to take what belongs to others; he still desires to steal. He still falls into the temptation to sin. And perhaps the temptation is even greater, now that the child knows it is wrong. It is a common experience that when we are told not to do something, we desire all the more to do it. When someone says to us, "Don't look," we want to look all the more! That's why Paul says here that sinful passions are **aroused by the law**.

6 **But now, by dying to what once bound us** (that is, by dying to the law), we are **released from the law**. Having been released from the law, we are now free to **serve in the new way of the Spirit**. In the beginning we were under the control of the **written code**, that is, the law. Now we live under the freedom of the Holy Spirit. Now when we obey God, we do so not out of obligation but freely and willingly from our hearts (see Jeremiah 31:33; 2 Corinthians 3:6; Hebrews 8:10).

Sin and the Law (7:7–13)

7 Just as a human father tells his children what is right and wrong, so the law tells men what is right and wrong. Even without the law, men have some knowledge of right and wrong, some knowledge of God (see Romans 1:19–20 and comment). But most of our knowledge of sin comes from the law.

For example, the last of the ten commandments is: **You shall not covet** (Exodus 20:17). If this commandment had never been written, no one would know that it was a sin to covet.

8 When Paul first learned about the command, "Do not covet," **every kind of covetous desire** arose in him. At that time, Paul had not yet believed in Christ.

Paul's experience was just like that of the first man and woman, Adam and Eve, in the Garden of Eden (Genesis 3:1–6). Every kind of fruit was available for them to eat; only the fruit of one tree was not to be eaten. Yet it was to that very fruit that they were drawn by their covetous desire. Of all the fruits, they desired most to eat the one fruit they had been forbidden to eat.

Therefore, as with Adam and Eve, Paul says that sin, **seizing the opportunity afforded by the commandment** (law), produced in him covetous desires. We could say, in other words, that the law brought sin **to life** (verse 9).

9 Paul, speaking of his childhood, says here: **Once I was alive apart from the law**. When Paul grew older, he

---

[33] Man's heart and mind are not sinful in themselves. But when they come under the control of our sinful nature, they too become sinful.

[34] In this verse, Paul is speaking not about believers in Christ but rather about non-believers. Non-believers are under the control of the law; they are **controlled by the sinful nature**. But believers are not controlled by the sinful nature (Romans 8:9).

became aware of the law; then he began to experience sin in his life. His happy and carefree life as a child was over. The sense of his sinfulness came upon him; in other words, **sin sprang to life**. Paul's conscience began to accuse him.

10 The law was meant to be a lamp that would light men's way (Psalm 119:105). The law was meant to lead men into righteousness, and thence into eternal life (Leviticus 18:5; Romans 10:5). But instead, the law condemns men to death, because it is impossible for anyone to obey every part of the law completely. The law does not forgive sin; the law does not give men the power to overcome sin. Therefore, through the law comes only condemnation and death.

Let us remember that, although Paul is speaking here of the Jewish law, what he says is true of the laws of all other religions as well. All religious laws result in condemnation and death. Except for Christians, the followers of all other religions try to get to heaven by observing various religious laws. Each religion has its own rules and commandments, but none of these can make a person righteous in God's sight. In this regard, the laws of other religions are just like the Jewish law. Men try by their own effort to obey these laws, but in the end these laws lead only to discouragement, condemnation, and death. Only by God's grace through faith in Christ can man be declared righteous in God's eyes and obtain salvation.

11 The experience Paul relates in this verse is the same as the experience of Adam and Eve described in Genesis 3:1–6. Eve was **deceived** by the serpent (sin). The serpent said to Eve: "Even if you eat the forbidden fruit, you will not die (Genesis 3:4). Instead, **you will be like God, knowing good and evil**" (Genesis 3:5).

12 But let us not blame the **law**, the **commandment**, for our sin. The law was given by God; it is **holy, righteous and good**. Rather, we must blame the "serpent"—that is, the sin in our heart. The law gives sin an opportunity; but sin itself, not the law, does the evil work. We must never blame God for the evil in our own hearts (James 1:13–15).

13 The law, **which is good**, did not bring death. It is sin that brings death, because sin makes man unrighteous and therefore deserving of the death sentence. When sin has brought us the death sentence, we can then recognize it more easily! At first, Eve did not recognize the serpent's deception. But after she had sinned by eating the forbidden fruit, she was able to see her sin.

Where there is no law, sin does not appear so sinful (see Romans 5:13,20). But **through the commandment** (law), sin is made to appear **utterly sinful**. That is, compared to God's holy law, sin appears all the more sinful.

Paul's Inner Struggle With Sin (7:14–25)

14 From verse 14 to the end of this chapter, Paul continues to speak of his own experience. Paul wanted to be a good Jew, to please God, to be righteous; but he could not. And Paul's experience is shared by all men who try by their own effort to become righteous by following some religious law or by doing good works: it is not possible.

As we read this section of Chapter 7, a question arises: Is Paul speaking here of experiences that took place before he became a Christian, or after? It is not easy to answer this question with certainty; some Bible scholars say one thing, some another.

However, we can say two things. First, many people who are not Christians sincerely seek God and try to please Him. They even confess their sins, and try—by their own power—to stop sinning. Many Jews in Paul's time were certainly like that. Therefore, what Paul writes here could possibly describe his experience before becoming a Christian.[35]

[35] Paul writes here: **I am . . . sold as a slave to sin**. Many Bible scholars believe that Paul must have been speaking here of the time before he was a Christian, because a true Christian would never have called himself a **slave to sin** (see Romans 6:18).

The second thing we can say is that all Christians experience the same thing Paul describes in this section. Even after we become Christians, we experience a struggle between our "new self" and our "old self," between our spirit (or spiritual nature) and our "flesh" (or sinful nature). In fact, the struggle usually becomes much greater after we have become Christians. Even though we have believed in Christ and "our old self has been crucified" (Romans 6:6), it still seems as if our old self was not completely dead. From time to time we sin (see 1 John 1:8). Therefore, some scholars think that Paul is speaking here of his experience after becoming a Christian.[36]

Whether we believe that Paul is speaking in this section about his experience before becoming a Christian or after, it is a fact that we all have experienced these same things at one time or another—either before we became Christians, or after. Probably most of us have experienced this inner spiritual struggle both before and after becoming Christians.

In verse 14, Paul writes: **I am unspiritual.**[37] He is speaking here of his "old self," which is under the control of his sinful nature. To be "unspiritual" is the same as to be **controlled by the sinful nature** (verse 5). All men are "unspiritual" from birth. That is, they are not controlled by the Spirit; rather, they are slaves to sin. When we believe in Christ, our old selves are crucified, **that we should no longer be slaves to sin** (Romans 6:6).

Paul writes: **I am . . . sold as a slave to sin**. In Paul's time, slaves were bought and sold like animals. They were the property of whoever bought them. Thus Paul's experience was like that of a slave who has been sold to a master—the master being sin.

15 We have all experienced what Paul writes in this verse. We know what is good, and we want to do it. But sin comes and we do evil instead. Afterward, we are upset with ourselves. We don't understand our own behavior. There is a struggle going on in our minds between our sinful nature and the Spirit (see Galatians 5:16–17 and comment).

16 Even though Paul does what he does not want to do (that is, evil), he still agrees in his inner being that the **law is good**.

17 The **sin living in me** that Paul mentions here is the impulse to sin, which arises from Paul's sinful nature. When Paul sins, it is not his spiritual self that is sinning; it is his old unspiritual self that is sinning, which is under the control of his sinful nature. Inside Paul's body, it seems as if there were two people—two laws—struggling with each other.

18 There is naturally no good in us—that is, in our **sinful nature** (see Romans 3:10–12). The desire to do good is present in Paul's **inner being** (verse 22); but Paul's sinful nature prevents him from carrying out his good desire. Paul's "inner spiritual being" doesn't have the power to overcome his sinful nature. Paul's body (eyes, arms, legs, etc.) obeys his sinful nature and not his inner being.

19 Here Paul repeats what he wrote in verse 15.

20 Here Paul repeats what he wrote in verse 17. Paul says that **it is no longer I** (my inner being) **who does it** (sin), **but it is sin** (my sinful nature) **living in me that does it**.

21 **So I find this law at work**. What law? The "law" that there is within Paul a continual struggle between **good** and **evil**. This struggle occurs in all men; it is like a principle or "law" of life.

---

[36] In verse 22, Paul writes: **For in my inner being I delight in God's law**. The Bible scholars who believe that Paul is writing here about his experience after becoming a Christian say that he could never have made that statement as a non-Christian (see 1 Corinthians 2:14).

[37] In place of the word **unspiritual**, some translations of the Bible say "carnal" or "fleshly." The meaning is the same.

22 The expression **inner being** means man's human spirit, together with his conscience.[38] From our "inner being" come our highest thoughts and aspirations. In God's sight, our inner being is more important than our "outer being,"—our outward appearance and behavior (Romans 2:28–29). **Man looks at the outward appearance, but the Lord looks at the heart** (1 Samuel 16:7).

If verses 14–24 describe Paul's experience before he was a Christian, then the term **inner being** would mean "conscience"; for all men have consciences, by which they can distinguish right from wrong. All men, through their consciences, know that they are sinners (see Romans 1:20; 13:5 and comments).

But if verses 14–24 describe Paul's experience after he had become a Christian, then the term **inner being** would mean Paul's new Spirit-controlled self. Both meanings are possible.

23 When Paul uses the word **law** in this verse, he means "principle." The expression **law of my mind**,[39] can also mean "rule of my mind"; and the expression **law of sin** can mean "rule of sin."

Paul writes: **I see another law at work in the members of my body**. This law is the **law of sin** mentioned later in the verse. This "law of sin" is **waging war against the law of** [Paul's] **mind**. The "law of Paul's mind" is the law or rule of Paul's spirit, or inner being (verse 22).

Thus in every one of us, there are these two "laws," (or principles, or forces): the "law of our mind" (that is, the law of our inner being), and the "law of sin" (that is, the law of our sinful nature).

The "law of sin" is at work in Paul's **members** (eyes, hands, feet, etc.), causing them to do evil. The "law of sin" works to make Paul a **prisoner** or slave of sin (verse 14).

24 **What a wretched man I am!** This is the cry of every man who recognizes his sin and wants to overcome it.

Who will rescue me from this body of death? The **body of death** is the "body of sin." They are the same, because sin leads to death. Here the word **body** means physical body (eyes, hands, feet). The physical body is not evil or sinful in itself. The desire to sin comes not from our physical body but from our sinful nature.

25 **Who will rescue me from this body of death**, from my sinful nature? Here Paul gives the answer: **Thanks be to God—**I will be rescued **through Jesus Christ our Lord!**

Our rescuer is Jesus Christ. He will rescue not only Paul, but every person who calls upon Him in faith. It is Christ who gives us the power to overcome the **law of sin** within us. It is Christ who rescues us from the punishment of sin, which is death. **Thanks be to God**!

In our Christian lives, this struggle between good and evil, between our old self and new self, between our sinful nature and spiritual nature, does not need to go on forever. Through Christ, that is, through the power of Christ given to us by the Holy Spirit, we can overcome the "law of sin" within us. In Chapter 7, Paul has described the inner struggle experienced by all of us. Now in Chapter 8, he will show us the way to obtain victory in that struggle, victory over sin. That way is to **live in accordance with the Spirit**

---

[38] Conscience is the "voice" of man's human spirit. Every man has a spiritual part, which responds to God's Holy Spirit. Our conscience tells us when we are disobeying God's Spirit. However, without God's Holy Spirit in our lives, our own spirit, or "inner being," is unable to overcome our sinful human nature. This is why sin reigns in the lives of those who do not have the Holy Spirit.

The term **inner being** can also mean man's "mind"—that is, a mind under the influence or control of man's spirit. Paul uses the word **mind** in this way in verse 23. Our mind can be under the control of either our sinful nature or our spirit. When our mind is under the control of our spirit, it represents our spiritual side, our "inner being." Such a mind is capable of being **transformed**, or **renewed**, and placed under the control of God's Holy Spirit (see Romans 12:2 and comment).

[39] Paul uses the word **mind** here to mean human spirit, or "mind under the influence of the spirit." For further discussion, see footnote to comment on verse 22.

(Romans 8:5), and to be **led by the Spirit** (Romans 8:14). Christ has given us the Holy Spirit; if we live by the Spirit, we **will not gratify the desires of the sinful nature** (Galatians 5:16).

CHAPTER 8

Life Through the Spirit (8:1–17)

1 Through the Jewish law comes **condemnation**. The law gives us the death sentence, because no matter how hard we try, we cannot fulfill all the requirements of the law. The law says: **Love the Lord your God with all your heart and with all your soul and with all your mind and with all your strength** (Deuteronomy 6:5; Mark 12:30). Who can obey that commandment fully? No one. The law says: **Do not covet** (Exodus 20:17; Romans 7:7). Who can obey that commandment fully? No one. Our heart, our nature, is evil and unholy. How can we ever be declared righteous in God's sight? We cannot. Instead, the law condemns us to death.

But here in verse 1, we find the means of escaping condemnation and death: If we are IN CHRIST, there is no condemnation!

To be **in Christ** means to believe in Him, to accept Him as our Lord and Savior, and to give Him the rule over our lives.

When we are in Christ, our sins are forgiven and washed away, and we are declared righteous in God's sight (see Romans 5:1). Whoever is not in Christ will be declared guilty and will receive eternal punishment.

Believers are declared righteous not on the basis of their own righteousness, but on the basis of Christ's righteousness. In Him there was no sin (Hebrews 4:15). He fulfilled the entire law perfectly. Having done that, He took upon Himself the punishment for our sins that we should have received. The law can no longer punish us. The punishment has already been given—to Christ; He received the punishment of death in our place. **Therefore, there is now no condemnation** for us who are in Christ. What amazing and wonderful news this is! All men throughout the world stand condemned before the one true God. But here, **in Christ**, God shows them the way to escape condemnation. By believing **in Christ**, their condemnation is removed.

But remember, even though we believers have escaped condemnation, sin still remains in our lives. Therefore, we are still guilty of sin and deserving of punishment. But if we repent of our sins, God will not count our sins against us; He will not judge us guilty (see 1 John 1:9 and comment).

2 Jesus is our Savior. The **Spirit of life** is the Holy Spirit (the Spirit of both God and Christ).

In his letters, Paul uses the word **law** in different ways; depending on the context, the word "law" has different meanings. Most commonly the word "law" means the Jewish law, the law God gave to Moses to pass on to the Jews. But in this verse, "law" has a different meaning: here it means "principle" or "rule" (as in Romans 7:21,23). Before the Holy Spirit entered us, only the **law** (rule) **of sin and death** was present in our lives. When the Holy Spirit entered us, that old "law of sin and death" was replaced by the **law** (rule) **of the Spirit of life**.

The Jewish law, which condemns men to death, places men under the **law** (rule) **of sin and death**. Christ's Holy Spirit has set us **free from the law of sin and death.**[40] The Holy Spirit sets us free not only from the guilt and punishment of sin

---

[40] Christ Himself, through His death on the cross, has set us free; but we experience that freedom through the Holy Spirit. Thus, to say that Christ has set us free and to say that the Holy Spirit has set us free is to say basically the same thing; both statements are true.

but also from the power and rule of sin (Romans 6:14).

3 In this verse, the word **law** means the Jewish law. The Jewish law was meant to lead men into righteousness and eternal life (Romans 7:10). But because of man's sinful nature, the law was **powerless** to make men righteous and to save them. The Jewish law could only condemn men for their sin; it could give men no help in overcoming their sin. **For what the law was powerless to do**—that is, set us free from the "law of sin and death"—God sent **his own Son** (Christ) to do. God sent Christ into the world to set us free from the law of sin and death—which the Jewish law could not do.

How did Christ set us free from the law of sin and death? He was sent **to be a sin offering;**[41] that is, He took the punishment for our sins by offering His life as a sacrifice. According to the Jewish law, if any Jew sinned, he had to offer an animal as a sacrifice.[42] In a sense, the sacrificed animal received the death penalty in place of the man who committed the sin. Similarly, Jesus Christ is like that sacrificed animal; through His sacrifice—the offering of His own body—we who committed the sin are now declared innocent. Christ, who never sinned, took both our guilt and our punishment upon Himself (see Mark 10:45; 2 Corinthians 5:21 and comments).

Christ came **in the likeness of sinful man**. He was not sinful Himself; He came only **in the likeness** of a sinful man. But in all other ways, Christ was fully a real man, just as we are. He experienced all the temptations that we experience—though He didn't fall into any of them (Hebrews 2:14–15,17–18; 4:14–15).

Christ **condemned sin in sinful man**—that is, He overcame sin and destroyed its power. How did He do this? In this way. The Jewish law is like a judge who must punish a man for his sin. After giving the punishment, that judge no longer has authority over the sinful man. When a man receives the death sentence, he becomes free of the judge and the law. He has paid the full price for his sin; there is no more left to pay. He is no longer guilty of sin. His sin is erased; it is finished. In a sense, his sin is **condemned** to death. This is what Paul means when he says that Christ **condemned sin in sinful man**. Christ, through the sacrifice of Himself, took our punishment and thereby "condemned" or erased our sin.

According to the Jewish law, every time a Jew sinned he had to offer an animal sacrifice in order to purify himself from his sin. Therefore, the Jews had to offer sacrifices repeatedly. After offering a sacrifice, they would momentarily be purified. But the next moment they would sin again, and thus become impure once more. In this way—one moment pure, next moment impure—the Jews could never really become cleansed of their sins. Their sins could never be completely erased. They remained guilty.

But Christ's sacrifice is different from the animal sacrifices of the Jews. Christ's sacrifice completely erases the sins of believers. His sacrifice remains in effect forever. Through His one sacrifice, sin is **condemned** and its power destroyed once for all (see Hebrews 7:26–27; 9:11–14,24–26; 10:1,4,11–14 and comments).

4 Paul says many things about the Jewish law—such as, the law is **powerless** (verse 3), it is the **law of sin and death** (verse 2). Nevertheless, it is God's law, which He gave to the Jews. Therefore, it is a just and righteous law. It must be obeyed. When the law is not obeyed, God must punish men for disobeying it. Christ Himself fulfilled all of the **righteous requirements of the law**. The law requires that men live a completely righteous life; Jesus **fully met** that requirment. The law requires that sin be

[41] In place of the words **to be a sin offering,** some versions of the Bible say "for sin," which is the literal translation of the Greek text. The meaning is the same.

[42] Not only that, once every year the Jewish high priest had to offer an animal as a sacrifice for both his own sins and for the sins of the people (Leviticus 16:6,15–16).

punished by death; Jesus, through His death on the cross, fully met that requirement also. In this way, He lived and died in order that the **righteous requirements of the law might be fully met in us**. We could not meet those requirements ourselves; so Jesus met them for us (see Matthew 5:17; Romans 3:31 and comments).

How were the righteous requirements of the law met? The answer is this: When Jesus took our guilt and punishment upon Himself, He at the same time gave us His righteousness, a righteousness which would satisfy the requirements of the law (2 Corinthians 5:21).

Who has received Christ's righteousness? Christ's righteousness has been received not by those who live **according to the sinful nature**, but rather by those who live **according to the Spirit**.

To live **according to the Spirit** means this: Once we have believed in Jesus, the Holy Spirit comes into our lives and gives us a new desire, a new power, to obey God. We are born again by the Spirit; we receive new spiritual life in Christ. Only by the help of the Holy Spirit within us can we fully meet the righteous requirements of the law. That is, only by the help of the Spirit can we lead righteous lives. To say that Christ is righteous is not enough; through the Spirit, Christ's righteousness must be demonstrated in our lives. This is what it means to live **according to the Spirit**.

The opposite of living according to the Spirit, of course, is to live **according to the sinful nature.**[43] To live according to the sinful nature is to live according to our sinful desires and thoughts (see Galatians 5:19–21). We cannot live according to the sinful nature and according to the Spirit at the same time; we must live according to either one or the other (see Galatians 5:16–18,24–25 and comment).

Here in these first four verses of Romans Chapter 8, Paul gives us a summary of the Gospel of Christ. In the first seven chapters of Romans, Paul gave us the background or foundation of the Gospel; now in Chapter 8, he gives us the Gospel itself. Now he tells us what it really means to be a Christian.

We can read these verses, study them, discuss them; we can even agree with them. (In fact, most people in the world agree that the Gospel is indeed "good news.") However, unless we actually experience the Holy Spirit living and working in our lives, these verses will be useless to us. The Holy Spirit is alive; He is real. And He is waiting to come into our lives. Let us hasten, therefore, to invite Him in!

5 How can we tell if we are living **in accordance with the Spirit** or not? We can tell by looking at what we have our **minds set on**. If our minds are set on worldly things—such as sinful desires, wealth, honor—then we are living **according to the sinful nature**, not according to the Spirit. But if our minds are **set on what the Spirit desires**—such as righteousness, love, humility, self-control—then we can be sure that we are living **in accordance with the Spirit**.

Let each of us ask ourselves: What is my mind set on?

6 **The mind of sinful man is death**—that is, when our minds are controlled by our sinful nature, the result is **death**. On the other hand, **the mind controlled by the Spirit is life** (eternal life) **and peace** (see Romans 7:5; 8:13; Galatians 6:7–8).

7 The **sinful mind**[44]—that is, the mind controlled by the sinful nature—is **hostile to God**. It is not just separated from God; it is actively opposed to God (James 4:4). It refuses to submit to **God's law**. (The term **God's law** in this verse does not mean the Jewish law, but rather "God's will" or "God's rule.")

---

[43] In the Greek language, the words **sinful nature** literally mean "flesh" (see Romans 7:5 and comment). Here in verses 3–13, the Greek word for "flesh" which Paul repeatedly uses is best translated by the term **sinful nature**.

[44] In the Greek language: "The mind that is set on the flesh."

8 No matter how many sacrifices we offer, no matter how many good works we do, if we are **controlled by the sinful nature,**[45] we cannot please God.

We must remember here that those who **live according to the sinful nature** (verses 4–5) or who are **controlled by the sinful nature** (verse 8) are not Christians; they have not received salvation (see Romans 7:5; 1 Corinthians 2:14). On the opposite side are those who **live in accordance with the Spirit** (verse 5) or who are **led by the Spirit** (verse 14). These are true Christians.

But in addition to these two main groups of people, there seems to be a third group in the middle. When you look at the lives of those in this third group, it is hard to tell whether they are Christians or not. These are unspiritual, immature Christians. In Corinthians 3:1–3, Paul calls such Christians **worldly,**[46] because they appear to live **according to the sinful nature**. Many Bible scholars believe that it is these worldly unspiritual Christians that Paul is talking about in Romans 7:14–24. In Romans 7:14, Paul calls himself **unspiritual**, or worldly.

However, whether Romans 7:14–24 is written about Christians or not, it is still true that many Christians today continue to experience the inner struggle between their spiritual and unspiritual natures that Paul describes in those verses. Their Christian lives do not fit the description given by Paul in Romans Chapter 8; instead, they fit the description given in Romans Chapter 7. Let this situation not continue! In Romans 8:2, Paul has been set free from the law of sin and death. The struggle between his sinful nature and the Spirit is over; the Spirit has won (see Galatians 2:19–21; 2 Timothy 4:7). Therefore, let us also leave the struggle of Romans Chapter 7 and enter into the victory of Chapter 8! Let us not remain worldly unspiritual Christians. Rather, let us be Christians who are controlled and led by the Spirit.

Some Christians believe that in order to become holy and spiritual it is necessary to receive some special grace all at once. Other Christians believe that we gradually become more holy and spiritual as we grow in our Christian life. However—whether quickly or gradually—let us leave behind the unspiritual condition described in Romans Chapter 7 and begin to experience the life of the Spirit described in Romans Chapter 8.[47]

9 Paul here reminds Christians that they are **controlled not by the sinful nature but by the Spirit.**[48] In this verse, the terms **Spirit, Spirit of God**, and **Spirit of Christ** all refer to the same Spirit—the Holy Spirit (1 Corinthians 3:16; 6:19).

A simple illustration about water will help us understand the relationship between God, Christ, and the Holy Spirit. God is the spring, the source of the water; Christ is the pipe or channel bringing the water to earth; and the Holy Spirit is the water itself, flowing down from God through Christ to us.

Only if the **Spirit of Christ** dwells in us do we belong to Christ. It's true that the Holy Spirit from time to time comes and calls non-believers, but He finds no dwelling place within them. Only when a person opens the door of his heart to the Holy Spirit can the Spirit enter that person and dwell within him (see Revelation 3:20 and comment).

10 **But if Christ** (Christ's Spirit) **is in you, your body** (your old sinful self) **is dead**. From now on, your **old self** is not your master (see Romans 6:6 and comment).

If Christ's Spirit is in you, your body is dead, **yet your spirit is alive**—that is,

---

[45] In place of the words **controlled by the sinful nature**, some versions of the Bible say "in the flesh," which is the literal translation of the Greek text. The meaning is the same.

[46] In the Greek language: "Men of the flesh."

[47] For further discussion of the life of the Spirit, see General Article: Holy Spirit.

[48] In place of the words **controlled not by the sinful nature but by the Spirit**, some versions of the Bible say, "not in the flesh but in the Spirit," which is the literal translation of the Greek text.

your new spiritual self is alive (Romans 6:11; Galatians 2:20).

Our bodies, our old selves, are dead **because of sin**. Our spirits are alive **because of righteousness**—that is, Christ's righteousness.

11 The One **who raised Jesus from the dead** is God. Through His **Spirit**, who dwells within us, God will **give life to** [our] **mortal bodies**. That is, He will give us spiritual life. God will not only give us new spiritual life in this world; but just as He raised Christ from the dead, so will He raise us from the dead at the end of the world so that we might live forever with Him. Here in this verse, then, we are given the promise that our bodies will be resurrected (see 1 Corinthians 15:42–49; Philippians 3:20–21 and comments).

12 Paul here reminds us of what he wrote in verse 4. Christians do not live **according to the sinful nature**. Rather, they live **according to the Spirit**. We have no **obligation** to our sinful nature; we are not obligated **to live according to it**. Our sinful nature has done nothing good for us; we don't owe it anything! Instead, we are obligated to Christ. It is Christ who paid the "debt" we owed because of our sin. Therefore, it is to Christ that **we have an obligation**—not to the sinful nature.

13 If we live according to the sinful nature, we will **die**—that is, we shall receive God's judgment, eternal death. Therefore, we must ask an extremely important question: How can we escape from eternal death and obtain eternal life?

Some people answer this question by saying that all we have to do is to believe in Christ, and then Christ will do everything else. These people say that all we need to do is say from our hearts, "I believe," and we will automatically be saved.

But here Paul gives a different answer. True, we must first believe in Christ. But then, through the help of the Holy Spirit, we must **put to death the misdeeds of the body** (sinful nature). Only if we do this will we **live**—that is, be saved. Why is this? Because we must live either according to the sinful nature or according to the Spirit; we cannot live according to both. If we live according to the sinful nature, we will die—that is certain. But in order to live according to the Spirit, we must do one thing: We must **put to death the misdeeds of the body**.

Here is an extremely important teaching. People mistakenly think that it is easy to follow Christ. They say that we Christians don't have to do good works or obey religious rules. They say that if we sin we don't have to worry about it, because we will automatically be forgiven. These statements are not true. To follow Christ is the most difficult road of all. Why? Because to follow Christ we must **put to death the misdeeds of the body**. That is like putting oneself to death. Is it easy to put oneself to death—to be crucified? Certainly not; there is nothing more difficult. Nevertheless, in order to live, it is necessary that our old sinful self be **put to death**. Before we can have new spiritual life, our old sinful self must die. Before there can be resurrection, there must first be death.

In order to "put to death" the misdeeds of our bodies, we first must put to death our sinful desires, because our misdeeds arise from our desires (see James 1:14–15 and comment). We must not only stop sinning; we must even stop thinking about sinning! We must be righteous not only on the outside, but also on the inside. We must "put to death" the secret parts of our hearts and minds, those places where sin first arises. This is one of the meanings of being crucified with Christ (see Romans 6:6,12; Colossians 3:5; Galatians 5:17,24 and comments).

It is not possible to live according to the Spirit and at the same time continue doing the misdeeds of the body. If we have not put to death the misdeeds of the body, the Holy Spirit is not in us and we do not belong to Christ. And if we do not belong to Christ, we have not received salvation.

But we must remember one thing: In order to put to death the misdeeds of the body, we need the help of the Holy Spirit. We cannot do it without Him. And the Holy Spirit is always with us, ready to help us lead righteous lives. This is the joyful news of Romans Chapter 8.

14 Only those who are **led by the Spirit** can be called the children of God. Some people say that God is the Father of all men. But that is not true. God is the Creator of all men, but He is the Father only of those who are led by the Spirit (see John 1:12 and comment).

15 The Spirit does not make us slaves; rather, He makes us the free sons of God. At first we were not sons; so the Spirit makes us adopted sons. The Holy Spirit is the **Spirit of sonship**,[49] or the Spirit of adoption. Through the Spirit, we are able to call God "**Abba**,"[50] which means "Father" (see Mark 14:36).

16 The Holy Spirit gives us the assurance that we are indeed God's children. If the Holy Spirit is in us, we shall not doubt that we are children of God (see Galatians 4:6–7; 1 John 3:1 and comments).

Paul says here that the **Spirit himself** (that is, the Holy Spirit) **testifies with our spirit** (that is, our own human spirit). What is the human spirit? The human spirit is the spiritual part of man. It is the part of us that the Holy Spirit makes alive when we believe in Christ. Some people call man's spirit his **inner being**, or conscience (see Romans 7:22 and comment). We can say that man is made up of three parts: spirit, soul, and body (1 Thessalonians 5:23). Through our human spirit, we experience the presence of God and the blessings of the Holy Spirit in our lives.

17 If we are children, then we are also **heirs**! The Holy Spirit within us is like a "deposit," a guarantee of our future inheritance in heaven (see 2 Corinthians 5:5; Ephesians 1:13–14 and comments).

But Paul here adds an important reminder. As **co-heirs with Christ**, we share not only in His life and in His glory, but also in His **sufferings**. If we are not willing to share in His sufferings, we shall not share in His glory (2 Timothy 2:11–12; 3:12; 1 Peter 4:12–14).

Christians have two kinds of crosses.[51] One cross is the cross on which our **old self** was crucified (Romans 6:6). The other "cross" is the suffering and persecution that comes as a result of following Christ. The first cross Jesus carried for us. The second cross we must carry for Him. If we want to be co-heirs with Christ and reign with Him, then we must carry this second cross (see Mark 8:34 and comment).

Future Glory (8:18–30)

18 Few men have endured more hardship and suffering than Paul endured (2 Corinthians 6:4–10; 11:23–28). Even so, compared with the glory that was to come, the suffering he endured wasn't worth taking into account (2 Corinthians 4:17).

Paul mentions here the **glory that will be revealed in us**. Whose glory will be revealed in us? Christ's glory. When we are raised with Christ, we shall receive His glory; we shall be like Him (1 John 3:2). For those who are being led by the Spirit, this glory has already begun here on earth (see 2 Corinthians 3:18 and comment).

19 The word **creation** in this verse means all living things, both animals and plants. The whole **creation** is waiting for the **sons of God** (believers in Christ) **to be revealed** (glorified). When will they be revealed? Except for God, no one knows. But according to the teaching of the Bible, they will be revealed at the end of the world, when Christ will come again to reign with glory (see Mark 13:23–27,31–32; 2 Peter 3:13; Revelation 21:1–4). The whole creation is waiting for that day, because on that day not only will

---

49 In place of the word **sonship**, some translations of the Bible say "adoption." For further discussion, see Word List: Adoption.

50 **Abba** is an Aramaic word meaning "Father," or "Daddy." It is an informal word expressing love and closeness.

In Jesus' time, Aramaic was the language most commonly spoken in the Middle East. Aramaic was the language that Jesus spoke while He was on earth. Today, however, Aramaic is spoken by only a few people in one small area of Syria.

51 For the Christian, the cross is a sign of suffering and death, because it was on a cross that Jesus was put to death. The cross was the chief method used by the Romans to execute criminals. Thousands of people were put to death in this way.

believers be revealed (glorified), but also the whole creation itself will in some way be made new.

20 When we look at the world, its situation in some ways seems futile; all of its activities seem to be in vain. Everything lives only for a moment; then it gets sick and dies. What is the point of life when it ends so quickly?

The creation was not like that in the beginning. After God created the world, He looked at it and saw that it was good (Genesis 1:31). Everything made by God was good and beautiful, but then God's creation was ruined by the sin of the first man and woman, Adam and Eve (Genesis 3:1–6). God said to them: "**Cursed is the ground because of you**" (Genesis 3:17–18). Thus in some way, because of man's sin, not only mankind but the entire creation was **subjected to frustration**—that is, subjected to death and decay. The **one who subjected it** was God.

But God did not plan that His creation should remain forever in such a "frustrated" condition. He subjected creation not only to frustration but also **in hope**. This **hope** was that at some future time the **creation itself** [would] **be liberated from its bondage to decay**, sickness, and death (verse 21).

21 When this present heaven and earth end, the whole creation will then in some way be resurrected and made new, and there will be no more **decay** and death. Paul calls this new resurrected condition the **glorious freedom of the children of God**—or, simply, eternal life. It is for this glorious freedom, this eternal life, that the whole creation **waits in eager expectation** (verse 19).

22 The **whole creation has been groaning as in the pains of childbirth**. We know from our own experience that this is true. In this world toil, strife, sorrow, sickness, and death are ever present in the lives of all of us.

But all of these troubles are like the **pains of childbirth**. The pain of childbirth is a sign that a new life is about to be born. Without the pain of childbirth, there can be no new life. In the same way, the pain that this creation is now enduring will in the end result in liberation **from its bondage to decay** (verse 21); it will result in a new birth, a new life, a new creation!

23 We believers are the children of God; we are led by the Spirit of God. Nevertheless, we also **groan inwardly** in this life. Our bodies, too, are in **bondage to decay**. Even though we already have the **firstfruits of the Spirit**—that is, new life in Christ—we still have not received our full inheritance, which is stored up for us in heaven (see 2 Corinthians 5:5; Ephesians 1:13–14 and comments). That inheritance is eternal life—the **glorious freedom** from decay and death (verse 21).

Believers in Christ are already "adopted children" of God (verse 15). But we have not yet come of age; we are not yet old enough to receive the full privileges of our ADOPTION **as sons**. We will receive the full privileges of our **adoption**, our full inheritance, on that day when the REDEMPTION **of our bodies** takes place—the day when our bodies are resurrected. On that day we will receive the full benefits of our **redemption**, of our salvation. We also, together with the whole creation, wait eagerly for that day! (see Ephesians 4:30).

24–25 For Christians **hope** is a very important thing. In this world we do not obtain our complete inheritance, our complete salvation; we obtain only an "advance" or **deposit** on our inheritance (Ephesians 1:14). Our complete inheritance, our complete salvation—**the redemption of our bodies**—will come later. Therefore, we **hope** for what is still to come.

For in this hope we are saved (verse 24). "This hope" is the hope of the **redemption of our bodies** (verse 23). Paul's meaning is that **in this hope** through faith we are saved. **Now faith is being sure of what we hope for** (Hebrews 11:1). Hope arises from faith. We have **faith** that God will fulfill His promises; therefore, we have **hope** that we will receive what He has promised.

26 One of the many things the Holy Spirit does for us is to help us pray. Sometimes we don't know what to pray for. We are like a small child who, not knowing better, asks his father for something unsuitable or even harmful. We do not always know what is best either for ourselves or for others.

Therefore, let us be thankful that the Holy Spirit is always ready to help us in our prayers. Just as Christ intercedes for us in heaven (Romans 8:34; Hebrews 7:25), so the Holy Spirit dwelling within us **intercedes for us with groans that words cannot express**. Some Christians pray in other tongues, that is, in a spiritual language.[52] Other Christians, with few words, simply cry out to God, laying their prayer burden entirely on Him.

If we ourselves do not make an effort to pray, the Holy Spirit certainly isn't going to help us! We must pray as best we can; that means we must spend time in prayer. There is a saying: Without God, we can't do anything; without us, God won't do anything. This saying is not only true for our prayer life; it's true for the rest of our life as well.

In 1 John 5:14, John writes: . . . **if we ask anything according to his will, he hears us**. It is the Holy Spirit who shows us what God's will is, so that we can then pray **according to his will**.

27 **And he** (God) **who searches our hearts knows the mind of the Spirit**. The **Spirit** is God's own Holy Spirit. Therefore, God will surely "know the mind" of His own Spirit. And because He is God's own Spirit, the Holy Spirit will always intercede for us according to God's will.

God can see into the very bottom of our hearts. He knows what we want before we even ask for it. God knows whether we are praying from our hearts, or only with our lips. Let it not be said of us that we worshiped God only with our lips! (Mark 7:6).

28 This verse surely ranks as one of the greatest verses in the New Testament. Millions of Christians over the centuries have drawn great comfort and hope from this verse. In **all things** God works for our good. The expression **all things** includes not only the pleasant and happy things in life, but the unpleasant and unhappy things as well. It includes evil, sickness, and death. God even uses the "bad" things in our lives to work for our **good**.

At those times when we are happy and things are going well, it is very easy to agree with this verse. But in times of trouble, this verse is hard to understand and still harder to believe. We must never treat this verse lightly—even in good times.

Here a question arises: If **in all things** God works for our good, does the term "all things" include Satan? Does God use Satan for our good? This is an important question. One could argue that if Satan's work can be used for our good, then Satan is not our enemy—he's our friend!

However, the Bible clearly teaches us that Satan is indeed our enemy—a powerful and terrible enemy. In this world Satan's work is not for our good but for our harm. For the thousands of Christians who have spent their lives in jail, or who have been killed—burned to death, crucified, fed to lions—how can we say that **all things** have been for their good in this world? We cannot.

Then how are we to understand this verse? We must understand it this way: All the things that happen to us here on earth God will work for our good in heaven. In verses 18–25, Paul has talked about our future hope and future glory. Therefore, in this verse the **good** that Paul is talking about is heavenly good, not earthly good. On earth Satan's power is great; but in heaven he has no power at all. In heaven all of Satan's earthly evil will be turned to our good.

But having said that, it is also true that God is concerned for our welfare in this life. He cares about our bodies, our health, even our food and clothing. Jesus said: "**. . . seek first** [God's] **kingdom and his righteousness, and all these things** (food, clothing, etc.) **will be given to you as well**" (Matthew 6:33). When God allows trouble to come into our lives, He usually uses that trouble to bring about some good result in our lives right here on earth (see Romans 5:3–4; James 1:2–4 and comments). It is through troubles

[52] "Speaking in other tongues" is mentioned in 1 Corinthians 14:2 and comment. For further discussion, see General Article: Holy Spirit Baptism.

that our faith is tested and made strong (1 Peter 1:6–7). Through various kinds of trouble God disciplines us, so that we might become more righteous (Hebrews 12:7,10–11). We must also remember that, even though Satan's power is great, God's power is much greater; Satan cannot alter God's ultimate plan for our lives.

The most important thing to remember about this verse, however, is that the promise given here is given only to those **who love** [God], **who have been called according to his purpose**. If we love God and are called according to His purpose, then we can fully trust Him to work for our good **in all things.** Our hope is in God; He is faithful and able to fulfill all He has promised (Hebrews 10:23).

If we do not love God and are not called according to His purpose, then the promise of this verse is not for us.

29 Here we see God's main purpose in working for our good in all things. His ultimate purpose for all of us who believe is that we might **be conformed to the likeness of his Son**. God **foreknew** each of us from before the creation of the world (see Ephesians 1:4–5 and comment). Before the world was even made, God had a plan for each of us; and that plan was that we should **be conformed to the likeness of his Son**—that is, that we should become like His Son Jesus. God's work of making us like Jesus begins when we first believe, and it is finished when our bodies are resurrected in heaven. If we love God and are called according to His purpose, then everything that happens to us on this earth—no matter how bad—will ultimately work toward this one great end of making us like Jesus.

When we are conformed to the likeness of Jesus, we become Jesus' **brothers**. And God desires that Jesus be the **firstborn among many brothers**. Paul is speaking here of the church, because the church is made up of many brothers (and sisters), among whom Jesus is the eldest.

30 God has had His eyes on us from before the creation of the world. His eternal purpose for us cannot be blocked. Even before we were born, He **foreknew** us (verse 29). Before we were born, He **predestined** us and **called** us. We heard God's call, and believed in Christ. Through faith we obtained Christ's righteousness, and God **justified** us. Then God **glorified**[53] us by making us His children—brothers and sisters of Jesus. And when we get to heaven, He will fully glorify us by resurrecting our bodies and making us fully **conformed to the likeness of his Son**. Thus in heaven our glory will be complete (see verse 18).

All of this that God has done and is doing for us is His great work of salvation. In verses 29–30, Paul has described the steps of salvation. From before the creation of the world, God's plan and purpose for us was that we might receive salvation and eternal life. How can we compare the troubles of this short life with such a great salvation! (verse 18).

More Than Conquerors (8:31–39)

31 **If God is for us, who can be against us?** Satan can be against us. But in the end, Satan cannot prevail against a true believer (see John 16:33 and comment).

32 God has given us many wonderful gifts—grace, love, joy, forgiveness, salvation, an inheritance in heaven—but the greatest gift of all is His Son Jesus Christ. If when we were still God's enemies He gave us His own beloved Son, now that we are His children will He not give us all these lesser gifts as well?

All these other gifts, in fact, are given to us in Christ. Every spiritual blessing is found in Christ (see Ephesians 1:3 and comment). And do we have to pay for any of these spiritual blessings? No. To those who believe in Christ, all these blessings are given free!

Paul says that God **gave him** (Christ) **up for us all**—that is, for **all** who love

---

[53] We are not fully **glorified** in this world; only in heaven will God fully glorify us. Therefore, why in this verse does Paul use the word **glorified** in the past tense, as if we had already been glorified? The reason is that Paul is so sure we are going to be glorified that he can speak of it as if it had already happened.

God and have been **called according to His purpose** (verse 28).

God **did not spare his own Son**. God has held nothing back from us. He has given us His most precious gift (His Son), and included in that gift He has given us all other spiritual blessings as well. Since God has held nothing back from us, He expects that we will hold nothing back from Him. As He gave Christ up for us, so we must give ourselves up for Him—ourselves and everything we have.

This essential truth is illustated by one of the most important events described in the Old Testament—Abraham's offering up of Isaac (Genesis 22:1–14). Abraham had waited many years to have a son; he was one hundred years old when Isaac was finally born! Then God commanded Abraham to offer Isaac as a sacrifice—to kill this son for whom he had waited so long! Yet Abraham obeyed God, and prepared to sacrifice Isaac. Then, just as Abraham was about to kill his son, God stopped him and provided a ram in Isaac's placc. God said to Abraham, "**Now I know you fear God, because you have not withheld from me your son, your only son**" (Genesis 22:12). Thus God's purpose in commanding Abraham to sacrifice his son was to test Abraham's faith and obedience.

Afterwards, God told Abraham: ". . . **because you have done this and have not withheld your son . . . I will surely bless you**" (Genesis 22:15–18).

Let us examine ourselves. Have we held anything back from God? Is there anything which we love or which is precious to us that we have not offered to God? Is there anything which we love more than God—such as our wealth, our family, our reputation? God has held nothing back from us. Let us, taking Abraham's example, hold nothing back from God (see Hebrews 11:17–19 and comment).

What happens when we offer up to God the things we love most? Very often God will give them back to us! Once God has seen that we are indeed willing to give them up, He often lets us keep them, just as He let Abraham keep Isaac.

33 Satan can **bring any charge** against us, but he can't condemn us. . . . **there is now no condemnation for those who are in Christ** (verse 1). True, in this world men can condemn us; but for those who are in Christ that condemnation will be erased in heaven. When Paul says that **there is now no condemnation**, he is talking about heaven, not earth.

34 **Who is he that condemns?** Ultimately, no one. Because God will not listen to Satan's charges against us. God will listen only to Jesus Christ, our advocate, who **is at the right hand of God and is also interceding for us** (see Ephesians 1:20–23).

35 **Who shall separate us from the love of Christ?** No one! Except for sin (see verses 38–39 and comment), there is no other circumstance in this life that can separate believers in Christ from God's love. Paul is not saying in this verse that troubles and persecution won't come upon us in this life. He is simply saying that these things will not separate us from God's love.

36 Here Paul quotes from Psalm 44:22. Just as Christ died for our sake, so we also must be ready to **face death all day long** for His sake (see 1 Corinthians 15:31; 2 Corinthians 4:8–12,16–17 and comments). Even death cannot separate us from God's love. Just as Christ offered up His body for us as a **sheep to be slaughtered**, so we also must offer up our bodies to God **as living sacrifices** (Romans 12:1). Whether we live or whether we die, we will remain in God's love.

37 Jesus Christ overcame the world (John 16:33). He overcame hostility, persecution, even death itself (2 Timothy 1:10). We, too, **in all these things . . . are more than conquerors**—not by our own strength but **through him who loved us**, that is, Christ (see 1 Corinthians 15:57 and comment).

38–39 From Paul's day to ours, these verses have given countless Christians tremendous comfort, encouragement, and hope. And these verses are completely true: There is nothing **in all creation** [that] **will be able to separate us from the love of God that is in Christ Jesus our Lord**.

Nevertheless, as Christians repeat these wonderful verses over and over, they tend to forget that there is, in fact, one thing—a thing which God did not create—that certainly can separate them from God's love. And that one thing is sin.

If we continue knowingly in some sin and refuse to repent of it, that sin will most definitely separate us from God's love and bring upon us God's terrible wrath and judgment. Before we were Christians, we were separated from God because of sin.[54] We were God's enemies (Romans 5:10). Then, after repenting of our sins and believing in Christ, we were reconciled to God. But if we fall back into sin and continue in it knowingly without repenting, we are in danger of again becoming separated from God (see Hebrews 10:26–27 and comment). And on the day of judgment, that separation will become permanent.

Of all the promises in the Bible, the promise of verses 38–39 is one of the greatest. But we must not think about a promise without also thinking about the conditions of that promise. It is good to remember the promises of the Bible—but we must not forget the warnings!

As we look back over this great Chapter 8 of Romans—a chapter which many would say is the greatest single chapter in the entire Bible—we see laid out before us the full and glorious Gospel of Jesus Christ. We see how we were once condemned, but now are justified. We see how we were once in bondage, but now are free. We see how we were once dead, but now are alive. We see that a new and victorious life is now possible for us through the Holy Spirit who dwells within us. We see that if we are led by that Spirit, we shall be accepted into God's family and be called His children and heirs. And finally, we see our eternal destiny—planned by God from before the creation of the world. And that destiny is summed up in the words of verse 29: our destiny is **to be conformed to the likeness of his Son** Jesus Christ forever.

Friends, let this be the one great burning passion of our lives: to be conformed to the likeness of Jesus Christ. There is no higher calling; there is no greater glory.

CHAPTER 9

Paul's Sorrow Over Israel's Unbelief (9:1–5)

1–3 Why did Paul have such **great sorrow and unceasing anguish**? Because most of the Jews, the people of his own race, had not believed in Jesus Christ. Even though the Jews were God's specially chosen people, they had lost the opportunity for salvation because of their unbelief. Christ had come first of all to be the Savior of the Jews (Matthew 15:24; Romans 1:16), but most of them had not accepted Him. Therefore, the Gospel was preached to the Gentiles. Paul himself was specially appointed to be an apostle to the Gentiles (Acts 9:15; Galatians 2:8). Thus the Gentiles began believing in Christ, and within a few years there were many more Gentile Christians than there were Jewish Christians.

Paul's sorrow was so great that he was himself willing to be **cursed**—if by that means his Jewish **brothers** might be saved. Paul's love and concern for others was so great that he was willing to give up his own eternal salvation for their sake! In the Old Testament, the great Jewish leader Moses offered to do the same thing in order to save the Jews from God's wrath (Exodus 32:30–32).

4 Paul here calls the Jews the **people of ISRAEL. Israel** was the original name of

---

[54] Before we were Christians, we were separated from God; but we were not separated from God's love. God's love reaches out to men even while they are His enemies. But on the day of judgment His love will no longer reach out to those who have refused to repent and believe in Jesus. On that day they will be separated from God's love forever.

the Jewish nation. The Jews were also called **Israelites** (Romans 10:1). God had chosen Israel to be His own special people; He had "adopted" them. He had given them the privilege of **adoption as sons**. The **divine glory**—that is, God's presence—was with them. God had established His COVENANTS with the Jews; in particular, He had made a covenant with Abraham, the first Jew (Genesis 17:3–8). God had given the Jews His **law**, in which His righteous will for them was clearly revealed. And He had given them **promises** that He would send them a Savior, Christ. Just as Abraham had been declared righteous because of his faith (Genesis 15:6), so the Jews also would be declared righteous and find salvation if they placed their faith in Christ.

5 Christ Himself was a Jew, descended from the Jewish **patriarchs**—Abraham, Isaac, Jacob, and Judah (Matthew 1:1–2). Surely Israel was a nation blessed by God!

Here Paul can't help adding a word about Christ: namely, that Christ is **God over all**. Let us always remember that Christ is not only a great man, a great leader, prophet, and teacher; He is also God Himself, **God over all**.

God's Promises Do Not Fail (9:6–13)

6 If Israel was such a blessed nation to begin with, what then happened to it? Why had the Jews lost their chance to find salvation? Had God's promises—**God's word**—to them **failed**, or been broken?

Not at all! God had not broken His promises to Israel. But those promises—the promises of a Savior and of salvation—had been given only to true Jews. And Paul says that not all who call themselves Jews are true Jews (see Romans 2:28–29). **For not all who are descended from Israel** (that is, Jews by birth) **are Israel** (that is, true Jews).

Therefore, the promises that God gave to the Jews had not been broken or cancelled, because most of the Jews were not, in fact, "true Jews." True Jews are only those Jews who believe in Jesus. In verse 8, Paul distinguishes between those Jews who are **natural children** (descendants of Abraham by birth) and those Jews who are **children of the promise** (those who have believed in the promise—in Jesus). Only for the "children of the promise"—that is, true Jews, believing Jews—are the promises of God fulfilled (see Romans 4:11–17 and comment).

The "children of the promise" are those who seek to become righteous through faith. The "natural children" are those who seek to become righteous by their own efforts, by good works (see Romans 9:32; Galatians 3:6–9 and comments).

7–9 To show that not all **natural children** (descendants by birth) receive an inheritance (the promise), Paul gives the example of Abraham. Abraham had two "natural children," Isaac and Ishmael. But only one of them, Isaac, was Abraham's "true son"; only Isaac received an inheritance. Abraham first had Ishmael by his wife's maid (Genesis 16:1–4,15–16). The descendants of Ishmael were not Jews.[55] The Jews were descended from Abraham's second son, Isaac, whom Abraham had by his wife Sarah. This was the son that God had promised to give Abraham (Genesis 18:14; 21:1–13; Galatians 4:22–23). God does not count true descendants only according to birth. In God's sight, true descendants are those who have come according to God's promise—that is, according to faith. Because it was on account of Abraham's faith in God's promise that God blessed Abraham and Sarah with a son.

Paul's main point here is that the Jews cannot claim to be **God's children** just because they are Abraham's **natural children** by birth. God's true children are the **children of the promise**. It is the **children of the promise who are regarded as Abraham's offspring**. Or, to put it another way, it is the children of faith, not of flesh, who are the true Jews. The true offspring of Abraham, then, are those who have faith in Christ. When the Jews (by birth) rejected Christ, they rejected them-

[55] Many people believe that the present-day Arabs are descendants of Ishmael.

selves, and lost their inheritance and their place in God's family.

10–12 In these verses, Paul gives a second illustration of how God does not choose His true heirs according to natural birth. Isaac's wife Rebecca gave birth to twins. According to Jewish custom, the firstborn twin, Esau, was supposed to receive the family inheritance. But God, according to His own purpose, caused the inheritance to be given to the secondborn twin, Jacob (Genesis 25:20–26; 27:1–35).

Here again we see that God does not give men an inheritance according to their birth, but rather according to His own will, so that His **purpose in election might stand** (verse 11). Even before he was born, God "elected" or chose Jacob to be the heir. Jacob had no chance to do any good works to prove he was worthy; he hadn't even been born yet! God's **election** is not based on **works**, but on His own sovereign will. God does not choose us because of our worth; He chooses us because of His grace.

13 In this way, God **loved** (chose) Jacob and his descendants, and **hated** (rejected) Esau and his descendants (Malachi 1:2–3). Jacob and Esau were both sons of Isaac, but only Jacob obtained the inheritance, and only from Jacob did the true Jews, the true Israel, descend.

Therefore, in this section Paul's main teaching is this: God did not choose those Jews to be His children who were Jews only by birth and who sought to be righteous by their own works. Instead, He chose those who, having heard His call, put their faith in His Son Jesus.

God Is Not Unjust (9:14–18)

14–16 Some people might think that God is unjust. They might ask: "Why did God love Jacob and hate Esau? Wasn't that unjust?" But we must not think such thoughts of God.

In verse 15, Paul quotes the words spoken by God to Moses in Exodus 33:19. God chooses men, calls men, and blesses men according to His own **mercy**, and not according to **man's desire or effort** (verse 16).

In these verses, Paul teaches that God's mercy is never unjust. Since every man and woman has disobeyed God in some way, no one is worthy to receive salvation. But God, by His mercy and grace, gave His own Son Jesus for our salvation. Except for God's mercy and grace, no one would ever be able to obtain salvation.

No man can receive God's grace and mercy by his own **desire or effort** (verse 16). True, God did say: "**You will seek me and find me when you seek me with all your heart**" (Jeremiah 29:13). True, we must look toward God with an open and humble heart. But even this we cannot do on our own without first receiving the promptings of God's grace (see John 1:12–13; 6:44). From beginning to end, our salvation is the work of God's grace.

17–18 Who was **Pharaoh**? In Moses' time, the rulers of EGYPT were called Pharaohs. The Pharaoh Paul refers to in these verses was Rameses II, a cruel and wicked ruler who persecuted the Jews living in Egypt at that time. God sent Moses to deliver the Jews from the hands of this wicked Pharaoh. To bring fear into the heart of this Pharaoh, God performed great signs and wonders through Moses, which are described in Exodus Chapters 7–12.

In verse 17, Paul quotes the words God spoke to Pharaoh (Exodus 9:16). God had raised up this evil ruler and hardened his heart so that God's power might be displayed and His name proclaimed. If Pharaoh's heart had not been hardened—if, for example, Pharaoh had repented—God would not have had the chance to demonstrate His power on that occasion. From this we can see that God shows **mercy** to some people, but the hearts of others He **hardens** so that they will not obtain mercy.

After reading this we are tempted to think that God really is unjust—that He was unjust to Pharaoh. God never gave Pharaoh a chance! He never showed Pharaoh a bit of kindness! But we must remember that no man is deserving of God's kindness; no man is deserving of God's mercy. No man can say to God: "I deserve a chance!" The reason is that we have all sinned against God repeatedly (see Romans 3:10–12). The only thing man deserves from God is punishment. God hardens men because of their sin. When God hardens a man, He is demonstrating His justice—not injustice.

Therefore, God hardened Pharaoh's heart because of Pharaoh's wickedness. God was totally just in hardening Pharaoh's heart.[56] Pharaoh deserved God's punishment.

Mercy, on the other hand, is not something anyone "deserves"; otherwise, it wouldn't be mercy. Mercy, by its very nature, is undeserved. It is given only to the undeserving. No one can complain about not receiving mercy, since no one deserves it! God is under no obligation to show mercy to anyone. But if God decides to show some people mercy, what is wrong with that? Is He unjust to do so? By no means.

So we see that God gives justice (punishment) to all. But to some, according to His eternal purpose, He shows mercy. And since the coming of Christ into the world, God has shown mercy to all those who believe in Him. God has not withdrawn the just punishment we deserve; instead, He has given it to Christ in our place. Thus we see together both the justice and the mercy of God.

Those who receive salvation have God alone to thank, because their salvation has come entirely as a result of His mercy and grace. But those who receive eternal punishment have only themselves to thank, because through their sin they have fully earned their punishment.

God Is Sovereign (9:19–29)

19–21 Just as a lump of clay has no right to complain against the potter, so we likewise have no right to complain against God for making us the way we are. We are not to blame God for our sin.

In Jeremiah 18:1–12, the prophet Jeremiah compares the nations of the earth to clay in the potter's hands. Through Jeremiah, God said that if any nation He planned to raise up did evil, He would change His mind and punish it instead. Likewise, if any nation He planned to destroy repented, He would forgive that nation and raise it up. Just as God deals with nations, so also does He deal with individuals.

22 What are the **objects of his** (God's) **wrath** that Paul mentions in this verse? They are disobedient men like Pharaoh, or like those who refuse to believe in Christ; they are deserving of God's **wrath**. God **bore with great patience** these disobedient men—these "objects of wrath"—so that they might have a chance to repent. But in the end He will show His wrath to all who do not repent. Such men are indeed **prepared for destruction**.

Here also some difficult questions arise: Who made these "objects of wrath" which were **prepared for destruction**,

---

[56] Here a difficult question arises: How does God harden a man's heart? Christians give two different answers to this question. The first answer is that God allows some men to continue in sin. As they continue in sin, they stop hearing God's voice; they can no longer repent. God "gives them over" to their sins (see Romans 1:24,26,28 and comment). Therefore, according to this first answer, God allows men, in effect, to harden their own hearts. Such men refuse to turn from their sins. Such men have first hardened their own hearts (Exodus 7:13–14,22; 8:15,32; Proverbs 29:1). In Hebrews 3:8, we are given the warning: "**. . . do not harden your hearts**." According to this first answer, then, the main responsibility for man's not obtaining salvation lies with man, not with God.

The second answer to the question about how God hardens man's heart is that in the very beginning God chose some men for salvation and some men He didn't. The choice was completely God's. According to this second answer, the main responsibility for man's not obtaining salvation lies with God, not with man (see Exodus 7:3; 9:12; 10:20,27; John 12:39–40 and comment; General Article: Salvation—God's Choice or Man's Choice?).

It is difficult to say which of these two answers is the correct one. But whichever answer is correct, we can never call God unjust. God accepts some men and rejects others, without looking at their work or worthiness. In particular, God accepts those who accept Jesus Christ, and He rejects those who reject Christ. How can we say that God is unjust in rejecting those who reject His own Son?

and when were they made? What was the clay like, from which these objects were originally made? Was the clay somehow bad, and that was the reason God made it into an "object of wrath"? Or did God simply set that clay aside in the beginning to be made into objects "prepared for destruction"? What was the basis for God's decision? Was it the quality of the clay? Or was it simply God's sovereign will? (see verses 17–18 and comment).

Again, Christians have two main thoughts on this subject. Many Christians think that God, from the very beginning, chose some men (clay) for destruction and other men for salvation. According to this first view, the responsibility for man's fate lies entirely with God.

But other Christians have a different thought. These Christians believe that God first made all men for salvation. But some men opposed God's grace and sinned against Him. As a result of their own opposition and sin, these men turned themselves into "objects of wrath." God **bore with great patience** their sin and disobedience. God waited patiently so that they might have a chance to repent. Even now, God continues waiting patiently for men to repent. There is still the chance for these disobedient men—these **objects of his wrath**—to repent and be made into **objects of his mercy** (verse 23). Thus, according to this second view, men themselves, not God, are primarily responsible for whether they are chosen for destruction or salvation, for whether they become objects of wrath or objects of mercy (see 2 Timothy 2:20–21 and comment).

It is not possible to say with certainty which of these two ideas is the correct one. There is clearly much truth on both sides. Perhaps, in some way that is beyond our understanding, both of these ideas are equally true and represent two sides of one great truth. But whichever of these ideas we prefer, there still remains one essential truth on which all believers can agree: namely, that salvation is granted to all men and women who truly repent of their sins and believe in Jesus Christ. This is the Gospel of Christ. More than this we do not need to know.

23–24 Who, then, are the **objects of** [God's] **mercy**? (verse 23). They are those men and women who have faith, who have been chosen by God from before the creation of the world—**even us, whom he also called** (verse 24). We believers are the "objects of God's mercy," to whom He has shown the **riches of his glory** (see Ephesians 1:18; 3:16).

25 Here Paul quotes from the Old Testament prophet Hosea. The Gentiles had not at first been God's **people.** But then, through faith, they became God's people. At first, only the Jews were considered by God to be "**my people**"; and only Israel was called "**my loved one**" (Hosea 2:23; 1 Peter 2:10).

26 But then the Gentiles, who were not God's **people**, became **sons of the living God** through faith in Christ. In other words, no longer did the "true Israel" consist only of Jews by birth, but it now included all those who believed in Christ (Hosea 1:10; Romans 9:6).

27–28 Here Paul quotes from the Old Testament prophet Isaiah. Isaiah says that only a few Jews, a **remnant**, will be saved—namely, those Jews who believe in Jesus Christ (Isaiah 10:22–23).

29 Here Isaiah says that if God had not left some descendants of Abraham—that is, a "remnant" of Jews—all the Jews would have come to destruction, like the inhabitants of the cities of **Sodom** and **Gomorrah** (Isaiah 1:9). God destroyed those two Old Testament cities, because of the wickedness of their inhabitants (Genesis 19:1–29)

The Reason for Israel's Unbelief (9:30–33)

30 The Gentiles did not **pursue righteousness** according to the written Jewish law; in the end, they obtained righteousness through faith (Romans 3:22).

31–33 **Israel** (the Jews), on the other hand, pursued a **law of righteousness** (verse 31), but didn't obtain it. Why didn't they obtain it? Because they did not have faith; rather, they tried to obtain righteousness **by works** (verse 32). They trusted in their own efforts. They said: "Because we are descendants of Abraham by birth, surely we must be children of God." But in thinking this, they had made a big mistake. Even though they were indeed God's chosen people on the basis of their natural descent from Abraham, in the end they lost the privilege of being God's people, God's children, because of their refusal to believe in Christ. Our election, our righteousness, our salvation are all by faith, not by works. Most of the Jews tried to obtain righteousness and salvation by their own religious **works**, and they failed. The Gentiles, who in the Jews' eyes didn't even pursue righteousness, ended up obtaining it—through **faith**.

In verse 33, Paul quotes again from Isaiah. **Zion** is another name for the Jewish nation of Israel. The Jews **stumbled over the "stumbling stone"** (verse 32). That "stumbling stone" was Jesus Christ. When the Jews rejected Christ, they lost their salvation—that is, they **stumbled** (Isaiah 8:14; 28:16). The Jews could not believe that their Savior—who the Old Testament had promised would come—would turn out to be the son of an ordinary carpenter and then, worse than that, end up dying on a cross like a lowly criminal. Instead of worshiping such a Savior, they despised Him. Therefore, Christ became for the Jews a "stumbling stone" over which they stumbled and fell (see 1 Corinthians 1:23; 1 Peter 2:8 and comments).

CHAPTER 10

Christ Is the End of the Law (10:1–4)

1 Why does Paul pray to God for the **Israelites,** the Jews? If, as Paul writes in Romans 9:18, **God has mercy on whom he wants to have mercy, and he hardens whom he wants to harden**, then what is the use of Paul's praying for the Jews' salvation? Is Paul going to influence God or change God's mind through his prayer?

The answer is yes. In some amazing way, God allows Himself to be influenced by our prayers. There are numerous examples of this throughout the Bible. Furthermore, through our prayers we can block the work of Satan. Prayer, next to the word of God, is the most powerful spiritual weapon we have (Ephesians 6:17–18). If we pray for anything in Jesus' name, God will grant our request (see John 15:16 and comment). Therefore, Paul prays for the Jews.

2 Many people are **zealous for God,** but if their zeal is not based on **knowledge** of the truth, it is in vain. Zeal based on falsehood is very dangerous and often leads to great evil.

3 Since the Jews did not know the **righteousness that comes from God**—that is, the righteousness that comes through faith in Christ—they did not submit to it. They didn't understand that Christ Himself was the embodiment of God's righteousness (see Romans 3:21–22 and comment).

4 When Paul says that **Christ is the end of the law,** he means that Christ has "ended" the law—that is, the Jewish law. The law has now been replaced by Christ Himself. No longer is the law necessary as a means of obtaining righteousness or salvation. Now Christ stands in place of the law. He is the new **way** for men and women to obtain righteousness; He is the new **way** to the heavenly Father for everyone who believes in Him (see John 14:6 and comment). Christ is not only the **end** of the law; He is also the fulfillment of the law (see Matthew 5:17 and comment).

The New Way of Righteousness (10:5–21)

5 Paul, quoting Moses, first describes the **righteousness that is by the law.** God said to Moses: "**The man who does these things**—that is, obey the commandments of the law—**will live by them**" (Leviticus 18:5). The Jewish law is able to give "life" (or salvation) to anyone who follows every provision of the law completely. Since no one has ever been able to do this, the law, then, has never saved anyone.

6 Paul now describes the **righteousness that is by faith**—which is essentially the way of salvation. We don't have to **ascend into heaven** to obtain this righteousness (Deuteronomy 30:11–12). Christ has already brought it from heaven down to us. We don't have to ascend into heaven **to bring Christ down**; He has already come down Himself.

7 Neither do we have to **descend into the deep** (into hell) to obtain this righteousness, that is, to find Christ (Deuteronomy 30:13). Christ has already risen from the dead; He has already come up from the grave.

8 **But what does it**—the righteousness that is by the law (verse 5)—**say?** It says that the **word of faith**, which shows men the way of salvation, has come **near.** It is not only **near**; it is **in your heart** (Deuteronomy 30:14).

9 What is this **word of faith**—this way of salvation? It is this: **That if you confess with your mouth, "Jesus is Lord," and believe in your heart that God raised him from the dead, you will be saved.**

This is the way of salvation. To obtain salvation, there are two things we must do: first, **confess** with our mouth; and second, **believe** in our heart. If we confess only with our mouth but do not believe, we are liars. If we think we believe but do not confess Christ with our mouth, we deceive ourselves: our faith is false. A person cannot be saved unless he is ready to confess with his mouth that "**Jesus is Lord.**" The so-called "secret Christian" who says he accepts Christ in his heart yet keeps on denying Him before men is not a true Christian (see Matthew 10:32–33 and comment).

10 Paul says that having believed with our heart, we will be **justified,** and having confessed with our mouth, we will be **saved.** But these are not two separate things. Believing and confessing always go together, just as justification and salvation always go together. Having believed, we confess our faith. Having been justified, we receive salvation. These things cannot be separated.

11 **Everyone** who believes in Christ, whether Jew or Gentile, **will never be put to shame** (Isaiah 28:16; Romans 9:33). Sometimes, however, we are ashamed of being Christians. We hide our faith. But how can this be? Is there something shameful about being saved, about being a child of God? Of course not! (2 Timothy 1:8,12).

12 The Jewish law has been replaced by Christ. For both Jews and Gentiles a new way of obtaining righteousness and salvation has been opened up. Now there is no difference between Jew and Gentile; Christ is **Lord of all** (see Romans 3:29; Galatians 3:28; Colossians 3:11 and comments). And Christ **richly blesses all who call on him**—that is, He gives them spiritual riches.

13 Paul here quotes Joel, one of the Old Testament prophets: "**Everyone who calls on the name of the Lord will be saved**" (Joel 2:32). This calling on the Lord's name doesn't mean just saying some words. To truly call on the name of the Lord, it is necessary to first believe in Him. Without faith, calling on the Lord is useless (see Hebrews 11:6). Calling on the name of the Lord always means believing in the Lord; that's why **everyone who calls** on His name **will be saved.**

14 Therefore, before calling on the Lord's name, there must be faith. But before there can be faith, there must be hearing. And in order to hear, there must be a preacher.

15 Who will be sent to preach? It's not only Paul but God Himself who is asking us that question. The feet of preachers (those who bring good news) are **beautiful**, Isaiah says (Isaiah 52:7). According to a Jewish saying, a man with "beautiful feet" is a man worthy to be welcomed.

16 But not all Jews **accepted the**

good news that was preached to them. Indeed, most of them did not. They refused to believe not only Christ but their own prophets as well (Isaiah 53:1). That is why Paul has such **great sorrow** concerning the Jews (Romans 9:2).

17 Here Paul repeats the thought of verse 14. Hearing should result in faith; but in the case of the Jews it did not.

18 Why didn't the Jews believe? Was it because they didn't hear the Gospel? No. Because the Gospel had been preached **to the ends of the world**. Here Paul quotes from Psalm 19:4. The Jews had heard, but they hadn't heeded.

19 Why didn't the Jews heed the Gospel? Was it because they didn't understand the word of Christ, the Gospel? No. They certainly understood it. Their own Scriptures (the Old Testament) spoke clearly of the coming of Christ. In Deuteronomy, which Paul quotes here, **Moses**,[57] predicted that the Jews would be made **envious by those who are not a nation**—that is, the Gentiles—and they would be made **angry by a nation** (the Gentiles) **that has no understanding** (Deuteronomy 32:21). And indeed that very thing happened: the Jews became envious and angry with the Gentiles because the Gentiles were receiving salvation and the Jews were not. Those who had understanding (the Jews) rejected the Gospel, while those with **no understanding** (the Gentiles) accepted the Gospel!

20 Here God says through the prophet Isaiah: **"I was found by those** (the Gentiles) **who did not seek me; I revealed myself to those** (the Gentiles) **who did not ask for me"** (Isaiah 65:1).

Is this not true for us also? God first found us when we weren't even seeking Him. He revealed Himself to us when we weren't even asking about Him. Such is His great mercy! (see Romans 5:8).

21 Therefore, the Jews both heard and understood the Gospel. Why then did they not heed it? Because they were a **disobedient and obstinate people** (Isaiah 65:2). Unbelief is always disobedience in God's eyes. If a man says, "I cannot believe," what he's really saying is, "I will not obey."

But notice the patience of God toward disobedient (unbelieving) men. God says: **"All day long I have held out my hands. . . ."**

CHAPTER 11

The Remnant of Israel (11:1–10)

1 **Did God reject his people**—the Jews, the nation of Israel? No, God didn't reject all the Jews. Because, says Paul, **I am an Israelite** (Jew) **myself**, and God hasn't rejected me (Psalm 94:14).

Paul was an Israelite of the **tribe of Benjamin**. Isaac's son Jacob had twelve sons, the youngest of which was Benjamin. From these twelve sons the twelve tribes of Israel are descended.

2–3 **Elijah** was one of the greatest Jewish prophets. Elijah complained to God about the Jews, because they had killed the prophets God had sent and they had torn down God's altars. Elijah thought that he was the only true Jew left—that all the other Jews had deserted God. **"I am the only one left,"** he told God (1 Kings 19:10).

4 But God told Elijah that there were seven thousand faithful Jews left, who had not gone after false gods (1 Kings 19:18). **Baal** was the name of a false god that many Jews worshiped during Elijah's time.

5 Just as in Elijah's time, so in Paul's time there was a **remnant** of Jews remaining, who had been **chosen by grace**—that is, those Jews who had been chosen by God according to His grace and brought to faith in Christ (Romans 9:27).

6 God **by grace** chose those Jews

---

[57] **Moses** wrote the first five books of the Old Testament.

who, like Paul, would believe in Christ. It was not because of their good works that God chose them to be saved; it was entirely because of His grace. Grace is never given according to man's work or effort. Man can never "earn" grace by his own labor. Man never deserves grace. Grace is something that is given only to the undeserving—otherwise it would not be grace. It is given freely; we don't have to pay for it. We receive grace simply because of God's mercy and love for us.

7 In this verse, who are the **elect**? The "elect" are those Jews and Gentiles who believe in Christ.

What did Israel seek so earnestly, but **did not obtain**? They sought righteousness, that is, salvation. But they didn't obtain it, because they refused to believe in Christ.

Those Jews who did not believe **were hardened** (see Romans 9:18). The great majority of Jews fell into this category; it was only a small **remnant** (verse 5) of Jews who believed.

8 Here Paul quotes from Isaiah 29:10 to show how God hardened the Jews. God gave them a **spirit of stupor**, which has remained **to this very day**. The Jews saw Christ, but did not believe; they heard His word, but they did not accept it (see Matthew 13:14–15; Mark 4:12 and comment).

9–10 In these verses Paul quotes the words of David, the great king of the Jews. David had spoken these words about his enemies (Psalm 69:22–23). But here Paul uses David's words to describe the unbelieving Jews of his own day. The Jews' **table** was the spiritual feast which God had originally prepared for the Jews—a "feast" of spiritual blessings, such as the law, the prophets, the promises, and their adoption as sons of God (see Romans 9:4). But now all these blessings had become for the Jews a **snare and a trap**—a curse—because they had not believed in Jesus. "**May . . . their backs be bent forever**," quotes Paul (verse 10), like the backs of disobedient slaves.

The Salvation of the Gentiles (11:11–24)

11 Have the Jews stumbled and fallen **beyond recovery**? Having rejected Christ, are they all now without hope? No, there is still hope for the Jews, says Paul. Because of the Jews' **transgression** (that is, their unbelief), the Gentiles have now had the opportunity to hear the Gospel and receive salvation (see Acts 13:44–47). Paul's hope is that as the Jews see the Gentiles receiving salvation, they will become envious (Romans 10:19), and eventually repent and turn to Christ.

12 And when the Jews finally turn to Christ, what a great blessing that will be for all men! Because, if through the Jews' **transgression** (unbelief) and **loss** (loss of salvation) great **riches** (blessings) have come to the world, how many more riches will come to the world through the Jews' **fullness**—that is, through their turning to Christ?

13–14 Even though Paul's primary calling was to be an **apostle to the Gentiles**, he nevertheless was always thinking about his **own people**, the Jews, and hoping for their salvation.

15 The falling away of the Jews resulted in the **reconciliation of the world**—that is, the reconciliation of the Gentiles. Because the Jews rejected the Gospel, the Gospel was preached to the Gentiles, and many were saved—reconciled to God (Romans 5:1). When the Jews finally become reconciled to God, for them it will be like coming to **life** after having been **dead**.

16 In this verse, Paul uses two illustrations to describe the Jewish nation, Israel. The first illustration is that of a loaf of bread. The Jews used to offer a part of every loaf—called the **firstfruits**—as an offering to God. If the "firstfruits" were considered holy, then the rest of the loaf would have to be holy too, since it all came from one batch of dough. The ancestors of the Jews were like the **firstfruits** of Israel; since they were holy, then the whole nation of Israel—even though it had mostly fallen into unbelief—must be basically holy too. So Paul still considers the Jews to be God's holy and beloved people. God will never reject them totally.

In the second illustration, Paul compares Israel with a tree and its roots. Again, the roots are the ancestors of the Jews, such as Abraham, Isaac, and Jacob. Even though the **branches** of the tree (Israel) had proved to be unfruitful, still the branches were holy because the roots were holy.

17 Paul here continues his illustration of the root and the branches. He says that **some of the branches have been broken off**—that is, some of the Jews have lost their salvation through unbelief. The **wild olive shoot** represents the Gentiles, who have been **grafted** into Israel, as one grafts a shoot onto a tree.

18 However, the Gentiles should never boast because they have been "grafted" into the tree of Israel. Let them not look down on the Jews; because the Jews are, in a sense, the roots of the tree. The Gentiles have been added onto the true Israel in an unnatural way. The true Israel is the church of Christ, whose roots are the Jews. Let the Gentile Christians not forget that.

19–21 Therefore, let the Gentile Christians not be **arrogant**; rather, let them be **afraid** (verse 20). It is because of faith they have been grafted into the tree. If they stop believing, they will be broken off even more quickly than the **natural branches** (the unbelieving Jews) were! Here again Paul reminds us that, for both Jew and Gentile, faith is all that is necessary to obtain salvation.

22 God shows **sternness to those who fell**—that is, to those who were disobedient, who did not believe. And He shows **kindness** (or grace) to those who believe. Yet Paul gives a condition for receiving God's "kindness." He says: God will show **kindness to you, provided you continue in his kindness**. If we do not continue in God's kindness, if we do not continue believing in Jesus (in whom God's kindness is fully demonstrated), then God will withdraw His kindness and we shall be **cut off**. In other words, if we do not remain in Christ, we shall be cut off from God's kindness and grace. We shall be thrown away like a dead branch (see John 15:6 and comment). Therefore, says Paul: **Do not be arrogant, but be afraid** (verse 20).

Many Bible scholars quote verses 19–22 to support the opinion that Christians can lose their salvation if they stop believing. But others say that true Christians can never lose their salvation. This second group says that anyone who becomes "cut off" could never have been a true Christian to begin with. According to this second group, Paul here is simply giving Christians a warning against being arrogant, but he is not saying that they would ever be completely "cut off." It is difficult to be certain which of these two interpretations is correct (see General Article: Can We Lose Our Salvation?).

23 If the Jews **do not persist in unbelief**, they will again be **grafted** back into the tree. They will again become citizens of the true Israel—that is, members of the church of Christ.

24 It is much easier to graft into a tree its own **natural branches** (the Jews), than it is to graft branches that are **wild by nature** (the Gentiles). Thus Paul is confident that one day the unbelieving Jews will repent, turn to Christ, and be grafted back into the tree from which they originally came.

The Salvation of Israel (11:25–36)

25 In verses 17–24, Paul has used the illustration of the olive tree and its grafted branches to explain to the Gentiles the **mystery** of Israel. His purpose in explaining all this to the Gentiles is so that they might **not be conceited** (see verses 17–18).

Israel has experienced a **hardening** until the **full number of the Gentiles has come in**. Only God knows what the "full number" of the Gentiles will be. But it will be such a large number of people that no one will be able to count them (see Revelation 7:9). During the time the Gentiles are being added to the church (which, of course, includes this present time) only a few Jews will believe. But after the **full number of the Gentiles** has believed, then the Jews will begin to believe also. Many people think that when this happens, the end of the world will be near.

26–27 Thus, in the end, **all Israel will be saved**, that is, all believing Jews. For without faith no one—neither Jew nor Gentile—can be saved.

Paul here quotes from Isaiah 59:20–21. **The deliverer** (Christ) **will come from Zion.**[58] Christ "comes from" Zion (Israel) because He himself was an Israelite, a Jew.

Christ will **turn godlessness away from Jacob,**[59] that is, from Israel. Christ will, in the end, turn Israel back to God.

28 The Jews of Paul's day were **enemies**. They were enemies of Christ and of all Christians. And they remain "enemies" to this day. Nevertheless, God originally chose the Jews to be His special people (Exodus 19: 3–6). God Himself created the nation of Israel. God called Abraham, the first Jew. God raised up Isaac, Abraham's son. Even though most Jews have not believed in Christ, God still loves them **on account of the patriarchs**—Abraham, Isaac, and Jacob.

29 God will never completely reject the Jews. He has given them great gifts, such as the law, the prophets, the promises. He called them to be His people. Even though they are disobedient, He will not abandon them; His **gifts and his call** to them are **irrevocable**—they cannot be changed.

30–31 Just as the Gentiles had once been disobedient and had received mercy (and salvation), so the Jews have become disobedient so that **they too may now receive mercy** (verse 31). If God has shown mercy to the Gentiles, He will surely show mercy to the Jews, His own people.

32 All men have been disobedient to God. All men, both Jew and Gentile, have "gone their own way" (Acts 14:16). God has **bound all men over to disobedience**—that is, He has "given them over" to disobedience (see Romans 1:24,26,28). But He has done this so that He might show mercy to **all**—that is, to both Jew and Gentile. If men were not disobedient, they wouldn't need mercy. Only sinners need mercy. But remember—we are all sinners (Romans 3:10–12). And to receive God's mercy, we must confess our sin.

Paul does not say here that God will show mercy to every person. Paul says that He will have mercy on **all**—that is, on **all** nations, on **all** who believe in Christ (see Galatians 3:22–29 and comment).

33 In Chapters 9–11, Paul has been talking about things which are not easy to understand. For example, why did the Jews fall away? Why does God harden some people, yet show mercy to others? We do not understand why. What God wants to do, He does! Yet whatever God does is also right, just, and wise. God has a plan and purpose for every person, both Jew and Gentile. Paul doesn't understand everything about God's purposes; nevertheless, he has complete confidence in God's **wisdom and knowledge**. God's purposes are amazing; through the fall of the Jews, the Gentiles have now been given the chance to enter the kingdom of God. Now God has given to all people the chance to find salvation. God's plan for mankind is so great and deep that Paul can only praise God, saying: **Oh, the depth of the riches of the wisdom and knowledge of God! How unsearchable his judgments** (see Colossians 2:2–3).

34 **Who has known the mind of the Lord?** (Isaiah 40:13–14). Only one man has fully known the mind of the Lord, and that man is Jesus Christ. But through Jesus' teachings, we too can know the mind of the Lord (1 Corinthians 2:16). We have knowledge of the Lord's mind, for Jesus **has made him known** (see John 1:18 and comment).

35 The Jews were envious of the Gentiles, because the Gentiles were receiving God's salvation. The Jews

---

[58] **Zion** is another name for Israel (see Romans 9:33).

[59] The nation of Israel was sometimes called **Jacob**, because Jacob was the father of the twelve sons from whom the twelve tribes of Israel are descended. Jacob himself was also given the name Israel by God (Genesis 32:28).

grumbled because they had lost God's blessing. They accused God of taking away their inheritance.

However, what God gives He has the right to take away. When Job was tested by Satan and lost his property, his honor, his family, and his health, what did he say? He didn't grumble; he didn't accuse God. He said: "**The Lord gave and the Lord has taken away; may the name of the Lord be praised**" (Job 1:20–21). And in Job 1:22, it is written: **In all this, Job did not sin by charging God with wrongdoing.**

And so, Paul quotes from Job 41:11, saying: "**Who has ever given to God, that God should repay him?**" No one as ever given to God; God is the Giver. God doesn't need to **repay** anyone. God is a debtor to no man. It is we men who are debtors to Him in all things. Let no man complain against God!

36 Why must we not complain against God? Because God is all–wise, all-good, all-powerful. **For from him and through him and to him are all things. To him be the glory forever! Amen** (see 1 Corinthians 8:6).

CHAPTER 12

Living Sacrifices (12:1–2)

1 In the first eleven chapters of Romans, Paul has presented the main doctrines and teachings of the Christian religion. He has laid the foundation of our faith. In brief, these teachings are as follows. We have been united with Christ. Through Christ's death, our "old self" has died, and the rule of sin in our lives has come to an end. Through Christ's resurrection, our "new self" has come to life. We have received Christ's Spirit, the Holy Spirit, through whom we receive the guidance and the power to lead holy and righteous lives.

Now in the next four chapters, Paul describes the holy and righteous life of a Christian. If we are indeed united with Christ, then there should be some visible evidence of it in our lives. If our inner being has been changed by Christ, then our outer behavior should be changed also. Therefore, Paul now begins to talk about the Christian's outer life, his work, his duties, his behavior (see Ephesians 2:10 and comment).

What is our first and greatest work as Christians? It is this: to offer our **bodies as living sacrifices . . . to God**. By the word **bodies**, Paul means our whole person—spirit, soul, and physical body together. However, this "body" (whole person) Paul is talking about is not our **old self** (Romans 6:6), which was under the control of our sinful nature. The "body" we must offer to God is our new transformed self, which is under God's control (Romans 6:13,19). The new transformed self that we present to God must be without sin, holy, spiritually alive (see 1 Peter 2:5). The "body" we offer must be a **living** sacrifice, without blemish.

We must offer ourselves as sacrifices in response to **God's mercy**. It was by God's mercy that Christ gave His own body as a sacrifice for us. Therefore, **in view of God's mercy** to us, we need to willingly offer ourselves to Him. That is the **spiritual worship** God wants from us. That is the service He expects from us. Such a sacrifice will be **holy and pleasing** to Him. Compared with what He has done for us, our service for Him is very small indeed!

Notice that, in God's sight, the body of a Christian is **holy**. From the beginning we were created by God to be **holy and blameless** (see Ephesians 1:4). The Christian's body is the **temple** of the Holy Spirit, the Holy Spirit's dwelling place (see 1 Corinthians 3:16; 6:19 and comments). It is because of the Holy Spirit dwelling within us that our bodies are made **holy and pleasing to God**.

2 **Do not conform any longer to the pattern of this world**. The word **world** in this verse means the "kingdom of Satan." Here in this world, Satan's power is great; he exercises authority over the lives of all non-believers. We must not cooperate with Satan or those who follow him. Let us not be like them; otherwise, we cannot be **holy and pleasing** to God (see 1 John 2:15–16 and comment).

How can we be "holy and pleasing" to God? Only by being **transformed by the renewing of** [our] **mind** can we become holy and pleasing to God. Paul in this verse is giving us a clear command: **Do not conform . . . be transformed**[60] (see Ephesians 4:22–24 and comment).

When we first believe in Christ, we are spiritually like newborn infants. We must grow. We must become more and more like Christ. How does our new spiritual self grow? It grows through the **renewing** of our minds. By the word **mind**[61] Paul means here our inner mind, or heart, from which all our thoughts, desires, and goals arise. From our **mind** come all the sinful thoughts and desires of our "old self"; and from our **mind** come all the good thoughts and desires of our "new self." As is our mind, so will be our thoughts and actions. Thus, when we become Christians, it is above all our **mind** that must be changed. This is why Paul says here: **. . . be transformed by the renewing of your mind.**

It is actually God who takes the leading part in renewing our minds. On our own strength, we cannot make our "old evil self" into a "righteous self." But even though God Himself creates our "new spiritual self," we must still **put on the new self** (Ephesians 4:24). Therefore, we can understand that Paul's expression, **renewing of your mind**, actually means "putting on your new self." That is, we must "put on" new thoughts, new desires, new goals, new actions—all of which are according to God's **good, pleasing and perfect will.**

What is God's **good, pleasing and perfect will**? It can be summed up in the two greatest commandments: **Love the Lord your God with all your heart and with all your soul and with all your mind and with all your strength. . . . Love your neighbor as yourself** (Mark 12:30–31). All other commands and rules of conduct are derived from these two great commandments (see Matthew 22:40; Romans 13:8–10; Galatians 5:14 and comments).

It is easy to say: "Love God; love your neighbor." All men agree that love is important. But in what way are we to love God and our neighbor in our daily lives? Every day we encounter many different situations. According to this law of love, what must we do in each situation?—that is the question. What is God's will in each of the small things that make up our daily life?

If our minds have been renewed—**transformed**—then we can know in each situation what God's **good, pleasing and perfect will** is. We learn through our **mind** what God's will is. When our mind is darkened and disobedient, we cannot discern God's will. But when our mind is transformed and renewed, we can then discern God's will in almost every situation. We are then **able to test and approve what God's will is.**

To discern God's will, two things are necessary. First, God must reveal His will. He does this in three ways: through the Bible, through the Holy Spirit, and through fellow Christians.

The second thing necessary for discerning God's will is that we must actively be seeking His will. How must we seek it? First, we must transform and renew our mind; that's the main step. Second, we must pray. Third, we must study the Bible. Fourth, we must listen to the advice of other Christians. Fifth, we must submit

---

[60] In the Greek language: "keep on being transformed."

[61] Here Paul uses the word **mind** in a different sense than he used it in Romans 7:23. There he used **mind** to mean "man's spirit," or a "mind controlled by man's spirit." Here in Romans 12:2, however, Paul uses the word **mind** in its most ordinary sense.

ourselves to God's will and agree to obey it—whatever it is.[62] When we have done all these things, then we shall know what God's **good, pleasing and perfect will is.**

The Proper Use of Spiritual Gifts (12:3–8)

3 Paul says here that he is writing **by the grace given to** him. The **grace**[63] given to Paul was his appointment from God to be an apostle (see Ephesians 3:7). Along with the appointment, Paul was also given **grace**—that is, the strength and ability—to do the work of an apostle. That work was to establish churches, to preach the Gospel, and to teach and admonish believers.

Here Paul writes: **Do not think of yourself more highly than you ought**. That is, we must think of ourselves **with sober judgment**—rightly, honestly, and as objectively as possible. We should not overestimate or exaggerate our weaknesses, nor should we unduly criticize ourselves; for this leads to a false humility.[64] On the other hand, we must not think too highly of ourselves, because this leads to pride.[65]

Paul shows us by what measure we must think of ourselves: . . . **think of yourself . . . in accordance with the measure of faith God has given you**. In this verse, the word **faith** has a special meaning which is different from its usual meaning. Here **faith** means a special gift of God which we use in faith. Some Christians are given the gift of preaching. Some are given the gift of teaching, or of hospitality. We must not despise these gifts of "faith" which God has given us; rather, we must use them with humility and thankfulness. Let us remember that all good gifts ultimately come from God; we are not entitled to boast of them as if they came from us!

Recalling Jesus' parable of the talents (Matthew 25:14–30), if we have received five talents from God, we should not act as if we had received only one or two. We should use all five talents for God **in accordance with the measure of faith God has given** [us].

4–5 God has given different functions and abilities to the various members of our bodies. Christ's church is like a human body: God has given to each Christian in the church a different function or ability—or perhaps more than one (see 1 Corinthians 12:12,27 and comment).

. . . **each member belongs to all the others** (verse 5). We Christians belong to each other just as the members of a body "belong" to each other. Therefore, we must use our gifts for the benefit of each other—not for our own benefit (see 1 Corinthians 12:7; 1 Peter 4:10 and comments).

Therefore, since we are all in one body, the church, it is essential that we think of ourselves and each other **with sober judgment** (verse 3). Let not the little finger think it is as big as the foot!

6 We all have been given different gifts **according to the grace given us** (see

---

[62] Many Christians are unsure of what God's will is because they are not willing to commit themselves totally to doing whatever God wants. God will not fully reveal His will to those who have not submitted themselves completely to Him. We must first say to God: "I will do anything you want." Then God will show us clearly what He wants us to do.

[63] In the New Testament, **grace** has two main meanings. Most commonly it means the undeserved love and mercy of God toward sinful man. But the second meaning of **grace** is a special appointment or gift, by which one is enabled to carry out a specific task for God. Here in this verse, Paul has this second meaning in mind. For further discussion, see Word List: Grace.

[64] Some people have a deeply rooted "inferiority complex," which is almost unconscious. While the humility of such people may not be false, their self-image certainly is. Such people need help in thinking "rightly" about themselves.

[65] The problem of thinking too highly of oneself is undoubtedly more common than the problem of thinking too lowly of oneself. If one is in doubt, it is better to err on the side of thinking lowly!

1 Corinthians 12:4–11 and comment). In this verse (as in verse 3) the word **grace** means a special "ability" or "calling."[66] In using this expression, **according to the grace given us,** Paul means the same thing that he meant in verse 3 by the expression, **in accordance with the measure of faith God has given** [us].

Notice that we Christians receive God's gifts **according to the grace given us,** or **in accordance with the measure of faith God has given** [us]. We receive gifts according to measurement, according to limits. However, Jesus Christ received the gifts of the Holy Spirit without measure, **without limit** (John 3:34), because He was God Himself.

In this verse Paul mentions the gift of **prophesying.** PROPHECY is a word that comes directly from God. A prophet, when he is prophesying, speaks only what God directly leads or inspires him to speak. The prophet must speak **in accordance with the measure of faith** given him; that is, he must speak to the extent that God has given him words to speak—no more, no less. A prophet does not speak on his own authority, but only on God's authority. Anyone who receives a word from God and speaks it is, in fact, prophesying. A prophecy isn't only a prediction about the future; it is often a word of encouragement or admonition for the present. Thus a preacher will sometimes prophesy in the course of his preaching (see 1 Corinthians 14:1,3; 1 Peter 4:11 and comments).

7 The gift of **serving** includes all the different kinds of assistance and service we offer to others. Christians need to "put on" the attitude of servants (see Mark 10:43–44 and comment). We need to serve with our whole heart. Indeed, whatever we do, we must do it whole-heartedly, as if we were doing it for the Lord[67] (see Ephesians 6:7). If, for example, our gift is **teaching, let** [us] **teach**—that is, let us teach whole-heartedly.

8 Notice that **encouraging**[68] others is also a gift, and it is an extremely important one. The gift of encouragement does not include rebuking and correcting others (though that may at times be necessary); rather, it means strengthening and comforting others. Encouragement or exhortation is always given for another person's welfare and benefit. When we meet and speak with each other, how often do we give a word of encouragement? When was the last time we encouraged a brother or sister? How important such encouragement might be for someone—even today!

. . . if it is contributing to the needs of others, let him give generously. When we give, let us not calculate the cost, but let us give liberally (see Matthew 6:3–4 and comment). That is how God has given His gifts to us (2 Corinthians 9:6–8; James 1:5). Let us not give to others in the hope of gaining something in return (Luke 6:33–34). We must give to others not for our own benefit but for theirs! In particular, we should give to those who can never repay us; if we do, we shall be repaid by God (see Luke 14:12–14).

. . . if it is leadership, let him govern diligently. The leaders of the church must govern with care and diligence; theirs is a big responsibility.

. . . if it is showing mercy, let him do it cheerfully. Sometimes when we are doing something merciful for someone else, we are not happy about it; we do it begrudgingly. We may be caring for a very sick person—someone with foul infected wounds, for example, which are repulsive to us—and our displeasure may show on our face. Furthermore, those who most need our mercy are usually not in a happy or pleasant state of mind themselves. All the more reason, then, that we should minister to these uncheerful people **cheerfully**!

---

[66] For further discussion, see footnote to comment on verse 3.

[67] Of course, whenever we serve others, we are also serving the Lord Jesus (see Matthew 25:34–40 and comment).

[68] In place of the word **encouraging,** some translations of the Bible say "exhorting."

Some Principles of Christian Living (12:9–21)

9 In verses 3–8, Paul has talked about different gifts and different kinds of work. Now he turns his attention to some of the general duties that apply to all Christians at all times.

In the Christian life, the first and greatest principle is always love. Our love must be **sincere**. True love arises from our inner being, from our spirit. If our love is just on the outside, then it is a false and hypocritical love, and it will not endure. A person whose love is false and hypocritical seeks only his own interests and welfare. On the other hand, a person whose love is **sincere** seeks only the interests of God and the welfare of others.

Hate what is evil. This world of men is evil; it is under the control of Satan. Therefore, to say, **Hate what is evil**, is the same as saying, **Do not conform any longer to the pattern of this world** (verse 2).

. . . cling to what is good. Hold it fast! Satan is always trying to draw us away from what is good; therefore, we must **cling** to it.

10 How should Christians love one another? We must love each other with **brotherly love** (see Hebrews 13:1). We must be **devoted** to one another like parents are devoted to their children. Christians should love all men, but they should especially love their brothers and sisters in the church (see Galatians 6:10; 1 Peter 4:8 and comments). We should love each other as Christ loved us (see John 13:34–35; 1 John 3:16–18 and comments).

Love is respectful; the person who loves his brother also honors his brother. We must always regard others as being above ourselves (see Philippians 2:3 and comment). If we do this, division and strife in the church will never arise. Let the other person have the honor, the position, the credit; let us not seek these things for ourselves.

Why is there division in our churches? Because each of us is seeking honor for himself and not giving it to others. We suppose ourselves to be "straight" and the other man "crooked." We imagine our work to be worthy, and the other man's unworthy. We are always elevating ourselves in our own eyes. When we do this, division is not far away.

11 **. . . keep your spiritual fervor**. Paul is referring here to both our own human spirit and to the Holy Spirit. To keep our **spiritual fervor** means that our human spirit must keep responding to God's Holy Spirit. Through the Holy Spirit our own spirits are made alive; through the Holy Spirit we are filled with **zeal**. Therefore, let us do nothing to hinder the work of the Holy Spirit in our lives (see 1 Thessalonians 5:19).

12 Because of our **hope**, we can be **joyful**. Because of our **hope**—that is, hope in salvation—we can persevere in times of trouble and suffering (Romans 5:2–4). And trouble and suffering are going to come one day to every Christian (2 Timothy 3:12). On that day, especially, we will need to remember this verse: **Be joyful in hope**.

In order to be **patient in affliction**, we will need to be **faithful in prayer**. Through prayer we will receive the strength and patience to endure affliction (Acts 1:14; 1 Thessalonians 5:17).

13 **Share with God's people who are in need**. We must never neglect our own Christian brothers and sisters who are in need; we must meet their needs before we go out and meet the needs of non-Christians. But we are only required to provide what they need, not what they want. Sometimes Christians can spend so much time caring for each other that they end up neglecting their neighbors outside the church.

To practice **hospitality** is an important Christian duty. We should always be looking for opportunities to practice hospitality—instead of doing it only when we have to! (1 Peter 4:9). And remember, let us not be hospitable only to those who can be hospitable to us in return. Rather let us be especially hospitable to those who will never be able to pay us back (see Matthew 5:46–47; Luke 6:32–34; 14:12–14 and comments).

14 In this verse, the word **bless** means to show kindness and love. We should pray that God will bless our enemies (see Matthew 5:43–44; Luke 6:27–28 and comment). It is not by our own strength but only by Christ's Holy Spirit that we can love our enemies in this way.

Christ is our example: instead of resisting, He prayed; instead of accusing, He forgave; instead of hating, He loved; instead of bringing death, He brought life (see Luke 23:34).

15 **Rejoice with those who rejoice.** Sometimes we are unhappy when our brother is happy or successful. This comes from envy (see Luke 15:25–30). Sometimes we are inwardly happy when our brother has failed, or is sad or in trouble. We are secretly pleased at his fall; because when he is "down," we feel "up."

But Paul says: Let this not be. When our brother is rejoicing, let us rejoice with him (see 1 Corinthians 12:26). When our brother is sad, let us share in his sadness. When our brother is burdened, let us help him carry that burden (see Galatians 6:2 and comment).

16 **Live in harmony. . . . Do not be proud.** In order to remain in harmony with one another we must remain humble; pride destroys unity (see Ephesians 4:2–3 and comment).

If we are of one body, then we must be of one mind (see 1 Corinthians 1:10; Philippians 2:2 and comments). Let us not look down on each other. Is the hand better than the eye? Is the tongue better than the foot? No. Therefore, let us respect one another (see 1 Corinthians 12:21–27 and comment).

. . . be willing to associate with people of low position.[69] This means to be willing not only to associate with those of lower position but also to do their work. Paul's point here is that Christians must never make differences between people according to such things as birth, caste, or financial status (see James 2:1–4 and comment). And especially they must not make such distinctions among fellow believers! Since we are all members of one body, those believers of higher position must willingly associate with those of lower position.

Do not be conceited. Let us not consider ourselves wise. It's good to be wise, but it's not good to think we're wise! Let us not always go around thinking, "I'm right." The man who is always sure he's right is very hard to teach; even God can't teach such a man.

People who are educated often become **conceited**—that is, wise in their own eyes. Let not the educated people look down on the uneducated. True wisdom isn't learned mainly in schools! It is learned mainly from God—from His Spirit, from His word (the Bible), and from fellow believers in the church. Often the uneducated members of the church will have more wisdom on certain matters than the educated will!

17 **Do not repay anyone evil for evil** (see Matthew 5:38–41; 1 Thessalonians 5:15; 1 Peter 3:9 and comments).

We must not only do what is right in the eyes of God; we must do what is right in the eyes of **everybody**[70] (2 Corinthians 8:21). Otherwise, we shall bring dishonor on Christ (see Romans 14:16; 1 Thessalonians 5:22 and comments).

18 It is not possible all the time to **live at peace with everyone**. We cannot live totally at peace with some people—evildoers, for example. We must oppose evil. We must oppose those who oppose Christ, especially those who dishonor Him and seek to block His work. But our opposition must be under God's guidance; we must not engage in conflict unless God is going to be glorified by it. Paul is here giving a general rule: **If it is possible,** live at peace—even with your enemies.[71]

However, within the church there must always be peace (see Romans 14:19; Ephesians 4:3 and comments).

19 **Do not take revenge.** This command is the same as Paul's command in

---

[69] In place of the words **willing to associate with people of low position**, some translations of the Bible say, "willing to do menial work."

[70] Sometimes what is "right" in the eyes of men is evil in the eyes of God. If that is the case, then we must do only what is right in God's eyes (see Acts 4:18–20; 5:29).

[71] For further discussion of this subject, see General Article: Resisting Evil.

verse 17: **Do not repay anyone evil for evil.**

We must never take any kind of revenge for any reason (Proverbs 20:22). When we are hurt in some way by another person, even by a Christian brother, our natural tendency is to find some way of getting even, of taking revenge. What kinds of things do we usually do to take revenge? We might refuse to speak to the person who hurt us. Not to speak is itself a form of revenge; by not speaking we are withdrawing our friendship and fellowship from that person. Our inner desire is to hurt him. And that is revenge. Instead of refusing to talk to the person who has hurt us, we should go to him and forgive him! We should try as quickly as possible to forget the wrong he has done.

Furthermore, it is not necessary for us to take revenge: God Himself will always avenge us. "**It is mine to avenge,**" says God (Deuteronomy 32:35). God will judge all men; He will reward every man according to his work—whether it be good or evil (see Romans 2:6; 2 Corinthians 5:10; Hebrews 10:30; Revelation 22:12 and comments).

20 Paul here quotes from Proverbs 25:21–22. The meaning of the proverb is that if we do good to our enemy, he will often become embarrassed and ashamed for the wrong he has done us. He will "burn with shame." This is one of the meanings of the words: **In doing this, you will heap burning coals on his head.** The **burning coals** are also a sign of God's judgment; if our enemy does not repent, our kindness to him will make his offense worse by contrast, and his judgment will be more severe.

There is an additional meaning in this proverb: namely, the best way to overcome your enemy is to turn him into your friend!

21 Evil is all around us. Sometimes Christians become discouraged and cast down by evil. They suffer on account of evil men. Sometimes they cry out, "I can't take it!" Their faith weakens; they become separated from God.

Let this not happen to us! Even though **evil** is all around us, we can with God's help **overcome evil with good**. Just as light always overcomes darkness, so good always overcomes evil.

Paul's words, **overcome evil with good,** are a command, not a suggestion! Whenever God gives a command, He always provides the means and the strength needed to carry out the command.

CHAPTER 13

Submission to Authorities (13:1–7)

1 All authority comes ultimately from God. No matter whose authority we're talking about—whether a king's, a president's, a general's, or anyone else's—their authority comes ultimately from God (Proverbs 8:15–16; John 19:10–11).

Therefore, whenever we disobey someone in authority over us, we are also disobeying God (verse 2). Instead, we should submit willingly to all authorities, as we would submit to God Himself. We must obey all authorities over us—no matter whether they be government officials, military officers, administrators, our employer, or our own parents. And certainly we must obey the leaders of the church, such as pastors and elders. However, in this section of Chapter 13, Paul is talking mainly about government authorities.

God has not only given authority to our leaders but He has appointed them all to their positions, that they might promote the well-being of the people under them (see 1 Timothy 2:1–2).

Here a question arises: What do we do if the one in authority over us is evil and disobeys God's law? Should we obey the authority under such circumstances? The answer is no. We should not obey the authority in that particular matter in which he is disobeying God's law. When God's law and man's law are opposed, we must always obey God's law (see Acts 4:18–20; 5:29).

However, most human authorities are not predominantly evil, and most of their laws do not oppose God's law. Therefore, we can follow the general rule given in this verse; namely, that we should submit to governing authorities (see Titus 3:1; 1 Peter 2:13–14).

If government officials oppose Christians and try to prevent them from preaching and witnessing, what should the Christians do? They must obey God and continue to witness and to speak His word whenever a suitable occasion arises. But, at the same time, they must be humble, cautious, and wise. They must not look for trouble; they must not oppose the government without good reason. As far as possible, Christians should obey all other government laws that are not opposed to God's law.

2 When we (without God's leading) oppose a government authority, we oppose God; and we shall be punished for it. But it will be God who punishes us, and usually He will use the very government authority we have opposed to carry out the punishment (verse 4).

If a government authority is evil and opposes God's law, then we must disobey him; but we shall still be punished—not by God, but by the authority himself. And we must be ready to accept that punishment without grumbling.

3–4 In this chapter, Paul is talking mainly about good rulers, not evil ones. Good rulers don't cause trouble for people who **do what is right** and who obey the law; rather, they punish only those who do wrong and break the law.

If we keep doing what is right, we will usually have nothing to fear from a ruler. **For he is God's servant to do you good** (verse 4). What **good** does the ruler do? He maintains peace (1 Timothy 2:2) and protects us from evil men.

If we do wrong, then the ruler becomes God's **servant** or **agent** to punish us. The **sword** mentioned in verse 4 is the sign of the ruler's authority. It is also the means of carrying out the ruler's authority. The ruler is given his sword (authority) by God, and the ruler will use it to punish wrongdoing.

The ruler **does not bear his sword for nothing**. That is, he does not exercise his authority for no purpose; he will not punish people without reason. Rather, the ruler "bears his sword" to punish and discourage evil.

Remember that in these verses Paul is referring primarily to good rulers who in most things do not actively oppose God. There are, of course, other rulers who are predominantly evil. But the authority of evil rulers also comes from God![72] Therefore, in most matters Christians must submit to evil rulers also. But if, in a particular matter, the evil ruler opposes God and demands that we oppose God too, then in that matter we must boldly refuse to obey the ruler.

5 Let us not obey our rulers only out of fear; let us also obey them **because of conscience**—that is, because of our love for God. Let us obey them from our heart (see Ephesians 6:6–7 and comment).

6 Let us also be happy to pay taxes to governing authorities. They are God's servants; therefore, through our taxes, we help them do God's work (Matthew 17:24–27; Mark 12:13–17).

7 We must pay to everyone whatever we owe them. If it's **revenue** we owe, then let us pay it. If it's **respect** we owe someone, let us pay it. If **honor**, let us pay it. We should owe no man anything (see verse 8).

Love Is the Fulfillment of the Law (13:8–10)

8 Having talked about our obligations to rulers and leaders, Paul now looks once again at our obligations to all men.

Let no debt remain outstanding.[73]

---

[72] All authority comes from God, even the authority of the most evil rulers (see verse 1).

[73] In place of the words, **Let no debt remain outstanding,** some translations of the Bible say, "Owe no one anything."

Does this mean that we should never borrow money or anything else? No, it can't mean that; because the Bible teaches that it is good to loan things to others (Psalm 37:25–26; 112:5; Matthew 5:42; Luke 6:35). Since it is good to loan, it must also be all right to borrow! But the meaning of this passage is this: We must pay back our loans as quickly as possible. If there is a time limit on the loan, we must pay it back within the time limit—or we become, in effect, thieves of the other's person's money or property. How often we borrow money and then are slow to pay it back, or fail to pay it back at all! This is very wrong. **The wicked borrow and do not repay** (Psalm 37:21). If someone has shown us love by lending something to us in time of need, then we must show our gratitude by paying the loan back—on time. We must not remain in debt to anyone; that is Paul's teaching. Whatever we owe people, whether money or something else—possessions, salaries to our workers, respect for others—we must pay it quickly.

There is one thing, however, that we can (and must) keep on owing; and that one thing is love. Love is a kind of debt. For example, we can never love God as much as He loves us; we will never be able to love Him enough to pay Him back for His love to us. Thus, we shall always be in debt to God—we shall always have a debt of love.

The same thing is true in our relations with our **fellow man**.[74] Following Christ's example, we must act toward other men as if we were "in debt" to them, as if we owed them love. And in doing this, we shall be obeying God's two great commandments to love Him and to love our neighbor (Mark 12:30–31). The entire moral law is based on these two commandments (see Matthew 22:40; Galatians 5:14 and comment).

Here one more question arises: Who is this **fellow man** we are supposed to love? Is he only our Christian brother? Is he only our fellow villager? No, our **fellow man**—our neighbor—is any person in need (see Luke 10:25–37).

9–10 Love is the **fulfillment of the law** (verse 10). The law teaches us how we must love. If we were able always and in all ways to love all men perfectly, then we would be fulfilling not only the two greatest commandments but all the other commands of the law as well.

Paul here repeats four of the ten commandments (Exodus 20:13–15,17). If we love our fellow man, how could we murder him? Or how could we steal from him? Thus we see that if we obey the command to love our neighbor, we will be obeying these other commands too. The command to love our neighbor as ourselves can be expressed in another form: **. . . in everything, do to others what you would have them do to you** (Matthew 7:12; Luke 6:31). This has been called the "golden rule."

Love is not just something hidden in our hearts. Love is practical; love manifests itself. Love not only **does no harm to its neighbor**; it also does its neighbor all kinds of good!

Here another question arises. The second greatest commandment says: **Love your neighbor as yourself** (verse 9). Does this mean that we should also love ourselves as much as we love our neighbor?

This is a profound question. Jesus said, "**If anyone would come after me, he must deny himself**" (Mark 8:34). But even if we deny ourselves, we still "love" and value our own bodies; that's natural. Loving our neighbor as ourselves means, then, that we love our neighbor as much as we naturally love our own bodies. We must not love ourselves more than our neighbor; to do that is selfishness. Instead, we must love our neighbor more than we love ourselves. Only when we do this will we love our neighbor as we naturally love ourselves. Since we naturally love ourselves most of all, then we'll have to love our neighbor "most of all" if we are going to truly love

---

[74] In place of the words **fellow man**, some translations of the Bible say "neighbor." The meaning is the same.

him "as ourself" (see Mark 12:31; Galatians 5:14 and comment).

How much must we love God? As much as we love ourselves? No, much more than that. The greatest commandment says: **Love the Lord your God with all your heart and with all your soul and with all your mind and with all your strength** (Mark 12:30). If we fulfilled this command, there wouldn't be any love left over for ourselves! And that's the point: All of our love should go to God and to our neighbor; we should save none for ourselves.[75]

The Day Is Near (13:11–14)

11 The word **slumber** in this verse means "spiritual slumber." The time of our **salvation**, which Paul refers to here, is the end of the world, when Jesus will come again and destroy the works of Satan, and when the bodies of all believers will be resurrected. That is the final step in our salvation—the resurrection or **redemption of our bodies** (Romans 8:23). To believe in Jesus was the first step; now as each day passes, that final stage of our salvation draws nearer. But exactly when that final day will be, no one knows but God (Mark 13:32).

We need always to keep in mind that one day Jesus will come again and then this world will end. Jesus could come tomorrow. He will come by surprise. That final day will come **like a thief in the night** (1 Thessalonians 5:1–2). Christ says to all believers: **"Be on your guard! Be alert! You do not know when that time will come. . . . Watch!"** (Mark 13:33–37). In other words: "Wake up!" It's time for us to wake up from our spiritual **slumber**; from now on we must remain alert and ready.

How can we remain ready? By always doing Christ's will. If we are walking according to His will, then we will be ready.

Imagine an angel from heaven coming and saying that Christ was going to return to earth in one month. If we received such news, would it make a difference in how we lived? Would our spiritual lives be any different during that last month than they were before we got the news? For most of us, the answer would be yes. But, in fact, receiving such news should not make that much difference in our lives.[76] We should right now be living each day as if Jesus was going to come tomorrow.

If Jesus came tomorrow, what would he find us doing? **If he comes suddenly, do not let him find you sleeping** (Mark 13:36).

12 The **night** of darkness and sin—the reign of Satan—is nearly over; **the day is almost here**, when Christ will come again and defeat Satan once and for all. Therefore, let us get up at once and **put aside the deeds of darkness**—that is, take off our **night** clothes—and put on the **armor of light**—that is, our **day** clothes (see Ephesians 4:22–24; 5:8–11; 6:11,13–17; 1 Thessalonians 5:4–8; James 5:8–9; 1 Peter 4:7–8 and comments).

When Jesus comes, which clothes will He find us wearing? Our night clothes, or our day clothes?

13 In this verse, Paul mentions a few of the **deeds of darkness**. More complete lists can be found in Romans 1:29–31 and Galatians 5:19–21.

14 **Rather, clothe yourselves with the Lord Jesus Christ** (see Galatians 3:26–27 and comment). Jesus is our **day** clothing. Jesus is our **armor of light** (verse 12). Jesus is all that we need.

Before we can clothe ourselves with Jesus, we must first put aside our night clothes, our old sinful self (Ephesians 4:22). To clothe ourselves with Christ is to live by the Holy Spirit. If we live by the

---

[75] Even though we Christians should not love ourselves, there is an important sense in which we should value ourselves as cherished and beloved children of God. We must not despise ourselves. If we have a negative and unhealthy image of ourselves, we will not be able to love God and others as we should.

[76] There would be some change in our activities, no doubt; projects of over a month's duration could safely be canceled!

Spirit, we will **not gratify the desires of the sinful nature** (Galatians 5:16). Normal bodily necessities—food, clothing, shelter, fellowship—we must make provision for. But for the **desires of the sinful nature**, we must make no provision.

CHAPTER 14

Do Not Condemn Your Brother (14:1–12)

1 In every church in every country there are those **whose faith is weak**, those who have trouble distinguishing between essential and non-essential beliefs. Those who are weak in faith are strongly influenced by non-essential beliefs and rules, and they live according to them. If they fail to follow these beliefs, such people begin to doubt if they are truly saved; their faith is indeed weak.

Paul says that we must accept such brothers and sisters without criticizing and judging them for these unnecessary beliefs. These beliefs concern **disputable matters**. It is no sin to believe in them, and it is no virtue not to believe in them; either way, these matters are not important to our salvation or to our fellowship in Christ. These matters are not worth arguing over.[77] Above all, we must not look down on our brothers or sisters whose faith is weak. We must not pass judgment on them for their beliefs about these disputable matters (Matthew 7:1). Rather, we should accept them in love just as they are.

In this section, Paul mentions two of the non-essential beliefs or rules that were followed by some of the Roman Christians whose faith was weak. The first rule was: We must not eat meat. The second rule was: We must regard certain days as "better" or more **sacred** than other days (verse 5). Paul mentions these two rules as examples. As we study this section, we should ask ourselves: Are there other examples of such "rules" which might exist in our own church? Because Paul's teaching here doesn't apply only to these two particular beliefs in the Roman church; it applies to any such beliefs in our own churches as well.

2 Those in the Roman church whose faith was strong knew that only by their faith could they please God; it was not necessary to observe all the Jewish religious regulations in order to please God.

But the weak in faith (mainly those who had formerly been Jews) thought that it was still necessary to obey all the Jewish regulations. Thus in the Roman church two opinions had sprung up: the weak in faith said it was wrong to eat meat; the strong in faith said it was all right to eat meat.

3 When two such conflicting opinions arise in a church, what usually happens? An argument develops, and then, eventually, a split comes in the church. "Let this not be!" is Paul's plea. The brother who is strong in faith **must not look down on** the brother who is weak in faith. And at the same time, the brother who is weak in faith **must not condemn** the brother who is strong in faith for breaking some non-essential rule. The strong brother can't be condemned, because he has been justified by his faith; **God has accepted him**. How common it is in our churches to see those of weaker faith condemning and criticizing those whose faith is stronger! How grievous this is to Jesus!

4 In this verse Paul speaks to the brother with weaker faith, and tells him not to judge the stronger brother.

We must never judge another Christian. He is not our servant, but Christ's

[77] It is wrong to argue over these matters, but it is not wrong to discuss them during a Bible study. We should not be afraid to discuss **disputable matters**, but we should do so only in a spirit of love and humility.

servant; and he will give an account of himself not to us but to Christ. Our job is to love and accept that Christian, just as Christ loves and accepts him. Let us not reject one whom Christ accepts; let us not criticize one whom Christ values.

How quick we are to judge each other! But let us not do so. We must leave all judging to Christ. He is the master of us all, and He will judge each one of us. Since we will all have to give an account of ourselves to Christ one day, we'd be better off now to concentrate on our own faults rather than on the faults of others.

5 In addition to the Sabbath day,[78] the Jews observed many other special days throughout the year. They considered these days to be more **sacred** than other days. On such days they would fast and observe other Jewish religious traditions. Some of the Jews who became Christians continued to observe these special days; they thought they must do so in order to please God. They didn't realize that Christians didn't have to observe such days. Their faith was weak; perhaps they didn't feel that God would be pleased with their weak faith alone. They thought they had to add something—some work or ritual—to make God happy.

Those Christians who are strong in faith consider every day the same. Every day they must give their lives fully to Christ's service. Every day must be spent completely for Christ—not more so on one day, or less so on another. Therefore, they say, how can one day be more **sacred** or important than another? It cannot. Are we to be more holy on one day than on the next? No. We are to be equally holy every day.

True, God commands us to rest one day a week (Exodus 20:8). On that day we have more time to worship Him and go to church. But that doesn't mean we are more holy on that day.

Furthermore, the Bible doesn't say which day of the week should be set aside as the day of rest, or Sabbath. The Bible only says we should work six days and rest the seventh. The Jews early in their history chose Saturday to be the Sabbath.

Some Christians believe that the day Jesus was born (Christmas) and the day He rose from the dead (Easter) are especially sacred days. But other Christians say that in our hearts we should celebrate Jesus' birth and resurrection every day of the year. Yes, on these special days it is suitable to have special services of praise and witness, and to spend extra time worshiping Christ. But we do this not because of some religious law or because the day is sacred in itself. Rather, we set these days aside by our own choice as special occasions to praise and worship Christ and to bear witness to Him. Christians do not celebrate days; they celebrate Christ.

There is nothing wrong with observing special days as long as we do it to the glory of God. There is nothing wrong with observing every day alike as long as we observe every day to the glory of God. If what we do is for God's glory, then it doesn't matter which of these two opinions we hold. **Each one should be fully convinced in his own mind**. That is, each Christian must decide what is right for him according to his own conscience. **To his own master he stands or falls** (verse 4). It is not our place to judge each other (see verses 10–13).

6 Therefore, whichever we do—eat meat or not eat meat, observe special days or not observe them—let us do it for Christ's sake, to glorify Him. Let the man who eats meat give thanks for his meat and glorify God. Let the man who eats

---

[78] The Jewish Sabbath day begins at sundown on Friday and continues until sundown on Saturday. The Jews regard the Sabbath as holy; on that day they worship at the synagogue and do no work (Exodus 20:8–11).

The early Christians also observed the Sabbath on Saturday; but later on in New Testament times, they began to observe the Sabbath on Sunday, the first day of the week (Acts 20:7). This practice still prevails among Christians in most countries.

vegetables give thanks for his vegetables and glorify God.[79]

The main thing to remember is that the Holy Spirit will guide each of us in these matters through our conscience and according to the strength of our faith. Each Christian must obey his conscience. We must not judge each other's conscience! The things of a man's conscience are between him and God alone (verse 22).

7–8 The one purpose of our lives is to please God. It is not to please ourselves. When we believe in Jesus, we give our lives to Him. Our life is no longer our own, it is His. Before we believed, we lived for ourselves. Now that we believe in Jesus, we **live** for Him (see 2 Corinthians 5:15 and comment). And we will also **die** for Him, because through death He calls us to be with Him in heaven.

Therefore, whatever we do, we each belong to the Lord Jesus. Both the brother weak in faith and the brother strong in faith belong to the Lord, and He accepts them both.

9 After Christ died, He descended into hell and became the Lord of the dead. Then, when He rose from the dead, He became the Lord of the living. Therefore, whether we are dead or alive, He is our Lord.

10 It is not right to judge another man's servant. Therefore, since we are all Christ's servants, we have no business judging one another. Christ will judge His own servants (2 Corinthians 5:10). We will all **stand before God's judgment seat**. In God's sight we are all worthy to be condemned; thus none of us has the right to judge another. If this is so, why, then, does so much condemning and judging go on among Christians? Let it stop! (see Galatians 5:15 and comment). Rather we ought to be so busy working on our own faults that we have no time left over for judging our brother (see 2 Corinthians 13:5).

One more thing needs to be said on the subject of condemning and judging. The condemnation and judgment that goes on among Christians is an almost unconscious habit; we are hardly aware we are doing it. For example, whenever we say about someone else, "He's not a good fellow," we are really judging him. We say, "I've not judged anyone." But the fact is that we do it all the time. Even if we don't say a word, we judge others by our critical or disapproving look. And even if we make no outward sign, we still judge the person in our thoughts. We need to pray constantly that God will guard our tongues and thoughts.

11–12 Here Paul quotes from Isaiah 45:23 (see Philippians 2:10–11). Every man—both Christian and non-Christian—will bow down before God on the day of judgment. On that day every one of us will have to confess his sins to God. That is, **each of us will give an account of himself to God** (verse 12). And we won't be giving an account of one another's sins; we'll be giving an account only of our own!

Do Not Cause a Brother to Fall (14:13–23)

13 The main teaching of Chapter 14 is summarized in this verse: Both the Christian who is weak in faith and the Christian who is strong in faith must stop judging each other. We must not judge either in word or in thought (see Matthew 7:1–5 and comment). From now on let us stop concentrating on whether it is right or not to eat meat, whether it is right or not to observe special days, or other such matters. Rather, let us concentrate on not putting a **stumbling block or obstacle** in our brother's way. That is the most important thing (see 1 Corinthians 8:4–

[79] Whatever we eat or drink, we must eat it and drink it for God's glory. Christians eat in order to live for God. Many people live in order to eat; they are called gluttons. Eating to keep our bodies healthy brings glory to God, if our bodies have been given to Him (Romans 12:1); a healthy body is more useful to God. But eating solely for pleasure or eating unhealthy food does not glorify God. Whatever we do, we need to ask ourselves: Is this going to glorify God or not? If what we do does not glorify God either directly or indirectly, then it is a sin.

13; 9:22–23; 10:23–33; Colossians 2:16 and comments).

14 The Jews regard many kinds of food to be ritually unclean, and in the Old Testament many laws are written about what the Jews can and cannot eat.

But Christ canceled all of those food laws. Therefore, even though he was a strict Jew himself, Paul says here that he is convinced that **no food is unclean in itself** (see Acts 10:9–16; 1 Timothy 4:4). Jesus taught that it's not what goes into a man's mouth that makes him unclean, but rather it's what comes out of his heart that makes him unclean (see Mark 7:14–23 and comment).

Paul here teaches another thing. If anyone whose faith is weak thinks that some particular food is unclean, **then for him it is unclean**. This means that that person should not eat that particular food, because according to his conscience, to eat it would be a sin. We must never go against the promptings of our conscience. If something seems like a sin to us, then we must not do that thing. Even though it is, in fact, not a sin, we still must not do it if we have any doubt about it. That is why Paul says that each person **should be fully convinced in his own mind** what is sinful for him and what is not (verse 5).

15 Paul now mentions the most important thing determining our relations with each other: we must act in love. For example, suppose that a brother believes in his conscience that he should not eat meat. And you believe in your conscience that it's all right to eat meat. Then suppose that you invite that brother to a meal and offer him meat. Not only that, suppose you pressure him into eating it—perhaps by making him feel bad if he doesn't eat it. Afterward, of course, that brother will be **distressed** in his conscience; his conscience will accuse him of having sinned. Because he believed it was a sin to eat meat, for him indeed it was a sin. Therefore, **because of what you eat**, you have caused your brother to sin. You have put a **stumbling block or obstacle** in your brother's path (verse 13). If you continue causing him to sin in this way, you will certainly **by your eating destroy your brother** spiritually.

If we love our brother, how can we act this way toward him? Not only that, Christ died for our brother! Are we going to **destroy** one whom Christ has saved? Heaven forbid! If Christ has given up His own life to save our brother, can we not give up a little meat for him? (see 1 Corinthians 8:13).

16 To be strong in faith is a **good** thing. To be free from the regulations of the Jewish law is also a **good** thing. But Paul writes here: Don't let what is **good** be spoken of as **evil**. That is, do not, by your **good**, do harm to your brother. If we do harm to our brother, then our "good" (our freedom, our strong faith) will be called **evil**. When this happens, both we and Christ are dishonored.

We know that no matter what we do, there will always be some people who will speak evil of us. However, let's not needlessly provide them with opportunities for doing so!

17–18 Here Paul gives another essential principle. It is not our outward behavior but our inner desires and motives that are most important to God. Whether to eat meat or not to eat meat isn't a very important matter. What is important is whether or not we love our brother. Our outward behavior arises from our inner mind, our heart, our character. If our mind, our heart, remains under the control of the Holy Spirit, both we and our brother will be led into **righteousness, peace and joy** (verse 17). This is **pleasing to God** (verse 18). God doesn't care what we eat or drink; what He cares about is whether there is **righteousness, peace and joy** in His church!

19 **Let us therefore make every effort to do what leads to peace** (see Romans 12:18; Ephesians 4:3 and comments).

Make every effort to do what leads to **mutual edification**. "Mutual edification" does not mean rebuking and accusing one another. Rather, it means teaching, advising, and strengthening one another, all for the purpose of building each other up in the Lord.

There can be no **peace** or **mutual**

edification when there is quarreling, accusation, and judgment going on among us.

20 Here Paul repeats the thought of verse 15. The **work of God** mentioned in this verse is "us"—mankind. We are God's creation, His **workmanship** (Ephesians 2:10). Therefore, let us not **destroy** our brother, who is a **work of God**.

To eat meat (for example) is not in itself a sin. But if by eating meat we might distress our brother or cause him to stumble, then to eat meat in that situation would be a sin (see 1 Corinthians 8:9–13 and comment).

21 To **eat meat** and **drink wine** are just examples of many activities that can cause our brother to stumble. Let us be constantly on the watch, not only in our own lives but also in the church, for any other activities which could **cause** [our] **brother to fall.**

22 The person who is strong in faith and is convinced it is all right to eat meat should eat his meat quietly in his own home. His eating meat should be a matter only between himself and God. In this way, he will **not condemn himself by what he approves**. That is, if his eating meat is **approved** between himself and God and gives no offense to others, his conscience will not **condemn** him for eating meat. But if, by doing something he approves of, he causes others to stumble, then he is committing a sin—and his conscience will indeed condemn him for it.

23 The word **faith** in this verse does not mean "faith" in Christ, but rather a deep certainty or conviction, about which one is **fully convinced in one's mind** (verse 5). One example would be the **faith** or conviction that it is all right to eat meat.

The **man who has doubts** is the man with weak faith, who believes he should not eat meat. Because he does not have the **faith** or conviction that it's all right to eat meat, he must not eat it. If we don't have the **faith** or conviction that something is all right to do, then we shouldn't do it. Even when something is not a sin in itself, if we have **doubts** about it and don't have **faith** that it's okay, then we must not do it—or for us it will be a sin.

CHAPTER 15

Pleasing Others, Not Ourselves (15:1–6)

1 In this verse, those **who are strong** are believers whose faith is strong. The **weak** are those whose faith is weak.

Those who are strong **ought to bear with the failings of the weak**. Not only must the strong **bear with** the failings of the weak, but they must also help to actually bear them. That is, the strong must encourage and strengthen the weak, not just tolerate them!

For example, suppose a weak brother has a problem controlling his temper. When he gets angry, his weakness is displayed. His weakness (quick temper) is a burden not only to himself but also to the church. Because when he gets angry, the members of the church also are troubled and embarrassed; they, too, are forced to "bear" his burden.

What is our responsibility toward a weak brother like this? Is it to rebuke and criticize him? No. That is not the answer. Our duty is to be patient with him, and to support and help him. In other words, our duty is to help him carry his burden (see Galatians 6:2 and comment).

Yes, one or two older brothers should privately, in love and humility, admonish and counsel the weak brother. It is the responsibility of older brothers and sisters in the church to admonish and correct the younger and weaker members. And the weak brother will listen to the older brothers, because they have come to him in love and for his good. However, more important than correcting that brother is to **bear with** him in love (see Ephesians 4:2 and comment).

Paul says we are **not to please ourselves**. Christ did not please Himself when He bore our sins on the cross. Let us behave toward our brother as Christ has behaved toward us (see 1 John 3:16 and comment).

2 Each Christian **should please his neighbor**, not himself. Here **neighbor** means a brother or sister in the church. We must please our "neighbor" **for his good, to build him up** (see 1 Corinthians 10:33). How do we build him up? By rebuking and criticizing him? No. We build him up by "pleasing" him.

In Chapter 14, Paul gave the example of eating meat. He taught that we must not rebuke or look down on the weak brother who thinks he should not eat meat. Instead, we must say to such a brother, "Okay, I won't eat meat either." Instead of pleasing ourselves, we must please our brother. In this way we can support and strengthen our weaker brother. In the end, because of our love, his faith will grow stronger. But if we argue with him and rebuke him, he will completely reject our counsel and friendship and become hurt and angry. We will have done nothing **for his good**—or for ours.

It is not necessary for us to advise and correct our brother in everything. Let us leave some place for the Holy Spirit to advise and correct him! Our main work is always to **bear with** our brother in love.

3 Paul here quotes from Psalm 69:9, which is written about Christ. Christ is an example for us. The Psalmist writes (as though Christ were speaking) that the **insults** that sinful men have given God "**have fallen on me**" (Christ). In other words, the **insults** or sins that we men have committed against God, together with the punishment that we should have received on account of them, have all fallen upon Christ. Christ has borne our punishment; He has died for our **insults** (sins). From this we know that **Christ did not please himself**, but instead "bore with the failings" of weak men (verse 1). Because of our wickedness, Christ received from us **insults**, hatred, and death. In view of this, can we not **bear with** a few failings of our weak brother!

4 Why does Paul quote so much from the **Scriptures**, that is, the Old Testament?[80] The reason is because the Scriptures have been written **to teach us** (see 2 Timothy 3:16–17 and comment). When we read in the Old Testament about men like Abraham, Moses and David, or when we read the prophecies of prophets like Isaiah and Jeremiah, then we learn to have the **endurance** which these men had, and from their example we receive **encouragement**, and from encouragement, **hope** (Romans 5:3–4).

5 It is God Himself who gives us **endurance** and **encouragement** through the Scriptures—which are, of course, His own living word. And in addition to that, He gives us **endurance** and **encouragement** directly through the Holy Spirit living within us.

Through the Holy Spirit, God also gives us a **spirit of unity**. Paul prays that the Roman Christians might be "of one mind" among themselves (see Romans 12:16; 1 Corinthians 1:10; 2 Corinthians 13:11; Philippians 2:2 and comments).

The expression, **as you follow Christ Jesus**, can also mean "in Christ Jesus." Our **unity of spirit** is always "in Christ." Only if we remain in Christ can we be "of one mind."

To have "one mind"—or **one heart and mouth** (verse 6)—means to be in agreement on important and essential matters. But on small non-essential matters it is quite all right to have different ideas. For example, let one man eat meat and another not. That is not an essential matter. But on important issues our minds should be united. For example, our minds should be united in our love for God and for our neighbor. With one mind—**with one heart and mouth**—we must strive to serve and **glorify** God and Christ. With one mind we must bear the fruit of the Holy Spirit—**love, joy, peace, patience**, etc. (Galatians 5:22–23). As an illustration, the branches of a tree grow as if they had "one mind," and they bear the

[80] In Paul's day, the New Testament had not been completed.

same tasty fruit. So should we do likewise!

6 Why is it so essential for us to be "of one mind"? It is essential because only when we are of one mind can we **glorify the God and Father of our Lord Jesus Christ**. If we are not of one mind, if there is quarreling and division among us, then we cannot glorify God. There are over sixty New Testament verses written on the subject of unity among believers; if our unity is so important to God, it should also be important to us!

Let us remember that unity among Christians is not just an external matter; it is also an internal matter, a matter of our minds. In order to have outward unity, there must first be inward unity. Oneness of mind rests on two foundations: first, faith in Christ; and second, mutual love and humility. Remember that wherever there is disunity of mind among Christians, sin will be always present; because only sin can destroy our unity.

Is there anybody today with whom we are not of one mind? If there is, then let us quickly do whatever is necessary to become united with that person, so that **with one heart and mouth** we might glorify God together.

The Gospel Is For the Gentiles Also (15:7–13)

7 How can we be of one mind? By accepting one another. Paul says here: **Accept one another.**[81] When we fully accept each other, our minds and hearts will be united. Does this mean that we must also accept another person's sins and mistakes? Yes, it does. Because that's how Christ accepted us. Christ fully accepted us—together with all of our sins and faults.

If we do not accept one another, how can we possibly glorify God? When we reject each other, we also reject Christ, who is present in every believer (see Matthew 10:40 and comment).

This accepting of one another must be from the heart, not just with the lips. We must accept one another as brothers and sisters of Jesus Christ. In this way our Lord will be glorified.

In Paul's time, the Christians of Jewish background had great difficulty accepting Christians of Gentile background, because the Jews, from their childhood up, had been taught to despise Gentiles. In a similar way, high-caste Christians have trouble accepting low-caste Christians, and educated Christians have trouble accepting uneducated Christians. The rich have trouble accepting the poor; the healthy have trouble accepting the sick. We all must fully accept and welcome each other. We are all in Christ's family.

Therefore, in verses 8–9, Paul explains that Christ came into the world not only for the Jews but also for the Gentiles—that is, for all people equally. The Jews have no grounds any longer for rejecting the Gentiles.

8 Christ came **to confirm the promises made to the patriarchs**—that is, Abraham, Isaac, Jacob, and others. The **promises** were the prophecies in the Old Testament which told of a Savior who was to come. But Christ not only "confirmed" the promises; He Himself was the fulfillment of the promises. Christ Himself was the Messiah,[82] the Savior, the One who was to come. Christ was the great king whose reign would never end. Christ was Abraham's **offspring**, or seed, through whom **all nations on earth** [would] **be blessed** (Genesis 22:18). Christ was first a **servant of the Jews**,[83] and His work at first was to show the Jews the way of salvation. Christ was a servant **on behalf of God's truth**, who, by fulfilling the promises in God's word, proved to the world that God's word was true.

---

[81] In place of the word **Accept**, some translations of the Bible say "welcome." The meaning in this context is the same.

[82] The name Messiah is the Hebrew word meaning "anointed one." "Christ" is the Greek word meaning the same thing. Thus Messiah is another name for Christ.

[83] In place of the word **Jews**, some translations of the Bible say "circumcision." The Jews were often referred to as "the circumcision," meaning a nation of circumcised people.

9 But Christ was not only a **servant of the Jews**; He also brought salvation to the Gentiles who believed in Him, so that the Gentiles also might **glorify God for his mercy**.

Here Paul quotes from Psalm 18:49. "**Therefore I** (Christ) **will praise you** (God) **among the Gentiles**." Here the Psalmist, King David, prophesies that the Gentiles will receive Christ's Gospel.

10 Here Paul quotes from Deuteronomy to show that the Gentiles will rejoice **with his people**—that is, with the Jews (Deuteronomy 32:43). The Gentiles will rejoice with the Jews, because they too have been given the chance to receive salvation through Christ.

11 Paul again quotes from the Psalms to show that the Gentiles will praise the Lord because of the salvation they have received in Christ (Psalm 117:1).

12 **Jesse** was the father of King David, from whom Christ was descended. Therefore the expression, **root of Jesse**, means Christ Himself. Christ arose **to rule over all the nations**, including the Gentile nations. Therefore, **the Gentiles will hope in him**—that is, in Christ (Isaiah 11:10).

13 The term **God of hope** means "God who gives hope." God gives us hope **by the power of the Holy Spirit**. What hope does He give? The hope of obtaining salvation, or eternal life.[84] Paul prays here that the Roman Christians might be filled **with all joy and peace**. Paul doesn't pray just for a little joy and peace; he prays for **all** joy and peace.

This **joy** is the spiritual joy given by Christ through the Holy Spirit; it is not the joy that comes from the world (see John 15:11 and comment). Likewise, this **peace** is the spiritual peace given by Christ through the Holy Spirit; it is not the peace that comes from the world (see John 14:27 and comment). No amount of trouble and suffering in this world can take away this spiritual joy and peace.

For the kingdom of God is ... righteousness, peace and joy in the Holy Spirit (Romans 14:17). A man will never find **all joy and peace** in any kingdom but the kingdom of God, in any religion but the Christian religion, in any god but the God Jesus Christ.

Let us not cease to pray for one another that we might be filled with **all joy and peace** through our Lord Jesus Christ.

Paul the Minister to the Gentiles (15:14–21)

14 If Paul wrote a letter addressed to our church today, how would he describe our church? Would he write about us, as he wrote to the Romans: **... you yourselves are full of goodness, complete in knowledge and competent to instruct one another**. Is that a description of our church? If not, it should be!

Christ wants us to have both **goodness** and **knowledge** together. Those who possess goodness and knowledge need to share those gifts with others.

At the time Paul wrote this letter, he had not yet been to Rome. But he was ready to believe good things about the Roman Christians. We, too, must always be more ready and eager to hear good things about each other than bad things.

15–16 Paul again reminds his readers that he has been given special **grace** (verse 15)—that is, a special anointing and power (see Romans 1:5; Ephesians 3:7 and comments)—for **proclaiming the gospel of God**.

What is the purpose of proclaiming the Gospel? The purpose, as stated in verse 16, is that those who accept the Gospel **might become an offering acceptable to God, sanctified by the Holy Spirit** (see Romans 12:1). If we have not been **sanctified by the Holy Spirit**, we cannot be an **offering acceptable to God**. And only by the work of the Holy Spirit living in us can we be **sanctified** (see 1 Corinthians 6:11 and comment).

That men and women might become sanctified offerings acceptable to God is the one chief purpose and goal of all preaching. Preaching is not a matter of dry discussion,

[84] Many great blessings are included in the word "salvation," but the greatest of them is eternal life with Christ. For further discussion, see General Article: Way of Salvation.

explanation, and teaching. It's a matter of persuading hearers to receive new life from Christ, and then to give their lives to Him in obedience and love.

17 Notice that Paul does not glory in himself, but **in Christ Jesus**.

18 Paul speaks only of **what Christ has accomplished through** [him]. Christ, through Paul's preaching, led the Gentiles **to obey God**. Obedience is the main sign and proof of true faith.

Notice that Paul says that the Gentiles have been led into obedience to God by what he (Paul) has **said and done**. Christ's ministers must serve not only by word but also by deed. People will often be more influenced by what we do than by what we say. However, they will be most influenced when we mix both words and deeds together.

19 The Holy Spirit worked mightily in Paul's life (see Acts 19:11; 2 Corinthians 12:12). Through the **power of the Spirit** Paul accomplished so much! We can say that Paul, through the Spirit, accomplished more than Jesus accomplished during His time on earth! Jesus had said: "**. . . anyone who has faith in me will do what I have been doing. He will do even greater things than these, because I am going to the Father**" (John 14:12). This is because only after Jesus went to the Father did He send the Holy Spirit to His followers. It is through the **power of the Spirit** that Paul was able to do all the things he did. And we too, through the Spirit's power, are able to do as much as Paul did!

The Holy Spirit works not only in the lives of believers; He also works in the lives of those who hear our words of testimony, our preaching. Our own words alone do not bring people to faith in Christ; it is the Holy Spirit, working in the hearts of those who hear our words, who brings them to Christ.

Illyricum was a province of the Roman Empire lying northwest of Greece. Today it is part of the modern nation of Yugoslavia.

20 Christians are not all called to the same work. Some Christians, like Paul, are called to travel from place to place. Other Christians are called to remain working in one place. Some Christians are called to proclaim the Gospel in new places where **Christ** [is] **not known**. And other Christians are called to build **on someone else's foundation**—that is, to teach and strengthen believers, to "water the seed" that someone else has planted (see 1 Corinthians 3:6–9 and comment). But the important thing to learn from this verse is that Christians should not compete with each other. We must never put another Christian down in order to advance our own work. We must never try to draw Christians away from other churches in order to make our own church bigger. We must never take for ourselves the honor or credit that belongs to someone else (2 Corinthians 10:15–16).

21 Here Paul quotes a prophecy of Isaiah, in which Isaiah says that those who have never heard of Christ **will see** and **will understand** (Isaiah 52:15). It was Paul's desire to help fulfill this prophecy by going and preaching to those who had never heard of Christ.

Paul's Plan to Visit Rome (15:22–33)

22 When Paul wrote this letter he had not yet visited Rome (Romans 1:13), because he had been busy preaching the Gospel in places **where Christ was not known** (verse 20).

23–24 Paul hoped to go to **Spain**, the westernmost part of the European continent. In Paul's time, Spain was a province of the Roman Empire. The Gospel had never been preached in Spain; that's why Paul wanted to go there.

Paul hoped that the Roman Christians would help him on his journey to Spain. In Paul's mind, the church in Rome was ideally situated to become a new center from which the Gospel could spread into western and northern Europe.

Paul had been **longing** to see the Roman Christians (Acts 19:21; Romans 1:11–12). Paul wanted to enjoy their **company**, their fellowship. However, a few years later when Paul finally arrived in Rome as a prisoner (Acts 28:16), these same Roman Christians refused to take his side; instead, at his trial, they all deserted him (2 Timothy 4:16).

25–26 **Jerusalem**[85] was the chief city of the province of **Judea**, the southern province of Israel. In New Testament times, all of Israel had fallen under the control of the Roman Empire. The **saints** (believers) in Jerusalem were very poor. Most of them had originally been Jews, but after becoming followers of Christ they had been opposed and persecuted by the other Jews around them. It's likely that many lost their property or businesses because of their faith in Christ. Probably many of them had to forfeit their inheritance. For these reasons, then, the Christians in Jerusalem were poor.

Twelve years earlier during a time of severe famine, Paul and Barnabas had taken up a collection in all the Gentile churches and had delivered that collection to the believers in Jerusalem (see Acts 11:28–30).

Now Paul was again on his way to Jerusalem to take to the Christians there a similar collection raised by the churches of **Macedonia** (northern Greece) and **Achaia** (southern Greece); the Jerusalem Christians were again in need of financial assistance from the wealthier Gentile churches of Greece (see 2 Corinthians 8:1–4; 9:1–2).

27 The churches of Macedonia and Achaia had been **pleased** to make a contribution. Yet in another way the Gentile Christians of Greece were under some obligation to help the Jewish Christians in Jerusalem. Why were they obligated? Because in the beginning the Gospel had come from the Jerusalem church. From Jerusalem the Gospel had been carried from one province of the Roman Empire to another—including, of course, the provinces of Macedonia and Achaia. Therefore, since the Gentile Christians in Greece had **shared in the Jews' spiritual blessings,** they certainly should be **pleased** to share with the Jewish Christians in Jerusalem some of their **material blessings,** their money. Indeed, Paul says, the Gentile Christians **owe it to the Jews** (Jewish Christians) to give them material help in exchange for the spiritual blessings they have received.

28–29 It is not known whether or not Paul ever reached Spain. However, we do know that when Paul finally arrived in Rome, he arrived as a prisoner of the Romans (Acts 28:16). But even though he was a prisoner, Paul came to Rome **in the full measure of the blessing of Christ** (verse 29). Wherever Paul went, in whatever circumstances he found himself, he always experienced the **full measure of the blessing of Christ**. Can we say that about ourselves?

30–31 Here Paul asks the Roman Christians to pray for two things on his behalf. First, he asks them to pray that he might **be rescued from the unbelievers in Judea** (verse 31). Paul was on his way to Judea to take the gift of the Gentile Christians to the believers in Jerusalem. But among the unbelieving Jews in Jerusalem Paul had many enemies. They would certainly try to kill him. And, indeed, shortly after Paul arrived in Jerusalem they did try to kill him, and almost succeeded! (Acts 21:27–32). Therefore, Paul asks prayer for his safety in Jerusalem.

Paul's second prayer request is that his **service in Jerusalem may be acceptable to the saints there**. Why should Paul have to pray for that? Why wouldn't his service be acceptable to the Jewish Christians in Jerusalem? The reason is that the believers in Jerusalem, being Jews, had never fully accepted the Gentile Christians. Furthermore, they were not happy that Paul, himself a Jew, had become an apostle to the Gentiles. Paul feared that these Jewish Christians in Jerusalem might not accept **his service**—this gift he was bringing from the Gentiles.

32–33 Paul writes that if these two prayer requests of his are fulfilled, then he will be able to come to Rome **with joy**

[85] Today **Jerasulem** is one of the main cities of Israel. It is regarded as a holy city by Jews, Muslims, and Christians.

(verse 32). But from reading Acts Chapters 21–28, we know that in Jerusalem things did not work out as Paul had hoped and prayed for. Paul prayed; but at the same time, he left his life in God's hands.

CHAPTER 16

Personal Greetings (16:1–27)

1–2 Some people believe that **Phoebe** carried this letter to Rome for Paul. She was a **servant,**[86] or "deaconess," of her own local church, and she had been a **great help to many** (verse 2). Like Phoebe, all Christians are called to be servants of one another.

3–5 **Priscilla**[87] **and Aquila** were a married couple, whom Paul met on his first trip to Corinth. Aquila, like Paul, made his living making tents. Therefore, while they were in Corinth they worked together (see Acts 18:1–3).

Priscilla and Aquila had **risked their lives** for Paul. It is not known exactly what event Paul is referring to here. The event is not mentioned elsewhere in the Bible. However, in Paul's day **all the churches of the Gentiles** (verse 4) knew about the event, because they were **grateful** to Priscilla and Aquila for saving Paul's life.

Priscilla and Aquila were mature Christians, who helped teach younger Christian leaders (see Acts 18:18–19,24–26).

In Rome a small "house church" met in Priscilla and Aquila's home. When they moved to Ephesus, there, too, a small church met in their home. In New Testament times, church buildings were very rare; most of the church services were held in people's homes (Colossians 4:15; Philemon 2).

6–15 Among the people whom Paul greets in this chapter are five Jewish Christians: namely, **Priscilla and Aquila** (verse 3), **Andronicus and Junias** (verse 7), and **Herodion** (verse 11). There are also two slaves included in Paul's list: **Ampliatus** (verse 8) and **Urbanus** (verse 9). **Aristobulus** (verse 10) was a grandson of King Herod, the former ruler of Judea.

In verse 13, Paul mentions the mother of **Rufus**; she had behaved like a mother to Paul. It is possible that the Rufus mentioned here is the same as the Rufus mentioned in Mark 15:21.

Notice that one third of the people mentioned in this chapter are women. Let no one say that women don't play an important role in the church! In fact, some Bible scholars believe that the apostle **Junias** (verse 7) was a woman; they say that in the Greek the name Junias is in the feminine form (see General Article: Women in the Church).

16 **Greet one another with a holy kiss.** Even today it is the custom in Middle Eastern countries for people to greet each other with a kiss. In 1 Peter 5:14, Peter tells those to whom he is writing to greet each other with a **kiss of love.**

17 **... watch out for those who cause divisions and put obstacles in your way.** Beware of them! Recall how many warnings Paul has given on this subject; it was always on his mind. And it should be on our minds too, because Satan's main method of destroying a church is by causing **divisions.** Paul tells us: **Keep away** from such people (see Galatians 1:8–9; 2 Thessalonians 3:6,14; 2 John 9–11 and comments).

18 What do these people do? They give false teaching. For example, they say

---

[86] The Greek word for **servant** used in this verse is the same as the Greek word Paul uses in 1 Timothy 3:8, where it is translated "deacon." That is why some translations of the Bible say "deaconess" in this verse.

[87] In place of the name **Priscilla,** some translations of the Bible say "Prisca," which is merely a short form of the name Priscilla.

that to be saved it is necessary to be circumcised. Or they say that to be a Christian it is necessary to be baptized in one particular manner. Such false and unnecessary teachings very quickly **cause divisions** in the church; and a division in the church is a wound in Christ's body.

False teachers always cause division. They try to entice others to become their followers. Do not be deceived by them, warns Paul. Such false teachers appear like sheep outwardly, **but inwardly they are ferocious wolves** (Matthew 7:15). Claiming to teach the truth, they present themselves as **apostles of Christ** and as **servants of righteousness** (2 Corinthians 11:13–15). Their teaching sometimes seems true and reasonable, but let us not be deceived; the truth never divides Christians. If Christians become divided because of some teaching, then that teaching will usually be false or distorted. Again, false teachers sometimes seem wise, but let us not be deceived. James said: **. . . the wisdom that comes from heaven is first of all pure; then peace loving, considerate, submissive, full of mercy and good fruit, impartial and sincere** (James 3:17).

For such people (false teachers) **are not serving our Lord Christ, but their own appetites**—that is, they are serving themselves. Their **appetites** are their desires and lusts, including their desire for fame and lust for power (Philippians 3:18–19).

19 Up until the time of this letter, the Roman Christians had not been deceived by false teachers. Paul is very thankful for this. That's why Paul is so anxious to warn them about the dangers of false teaching—he doesn't want to see their unity destroyed.

. . . be wise about what is good. This means: know all about doing good. Be **innocent about what is evil**. This means: know nothing about doing evil (see Matthew 10:16; 1 Corinthians 14:20 and comments).

20 Notice that Paul tells the Roman Christians: God will soon crush SATAN under **your** feet. That means God will crush Satan under our feet too. That is, God will use us to destroy Satan! (Genesis 3:14–15). Satan will be completely destroyed when Jesus comes to earth again.

21 Paul wrote this letter to the Romans from Corinth, the leading city of southern Greece.

Timothy was Paul's **fellow worker**; he was also Paul's spiritual son (Acts 16:1–3; Philippians 2:22). Timothy is mentioned many times in the New Testament. Paul wrote two letters to him, 1 Timothy and 2 Timothy, which are included in the New Testament.

A man named **Lucius** is also mentioned in Acts 13:1. It is possible that the Lucius of Acts is the same as the Lucius mentioned in this verse.

A man named **Jason** is mentioned in Acts 17:5–9. **Sosipater** is mentioned in Acts 20:4.

22 Paul usually didn't write his letters by his own hand; instead, he dictated them to a scribe, and the scribe wrote down what Paul said. The scribe who wrote this letter to the Romans was named **Tertius**, and here he gives his own greeting.

23–24 A man named **Gaius** is mentioned in Acts 19:29; 20:4; 1 Corinthians 1:14; 3 John 1.

25 Paul here calls the Gospel **my gospel**, because he preaches it. But, of course, it is really Christ's Gospel, the **proclamation of Jesus Christ**. Whenever we preach, the **proclamation of Jesus Christ** must be the central and pervading subject of our preaching (see 1 Corinthians 2:2). Through the preaching of the Gospel, Christ Himself will **establish** us (see Romans 14:4; 1 Peter 5:10 and comments).

What is the **mystery hidden for long ages past?** It is the "mystery" that men and women are saved not through their own works but through faith in Jesus Christ (see Ephesians 2:8–9; 3:4–6,8–9; Colossians 1:25–27 and comments). Now the full **revelation** of this mystery has occurred with the coming of Jesus Christ into the world.

26 The **mystery** concerning salvation through Christ was first revealed **through the prophetic writings** of the Old Testament prophets. But most people didn't truly understand what the prophets were saying. Only when Christ came was the mystery fully revealed (see Luke 24:25–27 and comment).

This **mystery** concerning salvation through Christ was revealed so that **all nations might believe** in Christ and **obey** Him. Notice again how believing and obeying must always go together (see John 14:15,21; Romans 1:5; James 2:14,17 and comments). Without obedience to Christ, there can be no true faith in Christ. Without faith in Christ, there can be no obedience; because obedience is the fruit and work of faith. We must not just listen to the Gospel; we must also obey it. Otherwise, there is no point in listening to it (see James 1:22 and comment).

27 Paul concludes this, the greatest of his letters, by saying that God will be glorified **through Jesus Christ** (see John 17:1,4 and comment). Through the life of Christ, God's righteousness, goodness, mercy, and love have been fully revealed. To this, the **only wise God**, and to His Son Jesus Christ, be glory forever. Amen.

1 Corinthians

INTRODUCTION

In Paul's time, Corinth was the most famous and important city in southern Greece.[1] Like Ephesus, Corinth was a commercial and cultural center. Corinth was also the capital of the Greek province of Achaia, which included most of southern Greece. Thus Corinth, because of its location and importance, was a strategic place in which to preach the Gospel.

In about 50 A.D., at the end of his second missionary journey, Paul traveled to Corinth and lived there for about eighteen months. At first Paul preached mainly to the Jews in Corinth; but when most of them rejected his teaching, Paul left the Jewish synagogue and began to preach among the Gentiles (see Acts 18:1,4–7,9–11).

After he had established a church in Corinth, Paul left the city in about 52 A.D. and went to Ephesus, where he stayed for over two years. Ephesus was located across the Aegean Sea, three hundred miles east of Corinth, in what is now modern Turkey. Since both cities were important, many people traveled by boat back and forth between them.

While Paul was in Ephesus, he heard some bad reports about the behavior of the believers in Corinth. In addition to that, Paul also received a letter from the Corinthian church asking him some practical questions about the Christian life. For these two reasons, therefore, in about 54 A.D. Paul wrote this, his first letter to the Corinthians. In the first part of the letter, Paul gives them some warning and advice concerning their improper behavior. Then, in the second part, Paul answers their questions.

Because of the stern warnings and rebukes that Paul wrote in this first letter, the Corinthians did not receive the letter happily. Many of them began to speak against Paul. Therefore, Paul sent them another letter from Ephesus (2 Corinthians 2:3–4). However, this second letter has been lost, and no copy of it exists today. (Perhaps, to express their displeasure at receiving the letter, the Corinthians themselves destroyed it.) Regardless of

[1] Greece is today an important country in southern Europe. In New Testament times, Greece was part of the Roman Empire. Before that, Greece had been the leading power in the Western world, as well as the birthplace of Western civilization.

what actually happened to this "lost" letter, once the Corinthians had received it, the situation in the Corinthian church began to improve. When Paul heard this good news, he then wrote a third letter to the Corinthians, which is the New Testament letter called 2 Corinthians.

For further information about Paul's life, see Romans: Introduction.

OUTLINE

A. Introduction (1:1–9).
  1. Greetings (1:1–3).
  2. Thanksgiving (1:4–9).
B. The Divisions in the Corinthian Church (1:10–4:21).
  1. The Fact of the Divisions (1:10–17).
  2. Divisions Concerning the Message (1:18–2:16).
  3. Divisions Concerning the Ministry (3:1–23).
  4. An Appeal to End the Divisions (4:1–21).
C. The Disorders in the Corinthian Church (5:1–6:20).
  1. The Absence of Discipline (5:1–13).
  2. Lawsuits before Non-Christian Judges (6:1–11).
  3. Immorality in the Church (6:12–20).
D. Paul's Answers to the Corinthians' Questions (7:1–15:58).
  1. Concerning Marriage (7:1–40).
  2. Concerning Meat Offered to Idols (8:1–13).
  3. Concerning the Rights and Duties of an Apostle (9:1–27).
  4. Concerning Questionable Practices (10:1–33).
  5. Concerning Women in Public Worship (11:1–16).
  6. Concerning the Lord's Supper (11:17–34).
  7. Concerning Spiritual Gifts (12:1–14:40).
  8. Concerning the Resurrection (15:1–58).
E. Final Instructions (16:1–24).
  1. The Collection for the Poor (16:1–4).
  2. The Planned Visit of Paul (16:5–12).
  3. Final Greetings and Prayer (16:13–24).

CHAPTER 1

Greetings and Thanksgiving (1:1–9)

1 Paul introduces himself as an **apostle of Christ Jesus by the will of God** (see Romans 1:1; Galatians 1:1; Ephesians 1:1 and comments).

Sosthenes was one of Paul's fellow workers. Sosthenes didn't actually write any part of this letter, but he had undoubtedly discussed the contents of the letter with Paul and had probably offered Paul advice concerning what to write.

When Paul had first arrived in Corinth, Sosthenes was the ruler of the Jewish synagogue there. Afterwards he had become a Christian (see Acts 18:17).

2 Paul writes to the CHURCH **of God** in Corinth. What is the **church**? The "church" is people—us—who are **sanctified in Christ Jesus**. This is why in the New Testament Christians are called "saints."

Who are the "sanctified in Christ"? They are all those **who call on the name of our Lord Jesus Christ** (see Romans 10:12–13). They are those who call not only with their lips but also from their hearts, who call out not only in words but also in faith—faith in Christ. Many people say, "Lord, Lord," with their lips, but in their hearts there is no change, no holiness (see Matthew 7:21 and comment). When we call on the name of Christ in true faith, Christ comes into our lives in the form of the Holy Spirit. Then through the power of the Holy Spirit, our lives become holy, or **sanctified**. We become "saints." The saints are those who have been "sanctified" in Christ—that is, those who have been declared righteous by God, who have been cleansed of their sins and have received forgiveness.

3 See Romans 1:7; Ephesians 1:2 and comments.

4 Paul always thanked God for all of his fellow Christians (Romans 1:8; Ephesians 1:15–16; Colossians 1:3–4). Paul here gives thanks for the Corinthian Christians because of the GRACE which God has given to them. Let us, also, not cease to offer thanks to God for each other, and for the gifts He has given to each of us.

5 The Corinthians were **enriched in every way**, but here Paul mentions two ways in which they were especially "enriched"—that is, in their **speaking** and in their **knowledge**. How rare is the person who has the gifts of both speaking and knowledge! Most people either speak well but have no knowledge, or they have knowledge but can't express it. The person who is rich in both gifts is able to give much blessing to others.

6 Here Paul gives the reason the Corinthian Christians had been so "enriched." It was because Paul's **testimony about Christ** had been **confirmed** in them. It is when we testify **about Christ** that others are enriched. Paul didn't testify about himself, but about His Lord.

7 Because of the **grace** God had given the Corinthian believers (verse 4), they didn't lack any **spiritual gift**. Here Paul is referring mainly to the special gifts of the Holy Spirit, about which Paul has written elsewhere (see Romans 12:6–8; 1 Corinthians 12:7–11,27–28; Ephesians 4:11). But the greatest "spiritual gifts" are Jesus Christ Himself, the Holy Spirit Himself, and our eternal salvation. All of God's blessings to us—His grace, His love, His mercy, His power, His Spirit, His Son—can be called "spiritual gifts."

Even though the Corinthians didn't lack any spiritual gift, they still were beset by many sins and weaknesses. They had no lack of spiritual gifts; but they had no lack of sins either! They were still far from mature, far from **perfect** (Matthew 5:48). Therefore, says Paul, let them wait eagerly **for our Lord Jesus Christ to be revealed**—that is, let them look for the second coming of Christ into the world, at which time their bodies will be redeemed (Romans 8:23), and their sins and weaknesses will be erased forever.

8 Christ **will keep you strong to the end**. Through His death on the cross,

Christ has taken away our guilt, our "blame," so that we will be **blameless** on the **day of our Lord Jesus Christ**—that is, on the day when Christ returns to earth to judge all men.

We are totally dependent on Christ's strength, which He gives us through the Holy Spirit. We cannot live a life pleasing to God by our own strength. Christ will keep us strong (see Philippians 1:6; 1 Thessalonians 5:23–24).

9 **God . . . is faithful**. God called us; He justified us; and He will glorify us (see Romans 8:30 and comment).

Some people, quoting verses 8–9, believe that Christians cannot fall away, that they cannot lose their salvation for any reason. But other verses in the New Testament suggest that Christians can indeed turn away from their faith (see Luke 8:13; Romans 11:22; 1 Timothy 4:1; General Article: Can We Lose Our Salvation?).

For what purpose does God call us? God calls us to have **fellowship with his Son Jesus Christ**. And as we have fellowship with Jesus, we become more and more like Him. This is God's ultimate purpose for us: that we might **be conformed to the likeness of his Son** (see Romans 8:29 and comment).

So, in view of such a great destiny, let us ask ourselves: Have we had fellowship with Jesus today? Without fellowship with Him, we shall become like a branch that is cut off from the tree and dies (see John 15:5–6 and comment).

Divisions in the Church (1:10–17)

10 Paul's prayer is that the Corinthian believers might **be perfectly united in mind and thought**. Does this mean that the Corinthians have to agree on every little matter? No, it doesn't mean that. But it does mean that they must agree on all major and essential matters—for example, that Jesus Christ is the Son of God, that the Bible is God's word which we must obey, that salvation comes through faith in Jesus Christ alone (see Introduction to the General Articles). We must be united in faith, in love, and in obedience to Christ. But in small matters, it is all right to have different opinions. Let one man eat meat, and another not (Romans 14:2,5). We needn't concentrate on these small matters. Even though we have different ideas and customs in small things, as long as we accept and respect each other, we will still be **perfectly united** in Christ. That is what is essential (see Romans 12:16; 15:5–6; 2 Corinthians 13:11; Philippians 2:2 and comments).

Oneness among Christians is like the "oneness" among leaves of a tree. From a distance, the leaves of a tree all look the same. But when you look closely, the leaves are all different. Just as leaves are united in a tree, so must we be united in Christ—united, but not identical!

Paul wasn't the only one who prayed for unity among believers. Christ Himself prayed that those who believed in Him might all be one (see John 17:20–23 and comment).

11 **Chloe** was a woman who lived in Corinth. Some members of her household had apparently traveled to Ephesus, where they had met Paul and informed him about the quarrels and divisions in the Corinthian church.

12 What had happened in the Corinthian church? The believers had become divided. Some believers had begun to follow Paul—probably those who had heard the Gospel from him in the beginning.

But then Paul had left Corinth, and some time afterward a leader named **Apollos** had come and taken Paul's place. So then, some of the Corinthians had begun to follow Apollos! Apollos was a learned Jew, and **he spoke with great fervor and taught about Jesus accurately** (Acts 18:24–25). While Apollos was at Corinth, **he was a great help** to the believers there (Acts 18:27–28).

Again, other believers had begun following **Cephas** (Peter), who was the chief among Jesus' original twelve disciples (see John 1:42). Perhaps the reason some believers were following Peter was that he was one of the original twelve disciples, while Paul and Apollos were not. Some people thought that only the original disciples should be considered true apostles.

And, finally, still another group said,

"We follow Christ." It was fine to say, "We follow Christ"; but what wasn't fine was that this group was looking down on all the other believers at Corinth. They considered themselves to be the only true Christians. But in thinking that, they were being proud; they were setting themselves above the others. What's more, their opinion was wrong: they weren't the only true Christians. The others were Christians too! Thus, because of their pride, those who called themselves "followers of Christ" ended up quarreling and causing division just like the other groups. They brought dishonor on Christ, because in claiming Christ was the Lord of their own little group, they were denying that He was the Lord of the whole church—which, in fact, He was.

Notice how much harm pride can do. It can even cause a division between Christ and His own apostles! The major cause of division in any church is pride. There is only one cure for division in the church: all members must humble themselves and begin to look to Christ instead of to themselves. Church leaders and their followers must concentrate on raising up, not themselves, but Christ alone.

13 How can the Corinthian Christians think about splitting into opposing parties like this? Paul asks. How can they give their loyalty to these different leaders? How mistaken they are! Christ alone died on the cross for them. These leaders may have baptized them, but they didn't baptize them in their own names; they baptized them in Christ's name.

14–15 Paul does not want the Corinthians to follow men; he wants them to follow Christ. Paul is happy that he only baptized two of the Corinthian believers, because that way no one can accuse him of trying to start his own party!

Crispus was the ruler of the Jewish synagogue in Corinth (Acts 18:8). **Gaius** is mentioned in Romans 16:23; perhaps the Corinthian church met in his house.

16 Paul suddenly remembers one more family he baptized, which he forgot to mention. Paul didn't want to forget anyone; every believer was important to him. But especially this family—**the household of Stephanas**—he didn't want to forget; they were the first people in the province of Achaia (southern Greece) to believe in Christ (1 Corinthians 16:15–18).

17 Paul now explains why he baptized so few people at Corinth. He says that his main calling was not to baptize but to preach. **Christ did not send me to baptize, but to preach the GOSPEL.** Most pastors and preachers do both kinds of work—baptizing and preaching—together, and in other cities Paul also did both. But in Corinth Paul concentrated mainly on preaching and left the baptizing to others. Paul is not opposed to leaders baptizing new believers; he is only opposed to creating parties and divisions in the church.

Paul does not preach **with words of human wisdom**—that is, words that come only from man's wisdom, not God's wisdom. In this, Paul is an example for all preachers to follow. For when a preacher speaks only with human wisdom—human eloquence—then the listeners are drawn to the preacher and not to Christ. They praise the preacher instead of praising Christ.

Paul wants people to believe the Gospel because it is God's truth, not because he preached it with eloquent words.

Some preachers appear to be very wise, and many people come to hear them. But these "wise" preachers don't say anything about how Jesus Christ died on the **cross**[2] for men. They don't say anything about how Christ, through His death on the cross, now has the **power** to forgive men's sins and give them eternal life. This is the "power of the cross" that Paul refers to here. And so, if these "wise" preachers don't say anything about Christ's **cross**, then the cross is **emptied of its power**—that is, it cannot benefit those who are listening. The listeners never have the chance to learn what Christ did for them on the cross, and so

---

[2] In the Roman Empire, the most common way to execute criminals was to hang them from a cross until they died. For further discussion, see Word List: Cross.

they cannot benefit from it. A preacher, no matter how wise, can't save anyone. Only the crucified and risen Christ can save us and give us eternal life. Through Christ's death on the cross we are made alive! That is God's wisdom. And that is what Paul preaches (see 1 Corinthians 2:1,4–5,13).

Christ the Wisdom and Power of God (1:18–31)

18 **For the message of the cross is foolishness to those who are perishing.** Who are the **perishing**? They are unbelievers. For them, the **message of the cross**—that is, the Gospel—**is foolishness**. Why? Because they think it's absurd that the Son of God, the Savior of mankind, would die on a cross like a criminal. They can't believe it. To them, any talk of Jesus' death on the cross is **foolishness**.

But all who know Christ and truly believe in Him have experienced in their own lives the same **power of God** which raised Christ from the dead. This is the power we receive when we accept the **message of the cross**, the glorious Gospel of Christ. Thanks be to God! (see Romans 1:16).

19 Paul quotes here from Isaiah 29:14. God, speaking through the prophet Isaiah, says that He will destroy the **wisdom of the wise**, which opposes the **message of the cross** (verse 18). How can man's wisdom be compared to God's wisdom? It can't be! (Psalm 33:10–11; Isaiah 55:8–9; Romans 11:33–34).

20 **Where is the wise man**? Nowhere. No one is wise except God. God gives His own wisdom to those who believe in the "message of the cross."

Where is the scholar . . . the philosopher? Men suppose that scholars and philosophers are very wise. Scholars and philosophers also read the Bible, though they don't believe what is written in it. But in sending His own Son to die on the cross, **God made foolish the wisdom of the world**—the wisdom of scholars and philosophers. The man with worldly wisdom will perish together with his wisdom; but the man who believes in Christ will live forever.

21 The wisdom of the world cannot know God's wisdom (see 1 Corinthians 2:14). The **world**[3] calls God's wisdom (the Gospel) foolishness. But God, by that so-called "foolishness," gives salvation to all who believe in Christ.

22 The JEWS were always demanding **miraculous signs** in order to believe (see Matthew 12:38; Mark 8:11; John 2:18 and comments). They needed proof; they had no faith.

Jesus gave them a sign. He rose from the dead—that was the sign (see John 2:19–22). But this, the greatest of all Jesus' signs—His own resurrection—the Jews refused to believe.

The **Greeks**[4] were always searching for **wisdom**, the wisdom of the world.

23 For the Jews, the crucified Christ was a **stumbling block**. That is, the cross was an obstacle that prevented them from believing. That their Savior would die on a cross was incredible, even contemptible, to the Jews. Even while Christ was hanging on the cross, they mocked Him (see Matthew 27:41–42; Mark 15:31–32).

For the GENTILES—that is, all the non-Jewish people of the world—the idea of a crucified Savior was **foolishness**. That the Son of God would come to earth and end up being executed as a criminal was ridiculous to them.

24 But for those who believe in Christ, the crucified Christ is **the power of God and the wisdom of God**.

Believers are **those whom God has called**. For those who accept God's call, the crucified Christ is not a sign of weakness, contempt, or foolishness. Rather, He is the **power** and **wisdom** of God. All power and all wisdom are in Christ (see Romans 1:16). And that power and wisdom is available to us also—the power to overcome sin and lead a new

---

[3] The **world** in this context means "unbelieving men of the world."

[4] The **Greeks** here include not only the inhabitants of Greece, but also all Gentiles, or non-Jews. In the New Testament, the word "Greek" is often used to mean Gentile.

life, and the wisdom to know God and find the way of salvation.

25 When Paul uses the expression **foolishness of God**, he is using the term an unbeliever would use. He means God's "foolishness" in sending His Son to be killed on a cross. By the expression **weakness of God**, Paul means Christ's "weakness"—that is, His death on the cross. Death is the ultimate sign of human weakness.

Yet compared to God's "foolishness" and "weakness," what can man's wisdom and strength do? The greatest wisdom and power of man cannot save a single soul. But God's foolishness and weakness can! And God's foolishness and weakness—that is, Jesus' death on the cross—saves not just one soul, it saves the soul of everyone who believes in Jesus.

26 Most people who are **wise**, **influential**, or **of noble birth** don't look to God. They think they don't need Him (see Mark 10:23 and comment). Such people don't want to be God's servants; they want to serve themselves rather than God (see Mark 10:42–44 and comment).

27–28 God's wisdom is the opposite of man's wisdom. What man considers to be wise, God considers to be foolish; and what man considers foolish, God considers wise.

Therefore, God has chosen those people whom men consider **foolish**, **weak**, and **lowly** to be His followers. The **foolish things**, the **weak things**, the **lowly** and **despised things** are us—believers! God has chosen people like us to **shame** the wise and the strong men of the world (see James 2:5).

The **things that are not** (verse 28) are also Christians like us. In the eyes of the non-believers in Corinth, the Christians were like "things that are not." The non-believers in Paul's time took no account of the church; they treated the church as if it didn't exist. And yet that church gradually spread throughout the Roman Empire, and later the world. And when the world passes away, the church of Christ will be remaining still.

29 Why did God choose us—the foolish, weak, and lowly? He chose the foolish, weak, and lowly so that no man would boast that he had been chosen because of his own wisdom and strength! (Ephesians 2:8–9). God doesn't want boasters. He chooses us because of His grace, not because of our worth. Besides, any wisdom and strength we might have has come from God in the first place! Man has absolutely nothing of his own to boast about.

30 Let us never forget that it was God who chose us in the very beginning, not we who chose God (see John 15:16; Ephesians 1:4–5 and comments). It is **because of him** that we are in Christ.

The greatest gift God has given us is Jesus Christ Himself. All the other blessings of God are included in Christ—such as, **RIGHTEOUSNESS**, **holiness and REDEMPTION**, or salvation (see Romans 3:24; Ephesians 1:6–8; Colossians 1:14 and comments). If we have received Christ, we have received every other spiritual blessing as well (see Romans 8:32; Ephesians 1:3 and comments).

Paul frequently uses the expression **IN CHRIST**. **To be in Christ Jesus** means to be joined with Christ like branches are joined to a tree (see John 15:4–7). When we are in Christ, Christ is also in us. And if Christ is in us, that means His power and wisdom and love—indeed, **all the fullness of God**—is in us also! (Ephesians 3:19). Christ is King and Lord of our life. We belong to Him.

31 Here Paul quotes from the Old Testament prophet Jeremiah. Jeremiah says that if we have something to boast about, then we must boast not in ourselves but **in the Lord** (Jeremiah 9:24). And indeed we do have something to boast about! Because Christ is in us, we are rich, wise, and strong. Surely we can boast—but not in ourselves. Every good thing we have has come from Christ; let us boast in Him (see Galatians 6:14).

CHAPTER 2

Paul's Preaching (2:1–5)

1 The Greeks placed great value on **eloquence** and **superior wisdom**—that is, worldly words and wisdom. There were many philosophers among the Greeks, who spoke **words of human wisdom** (1 Corinthians 1:17), and who tried to persuade men to believe in their teaching.

But Paul's preaching was not with **eloquence or superior wisdom**. Paul didn't teach his own philosophy, his own ideas. Instead, in plain language he proclaimed the **testimony about God**;[5] that is, he revealed the truth about Christ. God's **testimony** is about His Son Jesus. For those who do not believe, Christ's Gospel is something hidden, something hard to understand. It is a **mystery** that needs to be revealed (see Romans 16:25; Ephesians 3:4–6,8–9; Colossians 1:25–27). And Paul revealed this "mystery" of Christ in clear and simple language.

2 In all of Paul's preaching there was just one theme, and that theme was Jesus Christ. In this, Paul's desire was that men and women might be drawn to Christ and put their faith in Him.

Paul didn't preach only that Christ was God, but also that He was a man like we are, a man who died on a cross for our sins (see General Article: Jesus Christ). This was Paul's Gospel, and it was all he preached. Indeed, in his preaching, Paul **resolved to know nothing . . . except Jesus Christ**; that is, he resolved to preach the Gospel of Christ as if he knew **nothing** else.

If Paul had wanted to speak **with eloquence or superior wisdom** (verse 1), he would never have mentioned the cross of Christ in his preaching, because to the Greeks the cross was **foolishness** (1 Corinthians 1:18,23).

3 Corinth was a great city, and many rich and famous people lived there. Paul was an unknown foreigner, an ordinary man who went around preaching and making tents. He spoke in plain language (2 Corinthians 10:10). When Paul first went to Corinth, there was not a single Christian in the city. He was alone. Many opposed him (Acts 18:12). This is why Paul says here that he came to Corinth **in weakness and fear, with much trembling**.

4 But from Paul's plain preaching came a **demonstration of the** (HOLY) **SPIRIT's power**. When we are weak, then God's power is more clearly demonstrated in our lives (see 2 Corinthians 4:7; 12:9–10 and comments).

The **Spirit's power** was demonstrated in Paul's ministry in two ways. First, it was demonstrated in the many people who were moved to repent and to believe; that is, it was demonstrated in the building up of the church. Second, it was further demonstrated by the **signs** and **miracles** Paul performed as an apostle (see Romans 15:19; 2 Corinthians 12:12).

5 When we Christians witness and preach, many who hear us say that our words are pleasing and comforting. They like to hear the Gospel. But those who listen only to be pleased have not really understood the Gospel. They do not understand that the Gospel is, in fact, **the power of God for the salvation of everyone who believes** (Romans 1:16; 1 Corinthians 4:20).

Therefore, let our preaching and speaking not be **with wise and persuasive words, but with a demonstration of the Spirit's power** (verse 4), so that the FAITH, of those who hear us might not be based on human wisdom but on God's power. Only through the power of the Holy Spirit can men and women be brought to true faith in Christ. When our preaching is focused solely on **Christ crucified** (1 Corinthians 1:23), then we can know that our listener's faith will rest on the power of God.

[5] In place of the words **testimony about God**, some versions of the Bible say "mystery of God," which is a more literal translation of the original Greek text. The meaning is the same.

Wisdom From the Spirit (2:6–16)

6 For those who are **mature**, that is, spiritual, Paul's words are a **message of wisdom**. Paul does not speak the **wisdom of this age** or of its **rulers**. The **rulers of this age** are not only those rulers who exercise authority in this world, but also the **authorities, powers,** and **spiritual forces of evil in the heavenly realms** (Ephesians 6:12).

7 In one sense God's wisdom is **secret** and **hidden**. It is like a mystery. Natural or unspiritual men cannot understand God's wisdom. Only with the help of the Holy Spirit can we understand God's wisdom, the Gospel (verse 14). The Gospel is fully revealed only to those who believe in Christ.

The Gospel is God's wisdom, which He **destined for our glory**. Christ embodies God's wisdom; Christ Himself can be called the **wisdom of God** (1 Corinthians 1:24). Through Christ we will be glorified (see Romans 8:30; 2 Thessalonians 2:14 and comments). God made the decision to glorify us **before time began**—that is, before the creation of the world (Ephesians 1:4; 2 Thessalonians 2:13).

8 When Christ came into the world, God's wisdom became fully manifest. The "mystery" was revealed; God's wisdom was no longer hidden. But even though God's wisdom was made manifest, most people still didn't understand it. They rejected Christ. Their spiritual eyes were blind. Especially the **rulers of this age** were blind; otherwise, they would not have crucified Christ, the **Lord of glory**. The **rulers of this age** were the Jewish leaders and the Roman governor who actually put Christ to death; but the **rulers** also included the **spiritual forces of evil** (Ephesians 6:12), the forces of Satan. For those who crucified Christ were surely under the control of Satan; they did not do their evil work alone.

9 Paul quotes here from Isaiah 64:4. What is it that God **has prepared for those who love him**—but which has been hidden from those who do not? It is salvation, eternal life, and glory; this is what God has prepared for those who love Him. And what God has prepared for us who love Him is greater and more wonderful than we can even imagine (see Romans 11:33; Ephesians 3:20–21 and comments).

10 **God has revealed it** (His wisdom, the Gospel) **to us through his** (Holy) **Spirit**. The Holy Spirit knows the **deep things** of God, because the Holy Spirit is God's own Spirit. Nothing is hid from the Holy Spirit.

11 We men cannot know what is in another man's mind and heart; only that other man—that other **man's spirit**—can know what is in his mind and heart. But if that other man reveals to us what is in his mind and heart, then we also can know it.

In the same way, we do not know what is in God's "mind and heart." Only the Holy Spirit knows. But just as another man might tell us what is in his mind and heart, so the Spirit of God reveals to us what is in God's "mind and heart." This is how believers know the **thoughts** of God; they know them **by his Spirit**.

12 We have received the **Spirit who is from God**, that is, the Holy Spirit; and through the Spirit we can understand **what God has freely given us**: His own Son, and together with Him, salvation, eternal life.

13 Paul here repeats the thoughts of verses 1,4–5. We believers do not speak in words **taught by human wisdom**; rather, we speak in words **taught by the** (Holy) **Spirit**. Thus our words are **spiritual words**. And when we speak in spiritual words, we shall express **spiritual truths**. Spiritual truths can only be expressed in spiritual words. If our words are truly spiritual, **taught by the Spirit**, then we shall always express spiritual truths. A man who is not taught by the Spirit cannot express spiritual truths; he cannot even comprehend them.

14 The unspiritual or natural man does not have the Holy Spirit; therefore, he cannot understand the **things that come from the Spirit of God**. Only through the Holy Spirit can we understand God's thoughts (see John 8:47; 14:16–17; Romans 8:5,9 and comments).

15 The **spiritual man** is a true Christian. He has received the Holy Spirit. The "spiritual man" can understand and make judgments about both worldly things and spiritual things.

But the natural man, the **man without the Spirit** (verse 14), cannot understand the **spiritual man** nor make judgments about him. The spiritual man possesses the qualities of the Holy Spirit in his life, especially the fruits of the Spirit—love, joy, peace, etc. (Galatians 5:22–23). These things the natural man cannot fully understand; he cannot understand the source of these qualities. He cannot understand the concerns and priorities of the spiritual man. For this reason, the spiritual man **is not subject to any** (natural) **man's judgment**.

16 Here Paul quotes from Isaiah 40:13 (see Romans 11:34). Just as the natural or unspiritual man cannot know the mind of God, so he cannot know the mind of us who are Christians—because true Christians themselves have the mind of God. That is, **we have the mind of Christ**. What an amazing truth! And so, since we have Christ's mind, let us be diligent to use it!

CHAPTER 3

On Divisions in the Church (3:1–9)

1 When Paul first ministered in Corinth, he could not speak to the new Corinthian believers as he would to mature Christians; rather, he spoke to them as to spiritual **infants**. Even though they had believed in Christ and had received His Holy Spirit, they were still **worldly**.[6]

We must understand the meaning of this word **worldly**. A "worldly" man is a man who walks in the ways of the world. He loves the things of the world more than he loves God. The worldly man lives **according to the sinful nature** (Romans 8:4); that is, he remains under the control of his sinful thoughts and desires. His sinful nature rules in his life. The worldly man has not become free of his sinful nature (see Romans 6:11–12). The worldly man can also be called a "natural man," or a **man without the Spirit** (1 Corinthians 2:14). And he can also be called a man "of the flesh." All these expressions describe the same kind of man.

In this verse there is an essential teaching. Usually Paul refers to believers in Christ as "spiritual," and to non-believers as "unspiritual" or "worldly" (see Romans 7:14). But here Paul calls the Corinthian believers "worldly." The reason is this: New and immature believers are partly spiritual and partly unspiritual (or worldly). When a person believes in Christ, he receives new spiritual life through the Holy Spirit. But that person is spiritually like a newborn infant. He must grow spiritually. Even though he is a Christian, he is still partly unspiritual and worldly; he still has the habits and desires of the world. He still is drawn to the world. In his heart there is a struggle between his new spiritual self and his old worldly self (see Romans 7:19–21; Galatians 5:16–17 and comments). As we grow spiritually and become more and more mature, we gradually, with the help of the Holy Spirit, gain victory over our sinful nature; and in the end we will no longer be worldly but will be spiritual (see 2 Corinthians 3:18; Ephesians 4:13–15 and comments).

2 In the beginning Paul fed the new Corinthian believers **milk**, that is, the simple and basic and comforting truths of the Gospel—such as: God loves us and is willing to forgive us (John 3:16); Christ died for our sins (Romans 5:8); Christ gives us rest (Matthew 11:28). These teachings are like **milk**, suitable for spiritual infants (see Hebrews 5:11–14; 1 Peter 2:2).

On the other hand, **solid food** consists of the more deep and difficult teachings of Scripture. These would include the discourses of Jesus, such as those found in

---

[6] In place of the word **worldly**, some translations of the Bible say "carnal" or "of the flesh." The meaning is the same.

Matthew Chapters 5–7 and John Chapters 13–16. They would include the doctrinal teachings of Paul. They would also include the exhortation and warning passages, examples of which are found in Mark 8:34–35; Romans 8:13; 2 Timothy 3:12; Hebrews 10:26–31.

A wise pastor or preacher tries to get an idea of the spiritual "age" or condition of a person before deciding what kind of spiritual "food" to feed him—whether **milk** or **solid food**. Some need mainly "milk"; others need "solid food." To give a tiny child a big piece of meat is not helpful; it may become stuck in his throat!

When Paul first lived in Corinth, the new believers there were not ready to eat **solid food**; they were like **infants in Christ** (verse 1). Now as Paul writes this letter, three or four years have passed; what is the spiritual condition of these Corinthian believers now? They are still spiritual **infants**! They are still not ready for **solid food**; they are still not ready for the deeper teachings of the Gospel. They have not grown. They have been born of the Spirit, but they are not yet living by the Spirit (Galatians 5:16).

3 How does Paul know that the Corinthian believers are still spiritual "infants"? How does he know that they are still "worldly"? He knows because of the **jealousy and quarreling** among them. Jealousy and quarreling does not occur among mature spiritual Christians. These Corinthians were **acting like mere men**—that is, like natural, worldly men. They were still behaving as if they had never become Christians!

4 Here we see what the quarreling was about in the Corinthian church: the Christians had divided themselves into opposing parties (1 Corinthians 1:12). This was the proof that they were indeed worldly, or unspiritual.

Let us examine ourselves. How much are we like those Corinthian Christians? We need to ask ourselves: Am I worldly or am I spiritual?

We can learn another thing from these first four verses of Chapter 3: namely, Christians may not behave in accordance with the Spirit in everything all the time; nevertheless, they are still true Christians. Sometimes when we look at a brother who is behaving in a worldly way, we are tempted to think: "He is not a true Christian; he is worldly." However, only God knows for sure who is a true Christian and who isn't; it is not our place to judge our brother. Yes, we can look at our brother's behavior and say it is not like Christ's; but whether or not our brother belongs to Christ we cannot say. Yes, it is possible our brother is not a true Christian; it's possible that he has confessed Christ only with his lips. But it's also possible that he is indeed a true Christian in his heart. Therefore, even though our brother (who claims to be a Christian) may be leading a worldly life, we must still regard him as a Christian brother. Regardless of the actual state of his faith, we must not judge him; judging is only for God to do (see Matthew 7:1; Romans 2:1; 14:1 and comments).

5–7 Why should the Corinthians follow after Apollos or Paul? (1 Corinthians 1:12). Apollos and Paul are only men. They are servants, and their master is Christ. Paul plants the seed (Acts 18:1,4), and Apollos waters it (Acts 18:27). But that is only the work of gardeners. We Christians are only God's instruments; we are His "gardeners" who plant and water the seed, which is God's word (Mark 4:3,14). But the One who does the real work of making the plant grow is God Himself. It is God alone who produces the fruit—that is, new believers. God alone brings men to faith in Christ. Man is nothing; all the power is of God. Therefore, as Paul quoted earlier: **Let him who boasts boast in the Lord** (1 Corinthians 1:31).

Paul and Apollos are the servants of one master, Christ. If they have only one master, why should they each have a separate party in the Corinthian church? For one master, only one party is needed!

8 Paul and Apollos have one master, but that master has given them two different jobs to do. In the same way, we too have one master but do different jobs for that master (see 1 Corinthians 12:4–6). And each of us shall be **rewarded according to** [our] **own labor**—that is, we shall each receive a reward according to the particular job we have done. Notice that we are not rewarded primarily according to the success or failure of our work, but rather according to our **labor**, our effort and diligence. In Jesus' parable of the talents, the man who gained five additional talents and the man who gained two additional talents each received the same reward (Matthew 25:20–23). The Christian with only a few evident gifts and talents will receive the same reward as the Christian with many gifts and talents; they both will be rewarded primarily according to their effort and diligence. In Luke 19:16–19, Christ's illustration is slightly different, but the teaching is the same. According to Luke's version of the parable of the talents, the servants were all given the same gift—namely, one **mina**. But each servant received a different reward; that is, one servant received ten cities and another servant received only five. These servants received different rewards because their effort and diligence were different. In other words, each received a reward **according to his own labor**.

9 Paul describes himself and Apollos as God's **fellow workers**, God's field hands. And the Corinthian Christians, as a church, are **God's field**. Each one of them is a seedling planted in that field (Mark 4:20).

The church (that is, the body of believers) can also be described as a building—**God's building** (see Ephesians 2:22; 1 Peter 2:5 and comments).

God's Building (3:10–23)

10 Paul says: **I laid a foundation as an expert builder**. Is Paul boasting in himself here? No. He says he has done everything by the **grace God has given me** (see Romans 1:5; 1 Corinthians 15:10; Ephesians 3:7 and comments). God gave Paul the **grace** and skill to be an **expert builder**. Paul laid the foundation—and that foundation was Christ Himself (verse 11). That is why Paul is an **expert** builder; he chose the best foundation!

Paul was the first Christian to go to Corinth. He established the church there; that is, he laid the foundation. Now the Corinthians themselves had begun to help in building their church; that is, they had begun to build on Paul's foundation. Paul exhorts them, therefore, to make sure that what they build is as good as the foundation. Let them not build a hut on a foundation designed for a palace! **But each one should be careful how he builds** (on the foundation). Those Corinthians, in fact, were building a hut!

11 The foundation of all our work must be Jesus Christ (see Ephesians 2:19–22 and comment). If the sole foundation of a church is Jesus Christ, then divisions and parties will not arise.

12–13 We can build God's church using different materials, because we each have been given different gifts and skills. It is better, of course, if flammable materials are not used. But whatever material we use, we must **be careful** and build diligently.

The **Day** Paul refers to here is the day of judgment, which will occur at the end of the world. On that day God will examine all the work we have done. And He will test it **with fire** (verse 13). If we have built a church, God will allow **fire** or persecution to come upon that church to see if it will remain faithful (Job 23:10).

14–15 If what we have done is in some way displeasing to God, then our work will be **burned up**, and our reward in heaven will be less—that is, we will **suffer loss** (verse 15). But we ourselves will not lose our salvation.[7]

For example, if a builder builds a house poorly, that house will later fall down; and the builder, instead of earning his wages, will be forced to pay for the damage. But the builder himself will not be harmed; only his purse will suffer. In the same way, we may suffer the loss of our heavenly reward, but without losing our salvation.

We do not know what kind of heavenly reward God is going to give us for our

[7] In heaven we will receive a reward according to our work or labor; but salvation we receive only through faith (see Matthew 16:27; Ephesians 2:8–9; 2 Corinthians 5:10 and comments; General Article: Way of Salvation).

work. But if our work is good, then God will especially honor us in some way (see Matthew 7:24–27; 1 Corinthians 4:5; 2 John 8).

16 Each Christian has been built together into God's **temple**, or church. We believers are the stones of this temple (1 Peter 2:5). **God's Spirit** (the Holy Spirit) dwells within us, within our temple (see 1 Corinthians 6:19; Ephesians 2:22 and comments).

17 How can God's temple, or church, be destroyed? If we, the members—the stones—become worldly and unspiritual, our temple will be destroyed.[8] Our temple (church) can be destroyed by the sins, the worldliness, of its members. It is destroyed by false teaching, divisions, quarrels, and slander of one member against another. Therefore, let us beware! Whoever destroys God's church, God Himself will destroy.

18 The Corinthians considered themselves **wise**. Perhaps they were "wise" in worldly wisdom, but such wisdom is **foolishness** in God's sight (verse 19). It is much better to be foolish in the world's eyes than to be foolish in God's eyes! (see 1 Corinthians 1:27).

Let us not consider ourselves wise. Rather, let us be humble. Instead of relying on our own "wisdom," let us seek to learn from God. If the Corinthians had done this, such divisions would never have arisen in their church (see Isaiah 5:21; 1 Corinthians 8:2; Galatians 6:3)

19–20 Paul here quotes from Job 5:13 and Psalm 94:11 (see 1 Corinthians 1:19–20,25)

21 Therefore, says Paul, let there be no more **boasting about men**, men such as Paul and Apollos. Let the Corinthians stop following after men like Paul and Apollos. Rather, let them follow Christ alone (see 1 Corinthians 4:6). If they are going to boast, let them boast in Christ (1 Corinthians 1:29,31). God has given them **all things** in Christ (see Romans 8:32; 1 Corinthians 1:30; Ephesians 1:3). It is because they are in Christ that they have obtained **all things**. Where, then, is their boasting? Let them rather thank God for His unspeakable gift to them—the Lord Jesus Christ.

22 God gave to the Corinthians the apostles—Paul, Apollos, and Cephas (Peter). But the Corinthians had accepted one and rejected another. Yet they all were apostles; they all were God's gifts. Why should they have rejected a gift of God? The "wisdom" of the Corinthians was indeed foolishness!

All things are yours. The entire world is ours! The man who is not in Christ belongs to the world. But for the man who is in Christ, the world belongs to him! Christ has complete authority over all the earth, and He has given His authority to us (see Matthew 28:18). But we believers will not only **inherit the earth**; we will also inherit the **kingdom of heaven**! (Matthew 5:3,5,10).

23 **All things** are ours. Except one thing—our own self! All things are ours—but we are not our own. We are Christ's. We are His servants. He has bought us. He has bought us **at a price**, and the price was His own blood (see 1 Corinthians 6:19–20 and comment).

All things are ours because Christ is in us and we are in Christ (John 15:4–5). If we stop remaining in Christ, we shall lose all these things which we have been given (John 15:6).

Christ is of God. Just as Christ is in us, so God is in Christ (see John 17:22–23). But Christ is not only **of God**; He is God. **"I and the Father are one"** (John 10:30).

---

[8] The universal church of Christ cannot be destroyed, but a local church can be destroyed through the sins of its members.

CHAPTER 4

Apostles of Christ (4:1–13)

1 Paul writes that **men ought to regard us** (Paul, Apollos, and other apostles) **as servants of Christ**. Paul's point is that the apostles are not the leaders of independent groups in the church, but all are equally the servants of one master, Christ.

All Christians are **servants of Christ**. If we all behaved as servants of Christ, there would be no divisions in our churches (see Matthew 23:8,10).

The apostles have been entrusted with the **secret things** of God. These "secret things" make up the Gospel of Christ, the way of salvation. These secret things were once hidden, but are now revealed (Romans 1:17; 1 Corinthians 2:7). And these secret things have now been handed over to the apostles; the apostles are "stewards" of these things.

2 Stewards are men who have been entrusted with something, and anyone who has been entrusted with something must be faithful in the exercise of his responsibility. Because God has entrusted Paul with these secret things (the Gospel), Paul must faithfully preach these things to others, in order that **God's temple** (1 Corinthians 3:16)—that is, Christ's church—might be built up. Paul has been called to build the church, not his own party or faction.

3 In his work as an apostle, Paul does not seek the praise of men, but only the praise of God (see John 5:41,44; Galatians 1:10). Likewise, we too should not seek a good name among men. Of course, we don't need to seek a bad name either! Insofar as possible, we shouldn't let our name be stained, because this will then bring dishonor upon Christ's name. But if, as we carry out God's will, we are condemned by other men—that is, **by any human court**—let us not worry about it, says Paul. Men do not usually judge others fairly, because they don't have complete knowledge about what they are judging. But God always judges fairly. Therefore, Paul cares very much about God's judgment, but **very little** about man's judgment. **I do not even judge myself**, Paul says. That is, he doesn't even care about his own judgment of himself.

To examine oneself is good, but to judge oneself is useless. The reason is because we almost never judge ourselves accurately. Most of the time we judge ourselves to be innocent when, in fact, we are guilty (see 1 Corinthians 11:28,31 and comment).

4 Paul says here that he is not aware of anything against himself. That is, his **conscience is clear**. He has been a faithful "steward" of the Gospel; he has served Christ faithfully (2 Corinthians 1:12). But even though Paul's conscience is clear, that doesn't make him innocent. Often we do not see our own sins, or we quickly forget them. But God sees everything; He knows about our secret sins. We can never declare ourselves innocent, or righteous; only God can do that (see Romans 14:4).

It is the Lord who judges me. God has given to Christ full authority to judge all men (see John 5:22–23).

5 We have no business judging either ourselves or others. **At that time**—that is, at the day of judgment—Christ will judge each one of us (see Matthew 13:24–30,37–43). Only Jesus can judge correctly **what is hidden in darkness** (our sins); only Jesus can **expose the motives of men's hearts** (our secret desires and purposes). Thus, only Jesus is fit to be our judge (see Romans 2:16).

We are so ready to judge one another; it is even a habit with many of us. Yet should we not rather be afraid to judge each other? Because Jesus said that as we judge others, so also shall we ourselves be judged (see Matthew 7:1–2 and comment).

At that time each (person) **will receive his praise from God**. Here Paul is talking about believers. Unbelievers will receive condemnation on the day of judgment, but believers will receive **praise**. God will praise us (reward us) according to our labor (see 1 Corinthians 3:8,13–14). What are the praises of men compared to the **praise** of God! (see 2 Corinthians 10:18).

6 Paul here quotes a Jewish saying: **Do not go beyond what is written**—that is, do not teach beyond what is written in the Bible. (In Paul's time only the Old Testament existed; the New Testament had not yet been completed.) What is written in the Bible is the truth and wisdom of God. When we go beyond that, we will find only the wisdom of man, which is foolishness in God's eyes (1 Corinthians 3:19).

All man's blessings and gifts come from God. If that is so, why should we then **take pride in one man over against another**? Why should one man insist on following Paul, and another insist on following Apollos? (see 1 Corinthians 3:4–5,21). Taking pride in one man over another like this always leads to division; and such division is like a wound in Christ's body (the church).

7 Everything we have is from God. We have nothing we can call our own (except our sin). Therefore, we must not take pride either in ourselves or **in one man over against another**.

8 In this verse, Paul sarcastically repeats what the Corinthian believers think about themselves. Because the Corinthians had received some spiritual gifts, they were acting as if they were satisfied with themselves. "We have all we want," they thought. "We are already **rich**." They were acting like **kings**. But, in fact, they weren't rich at all. Spiritually they were poor; they were just **infants in Christ** (see 1 Corinthians 3:1–2; Revelation 3:17). Only in pride were they rich!

How backwards things were! These new Corinthian Christians had begun to think they were kings, while Paul and the other apostles were still mere laborers, lowly servants! If the Corinthians had truly been kings, what a nice thing that would have been, says Paul sarcastically; because then Paul himself could have been a king too! Paul, of course, did not want to be a king; in saying this, he was only trying to show the Corinthians how great their pride was.

9 Here Paul describes his own experience and that of his fellow APOSTLES. Because they were apostles, they had received all kinds of opposition not only from non-believers but from believers also. Instead of being like kings, they were like criminals sentenced to death. Every day they faced the risk of death.

In the time of the Roman Empire, criminals sentenced to die were forced to walk in a **procession** to the execution site; the criminals walked **at the end** of the procession. As the procession passed, other people would mock and insult the criminals. In other words, the criminals were put **on display**; they were **made a spectacle**. Each criminal had to carry his own cross, on which he was to be hung a few minutes later. Christ Himself had to carry His own cross in this way (John 19:17–18). Using an illustration taken from this same Roman custom of making criminals carry their own crosses, Jesus said to His disciples: "**If anyone would come after me, he must deny himself and take up his cross and follow me**" (Mark 8:34). Paul is saying here that he and his fellow apostles are like those condemned criminals; they had been **made a spectacle**; they had been put **on display** (see Romans 8:36).

10 Here again Paul writes sarcastically, repeating some of the things the Corinthians were saying about themselves. The Corinthians were acting as if they were better than the apostles. They regarded themselves as **wise, strong,** and **honored**, in contrast to the apostles who were **fools, weak**, and **dishonored**.

When Paul describes the actual situation of the apostles, he is not being sarcastic. The apostles had indeed become **fools** for Christ (2 Corinthians 12:11); they had indeed become **weak** and **dishonored** (1 Corinthians 2:3; 2 Corinthians 13:9).

11–13 In these verses, Paul continues to describe the life of an apostle. And this description doesn't apply only to the life of apostles; it applies to the life of every true Christian (see 2 Corinthians 6:4–10; 11:23–29). This description also applies to the life of Jesus Himself.

When we, like Paul, are **cursed, persecuted**, and **slandered** (verse 12), how do we behave in return? Can we say, like Paul, that when such trouble comes to us, we **bless**, **endure**, and **answer kindly**? For this is the behavior which God expects from every Christian (see Matthew 5:44; Luke 6:27; 1 Peter 2:21–23; 3:9 and comments).

Paul says in verse 12: **We work hard with our own hands**. In addition to preaching, Paul made tents as a profession (Acts 18:1–3). Wherever Paul went, he earned his own livilihood by making tents in his spare time (see 1 Thessalonians 2:9).

In writing these verses, is Paul complaining? No, he's not complaining. Paul is happy to **have become the scum of the earth, the refuse of the world** for Christ's sake (see Matthew 5:10–12; 20:16; 23:11–12; Mark 9:35; Philippians 3:7–8 and comments).

Warnings and Advice (4:14–21)

14–15 In verse 15, Paul writes that the Corinthian believers have **ten thousand guardians**.[9] A **guardian** in Paul's day was really a special high-ranking servant, paid to look after the master's children and take them to school. Thus Paul is saying that the Corinthians have many (ten thousand) of these spiritual "guardians" to look after them. However, these guardians are not the same as the children's own **father**. The Corinthians don't have many spiritual "fathers." Certainly Paul was their chief "father." Paul became their spiritual father **through the gospel**, which he had first preached to them. Therefore, Paul can call the Corinthian believers **my dear children** (verse 14).

16 Children should imitate their fathers. Paul imitated Christ; therefore, the Corinthian believers should imitate Paul (1 Corinthians 11:1). In doing so, however, they shouldn't become Paul's disciples; they should become disciples only of Christ. So closely did Paul imitate Christ that to imitate Paul was essentially the same as imitating Christ. How many of us, with Paul, can say that about ourselves?

What is involved in imitating Paul is described quite well in verses 11–13.

17 Paul plans to send **Timothy** to Corinth. Timothy was Paul's spiritual **son** (Acts 16:1–5; 1 Corinthians 16:10–11).

Paul writes here: . . . **my way of life . . . agrees with what I teach everywhere**. In other words, Paul practices what he preaches. As was his preaching, so was his life. Timothy will testify that this is true. Perhaps some of the Corinthians had falsely accused Paul of not practicing what he preached. But when Timothy gets to Corinth, he will take Paul's side and put an end to such false accusations.

Paul also says here that his teaching is the same in every church. He doesn't preach something to please people in one church, and then turn around and preach something different to please people in another church. Wherever Paul goes, he preaches the same truths.

Let us also imitate Paul. By our lives let us each give witness that we are faithful servants of Christ. Just as we preach, so let our lives be. And at all times, let us keep on boldly proclaiming the same truths of the Gospel, no matter whether people oppose us or not.

18 Some of the Corinthians who had become **arrogant** said that Paul didn't dare come to Corinth. Why doesn't he come himself? they asked. Why does he send Timothy in his place? Probably those who said this belonged to a party in the Corinthian church that opposed Paul and refused to accept his authority (1 Corinthians 1:12). Such people only wanted to increase their own authority.

19 But Paul wasn't afraid of his enemies at Corinth. He was planning to go himself to Corinth. Here he tells the Corinthians that he will come to them very soon—**if the Lord is willing.** All of Paul's plans depended on God's will; he didn't do anything according to his own will.

When Paul goes to Corinth, he will face those arrogant Corinthians. At that time

---

[9] In place of the word **guardian**, some translations of the Bible say "teacher." But the word "guardian" fits better with Paul's meaning.

he will find out if they have any real power or if they are only talking (2 Corinthians 12:11).

20 True apostles like Paul demonstrate God's power. One can identify true apostles, because they perform **signs, wonders and miracles** (2 Corinthians 12:12).

For the KINGDOM OF GOD is not a matter of talk only. We can listen to hundreds of sermons, and we can discuss the kingdom of God all day long; but for our lives to be holy, the thing we need is power, the power of the Holy Spirit.

21 Depending on the attitude and behavior of the Corinthian Christians, Paul will come either **with a whip**, or he will come **in love** (that is, with loving words) **and with a gentle spirit**. The choice is the Corinthians'. If their arrogant behavior continues, Paul will certainly come to them **with a whip**.

Like any other father, Paul continues to hope that his spiritual children at Corinth will repent. Paul doesn't want to use the "whip." He much prefers to meet them with a loving and gentle spirit.

But even if Paul has to bring the whip, he will still come to them **in love**. A father who truly loves his children will not hesitate, when necessary, to use the "whip" (see 2 Samuel 7:14; Hebrews 12:6 and comment).

CHAPTER 5

Immorality in the Church (5:1–13)

1 The citizens of Corinth were known for their sexual immorality, and this practice of immorality had come into the Corinthian church. Perhaps these new Corinthian Christians had supposed that having put faith in Christ and received salvation they could now behave in any way they pleased. If so, they would naturally begin to fall back into their old wicked customs.

One kind of sexual immorality that was present among the Corinthian Christians was so bad that even the ungodly citizens of Corinth didn't do it! That is, a man who called himself a Christian was living in adultery with his own stepmother! (Deuteronomy 22:30; 27:20). But there was another thing almost as bad: all the other Christians were tolerating this immorality; they didn't even care about it. That such a sin was present among them didn't seem to bother them at all.

2 In Chapter 4, Paul wrote about the arrogance of the Corinthians. Their arrogance was so great that they had begun to take pride in their own sins! Instead of being proud, they should have been mourning. Any man continuing in such a sin should have been immediately and publicly expelled from the church.

3 Paul was present with the Corinthians **in spirit** (see Colossians 2:5). All Christians can have spiritual fellowship with one another, even though they are not physically together.

Paul says that he has already **passed JUDGMENT** on the person who was committing adultery with his stepmother. What does Paul mean by this? Jesus Himself commanded: "**Do not judge**" (Matthew 7:1). Is Paul opposing a command of Jesus? Even Paul himself taught that Christians must not judge each other (Romans 14:4,13). Is he now opposing his own teaching?

No, Paul is not opposing Jesus' command or his own teaching. The confusion arises because there are two distinct kinds of judgment: One kind of judgment is the judgment of a man's outward work or behavior; the second kind of judgment is the judgment of a man's inward character and motives. Jesus' command, "**Do not judge**," refers to this second kind of judgment, the judgment of the inner man.

It is necessary and proper to "judge," or assess, a man's outward visible work and behavior; but it is wrong to judge the inner man himself. What Paul is really saying here is that he has **passed**

judgment not on the man himself but on his sin.[10]

4–5 Paul's "judgment" of the man committing adultery with his stepmother was not a final judgment of the man's soul. It was a judgment or decision concerning his sin at that particular time. Paul's judgment (decision) was that the man should be expelled from the church. But, says Paul, the Christians must expel the man only after assembling **in the name of our Lord** and only when the **power of our Lord Jesus is present** (verse 4).

The Corinthian Christians are to **hand this man over to SATAN** (verse 5). There are only two kingdoms a man can belong to—Satan's kingdom and God's kingdom—and a man belongs to either one or the other. If a man is expelled from one kingdom, he automatically ends up in the other. Any man who continues knowingly in sin does not belong to God's kingdom; he belongs to Satan's kingdom (1 John 3:8–9). Therefore, Paul says that this man must be transferred to Satan's kingdom.

Paul's hope is that this man, by being expelled, will come to hate his sin and repent of it, so that in the final judgment—**on the day of the Lord**—he might be saved (see 1 Timothy 1:20).

This man is to be handed over to Satan **so that the sinful nature may be destroyed**. Man's **sinful nature**[11] will be finally destroyed only at death. But through the sickness and suffering caused by Satan prior to death, a man can become repentant; and if he repents of his sins and turns in faith to Jesus he will be saved (Proverbs 23:14).

Thus we see there are two reasons why this sinful man should be expelled from the Corinthian church: first, to purify the church, which is God's holy temple (1 Corinthians 3:16–17); and second, to bring the sinful man to repentance, so that his eternal **spirit** might be saved.

Notice that, as far as a person's sin is concerned, there are two conditions necessary before any person is expelled from the church.[12] First, the person's sin must be a serious sin which is clearly visible and about which there is no question. Second, the person must be continuing in that sin with no sign of repentance. Those that repent of their sins should not be expelled from the church.

Remember, Paul does not despise this man who is to be expelled; he despises only his sin. There is a saying: It is not the child we beat, but the child's bad behavior. There is some truth to this saying. When we expel a person from the church, our purpose is not so much to expel the person as to expel his sin. It is primarily to cleanse the church of sin that we must expel the person. But the moment that person truly repents of his sin, we must forgive him and fully accept him back into the church. In fact, this is exactly what happened in the case of the man mentioned in this section (see 2 Corinthians 2:5–11 and comment).

---

[10] Some people believe that Paul, being an apostle, had received special authority from Christ to pass judgment in this particular situation. Such authority would not be given to ordinary Christians, these people say. However, others say there is nothing in the New Testament to support the idea that apostles are authorized to do things that other Christians are forbidden to do. Apostles are given special authority, it's true (Matthew 16:19; John 20:23), but not the authority to break Christ's commands.

[11] In place of the words **sinful nature**, some versions of the Bible say "flesh," which is a literal translation of the original Greek text. Paul uses the Greek word for "flesh" in two ways: first, he uses it to mean "body," which in itself is not sinful; and second, he uses it to mean "sinful nature," as in this verse. For further discussion, see footnote to comment on Romans 7:5; Word List: Flesh.

[12] In this paragraph, we are talking only about conditions relating to the person's sin. However, on the church's side, there are also two conditions necessary before a person can be expelled from the church. These two conditions are mentioned in verse 4: first, the church must have assembled **in the name of our Lord Jesus**—that is, in one mind and in accordance with Jesus' will; and second, the **power of our Lord Jesus** must be present. If these two conditions are not present, then the church should not take such severe action.

6 Paul here compares sin in the church to **yeast** in a **batch of dough**. Yeast is actually a microscopic organism, a fungus. If some of these yeast organisms are mixed with a batch of dough, they will spread throughout the entire batch and cause it to expand or swell up as the dough is baked. Thus a little bit of yeast changes the entire loaf. In the Bible, the word **yeast** is commonly used as a symbol of sin or evil (see Mark 8:15).

Paul has mentioned two main sins in the Corinthian church: pride and sexual immorality. Just as a **little yeast works through the whole batch of dough**, so these two sins (and other sins also) will spread through the whole church and defile it (see Galatians 5:9).

7–8 **Get rid of the old yeast** of sin and evil, Paul tells the Corinthian Christians. Expel not only this sinful man from your church, but also expel the sin from your own hearts!

Get rid of the old yeast, **that you may be a new batch without yeast—as you really are**. The Corinthian Christians (and all other Christians) have been made new spiritually; they are a **new batch** of dough. Therefore, they should be without the old yeast of sin. We Christians are a **new creation** (2 Corinthians 5:17). We are also **God's temple** (1 Corinthians 3:16–17). Therefore, there is no place in us for old yeast!

For Christ, our Passover lamb, has been sacrificed (verse 7). The word **Passover** means "deliverance." In Moses' time, the Jews lived in bondage in Egypt. To force the Egyptian ruler to set the Jews free, God sent many plagues upon the Egyptian people, the last of which was to cause the death of all the firstborn in Egypt, both of men and of animals. However, so that their own firstborn might be spared, the Jews sacrificed a lamb and painted its blood on their doorways (Exodus 12:6–8). Thus, when God sent His angel to kill all the firstborn of Egypt, the angel saw the blood on the Jewish homes and "passed over" their homes, sparing their firstborn (Exodus 12:12–13). In the morning the Egyptian ruler, filled with fear, let the Jews go free. Thus were the Jews delivered from bondage, and to this day they remember the event by celebrating the **Passover** (deliverance) festival.

On the night of their deliverance, together with the lamb they had sacrificed, the Jews also ate **bread made without yeast** (Exodus 12:8). God told them that they must thereafter, in remembrance of their deliverance, celebrate the Passover festival[13] each year (Exodus 12:14). During the period of the festival, they were to remove all yeast from their homes (Exodus 12:15). The reason was because the yeast was a sign of the sins of Egypt. In the same way, yeast was a sign of the sins in the Corinthian church.

Paul here calls Jesus Christ **our Passover lamb** (John 1:36). Through Jesus' death, through His blood, God has delivered us from bondage to sin, just as He delivered the Jews from bondage in Egypt (see 1 Peter 1:18–19). And just as those Jews had to eat their sacrificed lamb with bread made **without yeast**, so also must we **keep the Festival** (partake of Christ's life) **with bread without yeast**—that is, without the yeast of **malice and wickedness** (verse 8). The **bread without yeast** is the **bread of sincerity and truth**.

Instead of the Jewish Passover festival, Christians celebrate Jesus' death and resurrection. Jesus was put to death during the Passover festival. He Himself became the sacrifice for our "Passover," for our deliverance from sin.

But we Christians don't **keep** (celebrate) the Passover just one day or one week a year. We celebrate it continuously every day of the year. In fact, the Greek word **keep** which Paul uses here literally means "continue to keep." Therefore, if we are going to **keep the** (Passover) **Festival** each day of the year, we are also going to need to keep removing each day the old **yeast of malice and wickedness** from our hearts and from our church!

[13] The Passover festival is also called the Feast of Unleavened Bread. "Unleavened" means "without yeast."

9–10 Paul refers here in verse 9 to an earlier letter that has been lost. This is not the same as the other lost letter referred to in 2 Corinthians 2:3–4.

In the letter referred to here in verse 9, Paul had written to the Corinthians that they must not associate at all with sexually immoral people. Paul's meaning was that they shouldn't associate with sexually immoral people who called themselves Christians. However, when it came to associating with sexually immoral people who were not Christians and who were outside the church, that was a different matter. It was necessary to associate with these non-believers, because otherwise one would never get a chance to share the Gospel with them. Christ Himself associated with sinners (see Mark 2:15–17). If we had to avoid associating with all sinners in this world, we'd have to leave the world! (see John 17:15).

11 Here Paul further explains the meaning of his previous letter: The Corinthian Christians must not associate with **anyone who calls himself a** (Christian) **brother**, and who also continually does these other evil things listed in this verse (see 2 Thessalonians 3:6). **With such a man do not even eat**; that is, have no association with him whatever. Such a man must be expelled from the church (verse 13).

Sin coming into the church from the outside is indeed a great danger; but a far greater danger exists from sin that arises within the church. That sin is like yeast, which quickly spreads and makes the entire church impure.

12–13 Making judgments or decisions about people **outside the church** (unbelievers) is not the business of Christians. God will judge those **outside**. It is the believers' responsibility, however, to **judge** or make decisions about those **inside** the church. This responsiblity to "judge" fellow Christians applies only to judging their outward behavior, not their inward being (see verse 3 and comment).

This judging should be done only by those in the church who are properly authorized to give discipline—which in some churches could be the entire congregation acting as one body (verse 4). In the case of a church member who is living in sin, the other church members have the responsibility to expel that person in order to keep the church pure.

But remember that the judgment Paul is speaking of here involves only judging outward actions, not man's inner self. God alone is worthy and able to judge man himself.

CHAPTER 6

Lawsuits Among Believers (6:1–11)

1 In this section Paul brings up another problem in the Corinthian church, which had been reported to him by others: namely, some members of the church were going to court with charges against other church members; **one brother goes to law against another** (verse 6).

In any church it's possible for a dispute to arise between members from time to time. It shouldn't happen, but we all know that it does. Christ also knew that these kinds of disputes would arise. And He gave clear instructions as to what to do when they arose—and those instructions involved settling the dispute within the church (see Matthew 18:15–17 and comment). But the Corinthian Christians were going outside the church to law courts and accusing each other **before the ungodly**, that is, before unbelievers.

Why does Paul call unbelievers the **ungodly**? Because all men are ungodly until they believe in Jesus (Romans 3:10). It is only through faith in Christ that man can be declared "godly," or righteous (see Romans 5:1; Galatians 2:15–16 and comments).

Paul asks: How can the **ungodly** pass judgment on the SAINTS, that is, believers? Believers can only be judged according to spiritual criteria; the **spiritual man . . . is not subject to any man's judgment** (1 Corinthians 2:15).

Paul does not mean here that Christians should disregard the decisions of the judges and the courts. No indeed. Paul himself submitted to all civil authorities and respected them (see Romans 13:1–7). Paul is only saying here that those disputes that arise between Christians should be settled in the church and not in civil courts.

2 The **saints** (believers) **will judge the world.**[14] Since they are going to judge the world, they ought to be able to judge in such tiny things as disputes between brothers!

When will believers **judge the world**? They will judge the world when Christ comes again on the day of judgment (see Matthew 19:28; Revelation 3:21 and comments).

3 Believers will also judge ANGELS (see 2 Peter 2:4; Jude 6). Who are these **angels** whom we will judge? They are heavenly beings. Some angels have remained obedient to God and serve Him. Others, like Satan and his evil spirits, have rebelled against God and now oppose Him (see Revelation 12:9). On the day of judgment, these evil angels (evil spirits) will be judged and condemned. Paul's point is this: If the Corinthian Christians are one day going to judge heavenly beings like angels, then surely they ought to be able to judge earthly things like disputes between brothers!

4 Paul says here that since the Corinthian Christians are going to judge such big things as the world and angels, then surely **even men of little account in the church**[15] should be able to judge the disputes that arise between brothers. Anyway, it is better to appoint **even men of little account in the church** to judge disputes than to go outside the church to ungodly judges.

Who are these **men of little account in the church**? They are ordinary Christians. Paul is thinking here especially of the very humble and uneducated members of the church. Even these Christians **of little account** are more competent to judge church disputes than outside judges.

5 The Corinthian Christians took great pride in their "wisdom." They thought they were wiser than the apostles (1 Corinthians 4:20). Therefore, asks Paul sarcastically, how can there be no one wise enough in the church to judge these disputes between brothers?

6 To take your Christian brother to court is very wrong. When you do that, you become your brother's enemy. If you do that, where is love? Instead of disputing with your brother, it would be far better to give up the dispute and let your brother win—even if it meant

---

[14] This statement seems to contradict Paul's statement in 1 Corinthians 5:12–13, where he says it is not the business of believers **to judge those outside the church . . . God will judge those outside**. But in Chapter 5, Paul is not talking primarily of the last judgment, but rather of judging people here on earth. Whereas in Chapter 6, Paul is talking only about the last judgment at the end of the world.

Of course, at the last judgment the "chief" judge will be God. But God has entrusted the work of judgment to Christ (John 5:22); and Christ, in turn, will in some way give believers a share in that work. So it is in this sense that we **will judge the world**.

[15] The Greek text of this verse is difficult to understand. Bible scholars have two main ideas about what Paul means here. Any comment on this verse thus depends on which version of the Bible one is using.

The main difference in meaning concerns whether Paul is asking a question or giving a command. The version used in this commentary translates Paul's words as a command: . . . **appoint as judges even men of little account in the church**.

However, other versions translate the same words: ". . . why do you lay such cases before those who are least esteemed by the church?" If this second translation is chosen, then the **men of little account** are not believers, but rather the ungodly judges outside the church. According to this second translation, Paul's meaning is that the Corinthians should not be bringing disputes before these ungodly judges. Thus, whichever of the two translations one chooses, Paul's point is the same.

suffering loss (verse 7). That is the Christian way. Jesus taught that we should not even oppose an unbeliever in court (see Matthew 5:25,39–41). If that's so, how much worse it is to take our Christian brother to court and oppose him **in front of unbelievers!**[16]

7 Paul now goes to the heart of the Corinthians' sin in this matter. Their sin is to have the disputes in the first place; where they are settled is a secondary issue. Simply engaging in these disputes means that the Corinthians are spiritually **defeated already**. These disputes are proof that the Corinthians are still immature and worldly. In disputing with their brother, they are, in fact, sinning against him. They may have defeated their brother in court, but sin has defeated them in their hearts!

It is much better to suffer a little loss in this world than to suffer eternal loss on the day of judgment!

8 Even though our brother has cheated us or wronged us in some way, if we take him to court, we **cheat** and **wrong** him in return. Because when we do that, we are not forgiving and loving our brother; we are cheating him out of our love and forgiveness. And when we do not love and forgive our brother, we sin against him.

9–10 Who are the **wicked**? (verse 9). They are the same as the **ungodly** in verse 1; that is, they are unbelievers. They are those who are mentioned here in verses 9–10, those who continue in these sins without repenting. Such people **will not inherit the kingdom of God** (see Galatians 5:19–21). What is our inheritance in the kingdom of God? Salvation—eternal life.

11 The Corinthian Christians had once been **wicked**, unrighteous; they had once been sinners like those mentioned in verses 9–10. But now they were no longer unrighteous. Through faith in Christ and through the power of the Holy Spirit they had been converted, transformed.

How had they been transformed? First, they had been **washed**. They had repented of their sins and had been baptized with water **in the name of the Lord Jesus Christ and by the Spirit of our God**—the Holy Spirit (see Mark 1:4,7–8 and comment).

Then, having been **washed**, they were **sanctified**. They became a new creation in Christ (see 2 Corinthians 5:17 and comment).

Having been **sanctified**, they were then **justified**—or declared RIGHTEOUS,—in God's sight (see Titus 3:3–7).

All these things are included in our salvation. We receive this salvation **by grace** and **through faith** (see Ephesians 2:8 and comment; General Article: Way of Salvation).

Therefore, if the Corinthians, and we also, have truly been **washed, sanctified,** and **justified**, how then can we continue to behave as we did before we became Christians? If we are new creations, we must behave like new creations (see Romans 6:17–18; Ephesians 4:1 and comments).

Sexual Immorality (6:12–20)

12 "**Everything** (except sin) **is permissible for me**" was a common saying among the Corinthian Christians. But even though some action might not be a sin and therefore legally permissible, it still might not be beneficial for a person to do it. The action could result in harm both to the person himself and to his brother (see Romans 14:21; 1 Corinthians 8:9; 1 Peter 2:16 and comments).

Paul says: **I will not be mastered by anything.** Paul will allow no bodily desire to dominate him, or to "rule" over him. It is possible for us, through the very freedom we have found in Christ, to again allow ourselves to become slaves of our sinful desires. Our freedom in Christ is not for sinning, but for serving God! (see Romans 6:18,22; Galatians 5:13 and comments). Therefore, let us not again make sin our master (see John 8:34).

---

[16]Think of how doubly offended God must be when Christian couples divorce each other in public courts!

13 The Corinthians had another saying: "**Food for the stomach and the stomach for food.**" This saying is true. In this life, the stomach and food are indeed made for each other. But in heaven there will be no need for either food or stomach; God will **destroy them both**.

However, the Corinthians also said: "Just as the stomach is made for food, so the body is made for sexual pleasure"—and that saying is not true. God will do away with our stomachs in heaven, but He will not do away with our bodies. Instead, He will raise our bodies (verse 14).

Our bodies are not made for sexual pleasure, or any other kind of pleasure; our bodies are made to serve the Lord. Our body is the dwelling place of the Holy Spirit (verse 19). Therefore, we must not be mastered by any pleasure. To be mastered by pleasure is to make our body a slave to sin all over again.

Just as food and stomach are made for each other, so the Lord and our bodies are made for each other. The Lord is spiritual "food" for our bodies (see John 6:54).

14 God raised Christ; He will also raise us. He will raise not only our spirits, but He will raise our bodies as well (see Romans 6:5,8; 8:11; Ephesians 2:6; Philippians 3:20–21 and comments).

15 Our bodies are **members of Christ** (1 Corinthians 12:27). If we sleep with a prostitute, then we no longer belong to Christ but to the prostitute.

In Corinth, the prostitutes practiced their profession in the temple of the Greek goddess of love. Therefore, whenever a man had intercourse with a prostitute, he also became united with the goddess of the prostitute; he became, in a sense, an idol worshiper. According to the Bible, idol worshp is like adultery. When a man worships an idol, he is leaving the one true God and uniting himself with a false god or demon (Ezekiel 23:37: Hosea 5:4).

16 Just as a man and his wife become **one flesh** during intercourse, so a man who has intercourse with a prostitute becomes "one flesh" with that prostitute. Paul here quotes from Genesis 2:24, which is written about marriage. (Paul doesn't mean here that the man and the prostitute become "married" by having intercourse; they do not. In true marriage a man and wife are united not only in body but also in heart and mind and spirit.)

Paul's point is this: How can a man who is united with Christ in one spiritual body then go and unite himself in one body with a prostitute? This is a terrible sin against Christ. It is not only physical adultery; it is also spiritual adultery.

17 Just as a man and a woman become united in body, so does Christ become united in spirit with each believer (see John 17:20–23).

18 With the exception of **sexual immorality**, all sinful desires can be satisfied by objects that are not part of one's body. The desire to drink alcohol is satisfied by alcohol. The desire to become rich is satisfied by money. But the desire to have sexual intercourse is satisfied only by the stimulation of one's own body. Thus sexual immorality in a special way defiles one's body, because during fornication one's own body is given in sin to a prostitute or adulteress. This is what Paul means when he says that **he who sins sexually sins against his own body**.

Therefore Paul says: **Flee from sexual immorality**. Not only must we resist the temptation to sexual immorality; we must run away from it!

19 When we engage in sexual immorality, we are defiling not just our body but also God's temple—because the believer's body is itself God's temple. By our sin we "destroy" or ruin God's temple. If we do this, He will also destroy us (1 Corinthians 3:16–17).

It is not only God's temple that we destroy by sexual immorality; it is also the Holy Spirit's temple—because the body of each Christian is a temple of the Holy Spirit. We must not defile or make unholy the Holy Spirit's temple—that is, our body. If we do, the Holy Spirit will leave us; He will not dwell in an unholy place.

Our bodies are the temple of God and of His Holy Spirit; therefore, our bodies belong to God. **You are not your own,** Paul says. The Corinthian believers thought that their bodies were their own, and that therefore they could do as they pleased with their bodies. They thought that God didn't care that much about their bodies, but only cared about their spirits. How wrong they were!

20 How much does God care about our bodies? He cares so much that He bought our bodies! (see 1 Corinthians 7:23). What was the price God paid? The price He paid was the blood—the body—of his only Son Jesus Christ (see Mark 10:45; Acts 20:28; 1 Peter 1:18–19 and comments). God has bought us. Therefore, we must hand over our bodies, our lives, to Him (see Romans 12:1 and comment). Our bodies, our lives, are God's. All the parts of our bodies, our members, are not ours but God's. Therefore, we must use our members not according to our own will but according to God's will. In this world our lives have only one purpose, and that purpose is to glorify God with our entire selves—body, soul, and spirit.

CHAPTER 7

Teaching Concerning Marriage (7:1–24)

1 The Corinthian Christians had written to Paul asking some questions about marriage, and in this chapter, Paul gives the answers to their questions.

Paul starts out by saying: **It is good for a man not to marry.**[17] Why does Paul say that? Paul says it because, in the unmarried state, a man has more time to serve the Lord.

But in order to remain unmarried one needs from God a special **gift** (verse 7) of self-control; that is, one needs a special calling to remain unmarried. Most men and women do not have this gift, and therefore it is better that they marry.

2 One of the reasons that God established marriage was to prevent sexual immorality. All men and women have sexual desires and needs. But if every person has his or her own wife or husband, then there will be no need for anyone to engage in immoral sexual acts.

In this verse, Paul is not saying that every man must marry; he himself was not married! Paul is only saying this: Let each man who marries have his own wife, and let each woman who marries have her own husband.

3–4 The expression **marital duty** in verse 3 means "having sexual intercourse." Without sexual intercourse a marriage is not complete. One of the essential functions of marriage is that a man and a woman, through intercourse, become joined together as one body, as **one flesh** (Ephesians 5:31).

For this reason, a man and his wife must fulfill their duty to each other to engage in sexual intercourse. They must submit to one another in sexual matters (Ephesians 5:21). Their bodies should remain under each other's control. The wife's body belongs not only to herself but also to her husband, and the husband's body belongs not only to himself but also to his wife. They belong equally to one another.

In many cultures, the wife is considered to be the property of her husband. In such societies, all authority and all rights belong to the husband. The wife only has the "right" to honor and obey and serve her husband. The wife is like a slave. In God's eyes, such servitude is a corruption of true marriage. This was not God's intention when he established marriage between man and woman (see General Article: Christian Marriage).

5 In marriage, if the wife desires to have intercourse, the husband should agree (unless some legitimate reason prevents it). If the husband desires to have intercourse, the wife should agree. If the husband and wife refuse to fulfill each

---

[17] In place of the words **not to marry,** some versions of the Bible say, "not to touch a woman," which is the literal translation of the Greek text. The meaning is the same.

other's desire in sexual matters, then they **deprive each other**, and this is wrong. The husband and wife should always remain ready and willing to fufill each other's needs and desires.

For this reason, a husband and wife should not remain separated from one another unless absolutely necessary. Paul mentions only one suitable reason why a husband and wife should for a time **deprive each other**—that is, abstain from sexual intercourse—and that reason is so that they can both devote special time to prayer.[18] If they do abstain for this reason, it should be **by mutual consent**, and then only **for a time**. Otherwise, their sexual desire will build up, and the temptation to engage in sexual immorality may overcome them.

In many countries it is customary for the husband, in particular, to leave his wife and go away for a prolonged period to study or to work. According to the teaching of the Bible, this custom is not good. A Christian couple planning such a prolonged separation should diligently seek God's will in the matter. They should not go ahead with their plan unless they are convinced that it is God's will.[19] If it is essential that the husband move to a different place, every effort should be made to have the wife accompany her husband.

Some people believe that the only reason for having sexual intercourse is to produce children. But here Paul gives two other reasons why sexual intercourse in marriage is essential: first, to minimize the temptation to sexual immorality; and second, to enable a couple to experience the joy and intimacy which comes from fulfilling each other's sexual needs.

6 Paul says: I say **this** as a concession, not as a command. The "this" he refers to is what he said in verse 2: namely, that a man or woman should be married to his or her own spouse. Paul is not giving a **command** that everyone get married. Rather, he is only saying that most people need to get married in order to keep themselves from sexual immorality. After saying in verse 1 that it is **good for a man not to marry**, Paul then says in verse 6—**as a concession**—that, for most people, marriage will be necessary.

7 Paul writes: **I wish that all men were as I am**—that is, unmarried. Paul wishes this because unmarried people are able to devote more time and energy to serving Christ. **But each man has his own gift from God**. Paul had the **gift** of self-control; because of that, it was not necessary for him to marry. Others have different gifts. For example, those who marry will likely have the "gift" of raising children, or the gift of hospitality.

8 Paul here repeats the thought of verse 1: namely, that it is **good** to remain unmarried.

Paul again encourages those who have the gift of self-control to remain unmarried—**as I am**, Paul adds. It is not known whether Paul was previously married or not. Almost all Jewish men married, and Paul was a very strict Jew. It is possible that he had once been married but his wife had died. The only thing we know for sure is that at the time Paul wrote this letter, he was unmarried.

The word **unmarried** in this verse can have three meanings. First, it can refer to a person who has never married. Second, it can refer to a person who has once married but whose spouse has died—that

---

18 Many people believe that they should abstain from sexual intercourse during the wife's menstrual period (Leviticus 15:19,24; 18:19). However, this doesn't mean that a husband and wife must remain separated during this time. Furthermore, the Old Testament laws regarding intercourse during a wife's period are not binding on Christians. Those laws are among the Jewish purification laws, which Christ has canceled.

19 In the case of compulsory military service, of course, the husband must serve his required time. However, in many cases young men enlist voluntarily for financial reasons. In this case, a young Christian husband must have very clear direction from God before making such a decision. It would never be God's will for a man to jeopardize his marriage for financial gain. This would also be true for a husband who leaves his wife to work at some high paying job; only if absolutely necessary should a Christian husband ever consider doing this.

is, a widow or widower. Third, it can refer to a person who has been divorced from his or her spouse.[20] It is probable, however, that Paul is thinking mainly of the first meaning here, because he mentions **widows** (the second meaning) separately.

9 Paul advises the **unmarried and the widows** who **cannot control themselves** to marry rather than to **burn with passion**. That is, those without the gift of self-control should marry. This advice applies to both men and women.

To **burn with passion** is perfectly natural; it is not in itself sinful. However, if such passion remains unsatisfied, it can lead to temptation and then to sin. Therefore, one should not let such passion continue **to burn**; rather, one should get married.

10–11 Marriage is for a lifetime: that is Christ's command (Mark 10:6–9). **A wife must not separate from her husband** (verse 10). **And a husband must not divorce his wife** (verse 11). But if one of them has divorced the other (or is living separately from the other), they should make every effort to be reconciled to each other. If that proves impossible, then they will have to remain unmarried. There are only two conditions clearly given in Scripture under which it is lawful for divorced people to remarry. The first condition is when one's spouse has committed adultery; then it is lawful for the innocent spouse to remarry (Matthew 5:32). The second condition is when the divorced spouse dies; then also it is lawful for the surviving spouse to remarry (Romans 7:3; 1 Corinthians 7:39). If either of these two conditions do not exist, then a divorced person should not remarry; to do so would be to commit adultery.[21]

12–13 Here Paul turns to a different subject: the marriage in which one spouse is a believer and the other is not.

In verse 12, Paul addresses **the rest**. "The rest" are those believers who are married to unbelievers. There is no written teaching of Jesus on this subject. Because Jesus' ministry on earth lasted only three years, this problem of "mixed marriages" may not have arisen during His lifetime—certainly not for many people. Therefore, He would have had little occasion to teach about it. This is why, in this section, Paul speaks on his own authority as an apostle. He says: I **say this (I, not the Lord)**. Paul also speaks with the authority of the Holy Spirit (verse 40), because it is through the Holy Spirit's direct inspiration that Paul has written all of his New Testament letters.

Before looking at Paul's teaching on this subject of mixed marriages (in which only one spouse is a believer), it is important to reaffirm another of Paul's basic teachings: namely, that a Christian must never marry a non-Christian (2 Corinthians 6:14).

However, if one is already married and then afterward becomes a believer, what should one do? Paul's answer is this: If the unbelieving spouse is willing to live with the believing spouse, then the believing spouse must not divorce the unbelieving one. Such a marriage is still holy in God's sight.

14 **For the unbelieving husband has been sanctified through his wife, and the unbelieving wife has been sanctified through her believing husband.** This does not mean that the unbelieving spouse will receive salvation. It means

---

[20] Because the word **unmarried** can also mean those who are divorced, some Christian scholars believe that Paul teaches in verse 9 that it is all right under certain circumstances for divorced people to remarry. However, in verse 11, Paul says that a divorced woman should **remain unmarried or else be reconciled to her husband** (see Matthew 5:32; Mark 10:6–12 and comments).

[21] Some Christians say that there are still other conditions which permit a divorced person to remarry. One possible condition is mentioned in verse 15. However, these other conditions are not clearly stated in the Bible. We must not bend the verses of Scripture to make them say what we wish they would say. The subject, however, is complicated, and sincere Christian scholars have different opinions on the matter. For further discussion, see General Article: Christian Marriage.

that the purity and holiness of the believing spouse will in some way reflect on the unbelieving spouse and on their children. The spiritual blessings which God gives the believing spouse will also to some extent come upon the unbelieving spouse, their children, and even upon their entire household (Genesis 7:7; 39:4–5).

The **children . . . are holy**. This does not mean that children are automatically saved because of the faith of their parents. For we know that to be saved, each individual must believe for him or herself and be born again by the Holy Spirit (John 3:3). But the meaning of the above statement is this: The children of believing parents (or even of one believing parent) are in some way born into God's household, into God's family. But even though that is so, it is of course necessary that as soon as they are old enough they themselves put their faith in Christ. No person can be naturally born a Christian. A person is saved not through the faith of his mother or father but only through his own faith.

15 If the unbelieving spouse wants to leave, then the believing spouse should let the unbeliever leave. Why? Because God wants a husband and wife **to live in peace**. If the unbelieving spouse is always quarreling with the believing spouse, then let that marriage end! God is not pleased with a marriage full of strife.

If the unbelieving spouse leaves, the believing spouse **is not bound in such circumstances**. Many Christians think that Paul is saying here that it's all right for the believing spouse to remarry, because the **believing man or woman is not bound**.

16 The believing spouse must continually hope and pray that the unbelieving spouse will become a Christian and be saved (see 1 Peter 3:1–2). But if reconciliation is not possible, then the believing spouse should not force the unbelieving spouse to stay.

17 Paul now gives a general rule for everyone: **. . . each one should retain the place in life that the Lord assigned to him**. Even though we have been spiritually transformed as Christians, that doesn't mean we should expect our social and economic situation to be transformed as well.[22] For example, if a person was married when he first believed in Christ—that is, **when he was called** (verse 18)—then let him, if at all possible, remain married. If a person was **circumcised** (a Jew) when he first believed, then let him remain a Jew (verse 18). If a person was a slave, then let him remain a slave (verse 21).

18–19 No matter what our situation in life is, the most important thing is to remain obedient to God. **Keeping God's commands is what counts**, writes Paul (verse 19). Whether one is married or unmarried, CIRCUMCISED or uncircumcised, slave or free, is not the important thing (see Galatians 3:28; 5:6; 6:15). The most important thing is this—that we have been called to do God's will, to love and obey His Son Jesus Christ (John 14:21).

20–21 God can always change our outward circumstances; that is no problem for Him. If we are unmarried, and after becoming a Christian we want a husband or wife, God can provide one for us. If we are slaves, God can free us. But we ourselves must not try to change our situation by force or according to our own will. Instead, we must wait for God's leading and God's action (verses 20,24). God knows much better than we do what is best for us, and He certainly knows what is going to glorify Him the most. We have only one duty: to lead a life worthy of the calling to which we have been called (Ephesians 4:1).

22 Our outward situation—whether we are married, circumcised, or slaves—is of no account. The only thing that counts is that we belong to Christ. Nothing else matters more than this. A slave who believes in Christ is the **Lord's freedman**—and such a man is truly free (see

[22] Our social and economic situation will often improve after we have become Christians, but not always. God sometimes will withhold material blessings from us in order to give us greater spiritual blessings.

John 8:31–32,36). Or looked at another way, the free man who believes in Christ is, in fact, **Christ's slave**. Therefore, whether outwardly we're slave or whether we're free, inwardly we belong to Christ.

23 Once Christ has bought us, we are His "slaves." Even though outwardly we are another man's slave or servant, inwardly we belong to Christ and we must obey Him above all. He alone is our true master and Lord.

Christ has bought us. Just as, in Paul's day, slaves were bought and sold like property or cattle, so we also have been bought by Christ. What price did Christ pay for us? The price was His own blood, His own life (see 1 Corinthians 6:20; 1 Peter 1:18–19).

24 Paul here repeats what he wrote in verse 20.

Questions Concerning Virgins (7:25–40)

25 The word **virgin** in the Greek language[23] means a man or woman who has never been married. Therefore, in verses 25–28, we can understand that Paul is talking about both men and women who are virgins.

26 By the expression **present crisis,** Paul means the great difficulties and sufferings that were continually coming upon Christians in the Roman Empire during New Testament times.

Paul advises that under such circumstances it would be better to remain unmarried. People can usually endure persecution more easily if they don't have a wife and children to worry about!

27 Insofar as possible, let people remain in the situation they are in. Let them accept the circumstances in which God has placed them (see verse 17 and comment).

28 If anyone needs to get married, let him marry; that is no sin. But those who marry will experience more worry and trouble than the unmarried—such as, where they shall live, how they shall care for their family, etc. The married woman will have the additional troubles of giving birth, raising children, and remaining under her husband's authority. Paul urges the Corinthians to think twice before they get married under such circumstances!

29–31 One of the main reasons Paul advises Christians not to try to change their outward situation is that he believes **the time is short**. Paul's statement, **the time is short**, can have two meanings: first, that in this world our life is short; or second, that this world will soon end (see Romans 13:11–12). Whichever meaning we choose, one thing is sure: in a few short years our own lives on this earth will end—and, as a practical matter, that will be the "end of the world" for us. Because after that the next significant event for us will be the last judgment at the real end of the world.

Therefore, for all of us, the time is indeed short. In a few years, we who believe in Jesus will leave this earth to be with Him forever. So, then, why should we be filled with worry and care about our earthly situation? (see Matthew 6:31–33; Mark 4:19; Colossians 3:2). For example, in heaven we will not be married (Matthew 22:30). Therefore, those of us who have husbands and wives **should live as though** [we] **had none**. That is, we should not put so much concentration on marriage here on earth. Rather, let us concentrate most of all on keeping God's commands (verse 19).

By the same reasoning, whether we **mourn** or whether we are **happy** here on earth is not of great importance. Soon we will leave this earth; then all who have believed in Jesus will be **happy**, and those who have not believed will **mourn**. Therefore, let those who mourn and rejoice on earth do so as if their sadness or happiness will quickly pass—that is, let them mourn and rejoice **as if they did not** (verse 30).

Likewise, **those who buy something** should buy it knowing they can't keep it for long; let us not think we can store things up for ourselves (see Matthew 6:19–21; Luke 12:16–21 and

[23] Paul wrote all of his letters in the Greek language.

comments). We came into this world naked, and we shall leave naked (Job 1:21).

Likewise, **those who use the things of the world** should use them without being **engrossed in them**, or attached to them. That is, let us use the things of the world wisely, as good stewards. Let us use the things of the world—but not let the things of the world use us! The world is in our hands—but let it not be in our hearts (see John 2:15–17). **For this world in its present form is passing away** (verse 31).

32–34 In these three verses Paul again points out the advantages of remaining **unmarried**. The unmarried man or woman's duty is to Christ alone. Married men and women have duties both to Christ and to their spouses. The married person's attention is turned in two directions; it is divided. That is not a sin, because God has given married couples responsibilities for each other and for their children. But in Paul's opinion, it is better to remain single, so that one's entire care and attention can be given to the Lord.

35 Nevertheless, Paul does not want to **restrict** or lay any restraint upon the Corinthian believers. That is, let them be under no obligation either to marry or not to marry. Rather, let it be their one goal to **live in a right way in undivided devotion to the Lord**. On one side, if a person does not need to get married, it is better to stay single; otherwise, marriage could become an obstacle to that person's devotion to the Lord. On the other side, if a person does need to get married, it is better to marry; otherwise, "burning passion" (verse 9) could become an obstacle to that person's devotion to the Lord. If a person is always desiring to get married, how is he or she going to be devoted to the Lord without distraction? Such people will be able to serve the Lord much better if they marry! We each must live according to the gifts and calling which God has given to us (verse 7,17).

Therefore, whether we are married or unmarried—no matter what our situation is—let us as much as possible live **in undivided devotion to the Lord**.

36–38 There is uncertainty about how verses 36–38 should be translated. In the Greek text, it is not clear whether Paul is talking about a man and his fiancee, or whether he is talking about a father and his virgin daughter. The Bible translation used in this commentary follows the first meaning. The second meaning is mentioned in the footnote.[24]

According to the first meaning, a man who is engaged to a **virgin** is free to marry her or not to marry her. He should not feel under obligation to do one or the other. He should determine what the Lord's gifts and calling are to him, and then act accordingly. If the man **has control over his own will**—if he has been given the gift of self-control—and if he is convinced of the Lord's will, then he does right in not marrying the virgin he is engaged to.

Either way, the man **does right**, whether he marries or not. As usual,

---

[24] The alternate translation of verses 36–38 is as follows: "[36]If anyone thinks he is not treating his daughter properly, and if she is getting along in years, and he feels she ought to marry, he should do as he wants. He is not sinning. They should get married. [37]But the man who has settled the matter in his own mind, who is under no compulsion but has control over his own will, and who has made up his mind to keep the virgin unmarried—this man also does the right thing. [38]So then, he who gives his virgin in marriage does right, but he who does not give her in marriage does even better."

In most of the countries of Paul's day, as in many countries today, it was a father's duty to give his daughter in marriage. If the father did not arrange his daughter's marriage properly, she was put to shame. Thus, a father was "not treating his daughter properly" if he neglected to arrange her marriage. In such a circumstance, says Paul, the father should arrange for his daughter to marry. To do so would not be a sin (verse 36).

But if a father is convinced that his daughter should remained unmarried so that she might better serve the Lord, then he should not arrange her marriage (verse 37). Either way, the father "does right," whether he gives his daughter in marriage or not. However, Paul thinks it better if he does not give her in marriage (verse 38).

however, Paul thinks it better not to marry (verses 1,8).

39 A widow is always free to remarry (see Romans 7:2). But if she remarries, the person she marries **must belong to the Lord**; that is, he must be a believer.

This same teaching would apply also to a man whose wife has died, and who wants to remarry. He, too, must marry a believer.

40 In Paul's opinion, it is better if a widow (or widower) **stays as she is**—that is, stays unmarried and does not marry again. He believes she will be **happier** if she remains single. However, in 1 Timothy 5:14, Paul advises that widows who are young should usually get married again.

Paul's opponents in Corinth probably scoffed at Paul's letters, saying that the things Paul wrote were only his personal opinions and had no authority; therefore, it was not necessary to pay any attention to them. For this reason Paul reminds the Corinthians here that He has received the Holy Spirit as much as any of them—and surely much more so! Therefore, let them heed what he writes!

CHAPTER 8

Food Sacrificed to Idols (8:1–13)

1 The Corinthian Christians had written to Paul earlier asking him whether it was all right to eat food sacrificed to idols. In answering their question, Paul first talks about **knowledge** that **puffs up**. Why does he do that? Because the Corinthians had been arguing among themselves on this subject of food sacrificed to idols as if they knew everything. They were "puffed up" with what they thought was "knowledge." Some of them said it was all right to eat food that had been sacrificed to idols; others said it was not all right. Both sides were sure that they possessed **knowledge** of the subject; but what they didn't possess was love for each other. Without love, knowledge **puffs up**. But love **builds up** (see 1 Corinthians 13:2,8).

2 We are all familiar with the kind of man who thinks he knows everything and won't listen to anyone else. Such a man is puffed up with pride. He **does not know as he ought to know**.

How are we supposed to "know" things? With love and humility. We need to remember that we are only human, and that therefore our knowledge is limited. The wise man realizes how little knowledge he really has, and thus he remains humble (see 1 Corinthians 3:18–20).

3 If we want to obtain knowledge, we must first love God. That is the first and greatest commandment. If we do not **love** God, that means we do not **know** Him (1 John 4:8). And to know God is the highest knowledge of all. **The fear of the Lord** (God) **is the beginning of wisdom** (Psalm 111:10; Proverbs 1:7).

Thus we know God by two means. First, we know God when we love Him. Second, we know God when we know His Son, Jesus Christ. If we know Jesus, we will know God (see John 14:7–9 and comment).

However, in this verse Paul isn't talking mainly about our knowing God, but about God knowing us. The person who loves God is **known by God**. What does that mean? To be "known by God" means to be God's child; it means to be loved by God (see John 10:14,27). If we are not **known by God**, our situation is frightening indeed! (see Matthew 7:22–23).

Therefore, let us seek love first, not knowledge. If we have love, then we will have true knowledge also.

4 In Corinth, almost all the meat sold in shops had first been sacrificed to idols. The priests kept part of the meat, and then sold the rest to the shopkeepers. The question the Corinthian Christians had written to Paul about was whether it was okay to eat such meat.

Paul's answer is this: . . . **an idol is nothing at all**. If an idol is **nothing at all,** then there is no difference between meat sacrificed to an idol and meat that has not been sacrificed. And thus it makes no difference whether one eats such meat or doesn't eat it. Therefore, Paul is saying that it's all right to eat such meat (see 1 Corinthians 10:25–30 and comment).

Here we must understand an important thing. Eating food sacrificed to an idol is not the same as worshiping an evil spirit; these are two totally different things. There is nothing wrong simply with eating food that has been sacrificed to idols, because an idol itself is **nothing**. But if, as we eat, we are also worshiping that idol in some way, or worshiping the evil spirit or god that the idol represents, then that is a very great sin (Exodus 20:3–6; Romans 1:25). If anyone considers an idol to be a spirit or a god, then let that person not eat food offered to idols; otherwise, in his mind he will be worshiping and honoring the spirit or god represented by that idol.

But if someone considers that an idol has no meaning whatever—that it is just a dead piece of wood or stone or metal—then that person can eat food sacrificed to idols without sinning, because he is not worshiping a god or evil spirit when he eats such food. However, he must not eat such food in the presence of a brother or sister who believes that the idol is a spirit or god, because in their eyes it will seem as if he is worshiping an idol, and they will be offended. We must never act only according to our own opinion and understanding; we must also avoid doing those things which our brother or sister considers sinful and offensive. If one is going to eat food sacrificed to idols, let him do it in the privacy of his own home. He must not go to the temple or other public place to eat it, because a brother or sister might see him and take offense (see Acts 15:20,29; 1 Corinthians 10:18–22 and comments).

5 There are indeed many idols and **so-called gods**. Some are called **gods**, and some are called **lords**. Some, it is said, live **in heaven**, while others live **on earth**. However, none of these are God. They have no meaning; they have no real existence.

But even though idols are nothing, evil spirits (demons) are something—their existence and power is very real (1 Corinthians 10:20). These spirits or demons lead people to worship idols. When a person offers a sacrifice to an idol, he is actually offering a sacrifice to an evil spirit. However, the meat that is sacrificed to an idol doesn't change in any way; it still remains meat.

6 We have one God, our heavenly Father. And we have one Lord, Jesus Christ.

Paul says here that **all things** have come through Christ. God and Christ are one, and their work is one (see John 10:30 and comment). God has done **all things** through Christ. He created the world through Christ (see John 1:3; Colossians 1:16 and comments). He saved the world through Christ (see John 3:17 and comment). And, in the end, He will judge the world through Christ (John 5:22).

7 **But not everyone knows this**. That is, not everyone knows that **an idol is nothing at all** (verse 4). As a result, such a person's **conscience is weak**. A person with a weak conscience should not eat food sacrificed to idols. Even though such food is clean in itself, if a person thinks it is unclean, then for him it will be unclean. And if he eats it, his conscience will become unclean too (see Romans 14:14 and comment).

Food itself does not defile a Christian (Mark 7:18–19). It is doing something one thinks is wrong that defiles him; it defiles his conscience (see Romans 14:23).

8 It makes no difference to God whether we eat a certain food or not.[25] Food itself doesn't bring us closer to God; food itself doesn't make us better or worse (see Romans 14:17).

Some of the Corinthian Christians openly ate food sacrificed to idols right in the idols' temples in order to demon-

[25] However, we must not eat or drink anything that is harmful to our bodies. We must not become drunk with alcohol (Ephesians 5:18). We must not smoke tobacco, which has been shown to harm our bodies. Our bodies are God's temple, and we must do nothing that will destroy God's temple (1 Corinthians 3:16–17).

strate how strong their faith was—their faith that idols were nothing at all. But they were mistaken in doing this, because faith is not demonstrated by what people eat. Food is for man's body, not for his heart or spirit.

9 In this verse, the **weak** are those believers who have weak consciences; they do not know that idols are nothing (verse 7). Those who have the knowledge that idols are nothing are free to eat food sacrificed to idols. But they must not use their freedom to cause their weaker brother to stumble (see Romans 14:13,15,20–21 and comment). Our freedom is not the most important thing; rather, the most important thing is our love for our brother.

10 In New Testament times, the citizens of Corinth used to hold great feasts at the temples of various idols; here they would come not only to worship the idols but also to meet each other and have a good time. Some of the Corinthian Christians also went to these feasts to enjoy themselves.

However, warns Paul, a brother **with a weak conscience** might see a brother with strong faith eating at one of these feasts, and he might decide to follow the strong brother's example and eat also. But after eating, the weak brother may feel badly and think that he has sinned. And, indeed, if the weak brother thinks he is doing something wrong as he eats, then he is sinning. Thus those **who have this knowledge** (that an idol is nothing) will have led their weaker brother into sin because of their knowledge (verse 11)—that is, because of their freedom to eat anything. Let this not happen, says Paul. Let the stronger brothers not go to the temple to eat.

11–12 Our knowledge has made us free to eat food offered to idols. But our knowledge (or freedom) can destroy our weak brother. And when we sin against our brother in this way, we also sin against Jesus, who died on the cross both for us and for our brother. If Christ did that much for us, can we not give up a little bit of our freedom for our brother's sake? (see Mark 9:42; Romans 14:15).

So let us always remember that knowledge can destroy others, but love always **builds up** others (verse 1).

13 In this verse, eating meat is only an example of the kind of activity that can cause our brother to fall into sin. There are, or course, many other things that will cause our brother to stumble. Even if these things are not sins in themselves, we must never do them if there is any chance that they will cause our brother harm.

CHAPTER 9

The Rights of an Apostle (9:1–18)

1 Some of the Corinthian Christians had begun to speak against Paul. In particular, they said that Paul was not a true apostle. Therefore, in this chapter Paul tells about his life and work, so that the Corinthian believers might see that he is indeed a true apostle.

Am I not free? Yes, Paul is free; but he never lets his freedom cause his brother to stumble (1 Corinthians 8:13).

Am I not an apostle? Yes, Paul is an apostle, because he had seen the risen Christ with his own eyes (see Acts 9:3–6,17; 22:6–9).

What was the proof that Paul was a true apostle? The proof was in the fruit, the results, of his ministry. One fruit was the Corinthian church! Paul had done a great work among the Corinthians, and because of it the Corinthians should have known that he was a true apostle (2 Corinthians 12:12). Paul's work was always **in the Lord**, and therefore it always bore fruit.

2 The Corinthian Christians were themselves the **seal** or proof of Paul's apostleship. Just as a tree's fruit proves what kind of tree it is, so Paul's accomplishments proved that he was an apostle. The Corinthians should consider

Paul an apostle, because it was through his preaching that they first came to Christ.

3 The Corinthian Christians were very proud (1 Corinthians 4:18–19). They presumed to judge Paul, who was their spiritual father!

4 As an apostle, Paul had the right to expect the churches he visited to provide for his food and other living expenses (verse 14). The other apostles were provided for by the churches they visited. However, Paul never asked the Corinthians for anything; he never took advantage of this right. Instead, he earned his own living by making tents in his spare time.

5 If Paul had had a wife, he would have had the right to bring her to Corinth with him, and the Corinthian church would have been expected to provide for both of them.

The **Lord's brothers** mentioned in this verse are Jesus' younger brothers. Jesus was Mary's oldest son; He was born not by a human father but by the Holy Spirit (Matthew 1:18). After that, many Bible scholars believe that Mary had several other natural children by her own husband, Joseph. If this opinion is correct, then the **Lord's brothers** mentioned here are the true brothers of Jesus, the sons of Mary. Among them was James, who became the chief leader of the Jerusalem church. Most Bible scholars believe it was this James who wrote the New Testament letter called "James."

Cephas (Peter) was Jesus' chief disciple. Peter and Jesus' brothers usually took their wives with them when they traveled to other churches.

6 Among the apostles, only Paul and Barnabas earned their own living by working at a job. Paul made tents. They were not forced to work in this way; they did so voluntarily.

Barnabas was Paul's first colleague in ministry, and he accompanied Paul on his first missionary journey (see Acts 4:36–37; 11:22,24–26; 13:2–3).

7 In all other kinds of work, the worker receives a reward for his labor—either money or food or part of the harvest. The worker has a right to receive payment. But Paul asked for no payment or reward from the Corinthians for his work as an apostle.

8–9 It is not only Paul who says that a worker should receive payment; the **Law of Moses** (the first five books of the Old Testament) also says it. According to the Law of Moses, even an ox must be given "payment"—that is, its food. Therefore, one must not **muzzle** the ox that is **treading out the grain** (Deuteronomy 25:4).

10 If God cares that much for an ox, surely He cares for Paul even more! If an ox is entitled to receive a reward for its labor, surely men are entitled to receive payment for their labor (1 Timothy 5:17–18).

Apostles and preachers are like plowmen and threshers. Some plow the ground and sow the seed, while others reap and thresh the harvest.

11 Paul had planted **spiritual seed** at Corinth; and from this seed, spiritual fruit had sprung up in the lives of the Corinthian believers—the fruit of faith and eternal life. If Paul had given such a great gift to the Corinthians, could he not hope to receive from them some **material harvest**, that is, some material payment? (see Romans 15:27).

12 Other apostles had received help from the Corinthians. Didn't Paul, their spiritual father, have even more right to ask them for help? Nevertheless, he had asked them for nothing.

Why hadn't he asked them for help? Because Paul didn't want to hear the Corinthians complaining about having to help him. Perhaps they would have accused Paul of preaching only in order to get money or food from them. Such an accusation would surely have diminished the effectiveness of his preaching (see 2 Corinthians 6:3; 11:9).

13 According to the Jewish law, Jewish priests were given the sacrifices offered by the people (Numbers 18:8–9,12–14; Deuteronomy 18:1–5). Those serving in the Jewish temple were entitled to earn their living from the temple.

14 Again, according to Christ's teaching, apostles and preachers were entitled to receive payment or food for their work of preaching and teaching (Matthew 10:9–10; Luke 10:7).

15 Paul is not writing in hopes of getting **such things**—that is, help or payment—from the Corinthians, even though he has every right to expect such things from them. Paul wants to be able to "boast" that he has received nothing from them for his work as an apostle (verse 18).

16 Paul does not boast in his preaching, because he has been appointed by Christ to preach the Gospel; he has no choice but to preach. He is **compelled to preach**. He is under obligation to preach; therefore, he has nothing to boast about. Men don't boast about what they are compelled to do; they can only boast about things they do voluntarily.

Woe to me if I do not preach, Paul writes here. Not all Christians have been appointed to be preachers, but all Christians have been appointed to be witnesses of the Gospel as they have opportunity. Woe to the believer who refuses to witness for Christ!

One time, Paul proclaimed the Gospel to the Jews of a certain city, but they did not accept it. Therefore, Paul said to them: **"Your blood be on your own heads! I am clear of my responsibility"** (Acts 18:6). If Paul had not proclaimed the Gospel to them, he would have been responsible for their unbelief. Those who refuse to believe and repent will have to bear their own punishment; but those who should have witnessed to them but didn't will also receive a punishment. The "blood" of those non-believers will be "on the heads" of those who should have witnessed to them (Ezekiel 33:7–9); that is, the believers will be partly guilty of the unbelief of those non-believers.

17 If we preach **voluntarily**, we will receive a reward. But those who are specially called to preach do not preach "voluntarily"; rather, they are compelled to preach because of their calling. They have received a **trust**, and they must carry out that trust. And they shouldn't expect a reward for doing so—at least, not in this life.

18 In that case, what is Paul's **reward**? Paul's "reward" is the fact that he has preached the Gospel **free of charge**. Paul has received no personal benefit from his labor as an apostle. To be able to make such a statement is Paul's reward.

Paul's Efforts to Bring People to Christ (9:19–27)

19 Paul was **free**. In a spiritual sense, he was free from sin and from bondage to the world. In a financial sense he was free also; he owed no one anything. He earned his own living. He did not **belong** to any man.

But Paul voluntarily gave up his freedom and made himself a **slave to everyone**. He became a slave of others so that he might bring them to faith in Christ. First of all, Paul made himself a slave of Christ (1 Corinthians 7:22). Then, in the work of preaching, Paul made himself a slave of others, so that he might **win as many as possible** to Christ.

20 Paul tried as much as possible to adapt himself to those to whom he preached. Even though he was free from the customs and traditions of men, he voluntarily submitted to many of their customs and traditions in order not to give unnecessary offense to those he was trying to win.[26] For example, when Paul went into a Jewish synagogue, he followed the customs of the synagogue so as not to give any unnecessary offense to the Jews.

Those mentioned here who are **under the law** are Jews, especially those who were originally Gentiles but who then converted to the Jewish religion. The **law** is the Jewish law—in particular, all the ceremonial rules and traditions regarding sacrifices and cleanliness. Even though Paul was himself a Jew, he was no longer compelled to observe these rules and traditions. He was no longer under the control of the Jewish ceremonial law,

---

[26] Of course, Paul did not follow any customs or traditions that would bring dishonor to Christ.

because Christ had canceled the ceremonial law (see Ephesians 2:15; Colossians 2:14 and comments).

21 Those **not having the law** are the Gentiles, or non-Jews. When Paul was among them, he tried to behave according to their customs as much as possible. Paul preached the same Gospel both to Jews and to Gentiles, but his method and style of proclaiming the Gospel was different for the two groups.

Although Paul was no longer under the control of the Jewish ceremonial law (the Jewish ceremonial rules and traditions), he remained under **God's law**—that is, **Christ's law**—which is equivalent to the "moral" part of the Jewish law. Christ's law (the "moral" law) is summed up in the two greatest commandments: to love God and to love one's neighbor[27] (see Deuteronomy 6:5; Leviticus 19:18; Matthew 22:35–40; Mark 12:29–31 and comment).

22 The **weak** are those who are weak in faith and whose consciences are weak (Romans 14:2; 15:1; 1 Corinthians 8:9–13). If they are afraid to eat food sacrificed to idols, then Paul also will not eat such food when he is with them.

Paul did not want to offend people, lest they be turned away from accepting Christ. However, Paul did not "speak out of both sides of his mouth"; that is, he did not speak falsely to some people in order to flatter them. He spoke only the truth. But he tried to fit in as much as possible with the different kinds of people he preached to, in order that he might more readily **win** them to Christ. Paul had become **all things**—Jew, Gentile, weak, strong. Let us, likewise, follow Paul's example in this (see 1 Corinthians 10:33).

23 Paul became like other men so that he could proclaim the Gospel to them more effectively. And Paul shared in the joy and blessings of those who accepted the Gospel and received salvation.

24 The Christian life is like a race. And the "finish line" of the race is to **become mature, attaining to the whole measure of the fullness of Christ** (Ephesians 4:13). Or, in other words, the "finish line" is to **be conformed to the likeness of** [God's] **Son** (Romans 8:29). Our supreme goal in life is to be like Christ. All true Christians, through faith, will reach the finish line; that is, they will all reach heaven, where they shall be like Christ (see 1 John 3:2 and comment).

But here Paul says: Don't walk to the finish line as if you were going for a stroll; rather, run as hard as you can! Let us not be lazy; let us strive with all our soul and strength to be like Christ in this life—not just in heaven! Let as run as fast as we can and try to get the **prize** for first place (see Hebrews 12:1).

25 Christians are like those who are training for athletic **games**. Athletes set aside everything else in order to train for the games. Likewise, we Christians should be ready to give up all pleasures and conveniences in order to concentrate fully on serving Christ. We must keep our bodies under control—that is, we must exercise self-control—just as those who compete in the games exercise self-control. Let us remember that if we endure the training and discipline necessary to run the race, we shall obtain a prize, that is, a **crown**. In Paul's time, those who won the race received as their prize a "crown" made of a wreath of laurel leaves; they also, of course, received praise and honor from the spectators. The "prize" we Christians will receive is the praise of God for our faithful service to Him. Unlike the crown of leaves, our prize will never wither away; it will last forever (see 2 Timothy 2:4–5; 4:7–8; James 1:12).

---

[27] Even though Christians are free from bondage to the Jewish ceremonial law, they are not free from the moral law of the Old Testament, which consists primarily of the two great commandments and the ten commandments (Exodus 20:3–17). The ten commandments are, in a sense, a detailed version of the two great commandments to love God and to love one's neighbor. If one breaks any of the ten commandments, he is also breaking the two great commandments. Because if one disobeys any of the ten commandments, he is not showing love for God and for his neighbor (see Matthew 5:17–19; Romans 13:9; Galatians 5:14 and comments).

26 Paul does not run the race **aimlessly**; he runs the race in order to win. Paul does not want to reach the finish line behind the other racers.

In the Greek games of Paul's time, boxing was one of the sports that athletes competed in. Paul here uses the illustration of a boxer who, instead of hitting his opponent, keeps **beating the air**. It is "aimless" for a boxer to beat the air; he'll never overcome his opponent that way!

27 Paul says here: **I beat my body**. That is, Paul trains himself strenuously for the race. He exercises. He works constantly. He makes tents; he preaches and teaches; he travels from church to church; he writes letters. He is always working for God in one way or another (see 1 Thessalonians 2:9).

Paul makes his body his **slave**; that is, he subdues it. He keeps his body and the sinful desires of his body under control. Paul has self-control (Galatians 5:23). He denies himself (Mark 8:34). He does not want to lose his prize—that is, his reward for his faithfulness and good works (see 1 Corinthians 3:13–15).

Paul does not want to be **disqualified for the prize**. In the opinion of some Bible scholars, Paul is saying here that if he "runs the race" of the Christian life poorly, he might not get a "prize"—that is, he might lose his salvation. But other scholars say that the **prize** Paul is referring to here is not his salvation but rather the special praise and honor he hopes to receive from God for his faithful service.

How could a great preacher and apostle like Paul lose his prize? It's certainly possible. No matter how great a Christian leader, pastor, or preacher is, it's still possible for him to lose his prize. Even those who have led many others to heaven can lose the way themselves. Why? Because they too are human. They can fall into temptation. They can become lazy. They can become disobedient to Christ. Let us remember: if great apostles like Paul must keep running the race as hard as they can, surely we ordinary Christians must do so too!

CHAPTER 10

Warnings From Israel's History (10:1–13)

1 In this verse, the **forefathers** mentioned by Paul are the ancestors of the Jews, that is, the founders of the nation of Israel. Abraham was the first Jew, the father of them all. About three hundred years after Abraham's time, the Jews fell into bondage in the land of Egypt. These **forefathers** were, in a spiritual sense, the forefathers of the Corinthian Gentile believers too, because the Corinthian Christians were citizens of the new spiritual "nation" of Israel. In other words, all Gentile believers are citizens of the "new Israel"; they are spiritual descendants of Abraham; they have received a spiritual inheritance from Abraham (see Romans 4:11,16; Galatians 3:7,29 and comments). This is why Paul here writes "**our** forefathers," even though most of the Corinthian Christians were not Jews but Gentiles.

Moses led the Jews out of Egypt. These Jews, of course, were also the **forefathers** of Paul's generation. As they were led out of Egypt, the Jews journeyed **under the cloud** of God's presence and guidance (Exodus 13:21; Psalm 105:39).

As the Jews were escaping from Egypt, they **passed through the sea**. This was the Red Sea, which forms the eastern border of Egypt. God separated the water of the sea, and the Jews passed through it on dry land and thus escaped from the pursuing Egyptians (Exodus 14:21–31).

2 **Moses** was the greatest leader of the Jews. After he led the Jews out of Egypt, he continued to be their leader for forty years, during which time they remained in the Sinai desert between Egypt and Israel.

Paul says that all the Jews were **baptized into Moses**. Paul is not talking here about actual BAPTISM. Rather, he is using the experiences of the Jews to illustrate the meaning of Christian baptism. The **cloud** and the **sea** (verse 1) are symbols of God's presence and protection, blessings which believers also receive through Christian baptism. Just as the Jews were brought under the leadership and authority of Moses, so Christians are brought under the leadership and authority of Christ. This is why Paul says that the Jews were **baptized** into Moses.

3 While the Jews were in the Sinai desert, God fed them with "bread from heaven," or manna, which Paul here calls **spiritual food**[28] (Exodus 16:4,14–15,31,35; John 6:31).

4 God also gave the Jews water, or **spiritual drink**, while they were in the desert. That water came out of a rock in a miraculous way (Exodus 17:6). That rock was the visible sign of a "spiritual rock" that was always present with the Jews wherever they went. Paul says that **that** (spiritual) **rock was Christ**. All of these blessings—the **cloud**, the **sea**, the **spiritual food** and **drink**—actually came from Christ. Christ is the true bread that has come down from heaven (John 6:30–35). From Christ comes spiritual water, that is, the Holy Spirit (John 7:37–39). And even in the Sinai desert, Christ, the eternal Son of God, was with the Jews. Christ existed before the world began; He has always existed. All spiritual blessings are available in Christ (Ephesians 1:3). The person who has Christ has all the blessings of God (see Romans 8:32).

5 But what happened to the Jews? God had done so much for them. He had sent Moses to be their leader. He had delivered them from bondage in Egypt. He had given them, through Christ, all these spiritual blessings. But instead of being thankful, they complained against God (Numbers 11:1). Therefore, God punished most of them by causing them to die in the desert.

6 Let us be careful not to grumble against God. We who believe in Christ have received far greater blessings than those Jews received, yet how often we grumble and complain against God! God is not pleased with this. Let us not forget how severely the Jews were punished because of their grumbling!

Paul admonishes us to keep from **setting our hearts on evil things as** [the Jews] **did**. What **evil things** did the Jews do? Paul gives the answer in verses 7–10.

7 Some of the Jews were **idolaters** (Exodus 32:1–6). Paul quotes here from Exodus 32:6.

8 Some of the Jews committed **sexual immorality**, and God punished them by sending a plague upon them (Numbers 25:1–9). According to Numbers 25:9, twenty-four thousand Jews died. Here Paul writes that **in one day twenty-three thousand of them died**. The remaining one thousand died the next day.

9 **We should not test the Lord**. To "test the Lord" means to act or speak in opposition to God.

A good example of testing God in this way is found in Numbers 21:4–5. The result of such testing is described in Numbers 21:6.

10 God led the Jews from Egypt through the Sinai desert right up to the border of Canaan (present-day Israel), the land He had promised to give Abraham's descendants as an inheritance. God showed the Jews much love and mercy while they were in the desert, and He watched over them and protected them. In addition to that, God performed many amazing signs and miracles. Nevertheless, the Jews did not put their faith in God. Instead, they complained and grumbled against Him continually. Therefore, God prevented most of them from entering the promised land, and they perished in the desert (Numbers 14:1–33; 16:41,49).

The Jews were killed **by a destroying angel**, whom God sent to punish the Jews

[28] The manna was not only "spiritual food"; it was also actual food that the Jews could eat.

because of their complaining and grumbling (Exodus 12:23).

11 Paul describes the sins of the Jews and the punishment they received as an example and a warning for us. Therefore, let the Corinthian Christians not do as those Jews did; that is Paul's warning. There existed in the Corinthian church all the sins that those ancient Jews had been guilty of: idolatry, sexual immorality, testing God, complaining against Paul (as the Jews had complained against Moses). "Beware," Paul tells the Corinthians (and all other Christians), "or the punishment that fell upon those ancient Jews will also fall upon you!"

These things that happened to the Jews are warnings for us, **on whom the fulfillment of the ages has come**. What is the **fulfillment of the ages**? It is the time of Christ's first coming to earth. Christ Himself is the fulfillment of the ages (Galatians 4:4; Hebrews 1:1–2).

12 The Jews boasted that they were descendants of Abraham and thus were God's "chosen people." They were confident that God would always bless them. They thought they were **standing firm**. They thought they would never fall out of God's favor. They were proud. But in the end they fell more and more into sin, and God destroyed most of them in the desert.

The Corinthian Christians were also proud; they also supposed they were **standing firm** and would not fall. "We are free; we can do whatever we want," they thought. "Sin is no problem for us," they boasted.

Let us not think such things. The moment we think to ourselves, "I am standing firm," we will surely fall. It is only by God's grace given to us day by day that we can stand firm. Even mature and spiritual Christians can fall into temptation (Galatians 6:1).

. . . be careful that you don't fall. Some people believe that Paul is talking here about falling away from Christ altogether and losing one's salvation. Others say that Paul is only talking here about falling into sin.

If we follow Christ and obey His commands, He will keep us from falling. But if we stop following Christ, then we shall certainly fall. Christ cannot protect those who do not follow Him (see John 10:27–28 and comment).

13 All men experience TEMPTATION. If we are troubled by some temptation, let us not suppose that we are the only ones to have experienced that temptation. We can be sure that many others have struggled with the same temptation.

Temptations are of two kinds. First, there is the kind of temptation that comes from outside of us, such as persecution, abuse, hardship, illness.[29] The second kind of temptation arises from within us—namely, evil thoughts and desires, and lack of faith. In this verse, Paul has both kinds of temptations in mind.

God will not let us be tempted **beyond what** [we] **can bear**. This is an extremely important promise. We must never say that we can no longer resist a particular temptation, that we cannot stand firm. If we say this, we are calling God a liar. Because God has promised to give us the power to stand, to resist any temptation. If we have the will to resist, we shall be able to do so.[30] Either God will give us the power to resist the temptation, or He will **provide a way out**—that is, He will remove or lessen the temptation. God's grace is sufficient to enable us to overcome every temptation that comes to us. But we must pray for that grace whenever temptation comes.

Why does God allow temptation to come upon us? The answer is this: God allows us to be tempted so that our faith might be tested and so that we might become **mature and complete** (see James 1:2–4,12–15; 1 Peter 1:6–7 and comments).

---

[29] This kind of temptation is often called "testing." However, outward testing (or trial) always leads to the inward temptation to give up, to lose faith, to deny Christ. This is why outward testing can be called a kind of temptation.

[30] Sometimes to resist temptation means we must **flee** from it (see 1 Corinthians 10:14; 1 Timothy 6:11). In other words, we must actively take ourselves out of the way of temptation.

Idol Feasts and the Lord's Supper (10:14–22)

14–15 Let us recall that the first of God's ten commandments is this: **You shall have no other gods before me** (Exodus 20:3–5; 1 John 5:21). Let us also remember that **idolatry** includes more than just worshiping ordinary idols made of wood, stone, or metal. Idolatry means putting anything in God's place. It means giving something else besides God first place. It means loving something more than God—such as our money or possessions, our family, our work, our honor, etc. If we love anything more than God, then for us that thing becomes an idol.

16 The **cup of thanksgiving** is the third of the four cups of wine traditionally drunk during the Jewish Passover feast. Many Bible scholars believe that at Jesus' last supper it was this third cup that He raised when He said to His disciples, "**This is my blood**" (Mark 14:23–24).

Paul says here that the cup and the bread are a **participation** in the blood and body of Christ. Paul is talking here about the Lord's Supper. Some Christians believe that the cup (that is, the wine inside it) and the bread are actually Christ's blood and body in a physical way (Mark 14:22). Others believe that the cup and the bread are only symbols or representations of Christ's blood and body. Still others believe that the cup and the bread are only meant to be reminders of Jesus' death (see 1 Corinthians 11:23–26; General Article: Lord's Supper).

However, there is one thing that all Christians agree on, and that is that Christ gave His body and blood in order that our sins might be forgiven and we might receive salvation. When we drink from the cup and eat the bread during the Lord's Supper, we are sharers together in the great gifts of forgiveness and salvation that Christ has given to us. In the Lord's Supper, we in some way participate anew in Christ's death, through which death we receive new spiritual life that will never end (see John 6:33–35,48–56 and comment). We are sharers in the blood and body of the living God. How then, Paul asks, can we ever think of worshiping idols?

17 During the Lord's supper, the bread is broken into small pieces so that each one present can eat. But all the pieces come from one loaf. In the same way, even though we believers are many individuals, in Christ we are all one body (see Romans 12:4–5; 1 Corinthians 12:27 and comments).

Paul says that **we all partake of one loaf**. That is, we all are sharers together in the body of Christ. Just as the one loaf enters our bodies during the Lord's Supper, so Christ's one Holy Spirit enters each of us and makes us one spiritual "body," whose head is Christ Himself (see 1 Corinthians 12:12–13; Colossians 1:18).

18 Here Paul again cites the example of the people of ISRAEL, that is, the Jews. When the Jews offered sacrifices, the priests and the people used to eat the meat of the sacrificed animal (Leviticus 7:15–16; 10:12–14). When they did this, they were participating **in the altar**; that is, they were sharing in the meat sacrificed on the altar.

In the same way, when the Corinthian Christians ate at the temple of an idol, they were sharing and having fellowship with evil spirits, or **demons** (verse 20). Let this not be, says Paul. We cannot be sharers with Christ and sharers with evil spirits at the same time (see 1 Corinthians 8:4–5; 10:21 and comments).

19 Paul is not saying here that sacrifices offered by the Jews to the living God are the same as the sacrifices offered by the Gentiles to dead idols. An idol is nothing at all (1 Corinthians 8:4).

20–21 Idols are nothing, but DEMONS, (evil spirits) are something. When one worships an idol, he is really worshiping a demon (Deuteronomy 32:17). We must not be **participants** with demons.

22 If we become participants with demons, we are like adulterers. God is a jealous God (Exodus 20:5), and if we forsake Him to follow after demons, He will become angry with us. **Are we stronger than he?** Of course, not. It is surely foolish to anger God, who is so much stronger than we are!

The Believer's Freedom (10:23–33)

23–24 See Romans 14:19–20; 15:1–2; 1 Corinthians 6:12 and comments.

25 In Corinth in Paul's time, almost all the meat sold in shops had first been sacrificed to idols. But since an idol is nothing (1 Corinthians 8:4), such meat was not unclean; it was all right for a Christian to eat it.

26 Paul here quotes from Psalm 24:1. Everything that God has made is "clean," and can be enjoyed with thanksgiving (see Mark 7:19; Acts 10:13–15; Romans 14:14; 1 Timothy 4:4 and comments).

27 Christians should not go to feasts at the temples of idols; but it is all right for them to go to the homes of their non-Christian neighbors to eat. There they can eat whatever is served to them (Luke 10:8).

28–29 **But if anyone says to you,** "Look out, this food has been sacrificed to idols," then don't eat it (verse 28). When Paul says **anyone**, he means any Christian with weak faith or a weak conscience (see 1 Corinthians 8:7,9–13 and comment). If such a person of weak conscience knows that the food we are about to eat has indeed been sacrificed to idols and he warns us about it, then for the sake of that person's weak conscience, we must not eat that food.

It is for the sake of the **other man's conscience** (verse 29)—that is, the weak Christian's conscience—that Paul will not eat food sacrificed to idols. Paul will do nothing that might defile his brother's weak conscience and cause him to sin. Paul's own conscience says that he can eat such food freely and lawfully, but the weak brother's conscience does not allow him to eat it. Each man will be judged by his own conscience. Paul will be judged by his own conscience, not his weak brother's conscience. The weak brother's conscience cannot take away Paul's freedom. The weak brother is not entitled to judge Paul's freedom (see Romans 14:2–3). What would be a sin for the weak brother (eating food sacrificed to idols) is not a sin for Paul.

However, even though Paul has the freedom to eat food sacrificed to idols, he will voluntarily give up his freedom for his weak brother's sake, in order not to defile the weak brother's conscience and cause him to sin (1 Corinthians 8:13).

30 Anything we receive from God with thankfulness is clean and good, and can be lawfully enjoyed[31] (1 Timothy 4:4). We should not be denounced for partaking of it.

31 In this verse we see Paul's main point. Whatever we do, we must first ask ourselves: Why am I doing this? For whose sake am I doing this? And the answer must always be: I am doing it for God's sake, for His glory. If we cannot say that, then we shouldn't do that thing.

Anything we do must ultimately be **for the glory of God** (see Matthew 5:16; Romans 14:7–8). Anything that does not glorify God is not acceptable to Him.[32]

32 See Romans 14:13,20–21; 1 Corinthians 8:8,13 and comments.

33 Paul does not please others to gain advantage for himself. Rather, he tries to please others for their own spiritual benefit (see Romans 15:2; 1 Corinthians 9:22; 10:24 and comments).

---

[31] This does not include things that are harmful to our bodies or which lead us into temptation. Indulging in such things is not approved by God.

[32] Eating, resting, enjoying fellowship, and engaging in other such legitimate activities all ultimately bring glory to God, because these activities are necessary for our physical and emotional health. We can glorify God more when we are physically and emotionally healthy.

CHAPTER 11

Covering the Head During Worship (11:1–16)

1 Paul says: **Follow my example.** Can we, like Paul, say to our Christian friends: "Follow my example"? How good is our example?

Why could Paul say to others, "Follow my example"? Because Paul himself followed Christ's example. We can ask others to follow our example only to the extent that we ourselves follow Christ's example. It is Christ they need to follow, not us.

When others hear our good words, they may perhaps heed us; but when they see our good lives they will follow us. To give witness by word is good, but to give witness by one's entire life is better. Words and deeds together are more effective than words alone.

2 The **teachings** that Paul has passed on to the Corinthians are the teachings of the twelve apostles,[33] which teaching Paul had himself received from the apostles (see 2 Thessalonians 2:15). Almost all the teachings of Paul came either from the twelve apostles or by a direct revelation from Christ (Galatians 1:12). Only on a very few subjects did Paul give any teaching based on his own opinion (1 Corinthians 7:12,25,40).

Several times in this letter, Paul has had to rebuke the Corinthian Christians for their behavior. But in this verse he has some good words for them. Whenever it was necessary for Paul to rebuke others, he always tried to say something good about them as well. This is a good policy for all those in authority to follow.

3 **. . . the head of Christ is God.** Christ is equal to God (see John 10:30; Philippians 2:6–7). But while Christ lived on earth, He was also a man, God's Son, and God was His Father (see 1 Corinthians 3:23). This is why Jesus said, ". . . **the Father is greater than I**" (John 14:28).

Just as the head of Christ is God, so **the head of every man is Christ** (see Ephesians 1:22; Colossians 1:18). And just as the members of a body are under the authority of the head, so we, the "members" of Christ's body, are under the authority of Christ.

In the same way, **the head of the woman is man.** Here Paul is talking about married women. Unmarried women are not under the authority of men (see Ephesians 5:22–24 and comment).

This is how God created the world. God has the highest authority of all. Then comes Christ's authority. And then under Christ's authority, God has placed man. And under the husband, God has placed the wife.

Let husbands remember, however, that they must love their wives just as Christ loved the church (Ephesians 5:25). Wives must submit to their husband's authority, but husbands must not abuse their authority. The wife is not the slave of her husband; rather, she is his friend and helper.[34]

Let us also remember that in Christ the husband and wife are spiritually equal (see Galatians 3:28; 1 Peter 3:7 and comments). Some people believe that the wife must get the permission of her husband before she can be baptized. But this teaching cannot be correct, because both husband and wife equally and individually have been given the promise of salvation through faith in Christ. Each person is responsible for his or her own response to the call of God.

4 It was customary among the Greeks of Paul's time for those under the authority of others to wear some kind of covering on their heads. For example, slaves were required to wear hats. Wives covered their heads when they went outside their homes. But ordinary male

[33] These twelve men were Christ's original twelve disciples (minus Judas Iscariot), who become known as "apostles" after the Holy Spirit had come upon them.

[34] For further discussion, see General Article: Christian Marriage.

citizens did not cover their heads in public places.

Therefore, according to Paul's teaching, if a man covers his head while praying or prophesying in a church or other public place, he is acting as if he were under the authority of another person. But such a man is under the authority of Christ alone. Therefore, if he covers his head, he **dishonors his head**—that is, he dishonors Christ. He dishonors Christ because he is acting as if he were under the authority of someone else instead of Christ.

5 According to the custom of Paul's time, wives were required to cover their heads when they went outside their homes. Otherwise, they would be acting like men; that is, they would appear to be taking the authority that belonged to their husbands. Thus, a woman who worships in public without covering her head **dishonors her head**—that is, she dishonors her husband.

Not only that, in Paul's time only evil women such as prostitutes went outside without covering their head. Therefore, if an honorable housewife went outside without her head covered, she was acting like a prostitute, and was thus dishonoring both herself and her husband.

Christians have two main opinions about the teaching Paul gives in this section. Many Christians today believe that Paul's teaching is meant to apply only to the period in which he lived. These Christians say that Paul's teaching is based on the customs of his own time, and not on the customs of our time. According to this opinion, then, it is perfectly all right today for men to cover their heads in public and for women not to cover their heads in public.

All Christians agree that believers of each generation should follow the customs of their own time, as long as those customs are not opposed to God's law. If believers do not follow local customs, they will offend their neighbors unnecessarily and bring dishonor on Christ.

In each situation the important question is: What is God's law? Because God's law is unchangeable. The danger in holding the opinion of this first group of Christians is that we might begin to take other difficult Bible teachings and say that they don't apply to us either. Where does one draw the line?

The second group of Christians believes that in this section Paul is stating God's unchangeable law. They say Paul is writing here not just for his own time, but for all time. According to this second opinion, Christians of today must abide by the teaching Paul has given here. And Paul's central teaching in this section is that God has established different levels of authority: first God's own authority, then Christ's, then the husband's, and then the wife's.

Therefore, this second group of Christians believe that Christian wives should always cover their head during public worship as a sign that they are under the authority of their husbands. But husbands should not cover their heads during public worship, because they have authority over their wives.

Some Christians believe that a woman's long hair counts as a suitable covering for her head (see verse 15). If this is so, then a wife would need no other covering.

Let us remember that in this section Paul is talking about covering one's head during public worship—in particular, while praying and prophesying in public—whether in a home or church or some other meeting place. At all other times, a husband is free to cover his head, and a wife is free to leave her head uncovered.

6 In Paul's time, prostitutes and other evil women were punished by having their hair cut off and their heads shaved. Therefore, Paul says here that if any wife prays in public with her head uncovered, she is like a prostitute whose hair has been cut off; she is disgraced!

7 Except for slaves, Greek men of Paul's time did not wear hats. A man was free; he was the **image and glory of God**. Therefore, he didn't need to wear a hat.

According to Genesis 1:27, men and women were both created **in the image of God**. But because the man was created first, he is the **glory of God**, Paul says. And because woman was created from man, she is the **glory of man** (Genesis 2:18,21–23).

8–9 **For man did not come from woman, but the woman from man.** The first woman, Eve, was created from one of the ribs of the first man, Adam (Genesis 2:21–22).

God made the woman for the man, so that the man might have a **helper suitable for him** (Genesis 2:18).

10 After Eve sinned in the Garden of Eden, God placed her under Adam's authority (Genesis 3:16). That is why a wife must wear a sign of her husband's authority; that is, she must cover her head in public. If she does not cover her head, she is considered a dishonorable woman.

Paul says that a wife must also cover her head **because of the angels**. Many people believe that angels are present during the services of the church. Thus Paul's meaning is that wives must cover their heads during public worship in order not to offend the angels who are present.

11 God created man and woman to live together in dependence upon each other. They were created to become **one flesh** in marriage (Genesis 2:23–24). If they are "one flesh," how can they live independently of each other?

12 The man should not be proud and put down the woman. Let him remember that it was a woman who gave him birth!

But even though children are born from a woman's body, it is God alone who has the power to create life. ... **everything comes from God**.

13 The Corinthian Christians ought to have known that wives should cover their heads; even the non-believing Greeks knew that.

But remember: Paul's teaching about covering one's head applies only when one is praying and prophesying in a public worship service, not at other times (verses 4–5).

14 Throughout the Roman Empire in Paul's time, men wore their hair shorter than women did. A man was despised if he let his hair grow as long as a woman's.

Does Paul mean that men should never have long hair, no matter what generation they belong to or what country they live in? Some Christians think that Paul was only writing about his own time. But others think that Paul intends this teaching for all men of every generation; they say that a man's hair should always be shorter than a woman's hair.

It is possible for true Christians to have different understandings of Paul's teaching here. Each Christian, with the help of the Holy Spirit, must study these verses and decide in his own mind what Paul's meaning is. But we must not judge or condemn another believer who may have a different opinion from ours on these smaller matters. To differ with each other on small matters is all right; but to judge each other is not. Do not split the church by arguing over hair length!

15 Throughout history, women have usually worn their hair long. Paul says that the **very nature of things** (verse 14) teaches that this is suitable. A woman's long hair is like a covering provided by God. Indeed, many people think that this verse teaches that a woman's long hair is the only covering she ever needs (see verse 5 and comment).

16 The Corinthians should not become **contentious** over this matter; let them just accept what Paul says. Paul is not giving them some strange new teaching; he is giving them the same teaching he has given to all the other churches.

The Lord's Supper (11:17–34)

17–18 In verse 2, Paul praised the Corinthians; now he must correct them.

There were many divisions in the Corinthian church. Some of these divisions concerned which apostle to follow (1 Corinthians 1:11–12). Other divisions existed between the rich and the poor, between socially important believers and ordinary believers. When there are divisions like this, it is better not to meet at all! ... **your meetings do more harm than good**, Paul tells the Corinthians.

19 Among any group of Christians there will always be different ideas and points of view on many matters. This is not wrong. However, when such differences arise among Christians, it is essential that all sides act with love and humility toward each other. Only those demonstrating love and humility **have**

God's approval. Those who are proud and create strife and division in the church do not have God's approval. No harm comes from the humble expression of different ideas concerning smaller matters. Harm comes when believers judge each other and oppose each other over such matters.

20 In the Corinthian church, the LORD'S SUPPER was being celebrated together with an ordinary meal—just as Christ celebrated His last Passover meal with His disciples. Thus, when the Corinthian Christians met together for the Lord's Supper, they didn't eat and drink only the bread and wine, but they had a complete meal. But the Corinthians had forgotten the real meaning and purpose of the Lord's Supper. They were meeting together to have a good time, to eat their fill, and to get drunk on wine! (verse 21). Under such circumstances it was impossible to truly celebrate the Lord's Supper.

21 In the Corinthian church, each person who attended the Lord's Supper brought with him his own food from home. The rich brought much food; the poor brought little. But the rich did not share their food with the poor; therefore, the poor often went hungry. The more important members of the church went right ahead and ate **without waiting for anybody else**. (The church members who were slaves or servants usually came late, because they first had to serve their own masters at home before coming to the Lord's Supper.)

22 If the rich and important members of the church were going to act this way, says Paul, let them first eat their regular meal at home and then come to the Lord's Supper. The way they were behaving dishonored and grieved Christ. Where was their respect for the church, which was Christ's body? Where was their love for their poorer brothers? They may have called the Lord's Supper a "love feast," but the only love they were showing was for themselves.

23 Paul had received special instructions **from the Lord** concerning the Lord's Supper. Certainly Paul learned about Jesus' last supper from the twelve disciples. But Paul also must have received a direct revelation from Jesus concerning the Lord's Supper and how it was to be observed in the churches (see Galatians 1:11–12).

The first Lord's Supper took place **on the night** [Jesus] **was betrayed**. Seeing how much Jesus suffered for them, how can the Corinthian believers regard the Lord's Supper as a time for having fun and getting drunk?

24 The Lord Jesus took bread and said, "**This is my body**" (see Matthew 26:26; Mark 14:22; Luke 22:19; 1 Corinthians 10:16 and comments).

The Lord Jesus sacrificed His body for us, that through His death we might receive eternal life. We must never forget that tremendous fact. Indeed, one reason for celebrating the Lord's Supper over and over is so that we might always keep fresh in our minds what Jesus did for us.

Jesus said: "**. . . do this** (eat this bread) **in remembrance of me.**" Just as ordinary bread (food) is necessary for our bodies, so spiritual "bread" is necessary for our spirits. Jesus is our spiritual bread (see John 6:51,53–54).

25 Jesus said: "**This cup is the new** COVENANT **in my blood.**" According to Mark 14:24, Jesus also said: "**This is my blood of the covenant.**" The meaning of these two sayings is the same (see Matthew 26:28; Mark 14:23–24; Luke 22:20; 1 Corinthians 10:16 and comments).

By the word **cup** Paul means the contents of the cup. At Jesus' last supper, He and His disciples drank wine. But Paul is not saying here that we must drink only wine at the Lord's Supper. Many Christians drink some kind of fruit juice when they celebrate the Lord's Supper.

The **new covenant** mentioned here is the promise given to men and women by God that if they will believe in His Son Jesus, He will forgive their sins and give them eternal life. Under the old covenant, God had given men His law; under the new covenant, He has given men His Son. Now, through His Son and through the Holy Spirit, God has written a new "law," not on tablets of stone as the old covenant was, but on men's hearts (see Jeremiah

31:31–34; 2 Corinthians 3:6; Hebrews 8:8–10 and comments).

Therefore, the **blood** of Jesus is the sign of this **new covenant**. For it is through His blood (that is, His sacrificial death on the cross) that we receive salvation and eternal life.

As with the bread, Jesus took the cup and said: "**. . . do this** (drink this cup) **in remembrance of me.**"[35]

26 When we celebrate the Lord's Supper we **proclaim the Lord's death**; that is, we witness to all men that Christ died for our salvation and that He rose again. Let the whole world know what Christ has done; we are witnesses to it.

We must proclaim the Lord's death **until he comes**. That is, we must continue to observe the Lord's Supper until Jesus comes to earth again. After He comes we won't need to celebrate the Lord's Supper any more, because from that time on we shall be celebrating it with Him in heaven (see Matthew 26:29; Mark 14:25).

27 The Corinthians were celebrating the Lord's Supper **in an unworthy manner** (verses 20–22). To celebrate the Lord's Supper in an unworthy manner means to celebrate it without confessing one's sins, without loving one's brother, without humility. When we celebrate the Lord's Supper in such an unworthy manner, we are **sinning against the body and blood of the Lord**. It is as if we were crucifying Christ all over again, breaking His body and shedding His blood anew.

28 Therefore, before we celebrate the Lord's Supper we must carefully examine ourselves to see if there is any unconfessed sin in our life. If there is, we must at once confess it and repent of it, and then ask forgiveness from God (see 1 John 1:9). Only then will it be all right to eat the bread and drink from the cup at the Lord's Supper.

29 To eat and drink **without recognizing the body of the Lord** means to celebrate the Lord's Supper without honoring Jesus' body and without remembering His death. To eat and drink **without recognizing the body of the Lord** means to celebrate the Lord's Supper without caring about Jesus' suffering, His sacrifice. The Corinthians celebrated the Lord's Supper as if they were eating an ordinary meal. They celebrated the Supper, but they forgot the Lord!

If we celebrate the Lord's Supper without **recognizing**, or caring, about Christ's body, we will surely bring God's **judgment** upon ourselves; that is, God will punish us for sinning against the body and blood of Christ (verse 27). That **judgment**, or punishment, is not the same as the last judgment of unbelievers; rather, it is "discipline" (verse 32) given by God to those who partake of the Lord's Supper in an unworthy manner.

30 At the time Paul wrote this letter, God had already begun to discipline (or punish) the Corinthian Christians for their unworthy behavior. God had made many of them **weak and sick**; He had even allowed some of them to "fall asleep," that is, to die (see 1 Corinthians 5:5). What severe discipline the Corinthians needed! How severely will God have to discipline us?

31 **But if we judged ourselves, we would not come under judgement**—that is, we would not come under God's discipline. Here, to "judge ourselves" means to examine ourselves. Paul's meaning in this verse, then, is this: If we examined ourselves, we would not need to be disciplined by God. When we examine ourselves, we can discover our sin, and repent of it. And when we truly repent, we will not need to bear God's **judgment** or punishment for that sin. Because as soon as we have repented of a sin and asked for forgiveness, God will immediately forgive us (see 1 John 1:9 and comment). Then, after we have been forgiven, we can celebrate the Lord's Supper freely and joyfully, and we shall receive, not judgment, but blessing.

32 **When we are being judged by the Lord, we are being disciplined.** When Paul says we are "being judged,"

[35] For further discussion of the subject of the Lord's Supper, see General Article: Lord's Supper.

he is not talking about the last judgment that will come upon unbelievers. He is talking about the punishment or DISCIPLINE of believers. God disciplines us **so that we will not be condemned with the world**—that is, condemned with the **world** of unbelieving men at the last judgment. When we sin and do not immediately repent of it, God needs to discipline us (see Hebrews 12:5–7,10–11 and comment). Without God's discipline, it is possible to fall away from Christ. It is through God's discipline that we are kept on the right path; it is through His discipline that we are spared being condemned with unbelievers.

33–34 Having rebuked the Corinthian Christians for what they have done wrong (verses 20–22), Paul now tells them how they should celebrate the Lord's Supper. **If anyone is hungry, he should eat at home**. The Corinthians should not come to the Lord's Supper to fill their stomachs but to worship the Lord!

CHAPTER 12

Spiritual Gifts (12:1–11)

1 The Holy Spirit gives to believers two main kinds of blessings or gifts. First, the Holy Spirit causes His own fruit to grow within us—namely, **love, joy, peace, patience, kindness, goodness, faithfulness, gentleness, and self-control** (Galatians 5:22–23). These fruits are to be manifest in the lives of all Christians at all times.

The second main kind of blessings that the Holy Spirit gives us are the special **gifts** of the Spirit. Paul describes these gifts in this section. These gifts are given to selected Christians at special times. They are given to meet some special need or to enable one to accomplish some special task.[36]

2 Before the Corinthians had become Christians, they had been **influenced and led astray to dumb idols**. They had been led astray by false teachers and false prophets (see Ephesians 2:1–2; 4:17–18). An idol itself is nothing. But when the Corinthians worshiped an idol, they were in fact worshiping a false spirit, an evil spirit (1 Corinthians 10:19–20).

3 There is only one true Spirit, and that is the Holy Spirit. Only after receiving the Holy Spirit can a person know that Jesus is the Lord, the Son of God. If anyone is able to say from his heart, "**Jesus is Lord**,"[37] then it is certain that the Holy Spirit is in that person.

We must distinguish between false spirits and the Holy Spirit. A false or evil spirit says, "**Jesus be cursed**"; the Holy Spirit always honors Jesus (see John 16:13–14; 1 John 4:1–3 and comments).

4 The Holy Spirit gives the same fruits to all believers, but He gives different gifts to different believers. The Spirit gives one person one gift, and another person another gift. Nevertheless, these different gifts all come from one Spirit.

5 Each Christian has been given his own **service**, that is, his own work, his own responsibility. But these different kinds of "services" are all done for the same Lord.

6 **There are different kinds of working**. Here "working" means God's own working—calling people to faith, healing the sick, establishing His church. God works by different means, but He is the same God.

Here in verses 4–6, Paul mentions the three aspects of the triune God: **Spirit** (verse 4), **Lord** (verse 5), and **God** (verse

---

[36] For further discussion of the work of the Holy Spirit, see General Article: Holy Spirit.

[37] The expression **Jesus is Lord** means: "Jesus is the one and only Lord." Just as there is only one God, so there is only one Lord—namely, Jesus, the Son of God.

6). These three together are one God, and everything they do they do together.

7 Each believer is given the **manifestation of the Spirit**; that is, each believer is given one or more of the gifts of the Spirit. Why does the Holy Spirit give these gifts? He gives them not for our own personal benefit but **for the common good**.

When Paul writes that **to each one the manifestation of the Spirit is given**, what does he mean? Does he mean that every Christian is given one or more of the gifts of the Spirit? Some Bible scholars say "Yes," and some say "No." But whether Paul means that the gifts of the Spirit are given to "every" Christian or only to some, he at least means here that the Spirit gives gifts to **each one** of those He has chosen to give gifts to.

8 What are the gifts of the Holy Spirit? Here in verses 8–10, Paul gives nine examples of the Spirit's gifts. Paul gives other examples in Romans 12:3–8; 1 Corinthians 12:28; Ephesians 4:11.[38]

The first gift Paul mentions here is the **message of wisdom**. This is not ordinary wisdom, which God gives to everyone who asks (James 1:5). The "message of wisdom" mentioned here is a special spiritual wisdom given by the Spirit in particular situations to solve special problems.

The second gift is the **message of knowledge**. This is special spiritual knowledge given about a particular matter. For example, when a person is sick, someone else may receive a "message of knowledge" from the Spirit about that person's illness. Or, as another example, if some person secretly sins, someone else may find out about it through a special "message of knowledge" (see Acts 5:1–11).

9 The third gift, **faith**, is not the same as the faith in Christ through which we are saved. Rather, the **faith** mentioned here is a special kind of faith which is given in particular situations for some special work. For instance, if one believer has a special need for something—money, strength, health, etc.—some other believer may receive special faith to pray for that need. Such faith is usually given to us not for our own personal benefit, but for the benefit of someone else (see Mark 11:22–23 and comment).

The fourth example of the Spirit's gifts are **gifts of healing**. These are gifts given for the purpose of healing those who are sick or injured. When one has this gift, medicine and doctors are not needed; the sick person will be healed by the power of the Holy Spirit alone. In some cases two gifts may be necessary to heal a person: first, the gift of faith that the person will be healed; and second, the gift of healing itself.

10 The fifth gift is the gift of **miraculous powers**. This is different from the gifts of healing. In the New Testament, these "miraculous powers" are often given in special situations to inflict harm on someone. For instance, they might be given to make someone blind, or even to strike someone dead (see Acts 5:5; 13:6–12). But these miraculous powers are also given to bring blessing. For instance, during Jesus' ministry, such powers were used to turn water into wine and to feed the multitudes (Mark 6:30–44; John 2:1–11).

The next example of the Holy Spirit's gifts is the gift of PROPHECY. This is the gift of speaking a special word that has come directly from God. This gift is also given to predict future events.

The next gift, the **ability to distinguish between spirits**, is needed in order to deliver people from evil spirits. Also this gift is used sometimes to detect and block some hidden work of Satan[39] (see Matthew 24:24; 2 Corinthians 11:13–15 and comments).

---

[38] In verses 8–10, the gifts themselves are mentioned. But in 1 Corinthians 12:28 and Ephesians 4:11, it is not the gifts themselves that are mentioned, but rather special categories of workers with the corresponding gifts.

[39] This gift is also used in distinguishing between true prophets and false prophets; however, in most cases, this can be done without the help of a special supernatural gift (see 1 John 4:1–3).

The next gift is the **ability to speak in different kinds of tongues**—that is, the ability to speak in other languages (1 Corinthians 14:2). This gift has two forms. One form is the ability to speak in the languages of other countries (see Acts 2:4–12). The second form is the ability to speak in an unknown language, a language that is not spoken in any known country. Such a language is spiritual; it cannot be understood naturally (see Acts 19:6; 1 Corinthians 14:2,9,19). Whichever form of this gift a person receives, he is then able to speak in a language he has never learned; he speaks it not by his own understanding but by the power of the Spirit.

It is the Holy Spirit Himself that actually speaks through the mouth of the person who has the gift of speaking in tongues. But the person with the gift still has control over his own mouth; he can choose to open his mouth to speak, or choose not to open it. When a person speaks in a spiritual language, that person and those listening to him experience the Holy Spirit's presence and power. Speaking in other tongues is not screaming, moaning, or babbling. Rather, it is speaking in a language that has been given by the Holy Spirit Himself.

The **interpretation of tongues** is the ninth and last gift Paul mentions in this section. Whenever one person speaks in another tongue, someone else needs to "interpret" what has been said, so that others in the church will understand what the Holy Spirit is saying. If there is no one to interpret, then the church cannot receive any benefit from what is said (1 Corinthians 14:5–6,13). Sometimes the person who has spoken in another tongue will himself be the one to give the interpretation. Speaking in another tongue and interpreting what is said, when joined together, are equivalent to prophecy (see 1 Corinthians 14:4–6,13 and comment).

11 All of these gifts are given by one Holy Spirit, and they are given to individual believers **just as he** (the Spirit) **determines**. Therefore, there must be no conflict between believers who receive different gifts. All of the Holy Spirit's gifts are given for the purpose of building up the church and making its witness to the world more effective. If any believer uses a gift he has received in a way that divides the church, or in a way that puffs himself up and puts his brother down, then he is misusing that gift of the Spirit. The gifts of the Holy Spirit must always be used in love and in unity with other believers.

But there is one great danger in using the gifts of the Spirit that all Christians must be aware of: Satan can mimic all the gifts of the Holy Spirit. Sometimes a gift that is being misused is not a gift from the Holy Spirit at all, but a "gift" from Satan! Satan has the power to give men impressive gifts; and to those who are undiscerning, Satan's gifts can seem at first to be just like the Holy Spirit's gifts (see Mark 13:22 and comment). But, in the end, Satan's gifts always result in spiritual harm, not blessing.

Usually a believer receives only one or two gifts of the Spirit. But the apostles each received many gifts; these gifts were a sign or proof of their apostleship (2 Corinthians 12:12). With the help of these gifts, the apostles were able to establish the church of Christ throughout the Roman Empire.

One Body, Many Parts (12:12–31)

12 **The body is a unit, though it is made up of many parts. . . . So it is with Christ**—that is, so it is with Christ's body, the church (verse 27). Christ's body has many members (believers), but His body is one (Romans 12:4–5). The head of the body is Christ Himself (Ephesians 1:22–23; 5:23).

13 How do we become members of Christ's body? We become members of His body by being **baptized . . . into one body**—that is, by being baptized into Christ (see Galatians 3:26–27).

In this verse the word **baptized** means not only being baptized in water but also being "baptized" **by**[40] **one Spirit,** the Holy Spirit. When we believe in Christ, the Holy Spirit comes into our life; we can say that at that point Christ has "baptized" us with the Holy Spirit (see Matthew 3:11; Mark 1:8).

Therefore, some Christians believe that the moment one puts faith in Christ he is spiritually "baptized"—that is, he receives the "baptism of the Holy Spirit". But other Christians believe that the baptism of the Holy Spirit is a separate experience which occurs some time after one has put faith in Christ (see General Article: Holy Spirit Baptism). This second group of Christians calls this experience "the second blessing"; they say it is the same as being "filled" with the Spirit (Acts 2:4; 9:17), or "receiving" the Spirit (Acts 8:15,19; 10:47).

Whether the so-called "baptism of the Holy Spirit" is something that happens the moment we believe or whether it happens sometime after, the most important thing is that the Holy Spirit comes into our lives when we believe.[41] Because one thing is certain: If the Holy Spirit (Christ's Spirit) is not in us, we do not belong to Christ (see Romans 8:9). Only when the Holy Spirit is in us do we become members of Christ's body; it is the Spirit which makes us one body. The Holy Spirit is like blood; it circulates through every member of the body. Without blood, the body dies. Without the Holy Spirit, we also die—spiritually (see John 6:53).

Or, to use another illustration, the Holy Spirit is like **living water,** which we are invited to drink (see John 4:10,13–14). Here in verse 13, Paul writes that **we were all given the one Spirit to drink** (see John 7:37–39). When we drink of the Spirit's living water, we receive the power to serve Christ, and the fruit of the Spirit is manifest in our lives (Galatians 5:22–23).

Whether we are **Jews or Greeks, slave or free,** through the Holy Spirit we are all one in Christ (see Galatians 3:28; Colossians 3:11 and comments).

14 See Romans 12:4–5; 1 Corinthians 12:12,17–20 and comments.

15 Each believer is a distinct member of Christ's body. Just as the foot does the foot's work and the hand does the hand's work, so each of us has his own work to do. We should not seek to do the work of another member. Suppose, for example, that the foot says: "I am not happy being a lowly foot; I want to be a hand instead. The hand has much more interesting and important work to do. If I can't be a hand, I won't be part of the body!" Do we talk like that sometimes? Have we not sometimes said: "If I can't be on the church committee, I won't work in the church"? Or, have we not sometimes said: "I'm just a lowly person; I have no great gift; I have no part in this church"? Let us not think such things. Rather, let us each humbly and thankfully do the work that Christ has given us to do in His church, His body.

16 Paul here repeats the thought of verse 15.

17–20 In these verses, Paul adds to the thought of verse 14.

21 Each member of the body is dependent on every other member. Some Christians think that they can do everyone else's work, and that they don't need any help from others. But what a mistake! Can the eye do the work of the hand?

22 The eye is one of the **weaker** members of the body; nevertheless, it is **indispensable.**

23 The **less honorable** and **unpresentable** parts of the body are the excretory and reproductive organs. By

---

[40] The Greek word for **by** in this verse can also mean "with" or "in." Depending on which of the three meanings is chosen—"by," "with," or "in"—the meaning of the verse will be somewhat different. For further discussion, see General Article: Holy Spirit Baptism.

[41] It is not so important what we call the coming of the Spirit into our lives as long as He comes! The Holy Spirit manifests Himself in many ways in the lives of different believers. This is why there are so many terms given in the New Testament for the various ways in which the Holy Spirit manifests His presence in the lives of Christians.

covering these parts, Paul says, we treat them with **special honor.**[42]

In the same way, we should not despise the humble and less educated members of the church, but rather we should treat them with **special honor**. They are essential members of Christ's body. The church needs them (see Romans 12:16).

24–25 Like members of a body, the members of a church should have **equal concern for each other** (verse 25). God has given honor to all members of the body. Therefore, so should we. Let us not look down on any member of God's church.

26 If the foot is injured, the whole body suffers. If any member of the church suffers, the whole church shares in that member's suffering.

If a man receives honor because of the works of his hands or the words of his mouth, that whole man receives the honor, not just his hands or his mouth. So it is with members of the church: if one is honored, all are honored; if one rejoices, all rejoice (see Roman 12:15).

27 In each location, the local church constitutes the body of Christ. Every believer is a member of Christ's body, the local church. Let us examine ourselves. Are we behaving like members of Christ's body? Are we obedient to the head of the body, which is Christ? Is our local church doing the work of Christ's body—that is, the work that Christ Himself would do if He were here on earth? When non-believers look at our local church, do they see Christ working?

28 In this verse Paul gives some examples of different members of Christ's body. The two most important members are **apostles** and PROPHETS (see Ephesians 2:19–20). Some Christians believe that there are no apostles and prophets today. They say that the foundation of the church has already been laid by the apostles and prophets of the New Testament, and that, therefore, there is no need for any new apostles and prophets.

However, other Christians disagree. They say that there are still apostles and prophets in the church today, though they are not equal in authority to the original writers of Scripture. Their purpose is not to lay new foundations, but to continue building the church on the foundation that has already been laid. It is not clear from the Bible which of these two opinions is correct.

Having mentioned the two most important positions in the church—apostles and prophets—Paul next mentions a third position, that of **teachers**. After teachers, Paul mentions five other kinds of people that are needed in every church. These last five are probably not listed in any particular order—they are all equally important.

The Holy Spirit gives the necessary gift or gifts to all these members to enable them to do their particular jobs. Notice that some members of the church have supernatural gifts, such as the **gifts of healing** and the ability to perform **miracles** (see verses 10–12). Other members, however, have natural gifts, such as the **gifts of administration** and the ability to **help others**. Most members of the church have a combination of both natural and supernatural gifts. However, no matter what gifts one has been given, natural or supernatural, they all come from God's Holy Spirit. And no matter what kind of work one has been given, it can only be done through the Holy Spirit's power (verse 11).

Paul says at the beginning of this verse that **God has appointed** all these members to do their various jobs. God gives to each member different tasks and different responsibilities. We members do not choose our own work; our work is given to us by God. And whatever work God gives us to do, He will also give us the necessary strength and ability to do it. God will never order the hand to see, nor the eye to write.

All gifts are given for the upbuilding of the church, Christ's body (1 Corinthians 12:7; 14:26; Ephesians 4:12). They are not given for the personal benefit of the individual members receiving the gifts.

For further discussion on the subject of spiritual gifts, see Romans 12:6–8; 1

---

[42] Some people think that these "unpresentable" parts also include our internal organs, such as our liver, lungs, intestines, etc.

Corinthians 12:10–12; Ephesians 4:22 and comments; General Articles: Holy Spirit, Holy Spirit Baptism.

29–30 If everyone in the church did the same work, who would do all the other necessary work? If everyone were a teacher, who would do the healing? What use would there be of a body made up only of eyes!

31 **But eagerly desire the greater gifts**. It is good to desire spiritual gifts and to pray to receive them. However, the Holy Spirit will give His gifts according to His own plans and purposes (see verse 11).

What are the **greater gifts**? Bible scholars give different answers to this question. Some say that the **greater gifts** are the "gifts" of being apostles or prophets. Others say that the **greater gifts** are not the gifts listed in this chapter, but rather are the fruits of the Holy Spirit, such as love, joy, and peace. And still others say that both of the above answers are correct. It's not possible to be completely certain what Paul means by the term **greater gifts**.

The gift that the Corinthians desired above all others was the gift of speaking in other tongues. But this gift by itself does nothing to build up the church, because no one else can understand the other tongue. Therefore, the Corinthians needed also to pray for the gift of interpretation (see 1 Corinthians 14:12–13).

Up to this point, Paul has not mentioned the one "gift," or **way**, which is the highest of all. Without it, all the other gifts are worthless. And this highest gift is the gift of love.[43] Love is the **most excellent way**. Paul describes this way of love in Chapter 13.

CHAPTER 13

The Most Excellent Way (13:1–13)

1 By the expression, **tongues of men and of angels**, Paul is referring to two kinds of speech. First, he is referring to eloquent and powerful human speech, which he calls the **tongues of men**. (Paul himself was an effective speaker and preacher.) Second, Paul is referring to "other languages," or spiritual languages, which he here calls the **tongues . . . of angels** (see 1 Corinthians 12:10; 14:18).

Without love, both human eloquence and speaking in other tongues become just noise; they are worthless.

2 In this verse, Paul mentions three other gifts of the Holy Spirit: namely, **prophecy**, **knowledge**, and **faith** (1 Corinthians 12:8–10). Even if we receive these three gifts in the fullest measure—that is, even if we can **fathom all mysteries**, and even if we can **move mountains** (Mark 11:22–23)—if we do not have love we are nothing! Without love, these great gifts are nothing!

3 Without love, religious works are of no benefit. Followers of other religions seek to acquire religious merit by doing good works. They give money to the poor. They give their time to public works. They are even prepared to suffer pain and death. But why? For what? In the end, all these things are done to benefit the person doing them. They are done for the purpose of earning religious merit, so that the one doing them will be better off in the next life. These things are not done for others, but for oneself.

But Paul teaches here that such "good works" give no benefit to the one doing them. True, the poor may get a little help from such works, but the doer of the

---

[43] Love is different from the other "gifts" that have been described in this chapter. Love is a **fruit** of the Holy Spirit (Galatians 5:22). Indeed, it is the most important fruit. Whatever gifts we have received, we must use them in love. Without love, the Holy Spirit's other gifts are worthless, and can even lead to harm. In our Christian lives, the most essential thing of all is love.

works will not find the benefit he or she is looking for. Even Christians who are burned to death for the sake of the Gospel will receive no reward unless they also have the fire of love in their hearts.

4 In verses 4–7, when the word **love** is used, we can understand that Paul is talking about a "person filled with love."

Thus, in verse 4, we can read: The "person filled with love" **is patient**, the "person filled with love" **is kind**.

The word **kind** doesn't mean just being kind in one's heart; it also means showing that kindness to others. The man who is kind is always seeking to do good things for others.

Notice that the "man filled with love" who is **patient** and **kind** has three of the fruits of the Holy Spirit: **love, patience,** and **kindness** (see Galatians 5:22 and comment).

The "man filled with love" **does not envy** others. Instead, when others are happy and successful, he rejoices with them (see Luke 15:25–32 and comment).

The "man filled with love" **does not boast,** [he] **is not proud**. Instead, he is humble.[44] The proud man loves only himself, not others.

5 The "man filled with love" **is not rude**. His behavior is courteous and gracious at all times.

The "man filled with love" **is not self-seeking,** but seeks the good of others. He is filled with **goodness,** which is another fruit of the Holy Spirit (1 Corinthians 10:24,33; Galatians 5:22).

The "man filled with love" **is not easily angered**. If someone hurts him or insults him, he endures it quietly. The "man filled with love" **keeps no record of wrongs**—that is, he takes no account of wrongful acts that others do against him. Many of us, on the other hand, nurture hurts and offenses in our minds for years. When someone wrongs us and we keep remembering it, we are keeping a **record of wrongs**. We don't forget it; we don't forgive the other person for wronging us. Love is not like that. The man filled with love doesn't think about the wrong done to him. The man filled with love never seeks revenge.

6 The "man filled with love" **does not delight in evil**; he doesn't even want to hear about it. Many of us, on the other hand, are eager to hear something bad about someone else! Why? Because when others are put down, we feel raised up. But love is never like that.

The "man filled with love" **rejoices with the truth**. Love and truth always go together (see Ephesians 4:15 and comment).

7 The "man filled with love" **always protects**[45] others. In particular, he bears with and **protects** those who have weaknesses and faults. He doesn't reveal his brother's faults to others; instead, out of love he tries to cover them from view (see 1 Peter 4:8).

If we love someone, it is easy to bear that person's faults and weaknesses. But if we are finding it hard to endure a certain person, then we can be sure our love for that person is very small.

Love **always trusts**. When we love someone, we want to trust that person. True, in the end that person may betray our trust; but that is God's business, not ours. Our place is to trust others, not be suspicious of them.[46]

Love **always hopes**. When we love someone, we put hope in that person. We have hope for that person's welfare, his success, his happiness. We hope that his heart will be pure and his character strong. And even if that person should

---

[44] According to some translations of the New Testament, humility (or **gentleness**) is another fruit of the Holy Spirit (Galatians 5:23).

[45] In place of the words **always protects,** some translations of the Bible say, "bears all things." The meaning is similar.

[46] A Christian filled with love like this is called naive by worldly men—and even by some Christians. But we must understand that what the world calls "naivete" is often, in fact, a manifestation of Christ's love. Yes, it is good for Christians to be wise and discerning, but at the same time they must be filled with love.

disappoint us or betray us, we shall go on hoping in him.

Love **always perseveres**. Love always overcomes (see Romans 12:21). Love can never be destroyed. Love is the greatest force on earth.

In verses 4–7, Paul has given us a description of a man filled with love. This is how our own life should be! This should be our goal. But think for a moment: in these verses Paul has not just described some imaginary person; he has described Jesus Christ Himself. Our goal, then, is to be like Jesus, the man of love (Romans 8:29).

The love that Paul has been talking about in this chapter does not originate in man; it comes only from God (1 John 4:7). Love is the work of the Holy Spirit in men's lives (Romans 5:5). Let it be our earnest prayer that this love will continually flow from God into our lives and into our church.

Here we must understand something important. In this chapter, Paul has been talking about a spiritual love that comes only from God. There is a great difference between God's spiritual love and man's natural love. As far as it goes, man's natural love is good, but there is always selfishness mixed with it. The natural love between husband and wife, between parent and child, is pleasing to God; nevertheless, this love is mixed with motives that are fleshly and selfish. Because when we love our spouse or our child or a close friend, we are also, in a sense, loving ourselves[47] (see Ephesians 5:28–29). But God's spiritual love has no selfishness mixed with it. That is why this love can never come from man; it comes only from God.

There is another difference between God's love and man's love. We men love others according to their worthiness. We easily love our family and friends, because in our sight they are worthy of our love. But we find it difficult to love those who are unworthy or disagreeable or sinful. But God's love is not like our love; God loves even the most unworthy and unlovely people (see Romans 5:7–8). And with the help of the Holy Spirit working within us, we too can love these people. We must love them; indeed, Jesus has commanded us to love even our enemies! (see Matthew 5:44 and comment).

8 All of the gifts of the Holy Spirit—**prophecies, tongues, knowledge** (1 Corinthians 12:8–10)—will come to an end. In heaven these special gifts will not be needed. In heaven we shall know and understand everything; in heaven we shall all speak one heavenly language. But love will remain forever. Why? Because God Himself is love (1 John 4:8,16).

9–10 Even if we receive the gifts of the Holy Spirit in this life, our knowledge, our prophecies, and all our other works can never be perfect. But **when perfection comes**—that is, in heaven—then all our abilities and all our works will be perfect, because then we shall be like Christ (see 1 John 3:2).

11 For believers, this earthly life is like childhood. In heaven we will become fully mature. But in this life we must grow and, as much as possible, put **childish things** behind us.

The Corinthians were in many ways acting like children (1 Corinthians 3:1–3; 11:20–21; 14:20). They had received many spiritual gifts, but they had not become mature. Looking at these Corinthian believers, we can learn an important truth: namely, spiritual gifts in themselves don't make a person spiritual. It is not the gifts of the Holy Spirit but rather His fruits that make one spiritual (Galatians 5:22–23). A person is mature and spiritual when the fruits of the Spirit are manifest in his life. These fruits are absolutely essential for every Christian. The gifts of the Spirit are given individually, one to this person, another to that person. But the fruits of the Spirit are meant equally for every believer. We need both the fruits of the Spirit and the gifts of

[47] The same can also be said for a humanitarian concern for the poor and downtrodden. Such concern is always mixed with the selfish desire for merit or recognition—or, at least, self-approval.

the Spirit in our lives, but by far our greatest need is for His fruit.

12 When we look into an old and dirty mirror, we see a **poor reflection**. In the same way, our present knowledge and wisdom is like a "poor reflection" of reality. We do not see things clearly. In this life we **live by faith, not by sight** (2 Corinthians 5:7). But when we get to heaven, we shall see clearly; **we shall see face to face** (see 1 John 3:2). Then we shall know God just as He now knows us.

13 Everything on earth will pass away except these three things: **faith, hope and love** (see 1 Thessalonians 1:3). But among these the greatest is love—God's love. Everything comes from God's love. God's love was in the very beginning. It was God who first loved us (see John 3:16; Romans 5:8; 1 John 4:10,19 and comments).

From God's love comes our **love.** All of the spiritual love we have in our lives comes from God, who has **poured out His love into our hearts by the Holy Spirit** (Romans 5:5). Therefore, since God has given us His love, He expects us to love one another (see 1 John 4:7,11).

From God's love comes our **faith** (see 1 John 4:16). It is by God's love that we were first chosen and called to faith. Praise His name!

From God's love comes our **hope** (see 1 John 4:17). For what do we hope? We hope for salvation, for eternal life. We hope one day to meet our heavenly Father face to face, and to dwell in His love forever.

And in heaven there will be only **love,** because in heaven **faith** and **hope** will no longer be needed.

CHAPTER 14

Gifts of Prophecy and Tongues (14:1–25)

1 Love is the **most excellent way** (1 Corinthians 12:31). Therefore, Paul says: **Follow the way of love.** This is the greatest commandment (Mark 12:30–31). But at the same time, it is good to desire the **spiritual gifts** of the Holy Spirit (see 1 Corinthians 12:8–10,31).

Among the gifts of the Holy Spirit, Paul puts the **gift of prophecy** in the highest place. But, recall, the Corinthians mistakenly had been putting the gift of tongues in the highest place.

In the Bible, the word **prophecy** means much more than just a prediction of the future. It means the announcing of a special word or revelation from God on any subject.

2 When one speaks in a **tongue,** he is speaking in a language given by the Holy Spirit. Therefore, no one except God can understand what the person is saying. He is speaking **with his spirit**[48] (see 1 Corinthians 12:10 and comment).

3 Prophecy, like tongues, is also a word given by the Holy Spirit. But because prophecy is spoken in an ordinary human language, those listening are able to understand it. Thus, when others hear the prophecy, they receive **strengthening, encouragement and comfort.**

If someone speaks in a tongue (spiritual language) and then an interpretation is given, the tongue together with its interpretation will, in effect, be the same as a prophecy; it too will benefit the church (see 1 Corinthians 12:10 and comment).

4 The person speaking in another tongue receives much spiritual blessing himself, even though he can't understand what he is saying; he experiences in a special way the joy and presence of the Holy Spirit. However, the person listening to someone else speak in a tongue

---

[48] In place of the words **with his spirit,** some translations of the Bible say, "by the Spirit." Both meanings are possible, and both are true.

receives much less spiritual blessing. But if the tongue is also interpreted, then the listener will receive a much greater blessing.

5 Here Paul clearly states that the gift of prophecy is **greater** than the gift of speaking in tongues. But if the tongues are also interpreted, then speaking in tongues is essentially the same as prophesying.

Paul does not oppose speaking in tongues; indeed he wishes **every one** of the Corinthians spoke in tongues. But those Corinthians who did speak in tongues were misusing their gift. They were creating disorder in the church service. They were puffing themselves up because they had received the gift and others hadn't. They were speaking in tongues, not to honor Christ, but to receive honor for themselves. They were showing off.

6–9 We can recognize different songs because of a **distinction in the notes** (verse 7). Some songs are sad, some joyful. Some are love songs; others are war songs. We can tell them apart because their tunes, their notes, are different.

But speaking in tongues, Paul says, is like playing a song that has only one note. One can't tell what the meaning of the song is.

A **trumpet** also has different notes (verse 8). In the army, the trumpeter plays different notes on the trumpet to signal the soldiers when to get up, when to go to bed, when to eat, and when to **get ready for battle**. But the trumpeter must play the different notes clearly, or else the soldiers won't know what to do.

So then, says Paul, if the trumpet and other **lifeless** instruments can produce understandable sounds, surely we men ought to be able to!

10–12 If someone speaks to us in a foreign language that we can't understand, what that person says means nothing to us. In the same way, if someone speaks to us in a spiritual language without any interpretation, it means nothing to us; we are not benefited. All spiritual gifts—including the gift of speaking in tongues—are given for the benefit of others. They are given **for the common good** (1 Corinthians 12:7). They are given to **build up the church** (verse 12). Therefore, says Paul, let the Corinthians seek first those gifts that do most to build up the church.

13 Therefore, if a person has already received the gift of speaking in tongues, he should pray that he might also receive the gift of interpretation. If he has both gifts together, then he will, in effect, be able to prophesy, and thus bring great benefit to the church (verses 3–4).

14 The person who speaks or prays in a tongue (spiritual language) doesn't know what he is saying. His **mind is unfruitful**—that is, his mind is not being used. It is "turned off."

15 Therefore, when Paul sings or prays in church, he does so not only with his **spirit**—that is, in a spiritual language—but also with his **mind**, so that others in the church will be edified and blessed.

Some people believe that Paul is talking here about praying privately, not publicly. Nowadays many Christians have the gift of praying in tongues; they call this their "prayer language." They receive much spiritual blessing from praying in this way. They say that this is how the Holy Spirit helps us to pray, in accordance with Romans 8:26.[49]

16–17 Paul's meaning in these verses is this: When we pray in church **among those who do not understand**[50]—that is, among those who do not have the gift of interpreting tongues—we should pray in an understandable language. Otherwise, how would they be able to

---

[49] However, the private gift of praying in tongues isn't meant to benefit only the one praying. The gift should make the person's prayers for others more effective. And as a person's own spiritual life is blessed through praying in tongues, that person should be better able to serve and bless others.

[50] In place of the words **those who do not understand**, some translations of the Bible say "outsider," or "inquirer." The Greek text of this verse is difficult to translate.

say "**Amen**"[51] to our prayer? That is, how would they be able to agree with our prayer (for that is what saying "Amen" means)? How can we pray in a united way together and truly edify each other if we can't understand each other? Therefore, says Paul, when we are in church we must pray "with our minds" in an understandable language.

18–19 Paul himself spoke in tongues more than any of the Corinthians did. Therefore, the Corinthians shouldn't take such pride in having received the gift of tongues; others could speak in tongues too! But Paul says he will not use his gift of tongues during a church service unless someone is present who can interpret what he says. Instead, he will speak with **intelligible words** (verse 19).

20 The Corinthians were acting like children, because they were using the gifts of the Holy Spirit for their own individual benefit rather than the benefit of others. In their **thinking**, Paul says, they should be acting like **adults**—mature. **In regard to evil**, however, let them be like **children**—that is, innocent and inexperienced.

21 Here Paul quotes from Deuteronomy 28:49 and Isaiah 28:11–12. "**I will speak to this people**," the Lord says. The **people** are the Jews. Because the Jews had been disobedient, God sent prophets like Isaiah to warn them. But they did not listen to the prophets. Therefore, God sent **foreigners** to punish them—**men of strange tongues**. These foreigners were Assyrians. The Jews didn't listen to these foreigners either (since they spoke a foreign language), and the Jews suffered a severe defeat. The Jews should have listened to the prophets, whom they could understand!

22 Paul uses this quotation from Isaiah to show that tongues (or foreign languages) are a sign for disobedient and unbelieving men—a sign of God's power and judgment.

But for believers, prophecy is needed, not tongues. Prophecy is for believers, tongues for unbelievers. Therefore, in the church let there be prophecy instead of tongues.

23 Although speaking in tongues is a sign for unbelievers, the believers shouldn't all begin speaking in tongues at once when unbelievers enter their presence. Otherwise, the unbelievers will think the believers are out of their minds (see Acts 2:4,13). Speaking in tongues all at once like this can actually turn unbelievers away and harden their hearts, just as the Jews hearts were hardened when the Assyrians came speaking **strange tongues** (verse 21). If men don't listen to God's warnings when He speaks to them in understandable ways, they certainly won't listen to Him if He speaks in ways that are not understandable!

24–25 Although tongues are a sign for unbelievers (verse 22), unbelievers also receive more benefit from prophecy than from tongues. Remember, God first sent prophets to warn the unbelieving Jews; if they had listened to them, they would have been spared much trouble. For it was only after the Jews had rejected the prophets that God sent the foreigners with their **strange tongues** to attack them.

Therefore, even though Paul has said in verse 22 that tongues **are a sign . . . for unbelievers**, prophecy is still usually much more effective in leading unbelievers to repent and turn to God. Sometimes in a church service, God will give a believer a special word or prophecy about an unbeliever who is present, and as a result of that prophecy, the unbeliever will be brought to repentance and faith. Thus, in summary, prophecy is more beneficial than tongues, not only for believers, but for unbelievers also.

Orderly Worship (14:26–40)

26 Paul encourages the Corinthians to use the spiritual gifts they have been given whenever they meet together—whether in church, or in a house fellowship, or in a prayer meeting. Paul says that **everyone** has one or more gifts of the Spirit, through which the church can be

---

[51] The word **Amen** means, "May it be so!"

strengthened. Paul again mentions a few examples of these gifts. Two of the examples—the **hymn** and the **word of instruction**—can be natural gifts (Ephesians 5:19; Colossians 3:16). The other gifts—a **revelation**, a **tongue**, and an **interpretation**—are clearly supernatural gifts (1 Corinthians 12:8–10).[52]

27–28 Here Paul gives clear instructions about speaking in tongues during meetings of the church. In any one meeting, no more than three people should speak in tongues; and they should speak in turn, not all at once. In any church where tongues are spoken, there will usually be one or more persons who can interpret. If such an interpreter is not present at a particular meeting, then the one with the gift of tongues should not speak in tongues during that meeting (unless he himself can interpret what he says). Rather, he should **speak to himself and God** privately in prayer (verse 28).

Notice that the gift of speaking in tongues is under our control. In accordance with Paul's instructions and the Spirit's leading, we can choose either to speak or not to speak; the decision is ours.

29 Those with the gift of prophecy also should speak in turn. And **the others should weigh carefully what is said.** Why is that necessary? Because there is always the danger that false prophets might come into a church and deceive the believers (Matthew 7:15; Mark 13:22; Acts 20:29–30; 2 Corinthians 11:13–14). We must examine what every prophet says and determine whether or not it's true (1 John 4:1). In order to help believers recognize false prophets, the Holy Spirit gives to some in the church a special gift of **distinguishing between spirits**[53] (1 Corinthians 12:10). Those who have this gift can thus protect other believers from the teaching of these false prophets.

30–31 Before a prophet speaks, he must first receive from God a revelation of what he is to say. If such a revelation should come to someone during a church meeting, then that person should immediately be given the opportunity to share that revelation with the church. But if someone else is already speaking, that speaker should quickly finish what he is saying and sit down; then the one who has received the revelation can speak. Only one person at a time should address the congregation.[54]

32 Just as the person who speaks in tongues must control himself, so also the person who prophesies must control himself. God gives the revelation, but the prophet must speak in an orderly way.

The **spirits of prophets** are the human spirits of the prophets themselves. The Holy Spirit inspires the spirit of the prophet, but the prophet must use his mind and will to keep his spirit under control.

33 Why does Paul give all this teaching about order in the church? Because God **is not a God of disorder.** He is a God of **peace** and order, and He wants order to be maintained in His church. The last of the nine fruits of the Holy Spirit is **self-control** (Galatians 5:23). This fruit was lacking in the Corinthian church; that is why their meetings were filled with confusion. From this we can see once more that the fruits of the Spirit are much more important than the gifts of the Spirit. A man may have the Spirit's gifts, but if he

---

[52] Sometimes there is no clear line between what is a natural gift and what is a supernatural one. Often the Holy Spirit will add a supernatural element to a natural gift that someone already has. In a sense, this happens to all of us when we become Christians; the Holy Spirit takes our natural gifts and sanctifies them and begins to use them. The most important thing to remember is that all gifts—both natural and supernatural—come ultimately from God and are to be used **for the strengthening of the church** (verse 26).

[53] False prophets are under the control of evil spirits.

[54] In some churches a time of prayer is set aside during the service when everyone prays out loud at the same time. Since such prayers are addressed to God and not to the congregation, Paul's prohibition about more than one person speaking at a time would not apply to such prayer times.

does not also have the Spirit's fruits, his behavior will be displeasing to God.

34 . . . **women should remain silent in the churches**. These days there is much debate among Christians about the meaning of this verse. The verse cannot mean that women must remain completely silent all the time, because in this same letter Paul has written that women should cover their heads when they pray and prophesy publicly in church (1 Corinthians 11:5). Thus, according to Paul's own statement, it must be all right for women to pray and prophesy out loud in church; otherwise, Paul would never have said they needed to cover their heads.

So what does Paul mean when he says that women must remain silent in the churches? He means that women must not cause a disturbance during church meetings. **They are not allowed to speak**, says Paul; that is, they are not allowed to chatter. In Paul's time, the women sat in one part of the church and the men in another. Thus the women would often gossip and laugh among themselves and not pay any attention to what was being said in the meeting. They would often have small children with them, and the children would create a disturbance on their own. Paul would certainly instruct such women to keep their children under control, or take them outside. Otherwise, no one would be able to concentrate on what was being said.

Therefore, Paul is teaching here that women must not speak in a thoughtless or disorderly way in the church. They must remain **in submission** to the leaders in charge of the meeting (see General Article: Women in the Church).

This rule concerning women was applied even more strictly among the Jews of Paul's time. According to Jewish custom, woman were not allowed to speak at all in the synagogue. But because Christian men and women are equal in Christ, Christian women were allowed more privileges in the church. Even so, Paul teaches here that it is usually more suitable for women to remain silent during church services (see 1 Timothy 2:11–12; 1 Peter 3:1–4 and comments).

35 If a woman has a question she wants to ask, she must not suddenly jump up in the middle of the meeting to ask it; that would be **disgraceful**. It would create a disturbance. Rather, let her wait and ask her husband the question at a more suitable time.

In Paul's time, most women were uneducated. They couldn't understand everything that was being said in the church service. Therefore, it was the duty of their husbands to teach them, says Paul. The wives should not remain ignorant of spiritual matters. In spiritual understanding, the husband and wife should be equal. Let us ask ourselves: What is our own church like? Do women come freely? Do they receive teaching? Let the husbands not neglect their duty to teach their wives.

36 The Corinthians were proud. They followed their own rules for their church services. They acted as if their church were the only church on earth. Therefore, in this verse Paul reminds the Corinthians that they aren't the only Christians in the world. They should be following the rules that all the other churches followed (verse 33).

37 Anyone who claims to be a **prophet or spiritually gifted** among the Corinthians ought to know that these instructions that Paul has written are from the Lord Himself.

38 If anyone does not recognize or heed Paul's teaching, let that person **be ignored**;[55] let him be treated as an ignorant person.

39–40 Finally, in spite of all his warnings, Paul does not want to discourage the Corinthians from using the spiritual gifts they have been given. Let them be used! (verse 1). But let them be used **in a fitting and orderly way**.

---

[55] In place of the words **he himself will be ignored**, some translations of the Bible say, "let him ignore this," or, "let him remain ignorant." The exact meaning of the Greek text is uncertain. Any one of the three meanings is possible.

CHAPTER 15

The Resurrection of Christ (15:1–11)

1–2 **By this gospel you are saved, if you hold firmly to the word.** To believe means to **hold firmly to the word**, that is, to Christ. It means to remain in Christ (John 15:4–6). It means to **continue in** [God's] **kindness** (Romans 11:22). If we do not believe in this way, then we have believed **in vain**.

If we do not remain in Christ, there will be no spiritual fruit in our lives. If there is no fruit, that means our faith is **dead** (see James 2:14,17 and comment). If our faith is "dead," then surely we will have believed **in vain** (verse 2). Man cannot be saved by a faith that is dead!

True faith is a very deep thing. How easily we say: "I believe," but have no real faith. Let us always remember that true faith means to remain in Christ. If we do not remain in Christ, our faith will be lost—and so will we.

3 In verses 3–4, Paul briefly summarizes the Gospel which he has preached to them (verse 1). According to the **Scriptures**,[56] Christ **died for our sins** (Isaiah 53:1–12). He bore our punishment; and through His sacrifice—that is, through His death—we receive forgiveness for our sins (see Mark 10:45; 1 Peter 2:24 and comments).

4 But Christ did not die and remain buried like other men. His body remained in a tomb for three days, and then He rose from the dead. He came to life again. The tomb in which He had been buried was found empty! This is a fact of history. Because Jesus Christ rose from the dead—that is, because of His resurrection—we know that He is the living God. And because He rose from the dead, we know that He has the power to raise us from the dead also, and to give us eternal life (see Romans 8:11; Ephesians 2:4–7).

This is why Christ's resurrection is so important. If Christ had remained lifeless in the tomb, our faith would be worthless. Of what use to us is a dead Savior? (verse 14). For this reason let the whole world know that Jesus Christ has risen from the dead! He has conquered both sin and death.[57] He has obtained the victory; and through Him, we too have obtained victory over sin and death (verses 54–56).

According to the Scriptures, Jesus **was raised on the third day** (Psalm 16:10; Isaiah 53:10–12). Being raised on the **third day** is mentioned in the Old Testament book of Jonah (Jonah 1:17). The prophet Jonah was swallowed by a great fish. Jonah remained in the fish's stomach for three days. Then on the **third day**, the fish vomited Jonah up, and Jonah was saved. In Matthew 12:38–42, Jesus compares Himself with Jonah.

From the beginning, Christ knew that He would die and then be raised from the dead on the third day. At least three times He told His disciples in advance what was going to happen to Him (Mark 8:31; 9:31; 10:32–34).

5 How do we know for sure that Jesus rose from the dead? First of all, we know it because of the empty tomb. But the empty tomb in itself is not sufficient proof, because someone could argue that Jesus' body was not raised but stolen! (see Matthew 28:11–15). The greatest proof that Jesus rose from the dead is the fact that after His death He appeared to men.

Among the disciples, Jesus appeared first to **Peter** (Cephas), His chief disciple (Luke 24:33–34). Then Jesus appeared to all of His disciples together (Matthew 28:16; John 20:19). He did not appear in a vision or a dream; He appeared in His own body—His risen transformed body (see Luke 24:36–39; John 20:24–28).

6 Even having said this much, it could still be argued by an unbeliever that Jesus' twelve disciples were lying, that they had simply made up this story about Jesus' resurrection. But the five

56 In Paul's time, the only **Scriptures** were the Old Testament Scriptures.

57 Death is the punishment for sin (Romans 6:23).

hundred people mentioned in this verse who saw the risen Jesus with their own eyes could not have been lying. How could so many people have invented such a story and then stuck with it? That many people could never have agreed on what to say if their story had been false. No, what all those people reported was the truth: they had indeed seen the risen Jesus with their own eyes! Jesus had appeared to **more than five hundred of the brothers at the same time**—and that didn't even include women and children. And twenty years later, when Paul wrote this letter to the Corinthians, most of those five hundred witnesses were still alive. If Jesus had, in fact, not risen from the dead, Paul could not have written these words; there were too many people still around who would have called him a liar! And if anyone doubted Paul's word, there were all these witnesses to go to in order to check out Paul's story. Paul would never have dared to lie in this way—even if he had wanted to. No, Jesus' resurrection is an absolutely true and proven fact of history. Indeed, in all the history of the world there has never been a greater or more important event than the resurrection of Jesus Christ.

Paul says here that a few among those five hundred brothers **have fallen asleep**. Notice that when believers in Christ die, they don't really die; they just "go to sleep." And after they have "slept" for a while, they will be awakened (see 1 Thessalonians 4:13–18).

7 Jesus also appeared to **James,** His own brother, who later became the main leader of the church in Jerusalem (Galatians 2:9). He also wrote the New Testament letter called "James." At first James had not believed in Jesus (John 7:5). But after Jesus' resurrection, James and Jesus' other younger brothers believed in Him (Acts 1:14).

Jesus also appeared to **all the apostles**. Here Paul means not only the original twelve apostles (disciples), but also other leaders of the Jerusalem church who became known as apostles.

8 After His resurrection, Jesus remained on earth for forty days, during which time He appeared to all the people mentioned above. Then He ascended into heaven. Only after Jesus ascended did He appear to Paul. This is why Paul says here that **last of all** [Christ] **appeared to me also** (see Acts 9:1–9; 22:6–11; 26:12–18).

Paul says he was like **one abnormally born**. According to the context, Paul was born "late," because Christ appeared to him **last of all**. But Paul actually writes here that he was like one born suddenly "before" the proper time; that's the meaning of the Greek expression Paul uses. That is, he was born "prematurely." And just as a premature baby cannot be considered a normal baby, so Paul is saying that he cannot be considered a normal apostle—that is, he does not **deserve to be called an apostle** (verse 9). And the main reason Paul does not deserve to be called an apostle is because he **persecuted the church of God** (verse 9).

From verse 8 we can see the sign or stamp of a true apostle. Most of the apostles[58] saw the risen Christ with their own eyes, and from this experience they received a special inspiration and compulsion to go out into the world and witness to Christ and preach the Gospel.

So far, we have discussed two proofs that Jesus indeed rose from the dead, that His resurrection is indeed a historical fact: one, His tomb was empty; and two, He appeared to many people after His death. There is also a third proof, and this proof comes from the lives of Jesus' twelve disciples (apostles). Recall, at Jesus' arrest, His disciples all fled and hid (Matthew 26:56; Mark 14:50). They were filled with fear. Their leader had died. Now they were afraid that the Roman soldiers would come looking for them and put them to death too. Therefore, they hid in a house and locked the door (John 20:19).

But then what happened to those disciples? Somehow their lives were dramatically changed. One moment,

---

[58] Later on, a few apostles rose up who had not seen the risen Christ (see 1 Thessalonians 2:7).

they were filled with fear; the next moment they were fearless. One moment, they were hiding; the next moment they were out witnessing to Christ! And in Paul's case, one moment he was persecuting the church; the next moment he was preaching the Gospel throughout the Roman Empire. What happened to these men to change their lives so amazingly? There is only one answer possible: the risen Christ had appeared to them. And not only that, after Christ had ascended to heaven, He sent to them the Holy Spirit, from whom they received the power to be His witnesses throughout the whole world (Acts 1:8; 2:1–4,14,41).

Finally, there is a fourth proof of Christ's resurrection. For almost two thousand years millions upon millions of Christians have themselves experienced through the Holy Spirit the presence and power of the risen Christ. Let us ask ourselves: Is the risen Christ alive in us? If so, we are the greatest proof of all that Jesus has truly risen from the dead!

9 Paul could never forget how he persecuted Christ's church in the beginning (Acts 8:3; 9:1–2; 22:4–5; 26:9–11; Galatians 1:13). That is why he says he doesn't **deserve to be called an apostle**.

10 Even though Paul calls himself the **least of the apostles** (verse 9), still he was a true apostle. He spoke to the churches with the full authority of an apostle (1 Corinthians 1:1; Galatians 1:1). But Paul also says that it was solely by God's grace and mercy that he became an apostle (see Galatians 1:15–16). Not only that, God's grace was continuing to work in Paul's life. Paul had worked harder **than all of them**—that is, harder than all the other apostles. But Paul's great works had not really been done by him, but rather by the grace of God working in him (see Galatians 2:20).

11 However, says Paul, no matter who does the preaching, the Gospel is one. And for all who believe this Gospel, it is the **power of God** for salvation (Romans 1:16; 1 Corinthians 1:18).

The Resurrection of the Dead (15:12–34)

12 Because we know that Christ has been raised from the dead, we know that the dead will be raised also.

Some of the Corinthians did not believe in the RESURRECTION **of the dead**. Most Greeks believed that only man's spirit went to heaven. They believed that after death the body was completely destroyed forever. But Paul says here that that belief is false; because, when Jesus rose from the dead, His body rose too.

13–14 **And if Christ has not been raised** (verse 14), then where is the power of the Gospel to save us? The power doesn't exist. And if the power of the Gospel doesn't exist, then our faith is **useless**.

But because Christ has indeed risen from the dead, we know with certainty that He is God. We know that He is the living Lord. We know that His teaching is true. We can put our complete faith in Him. And our faith is not useless, because through our faith we too shall receive that same power which raised Christ from the dead and seated Him with God in heaven (see Ephesians 1:19–21).

15–17 **And if Christ has not been raised . . . you are still in your sins** (verse 17). To be **in your sins** means to be condemned, to be unsaved (Ephesians 2:1,4–5). It is because Christ has risen from the dead and conquered sin that He is able to save us from our sins. Christ's resurrection is the proof of His power to save men.

18 If there is no resurrection, then those believers who have died are **lost** indeed. They will remain buried. Their faith will have been a hoax! (see 1 Thessalonians 4:14).

19 If there is no hope of being resurrected after death, then Christians are certainly to be the most **pitied** of all men. After suffering abuse and persecution in this life, they then would have no hope of reward in the next. Rather, it would be better not to be a Christian!

However, in verse 20, Paul says: **But Christ has indeed been raised from the dead.** Let the Corinthians not doubt it.

Because the resurrection of Christ is their hope—and ours (1 Peter 1:3).

20 Christ was the first man to rise from the dead. Therefore, Paul calls Him the **firstfruits of those who have fallen asleep**. Because He rose from the dead, all Christians will also rise. They will be the "later" fruits (verse 23).

According to the Old Testament, the Jews offered the **firstfruits** of every harvest to God. By means of that offering, the rest of the harvest was made holy (Leviticus 23:9–14). Therefore, we can understand from this that Christ is the "firstfruits" of the harvest—that is, the church; and that through the offering of His body, the church is made holy.

21–22 Death came through **Adam**, the first man. In the same way, the resurrection of the body—or **redemption** of the body (Romans 8:23)—came through Jesus Christ. Because of Adam's sin, all men are born sinners and are condemned to die (Genesis 2:16–17; 3:6; Romans 3:9–10). Because of Christ's righteousness, all who are **in Christ** (verse 22)—that is, believers—will be made righteous and receive eternal life (see John 11:25–26; Romans 5:12,15–19; 1 Corinthians 15:45–49 and comments).

23 According to this verse, we believers will be raised up **when he** (Christ) **comes**—that is, at the end of the world.

24–25 When Christ comes again, He will destroy all the **dominion, authority and power** of evil, both in heaven and on earth (see Psalm 110:1; Mark 13:26; Ephesians 1:20–23; Philippians 2:9–11 and comments).

After conquering all His enemies, Christ will hand over His **kingdom** to God (verse 24); that is, He will give back to God all the authority which God had given Him (Matthew 28:18). Then, at that point, the world will end.

According to these verses, then, the end of the world will be like this. First, Christ will come again. Then Christ will reign until all His enemies are destroyed. Then all believers in Christ will be raised. After that, the world will end.

26 How will Christ "destroy" death? The answer is this: through the resurrection of the body. When believers die, they don't really die but rather "go to sleep." At the end of the world, we shall be "wakened up." That is when death will finally be destroyed. Thus, for believers, death has lost its **sting** (verses 55–56). From now on we need not fear, we need not despair.

27 Paul here quotes from Psalm 8:6. God **has put everything** (including death) **under his** (Christ's) **feet**—that is, under Christ's authority (see Psalm 110:1; Hebrews 2:6–9).

28 When all enemies are conquered—death, sin, Satan—then Christ will hand over His authority, His **kingdom** (verse 24), to God. And finally He will hand Himself over to God; He will make Himself **subject** to God. God has given to Christ all authority in heaven and on earth (Matthew 28:18). Therefore, after His work is finished, Christ will give His authority back to God.

Christ's entire purpose was to glorify God, so that God might be **all in all** (see Romans 11:36). This is the purpose of all creation—the creation of the world and the creation of each one of us—that God through the world and through us might be glorified, that He might be all in all (see Matthew 5:16; John 17:4; 14:12–13; Ephesians 1:12–13; Revelation 4:11).

29 This verse is difficult to understand. It's possible that some of the Christians in the Corinthian church were taking baptism on behalf of believers who had died before they'd had a chance to be baptized. Nothing else is written about this custom in the Bible.[59]

If there is no resurrection, there is no point in taking baptism for someone who has died. It certainly won't benefit the dead person!

30 If there is no resurrection, why should we Christians risk death? asks Paul. Rather, let us try to live as long as

---

[59] Paul doesn't say whether this custom of taking baptism for dead people is good or not. As far as is known, no other group of Christians has ever practiced this custom.

possible, because after we die there'll be nothing to look forward to (see verse 14).

31 **I die every day**, says Paul. This can have two meanings. First, it can mean that Paul is ready to die every day. He endangers himself **every hour** (verse 30). He faces death **all day long** (Romans 8:36).

The second possible meaning is this: Paul's **old self** is dying every day (Romans 6:6). That is, Paul is crucifying his old sinful self every day, so that he might live a righteous life. He is "denying himself" and "taking up his cross daily" (Luke 9:23).

Paul "glories over" the Corinthians. They are his spiritual children, and like any father, he is proud of his children. But he glories over them **in Christ Jesus**. The Corinthian church was the fruit of Paul's work in Christ; therefore, he is ready to die for them every day (see 1 Thessalonians 2:19–20).

32 If there is no resurrection, why should we take risks for Christ? Paul had faced great risks in Ephesus.[60] He had **fought wild beasts**. If he had done this **for merely human reasons** and not for spiritual reasons, he would have been foolish indeed. What would he have gained by becoming a meal for wild beasts!

Paul had suffered much at the hands of men. And according to this verse, he had even been forced to fight with wild animals. In the Roman Empire, one of the ways of executing criminals was to let lions eat them.

Here Paul quotes from Isaiah 22:13. "Let's enjoy ourselves today, because tomorrow our life will end." Even in Isaiah's time, this was a common saying among worldly men, and it has been a common saying ever since. And indeed, if there is no reward in the next life, it makes sense to follow this saying and get all the advantage one can out of this life!

What is to be gained by dying for Christ? Paul asks here. What will be gained is the resurrection of the body and eternal life. Therefore, it is better not to run after the pleasures of this life, lest we lose the reward that awaits us in the next.

33 When Paul mentions "bad company" here, he is thinking mainly of those who deny the resurrecton. Such people spend their lives eating and drinking and enjoying themselves. They are worldly; they love only the things of this world. **Do not be misled** by them. Do not associate with them, Paul advises, lest they corrupt your character.

But we believers seek our reward in heaven. Let us not be **misled** by those who say that the only rewards are here on earth.

34 **Come back to your senses**, Paul tells the Corinthians. Let the Corinthians not deny the resurrection. Let them not seek their reward in this life; to do so is a sin.

Those who deny the resurrection deny God's promises; they are **ignorant of God**.

The Resurrection Body (15:35–58)

35 How can a dead body come to life again? the Corinthians asked. Does the corpse itself rise up out of the ground where it was buried?

36 Paul calls this a **foolish** question. Then he gives the illustration of a seed. When we plant a seed in the ground, it's not the seed that rises up but a plant. That's how our resurrected bodies will be.

When we plant a seed in the ground, we "bury" it—much as we bury a corpse. In a sense, the seed dies; it is destroyed. But then, a little later, new life arises out of that seed.

Our physical bodies are like that seed. Whether our bodies are burned or buried, it makes no difference. No matter what happens to our physical bodies, we shall receive new resurrected bodies.

It's the same with our spiritual life. Like that seed, our old sinful self must die (see John 12:24; Romans 6:3–7 and comments). Only after that can we be

---

[60] Ephesus was an important city in the western part of present-day Turkey. Some of Paul's experiences in Ephesus are described in Acts Chapter 19.

spiritually reborn (John 3:3) and receive new spiritual life (Romans 8:11).

37–38 We are now like seeds. When we die, out of us will come a glorious resurrected body. Just as the plant is more glorious than the seed, so our resurrected body will be more glorious than our present body.

God will give each person a new body. God is the giver of both the seed and the plant. God is the Creator of every living thing; He is the source of all life. How can the Corinthians doubt that there is a resurrection? Every year they sow seeds and see new plants spring from the ground. If God can bring new life out of a tiny perishable seed, then He can surely bring new life out of our bodies.

39–41 There are many kinds of bodies, both **heavenly** and **earthly** (verse 40). Each kind of body has its own **splendor**. In the same way, each of our resurrected bodies will have its own splendor (verse 42).

42–44 Our present bodies are like seeds that will soon be sown in the ground—that is, burned or buried. A corpse is **perishable** (verse 42); it is characterized by **dishonor** and **weakness** (verse 43). Our new bodies will be **imperishable**; they will be characterized by **glory** and **power**.

Our new bodies will be **spiritual** (verse 44). What that means in detail is uncertain. For example, will we eat and drink in heaven? Christ ate and drank with His disciples after His own resurrection (Luke 24:39–43). What we do know for certain, however, is that our new bodies will never die (see John 6:40,63; 11:25–26).

45 **The first Adam became a living being**—that is, an ordinary earthly man (Genesis 2:7). The **last Adam** (Christ) became a **life giving spirit**—that is, a spiritual man (see John 5:21; 6:33–35). Christ was not only a **spirit**; He was also fully a man. Christ is God Himself, who came to earth in the form of a man (see General Article: Jesus Christ).

46 First we receive our natural bodies; afterward we receive our spiritual bodies.

47 Adam was made from the earth (Genesis 2:7). Christ was born of the Holy Spirit (see Matthew 1:18; John 6:33,38 and comments).

48–49 From Adam we receive our earthly body. From Christ we receive our heavenly body.

Now we are like Adam. After our resurrection, we shall be like Christ (see 2 Corinthians 3:18; Philippians 3:20–21; 1 John 3:2 and comments).

50 Paul says that **flesh and blood** (that is, unbelieving earthly man) **cannot inherit the kingdom of God**. Unspiritual earthly man will not enter God's kingdom; he will not be saved. Because in order to enter God's kingdom, man must first be **changed** (verse 53). And in order to be changed, the first step is to be born anew of the Spirit (see John 3:3,5–6 and comment).

All who truly believe in Jesus Christ are born again spiritually. Even in this world we begin the process of being changed, because when we are born again, we receive new life through the Holy Spirit. As soon as we believe in Jesus, we receive eternal spiritual life which begins right here on earth. But we will receive our resurrected bodies only after Jesus comes again at the end of the world (verses 22–23). At that time we shall be fully **changed**. Now we have received the Holy Spirit as an advance of what is to come (see 2 Corinthians 1:21–22; Ephesians 1:13–14). Later we shall receive our full inheritance: namely, the resurrection, or **redemption of our bodies** (see Romans 8:23 and comment).

There will be no redemption of the body for those who do not believe in Christ. For them there will be no resurrection in heaven. Their resurrection will be in hell (see John 5:29 and comment).

51 Here a new question arises. When Christ comes again, what will happen to the believers who are alive at that time? Will they be resurrected too? Yes, says Paul.

52 At the time of Christ's second coming, the **dead** will be raised instantly—**in a flash, in the twinkling of an eye**. And **we** (the believers living at that time) **will be changed**. For the dead, this is called a "resurrection." For the living, it is called a "change." But it's really the same thing. When Christ comes, both the dead and the living will get new bodies. This will occur **at the last trumpet** (Revelation 11:15)—that is, at the end of the world (see Matthew 24:27; Mark 13:26–27; 1 Thessalonians 4:14–17).

Jesus Himself was **changed** for a short time while He was here on earth (see Mark 9:2–10). At Christ's second coming, we shall be changed in the same way.

53–54 In these verses, Paul repeats the thought of verse 42.

When the dead are raised, then death will truly be defeated. Death will be **swallowed up in victory** (Isaiah 25:8).

55 Here Paul quotes from Hosea 13:14.

56 **The sting of death is sin**. Sin is like the **sting** of a hornet. It is sin that causes death, eternal death (see Romans 5:12; 6:23).

But Christ has removed the "sting," because He has forgiven our sin and taken our punishment—that is, death (see Mark 10:45; John 1:29; Colossians 1:14; 1 John 1:7; 2:2; 3:5 and comments).

The **power of sin is the law**. Sin receives its power to cause death from the law, because the law condemns to death all who sin (Romans 7:10–11).

57 Because Christ was resurrected, we also shall be resurrected. Because Christ obtained **victory** over death, we also shall obtain victory over death—that is, forgiveness of sins and eternal life. . . . **thanks be to God!** (see Romans 7:24–25; 8:1–2,10–11 and comments).

58 Here Paul comes to the final and main point of this entire chapter: **Therefore, my dear brothers, stand firm . . . your labor in the Lord is not in vain.** Why is our labor in the Lord not in vain? Because we shall obtain an eternal reward when our labor is finished: namely, the resurrection and **redemption of our bodies** (Romans 8:23)—or, more simply, SALVATION.

But, remember, it is not by our labor that we are saved, but by grace (Ephesians 2:8–9). We don't receive salvation because of our labor; we labor because of our salvation. We labor in gratitude for what Christ has done for us. And our reward is waiting for us in heaven.

Therefore, Paul says: **Let nothing move you**. Let us not be discouraged. Let us not be overwhelmed by trouble or sorrow or persecution. Because there is nothing that can overcome us—not even death (see Romans 8:35–39). God has given us the **victory through our Lord Jesus Christ** (verse 57). Hallelujah!

CHAPTER 16

The Collection for God's People (16:1–4)

1 Paul spent much time raising a collection for the poor Christians in Jerusalem, which he here calls **God's people** (see Romans 15:25–26 and comment).

2 Paul wanted the Corinthians to complete the collection before he came to visit them. One year after writing this letter, Paul wrote again to the Corinthians on the subject of this collection (see 2 Corinthians 9:1–5).

Paul here gives the Corinthians (and all Christians) two practical principles concerning the raising of money. First, it is better for people to give money regularly each week, rather than to try to raise money in a hurry all at once. Giving regularly to meet the needs of the poor is the duty of every Christian.

The second principle is that each Christian should give money **in keeping**

with his income.[61] Christians don't give because of a law. (The Jews gave a tenth of their income because the Jewish law said they had to.) Rather, Christians give because of love; they give from their hearts. Just as God has given generously to us, so we should give generously to others. Each Christian should ask God how much he should give (see Mark 12:41–44; 2 Corinthians 8:12 and comments).

3–4 Paul does not ask the Corinthians to turn the collection over to him. He doesn't want anyone to be able to accuse him of trying to raise the money for himself (see 2 Corinthians 8:19–21). Instead, he instructs the Corinthians to choose men from among themselves to take the money to Jerusalem.

Paul's Plans (16:5–12)

5 **Macedonia** was the main province of northern Greece; the Philippian and Thessalonian churches were located there. To go from Ephesus (where Paul wrote this letter) to Corinth by land, one would have to go through Macedonia. Corinth was in the southern part of Greece, in the province of Achaia.

6–7 Paul wants the Corinthians to understand why he can't come to them immediately. It's not because he doesn't care for them; rather, it's because he does care for them. He wants to be able to spend a long time with them, so he prefers to come when he has more time (see 2 Corinthians 1:15–16).

Paul will spend time with the Corinthians **if the Lord permits** (verse 7). Whatever Paul does, he does it only with the Lord's permission (see James 4:13–15 and comment).

8–9 Here Paul mentions a second reason why it is not suitable for him to go to Corinth immediately. In Ephesus a **great door for effective work** had opened for him. Paul was always seeking "open doors," that is, opportunities for spreading the Gospel. To preach the Gospel was his greatest obligation; therefore, he did not feel it was right to leave a place where there was so much opportunity **for effective work.**

Paul's "open door" in Ephesus is described in Acts 19:8–12,18–22. Notice that God, not Paul, opened the door. It is God's work to open doors; it is man's work to go through them.

Today, has any **great door for effective work** opened up for us? For our church? Are we going through that door?

Paul says: **. . . there are many who oppose me** (verse 9). Wherever there is an open door, there will also be many opponents. Satan will do his best to keep us from going through any open door. Some of Paul's opponents in Ephesus are mentioned in Acts 19:23–34.

Paul says that he wants to stay in Ephesus **until Pentecost**. The day of Pentecost falls fifty days after the last day of the Passover festival. It was on the first Pentecost after Jesus' death, that His disciples were filled with the Holy Spirit for the first time (Acts 2:1–4).

10–11 **Timothy** was Paul's colleague; Paul considered him his spiritual son (see Acts 16:1–5; 19:22; 1 Corinthians 4:17; Philippians 2:22).

12 **Apollos** was a great preacher, who took Paul's place at Corinth (Acts 18:24–28). Some of the Corinthians had begun to follow Apollos too eagerly, and as a result, had caused division in the church (1 Corinthians 1:12). Perhaps

---

[61] In place of the words **in keeping with his income**, some translations of the Bible say, "as he may prosper." The meaning is the same. Christians should give according to their income, not their fixed possessions. Christians are not expected to sell a percentage of their land or houses each year. However, in special circumstances, a Christian may be called by God to sell a piece of property or some other possession to further the Lord's work. And, of course, a Christian should sell any possession that he has begun to love more than God (see Mark 10:21).

Christians—even poor Christians—do well to give at least a tenth of their income for the work of the Lord. (Income can be either money or produce.) But Christians will receive greater blessing if they give more than a tenth. As one's income increases, that doesn't mean he'll have more to spend on himself; it means he'll have more to give to the Lord!

Apollos didn't want to go to Corinth at that time because he feared his presence would make the division worse.

Final Instructions (16:13–24)

13 See 1 Corinthians 15:58; Ephesians 6:10; 1 Peter 5:8–9 and comments.

14 See Romans 13:8; 1 Corinthians 14:1; Ephesians 5:2; Colossians 3:14; 1 John 4:7,11 and comments.

15–16 In New Testament times, entire households often believed in Christ at one time (see Acts 10:24,48; 16:29–34). Such was the case with **Stephanas** and his **household**.

... **submit to such as these**, Paul urges. In every church there are mature leaders like Stephanas who act as spiritual "fathers" in the church. In many cases such leaders, like Stephanas, were probably the first to be converted in a certain place. Or perhaps they were the first pastor or preacher in a certain church. It is essential for other church members to submit to these leaders, and to give them respect and **recognition** (see Ephesians 5:21).

How often we slander and oppose such leaders instead of respecting them! It's common in churches nowadays to see young and immature members criticize and attack those who are more mature and more experienced. Such immature members do the church great harm. If we ourselves have opposed any of our leaders, let us quickly repent of it and ask God for forgiveness.

17–18 Stephanas and his two colleagues, **Fortunatus** and **Achaicus**, had brought to Paul a letter from the church in Corinth, in which the Corinthians had asked various questions on such matters as marriage and food offered to idols (1 Corinthians 7:1). Paul has answered their questions in this first letter to the Corinthians.

Stephanas and his colleagues were themselves Corinthians. By coming to see Paul, they had **supplied what was lacking**—that is, personal fellowship and more detailed information about the church that the Corinthians had not written in their letter to Paul. These three men had **refreshed** Paul's spirit.

19 See Romans 16:3–5 and comment.

20 See Romans 16:16 and comment.

21 Paul customarily dictated his letters to a scribe (see Romans 16:22). However, Paul wrote the final four verses of this letter by his own hand. He did this to prove to the Corinthians that he was indeed the author of this letter (see 2 Thessalonians 3:17).

22 Those who do not love the Lord are **cursed**; that is, they have separated themselves from God. Those who do not love the Lord are those who do not obey His commandments (John 14:15,23–24). By their disobedience, some of the Corinthians have shown that they do not love the Lord. Let them be warned: the Lord will soon come and judge all men. Those who do not love Him will be condemned—**cursed**.

23 **The grace of the Lord Jesus be with you**. The Lord's **grace** includes the Lord's mercy, His love, the fruits of the Spirit, and the power of the Spirit. When we pray for the Lord's grace for ourselves and for others, all these things are given to us. May this be the experience of all of us!

24 Even though Paul has had to give the Corinthian Christians many severe warnings and rebukes, he still has great love for them **in Christ Jesus**. Paul loves them with a spiritual love. That is, he loves them with Christ's own love, which Christ has given to him. And so Paul ends this great letter thinking of his love for the Corinthians.

2 Corinthians

INTRODUCTION

Paul's second letter to the Corinthians was written from Macedonia, a province of northern Greece, in approximately 56 A.D., one or two years after his first letter.

Some time after writing his first letter to the Corinthians, Paul heard that the situation in the Corinthian church had become worse. Therefore, Paul, who was in Ephesus at the time, wrote a severe letter to the Corinthians, and sent it with his colleague Titus (2 Corinthians 2:3–4). This second letter has been lost; no copies of it exist.[1] When Titus did not return from Corinth promptly, Paul became worried and traveled to Macedonia to look for him (2 Corinthians 2:12–14). There Paul finally found Titus, and learned from him that the Corinthians had realized their mistakes and had repented of their sins. After hearing that good news, Paul wrote the Corinthians a third letter, which we now know as "2 Corinthians."[2]

2 Corinthians is the most personal of all Paul's New Testament letters. Here Paul opens his heart to the Corinthians—and to us. From this letter we can find out a great deal about what kind of man Paul was inwardly.

For further information about Paul's life, see Romans: Introduction.

OUTLINE

A. Paul's Recent Trials and Travels (1:1–2:11).
   1. Paul's Trials and Comfort (1:1–11).
   2. Paul's Change of Travel Plans (1:12–2:4).
   3. Advice Concerning the Former Offender (2:5–11).

B. The Nature of the Christian Ministry (2:12–7:16).
   1. The Greatness of the Gospel (2:12–4:6).

---

[1] Some Bible scholars think that this "severe" letter was actually Paul's first letter to the Corinthians. But most scholars think it was a different letter, which has now been lost.

[2] We call Paul's third letter "2 Corinthians," because the actual second letter he wrote has been lost.

   2. The Suffering and Glory of Ministry (4:7–5:10)
   3. The Work of Ministry (5:11–6:13).
   4. The Joy of Ministry (6:14–7:16).
- C. The Collection for the Poor (8:1–9:15).
   1. The Need for Generosity (8:1–15).
   2. Arrangements for the Collection (8:16–9:5).
   3. Principles of Christian Giving (9:6–15).
- D. Paul's Authority as an Apostle (10:1–13:14).
   1. The Rights of an Apostle (10:1–11:15).
   2. Paul's Defense of His Apostleship (11:16–12:10).
   3. Paul's Love and Concern (12:11–13:14).

CHAPTER 1

Paul's Trials and Comfort (1:1–11)

1 When Paul wrote this letter to the Corinthians, **Timothy**, Paul's young colleague and spiritual son, was with him (see Acts 16:1–5; 19:22; 1 Corinthians 4:17; Philippians 2:22). Therefore, Paul adds Timothy's name in the greeting, as if he and Timothy were writing the letter together. Paul writes not only to the church in Corinth, but to all SAINTS (Christians) in the province of **Achaia**,[3] the southernmost province of Greece.

Paul's greeting here is similar to that found in his other letters (see Romans 1:1; Galatians 1:1; Ephesians 1:1 and comments).

2 See Romans 1:7; Ephesians 1:2 and comments.

3–4 One of the most important teachings of the Gospel of Christ, one that we want all the people of the world to hear, is that God is a God **of compassion**, a God **of all comfort** (Psalm 86:5,15; 103:13–14). He **comforts us in all our troubles**—not sometimes, but always. Because of His comfort, we are able not only to endure our troubles but also to rejoice in them (2 Corinthians 12:10; James 1:2–3).

God comforts us for two reasons. First, He comforts us because He loves us as a human father loves his children. Second, God comforts us so that we might share His comfort with others who are in trouble. Just as God gives us comfort and blessing, so we must give comfort and blessing to others. We are like water pipes: as God's love flows into us, it must also flow out. **Freely you have received, freely give** (Matthew 10:8).

5 Together with God's love, the **sufferings of Christ** also flow into our lives. Christians are called to share in Christ's sufferings—His humiliation, His sorrow, His pain, even His death (see Philippians 3:10; 1 Peter 4:13 and comments). If we want to follow Christ, we must be prepared to suffer just as He suffered (see John 15:20; Romans 8:17; 2 Timothy 3:12 and comments).

But to whatever extent Christ's sufferings come upon us, to that same extent God's comfort and hope also come to us (Romans 8:18; 2 Corinthians 4:16–17).

Remember, when we suffer for Christ's sake, we receive comfort and other great blessings; but when we suffer because of our own sin and selfishness, then we receive, not comfort, but discipline.

6 Here, from his own experience, Paul states an important principle of the Christian life: **If we are distressed, it is for your comfort and salvation.** In order to preach the Gospel to the Corinthians and to bring them to faith, Paul had to endure much distress and suffering. His suffering was for their sake.

When we ourselves suffer, we receive through our suffering a special ability to comfort and heal others. In a way, this is a mystery. The one who has suffered the most is the one who is able to give the most help and comfort to others. It is written of Christ: **. . . by his wounds we are healed** (Isaiah 53:5). In suffering there is great power to heal others. This is an important spiritual truth.

Therefore, when we experience abuse, persecution, or distress of any kind, let us remember that through our suffering we are also being given the power to heal others. When we suffer, our love and humility can be more easily seen. When we ourselves are weak, then the power of Christ within us can more readily flow out to others (see 2 Corinthians 12:9–10 and comment).

If Paul is comforted, then the Corinthians should also be comforted. The Corinthians are sharers both in Paul's comfort and in his distress, both in his joys and in his sorrows (Romans 12:15). Through Paul's own suffering and comfort, the Corinthians should be better able to bear their own sufferings.

7 Just as the Corinthians shared in Paul's suffering and comfort, so each of

---

[3] Corinth was the capital of the province of **Achaia**.

us share in each other's suffering and comfort. We are all members of one body; when one member suffers, all the members suffer. When one member is comforted, all the members are comforted (1 Corinthians 12:26–27).

8–10 Paul mentions here the **hardships we suffered in the province of Asia**[4] (verse 8). It is not certain what these hardships were. Perhaps one of them is related to the episode described in Acts 19:23–41.

Through his sufferings, Paul learned to rely not on himself but on the God who is able to deliver us from all our troubles.

That which is a disaster for man is an opportunity for God; our disasters are an opportunity for God to show His power. When we are in despair, when we see no way out, when we can endure no more—then we can expect to see God do His greatest works.

11 Paul tells the Corinthians: . . . **you help us by your prayers**. God usually works according to the **prayers** of believers. All power is with God, but we obtain that power mainly through prayer. God can do all things, but He usually does only what we ask for. Let us not limit God's blessings by our small prayers!

Thus the Corinthians' prayers on Paul's behalf were extremely important. It's possible that if the Corinthians had not prayed for Paul, he would not have been delivered from all his troubles. Let us always remember that God desires to work according to the prayers of His people. Therefore, let us not neglect to pray for one another.

When we pray much, we receive much. When we receive much, we will have much to give thanks for.

Paul's Change of Plans (1:12–24)

12–14 Some of the Corinthian Christians opposed Paul and spoke evil of him. But here Paul reminds the Corinthians that he has behaved toward them with **holiness and sincerity**. He has behaved toward them **according to God's GRACE** (see 1 Corinthians 15:10). Paul wants all the Corinthians to understand this, so that **in the day of the Lord Jesus** (verse 14)—that is, when Jesus comes again—both he and they will be able to **boast** of each other (see 1 Thessalonians 2:19).

Paul says in verse 12 that his **conscience testifies** that he has behaved in holiness and sincerity. Paul's **conscience** was clear. He was in a right relationship with God; he was in fellowship with God. For this reason, God's power was always evident in Paul's life. If there is no spiritual power in our lives, it is most likely because our conscience is not clear—that is, there is some unconfessed sin in our lives, which we aren't willing to give up. If we don't give it up, God will not hear our prayers, and we shall receive no power or blessing from Him (Psalm 66:18).

15–16 Paul writes in verse 15: **Because I was confident of this** (confident that the Corinthians would be able to boast of Paul as their true apostle) **I planned to visit you first**. Because Paul had confidence that the Corinthians would accept him as their apostle, he desired to pay them an extra visit before going on to Macedonia. But after hearing of some new opposition to him among the Corinthians, he decided to cancel that extra visit and go to Macedonia first—which had been his original plan (1 Corinthians 16:5). Then, after visiting Macedonia and Corinth, Paul planned to go to **Judea**[5] to deliver the collection which had been raised for the poor Christians there (1 Corinthians 16:3–4).

17 Because of Paul's change of plans, some of the Corinthians began to speak against him, saying: "Paul says he'll come, and then he doesn't come. Today he says 'Yes,' and tomorrow he says 'No.' Who can trust what he says?"

18–20 Here Paul answers such statements. He says, in effect, to the Cor-

---

[4] The province of **Asia** was located in the western part of what is now modern Turkey. Its chief city was Ephesus.

[5] **Judea** is the southern province of Israel; Jerusalem is its main city.

inthians: "You can fully trust what I say. I didn't change my plans for no reason; I changed plans because of the guidance of the Holy Spirit."

But even though men's plans change, the Gospel of Christ, which Paul and Silas and Timothy preach, never changes. The Gospel of Christ is never "Yes" today and "No" tomorrow. The Gospel is always "Yes"; it is always true. **God is faithful** (verse 18). All the promises that God has given are **"Yes" in Christ** (verse 20); that is, all God's promises are fulfilled in Christ (Luke 24:44). And so we can say "**Amen**"[6] to all that Christ has done for us.

Silas (or Silvanus, his Greek name) was a leader of the Jerusalem church. Silas accompanied Paul on his second missionary journey (Acts 15:40). When Paul first went to Corinth to establish the church there, both Silas and Timothy were with him (Acts 18:1,5).

21–22 God makes us **stand firm** IN CHRIST. Just as God **anointed** Paul, so He "anoints" us with His Holy Spirit; that is, He appoints us, equips us, and gives us grace to do His work (see John 20:21; 1 John 2:20,27). He sets His **seal of ownership on us** (verse 22); that **seal** is the "seal" of the Holy Spirit (Ephesians 1:13; 4:30). In New Testament times, a seal was a sign of authority or ownership. When a person placed his seal on something, that proved that he was the owner of that thing. In the same way, when God sets the seal of His Holy Spirit on us, He is giving proof that He owns us—that we belong to Him, to Christ. Christ "bought" us with His own blood (see 1 Corinthians 6:16–20 and comment). Because we have received the Holy Spirit's seal, we know with certainty that we are Christ's (see Romans 8:16; 1 John 4:13).

God puts His HOLY SPIRIT in our hearts (verse 22). The Holy Spirit is like a **deposit**, a guarantee of our reward in heaven (see Ephesians 1:14). In this world, we receive only a part—a **deposit**—of our inheritance as children of God; but in heaven we shall receive our entire inheritance (Romans 8:23).

Thus, in summary, every believer in Christ is **anointed** with the Spirit, stamped with the **seal** of the Spirit, and given the Spirit as a **deposit** of his inheritance in heaven.

23 After writing his first letter to the Corinthians, Paul had made a quick visit to Corinth. That had been a **painful visit** (2 Corinthians 2:1). Therefore, Paul did not want to visit the Corinthians again immediately; because if he went immediately, he would have to discipline them. It would mean going to them **with a whip** (1 Corinthians 4:21); and he didn't want to do that. He didn't want to have another "painful visit."

24 Even though Paul had full authority as an apostle to discipline the Corinthians for their sins, he didn't want to **lord it over** them (see 1 Peter 5:2–3). Christ alone is Lord. Each man stands or falls before Christ alone (Romans 14:4). Paul didn't want to make himself a lord, a judge over the Corinthians' FAITH. Rather, he wanted only to strengthen their faith, because through faith they would be able to stand firm and to experience the **joy** of the Lord (see Philippians 1:25–26).

CHAPTER 2

Paul's Lost Letter (2:1–4)

1 After Paul wrote his first letter to the Corinthians, Paul made a **painful visit** to Corinth (2 Corinthians 13:2). At the time of that visit, there were many in the Corinthian church who opposed Paul. So after he had returned from Corinth, Paul wrote the Corinthians a severe letter. That letter has been lost (see 2 Corinthians: Introduction).

---

[6] In the Hebrew language, the language of the Jews, **Amen** is said in place of "yes."

2 Paul did not want to make another visit to the Corinthians at a time when there was so much ill feeling and opposition between himself and them. If Paul was going to visit them, he wanted it to be a time of giving and receiving joy. If he went **with a whip** (1 Corinthians 4:21), how would they be able to **make** [him] **glad**?

3–4 In these verses we see Paul's heart. Paul had the heart of a true Christian pastor or shepherd. He wrote and spoke to the Corinthians severely, but he did so with **great distress and anguish of heart**[7] (verse 4). Paul wrote severely to them because of his love for them. He wrote in that way so that the "painful" matter between them might quickly be made right, and so that they might share again in each other's joy.

Forgiveness for the Sinner (2:5–11)

5 Someone in the Corinthian church had **caused grief**—that is, he had sinned. This person had caused grief not only to Paul but to the whole church in Corinth. If one member brings dishonor upon himself, he brings dishonor upon the whole body—the whole church (1 Corinthians 12:26).

It is not certain who this person was who had caused grief to the church, but most Bible scholars believe it was the man mentioned in 1 Corinthians 5:1–5, who had committed adultery with his step-mother.

Paul tells the Corinthians that this man has grieved all of them **to some extent**. He says "to some extent" in order not to exaggerate. The expression **not to put it too severely** means "so as not to exaggerate."

6–8 Whoever the sinner was, Paul says that his punishment has been **sufficient** (verse 6). From this we can assume that the man has repented. Here Paul gives an important principle for all Christians to follow. We must always be ready to **forgive and comfort** a repentant sinner (verse 7), no matter how bad his sin has been. We must **reaffirm** [our] **love for him** (verse 8). When we do this, we are able to show the person that it was because of our love for him that we disciplined him. We show that it was not him but only his sin that we hated.

As part of reaffirming our love for the sinner, we must bring him back again into the full fellowship of the church. This is the whole purpose of discipline. Discipline is not for driving sinners out of the church, but rather for drawing them back in and leading them to repentance (see Galatians 6:1).

However, if the sinner refuses to repent, he must remain separated from the church; otherwise, the church will be defiled by his sin.

9 Paul had written before that the Corinthians must punish the man who had committed adultery with his step-mother (1 Corinthians 5:2–5). Now that they have indeed punished him, Paul is satisfied.

10 If the Corinthians now agree to forgive this sinner, Paul will forgive him also. As far as Paul is concerned, the matter will then be finished.

11 If we do not forgive a sinner after he has repented, but instead harbor resentment against him, then we are giving Satan a double opportunity. First, the sinner is likely to become discouraged and leave the church altogether; thus he will end up in Satan's kingdom. Second, we ourselves will be guilty of sin, because we have refused to forgive the sinner; whenever we refuse to forgive a repentant brother, we sin against him. And Satan will surely seize the opportunity afforded by our sin to defeat us. He is always seeking for ways to get into our hearts and cause us to turn against our brother. In this way he can cause division in the church.

Members of the church, having freely and fully forgiven one another, must stand united together in Christ. Mutual forgiveness and the unity that comes from it are the chief means we have of blocking Satan's **schemes** for dividing the church.

---

[7] Paul was like a father who is obliged to discipline his children. The loving father always feels the pain he inflicts upon his child.

In the church two things are essential: love (or unity) and purity (or truth). These two things must always remain in balance. If in order to preserve the church's purity we become too harsh, then where is our love? On the other hand, if because of our loving and tender heart we overlook or ignore the sins of others, where is our purity? Rather, we must always strive to preserve both our love and our purity together (see Hebrews 12:14 and comment).

The Fragrance of the Gospel (2:12–17)

12–13 **Troas** was an important city situated north of Ephesus on the west coast of present-day Turkey, about halfway between Ephesus and Macedonia. In Troas, Paul found another "open door" of opportunity for preaching the Gospel, which the Lord had opened up for him (see 1 Corinthians 16:9). But all the while Paul was preaching in Troas, he was also waiting for his colleague **Titus**[8] to return from Corinth. Paul had sent Titus to Corinth some time earlier to deliver a severe letter to the Corinthian church, and now Paul was eager to hear how the Corinthians had received his letter. But Titus did not return as quickly as Paul had hoped. Because of this, Paul had no peace of mind about the Corinthians; and so he decided to leave Troas and travel on to the province of **Macedonia**[9] in northern Greece in order to look for Titus.

14 Here in this verse, Paul suddenly interrupts his story to give thanks to God. Why? Because Paul did find Titus in Macedonia and found out from him that the Corinthians had received his severe letter with the right attitude (see 2 Corinthians 7:6–7). The Corinthians were filled with sorrow for having opposed Paul earlier. The devil's scheme to create a division between Paul and the Corinthians had been thwarted. Paul had been victorious over Satan once again. Indeed, Paul's life was like a **triumphal procession**. But Paul's victories were always **in Christ**; apart from Christ there can be no victory (John 15:5).

Through the victorious lives of the apostles, the **fragrance of the knowledge of him** (Christ) spread everywhere.

15–16 Christians who share the Gospel of Christ with others are like an **aroma**; they are the **aroma of Christ**. To those who are **being saved** through faith in Christ, the "aroma" of Christ is the **fragrance of life**. To those who are **perishing** on account of their lack of faith, the aroma of Christ is the **smell of death**, because all those without faith will be condemned and receive the sentence of death (see John 3:36; 1 Corinthians 1:18).

Each Christian needs to ask himself: Does my life have the **aroma of Christ**? Or does it have only the smell of sin and selfishness?

And who is equal to such a task? asks Paul (verse 16). That is, who has sufficient strength and wisdom for such a great responsibility as that of being an apostle? In a real sense, apostles hold in their hands the life and death of those who hear their words. What a great responsibility!

And so, who is equal to such a task? Paul gives the answer in 2 Corinthians 3:5: **. . . our competence comes from God**. Those whose competence comes from God will be equal to the task of carrying the "aroma of Christ" throughout the world.

17 Just as happens today, there were many people in Paul's time who preached the Gospel for their own advantage. They tried to get rich from their preaching. They sought to gain honor from men. They sought to turn men into their own disciples instead of making them disciples of Christ. They were false apostles.

But true apostles are not like that. True apostles do not appoint themselves. Rather, they are **men sent from God** (see Galatians 1:1). They always speak **in Christ**; they always speak **before**

---

[8] **Titus** was a close colleague of Paul (see Galatians 2:1,3 and comment).

[9] **Macedonia** was the main province of northern Greece. Together, Macedonia and Achaia (the southern province) made up most of the country of Greece.

God—that is, with the knowledge that God is listening; and they always speak **with sincerity**. This is how Paul and the other true apostles always conducted themselves (see 2 Corinthians 1:12; 4:2).

CHAPTER 3

Ministers of the New Covenant (3:1–6)

1 Some false apostles (2 Corinthians 2:17) went from church to church carrying **letters of recommendation**, in order to **commend** themselves in the eyes of the church members. These letters of recommendation were the "proof" of their authority as apostles, and so they showed these letters wherever they went.

Is Paul writing such a letter in order to commend himself? No. Does he need such a letter of recommendation? No.

2 What is the proof of Paul's apostleship? The Corinthian church itself is the proof of his apostleship. **You yourselves are our letter, written on our hearts,** writes Paul. Paul had brought the Gospel to Corinth; and through his preaching many people's lives had been changed. By the power of the Gospel, men and women had been turned from darkness to light. This was Paul's **letter of recommendation**. And it was a letter that was **known and read by everybody**; that is, everybody in Corinth was able to see the change that had taken place in the lives of the Christians there.

3 Paul's "letter of recommendation" was written not by man but by the **Spirit of the living God**. It was written not on paper **with ink**, or **on tablets of stone**; it was written on men's hearts. Ink fades; stones crumble to dust. But what is written on human hearts by the Holy Spirit remains forever.

The Old Testament law which God gave to the Jews was written **on tablets of stone** (Exodus 24:12; 31:18). But from Christ's time, a new law, or **new covenant** (verse 6), has been written by the Holy Spirit **on tablets of human hearts** (see Jeremiah 31:31–33; Hebrews 8:7–10 and comment).

Each one of us is like a **letter from Christ**. Can other people read our "letter"? What are they reading there?

4–5 Paul's confidence is not in any letter of recommendation; his confidence is **through Christ before God**. Paul's **competence** comes not from himself or any other man; it comes **from God** (see 1 Corinthians 15:10; 2 Corinthians 4:7).

6 In this verse Paul compares the old covenant (or law) with the **new** COVENANT, written by the Holy Spirit.

Both the old and new covenants are agreements or promises that God has offered to man. These covenants have been made by God.

Under the old covenant, God said to the Jews: "If you obey my law, I will make you my own special people and I will bless you." That was the old covenant.

But the purpose of the old covenant was not fulfilled. For a covenant to be fulfilled, both sides who take part in the covenant must keep their word. But the Jews didn't keep their word. They repeatedly broke God's law. They had to continually offer sacrifices to cleanse themselves from their sin.

But under the **new covenant**, through the sacrifice of Christ's own body we are cleansed from sin once for all (see Hebrews 9:15; 10:3–4,10–18 and comments). Through faith in Christ we are declared righteous (Romans 3:22–24). From now on, the old law (the Old Testament, or Jewish, law) cannot condemn us (see Romans 8:1 and comment).

Before Christ came, men were condemned by the law because they couldn't obey the law completely. The **letter**—that is, the written Old Testament law—**kills** men, because the law condemns them to death (see Romans 8:2 and comment). But now through the Holy Spirit men receive **life**, that is, eternal life

(Romans 6:23). And together with eternal life, men receive the power of the Holy Spirit which enables them to obey God's law. God's law has not changed. Only the place where it is written has changed. That is, instead of being written on tablets of stone, it is now written by the Spirit on men's hearts. For this reason Paul says here that he and the other apostles are **ministers of a new covenant—not of the letter** (the old law or covenant) **but of the Spirit** (the "writer" of the new covenant).

Does this mean that Christians no longer have to obey the Old Testament law? No, it doesn't mean that. We must continue to obey the "moral" law, that is, the law of love. (Christians are not required to obey the ceremonial law—the laws regarding sacrifices and purification—because Christ, through the sacrifice of His own body, has canceled those laws.) When we follow the two great commandments to love God and to love our neighbor, then we will also be fulfilling the moral law of the Old Testament (see Matthew 5:17–19; Mark 12:28–31; Romans 13:8–10; Galatians 5:14 and comments).

The Glory of the New Covenant (3:7–18)

7–8 The **ministry that brought death**—that is, the Old Testament (Jewish) law—doesn't itself cause death. Only sin causes death (see Romans 6:23; 1 Corinthians 15:56). But the law gives men the death sentence for sin (Romans 7:9–11).

Let no one despise the old covenant, the Old Testament law. Let us remember that it is God's law. In verse 7, Paul reminds us that it **came with glory** (Exodus 34:29–30).

9 The **ministry** of the old covenant (or law) condemned men (Romans 3:20). The **ministry** of the new covenant of Jesus Christ **brings righteousness** (see Romans 3:21–22; 5:16–17; 1 Corinthians 1:30 and comments). Thus the new covenant is much more glorious than the old.

10 The old covenant is glorious like the moon. But when the light of the sun (Jesus Christ) comes in the morning, the glory of the moon fades away.

11 Now the old covenant has passed away (Hebrews 8:13). In its place has come the new covenant, which will never pass away. Our salvation is eternal.

12–13 Therefore, because Paul has **such a hope**—namely, the hope of eternal salvation—he is **very bold**. He preaches the Gospel of Christ openly and with great boldness. He does not **put a veil over his face**, like Moses did (Exodus 34:33–35).

14–16 It was the custom every week in the Jewish synagogues to read the **old covenant**—that is, the Old Testament law[10]—and the custom still continues among the Jews. Paul says that when **Moses** (that is, the first five books of the Old Testament[11]) is read to the Jews, a **veil covers their hearts** (verse 15). That **veil** was the "veil" of unbelief; the Jews did not really believe Moses. That is why the Jews didn't believe in Christ either (see John 5:46–47). Because of their unbelief, **their minds were made dull** (verse 14); their hearts were darkened (see Romans 1:21; 11:8). Only through faith in Christ can the "veil" that covers men's hearts be removed. In Christ, the glory of God has been fully revealed without a veil (see Mark 9:2–7; John 17:5). When we follow Christ, we walk in the light and in the glory of God (see John 8:12 and comment).

17 The **Lord is the Spirit**. In this verse the word **Lord** can refer to both God and Christ. It is the same thing, because God, Christ, and the Holy **Spirit** are all one God. The Holy Spirit is both God's Spirit and Christ's Spirit.[12] And where the

---

[10] The first five books of the Old Testament are often called the "Law," or the "Law of Moses." Paul often uses the words "law" and "covenant" interchangeably. Both the Jewish law and the covenant relationship between the Jews and God are contained in those first five books of the Old Testament. For further discussion, see Word List: Law.

[11] The first five books of the Old Testament were written by Moses.

[12] For further discussion, see General Articles: Jesus Christ, Holy Spirit.

Spirit is, **there is freedom**. Therefore, when Christ's Spirit is in us, then we are truly free (John 8:36).

We are free from the old Jewish law (see Romans 7:6; 8:2). We are free from bondage to fear (Romans 8:15). We are free from **bondage to decay** (Romans 8:21). **It is for freedom that Christ has set us free. Stand firm, then, and do not let yourselves be burdened again by a yoke of slavery** (Galatians 5:1).

18 According to the Old Testament, only Moses was allowed to look upon the **glory** of God (Exodus 34:33–35). But we who believe in Christ can look upon God's glory **with unveiled faces**—that is, without putting a veil over our faces. That glory has been revealed in Christ (see John 1:14; 17:24; 2 Corinthians 4:6).

Not only that, we, too, **reflect the Lord's glory,**[13] just as the moon reflects the sun's glory. The glory of the moon is, in fact, the glory of the sun; the moon's light comes from the sun. In the same way, believers in Christ reflect not their own glory but Christ's glory.

But in another way, we are not like the moon. Our glory is brighter, because it comes from within us, from Christ's Spirit dwelling within us. Furthermore, our glory is ever increasing. By the help of the Holy Spirit, we are **attaining to the whole measure of the fullness of Christ** (Ephesians 4:13). And when Christ comes to earth again and we see Him face to face, then we shall be like Him (1 John 3:2). This is God's highest and final goal for all of us—that we be **transformed into [Christ's] likeness** (see Romans 8:29 and comment).

CHAPTER 4

The Light of the Gospel (4:1–6)

1 This **ministry**, which Paul and his colleagues have received, is the ministry of the **new covenant** (2 Corinthians 3:6). It is **through God's mercy** that Paul has received this great ministry (see 1 Timothy 1:12–14). Therefore, he does not **lose heart**.

2 Paul here gives the description of a true apostle. Paul does not follow the shameful ways of the false apostles, who **use deception** and **distort the word of God** (see 2 Corinthians 11:13–15; 1 Thessalonians 2:3–5). Like milkmen who add water to their milk before they sell it, these false apostles mix false teaching with the word of God.

On the contrary, writes Paul, **we commend ourselves to every man's conscience**. All men who have heard Paul ought to know in their hearts and consciences that his word is sincere and true. God also knows that Paul's word is true, because Paul does everything openly **in the sight of God** (see John 3:20–21).

3 The only ones who cannot see the truth of Paul's Gospel are those whose minds and hearts have been covered with the "veil" of unbelief (2 Corinthians 3:14–15). The veil is not covering the Gospel; it is covering the minds of unbelievers. Their spiritual eyes have been blinded to the truth. To proclaim the Gospel to such people is like giving a mirror to a blind man.

4 The **god of this age** is Satan (see John 12:31). He has **blinded the minds of unbelievers** (see John 8:42–47; 1 John 4:6). Because of their blindness, unbelieving men cannot see the **light of the GOSPEL of the glory of Christ**. Paul's main work as an apostle was to make blind men see, and to turn them from darkness to the glorious light of God (see Acts 26:17–18; 1 Peter 2:9).

Christ is the **image of God**. In Christ, the invisible God has been made visible

---

[13] In place of the words **reflect the Lord's glory**, some translations of the Bible say, "behold the Lord's glory." It is not certain in the original Greek text which meaning Paul intended. Both translations are possible and make good sense.

(see John 14:9; Colossians 1:15; Hebrews 1:3 and comments). But only those who have not been blinded by unbelief can recognize who Christ is.

5 Paul writes: **For we do not preach ourselves**. That is, Paul and his colleagues did not puff themselves up with pride, they did not seek honor from men (1 Thessalonians 2:6). Instead, **setting forth the truth plainly** (verse 2), Paul preached the Gospel of Christ and nothing else (see 1 Corinthians 2:1–5).

Even though Paul was an apostle, he was not the Corinthians' master; rather, he was their **servant** (see 1 Corinthians 4:1). In one way, Paul was the servant only of Christ, and not of any other man (1 Corinthians 7:23). But in another way, Paul made himself a servant of all men **for Jesus' sake** (1 Corinthians 9:19). In so doing, Paul was following the example of Jesus Himself, who, **being in very nature God . . . made himself nothing, taking the very nature of a servant** (see Philippians 2:5–8).

6 In the beginning, God said, "**Let there be light**" (Genesis 1:3). And even today God continues to say to all men: "Let there be light." **God is light; in him there is no darkness at all** (1 John 1:5).

God **made his light shine in our hearts**. At the time we first believed in Christ, God's light began to shine in our hearts. God makes His light shine in our hearts in order to reveal to us His own glory **in the face of Jesus Christ** (see John 1:14). Jesus said: "**I am the light of the world. Whoever follows me will never walk in darkness, but will have the light of life**" (John 8:12). One day on the road to Damascus, Paul himself had seen the light of Christ, and his life had been changed forever (Acts 9:3–5; 26:13–15).

The Apostles' Weakness and God's Strength (4:7–18)

7 We humans are like **jars of clay** (Isaiah 64:8). We are ordinary, weak, breakable jars. But in our "jars" we have **this treasure**: namely, the **gospel of the glory of Christ** (verse 4). Paul also refers to this "treasure" as the **light of the knowledge of the glory of God** (verse 6). In simplest terms, the **treasure** in our "jars" is the Gospel of Christ. This Gospel is the **power of God for the salvation of everyone who believes** (Romans 1:16). Such great power in such weak jars! Nevertheless, God desires to use weak "jars" like us, because when people see our own natural weakness they will know that the spiritual power within us comes from God and not from ourselves (see 2 Corinthians 12:9).

8–9 In these verses, Paul describes various trials he has experienced. Most Christians have experienced one or more of these difficulties that Paul mentions here. They have been **hard pressed** and **perplexed** (verse 8); they have been **persecuted** and **struck down** (verse 9). They have reached the point where there is no human solution to their problems, no way of escape. But God has always been with them. When human means end, then God's means begin (Deuteronomy 31:6).

Paul's life was filled with the kinds of trials he mentions here (see Acts 4:19; 2 Corinthians 11:23–28). Nevertheless, God always led him **in triumphal procession in Christ** (2 Corinthians 2:14). Christians even triumph in death! In death our body comes to an end, but we ourselves are not destroyed. Rather, through death we receive our heavenly inheritance, which is eternal life and a **crown of righteousness** (see 2 Timothy 4:6–8). There is nothing that can separate us from the love of God (Romans 8:35–39). We need not fear men who can kill only the body; we need fear only Him who is able to destroy both body and soul—that is, God (Matthew 10:28).

10–11 Paul writes: **We always carry around in our body the death of Jesus**. Paul and his colleagues **are always being given over to death for Jesus' sake** (verse 11). What does Paul mean by these statements?

Paul means that he and his colleagues are facing the risk of death every day (1 Corinthians 15:30–31). Like a sheep about to be sacrificed, Paul is, in a sense, facing death all day long for Christ's sake (Romans 8:36). In a way, Paul is being crucified **to the world** (Galatians 6:14). Just as Jesus had said to do, Paul is taking up his cross daily (Luke 9:23). Since Paul is Jesus' servant, he is receiving the same persecution that His Master received (John 15:20). Paul seeks the **fellowship of sharing in** [Jesus'] **sufferings** (Philippians 3:10–11).

To the extent that we die to ourselves, to that extent we shall live to Christ (see John 12:24–25). He who has died with Christ will also live with Christ (see Romans 6:4–5; Philippians 3:20–21; 2 Timothy 2:11–12 and comments).

Therefore, as we Christians suffer the various trials mentioned here, we are able not only to endure such trials but also to rejoice in them, **because great is** [our] **reward in heaven** (Matthew 5:11–12).

But let us remember one thing: When we suffer, it must be for Christ's sake that we suffer. If our suffering is not for Christ's sake, then there will be nothing to rejoice in.[14] In everything and at all times, we must live for Christ's sake and obey Him. If we do this, then no matter what kind of suffering comes upon us, we shall be able to rejoice in it and receive great spiritual blessing from it.

12 Paul tells the Corinthians: **So then, death is at work in us, but life is at work in you**. It is through Paul's suffering, through his daily **death** to self, that the Gospel of **life** has been brought to the Corinthians. Just as Jesus had done, Paul is offering his own physical life in order that the Corinthians might receive eternal life.

13 Here Paul quotes from Psalm 116:10. Psalm 116 is a hymn of thanksgiving to God for deliverance from death. Even when death is near, Paul's faith in God remains strong. Because of this **spirit of faith**, Paul always speaks with boldness no matter what his circumstances.

14 Why is Paul able to speak with such boldness? Because he knows that the **one who raised the Lord Jesus from the dead will also raise us with Jesus** (see Romans 6:5; 8:11; Ephesians 2:6; Colossians 3:3–4).

15 **All this**—that is, all Paul's trials and suffering—are for the benefit of the Corinthians. Paul is a minister of the **grace** of God,[15] and that grace (salvation in Christ) has been **reaching more and more people**. This means that there will be more and more people giving thanks to God. Thus God's grace will **cause thanksgiving to overflow to the glory of God.**

16 Although Paul's body **outwardly** is **wasting away**—growing old and tired and weak—his spirit **inwardly** is being **renewed** daily by the Holy Spirit within him.

17 Compared with the inheritance stored up for us in heaven, our suffering and troubles in this world are **light and momentary** (see Romans 8:18; 1 Corinthians 2:9). Paul is not saying here that we receive **eternal glory** (salvation) through our sufferings, or because of our sufferings. Salvation can only be received by grace through faith, not by any suffering we might endure. Some followers of other religions believe that man can achieve salvation through various kinds of suffering. That is not Paul's teaching. Yes, it's true that we will receive a "reward" when we suffer for Jesus' sake (see Matthew 5:12; 16:27; 1 Corinthians 3:13–14); but salvation itself can be received only by grace through faith (see Ephesians 2:8–9 and comment).

Let us not be surprised when suffering and troubles come upon us. Trouble and persecution will come upon all who follow Christ (2 Timothy 3:12; 1 Peter 4:12–13). **We must go through many hardships to enter the kingdom of God** (Acts 14:22).

18 If we look only at what can be seen, we will quickly become discouraged. Look at Paul's outward life. In the world's eyes, it was completely unsuccessful. In the beginning Paul was a well-

---

[14] When we suffer because of our own sin or stupidity, our suffering will then be a form of discipline given by God. If we repent of our sin and accept God's discipline, then even this kind of suffering will bring great spiritual benefit in the end (see Hebrews 12:11).

[15] In 2 Corinthians 3:6, Paul calls himself a "minister of a new covenant." That new covenant is the covenant of grace. Thus being a minister of the new covenant and being a minister of grace are the same thing.

known and influential Jew, but he gave up his position and reputation. After that, he spent his life enduring all sorts of suffering and hardship. All his friends abandoned him (2 Timothy 4:16). He had no home or property. He spent the end of his life in prison, and was finally put to death because of his faith in Christ. Such is the description of Paul's outward visible life.

But let us not look at these outward visible things. Let us look, instead, at Jesus (Hebrews 12:2–3). Let us remember that if we **share in his suffering,** we shall also **share in his glory** (Romans 8:17). Therefore, let us **press on toward the goal to win the prize for which God has called** [us] **heavenward in Christ Jesus** (Philippians 3:14).

CHAPTER 5

Our Heavenly Dwelling (5:1–10)

1 Here Paul calls our body an **earthly tent.** It is this "earthly tent" which Paul said in 2 Corinthians 4:16 was **wasting away.** Our earthly body will one day be **destroyed** by death. When our earthly body dies, then our spirit will leave our body. Our body will then be just a corpse.

But we know that even if our earthly body is destroyed, we will receive an **eternal house in heaven**—that is, a new spiritual body. That new body will be our redeemed body (Romans 8:23), our resurrected body (1 Corinthians 15:42–44,49).

Notice that Paul calls our earthly body a **tent.** A tent is not a permanent dwelling; it is only a temporary dwelling. In this world we men are merely **aliens and strangers** (1 Peter 2:11). We are waiting for the time when we shall dwell in our permanent house, our **eternal house in heaven,** which has been prepared for us by God (see Hebrews 11:8–10).

2 **Meanwhile** (in this "earthly tent") **we groan**—that is, in this life we suffer all kinds of trouble and pain. We wait eagerly for the day when we shall be **clothed with our heavenly dwelling**—that is, when we shall receive our new redeemed and resurrected bodies (see Romans 8:23).

3 Paul wishes he could be **clothed with** [his] **heavenly dwelling** quickly (verse 2), so that he will not be found **naked.** Because when we die we must remain "unclothed" or **naked** until Christ comes again; only after Christ comes will we receive our resurrected bodies, our **heavenly dwelling** (see 1 Corinthians 15:22–23). What Paul is really wishing, therefore, is that Christ will return before he dies.

4 **. . . we do not wish to be unclothed**—that is, to die. We see our earthly **tent** (body) slowly being destroyed; therefore, **we groan and are burdened** by our weak and dying bodies. In Paul's time, most Christians believed that Christ would return before they died. In that case, as soon as Christ came they would receive their new, resurrected, eternal bodies and thus would not have to remain "naked" (see 1 Corinthians 15:51–52; 1 Thessalonians 4:16–17). In this way, **what is mortal** (their earthly bodies) would be **swallowed up by life**—that is, would be resurrected and made eternally alive (see 1 Corinthians 15:54).

5 God will give all of us who believe a new resurrected body, so that we can live forever in heaven with Him. But already in this life God has given us the Holy Spirit, who is like a **deposit** guaranteeing **what is to come.** And "what is to come" is that we shall indeed receive new resurrected bodies and eternal life in heaven (see 2 Corinthians 1:22; Ephesians 1:13–14 and comments).

In a way, our new eternal life has already begun here on earth. Paul says that, even here, **inwardly we are being renewed day by day** (2 Corinthians 4:16). The Holy Spirit is working in us even now to **give life to** [our] **mortal bodies** (Romans 8:11). We can be confident that

he (God) **who began a good work in** [us] **will carry it on to completion until the day of Jesus Christ** (Philippians 1:6).

God has created us **for this very purpose,** that we might receive an eternal inheritance in heaven and live with Him forever. And the Holy Spirit within us testifies that this is true (see Romans 8:16–17 and comment).

6–8 **Therefore we are always confident.** As long as we live in this world **we are at home in the body**—that is, we have our earthly body. After we die, we shall receive our heavenly eternal body. That new body will be much better than our present earthly body, because now our earthly body is **away from the Lord** (verse 6)—that is, it is physically separated from the Lord. But our new heavenly bodies will be **at home with the Lord** (verse 8)—that is, they will be present with the Lord.

We live by faith, not by sight (verse 7). Christ is now in heaven, but we are on earth. Now we walk by faith; we cannot see Christ with our eyes. But in heaven we shall see Him face to face.

Either way, whether alive or dead, whether on earth or in heaven, Paul lives for Christ. Paul wrote to the Philippians: **I desire to depart and be with Christ, which is better by far** (Philippians 1:23). But Paul is also willing as long as necessary to serve Christ here on this earth (see Philippians 1:21–24).

9 Our chief goal is to **please** Christ. Whether we are alive or dead, whether we are in this earthly body or in our heavenly body—**whether we are at home in the body or away from it**—our goal is **to please him** (see Romans 14:8).

10 According to the New Testament, on the day of JUDGMENT God and Christ together will render two kinds of judgment. The first kind of judgment is for those who have not believed in Christ. **Whoever believes in him is not condemned, but whoever does not believe stands condemned already because he has not believed in the name of God's one and only Son** (John 3:18). The Christian is not condemned; he has been delivered from the judgment which will fall upon non-believers (see Romans 5:1; 8:1). The judgment which non-believers will receive is the sentence of death, eternal death in hell.

The second kind of judgment is for believers in Christ. This is the kind of judgment that Paul is talking about in this verse. We Christians, too, **must all appear before the judgment seat of Christ.** It is not we ourselves who will be judged; rather, it is our work that will be judged. Each Christian will receive **what is due him for the things done while in the body.** This is the judgment of our works. This judgment is not for giving punishment, it is for giving rewards (see Romans 14:10–12; 1 Corinthians 3:8,13–15 and comments).

We do not know what kind of reward we shall receive for our work. In 1 Corinthians 4:5, Paul says only this: **At that time each will receive his praise from God** (see Luke 19:15–19).

A Christian must not be content only to be saved. Rather, because he has been saved, because God has shown him such great love and mercy, the Christian must seek all the more to honor and to serve God with his whole heart. Jesus said: **"This is to my Father's glory, that you bear much fruit"** (John 15:8). He also said: **"You did not choose me, but I chose you and appointed you to go and bear fruit"** (John 15:16).

The Ministry of Reconciliation (5:11–21)

11–12 We **fear the Lord** (verse 11), because we know that one day we shall have to appear before His **judgment seat** (verse 10).

Some members of the church in Corinth were opposed to Paul. In verse 12, Paul says of these people that they **take pride in what is seen**—that is, they concentrate on what is seen. They take into account only those things that are outward, and do not pay attention to **what is in the heart.**

Paul says to the Corinthians: **We . . . are giving you an opportunity to take pride in us** (verse 12). Paul isn't trying to **commend** himself here; he only means that his own life has been upright and honorable, and that if the Corinthians would just use the example of his life, they would be able to refute those who speak against Paul. The Corinthians can indeed take pride in Paul, because he is their true apostle.

Notice here that Paul is prepared to argue with those who oppose him. Paul doesn't **commend** or defend himself for his own sake but for the church's sake. When Christians are spoken against, they usually should follow Jesus' example and remain silent (see 1 Peter 2:23). But when church leaders are spoken against, it is essential that they answer their opponents and refute their accusations. Because those who oppose their own leaders are also opposing Christ's church.[16] Therefore, just as Paul did, church leaders must defend themselves against such opponents in order to prevent harm to the church. But they must not defend themselves out of pride or anger; otherwise, they will be doing as much harm as those who oppose them.

13 Some of Paul's opponents said that he was "out of his mind." Perhaps they said he was too religious, that he was a fanatic. Paul answers such a charge by saying: "Okay, if I'm too religious, or if I seem to be out of my mind, it is all for your sake."

Some people had said that Jesus Himself was "out of His mind" (see Mark 3:20–22). Just as men spoke against Jesus, so they also spoke against Paul (see John 15:18,20 and comment).

14 The greatest compelling force in Paul's life was Christ's love. All Paul did was because of Christ's love. Christ gave up His own life for Paul. Therefore, Paul wants to give his life to Christ.

But Christ didn't only give up His life for Paul; He gave His life for all men. That is, He died in the place of all men, because all men were condemned to die. If Christ had not died in our place, we would all have been condemned to death in hell forever[17] (see Mark 10:45 and comment).

Paul says that **all died**. In one way, all believers have died with Christ (Romans 6:3). Our "old sinful self" has been crucified with Christ (see Romans 6:6–7 and comment).

15 Christ died to give us life. When we put faith in Christ, our old sinful self dies with Christ and we receive new spiritual life (see Romans 6:4–5,8; Galatians 2:20 and comments). What should we do for a man who gives up His life for us? We should live no longer for ourselves but for Him who died for us. We owe Christ our lives.

In verses 14–15, we see two important steps in the Christian life. First, Christ died for us (Romans 5:6,8). Therefore, through faith we are declared righteous and receive salvation (Romans 5:9–10). Second, our "old sinful self" dies with Christ (Romans 6:6,8; Galatians 5:24). When we put off our old sinful self, then we "put on" Christ and begin to live like Him (see Romans 13:14; Galatians 3:27; Ephesians 4:22–24 and comments; General Article: Way of Salvation).

16 So from now on we regard no one from a worldly point of view. Paul means that we should no longer evaluate anyone according to **worldly** standards, according to the flesh; rather, we should evaluate people according to spiritual standards (see Romans 8:5).

The Corinthians judged each other from a **worldly point of view**, according to worldly standards (see 1 Corinthians 3:3–4). But we must not make distinctions between people according to worldly standards, according to the flesh (see Romans 2:11; Galatians 3:28).

At first Paul had regarded Christ from a worldly point of view. We, too, before we believed, regarded Christ in this way. But now we have met the risen, living Christ Himself; therefore, we now regard

---

[16] Sometimes, of course, leaders fall into sin. When this happens, at least two witnesses are needed before any charge can be brought against a leader (see 1 Timothy 5:19–20). The charges must be clearly proven, or they should be dropped.

[17] Those in hell remain in a state which is like death, because in hell they are separated from God and Christ. Those who are separated from God and Christ can have no true spiritual life.

Him (know Him) according to a spiritual point of view, according to the truth.

It is not enough merely to obtain knowledge about Christ; we must know Him personally, spiritually. It does no good for a sick person to merely identify the right medicine; he must take it! In the same way, we must personally accept Christ through faith; we must take Him into our lives. For example, Thomas, one of Jesus' twelve disciples, did not believe at first that Jesus had risen from the dead. He said he would have to see and touch Jesus' wounds before he would believe. That is, he insisted on regarding Jesus from a worldly or fleshly point of view. But Jesus said to Thomas, "**Stop doubting and believe.**" And Thomas' spiritual eyes were opened, and he saw the risen, living Christ, and accepted Him (see John 20:24–29).

17 This verse contains one of the greatest statements in the entire New Testament. In the teaching of no other religion do we find that a person can become a **new creation**. But when a person is **in Christ**, he or she does indeed become a **new creation**. Our "old self" dies, and our "new self" is born (see John 3:3; Romans 6:8 and comments).

The most important words in this verse are the words **in Christ**. To be **in Christ** means to have faith in Him, to obey Him, to love Him, to know Him personally, and to make Him the Lord of one's life. Just as a branch is "in the tree," so we must be "in Christ" (see John 15:4–6).

If we are in Christ, Christ will be in us; and through His Holy Spirit living within us, we shall become "new creations" (Romans 8:11).

In order for our "new creation," our new spiritual life, to arise, our "old sinful self" must die (Romans 6:6; Galatians 5:24). We must put off our old self (Ephesians 4:22). Before we can receive a new heart, our old sinful heart must be removed (Ezekiel 11:19). Before new leaves can come, the old leaves must fall.

But to be a "new creation," we must be **in Christ**. And if we are new creations in Christ, it means that all our old sinful desires and habits must be done away with; **the old has gone, the new has come!** If our lives are filled with old sins and habits, how can we say that we are new creations?

Looking at ourselves, can we indeed say that we are a **new creation**? Is our life, our behavior, like that of a new creation? If the answer is no, then the reason can only be that we are not **in Christ**. Let us examine ourselves.

18 All things have their origin in God; all work begins with Him. First, He **reconciled us to himself**, and then He gave us the ministry of calling others to be reconciled also.

Why does man need to be reconciled to God? Man needs to be reconciled to God because of man's sin. Because of man's sin, God's wrath has come upon mankind (Romans 1:18).

But how, then, can a person be reconciled? The answer is: **through Christ**. God's wrath fell upon Christ instead of upon us. Christ Himself took our punishment for sin (Isaiah 53:5–6). Through Christ's sacrifice of His body on the cross—that is, through His death—He brought about our reconciliation with God. He made peace between us and God (Romans 5:1). Christ is the one and only **mediator** between man and God (1 Timothy 2:5). Only through Christ can we come to the heavenly Father (John 14:6).

Let us ask ourselves this: In our village, in our city, in our country, what is man's greatest need? Is it clean water? Is it a good diet? Is it good health, or good schools? Improved agriculture? Roads and cars? No, it is none of these things. The single greatest need of every man, woman, and child is to be reconciled to God! Besides this, what else is important? And what is amazing is that God has committed to us—weak and ordinary "jars of clay"—the tremendous task of proclaiming this **message of reconciliation**, of proclaiming to men and women that through faith in Christ they too can be reconciled to God.

19 The **message of reconciliation**, in brief, is this: **that God was reconciling the world to himself in Christ** (see Colossians 1:19–20). Through Christ our sins are forgiven and our punishment taken away. Christ was the sacrificial lamb that takes away the sins of the world (see John 1:29 and comment). **Therefore, there is now no condemnation for those who are in Christ Jesus** (Romans 8:1). In other words, the **message of reconciliation** is simply the Gospel of Jesus Christ.

And God has **committed to us** this message; He has given us the responsibility of proclaiming this message to the world. God hasn't given this responsibility only to Paul and the other apostles; He has given it to every Christian. What have we done with the message? Have we shared it with others, or have we kept it for ourselves? Are we remaining silent while our family, friends, and neighbors are being condemned to eternal punishment?

20 Let us not remain silent! Like Paul, we too are **Christ's ambassadors.** We are God's spokesmen, His representatives on earth. God did not reconcile us to Himself only for our own sake, but also so that others might be reconciled through our testimony.

To be the ambassador of a king is a great honor and responsibility. But to be the ambassador of the **King of kings,** Jesus Christ, is incomparably greater (see 1 Timothy 6:15). And every Christian—whether rich or poor, educated or uneducated, high or low—every one is an ambassador of Christ.

As Christ's ambassadors, our job is to **implore** men and women: **Be reconciled to God**. Or, in other words: Accept by faith the reconciliation that Christ has already worked out for mankind through His death on the cross (see Romans 5:1,10–11 and comment).

21 Christ never committed a sin (Hebrews 4:15; 1 Peter 2:22; 1 John 3:5). It was because Christ was completely innocent, completely without sin, that He was able to take our punishment. If Christ had been sinful Himself, He could only have taken His own punishment, not ours. God made Christ **to be sin for us**; that is, God sent Christ to stand as a sinner in our place before God's judgment seat (Isaiah 53:12).

By taking upon Himself the punishment for our sins, Christ has taken away our guilt, our unrighteousness. Therefore, we are now declared righteous in God's sight. Paul says here that **in him** (Christ) we have **become the RIGHTEOUSNESS of God**; that is, through faith we have obtained the righteousness of God (see Romans 1:17; 3:21–22 and comments).

CHAPTER 6

A Description of Paul's Life (6:1–13)

1 Here and in 1 Corinthians 3:9, Paul calls himself and his fellow apostles **God's fellow workers**. Since Paul is God's fellow worker, the Corinthians (and we also) need to heed what Paul says.

Paul urges the Corinthians **not to receive God's grace in vain**. This can have two meanings. Some Christians think that even after receiving God's grace it is still possible to lose it again. Those who lose God's grace would certainly have received it **in vain**! (see 1 Corinthians 15:2; 1 Timothy 1:18–20; Hebrews 6:4–6; 10:35–39). Jesus Himself taught about the seed that fell on rocky soil and quickly sprouted, but then later died (Mark 4:5–6,16–17).

Other Christians believe that God's grace—God's salvation—can never be lost (see General Article: Can We Lose Our Salvation?). They say, however, that a believer's life can become unfruitful because of sin or because of ignorance of the Bible's teachings. In such a case also, one could rightly say that the unfruitful believer had received God's grace **in vain** (see Mark 4:7,18–19). In 1 Corinthians 3:10–15, Paul teaches that our work will be tested; if our work is no good, it will be destroyed, but we ourselves will be saved (see 2 Corinthians 5:10).

Whichever meaning Paul intended here (and perhaps he intended both), let us not be among those who **receive God's grace in vain.**

2 Paul wants to remind the Corinthians how they had first received God's grace. He quotes here from Isaiah 49:8. In this verse the prophet Isaiah, speaking God's words, is prophesying about the coming of the Savior Christ. Isaiah describes Christ's coming as the **time of** [God's] **favor,** the **day of** SALVATION. Paul says that that **day** has now arrived. Now the time has come when men and women can receive salvation through faith in Christ. Let no one delay. Do not even wait until tomorrow. Now, today, the opportunity to receive salvation has come; it may not come again tomorrow. Tomorrow may be too late. A heart that is open and tender today may become closed and hard tomorrow. A man who is alive today may be dead tomorrow. Therefore, **now is the day of salvation.**

3 Paul does not want to put a **stumbling block in anyone's path;** that is, he does not want to do or say anything that will block people from coming to Christ. Paul always makes sure that his own life and behavior are in accordance with his teachings; otherwise his ministry would be **discredited,** and people would stop listening to him. In this, Paul has given us all an example to follow (see 2 Corinthians 1:12).

Why doesn't the church of Christ grow faster? Because other people look at us and see that our daily behavior does not correspond to the Bible's teachings. Looking at our lives, they can't even tell what it means to be a Christian. So, naturally, they ask: "Why should I become a Christian?"

Our bad behavior is a **stumbling block** to others; our behavior hinders others from coming to Christ. When people hear us talk one way but act another, they are turned away from Christ. Even if our lives are pure, our testimony about Christ is sometimes poorly presented, inaccurate, or even false; this can also be a "stumbling block" to others.

However, it is also true that people are looking for an excuse not to become Christians; they don't want to submit to the demands of Christ. So they use our bad behavior as an excuse not to believe in Christ. But in God's sight, our bad behavior will not completely excuse them. Ultimately, they alone are responsible for their lack of faith. They should have looked at Christ Himself. Regardless of the behavior of His followers, Christ is the sinless Son of God, and those who reject Him will be condemned (John 3:18). Thus, in everything we do and say, let us seek to point people to Christ rather than to ourselves. But, at the same time, we must not put them off by our bad behavior.

4–5 Paul says in verse 4: **... as servants of God we commend ourselves in every way.** That is, Paul shows himself to be a true servant of God in every way. How? By his **endurance** of many trials—**troubles, hardships and distresses**—for Christ's sake. For Christians, such trials develop **perseverance** (James 1:3). For non-believers, or worldly men, trials lead to bitterness and despair. But for Christians, trials lead to **perseverance, character,** and **hope** (Romans 5:3–4). Trials test and strengthen our faith (1 Peter 1:6–7).

Therefore, because Paul has endured such trials and suffering, the Corinthians can be sure that he is indeed a true servant of God (see Acts 14:19; 16:22–23; 18:12; 2 Corinthians 11:23).

6 Here Paul describes some of the gifts and fruits of the Holy Spirit that are apparent in his life. Paul shows he is a true servant of God because he is **in the Holy Spirit,** which means that he lives in dependence upon and under the authority of the Holy Spirit. It also means that Paul has received from the Holy Spirit the strength necessary to endure these trials and the gifts necessary to do Christ's work.

7 In this verse, **truthful speech** can refer to the Gospel of Christ, or it can refer to Paul's truthful speech—or both. Paul has always spoken the truth; the Corinthians know that (2 Corinthians 2:17).

Paul has always worked **in the power of God,** or, in other words, through the power of the Holy Spirit (see 1 Corinthians 2:3–5).

The **weapons of righteousness in the right hand and in the left** refer to parts of the **armor of God** described by Paul in Ephesians 6:11–18. In the **left** hand would be the **shield of faith** (Ephesians 6:16), and in the **right** hand would be the **sword of the Spirit** (Ephesians 6:17). Paul's weapons are not like the weapons of the world; they are spiritual weapons (see 2 Corinthians 10:4).

8 It is easy to be a servant of Christ when others give us a **good report**, that is, when they speak well of us. But when we receive **dishonor** from others, or if others give us a **bad report** or call us **impostors**, then what do we do? Do we continue serving the Lord with **great endurance** (verse 4) and with **patience and kindness**? (verse 6).

Jesus said to His disciples: **"If they** (men of the world) **persecuted me, they will persecute you also"** (John 15:20). Let us follow the example of Jesus: **When they hurled their insults at him, he did not retaliate. . . . Instead, he entrusted himself to him** (God) **who judges justly** (1 Peter 2:21–23).

9 Paul was **known** in the churches he had established, and he was **known** by God. Paul wrote to Timothy: **The Lord knows who are his** (2 Timothy 2:19). But to unbelievers, Paul was **regarded as unknown**; they considered him a "nobody." When he chose to follow Christ, Paul lost his name, his fame, and his honor. Paul gave up everything for Christ's sake.

Paul says he was **dying**. Paul was always close to death; **outwardly** he was **wasting away** (2 Corinthians 4:16). Daily he faced the risk of **dying** (see Romans 8:36; 1 Corinthians 15:31; 2 Corinthians 1:8–10; 11:23–26). Through such "dying," the life of Christ was more clearly manifested in Paul's life (see 2 Corinthians 4:10–12).

Even though Paul was **beaten**, he did not lose hope; he had not yet been **killed** (see Acts 14:19–20; 2 Corinthians 4:8–9). When Paul mentions being **beaten, and not yet killed**, perhaps he was thinking of Psalm 118:18, where the Psalmist writes: **The Lord has chastened me severely, but he has not given me over to death**.

10 In the eyes of the world, Paul appeared **sorrowful**. Yet, in fact, he was always **rejoicing** (see Matthew 5:11–12; Romans 5:3; Philippians 4:4).

In the eyes of the world, Paul appeared **poor**; he appeared to possess **nothing**. Yet, in fact, Paul was immensely rich (see Ephesians 1:7; 2:7; Philippians 3:7–8; 4:19). In Christ, Paul possessed **everything** (see Romans 8:32). He preached to others the **unsearchable riches of Christ** (Ephesians 3:8,16). Paul followed the example of Christ: **though** [Christ] **was rich, yet for your sakes he became poor, so that you through his poverty might become rich** (2 Corinthians 8:9).

We Christians may have no "silver and gold" to give to others, but that which we have we can give in abundance: namely, the **unsearchable riches** of Christ (see Acts 3:1–8,16).

Let us ask ourselves: How much is our life like Paul's life? Do we act as though we possessed these spiritual riches? Do we persevere when trials and persecution come? Do we endure in silence when others revile us? Paul has set for us such a high standard, such a high example! But even though Paul's example is high, through God's grace and the Holy Spirit's help we can follow it; we not only can, we must!

11 Paul has **spoken freely** to the Corinthians; in every matter he has spoken plainly and openly. Paul's heart is **opened wide** to the Corinthians; that is, his heart is filled with love for them.

12 Paul writes to the Corinthians: **We are not withholding our affection from you**; we are not restricting our affection for you. But, says Paul to the Corinthians, **you are withholding** [your affection] **from us**; it is your affections that are restricted. Paul's love for the Corinthians is "wide"; but their love for him is "narrow."

13 Just as a father would ask a favor from his children, so Paul asks the Corinthians to **open wide** [their] **hearts** to him—to enlarge their love for him.

Do Not Be Yoked With Unbelievers (6:14–18)

14 Do not be yoked together with unbelievers—with **wickedness**, with **darkness**. What does Paul mean here? His meaning is this: Christians must not live and work in partnership with those who deny Christ.

For example, a believer must not marry an unbeliever (see 1 Corinthians 7:39). But if one becomes a Christian after being already married, the believing partner should not leave his or her spouse (1 Corinthians 7:12–13).

Paul has written that it is all right for Christians to eat with unbelievers (1 Corinthians 10:27). Furthermore, it is necessary to have some association with sinful and evil people (1 Corinthians 5:9–10). But we must take no part in their sin and evil. Especially we must not take part in the worship of idols.

It is impossible for **light** to have "fellowship" with **darkness**. **God is light; in him there is no darkness at all** (1 John 1:5–7). We must live **as children of light** (Ephesians 5:8). Jesus Christ is the **light of men** (John 1:4–5); He is the **light of the world** (John 8:12). Believers in Christ have been called **out of darkness into his wonderful light** (1 Peter 2:9). To reject Christ is to walk in darkness (see John 3:19–20).

15 **What harmony is there between Christ and Belial?**[18] **What does a believer have in common with an unbeliever?** The believer's life is lived for Christ; the unbeliever's life is lived for self. The believer's treasure is in heaven; the unbeliever's treasure is on earth. The believer seeks the praise of God; the unbeliever seeks the praise of men. How, then, can the believer and unbeliever work together?

16 We believers are God's holy **temple** (1 Corinthians 3:16; 6:19; 1 Peter 2:5). The word "holy" means to be separated from evil and sin. There must be no evil, unholiness, or idol worship in us, in our "temple" (see 1 Corinthians 10:20–21). Our temple (body) must remain holy, because God is living there.

Paul here quotes from Jeremiah 32:38 and Ezekiel 37:27. Where God's **people** are, there will God also be. Therefore, God's people (the church) must be holy, because God can tolerate no unholiness.

17 **Therefore come out from them and be separate** (Isaiah 52:11). From whom must we come out and be separate? From unbelievers, from evil doers, from those who walk in darkness. **Have nothing to do with the fruitless deeds of darkness** (Ephesians 5:11). . . . **you must not associate with anyone who calls himself a brother but is sexually immoral or greedy, an idolater or a slanderer, a drunkard or a swindler. With such a man do not even eat** (1 Corinthians 5:11). One sin can make a person's entire life impure; one unrepentant sinner can make the entire church impure (see 1 Corinthians 5:6–7).

Even though all of this is true, we must be careful how we act upon it. Because these verses do not tell us to separate from a brother simply because we have a disagreement with him over some matter. No, we must not separate in this way. One of Satan's chief methods for dividing the church is to lead Christians to judge each other, to condemn each other, and to accuse each other of being false Christians. Many churches have been split apart because of this. And those people who split the church in this way often quote this very verse to justify their actions: . . . **come out from them and be separate**. But along with this verse, those people should remember another verse, the command of Jesus: **"Do not judge"** (Matthew 7:1).

In Christ's church both purity and unity are essential. We need the very clear guidance of the Holy Spirit to know when to separate from a brother, or to come out from a church. If for any selfish, impure, or false reason we condemn a brother or a church, we are committing a far greater sin against the body of Christ than the sin we are accusing our brother of. In these matters let us be humble; and let us also remember that as we judge others, so God will judge us (Matthew 7:2).

Therefore, we must understand the basic teaching of this verse to be this: It is not man we must separate from, but man's sin. On the one hand, there must be no sin in the church; on the other hand,

---

[18] **Belial** is another name for Satan.

there must be no disunity or conflict. We must try to persuade the sinner and the false teacher to repent; only if they refuse to repent are we to discipline them or separate from them. And whatever we do, we must do it in love and humility and under the direction of the Holy Spirit.

18 Paul here quotes from 2 Samuel 7:14. If we remain pure, God will be a Father to us, and we will be His children.

CHAPTER 7

Paul's Joy and Comfort (7:1–7)

1 When Paul says, **we have these promises,** he is referring to the promises mentioned in 2 Corinthians 6:16,18. Since God is our Father and we are His children, **let us purify ourselves from everything that contaminates body and spirit.** God is holy; therefore, we too must be holy (see 1 Peter 1:14–16). There are sins of the **body** and sins of the **spirit;**[19] we must be cleansed from both types of sin. Our **holiness** must be "perfect."

2–4 Paul here continues the thoughts he wrote in 2 Corinthians 6:11–13. We can see from these verses what a great love Paul had for the Corinthians. Paul is ready both to **live** with the Corinthians and to **die** with them.

5 Why is Paul so joyful? Because he has just heard good news about the Corinthians from his colleague Titus (verse 6).

According to 2 Corinthians 2:12–13, Paul had gone to **Macedonia** (northern Greece) to meet Titus. Titus was returning from a visit to Corinth, and was bringing with him news of the Corinthian church. Titus earlier had taken to the Corinthian Christians a severe letter that Paul had written, and Paul was very worried about how the Corinthians had reacted to his letter (2 Corinthians 2:3). Had the Corinthians become angry and rejected Paul completely? Or had they repented and agreed to obey Paul's words—as they used to do in the beginning when Paul first worked among them. These were the questions in Paul's mind as he journeyed to Macedonia to find Titus.

6–7 Titus had brought with him good news from Corinth: The Corinthians longed for Paul and cared for him! Not only that, they felt **deep sorrow** for the distress they had caused him.

Sorrow That Leads to Repentance (7:8–16)

8–9 Paul's first thought had been: "I wish I hadn't sent that severe letter to the Corinthians; it has hurt them." But after he had received the good news from Titus, Paul was happy. He was happy because even though his letter had caused them sorrow, it had also led them to repentance (see 2 Corinthians 2:2–4).

Here we can see the purpose of disciplining and punishing Christians within the church. Such discipline is never given in order to hurt or harm a person; rather, it is given to lead that person to repentance and greater holiness. True Christian discipline is never harmful; it is always beneficial—if it is accepted in the right spirit.

10 **Godly sorrow** is discipline from God, and it leads men to REPENTANCE. And repentance leads to forgiveness, and then to **salvation**.

Godly sorrow comes because of our sin. On the other hand, **worldly sorrow** comes because of worldly troubles and disappointments. If we harden our hearts and reject God's discipline, our sorrow will turn to worldly sorrow, which gives

---

[19] The sins of the **spirit** are such things as unbelief, pride, discontent, criticism, idol worship, etc. The **spirit** mentioned here is the human spirit. All sins arise in man's heart and mind, but some sins especially involve man's **body,** while other sins especially involve man's **spirit**.

no benefit. Instead, such worldly sorrow brings despair and eternal punishment—**death**.

11 Here we see what the Corinthians thought after receiving Paul's severe letter, and how they then reacted to it. In that letter, Paul had warned the Corinthians about a man in the church who had committed a great sin. According to this verse, the Corinthians had then given this man some kind of punishment, or had in some way removed his sin from their midst. So they had now become **innocent** of any involvement in this man's sin. That bad situation had now been corrected.

12 The Corinthians had at first refused to follow Paul's instructions; they had rebelled against Paul's authority. They at first didn't give that sinful man any discipline or punishment; they tolerated his sin (see 1 Corinthians 5:1–2). The Corinthian Christians were proud. Therefore, Paul wrote them that severe letter in order to bring them to repentance. Paul hoped that they would respect his authority and obey his words (see 2 Corinthians 2:9). Now his hope had been fulfilled.

Godly sorrow and the **repentance** that comes from it always lead in the end to joy for all concerned. Paul was joyful; Titus was joyful; and the Corinthians were also joyful. Let us not be surprised at all this joy. Jesus said: "**. . . there is more rejoicing in heaven over one sinner who repents than over ninety-nine righteous persons who do not need to repent**" (Luke 15:7).

13 Paul is particularly delighted at the way the Corinthians treated Titus; they had treated him with kindness and respect. As a result, Titus' spirit had been **refreshed**. One of the most important things we can do for one another as Christians is to encourage and refresh each other.

14–16 Paul had told Titus many good things about the Corinthian Christians. He had **boasted** about them (verse 14). Paul is happy that the Corinthians have not **embarrassed** him by behaving badly to Titus. They had proven by their good behavior that the good things Paul had said about them were indeed true. They had behaved towards Titus just as Paul had predicted they would.

The Corinthians had received Titus as if he had been Paul himself, that is, **with fear and trembling** (verse 15). From this, we can see what a great change had taken place in the hearts of the Corinthians!

CHAPTER 8

Generosity Encouraged (8:1–15)

1–2 Among the **Macedonian churches**, the two most well-known were the Philippian church and the Thessalonian church. The Thessalonians had become a **model to all the believers in Macedonia and Achaia** (1 Thessalonians 1:7).

Even though the Philippians and Thessalonians were themselves extremely poor and were experiencing severe trials, still they were filled with **rich generosity** toward other Christians in need (verse 2). In particular, they had contributed generously to the collection that Paul had been raising in the churches of Greece to send to the poor Christians in Jerusalem. Paul hopes that the Corinthians will follow the example of the Macedonian churches and contribute to the collection for the Jerusalem Christians with equal generosity.

Generosity is not measured only by how much one gives; it is also measured by how much one keeps! A poor man can never give as much as a rich man; nevertheless, the poor man's generosity may be much greater than that of the rich man. Remember the poor widow whom Jesus talked about; she put into the temple treasury **only a fraction of a penny**. But Jesus said of her: "**I tell you the truth, this poor widow has put more into the treasury than all the others. They gave out of their wealth; but she,**

out of her poverty, put in everything—all she had to live on" (Mark 12:41–44).

3–4 The Christians of Macedonia had **urgently pleaded** with Paul for the opportunity to send money to the **saints**—the believers—in Jerusalem (verse 4).

Are we like those Macedonian Christians? Or rather do we complain about how poor we are and try to give as little as possible? We need to remember that our money is not our own; it belongs to the Lord Jesus. We must decide how much to give, not according to our own wish or calculation, but according to His.

Remember this: If we are generous toward others, God will be generous toward us. The more we give, the more we will receive (see 2 Corinthians 9:6). **A man reaps what he sows** (Galatians 6:7). Let us not be stingy. **God loves a cheerful giver** (2 Corinthians 9:7). When we give, let us not worry about ourselves, because **God will meet all** [our] **needs according to his glorious riches in Christ Jesus** (Philippians 4:19).

5 The Macedonian Christians gave not only their money, but **they gave themselves** as well. They are an example for us to follow. More than our money, God wants us. Paul wrote: **I urge you . . . to offer your bodies as living sacrifices . . . to God** (Romans 12:1). If we belong to Christ, then our money belongs to Him also. That is why the Macedonian Christians were so generous: they had given themselves **first to the Lord**. They had also given themselves—submitted themselves—to Paul, as an apostle of the Lord, which was **in keeping with God's will**. Paul hopes that the Corinthians will do the same.

6 Paul had appointed Titus to bring to completion **this act of grace**. This **act of grace** was the collection for the poor that Paul was raising to send to Jerusalem. Paul calls it an "act of grace," because just as God shows His grace to us, so we must show that grace to others (see verse 1). Grace consists of love, mercy, kindness, and generosity. All grace comes first from God. Let us be diligent to share God's grace with those around us—especially the poor.

7 The Corinthians had been given an abundance of God's grace, God's gifts (see 1 Corinthians 1:4–7). Therefore, let them now **excel in this grace of giving** to others.

8 Paul does not want to force the Corinthians to give their money. But Paul is testing the sincerity of the Corinthians' love **by comparing it with the earnestness of others**—namely, the Macedonian Christians (see 1 John 3:17–18).

9 For us the greatest example is always Jesus Christ Himself. He was rich beyond measure. He possessed all the riches of God. Yet He gave it all up. For our sakes, He became **poor** (see Philippians 2:6–7). Through His **poverty**—that is, through His death[20] on the cross—we have become spiritually rich.

If Christ has done that much for us, how can we not follow His example and give both our possessions and ourselves for the sake of others?

10–11 Among all the Greek churches, the Corinthians had been the first to contribute to Paul's collection for the poor in Jerusalem. But then they fell behind in their contributions; the collection was forgotten for a time. Now Paul urges them to **finish** what they had started.

12 How much the Corinthians give is not the main thing, says Paul. They can't give what they don't have. Rather, the main thing is their **willingness** to give. If they have the willingness, then their gift will be **acceptable**. Paul's advice in verse 11 is this: Give **according to your means** (see 1 Corinthians 16:2 and comment).

13 Paul doesn't want the Corinthians to give so much that they themselves become **hard pressed**. They should not go into debt in order to contribute to the collection.

14 For Christians, giving to those in need is a natural and reasonable thing to do. Today we supply someone else's

[20] Death, in a material sense, is the ultimate state of poverty. Through death we lose not only our possessions but also our bodies.

need; tomorrow he will supply our need. This is what Paul means by **equality**.

This is not the same as the communist system, in which the government takes from one and gives to another. In Christianity, it is love that causes us to give to others, not the government. We give freely, not by law. And, relative to our means, how much we give will depend on the needs of others (see Acts 2:44–45; 4:34–35).

Paul doesn't say that all Christians must have exactly the same amount of money and possessions. God has assigned to Christians different ranks, different jobs, and different gifts. Some are rich, some are poor. But there must always be generous sharing between those who have enough and those who don't. No Christian should ever remain in need. Those who have enough should give according to their means, and those who don't have enough should receive according to their needs. All that we have has come from God (see 1 Corinthians 4:2). Whatever we have is God's, not ours.

15 Paul here quotes from Exodus 16:18. This verse describes how the ancient Jews gathered **manna** from the desert. "Manna" was a kind of bread, which God sent down from heaven to the Jews so that they wouldn't starve in the desert. Each day the Jews gathered the "manna." Those Jews who were younger and stronger gathered more than those who were old and weak. But when all the "manna" had been gathered, it was distributed equally to all. Therefore, **he that gathered little did not have too little.** If any Jew tried to keep for himself more than his share of "manna," it quickly spoiled and could not be eaten (Exodus 16:14–20,32).

Titus Sent to Corinth (8:16–24)

16–17 Titus volunteered to return to Corinth to help make the final arrangements for completing the collection.

18 In this verse, Paul mentions a **brother** who was praised by all the churches. It is not certain what brother Paul is referring to here. Some think it is Luke; others think it is Tychicus (Acts 20:4; Ephesians 6:21).

19 Whoever this **brother** was who accompanied Titus to Corinth, he was chosen, not by Paul, but by the churches who were taking part in the collection.

20 It was important for the churches themselves to choose their own representatives to join in taking the collection to Jerusalem (1 Corinthians 16:3). Otherwise, people could falsely accuse Paul and his colleagues of taking the collection for themselves, and they would have no witnesses to deny the charges. Satan is always looking for an opportunity to bring evil out of a good work.

21 Concerning the collection, Paul wanted to do what was right, **not only in the eyes of the Lord but also in the eyes of men**. Paul doesn't mean here that he was looking for praise from men. Paul sought praise only from God. Whatever Paul did, he did it for the Lord alone (see Romans 14:7–8; Ephesians 6:5–8).

But Paul knew that if he brought dishonor upon himself, this would also bring dishonor upon Christ. Therefore, he wanted to avoid anything that would appear dishonorable in men's eyes. He wasn't worried about his own reputation, but about Christ's reputation.

In the same way, every Christian, insofar as possible, must protect his reputation from dishonor—even the appearance of dishonor. This doesn't mean that we should avoid being dishonored for Christ's sake; all believers can expect to be dishonored because of their faith in Christ. But it means that we should avoid the dishonor that comes from wrongdoing, or the appearance of wrongdoing. Paul wrote: **Avoid every kind of evil** (1 Thessalonians 5:22). We must not give people any unnecessary opportunity to speak against Christ and His Gospel[21] (see 1 Corinthians 9:12).

[21] The particular matter that Paul is referring to in this verse is a financial matter. All church leaders must make themselves and their work accountable to other Christians, especially in financial affairs. It is not enough to say, "I am accountable only to God." Satan will surely trip up the leader who refuses to be accountable to other believers.

22 Here Paul mentions another brother—**our brother**—who also accompanied Titus to Corinth. It is not known who this brother was.

23–24 Paul tells the Corinthians that Titus and these two brothers are worthy of their love and respect. Titus himself was Paul's **partner and fellow worker** (verse 23). These two brothers who accompanied Titus to Corinth were **representatives of the churches**. But more than that, they were an **honor to Christ**.

If Paul were here today, would he be able to say about us that we were an **honor to Christ?**

CHAPTER 9

The Service for the Saints (9:1–5)

1–2 In these verses, Paul adds to what he said in 2 Corinthians 8:10 about **this service to the saints**—that is, the offering (or collection) for the poor Christians in Jerusalem. **There is no need** for Paul to write any further to the Corinthians about this **service**, or offering, because he already knows about their **eagerness to help** (verse 2). At first the Christians in Corinth and the surrounding province of **Achaia** had been eager to raise this offering. When the Christians in Macedonia saw the Corinthians' **enthusiasm**, they too became eager to help.

3–4 Now, Paul says, the Corinthians should complete the work of raising money for the offering; otherwise, all the **boasting** Paul has done about the Corinthians' enthusiasm would in the end **prove hollow** (verse 3); it would prove empty and false. Therefore, Paul is going to send Titus and two brothers to Corinth to help the Corinthians complete the collection. Paul does not want to be **ashamed** because the Corinthians are not ready to send their offering to Jerusalem.

5 Furthermore, Paul does not want the Corinthians to give their money for the collection **grudgingly** (see verse 7). Let them give generously from their hearts.

Sowing Generously (9:6–15)

6 **Whoever sows sparingly will also reap sparingly**. Giving our money and possessions for the Lord's work is like sowing seed in the ground. If we give (sow) generously, God will give to us generously in return (Proverbs 22:9). **One man gives freely, yet gains even more; another withholds unduly, but comes to poverty. A generous man will prosper; he who refreshes others will himself be refreshed** (Proverbs 11:24–25).

As a man sows, so will he reap. This principle applies not only to material things, but to spiritual things as well—such as forgiveness, judgment, and sin (see Matthew 6:12,14–15; 7:1–2; Galatians 6:7–10 and comments).

Jesus said: "**And if anyone gives a cup of cold water to one of these little ones . . . he will certainly not lose his reward**" (Matthew 10:42). But if we selfishly give to others only to gain a reward, we shall lose the reward. We must give unselfishly and generously, without any thought for our own benefit. If we give in this way, God will surely bless us both in this world and the next (see Proverbs 19:17; Matthew 25:34–40; Luke 6:34–35; 14:12–14).

7 The Corinthians should not give **reluctantly or under compulsion**, but rather from their hearts and by the guidance of the Holy Spirit (see verse 5).

Let us not give in order to obtain praise from men (Matthew 6:1–4 and comment). And certainly let us not say we have given when we haven't! (see Acts 5:1–11).

Our service, our giving, must be done **generously**; our acts of mercy must be done **cheerfully** (Romans 12:8). If when we give we are not happy about it, then we are not giving in the right way. Let us remember Jesus' words: "**It is more blessed to give than to receive**" (Acts 20:35). Jesus said: "**Freely you have received, freely give**" (Matthew 10:8).

8 Let us never think that if we give to the Lord we will suffer loss. When a farmer sows seed in the ground, the seed is not lost—it turns into a harvest! God is able **to make all grace abound** to us—**in all things at all times** (see Matthew 6:31–33; Philippians 4:19 and comments). What an amazing promise! God be praised!

9 Paul here quotes from Psalm 112:9. When a man gives generously to the poor, **his righteousness endures forever**.

10 God supplies both the **seed** and the **bread**. All things come from God's grace. As much as we give to others, that much more will God **increase** [our] **store** and **enlarge the harvest of** [our] **righteousness**. In other words, when we give to others, God will give us both material[22] and spiritual blessings in return.

Let us always remember how great God's power is (Ephesians 3:20–21). From a tiny seed, God can make a great tree. But we have to let go of that seed; we have to bury it in the ground. If we keep that seed in our pocket, no tree will come from it. In the same way, a small boy once gave away five loaves and two fish to Jesus, and Jesus turned them into a feast for five thousand men! (see Mark 6:35–44).

11 We will be made **rich in every way**. To the degree that we ourselves are generous toward others, God will make us **rich**—both spiritually and materially—**in every way**.

Why will God make us "rich"? He will make us rich so that we can then be more generous, so that we can be generous continuously. The moment we stop being generous, God will stop making us rich!

Paul tells the Corinthians that **through us your generosity will result in thanksgiving to God**. That is, when Paul and his colleagues bring the Corinthians' offering to Jerusalem, the believers there will thank God for the generosity of the Corinthians.

12 It is necessary to thank other people for their gifts to us. But it is even more necessary to thank God for their gifts, for their generosity. Because all generosity arises out of the grace of God. God gives both the "seed" of generosity and its "harvest."

13 Through this **service** (the offering), the Corinthians are giving proof of their **obedience that accompanies** [their] **confession of the gospel**. Obedience must always accompany our confession of faith; otherwise, our confession will be shown to be false. To obey the gospel is to give help to our brothers and sisters in need (see James 2:14–17). Such obedience is the proof that our faith is real.

14 Because of the **surpassing grace** (the grace of generosity) that God has given to the Corinthians, the hearts of the believers in Jerusalem **will go out** to the Corinthians. The Jewish Christians of Jerusalem and the Gentile Christians of Corinth will be drawn to each other in love. This is why Paul considers this offering to be so important.

15 **Thanks be to God for his indescribable gift**—the gift of His grace! But what exactly is the gift of God's grace? Above all, it is Jesus Christ. All of the grace and blessings of God come to us in Christ (see John 3:16; Romans 8:32; Ephesians 1:3 and comments). **Dear friends, since God so loved us, we also ought to love one another** (1 John 4:11).

---

[22] Although God usually gives Christians material blessings along with the spiritual blessings, He doesn't always do so. Sometimes God leads us through periods of hardship in order to test us or in order to give us even greater spiritual blessings.

CHAPTER 10

Paul's Defense of His Ministry (10:1–18)

1 Paul appeals to the Corinthians by the **meekness and gentleness of Christ**. Meekness and gentleness are qualities of a mature Christian. Many people think that a meek and gentle man is a weak man, but that is not true. Meekness and gentleness are signs of strength. The greatest and strongest man in history, Jesus Christ, was meek and gentle. And so was Paul, because he had received Christ's Spirit.

But even though Jesus Christ was meek and gentle, He was bold and severe in His opposition to sin (see Matthew 23:13–36; John 2:14–16). In the same way, though meek and gentle, Paul boldly rebuked the Corinthians for their sins. But Paul's boldness did not come from himself; it came from Christ.

Paul's enemies in the Corinthian church criticized Paul by saying that when he was away from Corinth he was **bold**, but when he was in Corinth he was **timid**. That is, he was **bold** in his letter writing but not in person (verse 10). Like a cowardly dog who barks only from a distance, Paul didn't have the courage to speak to the Corinthians face to face. Here in this verse, Paul sarcastically repeats their criticism.

In one way, the criticism of Paul's enemies was true, because when he had first come to Corinth he had come **in weakness and fear** (1 Corinthians 2:3). But these enemies had forgotten one thing: namely, that Paul's preaching had been **with a demonstration of the Spirit's power** (1 Corinthians 2:4). By leaving out one part of the truth, Paul's enemies were making a false accusation against him. This is the habit of slanderers: they do not speak the whole truth, but only part of it. Let us take heed, so that we ourselves do not speak in this way against others.

2 Paul's enemies at Corinth said that Paul lived **by the standards of this world**. Now, if necessary, Paul is ready to be **bold** in dealing with these enemies. However, Paul doesn't want to behave boldly and severely with the Corinthians. Instead, he hopes that these enemies will repent before he comes to Corinth, so that he won't have to rebuke them.

3 Living **in the world** is different from living **by the standards of this world** (verse 2). When Paul says that **we live in the world**, he means that, as men, we have bodies and therefore must endure the weakness of the body. Paul must eat; he must sleep. He gets tired; he gets worried. But although Paul lives **in the world**—in the body—he does not live **by the standards of this world**, nor does he wage war **as the world does** (verse 3). The expression "to live by the standards of this world" means to live according one's **old self** (Romans 6:6) or according to one's **sinful nature** (Romans 8:4–5). Before Paul became a Christian, he had lived and "waged war" according to his "old self," according to his sinful nature. But now **in Christ** Paul has become a **new creation** (2 Corinthians 5:17); therefore, he lives not by the standards of this world but **by the Spirit** (Galatians 5:16). However, Paul's body is not new. Until he dies, Paul must remain in his body—**in the world.**

Paul does not **wage war as the world does**—that is, he does not wage war with the weapons of the world. Paul doesn't fight as other men do. He does not use deception; he does not slander others. He does not fight with swords and arrows.

4 Paul does not fight with the **weapons of the world**; his weapons are spiritual (see Romans 13:12; 2 Corinthians 6:7; Ephesians 6:13–18). These spiritual weapons **have divine power**. They have the power to **demolish** (Satan's) **strongholds**. They ruin Satan's **schemes** (Ephesians 6:11). Our enemy is not man, but Satan (Ephesians 6:12). It is useless to fight Satan with weapons that only work against men.

5 The thoughts of men who live **by the standards of this world** are not like the thoughts of God. Only a new man in Christ can have the thoughts of Christ and God (see 1 Corinthians 2:16). The **arguments and every pretension** of natural, worldly men are opposed to the **knowledge of God**. We can say that, in a sense, the mind of natural man is Satan's "stronghold," and the thoughts of natural man are Satan's messengers and soldiers. Only with God's spiritual weapons can Paul demolish Satan's stronghold and **take captive** (bring under control) man's evil thoughts.

Let us ask ourselves: Have all our thoughts been "taken captive" and brought under the control of Christ? Perhaps outwardly we obey Christ; but do we also obey Him in our thoughts?

Everyone agrees that to speak evil thoughts is wrong. But to keep such thoughts in our minds is also wrong. We can hide our thoughts from other men, but we cannot hide them from God.

But from time to time evil thoughts come suddenly into our minds. How can we get rid of these thoughts? We can "take them captive." That is, we can bring them under the control of Christ. Evil thoughts are Satan's soldiers. We can overcome these thoughts with the spiritual weapons of righteousness, light, and faith, together with the **sword** of God's word (Ephesians 6:17).

For example, these evil thoughts—thoughts of anger, jealousy, greed, unrighteousness, worry, etc.—are like birds flying around our heads. We can't stop the birds from flying over our head, but we can certainly stop them from building nests in our hair! (see James 1:15 and comment).

6 Paul hopes and believes that most of the Corinthians will reject the false teachers who have come into their church. Paul is waiting for the true Christians among the Corinthians to repent and turn from the false teachers; that is, he is waiting for their **obedience to be complete**. Only after the Corinthians have turned from these false teachers will Paul go to Corinth. And when Paul goes to Corinth, he will certainly punish those false teachers and expel them from the church.

7 Some in the Corinthian church said: "We belong to the party of Christ." In saying this, they looked down on others in the church; they considered themselves the only true Christians (see 1 Corinthians 1:12). These same people, in judging Paul, were **looking only on the surface of things**; they were judging on the basis of outward things alone. "Don't judge me," Paul tells them; "I belong to Christ just as much as you do."

In this verse, there is an important lesson for us all. We look mainly at outward things. Perhaps we look at a brother and we don't like what he does, we don't like his manner. We judge him; we say, "He is not one of us." Or we say: "He is no good." But we forget that that brother belongs to Christ too. He is Christ's servant, just as we are. The Holy Spirit is in him also. Therefore, let us not look only at outward things, but as much as possible, let us look at inner things. Let us consider our brother's motives, his purposes, his desires. If we do this, we shall understand better why our brother does the things he does. We won't be quite so ready to judge him!

8 Paul boasts of his authority, because it has been given to him by the Lord. Paul's authority is not his own; it comes from Christ.

Notice that Christ gives His authority to pastors, elders, and preachers so that they might build Christians up, not tear them down (see 2 Corinthians 13:10).

9–11 Paul had formerly behaved toward the Corinthians with **meekness and gentleness** (verse 1); he had come to them **in weakness and fear** (1 Corinthians 2:3). But let the Corinthians not think he is afraid of them. Paul is going to **punish every act of disobedience** (verse 6). However, Paul hopes he will not have to be harsh with them when he comes to Corinth.

12 In this verse, Paul again writes to the Corinthians in a sarcastic manner. He says that he is not as "great" as those people at Corinth who make themselves out to be great.

The false teachers at Corinth "commended" themselves. They were puffed up with pride. They measured themselves **by themselves**—that is, they measured themselves by their own measurement, by their own standards, the standards of this world. But how foolish they were!

There is only one measurement, one standard, by which we should measure ourselves; and that is the standard of Jesus Christ. Only when we compare ourselves with Christ will we be able to measure ourselves accurately. And when we compare ourselves with Christ, how unworthy we appear!

13–14 Paul does not boast in himself. He does not boast **beyond proper limits** (verse 13). Rather, he limits his boasting to the **field** God has assigned to him. That is, he boasts only in the area of work which God has given him. That area of work is to preach the Gospel to the Gentiles (see Acts 9:15; Romans 1:5). Paul's "field" has extended all the way to Corinth.

15–16 Paul does not boast in or take credit for the work of other apostles and preachers. He goes only to those places where others have not gone (Romans 15:20). Paul's hope is that Corinth might become a center from which the Gospel could then spread further westward. But first it will be necessary for the Corinthians' faith to grow; they must become more mature. Otherwise, their church will not become a center for spreading the Gospel, and they will not be able to give much help to Paul in the work of preaching. The reason is because Christ cannot work effectively in a church that is divided into factions, or which is filled with sin and false teaching.

17–18 Paul here quotes from Jeremiah 9:24 (see 1 Corinthians 1:31).

Let us not commend ourselves. That is the practice of proud and worldly men. Furthermore, let us not seek the commendation and praise of men (see John 5:44; 12:43). Instead, let us seek the commendation of God alone, because it is only by God that we can truly be **approved**.

CHAPTER 11

Paul and the False Apostles (11:1–15)

1 Paul's **foolishness** is to talk about himself. Paul is now about to open his heart to the Corinthians. Usually we don't talk about ourselves in this way, for fear of appearing "foolish." But Paul loves the Corinthians so much that he is willing to appear foolish in their eyes by opening his heart to them.

2 The church is Christ's bride (see Ephesians 5:23–27). Because Paul had founded the Corinthian church, he was like a father to it (1 Corinthians 4:15). Therefore, it was his duty to present his "daughter," the Corinthian church, **as a pure virgin** to her bridegroom Christ. It was Paul's great concern that the Corinthian church should remain **pure** until Christ's coming.

3 Paul fears that the Corinthians will not remain pure, that they will not remain faithful to Christ. The reason he is fearful is because false teachers have entered the church and are trying to lead the Corinthians astray (verses 13–15), just as the serpent deceived Eve in the Garden of Eden (Genesis 3:1–3).

4 The Corinthians, like other Greeks, were always eager to hear any kind of new teaching (see Acts 17:18–21). Therefore, they were easily fooled and drawn away from the true teaching given by Paul (see 2 Timothy 4:3–4). But there is only one Christ, and one Spirit (the Holy Spirit), and one Gospel. Let the Corinthians not follow after false Christs and false spirits, warns Paul (see 1 John 4:1–3). Paul does not want the Corinthians to be turned away from the true Gospel, as the Galatians had been (see Galatians 1:6–9). Paul's meaning is this: the Corinthians have too easily **put up with**, or tolerated, false teachers, and in so doing they are making a great mistake.

5 Here Paul, again being sarcastic, calls the false teachers **super-apostles** (see verse 13). In fact, these teachers were not "super-apostles"; they were false apostles.

6 Paul's language was clear and simple. Therefore, some of the Corinthians, when they heard Paul, supposed that he was not so wise. But Paul had true **knowledge**—a knowledge and wisdom that came from God (see 1 Corinthians 2:4–7).

7 In Paul's time, most philosophers and teachers received payment for their teaching (2 Corinthians 2:17). Because Paul didn't demand payment for his teaching (he earned his living by making tents), his enemies among the Corinthians said that his teaching was worthless.

Therefore, Paul here asks the Corinthians sarcastically: **Was it a sin for me** not to demand payment for my teaching? Paul had the right to demand payment (1 Corinthians 9:14). But Paul had given up that right, so that no one would be able to accuse him of being greedy for money (see 1 Corinthians 9:12,15,18; 1 Thessalonians 2:9; 2 Thessalonians 3:7–9).

8 Paul received **support**, financial help, from other churches. Here he says he **robbed** these churches. Paul didn't like to receive help from the churches he established; in his mind it was like "robbing" them.

9 Even while Paul was at Corinth, he received help in times of need from the Macedonian Christians (especially the Philippians), and not from the Corinthians (see Philippians 4:15–16).

10 See 1 Corinthians 9:15 and comment.

11 By refusing to take money from the Corinthians, Paul has proven his love for them. **God knows** that Paul loves the Corinthians.

12 The false teachers at Corinth wanted an **opportunity to be considered equal** with Paul; that is, they wanted to appear equal to Paul. They took payment for their teaching; therefore, they wished that Paul would take payment too, so that there would be no difference between Paul and them. But Paul will not agree to accept payment as they do. He doesn't want to give these false teachers any chance to appear equal with him.

13 These false teachers, in fact, were not equal with Paul. Paul was a true apostle, but they were **false apostles**.

From Paul's time up until the present, many false apostles have passed into the church of Christ (see Mark 13:22; Acts 20:29–30; Romans 16:17–18; Galatians 1:7; 1 Timothy 4:1–2; Titus 1:10–11). How can we keep ourselves from being deceived by these false apostles? The answer: By studying God's word—the Bible—and by keeping His word in our hearts.

14 These false apostles are servants of SATAN. Satan himself **masquerades as an angel of light**, and by this means deceives many (see Matthew 7:15 and comment).

15 These false apostles, like their master Satan, **masquerade as servants of righteousness**. How can we recognize them? We can recognize them by their works, **by their fruit** (see Matthew 7:16–20 and comment).

On the day of judgment, these false apostles will receive the punishment they deserve (Matthew 7:19; 2 Thessalonians 1:8–9).

Paul Boasts About His Sufferings (11:16–33)

16 Paul is not a **fool**. But if the Corinthians want to think he's a fool, then let them think it. Paul here says to the Corinthians: "Since you think I'm a fool, I'm going to talk like a fool and boast further about myself" (see verse 1).

17–18 Paul says that in this section he is not talking as Christ would talk; he is talking like a fool. Indeed, he is talking as those false apostles would talk. The false apostles boasted about themselves. In order to expose the foolishness of the false apostles, Paul in this section imitates their own manner of speaking and reasoning. This is why Paul boasts about himself here: he is only imitating the false apostles. At the same time, we must remember that everything Paul boasts about is, in fact, true.

19 Here Paul again speaks to the Corinthians sarcastically. Because they liked to listen to all kinds of teachers, the Corinthians considered themselves **wise**. But even though they were "wise," they had accepted the foolish teaching of the false apostles, and that teaching had done them great spiritual harm.

20 Through their teaching, the false

apostles were bringing the Corinthians into bondage to Satan. The Corinthians were being "enslaved." The false apostles were turning the Corinthians away from their freedom in Christ (see Galatians 5:1).

By taking payment for their teaching, these false apostles were "exploiting" and "taking advantage" of the Corinthians, Paul says. By their false teaching, these false apostles were, in a sense, "slapping" the Corinthians in the face.

21 Paul here says sarcastically: "I am **too weak** to do what those false apostles are doing; I am not strong and bold like they are." Paul means by this that he himself has not exploited or enslaved the Corinthians in any way. This shows how "weak" Paul is!

But if these false apostles are going to boast about themselves, then Paul is going to boast about himself. He is ready to prove that they are no better than he is. He will speak in the same proud and foolish way they do!

22 The false apostles boasted that they were true **Hebrews**—that is, **Israelites** (Jews). Paul says: "I also am a true Jew."

23 The false apostles claimed to be apostles of Christ (verse 13). But they had not suffered for Christ the way Paul had. Paul was a true apostle of Christ, because he had suffered for Him.

According to the book of Acts, Paul was imprisoned at least four times (Acts 16:23; 22:29; 23:35; 28:16). Some historians say that Paul was imprisoned as many as seven times.

Paul's floggings are mentioned here in verse 24 and in Acts 16:22–23.

Paul was **exposed to death** again and again; that is, he constantly faced the risk of death (see Acts 14:19; Romans 8:36; 1 Corinthians 15:30–31; 2 Corinthians 1:8–9).

24 According to Deuteronomy 25:2–3, a criminal was never to receive more than forty lashes with a whip. Therefore, so that they would never accidentally (by miscounting) give more than forty lashes, the Jews always used to give **forty lashes minus one**—that is, thirty-nine lashes.

Jesus warned His disciples that they would be flogged by the Jews (Mark 13:9). Before he met the risen Christ, Paul himself had caused Christians to be flogged in the Jewish synagogues (Acts 26:11).

25 The Jews used to beat people with whips. The Gentiles (the Greeks and Romans) beat people with rods (Acts 16:22).

The Jews carried out the death sentence against criminals by stoning them (Leviticus 24:16; Acts 7:57–58). Paul's stoning is mentioned in Acts 14:19.

26 Paul was constantly in danger (see 2 Corinthians 4:8–9). Notice that the last danger Paul mentions is the **danger from false brothers**. Many Christians can testify from their own experience that this is the most grievous danger of all (Psalm 55:12–14).

27 In verse 26, Paul has mentioned various dangers. Here in verse 27, Paul mentions some of the hardships he has faced. From this we can see how much Paul suffered. Paul had not only experienced **hunger and thirst**, but he had also been **cold and naked** (see 1 Corinthians 4:11–13; 2 Corinthians 6:4–10; 1 Thessalonians 2:9).

28 In addition to these "outward" dangers and hardships, Paul experienced the "inward" **pressure of . . . concern for all the churches**. Just as a father is concerned for his children, so Paul was concerned for the churches. Paul worried most of all about the false apostles and teachers—the **ferocious wolves**—who were always trying to enter the church (see Matthew 7:15; Acts 20:29).

29 Here again we can see inside Paul's heart. The Corinthians were like Paul's spiritual children. If they are **weak**, then Paul feels their weakness. If they are **led into sin**, then Paul will **inwardly burn** with anger against the person who led them into sin.

30 Paul does not boast of his own strength. Instead, he boasts of the **things that show** [his] **weakness**—such as his sufferings, his worries, his dangers, his hunger and thirst.

Paul does not boast in himself. Yes, he told the Corinthians: **I worked harder than all of them**. But he quickly added: **. . . yet not I, but the grace of God that was with me** (1 Corinthians 15:10). There are times when it is appropriate for Christians to "boast" of what God has done in their lives. But always we must boast of what God has done, not what we have done.

31 Paul's enemies in Corinth may say that Paul is lying about all his sufferings and hardships. But God knows that he is not lying.

32–33 Here Paul remembers still another experience, and so he mentions it in these verses. This was an important event in Paul's life. Paul had just met the risen Christ on the road to **Damascus,**[23] and had been converted (see Acts 9:1–8). After he arrived in Damascus and was baptized, Paul began to preach about Christ. But he had originally gone to Damascus to arrest and punish the followers of Christ. What a dramatic change had taken place in his life! When he had set out for Damascus, he was a proud Jew searching for Christians. But when he left Damascus, he was a humble Christian hiding in a basket! (see Acts 9:20–25).

CHAPTER 12

Paul's Vision and His Thorn (12:1–10)

1–2 Fourteen years before writing this letter, Paul had a vision or revelation of heaven. That revelation was so amazing that Paul can't even speak about it in an ordinary way. Instead of saying, "I had a vision," Paul says: **"I know a man in Christ** who had a vision" (verse 2). We know that Paul is referring to himself when he says this, because in verse 7 he writes: **To keep me from becoming conceited because of these surpassingly great revelations, there was given me a thorn in my flesh.**

The revelation was this: A **man** (Paul) **was caught up to the third heaven** (verse 2). The **third heaven** is a Jewish expression, which means a place where God is present. According to Jewish belief in Paul's time, the "first heaven" was the sky and the "second heaven" was the universe. According to that belief, then, the "third heaven" signifies the spiritual heaven where Christ sits on the right hand of God (see Acts 1:10–11; Ephesians 1:20), and where believers in Christ will live with God forever.

In this revelation Paul is not sure whether his body was taken up into this third heaven, or whether only his spirit was taken up.

3–4 What is **Paradise**? (verse 4). **Paradise** is mentioned also in Luke 23:43 and Revelation 2:7. Many Bible scholars think that Paradise is a place believers in Christ go to as soon as they die. There, without a body, the souls and spirits of believers remain until the end of the world, at which time Jesus will come again and give each believer a new resurrected body (see Romans 8:23; 1 Corinthians 15:42–44; 1 Thessalonians 4:16–17). Then, when they have received their new resurrected bodies, believers will enter heaven—the **third heaven**—where they will live with God and Christ forever.

Notice, in verse 4, that Paul says he was caught up **to** (into) **Paradise**; but in verse 2, he says he was caught up **to** (as far as) **the third heaven**. In the Greek, Paul uses two different words for "to" in these verses. He seems to be saying that he was taken "into" Paradise, but that he only reached "as far as" the third heaven but not into it. Many Bible scholars believe that this shows that Paradise and the third heaven are two different places.

But other scholars believe that Paradise and the third heaven are really the same place. The Bible gives us very little description of life after death. Therefore, it is not possible to be certain about this matter. Paul says that he is **not permitted** even to talk about it! (verse 4).

---

[23] **Damascus** is the capital of the Middle Eastern country of Syria.

5 Paul writes: **I will boast about a man like that**; that is, Paul will boast about the revelation that God had given to him. But Paul will not boast about himself. If Paul boasts about himself, it will be about his **weaknesses** (see verses 9–10).

6 Paul could legitimately have boasted about his accomplishments, because his boasting would have been completely true. Paul's accomplishments were surely great. He had established many churches. He had received many gifts from the Holy Spirit. He had performed many **signs, wonders and miracles** (verse 12). But even though all this was true, Paul will not boast about it, lest others begin to praise him instead of praising God (2 Corinthians 3:5). Paul does not want to exalt himself. He remembered Christ's teaching: "**For whoever exalts himself will be humbled, and whoever humbles himself will be exalted**" (Matthew 23:12; Luke 14:11).

7 The **thorn** in Paul's flesh and the **messenger of Satan** mentioned here are the same thing. Paul does not say what the **thorn** in his flesh was. But we can understand that it was some kind of special trial or human weakness that afflicted Paul. Some believe it was an eye disease; others think it was malaria, or epilepsy, or some form of depression. Some believe it was the same malady which Paul referred to in Galatians 4:13–14, whatever that malady was. Others believe Paul's **thorn** was some temptation that kept coming upon Paul during times of difficulty.

It is to our advantage that Paul does not tell us exactly what his **thorn** was. Because if we knew exactly what Paul's thorn was, we might then be tempted to say: "I don't have any 'thorn' like that; therefore, Paul's teaching here about his thorn has no relation to me."

But, in fact, this teaching about Paul's thorn is extremely important for us, because every Christian has some kind of "thorn" or "thorns." That is, every one of us has some kind of bodily or mental weakness. Through this weakness, we are made humble. God cannot easily work through a person who is conceited and proud. Thus we can see that although God gave Paul amazing gifts and experiences, He at the same time gave Paul a "thorn" to keep him humble.

Let us, therefore, not complain about our "thorn," whatever it might be. That thorn has been given to us for our spiritual benefit (Hebrews 12:10–11). Because of our thorn, our weakness, God's power will be more visible in our lives (see 2 Corinthians 4:7 and comment).

Paul says here that his thorn is a **messenger of Satan**; that is, his thorn has been sent by Satan. For example, we know that Satan can cause various diseases (Luke 13:16). But let us not forget that Satan is always under God's ultimate control. Satan cannot send us any kind of "thorn"—any kind of trouble or suffering—without God's permission (Job 1:6–22; 2:1–10). God always overcomes evil with good in the lives of those who love Him (see Genesis 37:28; 45:4,8; 50:20; Romans 8:28 and comment).

8–9 In the garden of Gethsemane Jesus prayed three times: "**My Father, if it is possible, may this cup** (death on the cross) **be taken from me**" (Matthew 26:39,42,44). Didn't God answer Jesus' prayer? Yes, He answered it. But He answered it not with a "Yes," but with a "No." God gives us an answer to all our prayers, but He may not give us the answer we hoped for. His answer will be better for us than what we had hoped for. God answers our prayers not in the way we ask, but in a way that will lead to our greatest good. And He knows far better than we do how to achieve our greatest good. God always gives His children **good gifts** (Matthew 7:9–11). For Paul, that **thorn** was a "good gift."

Is it suitable for us to pray for our "thorn" to be removed? Yes, it is suitable. Like Paul, we can pray that our thorn might be taken away. Perhaps God will take away one or more of our thorns. But God will leave at least one thorn with us, that we might remain humble and always dependent on God's power.

No matter what our weakness is, God will always give us sufficient grace to do His will (Philippians 4:13). The weaker we are, the greater will God's power appear in us (2 Corinthians 4:7). Therefore, Paul **all the more gladly** boasts about his weaknesses (verse 5).

Let us never complain against God. Rather, let us praise and thank Him for every difficulty, every trial, every need that He allows to come into our lives (Job 1:21–22).

10 Paul not only endures **weaknesses . . . insults . . . hardships . . . persecutions . . . difficulties**; he takes **delight** in them! Paul delights in them, because when he is **weak**, then he is **strong**. Paul delights in all these hardships, because through them the comfort of Christ **overflows** in his life (2 Corinthians 1:5). Paul delights in them, because through them the **life of Jesus** is being **revealed** in his body (see 2 Corinthians 4:8–10).

Paul delights in his weaknesses **for Christ's sake**. Paul does not seek such hardships and difficulties for his own spiritual benefit, as the followers of other religions do. Rather, everything Paul seeks is for Christ's sake alone. God will reward us only for what we do and endure for Christ's sake (see Matthew 5:11; 19:29).

Paul's Concern for the Corinthians (12:11–21)

11 Paul has made a "fool" of himself by boasting. Yet the Corinthians themselves forced Paul to write that way. They are the ones who should have been boasting about Paul! Because they didn't commend Paul, Paul had to commend himself; he had to "boast" about himself. Otherwise, there would have been no one to refute the statements of those false apostles, those "**super-apostles.**"

Paul himself is **nothing**; that is, he is only a weak and frail man. Nevertheless, he is **not in the least inferior** to those "super-apostles" (2 Corinthians 11:5).

12 Paul has proven that he is a true apostle by the **signs, wonders and miracles** that he has performed, and also by the fruit that has resulted from his preaching (see 1 Corinthians 9:2).

13 Many of these signs and wonders had been done at Corinth. The church at Corinth had been founded by a true apostle of Christ. Therefore, the Corinthian church was not inferior to any other church—except in one thing: they had not given any support to their apostle Paul. In refusing to take any help from them, Paul had deprived the Corinthians of the chance to boast that they had helped him. Because he has deprived them of this chance to boast, Paul sarcastically asks them to forgive him for **this wrong**.

14 It was on Paul's first visit to Corinth that he founded the church there (Acts 18:1). Paul's second visit to Corinth was the **painful visit** (2 Corinthians 2:1).

Paul does not seek the Corinthians' possessions. Rather, Paul seeks the Corinthians themselves—that is, their love, their hearts. As their spiritual father, he is coming to Corinth not to receive help from them but rather to give help to them.

15 Any human father desires to be loved by his children. He hopes that just as he has loved his children, his children will return his love. But even if the children do not show any love to their father, he will nevertheless, with tears, keep on loving them all the more. Paul's love for the Corinthians was like that.

16 Paul did not take any money from the Corinthians (2 Corinthians 11:9). Yet his enemies accused him of being **crafty**. They said that the collection Paul had been raising for the poor believers in Jerusalem was **trickery**—that is, Paul was raising the money for himself! In this verse Paul sarcastically repeats their false accusation as if he agreed with it.

17–18 Paul had sent **Titus** and **our brother** to Corinth to help the Corinthians complete the collection (2 Corinthians 8:16–18; 9:5). Paul asks the Corinthians: Did Titus or this brother **exploit** you or in any way take advantage of you? The answer is no.

19 Paul has not been defending himself before the Corinthians in the same way he would defend himself before a judge (see 1 Corinthians 4:3). Paul here has been speaking only **in the sight of God**. Paul has spoken in this way not for his own sake, but for the **strengthening** of the Corinthians.

20 Paul is afraid that when he meets the Corinthians he is going to find that they are still **worldly** (see 1 Corinthians 3:1–3). If this should be the case, then the Corinthians are not going to find Paul the way they like him either! Because Paul will be coming **with a whip** (1 Corinthians 4:21).

Let us examine the list of sins which Paul writes here. Are any of these sins in our church? (see Mark 7:21–23; Galatians 5:19–21).

21 Paul has taken much pride in the Corinthians (2 Corinthians 7:4). But if they refuse to repent of their sins and harden their hearts against Paul, then Paul will certainly be made **humble** before them; he will be **grieved**. Paul fears that just as a human father grieves over a wayward and rebellious son, so he will be made to grieve over his beloved Corinthians.

CHAPTER 13

Final Warnings (13:1–10)

1 In this section Paul gives his final warnings to the Corinthians. When Paul comes to Corinth, he will punish those who have not repented of their sins. But he will not listen to unproven charges. **Every matter**—that is, every accusation—will have to be proven by the **testimony of two or three witnesses** (Deuteronomy 19:15; Matthew 18:16). Paul will not listen to any accusation brought by only one person.

It needs to be said here that a true "witness" is not someone who merely repeats someone else's accusation; rather, he is a person who has seen something with his own eyes or heard it with his own ears. Those who repeat someone else's critical talk are not **witnesses**; rather, they are **gossips** and **slanderers** (see Romans 1:29–30; 2 Corinthians 12:20).

Not only that, but witnesses must be of one mind; their testimony must be in agreement. When the witnesses are not in agreement with each other, then no judgment or decision should be made. There is always a danger that a witness will try to falsely accuse a believer (see Psalm 27:12; Mark 14:55–56; Acts 6:12–13). False witnesses who accuse other Christians can even be found within the church; they do the church great harm.

2 Paul had warned the Corinthians earlier that when he came he would punish the unrepentant sinners. Now Paul gives them a final warning.

God will bear with an unrepentant sinner for a long time, but not forever!

3 The Corinthians had demanded proof that Paul was a true apostle of Christ. "Okay," says Paul, "I'll give you proof. If you do not repent, you will soon discover that I have the full power and authority of Christ! That will prove to you that I am His true apostle."

4 When Christ was **crucified**, He appeared weak like other men. But Christ was raised from the dead by God's great power, and now He lives by God's power. In the same way, Paul appears weak; but he, too, lives by God's power (see Romans 6:5,8; Galatians 2:20). At first Paul came to the Corinthians in weakness, in **meekness and gentleness** (1 Corinthians 2:3; 2 Corinthians 10:1). But now Paul is ready to come to the Corinthians with the power and authority of Christ Himself.

If Paul came to our church today, what would he find? How would he come? Would he come **with a whip**, or **with a gentle spirit**? (1 Corinthians 4:21).

5 In our Christian lives one of the most important things we must do is to regularly examine ourselves (see 1 Corinthians 11:28). Are we **in the faith**? Are the fruits of our faith visible in our lives? Do we experience Christ living within us? Or do we **fail the test**? We must ask ourselves these questions.

But instead of examining ourselves, we spend more time examining our brother! Instead of looking for our own sin and confessing it, we prefer to look for our brother's sin. We consider ourselves "straight," and our brother "crooked."

When we do these things, how great is our sin!

6 If, when the Corinthians examine themselves, they discover that they do not **fail the test**, they will at the same time discover that Paul has not failed the test either. The reason is, of course, that their faith has come from Paul's preaching. If their faith is genuine, then Paul's faith also must be genuine. If they are in Christ, then Paul also must be in Christ.

7 Paul prays that the Corinthians will not do anything **wrong**—that is, he prays that they will repent of their sins and keep their church pure. If they do this, then Paul won't have to use his power and authority to punish sinners. If Paul doesn't use his power, it will seem as if he has no power. That is, it will seem as if Paul is not in Christ; it will seem as if he has **failed the test**. Well, if it seems that way to people, so be it. Paul's only desire is that the Corinthians repent, so that he won't have to come to them "with a whip."

8 If the **truth** has been established in the Corinthian church by the time Paul comes, then he won't have to use his power and authority. Paul's power is not for opposing the truth but for opposing sin and falsehood. If the Corinthians are not sinning, then Paul **cannot do anything against** them.

9 Paul's hope and prayer is that the Corinthians might be **strong**—that is, perfect and holy and strong in faith. If the Corinthians are strong in this way, then Paul will not have to use his own authority; that is, he will appear **weak**. That's why Paul says he is **glad** when the Corinthians are "strong" and he is "weak."

Notice that Paul doesn't use his authority just as he pleases. Those with authority must be very careful not to misuse it. Authority is not something to be taken and used for oneself. All authority comes from God, and it is to be used only in the service of others (see Mark 10:42–45).

10 Paul's main purpose in writing to the Corinthians can be seen here: namely, that the Corinthians might repent and that he might not have to be **harsh** with them.

Again we see the purpose of authority: it is for building people up, not for tearing them down (see 2 Corinthians 10:8).

Final Greetings (13:11–14)

11 **Aim for perfection**. That is, make perfection your goal. In verse 9, this is Paul's prayer for the Corinthians. Not only that, it is also the command of Christ: "**Be perfect, therefore, as your heavenly Father is perfect**" (Matthew 5:48).

. . . **be of one mind** (see Romans 15:5; 1 Corinthians 1:10 and comments).

12–13 **All the saints** are all the Christians with Paul at the time he is writing this letter (see Romans 16:16; 1 Corinthians 16:20).

14 This verse is perhaps the most quoted verse in the entire Bible. Here are mentioned the three forms or persons[24] of the one true God: namely, Jesus Christ the Son, God the Father, and the Holy Spirit. These three are one. Whatever they do, they do together.

Notice what Paul writes here. First comes the **grace of the Lord Jesus Christ**; second comes the **love of God**; and third comes the **fellowship of the Holy Spirit**. In a sense, we can say that we experience God in that order. First, we receive the **grace** of Christ, His forgiveness, His righteousness. Next, we experience the **love** of God filling our hearts. And third, we receive the Holy Spirit, who lives within us and gives us **fellowship**. But we need not separate grace, love, and fellowship. These are all the one work of the one God. And we need all three—**grace, love,** and **fellowship**—every minute of our lives.

May the grace of the Lord Jesus Christ, and the love of God, and the fellowship of the Holy Spirit be with you all.

---

[24] When referring to God, it is more accurate to speak of His three "modes of existence," rather than His three "forms" or "persons." For simplicity's sake, however, this commentary generally uses the word "form."

Galatians

INTRODUCTION

Galatia was a province of the Roman Empire located in the center of what is now modern Turkey. Paul's letter to the Galatians was written not to just one church but to several churches, all of which Paul himself had founded some years earlier. It is not certain exactly which churches Paul wrote to, as none are mentioned by name in this letter. Also, it is not certain what year this letter was written: Some say 54–56 A.D., while others say 48–49 A.D.

Paul's reason for writing is evident from the letter itself. No sooner had he founded these Gentile churches than certain Jewish Christians came and began to oppose Paul's teaching. Paul taught that man is saved by grace through faith alone (Ephesians 2:8), but these Jewish Christians said that to be saved it was also necessary to follow the Jewish law. If the teaching of these Jewish Christians prevailed, then Paul's Gospel of grace would become of no account. Thus Paul felt constrained to write this letter to counter the false teaching of the Jewish Christians and to protect the young believers of the Galatian churches from being led astray. If the Galatians were to begin seeking salvation through works of the law, they would be in danger of losing the grace they had received.

In the history of the Christian church, Paul's letter to the Galatians has been extremely important. It was after studying this letter that Martin Luther in the sixteenth century recognized the false teaching of the Roman Catholic church at that time, and started the Protestant movement. For it was by studying this letter that Luther discovered the central truth of the Christian Gospel: namely, that man obtains salvation not through any church or by following any law; rather, man obtains salvation solely by God's grace received through faith.

Worldly men seek salvation by their own work and effort. They try to please God by following various religious rules and rituals. They attempt to become holy by their own power. But their efforts are all in vain. It is only by grace that man becomes acceptable in God's sight. Out of His great love and mercy God has opened a door into heaven for sinful men. By believing in Christ we can pass through this door. This is the main teaching of this letter to the Galatians.

For further information about Paul's life, see Romans: Introduction.

OUTLINE

A. Introduction (1:1–10).
   1. Greetings (1:1–5).
   2. Reason for the Letter (1:6–10).
B. Paul's Defense of His Apostleship (1:11–2:21).
   1. Paul's Gospel Received Directly from God (1:11–24).
   2. Paul's Relationship to the Other Apostles (2:1–14).
   3. Failure of the Jewish Law (2:15–21).
C. Paul's Defense of the Gospel (3:1–4:31).
   1. Justification by Faith (3:1–14).
   2. The Law and the Promise (3:15–29).
   3. Paul's Appeal to the Galatians (4:1–31).
D. Call to Godly Living (5:1–6:18).
   1. Danger of Falling from Grace (5:1–12).
   2. Life by the Spirit (5:13–26).
   3. Two Practical Exhortations 6:1–10).
   4. Conclusion (6:11–18).

CHAPTER 1

Greetings (1:1–5)

1 Paul was an APOSTLE appointed directly by God and by Jesus Christ. He did not receive this appointment through any man. In the New Testament, an apostle was one who had received special authority from Christ to preach the Gospel and to establish churches. Most of the New Testament apostles had seen the resurrected Christ with their own eyes. Paul had seen Jesus while traveling to the city of Damascus to persecute the Christians there (see Acts 9:3–6; 26:12–15; 1 Corinthians 15:8). At that time he received from Jesus the appointment to be an apostle to the Gentiles, that is, to all non-Jews (Acts 9:15; 26:16–18). And now Paul writes to the Galatians—and to us—with the full authority of the Lord Jesus Christ. Let the Galatians, therefore, heed Paul's word. And let us do likewise (see Romans 1:1; Ephesians 1:1 and comments).

Notice here that Paul has been called by both **Jesus Christ and God the Father**. Christ and the Father are one God. They always do everything together. Even though in some verses only Christ is mentioned and in other verses only God is mentioned, we must remember that they always work together.

We Christians today have also, like Paul, been called to serve Christ. Even though we do not have the special authority that Paul received, nonetheless we have all been appointed to be disciples and co-heirs of Christ. Let us not suppose that it is only special apostles who can do Christ's work. God has given each of us our own work to do for Him, and He also through the HOLY SPIRIT gives us the necessary grace and strength to do that work. Jesus Himself said: "**. . . anyone who has faith in me will do what I have been doing. He will do even greater things than these, because I am going to the Father**" (John 14:12).

2 It is not certain which Galatian churches Paul is addressing in this verse. Many Bible scholars believe that Paul is writing to the churches in the southern Galatian cities of Pisidian Antioch, Iconium, Lystra, and Derbe (see Acts 13:14; 14:1,6,21–22; 16:1–2). Paul had visited all these cities on his first and second missionary journeys.

3 Paul prays for GRACE and PEACE for his readers. Grace and peace are the two main pillars of the Gospel. First grace; then peace. Grace is always first. Everything ultimately comes from the grace of God. By grace we are called. By grace our sins are forgiven. By grace we are saved. By grace we are justified and made holy, and by grace we have **peace** with God. Without grace there is no Gospel of Christ. Because of God's grace, Christ came to earth and **gave himself for our sins** (verse 4). Grace is the undeserved, unlimited, freely given love and mercy of God. Let us never stop praising God for the glory of His grace (see Romans 1:7; Ephesians 1:2,6 and comments).

Again notice that grace and peace come from both **God the Father and our Lord Jesus Christ** together. God and Christ are one (see John 10:30 and comment; General Article: Jesus Christ).

4–5 Christ **gave himself for our sins**. His sacrifice is complete and fully sufficient for our salvation. We need do nothing but place our faith in Christ.

Christ rescues us from the **present evil age**—that is, the world. The world is Satan's kingdom; Satan is the **prince of this world** (John 16:11). Christ doesn't take us out of the world; rather, He rescues us from the evil of the world (John 17:15).

No Other Gospel (1:6–10)

6–7 Paul is **astonished** at the behavior of the Galatians. The Galatians had only recently received the Gospel of grace, and now **so quickly** they had begun to turn from it.

Some Jewish Christians had come from Jerusalem and were trying to persuade the new Galatian believers to follow a **different gospel**, a "gospel" of salvation by works instead of by grace, and were thereby throwing the Galatians **into confusion** (verse 7). But their "gospel" is no gospel at all, says Paul. There is only one GOSPEL—the Gospel of salvation by grace.

What a sad and frightening thing these Galatians were doing! They had received the free and unlimited grace of God through the preaching of Paul. Now they were deserting both Paul and the God who had called them. They were denying and throwing away God's grace.

Paul is writing to oppose these false teachers who were **trying to pervert the gospel of Christ**. They were teaching that Christ alone could not save men, but that to be saved it was necessary also to obey the Jewish law. Such teaching makes the grace of Christ of no account. When grace is taken out of the Gospel, no Gospel remains. Paul does not want to see his spiritual children turned from the true Gospel in this way.

There is something that we must keep in mind as we read this letter. Paul is writing here about some Jewish Christians who were giving the Galatians the false teaching that it was necessary to follow the Jewish law to be saved. For us, this serves as an example of similar kinds of false teaching that continue to threaten Christian churches right up to this present time. No matter what country we are from, there are always those who teach that it is necessary to follow some law, or some religious custom or ritual in order to be saved. This is an utterly false and dangerous teaching. The truth is that only by God's grace is man saved. This is the essence of the Gospel of Christ.

8–9 From these verses we learn how great, how important is God's work, God's Gospel. We dare not change God's Gospel in any way. No preacher or teacher—not even an ANGEL—has the authority to change God's word. To preach and teach God's word is a heavy and awesome responsibility. We must preach and teach it faithfully, because if we preach a Gospel contrary to what is in the Bible, we shall be **eternally condemned** by God.

Let those who hear the word also take heed to hold fast to the one true Gospel, and not let themselves be deceived by false teachers.

10 Paul's opponents in Galatia, that is, these Jewish Christians, accused Paul of trying only to please men. They said that when Paul taught that it was not necessary to follow the Jewish law, he was merely trying to make the Galatian Gentile believers happy; he was trying to make it easy for them to obtain salvation.

But Paul says here that he is not trying to please men (see 1 Timothy 2:6). Indeed, Paul is about to sternly rebuke the Galatians in this letter. Paul says here that it is a very difficult thing to please men and at the same time be a **servant of Christ**. No matter what other men think, a servant of Christ must preach the Gospel faithfully (1 Thessalonians 2:4). The preacher's supreme purpose is this: to honor Christ and to lead men on the path to salvation (1 Corinthians 9:19,22–23).

Paul Called by God (1:11–24)

11–12 In these verses, Paul tells the Galatians that he is a true apostle. He preaches the true Gospel, which he received directly **by revelation from Jesus Christ** (verse 12). Paul first received this revelation when the risen Christ appeared to him on the road to Damascus (Acts 9:3–5).

The Gospel of Christ is not something that man made up. Apart from Judaism and Christianity, the other religions of the world are derived from the philosophy and ideas of men. But the Gospel of Christ is not like that. It is the good news of what God Himself has done. It is the full and final truth about God and about the way to obtain salvation.

Usually we Christians first receive the Gospel from hearing the preaching of other men or from reading the Bible. Sometimes we receive teaching directly from Christ through His Holy Spirit. Whenever we receive direct teaching through the Holy Spirit, it is never a new or different teaching. The Holy Spirit always agrees with what is written in the

Bible.[1] Paul, however, received the Gospel from Christ Himself, before the New Testament was written. If Paul had received the Gospel from some other man, he would have in a way been "lower" than that man. He would have been a "student apostle," or an "under-apostle." But Paul is fully equal with the other apostles like Peter (Cephas), John, and James (verse 9). No man has taught him the Gospel. He is a true apostle, and he teaches the true Gospel. Let the Galatians not doubt that!

And let us who study this letter of Paul not doubt it either. In the world today there are many doubters and agnostics. They say: "How can man know the truth? He can't." They also say: "All religions are good and beneficial, and all lead men to heaven." But such people think wrongly. The Gospel of Christ is the one and only true Gospel. Jesus said: "**I am the way and the truth and the life. No one comes to the Father except through me**" (John 14:6).

13–14 Paul here reminds the Galatians of the great change that had taken place in his life. With such great severity and violence he had persecuted the church of Christ in the beginning! (Acts 8:3; 9:1–2; 22:4). How strictly and zealously he had followed **Judaism**,[2] the religion of the JEWS (Acts 22:3; Philippians 3:4–6). The Jews believed that only through obeying the Jewish law could man be saved, and Paul had shared completely in this belief. But now Paul's main message is that man is saved only by grace through faith in Christ—this same Christ whose followers he had initially persecuted so intensely. Only God Himself could have brought about such a great change in Paul's life.

15 God had appointed Paul to be His apostle before he was even born. In the same way, God appoints each one of us from birth—indeed, from before birth (Psalm 139:13–16). In fact, He has chosen us from **before the creation of the world** (Ephesians 1:4). God does not choose us according to our own works or worthiness, but only according to His grace. Paul says here: God **called me by his grace** (see 1 Corinthians 15:9–10). We do not earn or merit our calling; God calls us before we are born.

For what does God call us? First, He calls us to be saved. Second, together with being saved, He calls us to be His adopted children (Ephesians 1:5), to be **co-heirs with Christ** (Romans 8:17). Third, God calls us to some task or service that He has prepared for us to do (Ephesians 2:10). Paul's special service was to preach the Gospel to the GENTILES (verse 16).

16 Paul writes here: God was pleased to reveal His Son **in me**.[3] It is not enough that Christ be revealed "to" us; He must also be revealed **in** us. Christ—that is, Christ's Holy Spirit—must dwell **in** us, or else our religion will be but a hollow form and our lives will have no spiritual power.

17 For three years after his conversion, Paul did not meet with the other apostles such as Peter and James, the Lord's brother. He did not receive teaching from any other man. He was taught directly by God and by Christ.

After his conversion, Paul went away into Arabia for a period, but it is not known what he did there. Perhaps he

---

[1] The Holy Spirit always agrees with the Bible, because the Bible was written through the Holy Spirit's inspiration in the first place. For further discussion, see General Article: How We Got Our Bible.

[2] **Judaism** is the religion and way of life of the Jewish people. About two thousand years before Christ, God called Abraham to be the father of the Jewish people. God chose the Jews to be His own special people. He gave them His law—the Jewish law—to obey. The Scriptures of the Jewish people are contained in the Old Testament. The Old Testament describes the history of the Jews; and it contains the Jewish law, as well as the writings of the Jewish prophets (see General Article: Summary of Old Testament).

[3] In place of the words **in me**, some translations of the Bible say "to me." However, in the Greek language, the words mean **in me**. This is what Paul actually wrote.

spent the time in prayer and in meditation on the Old Testament Scriptures, in the course of which he learned further about the work God had called him to do.

After his time in Arabia, Paul returned to **Damascus,**[4] which is where he had first gone after his conversion. Then, after three years in Damascus, Paul finally went up to **Jerusalem**[5] (verse 18).

We see from this that for Paul a time of preparation was needed. This is surely true for all of us. We do not immediately become mature Christians. God wants to prepare each one of us, and that takes time. For Moses, the great Old Testament leader of the Jews, the special time of preparation lasted forty years. In fact, it wasn't until Moses was eighty years old that he was ready to do the work that God had called him to do (Exodus 7:7; Acts 7:23,30). Let us not think, therefore, that we can be ready immediately!

By God's grace we are called. By God's grace we are prepared. Each of us is being prepared continually day by day, and so we shall continue to be prepared until we die. All of us need to learn more and more of the depths and the glory of God's grace.

All is by grace. By God's grace the stars and planets are held in their courses. By God's grace the right distance is preserved between earth and sun, so that we neither melt with heat nor freeze with cold. By God's grace we breathe, we eat, we laugh, we live. God does not need man's puny efforts to accomplish His purposes. All is accomplished by His grace. Neither does God's love for us depend on what we do for Him. He doesn't love us because of what we do; He loves us because of what we are—that is, His own children. And we are His children purely through His grace. Therefore, brothers and sisters, let us seek to live our whole lives **to the praise of his glorious grace** (Ephesians 1:6).

18 Three years after his conversion Paul finally met **Peter.**[6] Paul did not learn to be an apostle from Peter. Paul and Peter were equal in apostolic authority. But why does Paul feel the need to write this? The reason is because Paul's enemies in Galatia were saying that Peter was a genuine apostle, but that Paul was not.

This first visit of Paul to meet Peter is also described in Acts 9:26–30.

19–20 The **other apostles** mentioned here are mainly the original twelve disciples of Jesus (minus Judas Iscariot). But in addition to the Twelve, there were other apostles also, among whom was **James,** the brother of Jesus (1 Corinthians 15:7). At the time Paul wrote this letter to the Galatians, James was the main leader of the "mother church" in Jerusalem (Acts 21:18; Galatians 2:9). Here Paul says that on that visit he did not meet with any of the other apostles except James.

21 Paul stayed in Jerusalem for only fifteen days (verse 18). He did not preach in the surrounding province of Judea. Instead, he left the area and went to preach to the Gentiles in **Syria** and **Cilicia.**[7]

22–24 The churches of **Judea,** the southern province of Israel, remembered Paul (or Saul) as a persecutor. They had heard all about his evil deeds. But because Paul did not preach in Judea, the Judean Christians did not get the chance to become acquainted with the new Paul, the apostle of Christ. Nevertheless, they heard about Paul's preaching in Syria and Cilicia, and they praised God because of him. Those whom Paul had once persecuted were now thanking God for him. But the new Galatian

---

[4] **Damascus** is the capital of the Middle Eastern country of Syria.

[5] **Jerusalem** was the capital of the province of Judea, the southern province of Israel. Jerusalem was the chief city of the Jews; it was their holy city, the center of their religious life. And it remains so for the Jews up to this present day. Today Jerusalem is an important city in the modern nation of Israel.

[6] In place of the name **Peter,** some translations of the Bible say "Cephas." Cephas is the Greek word for Peter.

[7] **Cilicia** was a Roman province north of Syria (now southern Turkey).

Christians, whom Paul had never persecuted, were turning away from him. Those whom he had loved like a father from the beginning had begun to reject him.

CHAPTER 2

Paul Accepted by the Apostles (2:1–10)

1 Many Bible scholars believe that the journey to Jerusalem mentioned in this verse is the same as the journey described in Acts 15:1–29.[8] One of Paul's companions on this journey was **Barnabas**, a close colleague who had accompanied Paul on his first missionary journey (see Acts 9:27; 11:22–26; 13:2–3). The other companion, **Titus**, was a younger colleague of Paul, who is mentioned in 2 Corinthians 7:6–7,13; 8:16–17,23. Later, Paul wrote to him the New Testament letter called "Titus."

The reason for this trip to Jerusalem is clearly described in Acts 15:1–2. In Paul's time a major disagreement arose between those Christians who had originally been Jews and those Christians who were Gentiles. The Jewish Christians argued that it was necessary for the Gentile Christians to obey the Jewish law, the law of Moses (Acts 15:1,5). But Paul, taking the side of the Gentile believers, strongly opposed the teaching of the Jewish Christians. He argued that the Gentile Christians should not be forced to follow the Jewish law. Therefore, when Jewish Christians from Jerusalem and the surrounding province of Judea came to Galatia and began to teach the Gentile Galatian believers that they must obey the law of Moses, Paul decided to go to Jerusalem to refute their false teaching before the leaders of the Jerusalem church.

2 Paul went to Jerusalem **in response to a revelation**; that is, he had received a revelation from the Holy Spirit indicating that he should go to Jerusalem. Throughout his life, Paul was frequently guided in major matters by special revelations from the Holy Spirit (see Acts 16:6–10; 22:17–18; 27:23–26).

Paul set before the leaders of the Jerusalem church the **gospel that I preach among the Gentiles**. What Gospel was that? It was the Gospel of the grace of Christ, which states that man is saved not by observing the Jewish law but rather by grace alone, received through faith. If the Jewish Christian leaders in Jerusalem did not accept Paul's teaching, then indeed his preaching would be to no avail. He would truly be **running . . . his race in vain**.

Paul spoke **privately** to the leaders of the Jerusalem church. He did not want to stir up any unnecessary commotion or opposition among the ordinary Jewish Christians of that city.

3 Paul's meeting with the Jerusalem leaders was successful. One of the main points at issue was whether or not Gentile Christians had to be **circumcised**[9] according to the Jewish law. The Jewish Christians said it was necessary, and Paul said it was not. In the end, the leaders of the Jerusalem church took Paul's side. As evidence of this, they did not force Titus to be circumcised. (Titus

[8] Some Bible scholars, however, do not agree with this opinion. They say that the journey mentioned in this verse is the same as the one described in Acts 11:29–30.

[9] Circumcision is a minor surgical procedure in which the excess skin at the end of the penis is cut away. All Jewish males are required to be circumcised on the eighth day of life (Genesis 17:9–14). In Paul's time, circumcision was the chief outward sign of being a Jew. For further discussion, see Word List: Circumcision.

was a **Greek**[10] Gentile, not a Jew.) They accepted him as a full Christian brother even though he was not circumcised.

To us today this seems like a small matter. But in the history of the Christian religion, this meeting in Jerusalem was an event of great importance. Because from that time on it was officially established by the entire church—both Jewish Christians and Gentile Christians—that man is not saved by the observance of any law or man-made ritual, but only by grace through faith. This is the Christian Gospel. This is what makes the Christian religion different from all the other religions of the world. According to the teaching of all other religions, man must perform certain duties and observe certain customs and regulations in order to be saved. These religions are based on obtaining merit by one's own efforts. But the Christian religion is totally different. According to the Gospel of Christ, no one can earn salvation by his own works. Salvation is a free gift of God's grace, received through faith in the Lord Jesus Christ.

4 Those who were teaching that observance of the Jewish law was necessary for salvation Paul calls **false brothers**. They were not true Christians. Paul writes: they **had infiltrated our ranks**; that is, they had slipped into the churches like spies. They were like **wolves** dressed in **sheep's clothing** (Matthew 7:15). They were servants of Satan. They were trying to force new Christians who had only recently escaped from Satan's kingdom to again become **slaves** of Satan. They were trying to take away the new Christians' freedom and bring them again into bondage to the law. Satan knows he can never take away our salvation (John 10:27–29). Therefore, he tries to take away our freedom and our joy instead.

How can we recognize **false brothers**, or false prophets and teachers? There are two ways. First, we can recognize them by what they say (1 John 4:1–3). Anyone who acknowledges by faith that Christ is the Son of God and that He has come in the flesh is a true brother (see Romans 10:9). Second, we can recognize false brothers by what they do—that is, by their fruit, by their work (Matthew 7:16–18).

Is it possible for true brothers to fall into erroneous thinking? Yes, of course it is. Peter himself, Jesus' chief disciple, together with Barnabas, was later led astray by these same false Jewish teachers (verses 11–13). Yet Peter and Barnabas did not become false brothers just because they were in error on one point.

In this matter we must exercise great caution. It is our duty to correct a brother when he falls into error, but we must not be quick to call him a false brother. We may only call false brothers those who deny that Jesus Christ is God come to earth in the flesh.

Nevertheless, there are always some in the church who are ready at once to label a brother false if any disagreement arises between them. We must not judge our brother in this way (Matthew 7:1). In the end, it is only God who knows a man's heart (see Matthew 13:24–30).

5 Paul stood firm in his opposition to the false teaching of the Jewish brothers. He defended the truth of the Gospel, so that that truth might be preserved, not only among the Galatians but among all generations of Christians.

6 When Paul went to Jerusalem, those **who seemed to be important**—that is, the leaders of the Jerusalem church—**added nothing** to Paul's message. They accepted Paul's position. They did not insist that Gentile Christians follow the Jewish law.

Notice here that Paul does not consider these Jerusalem leaders and apostles to be above himself. Paul did not receive his apostolic authority from them. He received his authority directly from God.

---

[10] The Greeks were the inhabitants of the southern European country of Greece. In New Testament times, Greece was part of the Roman Empire. The Greeks were Gentiles—that is, non-Jews. The Greeks were a highly cultured people. In Paul's time, most of the educated people throughout the Middle East spoke Greek. The New Testament was originally written in the Greek language.

They perhaps **seemed to be important** in the eyes of men, but that doesn't mean anything to Paul. God looks on men according to their inner spiritual state, and not according to their outward position in the world.

Paul is not teaching here that we don't have to obey and respect our leaders. Rather, Paul is asserting that he himself is a leader and apostle, equal to Peter, James, and the other apostles in Jerusalem. Therefore, he is not obliged to follow their decisions. However, we ordinary Christians are expected to obey our leaders. We must obey not only our leaders within the church, but we must also obey our employers and government leaders in the places where we live and work (see Romans 13:1–2; 1 Peter 5:5).

7–8 Just as Peter and the other Jerusalem leaders had been entrusted with the Gospel, so likewise had Paul. Just as the Jerusalem apostles had been appointed to preach among the **Jews**,[11] so had Paul been appointed to preach among the **Gentiles**.[12] Therefore, in the same way that God was working through the other apostles, He was working also through Paul. Paul and the others preached the same Gospel, not two gospels.

9 Happily, the Jerusalem church leaders fully accepted the apostleship of Paul and Barnabas, and extended to them the **right hand of fellowship**.[13] Paul says: **. . . they recognized the grace given to me**—that is, the grace of apostleship (see Ephesians 3:7–8).

The chief leaders of the Jerusalem church at that time were **James**, **Peter** (Cephas), and **John**. These were the ones who Paul said were **reputed to be pillars** of the church. **John** was known as Jesus' beloved disciple; he later wrote the Gospel of John and the three New Testament letters bearing his name.

These Jerusalem leaders also agreed that Paul and Barnabas should work mainly among the Gentiles, and that the Jerusalem apostles should work mainly among the Jews. This was a completely reasonable arrangement. Some Christians are called to one kind of work, while others are called to a different kind of work. We each have a different assignment from God. Where He sends us, there we must be prepared to go.

10 The Jerusalem church leaders made only one request of Paul: namely, that he would continue to **remember the poor**. The leaders meant by that the **poor** believers in Jerusalem. We know from reading elsewhere in the New Testament that Paul indeed spent much time and effort in raising collections among the Gentile churches to send to the needy believers in Jerusalem (see Acts 11:29–30; Romans 15:25–26).

Paul Opposes Peter (2:11–14)

11 **When Peter came to Antioch,**[14] **I opposed him to his face**. In this section we read about a major disagreement between Paul and Peter. Let us notice that Paul opposes Peter **to his face**, not behind his back. Let us likewise, in the event of any disagreement with a brother, be sure always to speak directly with him face to face. Let us never fall into the sin of speaking against a brother behind his back.

Peter **was in the wrong**. He stood condemned—that is, self-condemned. His error was obvious to all—even to himself.

12 The disagreement between Paul and Peter was not primarily over doc-

---

[11] In place of the word **Jews**, some translations of the Bible say "circumcised," which is the actual word used in the original Greek text. The meaning, of course, is the same.

[12] Here also, instead of **Gentiles**, the actual word in the Greek text is "uncircumcised." The meaning is the same.

[13] The shaking of one another's right hand is a sign of fellowship among many people of the world. It was also so in Paul's day.

[14] **Antioch** is an important city in northern Syria. The establishment of the church at Antioch is described in Acts 11:19–26.

trine; it was mainly about social behavior. Peter had already agreed that the Gentile Christians did not need to obey the Jewish ceremonial regulations. In fact, Peter, a Jew himself, was not following Jewish customs. Indeed, he had been living like a Gentile (verse 14).

In what way was Peter wrong? Simply, he had stopped eating with the Gentile Christians at Antioch. And why had he done this? Because some Jewish "brothers" from Jerusalem had come to Antioch, saying that it was not right for Jews to eat with Gentiles. These men belonged to the **circumcision group**. That is, they were Jews; they taught that to be saved a man had to be circumcised. And Peter, for fear of these men, **began to draw back and separate himself** from the Gentile Christians.

In the Jews' mind, Gentiles were unclean. Therefore, the Jews supposed that by eating with Gentiles they themselves would become unclean. Even after a Jew became a Christian, such wrong ideas did not immediately vanish away. Peter knew that he was wrong to separate himself from Gentile Christians. He knew that Jewish and Gentile Christians were equal in God's sight; they were one in Christ (see Acts 10:27–28; 15:7–9; Galatians 3:28; Colossians 3:11). But Peter's old fears and customs overcame him, and he fell into error. We, too, sin against Christ if we refuse to associate or eat with a fellow Christian because of his caste or the color of his skin.

13 The other Jewish Christians at Antioch also joined Peter's **hypocrisy**. It was hypocrisy because in their speech they said that Jews and Gentiles were one in Christ, but in their actions they treated the Gentile Christians as if they were inferior and unclean.

From this sad incident let us learn how easy it is for us also to be led astray in various ways. Even great leaders like Peter and Barnabas can fall into error. And when leaders fall into error, they lead many others into error also. How important it is for leaders to set good examples—especially for the sake of new Christians (Mark 9:42).

14 According to Acts 15:13–14,19, the Jerusalem leaders agreed that it was not necessary for Gentile Christians to follow the Jewish law. The **truth of the gospel** is that both Jews and Gentiles are saved by grace through faith in Christ. Peter had agreed with this (Acts 15:7–11). What's more, he had even been living **like a Gentile**. But now he was again refusing to eat with the Christian Gentiles because they were uncircumcised and ritually "impure." By his behavior Peter was saying to the Gentiles, "If you do not follow the Jewish law, I will not eat with you." In this way he was, in effect, forcing the Gentile Christians **to follow Jewish customs**.

The Failure of the Jewish Law (2:15–21)

15–16 Paul here continues to speak to Peter and to the other Jewish Christians in Galatia. He says, "Yes, we are Jews, and **not Gentile sinners**." (The Jews considered all Gentiles to be sinners because they did not follow the Jewish law. Paul is here talking in the manner of the Jews.) "But," Paul goes on to say, "even we Jewish Christians **know that a man is not justified by observing the LAW**." Jews also, together with Gentiles, are **justified**—that is, declared RIGHTEOUS—only **by FAITH in Jesus Christ** (see Acts 15:11). This is the true Gospel that from the beginning Paul had taught to the Galatians. Having already been justified by faith in Christ alone, how can these Galatians now believe that to be justified it is necessary to obey the Jewish law? Let this not be!

At this point it is well for us to review exactly what is necessary for a man or woman to obtain salvation. The first and most important thing to remember is that all good things come from the grace of God. Because of God's grace, that is, because of His love, Christ came to earth to save men and women (John 3:16). All men are sinners, whether Jew or Gentile (Romans 3:9–10); therefore all men equally need a Savior to save them from the punishment for their sins, which is eternal death (Romans 6:23). While we were still undeserving sinners, Christ died for us (Romans 5:6,8). Because

Christ took upon Himself the punishment for our sins, we who believe in Him no longer stand condemned, but are declared righteous in God's sight (Romans 3:23–24). All this is the result of God's grace.

What, then, does a person have to do in order to be saved? He must believe in Christ—that's all. He must receive—appropriate—God's grace. God holds out His hand, but we must take the gift from His hand. Faith is the simple act of reaching out and taking God's gift of grace. This is why Paul wrote to the Ephesians: **For it is by grace you have been saved, through faith—and this not from yourselves, it is the gift of God** (Ephesians 2:8). Both our faith and God's grace are necessary for our salvation.

When we believe in Christ, we receive His righteousness; that is, we are declared innocent, we are **justified** (Romans 5:1–2). Therefore, it is no longer necessary for God to punish us for our sins. Instead, He pardons us and makes us His children. At the instant we are justified we obtain our salvation (Romans 5:9–10). And with salvation, we receive eternal life.

Therefore, to be saved we must first be declared righteous—**justified**. To be justified we must believe in Christ. In order to believe in Christ, we must first have received the grace of God. God has called us from before the creation of the world (Ephesians 1:4). Our salvation, our justification, our faith, our calling all begin in the infinite depths of God's grace. All this is one great work of grace (see General Article: Way of Salvation).

Therefore, let us never attempt to obtain salvation by following any law or man-made custom. We cannot gain salvation by accumulating merit. It will never work. Whenever we seek to obtain salvation through our own works, we are in effect denying Christ's work of grace (see Romans 3:20,28).

Paul says at the end of verse 16 that **by observing the law no one will be justified** (declared righteous). Why is that so? Because no one can faithfully keep every point of the law all the time. James wrote: **For whoever keeps the whole law and yet stumbles at just one point is guilty of breaking all of it** (James 2:10). What is the one commandment, in particular, that we can never fully obey? **You shall not covet** (Exodus 20:17). We perhaps can obey the first nine of the ten commandments, but we cannot always obey the tenth. **You shall not covet** essentially means that we must have no evil desires. Who has ever fully obeyed that command? No one! Therefore, no one can ever be justified by obeying the Jewish law, or any other law; it is impossible (see Romans 7:6–11).

17 Here Paul is still talking to Jewish believers. The Jewish Christians feared that if they stopped following the Jewish religious regulations their sins would surely increase. If this were true, then it would appear that faith in Christ only leads to more sinfulness. In other words, it would appear that **Christ promotes sin**. But this is not so, says Paul; indeed, the opposite is the case. If they stop seeking to be justified through faith in Christ alone, then in God's sight they will be even greater sinners. The only means of being made holy and pure is to put faith in Christ and receive His righteousness.

18 To put reliance on the law will make us worse sinners, says Paul. Paul will not **rebuild** what he has **destroyed**. In other words, Paul will not set up laws and regulations again which he has "torn down"—that is, declared unnecessary. If he were to set these laws up again, he would be rendering the "law of grace" of no account. He would be denying the work and sacrifice of Christ, by which alone man can be justified. He would be giving up the righteousness of Christ and looking to be justified by the law, the ineffective law. If he were to do this, he would surely become a **lawbreaker** in God's eyes, because **by observing the law** no one can be justified (verse 16).

19 The law cannot give sinful man new life; all it can do is to condemn man. The law gave Paul the death sentence. Paul says: **For through the law I died**. But when he died, he became free of the law. Once a judge gives the sentence, his work is finished. His power over the criminal ends. By serving his sentence, the criminal becomes "free" of the judge. In a similar way, Paul has become free of the law; Paul has **died** to the law. Having given Paul the death sentence, the law can no longer touch him. Paul is like a slave who through death becomes free of his master. And now, being free of his old master, the law, Paul is free to serve Christ, to **live for God** (see Romans 7:4,6–7; 8:1–2 and comments). Not only is Paul now free to live for God, but he also has the power to live for God, because Jesus Christ now dwells within him (verse 20).

20 **I have been crucified with Christ**. What a deep and amazing testimony Paul gives here! Before anyone can receive new spiritual life, he must first die. That is, his **old self** must die; it must be placed on the CROSS (Romans 6:6). To be crucified with Christ means that our old sinful self dies. Then Christ's nature and character can fill our lives. His Spirit, the Holy Spirit, enters us, and through the Holy Spirit we receive power to lead holy and righteous lives. But it is not we—that is, our old self—that is living; it is Christ who is living in us. Our old sinful self is dead. We are free of it. We are no longer under the power of our sinful nature (see Romans 6:3–8 and comment).

Paul says: **I no longer live, but Christ lives in me**. Can we also say that about ourselves? Let each of us ask ourselves: Who is living in my body? Is it my old self, or is it Christ? Can we say with Paul: **Christ lives in me**?

This is the real meaning of the Christian life: It is Christ living in the believer. We don't have to live our lives on our own. Instead, through faith we let Jesus live in us. Jesus said: "**Remain in me, and I will remain in you**" (see John 15:4–5). Because Jesus lives in us we shall be able to live like Jesus. Then other people will be able to see Christ in us, and want to become Christians too.

Paul says: **The life I live in the body,**[15] **I live by faith in the Son of God**. The **Son of God** is Jesus Christ, who came to earth to die for our sins, so that we might receive salvation and eternal life (see Mark 10:45 and comment).

21 **I do not set aside the grace of God**. That is, Paul will not again attempt to gain salvation by the works of any law. If man could be saved by the law without faith in Christ, then Christ would certainly have **died for nothing**!

CHAPTER 3

Faith or Observance of the Law (3:1–14)

1 The foolish Galatian believers have been bewitched. Paul had clearly taught them that they had been saved through Christ's death on the cross. Before their very eyes **Christ was clearly portrayed as crucified** (see 1 Corinthians 1:23–24; 2:2). Why should they now begin to put reliance on their own works?

2 Paul asks the Galatians just one question: "How did you receive the Spirit? That is, how did you become Christians?" The Galatians knew the answer. They received the Spirit **by believing what they heard**—that is, by believing Paul's message. First we hear, then we believe; and then we receive the Holy Spirit (see Acts 2:38; Romans 10:14; Ephesians 1:13).

3 In the beginning the Galatians had received the Holy Spirit through faith. They had received new life in Christ. Therefore, Paul asks, "Why are you now **trying to attain your goal by human**

---

[15] In place of the word **body**, some translations of the Bible say "flesh." Here the meaning is the physical body. In other verses in the New Testament, the word "flesh" is used to mean man's sinful nature (Romans 8:3–13; Galatians 5:16–19); but that is not the meaning here. For further discussion, see Word List: Flesh.

effort?"[16] That is, why are the Galatians now trying to become holy by their own effort, by their own works? They have already learned that man can become holy (or justified) only through faith. Now these Galatians are turning from the power of the Spirit and relying instead on the weakness of man. They are trying to prove to God how righteous they are by their own works. But in God's sight, no one is ever righteous because of works (Galatians 2:16).

4 The Galatians had already suffered much because of their faith in Christ. Now if they give up that faith, they will have suffered for nothing. Paul then adds: **. . . if it really was for nothing**. In saying this, Paul is expressing the hope that indeed their suffering will not have been for nothing.

5 Paul here repeats the question of verse 2. The Galatians know that it is because of their faith, not works of law, that God has given them His Spirit and worked miracles among them. Paul is reminding them of what they already know. After receiving such blessing from God and seeing His mighty works of grace among them, how can the Galatians now reject His grace and put their reliance on the law?

6 **ABRAHAM**, the father of the Jews, serves as an example for all men. He was declared righteous by faith, not by works. Paul here quotes from Genesis 15:6. Abraham's faith **was credited to him as RIGHTEOUSNESS** (see Romans 4:1–3 and comment).

The Jewish teachers in Galatia were teaching that to be declared righteous it was necessary for one to be circumcised and to obey the Jewish law. They also claimed that to be righteous in God's sight, one had to be a descendant of Abraham according to the flesh; that is, one had to be a Jew. But Paul shows from the Jews' own Scriptures (the Old Testament) that only by faith is a man declared righteous by God.

7 All those who place faith in Christ are Abraham's spiritual descendants. Through faith, Gentiles inherit the blessings that God promised to Abraham and his descendants. Therefore, the true descendants of Abraham are not those who are natural descendants according to the flesh (that is, Jews), but those who believe in Christ (see Romans 4:11,13,16 and comment).

8 Paul quotes from the book of Genesis to show that God promised Abraham that all nations would be blessed through him (Genesis 12:3; 18:18; 22:17–18). **All nations** means not only Jews but Gentiles as well. The Jews believed that only they would inherit the blessings promised to Abraham, because only they were his natural descendants according to the flesh. But one cannot inherit spiritual blessing through the flesh, that is, through one's natural birth. Only through faith can man receive spiritual blessings. Therefore, believing Gentiles will receive all these blessings through faith.

9 Paul here repeats the thought of verse 7.

Let us remember that Abraham was not justified (declared righteous) on the basis of circumcision, because when Abraham first believed he had not yet been circumcised (Romans 4:9–11). Again, he was not justified by obeying the law, because in Abraham's time the law had not yet been given (Romans 4:13). The law came only in Moses' time, 430 years later (verse 17). Therefore, only by faith was Abraham declared righteous. In the same way, only through faith in Christ can we too be declared righteous in God's sight (see Acts 13:38–39; Romans 5:1).

10 If we do not obey everything in the law, the law will condemn us (see James 2:10). Therefore, if we rely on the law, we will be **under a curse**—that is, under the death sentence. We shall receive the sentence of death. Why? Because no one can obey everything in the law continuously without slipping.

[16] In place of the words **trying to attain your goal by human effort**, some versions of the Bible say, "ending in the flesh," which is the literal translation of the Greek text. The meaning is the same. In this verse, the Greek word for "flesh" means our sinful nature. For further discussion, see footnote to comment on Galatians 2:20; Word List: Flesh.

Paul quotes here from Deuteronomy 27:26.

11 No one is justified by the law because no one can fully obey it. Paul quotes from the Old Testament prophet Habakkuk: **The righteous will live by faith**, not by the law (Habakkuk 2:4; Romans 1:17).

12 Here Paul quotes from Leviticus 18:5. **The man who does these things** (the works of the law) **will live by them** (see Romans 10:5). If any man obeys the law perfectly (which is impossible), he shall live. If not, he will be condemned. Therefore, the law is not based on faith, but on man's works and obedience.

13 The **curse of the law** mentioned here is the death sentence. Christ **redeemed us** by taking upon Himself our death sentence. Since the sentence is removed from us, we become innocent and righteous in God's sight.

God says: "Man must be punished for sin. Whom shall I punish?" Jesus, standing in our place, says: "Punish me instead of them. Let them go free" (see Mark 10:45).

Christ redeemed us from the curse of the law. We can better understand this by using another illustration. We were once like slaves in bondage, and the Jewish law was our master. In order for us to gain freedom, it was necessary for someone to pay our master a price, a ransom. Jesus paid that price for us. The price He paid was His own blood, that is, His own life. He gave His life for us. Now we are no longer under the authority of the law; we belong to Christ. He paid the price for us; He bought us. We are His (see 1 Corinthians 6:19–20; 7:23; 1 Peter 1:18–19).

Paul quotes here from Deuteronomy 21:23. This is a prophecy concerning Christ's death on the cross—the **tree**. Through His death He became a **curse for us**. At the time the book of Deuteronomy was written, executed criminals were hung on trees as a sign of their "curse," their shame. Instead of a tree, Christ was hung on a wooden cross; however, the principle is the same.[17]

14 Because of the **curse of the law** (verse 13), the blessing promised to Abraham in Genesis 12:3 was never fulfilled in the time of the Old Testament. But Christ has come and removed the curse. Now, because of the sacrifice of Christ's body on the cross, we can receive through faith in Him the blessings promised to Abraham. Through faith in Christ we become not only the true children of Abraham; we also become the true children of God (Romans 8:16). Not only that, but we also receive the promise of the Holy Spirit, which is like an advance on the inheritance stored up for us in heaven (see 2 Corinthians 1:21–22; 5:5; Ephesians 1:13–14).

From this verse we can see what the promise is that God gave to Abraham and his descendants. It is salvation. It is new spiritual life in Christ through the Holy Spirit, a new life which begins as soon as we believe and which will never end.

The Law and the Promise (3:15–20)

15 In order to describe the promise God made to Abraham, Paul uses an illustration from ordinary life. Men make various kinds of covenants with each other other. Once a COVENANT is made, it is fixed, it is **established**. It cannot be easily changed.

16 In the same way, God made a covenant with Abraham. God made sure promises **to Abraham and to his seed**. The promise was that Abraham's descendants would receive salvation and the Holy Spirit. Therefore, the **seed** (offspring) means Christ and all those who place their faith in Him. Christ is the firstborn, the firstfruit of a new spiritual family or nation (see Romans 8:29; 1 Corinthians 15:20). The promises were not made to all the **seeds**—that is, to all the natural offspring of Abraham—but only to Christ, and through Christ to those who believe. God said to Abraham: "**. . . through your offspring all nations on earth will be blessed** (Genesis 22:18).

---

[17] In the time of the Roman Empire (that is, Christ's time), criminals were executed by hanging them on a cross.

In Christ, therefore, the promise God gave to Abraham is fulfilled.

17 Here Paul makes his main point. God gave the promise of salvation to Abraham 430 years before the law was introduced (Exodus 12:40). How, then, can those Jewish teachers in Galatia say that the law is necessary for salvation? The promise of salvation in no way depends on the law; nor does the coming of the law in any way affect the promise.

18 If the law were necessary to obtain the **inheritance** (that is, salvation), then the promise God gave Abraham would become void. If the law were necessary for salvation, then the covenant God made with Abraham would be altered—in fact, canceled. But that cannot be done (verse 15). God's promise can never be canceled. Paul is saying that God gave Abraham and his spiritual descendants an inheritance (salvation) not through the law that would come afterward, but **through a promise** which arose out of God's grace and is received through faith (see Romans 4:14,16). Salvation is given to man by grace alone. We cannot earn it by obeying the Jewish law, or any other law (see Romans 11:6).

19 Therefore, it is natural to ask, what was the purpose of the law? **It was added because of transgressions**. The law was given by God to manifest sin, to bring sin into the light (see Romans 5:20 and comment). Before the law was given, there were sins that man did not recognize, such as covetousness. God gave the law so that all men could see their own sin, so that each man could understand that he was a sinner (see Romans 3:20; 7:7).

The law clearly demonstrated that man cannot save himself nor make himself righteous. The law showed that all men are in need of a Savior, that is, Christ. In other words, the law pointed to Jesus Christ, and the law remained in effect **until the Seed** (Christ) **to whom the promise referred had come**. After Christ came, the law was no longer necessary.

Nevertheless, the law continues to serve an important function: It shows us what sin is. Jesus Himself based much of His teaching on the Jewish law (see Matthew 5:21–22,27–28,38–39,43–44).

The law is inferior to the promise. The law was temporary. It remained in effect only until Christ came. Now Christ has saved us from the condemnation, the **curse**, of the law.

The law was not given directly from God to man, as the promise was. The law was given through a **mediator**—that is, Moses[18]—together with the help of **angels** (Exodus 31:18; Acts 7:53). Therefore, since the promise came directly from God (instead of through a man), it is superior to the law, which came through Moses and the angels.

20 A **mediator** represents not one party but two. By taking the side of both parties, the mediator helps bring them to an agreement. The giving of the law to the Jews through Moses, the mediator, was like an agreement between two parties. God gave the law: man had to obey it. God did something, and man had to do something in return—that is, obey. In order for a covenant to be made, both parties must take part. Thus, when the old covenant between man and God was made, a **mediator** (Moses) was needed.

But a promise is different from a covenant or agreement. To make a promise, only one party is necessary—that is, God. When God makes a promise, He acts alone. He gives the promise freely. All that we men and women have to do is to accept the promise. Without any human or angelic mediator,[19] God comes to us

---

[18] Moses was one of the greatest leaders of the Jews. He was born about four hundred years after Abraham's time. He received the law from God on top of Mount Sinai, and passed it on to the Jewish people. It was through Moses, then, that the Jews received the law. This is why Moses is called a **mediator**.

[19] In 1 Timothy 2:5, Paul writes: **For there is . . . one mediator between God and men, the man Jesus Christ**. But remember, Jesus Christ was not only a man; He is also God Himself. Therefore, God Himself is the "mediator" of the promise of salvation given to men. No other mediator is necessary.

and offers the promise of salvation and the Holy Spirit. And through the Holy Spirit, that is, through Christ dwelling within us, we receive the power to obey the law. With the promise comes power.

The Purpose of the Law (3:21–29)

21 The law does not oppose the promise. The difference between the law and the promise is only this: The law has no power; the promise has. The law cannot **impart life**, but the promise can. To **impart life** means to make alive—to make spiritually alive, spiritually powerful. If the law could have given us spiritual life and power, then we could have become righteous through the law. But the law could not (see Romans 8:3). And because the law could not impart life and power, no one could become righteous by observing it. Only by grace through faith in Christ can one be made righteous in God's sight and obtain salvation (Ephesians 2:8).

22 **But the Scripture** (God) **declares that the whole world** (all mankind) **is a prisoner of sin**. In other words, because men rebelled against God, He placed them under bondage to sin (Romans 3:9–10; 11:32). Because men sinned against God, He condemned them through the law. But now God has given man a way of escape, a promise of salvation, which promise we receive through faith in Christ.

Therefore, how can the Jewish teachers at Galatia say that following the law is a means of salvation? The law can only condemn (Romans 7:10). Their teaching is the opposite of the truth.

23 Paul here repeats the thought of verse 22. **Before this faith** (the Gospel of Christ) **came, we were held prisoners by the law**. In verse 22, Paul said that we were prisoners **of sin**. The meaning is the same: to be held prisoner **by the law** and to be a prisoner **of sin** is the same thing. Sin and the law work together to condemn us. Sin gets its power from the law (see Romans 7:8–11; 1 Corinthians 15:56).

24 Because of man's sin, it was necessary that man remain under someone's control. In Paul's day, wealthy families hired special tutors or custodians to look after their children. The children were placed under the authority of the custodian. In the same way, the law **was put in charge** of us; it was our "custodian." Just as a custodian brings up the students under his charge, so the law became our custodian **to lead us to Christ**.

25 Now that the Gospel has come and we have believed in Christ, we no longer need to be under the **supervision of the law**—that is, we no longer need a custodian.

26 In Paul's time, a son did not receive his full rights and authority as a son until he reached the proper age. Before that, he remained under the authority of the custodian (Galatians 4:1–2). Those who have placed faith in Christ are like sons who have come of age; they are now fully sons. They are sons of God (John 1:12–13; Galatians 4:7). Paul says to the Galatian Christians: **You are all sons of God**—whether you are Jew or Gentile, slave or free, male or female (see verse 28).

27 When we come of age and become full sons, we take off our old student uniform and put on new clothes. In the same way, when we believe in Christ we take off our old clothes and put on Christ—that is, we put on His righteousness. When we are **baptized into Christ**, we become **clothed . . . with Christ**. This is the real meaning of BAPTISM.. When we are **baptized** in Christ's name, we put off our old sinful life, our old self, and put on a new self, new spiritual life in Christ (see Romans 6:3–4,6; 2 Corinthians 5:17; Ephesians 4:22–24 and comments).

28 Who, then, can come to Christ in faith? All can come. Spiritually there is no difference between people. All are equally entitled to be sons and daughters of God through faith. And when we are baptized in Christ, when we have been **clothed . . . with Christ**, we become one family, even one body (see 1 Corinthians 12:13 and comment). We all—**Jew** and **Greek** (Gentile), **slave** and **free**, **male** and **female**—become **one in Christ Jesus**.

Think of the great difference there was

in Paul's time between Jew and Gentile, master and slave, men and women. The Jews despised the Gentiles; slaves were crushed under the power of their masters; men looked down on women, regarding them as inferior. Yet in Christ there was no difference between any of them. In Christ, all became one (see Colossians 3:9–11).

Among Christians there can be no difference between high caste and low caste, between rich and poor, between foreigner and national. As we each look about us within our own churches, do we see any of these differences? Are those of low caste treated with the same respect as those of high caste? Are women treated as respectfully as men? Are there differences made between foreigners and nationals? Do the nationals say: "This is our church; the foreigner is only a visitor"? But such differences should not be. The church does not belong to one group or another; it belongs to Christ! The church is Christ's body (1 Corinthians 12:27; Ephesians 1:22–23). In each local church we are all one in Christ. Where is the difference between high caste and low caste, between foreigner and national? Our citizenship is in heaven, not in this world. In heaven there are no castes, and no foreigners. If we allow any of these differences to remain in our churches, we are guilty of dividing Christ's body into pieces.

29 Christ is the true **seed** (offspring) of Abraham (verse 16). Therefore, when we put faith in Christ we also become true seed of Abraham (verse 7). We become **heirs—co-heirs with Christ** (Romans 8:17). We inherit the **promise**—the promise of salvation, of eternal life.

CHAPTER 4

Heirs Through Faith (4:1–7)

1–2 In Paul's time, an heir who was not of age had no more authority than a household slave. He remained completely under the authority of **guardians and trustees**.

3 Before Christ came, we also were **in slavery under the basic principles of the world**. That is, we were slaves to worldly beliefs and practices; we were slaves, in fact, of Satan and his evil spirits (Galatians 3:23; Colossians 2:20). We were like heirs who had not come of age. We were under the authority of a "guardian," that is, the law. But at the same time, we were slaves under the **basic principles of the world**.

These **basic principles** that Paul mentions here are all man's rituals, traditions, and customs. Included here would be idol worship, and all the religious laws and regulations established by men. Included also would be all of man's works of law, all his attempts to become holy by his own effort. Also included would be evil spirits, under whose servitude man does all these works (see Galatians 4:8–9; Ephesians 2:1–2).

4 **But when the time had fully come**—that is, when we heirs had come of age—**God sent his Son**, Christ (see Romans 5:6). Christ was **born of a woman**, just as we were (see Matthew 1:18; Philippians 2:6–8). He experienced all man's temptations and weaknesses (Hebrews 2:15,18; 4:15). He was **born under law**. God, the lawgiver, came to earth as a man, and put Himself under His own law. In this way He was able to completely fulfill the law. Not only that, He also paid the price for our sins according to the law. That price was his own life—because the **wages of sin is death** (Romans 6:23).

5 Why did God send His Son? He sent Him **to redeem those under law**—that is, those under the **basic principles of the world**, both Jews and Gentiles. We were once like slaves, and our master was Satan, the **prince of this world** (John 12:31). Therefore, because we were Satan's "property," Christ had to pay a price to **redeem** us from Satan (Galatians 3:13).

But when Christ "purchases" us, we are no longer slaves as before. We become Christ's brothers and sisters, that is, adopted children and full heirs of God (Ephesians 1:5; 1 John 3:1).

What does it mean to be an adopted child of God? An adopted son is one who has been made the heir of someone who is not his natural father. Even though he is the natural son of another man, the adopted son receives the full inheritance of his new father.

Similarly, in a spiritual sense, believers in Christ are also adopted children. First, according to the flesh we were children of darkness, that is, children of Satan (Ephesians 2:3; 5:8). But now we are children of God, not according to the flesh but according to the Spirit. We have received the **full rights of sons**—that is, we have been adopted as sons (see John 1:12–13).

Here let us remember one thing. If we choose not to leave the **basic principles of the world**—that is, Satan's kingdom—Christ will not purchase us. He will only **redeem** those who turn to Him in faith. He never forces people to enter His kingdom against their will.

6 Having become adopted children, what is our inheritance? Our inheritance is eternal life in heaven. Do we also get any inheritance in this life? Yes, we receive the Holy Spirit now as an advance on our full inheritance. And the Holy Spirit is not only an advance on our heavenly inheritance; He is also like a sign, a seal, placed on us, which gives proof that we are God's adopted children, now and forever (see 2 Corinthians 1:21–22; Ephesians 1:13–14).

As soon as Christ redeems us, God sends the **Spirit of his Son** (the Holy Spirit) **into our hearts**. To obtain salvation, to become adopted children of God, to receive the Holy Spirit—these always go together. They are all aspects of the same salvation. Through the Holy Spirit we know with complete certainty that we are God's children. We personally experience the heavenly Father's presence in our lives. We can call out to Him: "**Abba,**[20] **Father.**" Because of the witness of the Holy Spirit in our hearts, we have no doubt that we are fully children of God (see Romans 8:14–16).

7 As soon as the Holy Spirit (the Spirit of Christ) enters our hearts, we are set free. We are no longer slaves, but sons. And if we are sons, we are also heirs (Romans 8:17). Think of the greatness of God's possessions. And we are the inheritors of them!

Let us reflect for a moment on what it means to be an adopted son or daughter of God Himself. It is the highest of all the blessings God gives to us. Some people believe that all men are children of God, but this is not true. Yes, God is the Creator of all men, but He is not the Father of all men. Only those who believe in Christ can legitimately call God their Father (see John 1:12–13; Galatians 3:16).

In no other religion is God called Father. The followers of other religions cannot fully know God, because they do not know Him as Father. Yes, they know that God is living, holy, all-powerful, all-knowing. But God is more than all this. God is also our loving and merciful heavenly Father. And we who believe in Christ are His children.

Paul's Concern for the Galatians (4:8–20)

8–9 The Galatians were formerly slaves of Satan and his evil spirits. They worshiped idols, who were no gods (1 Corinthians 8:4), and who could neither hear them nor help them in any way. They were slaves of the **basic principles of the world** (verse 3).

But now they know the true living God. He is their Father. He has made them His own children, and the inheritors of all His spiritual possessions. He has given them freedom. He has given them eternal life. How then can the Galatians turn back and allow themselves to be

[20] **Abba** was an informal Aramaic expression meaning "my father." Aramaic was the language spoken by most of the common people in the Middle East during New Testament times; it was the language spoken by Jesus and His disciples (see Mark 14:36).

enslaved again by those **weak and miserable principles** (verse 9), which have no power to save them? (see Colossians 2:8). The **weak and miserable principles** Paul mentions here are the same as the **basic principles of the world** he mentioned in verse 3. In particular, Paul is thinking here of the ceremonial regulations of the Jewish law.

Here an important question arises: What is the reason that men seek to please God? The followers of other religions seek to please God in order to obtain blessings for themselves. But we who believe in Christ seek to please God because of the blessings He has already given us. We desire to show our gratitude. Because we are His children we want to act like His children. Paul wrote to the Ephesians: **. . . you are light in the Lord. Live as children of light** (Ephesians 5:8). From this we can see the difference between the Christian religion and all other religions. Other religions say: Obey, so that you might be saved. The Christian religion says: Obey, because you have been saved. On the one hand men obey God in order to receive some benefit. On the other hand Christians, having already received the benefit, obey God in order to show their gratitude.

But the followers of other religions are misled, because it is not possible for man to be saved by obeying religious rules and regulations. To seek salvation by following a religion is of no avail. Salvation is obtained only by grace through faith (Ephesians 2:8). The Galatians had already begun to forget that.

Let us, therefore, ask ourselves: Why do we try to please God? Why do we try to do His will? Is it in order to obtain salvation? In order to obtain some blessing? If so, then we are acting like the **foolish** Galatians (Galatians 3:1). Rather, we should be obeying God because of the grace He has showered upon us. The Apostle John has written: **We love because he first loved us** (1 John 4:19). If God's love and grace had not first been poured out upon us, we would never have been able to please Him.

Outwardly the behavior of Christians and the behavior of followers of other religions may appear to be similar. They both are trying to please God. But the difference lies in their reason or motive for pleasing God. The followers of other religions try to please God for their own sake. The followers of Christ try to please God for God's sake.

10–11 In these verses Paul expresses his despair over the Galatians. They have begun again to follow the Jewish customs and rituals. They are observing all the Jewish special days and ceremonies (see Colossians 2:20). Paul fears that his work among them has been in vain.

12 **. . . become like me** (see 1 Corinthians 11:1). "Become like me," says Paul. "I am free of the law, free of the **basic principles of the world** (verse 3). You can be free too. Don't seek to become like the Jews."

Then Paul adds: **. . . for I became like you**. That is, Paul is saying, "I, a Jew, have become like you Gentiles. I no longer rely on the works of the law; I have accepted Christ through faith alone, just as you Gentile Galatians have done."

The Galatians had done Paul **no wrong**. Rather, they had loved him. Paul now asks them not to oppose him, but to love him as they did at first.

13 When Paul first went to Galatia, he developed an **illness**. Perhaps because of this illness he was not able to travel on, but was obliged to remain in Galatia to recover. Thus, the Galatians gained the opportunity to hear Paul's Gospel.

What Paul's illness was is not known with certainty. Some think it was the result of being stoned in the Galatian city of Lystra (Acts 14:19–21). Others think it was the **thorn** in Paul's flesh that Paul mentions in 2 Corinthians 12:7.

14 In spite of his illness and weakness, the Galatians could see the power of Christ in Paul's life and speech (1 Corinthians 2:3–4; 2 Corinthians 4:7). God had told Paul: "**My grace is sufficient for you, for my power is made perfect in weakness**" (2 Corinthians 12:9–10). The Galatians had regarded Paul as if he were an angel, as if he were Christ Himself (see Acts 14:8–15). Why, then, do they now turn away from him?

15–16 **What has happened to all your joy?** asks Paul. In other words, what had become of the Galatians' joy in their new freedom, in their salvation? They had once been joyful and free. Now Satan was taking away their joy and freedom. Satan cannot take away a Christian's salvation (John 10:18), but he surely can take away a Christian's joy and his sense of freedom.

When Paul speaks of **joy** here, he is really talking about spiritual joy, a joy that does not depend on worldly circumstances. Joy is one of the fruits of the Holy Spirit (Galatians 5:22). We experience joy because we are no longer in bondage to the law, to the world. But now these Galatians had begun to turn back to the "basic principles" of the world, to the Jewish rules and regulations; and, as a result, they had lost their joy.

When we observe followers of other religions carrying out their various rituals, do we see joy and satisfaction on their faces? No, more often we see fear. They fear lest they fail to observe some rule or ritual, and thereby incur the anger of their gods.

But those who are in Christ have no such fear. God is their loving Father. For them rules and rituals are no longer necessary. There is freedom and joy in God's family. Paul does not want to see the Galatians lose this freedom and joy.

Those of other religions often suppose that the Christian religion is very easy to follow: There are no rules! And in one way they are right (see Matthew 11:28–29). But it is not because there are no rules that it is easy to follow Christ. Rather, it is easy to follow Christ because He gives to us through the Holy Spirit the power to follow Him, as well as the joy of doing so.

In the beginning the Galatians had been so joyful and grateful for hearing Paul's Gospel that they would have done anything for him. They would even have **torn out** their own eyes[21] and given them to him, had it been possible. Paul hopes that they will not now become his enemies simply because he has told them the truth about their errors.

How easy it is for those who were once our friends to become our enemies! And how quick we are to count as enemies those who tell us the truth about our faults!

Nevertheless, we must always be prepared to speak the **truth in love** (Ephesians 4:15), even if in so doing we sometimes make an enemy. But let us be sure it is the **truth** that we speak! And let us be sure that we speak it **in love**, face to face, and not behind a person's back. If we follow these precautions we shall avoid speaking many unwise and harmful words.

17 Paul says: **Those people** (the false Jewish teachers) **are zealous to win you over**. These teachers were zealous to persuade the Galatians to follow them. They wanted to be big and important and to have many disciples. They wanted the Galatians to serve them instead of serving Paul. Therefore, they tried to **alienate** the Galatians **from us**; that is, they tried to separate the Galatians from Paul, so that the Galatians would **be zealous for them**.

18 In the beginning the Galatians had been **zealous** for Paul. They had zealously sought to hear his Gospel. But now Paul was no longer with them, so they were beginning to be zealous for these false teachers, whose **purpose** was **no good** (verse 17). Let this not be, urges Paul. Even though he is now absent from them, let them not abandon the true teaching he has given them.

19–20 Paul, like a mother, has given birth to the churches in Galatia. But now again he is **in the pains of childbirth**. The reason is because the Galatians have turned from the Gospel. They will have to be "born" all over again.

Paul's main goal and desire is that Christ be **formed** in the Galatians (verse 19). This is the goal of every true pastor and preacher. Just as a mother's birth pains do not cease until the child is **formed** (delivered), so Paul's pain will not cease until Christ is formed in the Galatians.

. . . **until Christ is formed in you**. To

---

[21] This is a common saying in countries of the Middle East. It means that one would do anything for another person.

have Christ **formed** in us means to have Christ live in us through His Spirit (Romans 8:10–11). It also means to **be conformed to the likeness** of Christ (Romans 8:29; 2 Corinthians 3:18). And finally, it means to **become mature, attaining to the whole measure of the fullness of Christ** (Ephesians 4:13).

The Example of Hagar and Sarah (4:21–31)

21 If the foolish Galatians really want to live under the Jewish law again, then they had better learn **what the law says**! Here, by the word **law** Paul means the first five books of the Old Testament.[22]

22–23 Here Paul mentions two women, one slave, one free. The **slave woman** is Hagar, who was the slave of Abraham's wife Sarah. Abraham's first son, Ishmael, was born from Hagar (Genesis 16:1–4,15).

The **free woman** is Sarah. Sarah had been barren all her life. She had reached ninety years of age. It was physically impossible for her to have a child (Genesis 16:1; 17:17). Yet God had promised that she would conceive and bear a son for Abraham (Genesis 17:15–16). Sarah's son was born **by the power of the Spirit** (verse 29), that is, by God's power. His name was Isaac (Genesis 21:1–3).

24–25 **Hagar** represents the law, that is, the old covenant (or Old Testament). Sarah represents grace, that is, the new covenant (or New Testament).

Now Hagar stands for Mount Sinai (verse 25); that is, she represents Mount Sinai. It was on top of Mount Sinai that God gave the Jewish law to Moses (Exodus 31:18). Hagar, therefore, represents all those who are under the law, namely, the Jews. She also represents Jerusalem, because Jerusalem is the holy city of the Jews. (Recall that it was from Jerusalem that the false Jewish teachers had come to Galatia in the first place; it was because of them that Paul has written this letter.)

Because Hagar was a slave, her children are slaves also. They are slaves to the law. The Jews prided themselves that they were the true sons of Abraham according to the flesh, that is, by natural descent. But here Paul says that they are not sons, but slaves. They are like the sons of the slave woman.

26 **But the Jerusalem that is above is free.** The **Jerusalem that is above** is the heavenly Jerusalem—that is, the kingdom of God (see Hebrews 12:22; Revelation 21:2). It is the city where Christ lives, and where there is freedom from the law.

Sarah corresponds to the Jerusalem that is above. She is the "mother" of all believers in Christ. She is the mother of all true heirs of Abraham born **as the result of a promise** (verse 23)—that is, born as a result of the promise God gave to Abraham and Sarah that they would have a child.

27 Here Paul quotes from Isaiah 54:1. The **barren woman** is Sarah. Let her **break forth and cry aloud** with joy. Because she will have more descendants than Hagar **who has a husband.**[23]

28 God's promise—that is, His word—is powerful. It is a living word. It gives life. Through God's word Sarah gave birth to a child, Isaac, even though she was ninety years old! In the same way, through God's word of grace, the Galatians have been born **by the power of the Spirit** (verse 29). They too are citizens of the heavenly Jerusalem, the true offspring of Abraham, not by natural descent but by the grace of God. Why should the Galatians now turn back and seek to live like children of Hagar the slave woman?

29 According to Genesis 21:9, Hagar's son Ishmael, who was born **in the ordinary way** according to the flesh, **persecuted** Sarah's son Isaac, who was born **by the power of the Spirit. It is the**

---

[22] The first five books of the Old Testament are often called the Law, or the Law of Moses.

[23] Abraham took Hagar to be his second "wife" when Sarah had no children (Genesis 16:1–4). Therefore, Sarah became like one "without a husband," while her slave Hagar became like one **who has a husband**.

same now, Paul says. In Paul's time, believers in Christ, born according to the Spirit, were being persecuted by the Romans and Jews, who had been born according to the flesh. The heirs of the flesh always persecute the heirs of the Spirit.

30 According to Genesis 21:10, which Paul quotes here, Sarah said to Abraham, "**Get rid of the slave woman** (Hagar) **and her son** (Ishmael)." And Abraham did as Sarah said (Genesis 21:12–14). In the same way, the Galatians should **get rid of** the false Jewish teachers, who were sons of the flesh.

31 We who believe in Christ are children of the **free woman,** Sarah. We are **children of promise** (verse 28). We are God's children by grace, that is, by the gift of God. We have been made His children by the power of the Holy Spirit (Romans 8:14), which we have received through faith in Christ (Galatians 3:26).

Therefore, let us not throw away so great a gift. Let us not throw away the grace of God by putting our faith in the works of any law or any religion. Let our faith be in Christ, and in Christ alone.

CHAPTER 5

Freedom in Christ (5:1–12)

1 **Christ has set us free.** He has delivered us from the curse of the law, that is, the death sentence (Galatians 3:13). We were like prisoners in jail waiting to die. Then Christ, by dying in our place, set us free (Romans 7:6). For anyone set free in this way, to try to get back into jail would indeed be crazy! But the Galatians were doing that very thing. Having been set free from the prison house of the law, they were once again putting themselves back under the same bondage. **Stand firm, then,** says Paul. Do not let this happen!

2 One kind of bondage the Galatians were putting themselves under was circumcision. It is not wrong to be circumcised (see Acts 16:3). But it is wrong to be circumcised thinking thereby to obtain salvation. If we suppose that we can be saved by circumcision or any other works of law, then we make Christ's work of no account. We are denying Christ. There will no longer be any **value** in having accepted Christ. If we do not put faith in Christ alone, He will not save us. We are not saved by Christ plus the law; we are saved only by Christ.

3 Paul reminds the Galatians that circumcision by itself has no value. If they are hoping to be saved by the law, then they must keep the whole law, not just part of it. And there are over six hundred different commands and regulations in the Jewish law. To obey every one of these perfectly all the time is impossible (see Galatians 2:15–16; 3:10).

4 Law and grace oppose each other. We cannot mix law and grace together. The Galatians had been justified and saved by grace. But now they had begun to put their trust in the law, in their own work and effort. If they persist in this, they will lose their grace. They will be **alienated from Christ,** who is their Savior.

There are some people who receive Christ by grace, but after a little while turn away (Mark 4:16–17). They return to their former religion. Those who do this, like the Galatians, **have fallen away from grace. Stand firm,** says Paul (verse 1). Do not let this happen.

We cannot mix Christianity with other religions. We cannot merely add Christ to the other gods we previously worshiped. Either we place faith in Christ or we place faith in our old religion, but not both. Christ is not one of several roads to heaven; He is the only road (see John 14:6 and comment).

A man cannot walk on two roads at the same time. A man who thinks he can trust Christ for salvation and continue to trust in his old religion is fooling himself. Anyone who tries to do this is not truly believing in Christ. Such a person will not find salvation.[24]

5 The Jewish teachers in Galatia taught that man becomes righteous by obeying the law. But Paul says that only **by faith . . . through the Spirit** can righteousness be acquired—that is, Christ's righteousness. It is through faith in Christ that we are declared righteous (Romans 5:1–2), and thereby escape **condemnation** (Romans 8:1).

6 To obtain salvation **in Christ Jesus,** it makes no difference whether one is circumcised or not circumcised. There is no advantage in being circumcised, and no disadvantage in being uncircumcised (Galatians 6:15). We are saved only through faith in Christ.

Here an important question arises: What is faith? Many people say, "I believe, I believe," but it means nothing (see Matthew 7:21 and comment). Why does it mean nothing? Because their faith is not genuine. Faith must express itself **through love,** or else it is a false faith (see James 2:14,17 and comment).

When we believe in Christ, the Holy Spirit comes into our lives, and through the Spirit God's love is **poured out . . . into our hearts** (Romans 5:5). Love is the first and most important fruit of the Holy Spirit (verse 22). Therefore, true faith always produces in our hearts love for God and for our neighbor. And if love is in our hearts, it must flow out of our life into the lives of others. In other words, we must demonstrate our inward love to our neighbor. Genuine faith is always **expressing itself through love.**

7 The Christian life is like a race (2 Timothy 4:7; Hebrews 12:1). The Galatians had started well. But the false teachers had hindered them. Not only that, the Galatians had even begun running in the wrong direction! They had taken their eyes off Jesus (Hebrews 12:2). The Galatians had stopped **obeying the truth** of the Gospel. The **truth** is not only to be believed; it is to be obeyed.

8 Paul says to the Galatians: **That kind of persuasion** (the false teaching that works of the law are necessary for salvation) does not come **from the one who calls you**—that is, God.

9 Even a small amount of such false teaching can do immeasurable harm. **A little yeast** (false teaching) **works through the whole batch of dough.** It spreads through the whole church (see 1 Corinthians 5:6 and comment).

10 Yet Paul has not given up hope for the Galatians. He has confidence that they will **take no other view** than his, that they will not turn away from the true Gospel. The false teachers who are **throwing** [the Galatians] **into confusion** will **pay the penalty**—that is, they will be punished by God.

11 Some Galatians were so confused that they had accused Paul of preaching that it was necessary to be circumcised! But if that were true, answers Paul, the Jews would not be persecuting him. Yet the Jews were continually persecuting him; therefore, that accusation must be false.

If Paul preached circumcision, the **offense of the cross** would be removed. If men could be saved by being circumcised, there would be no need to preach about Christ's death on the cross. For the Jews, the cross of Christ was an **offense,** that is, a **stumbling block** (1 Corinthians 1:23). The Jews scoffingly said, "How can a dead criminal hanging on a cross save us? That's absurd!" Therefore, they opposed Paul, because he preached that man is saved, not by circumcision, but through faith in the crucified Christ.

Men do not like to hear about the cross.

---

[24] In most cases, when a person becomes a follower of Christ, he must completely turn from his old religion. However, there is an exception to this rule. Jews who become Christians do not have to "turn from" Judaism. Paul and the other apostles all remained "Jews." Christ Himself was a Jew. The thing a believing Jew must turn from is his reliance on the works of the law as a means of salvation; he must put his entire trust in Christ.

There is a second possible exception: Islam. Some Christians believe that a Muslim does not have to give up all Islamic practices when he becomes a follower of Christ. But the Muslim (like the Jew) must change his belief about Christ. To be a true Christian one must believe that Jesus is God incarnate, the one and only Savior of mankind.

Christ looks down from the cross and says: "Believe in me, and I will save you." But man replies: "I can save myself. I don't need anyone's help. I'm worthy enough. I can keep the law." And therefore, so saying, man opposes the message of the cross. The cross has become a "stumbling block" for him.

12 Paul has some harsh words for those **agitators**, the Jewish teachers who were unsettling the Galatians by telling them that they must be circumcised to be saved. Paul says: "Let such teachers not only be circumcised, but let them castrate themselves as well!" In Paul's time, some people among the pagan nations used to castrate themselves in order to please their gods. Let the false Jewish teachers do likewise!

Life by the Spirit (5:13–26)

13 God created man to be free. Man was made for freedom, not for slavery (John 8:32,36; Romans 8:2; Galatians 5:1). But, says Paul, **do not use your freedom to indulge the sinful nature.**[25]

As Christians we are indeed free. However, we are not free to sin (Romans 6:1–2,12–14). We are free from bondage to the law, but we are not free to break the law. Even though we are free, our lives must remain holy and perfect (Matthew 5:48; 1 Peter 1:15–16).

Followers of other religions often accuse Christians of leading loose lives, lives without any law. They accuse Christians of bad behavior, of doing whatever they please without regard for others. And it must be said that all too often such accusations are true! But it should not be so.

We Christians are free, but we do live according to a law. And that is the law of love (see Mark 12:29–31; John 13:34–35 and comments). We are free to serve one another in love. A slave does not serve his master out of love, but rather out of duty and fear. But we, being free, serve one another in love. Only free men can love freely.

We Christians have been **set free from sin**, but at the same time we have made ourselves **slaves to God** (Romans 6:22). We have been set free from our old master, the law, which leads us to death; but we have become servants of a new master, Christ, who leads us to life. We used to obey the law because of fear. But now we obey Christ, not because of fear, but because we love Him (John 14:15,21; 1 John 4:18).

14 The Jewish teachers in Galatia should have known all about love. Their own Jewish law is **summed up in a single command: "Love your neighbor as yourself"** (Leviticus 19:18; Matthew 22:35–40; Mark 12:31; Romans 13:8–9; Galatians 6:2).

A question arises: Is Paul giving us here a new law that we must follow, like the Jewish law? If he is just giving us another law, then we Christians are no different from the Jews.

But this new law of love is not like the old Jewish law, nor is it like the laws and regulations of other religions. In the first place, the Jews and the followers of other religions follow their laws and traditions in order to be saved. But we Christians do not follow the law of love in order to be saved. Rather, it is because we are already saved that we follow it. We are saved through faith in Christ, not because we follow any law. It is not because we follow the rules of the Christian religion that we are saved. We are saved because we follow Christ the Savior. Our salvation is not from a religion, but from a person—Jesus Christ.

The second difference is this: The Jews and those of other religions attempt to follow their laws and traditions in their own strength. But we Christians do not follow the law of love in our own strength. We have received Christ's Holy Spirit; it is by the Spirit's power alone that we follow the law of love. Our love does not come from our own nature, but from

---

[25] In place of the words **sinful nature**, some versions of the Bible say "flesh," which is the literal translation of the original Greek text. The meaning is the same. In this chapter, the Greek word for "flesh" is translated **sinful nature**, as it is also in Romans Chapter 8. For further discussion, see Word List: Flesh.

the Holy Spirit who dwells within us. We love others because of the love that has been **poured out . . . into our hearts by the Holy Spirit** (Romans 5:5).

Yes, Christians indeed must obey the law of love. But through the Holy Spirit God gives us the strength to do so. Everything we do is done through the grace and power of God.

Here another question arises. The law says: **Love your neighbor as yourself**. What is the meaning of **as yourself**? Does it mean that we love ourselves and our neighbors equally?

No, it doesn't mean that. We are to love our neighbor more than we love ourselves. Christ said: **"If anyone would come after me, he must deny himself and take up his cross and follow me"** (Mark 8:34). Following the example of Jesus Himself, we should be prepared to give even our own lives for the sake of others (John 15:13).

Therefore, the expression **as yourself** means this: We who are spiritual should love others as much as the natural man loves himself. The natural man loves himself first of all—above others. Therefore, we who are spiritual should love others first of all—above ourselves.

Paul does not mention the first commandment here: **Love the Lord your God with all your heart and with all your soul and with all your mind and with all your strength** (Mark 12:30). Every Jew knew that that was the first and greatest commandment. Paul doesn't even need to mention it. However, we need to remember that if we don't love God, we certainly won't be able to love our neighbor. Love for God always comes first.

Yet, on the other hand, we cannot say we love God if we do not love our neighbor. True love for God is always followed by love for our neighbor (1 John 4:20–21). And who is our neighbor? Our neighbor is anyone in need (see Luke 10:25–37). Everyone, therefore, is our neighbor.

15 Where there is no Holy Spirit, there is no love. Where there is no love, men will **keep on biting and devouring each other**—that is, they will oppose, accuse, and slander each other.

If we accuse and slander each other, our church will be **destroyed**. Jesus said: **"If a house is divided against itself, that house cannot stand"** (Mark 3:25). Even if the negative things we say about someone else are true, it will still destroy the church. It is still slander. Slander is anything we say against our brother, whether true or false. If our brother has fallen into error or sin and we are obliged to accuse him, we must first do it to his face privately. We must give him a chance to answer for himself (see Matthew 18:15 and comment). Only after that are we entitled to go to the elders in the church with our complaint (see Matthew 18:16 and comment). But among ourselves, we are never entitled to speak against another brother or sister.

16 We who have received the Holy Spirit must therefore **live by the Spirit**. We must be led by the Spirit. We must place our **sinful nature** (our flesh) under the control of the Spirit. If we do this, the Spirit will restrain us from gratifying the **desires of the sinful nature**. In other words, the Spirit will keep us from falling into sin. But in order to avoid falling into sin, we must continuously submit to the Spirit. We must at all times walk in dependence upon the Spirit.

And finally, if we do not **live by the Spirit**, if we are not **led by the Spirit**, we shall not be able to call ourselves sons and daughters of God (see Romans 8:14).

17 Even though we have put our faith in Christ and have received the Holy Spirit, our old sinful nature does not completely die and disappear. Even though it has been placed under the control of the Spirit, it is always present with us. And it always opposes the Spirit. It opposes the new self, the new spiritual life, which we received when we believed.

Therefore, there is continual warfare in our souls, and this warfare lasts until we die. The new spiritual self seeks to do good, but the old sinful self prevents him (Romans 7:18–19).

As long as we **live by the Spirit** (verse 16), our **sinful nature** is kept under control. When we live by the Spirit, our

sinful nature is crucified; that is, it is made powerless (see Romans 6:6–7,12–14; Galatians 2:20; 5:24 and comments). When we live by the Spirit, we do not need to **gratify the desires of the sinful nature** by sinning, because the sinful nature has no power over us. We are free from the power of sin. This is the deepest meaning of our freedom in Christ.

However, if we stop living by the Spirit, if we stop depending on the Spirit, immediately our old sinful nature will spring to life and come down from the cross where we had placed it; then, once again, we will come under its control. If this happens, we will lose our freedom and become slaves to sin all over again.

18 **But if you are led by the Spirit, you are not under law**. The law here is the Jewish law, which Paul elsewhere calls the **law of sin and death** (Romans 8:2). To be under this law is to be under a **curse** (Galatians 3:13); it is to be under a death sentence; it is to be under the power of sin. Paul says that if we are led by the Spirit, we no longer need to remain under such a law. Yes, in our soul there is warfare between flesh and Spirit, but we can be victorious in that warfare every day. We do not need to be defeated by sin.

How then do we obtain this victory over sin? We obtain victory by continually letting the Spirit lead us. We do not have to struggle on our own. But we must place ourselves under the control of the Spirit (Romans 8:9). Through the Spirit's power we shall remain victorious.

The Jews and the followers of other religions believe that by obeying laws and traditions they will be prevented from falling into sin. But this is not true. Laws have no power to keep men from sin. Yes, perhaps laws can keep men from committing some outward sins, but laws cannot keep men from committing inward sins. Laws cannot cleanse men's hearts from sinful desires. Only through the power of the Holy Spirit dwelling in us can we be victorious over the inner sins of our hearts. And let us remember this: God looks primarily on our hearts, not our outward actions (1 Chronicles 28:9; Jeremiah 17:10; Mark 7:6).

We must ask here: Why do Christians sin so often? They sin because they want to sin. They sin because they decide to sin. When temptation comes, the Spirit says to us: "Come to me." But we refuse. And at once we fall into sin. And not only do we fall into sin, but something else happens: The Spirit withdraws from us. The Holy Spirit does not want to live in an unholy body. The Spirit is grieved. This is what Paul meant when he wrote to the Ephesians: **. . . do not grieve the Holy Spirit of God** (Ephesians 4:30). Only when we have confessed our sin and repented of it will the Spirit return to us.

Is there anyone among us whose spiritual life is dried up or wilted, who is without spiritual power? If so, let him look into his heart and find there the hidden sin which has caused the Spirit to depart. And let him bring that sin into the light, and then let him turn from it. Because whenever we grow distant from God, the reason is never far to find: It is always because of some hidden (or not so hidden) sin in our heart (see General Article: Revival).

19–21 Now Paul lists some of the sins that separate us from God. Let us look carefully at each of these **acts of the sinful nature**. Can we recognize any of them in our own lives? (see Romans 1:29–31).

We quickly and easily see sins in other people. But we are not so quick to see the same sins in ourselves. In our own eyes we seem righteous.

But we ought not to look at the sins of others—we should look only at our own. And let us pray that the Holy Spirit will clearly show us all of our hidden sins (Psalm 139:23–24).

Of the fifteen sins mentioned here, eight of them have to do with division and strife among Christians; that is, they have to do with our **biting and devouring each other** (verse 15).

Within the church there are only two legitimate reasons for opposing a brother or for remaining separate from him. The first is when a brother continues in a public and grievous sin without repenting (1 Corinthians 5:11). The second is when a brother denies that Jesus is God Himself, who has come in the flesh; that is, when a brother does not teach the truth about Jesus Christ (1 John 4:2). If we oppose any brother for reasons other than these two, we shall be guilty of committing one or more of the sins that Paul has mentioned in these verses.

. . . those who live like this will not inherit the KINGDOM OF GOD. That is, those who commit these sins habitually without repenting will not enter the kingdom of God. From time to time we all fall into some of these sins, and when we do we can quickly repent and ask forgiveness, and God will cleanse us (1 John 1:9). But he who knowingly continues in sin without repenting will not inherit the kingdom of God—that is, he will not be saved.

22–23 Those who **live by the Spirit** (verse 16) will manifest the **fruit of the Spirit** in their lives. This **fruit** will appear in the lives of those who remain in Christ (John 15:4–5). Here in these important verses, Paul tells us what these fruits are.

Let us first remember, however, that the fruits of the Spirit are different from the **gifts** of the Spirit. The gifts of the Spirit are given to various Christians at various times according to the will of the Holy Spirit (see 1 Corinthians 12:7–11). But the fruits of the Spirit are to be manifested by all Christians at all times. Both in the church and in our individual lives, the fruits of the Spirit are more important and more essential than the gifts of the Spirit.

The first fruit Paul mentions is **love,** love for God and love for neighbor (see verses 13–14 and comment).

The second fruit is **joy**—that is, spiritual joy. This joy continues even in the midst of hardship and suffering. This is the joy that comes to us by God's grace; it is the joy of our salvation (John 15:11; Philippians 4:4).

The third fruit, **peace,** is first of all peace with God. We have this peace through faith in Christ (Romans 5:1; Philippians 4:7). Having first found peace with God, we then must strive to promote peace with our brothers and sisters in the church (Romans 14:19; Ephesians 4:3).

The fourth fruit, **patience,** is endurance in trial and hardship. It also means having sympathy and understanding for our brother. We must be patient with our brother's weaknesses and sins (Ephesians 4:2). Just as Jesus has been patient with us, let us be patient with each other (1 Timothy 1:16).

Paul next mentions **kindness, goodness,** and **faithfulness.** Kindness means being merciful and forgiving (Matthew 18:21–22). Goodness means seeking opportunities to do good to all men. Faithfulness means being faithful and reliable.

Then, in verse 23, comes the eighth fruit: **gentleness.** Gentleness involves being gentle not only in our outward behavior but also in our inward spirit. Inward gentleness is the same as humility. This is the most delicate of the fruits of the Spirit; it easily perishes. The hardest sin for man to overcome is pride, which is the chief enemy of gentleness or humility. We usually don't even recognize our pride, but it is always present. And if we think we have overcome it, that merely proves we haven't!

Or perhaps we think we are humble, but then suddenly someone insults us and at once we are hurt and offended. Why? Because of pride. If we had no pride, we would take no offense. Whenever we seek to preserve our honor, we do so because of pride. A humble man, a man with a gentle spirit, does not care about his own honor. He cares only about the honor of Christ.[26]

We can't drive out our pride; only the Holy Spirit can do that. Only the Spirit can make us inwardly gentle and humble.[27] We need to pray continually for humility. But we must also keep in mind that in order to make us humble the Spirit will have to inflict some pain upon our pride. Are we ready to bear the humbling work of the Spirit?

The final fruit of the Spirit is **self-**

---

[26] However, it's true that when we are dishonored, Christ is dishonored also. Therefore, for Christ's sake (not ours) we should try to avoid bringing dishonor upon ourselves.

[27] The Spirit's work is to make us humble. Our work is to humble ourselves (1 Peter 5:5–6).

control. This means placing our old sinful self under the control of the Spirit. It means refusing to **gratify the desires of the sinful nature** (verse 16).

How can we tell if the fruit of the Spirit in our lives is fully "ripe"? We can tell by the same means we use to tell if any fruit is ripe: by squeezing it. As long as our circumstances are happy, it is easy to be a Christian. The fruits of the Spirit in our lives may appear to be completely ripe. It is only when trouble comes—when we are "squeezed"—that we can test whether the Spirit's fruit in us is ripe or not. When abuse, slander, persecution, and other hardships come upon us, how do we react? When our fruit is squeezed, what kind of juice comes out? The bitter juice of hurt or pride? Or the sweet juice of love, joy, patience, humility? Our lives are tested only when we are squeezed.

Let us remember that these nine fruits are produced not by our work and effort, but by the Holy Spirit dwelling in us. If these fruits are visible in our lives, then we are fulfilling God's law in our lives. If these fruits are present in our lives, we will be holy and righteous, and no law will be able to condemn us. There is no law which says these fruits are evil. **Against such things** (these nine fruits of the Spirit) **there is no law** (verse 23).

24 For the Holy Spirit to fully come into our lives, our **sinful nature** must be put on the cross. According to Paul's teaching in Romans, it is our **old self** (which is under the control of the sinful nature) that is placed on the cross (Romans 6:6). Here, Paul says that our **sinful nature** itself must be placed on the cross. In one sense, our old self must die. But in another sense, our **sinful nature** does not die completely. We must continually "crucify" our sinful nature. Daily we must hang our old nature on the cross (Luke 9:23). And we must keep it there![28]

Does our old nature enjoy being crucified? Of course, not! It is not a pleasant thing to be hung on a cross. It is not easy to endure. Therefore, it is not easy to live a Christian life. In fact, it is impossible!

But God doesn't demand that we "live a Christian life." God only says that we must **live by the Spirit** (verses 16,25)—one day at a time. We must walk in dependence on the Spirit—one step at a time. It is only **by the Spirit** that we can lead lives that are pleasing to God.

25 **Since we live by the Spirit, let us keep in step with the Spirit**. If we are under the control of the Spirit, then we should act as if we were! If we are indeed the children of God, then we should act like children of God!

Here an important question arises. We know that as soon as we believe in Christ we are declared righteous in God's sight. This is completely true. But we also know from experience that our daily behavior is not always righteous. We can explain both of these facts by a simple illustration. We are like fruit ripening on the tree. At first the fruit is green and hard. But gradually, with sun and rain, the fruit becomes ripe. God knows that, just as the fruit will ripen, so we also in the end will become fully ripe. For this reason He can regard us even now as if we were already fully ripe. But in our own eyes, we remain hanging on the tree, parts of us still green and hard.

It is by God's grace that we began our Christian life. It is by God's grace, by His rain and sun, that we are ripening—that is, becoming holy and perfect. And it is by God's grace that the day will come when we shall be fully ripe and perfect, even as Christ is perfect, and we shall enter with joy into His kingdom. Brothers and sisters, let us never stop praising God for the glory of His grace! (Ephesians 1:6).

26 Paul here gives three examples of behavior that is not of the Spirit. First, being **conceited** means wanting to look good in other people's eyes. Second, **provoking** other people means, in this context, putting them down. Third, **envying** means resenting that others

[28] The New Testament speaks of two kinds of crucifixion for the believer: active and passive. In Romans 6:6 and Galatians 2:20, our old self is crucified through faith in Christ; this is our "passive crucifixion." But in addition, according to Mark 8:34, Romans 8:13, and here in Galatians 5:24, there is also an "active crucifixion" of our sinful nature, which we ourselves must carry out daily.

appear better or more fortunate than we. Because of conceit and envy, we seek to provoke others, to put them down. By doing this, we think to elevate ourselves.

But Jesus taught that if we do this, the result will be the opposite of what we had hoped: **"For whoever exalts himself will be humbled, and whoever humbles himself will be exalted"** (Matthew 23:12). Therefore, let us exalt our brother and sister, and let us humble ourselves.

CHAPTER 6

Doing Good to All (6:1–10)

1 **Brothers, if someone is caught in a sin, you who are spiritual should restore him gently.** Those **who are spiritual** are those who **live by the Spirit** (Galatians 5:16,25). We who are spiritual must take responsibility for our fellow believers in the church. When they fall into sin, we should first try to restore them gently, not rebuke them. We must never secretly rejoice when our brother falls. Rather we must restore him humbly, looking to ourselves—that is, keeping our own weaknesses in mind. Because the temptation that comes upon our brother today can come on us tomorrow. When we see a brother fall into sin, let us always remember that there but for God's grace go I (see 1 Corinthians 10:12). Let us think: "How would I like to be treated if I were to fall into sin?" In that way, then, let us treat our brother.

2 **Carry each other's burdens.** What are these **burdens**?

Some burdens are caused by one's work and responsibilities. Perhaps our brother's work is hard. He is tired. Therefore, we must help him carry his work burden.

Other burdens are things like anxiety, disappointment, sadness, weakness, sickness. These burdens can be both of body and of spirit.

The third kind of burden is sin. For our brother, his sin is a burden. Perhaps he has a temper. He knows it is a sin to lose his temper. Nevertheless, from time to time he gets angry. For him it is a great burden. How can we help him carry that burden?

We can help him carry his burden by forgiving him, advising him, restoring him gently, and accepting him lovingly—along with his sin. Let us never say: "Only after my brother's bad temperament and bad habits are corrected will I accept him." Remember, Christ did not say that to us. He accepted us with all our weaknesses and sins. Christ bore our burdens on the cross.

When our brother sins, shame and disgrace come upon him. But sometimes, because of his sin, shame and disgrace fall upon us also—upon the church. The church is dishonored. In this way our brother is also sinning against us. We receive trouble and grief as a result of his sin. Must we bear that, too?

Yes, we indeed must bear it. This is the deepest meaning of this verse. That is, we must not only bear our brother's burden of sin, but we must also be prepared to suffer because of it. That is exactly what Christ did for us. Therefore, let us be ready to suffer for our brother's sin. If we do, we shall **fulfill the law of Christ**. For Jesus said: **"Love each other as I have loved you"** (John 15:12).

3 Compared with God, man is **nothing** (Psalm 8:4). Therefore, let us not think we are **something** when we are not. Let us not think we are good, worthy, important, or we shall deceive ourselves through pride.

Let us never compare ourselves with other people. If we do so, we shall always be striving to appear better than they. Rather, let us compare ourselves only with Jesus. If we do this, we shall remain more humble!

4 We are each responsible for our own **actions**, that is, our own behavior. We must test our actions. Just as the fruit is proof of the tree, so our actions, our behavior, is proof of our faith. If a person's work and actions are good, he will be able to **take pride in himself,** Paul says. Paul does not mean here that we should put pride in ourselves, because we know that all our good works are done only through God's grace (1 Corinthians 15:10). Paul simply means that we must not compare ourselves with others. We cannot **take pride** in the fact that our brother is weaker or more sinful than we are. Rather, we can **take pride**—that is, rejoice—only if our work and actions are pleasing to God (2 Corinthians 10:17–18).

Let us compare ourselves only with Christ. When we compare ourselves with Christ, then we shall be able to see how weak and sinful we really are; and, as a result, we shall not be so quick to look down on others.

5 In verse 2, Paul says: **Carry each other's burdens**. Here he says: Each one **should carry his own load**. Is Paul contradicting himself? No. The **load** mentioned here in verse 5 is different from the **burden** mentioned in verse 2. Here in verse 5, **load** means duty or responsibility. We each must do our own duty, whatever it is. We each must fulfill the responsibility which God has given to us. Each of us alone will have to give an account to God of what we have done on this earth (Romans 14:12; 2 Corinthians 5:10).

6 Preachers or pastors or others who teach the word of God may be poor. They may fall into physical need. If that should happen, we who have been blessed by their instruction should be ready and eager to help them, and to **share all good things** with them (see Romans 15:26–27; 2 Corinthians 9:11–12).

7 **A man reaps what he sows.** This rule is established both in the natural world and in the spiritual world. This rule applies to all men. We cannot fool God: He knows what we have sown.

As much as we give to others, that much we shall receive again from God. **A generous man will prosper; he who refreshes others will himself be refreshed** (Proverbs 11:25; 2 Corinthians 9:6).

8 He who **sows to please his sinful nature**—that is, he who serves his sinful nature—will receive the sinful nature's reward: **destruction** (death). He who **sows to please the Spirit** will receive the Spirit's reward: ETERNAL LIFE (see Romans 6:21–23; 1 John 2:17).

If one wants to reap spiritual fruit, one must do spiritual work. If one wants to reap the sinful nature's fruit, which is death, then let him do the **acts of the sinful nature** (Galatians 5:19–21). God is always just. God rewards us according to our work. He will always give us what we have worked for!

9 Many Christians begin their Christian lives with eagerness and enthusiasm. But then they slowly **become weary**. Some even stop running altogether (Galatians 5:7).

Are there any among us who are **weary**? Let them call upon the Lord, who **gives strength to the weary** (Isaiah 40:29–31). Let them fix their eyes upon Jesus, that they might **not grow weary and lose heart** (Hebrews 12:3). Let them remember their reward, preserved for them in heaven (1 Peter 1:3–4). If they do **not become weary,** they will reap a harvest of righteousness in this world, and in the world to come, life eternal (see 2 Timothy 4:7–8).

10 In verse 9, Paul says: **Let us not become weary in doing good**. "Doing good" means to **do good to all people**; in other words, it means loving our neighbor as ourself (Galatians 5:14).

We must do good to all people **as we have opportunity**. That does not mean at our convenience. How many opportunities for doing good have we lost today? May God forgive us!

We must do good to all people, but **especially to those who belong to the family of believers**—that is, the family of God, the church (see John 13:34–35).

Not Circumcision but a New Creation (6:11–18)

11 From here on, Paul has written the rest of this letter in his own hand (see 1 Corinthians 16:21; 2 Thessalonians 3:17).

12 The false teachers who had come from Jerusalem (Galatians 2:4,12) were trying to make a **good impression out-**

wardly on the Jews who lived in Galatia. They were trying to gain their favor and approval, because they wanted to avoid being persecuted by them. For this reason these teachers taught the Galatian Gentiles that they should be circumcised in order to be saved. The Jews believed that only by being circumcised and obeying the law could a man be saved. But according to the preaching of the **cross of Christ**, man is saved only through faith in the crucified Jesus. Therefore, the cross was an offense to the Jews, and they persecuted all who preached it (see Galatians 5:11).

13 The false Jewish teachers—that is, **those who are circumcised**—did not obey the Jewish law themselves. They persuaded the Galatian Gentiles to be circumcised not out of respect for the law, but only in order to boast that they had made the Galatians like Jews. These teachers were hypocrites. By teaching that circumcision was necessary for salvation, they were in fact stopping the Galatians from obtaining true salvation by grace (see Matthew 23:13; Luke 11:46).

14 The Jews boasted in circumcision and the works of the law. Paul, however, boasts only in the cross of Christ—that is, in Christ's work, in His sacrifice.

Let us think about the cross. In the eyes of the Roman world, the cross represented all that was shameful, contemptible. The cross was a sign of weakness, defeat, death. Nevertheless, it is this same cross that Paul boasts in! Because only through Jesus' death on the cross can men and women obtain salvation.

For Paul, **the world has been crucified**—that is, for him all worldly thoughts and desires have died. Paul places no confidence in the world nor anything in it. He puts his faith only in the cross (see 1 Corinthians 1:18; Philippians 3:7–8).

Not only has the world been crucified to Paul, but Paul has also been **crucified . . . to the world**. By this, Paul means that his old self has died on the cross with Christ (Romans 6:6; Galatians 2:20).

15 In Galatians 5:6, Paul says that the only thing that counts for obtaining salvation is faith (see Galatians 5:6 and comment). Here, in different words, Paul says the same thing. Through faith in Christ, we become a **new creation**—that is, we become a new spiritual person, a child of God (see 2 Corinthians 5:17 and comment). We are born again (John 3:5). Salvation means becoming a **new creation**; that is all that counts.

16 All **who follow this rule** are all those who obey the teaching of this letter. What Paul has written is the true Gospel of Christ. Those who walk by **this rule** are the true **Israel**[29] **of God**—that is, they are the true family of God. The true Israel are not those who have descended from Abraham according to the flesh, but rather those who have put faith in Christ.

17 **Finally, let no one cause me trouble**, writes Paul. Paul bears on his body the **marks of Jesus**, that is, the scars from the whippings and beatings he has received for Christ's sake (2 Corinthians 11:23–28). Anyone who troubles Paul also troubles Christ. Therefore, let the Galatians stop opposing Paul. Let them turn from the false teachers, and follow once again the true Gospel.

18 Even though Paul has severely rebuked the Galatians in this letter, in this last verse Paul calls them **brothers**. They are like sheep who have gone astray. They have followed after false shepherds. But Paul loves them still. And he prays that they may receive the highest blessing of all—the **grace of our Lord Jesus Christ**.

---

[29] **Israel** is the name of the Jewish nation. But now, believers in Christ are called the "true Israel," because it is they who are truly the people of God.

Ephesians

INTRODUCTION

Paul wrote this letter to the Ephesians in 60–61 A.D., while he was a prisoner in ROME. During that same period of imprisonment, Paul also wrote the New Testament letters to the Philippians, to the Colossians, and to Philemon.

In New Testament times, Ephesus was an important city of the Middle East. It was the chief city of the Roman province of Asia, (now the western part of present-day Turkey). Ephesus was also a major commercial center, and people came there on business from all over the Middle East (see Acts 18:19).

Paul himself had lived in Ephesus from 53 to 55 A.D. During that time he taught daily in a lecture hall, and many people came to listen to him. Some believed in Christ, and soon a church was established in Ephesus. Not only that, but many of those who came from outside of Ephesus on business also heard Paul and believed, and then took the Gospel back to their own cities. In this way, the Gospel of Christ spread throughout a wide area around Ephesus (Acts 19:8–10).

Many Bible scholars believe that Paul's letter to the Ephesians was written not only to the Ephesian Christians, but also to the churches in the surrounding cities which had sprung up as a result of Paul's two years of teaching in Ephesus. Most of Paul's other New Testament letters are written in a personal style to individual churches; but this letter is different. In this letter Paul writes about broad and general subjects with almost no reference to the Ephesians themselves.[1] Many scholars believe that this letter was written as a circular letter to be passed from church to church.

[1] The words **in Ephesus** in verse 1 are not found in all ancient manuscripts. This suggests that this letter was meant to be read in other churches besides the church in Ephesus.

For further information about Paul's life, see Romans: Introduction.

OUTLINE

A. The Believer's Position in Christ (1:1–3:21).
   1. Spiritual Blessings in Christ (1:1–14).
   2. A Prayer of Intercession (1:15–23).
   3. Salvation by Grace through Faith (2:1–10).
   4. Jews and Gentiles Reconciled in Christ (2:11–22).
   5. The Revelation of the Mystery (3:1–13).
   6. Paul's Second Prayer (3:14–21).

B. The Believer's Conduct in the World (4:1–6:24).
   1. The Unity of the Church (4:1–16).
   2. The Changed Life (4:17–32).
   3. Living as Children of Light (5:1–21).
   4. Christian Marriage (5:22–33).
   5. Christian Parenthood (6:1–4).
   6. Christian Employment (6:5–9).
   7. Christian Warfare (6:10–24).

CHAPTER 1

Spiritual Blessings in Christ (1:1–14)

1 Paul writes this letter as an APOSTLE **of Christ Jesus**; he writes with the full authority of Christ. Paul was appointed to be an apostle not according to man's will, but by God's will. As we study this letter, we must understand that God Himself is speaking to us through His apostle.[2]

Paul addresses this letter to the SAINTS in Ephesus, that is, to those who are **faithful in Christ Jesus**. In the New Testament, believers in Christ are often called "saints." A saint is anyone who through faith in Christ has been forgiven and cleansed of his sins (see Romans 1:7; Philippians 1:1).

Let us remember that this letter is written not only for the churches in and around Ephesus; it is written for our own church as well. This is a living letter, as important to us today as it was to the believers of Paul's time. As we read it, let us listen to what God is saying to us.

2 Paul prays that his readers might experience God's grace and peace.

GRACE is the mercy and love of God, which God gives freely to men. Man does not deserve God's grace, nor can he earn it by doing good works; God showers His grace upon men and women simply because He loves them.

By this grace of God, men can find PEACE with God and with each other. This letter of Paul to the Ephesians could be named "Peace through Grace," for that is its main theme from beginning to end.

3 God has blessed believers **with every spiritual blessing**. Paul doesn't say that God "will bless us"; he says that God **has blessed** us already. God has blessed us IN CHRIST. Every spiritual blessing comes to us through Christ.

Only because we are **in Christ** can we receive these blessings; if we are not in Christ, we shall not receive them. To be "in Christ" means that we accept Christ as our Lord and Savior, and through faith become united with Him and put our lives under His authority.

Even though God has already made these blessings available to us, we still must "reach out" and take them by faith; in other words, we must appropriate by faith what has been given. If we do not exercise faith, we shall receive nothing.

What are these spiritual blessings? The first blessing is that God **chose** us (verse 4) and **adopted** us (verse 5). The second blessing is that God has **freely given us** His **grace** (verse 6), by which grace we receive **redemption** and the **forgiveness of sins** (verse 7). The third blessing is that God has **made known to us the mystery of his will** (verse 9). Fourth, we have **heard the word of truth, the gospel** (verse 13); and fifth, we have been **marked** with the **Holy Spirit** (verse 13), which Spirit is a **deposit guaranteeing our inheritance** (verse 14). These, then, are the spiritual blessings **in the heavenly realms**, which we obtain through faith in Christ.

4 God chose us **before the creation of the world**. Think about that! Then there was no earth; there was only God. At that time, **in accordance with his pleasure and will** (verse 5), God made an eternal plan; and part of that plan involved "choosing" us who believe in Christ. According to verse 5, God **predestined** us to be His children; this is what being "chosen" means. This is an important truth. First, before anything else happened, God chose us. Sometimes we think that it is we who have chosen God first; but this is not so. He has first chosen us; and only because of this can we then turn to Him and "choose" Him. And we have no cause to take pride in God's having chosen us in this way. We did nothing to deserve it; God chose us long before we were born! We didn't earn our place in God's family; it is according

---

[2] Indeed, this same principle applies to our study of the entire Bible. The Bible is God's own word, and He speaks to us through every verse.

to God's own **pleasure and will** (verse 5) that He has predestined us to be His children. Therefore, we are in fact "debtors" to God. Instead of taking pride in ourselves, we should humbly thank and praise God for the great grace He has shown to us.

In some religions there is a belief that when a child is born, a spirit comes and determines the child's future. But this is not true. From before the creation of the world, the one true God has determined the future of every human being.

Many Christians take this verse to mean that God "chooses" some people to be His children, but not others. The reason why God should choose some and not others is very difficult for people to understand and accept. In 1 Timothy 2:4, Paul writes that God **wants all men to be saved**; and yet, according to many other verses, not all men will automatically be saved. The important thing to remember here, however, is that every person who believes in Christ is chosen by God (see Romans 9:14–21 and comment; General Article: Salvation—God's Choice or Man's Choice?).

The question arises: Why did God choose us? He chose us **to be holy and blameless**. Let us never think that because we have been chosen by God we can now do anything we please; this is not so. There must be no sin or impurity in our lives, because God has called us to be **holy and blameless** (see 1 Peter 1:15–16).

5 God has predestined us **to be adopted**[3] as his children. In a spiritual way, believers in Christ become the sons and daughters of God.

On the one hand, as adopted children of God we receive forgiveness, salvation, an inheritance in heaven, and many other great blessings. But on the other hand, as children we have been given a great responsibility: to be **holy and blameless** (verse 4).

We have been adopted as children **through Jesus Christ**. It is only when we receive Christ as our Lord and believe in His name that we are adopted by God and become members of His family (see John 1:12; Galatians 3:26; 4:5 and comments).

6 As Paul thinks of the marvelous grace of God in making us His own children, Paul's heart is filled with praise. God has done all this, Paul says, **to the praise of his glorious grace**. God **has freely given us** this glorious grace; we didn't do anything to earn it. And God has given us this grace **in** (through) **the One he loves**—that is, Christ.

7 The main reason God sent His Son Jesus Christ to earth was to make possible our **redemption**,[4] or salvation. Jesus was sent to earth to save men and women. Without redemption, we cannot be God's adopted children. God's work of redemption is even greater than His work of creation, because to create the world all God had to do was speak, but to redeem men God had to die; He had to give His own Son Jesus as a sacrifice for our redemption.

In him we have redemption, says Paul. How often Paul writes "in Him," or "in Christ," or "in the One He loves" (see verses 2,3,4,6,7,8,10,11,13). This is one of the main teachings of Paul: namely, that our lives are centered "in Christ." Every kind of spiritual blessing is **in Christ**. All power is also in Christ. And here, according to verse 7, our redemption is also in Him. Our redemption is **through his blood**, that is, through His death as a sacrifice. Jesus Christ died on the cross in order to take upon Himself the punishment for our sins; He is the atoning

---

[3] To be **adopted** in a natural sense means to become the legal child of someone who is not one's natural parent. The adopted child receives all the rights and privileges that a natural heir would receive. In the spiritual sense, to be "adopted" by God is to become entitled to all the blessings of heaven; it is to become a member of God's own family. For further discussion, see Word List: Adoption.

[4] The word **redemption** in the New Testament means the setting free or delivering of a person from the penalty of sin by paying a ransom or offering a sacrifice. It is one aspect of our salvation. For further discussion, see Word List: Redemption.

sacrifice for our sins (see Mark 10:45; Romans 3:23–25; 1 Peter 1:18–19 and comments).

One aspect of our **redemption** (or salvation) is the **forgiveness of sins**. Again, from this verse, we can see that we receive forgiveness through God's grace, even though we ourselves are not worthy of it.

8 When God pours out His grace upon people, He doesn't send it in small trickles. God has **lavished** on us the **riches** of His grace. Let us never fail to praise Him for his **glorious grace** (verse 6).

9–10 God has made known to us the **mystery of his will** through the teachings of Christ. God's **will** is to **bring all things . . . together under one head, even Christ** (verse 10). That is, God's purpose is to bring everything in heaven and on earth under the lordship and authority of Christ (see Philippians 2:9-11; Colossians 1:15–20).

When will this happen? It will happen **when the times will have reached their fulfillment**—that is, at just the right time selected by God. No one but God knows when that time will be.

How great is Paul's vision! It extends from **before the creation of the world** (verse 4) right up until the **fulfillment** of the **times**. Everything in heaven and on earth is included in Paul's vision. Yet when Paul wrote this letter he was sitting in a jail cell. With his physical eyes he could see only the four walls of his cell. With his spiritual eyes, however, he could see the entire will and purpose of God!

Sometimes our lives become like the inside of a jail. We need to open our spiritual eyes and see the **mystery of** [God's] **will**. The **mystery** is this: God sent His only Son Jesus Christ into the world that we might receive redemption and forgiveness of sins and become holy and blameless adopted children of God. That such weak and sinful people as we should receive these glorious blessings is a mystery indeed!

11–12 In these two verses Paul speaks about the Jews.[5] Paul was himself a Jew. Paul says in verse 11: **In him** (Christ) **we** (the Jews) **were also chosen.**[6] Then in verse 12, Paul explains that the Jews were chosen **in order that they . . . might be for the praise of his glory.** From long before Christ's time, the Jews had been waiting for a Savior to come; the coming of a Savior had been foretold by the Jewish prophets of the Old Testament. This is why Paul says in verse 12 that the Jews **were the first to hope in Christ**.

13 Now Paul turns his attention to the Ephesians, who were not Jews. Paul writes: **And you also were included in Christ**. That is, the Ephesians also had been given the chance to receive salvation through faith in Christ. The Ephesian believers had been included in Christ because they had **heard the word of truth, the GOSPEL of** [their] **SALVATION**, and had **believed** it.

The proof that the Ephesians had been included in Christ is that they had been **marked in him** (Christ) **with a seal**. That "seal" is the **promised HOLY SPIRIT**. Paul says the Spirit is **promised**, because Jesus had promised His disciples that the Spirit would be sent from God (see John 14:26).

What, then, is the **seal** of the Holy Spirit? In New Testament times, a king would stamp his seal on his letters, so that a person receiving the letter would know without doubt that it was indeed the king's letter. Any letter stamped with the king's seal had the king's authority. In the same way, when any person has been "stamped with the seal" of the Holy Spirit, we can know that that person belongs to Christ and has Christ's authority.

Also notice here that in order to be a Christian and to receive the Holy Spirit (to be "stamped with the seal" of the

---

[5] The Jews were a race of people living in the Middle East, who from the beginning worshiped the one true God. God had chosen the Jews to be His own special people. Jesus Himself was a Jew. For further discussion, see Word List: Jew.

[6] In place of the words **were chosen**, some translations of the Bible say, "were made heirs." The meaning is the same. The Jews were "chosen to be heirs."

Spirit), two things are necessary. First, we must have **heard** the Gospel. Second, we must have **believed** in Christ.

14 The **Holy Spirit** is both the Spirit of God and the Spirit of Christ. It can be said (in simple terms) that the Holy Spirit is one of God's forms.[7] It is in the "form" of the Holy Spirit that God enters our hearts and changes our lives. Through the Holy Spirit we can experience a foretaste of heaven; that is, the Holy Spirit is like a **deposit**, or advance, on the full inheritance that awaits us in heaven. In this world we do not receive our full heavenly inheritance; but we do receive an advance on it, a **deposit guaranteeing** that we shall receive the rest of it in heaven. Having received the **deposit**—the Holy Spirit—we can know without doubt that we shall one day receive our full inheritance (see Romans 8:16–17; 2 Corinthians 1:22).

As Paul speaks about our heavenly inheritance, he once again reminds us that the blessings we have already received and the blessings we will yet receive in heaven are **to the praise of his** (God's) **glory**. Paul has repeated this expression three times in this chapter (verses 6,12,14). Paul has also repeated three times the expression "according to His (God's) **pleasure, will**, or **plan**" (verses 5,9,11). In emphasizing these points, Paul shows us that everything begins with God's **pleasure** and **will**, and everything ends in God's **glory**. Here, too, we can see the entire meaning and purpose of our lives. According to God's pleasure and will, we have believed in Christ and have been brought into God's family. And now, therefore, we must live **to the praise of his glory**.

Worldly men[8] say: "I will live my life according to my own will and for my own glory." But believers in Christ say: "I will live my life according to God's will and for His glory." How different is the mind of the worldly man and the mind of the Christian!

Thanksgiving and Prayer (1:15–23)

15–16 Even though Paul has written this letter to the Ephesians almost two thousand years ago, it is also written for us today. Here Paul's prayer is not only for the Ephesians; it is for us too.

If Paul were alive today, what would he have heard about our **faith** and about our **love for all the saints**? Would he be able to give thanks for our faith and love?

17 In this prayer for the Ephesians (and for us), what does Paul pray for? He prays that we and the Ephesians might be given the **Spirit**[9] **of wisdom and revelation**. This **wisdom** is needed so that we might know God better. Spiritual **wisdom and revelation** always come from God, not from man.

Paul further prays that through this wisdom, we and the Ephesians might know three things: first, the **hope** to which God has **called** us (verse 18); second, the **riches of his glorious inheritance** (verse 18); and third, **his incomparably great power** (verse 19).

18 What is the **hope** to which we have been **called**? Our hope is in the things which Paul has already mentioned in this chapter. We hope to be free of sin; we hope to be children of God; we hope to be holy and to remain in Christ. We have been **called** to all of these things, and thus we can place our **hope** in them.

What is the **glorious inheritance** which God has promised us? We have already received the **deposit** of this inheritance—that is, the Holy Spirit (verse 14). The remainder of our inheritance is waiting for us in heaven. The most wonderful

---

[7] In place of the word "forms," it is more accurate to say "modes of existence." For further discussion of the Holy Spirit, see General Article: Holy Spirit.

[8] Worldly men are those men who love the world and the things of the world more than they love God.

[9] It is not certain whether Paul is referring to the Holy **Spirit** here, or only to a "human spirit" of wisdom and revelation. In the original Greek text, there is no way to distinguish between Spirit with a capital "S" and spirit with a small "s." However, there is not much difference in the meaning either way, since all true wisdom and revelation comes from the Holy Spirit in the first place.

part of our heavenly inheritance will be living forever with God and Christ. In addition to that, we will be like Christ (1 John 3:2), and we shall reign with Christ (2 Timothy 2:12).

19 At the beginning of our Christian lives, we were **called**. At the end of our Christian lives, we shall receive a **glorious inheritance**. And between the beginning and end of our lives, we are sustained by God's **incomparably great power . . . his mighty strength**. God's power has no limit, and this power is available to us throughout our Christian lives.

20–21 How great is that power! By that power God raised Jesus Christ from the dead. By that power Jesus reigns in heaven over **all rule and authority, power and dominion** (verse 21). He reigns over Satan, and all his spirits and demons. He reigns over evil and over death. He reigns over all things, both of heaven and of earth, both present and future. He is reigning today, and He will reign forever—all through the power of God.

Can any human power bring a dead person to life? No. But God's power can. For God, nothing is impossible (Mark 10:27). And that same power that raised Christ from the dead is available to us who believe. Through that same power, we who were once dead in our sins (Ephesians 2:1) have now been made alive in Christ (Ephesians 2:4–5) and have been seated with Him in the heavenly realms (Ephesians 2:6). And that power is available to us day by day through the Holy Spirit; therefore, let us not fail to ask for it.

22–23 All things have been placed **under his** (Christ's) **feet**—that is, under His authority (verse 22). When we feel overwhelmed by sin, by weakness, by fear and anxiety, let us remember that all these things have already been put under Christ's feet. And if they are under Christ's feet, they are under our feet too!

Paul says here that Christ is the **head over everything for the** CHURCH. In Ephesians 5:23, Paul calls Christ simply the **head of the church**. If Christ is the **head**, then the church is His **body** (verse 23). And if the church is Christ's body, then we believers are members of His body (see Romans 12:4–5; 1 Corinthians 12:12,27 and comments).

The church is Christ's **fullness**. Just as a kingdom can be called the "fullness" of a king, so the church is the "fullness" of Christ. But it is not the church that does the "filling"; it is Christ Himself who **fills everything in every way** (verse 23). **From the fullness of his** (Christ's) **grace we have all received one blessing after another** (John 1:16). This should not surprise us, because Christ is God Himself (see John 10:30; Colossians 1:15–20; General Article: Jesus Christ).

CHAPTER 2

Made Alive in Christ (2:1–10)

1 Here Paul reminds the Ephesians that they had once been **dead in** [their] **trangressions and sins**. In what way were they **dead**? They were spiritually dead; that is, they were separated from God (see Ephesians 4:18). Our sins separate us from God; it is impossible for sinful man to have fellowship with God. To remain apart from God is spiritual death.

2 Before they believed in Christ, these Ephesians had been in a wicked and miserable state. Their entire nature was evil. They followed the ways of the world. That means they lived according to their own will and for their own glory (see Ephesians 1:14 and comment). Worldly men live to please themselves; but God says that man must live to please Him. Therefore, if we walk according to the ways of the world, we shall be disobeying God. We shall be God's enemies.

The **ruler of the kingdom of the air** which Paul mentions here is Satan, who is the chief of all the evil spirits. Jesus calls

Satan the **prince of this world** (John 12:31), because Satan rules in the lives of those who follow the ways of the world and do not obey God.

3 We Christians, too, lived in sin like this before we believed in Christ. We, too, were **by nature objects of wrath**—that is, we were deserving of God's wrath and punishment. God's **wrath** is not like man's anger. God does not get angry with sin one day and forget it the next. God is completely holy; He cannot tolerate unholiness. Therefore, He is determined to destroy evil and all those who persist in doing evil.

From this we can understand that the situation of natural[10] and worldly men who refuse to accept Christ is very dangerous and frightening indeed. All our friends and neighbors and relatives who have not accepted Christ are spiritually dead, separated from God, deserving of God's wrath. Yes, they appear alive and their bodies are active, but spiritually they are dead. They will not receive eternal life in heaven. And yet, to become alive and to obtain eternal life, all they have to do is hear the **word of truth, the gospel of . . . salvation** (Ephesians 1:13), and having heard it, believe. We who already believe need to do all we can to give them the chance to hear!

A question arises here: Are non-believers and those who follow the ways of the world completely evil? Is man by nature completely bad? The answer is no. All men are made in God's image (Genesis 1:27). Many people seek after God diligently and strive to please Him. But the main point is this: Without putting faith in Christ, who died on the cross to take away man's sins, no man can please God (see John 3:18,36; 14:6; Acts 4:12 and comments).

4–5 We have seen how evil and corrupt man is by nature (Romans 3:10–12). We have seen how "sick" he is spiritually—indeed, he is already dead! No ordinary medicine or ordinary doctor is going to help such a hopeless patient. There is only one "doctor" who can help a dead patient, and that is God. And God's medicine is love. Because of His great love, He is ready to pour out His grace and mercy upon sinful men. These three words—love, grace, and mercy—always go together; they are like one great work of God's love. How different is the one true God from the gods and goddesses of other religions! God loved us so much that He sent His only Son to earth to die for us (see John 3:16 and comment).

6 God not only makes us alive here on earth, but He also seats us with Christ in heaven. And if we are sitting with Christ in heaven, what are we sitting on? Thrones! (see Revelation 3:21). Paul is so confident of the believer's place in heaven that he writes here in the past tense. He says that God **seated** us with Christ in the heavenly realms, as if we had already been seated there (see Romans 8:30 and comment).

7 Why does God raise us up with Christ and seat us with Him in the heavenly realms? He does it to show future generations **in the coming ages** His great love—to show them the **riches of his grace**.

8 Here we come to one of the most important verses in the entire Bible. In this verse there are two main words: **grace** and FAITH. To put it in simple terms, **grace** is God's free gift of salvation in Jesus Christ; **faith** is receiving that gift. Faith is not "doing"; it is "receiving." Faith itself is a gift of God, and it comes from hearing God's word (Romans 10:17). Therefore, we can see from this that salvation is totally a gift of God. We can do nothing to earn it; we can do nothing to make ourselves worthy of it.

We can also see from this how different Christianity is from other religions. Other religions teach that in order to be saved man must earn merit by doing good works. They teach that man's sinful nature can be "purified" by following certain rules and rituals. But these teachings are not true. Our inner being cannot be purified by outward works.

---

[10] Natural man follows the natural and selfish desires of his heart. He knows of no other rule but to gratify the desires of his sinful nature. All men by nature are sinful (see Romans 3:10–12).

And no matter how many good works we do, until our inner being has been purified or made righteous, we cannot please God or obtain salvation (see Galatians 2:15–16 and comment; General Article: Way of Salvation).

9 Paul again repeats here that we cannot obtain salvation by our own work or effort. No one can ever say: "I have got to heaven by my own work." Only through faith in Christ can one obtain salvation; Christ alone is our Savior. He saved us by receiving the death penalty for our sins; He died in our place. By believing in Christ, we can receive forgiveness for our sins and be declared righteous in God's sight (see Romans 3:22–24; 8:1 and comments). It is only when we have been cleansed and made holy that God will accept us as His children. And how are we cleansed and made holy? Through faith in Jesus Christ.

10 In this verse we see the second purpose God has in saving us. (The first purpose, mentioned in verse 7, is to demonstrate His grace to future generations.) The second purpose for our salvation is that, once saved, we might **do good works**. Notice here that we don't do good works in order to be saved. Rather, we are saved in order to do good works. We are not saved because of our good works; rather, we do good works because we have been saved.

God has prepared in advance **good works** for every Christian to do. Let no Christian think: "I have been saved by grace; therefore I don't need to do any good works." Yes, salvation comes first; but after salvation there must be good works. First, we obtain new life in Christ; then we must begin to live a new life (see 2 Corinthians 5:17; Ephesians 4:1 and comments).

One in Christ (2:11–22)

11 GENTILES are all those people who are not Jews. In Paul's time, the Jews called Gentiles **uncircumcised,** because they didn't undergo the ceremony of CIRCUMCISION, as the Jews did. According to God's command, on the eighth day of life every Jewish male has the excess skin at the end of his penis cut off: this is called circumcision (Genesis 17:9–14). Circumcision is the outward sign of being a Jew; thus the Jews of Paul's day called themselves **the circumcision**.

12 In this verse, Paul reminds the Ephesians of their former state. First of all, they had not heard of Christ. Second, they were not citizens of ISRAEL, that is, the Jewish nation. Third, they had no part in the COVENANTS **of promise** that God had made with the Jews. The greatest **promise** that God made to the Jews was that He would send them a Savior. For these three reasons, therefore, in the Jews' sight these Ephesian Gentiles were **without hope and without God**. They did not know the one true God. They were **far away** (verse 13).

13 But Jesus Christ, even though He was Himself a Jew, came to save not only Jews but also Gentiles. Jesus came into the world to be the Savior of all people—both Jew and Gentile. Through the **blood of Christ** (through Christ's sacrificial death) all believers are **brought near**—that is, they are brought into the family of God. Thus both Jews and Gentiles, once they have believed in Jesus, become joined together in one spiritual family (see Galatians 3:24 and comment).

14 Christ is our **peace**. Christ makes peace between man and God, and also between man and man. He makes peace between Jew and Gentile. He has broken down the **barrier, the dividing wall of**

hostility[11]—the division, prejudice, and enmity—between Jew and Gentile, between high caste and low caste, between rich and poor, between different races, and between different nations. In this verse, of course, Paul is thinking mainly of the **hostility** between Jews and Gentiles. The Jews considered themselves to be superior to Gentiles. The Jews didn't even associate with Gentiles, because in their sight the Gentiles were unclean.

15 The Jews obeyed many **commandments and regulations**, which were contained in the Jewish LAW. The Jews thought that by obeying the law they could find salvation. The Jewish law had two main parts: first, the "moral law," in particular the ten commandments (Exodus 20:1–17); and second, the "ceremonial law," which consisted of all the regulations about eating and washing, and about offering sacrifices. By the standard of the ceremonial law, the Gentiles were unclean; thus they were not permitted to enter the inner part of the Jewish temple, lest they defile it. For this reason, the Jewish law itself was like a **barrier**, or **dividing wall of hostility** (verse 14).

Christ destroyed that barrier **by abolishing . . . the** (ceremonial) **law.**[12] Christ taught that man is saved, not through obeying the law, but only through faith in Him (see Galatians 2:15–16 and comment). Therefore, by **abolishing** the ceremonial law and destroying the **barrier** between Jew and Gentile, Christ created **in himself one new man out of two**. That is, He created one new people (believers) out of two peoples (Jews and Gentiles). All who believe in Christ—whether Jew or Gentile, high caste or low caste, male or female—all are now one in Him (see Galatians 3:28). They are all members of **one body** (verse 16), whose head is Christ (see 1 Corinthians 12:13,27; Ephesians 5:23).

16 Christ didn't only make peace between Jew and Gentile; He also made peace between both of them and God (see Romans 1:18–20; 5:1 and comments). Christ, **through the** CROSS (through His death on the cross), has brought all believers into God's family, the church. God treats all of His children equally; He shows no partiality toward one over another. And He wants no barrier, no **dividing wall of hostility** to arise among them.

Therefore, let us make sure that no "dividing walls of hostility" arise in our church. And if they do arise, let us quickly tear them down! If we are not watchful, such dividing walls can easily arise between rich and poor, educated and uneducated, men and women, foreigner and national, high caste and low caste. Let this not happen!

17–18 Those **who were far away** (Gentiles) and those **who were near** (Jews) are now equally able to draw near to God; they have equal **access** to God.

In verse 18, Paul mentions the three forms or modes of existence of God: **For through him** (Christ, God the Son) **we both have access to the Father** (God the Father) **by one Spirit** (God the Holy Spirit). But even though God has three forms—Father, Son, and Holy Spirit—He

---

[11] Surrounding the inner court of the Jewish temple in Jerusalem, there was a wall or **barrier** through which Gentiles were not permitted to pass. In this verse Paul calls it a **dividing wall of hostility**, because that wall was, in a sense, a sign of the hostility between Jews and Gentiles. It was also a sign that the Gentiles were **far away** (verse 13), that they could not come near to God.

When Paul says Christ **destroyed** that wall, he means that Christ destroyed the significance of the wall, not the wall itself. The original purpose of the wall was to keep the unclean Gentiles from coming into the presence of a holy God. Now Christ has made it possible for the Gentiles to be cleansed through faith and thus to come into God's presence. The wall is no longer necessary. Thus Christ has removed the barrier keeping the Gentiles away from God; through His death the Gentiles are now **brought near** to God (verse 13).

[12] However, Christ did not abolish the "moral law." For further discussion, see Matthew 5:17–20 and comment.

is one God. Christians refer to these three forms of God together as the "Trinity."

19 Here Paul tells the Ephesian Gentiles that they are now **fellow citizens with God's people** (the Jews) **and members of God's household** (the church). And Paul is saying the same thing to us today. We too were once **foreigners and aliens**. We too did not know Christ. But now, through faith in Him, we have become **members** of God's family and **citizens** in His kingdom (Luke 12:32).

20 In this verse, Paul says some important things about **God's household**, the church. It is built upon the **foundation of the apostles and prophets**—that is, the New Testament **apostles** and the Old Testament PROPHETS. In other words, the church is built upon the foundation of the Old and New Testaments—the Bible. In simplest terms, the foundation of the church is God's word. And this word (foundation) has been written down for us by the apostles and prophets.

Then Paul says that the **chief cornerstone**[13] of the church is Jesus Christ Himself. Without such a cornerstone, a building will fall down.

21 The Jewish temple in Jerusalem no longer exists; the church is now God's **holy temple**. And this temple is joined together in Christ; it is held together by Him. Christ is not only the church's "cornerstone"; He is its head.

22 We believers are like stones, from which God has built His temple. We have been **built together** into one building, one church. We are united with each other. And God's Holy Spirit lives in this temple, of which we are the stones (see 1 Corinthians 3:16; 1 Peter 2:5 and comments). God has built His temple so that He can dwell in it!

Today what is our church like? Are its members joined together in unity? Is there peace in our church? Are we living together in love as in one family? When other people look at our church, what do they see? What does God see?

CHAPTER 3

Paul the Preacher to the Gentiles (3:1–13)

1–2 Paul calls himself a **prisoner**, because he is writing this letter while imprisoned in a Roman jail. He was a prisoner **for the sake of you Gentiles**, he tells the Ephesians. It was because of his preaching to Gentiles that Paul had been imprisoned.

In another sense, Paul was a "prisoner" of Jesus Christ whether he was in jail or not. He had made Jesus the ruler and Lord of his life at all times and in all places.

Paul's special work was to preach to the Gentiles (see Acts 22:21; Romans 15:15–16). Paul had received a special **administration of God's grace** to do this work (verse 2).

3 Here again Paul talks about the **mystery** that had been revealed to him, and which he has mentioned already in Ephesians 1:9–10; namely, the "mystery" that God will one day unite all things in Christ. In Ephesians Chapter 2, Paul has shown how Jews and Gentiles have already been united in Christ. Paul did not learn of this **mystery** from any man; rather, the mystery was made known to him **by revelation** directly from God.

4 After reading Ephesians Chapters 1–2, the Ephesians would surely know that Paul did indeed have **insight** into what this **mystery** was all about. This mystery was the **mystery of Christ**: namely, that Christ is the **head over everything** (Ephesians 1:22), and that in Christ Jews and Gentiles are now united

---

[13] The kind of **cornerstone** which Paul refers to here is a capstone which covers the right angle where two walls join together. Without such a capstone, the walls will fall down.

in **one body**, the church (1 Corinthians 12:12–13,27; Ephesians 2:16–17; 3:6).

5 This mystery **was not made known to men in other generations**. That is, this **mystery of Christ** was not revealed to the people who lived before Christ's time. Only when Christ came to earth was the mystery fully revealed to **God's holy apostles and prophets**.[14] The mystery was revealed to them **by the** (Holy) **Spirit**.

6 Here Paul states again what the **mystery** is: Gentile believers have become **heirs together . . . members together . . . and sharers together** with Israel, with the Jews (see Ephesians 2:19 and comment). Jewish and Gentile believers have become one in Christ; they are equal in God's sight. This means that in God's sight there is no high caste and low caste, high class and low class. The Jews considered the Gentiles "low caste" and themselves "high caste." But now, in Christ, there are no castes; all have become one.

The Gentiles are **heirs together with Israel**. This means that, together with the Jews, they are fellow citizens of God's kingdom. Now the Gentiles have a part in the covenant that God established with Israel. According to that covenant, the Jews were supposed to worship and obey God, and in return God would make them His special people. Now believers in Christ—both Jew and Gentile—have become God's special people.

The Gentiles are **members together of one body**. This means that Gentile believers, together with Jewish believers, are members of Christ's body (1 Corinthians 12:27).

The Gentiles are **sharers together in the promise**—that is, the **promise** of salvation through faith in Christ. God had promised the Jews that He would send a Savior to them. But when the Savior (Christ) finally came, most Jews rejected Him; therefore, God made Christ's saving work available to the Gentiles through faith. In this way, the Gentiles became sharers in the promise of salvation.

7 Paul was made a **servant** of the gospel **by th**[illegible]
the **workin**[illegible]
us who bel[illegible]
have, like P[illegible]
Gospel thr[illegible]
God. God [illegible]
need to be His servants. We need to ask ourselves: "Whose servant am I? Who do I spend most of my time serving? How much do I love my master Christ and His Gospel?"

8 Paul does not exalt himself. If Paul were to appear among us today, he would surely say: "I am **less than the least** of you."

The special work that God gave Paul to do was this: **to preach to the Gentiles the unsearchable riches of Christ**. Christ's spiritual riches are **unsearchable**—without limit and without number! These **unsearchable riches** are the same as the spiritual blessings that Paul mentioned in Ephesians 1:3 (see Colossians 1:24–27).

When we are talking with our friends and neighbors, do we ever tell them about the **unsearchable riches** of Christ? Do we tell them about the **riches of his glorious inheritance**? (Ephesians 1:18). Or about **his incomparably great power**? (Ephesians 1:19). Have we ourselves received these riches? Or are we like the guest invited to a great banquet who sits down at the table but does not eat?

The men of the world seek after riches that spoil; but we have found riches that will last forever. Should we not tell others about these riches?

Sometimes we act as if we had no spiritual riches at all! We say, "What can we do? Our church is so poor and weak." Poor and weak? How can that be? Each church possesses the **unsearchable riches of Christ**; it possesses His **incomparably great power**! We have enough spiritual wealth and power to share with everyone; our supply is infinite!

What are the riches of Christ we have to share? They include all of His grace and gifts and spiritual blessings (Ephesians 1:3), together with His Gospel of salvation, which is the power of God (1 Corinthians 1:18). But the greatest thing

[14] These are New Testament, not Old Testament, **prophets**.

we have to share is Christ Himself; He is the sum of all spiritual blessings (see Romans 8:32).

9 Together with preaching to the Gentiles, Paul was appointed by God **to make plain to everyone the administration of this mystery**. Before Christ's time, this **mystery** had been **kept hidden**, but now at last it was revealed (verse 5). As we have seen before, the **mystery** was that God was going to **bring all things** under Christ (Ephesians 1:10). That involved creating a new spiritual people, the church, of which all men on earth can be members through faith in Christ. This, then, is God's **eternal purpose which he accomplished in Christ Jesus our Lord** (verse 11).

10 What was God's intention in revealing this mystery? His intention was to show His wisdom to the **rulers and authorities in the heavenly realms**. These "rulers and authorities" include both angels and evil spirits (see Ephesians 2:2).

And how will God show His wisdom to these rulers and authorities? He will do it **through the church**. Think of it! Through every little church, God is showing forth His **manifold wisdom** to all the rulers and authorities in heaven! In the church, God's wisdom can be seen not only by men but also by angels and spirits—even by Satan himself. The church, which is Christ's body, has overcome the authority of Satan.

11–12 God's **eternal purpose** is that all people—both Jew and Gentile—might enter with boldness into His presence and become members of His family, the church (see Hebrews 4:16; 10:19–22 and comments).

Let us think about this church. The church is the most important thing in the world, because it is the fulfillment of God's **eternal purpose**. Second only to Christ's death and resurrection, the establishing of Christ's church has been (and continues to be) the most significant development in the history of mankind.

Historians of the world write about kings and queens, ministers and noblemen and other famous people. But Bible historians[15] write about common and ordinary people like us.

Historians of the world write about wars, peace treaties, and then more wars. But Bible historians write about the war between Christ and Satan—the war between good and evil—a war which was won by Christ. And in the Bible we read about the greatest "peace treaty" of all, the peace treaty between God and man, which was mediated by Jesus Christ.

Historians of the world write about kingdoms which rise and fall like the sun. But Bible historians write about a spiritual kingdom, which is always rising and will never fall. This kingdom has no boundary; it extends throughout the world. This kingdom is the church of Christ.

13 Even though Paul is in jail, the Ephesians should not be discouraged. Rather, they should meditate on the unsearchable riches of Christ, which is their glory.

Paul's Prayer for the Ephesians (3:14–21)

14–15 The **whole family in heaven and on earth**—that is, the whole family of believers, which is the church—takes its name from God the Father. The church is God's family, so it takes God's name.

Since the church is God's family, Paul prays here to the **Father** of the family. Paul's prayer is that God will **strengthen** the Ephesians **through his Spirit in** [their] **inner being** (verse 16), and that **Christ may dwell in** [their] **hearts through faith** (verse 17). And, of course, as we read this prayer, we must keep in mind that it is written not only for the Ephesians, but also for us.

16 The strength for which Paul is praying here is spiritual strength. This kind of strength is always inward, in a person's heart, in his **inner being**; and it comes only **through** [God's] **Spirit**. This

[15] We must remember that the Bible is not only a book of laws and prophecies; it is also a book of history. And the history written in the Bible is completely accurate.

strength is the **mighty strength** that Paul mentioned in Ephesians 1:19, and which Paul himself continually experienced (Philippians 4:13).

17 The second part of Paul's prayer for the Ephesians is that Christ (that is, Christ's Spirit, the Holy Spirit) might dwell in their hearts. When Christ dwells in our hearts, we become more and more like Him. Through Christ's Spirit within us, our hearts are filled with His love (see Romans 5:5).

18 If Christ dwells within us, we indeed shall be **rooted and established in love**. We shall be like a tree, whose roots are implanted in love. Or we shall be like a house, whose foundation is embedded in love. Paul prays that the Ephesians might understand how great—how **wide and long and high and deep**—Christ's love is. Christ's love is **wide** enough to embrace all men. His love is **long** enough to last forever. It is **deep** enough to reach down to the lowest sinner. And it is **high** enough to lift that sinner up to heaven.

The cross is the greatest sign of Christ's love. The horizontal beam of the cross reaches from the East to the West. The upright post of the cross reaches from earth to heaven. The love of Christ is great enough to reach everyone everywhere.

19 Paul here prays that the Ephesians might not only understand how great Christ's love is, but that they might also **know this love**—that is, that they might experience this love in their lives. Christ's love (God's love) is so great that it **surpasses knowledge**. However, we can each experience this love in our hearts. And having experienced it, we shall be **filled to the measure of all the fullness of God.**

What is it like to be filled with **all the fullness of God**? The fullness of God includes **every spiritual blessing** in the heavenly realms (Ephesians 1:3); it includes the **riches of his glorious inheritance** (Ephesians 1:18); it includes His **incomparably great power** (Ephesians 1:19); it includes His **unsearchable riches** (verse 8). Finally, it includes His great love, which He has poured out into our hearts by His Holy Spirit (Romans 5:5). And if Christ dwells in our hearts through faith, all this—**all the fullness of God**—will be ours!

Let it be our constant prayer for our church and for each other that we might be continuously filled with **all the fullness of God**. Let us not limit our prayers to small things; rather, let us, like Paul, pray for the greatest thing it is possible to imagine—**the fullness of God**!

What an amazing prayer Paul has prayed for the Ephesians—and for us! He has prayed for strength, for love, for knowledge, for all the fullness of God. Can God answer a prayer like that? Does God have the power to fulfill such a prayer? He certainly does! (see verse 20).

20–21 God's power is great enough to do anything we can ask. Not only that, God can do more than we can even imagine. And this same power of God **is at work within us** (verse 20). Just as God's love is beyond our knowledge (verse 19), so His power is beyond our imagining. Infinite love; infinite power. How great is our God! He is worthy of infinite praise! To Him **be glory in the church and in Christ Jesus throughout all generations, for ever and ever!**

CHAPTER 4

Unity in the Body of Christ (4:1–16)

1 In the first three chapters of this letter, Paul has written about God's **eternal purpose** (Ephesians 3:11), about the **one new man**—the church—which God has established (Ephesians 2:15), and about our calling to be God's children (Ephesians 1:5). Now in these last three chapters, Paul writes about how we should live our daily lives. Since we have been called to be God's children, we need to know how God's children should act. Because if we are God's children, we must act like God's children!

Therefore, here in verse 1, Paul exhorts us to live lives **worthy of the calling** that we have received from God—the calling to be His children (see Philippians 1:27; Colossians 1:10). And then in verses 2–16, Paul reminds us that we have been called to be one new people, members of one family, the church. In order to be worthy of this calling we must remain united!

2 How do we Christians remain united with one another? First, by being **humble.**[16] Why do divisions arise in our churches? It is usually because of pride. Two bad things arise from our pride. First, some of us seek to be leaders out of pride, and when we are not given leadership, we become angry and cause division in the church. The second thing to arise from our pride is this: If someone should oppose us or betray us in some way, our pride is hurt and we become angry with that person and refuse to have fellowship with him. Whenever we feel hurt in this way, it is because of pride; it is because we lack humility. Therefore, Paul says, in order to maintain unity in the church and with each other, the first thing we need is humility.

Some people suppose that a humble man is a weak man. But that is totally false. The humble man is, in fact, a strong man. He is the master of himself. At the same time, he happily makes himself the servant of others.

How can we tell if we are humble? How can we test our humility? When we pray, it is easy to call ourselves sinners. That is no test. The test comes when someone else calls us a sinner—especially in front of others! How do we accept it? Do we accept it happily and graciously? If we do not, we are not humble. We have failed the test.

The second thing necessary for preserving unity in the church is patience. To remain united with each other, we must be **patient** with each other. Every one of us has faults and weaknesses. We naturally want others to be patient with our defects; we want others to accept us in spite of our defects. Therefore, we need to be patient with others and to accept them in spite of their defects. After pride, criticism and slander is the second major cause of division in the church. This is one of Satan's chief methods of destroying our unity. We must be patient with others even when they speak against us. Such opposition can usually be overcome with patience.

There is a third thing necessary for preserving unity, and that is love. Paul tells us here to bear with one another **in love,** just as Christ bears with us in love. We must forgive one another, just as Christ has forgiven us (Ephesians 4:32).

Thus, to maintain our unity three things are necessary: humility, patience, and love. Paul earlier wrote that believers were like the stones of God's temple (see Ephesians 2:22). If we are the stones, then humility, patience, and love are the mortar or cement which holds us together (see Colossians 3:12–14).

3 Our unity is **of the Spirit**. God's Holy Spirit dwells in our church (Ephesians 2:22); it is the Spirit who makes us one. Therefore, our unity is a spiritual unity. Our work and manners and customs may be different, but in the Spirit—in our inner hearts and minds—we must be completely one.

Unity doesn't happen automatically. To remain united takes work on our part. Satan is always trying to divide us. We need to make **every effort** to preserve our unity (see 1 Corinthians 1:10 and comment).

To remain united, we must bind ourselves in the **bond of peace**. Jesus Christ is our **peace** (Ephesians 2:14); He binds us together. Let us, therefore, bind ourselves together in Christ.

4 We were **called to one hope**. Our **hope** is that, as God's children, we shall receive an inheritance in heaven and live forever with Him. This is the hope of every believer.

[16] Paul says that we should be **humble and gentle**. Gentleness always goes together with humility. The eighth fruit of the Holy Spirit is **gentleness** (Galatians 5:23). Indeed, some translations of the Bible call the eighth fruit of the Spirit "humility" instead of "gentleness."

There is one **Spirit**, and there is one **body**. Because there is one Spirit in all of us, we are one body. First, one Spirit; then, through the Spirit, one body (see 1 Corinthians 12:13 and comment).

5 Because we have one **Lord**, we have one **faith**—that is, we believe in the one Lord Jesus Christ. And because we have only one Lord, we also have only one BAPTISM—that is, we are baptized in the name of that one Lord.

6 There is only one true **God** (see 1 Corinthians 8:5–6 and comment). God is our **Father**. From one Father comes one family, one church. Between the Father, the Son (the Lord Jesus Christ), and the Holy Spirit there is complete unity. Because of the unity of God, there must be unity in the church.

The true spiritual church cannot be divided. Nevertheless, when we look at our own church we see division and disunity. How is that possible? On the one hand, our church is one spiritual body which cannot be divided. But, on the other hand, when we look at it, it appears divided. How can that be?

We can explain the problem by using the illustration of an ordinary human family consisting of a father and mother and their children. Let us suppose that the father and mother become divorced. Let us also suppose that the children fight among themselves and each go their own way. The family thus becomes completely split up. Are they still one family, or not? Are those children still the children of their mother and father? Yes, they are. The family is still one family; only it has been split apart.

Our church is like a human family; even when there is strife and division, we are still one church. Sometimes there is a division within a single congregation. Sometimes there are divisions between several different congregations. Sometimes the churches of one place refuse to accept the churches of another place. But whatever type of disunity arises, the church in all these situations is still one; it is still the one church of Jesus Christ.

But, just as in a human family, the members of the church must make **every effort to keep the unity of the Spirit** (verse 3). Just as division in a family is distressing to a human father, so division in the church is distressing to our heavenly Father. Division in the church is always Satan's work. Wherever Satan finds a lack of humility, patience, and love among the church members, there he will find an opportunity to cause division.

It is right to establish different congregations in different places. Each village needs its own church. In a larger city or town, several congregations are needed in different areas. In this way, believers can easily belong to a local congregation near them. It is even all right in special circumstances to have several types of church in one location—as long as there is no disharmony or opposition between them.

But when two or more congregations in an area stop having fellowship with each other, or refuse to cooperate with each other, then there is division. And God is displeased. May God forgive us and cleanse us and heal us!

7 **But to each one of us grace has been given as Christ apportioned it.** Paul uses the word **grace** in this letter in two different ways. The usual meaning of the word **grace** is "saving grace," as in Ephesians 2:8, which every believer receives equally. But a second kind of grace is the "grace of **gifts**" (verse 8), which is given to believers as Christ apportions it. It is not given equally to all believers. The **gifts** referred to here are special skills and abilities, such as the gift of preaching and teaching, the gift of healing, the gift of hospitality, etc. Christ has **apportioned** these gifts to us in order that we might serve others.

Because of "saving grace," we believers are all equally God's children. Because of the "grace of gifts" (or grace of service), we each have different gifts and different tasks assigned to us—just as children in a family have different gifts and abilities.

These two kinds of grace—"saving grace" and the "grace of gifts"—are both given by the Holy Spirit. From this we can see that the highest gift of all which Christ gives to us is the Holy Spirit Himself, because it is from the Holy Spirit that all other gifts are distributed. God gave us Christ; Christ gave us the Holy Spirit; and all three together—Father, Son, and Holy Spirit—give us all these other **gifts**.

8 Here Paul quotes from Psalm 68:18. In this quotation, God, through the Psalm writer, is prophesying about Christ's ascension into heaven.

When Christ ascended to heaven, **he led captives in his train**. That is, Christ made **captives** of all those things that formerly made us captives—such things as sin, death, and Satan. Christ overcame all these things and took them captive. And when He reached heaven, He **gave gifts to men**—to the church.

9–10 When Christ died, He first **descended to the lower, earthly regions** (verse 9). And after three days, He **ascended higher than all the heavens** (verse 10), where He now rules with God over all things in heaven and on earth (see Ephesians 1:22–23).

11–12 In these verses, Paul mentions five "gifts" or appointments, which Christ has given to different individuals in the church. He has given some to be **apostles**, some to be **prophets**, some to be **evangelists**, and some to be **pastors and teachers**. There are more gifts than these five, of course; these are only examples (see 1 Corinthians 12:27–28; Romans 12:4–8 and comments). But the five appointments which Paul lists here are the most important ones for the church.

The five "gifts" listed here are really five different kinds of leaders which Christ has given especially for the establishing and building up of the church. Some Bible scholars say that these five "gifts" are not related to the gifts of the Spirit mentioned in 1 Corinthians 12:7–10. But whether they are related or not, all gifts and all appointments are given by both Christ and the Holy Spirit together, and all of them are given for the building up of the church.

Here a question arises: Are these gifts mentioned here natural gifts, that is, given at birth; or are they supernatural, that is, given later by the Holy Spirit? The answer is that these gifts have a natural part and also a supernatural part. God has given to every person at birth certain natural gifts and abilities. But when a person becomes a Christian, then the Holy Spirit begins to use those natural gifts. And in doing so, the Holy Spirit enlarges and refines those gifts, and sanctifies them for God's service.

However, there are other gifts, particularly those mentioned in 1 Corinthians 12:8–10, which are primarily supernatural, and are given to a person only after he has become a Christian (see 1 Corinthians 12:7–11 and comment; General Article: Holy Spirit Baptism).

Why are these gifts given? They are given **to prepare God's people for works of service** (verse 12). In this way, the body of Christ (the church) will be **built up**. These gifts are not given to us primarily for our individual benefit, but rather they are given for the building up of the church; they are given **for the common good** (1 Corinthians 12:7). These gifts are given to us so that we might use them to serve others. For example, a **pastor** is not the ruler of his church; rather, he is its servant! The teacher is not the master of his students; he is their servant. Christ is our example: Even though He was our Lord, He came to earth to serve, not to be served (see Mark 10:43–45 and comment).

If we do not use the gifts we have received to build up the church, then we are misusing our gifts, and God will not be pleased.

13 In this verse we see the two ultimate goals of these gifts to the church. The first goal is that we—each member of the church—might **reach unity in the faith and in the knowledge of the Son of God**. The second goal is that we might **become mature, attaining to the whole measure of the fullness of Christ**. This second goal is the final and greatest goal God has set for every one of His children; this is the end and purpose of our life—**to be conformed to the likeness** of Jesus Christ (see Romans 8:29 and comment).

In this life we will never completely attain to the **whole measure** of Christ's fullness; in this life we are growing, always growing. But even though on earth we cannot attain to all of Christ's fullness, we must keep moving toward that end. We must keep on growing more and more **mature**; we must not remain children spiritually (verse 14).

14 Children are unstable. They believe whatever they hear. They are easily deceived. They are like leaves blown here and there by the wind. Don't be like immature children, says Paul.[17]

15 The **truth** makes us stable. But the truth must be spoken **in love**. Some people speak the truth without love; such people create strife and divide the church. Other Christians make the opposite mistake. They believe that truth is not as important as love; as a result, they often avoid speaking the truth lest they hurt someone's feelings. The fact is that both **truth** and **love** are equally necessary. Truth without love is too hard; love without truth is too soft. If there is both truth and love in a church, that church and its members will be able to **grow up into . . . Christ**.

Some people believe that in order to avoid hurting others it is necessary from time to time to tell little falsehoods. But this belief is not correct. It is all right to keep silent about a hurtful matter; but if we are going to speak about it, we must speak only the truth.

16 Here again Paul compares Christ's church to a body, whose head is Christ. All of the body's parts are under the control of Christ, the **Head** (verse 15). Just as a small child grows, so grows the church, each part growing together in love. Each **supporting ligament** joining the parts of the body together helps the body to grow in harmony. Each ligament is like a **bond of peace** (verse 3) between members of the body. And as with an ordinary body, if the members of a church are not **joined and held together** in peace, the church cannot function properly and it will cease to grow.

The Old Self and the New Self (4:17–32)

17 In this section Paul begins a new subject. In verses 1–16, He has talked about the unity of the church. Now, from this verse through to Ephesians 5:21, Paul talks about the purity of the church. These are the two things above all that are essential for the church: unity and purity.

Paul exhorts the Ephesian Christians to no longer **live as the Gentiles do**. Most of the Gentiles of Paul's day did not believe in the one true God; rather, they worshiped idols and engaged in all kinds of immoral practices. Their minds were filled with vain and futile thoughts; their **thinking** was characterized by **futility**. Indeed, worldly men of every generation are like the Gentiles of Paul's day. Let us not be like worldly men. We are no longer children of the world; we are children of God. Therefore, we must act like children of God. We are a new people, and new people need to lead new lives (see Galatians 3:27 and comment).

18–19 From these verses we can see what eventually happens to worldly men. They become more and more separated from God. Their hearts become hardened (verse 18). Because of this **hardening** of their hearts, they lose all **sensitivity**; they no longer care about distinguishing right from wrong. They seek pleasure in **every kind of impurity**, but they cannot find satisfaction. Therefore, they continually **lust for more** (verse 19).

20–21 **You, however, did not come to know Christ that way**. That is, the Ephesians did not learn such behavior from Christ's teachings or from His example. Such behavior is based on falsehood; it is based on denying the **truth** of Christ's teachings. Let the Ephesians hold fast to that truth, and not follow after the false ways of the world.

22 What did the Ephesians learn from Christ? They learned that they must **put off** their **old self**—that is, they must put away the thoughts and desires and actions of their old sinful self. Every one of us is born with a sinful nature, and until we accept Christ we live under the control of that sinful nature. Our **old self** is simply the person we were when we

[17] In another sense, however, Christians should be like children. In particular, we should have the open and trusting attitude of children. We need to have a child's faith (see Mark 10:15 and comment).

lived under the control of our sinful nature. Therefore, before we can **put on the new self** (verse 24), we must first **put off**, or put to death, our **old self** (see Romans 6:6; 8:13 and comments).

23 Paul next tells the Ephesians to **be made new in the attitude**[18] **of** [their] **minds** (see Romans 12:2 and comment).

Remember, Paul is writing here to people who were already Christians. These Ephesian believers had already received new spiritual life through faith in Christ. They had already been **born again** (see John 3:3–5 and comment). There is no use in saying to people who haven't been born again: "**. . . be made new in the attitude of your minds**." It's impossible. They can't create a "new mind" by themselves. First they must believe in Jesus and receive new spiritual life; after that, it will be possible for them to have a new mind as well.

Because these Ephesian Christians had new spiritual life, they now needed new minds. New birth; new life; new mind. With a "new mind" we are better able to understand God's word; we are better able to walk in the light and not in darkness, to walk in truth and not in ignorance.

24 Having put off the old sinful self, we must then **put on the new self**—that is, we must "put on" the thoughts, desires, and actions of our new spiritual self, which is under the control of the Holy Spirit. If we take off the old self and don't put on the new self, we shall be naked! Many people try to put off the old self, but they hesitate to put on the new self. They leave their old religion, their old beliefs, their old ways, but then they don't follow a new way. They are neither here nor there; they drift without purpose; and eventually they are pulled back into their old life. And their final condition will be worse than their first (see Matthew 12:43–45; 2 Peter 2:20 and comments).

All of us who have believed in Jesus and been born again are already "new people," new creations (2 Corinthians 5:17). But now we must live like new people—new people who are **created to be like God in true righteousness and holiness**.

Paul says to **put on the new self**. We can compare this "new self" to a new uniform. Nurses in a hospital wear their own special uniforms. Police have their uniforms. Prisoners in jail have their uniforms. And Christians—that is, new men and women—have their "uniforms." The "uniform" of a Christian is Jesus Christ Himself—Christ's mind, Christ's behavior. Christians must "clothe" themselves with Christ.

Just as one's uniform must match his profession, so a Christian's behavior (uniform) must match his "profession," which is to be a child of God. We can tell a person's profession by the uniform he wears. If we Christians do not wear the "uniform" (behavior) of a Christian, how will people tell we are Christians? They won't be able to. A "new man" must wear new clothes. What's the first thing a prisoner does when he is released from jail? He takes off his jail clothes, and puts on new clothes! In the same way, we believers, who have been released from the "jail" of sin and Satan, should take off our jail clothes and put on Christ—our new clothes (see Romans 13:14 and comment).

25 Now Paul gives some examples of old behavior that we must "put off," and the corresponding new behavior that we must "put on."

First, Paul says, **put off falsehood**. Instead, **speak truthfully**. We must speak the truth always, in every situation. How often we twist the truth in order to hide our mistakes and sins! Let this not be; to twist the truth is to lie.

It is not enough simply to refrain from lying; we must speak the whole truth. When we withhold part of the truth, we often lead others to believe a falsehood—even though we have not actually lied. We deceive others by hiding part of the truth. To deceive others deliberately in this way is the same as to tell a lie.

To **speak truthfully** has another mean-

[18] In place of the word **attitude**, some translations of the Bible say "spirit." In this context, the meaning is the same.

ing: it means to keep our word, our promises. There must be trust between us, and the foundation of trust is keeping one's word.

26 **In your anger do not sin**. This is a quotation from Psalm 4:4. When we are angry, we must make sure it is the offense we are angry with, not the offender. To be angry with a person—no matter how great his offense—is always a sin on our part.[19] We must forgive the offender, not be angry with him. We must hate the sin but love the sinner. That was how Christ treated us!

Even when we are properly angry with someone's sin or offense, we must not drag out our anger for a long time. Our anger should end by the time the sun goes down. Otherwise, Satan will find an opportunity to enter our heart and turn our righteous anger into sinful anger. How can we end our anger? By completely forgiving the offender from our heart.

27 The **devil**—that is, SATAN—is always looking for an opportunity to use our anger for his purposes. When we are angry, we naturally begin to speak against the person who has angered us. Others hear us, and spread around our evil report about that person. When this happens, Satan is very happy, because soon more and more Christians will begin to talk against one another. This is Satan's most effective method of splitting apart a church or a Christian team.

It is not only wrong to talk against others; it is also wrong to even listen to such talk. To speak negatively about another person—even if it's the truth—is slander. And slander is a grave sin (Romans 1:30; 1 Corinthians 5:11; Ephesians 4:31). Satan will always use our slander as a weapon to destroy the church.

28 The second example of "old behavior" that Paul gives is **stealing**. The new behavior is work—**doing something useful**. It is not enough just to give up stealing; one must begin to work. There is no place for laziness. We should work not only to provide for our families, but also to provide for others in need. From stealing one moment, to giving the next: only the power of Christ can change a man like that!

29 The third example of "old behavior" is **unwholesome talk**. The new behavior is talk that is **helpful for building others up according to their needs**. Let everything we say be judged by this standard: does it help build others up, encourage them, or benefit them in some way? If so, then let us say it; if not, then let us keep silence.

30 The next example of "old behavior" is very broad; it is really a joining of all our "old behaviors" into one. Paul calls it "grieving" the Holy Spirit. **And do not grieve the Holy Spirit**, Paul writes. Whenever we sin, we **grieve** the Spirit; that is, we trouble and disappoint and insult the Spirit. The Spirit is grieved by every kind of unholiness.

Whenever we **grieve** the Spirit, the Spirit draws away from us. Whenever we Christians grow lukewarm in our spiritual lives, whenever our zeal or joy decreases, it is almost always because we have grieved the Holy Spirit in some way (Isaiah 63:10). Remember, we have been stamped with the **seal** of the Holy Spirit (Ephesians 1:13). Here Paul says we have been **sealed** with the Spirit. It's the same thing. We have been sealed with the Spirit **for the day of redemption**[20]—for the day of salvation. The Holy Spirit's seal is our passport to heaven. Let us not lose it!

31–32 In verse 31, Paul gives other examples of old behavior; in verse 32 he gives the new behavior (see Colossians 3:12–13 and comment).

God loved us when we were still sinners (see Romans 5:8 and comment). For Christ's sake He forgave our sins. But Jesus warned us that if we do not forgive others, God will not forgive us (see Matthew 6:12,14–15 and comment). Let us heed this warning.

---

[19] When we are angry with the offense, we use our anger to benefit the offender. But when we are angry with the offender, we desire to hurt him, not benefit him. And that is a sin.

[20] For further discussion of redemption, see comment on Ephesians 1:7 and footnote to comment.

CHAPTER 5

Living as Children of Light (5:1–21)

1–2 Just as God has acted with grace toward us, so must we, imitating God, act with grace toward others. Just as Christ loved us, so we must love others. The greatest proof of Christ's love was that He **gave himself up for us** as an offering and sacrifice to God. We likewise must give ourselves up for others, and present our lives, our bodies, as an offering and sacrifice to God (see Romans 12:1 and comment).

3 In this verse Paul mentions **sexual immorality, impurity,** and **greed.** He doesn't merely tell the Ephesians to avoid such evils; he says there mustn't be even a trace or hint of these evils in their lives. These evils shouldn't even be named among them.

Because we are God's children, we have been made holy. Therefore, we must lead holy lives. The moment we are tempted to do something unholy, we should at once remember who we are. We are **God's holy people.** We are His children. If we keep this always in our minds, we will find help in overcoming temptation. God says to each one of us: "You are my child; therefore, act like my child" (see 2 Corinthians 6:17–18 and comment).

4 Christians must not engage in **obscenity, foolish talk, or coarse joking.** The kind of **joking** that Paul is referring to here is the kind which is rude, which hurts and ridicules others. However, Paul does not mean that Christians are never to make jokes of any kind. There is a kind of joking that makes everyone laugh—even the person who is the butt of the joke. Christians do not always have to remain somber and serious. It is perfectly proper for Christians to laugh and have a good time and play jokes on each other. The only rule is that our joking must not be coarse and hurtful.

In this verse, Paul is cautioning Christians to avoid all ungodly conversation. God is going to take into account every careless word we have spoken (see Matthew 12:36–37 and comment). Instead of engaging in pointless worldly conversation, we ought to be giving joyful thanks to God for the great love and grace that He has shown to us in Jesus Christ.

5 A **greedy person** is an **idolater,** says Paul. A greedy person "worships" money and possessions instead of God. For him, money and possessions are like an idol (see 1 John 5:21 and comment).

No immoral, impure or greedy person will be able to enter the **kingdom of Christ and of God** (see 1 Corinthians 6:9–11; Galatians 5:19–21 and comments). Certainly we believers must not engage in such evildoing, or we shall risk losing our own inheritance in heaven (see Matthew 7:21; 1 John 2:15–17 and comments).

6–7 Men are always trying to deceive us with **empty words** (verse 6). They say: "It's okay to do what you want, to enjoy yourself. So what if you sin a little bit. Don't worry about it. Nothing will happen."

But such words are utterly false. Something will indeed happen if we sin: God's **wrath** will fall on us! Our sins have eternal consequences. God will judge all men—both believers and non-believers—for every sin they commit (see Romans 14:12; 2 Corinthians 5:10 and comments). Therefore, let us not be deceived by **empty words.**

Nevertheless, Christians do sin from time to time; none of us is without sin (1 John 1:8). But if we immediately repent of our sin, we shall receive forgiveness and be cleansed, and God's wrath will not fall upon us (Proverbs 28:13; 1 John 1:9). But God's wrath will indeed fall upon all those who refuse to repent and who continue to walk in disobedience.

Those who do evil often try to persuade Christians to join them in their evildoing. Before we believed in Christ, we too were evildoers. Especially our old friends will try to get us to do again the things we used to do with them. We must refuse to do so. We must not be **partners with them** in evil (verse 7).

8–9 **. . . you were once darkness**—that is, you once lived in darkness. Paul wrote earlier that the Ephesians were **darkened in their understanding** (Ephesians 4:18).

Jesus Christ is the light of the world. Therefore, those who follow Him walk in the light (see John 8:12 and comment). Not only that, as we follow Christ, His light shines out from our lives, and lights the way for other men to follow. Therefore, Paul says here that we are **light in the Lord** (verse 8). We are **children of light** (see John 12:35–36; 1 Thessalonians 5:5; 1 Peter 2:9 and comments).

10 Christians do good, not out of fear, but out of a desire to please the Lord. They are like obedient children who desire to make their parents happy. Therefore, Paul says, **find out what pleases the Lord**. And what pleases the Lord is this: that His children walk in the light and have nothing to do with the works of darkness. Instead, by our light we must expose the works of darkness (verse 11). Evil men work in the darkness; they do not like to come into the light lest their evil deeds be exposed (see John 3:19–20 and comment).

11 **Have nothing to do with the fruitless deeds of darkness, but rather expose them**. What must we do to **expose** the deeds of darkness? We must simply let our light shine—that is, we must quietly set an example of righteousness. This alone will be sufficient to expose the deeds of darkness, of evil. Yes, from time to time it is necessary to speak out openly against evil. But usually all we need to do is to let our light shine; that is always our main means of exposing evil.

Notice that Paul says we are to have nothing to do with the **deeds of darkness**; he doesn't say we are to have nothing to do with the doers of such deeds. Some Christians are so offended by the evil actions of other people that they refuse even to speak to them; but that is not what Paul is saying in this verse. After all, Jesus Himself ate with sinners (see Mark 2:15–17; 1 Corinthians 5:9–11; 2 Corinthians 6:14–18 and comments).

12 Sometimes a man's evil work is so bad that it is embarrassing to even talk about it!

13–14 In verse 14, Paul quotes the words of a poem written in his time. The **sleeper** mentioned in the poem is a person who is dead in his sins (Romans 13:11; Ephesians 2:2).

15 **Be very careful, then, how you live**. "How" we live is, of course, the most important practical issue in our lives. We must be **careful**—diligent—to live wisely. A foolish man doesn't care how he lives; the wise man does.

16 Paul tells us to use our time to the full, to make the most of **every opportunity** that comes to us. That is, we must not lose any opportunity to please God and do His will. Once time goes by, it never comes back; an opportunity lost will never return. (Another opportunity may come again, but not the one that was lost.) The wise man thinks about how he uses his time. Time is a gift given by God; we must not waste it.

Today, have we used our time wisely? God will one day demand an account of how we have used our time during this life.

. . . because the days are evil. This means that man's days on earth are filled with sorrow and suffering. In Paul's time especially, many Christians were being imprisoned and put to death. Therefore, says Paul, as long as the chance to serve God lasts, let Christians take every opportunity to do so. Because the day may quickly come when we no longer have the chance (John 9:4).

17 We must **understand** what the Lord's will is. The first step in understanding God's will is to **fear** Him. **The fear of the Lord is the beginning of wisdom** (Proverbs 1:7). The foolish man neither fears God nor cares about God's will; the wise man does.

How can we understand what God's will is for our lives? How can we know His will day by day? God's will has two parts: first, His "general will"; and second, His "specific will." God's general will is the same for all Christians; that is, He wants us to be holy, to be like Christ. We can find out what God's general will is by reading the Bible, God's word.

But the second part of God's will, His specific will, is not the same for every Christian. It varies for each Christian, and it varies in each situation. For example: Who should one marry? What course should one study? What should one do today? Where should one go? In matters like these, God's will is going to be different for each Christian. Direct answers to questions such as these are not found in the Bible.

Therefore, how can we understand what God's "specific will" is in such matters? First, by praying. The Holy Spirit will guide us if we ask Him. Second, by consulting our pastor, our parents,[21] or other Christian friends and elders. Third, by studying the Bible. When we study the Bible, we shall better understand God's "general will," and this in turn will help us discern His specific will. For example, the Bible doesn't tell us which girl or boy to marry, but it does tell us that we must marry a believer (2 Corinthians 6:14).

As we pray, consult, and study the Bible, we must use our minds to determine what God's will is. God gave us minds and reasoning power. He does not lead us as if we were a horse or mule with no understanding (Psalm 32:8–9). God will give us wisdom and guidance, but we must use our minds to receive it.

18 Christians must **not get drunk on wine**—or on any other alcoholic drink. Paul does not say that a Christian must never drink any wine at all (Psalm 104:15); he only says that a Christian must never get drunk.[22] A Christian must not even get a tiny bit drunk. Some people, especially some tribes, are heavy drinkers by custom; but God says to them as well: Do not get drunk. To get drunk is a sin. And once a person becomes drunk, he is led to commit even worse sins. And his desire to drink will grow and grow, and eventually it will enslave him.

People drink in order to find happiness or encouragement, but of course their happiness and encouragement lasts only a very short time. And they pay a high price for such momentary pleasure; drinking squanders not only their money but also their health. There is only one way to find permanent joy, happiness, and encouragement, and that is by being **filled with the** (Holy) **Spirit**.

. . . be filled with the Spirit.[23] That's not a suggestion; that's a command. And Paul actually wrote here that we should "keep on being filled" with the Spirit—not only today and tomorrow, but all week, all month, all year, all our lives!

How will we know if we are filled with the Spirit? We will know that we are filled with the Spirit when we see the fruits of the Spirit in our lives—that is, **love, joy, peace, patience, kindness, goodness, faithfulness, gentleness and self-control** (Galatians 5:22–23).

A man filled with liquor is under the liquor's control; a man filled with the Spirit is under the Spirit's control. A man filled with liquor cannot control himself; he has no self-control. But the man filled with the Spirit has self-control, which is the ninth fruit of the Spirit. Commotion and wild behavior among men is never produced by the Holy Spirit.

19 However, what the Spirit does produce in us is great joy; the Spirit makes us want to sing and make music to the Lord. Let us, therefore, praise God together with **psalms, hymns and spiritual songs**, not only with our lips but from our hearts (Colossians 3:16).

20 We must **always** give thanks to God **for everything**. For everything? For sickness? For hurricanes and hailstorms? For sorrow and trouble? Yes, for all of these. We must thank God **for everything**—whether good or bad. Why?

---

[21] If our parents are not Christians and give advice that is opposed to God's word, then we must not follow their advice in that particular matter.

[22] God leads some Christians to completely abstain from any kind of alcoholic beverage (see Luke 1:15). Certainly, any believer who had a drinking problem before becoming a Christian must stop drinking altogether.

[23] In the Greek text, the words **be filled** mean "keep on being filled."

Because God is our loving heavenly Father. No matter what troubles and difficulties He allows us to go through, we can know with certainty that in the end God will work it out for our good. God does only good to His children who love and serve Him (see Romans 8:28 and comment). This is why we must give thanks to God **for everything**.

21 When we try to control others, arguments and divisions arise. Therefore, instead of trying to control each other, let us rather put ourselves under each other's control. In this way, there is no chance for argument and division. Let us make ourselves each other's servant. This is the example that Jesus gave us when He washed His disciples' feet (see John 13:12–15 and comment).

Wives and Husbands (5:22–33)

22 God has given husbands authority over their wives. In a similar way, He has given parents authority over their children (Ephesians 6:1), and He has given employers authority over their employees (Ephesians 6:5). In each of these three cases—husbands and wives, parents and children, employers and employees—each person as an individual is equal in God's sight. But God has not given each person the same authority, the same responsibility, the same work. Paul does not say that the husband is better than the wife; he only says that God has given the husband greater authority in the family (see General Article: Christian Marriage).

The husband is given authority over his wife not for his own benefit but rather for the benefit of the whole family. His authority is to be used to maintain discipline, order, and peace within the family. The husband has no authority to maltreat or abuse his wife. Instead, he is to behave toward her with love and mercy, just as Christ behaved toward us. God has given husbands authority to do good, not to do ill.

23–24 Just as Christ has authority over the church and each of its members, so husbands have authority over their wives. And just as all Christians must remain under the authority of Christ, so wives must remain under the authority of their husbands (see Colossians 3:18; 1 Peter 3:1–2 and comments). The husband's authority is not his own; it is Christ's. Wives need to be able to see Christ—that is, Christ's qualities—in their husbands. If a wife can see Christ in her husband, then she should not have any difficulty remaining under his authority!

Remember, wives are under the authority only of their own husbands, not of other men. Furthermore, wives are not to be treated as servants or slaves; they must not be regarded as if they were a piece of household property. Together with her husband, a wife is an equally beautiful and valuable creation of the living God; she must not be treated as inferior in any way. Rather, the husband must love and cherish his wife as he would his own body (see Ephesians 5:28; 1 Peter 3:7 and comments).

But here a question arises: How should a wife behave toward a husband who is evil? Suppose that he gets drunk and beats her, and tells her to do things that are contrary to God's word. Should she obey him in such a situation, or not? No, she should not obey any command of her husband's that is against God's word. She must remember that her husband's authority over her is really God's authority. When the husband tries to force his wife to do something contrary to God's will, then he can no longer claim to have God's authority in that matter. In such a situation, the wife must obey God rather than her husband.

This same principle applies also to the relationship between parent and child, between employer and employee, and between any government and its citizens. As long as those in authority—whether parents, employers, or government officials—continue to obey God's law, then we must submit to their authority **in everything** (verse 24)—that is, in all matters over which God has given them authority. But if they order us to do anything that is against God's word, then we must not agree to do that thing. God's command is always higher than man's command (see Acts 4:18–20; Romans 13:1–5 and comments).

25 Notice that in verses 22–24, Paul

has talked about the wife's duty: to submit to her husband. Now in verses 25–28, Paul talks about the husband's duty to his wife: to love her! How must the husband love his wife? He must love her **as Christ loved the church**. The husband must "give himself up" for his wife in the same way that Christ **gave himself up** for the church. Think about that; the husband's duty is not so easy to fulfill! (Colossians 3:19).

26–27 Christ and His church can be compared to a husband and his bride. Paul wrote to the Corinthian church: **I promised you to one husband, to Christ, so that I might present you as a pure virgin to him** (2 Corinthians 11:2).

Christ loved His church, in spite of her impurity and imperfection. But more than that, He cleansed and purified her **by the washing of water through the word** (verse 26)—that is, through baptism[24] and through His word (see John 15:3 and comment). Christ desires that His church be **without stain or wrinkle or any other blemish** (verse 27).

28–29 Here Paul describes a second way in which husbands must love their wives—that is, **as their own bodies**. After marriage, the husband and wife become **one flesh** (verse 31); therefore, the husband is expected to love his wife as he loves his own body, as he loves himself.

30 Just as we care for the members of our own bodies, so in the same way does Christ care for the members of His own body, the church.

31–33 Paul quotes here from Genesis 2:24, in which God established the marriage relationship between men and women. The relation between husband and wife is the closest human relationship of all, closer even than that of mother and child.[25]

Just as a man leaves his mother and father and becomes united with his bride, so, in a sense, did Christ leave his heavenly home and come to earth to be united with His bride, the church. Let there be the same relationship between husband and wife that exists between Christ and His church. That is, let the wife submit to her husband as the church submits to Christ; and let the husband love his wife as Christ loves the church. This is the one guaranteed prescription for a happy and successful marriage.

From this comparison of the church with a bride, we can learn something about the church's position also. The church that disobeys her Lord is like an unfaithful wife who commits adultery. Let this not be true of our church!

CHAPTER 6

Children and Parents (6:1–4)

1 This verse applies primarily to young children, not adult children. Paul does not mean here that grown-up children must **obey** their parents. Paul is saying that only younger children who are still dependent must remain obedient to their parents (Proverbs 8:32–33; 15:5).

2–3 However, no matter how old we are, we must continue to honor our parents. Among the ten commandments of the Old Testament, the command to honor one's parents comes fifth (Exodus 20:12; Deuteronomy 5:16). But it is the first commandment that has a promise attached to it. If one obeys this commandment, God promises that it will **go well** for that person and he will **enjoy long life** (verse 3).

4 Having talked about the duties of children, Paul now talks about the duties of parents. That is, parents must bring their children up **in the training and**

---

[24] For further discussion of the role of baptism in cleansing us from sin, see General Article: Water Baptism.

[25] After birth, mother and child become two flesh, not one.

instruction of the Lord. The parents' goal is to teach the children obedience, so that when they grow up they will obey Christ, just as they obeyed their parents when they were young (Proverbs 22:6).

Together with teaching them obedience, parents must also be loving and tender toward their children. They must treat their children with fairness. They must not **exasperate** their children; that is, they must not needlessly rebuke or punish them, or inflict other unnecessary hardship upon them. Parents must not make their children angry without cause. Yes, we must discipline our children, but this is always in order to insure their future welfare. And we must always discipline them in love; love and discipline must always go together equally. We must discipline our children only after explaining what they have done wrong and why we are punishing them. Our discipline should not be overly severe; we must be careful not to grieve or harden the tender hearts of our children. We must never discipline our children in anger or impatience. If we are angry or upset with our children for doing something wrong, we must wait until our anger is over before we discipline them (Colossians 3:21). Just as God has given husbands authority to be used for the benefit of their wives, so God has given parents authority to be used for the benefit of their children (Deuteronomy 6:6–7; 2 Corinthians 12:14; 1 Timothy 3:4; Titus 2:4).

Slaves and Masters (6:5–9)

5 During New Testament times, the practice of slavery was widespread throughout the Roman Empire. Slaves were treated very badly. They had no freedom, no rights; they were treated like animals. They had to obey their masters in everything. Many slaves became Christians, because they received peace and hope from the Gospel of Christ, from Christ's promise of salvation and eternal life.

However, even though their situation as slaves was very grievous, Paul still tells them that they must remain obedient to their masters.

In today's world, the practice of keeping slaves is rarely found. However, the same principles that applied to masters and slaves in Paul's day can be applied to employers and employees in our day. Christian employees should obey their employers (in the work situation), just as they obey Christ (Colossians 3:22–24).

6 We must not do good work to win the approval of men; we must do it to win the approval of God. We must work **with sincerity of heart** (verse 5), not to appear good in the eyes of others, but rather to please God.

7–8 The master or employer's authority comes from God. **There is neither . . . slave nor free . . . for you are all one in Christ Jesus** (Galatians 3:28). All Christians are equal in the sight of God. On earth, their positions and ranks may be different, but in heaven they will all be equally the servants of one Lord (verse 9). God has appointed people to different callings; some He called to be employers, others He called to be employees.[26] Therefore, let us not grumble or complain against authorities which God has appointed. Just as we submit to Christ's authority, so must we **wholeheartedly** submit to the authority of our employer, or to the authority of our leaders in government or in the church (see Titus 2:9–10 and comment). If we willingly fulfill all our duties to our masters, God has promised that we shall be rewarded (see Matthew 16:27; 2 Corinthians 5:10).

9 The duty of the employee is to obey. Now Paul tells us about the duty of the employer, or master. The duty of the master is to treat those under him **in the same way** that he hopes the heavenly Master, Christ, will treat him. That is, the

[26] During their lifetime, God gives most Christians opportunities to advance. It is right for Christians to take these God-given opportunities to improve their life situation. But the main thing is this: We must accept God's will for our lives no matter what that will turns out to be. We must never grumble against God (see 1 Corinthians 7:17–24; 10:10 and comments).

employer must treat his employees with kindness and respect. The employer must give his employees a fair wage; he must not exploit them. He must give them suitable work and provide them with proper working conditions. The employer or master must not make people work to satisfy his own selfishness or greed. God has granted to us mercy, love, and forgiveness; the employer or master should treat his workers **in the same way**. Just as the worker will receive a reward for fulfilling his duties in obedience to his master, so the master also will receive a heavenly reward for fulfilling his duties toward his workers. Let earthly masters always remember that they have a Master in heaven! (Colossians 4:1). We are all fellow servants of Christ, and each of us—whether master or servant, employer or employee—will be rewarded in heaven according to how well we obeyed Christ here.

Let each person think only about his duty to others. Let us not think about what we can get from others, but rather what we can give to them. Let employees not think primarily about what wages and benefits they can get, but rather let them think about how they can do the best work for their employer. Let employers not think about how much work they can squeeze out of their workers, but rather let them think primarily about giving their workers a fair wage and good working conditions. This is the Christian way. If the people on each side would concentrate mainly on their duties instead of always worrying about their rights, then there would no longer be complaints, disagreements, demonstrations, and strikes. Jesus taught all of us to put the interests of others above our own.

The Armor of God (6:10–24)

10 . . . **be strong**. That is not a suggestion; it is a command. How can we obey this command? How can we be strong? By putting on the **full armor of God** (verse 11).

11 There is no point in thinking about how weak we are. Of course, we're weak! That's why God has given us His armor, so that we might be strong and equipped to fight the enemy. Therefore, Paul says to us: **Put on** [this] **armor**.

God has given to us His armor. It is spiritual armor, and it will protect us from our chief spiritual enemy, the **devil**—that is, Satan.

12 Our Christian life in this world is like a **struggle** or battle. In order to be victorious in battle, the first thing that's necessary is to put on one's armor. The second necessary thing is to understand one's enemy and know how strong he is. Let us not make the mistake of supposing that Satan is not strong; he is very strong. If we think Satan is not strong, he will surely overcome us. He is much stronger than we are! If we are without our armor, Satan will easily defeat us.

And Satan is not alone. Allied with with him are **rulers, authorities, powers** on earth, and **spiritual forces of evil** in heaven. These are the same authorities and powers over which Christ now reigns in heaven (Ephesians 1:20–21); they are the same **rulers and authorities** to whom God, through His church, is making known His **manifold wisdom** (Ephesians 3:10). However, here on earth the power of all these rulers and authorities is still very great, and thus we need God's armor to stand against them.

Therefore, having put on our armor, what do we need to know about our terrible enemy, Satan? First, he is invisible; he is a spirit. Second, as we have already said, he is powerful. Third, he is wicked and evil; he is the leader of all the **spiritual forces of evil**. There is no good, no mercy in Satan. His one desire and goal is to destroy, by any means possible, the spiritual life of every Christian. The fourth thing to know about Satan is that he is crafty and cunning. Peter says that Satan is **like a roaring lion looking for someone to devour** (1 Peter 5:8). That is true; but more usually Satan does not roar. He sneaks up on us quietly when we are not watching. Or he disguises himself, so that we can't recognize him (2 Corinthians 11:14). He is like a wolf who puts on sheep's clothing; the sheep think he's just another sheep, and let him into the flock (see Matthew 7:15 and comment).

How can we fight against such a terrible enemy?

13 We can fight against Satan with God's strength, because God's strength is far greater than Satan's (see 1 John 4:4 and comment). By putting on God's armor and standing our ground, we can cause Satan to flee (see James 4:7 and comment). Here again, as in verse 11, Paul tells us to put on the **full armor** of God. If even one piece of the armor is missing, Satan will immediately wound us in that unprotected area.

Paul tells us here to be ready to stand against Satan **when the day of evil comes**. The **day of evil** is the day of temptation, the day of persecution. In particular, it is any day when Satan especially attacks us.

14 In verses 14–17, Paul mentions six parts of God's armor: the **belt** and the **breastplate** (verse 14), "shoes" for the feet (verse 15), the **shield** (verse 16), the **helmet** and the **sword** (verse 17). In Paul's day, a soldier's armor consisted of these six pieces. Paul wrote this letter while a prisoner in Rome; he was probably being guarded by a soldier who was wearing just this kind of armor. Perhaps Paul's description of God's armor was based on the armor of his guard.

Now let us examine each piece of this armor. First, Paul mentions the **belt of truth**. Satan is the **father of lies** (John 8:44), and only the truth can defeat his lies. Truth also means trustworthiness, because in our battle with Satan we must be able to trust one another.

The second piece of armor is the **breastplate of righteousness** (Isaiah 59:17). God has declared believers in Christ to be righteous; we have received Christ's RIGHTEOUSNESS. We are declared righteous because Christ took upon Himself the punishment for our sin; through faith in Him, we are no longer guilty of sin (see Mark 10:45 and comment). We must put on the **breastplate of righteousness**; otherwise, Satan will accuse us of being unrighteous. Without righteousness, we shall lose our standing with God. Satan is a great accuser; he is called the **accuser of our brothers** (Revelation 12:10). Satan will try to make us doubt if we are really saved. One of Satan's main tactics is to shake our faith by creating all kinds of doubts in our minds. He tries to make us doubt our standing with God; he tries to make us doubt that God is on our side. He says to us: "You're just a sinner; you are unrighteous. God isn't going to take your side." Let us not listen to Satan when he talks like this. Rather, let us put on the **breastplate of righteousness**; let us hold fast to our faith that through Christ we have indeed been declared righteous in God's sight.

15 The third part of God's armor is footwear. We need to put on the "shoes" of **readiness that comes from the gospel of peace**. That is, we must be ready to carry the Gospel of Christ to others. A farmer doesn't need shoes, but a soldier does. Shoes help keep us from stumbling. Shoes help us to be ready; they put us in **readiness**. With our shoes on, we shall be ready to carry the Gospel, and we shall not stumble on the way. Wherever our shoes go, there also will go the **gospel of peace**—the Gospel of Christ! Here Paul calls the Gospel the **gospel of peace**, because through it peace can come between man and God (see Romans 5:1 and comment).

16 The fourth piece of armor is the **shield of faith**. This **shield** is our faith in God. When we raise our shield, we can have complete confidence in God's power. In Paul's day, the shield of a soldier was four and a half feet high and two and a half feet wide; it was big enough to protect the entire body. In the same way, when we raise our "spiritual shield," we are fully protected from Satan's **flaming arrows**. Satan's "flaming arrows" are such things as fear, discouragement, confusion, and doubt. When our shield of faith is raised, these things will not be able to touch us.

17 The fifth piece of God's armor is the **helmet of salvation** (Isaiah 59:17). The steel helmet of a soldier protects his head, so that his enemy cannot kill him. In the same way, the helmet of salvation protects us from being spiritually "killed" by Satan. The helmet is the guarantee of our salvation, our eternal life. With our helmet on, Satan cannot take away our eternal life.

The sixth part of God's armor is the **sword of the Spirit**. Notice that the first five pieces of the armor are defensive in nature. But the sixth part, the sword, is offensive. It is for attacking Satan. Without the sword, we cannot defeat Satan. What is the sword? It is the **word of God**.

Remember, by His **word** alone, God created the whole earth, the whole universe. By His word He also created all the **rulers**, **authorities**, and **powers** mentioned in verse 12, who afterward began to oppose Him. The **word of God** is effective; it's powerful! It has far more power that anything on earth. And when we hold the **sword of the Spirit** in our hands, that power is ours!

That **sword** is the sword of the Holy Spirit. The Holy Spirit reminds us of God's word (John 14:26). God intends that we use His word to defeat Satan. The best example of the use of God's word as a "sword" can be seen in Jesus' answers to Satan during His temptation (see Matthew 4:1–11).

18 We must put on all of our armor with **prayer**. Some people call prayer the seventh part of our armor. Without prayer, our armor will be useless. Our prayers should not only be for ourselves, but for our other Christian brothers and sisters, that they might be able to stand against the attacks of Satan and overcome him. If we neglect to pray for them, they will be defeated. We must pray **on all occasions ... and always keep on praying for all the saints**.

Paul tells us to pray **in the Spirit**—that is, with the help and inspiration of the Holy Spirit. The Spirit inspires our prayers and teaches us what to pray (Romans 8:26).

19–20 Even the greatest Christian leaders and preachers need our prayers. Paul was able to do the great works he did because of the prayers of fellow Christians.

In verse 20, Paul calls himself an **ambassador** (2 Corinthians 5:20). Yet even though he is an ambassador of the King of kings, Paul has ended up **in chains** in a Roman prison!

21–22 **Tychicus** was one of Paul's colleagues, who was with him during part of his imprisonment in Rome. In addition to delivering this letter to the Ephesians, Tychicus also delivered Paul's letter to the Colossians (Colossians 4:7–8).

23–24 Paul began this letter by expressing his desire that the Ephesians might experience the **grace** and **peace** of God (Ephesians 1:2). Now Paul ends the letter by giving to the Ephesians a benediction of **peace** (verse 23) and **grace** (verse 24). From this we are again reminded of the great theme of this great letter: Peace through grace (see Ephesians 1:2 and comment). Even though we are in the midst of a great spiritual struggle, we have peace with God, and peace within our church and within our hearts.

Grace to all who love our Lord Jesus Christ. Those who do not love the Lord have not experienced His love, His grace. Anyone who has received the grace of God will love His Son Jesus, for it is through Jesus that God's grace has come to us. Therefore, let us love our Lord **with an undying love**. And let us live our lives to the praise of the glory of His grace!

Philippians

INTRODUCTION

Philippi was a leading city of Macedonia, the northern province of Greece.[1] Because many Roman citizens and Roman soldiers had settled there, it had been made a Roman colony (see Acts 16:12 and comment).

Paul first came to Philippi during his second missionary journey. That was the first time the Gospel of Christ had been preached in the continent of Europe. It was here at Philippi, then, that the Gospel first spread to Europe from Asia. Remember, Christianity is not a European or Western religion: it began in Asia.

Paul first went to Philippi because of a vision he received, in which a man from Macedonia said to him: "**Come over to Macedonia and help us**" (Acts 16:9–10).

Paul's first visit to Philippi is described in Acts 16:11–40. Later, Paul visited Philippi again during his third missionary journey (Acts 20:1,6).

Most Bible scholars believe that Paul wrote this letter to the Philippians in about 60–61 A.D., while he was a prisoner in ROME. These scholars believe that Paul wrote his letters to the Ephesians and Colossians and to Philemon during that same imprisonment.

For further information about Paul's life, see Romans: Introduction.

[1] Greece is an important country of southern Europe. In New Testament times, it had fallen under the rule of the Roman Empire. Nevertheless, it had remained a center of culture and learning. Most educated people in New Testament times spoke the Greek language. The New Testament itself was originally written in Greek.

OUTLINE

A. Introduction (1:1–26).
   1. Thanksgiving and Prayer (1:1–11).
   2. Paul's Situation in Rome (1:12–26).
B. Exhortations (1:27–2:18).
   1. Exhortation to Steadfastness and Unity (1:27–2:4).
   2. The Example of Christ (2:5–2:11).
   3. Exhortation to Work Out One's Salvation (2:12–2:18).
C. Plans and Warnings (2:19–3:21).
   1. Plans for Coming Visits (2:19–30).
   2. Warnings Against False Teachers (3:1–21).
D. Concluding Remarks (4:1–23).
   1. Final Exhortations (4:1–9).
   2. The Philippians' Gifts to Paul (4:10–23).

CHAPTER 1

Thanksgiving and Prayer (1:1–11)

1 As in his other letters, Paul begins this letter by sending a greeting to the Philippians (see 2 Corinthians 1:1; Ephesians 1:1 and comments). **Timothy** was with Paul when he wrote this letter (see Colossians 1:1).

Notice that Paul and Timothy are not masters in the church; rather, they are **servants** of Christ. There is no position higher than that of being a servant of Christ.

This letter is addressed to all the SAINTS—that is, believers—at Philippi. Christians in themselves are not "saints," they are not holy. It is only IN CHRIST that they are holy. Believers receive Christ's holiness or righteousness not according to their own worthiness but by the grace of God. To be a **saint** or to be holy means to be separated from all evil and impurity and to be set apart for God.

This letter is also addressed to the **overseers**[2] **and deacons** of the Philippian church. The **overseers** were the chief leaders in the church; sometimes in the New Testament they are called **elders** (see Acts 14:23; 20:17; 1 Timothy 3:1; Titus 1:5–7 and comments; General Article: Church Government). The **deacons** are specially appointed members of the church, who have been given responsibility for the financial affairs and charitable work of the church (see Acts 6:1–6; 1 Timothy 3:8 and comments).

2 See Romans 1:7; Ephesians 1:2 and comments.

3–5 In verse 3, Paul gives thanks for the Philippian believers (see Romans 1:8–10; 1 Corinthians 1:4; Colossians 1:3–4,8 and comments). They have been partners with Paul **in the** GOSPEL—that is, in the preaching of the Gospel (verse 5). In the Greek language (the language in which Paul wrote all of his letters), the words for **partnership** and fellowship come from the same root. From this, we can understand that "fellowship" isn't just meeting together; it's working together—working together for the Gospel. Fellowship isn't just having a good time; it is being yoked together under Christ's yoke in order to serve Him.

Paul prays for the Philippians **with joy** (verse 4). This letter has been called the "epistle of joy," because in it Paul mentions the word "joy" fifteen times.

6 God, by His grace, has begun in each one of us a **good work**. That "good work" began with God's imparting to us Christ's Spirit, Christ's righteousness. God's "good work," in other words, was to make us a **new creation** (2 Corinthians 5:17). That was the beginning of God's work. And in the end, just as fruit ripens on a tree, God will bring His "new creation" **to completion**—to perfection.[3]

When we look at ourselves and at each other, we can see that our lives are far from "complete" or perfect. But we must be patient both with ourselves and with each other. It takes time for fruit to ripen. In the same way, it takes time for God to perfect us and to make us holy (Philippians 3:12). True, as soon as we believe, God declares us to be righteous, to be holy **in Christ** (verse 1). That's because God knows that in time we shall "ripen." He knows that in the end we shall become perfect. Therefore, God regards

[2] In place of the word **overseers**, many translations of the Bible say "bishops." The meaning is the same; "bishop" is simply a name for an overseer. In later church history, however, the word "bishop" came to mean a special high-ranking leader of the church.

[3] In this one short verse, we can see the two great doctrines of justification and sanctification. Justification is the **good work** that God has begun in us. We have been **justified freely by his grace** (Romans 3:24). Sanctification is the bringing of that work **to completion**, to perfect holiness. Our justification has already taken place—by grace through faith. Our sanctification continues to take place throughout our lives—by grace through faith. For further discussion, see General Articles: Way of Salvation, Holy Spirit.

us now as if we were already holy and righteous. But He works gradually to make us actually perfect in our daily lives.

From this verse we can take great hope. Perhaps some among us have become discouraged, because we see that our daily life is so imperfect. Perhaps we have a bad or sinful habit that we just can't seem to overcome. But let us remember that God is constantly working in us (Philippians 2:13). And if we do not lose faith, God will surely complete the work of making us holy (see Romans 11:22; Colossians 1:22–23,28 and comments).

When will God's work in our lives be completed? It will be completed on the **day of Christ Jesus**—that is, the day when Jesus comes again at the end of the world.[4] Only after Christ comes again in glory will the work God has begun in our lives be complete. At that time the **redemption of our bodies** will take place (Romans 8:23), and we shall become like Christ (see Romans 8:29; 2 Corinthians 3:18; 1 John 3:2 and comments).

7–8 From these verses we can see how much Paul loved the Philippians. Paul loved them not just with a human love, but **with the affection of Christ Jesus** (verse 8). Paul calls the Philippians not only partners but also sharers with him **in God's** GRACE. Whether Paul is in prison or not, the Philippians are Paul's partners and fellow sharers in all things—in his joy, in his sufferings, and in the work of the Gospel (see verses 29–30).

9 Paul prays that the Philippians' **love may abound more and more**. Paul prays that they might not love mindlessly or in ignorance, but that they might love with **knowledge and depth of insight**. It is not enough only to love; we must also love wisely (see Colossians 1:9).

10 Why do we need **knowledge and depth of insight**? (verse 9). The answer is so that we might **be able to discern what is best**. Before we can do what is best, we need to know what is best! Only then can our life be **pure and blameless**; only then can it be **filled with the fruit of righteousness** (verse 11). Thus Paul prays that the Philippians might remain pure and blameless **until the day of Christ**, when Christ will come again at the end of the world to judge all men (see 1 Corinthians 1:8; Philippians 1:6).

11 God has appointed us to bear **fruit** (John 15:16). What kind of fruit? There are two kinds of fruit we are expected to bear. The first kind of "fruit" is new disciples, those who come to faith in Christ through our witness. The second kind of fruit, the kind that Paul is mainly thinking about here, is the **fruit of righteousness**, which comes only through Christ (John 15:4–5). Our own righteousness is worthless in God's sight; to Him, **all our righteous acts are like filthy rags** (Isaiah 64:6). Only the righteousness we have received **through Jesus Christ** will be **to the glory and praise of God**. The **fruit of righteousness** is the same as the fruit of the Holy Spirit (Galatians 5:22–23). This fruit is manifested in our good attitude and in our good works, in the blessings and loving help we give to others. Paul prays for the Colossians that they will **bear fruit in every good work** (Colossians 1:10). Let that be our prayer as well, both for ourselves and for each other!

Paul's Chains Advance the Gospel (1:12–26)

12–14 At the time Paul wrote this letter, he was a prisoner in Rome (Acts 28:16; Philippians: Introduction). But even though Paul's personal circumstances were bad, God was bringing good out of them. Paul's sufferings had **served to advance the gospel** (verse 12). Furthermore, because of Paul's imprisonment, his fellow Christians in Rome had been **encouraged to speak the word of God more courageously and fearlessly** (verse 14). When we ourselves are facing trouble and persecution for Christ's sake,

---

[4] The **day of Christ** also means the day of judgment, when Christ will judge every man (John 5:22; 2 Corinthians 5:10). The day of judgment will take place at the end of the world, when Christ comes again.

let us remember these words of Paul. Because God will surely bring great good from our suffering also (see 2 Timothy 2:9).

15–17 Among the preachers of the Gospel in Rome, Paul, being an apostle, was the most famous. Therefore, some of the other preachers were jealous of Paul. They looked for an opportunity to pull Paul down and at the same time puff themselves up. They did indeed **preach Christ** (verse 15)—that is, they preached the true Gospel of Christ—but their purpose and motives were wrong. They preached **out of selfish ambition, not sincerely** (verse 17).

Let all preachers and servants of Christ examine themselves. Why are we preaching? Why are we working? Is it to enhance our own glory or Christ's glory? Let there be no **envy and rivalry** among us! These are the works of the sinful nature, and those who indulge in such things **will not inherit the kingdom of God** (Galatians 5:19–21).

There were other preachers in Rome, however, who preached **in love** (verse 16). They showed respect for Paul. They knew that Paul had been imprisoned because of his labor for the Gospel of Christ.

18 Paul's heart is big. If Christ's Gospel is preached, he is happy—even if it is being preached by his enemies. He will do nothing to oppose them.

Let us follow Paul's example in this. Suppose we learn that a Christian brother is wrongfully opposing us for some reason. If he, at the same time, is truly working for the Lord, we must not oppose him in return or speak against him. We must not try to "get even." Rather, forgetting our own honor and reputation, we must support and encourage that brother in his work for the Lord.

19 Paul has complete faith that whatever happens to him will work for his good, for his **deliverance**,[5] or salvation (Romans 8:28). By "deliverance," Paul means not only deliverance from prison but also salvation in the next life (see 2 Timothy 4:18). Paul's salvation will come through the **prayers** of his friends (like the Philippians) and through the **help given by the Spirit of Jesus Christ**—that is, the HOLY SPIRIT.

After reading this verse, let us always keep in mind how important our prayers are in the fulfilling of God's purposes. Here we see the **prayers** of Christians mentioned right alongside the work of the Holy Spirit Himself.

20 Whether he lives or is condemned to death, Paul expects and hopes that Christ will be **exalted** in his body. If he lives, his life will be for Christ's glory; if he dies, his death will be for Christ's glory (Romans 14:8).

21 **For to me, to live is Christ.** Everything Paul did, he did for Christ's sake and through Christ's Spirit. Without Christ, Paul was nothing. Paul's entire purpose in life was to serve and glorify Christ. Without Christ's grace and power, Paul could not live (Galatians 2:20).

Nevertheless, Paul is also happy to die for Christ. For believers in Christ, it is more advantageous to die than to live (verse 23). Paul will go to heaven. In heaven there will be no chains, no prisons, no pain, no sin or weakness. There will be only eternal joy and fellowship with Christ. That is **gain** indeed! (see 2 Corinthians 5:8).

22–23 If Paul lives, he will continue to engage in **fruitful labor** (verse 22). If he dies, he will be **with Christ** (verse 23), which for him will be **better by far**. Paul can't choose between living and dying; they are both good.

24 But Paul thinks about the Philippian church and the other churches he has established. For their sakes, Paul decides it would be better for him to live—to **remain in the body**. For his own sake it would be better to die; but for their sakes, it is necessary that he live.

25–26 Here Paul expresses the hope that he will be able to visit the Philippians again (see Philippians 2:24). As a result of his presence with them, Paul hopes they will progress still further in joy and faith.

It is not known whether or not Paul ever obtained his freedom. Many Bible

---

[5] In place of the word **deliverance**, some translations of the Bible say "salvation."

scholars believe that Paul was freed for a few years. Perhaps he was able to visit the Philippians one or two more times. But the Bible does not say definitely what happened to Paul after this letter was written. The last thing we know for sure about Paul comes at the end of the book of Acts, when Paul is still a prisoner in Rome (Acts 28:16,30–31).

Exhortation to Steadfastness (1:27–30)

27 **. . . conduct yourselves in a manner worthy of the gospel of Christ.** To conduct ourselves in a manner worthy of the Gospel, we must imitate Christ and lead a holy life. The Gospel of Christ is most effectively "preached" not with our tongues but with our lives (see Ephesians 4:1 and comment).

If the conduct of the Philippians remains worthy of the Gospel, then Paul will know that they are standing **firm in one spirit, contending as one man for the faith**—that is, for Christ and His Gospel.

To conduct ourselves in a manner worthy of the Gospel, we must be united. We must stand firm **in one spirit**, and we must contend for the faith **as one man**.

Before we can contend for Christ **as one man**, we must first be united **in one spirit**. Yes, in one sense, we are already spiritually united in Christ through the Holy Spirit. But, in another sense, we ourselves, as we live and work together, must maintain and preserve that spiritual unity (Ephesians 4:3).

To preserve our spiritual unity, there must be personal love and harmony between each member of the church. Many people mistakenly suppose that, if we just begin to work on some project or program together, unity will automatically come. But that is not so. First of all, we must get rid of all personal hurt, anger, envy, and slander that may have arisen among us. We must ask forgiveness of each other—and we must grant forgiveness to those who ask for it. Only after that will we be able to contend and work together **as one man**. Only after we are joined together **in one spirit** will our work be pleasing to God (see Matthew 5:23–24).

28 In order to conduct ourselves in a manner worthy of the Gospel (verse 27), we must be courageous and strong in Christ (1 Corinthians 16:13; Ephesians 6:10). Paul tells the Philippians not to fear those who oppose them. The Philippian church was a new church; it was small. Philippi was a great and important city; it was a Roman colony. The Romans strongly opposed the Christians. Thus the Philippians were surrounded on all sides by powerful enemies. But Paul is confident that their faith and steadfastness will serve as a **sign** or proof that they will be saved and their enemies will be destroyed. Those who oppose the Philippians also oppose God (Acts 5:38–39).

29–30 It had been **granted** to the Philippians to **suffer** for Christ. Let them rejoice in this (see Matthew 5:10–11; Acts 5:41; Philippians 2:17–18; Colossians 1:24). If we **share in** [Christ's] **sufferings**, we shall also **share in his glory** (Romans 8:17).

Paul was an example for the Philippians. They had seen the suffering he had endured when he first came to Philippi (Acts 16:19–24; 1 Thessalonians 2:2). Now Paul is in chains. Yet he continues to be filled with joy and hope. Let the Philippians be encouraged by his example! (see verse 14).

CHAPTER 2

Exhortation to Unity (2:1–4)

1–2 In these verses, Paul pleads urgently with the Philippians that there might be unity among them. In one way, all Christians are united in Christ; that is, they are all members of His body, the church (1 Corinthians 12:13,27). But in their daily lives, especially in their behavior toward each other, Christians do not act as if they were united. Just as two brothers, though of one family, can be divided against each other, so the members of a church, though of one spiritual family, can be divided against each other in their behavior.

For this reason Paul exhorts the Philippians to be **like minded** and to be **one in spirit and purpose** (verse 2). We must be **like-minded** in all major matters. On small, secondary matters it is all right to have different opinions; but even though our opinions on small matters may differ, we still must remain **one in spirit and purpose**. We must make **every effort to keep the unity of the Spirit through the bond of peace** (Ephesians 4:3).

To be **like-minded** and **one in spirit,** we must have the same goal and purpose: namely, to love and obey Christ, and to glorify Him. This must be the life-purpose of each one of us. But, of course, to achieve this purpose, there are many different means (see 1 Corinthians 1:10 and comment).

In verse 1, Paul mentions four blessings that all Christians should experience through the Holy Spirit: **encouragement from being united with Christ . . . comfort from his love . . . fellowship with the Spirit . . . tenderness and compassion**. Paul knows that the Philippians have already received these blessings. They have experienced the working of the Holy Spirit in their midst. If this is so, then let them act as if they were united. If they have truly received the Holy Spirit, let them act as if they have received the Spirit! Let them share with each other these blessings of the Spirit. If the Philippians will do this, they will make Paul's **joy complete**.

When Jesus looks at our church today, what gives Him joy? Our programs? Our work? Our church's size? No, not these things. What gives Him joy is our unity.[6] Therefore, let us be **like-minded, having the same love, being one in spirit and purpose**.

If we have no unity of mind, we shall have no unity in our work. Unity arises out of a personal love and closeness between brothers and sisters in the church. If we say we are united spiritually, but there is no personal unity among us, our so-called "spiritual unity" is meaningless. Just as good works are the proof of our faith (James 2:14,17–18), so our loving acceptance of one another is the proof of our unity.

3 In order to preserve and maintain our unity, the most important quality we need is humility. Whenever there is a personal division between brothers or sisters in the church, the main cause will almost always be pride. Pride usually remains hidden in our minds; thus we cannot see our own pride. Because of our inner pride, we give offense to others. Not only that, because of our inner pride we also take offense at others. It is because of pride that our feelings are hurt or we feel slighted. Therefore, when it comes to both giving offense and taking offense, pride is the major cause (see Ephesians 4:2).

It is not enough to consider others equal with ourselves; we must consider them **better** than ourselves (see Romans 12:10). We must judge our own faults and sins severely; but we must look on our brother's sins and weaknesses with sympathy and understanding.

4 We should look not only to our own interests, **but also to the interests of others**. What are these interests that we

[6] The other thing besides unity that gives Jesus special joy is our purity. Purity and unity are both equally essential for the church.

should look to? They are the needs, the welfare, of others (Romans 15:2; 1 Corinthians 10:24,33; Galatians 6:2). Paul doesn't mean here that we must always be interfering in the affairs of others or trying to dominate them. Rather, he means that we should seek every opportunity to help and encourage others.

The Example of Christ (2:5–11)

5 The greatest example of humility is Jesus Christ Himself. Even though He was the highest man of all—yes, even God Himself—He nonetheless lowered Himself and made Himself a servant for our sakes. Let the attitude that was in Christ be also in us!

6–7 Christ is **in very nature God**. This means that God's entire nature, character, and qualities are in Christ. But even though Christ was equal with God, He voluntarily emptied Himself of all these divine qualities and **made himself nothing**. Even though He was fully God, He became fully man. That is, he took the nature of a man—indeed, the **nature of a servant** (see Mark 10:43–45; 2 Corinthians 8:9 and comments).

Christ did not have to **grasp** His equality with God; it was His to begin with. Christ was and is equal with God; He is God. An heir doesn't have to **grasp** at his inheritance; it is his; it has been preserved for him.

Christ came to earth **in human likeness** (verse 7). Christ was a man like us in every way—except for one thing: He never sinned (Hebrews 2:14; 4:15).

But even though Christ was **in human likeness** while He was on earth, He didn't stop being God. For it was God Himself who came to earth in the form of the man Christ. God and Christ are one (see John 1:1,14; 10:30 and comments; General Article: Jesus Christ).

8 Christ not only took the nature of a man; He made Himself even lower than that. He allowed Himself to be killed on a CROSS as a criminal. In Christ's time, to be put to death on a cross was the most contemptible thing that could happen to a man. The Romans used to crucify only the worst criminals on crosses. There was nothing lower than a crucified criminal. And yet Christ came down from the highest position of all and put Himself in the lowest position of all—for our sakes.

9–11 **Therefore God exalted him to the highest place**. It was because Christ had first lowered Himself that God exalted Him (Matthew 23:12; James 4:10; 1 Peter 5:6). That **highest place** is at the right hand of God in heaven, where Christ is now seated (see Ephesians 1:20–23; Hebrews 1:8–9 and comments).

At the end of the world, **every knee** (every person)—whether living or dead, whether a believer in Christ or an unbeliever—will **bow** (verse 10); and **every tongue** (every person) will **confess that Jesus Christ is Lord**.

Shining as Stars (2:12–18)

12 For us, Christ is not only an example of humility, but also of obedience (Philippians 2:8; Hebrews 5:8). Here Paul exhorts the Philippians to be obedient. When Paul says, **continue to work out your** SALVATION, he means that we must obey Christ and do God's will. We must continue to follow Christ's example. Our lives must become more and more holy. Jesus said: **"Be perfect, therefore, as your heavenly Father is perfect"** (Matthew 5:48). This is what it means **to work out** [our] **salvation**.

We must work out our salvation **with fear and trembling**. We are weak and sinful. We stumble and go astray. We need to "fear" our own sins and weaknesses. Just as a child is afraid of displeasing his father, so we need to be afraid of displeasing God.[7] Because one day we are going to be judged by Jesus Christ for everything we have done in this life (2 Corinthians 5:10). We must continually confess to God our weakness and unworthiness. But at the same time we must continually praise and thank

[7] Christians do not need to be afraid of God's condemnation, but they do need to be afraid of displeasing and disappointing God. For further discussion, see 1 John 4:18 and comment.

God for His grace, by which we have been declared worthy and righteous in Christ.

13 We cannot "work out our salvation" by our own strength. Only because God is working in us are we able to do so (John 15:5). God not only gives us the strength to do His will; He also gives us the desire to do it. Yes, we are the ones that must carry out His will; we are the ones that must actually do the work. But it is only through God's grace and strength that we can do it. Everything we do is done by the grace of God (1 Corinthians 15:10). To God goes all the praise!

But remember this: We are free to reject God's grace. We can refuse to obey God's will. We can continue in sin without repenting. That is dependent on us; that is our choice. But if we choose to accept God's grace and to obey Him, then God has promised to help us.

Let us examine our hearts. Is there any area of our life in which we are refusing to obey God? Let us repent of that disobedience. Let us not despise the grace of God!

14 In God's sight, our inner minds and spirits are far more important than our outward actions (1 Samuel 16:7). There must be no silent **complaining or arguing** in our minds and spirits. Because that is really the same as complaining and arguing against God. And when we complain and argue against God, we are rejecting His grace and His will for our lives.

15 If there is no **complaining or arguing** in our minds and spirits, then we shall be **blameless and pure**. We were chosen, as God's children, to be **holy and blameless** (Ephesians 1:4). If we are blameless and pure in our inner minds and spirits, then we shall also be blameless and pure in our outward behavior. The holiness of our outward behavior is both the proof and the result of our inward holiness.

Let us examine ourselves. Are we **blameless and pure**? Do we **shine like stars in the universe**? That is Paul's hope and expectation for the Philippians. And it is also Christ's hope and expectation for us (Matthew 5:14,16; Ephesians 5:8).

16 Not only must we "shine like stars" for other men to see, but we must also **hold out**[8] **the word of life** for other men to hear. The **word** is Christ's word, which gives life (John 6:63). The **word** is also the Gospel, which is the **power of God for the salvation of everyone who believes** (Romans 1:16). However, there is little use in our preaching the **word** of Christ to others if the light of Christ is not visible in our lives.

If the Philippians "shine like stars" and proclaim the word of life, then Paul's labor among them will not have been in vain. He will be able to **boast** about the Philippians on the **day of Christ** (see Philippians 1:6; 1 Thessalonians 2:19–20).

17–18 The Philippians have already been offering to God their **sacrifice and service** (verse 17). Now, in addition to their sacrifice, Paul may have to offer his own life as a sacrifice. But he is happy to do so. He may be about to receive the death sentence. But even though he is sentenced to death, Paul can be **glad and rejoice** that, through his death, Jesus Christ will be glorified (Philippians 1:20). Whether Paul is sentenced to death or not, let the Philippians rejoice with him!

Timothy and Epaphroditus (2:19–30)

19 **Timothy** helped Paul establish the church at Philippi (Acts 16:1–3). At the time Paul wrote this letter, Timothy was with him in Rome (Philippians 1:1).

Paul hopes **in the Lord** to send Timothy to Philippi. All Paul's hopes are **in the Lord** (verse 24). But whatever the Lord wills, Paul is ready to accept (see James 4:13–16).

20–22 Why was Timothy such a valuable colleague for Paul? Because

[8] In place of the words **hold out**, some translations of the Bible say "hold on to." Although the two meanings are different, they are both true. It is not certain which meaning Paul intended.

Timothy was always looking out for the interests of others, for the welfare of others. Timothy cared deeply for the Philippians. Timothy had served with Paul **as a son with his father** (verse 22). Notice that Paul doesn't say here that Timothy "served" him, but rather that Timothy "served with" him. Timothy did not serve Paul; rather, together with Paul, he served Christ.

Paul writes that everyone else **looks out for his own interests**; that is, they selfishly seek first their own advantage in everything. Timothy was not like that. Timothy looked out for Christ's interests first of all.

How many people like Timothy are there in our church? Whose interests do we look out for first—ours or Christ's?

23–24 Timothy will be able to give news to the Philippians about **how things go with** [Paul]—that is, whether he is released or sentenced to death. Paul is **confident in the Lord** that he will be released and will be able to come to the Philippians himself (Philippians 1:25).

25 **Epaphroditus** was a Philippian, who had been sent to Rome by the church in Philippi to give help to Paul and to bring Paul a gift from the church (Philippians 4:18). Epaphroditus stayed for some time in Rome with Paul; that's why Paul calls him **my brother, fellow worker and fellow soldier**.

26–28 While he was in Rome, Epaphroditus became ill. When the Philippians heard about it, they were greatly worried. After his recovery, Epaphroditus wanted to return to Philippi so that he could dispel the anxiety of the Philippians on his behalf. For the Philippians' sakes, Paul was willing to let his helper Epaphroditus go.

29–30 All those who risk their lives for Christ deserve the respect of other Christians. It was always Paul's custom to give honor to each servant of Christ. Paul always speaks well of all those who serve Christ faithfully.

Paul writes that Epaphroditus risked his life **to make up for the help you** (the Philippians) **could not give me** (verse 30). Paul means that since all the Philippians could not personally come to Rome to help Paul, they had sent their representative Epaphroditus to do what they could not do in person.

CHAPTER 3

No Confidence in the Flesh (3:1–11)

1 **. . . rejoice in the Lord!** Why is it so important for us to rejoice? There are three reasons. First, joy is one of the fruits of the Holy Spirit (Galatians 5:22); therefore, our rejoicing is proof that the Holy Spirit is dwelling within us. Second, if we continually rejoice, we will more easily avoid the sin of complaining and grumbling against God when things don't go well. Third, because of our joy, others will want to know Jesus Christ too. If our face is always dark and sad, who will want to become a Christian?

In many countries of the world, Christ's church is growing rapidly. One of the main reasons for this is that the Christians in those countries are joyful—even though they are being persecuted!

In what is our joy? It is **in the Lord**. It is in His blessings, in His grace, in His fellowship. That's why trouble and persecution can't take away our joy. Our joy is not in this world; it is in Christ.

2 In this verse, Paul mentions **dogs . . . men who do evil . . . mutilators of the flesh**. These are simply three different names for the same group of people: namely, false teachers and false prophets. In Paul's time, most of the false teachers in the church were Jews who tried to teach new believers that in order to obtain salvation they must be circumcised. But Paul clearly taught that there was no spiritual advantage in being circumcised (1 Corinthians 7:19; Galatians 5:2,6).

3 **For it is we who are the**

CIRCUMCISION. That is, says Paul, we believers in Christ are the true **circumcision**, the true Israel. The Jews believed that because they were the natural descendants of the first Jew Abraham and because they had been circumcised, they were therefore the only "true Jews," the "people of the circumcision." But Paul denied this. He taught, rather, that the "true circumcision" are those people whose hearts have been "circumcised"; that is, those who have been circumcised inwardly, spiritually. The "true circumcision" are those **who worship by the Spirit of God, who glory in Christ Jesus**. The "true circumcision" are those **who put no confidence in the flesh**—that is, they put no confidence in the act of circumcision itself, the cutting away of the "flesh" at the end of the penis. They put their confidence only in Jesus Christ (see Romans 2:25–29; Colossians 2:11 and comments).

4 The false Jewish teachers put their confidence **in the flesh**; that is, they put confidence in the fact that they were natural descendants of Abraham and that they had been circumcised. "We are the true Jews," they boasted.

But Paul was also a true Jew according to the flesh. If these false Jewish teachers thought they could put confidence in the flesh, Paul could put even more confidence in the flesh.

5 According to Jewish law, Paul had been circumcised on the eighth day of life (Genesis 17:12). Paul belonged to the nation of ISRAEL, the Jewish nation; that is, he was a Jew according to the flesh. Paul was descended from **Benjamin**, the youngest son of Jacob. Jacob was Abraham's grandson, and he had twelve sons, from which the twelve tribes of Israel are descended. Paul was a **Hebrew of Hebrews**;[9] that is, he was as true a Hebrew (Jew) as one could be. He spoke the Hebrew language and followed Hebrew customs (2 Corinthians 11:22). Not only that, Paul was also a PHARISEE; the Pharisees were the strictest sect of the Jews.

6 Paul was so strict and zealous a Jew that he persecuted the CHURCH, that is, the believers in Christ (see Acts 9:1–2; 22:3–4; 26:9–11; Galatians 1:13–14).

Paul says that **as for legalistic righteousness**, he was **faultless**; that is, outwardly he obeyed all the rules and regulations of the Jewish law.

7 **But whatever was to my profit**—that is, all the things Paul wrote in verses 5–6—Paul now considers to be of no profit. In fact, Paul now considers them **loss**; he considers them harmful, disadvantageous. These things (being a Jew, Hebrew, Pharisee, etc.) were disadvantageous because they had kept Paul from putting his confidence in Christ. Now, **for the sake of Christ**—or, because of Christ—Paul has left all these old Jewish things.

8 There is nothing on this earth more valuable than knowing Jesus Christ personally. Nothing else can give a person salvation and eternal life. Only by knowing and accepting Christ as our personal Savior can we obtain salvation.

As an illustration, let us imagine a boat. The boat is loaded with valuable goods. The boat is crossing the sea when a great storm comes up. The boat begins to sink. What must the sailors in the boat do to be saved? They must throw all those valuable goods overboard. Yes, the goods are valuable; but because of the weight of the goods, the boat is sinking and the men are about to drown.

In the same way, Paul has had to "throw overboard" all his old religious "goods"—such as, his Jewish background, his circumcision, his **legalistic righteousness** (verse 6). Paul has lost all these things so that he **may gain Christ**—so that he might be saved.

On this subject, Jesus told two parables of men who sold everything they had in

---

[9] The **Hebrews** were Jews who spoke either the Hebrew or Aramaic languages. In Paul's time, there were two main kinds of Jews: those who spoke the Greek language, and those who spoke Hebrew or Aramaic (Acts 6:1). Even though Paul could also speak Greek, he was himself a Hebrew. The Hebrews considered themselves to be the purest and truest Jews of all.

order to buy something else of even greater value (Matthew 13:44–45). Jesus Christ is that "something;" He is more valuable than everything in the world put together.

9 Paul does not want a RIGHTEOUSNESS ... **that comes from the** LAW—that is, that comes from obeying the law. Such righteousness is not true righteousness (see Galatians 2:15–16). Rather, Paul wants to receive Christ's righteousness—**the righteousness that comes from God and is by** FAITH (see Romans 1:17; 3:21–24 and comments). Only this is true righteousness. True righteousness is always a gift of God. It is not given to us on the basis of our own work or effort; it is given to us by God's grace (see Ephesians 2:8–9 and comment).

10 Paul seeks not only Christ's righteousness, but he seeks also to know Christ—**to know Christ and the power of his** RESURRECTION. Paul wants to know Christ personally; he wants Christ to dwell within him (John 15:5). Paul wants to experience the power of the resurrected Christ, which is given through Christ's Holy Spirit. Paul, in short, wants to have a new life (see Romans 6:4; 8:11; Ephesians 2:4–6).

In order to share in Christ's life and in His power, we must also share in His sufferings. Therefore, Paul wants to know the **fellowship of sharing in his sufferings**.

Not only that, Paul wants to become **like him** (Christ) **in his death**. This has two meanings. First, Paul wants his "old sinful self" to be crucified with Christ (see Romans 6:6; Galatians 2:20; 5:24 and comments). Second, Paul is ready every day to die with Christ (1 Corinthians 15:31). Paul wrote: **We always carry around in our body the death of Jesus** (2 Corinthians 4:10–11). Paul is ready to lose his life for Jesus' sake (Mark 8:34–35).

Therefore, to know the **fellowship of sharing in** [Christ's] **sufferings** means not only to outwardly suffer trouble and persecution for Christ's sake, but also to inwardly crucify the old sinful nature and its desires—to **put to death the misdeeds of the body** (Romans 8:13).

11 Having died with Christ, Paul hopes to **attain to the resurrection from the dead** (see Romans 6:4–5,8 and comment).

Pressing on Toward the Goal (3:12–16)

12 Paul has not yet obtained the full knowledge and the full righteousness of Christ. He is not yet **perfect**. But Paul presses on **to take hold of that for which Christ Jesus took hold of** [him]—that is, to take hold of holiness, perfection, and maturity (Ephesians 4:13). Because it is for this reason—that Paul might be **holy and blameless** (Ephesians 1:4)—that Christ **took hold of** Paul.

Remember, Christ first "took hold" of us. Because of that, we can "take hold" of Him; we can obtain Him and hold on to Him in a spiritual sense. And even though, as we take hold of Him, our grip is weak, His grip on us is strong; He will not let us slip out of His hands.

13–14 **But this one thing I do**. Paul is completely single-minded. He does not allow himself to be distracted from his purpose. He does not waste his energy on secondary issues. **Forgetting what is behind ...** Paul forgets **what is behind**. That is, he doesn't look back; he doesn't mope over his failures, his mistakes and sins. It is useless to keep thinking about these past things. Paul is like a runner in a race: he looks only ahead (see Luke 9:62; Hebrews 12:1–2). A runner is slowed down if he looks back.

Paul then says: ... **straining** toward what is ahead, I **press on** toward the goal. Paul is not a passive Christian; he is actively—strenuously—pursuing the goal of becoming like Christ.

Many Christians are confused about this point. They say: "Everything is by God's grace. Not only our justification is by God's grace, but also our sanctification. Just as fruit ripens on a tree, so will we become like Christ. We don't need to strive and struggle."

In saying this, these Christians are in part correct. It is indeed correct to say that all is by grace, and that we do not need to strive and struggle on our own strength.

However, there is another side to the truth—a side which Paul presents in these verses. Men are not quite like fruit on a tree. Fruits submit naturally to the ripening process; men do not. Men must actively submit to God and obey Him; they must actively **throw off everything that hinders . . . and run with perseverance the race marked out** for them (Hebrew 12:1). The Christian life is a race, and we must run it. No one ever won a race by sitting on the sideline.

The **prize** (verse 14) that Paul wants to win at the end of the race is full fellowship with Christ. Paul also hopes to be a "co-heir" with Christ and to share in his glory (Romans 8:17; 1 Corinthians 9:24–25; James 1:12).

15 Who are the **mature** whom Paul mentions here? In verse 12, Paul says that he has not yet been made **perfect**. Christians cannot be "perfect" in this life, but they can be "mature." The **mature** are those who forget **what is behind** and strain **toward what is ahead** (verse 13); they believe that looking back is useless, even harmful. The **mature** are those who are single-minded, who, like Paul, have only one consuming passion in life: namely, to **know Christ** (verse 10) and to be like him (Romans 8:29). All mature Christians **should take such a view of things**. If any among the Philippians take a different view of the matter, Paul is confident that God will **make clear** to them that Paul's teaching is correct.

16 **Only let us live up to what we have already attained**. Paul means by this that each of us should live according to the grace he or she has received. We do not receive God's full grace all at once; we do not become mature at once. Through the Holy Spirit, God shows us our hidden sins and weaknesses one by one. We cannot correct sins and faults we don't know about.

Therefore, Paul says here that we must walk according to the grace, knowledge, and power we have each been given. If the Holy Spirit reveals to us a particular sin in our life, we must turn from that sin. Day by day God will give us enough grace to overcome sin. We must live according to that grace. We must **live up to** [the grace] **we have already attained**.

The Enemies of the Cross (3:17–21)

17 It is not enough to preach about Christ; we must also live like Christ. New Christians, especially, need examples of Christ-like living to follow (see 1 Corinthians 11:1).

The Philippians should follow not only Paul's example but also the example of those **who live according to the pattern** given by Paul. Paul's own example has influenced many to live like Christ; now they in turn are influencing still others. The influence of our example will spread to those we have never even met! Therefore, we need to ask ourselves: What kind of example am I setting?

18 Let the Philippians not follow the example of the **enemies of the cross**. The **enemies of the cross** are those who say that Christ's death on the cross is not sufficient to save men. Such **enemies** say they are Christians, but they are not; they are false teachers (Matthew 7:15; Mark 13:22; Acts 20:29–30; 2 Corinthians 11:13; 2 Timothy 4:1–2). They are those who look out only for their own interests (Philippians 2:21).

19 Here Paul writes four things about these **enemies of the cross**. First, they will be destroyed. **Their destiny is destruction**. They will receive eternal punishment on the day of judgment. Second, **their god is their stomach**—that is, they serve their own desires and appetites; they do not serve Christ (Romans 16:18). Third, **their glory is in their shame**; that is, they glory in their shameful lusts and shameful acts.[10] Fourth, their minds are on **earthly things**, or worldly things, not on spiritual things (Romans 8:5–6). Such men are indeed enemies of Christ's cross.

20 But Christians should not be like this. Let the Philippians set their minds

---

[10] Among the enemies of the cross, those who are Jews glory also in their flesh, that is, in their circumcision (verse 3).

on things above, not on earthly things (Colossians 3:2). Paul says that **our citizenship is in heaven.** God **has seated us with** [Christ] **in the heavenly realms** (Ephesians 2:6). In this world we are only **aliens and strangers** (1 Peter 2:11). Therefore, let believers not put any significance on what their nationality is, on whether they are "nationals" or "foreigners." Because, in this world, all believers are foreigners. But in heaven we will all be "nationals," for that is where our **citizenship** is.

And we eagerly await a Savior from [heaven]. Christians know that Jesus Christ will come again at the end of the world. Let us eagerly watch for His coming.

21 After Christ comes again, our **lowly bodies** will be transformed. In other words, it is then that the **redemption,** or resurrection, of our bodies will take place (see Romans 8:23; 1 Corinthians 15:42–44,49; Colossians 3:4; 1 John 3:2 and comments). Our resurrection will take place through the **power** of the risen Christ (Ephesians 1:19–22).

CHAPTER 4

Final Exhortations (4:1–9)

1 Having described in Philippians 3:12–21 how the Philippian believers should "press on" and not look back, how they should follow the example of mature Christians, how they should "eagerly await" the coming of Christ, Paul now writes: **Therefore . . . that is how you should stand firm in the Lord.**

We must stand firm **in the Lord,** in His strength and in His grace. One of the biggest helps in standing firm is our faith that Jesus will return and transform our bodies into His likeness (Philippians 3:20–21).

The Philippians are Paul's **joy and crown** (see 1 Thessalonians 2:19). They are the fruit of Paul's labor. They are his "crown of victory," the crown the runner receives when he wins the race (1 Corinthians 9:25).

2 Here we read that two leading women in the Philippian church have had a disagreement. Paul doesn't tell us what the disagreement is about. He only pleads with them that they agree with each other and become of one mind (see Philippians 2:2). Paul's great desire is that there be unity in the church.

Unity in the church depends on two things: true teaching and purity of life. It is essential to oppose those who teach falsehood and those who live in sin without repenting. Such people are like a "cancer" in Christ's body, the church; and that "cancer" needs to be cut out and removed.

But it is a sin to oppose those in the church who have a disagreement with us over a personal matter. To oppose a brother or sister for such a reason is a work of the sinful nature, a work of impurity. Such opposition wounds Christ's body. It can destroy the church. Whenever we feel impelled to oppose some brother or sister in the church, let us make very certain that we are opposing that person for Christ's sake and not our own sake. Otherwise, we shall be opposing Christ Himself.

Paul asks these two women to agree with each other **in the Lord.** In order for there to be true agreement between Christians, each side must accept the lordship and authority of Christ. Only as brothers and sisters **in the Lord** can we truly be of one mind with each other. We cannot be of one mind on any major matter with those who are not in the Lord.

3 Paul here asks another member of the Philippian church to help the two women mentioned in verse 2 to resolve their differences. Paul calls this person his

loyal yokefellow. It is not known who this person was. Paul also mentions **Clement**[11] and other fellow workers, whose names are written **in the book of life** (see Luke 10:20; Revelation 3:5).

4 Paul again tells the Philippians to rejoice in the Lord (see Philippians 3:1 and comment).

Rejoice! This is not a suggestion; it's a command. When we are continually sad, we are disobeying God's word. Nevertheless, there are times when it is appropriate to mourn, and at such times it is not a sin to be sad. And we must always mourn for sin, both for our own sins and for the sins of others (see Matthew 5:4; Romans 12:15 and comments).

5 The word **gentleness** that Paul uses here is a very broad word. Its meaning includes not only **gentleness**, but also **patience**, **kindness**, and **goodness**—all fruits of the Holy Spirit (Galatians 5:22–23). A gentle man is also a generous man. Such a man looks out not for his own interests but for the interests of others (Philippians 2:20–21). Let our **gentleness** be apparent to all men. Gentleness is one proof of our love for each other (see John 13:35).

The Lord is near. Paul means that Christ is near to the Philippians and has His gaze upon them. Christ is constantly purifying His church in Philippi.

But there is a second meaning to Paul's statement that the **Lord is near**: namely, that the Lord is about to come again (James 5:8). Some people ask: "Is the Lord late in coming? If when Paul wrote this letter the Lord's coming was **near**, why has He not come?" But let us not doubt about His coming. Rather, let us remember that in the Lord's sight **a day is like a thousand years, and a thousand years are like a day** (2 Peter 3:8).

6 **Do not be anxious about anything**. This is a command. To be anxious is always a sin, because anxiety is a sign of lack of faith (Romans 14:23). God is our loving and all-powerful heavenly Father. He will take care of His children (1 Peter 5:7). We are not to worry (see Matthew 6:25–34).

However, when we have a need for something, we must ask God for it (Matthew 6:11; 7:7–8). God knows what we need before we ask for it. Nevertheless, just as a human father wants to hear his children's requests, so our heavenly Father wants to hear our requests. But we must ask God in faith (James 1:6–8). Not only that, we must ask with thanksgiving (Ephesians 5:20; Philippians 1:3). God hears our requests, and He always gives us an answer. Therefore, even as we pray, we can thank Him for answering (see 1 John 5: 14–15 and comment).

7 The **peace of God** is one of the nine fruits of the Holy Spirit (Galatians 5:22). When God's peace comes into our minds, anxiety goes out. Peace and anxiety are opposites. God's peace is greater than our understanding. It **transcends all understanding**. With our understanding, we see things that make us anxious; but when God's peace comes, our anxiety is overcome. God's peace will **guard** our hearts and minds from every anxiety. Anxieties are weapons of Satan.

But the peace of God is available only **in Christ Jesus**. Apart from Christ, the Holy Spirit does not dwell within us. And if the Holy Spirit is not in our life, there will be no peace either.

8 What kinds of things do we think about, what do we concentrate on? Do we spend a lot of time finding fault with others? Or grumbling among ourselves? Let us stop that. Instead, let us think about things that are **true, noble, pure, lovely,** and **admirable. . . . think about such things**.

9 Whatever true teaching from the Bible we read or hear about we must put into practice. **Do not merely listen to the word. . . . Do what it says** (James 1:22,25). If we obey God's word, not only the **peace of God** (verse 7) but the **God of peace** will be with us—God Himself!

---

[11] **Clement** is not mentioned elsewhere in the New Testament. It is not known who he was.

Thanks for Their Gifts (4:10–23)

10 Paul rejoices in the love and generosity that the Philippians have shown to him. Epaphroditus has just recently brought to Paul a gift from the Philippians (verse 18).

11–12 But Paul has not written verse 10 because he is still in need and hopes to get even more help from the Philippians. He is not writing to flatter the Philippians, but merely to express his gratitude. Paul has learned to be **content** whatever the circumstances (1 Timothy 6:6). In other words, Paul's state of contentment does not depend on outward circumstances. He possesses the peace of God (verse 7). Let us, like Paul, learn to always be **content**. If we have plenty, let us humbly accept it with a clear conscience, giving thanks to God. If we have little, let us not complain against God; rather, let us fully accept His will in all things (Job 1:21–22).

Worldly men—those who love the world more than they love God—are always seeking bodily comforts and pleasures. But we believers in Christ should seek only our bodily necessities. As far as our physical lives are concerned, we should ask God only for those things which are necessary for our well-being. But as far as our spiritual lives are concerned, there is no limit to what we can ask for from God. God is ready to give us spiritual gifts and blessings in abundance.

13 In verse 12, Paul said that he has learned the **secret** of remaining content. What is that "secret"? In Paul's words, the secret is this: **I can do everything through him** (Christ) **who gives me strength**. There's nothing that Christ cannot give. There's no work that Christ cannot enable us to do (see 2 Corinthians 12:9). Because of this, we can do **everything** through Christ (see Ephesians 3:20–21).

14 Even though Paul could have managed without the Philippians' help, he is grateful that they have been sharers in his troubles.

15–16 Here Paul recalls with appreciation the Philippians' former generosity and assistance (Philippians 1:4–5).

17 Paul is not praising the Philippians in order to get more help from them. Rather, he is seeking that they might receive spiritual fruit as a reward for their generosity to him. He wants them to be spiritually blessed for their generosity; he wants their generosity to be **credited to their account**.

18 Because of the gift that Epaphroditus has recently brought from the Philippians, Paul is now abundantly supplied. Paul says that their gift is a **fragrant offering, an acceptable sacrifice, pleasing to God**. Whenever we help others, especially those who are in Christian work, we are presenting a **fragrant offering**[12] to God (see Hebrews 13:16). This kind of sacrifice is pleasing to God. Whatever we do for our brothers, we do also for Christ (Matthew 25:40). But even more than the sacrifice of our money, God wants the sacrifice of ourselves, our own lives. He wants us to offer ourselves as living sacrifices in obedience to Him (Romans 12:1; Hebrews 10:5–7).

19–20 The promise Paul has written in verse 19 is one of the greatest promises in the Bible: **God will meet all your needs according to his glorious riches in Christ Jesus**. God will meet **all your needs**—both physical and spiritual! Brothers and sisters, are any of you in any need? Simply trust in God and in His promises. He says: "I will meet **all your needs**" (see 2 Corinthians 9:8).

God will meet all our needs **in Christ Jesus**. Apart from Christ, we shall not receive any of God's promises. All of our needs are met in Christ and through Christ. Together with Christ, God freely gives us all things; but if we are not in Christ, we shall receive nothing (see Matthew 6:33; Romans 8:32 and comments).

And does God only give us a little? Does He give us only barely enough? No, He gives to us **according to his glorious riches**! (see Ephesians 1:3; 3:8,20–21).

---

[12] In accordance with Jewish law, the Jews burned fragrant incense when they offered sacrifices.

There is no limit to the glorious riches of Christ. And these riches are ours in Him! May God be praised!

But a word of caution is necessary here. The **glorious riches** Paul refers to in verse 19 are primarily spiritual riches, not material riches. In material things, God has promised to supply only our **needs**—not our wants! But in spiritual things, God is ready to bless us in abundance.

21–22 Paul here sends the Philippians greetings from various Christians in Rome. Those **who belong to Caesar's household** are some of the servants and household officials of **Caesar**[13] who had become believers. Because Paul was a prisoner of Caesar, he had contact with some members of Caesar's household. Through his witness, some had become Christians (see Philippians 1:13).

23 See 1 Corinthians 16:23 and comment.

[13] All Roman emperors were given the title **Caesar**. "Caesar" means emperor.

Colossians

INTRODUCTION

Colosse was a small city of the ROMAN EMPIRE located in what is now modern Turkey. It was about one hundred miles from Ephesus. While Paul was staying in Ephesus, some people came from Colosse and heard his teaching (see Ephesians: Introduction). One of these visiting Colossians, whose name was Epaphras (Colossians 1:7–8), believed Paul's Gospel and returned to Colosse and started a new church there.

Evidently some false teaching had arisen in this new Colossian church. Therefore, Epaphras asked Paul to send the church a letter refuting the false teaching and presenting the true Gospel of Christ. Since all Christians throughout the Middle East had heard of Paul, Epaphras hoped that the believers in Colosse would heed the instruction of such an important leader.

Therefore, in the first two chapters of this letter to the Colossians, Paul gives the basic teachings of the Gospel and refutes the false teaching that had arisen at Colosse. Then, in the last two chapters, Paul gives practical advice about how one should live the Christian life.

Most Bible scholars believe that Paul wrote this letter in about 60–61 A.D., while he was imprisoned in Rome. Tychicus, a colleague of Paul, carried this letter to Colosse; along with it, he also carried Paul's letter to the Ephesians.

For further information about Paul's life, see Romans: Introduction.

OUTLINE

A. Thanksgiving and Prayer (1:1–14).
   1. Thanksgiving for the Colossians' Faith (1:1–8).
   2. Prayer for the Colossians' Spiritual Growth (1:9–14).
B. The Supremacy of Christ (1:15–2:23).
   1. Christ the Lord of Creation (1:15–23).
   2. Paul's Ministry for Christ (1:24–2:5).
   3. The Fullness of Life in Christ (2:6–23).
C. Rules for Holy Living (3:1–4:18).
   1. Abandoning the Sins of the Old Life (3:1–11).
   2. Putting on the New Life (3:12–17).
   3. Rules for Christian Households (3:18–25).
   4. Further Instructions (4:1–6).
   5. Final Greetings (4:7–18).

CHAPTER 1

Thanksgiving and Prayer (1:1–14)

1–2 **Timothy** was a close friend and disciple of Paul, who shared in much of Paul's work as an apostle (see Acts 16:1–3; 1 Timothy 1:2). Timothy was with Paul when Paul wrote this letter; thus Paul has included his name in his salutation to the Colossians (see Ephesians 1:1–2; Philippians 1:1–2 and comments).

3–4 Paul gives thanks for the faith and love of the Colossians. We too, like Paul, need to develop the habit of thanking God for each other. How often we only complain about each other! This is a sin in God's eyes; He does not want to hear our complaints about others. Instead, let us give thanks to God for every believer (see Ephesians 1:15–16 and comment).

Paul gives thanks especially for the FAITH of the Colossians and for the **love** that they have for all the SAINTS. Faith and love always go together. Faith without love—or faith without works—is a false faith; the proof of our faith is love and good works. If there are no works of love, then there is no faith (see Galatians 5:6; James 2:14–17 and comments).

Let us ask ourselves: If Paul were alive today, would he be able to give thanks to God for our faith and love?

5 Paul says that faith and love **spring from the hope stored up . . . in heaven**. What **hope** is that? It is the hope of salvation, of eternal life, of an inheritance in heaven; it is for these things that Christians hope. Our hope is not weak and uncertain; it is strong and firm. Our hope is strong because it comes from Christ and is in Christ. Christ Himself is our hope, because it is from Him and in Him that we receive every spiritual blessing (Ephesians 1:3). If we have received Christ, then we have received every other spiritual blessing as well (see Romans 8:32 and comment).

The Colossians received their hope when they heard the **word of truth, the** GOSPEL. The Gospel of Christ is the **truth**. It does not come from man's thoughts. It is not something invented or imagined by man. The Gospel is God's true word. It is the central message of the Bible. The Bible is not an ordinary book written according to man's wisdom and knowledge. Rather, the Bible is God's own word.[1] Therefore, we can place our complete reliance and faith in the Bible. From it we receive our hope of salvation and eternal life (see John 5:39–40; 6:68 and comments).

We Christians would do well to think more about the hope stored up for us in heaven. If we did so, we might think less about the wealth and possessions we try to store up for ourselves on earth (see Matthew 6:19–21; Colossians 3:1–2; 1 Peter 1:3–4 and comments).

Here in verses 4–5, then, we see the three greatest gifts or graces that God gives to us, and for which Paul here gives thanks: namely, **faith, love,** and **hope** (see 1 Corinthians 13:13; 1 Thessalonians 1:2–3 and comments).

6 Paul says here: **All over the world this gospel is producing fruit and growing**. And Paul adds that the Gospel has been producing fruit and growing among the Colossians as well.

We need to ask ourselves: In our own area and in our own church, is the Gospel producing fruit and growing? If we have truly received and believed the Gospel, then its fruit should be increasing in our lives and in our churches.

Paul reminds us here that the Gospel is founded in God's GRACE, in God's freely given love and mercy. When we hear the Gospel, we can understand **God's grace in all its truth**. The Gospel is the "Good News" of God's grace to men and women.

7–8 **Epaphras** was a **faithful minister of Christ**; that is, he had received Christ's full authority to preach the Gospel. Epaphras was Paul's **fellow servant**; Paul and Epaphras were the servants of one Master, Christ. Bible scholars believe that it was Paul who

[1] For further discussion, see General Article: How We Got Our Bible.

originally sent Epaphras to establish the church at Colosse.

Paul heard from Epaphras about the Colossians' **love in the Spirit** (verse 8). For this kind of love to be present in our lives, the Holy Spirit must be present also. It is by the Holy Spirit that God pours out this love into our hearts (Romans 5:5). This love is the first of the nine fruits of the Spirit (Galatians 5:22–23).

Paul heard good things from Epaphras about the Colossians. Let us think about what kinds of things others are hearing about us!

9 Paul now prays that the Colossians might be filled with the **knowlege of his** (God's) **will**. There are many kinds of knowledge, but the most important of all is the knowledge of God's will. If one does not have a knowledge of God's will, all other knowledge will be useless (see Ephesians 1:15–17 and comment).

To obtain spiritual knowledge or wisdom, the first step is to fear God (Psalm 111:10; Proverbs 1:7). But remember, Satan and his evil spirits also fear God (James 2:19); therefore, they too have the first part or "beginning" of wisdom. But that is all they have, because they refuse to heed that wisdom. They fear God, but they do not obey Him.[2] The second step, then, in obtaining spiritual knowledge or wisdom is to obey God. Only those who obey God and who walk in His way will obtain **all spiritual wisdom and understanding**.

10 Thus we see that it is not enough to have a knowledge of God's will; we must also obey His will (see James 1:22). A knowledge of God's will is useless unless we live according to that knowledge. What is God's will? It is to **live a life worthy of the Lord** (see Ephesians 4:1 and comment). And what does it mean to live a life "worthy of the Lord"? It means **bearing fruit in every good work**, and **growing in the knowledge of God**.

What kind of **fruit** does God want us to bear? First, he wants us to bear the nine fruits of the Holy Spirit (see Galatians 5:22–23 and comment). Second, through our own witness and example, God wants us to "bear" or raise up new believers, new disciples, new children for Him; this kind of "fruit" is also pleasing to God (see John 15:16; Philippians 1:9–11 and comments).

Notice that Paul says that we must keep **growing in the knowledge of God**. A tree either grows, or it dies. If we see a tree that has stopped growing and has stopped bearing fruit, then we know that that tree is about to die. Let our Christian lives never reach that state!

11 First, Paul has prayed that the Colossians might have a **knowledge of** [God's] **will** (verse 9). Now he prays that they might be **strengthened with all power** in order to carry out God's will. Paul prayed the same thing for the Ephesians (see Ephesians 3:14–16,20–21).

All we need to do is to pray in faith for this **power**, and God will give it to us. But, in another sense, we have already received this power. This is why Paul has given us this command: . . . **be strong in the Lord and in his mighty power** (Ephesians 6:10). True, on the one hand, we must continually ask God for power. But, on the other hand, God says to us: "I have already given you power; use it!"

Having been **strengthened with all power**, we shall be able to bear all kinds of trouble with **great endurance and patience**—and do so **joyfully**.

12–14 Paul here mentions three things for which the Colossians—and we also—should thank God. First, we should thank God that we have been **qualified . . . to share in the inheritance of the saints in the kingdom of light**—the KINGDOM OF GOD. That is, we have been made full citizens of God's kingdom.

The second thing we should thank God for is that we have been **rescued . . . from the dominion of darkness** (verse 13)—that is, from the kingdom of Satan. And

[2] Satan and his evil spirits fear God, because they know that in the end they will be punished and destroyed. Believers, however, have the assurance of salvation and eternal life. Thus they have no fear of eternal punishment. Fear of God is only the first step of wisdom; once we have believed, our fear of God is replaced by love for Him (Psalm 2:11; 1 John 4:18 and comment).

we have been brought into the **kingdom of the Son** (Christ), which is the same as the kingdom of God (1 Peter 2:9).

The third thing to thank God for is that **we have REDEMPTION, the forgiveness of sins** (verse 14). The word **redemption** means deliverance from the penalty of sin through Christ's sacrifice; it is one of the main aspects of our salvation (see Romans 3:24; Ephesians 1:7 and comments). We are no longer servants of Satan; we are no longer prisoners in his kingdom. We have been set free, and have become citizens in the kingdom of God (see Ephesians 2:19 and comment).

These three great blessings are not something we shall obtain only in the future; we have already received these blessings! Let us indeed give thanks and praise to God!

The Supremacy of Christ (1:15–23)

15 **He** (Christ) **is the image of the invisible God**. No man can see God with his natural eyes; but men could clearly see Jesus Christ while He was on earth (see John 1:18; Hebrews 1:3 and comments). By looking at Jesus, we can see the character and qualities of God Himself. But more than this, when we see Jesus, we are actually seeing God Himself, as revealed in the form of His only Son (see John 14:9 and comment). Christ is not only the **image** of God; He is God's one true incarnation. He is the one true God come down to earth. He is God Himself (see John 10:30 and comment; General Article: Jesus Christ).

God has made man in His image (Genesis 1:27). That's why, when God chose to come down to earth, He came in the form of a man—Jesus Christ. Jesus is the **firstborn over all creation**; He is our older brother (Romans 8:29). Because Jesus is the **firstborn**, He receives the Father's inheritance. Jesus is the **heir of all things** (Hebrews 1:2).

We too have been created in God's image, and through faith in Christ we can become **co-heirs** with Him (see Romans 8:17 and comment).

16–17 Christ is not only the **firstborn over all creation** (verse 15); He is the Creator. **For by him all things were created**. Christ existed from before the creation of the world (see John 1:1–3 and comment).

Christ has created all things. Therefore, He has authority over all things—both in heaven and on earth. Christ rules over all **thrones, powers, rulers,** and **authorities** in the universe (see Ephesians 1:21). He rules over evil spirits, and gods and goddesses; He rules over Satan himself. In everything, God has given Him the **supremacy** (verse 18). Christ is truly the **Lord of lords and King of kings** (Revelation 17:14).

18 Christ is the **head of the body, the** CHURCH (see Ephesians 1:22–23 and comment). No body can live without a head. If we lose one member of our bodies—such as an arm or a leg or an eye—we will still live. But if there is no head, there is no life!

Christ not only created the universe and everything in it, but He also created a "new man," a "new people"—that is, the **church**. Through His church, Christ continues working in the world today. Today men can't see Christ (because He has ascended into heaven), but they can see us, Christ's church. Therefore, they must be able to see Christ in us. And that must be our goal. We must live as Christ did, so that when other people look at us, they will indeed see Christ in our lives. The indwelling Holy Spirit of Christ must shine forth in our daily speech and behavior. Men know God through Christ. And men know Christ through us—that is, through the Holy Spirit dwelling within us (see 1 Corinthians 3:16; Galatians 2:20; Ephesians 2:22 and comments).

Let us examine ourselves: Can others see Christ in our church? In each one of us? Is Christ truly our Head? Or are we like a chicken with its head cut off, running here and there and soon to die? (see 1 John 5:12).

Christ is the firstborn **from among the dead**. God raised Christ from the dead. And God will raise up from the dead all who truly believe in Christ. Those who believe have been chosen by God to be His children, to be members of His family. And since we are God's children, Christ is our older brother (see Romans 8:11,29 and comment).

19 God has given all of His power, authority, and lordship to Christ (see Colossians 2:9–10 and comment). That is, God has given to Christ **all his fullness**. And through the Holy Spirit living within us and filling us, we too can possess that **fullness**.

20 Here we can see God's purpose in giving Christ the **supremacy** (verse 18). God's purpose was **through him** (Christ) **to reconcile to himself** (God) **all things**.

Through the sacrifice of Christ's body—that is, through Christ's death on the cross—God transferred the punishment for our sins to Christ. Therefore, we who believe in Christ are no longer held guilty; we have received forgiveness for our sins (see Ephesians 1:7; Colossians 1:14 and comments). Not only are our sins washed away, but we have also been reconciled to God. There is now **peace** between us and God. Thus we can see here two major aspects of our salvation: forgiveness of sin, and reconciliation with God. And all this—our forgiveness and our reconciliation—have been made possible **through** [Christ's] **blood**—that is, through Christ's death on the cross (see Romans 5:9–11; Ephesians 2:13 and comments).

Paul says here that God's purpose was **to reconcile to himself all things**. What does this mean? Does it mean that Satan and his evil spirits will be reconciled to God and receive salvation? No, it doesn't mean that. It means that the entire creation is going to be placed under Christ's authority and lordship. Therefore, Satan and his evil spirits, having received eternal punishment, will also be brought under the authority of Christ (Ephesians 1:22).

21 All men at first are **alienated from God**. Because of their evil and self-centered behavior, men are **enemies** of God in their minds. Some people think that all men are basically good by nature, but Paul does not agree. Paul says that at one time all of us were by nature **enemies** of God.

22 Now, however, through the death of Christ's body on the cross, we have received forgiveness for our sins, we have been cleansed of our impurities, and we have been delivered from the punishment we deserved. Thus we have now been completely reconciled to God (see Ephesians 2:13 and comment).

23 Is it possible, once having been reconciled to God, to later lose our salvation? This verse seems to say that if we stop believing, we can indeed lose our salvation. We must **continue in** [our] **faith**, or else Christ's death will be of no benefit to us. We are saved **through faith** (Ephesians 2:8); therefore, if we leave the faith, we will forfeit our salvation.

But many Christians believe that once a person is truly saved, his salvation can never be lost. They quote John 10:28, where Jesus says: "**I give them eternal life, and they shall never perish; no one can snatch them out of my hand.**" This is true. But others answer that even though **no one can snatch** us out of Jesus' hand, we ourselves can choose to jump out of His hand: that is, we can choose to stop believing.[3] This much can be said with certainty: If we leave our faith, our situation will be extremely dangerous (see Luke 9:62; 2 Peter 2:20–22 and comments; General Article: Can We Lose Our Salvation?).

Here another question arises. Some Christians at first seem to be very strong in their faith, but then later they appear to fall away; they stop coming to church, they do not behave like Christians, they no longer do the works of faith. But they say, "I believe; I have not stopped believing." But what kind of "faith" do they have? It is a false faith. True faith always gives rise to good works, to works of love. If our faith doesn't result in good works, it is a dead faith (see James 2:14–24 and comment).

Therefore, let us continue in our faith, **established and firm**; let us not be **moved**

[3] Some people would answer that anyone who "stops believing" never truly believed to begin with. This may be true; there is no way to prove it one way or another. Only God knows who has truly believed; only God is in a position to judge men's hearts.

from our **hope** (see Hebrew 10:23). Our hope has been revealed or **held out in the gospel** of Christ. And this Gospel of Christ has been proclaimed to **every creature under heaven**. That is, the Gospel of Christ is for every man and woman on earth.

Paul's Labor for the Church (1:24–29)

24 God's true servants **rejoice in what** [they have] **suffered** for Christ and His church (see Matthew 5:11–12; Acts 5:41–42; Romans 5:3 and comments). Even though Paul is in jail as he writes this letter, he is rejoicing!

There is nothing **lacking** in Christ's suffering for us. He took the whole weight of our sins upon Himself, and suffered a slow and painful death on the cross. His suffering is complete. But Paul's suffering is not yet complete; he has still more to suffer.[4]

Paul has suffered much for the sake of the church, Christ's body (1 Corinthians 4:9–13; 2 Corinthians 11:23–28). Even though Paul has never met the Colossians (he only knows about them through the report of Epaphras), he has suffered for them also.

We must learn something here from Paul's life: namely, that if we want to follow Christ we must be ready to suffer for Him. Paul wrote Timothy: **. . . everyone who wants to live a godly life in Christ Jesus will be persecuted** (2 Timothy 3:12). Are we ready to suffer? Not only that, will we be able to rejoice when trouble and suffering come? It's easy to say yes—before the suffering comes! And suffering comes not only from our enemies; it often comes from those who are supposed to be our friends, from our own brothers and sisters in the church. Such was Paul's own experience (2 Timothy 1:15).

25 In order to overcome the false teaching that had arisen in the Colossian church, Paul here reminds the Colossians of his apostolic authority; he reminds them that he has been specially appointed to preach the full Gospel of Christ and to expose error in the churches. Everything Paul writes is completely true and trustworthy; therefore, let the Colossians heed what he has written in this letter! (Ephesians 3:7; 2 Timothy 1:11).

26–27 In one way, the word of God is like a **mystery**, because its meaning is hidden from many people. But the "mystery" has been **disclosed to the saints**—that is, to those whose hearts are open and who are ready to believe.

In another letter Paul has clearly written what this **mystery** is: namely, **that God was reconciling the world to himself in Christ** (2 Corinthians 5:19). And even now, through His Holy Spirit living within us, Christ is reconciling us to God and to each other. And this Gospel, from which we obtain the hope of salvation—**the hope of glory** (verse 27)—is not only for the Jews, but is also for the **Gentiles**, such as the Colossians (Ephesians 3:8–9).

28 Here we see the main subject of all Paul's preaching: Jesus Christ. **We proclaim him** (Christ). And the chief goal and purpose of all preaching and teaching can also be seen here: namely, **that we may present everyone perfect in Christ**. The word **everyone** here means "every believer," since it is impossible for a non-believer to be presented perfect in Christ. And we believers will be presented **perfect in Christ** on the day when we stand before Christ's throne in heaven.

29 Paul labors and struggles. But he labors and struggles not with his own energy, but with Christ's energy. Let us too, like Paul, attempt nothing in our own strength; otherwise, what

[4] There is a difference between Christ's suffering and the believer's suffering. Christ's suffering was for our redemption, for our salvation. Our suffering, on the other hand, is for the propagation of the Gospel. Our suffering is not complete because there is still much work to do to spread the Gospel throughout the world. The Gospel spreads most rapidly through the suffering of believers.

we do will come to nothing. Without Christ's power, we can do nothing worthwhile for God (see John 15:5 and comment). But with Christ's power, we can do anything (Philippians 4:13).

CHAPTER 2

Paul's Struggles for the Colossians (2:1–5)

1–3 Paul had never met the Christians in the cities of Colosse and **Laodicea**;[5] nevertheless, he labored and struggled for them. Especially the Colossian believers were on his heart. He writes this letter as if he were their own pastor.

The purpose of Paul's **struggling** is that these believers whom he has never met might **be encouraged in heart and united in love**, and that they might **know the mystery of God, namely, Christ** (verse 2).

The essence of the Christian religion is to **know . . . Christ**. We Christians are not followers of a religion; we are followers of a person, Jesus Christ. Our religion is not some philosophy or system of ideas; it is a person, Christ, whom we can know personally. If we do not know Christ personally, we cannot call ourselves Christians.

We can know Christ through faith. To the person without faith, Christ is only a **mystery**. But when we have faith, that "mystery" is disclosed. As soon as we believe, Christ's Spirit (the Holy Spirit) enters our lives; then, through the Spirit, we experience a personal relationship with Jesus Himself.

When we know Christ, we receive **all the treasures of wisdom and knowledge**, which are **hidden** in Him (verse 3). Thus, to know Christ is to know everything we'll ever need to know!

4 Paul wants his readers to know Christ, so that they will not be deceived by false teachers. What kinds of things do false teachers teach? They teach that Christ is not the Son of God. Or they teach that we can obtain spiritual wisdom and knowledge without knowing Christ. Such teachers use **fine-sounding arguments**; but their "wisdom" is not from God, it is from man (verse 8).

5 Paul cares so much for the Colossians that he feels almost as if he was present with them; and indeed Paul was with them **in spirit**. In the same way, when we love and care for other believers, we are with them **in spirit** even though we are many miles apart—and even though we have never met.

The Fullness of Life in Christ (2:6–23)

6–7 **. . . just as you received Christ Jesus as Lord, continue to live in him.** Just as we received Christ through faith, so we must **continue to live in him** through faith.

Can we remember when we first received Christ as our Lord? What was it like? We were filled with joy, peace, and love, were we not? Now, says Paul, keep on living like that! Continue to live **just as you received Christ**.

We must continue to live **rooted and built up in him** (verse 7). Christ is the vine; we are the branches. If we become separated from Him, we shall die (see John 15:4–5 and comment).

Let us not be like rocky soil, where the seed (God's word) that is sown springs up quickly, but soon dies because the soil is too shallow (see Mark 4:5–6,16–17 and comment). Or let us not be like thorny soil, where the seed grows rapidly, but then is choked by the thorns—that is, by the **worries of this life, the deceitfulness of wealth and the desires of other things** (see Mark 4:7,18–19 and comment).

---

[5] **Laodicea** was eleven miles from Colosse; Paul wanted this letter read in the church there also (see Colossians 4:15–16 and comment).

8 Paul mentions two kinds of knowledge here: first, the knowledge that comes from Christ; and second, the knowledge that comes from the world, from man. Human or worldly **philosophy** is all around us, but compared to the wisdom and knowledge that is in Christ, the philosophy of the world is **hollow and deceptive**. There are many kinds of so-called "Christian" philosophies, which are put forward by people who claim to be Christians but whose teaching is false. These people deny that Jesus is the Son of God, the one true incarnation of the living God. Even true Christians can be deceived by the **hollow and deceptive philosophy** of such people.

9 In this verse Paul tells us what it means to be the true incarnation of God: **. . . in Christ all the fullness of the Deity lives in bodily form.** Jesus Christ is not an image of God. He is not a form or an example of God. He is not an ambassador or representative of God. He is none of these things. Jesus Christ is God Himself! In Christ **all the fullness of the Deity lives** (see Colossians 1:19).

What is God's **fullness**? It is all His qualities taken together—such as, love, light, truth, power, wisdom, holiness, etc. All of these qualities of God are also in Jesus Christ. Notice here that the fullness of God **lives** in Christ. God still lives in Christ. Christ continues to be God's one true incarnation. Christ is the living God; He has existed from the beginning and He will exist forever.

10 We also, through faith in Christ, can share in that **fullness** (Ephesians 3:19). Through the Holy Spirit, we too can be filled with all the qualities of God. And if we are filled with God's qualities, we shall be fulfilled and complete indeed! Compared with this, life apart from God and Christ is hollow and meaningless.

Paul writes many times that Christ is the **head**, the master, the Lord. Christ is supreme; He is over every **power and authority** (see Ephesians 1:20–22; Philippians 2:9–11 and comments). Many people mistakenly think that Christ is just one of many imagined incarnations of God, or that He is just another religious leader like Buddha or Mohammed. Still others mistakenly think that Christ is only a great teacher, a great prophet. But Paul says that Christ is above all; there is no power or authority like Christ's; all things are **under his feet** (Ephesians 1:22). He cannot be compared to any other (see Mark 8:27–29 and comment).

11 **In him** (Christ) **you were also circumcised.** CIRCUMCISION is the cutting off of the excess skin at the end of the penis. According to Jewish law, all males must be circumcised on the eighth day of life. In Paul's time, circumcision was the special outward sign of being a Jew (Genesis 17:9–14).

Here Paul uses circumcision as an illustration for the "cutting away" of our **sinful nature**,[6] or sinful flesh.[7] To be **circumcised** by Christ is to be spiritually "circumcised," to be made holy in our hearts (See Jeremiah 4:4; Romans 2:28–29 and comment).

12 Not only is the believer **circumcised** in Christ; he is also **buried with him** (Christ) **in** BAPTISM. Baptism signifies the washing away of our sins. In baptism, we are cleansed of sin through faith; we are made pure.

Thus Paul is using the examples of **circumcision** and **baptism** to describe the "cutting" or "washing away" of our old nature and its sins, so that we can begin a new life in Christ.

---

[6] In place of the words **sinful nature**, some versions of the Bible say "flesh," which is the literal translation of the Greek. For further discussion, see Galatians 5:13,16–17,24; Word List: Flesh.

[7] There is a sense in which we cannot completely "cut away" or "put off" our sinful nature as long as we are alive on this earth. Without the overruling power of the Holy Spirit in our lives, our sinful nature will always try to reassert itself.

But, in another sense, through the Spirit, we can render the sinful nature powerless, lifeless; we can "crucify it" (Galatians 5:24). This is what Paul means here by the **putting off of the sinful nature**. It means **putting off** the power and control of the sinful nature in our lives.

In the context of this verse, baptism has a second and related meaning: it signifies the "death" of our old self. Believers are **buried . . . in baptism**. Thus we see that before we can enter into new life in Christ, we must not only be cleansed; we must also die! Only when our old sinful self is dead can we receive new spiritual life. Our old self must be "buried with Christ" before our new self can rise with Him (see Romans 6:3–6,8; Galatians 2:20; Ephesians 4:22–24 and comments).

Thus we see here the true meaning of spiritual conversion. We see why no one is ever "born" a Christian. For to become a Christian, one must first die, and then be **born again** (see John 3:3,5 and comment).

Having been buried with Christ in baptism, Paul then says that we are **raised with him through . . . faith in the power of God**. The same **power of God** that raised Jesus from the dead will also raise us from spiritual death into new life. And this will happen through our **faith**.

13 Before we believed in Christ we were spiritually dead. We were **dead in** [our] **sins and in the uncircumcision of** [our] **sinful nature**. The **uncircumcision of** [our] **sinful nature** is the condition we were in before our sinful nature was "circumcised" or "cut away" by Christ. Then, by His grace, God **made** [us] **alive** and **forgave us all our sins**. By His grace, through faith, we have received new life, eternal life (see Ephesians 2:1–2,4–6,8 and comment).

14 The **written code** mentioned in this verse is the Jewish law, which is written in the Old Testament.[8] According to this law, if anyone broke even one of its **regulations**, he was to be considered guilty of breaking the whole law (James 2:10). Such a man was condemned; the law did not forgive him.

But God, because of His great mercy and love for us, **canceled the written code**—that is, He canceled the penalty and the condemnation of the Jewish law. Just as Christ was nailed to the CROSS, so that **written code** and its condemnation have been "nailed to the cross"—that is, **canceled**, rendered void.

But the law couldn't simply be canceled; someone had to pay the penalty that the law demanded; someone had to receive the condemnation for man's sin. And someone did—and that someone was Jesus Christ. Thus when He was nailed to the cross, the law was nailed to the cross with Him. He took our punishment upon Himself. The law can now no longer condemn us (see Romans 8:1 and comment).

15 When Christ rose from the dead, He **disarmed** and overcame all **powers and authorities**. These powers and authorities are Satan and his evil spirits (Ephesians 6:12). We were once their prisoners; now that Christ has overcome them, we have been set free from their control. When we were under Satan's control, we were spiritually dead. But on the cross Jesus overcame death (Romans 6:9; 2 Timothy 1:10), and in so doing He also saved us from spiritual death. In this way, Christ **made a public spectacle** of Satan and his evil spirits—of these **powers and authorities**. In other words, He put them to shame.

16–17 The Jewish law had two main parts: the "moral law" (such as the ten commandments); and the "ceremonial law," which consisted of all the regulations concerning sacrifices, purification rituals, and the proper observance of Jewish festivals. The ceremonial law contained hundreds of these regulations (see Mark 7:1–4; Ephesians 2:15 and comments).

Christ canceled this ceremonial law and all its regulations (verse 14). However, some of the believers at Colosse were still observing these regulations. Not only that, they were judging and condemning those in the church who were not observing them. They were teaching that unless a person observed all these regulations, he could not be saved.

But Paul says: Do not listen to those

[8] The Jewish law is written in the books of Exodus, Leviticus, Numbers, and Deuteronomy. It is the law that God gave to the Jewish people. For further discussion, see Word List: Law.

who teach such falsehood! Man is saved by God's grace through faith in Christ alone. Christ has canceled these regulations; these rules have no more meaning. They are a **shadow of the things that were to come** (verse 17); that is, they are nothing but a "shadow" of Christ. We have only one rule, one law, and that is to obey Christ Himself.

In this we can see the great difference between Christianity and all other religions. Other religions have many rules and rituals. The followers of these religions believe that by obeying such rules they can reach heaven. In other words, for them these rules are like a road to heaven.

But in the Christian religion, such rules are not the important thing: only Christ is important. Christ Himself is the way to heaven (see John 14:6 and comment). Man does not reach heaven by following rules, but only by following Christ. Apart from Christ, there is no other way a man can be saved (Acts 4:12).

18 Some of the false teachers at Colosse were saying that in order to be saved it was necessary to do some special penance or to undergo some special hardship or humiliation. Along with that, these teachers said it was necessary to worship ANGELS; the angels, they claimed, acted as mediators between God and man. These teachers also claimed to have had special visions and ecstatic experiences, and they looked down on those who had not had such experiences.

But Paul says that such teaching and such behavior is wrong. Man is not saved by **false humility**, the **worship of angels**, and special spiritual experiences. Man is saved only by believing in Christ. Angels are not mediators between God and man; there is only one mediator between God and man, and that is Jesus Christ (see 1 Timothy 2:5; 1 John 2:1 and comments). Let us not be deceived. Let us not take our faith away from Christ and put it on these false and worthless things. If we do, we shall be in danger of losing our reward, our salvation.

19 False teachers, such as Paul has described in verse 18, have **lost connection with the Head**, that is, Christ. They are following after **idle notions** (verse 18). False teachers like this do great harm in the church. The church is like a body; it is essential, therefore, that each member remains under the control of the head, Christ. Otherwise, the members of the body cannot work together, and the body will not grow (Ephesians 4:15–16).

20–21 In New Testament times, there were many slaves. These slaves had no freedom at all; they were owned by their masters, and they were required to serve their masters for life. In fact, there was only one way they could gain their "freedom," and that way was to die! Once they died, they were "free" of their masters.

Here Paul uses this condition of slaves to illustrate what was happening to the Colossians spiritually. Paul says to them: "You have **died with Christ** (verse 20); therefore, you are now free from your old master, Satan. You are free from the world, from the kingdom of Satan.[9] Therefore, why are you still making yourselves slaves of Satan? You have been freed from the **basic principles of this world**—that is, the law and all its rules. Therefore, why do you continue to **submit to its rules**?" (see Romans 6:6–7; 7:4–6; 8:1–2; Galatians 4:8–11 and comments).

Many people, even after they have believed in Christ, still find it hard to give up all the rules and rituals of their old religion. They say they believe in Christ, but they do not leave their old ways. But it is impossible to have faith both in Christ and in one's old religion at the same time. Once we have become Christians, we must put away the **basic principles of this world**. That is, we must stop trusting in our old religious laws and rituals as a means of getting to heaven.

22 The traditions and regulations of men have to do with perishable things like food, things which do not last. And neither do these traditions and regula-

---

[9] Satan is the **prince of this world** (John 12:31). For further discussion, see Word List: Satan.

tions last; they will all pass away. Only God's word will remain forever.

The Jewish leaders tried to condemn Jesus and His disciples, because they did not follow all the Jewish religious rules and regulations. But Jesus said to the Jews: **"You have let go of the commands of God and are holding on to the traditions of men"** (Mark 7:8).

23 When we look at holy men, monks, and pilgrims, we sometimes think: "How religious they are!" They humble themselves; they do good works; they discipline their bodies; they follow very strict rules. Surely they must be very holy and wise, we think. But they have only the appearance of holiness, the **appearance of wisdom**. Their practices are not spiritual; rather, **they are based on human commands and teachings** (verse 22).

Furthermore, their practices are of no value in **restraining sensual indulgence**; that is, they are of no value in overcoming our sinful nature. They are of no value in obtaining salvation. If we rely on our own efforts and good works to be saved, we shall become either very discouraged or very proud; in either case we shall be relying on something worthless. Only by relying on Christ and on His righteousness will we be able to overcome our sinful nature and obtain salvation.

CHAPTER 3

Rules for Holy Living (3:1–17)

1 The raising of Christ from the dead was an amazing event. But just as amazing is the fact that we believers are also **raised**! (See Romans 6:8; Colossians 2:12). And having been raised, we receive new life, life that will never end. Through faith in Christ, we are translated from death to life, from darkness to light, from the kingdom of Satan to the kingdom of God. Therefore, Paul says here: **Since, then, you have been raised with Christ, set your hearts on things above**—that is, on things of the kingdom of God. Especially, let us set our hearts on Christ. Let us not love this world, nor worldly pursuits and possessions, because the more we love the world the less we shall love God. It is not possible to love both God and the world at the same time (see Matthew 6:19–21,24; 1 John 2:15–17 and comments).

2 Having received new life in Christ, we need to receive a new mind also. We must no longer think as we once did, when we belonged to the world. When we belonged to the world, we walked according to our old worldly nature. But now, Paul says, having received a new spiritual nature through the Holy Spirit, we must walk according to that new nature (see Galatians 5:25 and comment).

3 Does a dead man have any desire or longing for the things of the world? No, he doesn't. And neither should we. For we too have died to the world. Therefore, we must not set our minds on the things of the world. Our old sinful life has ended; now we have received a new spiritual life, which is **hidden with Christ in God**.

Paul says that our new life is **hidden** with Christ in God. Spiritual things are "hidden" from worldly men.[10] Worldly men cannot see Christ, and they cannot see our new spiritual life in Christ. But they can see the fruit of our new life; that is, they can see our good works, our love, and our joy.

Worldly men cannot see Christ, but we can see Him (see John 14:19–20 and comment).

4 Christ is now hidden from men's physical eyes; but one day He will come again, and at that time He will appear to all men (see Mark 13:26; 14:61–62 and comments). And we, too, **will appear**

---

[10] Worldly men are men who love the world more than they love God.

with him in glory. After that, nothing will be hidden (Romans 8:18–19).

Christ is our life, says Paul here. Christ is the source of our life; He is the goal, the purpose, the fulfillment, the blessing of our life. Our life is in Him; His life is in us.

If this is so, then let us set our hearts on Him! Our Lord, our eternal home, our inheritance and reward are all in heaven. Therefore, let us set our hearts and minds **on things above**. Why look to **earthly things**? (verse 2).

5 Put to death, therefore, whatever belongs to your earthly nature—that is, "put to death" your old sinful desires and actions. Sin begins in our hearts, in our sinful natures. But then the various members of our bodies actually carry out the sin. Therefore, most important of all, we must "put to death" our sinful nature with its passions and desires (see Galatians 5:24 and comment). But we must also restrain and subdue our members; we must, in a sense, "put them to death" too. Jesus said, "**If your hand causes you to sin, cut it off**" (Mark 9:43). Thus Paul's meaning here is that we must subdue or "put to death" every part of us that is leading us into sin.

Our members once did evil; they were used to serve Satan. But now we have been called from the world into the kingdom of heaven. Our **old self** (verse 9) has died with Christ (see Romans 6:6; Ephesians 4:22 and comments). Therefore, if our old sinful self has died, our old passions and actions should be put to death too—that is, they should be subdued (see Mark 9:43–47; Romans 6:11–13; 8:13 and comments).

Paul mentions here some of the major sins. He says that **greed** is the same as **idolatry**, because to be greedy for something means that we love that thing more than we love God; and whenever we love a thing more than God, that thing becomes for us an idol (see Ephesians 5:5).

Here a question arises. In verse 3, Paul says: **For you died**. But in verse 5, he says: **Put to death . . . whatever belongs to your earthly nature**. If our earthly nature has died, how can we then "put it to death"? Why does Paul tell us to subdue something that is supposed to be already dead? In verse 3, our old self has died; in verse 5, it is committing all sorts of sins! One moment it is dead; the next moment it seems very much alive. Is that possible?

Yes, both things are true. In one way, our old self has died; we have been forgiven; we have received salvation and have been delivered from Satan's kingdom. But even though this is all true, our physical bodies remain on earth until we actually die. Thus we continue to be surrounded by sin on all sides. Sometimes we fall into sin. Temptation comes. Satan is always trying to defeat us; we are in a battle. In a sense we are in two worlds at once: the spiritual world, or kingdom of God; and the physical world, or kingdom of Satan.[11] In a bodily sense, we are part of the physical world. But the main thing is that, in a spiritual sense, we are alive in Christ; we have become a new people; we are citizens of God's kingdom; we have been made children in God's family.

Therefore, if we are indeed citizens of God's kingdom and children in His family, then we must behave like His citizens, like His children. True, Satan will keep trying to lead us into temptation, and he will try to make our bodies do evil. But we must not submit to him; we must resist him (see James 4:7 and comment). Instead of submitting to Satan, we must submit to God. We are God's children, and God's children must reflect the nature of their Father (see 1 Peter 1:15–16).

The story is told about an English king some years ago, whose somewhat rebellious son wanted to go and have fun with his friends and do all the things they did. The king, when he heard about it, called

---

[11] The expression "kingdom of Satan" has two meanings, which are closely related. First, it means Satan's authority and power. Second, it means the world; because it is in the world that Satan exercises his authority.

It should be noted, however, that the "kingdom of Satan" is not limited to this physical world. Satan also rules over **spiritual forces of evil in the heavenly realms** (Ephesians 6:12).

his son and said to him just one thing: "Remember who you are."

Likewise, we who believe in Christ need to remember who we are. We are the children of the Great King—the King of kings! Are we acting like His children?

6 **... the wrath of God is coming.** We Christians like to talk mostly about the love of God; and that is perfectly proper, because God is love (1 John 4:8). It was because of His love that God sacrificed His own Son for us (John 3:16). But let us not forget about the **wrath of God.** Because the **wrath of God is coming** upon all those who are disobedient, who do evil, who refuse to believe in His Son (see Ephesians 5:6). God will certainly punish all these people.

7 We, too, were once disobedient, and used to engage in the sins mentioned in verse 5 (see Ephesians 2:1–3 and comment).

8–9 **But now you must rid yourselves of all such things** (verse 8), because **you have taken off the old self** (verse 9). According to verse 8, we must rid ourselves of the ways of the old self; but according to verse 9, we have already put off the old self. What Paul means here is that because we have put off the old self, we must now put off its bad deeds also.

10 Our **old self** has died with Christ. Now we have become new people, new creations; that is, we have put on the **new self** (see 2 Corinthians 5:17; Ephesians 4:22–24 and comments). Our new self is to be **renewed ... in the image of its Creator**—that is, in the image of both God and Christ.

As in his letter to the Ephesians, Paul here describes our daily behavior as a set of clothing. Just as we take off dirty old clothes and put on clean new clothes, so we must "take off" our old behavior and "put on" new behavior. Our new behavior is to be like Christ's behavior; in other words, we are to **clothe** ourselves with Christ (see Romans 13:14; Galatians 3:27 and comments). When men look at our lives, they must be able to see Christ.

Our new self is **being renewed in knowledge**. A "new man" not only needs new clothes and new behavior; he also needs new **knowledge**. After becoming Christians, we do not think like other people; not only is our outward behavior changed but our inward attitudes are changed as well. Not only is our outer self changed, but our inner self—our mind—is changed also. When we clothe ourselves with Christ, we also clothe ourselves with His mind and with His **knowledge** (see Romans 12:2 and comment).

11 After we have put on our new "clothes" (new behavior and new mind), we believers will to some extent all look alike. We will look like Christ, because our new clothes are, in fact, His clothes. Because of our old clothing we were divided: high caste and low caste, educated and uneducated, rich and poor, male and female. But after we have clothed ourselves with Christ, we will no longer be divided by these things. We will all be as one, united together in one family. Among Christians there are no divisions (see Galatians 3:26–28 and comment).

How amazing is our unity in Christ! In Paul's time, great distinctions were made between different classes of people: between **circumcised** (Jew) and **uncircumcised** (Gentile), between **slave** and **free**, between the highly civilized **Greek** and the uncivilized **barbarian**[12] and **Scythian.**[13] Furthermore, there was much ill feeling between these groups. How, then, can such different classes of people be united together in one family, in one body? How can such great divisions be removed? Only through

---

[12] In place of the word **barbarian,** some versions of the Bible say "speakers of other languages," which is the literal translation of the Greek text. The meaning is essentially the same. The educated Greek-speaking people of New Testament times considered anyone who didn't speak Greek to be a **barbarian.**

[13] The Scythians were residents of the uncivilized country of Scythia, which is now part of southern Russia.

Christ is it possible. It is Christ Himself who unites us. **Christ is all**—that is, Christ is all one body. And Christ **is in all**—in all the members of the body. We are in Christ, and Christ is in us. Therefore, we are all **one in Christ** (Galatians 3:28).

But even though we are one in Christ, equal and united members of one family, and even though the divisions that once existed between us have been removed, we are, however, not all exactly alike. We each have been given different gifts and different responsibilities. Our situations are different also. Indeed, among Christians there are some who are rich and some who are poor; some who are educated and some who are uneducated; some who are men and some who are women. However, these different groups are not divided; there is no elevating of one group over another. Spiritually they all have equal standing in the church and before God; they are all one in Christ.

When we look at our own church, what do we see? Are there divisions? Are there divisions in our hearts between one another?

12 In verse 10, Paul says that we have **put on the new self**. Now in verses 12–17, Paul describes this "new self."

Notice that the qualities of the new self listed here in verse 12—**compassion, kindness, humility, gentleness and patience**—are the opposite of those qualities of the old self that Paul listed in verse 8. These new qualities are the fruits of the Holy Spirit (Galatians 5:22–23). These new qualities are essential for preserving our unity; they are essential for our church (see Ephesians 4:2–3 and comment).

Why should we Christians clothe ourselves with these qualities? Because we have been **chosen** by God to be His **holy and dearly beloved** people. God chose us **before the creation of the world to be holy and blameless in his sight** (Ephesians 1:4). Let us not refuse what God has chosen for us!

13 Each of us has some bad qualities which others have trouble tolerating. Do we want others to tolerate us, to bear with us, to accept us? Yes, of course we do. Well, if we want them to bear with our bad qualities, we must be willing to bear with theirs (Ephesians 4:2–3).

Do we want others to forgive us? Of course, we do. Well, if we want them to forgive us, we will have to forgive them. Forgiveness is not given with the lips alone; it is given from the heart. After we have forgiven our brother for some wrong, does the matter still linger in our hearts? Do we remain a little angry, a little hurt? If so, then we have not completely forgiven our brother.

When we refuse to forgive others completely, we are really hurting ourselves. Instead of peace, there is anger and bitterness in our hearts. Not only that, if we do not forgive others, God will not forgive us (see Matthew 6:12,14–15 and comment).

Think for a moment: How many times has God already forgiven you? How many more times do you want God to forgive you? Well, as many times as you want God to forgive you, that many times you must forgive your brother! (Matthew 18:21–22).

Let us not forget how much mercy God has shown to us. Let us show, then, that same mercy to others. **Forgive as the Lord forgave you** (see Ephesians 4:32).

14 **And over all these virtues, put on love**. Love is like a "rope" that **binds** [these virtues] **together**. In other words, all the qualities of the new self (verses 12–13) are included in **love**. Love is the chief quality of God and of Christ. All other virtues flow out of love; love is the source of them all. Likewise, the two greatest commandments are to love God and to love our neighbor (Mark 12:30–31), and from these two commandments all other commands are derived (see Romans 13:9–10; Galatians 5:14 and comments).

15 Like love, **peace** is a "rope" that binds us together in unity (Ephesians 4:3). Wherever there is love, there will also be peace. If there is a lack of peace in our church, there must be a lack of love as well.

Peace is also a freedom from worry and fear. Peace is a gift of Christ (see John 14:27 and comment). If the peace of Christ "rules" in our hearts, then worry, fear, and strife cannot arise.

And be thankful. Why should we be thankful? Because of all that God has done for us! He has given us new life; He has given us grace, love, peace, forgiveness, salvation. But more than all these, He has given us His one and only Son Jesus Christ, and with Him, He has given us **every spiritual blessing** (see Romans 8:32; Ephesians 1:3 and comments). Therefore, how can we not thank God?

16 In this chapter, Paul has described the "new spiritual man." But a spiritual man needs spiritual food. What is spiritual food? It is the **word of Christ**—that is, the word of God, our Bible. How can we let the word of Christ **dwell** in us? By reading and studying the Bible (Joshua 1:8; Psalm 1:2). Through studying the Bible, we will be able to **teach and admonish one another with all wisdom**.

Here we see how our church services and house fellowships should be! Not only are we to teach and admonish one another, but we are also to **sing psalms, hymns and spiritual songs with gratitude . . . to God** (see Ephesians 5:19–20).

17 Paul says to the Colossians: **And whatever you do . . . do it all in the name of the Lord Jesus**. "Whatever" we do means "everything" we do. That is, we must not only pray in Jesus' name; we must do everything—**whether in word or deed**—in His name. (Except, of course, we must do nothing that will dishonor His name!) Our entire lives must be worthy of His name.

. . . in the name of the Lord Jesus. This is not some kind of magic formula. "In the name of the Lord Jesus" means "for the sake of Jesus," and "with the authority of Jesus."

Remember, all of us who believe in Jesus are His ambassadors or representatives here on earth (2 Corinthians 5:20). Jesus has given us full authority to do His work in His name. Just as any ambassador must do everything in the name of his king or president, so in the same way must we Christians do everything in the name of Jesus.

In verses 12–17, we are given a description of the "new man," the man raised with Christ. Are we like the "new man" described here? Let each one examine himself.

Rules for Christian Households (3:18–25)

18 See Ephesians 5:22–24 and comment.

19 See Ephesians 5:25,28 and comment.

20 See Ephesians 6:1 and comment.

21 See Ephesians 6:4 and comment.

22–24 Just as we obey the Lord Jesus, so we must obey our **earthly masters**—the authorities and employers whom God has placed over us. The Lord sees everything we do. It is no advantage to do good only when our "earthly master" is looking—because our heavenly Master is always looking! Therefore, let us always do everything **with all** [our] **heart, as working for the Lord** (see Romans 12:11; Ephesians 6:5–8; Titus 2:9–10 and comments).

Slaves in Paul's time had no rights and no property; they received no inheritance. But here Paul gives them a great promise: If they will serve their earthly master faithfully, they will receive an **inheritance from the Lord as a reward**. Though they have no inheritance on earth, they will receive from God an eternal **inheritance** in heaven.

Here a question arises: Why didn't Paul more clearly oppose the custom of slavery in his writings? We can be sure that Paul was personally opposed to slavery. However, Paul's main goal was not to change society, but to change people's hearts. If people's hearts are changed, their society will be changed too. Therefore, Paul was mainly concerned that masters treat their slaves with kindness and fairness (Colossians 4:1), and that slaves serve their masters faithfully and **with sincerity of heart** (verse 22). Paul knew that if the relationship between master and slave were based on mutual love and respect, the custom of slavery would soon come to an end (see 1 Timothy 6:1–2; Titus 2:9–10 and comments).

25 God will judge all men equally, whether husband or wife, parent or child, master or slave. In Christ we are all equal, and we shall be **repaid** equally by God. With God, **there is no favoritism**. We shall be repaid not only according to the

good we have done (Ephesians 6:8), but also according to the **wrong** we have done.

CHAPTER 4

Further Instructions (4:1–6)

1 In the world's eyes, some men are masters and some are slaves, or servants. But in God's eyes, all men are servants. Therefore, let earthly masters beware! Just as they behave toward their servants on earth, so will God behave toward them in heaven (see Ephesians 6:9 and comment).

2 Here Paul tells the Colossians: **Devote yourselves to prayer.** Christians should take every opportunity to pray whenever there is a suitable occasion. This is the responsibility of every Christian. If we do not pray, we shall receive little help or blessing from the Holy Spirit. If there is no prayer, there certainly won't be any answers to prayer!

As we pray, we must be **watchful**. Watchful for what? First, we must watch for those—both believers and non-believers—who need our prayers; we must be **watchful** for the needs and welfare of others. Second, we must be **watchful** for Satan, lest he trip us up (see Mark 14:38; Ephesians 6:18; 1 Peter 5:8 and comments).

3 All Christians must pray continually that **God may open a door** of opportunity for preaching His word, the Gospel, so that the Gospel of Christ might reach into every corner of the world, and so that every man and woman might have the chance to hear about Christ.

4 Paul was a great and effective preacher and teacher. But Paul knew very well that his effectiveness was due to the prayers of fellow believers. Therefore, Paul continues to ask the Colossians for their prayers, knowing that if their prayers for him lessen, his effectiveness will also lessen.

God has placed His work into our hands. Yes, God can do everything by Himself, but He has chosen to do His work through us, His children. If we fail to carry out our responsibilities to work and to pray, then God's work will suffer loss.

Therefore, let us continue to pray diligently for one another and, like Paul, continue to ask for prayer for ourselves that we might effectively do God's work (Ephesians 6:19–20).

5 Paul says here that we should **make the most of every opportunity**—that is, every opportunity to witness. Let us not miss opportunities that arise. We must take every opportunity to share the Gospel with **outsiders**—that is, with unbelievers (Ephesians 5:15–16; 2 Timothy 4:2).

6 One's speech can either be loving and gracious, or it can be harsh and bitter. Let our speech always be **full of grace**.

Our speech also needs to be **seasoned with salt**. Speech that is "seasoned with salt" is speech that is wise, uplifting, and challenging. In particular, our speech needs to be "seasoned" with wisdom. We need to witness wisely. There are different ways of presenting the Gospel, and one way works well with one person and another way works well with another person. Therefore, we must understand the person we're talking to, so that we can speak in the most effective way. Let people not be turned away from Christ because of our inappropriate speech (see 1 Peter 3:15).

Final Greetings (4:7–18)

7–8 Paul wrote this letter to the Colossians while in prison in Rome. Paul's fellow worker **Tychicus** then delivered it to the Colossians (Ephesians 6:21–22).

9 **Onesimus** was a slave from Colosse who had fled to Rome after running away from his master Philemon. In Rome he met Paul, and became a believer. Now Paul is sending Onesimus back to his master Philemon (see Philemon 10–16).

10–11 **Aristarchus** was with Paul in

Ephesus (Acts 19:29). After that, he went with Paul to Rome (Acts 27:2).

Mark is the writer of the Gospel of Mark. Some years earlier, Paul had become very displeased with Mark, because Mark had deserted Paul in the middle of a preaching journey. After that, Paul refused to take Mark with him on any more of his travels (Acts 15:36–40). Now, from this letter, we can see that Paul has forgiven Mark and forgotten about Mark's earlier mistake.

From this we can learn an important lesson. Even though someone makes a great mistake or commits a great sin, we must not always hold it against him. We must not only forgive the person for his mistake—we must then forget it!

Consider what happened to Mark after he made that earlier mistake. Having been forgiven, he eventually went on to become Paul's faithful fellow worker (2 Timothy 4:11). And God chose Mark to be the first to write down the story of Jesus' life.[14]

We must never keep on accusing someone of a past sin. If we do this, it is we who are committing the sin! When we refuse to forgive, we are opposing God and inviting judgment upon ourselves (see Matthew 6:14–15).

As for **Jesus, who is called Justus** (verse 11), nothing else is known about him except what is written here.

12–13 **Epaphras** was one of the founders of the church at Colosse (Colossians 1:7). Let us also, like Epaphras, always be **wrestling in prayer** for each other (verse 12). To overcome Satan, we must "wrestle" in prayer; we are in a spiritual battle with Satan, and prayer is one of our most effective weapons (see Ephesians 6:18 and comment). And may Epaphras' prayer for the Colossians also be for us: that we might **stand firm in all the will of God, mature and fully assured**.

14 **Luke** is the writer of the Gospel of Luke and the book of Acts. He was a close colleague of Paul, and journeyed with Paul to Rome.

Demas later deserted Paul, **because he loved this world** (2 Timothy 4:10). It is not written anywhere that Demas repented and began serving the Lord again. Some, like Mark, return to serve the Lord; others, like Demas, fall away and do not return.

Let us beware that none of us becomes like Demas. For us, he is a warning.

15 **Laodicea** was a city near Colosse, where there was also a church. The Laodicean church is one of the seven churches mentioned in the book of Revelation, to which Jesus, through the Apostle John, sent letters of warning (Revelation 3:14–22).

In New Testament times, most of the Christian churches were "house churches" or "house fellowships" (Philemon 1–2). Perhaps in places where there was much persecution against Christians, the believers met in homes so as not to attract attention. But probably in most cases they met in homes because there was not enough money to build a separate church building.

16 The letter mentioned here which Paul wrote to the Laodiceans has been lost.

17 Paul here gives a special admonition to **Archippus**, a member of the Colossian church. Let Paul's word to Archippus be for every one of us: **See to it that you complete the work you have received in the Lord**. And let us, like Paul, be able to say at the end of our lives: **I have fought the good fight, I have finished the race, I have kept the faith** (2 Timothy 4:7).

18 Up through verse 17, Paul has dictated this letter to a scribe. But now in verse 18, he writes in his own hand, so that the Colossians may know that this letter has truly been sent from Paul.

Paul writes: **Remember my chains**. In most of his letters, Paul asks for the prayers of his readers. We must not neglect to pray for our fellow workers in Christ. Especially we must pray for those in prison, and minister to their needs whenever we can (see Matthew 25:36; Hebrews 13:3).

---

[14] Even though Mark's Gospel is the second Gospel in the New Testament, most Bible scholars believe that it was actually the first to be written.

1 Thessalonians

INTRODUCTION

Thessalonica was the capital of Macedonia, the northern province of Greece. Paul's first visit to Thessalonica, which took place during his second missionary journey, is described in Acts 17:1–9.

This letter was written from Corinth in about 50 A.D., shortly after Paul's first visit to Thessalonica. Because of the opposition of the crowds, Paul had been able to spend only a few weeks in Thessalonica; he had been forced to leave the city quickly. After he left, trouble and persecution came upon the new Christians there. Paul wrote this letter to give them encouragement and further teaching on a number of points.

In addition to that, Paul had many enemies in Thessalonica, both Jews and Gentiles. In order to discredit the Gospel of Christ, these enemies had begun to slander Paul and make false accusations against him. Paul feared that if he was dishonored by these false accusations, the new Thessalonian believers would be weakened in their faith. Therefore, in this letter Paul opposes his enemies and refutes their false charges.

This letter and 2 Thessalonians, together with Galatians, are the earliest letters Paul wrote. These three letters were the first New Testament books to be written.

For further information about Paul's life, see Romans: Introduction.

OUTLINE

A. Personal Reflections (1:1–3:13).
   1. Thanksgiving for the Thessalonians (1:1–10).
   2. Paul's Founding of the Church at Thessalonica (2:1–20).
   3. Timothy's Strengthening of the Church (3:1–13).

B. Practical Exhortations (4:1–5:28).
   1. Exhortation Regarding Holy Living (4:1–12).
   2. Exhortation Regarding Christ's Second Coming (4:13–5:11).
   3. Final Instructions (5:12–28).

CHAPTER 1

Thanksgiving for the Thessalonians (1:1–10)

1 **Silas** (or Silvanus) and **Timothy** were with Paul when he wrote this letter (see 2 Corinthians 1:1–2,19 and comment).

2 See Ephesians 1:15–16; Colossians 1:3–5; 2 Thessalonians 1:3 and comments.

3 Here Paul recalls three things about the Thessalonians. First, he recalls their **work produced by** FAITH—that is, the work they have done as the result of their faith (see James 2:17). Second, Paul recalls their **labor prompted by love**. Just as true faith must be manifested by good works, so must true love be manifested by **labor** or works of love. Third, Paul recalls their **endurance inspired by hope**. Those whose hope is placed on Christ will have **endurance**. Thus the **work, labor,** and **endurance** of the Thessalonians are the result of their **faith, love,** and **hope,** which Paul says are the three most important things in our Christian lives[1] (see 1 Corinthians 13:13 and comment).

4 Paul reminds the Thessalonians that they have been **chosen** by God, and that they are **loved** by Him (see Ephesians 1:4–5; 2 Thessalonians 2:13 and comments). Paul calls the Thessalonians "brothers," because they have been chosen by God to be His children. Since Paul is also a child of God, that makes him and the Thessalonians spiritual "brothers." However, all men cannot be said to be brothers; only those who belong to God's family through faith in Christ are true spiritual brothers and sisters to one another. There can be no "brotherhood of man" for those who do not acknowledge the "fatherhood of God."

5 Paul here calls the Gospel **our** GOSPEL; that is, it was the Gospel of Christ preached by Paul, Silas, and Timothy.

This **gospel** came to the Thessalonians **with power**. The Gospel is the **power of God for . . . salvation** (Romans 1:16). When Paul preached the Gospel, his words came with God's **power** (see 1 Corinthians 2:4–5 and comment).

This **gospel** also came to the Thessalonians **with the** HOLY SPIRIT. Any word that does not come with the Spirit is a dead word, or dead letter. And the **letter kills, but the Spirit gives life** (2 Corinthians 3:6). The power of the Gospel comes from the Holy Spirit. The Spirit was in Paul. And when the Thessalonians accepted the Gospel and believed in Christ, the Holy Spirit began to dwell within them also.

Paul preached the gospel **with deep conviction;** and the Thessalonians believed it **with deep conviction.**

The Thessalonians know what kind of men Paul, Silas, and Timothy are. They have seen that they are men filled with the Spirit (see 1 Thessalonians 2:10).

6 The new believers in Thessalonica at first became **imitators** of Paul, Silas, and Timothy. Then, from these three men, the Thessalonians learned to imitate Christ Himself. They could see how Paul, Silas, and Timothy themselves imitated Christ (1 Corinthians 4:16; 11:1).

What kind of example do we ourselves give to new believers? Can any of us say to another person, "If you imitate me, you'll be imitating Christ"? We ought to be able to say that! Yes, the witness of our lips is very important; but the witness of our lives is even more important.

From the beginning, the new believers in Thessalonica were persecuted by the society around them. Even while Paul was there preaching, a great uproar arose against the Christians (Acts 17:5–7). Nevertheless, the Thessalonian believers received Paul's message **with the joy given by the Holy Spirit** (see John 16:22; Galatians 5:22).

We Christians do not like to face trouble or persecution. In every country

[1] The two most important things are **faith** and **love** (see Galatians 5:6; 1 Thessalonians 3:6 and comments). The third most important thing is **hope**.

of the world, Christians seek for religious freedom, so that they can practice their religion without being persecuted. But according to the teaching of the New Testament, to endure persecution for the sake of Christ is a joyful privilege (Acts 5:41; 1 Peter 4:13). The church that endures persecution with joy is a strong church, and its witness is powerful. Let us not seek the easy road (see Matthew 7:13–14). Through the suffering we endure for Christ's sake, God will be glorified and our church will be made strong.

7 Because these Thessalonian Christians had endured persecution with such joy and were imitating Christ so faithfully, they had become a **model**, an example, for all the other believers living in **Macedonia**, the northern province of Greece. Let these Thessalonian Christians be a **model** for us too! Then, in turn, we too will become a model for others.

8 Paul says that the Lord's message **rang out** from the Thessalonian church. Now, as a result, **their faith in God has become known everywhere**—not just in **Macedonia** and **Achaia**,[2] but in other countries as well. Remember, this church was less than a year old at the time Paul wrote this letter. It was a tiny, persecuted church. Nevertheless, their faith had **become known everywhere**!

How do our churches today compare with that little Thessalonian church? Our churches are bigger, richer, and older; but does the Gospel "ring out" from our churches as it did from that Thessalonian church? O brothers and sisters, if not, then let it begin to do so without delay!

9 Wherever Paul goes, he hears other people talk about the faith of the Thessalonians, especially how they **turned to God from idols to serve the living and true God**.

What a powerful witness the Thessalonians had! What do people say about us?

10 The Thessalonians had turned from idols **to serve the living and true God** (verse 9) and **to wait for his Son** (Christ) **from heaven**. Their eyes were raised toward heaven. Their hope was not in this life. Their hope was in Jesus, whom God **raised from the dead**, and who would return to rescue them **from the coming wrath**—from God's judgment. No wonder the Gospel **rang out** from them!

CHAPTER 2

Paul's Ministry in Thessalonica (2:1–12)

1–2 Some of Paul's enemies were falsely saying that Paul preached only to get money. In New Testament times, there were many false preachers who were greedy for money, and who preached only to gain benefit for themselves. But the Thessalonians knew that Paul's preaching was not like that. His preaching was with the power of the Holy Spirit (1 Thessalonians 1:5). They knew that Paul's visit to Thessalonica had not been a **failure** (verse 1); it had resulted in a church being established there. Furthermore, because of the way Paul suffered for the Gospel, they could see that he didn't preach for his own advantage. They knew that in Philippi Paul had suffered a great deal (Acts 16:19–24). But in spite of that, Paul had come immediately to Thessalonica and had fearlessly begun to preach there **in spite of strong opposition** (Acts 17:5–6). No false preacher would have done that.

3 Here Paul refutes the false accusation that his motives for preaching were selfish and impure. Paul's **appeal**—that is, his preaching of the Gospel—did not spring from **error or impure motives**, or a desire to **trick** people.

4 Paul spoke nothing untrue, because

---

[2] **Achaia** was the southern province of Greece. Thus Macedonia and Achaia together made up most of the country of Greece.

God had **entrusted** His truth, His Gospel, to Paul. The words that Paul spoke were God's words, not his own words. Furthermore, Paul's motives were not impure, because he had been **approved by God** (see Romans 1:1,5; 1 Corinthians 4:1; 2 Corinthians 2:17; Ephesians 3:7).

Paul never tried to **trick** or deceive people; he sought to please only God, not men. In other words, he never tried to put on a false front in order to **please men** or to win their approval (see Galatians 1:10).

The Gospel of Christ never "pleases" natural or sinful man. Natural, worldly man always opposes the Gospel. When we preach Christ, we must never try to **please men**; if we do, our "gospel" will be not the true Gospel but a false gospel. We must speak the truth boldly; we must speak out against sin and evil. We must not fear the opposition of men (see 2 Corinthians 4:1–2,5).

5 Paul never **used flattery**. He never tried to flatter people by minimizing their sins, by telling them that their sins were nothing to worry about. He never gave people false hope, nor did he give them false promises. He never told people that following Christ was easy.

6 Paul and his fellow preachers sought praise only from God, not from men (see John 12:42–43).

In verse 7,[3] Paul calls Silas and Timothy APOSTLES, together with himself. In the New Testament, the apostles were men appointed by God to preach the Gospel and to establish churches (Acts 14:4; 1 Corinthians 15:5,7).

Because they were apostles, Paul, Silas, and Timothy had the right to expect support from the new believers in Thessalonica (1 Corinthians 9:12–14; 2 Thessalonians 3:8–9). However, they had not burdened anyone by demanding support (verse 9). Therefore, no one could accuse them of preaching for money!

7–8 Let us look at the conduct of Paul, Silas, and Timothy, which is described in these verses. Let all pastors, preachers, and elders follow their example. These apostles not only shared the Gospel with the Thessalonians; they also **shared** [their] **lives** with them (see 2 Corinthians 12:15; 1 John 3:16).

9 Wherever he traveled as an apostle, it was Paul's custom to earn his own living. He did not ask for money or support from the churches that he established (see Acts 18:3; 20:33–34; 2 Thessalonians 3:8).

10–12 Here again, we see the behavior of Paul, Silas, and Timothy. Let all Christian leaders follow their example.

God calls us **into his kingdom and glory** (verse 12). As soon as we believe in Christ, we enter God's **kingdom**; that is, we come under God's rule and authority. And when Christ comes again, we shall enter God's **glory** (see 1 Peter 5:10).

But let us remember this: if to enter into God's kingdom and glory is our privilege, then **to live lives worthy of God** is our duty! If we want to enter into His kingdom and glory, we must live lives worthy of Him who has called us. If we don't, instead of glory we shall receive punishment.

The Thessalonians Are Paul's Glory (2:13–20)

13 The Thessalonians had accepted Paul's preaching as the word of God. Paul's purpose was to communicate God's word, not man's word. Thus it was always his hope that his listeners would receive his teaching as coming from God (1 Corinthians 2:4–5; Galatians 1:11–12).

God's word is a living word, **which is at work in** [those] **who believe** (see Hebrews 4:12; 1 Peter 1:23).

14 All Christians must be ready to suffer for Christ (2 Timothy 3:12). Our faith is tested through suffering (James 1:2–3; 1 Peter 1:6–7). Thus Paul knows that the Thessalonians' faith is true, because even through much suffering their faith has remained firm.

The Thessalonians had become **imitators of God's churches in Judea. Judea** was the southern province of Israel; its capital was Jerusalem. The churches in

[3] In some versions of the Bible, this reference to **apostles** is included as part of verse 6.

Judea had suffered severe persecution from the JEWS. One of the main persecutors had been Paul himself (Acts 8:1,3). Just as the **churches in Judea** had endured persecution, so had the Thessalonians endured persecution. In this way, then, the Thessalonians had become **imitators** of the Christians in Judea.

15–16 Wherever Paul went, the Jews bitterly opposed him (Acts 9:23; 13:45; 14:19; 18:12; 21:27). The Jews especially hated Paul because he had once been one of them but had now become a Christian; in their minds, he was an apostate, a traitor.

The Jews **killed the Lord Jesus** (verse 15); that is, the Jews accused Jesus before the Roman governor and persuaded the governor to execute Him (Mark 15:1; John 18:28; Acts 2:22–23). The Jews were fully responsible for Jesus' death. The Jews had also killed their own Old Testament **prophets** (Acts 7:51–52). Wherever the apostles went, the Jews opposed them and tried to drive them away from that place (Acts 13:50; 17:5,13–14). The Jews tried to stop Paul from preaching to the GENTILES. In doing these things, the Jews opposed God Himself. **The wrath of God has come upon them,** Paul says (verse 16). Paul is talking here about the final judgment of God; for the Jews, God's judgment will seem like **wrath**. It is so certain to come upon them that Paul talks as if it had already happened. Indeed, the Jews experienced a foretaste of God's judgment twenty years after this letter was written, when the Jewish capital of Jerusalem was utterly destroyed by the Romans, and the few Jews who escaped death were scattered.

17–18 Paul was **torn away** from the Thessalonians, because his enemies there forced him to leave the city (see Acts 17:5–9).

SATAN always opposes God's servants, and tries to keep them from doing God's work. Satan is under God's ultimate authority—because everything in the universe is under God's authority. Nevertheless, Satan has great power, and he uses it to interfere with God's work.

Why couldn't Paul return to Thessalonica? Because Jason and some other Thessalonian believers had "posted bond" in order to free Paul from custody and allow him to leave the city (Acts 17:9). If Paul returned to Thessalonica, that bond would have to be forfeited, and Jason and his companions would suffer great loss. Thus, by means of the bond, the city officials were able to keep Paul from returning to their city.

19–20 When Paul stands before the judgment seat of the Lord Jesus, he will be able to glory in the Thessalonian believers. They will be his **joy** and **crown** (Philippians 2:16; 4:1). In Paul's time, the winner of a race was given a "crown" made of special leaves. But unlike a crown of leaves, which soon withers, Paul's crown will last forever. And so will the crown of each believer (1 Corinthians 9:24–25).

CHAPTER 3

Timothy's Strengthening of the Church (3:1–13)

1 From Thessalonica, Paul had been taken to the city of Berea. From there, he journeyed to **Athens**, the capital of Greece (Acts 17:13–15).

Paul cared deeply about the new believers in Thessalonica. Paul had been forced to leave them so quickly. They were only infants in Christ; already persecution had come upon them, and Paul couldn't be there to help them. Paul was filled with worry about whether they were standing firm in the faith or not.

2 Therefore, Paul sent Timothy to **strengthen and encourage** them.

3–4 The Thessalonians knew that trials must come; Paul had warned them it would be so. And trials did come. So let the Thessalonians not be surprised or discouraged. We have been **destined** to endure trials; indeed, such trials are for our good (see Romans 5:3; James 1:2–3; 1

Peter 3:12–13). Those who suffer for Christ on earth will share in His glory in heaven (Matthew 10:22; Acts 14:22; Romans 8:17–18; 2 Timothy 2:12).

Therefore, let us rejoice in our suffering for Christ, for great will be our reward in heaven (Matthew 5:10–12; John 16:33).

5 The **tempter** Paul mentions here is Satan (Matthew 4:3,10). Satan tries to tempt believers to leave their faith. Satan is always working. He especially attacks new believers, those who have only recently escaped from his kingdom and whose faith is still weak.

Satan works by leading believers into TEMPTATION (Matthew 6:13). Temptations are of many kinds. For example, a new believer may be pressured into performing some ritual connected with his former religion. He may fear he'll lose his family inheritance if he refuses. Thus he is **tempted** to turn back and worship his old gods. But he must resist such a temptation. It's much better to lose our earthly inheritance than to risk losing our heavenly inheritance.

There are other temptations for new believers, such as fear of imprisonment, fear of losing a job, fear of ridicule from one's friends. All of these temptations come from Satan. Yet God, according to His eternal purposes, allows these temptations to come upon us in order to strengthen our faith.

There are, of course, many other temptations: doubt, fear, sickness, etc. Satan uses different methods to try to destroy our faith and block Christ's work (see Matthew 13:39; Mark 4:15; Luke 22:3; 1 Corinthians 7:5; 2 Corinthians 4:4; 12:7; 2 Thessalonians 2:9).

Yet this great enemy Satan has already been defeated by Jesus Christ (Colossians 2:15). And in Christ's strength, we too, taking the **shield of faith**, can defeat Satan (Ephesians 6:16).

6–7 The main goal of a true pastor or preacher is to lead people to Christ and then help them grow in **faith** and in **love**. A pastor or preacher is like a parent to new believers (Galatians 4:19; 1 Thessalonians 2:8,11). This is why Paul was so overjoyed to hear good news about his spiritual children in Thessalonica.

Notice that Timothy brought good news concerning the Thessalonians' **faith and love** (verse 6). Faith and love are the two most necessary and important things in our lives. If we had to describe the Christian life in just two words, we could do it by choosing the words **faith and love** (see Galatians 5:6 and comment).

8 **For now we really live.** On the one hand, Paul said: **For to me, to live is Christ** (Philippians 1:21). On the other hand, Paul "lives" in his spiritual children. If they remain strong in the Lord, that will be like "life" to Paul.

9–10 Paul desired to visit the Thessalonians again in order to **supply what was lacking** in their faith (see Romans 1:11). These new believers needed more spiritual wisdom; they needed **solid food** (see Hebrews 5:13–14; 6:1). They needed to go on to maturity in Christ (Ephesians 4:12–13).

11 Paul here calls God **our God and Father.** Christians are entitled to call God "our Father." God is the Creator of all men, but He is not the Father of all men. He is the Father only of those who are adopted into His family through faith in Christ (Romans 8:15–16; Galatians 4:6–7).

Paul prays that God will **clear the way** for him to come to Thessalonica. Paul didn't travel here and there according to his own desire and plan. Paul went only where God had "cleared the way"; he went only according to God's guidance.

12 Paul prays that God might make the Thessalonians' love **increase**. We Christians must always be increasing in spiritual qualities; we must always be growing. We cannot remain in the same condition. We must either grow or die. And as our love grows, it must grow not only for **each other** but also **for everyone else**.

13 **May he strengthen your hearts so that you will be blameless and holy.** To strengthen one's heart means to strengthen one's faith (see 1 Corinthians 1:8). Our goal is to be **blameless and holy;** God will not be satisfied with anything less (see Matthew 5:8,48; Ephesians 1:4 and comments). To be **holy** means to be "set apart" for God. This is why, in the New Testament, Christians are often called "saints," or "holy ones."

Angels also are called **holy ones** in the

New Testament. When **our Lord Jesus comes** to earth again, the angels will be with him (Mark 8:38; 2 Thessalonians 1:7). Jesus will come to judge all men (John 5:22; 2 Timothy 4:1). Therefore, let us go on striving in Jesus' strength to be **blameless and holy**, remembering this, that one day we will all have to stand before His judgment seat (Romans 14:10; 2 Corinthians 5:10; 1 John 2:28)

CHAPTER 4

Living to Please God (4:1–12)

1–2 There is only one ultimate purpose to man's life, and that is to please and glorify God. Paul had taught the Thessalonians how they should live in order to please God, but now he urges them to live in that way **more and more** (verse 1). Here again, as in 1 Thessalonians 3:12, Paul exhorts his spiritual children to grow in the Lord.

Paul reminds the Thessalonians that he does not speak by his own authority, but **by the authority of the Lord Jesus**.

3 What kind of life is pleasing to God? The life that is pleasing to God is a **holy** life (verse 7). It is God's will that we be holy. He has chosen us to be **holy and blameless** (Ephesians 1:4). Only those who are holy and pure in heart will get to see God (Matthew 5:8; Hebrews 12:14). God says: **"Be holy, because I am holy"** (1 Peter 1:15–16).

. . . **avoid sexual immorality**. In Paul's day, the Greeks regarded sexual sins lightly; they did not consider them very great sins. Every kind of sexual immorality was practiced among them. Therefore, it was necessary for these new Greek believers in Thessalonica to completely give up all these sinful sexual practices that were considered acceptable by the society around them (Ephesians 4:17–19; 1 Peter 1:14). God condemns all kinds of sexual immorality. The Thessalonians must follow God's law, and do what is pleasing to Him (1 Corinthians 6:18–20; Galatians 5:19; Ephesians 5:3,5).

4 . . . **each of you should learn to control his own body.**[4] It is necessary for each Christian to learn how to keep his own bodily passions under control, especially his sexual passions. We must keep our bodies **holy and honorable**. Any impurity or unholiness in our lives brings dishonor upon our bodies and upon the Lord. Let us remember that we belong to Christ; we are not our own (1 Corinthians 6:19).

5 Paul uses the word **heathen** in this verse to mean Gentiles who do not believe in Christ. Christians must not live as the "heathen" do. The heathen live **in passionate lust**. They do not know God. Yet they have no excuse for not knowing God, because God has revealed Himself to all men (Romans 1:18–20). But the heathen reject the knowledge of God. Therefore, God has given them over to **sexual impurity** (Romans 1:24) and to a **depraved mind** (Romans 1:28).

6 . . . **in this matter**—the matter of sexual impurity—**no one should wrong his brother or take advantage of him**. If, for example, we commit adultery with another man's wife, we **wrong** that man.

---

[4] In place of the words **control his own body**, some versions of the Bible say, "learn to live with his own wife," or "learn to acquire a wife." The original Greek text can mean any of these things; it is not certain how it should be translated. However, no matter which translation is used, Paul's meaning is essentially the same: a man must control his sexual impulses. God has given us a natural way to do this: namely, to acquire a wife and learn to live with her in mutual consideration and respect (1 Peter 3:7).

If we have sexual relations with an unmarried person, we not only **wrong** that person, but we also wrong whomever that person might later marry. God will **punish**[5] the person who does such things (Ephesians 5:5–6; 2 Thessalonians 1:8; Hebrews 13:4).

7 Here Paul repeats the thought of verse 3.

Remember, we ourselves did not first decide to live a holy life. It was God who first called us in the beginning. **While we were still sinners, Christ died for us** (Romans 5:8).

In one way, we have already been made holy or righteous in God's sight through faith in Christ (Romans 3:24,28). But in another way, through the power of the Holy Spirit, we must lead increasingly holy lives. That is our responsibility. If God has chosen us to be holy, then we must determine to manifest that holiness in our lives (Ephesians 5:3).

8 If we reject **this instruction**—that is, Paul's teaching in the above verses—we will be rejecting God; we will be disobeying God. We will be "grieving" the **Holy Spirit**, whom God has given to us (Ephesians 4:30). It is the Holy Spirit who makes us holy (2 Thessalonians 2:13). Thus whenever we "grieve" the Holy Spirit, we cease being holy and separate ourselves from God. Therefore, the Thessalonians—and we also—must completely turn away from all impurity and unholiness, and devote ourselves totally to what is pleasing to God.

9–10 The **love** mentioned in the New Testament is spiritual love. It is God's love. When we believe in Christ, God then pours out His love into our hearts by the Holy Spirit (Romans 5:5).

God loved us even though we were sinful and unworthy (Romans 5:8; 1 John 4:9–10). Just as God loved us, so we must love our neighbor—whether our neighbor is worthy of our love or not! We must even love our enemies (Matthew 5:44). But even more than our neighbors and our enemies, we must love our Christian brothers and sisters (1 Thessalonians 3:12; 1 John 4:11). This is the third great commandment that Jesus gave us (John 13:34). When we obey this third great command to love our fellow believers, then all men will know that we are Jesus' disciples (John 13:35). When we love our brother, we **know that we have passed from death to life** (1 John 3:14).

11–12 Here Paul gives some important advice to all of us: **Make it your ambition to lead a quiet life** (verse 11). That means: Try not to let your life be filled with restlessness, turmoil, or anxiety. Then Paul says: **... mind your own business**. That is, don't always be criticizing other people and interfering in their affairs. Next Paul says: **... work with your hands**. That means: Earn your living through the labor of your own hands. Perhaps the Thessalonians were surprised at this last piece of advice, because most Greeks, being highly educated, despised working with their hands. They gave such work to their slaves! But Paul says to them: **... work with your hands!** (see 2 Thessalonians 3:11–12).

When Christians become educated, they too, like the Thessalonians, begin to look down on manual labor, such as farming and crafts. But let this not be. Paul made tents for a living (Acts 18:3). And Jesus Himself spent most of his life as a carpenter (Mark 6:3).

In all things our daily life must **win the respect of outsiders**—that is, non-believers (verse 12). In all things, our lives must be honorable and praiseworthy. Let us not be people who are lazy, who waste time, who indulge in idle gossip. Rather we must apply ourselves diligently to the work which God has given us to do. We must not always be hoping that someone will help us, or give us a handout. We should **not be dependent upon anybody**—except God.

The Coming of the Lord (4:13–18)

13 The Thessalonians had supposed that Christ was going to return again before any of them died. However, a few

[5] In place of the word **punish**, some versions of the Bible say "avenge," which is the literal translation of the Greek text. The meaning is the same.

of the Thessalonian believers had recently died. Therefore, the Thessalonians were perplexed, and wanted to know what was going to happen to those who had died. In this section, Paul gives them the answer to their question.

When Paul mentions **those who fall asleep**, he is referring to those believers who have died. They will not remain "dead" forever. We Christians have the sure hope and faith that after our earthly bodies die, we shall live again. Therefore, the Thessalonians do not need to have any anxiety about those who have died. They are "sleeping" now, but will soon "wake up."

In one sense, then, we don't need to grieve for believers who die. When we grieve over the death of a fellow believer, we are really grieving over our own loss, and that is natural. But even as we grieve, let our hope of eternal life overcome our grief. Let us rejoice that our loved one is now in Christ's hands.

14 How do we know that we will be raised? We know, because Christ Himself died and rose again. If Jesus died and rose (and we know that He certainly did rise), then we too, after we die, shall certainly rise again (Romans 8:11; 1 Corinthians 15:17–18,20,22–23; 2 Corinthians 4:14).

15 Here and in verse 16, Paul says that when Christ comes again, believers **who have fallen asleep** (who have died) will rise and be carried into heaven first; then, after them, those who are alive at Christ's coming will be taken up into heaven. Thus, those who have died will enter heaven first of all; they are at no disadvantage! The Thessalonians don't need to be anxious about them.

Paul says that what he has written here is according **to the Lord's own word**. This is the only place in the New Testament where the Lord's word on this subject is mentioned.

16 In this verse, Paul briefly describes what will happen at Christ's second coming (see Mark 13:24–27; John 5:28–29; 1 Corinthians 15:51–52 and comments).

17–18 Those who are alive at Christ's coming will be **caught up** and taken to heaven. At that time, those who are living will be joined again with those who have died, and from then on, all believers will live together with the Lord forever. **Therefore encourage each other with these words** (verse 18).

The New Testament does not tell us in detail what will happen when Christ comes again. In fact, the New Testament contains very little teaching on this subject. We simply do not know all the things that will take place; and it is pointless to speculate and argue about it.

No one knows the day when Christ will come again. But there is one thing we do know, and that is that all believers must always be ready for that day (see Mark 13:32–33; 1 Thessalonians 5:1–2 and comments). What will the Lord find us doing when He comes?

CHAPTER 5

Christ's Second Coming (5:1–11)

1–2 No one knows what hour in the night a thief is going to come. A thief comes by surprise. The **day of the Lord**—Christ's second coming—will be like that (see Matthew 24:42–44; Mark 13:34–36; Acts 1:7; Revelation 3:2–3).

Here in verse 2, Paul calls Christ's second coming the **day of the Lord**. In other verses in the New Testament, it is called the **day of judgment** (2 Peter 2:9), the **great day of . . . wrath** (Revelation 6:17), the **day of redemption** (Ephesians 4:30), the **last day** (John 6:39), and the **great Day** (Jude 6).

3 Worldly men don't think about the day of judgment; they don't care about it. They think only about the world and its pleasures. They say: "**Peace and safety**. All is well; there's nothing to worry about."

But **destruction**, or God's wrath, will fall upon them suddenly (2 Thessalonians

1:9). Just as labor pains will inevitably come upon a woman who is pregnant, so will God's wrath come upon those who do not believe in Christ (see Mark 13:8).

4–5 The Thessalonian Christians do not need to fear the day of the Lord. They are God's children; they are **sons of the light**, they are **sons of the day** (the day of the Lord). They do not belong to the kingdom of **darkness**, upon which God's wrath will come (see Ephesians 5:8 and comment).

6–8 Let us not be like those who are spiritually asleep. They are unaware of the coming wrath. Let us not be like those who are drunk, who are "drunk" with the desires and passions of this world. Rather, let us put on the **armor of light** (Romans 13:12).

What is our armor? Paul says here in verse 8 that our "armor" is **faith, love,** and **hope** (see 1 Corinthians 13:13; 1 Thessalonians 1:3). In Ephesians 6:14–17, Paul gives a slightly different description of our armor than the one he gives here, but the basic idea is the same. Paul uses the illustration of the soldier's armor to describe the spiritual qualities we need in our lives.

In verse 8, Paul mentions the **hope of SALVATION**. In one way, we have already obtained salvation; therefore, there is no need to hope for it! But in another way, we have not yet received our complete salvation; only after Christ comes again will we receive our full salvation, our full heavenly inheritance. It is for this full heavenly inheritance that we hope. And our hope is not like the hope of other men. The Christian's hope is not in something uncertain; it is fixed on something that is absolutely certain and sure: namely, that just as Jesus rose, we too shall rise and live with Him forever.

9 In this verse, Paul gives us a one-sentence summary of the glorious Gospel of Christ: Those who believe in Christ will not suffer God's **wrath**, but will **receive salvation through our Lord Jesus Christ**. According to the teaching of other religions, man must do good works or obey certain laws in order to obtain salvation. But salvation cannot be obtained by these means. Only through faith in Jesus Christ can salvation be obtained. But let no one boast in his faith, saying: "I myself have believed." Because faith does not arise from man; **it is the gift of God** (Ephesians 2:8). Paul says here that God has "appointed" us to believe and to receive salvation.

10–11 Christ **died for us** (see Romans 5:6,8). He suffered God's wrath in our place (see Mark 10:45; Romans 3:23–25; 5:9; 1 Thessalonians 1:10 and comments). Christ died for us **so that . . . we may live together with him**. At His second coming, whether we have died or are alive, we shall all rise (Romans 14:9), and we shall live with Him in heaven forever. Hallelujah!

Final Instructions (5:12–28)

12–13 In verse 12, Paul gives a description of church leaders, and tells the Thessalonians to **respect** them. Paul says: Those who **work hard among you**, and who **are over you in the Lord**, and who **admonish you**, **deserve** your respect.

In many churches one finds young and immature Christians who do not respect their leaders. These immature Christians see faults and weaknesses in their pastor or their elders, and are always quick to accuse and criticize them. In their own minds they are sure they are doing the right thing, but in fact they are doing great wrong. If anyone wants to accuse a leader of the church, let him first meditate on these verses.

There is only one situation in which we can properly accuse or oppose a leader, and that is when the leader has clearly broken one of God's commands. But before we can accuse or oppose that leader, we must have proof of his wrongdoing. Two or more reliable eyewitnesses are required to confirm an accusation. We must not even listen to rumors or second-hand gossip! (1 Timothy 5:19).

If all Christians would obey the rules Paul has given here, there would be peace in our churches. Remember, these leaders are our leaders **in the Lord** (verse 12). Their authority is the Lord's authority. It is meant to be used for our spiritual good.

When we oppose our leaders, we oppose Christ (see Romans 13:1–3 and comment).

Why must we hold our leaders **in the highest regard in love**? (verse 13). The reason is: **because of their work**. Even if we do not personally like a particular leader, and even if that leader has faults and weaknesses (every leader has faults and weaknesses), we must still hold that leader **in the highest regard in love—because of** [his] **work**. If we criticize or oppose our leaders, they cannot do their **work** successfully. As a result, the work of Christ will suffer. We should fear to oppose our leaders! Do we want to destroy the work of Christ? (see 1 Timothy 5:17; Hebrews 13:17).

If it is essential to oppose something a leader has said or done, then we must first go to that leader alone, face to face, and talk with him about it (see Matthew 18:15 and comment). Otherwise, we are opposing Christ.

14 **... warn those who are idle** (see 1 Thessalonians 4:11 and comment).

... encourage the timid, help the weak (see Romans 15:1–2; Galatians 6:2; 1 Thessalonians 2:11–12 and comments).

... be patient with everyone (see Ephesians 4:2 and comment).

15 **Make sure that nobody pays back wrong for wrong** (see Matthew 5:38–42; 18:21–22; Romans 12:17,19–21; 1 Peter 3:9 and comments). Instead, **always try to be kind to each other**. Paul's meaning here is that we must **be kind** to those who do us wrong.

16–18 **Be joyful always** (see Philippians 3:1; 4:4 and comments).

... pray continually. We live in complete dependence upon God every hour of every day. We should not stop praying even for one day (see Matthew 7:7–8; Ephesians 6:18; Philippians 4:6 and comments).

... give thanks in all circumstances (see Ephesians 5:20; Colossians 3:17; 4:2 and comments).

To be joyful **always**, to pray **continually**, and to give thanks **in all circumstances**—this is **God's will for** [us] **in Christ Jesus**.

19 **Do not put out the** (Holy) **Spirit's fire** (see Ephesians 4:30). The Holy Spirit is like a fire (Matthew 3:11; Acts 2:3–4). We must not put out that fire! What puts out the fire? Sin. Sin always puts out the fire of the Spirit in our lives. And what makes the fire burn more brightly? Joy, prayer, and thanksgiving (verses 16–18).

There is a second meaning to this verse. The Holy Spirit gives different gifts to men (1 Corinthians 12:7–11). We must use the gifts the Spirit gives to us. If we fail to use them, we will put out the **Spirit's fire**.

20–21 Some of the Thessalonian believers had been given the gift of prophecy (1 Corinthians 14:1,3). But others in the church were not heeding these PROPHECIES. Thus Paul admonishes the Thessalonians not to treat prophecies **with contempt**.

However, they must not automatically accept every prophecy; it is first necessary to weigh and examine each prophecy (1 Corinthians 14:29; 1 John 4:1). Today we also must weigh and examine each prophecy we hear or read by comparing it to what is written in the Bible. If the prophecy is in agreement with Biblical teachings, then we can be sure that the prophecy is from the Holy Spirit. The Holy Spirit never does anything that opposes God's written word, the Bible.

There is a second meaning of the word **prophecies**, as it is used in this verse: namely, preaching. We must not treat **with contempt** the sermons we hear preached. Even if the preacher's manner doesn't please us, or even if we've learned nothing new, we still must respectfully heed his words.

22 **Avoid every kind of evil** (see Romans 1:29–31; Galatians 5:19–21: Ephesians 4:31; 5:3–4 and comments).

23 God's people must be holy. But here in this verse we see that it is God Himself who makes us holy, or "sanctifies" us. We cannot **sanctify** ourselves by our own efforts. We need the help and power of God's Holy Spirit to become holy (see Philippians 1:10; 1 Thessalonians 3:13 and comments).

Our **whole spirit, soul and body** must be kept blameless. Paul's meaning is that every part of our lives, every part of us—**spirit, soul and body**—must remain holy.

Some Christian scholars believe that this verse teaches that man is made up of three distinct parts: spirit, soul, and body.

Our **spirit** is that part of us which has direct contact and fellowship with God (Romans 8:16). Our **soul** is that part of us from which our feelings, thoughts, and desires arise. Sin also arises in the soul (James 1:14–15). The Bible often calls the soul the "heart" or the "mind." Then, the third part, our body, is the physical part of us. Our body is under the direction of our spirit and soul; whatever our spirit and soul say to do, that will our body do (Romans 6:13).

In order for us to be fully holy and healthy in God's sight, all three parts of our lives must be holy and healthy. It does little good to take medicine to make our body well, if our soul is sick with sin and our spirit is separated from God. In fact, our physical body is the least important part of us; it is much more important that our spirit and soul be healthy, because they are the parts of us that will remain forever. We don't need healthy bodies to enter heaven! (see Mark 9:43–48).

24 God has chosen us **to be holy and blameless** (Ephesians 1:4). He has called us **to live a holy life** (1 Thessalonians 4:7). God is **faithful**. He will surely complete the work He has begun in us (see Numbers 23:19; 1 Corinthians 1:8; Philippians 1:6; 2:13; Jude 24–25 and comments).

25–27 See Romans 16:16 and comment.

28 See 1 Corinthians 16:23 and comment.

2 Thessalonians

INTRODUCTION

Paul's second letter to the Thessalonians was written from Corinth not long after he wrote his first letter.

Some of the Thessalonian believers, after reading Paul's first letter, had got the idea that Jesus was about to come again very soon. Paul had written that the end would come **suddenly** (1 Thessalonians 5:3); but the Thessalonians understood from this that Jesus was coming immediately. For this reason, many of the Thessalonians had completely stopped working, and were simply sitting around waiting for the Lord to appear! Therefore, Paul wrote this second letter to correct the Thessalonians' mistaken thinking and behavior. Paul writes to them saying, in effect: "Get up; go back to work; don't be lazy."

OUTLINE

A. Thanksgiving and Prayer (1:1–12).
   1. Thanksgiving for Perseverance in Persecution (1:1–10).
   2. Prayer for the Thessalonians (1:11–12).
B. Instructions and Exhortations (2:1–3:18).
   1. Instructions Concerning the Coming of the Lord (2:1–17).
   2. Exhortations to Pray and Work (3:1–18).

CHAPTER 1

Thanksgiving and Prayer (1:1–12)

1–2 See 1 Thessalonians 1:1 and comment.

3 According to this verse, Paul's prayer in 1 Thessalonians 3:12 has been completely answered (see Ephesians 1:15–16; Colossians 1:3–4; 1 Thessalonians 1:2–3 and comments).

4 The Thessalonian believers had received much persecution, yet their faith had not wavered; they had persevered. This was a cause of great joy for Paul, who was their spiritual father (see 1 Thessalonians 1:6). Not only had their faith remained firm, but it was growing even stronger because of the persecution they were still enduring (James 1:2–3).

5 Paul says here that the persecution that has come upon the Thessalonians is **evidence that God's** JUDGMENT **is right**. What is Paul's meaning? Paul means that according to God's eternal purpose and judgment, suffering and persecution must at some time come upon every Christian (1 Thessalonians 3:3; 2 Timothy 3:12).

Through our trials and sufferings, God brings great benefit not only to ourselves but also to others. Through Christ's sufferings, God healed us (Isaiah 53:5). Through our sufferings, other men can see our perseverance and faith more clearly. The **perseverance** and **faith** of the Thessalonians was also clearly visible (verse 4), and this is why they were such a good example for other believers to follow (1 Thessalonians 1:7). Through suffering, God also disciplines us and makes us holy and perfect (Hebrews 12:10). Even Christ Himself was perfected through suffering (Hebrews 5:8–9).

For all these reasons, therefore, the trials and sufferings of the Thessalonians are **evidence that God's judgment is right**. In fact, suffering and persecution are **evidence** that God is for us, not against us (1 Peter 4:14).

Thus the Thessalonians had not merely endured suffering; they had endured it with perseverance. This is additional evidence that God was fulfilling His eternal purposes in the lives of the Thessalonians. Because of their perseverance in persecution, the Thessalonians would be **counted worthy of the** KINGDOM OF GOD (see Matthew 5:10–12; Romans 8:17).

Remember, Jesus Christ is worthy. He is worthy to have us suffer for Him. And if we suffer for Him, we ourselves shall become worthy of Him.

6 When we look at the world, we see much injustice all around us. The strong oppress the weak. The rich exploit the poor. The wicked persecute the innocent. However, we must not call God injust. On the final day of judgment, every man will be rewarded according to his works (Matthew 16:27; 2 Corinthians 5:10; Colossians 3:25). God will avenge all evil (Romans 12:19).

7 Therefore, let the Thessalonians be patient and steadfast. After persecution and suffering comes **relief**. But notice, God does not promise to send **relief** in this life. Our **relief** will come **when the Lord Jesus Christ is revealed from heaven**—that is, when the Lord Jesus comes again. Our **relief**—our "reward" or salvation[1]—will be far greater than all the sufferings that come to us on this earth (Romans 8:18).

It is necessary to add something here: Even though God may not give us full "relief" here on earth, He will certainly give us peace in our hearts. Peace is one of the fruits of the Holy Spirit. For the Christian, even when there is no outward peace, there is always inward peace (see Philippians 4:7).

The Lord Jesus will be **revealed from heaven**. At the present time, Jesus is hidden from those who do not have faith. But when He comes again, He will be fully revealed to all men. On that day, **every tongue**—that is, every person—will

[1] For believers, heavenly rewards for good works are in addition to their salvation. Salvation itself does not depend on good works, but on faith.

confess that Jesus Christ is Lord (see Philippians 2:9–11).

Jesus will be revealed **in blazing fire with his powerful** ANGELS (see Mark 8:38; 1 Thessalonians 3:13; 2 Peter 3:10). In the New Testament, **fire** is a sign of the presence of God's Holy Spirit (see Acts 2:3). This **fire** will destroy all those who do not believe in Christ, but it will purify all those who believe. Non-believers will be terrified at Christ's coming, but believers will rejoice and "marvel" (verse 10).

8 Those people who **do not know God** and those who **do not obey the gospel of our Lord Jesus** are the same group of people. Not to obey the Gospel is the same as not to believe. Those who don't believe in Jesus cannot know God (John 1:18; 14:7,9). Therefore, Paul is saying here, in effect, that God will punish all those who do not believe in Jesus (John 3:18,36).

9 What is God's punishment? It is **everlasting destruction**. It is the opposite of eternal life. It is existence in hell, separated from God. Such existence is like death.

Therefore, we can understand that to reject Christ and disobey His Gospel is a frightful thing indeed; for the result of rejecting Christ is eternal death—**everlasting destruction**.

10 That **destruction** will come upon unbelievers **on the day he** (Jesus) **comes to be glorified**.

Jesus will be glorified **in his holy people**—that is, in believers. He will be glorified in us, and we will be glorified with Him (Romans 8:17,19). Christ is even now being glorified by those who persevere in their faith (John 17:10).

11 **With this in mind**—that the Thessalonians might share in Christ's glory—Paul prays constantly for them. Paul first prays that God will count the Thessalonians **worthy of his calling** (see Ephesians 4:1; 1 Thessalonians 2:12 and comments). Let us never forget that we have been called by God. We are His sons and heirs (Galatians 4:7; Ephesians 1:5). We have been called to share in Christ's glory (2 Thessalonians 2:14; 1 Peter 5:10). Let it be our constant prayer that we might remain worthy of such a calling!

Second, Paul prays that God **by his power . . . may fulfill every good purpose of** [the Thessalonians] **and every act prompted by** [their] **faith** (see Philippians 2:13 and comment). God will fulfill His purposes in us **according to his power that is at work within us** (Ephesians 3:20–21).

12 Why does Paul pray this? He prays this so that the **name of our Lord Jesus may be glorified in** [the Thessalonians]. This is why we have been called. To glorify the name of Jesus Christ is our duty and our calling (see Matthew 5:16). When we stand firm in faith, when we love others with Christ's love, when we suffer patiently for Christ, then we bring glory to His name. And if Jesus is glorified in us, we too will be glorified in Him (Romans 8:30). We will be glorified **according to the** GRACE **of our God and the Lord Jesus Christ**. May our lives each day reflect the glory of His grace! (Ephesians 1:6).

CHAPTER 2

The Man of Lawlessness (2:1–12)

1–2 The Thessalonians had heard some things that made them think the **day of the Lord** had already begun (verse 2). They supposed that Christ was coming immediately. But Paul tells them not to be deceived by such talk. "Such talk has not come from me," says Paul (see 1 Thessalonians 5:1–2 and comment).

In Paul's time, there were many ignorant and false teachers, who by **prophecy,**[2] **report or letter** troubled and confused new believers. The Thessalonians had been confused by such teachers.

3 Here Paul states the reason why **that day**—that is, the **day of the Lord** (verse 2)—has not yet come: namely, before **that day** can come, the **rebellion** must first occur. Since the **rebellion** has not occurred, the Thessalonians can know that the day of the Lord has not yet come. At the time the **rebellion** occurs, the **man of lawlessness** will be revealed (Daniel 8:23–25).

Many Bible scholars believe that Paul is talking here about the end of the world. Just before Christ comes again at the end of the world, a **rebellion** against God will occur, and the leader of the rebellion will be an evil and powerful person whom Paul calls the **man of lawlessness**. Paul doesn't tell us exactly who this "man of lawlessness" is. He is probably the same as the **antichrist** mentioned by the Apostle John (see 1 John 2:18).

Paul also calls the "man of lawlessness" the **man doomed to destruction**. That is, this person will not only cause the destruction of many people, but also he himself will be destroyed. He will not be able to overcome Christ (verse 8).

4 This **man of lawlessness** will call himself God. He will sit in God's holy place, in **God's temple.**[3] He will oppose God (see Daniel 11:36; Mark 13:14).

5–6 Paul has taught the Thessalonians some things about the day of the Lord, but in these verses Paul tells us only a small part of what he has taught them. For example, the Thessalonians know **what is holding him** (the man of lawlessness) **back**; but Paul doesn't say in this letter what or who it is.[4] The only thing we can tell is that something or someone is holding back the **man of lawlessness** in some way; something or someone is keeping him under control. This is why the **man of lawlessness** has not yet been fully revealed.

7 Paul says here that the **secret power of lawlessness**[5] is already at work in the world. The Apostle John says the same thing when he writes that **even now many antichrists have come** (1 John 2:18). John also repeats the same idea when he writes: **This is the spirit of the antichrist, which you have heard is coming and even now is already in the world** (1 John 4:3).

But for the present, says Paul, the **one who now holds . . . back** the "man of lawlessness" will continue to hold him back and block his work **till he** (the one holding him back) **is taken out of the way.** But the day will come when the one holding back the "man of lawlessness" will be taken out of the way, and after that the "man of lawlessness" will be fully revealed.

It is not known who this **one** is who holds back the "man of lawlessness." Some Bible scholars think that Paul is referring to the Roman Empire or one of the Roman emperors. Other scholars think that the one holding back the "man of lawlessness" is an angel. Others think it is the Holy Spirit. But Paul does not tell us, and so we cannot be sure of his meaning.

8 Here Paul calls the "man of lawlessness" the **lawless one**. The Lord Jesus will overthrow the "lawless one" **with the breath of his mouth**—that is, with His word—and He will destroy him **by the splendor of his coming**. The "lawless one" will be destroyed by Christ's

---

[2] In place of the word **prophecy,** some translations of the Bible say "spirit," that is, man's human spirit. Prophecy that comes from man's spirit is likely to be false prophecy; only the prophecy that comes from God's Holy Spirit can be trusted. For further discussion, see Word List: Prophecy.

[3] It is not certain what **temple** Paul has in mind here.

[4] The thing or person who is "holding back" the man of lawlessness is the same as the **one who now holds . . . back** the power of lawlessness in verse 7 (see verse 7 and comment).

[5] In place of the words **secret power of lawlessness,** some translations of the Bible say, "mystery of lawlessness." The meaning is the same.

presence alone. The "lawless one" is indeed **doomed to destruction** (verse 3).

9–10 The **lawless one** (the "man of lawlessness") is not the same as SATAN, but his work will be **in accordance with the work of Satan**. The **lawless one** is a representative of Satan.

The coming of the **lawless one** will be accompanied by **all kinds of counterfeit miracles, signs and wonders**. He will deceive many people (Mark 13:22). But he will deceive only **those who are perishing**—that is, those who refuse to accept and **love the truth** (Christ's Gospel). All those who follow the lawless one will be destroyed with him.

11 God will send a **powerful delusion** on all those who follow the **lawless one**. God will blind their understanding, **so that they will believe the lie**—that is, the lie that the "lawless one" is God.

From all of this, we can understand that God is more powerful than all the forces of evil. Furthermore, God takes the evil of evildoers and uses it to punish them. Thus evildoers, by their own evil, bring punishment upon themselves. God has all power. God, in the end, makes even Satan fulfill His purposes.

12 One of God's purposes is that **all will be condemned who have not believed the truth**. The **truth** is not only Christ's Gospel, it is also Christ Himself (John 14:6). All who do not believe in Him will be condemned (see John 3:18–19,36).

There are basically only two kinds of people in the world: those who believe the truth, and those who delight in wickedness. If a man begins by rejecting the truth (Christ), he will end by delighting in wickedness. This is a spiritual principle. If we begin walking on the wrong road, we shall get farther and farther from God. If we reject the light, we will pass deeper and deeper into darkness. God will "give us over" to wickedness (see Romans 1:21,24–26,28 and comment).

Stand Firm (2:13–17)

13 Paul calls the Thessalonians **brothers loved by the Lord**. We, too, are "brothers (and sisters) loved by the Lord." Therefore, before we criticize or accuse a brother, let us remember that he is **loved by the Lord**!

From the beginning God **chose** us **to be saved**. Our SALVATION arises from God's grace. We didn't first choose Him; He first chose us (Ephesians 1:4). God chose us not because we were holy; He chose us in order to make us holy.

Here Paul writes two things about our salvation. First, we are saved **through the sanctifying work of the Spirit**. The HOLY SPIRIT is continually making us more and more holy and blameless. The Holy Spirit is preparing us to meet Christ. We are not yet perfect. But when we receive our full salvation at Christ's second coming, then at that time the Spirit will have made us perfect (see Philippians 1:6 and comment; General Article: Way of Salvation).

The second thing Paul says about our salvation is that we are saved **through belief in the truth**. To believe is man's responsibility. We must believe **in the truth**—that is, in Christ. The work of saving man is from beginning to end God's work. But if God's work of salvation is to be completed, we must believe in His Son Jesus (see General Article: Salvation—God's Choice or Man's Choice?).

14 **He** (God) **called you to this**; that is, He called you to be saved. God's purpose for us is that we might **share in the glory of our Lord Jesus Christ**. That is the final stage of our salvation (see Romans 8:17,30; 2 Thessalonians 1:12; 1 Peter 5:10 and comments).

15 Because of this great hope of salvation and glory, let the Thessalonians **stand firm**, says Paul. In the New Testament, we are urged again and again to stand firm (Matthew 10:22; 1 Corinthians 16:13; Galatians 5:1; Ephesians 6:10,13; Philippians 4:1).

In order to stand firm, we must **hold to the teachings** of the Bible. Paul tells the Thessalonians to hold to the teachings **we passed on to you**. In Paul's time the New Testament had not yet been fully written; therefore, the Thessalonians needed to hold to the words Paul spoke (see 1 Corinthians 11:2).

16–17 In order to stand firm, we need the grace, strength, and encouragement of God and Christ. Let us continually pray for one another the prayer written here in these verses (see 2 Corinthians 1:3–4; 1 Thessalonians 3:13; 1 Peter 5:10).

CHAPTER 3

Final Exhortations (3:1–18)

1 Paul was a great and influential apostle. Nevertheless, his success did not depend on his own strength and ability; rather, it depended on God's grace and on the prayers of other Christians (see Colossians 4:3–4 and comment).

2 The **wicked and evil men** Paul mentions here are mainly the Jews, who opposed the Gospel and persecuted Paul wherever he went. Paul wrote this letter from Corinth, where he had received great trouble from the Jews (Acts 18:12). Later on, Paul asked the believers in Rome to pray that he might be **rescued from unbelievers**—that is, from the Jews in Judea (Romans 15:31).

3 Paul had confidence that the Lord would strengthen and protect the Thessalonians from the **evil one**—that is, from Satan (Matthew 6:13).

4 Paul always praises his fellow Christians. But notice, his confidence is not in the Thessalonians themselves, but **in the Lord**. It is the Lord who will strengthen the Thessalonians and protect them from Satan. And the **Lord is faithful** (verse 3).

5 Paul prays that the Thessalonians' hearts may be filled with **God's love**, and that they may be strengthened by **Christ's perseverance.**

6 Paul here writes with the full authority of an apostle of Christ; that is, he writes with Christ's own authority. Paul commands the Thessalonians to **keep away from** every brother who is **idle**. Such brothers are the same as those mentioned by Paul in 1 Thessalonians 5:14. They did **not live according to the teaching** that Paul had given. They were expecting the Lord to come immediately. Therefore, they had stopped working; they no longer earned their own living. They had become lazy, and were asking for help from the others who continued to work. They had already received teaching from Paul on these matters in his first letter to the Thessalonians. Now, if they refuse to obey Paul's command, they must be put out of the fellowship of the church. We must have no fellowship with those who refuse to repent and continue knowingly in sin (see 1 Corinthians 5:11).

Here a question arises. For what kind of sin must we keep away from our brother? Because many verses in the New Testament tell us to remain at peace with our brother, but only a few tell us to separate from him. This is a difficult question. Each case must be looked at individually. There are two purposes for remaining separate from our brother: first, to bring our brother to repentance; and second, to keep the church pure. In order to decide how to behave toward a brother who is sinning, we need the wisdom and guidance of the Holy Spirit.

7–9 During the time they stayed in Thessalonica, Paul, Timothy, and Silas earned their own living. Surely, then, the Thessalonians ought to do the same! In fact, Paul tells the Thessalonians that they should be following his example. Paul taught not only by word, but also by the example of his own life. If our lives match our preaching, then people will be much more likely to heed what we say (see 1 Corinthians 9:4,12,14; 1 Thessalonians 2:7–9 and comments).

10 According to the teaching of the Bible, begging is wrong. If a man has the strength to work, then he must work. If a man strong enough to work refuses to do so, then let him not eat, says Paul. Let all Christians remember that to be lazy is a sin.[6]

11 Some of the Thessalonians were lazy and simply sat or wandered about doing nothing; they were **idle**. Whenever a man has no work of his own to do, he usually ends up interfering with his neighbor's work. If we remain idle, Satan will always find us something to do! Our minds are constantly running. If we are not busy doing good, we will soon be busy doing evil!

12 Here Paul especially exhorts those who are idle. **Such people we command and urge . . . to settle down and earn the bread[7] they eat** (see 1 Thessalonians 4:11). Paul did not admonish people just to put them down, but rather to help them improve their lives. Paul did not want to drive anyone out of the church permanently.

13 Even if the lazy and idle people don't heed Paul's admonition, at least let the other Thessalonians heed it and continue doing good; let them continue to follow Paul's example and work hard (see Galatians 6:9).

14 Paul here repeats the thought of verse 6. We must remain separate from a brother who knowingly keeps on sinning, **in order that he may feel ashamed**. The hope is that once he feels ashamed, he will repent and be cleansed of his sin.

15 However, we must behave toward the sinning brother, not as an enemy, but as a brother. He is still a beloved brother in the Lord. All discipline must be given in love and because of love.

16 See Philippians 4:7 and comment.

17 See Galatians 6:11; Colossians 4:18 and comments.

18 See 1 Corinthians 16:23 and comment.

---

[6] Even those who are handicapped can usually do something to help earn their living. Those, of course, who are truly unable to meet their own needs will require assistance from others. But if they are believers, they should not resort to begging.

[7] Bread is the main food of the Middle East.

1 Timothy

INTRODUCTION

Timothy was a young man from the city of Lystra, which was located in what is now southern Turkey. Timothy was Paul's beloved companion and co-worker (Acts 16:1–4). Timothy became Paul's closest disciple; Paul called him his **true son in the faith** (1 Timothy 1:2).

Most Bible scholars believe that Paul wrote his two letters to Timothy after the events described in the book of Acts had all taken place. Some of these scholars believe that after spending two years under house arrest (Acts 28:16,30), Paul was then released, and for one or two years continued his preaching and traveling. He could have written these letters to Timothy during that period.

Paul was getting to be an old man when he wrote to Timothy. He realized that he needed to pass on his apostolic authority to some younger leaders such as Timothy and Titus. Even before writing this letter, Paul had appointed Timothy to be the leader of the church in Ephesus (1 Timothy 1:3). Paul wrote this first letter to Timothy in order to encourage him and instruct him in his duties. That is why, from Timothy's time until the present, this letter has been very important and helpful for church leaders—and not only for leaders but also for those under them.

For further information about Paul's life, see Romans: Introduction.

OUTLINE

A. Timothy's Task at Ephesus (1:1–20).
   1. Warning Against False Teachers (1:1–11).
   2. Paul's Thanksgiving to God (1:12–20).

B. Instructions and Advice (2:1–5:25).
   1. Instructions to the Church (2:1–3:16).
   2. Instructions to Timothy (4:1–16).
   3. Advice Concerning Special Groups (5:1–25).
C. Final Admonitions (6:1–21).
   1. Various Teachings (6:1–10).
   2. Paul's Charge to Timothy (6:11–21).

CHAPTER 1

Warning Against False Teachers (1:1–11)

1 Paul says here that he is an APOSTLE of Christ **by the command** of God and Christ. Paul was not an apostle by his own choice or desire, or by any other man's desire. Rather, God Himself had commanded Paul to be a **servant of Christ Jesus** (Romans 1:1). Paul was Christ's soldier; he was under His authority.

Paul here calls God **our Savior**. Usually in the New Testament it is Christ who is called the Savior. But it is also correct to call God "our Savior," because God and Christ are one (see John 10:30 and comment; General Article: Jesus Christ).

2 Timothy was Paul's **true son** in the faith. Timothy had already become a Christian by the time Paul first met him (Acts 16:1). But Paul had nurtured and strengthened Timothy in the faith; he had loved and cared for Timothy like a father would love and care for his own natural son (see 1 Corinthians 4:17). Now Timothy had become a mature man, and was ready to stand in Paul's place as a leader in the church.

Paul prays that Timothy might experience GRACE, **mercy and** PEACE from God (see Romans 1:7; Ephesians 1:2 and comments). Here and in Paul's second letter to Timothy, Paul adds the word **mercy** to his usual prayer for grace and peace. Mercy is one part of God's grace. Because of God's mercy, we have received forgiveness for our sins. Without God's mercy and forgiveness, we cannot obtain God's **peace**.

3 Paul had founded the church at Ephesus about ten years before this letter was written (see Acts 19:1–10). But even within that short time, some men had begun to teach **false doctrines**—false teachings that were different from the truth that Paul had taught. Here Paul gives Timothy, as leader of the Ephesian church, complete authority to stop men from teaching such false doctrines in the church.

4 In addition to teaching **false doctrines**, these men were also teaching Jewish **myths** and **endless genealogies**. For the Jews, genealogies were very important; it was important for a Jew to be able to trace his genealogy right back to the first Jew, Abraham. The Jews believed that, because they were the natural descendants of Abraham, they would thereby obtain salvation. But Paul says that it is useless to put any reliance upon genealogies or upon who one's ancestors were. Genealogies do not promote good works; they do not lead to salvation. **God's work**—that is, God's work of saving men—depends on FAITH, not on who our ancestors were. Instead, things like myths and genealogies lead only to **controversies**, and such controversies profit no one.

People are always eager to hear new and interesting things. But we must always compare any new teaching we hear with what is written in the Bible. If a new teaching does not agree with what is written in the Bible, then we must reject that teaching; we must not listen to it.

Some people are always seeking the truth, but never finding it. They ask questions but receive no answers, because they do not accept the truth written in the Bible. Such people not only fall into error themselves, but they lead others into error as well. Thus Paul forcefully instructs Timothy to eliminate such false teaching from the church, so that the believers might not fall into error but hold fast to the truth and grow in faith and in works of love.

5 **The goal of this command is love.** Here **this command** is the command to stop teaching false doctrines in the church. The **goal** of the command is that believers might grow in **love**. True doctrines lead men into a life filled with love (see Galatians 5:6). For God's love to fill our lives, three things are necessary: a **pure heart**, a **good conscience**, and a **sincere faith**. Our **faith** must be in Christ and in His truth, not in false doctrines. Through faith in Christ our hearts are made **pure** (see John 15:3; Acts 15:9). Together with a pure heart, we must have a **good conscience**—that is, we must keep a clear conscience (Acts 24:16); otherwise, the Holy Spirit will not be able to work in our lives and our love will dry up.

6 Without a pure heart, a good conscience, and a sincere faith, men will "wander" from the truth and lose the way. They will turn instead to **meaningless talk**, such as the false doctrines and controversies mentioned in verses 3–4 (see 1 Timothy 6:3–5).

7 Most false teachers are smooth and skillful talkers. They seek positions of importance. They desire to be **teachers of the** LAW. But, in fact, they do not know the truth. Such teachers do great harm in the church. They are like wolves in sheep's clothing (Matthew 7:15).

8 Having just condemned false teachers who seek to be **teachers of the law**, Paul now reassures Timothy that the law itself is **good**. But the law must be used properly. The proper use of the law is to restrain men from doing evil.

9–11 Rules and laws are not given for those who are obedient; rather, they are given to correct those who are disobedient.

Paul here gives examples of different kinds of evildoers. Then, at the end of the list, Paul writes: **. . . and for whatever else is contrary to the sound doctrine** (verse 10). Everything—no matter how small—that is **contrary** to the teaching of the Bible is evil. But **sound doctrine** conforms to the **glorious** GOSPEL of God, that is, to the teaching of Christ and His apostles.

The Lord's Grace to Paul (1:12–20)

12–13 Paul can never forget how he once persecuted the church of Christ (Acts 8:3; 9:1–2; 26:9–11; Galatians 1:13). Nevertheless, because he had acted in ignorance, God had shown him mercy. God not only forgave Paul's sins; He also **considered him faithful** (verse 12). God considered Paul so "faithful" that He appointed him to be an apostle. If God could make such a great change in a hardened enemy of Christ like Paul, then surely He can change any man!

But we must remember that God does not show mercy to those who knowingly continue to sin against Him. According to the teaching of the Old Testament, there was no sacrifice that would take away sins committed knowingly (see Hebrews 10:26–29 and comment). Because Paul had persecuted the church **in ignorance and unbelief** (verse 13), he had obtained mercy and forgiveness from God.[1]

14 Paul never failed to be amazed at the **grace** which God had so abundantly poured out into his life, and he never stopped thanking God for it. Because of that grace, Paul's life was filled with the **faith and love that are in Christ Jesus**.

15 Here Paul gives a one-sentence summary of the Gospel of Christ: **Christ Jesus came into the world to save sinners** (see Mark 2:17). All men are sinners (Romans 3:9–10). Therefore, all men need a Savior. Jesus came to save every man and woman of every nation and tribe on earth. All who believe in Him will be saved (John 3:16).

16 Paul serves as an example for all those who seek God and who believe in Christ. If Christ showed such great patience toward Paul, the **worst** of sinners, He will certainly show patience toward us.

Paul was a devout and righteous apostle of Christ. Nevertheless, he calls himself here the **worst** of sinners. This is not false humility. The more holy a Christian becomes, the more unholy he will consider himself. The reason is that the nearer we come to God, the clearer we see our own unholiness. In the light of God's holiness, our own lives appear unholy and unrighteous—as indeed they

[1] Paul is not saying here that all men who act **in ignorance and unbelief** will automatically receive mercy. No man is completely ignorant of right and wrong; no man is completely ignorant of God (see Romans 1:18–21 and comment). Paul still needed to repent of his sins and believe in Christ. But God will show more leniency, more mercy, toward those who have less knowledge; and He will judge more severely those who have more knowledge (see Luke 12:47–48 and comment).

are. Whoever says, "I am not a sinner; I am holy," is far away from God.

17 As Paul thinks about the mercy and grace which God has showered upon him, he cannot keep from praising such an amazing and wonderful God—**the King, eternal, immortal, invisible, the only God**! To Him be **honor and glory for ever and ever**!

18 Paul had previously received PROPHECIES concerning Timothy, and because of these prophecies Paul knew with certainty that Timothy had been selected by God to be a leader in the church. Now Paul reminds Timothy of these **prophecies**, so that Timothy might be encouraged. Paul knew that Timothy, being a young pastor, would have to face many battles. But if Timothy remembers that God Himself has appointed him to leadership, he will be strengthened to **fight the good fight**.

19–20 By remembering the prophecies concerning himself, Timothy will not only be better able to **fight**, but he will also be better able to hold fast to his **faith** and to keep a **good conscience** (verse 19). Faith and a clear conscience always go together. If our faith is not genuine, we will be led into sin and we will lose our clear conscience. At the same time, if we sin and do not repent, we will be turned away from true faith toward false doctrines. Our faith and our behavior must always agree.

Paul here mentions two men, **Hymenaeus** and **Alexander**, who had **shipwrecked their faith**—that is, they had turned from the true faith. These two men had lost their good conscience and had begun to blaspheme against God. Paul had expelled them from the church and had **handed** (them) **over to SATAN** (see 1 Corinthians 5:5 and comment). Paul expected that Satan would afflict them with some illness or other trouble (see Acts 13:9–11). Paul's hope was that, as a result of this punishment, they would then be led to repentance.

Nothing else is known about these two men. Two other Alexanders are mentioned in the New Testament (Acts 19:33; 2 Timothy 4:14), but many scholars believe they are different from the Alexander mentioned here.

A **good conscience** (or clear conscience) is essential for every Christian. Why do our spiritual lives so quickly become dry? Why do we lose our zeal for the Lord? Why does our love so easily grow cold? The reason is always the same: namely, our conscience has become unclean because of some sin. If we have sinned and not repented, we will lose the desire and the power to love and serve the Lord.

CHAPTER 2

Instructions on Worship (2:1–8)

1 In this section Paul gives Timothy instructions about worship in the church. In his instructions, Paul starts **first of all** with prayer. In Paul's mind, there is nothing more important than prayer in the life of the church and in the life of the individual.

Just as true doctrine and teaching are essential for the church, so prayer is also essential. There are different kinds of prayer. The first kind that Paul mentions are **requests**, which are the simple statements of a desire or need. God is always ready to hear our requests. Paul then mentions **prayers**, a general word for private and public prayer to God. Then Paul mentions **intercession**, which is prayer primarily for others. Intercession is a very bold and free kind of prayer, in which the intercessor pleads with God on someone's behalf.

Finally, Paul ends with **thanksgiving**, which is an important part of every prayer (see Romans 1:8; Ephesians 5:20; Philippians 1:3; 4:6; 1 Thessalonians 5:17–18). Paul says that we must pray for all people everywhere (see Luke 6:27–28).

2 Among all the people we should pray for, Paul mentions here **kings and all those in authority**. Both Paul and

Peter in other letters have taught that we must submit to those in authority (Romans 13:1–5; 1 Peter 2:13–17). But here Paul teaches that we must also pray for them. And we must pray not only for good leaders, but also for evil and corrupt leaders. We must pray that they will turn to God and begin to do His will, so that we may **live peaceful and quiet lives in all godliness and holiness.** The main purpose for praying for our leaders is not that we might live easy and comfortable lives, but that we might live **in all godliness and holiness.**

3–4 To pray **for everyone** (verse 1) is **good** in God's sight. It **pleases** Him, because He wants **all men to be saved**—to receive SALVATION. This does not mean that God has determined that every man and woman will, in fact, be saved. It means only that God's general desire is to see all people saved.[2] God's salvation is not for one race or nation alone—as the Jews mistakenly thought. Instead, God's salvation is for everyone who believes. That's why we must pray for all people, says Paul, so that they might **come to a knowledge of the truth**—that is, the truth of Christ—and thus find salvation (see 1 Timothy 4:9–10 and comment).

5–6 Christ is able to save us because He is the **one mediator between God and men**. Only through faith in Christ can we receive God's pardon and be reconciled to Him (Romans 5:1).

How did Christ become our **mediator**? He took the punishment for our sins upon Himself. By offering Himself up, He paid the price for our sins. And that price was His own life, which He gave for us that we might be saved from punishment—from eternal death (see Mark 10:45; Romans 6:23; Hebrews 9:15 and comments). The **testimony** of Christ is that He offered Himself at the **proper time** to save sinners (see Galatians 4:4–5 and comment). The price or **ransom** that Christ paid—that is, His own life—is great enough to save all men. But all men, sadly, do not appropriate what Christ has done for them. They do not believe in Him; they refuse to obey God.

Salvation can be compared to a great feast. The feast is all prepared; but unless a man eats, he will remain hungry. Salvation can also be compared to a powerful medicine. The medicine can cure any disease; but unless a man takes the medicine, he will remain uncured.

Notice that Paul in verse 5 calls Christ the **man Christ Jesus**. Jesus was both fully **man** and fully God (Colossians 2:9). Because of this, Jesus is the sole and perfect mediator between us and God.

7 Christ came to save all people, not only Jews. For this reason, Paul was appointed to preach the Gospel of Christ to non-Jews, or **GENTILES** (see Galatians 2:7).

8 God wants us to pray, but He doesn't want us to pray only with our lips. He wants us to pray also with **holy hands**—that is, with pure hearts. If we have kept any sin or evil in our hearts, God will not hear our prayer (Psalm 26:6–7; 66:18; Mark 7:6). If we are angry with our brother or have sinned against him in any way, we must first go to that brother and be reconciled with him; we must forgive and be forgiven. Only after that will God accept our prayers and offerings (see Matthew 5:23–24).

Suitable Behavior for Women (2:9–15)

9–10 In Paul's time, vain and worldly women used to braid their hair and tie it up with ribbons. They wore expensive jewelry and fancy clothes. Such women did this to show others how wealthy and important they were. Paul teaches here that such proud and ostentatious behavior is wrong. Rather, let women wear ordinary and suitable clothing. A woman's finest "clothing" is her **good deeds** (verse 10); let her clothe herself with these (see 1 Peter 3:3–4).

11 Paul says that women must remain in submission to men. This rule applies to husbands and wives (see

[2] For further discussion, see General Articles: Way of Salvation, Salvation—God's Choice or Man's Choice?

Ephesians 5:22–24 and comment). It also applies within the church (see 1 Corinthians 14:34–35 and comment).

12 Paul writes here that it is right for women to learn, but it is not right for women to teach men. In the church, women must not exercise authority over men; in this context, being a teacher implies the exercise of authority. However, Paul does not prohibit women from teaching children or other women (Titus 2:3–4).

Many Christians believe that in verses 9–12 Paul's words refer only to the time and culture in which he lived; they say that his teaching in these verses does not apply to every culture and to every period of history. In Paul's time, women were generally oppressed and put down by a male-dominated society. Therefore, it would obviously have been against the culture and practice of that time for women to teach men. According to this first opinion, then, Paul in these verses is simply reflecting the attitudes of his own time.

However, many other Christians disagree with this viewpoint. They say that Paul's teaching here is for all times and for all cultures. They say that we too, in this present time, must follow what Paul wrote (see 1 Corinthians 11:5; 14:34–35; 2 Timothy 3:6–7 and comments; General Article: Women in the Church).

13 Paul now gives the reason why women should remain under the authority of men in the home and in the church: namely, because they were created after man was created. God created the first woman, Eve, from the rib of the first man, Adam (Genesis 2:21–22; 1 Corinthians 11:8–9). Therefore, man is the **head** of the woman (see 1 Corinthians 11:3 and comment).

14 Paul here gives a second reason why women should not teach and have authority over men: namely, because women are more easily deceived by false teaching than men are. In the Garden of Eden, that evil serpent Satan deceived Eve, not Adam (Genesis 3:1–6). True, Adam shared in Eve's sin; but they fell into sin because Eve had first been deceived.

However, we cannot say on the basis of this verse that women are more sinful than men! Because even before Eve had been created, God had directly told Adam not to eat the fruit of that one particular tree (Genesis 2:16–17). Adam knew full well that it was a sin to eat that fruit; we cannot say that Eve deceived him. Adam was without excuse.

15 Because of Eve's sin, God punished her, saying to her: **"I will greatly increase your pains in childbearing"** (Genesis 3:16). But now Paul promises women that if they will continue **in faith, love and holiness**, God will preserve them through the pain of childbirth. And indeed, this has proved true. From Paul's time right down to this present time, women—to a greater degree than men—have demonstrated in their lives these three supreme qualities of faith, love, and holiness. Thus there is much truth in the saying: Women who aim for equality with men are aiming too low!

CHAPTER 3

Overseers in the Church (3:1–7)

1 In Chapter 3, Paul writes about how each local church is to be administered. In this section, Paul calls the chief leader of the church an **overseer**,[3] or "bishop." In other places in the New Testament, such a leader is also called an "elder." Today, he is sometimes called a "minister" or "pastor" (see 1 Timothy 4:6; 1 Peter 5:2 and comments; General Article: Church Government).

To be an overseer or pastor is a high

---

[3] In place of the word **overseer**, some translations of the Bible say "bishop." The meaning is the same. In the Greek language, "bishop" means **overseer**.

calling. It is good to desire to be a leader in the church if one has truly been called by God to that task. But it is not right to seek such a position because of pride. Pride is probably the greatest temptation for those who desire leadership in the church. Rather, it is best to let God choose the leaders for His church. Let us never strive or struggle for a high position. Let us never criticize or put down a brother in order to advance ourselves. God will not be pleased by such behavior.

2–3 What kind of men are suitable to be overseers or pastors? First, they must be men who are **above reproach**. That means there must be no unrepented sin or wrongdoing in their lives. Not only that, they should have no obvious bad habit or weakness of character. Otherwise, they would be subject to accusation by others, and this would bring discredit on themselves and on the church.

Second, an overseer or pastor must be the **husband of but one wife**—that is, he must not have more than one wife. In Paul's time, many Gentiles kept more than one wife. When such people became Christians, they were not allowed to become overseers or pastors. Paul does not say that people with more than one wife must get rid of their extra wives; nowhere in the Bible does it say to do that. That would be like trying to correct one wrong by committing a second wrong. Paul says only that a man with more than one wife cannot be an overseer or pastor in the church; he cannot even be a **deacon** (verse 12).

The remaining qualities that Paul lists in verses 2–3 are all equally important. They are all necessary if one is to be an overseer in the church (see Titus 1:6–9).

4–5 Before choosing an overseer, it is necessary to look at his family. If he cannot control his own children and exercise authority properly in his own family, then he will not be able to exercise authority properly in the church (Titus 1:6). God tests potential leaders by first giving them a small responsibility—such as responsibility for their family. If they can successfully fulfill the small responsibility, God will then give them a greater responsibility—such as leadership in the church (see Matthew 25:21).

6 It is not good to give leadership to a **new convert**, one who has only recently become a Christian. All Christians should first learn to submit humbly to the authority of others. Only after that will they be ready to exercise authority themselves.

If a **new convert** receives a position of leadership too quickly, he will almost always become proud. Then he will receive the same judgment that the **devil** (Satan) received because of pride.[4]

7 An overseer or pastor must have a good name among those outside the church also. Non-Christians are always looking for faults among us, and when they find them they are quick to accuse us. Whenever Satan, the slanderer and **accuser of our brothers** (Revelation 12:10), finds any fault in a Christian—especially in a leader—he immediately begins to stir up grumbling and evil talk against that person; in this way that person falls **into the devil's trap**. Such grumbling and evil talk does not arise only among those outside the church; sadly, it also arises within the church! This is one of Satan's greatest weapons: If Satan can get Christians to grumble and talk against their own leaders, then he can destroy the work and effectiveness not only of those leaders but also of the church. That is why it is so important that church leaders be **above reproach** (verse 2). Insofar as possible, we must not give Satan any opportunity to make accusations.

Other Leaders in the Church (3:8–16)

8 **Deacons** are the second main group of leaders in the church. Their main work is to help people in need and

---

[4] In Isaiah 14:12–15, the prophet Isaiah describes how the **devil**, or Satan (also called by Isaiah the **morning star** and **son of the dawn**) tried to make himself equal with God. Because of this, God's judgment fell upon Satan, and he was thrown out of heaven.

to take care of the property and the financial affairs of the church. By doing these things, the deacons free the overseers and elders for their main work, which is to pray, to preach, and to teach (see Acts 6:1–4).

Like overseers, the deacons must be men of good character. Because they have responsibility for the finances of the church, they must not have any desire for **dishonest gain**—as Judas did, who handled the money of Jesus and His disciples (John 12:4–6).

9 Even though deacons usually do not preach and teach,[5] they still must hold fast to the true faith; they must **keep hold of the deep truths**[6] **of the faith**. They must also have a **clear conscience**—that is, there must be no unrepented sin in their lives (see 1 Timothy 1:19).

10 Some people mistakenly think that a deacon's work is not so important, and that therefore anyone can be a deacon. But that, of course, is not true. A deacon's work is extremely important. Before anyone is appointed to be a deacon, he should be carefully **tested**, or examined. Only if he is found blameless should he be appointed. This examination is to be carried out by the congregation (see Acts 6:3). Deacons are ordinarily chosen by the congregation; pastors and overseers, however, are ordinarily appointed by other overseers (see Acts 14:23; Titus 1:5).

11 In this verse Paul mentions the **wives** of deacons. However, it is also possible that Paul is referring here to any woman who is called to do the work of a deacon; the Greek text can have both meanings. Either way, such women, like their male counterparts, are to be **worthy of respect**. In particular, the wives of deacons (and the wives of overseers) must be women of good character. They must not be **malicious talkers**; rather, they should be **temperate and trustworthy in everything**. Otherwise, they will bring discredit upon their husbands and thereby destroy their ministries.

12 See verses 2,4–5 and comment.

13 Just as the overseer's task is a **noble** one (verse 1), so is the deacon's task. Deacons who serve faithfully will receive a reward for their faithfulness: namely, a sure place in the kingdom of heaven and a **crown of glory** (1 Peter 5:1–4). They will also **gain an excellent standing** in the eyes of men, and they will have **great assurance in their faith** as they bear witness to Christ.

14–15 It is very important that the church be governed well, and that those in leadership should be men of good reputation. This is because the church is not the dwelling place of some dead idol; it is the **church of the living God** (verse 15). It is **God's household**; God Himself dwells in the church (see Ephesians 2:19–22).

The church is also the **pillar . . . of the truth**. The church proclaims the truth, and thus stands among men as a "pillar" supporting justice and righteousness. The church is also a **foundation** of the truth; that is, it maintains and defends the truth.

16 In this verse, Paul has written a poem or psalm praising Christ. The **mystery of godliness** is Christ Himself. Christ is like a "mystery," a mystery which is hidden from unbelieving men but is revealed to those who believe (see Colossians 1:26–27).

He (Christ) **appeared in a body** (see John 1:14). He was **vindicated by the Spirit**; that is, He was shown to be God's Son when He was raised from the dead (Romans 1:4). He was **seen by** ANGELS. God has manifested the risen Christ to all the angels of heaven (Ephesians 3:10).

But Christ has not only been manifested in heaven. He has been **preached among the nations**. This Jesus—a Jewish carpenter, executed as a criminal—has

---

[5] Being **able to teach** (verse 2) is not listed here among the qualifications of deacons. Nevertheless, there are many deacons who are also excellent teachers, and they should use their teaching gifts. Many of these deacons later become overseers and pastors.

[6] In place of **deep truths**, some translations of the Bible say "mystery." The meaning is the same. The deep spiritual truths of the Christian faith seem like a "mystery" to unspiritual, worldly men.

been made known throughout the world. Men and women from every nation on earth have believed in Him. He is the Savior of all people of every age.

Finally, at the end of His life on earth, Jesus was **taken up in glory**. And now He is seated at the right hand of God Himself (Ephesians 1:20–21).

CHAPTER 4

Concerning False Teachers (4:1–5)

1 All false teaching comes from Satan and his DEMONS. Satan is the **father of lies** (John 8:44). The main danger in false teaching is that men are deceived by it. Here Paul calls Satan's demons **deceiving spirits**. Their teaching has the appearance of truth; therefore, men are deceived into following it (see 2 Timothy 2:17–18 and comment).

The **later times** mentioned here are the times following Paul's time. From Timothy's time until this present time, false teachers and false prophets have been trying to deceive Christians and lead them astray. Jesus Himself clearly warned that this would happen (Mark 13:22). In other New Testament verses also, we are given warnings about false teachers (Acts 20:29–31; 1 John 4:1–3).

2 These **deceiving spirits** mentioned in verse 1 teach through human teachers; Paul here calls such teachers **hypocritical liars**. Such men do not have clear consciences. Rather, their consciences have been **seared as with a hot iron**. When a hot iron first touches the skin, the pain is very great. But after a while the pain grows less, because the pain nerves are being destroyed by the heat. In the end, the hot iron causes no pain at all. Our consciences are, in a way, like skin. At first our conscience can detect and "feel" every sin. But if some sin remains in us for a while, then our conscience gradually stops "feeling" that sin. Eventually our conscience no longer feels anything; it is destroyed—**seared**. When that situation occurs, a man can no longer tell right from wrong—and no longer cares. He thus goes deeper and deeper into sin.

3 These false teachers teach that in order to be acceptable to God one should not get married or eat certain foods. But this teaching is completely false. First of all, man is made acceptable to God only through faith in Christ. Second, marriage and food are given to us by God for our benefit; thus it is right for us to receive and enjoy these gifts with thanksgiving. God has created these things for all men; certainly, therefore, God's own children—**those who believe and who know the truth**—can rightfully partake of them.[7]

4 But we must partake of God's gifts **with thanksgiving**, remembering that God is the creator of all things. Everything created by God is pure and good (see Mark 7:18–19; Romans 14:14).

5 Everything Christians do should be done with **thanksgiving** (verse 4), and with **prayer** and the reading of the **word of God**. The word of God cleanses us and all things (John 15:3). Whatever we do (except for sin) and whatever we eat is **consecrated** or cleansed by prayer and by God's word. This is one reason why Christians pray before eating.[8] Some scholars say that in Paul's time the Christians also read from the Old Testament before they ate.

Instructions to Timothy (4:6–16)

6 If Timothy warns the **brothers** (believers) about these false teachers and faithfully continues to teach the truth, he

---

[7] Even though all this is true, it must be said that some Christians do receive a special calling from God not to marry. Such people will be better able to glorify God by remaining single (see Matthew 19:12; 1 Corinthians 7:7–8 and comments).

[8] The second reason Christians pray before eating is to offer **thanksgiving** (verse 4).

will be a **good minister of Christ Jesus.** It is not enough only to refute false teaching; it is also necessary to teach the truth clearly and forcefully.

Paul here calls Timothy a **minister.** Today in many churches the pastor is called a "minister," which means servant. This is appropriate, because Jesus Himself taught that in order to be a leader one had to become a servant (see Mark 10:43–45). All true Christian leaders are the servants of the people they lead.

7–8 In verse 7, Paul calls false teaching **godless myths and old wives' tales** (see 1 Timothy 1:3–4). These false teachings are like the stories and gossip that ignorant and unbelieving women like to listen to. Timothy must reject all such teaching.

Instead, Timothy must concentrate on the **truths of the faith** in which he was brought up (verse 6). He must not only teach these truths to others, but he must follow them himself. Timothy must train himself **to be godly** (verse 7). Christians need spiritual training and exercise. Following Christ is not like taking a leisurely stroll! At times our Christian life is like a military battle; at other times it is like a race (see 1 Corinthians 9:24–27; 2 Timothy 4:7). If physical training makes our bodies healthier, then spiritual training in godliness will make us completely healthy in body, soul, and spirit—both in this life and also in the next.

9–10 Paul here reminds Timothy that Christians have put their hope—not in **myths and old wives' tales** (verse 7)—but in the **living God.** It is because of that hope that **we labor and strive.**

Here again Paul calls God the **Savior** (see 1 Timothy 1:1; 2:3). In this verse, however, the meaning is different. Here "savior" means the preserver and sustainer of all living things (Matthew 5:45; 6:26). But as far as believers are concerned, God not only preserves and sustains them physically; He also gives them spiritual life that lasts forever.

11–12 In every generation, older people are inclined to look down on younger people. Young people are not respected. But among Christians, says Paul, let this not happen. Let Timothy earn the respect of his elders by his good life and example.

There are five areas in which Timothy must set a good example: **in speech, in life, in love, in faith and in purity** (verse 12). Leadership in the church is not given to a person according to his age, but rather according to the quality of his character in these five areas. Let any young man who aspires to leadership first examine himself in these five areas.

Paul not only admonishes Timothy; he also encourages him. Paul tells him: **Don't let anyone look down on you because you are young.** Timothy was a timid person; Paul knew that he needed encouragement and support (see 1 Corinthians 16:10–11).

13 Paul describes here three important parts of the job of overseer or pastor: first, the **reading of Scripture,** which in Paul's day meant the Old Testament (the New Testament had not yet been written); second, **preaching**—that is, giving a sermon on the subject of the Old Testament reading; and third, **teaching** true Christian doctrines. The first two of these activities took place every Sabbath day (Saturday) in the Jewish synagogues of Paul's time, a custom that the new Christian churches also followed (Luke 4:16–21; Acts 13:14–15). But the third activity, the **teaching** of Christian doctrine, became a new and distinctive feature of Christian worship services.

Paul instructs Timothy to **devote** himself to these three activities; that is, Timothy must "give himself" to these activities. A pastor or other church leader must give himself totally to the service of Christ and the church (see verse 15).

14 Timothy had been given a **gift,** the gift of preaching, teaching, and leading. Although the gift was given freely by God, Timothy must now take it and use it (2 Timothy 1:6). If we do not use the gifts that God gives us, they will produce no fruit (see Matthew 25:14–18).

At the time Timothy was first called to serve in the church, prophecies were spoken concerning him (see 1 Timothy 1:18). At that time elders laid their hands on him and appointed him to be a leader (see Acts 6:6; 13:1–3 and comments).

15–16 Now Paul tells Timothy how

he can nurture and increase his gift. Timothy must be **diligent** to use his gift (2 Peter 1:10). He must give himself wholly to the **reading** of Scripture, to **preaching**, to **teaching** (verse 13), and to being **godly** (verse 7). Even though he is a leader, there must be **progress** in his Christian life that can be seen by others (verse 15). Not only must Timothy be skillful in preaching, but his character and behavior must agree with what he preaches.

Watch your life and doctrine, Paul tells Timothy (see 1 Thessalonians 5:6; 1 Peter 5:8). **Persevere in them**; that is, remain firm in the faith (1 Corinthians 15:58; 16:13; Galatians 6:9; 2 Thessalonians 5:21). If Timothy does this, not only will he bring his hearers to salvation, but he will also **save** himself—that is, he will **work out** his own salvation (see Philippians 2:12 and comment). Even Paul had to remain watchful, lest after preaching to others he should himself be **disqualified for the prize** (1 Corinthians 9:27).

CHAPTER 5

Advice About Widows, Elders and Slaves (5:1–25)

1–2 In this chapter, Paul gives Timothy many instructions on how to deal with various groups within the church.

It is the responsibility of overseers (elders) and pastors to reprove sin in the church and to discipline church members. However, it is never suitable to harshly rebuke an older person. Rather, the pastor should treat older people with the respect he would show to his own parents.

Timothy should advise and admonish younger members of the church as he would his own brothers and sisters. However, with the young women he must act **with absolute purity**. It is best for a pastor to give most of the responsibility for teaching and counseling young women to the older women in the church; in this way the pastor can avoid temptation (Titus 2:3–5).

3 Caring for widows is a very important Christian duty (James 1:27). Many widows have no way to support themselves. If a widow has no family members who can take care of her, then the church must take responsibility for her welfare. When Paul says here to give widows **proper recognition**, he means that the church should care for widows and meet all their legitimate needs. But the church only needs to care for those widows **who are really in need**.[9]

4 If a widow has children or grandchildren, then they are the ones who should care for her, not the church. It is the duty of children to honor and care for their aging parents and grandparents (Exodus 20:12; Ephesians 6:2). We cannot say we honor our parents if we do not care for their needs.

5 For a widow to receive help from the church, she must first be **really in need**,[10] and second, she must herself be worthy to receive help. She must be one who puts her hope in God and prays continually.

6 Some widows, however, lead immoral lives. Some may even become prostitutes in order to earn their living. Such widows are not worthy to receive help from the church. Even though their bodies are alive, their spirits are **dead**.

7 Timothy is to give these instructions both to widows and to their families, so that everyone may act properly and remain blameless.

8 Any Christian who does not provide for his parents and grandparents

---

[9] In place of the words **who are really in need**, some versions of the Bible say "who are real widows," which is a literal translation of the Greek text. In the context of this verse, the meaning is the same. This same phrase is also found in verses 5 and 16.

[10] See footnote to comment on verse 3.

and other close relatives is **worse than an unbeliever**. Even unbelievers take care of their own families.

9–10 In Paul's time, widows who were worthy to receive help from the church were put on a **list**. In order to be put on the list, a widow had to have the following qualifications: she had to be over sixty years old, she had to have been faithful to her husband, and she had to be known for her good works. Widows who had these qualifications were given special duties to perform in the church. Perhaps the work they were given to do in the church was the same kind of work that they had already become known for—such as caring for children, providing hospitality, helping those in need, or teaching other women.[11]

11–12 Those widows who were on the list were expected to remain totally devoted to Christ's service. It appears that they made some kind of vow or promise not to get married again. Therefore, it was better not to put younger widows on the list, because they usually desired to remarry. If, having been put on the list, they then broke their vow and remarried, they would **bring judgment on themselves**.[12] Therefore, Paul advises Timothy not to put younger widows on the list to begin with.

13–14 Furthermore, Paul says, younger widows often become lazy and spend their time gossiping and talking unsuitably. Rather, let these young widows remarry and get busy taking care of their homes; in this way, they will avoid falling into sin, and Satan will not have opportunity to accuse them (see 1 Corinthians 7:39–40).

15 Apparently some young widows had already been put on the list, and had subsequently **turned away to follow Satan**—that is, they had fallen into sin. This is why Paul urges Timothy not to put young widows on the list: he doesn't want any others to be tempted to break their vow to God and fall into sin.

16 Just as children must care for their widowed mothers and grandmothers, so must the women of a family take care of any other widows in their family, such as widowed sisters, sisters-in-law, daughters, daughters-in-law, etc. Paul says that such widows who have another woman in the household who can care for them should not be put on the church list of widows. The church should only be responsible for those widows **who are really in need**.[13]

17 Timothy is also responsible for supervising and paying the **elders** of the church. Together with the pastor, the elders are the main leaders of the local church[14] (see Acts 20:17,28; Titus 1:5–9; 1 Peter 5:1–3 and comments). Those elders who do their work well are worthy to receive **double honor**—that is, they are worthy both to be honored for their work and to receive payment for it.

18 Workers in the church deserve to be paid for their work. To affirm this principle, Paul quotes from Deuteronomy 25:4 (see 1 Corinthians 9:7–9 and comment). If it is right to feed the ox which treads grain that perishes, it is certainly right to pay the pastor or elder who feeds us the true bread of life that never perishes.

Paul also quotes here from Luke 10:7 (see 1 Corinthians 9:14). True, elders

---

[11] In some churches, there is a special group of women who have been given responsibility and authority to carry out various works of service (see General Article: Women in the Church).

[12] If we make any kind of vow or promise to God, we must be careful not to break it; otherwise, we will come under God's judgment (Numbers 30:2; Deuteronomy 23:21–22; Ecclesiastes 5:4–5; Acts 5:1–5).

[13] See footnote to comment on verse 3.

[14] Some Bible scholars think that in this verse Paul is talking about two different kinds of elders: the elders **who direct the affairs of the church**, and the elders **whose work is preaching and teaching**. It is reasonable that there be different kinds of elders who are given different responsibilities according to their gifts. For further discussion, see General Article: Church Government.

should not work for the love of money (1 Peter 5:2); but the church has a responsibility to pay them fairly.

19 From time to time accusations may be brought against an elder. Such an accusation should not even be **entertained**—that is, not even listened to—unless it is confirmed by two or three eyewitnesses (see Deuteronomy 19:15; Matthew 18:16; 2 Corinthians 13:1)

20 If a charge against an elder is proven, that elder must be **rebuked publicly**.[15] This will provide a warning to others not to sin.

21–22 Timothy must not show any **partiality** or **favoritism** in dealing with others. Before **laying on** hands—that is, before appointing anyone to an office in the church—Timothy must carefully examine that person to see that he is worthy (see Acts 6:6 and comment). If later on he proves to be a sinner, then Timothy will have to take responsibility for his sin, since he was the one who appointed him. Because of that person's sin, Timothy's own service will be dishonored. And certainly, Timothy himself must take no part in someone else's sin; he must keep himself **pure**.

23 From this verse we learn that Timothy was not a strong and healthy man physically. He had many illnesses. In New Testament times, a little wine was considered good for one's stomach.[16]

24–25 These verses are connected with verse 22. In appointing men to office in the church, it is easy to be deceived. Some men's sins can be readily seen. The sins of such men come immediately to the attention of the court.

Other men, however, seem good on the outside, but inwardly they are sinful. The sins of these men come to light only later on. Many such men have been appointed to leadership in the church, and the church has suffered great harm as a result.

In the same way, some good deeds are immediately seen, while other good deeds come to light only later on. Thus many men who are worthy to be leaders are not chosen, because their good deeds are not at first apparent. Only later does it become clear that they are indeed worthy to be leaders.

Finally, there are many people whose worthiness will only be fully manifest in heaven. How many Christians there must be who quietly do good, who sacrifice, who pray—but no one hears about them! Surely these saints will one day receive their full reward.

CHAPTER 6

Various Teachings (6:1–10)

1 Slavery was widespread throughout the Roman Empire, and in New Testament times there were many slaves. Slaves who were believers in Christ were equal with everyone else within the church. But in their master's home, they were treated little better than animals.

Paul here tells believing slaves that they must obey and respect their masters. Even if the master was evil and cruel, a Christian slave still had to show respect for him. A slave who did not respect his master would be considered guilty of wrongdoing, and thus would bring dishonor upon **God's name** and upon the apostles' **teaching** (see Ephesians 6:5–8; Titus 2:9–10 and comments).

---

[15] In place of the word **publicly**, some translations of the Bible say "in the presence of all." It is not certain whether Paul means that the guilty elder should be rebuked in the presence of "all" the members of the church, or only in the presence of "all" the other elders. Both meanings are possible.

[16] Nowadays, there are many kinds of medicine for one's stomach; therefore, it is not necessary to drink wine. Notice that Paul tells Timothy to drink only a **little** wine—not a lot!

2 The masters of some Christian slaves were believers also. Some of the Christian slaves did not show full respect to their Christian masters; they behaved toward their masters like brothers instead of servants. These slaves did not work hard for their Christian masters. But Paul says here that believing slaves should show Christian masters even more respect than non-Christian masters. The believing slave should work even harder for a Christian master, simply because he is a fellow Christian. He should serve his master not out of obligation but out of love. He should serve his master not because he has to but because he wants to.

3–5 Whoever does not heed the teaching of Christ is **conceited** (verse 4). A conceited man is usually an ignorant man. He thinks he knows a lot, but in reality he **understands nothing** (see 1 Timothy 1:7).

A bad tree bears bad fruit (Matthew 7:17–18). Likewise, a false teacher bears the "fruit" of **envy, quarreling, malicious talk, evil suspicions and constant friction** (see 1 Timothy 1:3–4). If our teaching and doctrine are false and impure, our lives also will be false and impure. Likewise, if a man's life is full of **envy, quarreling**, and **friction**, then we can be sure that his teaching will be false and impure. Jesus said: "**Thus, by their fruit you will recognize them**" (Matthew 7:20).

Many false teachers are interested only in winning arguments or in exalting themselves at the expense of others. They are not concerned about defending the truth. Other false teachers are mainly interested in making money from their teaching. In their minds, **godliness is a means to financial gain**.

Envy, quarreling and malicious talk doesn't come only from false teachers; it arises also from immature Christians within the church. When such behavior occurs, the church is weakened and ceases to bear fruit.

6 Certainly, **godliness** does produce much **gain**—but the gain is spiritual, not material. The **gain** that comes from godliness does not depend on outward or material circumstances. Only when we are **content** do we become free of greed, anxiety, and the love of possessions; and only then can we obtain the full benefit and blessing of godliness (see Mark 4:18–19; Philippians 4:11 and comments).

7 It is vain to try to store up possessions on earth. On the day we die, we shall lose them all (see Job 1:21; Ecclesiastes 5:15; Luke 12:16–21 and comment).

8 If we have necessary food, clothing, and shelter, we should be content. To desire to obtain more than we need is not right. God has promised to meet our needs (see Matthew 6:33 and comment). To be discontent with the material gifts that God has given us is a sin. To be discontent is to grumble against God.

However, we should not be "content" with the spiritual gifts we have received; we should earnestly desire to receive more and more (1 Corinthians 14:1). God wants to pour out greater and greater spiritual blessings upon us. We should not remain satisfied with our spiritual state; rather, we should seek to be more and more filled with the Holy Spirit, so that His fruit and His gifts might be more abundantly manifest in our lives (1 Corinthians 12:7–11; Galatians 5:22–23).

9 Possessions themselves are not evil. What is evil, however, is the love of possessions and the desire to accumulate them (verse 10). Three things happen to people who love and accumulate possessions: first, they **fall into** TEMPTATION; **then, second, they fall into Satan's trap**—that is, they are entrapped by **many foolish and harmful desires**; and finally, third, they are plunged into **ruin and destruction**, from which their lives cannot be restored (see James 1:14–15).

10 **For the love of money is a root of all kinds of evil**. When that **root** grows, it produces all kinds of evil fruit. Notice that Paul says it's the love of money, not money itself, that leads to evil.

Those who love money will always wander from the faith (see Mark 10:23–25). It is not possible to love both God and riches at the same time (see Matthew 6:24–25 and comment). Not only that, no matter how rich a person gets, he will never be satisfied. One can never find true peace or joy or contentment through riches. Instead, riches lead to anxiety; the person with riches will constantly be worried about losing them. His riches will be a curse, not a blessing. He will be **pierced . . . with many griefs**.

Paul's Charge to Timothy (6:11–21)

11 **But you, man of God . . .** Paul here writes not only to Timothy, but also to all of us who believe. . . . **flee from all this**—that is, from love of money and possessions—**and pursue** spiritual "possessions"—namely, RIGHTEOUSNESS (Matthew 6:33), **godliness** (1 Timothy 4:7–8), **faith** (Hebrews 11:6), **love, endurance and gentleness** (Galatians 5:22–23). Paul here uses the strong word **flee**. Flee—run away—from the love of things of the world. Flee from every kind of evil (2 Timothy 2:22). Satan is always seeking to lead us into temptation—into his trap—where he can then devour us (1 Peter 5:8).

At the same time we are fleeing from the love of material possessions, we must eagerly **pursue** spiritual possessions. It's not enough to say, "If spiritual blessings are given to me, I'll accept them." No, we must actively **pursue** spiritual blessings, and then God will give them to us (see Matthew 7:7–8,11; Luke 11:13; Philippians 3:12–14 and comments).

12 **Fight the good fight of the faith**. Christians are engaged in a continuous spiritual battle (see Ephesians 6:10–12; 2 Timothy 4:7). In this verse, the word **faith** means the teachings of Christ, the Gospel. But it can also mean our personal **faith**; Satan is always seeking to destroy our faith by creating doubt in our minds. In our battle against Satan, faith is one of our main weapons (Ephesians 6:16). Doubt is Satan's weapon.

Take hold of the ETERNAL LIFE. Our **eternal life** begins from the time we believe. However, we must "take hold" of it through faith. Satan will try to take our eternal life from us; but if we hold on to it by faith, Satan will not be able to succeed (see John 10:28–29 and comment).

Timothy was **called** to eternal life when he made his **good confession**—that is, when he was baptized.

13–14 Paul charges Timothy to **keep this commandment without spot or blame** (verse 14). This **commandment** refers to the command to flee evil and pursue righteousness, which Paul has written in verses 11–12. This **commandment** can also refer to the command to follow Christ, which was given to Timothy at the time of his baptism.

Paul gives this **commandment** to Timothy in the **sight of God . . . and of Christ Jesus** (verse 13). God is always present as a witness of everything we do. Christ is also a witness. Christ made His **confession** as a witness when He suffered for our sins at the hands of the Roman governor **Pontius Pilate** (John 18:37). Let Timothy follow Christ's example and faithfully confess Christ and be prepared to suffer for Him.

Timothy must keep this commandment **without spot or blame** until Christ's second coming. Timothy must not only keep this commandment perfectly, but he himself must remain blameless (see 1 Thessalonians 3:13; 5:23).

15–16 God will send Christ back to earth **in his own time**, and other than God Himself, no one knows when that time will be (Mark 13:32).

Here in these two verses, Paul interrupts his practical instructions and praises God. Paul's God is not a stone, not an idol, not a myth. Instead, Paul's God is the **King of kings and Lord of lords** (Revelation 17:14; 19:16). This same name is also given to Christ, because Christ and God are one (John 10:30).

God is **immortal**. He has no beginning and no end; He lives forever. God is so great, so high, and so holy that we cannot even approach His light (Exodus 33:18–23). No one **has seen or can see** God (verse 16). But Christ the Son of God, **who is at the Father's side, has made him known** (John 1:18). **To him be honor and might forever**.

How big is the God you worship? If we believe in a small God, our faith will also be small. If we believe in a weak God, our lives will also be weak. But our God is not small and weak. He is the King of kings and the Lord of lords. He is the God **who**

gives life to everything (verse 13). Let His name be praised! **Now to the King eternal, immortal, invisible, the only God, be honor and glory for ever and ever** (1 Timothy 1:17).

17 In verses 9–10, Paul wrote of those who wanted to get rich. Here Paul speaks to Christians who are already rich. Let them not be **arrogant**. Everything they have has been given to them by God. They must not **put their hope** in their wealth (see Matthew 6:19–21 and comment).

Money and wealth are not in themselves evil. God has provided us **with everything for our enjoyment**. Therefore, we can receive His material gifts with thanksgiving. But if we begin to love our material possessions, it would be best to sell them; otherwise, we risk losing the spiritual possessions stored up for us in heaven (see Mark 10:21–23 and comment).

18–19 Let a man be rich in good deeds rather than in money. The riches of this world will perish, but every good deed done for God will remain forever. By doing good deeds in this life, the believer stores up for himself treasures in heaven.[17] Therefore, let the rich believer be **generous and willing to share** (verse 18). If he heeds this, he will receive **life that is truly life**—that is, eternal life in heaven.

When Paul talks about the **rich** of this world, who does he mean? He means all those who have more than they need. By New Testament standards, anyone who has more than he needs is rich.

20–21 Timothy must guard what has been entrusted to him; that is, he must guard the true doctrines and teachings of Christ that have been handed down to him by the apostles. He must not let them be changed or twisted. He must not let any false teaching enter the church. Rather, he should immediately refute any false teaching and turn away from it (see 1 Timothy 1:3; 4:7; 2 Timothy 2:16–18).

---

[17] But man is not saved by doing good deeds; he only is rewarded for his good deeds (Matthew 16:27). Salvation is by grace through faith alone (see Ephesians 2:8–10 and comment).

2 Timothy

INTRODUCTION

Many Bible scholars believe that Paul wrote his second letter to Timothy during a second and final imprisonment in ROME. At that time Timothy was a chief leader in the church of Ephesus (see 1 Timothy: Introduction).

These scholars believe that Paul was released from his first imprisonment in Rome (Acts 28:16,30). But after some time, they say, Paul was again imprisoned and eventually put to death by the Romans.

As Paul wrote this letter, he knew that his death was near (2 Timothy 4:6). This is the last of Paul's New Testament letters.

OUTLINE

A. Introduction (1:1–18)
   1. Greeting and Thanksgiving (1:1–7).
   2. Encouragement to be Faithful (1:8–18).
B. The Christian Leader (2:1–3:17).
   1. A Soldier of Christ (2:1–13).
   2. A Workman Approved by God (2:14–26).
   3. A Guardian of the Gospel (3:1–17).
C. Conclusion (4:1–22).
   1. Paul's Final Charge to Timothy (4:1–8).
   2. Personal Remarks (4:9–22).

CHAPTER 1

Thanksgiving and Encouragement (1:1–18)

1 In most of his letters, Paul reminds his readers that he has been made an APOSTLE not by man's will but **by the will of God** (see 1 Corinthians 1:1; Ephesians 1:1; 1 Timothy 1:1 and comments).

2 See Romans 1:7; Ephesians 1:2; 1 Timothy 1:2 and comments.

3 Paul here gives thanks for Timothy (see Romans 1:8; Ephesians 1:15–16; Colossians 1:3–4 and comments). Paul remembers Timothy in his prayers **night and day** (Acts 20:31). As in his first letter to Timothy, Paul here again mentions a **clear conscience**. In Paul's experience, having a clear conscience was absolutely essential for leading a fruitful and Spirit-filled Christian life (see 1 Timothy 1:5,19 and comment).

4 Paul remembers Timothy's tears. It's possible that Paul is thinking here of the time he gave a final farewell to the elders of the Ephesian church; Timothy was probably among those elders (Acts 20:37).

5 Many Christians testify that they first believed in Christ through the influence and example of devout parents. It was so with Timothy. Paul here recalls the faith of Timothy's mother and grandmother; it was through their faith that Timothy had himself been led to believe in Christ (Acts 16:1).

One does not automatically become a Christian because of the faith of his parents. We must each believe for ourselves and receive new spiritual life (John 3:3). But even though this is true, it is still God's desire and plan that children follow the example of their believing parents.

6 Paul exhorts Timothy to **fan into flame** the gift that God has given him. Timothy doesn't need a new gift for being a church leader; he needs only to keep alive the gift he has already been given. He needs to keep its **flame** burning. We, likewise, must use and develop the gifts that God has given us. The man who doesn't use his gifts is like a man who receives a lamp and then, having let it go out, remains sitting in darkness.

Timothy received his gift or anointing for leadership when Paul, together with some other elders, laid their hands on him and appointed him to be a leader in the church (see 1 Timothy 4:14 and comment).

Every Christian has been given the necessary spiritual and natural gifts to do the work that God has appointed him or her to do. God will never ask us to do a work for which He has not prepared and equipped us.

7 Timothy was by nature a timid and fearful man. Paul here reminds Timothy that in place of his natural timidity God, through the Holy Spirit, will give him a **spirit of power, of love and of self-discipline**. Throughout history, God has accomplished great and amazing things through naturally timid people who have been filled with the Holy Spirit.

For any leader **self-discipline** and self-control are very important. Before a leader can discipline others, he must first be able to discipline himself.

8 Therefore, Paul encourages Timothy to put away any fear and shame he might naturally feel and to testify boldly about Christ. Let Timothy be prepared to join Paul **in suffering for the** GOSPEL. In Paul's day, Christian preachers and pastors were imprisoned, beaten, and even killed. But Timothy will be able to endure such suffering **by the power of God**—that is, by the power given to him by the Holy Spirit (verse 7).

Notice Paul's personal request to Timothy. The great apostle, a prisoner in Rome, writes to his spiritual son Timothy and asks him not to be **ashamed** of him. Like Jesus before him, Paul was about to be condemned to death as a criminal. In the world's eyes, Paul was a man to be shunned and despised. But let Timothy not despise Paul. Rather, let him follow in Paul's footsteps and be prepared to suffer for Christ.

9 In verses 9–10, Paul briefly interrupts his teaching in order to praise God, **who has saved us** through Jesus Christ (see 1 Timothy 1:1 and comment). God has not only saved us, but He has also **called us to a holy life** (see Ephesians 1:4; 2:10; 1 Peter 1:15–16 and comments). He has called us not because of anything we have done but **because of his own purpose and** GRACE (see Ephesians 1:4–5,11; 2:8–9 and comments). This **grace** was given to us **before the beginning of time**—that is, before the creation of the world (Ephesians 1:4).

10 This grace was first revealed in the world **through the appearing of our Savior, Christ Jesus**; that is, God's grace came into the world in the person of Christ (Titus 2:11). Christ destroyed death, our **last enemy** (1 Corinthians 15:26). Now we no longer need to fear death (1 Corinthians 15:55–56; Hebrews 2:14–15). Jesus **has brought life and immortality**—that is, eternal life—**to light**. This eternal life, or salvation, was at first hidden from men; it was like a "mystery." But now for all who believe, this mystery has been revealed; it has been brought **to light** (see Romans 16:25–26; Ephesians 3:4–5). This mystery has been brought to light **through the gospel**. Indeed, verses 9–10 themselves are a brief summary of the Gospel of Christ.

11 Paul can never forget how he had been appointed to be a **herald and an apostle and a teacher** of this great Gospel (1 Timothy 2:7). But now, Timothy must step into Paul's place.

12 It is because of Paul's preaching of the Gospel of Christ that he has had to suffer. However, there is nothing shameful in suffering for Christ; it is the highest privilege a man or woman can have (see 1 Peter 4:12–16).

Paul knows the One in whom he has believed. He knows God personally; he has met Him! Paul has complete confidence in God. Therefore, Paul has entrusted his spirit, his soul, his salvation, and all his work and labor completely to God. Paul knows that God will **guard** all that Paul has entrusted to Him. God will guard it **for that day**—that is, for the day when Christ comes again at the end of the world. On that day, Paul will receive his full reward.

13 Paul has given to Timothy the **pattern of sound teaching**; he has passed on to Timothy the basic doctrines of the Christian faith. Now Timothy must hold on to that **pattern** and faithfully preach it and teach it to others **with faith and love**.

14 The **pattern of sound teaching** (verse 13) is the Gospel of Christ itself, which Paul here calls the **good deposit**. Timothy is to guard this Gospel, this **deposit**, from error and from false teachers. In guarding the gospel, as in preaching it, Timothy is to rely on the help of the HOLY SPIRIT.

15 Nowadays, when we read about Paul, we all agree that he was a great apostle—probably the greatest. But in Paul's time, most people did not have that opinion. Most people despised Paul and did not accept his teaching or his authority. His own Christian brothers betrayed him. He writes here: . . . **everyone in the province of Asia**[1] **has deserted me** (see 2 Timothy 4:16).

Christ was also deserted by His disciples (Mark 14:50). But let not such a thing happen in our churches today. Let us never desert or oppose our leaders, or speak evil of them. Great harm comes to the spiritual lives of Christians who oppose or speak against their leaders; many will even leave their faith.

Phygelus and Hermogenes were two such men. Nothing is known of them except what is written in this verse. They are remembered only because they deserted their leader Paul. Let this not be the reason that people remember us!

16–18 Instead, let us, like **Onesiphorus**, be remembered for our faithfulness, so that we too might find mercy **on that day**—the day when Christ comes again.

---

[1] **Asia** was a province of the Roman Empire, located in the western part of present-day Turkey. Its chief city was Ephesus.

CHAPTER 2

The Soldier of Christ (2:1–13)

1 Paul tells Timothy to **be strong** (see Ephesians 6:10 and comment). Timothy is to be strong not in himself but **in the grace that is in Christ Jesus**. All of God's gifts to us are included in His **grace**: the Holy Spirit, salvation, mercy, strength, all kinds of help—all these come from God's grace. And God's grace is given to us **in Christ Jesus**. The greatest gift of all is Jesus Christ Himself.

2 Over the years, Paul has taught Timothy many things in the presence of many people, or **witnesses**. Now Timothy must pass on these teachings to other select men who themselves will teach yet others. These men must have two qualifications: first, they must be **reliable**; and second, they must be **qualified to teach others** (see 1 Timothy 3:2). In this way the Gospel and the true doctrines of the faith will be passed down accurately from generation to generation.

3–4 Here Paul writes that Timothy must be able to endure hardship like a soldier. Not only that, just as a soldier must not become **involved in civilian affairs**, so a leader in the church must not become entangled in the things of this world. Worldly affairs in themselves are not evil; but if they entangle and distract us, they must be cast off (see Mark 4:18; Hebrews 12:1). Just as a soldier seeks first of all to please **his commanding officer**, so the "soldier" of Christ must first of all seek to please Christ. A true soldier is always ready and willing to go anywhere and do anything, no matter what his own personal desire might be. Christ's soldiers must be like that.

5 Here Paul says the Christian is like a person who **competes as an athlete**. An athlete competing in sports must train himself rigorously; he must be single-minded. In the games he must compete with all his energy and skill. In Paul's time, all athletes trained for a certain length of time and in a certain way. An athlete who did not train **according to the rules** would not be able to win in the games. In the same way, Christians must live **according to the rules** laid down by Christ and His apostles. Those who do so will receive the **victor's crown** (1 Corinthians 9:25; 2 Timothy 4:7–8).

6 Here Paul gives a third description of the Christian worker: he is like a **hardworking farmer**. A farmer deserves to receive a share of the crops. This means that a pastor or other full-time Christian worker is entitled to receive a suitable salary or living allowance from the church (see 1 Corinthians 9:10–11,14).

However, if the farmer is not **hardworking**, there will be no crop for him to share in. And so it is with Christian workers. Without hard work, there will be no spiritual fruit.

7 **Reflect on what I am saying**, Paul writes Timothy. To the extent we reflect and meditate on the teachings of the Bible, to that same extent God will increase our understanding. But we ourselves must apply ourselves and study the Bible; and as we do so, God will continue to open our minds to receive more and more of His truth.

8 In accordance with the prophecies of the Old Testament prophets, Jesus Christ was descended from **DAVID**, the most famous king of the Jews (see Matthew 1:1; Luke 1:32; Romans 1:3–4 and comments).

Remember Jesus Christ. In everything we do, no matter what kind of work it is, let us remember Jesus and keep our eyes fixed on Him (Hebrews 12:2).

9 The Romans could put Paul in chains, but they couldn't put God's word, the Gospel, in chains. Pastors and preachers may be put in prison, but God's word will continue to spread all the more (see Philippians 1:12–14).

10 Paul endures everything **for the sake of the elect**. In this verse, the **elect** are those who have been chosen by God to be saved, but who as yet have not believed in Christ (see Acts 13:48 and comment). It is the duty of every Christian to share the Gospel with others and to witness to Christ, so that those whom God has called from before might hear and believe. God has given to us the responsibility of actually bringing the **elect** to faith, so that they might receive salvation (see Matthew 9:36–38 and comment).

11 If we have died with Christ through baptism, **we will also live with him** in His resurrection (see Romans 6:3–5 and comment).

12 To reign with Christ, we must stand firm under trials and endure to the end (see Mark 13:13; Romans 8:17; Revelation 3:21 and comments).

If we disown Christ, **he will also disown us** (see Matthew 10:32–33 and comment).

13 Even **if we are faithless, he will remain faithful**. This saying can have two meanings. First, it can mean that even when we stumble and fall into sin, God will be **faithful** to forgive us and cleanse us—if we repent (1 John 1:9). The second possible meaning is this: If we disown God, He will surely disown us, because God must be **faithful** to Himself; He cannot accept anyone who rejects Him (see Romans 3:3–4 and comment). These two meanings are not contradictory; both are true.

A Workman Approved by God (2:14–26)

14 Timothy must keep reminding the members of the church of **these things**—that is, the things that Paul has been writing in this letter.

Paul here is thinking especially about those people who spend time **quarreling about words**. As we seek to understand the truth together, it is proper—in love—to discuss and debate the meaning of Biblical words; but we must not quarrel over them. The **letter kills, but the Spirit gives life** (2 Corinthians 3:6). We must learn to discuss and debate without **quarreling**. Quarreling grieves the Holy Spirit and destroys our fellowship. Such quarreling leads people astray and **ruins** those who listen (see 1 Timothy 1:3–6 and comment).

15 If something that a workman makes is later shown to be defective, the workman is ashamed. So it is with leaders of the church. Let their work not be defective. Especially, let them handle the word of truth correctly; that is, let them preach and teach the word of God faithfully and accurately.

16 Paul here repeats the thought of verse 14 (see 1 Timothy 6:20–21). Those who indulge in **godless chatter** get farther and farther away from God.

17–18 In these two verses, Paul is thinking not only of **godless chatter** (verse 16), but also of false teaching. Why is false teaching so dangerous and harmful? The reason is this: People do not easily recognize that false teaching is, indeed, false; they are deceived by it. It seems like the truth. They are easily led astray by false teachers. If we could immediately recognize false teaching, it would do no harm (see 1 Timothy 4:1 and comment).

This is why Paul says that the teaching of false teachers **will spread like gangrene** (verse 17). How does gangrene spread? Slowly, insidiously. In the same way, the "gangrene" of false teaching spreads through our minds, and before we are aware of it, it has destroyed us.

Jesus compared false teaching to leaven (Matthew 16:6,11–12). A little bit of leaven spreads slowly and insidiously throughout the whole loaf (Galatians 5:9).

False teaching is also like poison. One drop of poison in a jug of water will make all the water in the jug poisonous, and he who drinks of it will die.

Two such false teachers in Paul's time were **Hymenaeus** (1 Timothy 1:20) and **Philetus**. They taught that the RESURRECTION had already occurred; that is, they taught that there was no real resurrection of the body. They said that the so-called "resurrection" was only a spiritual experience that all believers had already received. But their teaching was completely false. If there is no resurrection of the body, then Christ Himself was not raised from the dead. And if Christ was not raised, then our faith is in vain. Such false teaching will certainly destroy men's faith (see 1 Corinthians 15:12–17).

19 False teachers will deceive men, but they cannot deceive God. God's church and its foundation will not be shaken (Ephesians 2:19–22). God knows who are His true servants. **The Lord knows those who are his.** He knows who are true Christians and who are false Christians. Those who do not turn away from **wickedness** are false Christians; they are not true members of God's church.

20 In any church, there are some members who are worthy and **noble,** and other members who are unworthy and **ignoble.**

21 Let every true believer cleanse himself **from the latter**—that is, from those church members who are false and **ignoble.** By cleansing himself from false brothers and false teaching, the true believer can become an **instrument for noble purposes, made holy, useful . . . and prepared to do any good work.**[2]

22 Therefore, Paul writes to Timothy: **Flee the evil desires of youth**—such as, immorality, pride, quarreling, etc. Instead, together with other true Christians, **pursue** RIGHTEOUSNESS, **FAITH, love and** PEACE (see 1 Timothy 6:11; 1 Peter 2:11 and comments).

23 We must avoid vain discussions and arguments, because they do not lead to edification but to quarreling (see 1 Timothy 6:20–21; 2 Timothy 2:14,16 and comments).

24 The **Lord's servant**—that is, the pastor or leader of a church—should never enter into arguments and quarrels. Instead, he should be **kind.** Instead of quarreling, he should be **able to teach.** When others oppose him, he shouldn't be harsh and **resentful**; otherwise, their opposition will increase.

25–26 The church leader should **gently instruct** those who oppose him and who fall into error. It is essential to do this with humility; otherwise, those whom the leader is trying to instruct will become angry and resistant, and it will be even harder to become reconciled with them. The leader's hope must be that they might come to REPENTANCE and return to the truth, and thus escape from Satan's trap.

Notice here that **repentance** is "granted" by God; it is a gift of God. Just as we first believed by God's grace, so in the same way do we repent by God's grace. Without God's grace, we can do nothing that is pleasing to God.

The first gift that a person receives from God is the ability to recognize his sin and to repent of it (see Mark 1:4 and comment). The first essential step in pleasing God and leading a holy life is to confess and repent of one's sin (see 1 John 1:9 and comment). Therefore, one of the church leader's main duties and goals is to bring those who have gone astray to repentance.

CHAPTER 3

Godlessness in the Last Days (3:1–9)

1 In the New Testament, the expression **last days** usually means the period just before the second coming of Christ. But here Paul writes as if these "last days" had already begun. In fact, the description of these "last days" that Paul gives here could easily apply to every generation of men from Paul's time right down to the present. Therefore, in this verse, the expression **last days** means the period of time between Christ's first coming and His second coming. This is the second meaning of "last days" found in the New Testament (see Hebrews 1:2).

2–5 Paul here gives some examples

---

[2] There is a second possible interpretation of this verse. To cleanse oneself **from the latter** can mean to cleanse oneself from **purposes** that are ignoble (instead of from **articles** that are ignoble). Then Paul's meaning would be that we should cleanse ourselves from false teaching (instead of from false teachers). It is possible, of course, that Paul intended both of these meanings.

of different evil works. These evil works were already widespread in Paul's time. In fact, most of them have been found among men since the beginning of the world (see Genesis 6:5; Romans 1:29–31). Paul warned the Galatians that those who do such things will not inherit the kingdom of God (see Galatians 5:19–21). And Paul had written earlier to Timothy that Christians **must turn away from wickedness** (2 Timothy 2:19).

Here also Paul says that Christians should have **nothing to do** with evildoers (verse 5). However, in 2 Timothy 2:25, Paul has written that the church leader must **gently instruct** those who oppose him and the truth. Both things are true. First, the leader must try to bring to repentance those who have fallen into sin and error. But if they refuse to repent, then the leader should have nothing to do with them.

In verses 2–5, Paul is writing not only about evildoers outside the church but inside as well. In fact, he is particularly thinking of so-called Christians who refuse to repent and who continue living in sin; it is these false Christians that we must have nothing to do with (see 1 Corinthians 5:9–11 and comment). Christ's most dangerous enemies are those within the church! Two enemies within the church can do more harm then two thousand enemies outside the church.

In verse 5, Paul writes that these evildoers have a **form of godliness**. They appear righteous. But because of the evil in their hearts, the Holy Spirit will not dwell in them. For this reason they have no true spiritual power. They do not have the power to be holy or to obey God's will. Only when the Holy Spirit dwells in us do we receive spiritual power. If we grieve the Holy Spirit by continuing in sin without repenting, He will leave us (see Proverbs 1:24–28; Isaiah 63:10; Ephesians 4:30 and comment).

Evildoers may sometimes preach with great effectiveness and perform great miracles. They may even do these things in Christ's name. They call themselves Christians; they are members of the church (Titus 1:16). But in the end Christ will reject them (see Matthew 7:22–23; 13:24–30,47–50 and comments). **The Lord knows those who are his** (2 Timothy 2:19).

Therefore, such evildoers not only display a false power, but they also deny the true power of the Holy Spirit. When one looks from the outside they appear godly, but inside they have no spiritual power; they are spiritually dead.

6–7 Nevertheless, these false Christians deceive many people. They especially deceive women (1 Timothy 2:14), in particular those women whose faith is weak and who have not learned the truth of Scripture. Such women are **loaded down with sins** (verse 6)—that is, they are burdened with guilt and with an unclean conscience. These women are **swayed by all kinds of evil desires** and also by all kinds of new teaching. They are always learning, but they cannot recognize the truth.

In Paul's day, women were easily misled by false teachers, because they did not receive the same opportunity that men received to learn the truth of Scripture. In New Testament times, women were considered ignorant and weak in understanding. But in those countries where women are given an equal chance to learn, they are not so easily deceived. And we must remember also that there are many men who are just as easily deceived as the women Paul mentions here!

8 According to the opinion of some ancient historians, **Jannes** and **Jambres** were magicians of Pharaoh who tried to oppose MOSES (Exodus 7:10–12).

Evildoers and false Christians are **men of depraved minds**—that is, they neither know the truth nor seek it (Romans 1:21; Ephesians 4:17–18). God will totally reject such men.

9 For some time these evildoers and false Christians can deceive other people, but in the end their evil work and evil character will become clear to everyone.

Final Instructions (3:10–17)

10–11 Timothy knows what Paul's life and behavior have been like. Paul offers his own example for Timothy to follow. Paul does not boast in himself; all of his good qualities and good works are the result of God's grace alone (1 Corinthians 15:10).

Paul mentions his **teaching** first of all. All the other things in Paul's life arise out of his teaching. Paul follows in his own life the same teaching he gives to others. Timothy knows that Paul has lived as he has taught. May all teachers do the same.

Paul reminds Timothy of what happened to him in **Antioch, Iconium and Lystra** (Acts 13:49–52; 14:1–20). Timothy had been in Lystra at that time (Acts 16:1). Surely Timothy had heard Paul speak and had seen him stoned by the crowd (Acts 14:19). Paul endured many persecutions (2 Timothy 2:12); but, he says to Timothy in verse 11, **the Lord rescued me from all of them** (Psalm 34:17).

12 Here Paul reminds Timothy of a very important thing: Every true follower of Christ sooner or later **will be persecuted**. Many years earlier, Timothy may have heard Paul say at Lystra: **"We must go through many hardships to enter the kingdom of God"** (Acts 14:22). From Christ's time until the present, all true Christians have faced trials and suffering of some kind. Jesus said to His disciples: **"All men will hate you because of me"** (Matthew 10:22). **"If they persecuted me, they will persecute you also"** (John 15:20).

13 When once a man starts on an evil path, his life becomes more and more evil (see Romans 1:21,28; Ephesians 4:17–19 and comments).

14–15 But, Paul says to Timothy, **continue in what you have learned**. It is not enough only to learn; we must **continue** in what we have learned. Timothy can trust that what he has learned is true, because he can trust his teachers—such as Paul, his mother, and his grandmother (2 Timothy 1:5). Again, Timothy can have confidence in what they have taught, because it agrees with what is written in Scripture. Timothy can be sure that if a teaching agrees with Scripture, it will be a true teaching.

Paul writes that the **holy Scriptures**[3] **. . . are able to make you wise for SALVATION** (verse 16). That is, the Scriptures teach us how salvation can be obtained. How can salvation be obtained? It can be obtained **through faith in Christ Jesus**. And the **Scriptures** Paul is talking about here is the Old Testament. If the Old Testament can show us the way of salvation, how much more will the New Testament show us the way!

16 This is one of the most important verses in the entire Bible. **All Scripture**—that is, every verse of the Bible, both Old Testament and New Testament—has been written by the inspiration and guidance of God (see 2 Peter 1:20–21 and comment). There is no other book like the Bible in all the world. Other books may contain things that are true, that are wise, that are helpful; but there is only one book that contains the words of God Himself, and that is the Bible. Only the Bible has been written by the direct inspiration of God; it is **God-breathed**. We can fully trust every word in the Bible. It is truly God's own word (see General Article: How We Got Our Bible).

Because the Bible is God's word, it is useful for **teaching, rebuking, correcting and training in righteousness**. The Bible shows us the true way of righteousness and, in addition, helps us to walk in it.

17 Through the teaching, rebuking, correcting and training that comes from studying the Bible, the **man of God** will become equipped for every good work. Here, the expression **man of God** especially means a church leader or teacher like Timothy. But this verse is also equally true for all Christians everywhere, both men and women.

---

[3] In Paul's time, the **holy Scriptures** consisted of the Old Testament alone. The New Testament had not yet been written.

CHAPTER 4

Paul's Charge to Timothy (4:1–8)

1 As Paul gives Timothy this final charge, he reminds Timothy that he is giving it in the **presence of God and of Christ Jesus**. That is, God and Christ give their approval to this charge which Paul is about to give. They will see whether or not Timothy heeds Paul's words. Let Timothy remember that one day he will have to give an account of his work to God and to Christ (see Romans 14:12; 2 Corinthians 5:10 and comments).

Jesus Christ is not only the Savior of the world; He is also the final Judge of the world (John 5:22–23; Acts 10:42; 17:31). When He comes again, He will judge both those who are alive at that time and those who have already died.

2 Paul here gives five charges to Timothy—and not only to Timothy but to all Christian leaders. **Preach the Word**—that is, the Gospel; **be prepared** at all times—remain on duty; **correct, rebuke and encourage**.

The church leader must be prepared to preach the Gospel **in season and out of season**. Many Christians wait for just the right occasion before sharing the Gospel with someone; but that "right occasion" often never comes, and thus that person loses the chance to hear about the way of salvation. Therefore, under the guidance of the Holy Spirit, we must be always ready to share the Gospel with others, even at difficult and inconvenient times.

The church leader must be ready when necessary to **correct** and **rebuke** those who do wrong. This may sound harsh to our ears; nevertheless, this is one of the main duties of a leader (1 Timothy 5:20; Titus 1:13; 2:15). Without such discipline a church becomes weak, and evildoers and false Christians are able to enter the church and grow in numbers. However, when a leader corrects and rebukes others, he must do so **with great patience and careful instruction**. The leader must not only tell a person he's on the wrong road, but he must also show that person the right road. And he must do this with **patience**. Just as a father rebukes his children with love and patience, so also the church leader should correct and rebuke those who have gone astray with love and patience.

3–4 Timothy must preach the Gospel diligently, because the **time will come** when men will not accept the truth (see 1 Timothy 4:1; 2 Timothy 3:1 and comments). They will listen only to what they want to hear. They will have **itching ears** (verse 3)—that is, ears eager to hear any new and interesting teaching. They will turn aside to **myths**, because myths are pleasant and enticing. They will not even know that they have wandered from the truth.

5 But Timothy must not be misled by such new and enticing teaching; he must speak and teach only the truth. He must endure hardship and opposition (2 Timothy 2:3). He must fulfill all the duties of a pastor (verse 2). Since Paul's time of departure is near (verse 3), Paul exhorts Timothy to follow in his footsteps, and to carry on in his place.

6 Paul is about to be sacrificed like a **drink offering** (see Philippians 2:17). Christ also was sacrificed as an offering for our sakes (Hebrews 9:14,28; 10:10). In the same way, Christ's servants must sacrifice themselves for His sake and for the sake of others.

7 Paul can now look back on his life with satisfaction. He has fulfilled all the work that Christ had appointed him to do. His **fight** is over; now Timothy must fight on in Paul's place (1 Timothy 6:12). Paul has **finished the race**; he has remained faithful to death (Acts 20:24).

I have kept the faith, says Paul. This can mean that Paul has guarded the **faith**—that is, the Gospel.[4] He has let no error or falsehood come into his preaching.

[4] In addition to its usual meaning, the word **faith** can also mean the Gospel, or the true doctrines of the Christian religion.

He has kept the Gospel pure and true (see 2 Timothy 1:14 and comment).

But when Paul says, **I have kept the faith**, he also means that he himself has remained faithful to the end; his faith in Christ has not wavered. For Paul, the promise of Jesus will soon come true: "... **he who stands firm to the end will be saved**" (Mark 13:13).

8 The Lord Jesus, who will judge all men righteously and fairly, will reward Paul **on that day**—that is, on the day of judgment. And Paul adds that Jesus will also reward **all who have longed for his appearing**—that is, all who love Jesus and follow Him.

Paul calls this reward a **crown of righteousness**. In Paul's day, the winner of a sporting contest was given a crown of leaves (1 Corinthians 9:25). Rulers used to give people crowns for rendering some special service to the state. Thus in New Testament times, people received a **crown** for a reward instead of a medal. The **crown of righteousness**, therefore, is the reward given to all those who are righteous. The reward is eternal life with God.

Personal Remarks (4:9–22)

9–12 Let us imagine Paul's situation. He is old and weak, imprisoned in a Roman jail. He has probably already received the death sentence. Except for **Luke**,[5] Paul is alone (verse 11). Paul's former colleague **Demas** (Colossians 4:14) has deserted him. Paul has sent his other colleagues **Crescens**,[6] **Titus**[7] and **Tychicus**[8] to other places for various reasons.

Paul asks Timothy to come to him, and to bring **Mark** with him (verse 11). When Mark was younger, he had caused Paul much grief (Acts 15:37–40). But now he has become a faithful and **helpful** disciple (Colossians 4:10).

13 Winter was coming; therefore, Paul needed his cloak. Nothing is known of the **scrolls** and **parchments** that Paul asked for. Perhaps the scrolls were copies of Old Testament books, or articles that Paul himself had written. Among the parchments, perhaps, was Paul's certificate of Roman citizenship.

14–15 A person named **Alexander** is also mentioned in Acts 19:33–34 and 1 Timothy 1:20.[9] Alexander may have testified against Paul at his trial. He also opposed the Gospel. **The Lord will repay him** (see Psalm 62:12; Romans 12:19 and comment).

16 According to Roman law, every prisoner or defendant was given the opportunity to present his defense before the court. At that time, the defendant could call witnesses who would speak on his behalf. But Paul could find no witnesses who would take his side; at his trial he had been left completely alone. The other Christians living in Rome at the time were afraid to speak out in Paul's defense. Paul asks that they might be forgiven (see Luke 23:34; Acts 7:60).

17 But even though Paul's colleagues and fellow Christians had deserted him, the Lord did not. **But the Lord stood by my side**, Paul writes. With God's help, Paul was enabled to proclaim the Gospel not only inside the court but outside the court as well, so that **all the Gentiles might hear it** (see Romans 1:5). Paul didn't care about defending himself; he cared only about defending the Gospel. Right there in Rome, the center of all the Gentile nations and the capital of the Roman Empire, the Apostle Paul, even as a prisoner, **fully proclaimed** the Gospel of Christ (see Acts 28:30–31).

Paul says: **I was delivered from the lion's mouth**—that is, from the death sentence. It is not certain when and how

---

[5] **Luke** was Paul's **dear friend, the doctor** (Colossians 4:14). He was also Paul's colleague on some of his missionary journeys. Later he wrote the Gospel of Luke and the book of Acts.

[6] **Crescens** is not mentioned elsewhere in the New Testament.

[7] **Titus** was a close colleague of Paul's, to whom Paul wrote the New Testament letter called "Titus" (see Titus: Introduction).

[8] **Tychicus** is also mentioned in Ephesians 6:21 and Colossians 4:7.

[9] Some Bible scholars believe that these three Alexanders are all different men.

this deliverance took place. Most likely Paul is referring here to deliverance from his first imprisonment in Rome (see Acts 28:30; 1 Timothy: Introduction; 2 Timothy: Introduction).

18 Now Paul was in a Roman prison for the second and final time. He now had no hope of being delivered from prison and from death. He was prepared to die (see verse 6). But Paul had complete faith that God would rescue him **from every evil attack** of Satan, and in the end would bring him into His kingdom. For Paul, death was not the end, but the beginning. It was not defeat, it was victory; it was salvation (see 1 Corinthians 15:54 and comment).

19 **Priscilla and Aquila** are mentioned in Acts 18:2,18,26 and Romans 16:3. **Onesiphorus** has already been mentioned in 2 Timothy 1:16.

20 **Erastus** is mentioned in Acts 19:22; and **Trophimus** is mentioned in Acts 20:4 and 21:29.

21–22 Paul again asks Timothy to come quickly. Winter was near, and it soon would be impossible to sail across the Mediterranean Sea from Ephesus because of the winter storms (see Acts 27:9–12 and comment).

The four persons mentioned in verse 21 are mentioned nowhere else in the New Testament. In addition to these four, **all the brothers** also send greetings to Timothy. Nevertheless, these same brothers had refused to take Paul's side at his trial. Perhaps they had now repented for deserting Paul at his time of need. In any event, they have not left the faith. They are now with Paul, and they send Timothy their greetings.

Titus

INTRODUCTION

Like Timothy, Titus was a young colleague of Paul's, whom Paul called, in a spiritual sense, a **true son** (Titus 1:4). Paul also called Titus **my partner and fellow worker** (2 Corinthians 8:23). Paul had sent Titus to Corinth to help the Corinthians complete the collection they had started to raise for the poor Christians in Jerusalem (2 Corinthians 8:16–17; 9:5; 12:18). After that, Paul had left Titus on the island of Crete to take care of various matters and to appoint elders in the churches they had recently established there (Titus 1:5).

This letter was sent to Titus while he was still in Crete. According to 2 Timothy 4:10, when Titus had finished his work in Crete, Paul sent him to Dalmatia (present-day Yugoslavia). In the New Testament, Dalmatia is also called Illyricum (Romans 15:19).

OUTLINE

A. Concerning Elders and False Teachers (1:1–16).
   1. The Appointment of Elders (1:1–9).
   2. The Refutation of False Teachers (1:10–16).
B. The Work of Elders (2:1–3:15).
   1. Proclamation of Sound Doctrine (2:1–15).
   2. Demonstration of Sound Doctrine (3:1–15).

CHAPTER 1

Titus' Task on Crete (1:1–9)

1–3 The greeting in these verses is long and formal, considering that this is a personal letter. However, Paul probably meant this letter to be read in the churches under Titus' authority; that is why the greeting is longer than usual.

In verse 1, Paul calls himself a **servant of God and an** APOSTLE **of Jesus Christ** (see Romans 1:1 and comment). Paul was appointed an apostle **by the command of God our Savior** (verse 3) to bring **God's elect** to FAITH and to a **knowledge of the truth** (verse 1)—that is, to a knowledge of Christ (see Acts 13:48; 1 Timothy 1:1; 2 Timothy 2:10 and comments). That **faith** and **knowledge . . . leads to godliness** and gives **hope of** ETERNAL LIFE (verse 2), which God has promised to all those who believe in Christ.

4 In verse 3, Paul calls God **our Savior**. Here in verse 4, he calls Jesus **our Savior**. Both are equally correct, because God and Jesus are one (John 10:30).

Paul calls Titus **my true son in our common faith**. Paul was a Jew, and Titus was a Greek (Galatians 2:3); however, in Christ there is no distinction between Jew and Greek (Galatians 3:28). In God's family Paul and Titus were spiritually father and son.

5 Many Bible scholars believe that after Paul was released from his first Roman imprisonment, Paul and Titus went together to **Crete**[1] to preach the Gospel (see Titus: Introduction). Now, at the time of writing this letter, Paul has left Titus in Crete to **straighten out** some matters in the churches they had recently established there. Notice that Titus has received authority from Paul to **appoint elders in every town** where there was a church. There is no mention here of elders being elected by the church members. According to this verse, the elders' authority does not come from the congregation; it comes from the Apostle Paul through his disciple Titus (see Acts 14:23 and comment).

6–7 In the New Testament, church leaders are most commonly called **elders.**[2] Another name is **overseer** (see 1 Timothy 3:1 and comment). The qualifications for overseers mentioned in 1 Timothy 3:2–5 are essentially the same as the qualifications for **elders** that Paul lists here.

Elders and overseers must be **blameless,** because they are **entrusted with God's work** (verse 7)—that is, they have been entrusted with the responsibility for God's church.

Notice in verse 6 that the children of elders must not be **wild and disobedient**; furthermore, they must **believe** in Christ (see 1 Timothy 3:4).

8–9 In verse 7, Paul lists some bad qualities which must not be present in church leaders. Now in verses 8–9, Paul mentions some of the good qualities a church leader must have (see 1 Timothy 3:3). The leader must **hold firmly to the trustworthy message** as it has been taught by Paul and the other apostles (see 2 Timothy 3:14). The leader must be able to teach that **message** to others (2 Timothy 2:2). That **message** is the word of God, by which the leader is able to instruct others in the way of righteousness and to refute false teaching.

Concerning the Men of Crete (1:10–16)

10–11 As in almost all the other churches mentioned in the New Testament, false teachers had also begun

---

[1] **Crete** is a large island in the Mediterranean Sea south of Greece (see Acts 27:7–8,12–13).

[2] Some Bible scholars believe that the title **elder** mentioned in verse 5 and the title **overseer** mentioned in verse 7 refer to two distinct kinds of church leader. The reason they believe this is because the word **blameless** occurs both in verse 6 and verse 7—as if Paul was talking about two different types of leader, both of whom had to be blameless. These scholars say that if Paul had been talking about only one type of leader, he wouldn't have mentioned twice that they must be "blameless." For further discussion, see General Article: Church Government.

teaching in the churches of Crete. Among them were some Jewish believers of the CIRCUMCISION **group** (verse 10), who were falsely teaching that in order to be saved one had to obey the Jewish law (see Galatians 2:11–14 and comment). Outwardly these false teachers seemed like Christians, but inwardly they were **rebellious**—that is, they did not heed the truth of the Gospel and they did not submit to the leaders of the church. They taught only in order to get money from the gullible people who believed their teaching (verse 11). These false teachers must be **silenced**, says Paul.

12 Paul here quotes something written by one of Crete's famous philosophers, whom the Cretans themselves regarded as a prophet. Even their own prophet had called the Cretans **liars, evil brutes**, and **lazy gluttons**!

13–14 Paul affirms that what this prophet has written about the Cretans is indeed true. Therefore, Paul instructs Titus to **rebuke them** (the Cretan believers) **sharply**, so that they will be **sound in the faith** and avoid following false teaching. On occasion it is necessary to rebuke some people **sharply**; but usually it is best to admonish them gently. The church leader rebukes people not to hurt them but to help them. He does it for their good, not for their harm (see 2 Timothy 2:24–25; 4:2 and comments).

15 For those who are inwardly **pure**, all things—food, marriage, etc.—are also pure (see 1 Timothy 4:3–4 and comment). Purity comes from within us; outward things such as food do not make us impure (see Mark 7:15–23 and comment).

Similarly, if a man is inwardly impure, he will remain impure no matter how much he washes himself outwardly. Neither outward washing nor any other religious ritual or sacrifice can ever make a man's heart pure (Matthew 23:25–26; Hebrews 10:1–4,11).

Those who are impure in heart make everything they do impure. If a man's motives are impure, his actions will also be impure. Not only are the minds of such people impure, but their **consciences are corrupted** as well. The man whose conscience has been corrupted cannot hear God; he cannot discern the truth. Therefore, no matter what he does it will be impure and corrupt (see 1 Timothy 4:2 and comment).

16 These false teachers and evildoers say they know God, but **by their actions they deny him** (see Matthew 7:21; Mark 7:6–7; Romans 1:21–22 and comments). Such hypocrites are **detestable** in God's sight; they are unfit for any good work.

CHAPTER 2

Sound Doctrine (2:1–15)

1 See Titus 1:9 and comment.

2 Older men in the church must behave like mature fathers and elder brothers. They should demonstrate the same qualities required of overseers and deacons (see 1 Timothy 3:3,8–9). In fact, all believers should demonstrate these qualities; but it is especially important for the church leaders and the older men to do so, because they set an example for everyone else.

3 Paul has written that women are not to teach men in the church (see 1 Timothy 2:12 and comment). But it is right for older women to teach younger women and children. The older women must be **reverent in the way they live**. They must not be **slanderers** of others (1 Timothy 3:11). Sadly, the sin of slander is found not only among the women of the church but among the men as well. Let this not be! (see Titus 3:2 and comment).

4–5 Paul here describes the qualities necessary in a Christian woman. The older women must teach the younger women how to develop these qualities and how to lead godly lives. The main responsibility of young married women is to help their husbands and to raise their children. And that is such an important responsibility! Let no one look down on the work of a woman in her home.

Remember, it was through the faith of Timothy's mother and grandmother that Timothy himself believed (2 Timothy 1:5). And it has been the same for countless Christians down through history.

If young women neglect their duties and wander about gossiping and slandering people, others will **malign the word of God** because of their behavior. The word of God will be dishonored (1 Timothy 5:13–14). When Christ's followers do not live godly lives, Christ's name is dishonored. Unbelievers are always watching us to see how we act. Do they see anything about our lives and our behavior that sets us apart from other worldly men? Or do we act the same as unbelievers? (see Matthew 5:46–48 and comment).

6 One of the most important requirements for young men is to be **self-controlled**. Self-control is one of the fruits of the Holy Spirit (Galatians 5:23).

7–8 **In everything** Titus must set an example for others in the church (see 1 Timothy 4:12 and comment). Both Titus' life and his teaching must be blameless, so that his enemies will have nothing bad to say about him and thus be put to shame (see Romans 12:20–21; 1 Peter 2:15; 3:16 and comments).

9–10 Paul here gives some teaching concerning slaves that is similar to that found elsewhere in the New Testament (see Ephesians 6:5–8; 1 Peter 2:18–20 and comments). Most of Paul's teaching about slaves applies also to other kinds of workers and employees.

In Paul's time, slavery was widespread; it was oppressive and evil. But the New Testament says little that is directly opposed to slavery. The reason is that before an evil custom like slavery can be changed, it is necessary to change men's hearts and motives. Therefore, the New Testament writers concentrated first of all on getting people to change their inward lives.

When a person's inward condition is right in God's sight, then God will usually change that person's outward condition. Slaves should concentrate on their own duties and on doing what is right. The duties of a slave were to obey and respect his master, to be trustworthy, and to work diligently. However, if a slave, in order to improve his outward circumstances, were to rebel against his master, he would bring dishonor to Christ and His Gospel (see 1 Corinthians 7:17,20–22; 1 Timothy 6:1 and comments). But, says Paul, if the Christian slave does his work well, his unbelieving master will see that his faith has made him different from other slaves. Because of this, Christ's Gospel and doctrine will be made **attractive** in men's eyes, and Christ will be honored (Matthew 5:16; 1 Peter 2:12).

The slave must submit **in everything** to his master. However, if a master orders the slave to disobey a command of God, the slave must not obey his master in that matter; rather, he must obey God (see Romans 13:1–2 and comment).

Paul says here that a slave must not **talk back** to his master. For example, if a slave (or other worker) makes some mistake, he shouldn't try to deny it or make excuses for it; if he does, it makes his mistake twice as bad. And this rule applies not only to slaves but also to any worker or employee.

11 In verses 1–10, Paul has taught about the correct behavior of various groups in the church. Now in verses 11–14, Paul gives the reason for that correct behavior: **For the GRACE of God that brings SALVATION has appeared to all men**—to men and women, to slave and free, to Jew and Gentile (see 2 Timothy 1:9–10). The **grace of God** saves us, and produces within us godliness and new spiritual life. Our transformation doesn't take place only after we get to heaven, but by grace it begins here in this life. If there has been no change in our lives, then we have not yet received God's grace.

In everything we are completely dependent on God's grace (1 Corinthians 15:10). There is no salvation, no good work, apart from God's grace (see Ephesians 2:8–10 and comment; General Article: Way of Salvation).

12 Since God has given us His grace, we must live according to it. We must love God and obey Him (John 14:15). We must **say "No" to ungodliness and worldly passions**. We must flee from these things and pursue righteousness (see 1 Timothy 6:11; 2 Timothy 2:22 and comments).

13 God's grace has been revealed in Jesus Christ. When Christ came to earth, grace came to men and women. Now we are waiting until **our great God and Savior, Jesus Christ** comes again to earth a second time. Christ is our **blessed hope** (1 Timothy 1:1). Through faith in Him we receive salvation. Through Him we have eternal life.

14 Why did Christ give Himself for us? That is, why did Christ die as a sacrifice for us? First, He died in order to **redeem us from all wickedness** (see Mark 10:45; 1 Timothy 2:6 and comments). Second, He died that we might be inwardly purified through His word, that we might become His pure and spotless **people** or church (see Deuteronomy 14:2; Ezekiel 37:23; Ephesians 5:25–27; 1 Peter 2:9 and comments).

15 **Encourage and rebuke with all authority** (see 1 Timothy 4:12; 2 Timothy 4:2 and comments).

Paul writes to Titus: **Do not let anyone despise you**. Let Titus' life be pure and his teaching true, and in that way men will find no legitimate reason to despise him (verses 7–8).

CHAPTER 3

Doing What Is Good (3:1–15)

1 As is taught elsewhere in the New Testament, Paul here teaches that believers must be **subject to rulers and authorities** (see Romans 13:1–5; 1 Peter 2:13–14 and comments).

Remind the people . . . to be ready to do whatever is good. Christians should look for ways to contribute to the welfare of their villages and communities. They should support worthy community projects. They should be thinking of how they can be helpful to others.

In Paul's time, many people mistakenly considered Christians to be enemies of the Roman Empire. Even today in some countries, Christians are regarded as enemies of society. Unfortunately, in some cases Christians themselves have given that impression by their misguided opposition to their governments. But Christians should rightly be recognized as law-abiding citizens. Therefore, insofar as possible, it is essential that Christians obey the law and support their government. We must try to be good citizens in every way.

2 **. . . slander no one**. We are not to slander or speak evil of anyone—neither believer nor unbeliever. Satan uses slander, murmuring, and evil talk to divide Christians; it is his most effective and dangerous weapon for destroying the church. We are never to talk against a person behind his back—even if what we say is true—because that is slander (see Matthew 18:15–16 and comment).

3 We must be patient with unbelievers and seek their good. Because we must remember that we too were once unbelievers. Even though we did not deserve it, God showed us mercy. Therefore, we must show mercy to others. We, too, were once **foolish**; that is, we were without spiritual understanding. We were in bondage to sin; we were **enslaved by all kinds of passions and pleasures**. But now we have become free. Only when a man has been a prisoner or slave does he know the full blessing of being free; therefore, let us never forget how we once were! (see 1 Corinthians 6:9–11; Ephesians 2:1–3; 4:17–19 and comments).

4–5 Here in verses 4–7, Paul gives us a summary of the entire Gospel of Christ. Into the darkness and evil of this world, in which we were prisoners, came **God our Savior**, that is, Jesus Christ. He **saved us**, not because we obeyed some religious law or did some religious work, but because He loved us and had **mercy** upon us (see John 3:16; Galatians 2:15–16; Ephesians 2:8–9; 2 Timothy 1:9–10; 1 John 4:9–10 and comments).

Christ saved us **through the washing of rebirth** (verse 5). Here **washing** refers to baptism. There is a sense in which

Christ has saved us through baptism[3] (see 1 Peter 3:21 and comment). The **rebirth** is the new birth or new life that comes from the HOLY SPIRIT (see Mark 1:8; John 3:3–5; 1 Corinthians 6:11 and comments).

Christ saved us also through the **renewal by the Holy Spirit**. The **rebirth** mentioned above happens just once at the beginning of our Christian lives; but the **renewal** by the Holy Spirit continues from the time we believe to the end of our lives (see 2 Corinthians 4:16; Philippians 1:6 and comments).

6–7 God **poured out** His Holy Spirit upon us **through Jesus Christ our Savior**[4] (see John 7:37–39; Acts 2:1–4,32–33; Romans 5:5 and comments).

We have been **justified by his grace** (see Romans 3:23–24; 5:1 and comments). God has declared us righteous in order that we might be co-heirs with Christ and receive eternal life. Without having been justified by God, no one is worthy to enter the kingdom of heaven (see John 1:12; 6:40; Romans 6:23; 8:15–17; Galatians 3:26,29; 4:4–7; 1 John 5:11–13 and comments).

8 In verses 4–7, Paul has described the great work of God's grace—our salvation—which has been carried out for us. Now in this verse, Paul instructs believers to **be careful to devote themselves to doing what is good**. In the Bible, the great doctrines of the Gospel always come side by side with practical instructions for daily living. On one side, we see God's great love and grace; on the other side, we see our duty. These two sides must never be separated.

In this verse, Paul twice writes the words **these things**. "These things" are all the teachings written in this letter.

9 See 1 Timothy 1:3–4; 4:7; 6:20; 2 Timothy 2:14,23 and comments.

10–11 Paul tells Titus to give just two warnings to the person who is **divisive**, who persists in quarreling and arguing. If he doesn't heed the two warnings, then Titus should have **nothing to do with him**.[5] He should not try to argue with such a person; it will do no good. Such a person is **warped and sinful** (verse 11). It is not possible to reason with him. He will not listen to any further warnings. Because of his divisiveness and his opposition to others, such a man sins against the church. He is **self-condemned**; that is, he is condemned by his own words and actions.

Men leave true doctrine and teaching because they want to walk in their own way and do as they please. Such men are selfish, proud, and ignorant. And after they leave the truth, they become even more enslaved by sin and their minds become even more hardened and corrupt (see 1 Timothy 6:3–5; 2 Timothy 2:16 and comments).

12 Paul was about to send **Artemas**[6] or **Tychicus**[7] to Crete, so that Titus might then be free to come to Paul in **Nicopolis**.[8]

13 Paul asks Titus to help **Zenas** and **Apollos** on their journey. Apollos was a famous preacher; he was a colleague of Paul's (Acts 18:24–28; 1 Corinthians 3:4–6). Nothing else is known about Zenas.

14–15 **Our people**—that is, the believers in Crete—must be ready to help each other in all practical ways. They must especially give help and hospitality to travelers, such as Zenas and Apollos.

---

[3] The ceremony of baptism in itself does not save us. But true baptism in faith signifies the **washing** away of our sins, in which we were once dead (Ephesians 2:1), and our resulting spiritual **rebirth**. The washing away of our sins and our being reborn by the Spirit always go together. For further discussion, see Word List: Baptism.

[4] Here we see that we have been saved by all three persons of the triune God—Father, Son, and Holy Spirit—working together. For further discussion, see General Articles: Jesus Christ, Holy Spirit.

[5] Paul does not say here that such a person must be expelled from the church after two warnings; but certainly if he continues being divisive, he should be expelled (see 1 Corinthians 5:11,13 and comment).

[6] **Artemas** is not mentioned elsewhere in the New Testament.

[7] **Tychicus** is mentioned in Ephesians 6:2; Colossians 4:7; 2 Timothy 4:12.

[8] **Nicopolis** is a city in western Greece.

Philemon

INTRODUCTION

Paul wrote this letter to Philemon in about 60–61 A.D., while he was a prisoner in Rome. Paul sent this letter at the same time he sent his letter to the Colossians (see Colossians: Introduction).

Philemon was a Christian who lived in the city of Colosse. A "house church" used to meet in his home (verse 2). Some time earlier, Philemon's slave Onesimus had stolen some of his master's goods and run away. Onesimus eventually arrived in Rome, where he met Paul; as a result, Onesimus became a believer.

Paul knew that he had to return Onesimus to his master, Philemon. In Paul's day, the custom of slavery existed throughout the ROMAN EMPIRE. According to Roman law, a slave was the property of his master. But to return Onesimus to his master created a great problem for Paul, because according to law, runaway slaves were given a very severe punishment. Some runaway slaves were even put to death. Therefore, Paul wrote this letter to Philemon, asking Philemon to have mercy on Onesimus and to forgive him. On the one hand, Onesimus needed to repent and restore the stolen property. On the other hand, Philemon needed to fully forgive Onesimus from his heart. Both of them were now Christian brothers. Even though according to Roman law they were still master and slave, they were now, in fact, equal in Christ.

Slavery was indeed an evil and unjust system. In this letter, we see Paul's method of overcoming this great evil: the method of love, repentance, and forgiveness between master and slave.

Paul could have kept Onesimus with him in Rome. Paul could have encouraged and helped other slaves to escape. He could have opposed slavery openly by breaking Roman law. But that was not his method. Paul's method was to follow the law of love. The highest law is not man's law, but God's law—Christ's law—

especially the law of love (Mark 12:30–31). Love is a stronger force than all the laws of the world. In Christ's love, master and slave become equal; they become one (Galatians 3:28).

OUTLINE

A. Introduction (1–7).
   1. Salutation (1–3).
   2. Thanksgiving and Prayer (4–7).
B. Main Part of Letter (8–25).
   1. Paul's Plea for Onesimus (8–22).
   2. Final Greetings (23–25).

PHILEMON

Greetings and Prayer (1–7)

1–2 Paul calls himself a **prisoner**, because at the time of writing this letter to Philemon he was imprisoned in Rome. **Timothy** was with Paul as he wrote this letter (see Philippians 1:1; Colossians 1:1).

Some scholars think that **Apphia** was Philemon's wife. **Archippus** was a leader in the Colossian church (Colossians 4:17).

A "house church" met in Philemon's home. It is likely that this "church" was mainly made up of members of Philemon's household; but it is possible that believers outside his household attended the church as well. In New Testament times, there were two kinds of house churches: those consisting of one large household, and those made up of several households (see Romans 16:5; 1 Corinthians 16:19; Colossians 4:15).

3 See Romans 1:7; Ephesians 1:2 and comments.

4–5 See Romans 1:8; Ephesians 1:15–16; Colossians 1:3–4 and comments.

6–7 Paul has surely prayed for many things for Philemon in the past, but in verse 6, Paul only mentions one thing: namely, that Philemon **may be active in sharing** [his] **faith**—that is, that he may actively witness to others about Christ.

That we might be **active in sharing** [our] **faith** is a prayer for all of us. We who have received Christ are not meant to keep Him for ourselves; the good news of Jesus Christ is meant to be shared with others. And we must share our faith—share the Gospel—actively, effectively, and frequently. Let us ask ourselves: When was the last time we shared our faith with a non-believer? Do we hide our faith? Do we remain silent? The work of witnessing is not only for pastors and preachers; it is for every Christian!

Paul's Plea for Onesimus (8–25)

8–9 Because Paul was an apostle, he had the authority to command Philemon to forgive Onesimus. However, in this letter Paul does not use his authority to force Philemon to do as he asks; rather, Paul tries to persuade Philemon by love. Love, to be effective, does not require force. There is nothing stronger than love (see Philemon: Introduction).

10–11 Onesimus became Paul's **son while** [Paul] **was in chains**. That is, during Paul's imprisonment Onesimus somehow met Paul and through his witness believed in Christ. Now, because he had become a Christian, Onesimus was **useful**[1] both to Paul and to Philemon. Because Onesimus had run away from Philemon, he had been for a time **useless** to Philemon; but now he had become **useful** again.

12–14 Paul personally wanted Onesimus to stay with him and be his helper. Paul was not simply **in chains** like other prisoners; he was **in chains for the gospel** (verse 13). He desired the fellowship and help of Onesimus, who being a slave, was also "in chains." But Paul, forgetting his own desires and needs, is prepared to send Onesimus back to Philemon. If Paul had kept Onesimus with him without Philemon's consent, then any **favor** Philemon might have done (in allowing Onesimus to stay with Paul) would have been **forced** and not **spontaneous** (verse 14).

15–16 God is always able to overcome evil with good. Onesimus had run away. Philemon had suffered loss. But now Onesimus had received salvation, and Philemon had gained a new **brother in the Lord**.

17–18 Notice how strongly Paul pleads with Philemon on Onesimus' behalf. See how much Paul loves this lowly runaway slave! Paul is even ready to personally pay back whatever loss Philemon has suffered on account of Onesimus' bad behavior.

19 Let Philemon remember that he too owes his salvation to Paul's witness, because he too, like Onesimus, had first

---

[1] In the Greek language, the name Onesimus means **useful**.

heard the Gospel from Paul. Since Philemon has received such grace—such great mercy—from God, he must now show mercy to Onesimus (see Matthew 18:23–35).

20 What **benefit** does Paul seek from Philemon? The benefit Paul seeks is that Philemon might **refresh** [his] **heart**. How? By loving and forgiving Paul's spiritual son Onesimus.

21 Paul is confident that Philemon will obey Christ in this matter. Having said that, Paul shows his confidence by adding that he knows Philemon will do **even more than I ask**. In saying this, Paul is really praising Philemon. In this, we can learn something from Paul. If we want to persuade someone to do something, the best way to get that person to do it is to praise him! But, of course, the praise must be true, and not just false flattery.

22–24 All the people mentioned in these verses are also mentioned in Paul's letter to the Colossians (Colossians 4:10,12,14).

25 See 1 Corinthians 16:23; Philippians 4:23 and comments.

Hebrews

INTRODUCTION

It is not known who wrote this letter to the Hebrews. Unlike Paul, who started all of his letters by giving his own name, the writer of Hebrews has not written his name anywhere in the letter. According to Hebrews 2:3, the writer of this letter learned of the Gospel from **those who heard** [Christ]—that is, from the apostles. Paul cannot have been the writer of this letter, because he would never have written that verse; Paul had received the Gospel directly from Christ Himself (Acts 9:4–6).

This letter was written sometime between 60 and 70 A.D. It is not known who the "Hebrews"[1] were to whom this letter was addressed. Most Bible scholars believe that they were Aramaic speaking Jewish Christians. But what city they were from, no one knows.

But we need not be troubled that we don't know the author of this letter, or to whom it was written. Because there is something we do know—the most important thing of all: the real author of this letter is God, and it was written to us.

Why did the author write this letter to these Hebrews—to these Jewish Christians? These Christians—whoever they were—had recently begun to fall into temptations of various kinds, and the author is writing to exhort them not to fall into these temptations. What temptations? These Hebrews were becoming **lazy** (Hebrews 6:12). They had begun to **grow weary** and **lose heart** (Hebrews 12:3). Their initial enthusiasm and zeal was beginning to cool (Hebrews 3:14; 10:23,35). They had not matured in their faith (Hebrews 5:12–14). Some of them had stopped meeting together (Hebrews 10:25). They were opposing

[1] Hebrews were Aramaic (or Hebrew) speaking Jews. (The Hebrew and Aramaic languages were almost the same.) In New Testament times, the Aramaic language was the most commonly spoken language in the Middle East.

their own Christian leaders (Hebrews 13:17). Some of them were even about to give up their faith completely (Hebrews 3:12; 10:26).

As we think about the spiritual condition of these Hebrews, let us also examine ourselves. Have we become like them in any way? Because if we have, then this letter is certainly written for us!

In summary, the Hebrew Christians were about to fall into a very great temptation. They were about to leave their new Christian faith and return to their former Jewish religion.

Thus, the author of this letter has four purposes in writing. First, he writes to remind these Christians about the salvation and eternal life that comes only through Christ. Second, he writes to remind them of the immeasurable blessings that are available in Christ through faith. Third, he writes to tell them that to reach heaven believers must expect to suffer, even as Christ suffered. And fourth, the author writes to warn these Hebrew Christians that if they turn from their faith in Christ, God's fearful judgment will fall upon them.

OUTLINE

A. The Excellence of Christ (1:1–7:28).
   1. Introduction (1:1–4).
   2. Christ Superior to Angels (1:5–14).
   3. A Warning to Pay Attention (2:1–4).
   4. Christ the Perfect Man (2:5–18).
   5. Christ Superior to Moses (3:1–6).
   6. The Rest that Christ Promises (3:7–4:11).
   7. Christ the Great High Priest (4:12–5:10).
   8. A Warning Against Apostasy (5:11–6:20).
   9. Christ's Priesthood Superior to the Priesthood of Melchizedek (7:1–28).

B. A New and Better Covenant (8:1–10:18).
   1. The New Covenant (8:1–13).
   2. The New Sanctuary and the Blood of Christ (9:1–28).
   3. Christ's Sacrifice Once for All (10:1–18).

C. The Life of Faith (10:19–13:25).
   1. Description of the Life of Faith (10:19–25).
   2. The Fate of Those Who Fall Away (10:26–39).
   3. Men of Faith (11:1–40).
   4. Christ Our Example (12:1–3).
   5. Discipline (12:4–13).
   6. Christian Living under the New Covenant (12:14–29).
   7. Daily Christian Living (13:1–17).
   8. Conclusion (13:18–25).

CHAPTER 1

The Excellence of the Son of God (1:1–4)

1 **In the past**—that is, before Christ came to earth—God spoke to **our forefathers** (the JEWS) **through the** PROPHETS of the Old Testament.
2 **. . . but in these last days** [God] **has spoken to us by his Son** (Christ). These **last days** are the days since Christ came to earth.

The writer of this letter isn't saying here that the words of the prophets are less true or less worthy than the words of the Son. But the difference is this. The Old Testament prophets pointed the way to Christ; they prophesied about the coming of Christ's kingdom. But Christ was Himself the fulfillment of those prophecies. The New Testament is the fulfillment of the promises and prophecies of the Old Testament (see 2 Corinthians 1:20).

What kind of person is God's Son, Christ? First, He is the **heir of all things**. All power and authority belongs to Christ (Matthew 28:18). It was **through** Christ that God **made the universe** (see John 1:3; Colossians 1:16). From before the creation of the universe Christ was with God. Everything that God created He created through Jesus Christ.
3 Christ is the **radiance of God's glory**. Just as the radiance of the sun shines on the earth, so the radiance of Christ shines in men's hearts.

Christ is the **exact representation of** [God's] **being**. Christ is the **image** of God (2 Corinthians 4:4; Colossians 1:15). He is the manifestation of God. When we spiritually see and know Christ through faith, then we also see and know God (see John 1:18; 14:7–9). **For in Christ all the fullness of the Deity lives in bodily form** (Colossians 2:9).

Christ sustains **all things by his powerful word. . . . in him all things hold together** (Colossians 1:17). Christ is not only the creator of the universe; He is also the sustainer of the universe. He is the One who holds the universe together; He is the One who holds the stars and planets in their courses. And He does all this by His **powerful word**. The **word** that Christ speaks is God's word. In the Bible, God's **word** means both word and action together. God doesn't merely speak; whenever He speaks, He also acts. Whatever He says, He accomplishes. **God said, "Let there be light," and there was light** (Genesis 1:3).

Christ **provided purification for sins**. He offered Himself as a sacrifice for our sakes so that we might be forgiven of our sins and made clean. He bore in our place the punishment of our sins (see Mark 10:45 and comment). Christ became a **sacrifice of atonement** for us (Romans 3:25). Through Christ—through His blood, through His sacrifice—believers in Him are declared pure and RIGHTEOUS in God's eyes (see Romans 3:24; 5:1,9 and comments).

Three days after Christ was killed, He rose from the dead, and now He sits at God's **right hand in the heavenly realms** (see Psalm 110:1; Luke 22:69; Ephesians 1:20–21).

From these first three verses of Hebrews, we can see that Christ is the greatest "prophet" of all, through whom God has spoken His final word to the world. Not only that, Christ is also the greatest "priest" of all, through whose self-sacrifice God's people—that is, we believers—have been declared pure and righteous in God's sight. And Christ is not only a prophet and a priest; He is also the King of kings, who sits on His throne in heaven at the right hand of God. This is the Christ, about whom the author of this letter writes in these opening verses. This is the Christ in whom these Hebrew Christians have put their faith.[2]
4 Christ is also **much superior to the** ANGELS. Christ's **name** is above every name (see Philippians 2:9–11).

---
[2] For further discussion, see General Article: Jesus Christ.

Christ Is Superior to Angels (1:5–14)

5 In verses 5–13, the writer of this letter quotes seven passages from the Old Testament to show his readers that Christ is indeed superior to the **angels**. Notice that in all of these Old Testament quotations it is God who is speaking. Let us keep in mind that the entire Old Testament (as well as the New Testament) is God's own word (verse 1). Through the Bible, God continues to speak to us today.

God has never said to any angel: "**You are my Son**." God has only one Son, and that is Jesus Christ. Jesus has always been God's Son (see John 1:1–2,14).

In this verse, the writer quotes from Psalm 2:7 and 2 Samuel 7:14. These Old Testament verses are prophecies which were written about Christ.

6 Christ is God's **firstborn**. Christ is the **firstborn** in two ways. First, He is God's **one and only Son** (John 1:14). Second, He was the first to rise from the dead; therefore, He is the "firstborn" of all those who will be resurrected (see Romans 8:29; 1 Corinthians 15:20).

In this verse, the writer quotes from Deuteronomy 32:43 and Psalm 97:7. **Let all God's angels worship him** (Christ). Since the angels worship Christ, we know that Christ must be above the angels.

7 Here the writer quotes from Psalm 104:4. Angels serve God like **winds** and **flames of fire**. That is, they appear when God has a special assignment for them to do, and when they have completed it, they disappear again—just as wind and fire come one moment and go the next. The angels have no independence; they are only **servants**.

8–9 But Christ is not only a servant of God; He is also God's Son. Christ does not come and go like an angel. Christ's **throne**—that is, His kingdom—**will last for ever and ever** (verse 8). Notice here that Christ is called **O God**. And RIGHTEOUSNESS will be the **scepter**, or rule, of His kingdom. Among kings, only Christ rules with complete righteousness. In these verses 8–9, the writer quotes Psalm 45:6–7.

God has set Christ **above** [His] **companions**—that is, above believers—**by anointing** [Him] **with the oil of joy** (verse 9). The **oil of joy** is the joy of the Holy Spirit (see Hebrews 12:2). Therefore, this verse means that God has given Christ His Holy Spirit without measure (John 3:34; Acts 10:38). We believers, however, are given the Spirit according to measure (Romans 12:3; Ephesians 4:7).

10–12 In these verses, the writer quotes from Psalm 102:25–27. Notice that God here calls Christ **O Lord**. Christ is the creator of heaven and earth. Heaven and earth **will perish**, but Christ will **remain** (verse 11); He will **remain the same** (verse 12).

13 This verse is quoted from Psalm 110:1 (see 1 Corinthians 15:25; Ephesians 1:20–22; Hebrews 10:12–13). God has never told an angel: "**Sit at my right hand**." That place is reserved for Christ alone. From His throne at the right hand of God, Christ now reigns with all authority and power.

14 God's Son Christ rules on the throne. Angels are **ministering spirits**. These angels have been **sent to serve those who will inherit salvation**—that is, believers in Christ. Angels stand in the presence of God, but they are only messengers of Christ (see Luke 1:19). Christ is supreme.

Believers are those **who will inherit** SALVATION. We who have believed in Christ already have been saved. But only after Christ has come again at the end of the world will we receive our full inheritance, our full salvation (see General Article: Way of Salvation).

CHAPTER 2

Warning to Pay Attention (2:1–4)

1 Why do we need to study the Bible? Why is it necessary to **pay careful attention** to the words of preachers and pastors? Because if we do not pay attention to **what we have heard**—that is, God's word—we shall **drift away** from the truth. We will drift away from Christ; we will turn from true faith in Him. And if we turn from Christ—**if we ignore such a great salvation**—we shall not escape God's wrath and judgment (verse 3). Apart from the Gospel, apart from the salvation that comes through faith in Christ, there is no other way to escape from the **just punishment** (verse 2) that God will give to those who do not believe in Christ. **We must pay more attention, therefore, to what we have heard!**

2 That which **we have heard** is the Gospel of Christ. If the **message spoken by angels**—that is, the Old Testament, or Jewish LAW—**was binding**, then the Gospel of Christ—the New Testament—is even more binding. Why? Because the Old Testament law was **spoken by angels** (Acts 7:53); but the New Testament was spoken by Christ and through Christ (Hebrews 1:2). And in Chapter 1, the writer of Hebrews has shown that Christ is superior to angels. For this reason, then, the New Testament is superior to the Old Testament. The Jews received a **just punishment** for **every violation** of the Jewish law that they committed. If men were punished for violating even the tiniest rule or regulation of the Old Testament law, certainly we shall be punished for rejecting the Gospel of Christ, spoken by God's own Son.

3 **This salvation** was first announced **by the Lord**, that is, by Christ. The Old Testament prophets prophesied about the coming of Christ, but Christ Himself announced the fulfillment of their prophecies (see Mark 1:14–15; Luke 4:17–21). Christ didn't only announce the fulfillment of the Old Testament prophecies; He was their fulfillment!

This salvation that Christ announced **was confirmed** by the apostles who heard Christ. This Gospel of salvation was no rumor or man-made tale. Both the writer and the readers of this letter had heard the Gospel from men (the apostles) who had themselves heard and seen Christ with their own ears and eyes.

4 It wasn't only the apostles who testified to the Gospel by their preaching; God Himself also **testified to it**—or proved it—by **signs, wonders and various miracles, and gifts of the HOLY SPIRIT**, which God distributed **according to his will** (see Acts 2:22,43; 1 Corinthians 12:7–11). How, then, can anyone ignore such a great salvation?

In the time of the apostles, everyone knew about these signs and miracles. Many people had seen God's powerful works with their own eyes. But here a question arises. Is God, in this present time, still doing these powerful works and distributing these gifts of the Spirit?

The answer to this question is yes. Today all over the world, in answer to the prayers of believers, God is performing miracles, healing the sick, and giving millions of people new spiritual life through the power of His Holy Spirit. Let us not doubt that God's great power is at work today, as it always has been. Rather, let us go on increasing in faith. Just as the author has written to these Hebrews, so he writes also to us: **We must pay more careful attention . . . to what we have heard, so that we do not drift away** (verse 1).

Christ Made Like His Brothers (2:5–18)

5 This present world has been **subjected** to the administration or control of **angels**, some of whom are good angels, and some of whom are evil (see Daniel 10:20–21; 12:1; John 16:11; Ephesians 6:12). But the **world to come** will not be subjected to angels; it will be subjected to God's Son Christ. This **world to come** is the KINGDOM OF GOD, over which Christ will reign from His throne at the right hand of God. In one way, the kingdom of God began when Jesus came to earth the first time (see Matthew 12:28; Luke 17:20–21). But only after Jesus comes again at the end of this present world will the kingdom of God be fully established.

6–8 Even though Jesus Christ, being God's Son, is higher than all the angels, God for a time made Him a **little lower than the angels** (verse 7). When Jesus came to earth the first time, He came in the form of a man—that is, lower than an angel. After that, God **crowned him with glory and honor**; that is, God raised Him from the dead. And God **put everything under** [Christ's] **feet**—that is, under His authority (see Ephesians 1:20–22; Hebrews 1:13).

Here the writer of Hebrews quotes from Psalm 8:4–6. This passage from the Psalms was originally written about an ordinary man, that is, about mankind. But the writer of Hebrews reinterprets this passage from Psalms and gives it a new meaning: he interprets this passage to be referring, not to an ordinary man, but to the perfect man, Jesus Christ. And this passage could also refer to all of us who have put our faith in Christ. Because of our faith, we also will be crowned **with glory and honor**.

In verse 8, there is an important truth that we must understand. Christ already has all power and authority. Christ already is seated at God's right hand. Everything is now subject to Him. However, we can still see Satan and his evil spirits at work in the world. We can see sin in our own lives. Even though Christ has triumphed over Satan, He still allows Satan to continue doing evil in the world. Only when Christ comes again will Satan be completely destroyed. Yet even now, in spite of Satan's activities, Christ is reigning in the world. **For he must reign until he has put all his enemies under his feet** (1 Corinthians 15:25). It will be only then—when His enemies are under His feet—that Christ finally **hands over the kingdom to God the Father** (1 Corinthians 15:24).

9 The writer here adds to the thought of verse 7. It was **because he suffered death** that Christ was crowned with glory and honor (see Philippians 2:8–9 and comment). Christ came to **taste death** for all men; that is, He came to suffer the death penalty that we ourselves should have received because of our sin. Jesus died in our place; He "tasted death" for us. Thus, because Jesus, in obedience to God, gave up His own life as a sacrifice for sin, God raised Him from the dead and **crowned him with glory and honor** (verse 7).

10 Jesus not only **announced** our salvation (verse 3); He also is the **author** of our salvation. Through His sufferings Jesus gained salvation for us. Through His sufferings He brought **many sons** (believers) **to glory** (to salvation). Jesus led the way for us; He showed us the way of salvation. Because Jesus suffered for us, we now, through faith in Him, will get to share in His glory. But just as Jesus' way to glory led through suffering, so our way to glory must also lead through suffering.

Why did God need to **make** [Jesus] **perfect through suffering**? Jesus was already "perfect." But here the meaning is this: God needed to make Jesus **perfect**, or prepared, for being the Savior of mankind. Without having suffered, Jesus could not have saved men and brought them **to glory**. In this way, God made Jesus a **perfect** Savior through suffering.

11 Jesus is the **one who makes men holy**. He makes us holy by His death, by the sacrifice of His body (Hebrews 10:10). Through faith in Him, we become children of God (John 1:12). In this way we become **brothers** of Christ; together with Him we are **of the same family**. This is why **Jesus is not ashamed to call** [us] **brothers** (see Romans 8:29).

If we are not ashamed of Jesus, He will not be ashamed of us. But if we are ashamed of Him, He likewise will be ashamed of us (see Matthew 10:32–33; Mark 8:38).

12 This verse is a quotation from Psalm 22:22. Here Christ is speaking through the words of the Psalm writer. Christ says: "**I will declare your** (God's) **name to my brothers**." Thus, He is calling us His **brothers**.

13 Here the writer of Hebrews quotes from Isaiah 8:17–18. Here again, Jesus is speaking through the words of the prophet Isaiah: **"I will put my trust in him** (God)." Even while Jesus was dying on the cross, He put His **trust** in God. And then God raised Him up to heaven. Now Jesus can say: **"Here am I, and the children God has given me."** We believers are the **children** whom God has given to Jesus. We are the **sons** whom Jesus is bringing **to glory** (verse 10).

14–15 The **children**—we believers—are made of **flesh and blood**. In order for Christ to save us, He had to become like us. He had to share in our **humanity** (verse 14). Only by becoming a man and dying and then rising again could Christ destroy the **devil**, SATAN, **who holds the power of death** (see 2 Timothy 1:10; Revelation 1:18). Satan has the **power of death** because he leads men into sin, for which the punishment is **death** (Romans 6:23).

Therefore, when we see Jesus in the form of a man dying like us and then rising again from the dead, we know that we too, through faith, will rise again after death (2 Corinthians 4:14). Death no longer has any power over us (1 Corinthians 15:55,57). We are now free from the **fear of death** (verse 15).

Why do we no longer need to fear death? Because for believers in Christ death leads to liberation, to glory, and to eternal life with Christ in heaven. But for non-believers, death leads to eternal punishment in hell.

16 Christ became a man and came to earth not to help angels but to help—to save—men. What men? **Abraham's**[3] **descendants**. Here the writer is referring not to Abraham's natural descendants according to the flesh (the Jews), but rather to his spiritual "descendants" according to faith. All who believe in Jesus are the true **descendants** of Abraham (see Galatians 3:7,9,29 and comment).

17 In order to make ATONEMENT for our sins, Jesus had to become like us in every way—except that He never sinned (Hebrews 4:15).

To understand this verse, we need to know about the Jewish **high priest** in Old Testament times. Each year the Jewish high priest used to offer an animal sacrifice to God to atone for the sins of the people. The high priest went before God as the representative of the people. In order to be a representative of men, the high priest needed to be a man himself. In the same way, in order to be our **high priest** and Savior, Jesus had to become a man also. He had to come down to us in order to make atonement for our sins. Only a man can atone for the sins of men.

Jesus was a perfect **high priest**, because He Himself was sinless. Therefore, He could come directly into the presence of a holy God. Because He was a man, He was a **merciful** high priest, who could **sympathize with our weaknesses** (Hebrews 4:15).

The sacrifice that Jesus offered was not a goat or a buffalo, but His own body. It was a perfect sacrifice, without spot or blemish or sin. It was fully acceptable to God. In this way, through His perfect sacrifice, Jesus was able to make full atonement for our sins (see Romans 3:24–25 and comment).

18 People who have themselves suffered are best able to help and comfort others who are suffering. If today we are suffering for Christ, let us remember that He Himself first suffered for us. And He is with us now; He will help us stand firm. He will strengthen us. And He will give us inner joy and peace (see 2 Corinthians 1:3–5).

Therefore, Jesus Christ is in every way a perfect High priest and perfect Savior. He has brought about peace between us and God (Romans 5:1). He has made atonement for our sins, and as a result, we are now justified in God's sight (Romans 3:24). But that is not all. Because Jesus Himself suffered and was tempted, He is now fully able to comfort and strengthen those of us who are suffering and being tempted. How can we not praise and worship and love such a Savior!

---

[3] **Abraham** was the first Jew; he is therefore the original ancestor of all the Jews according to the flesh. Christ Himself, being a Jew, was descended from Abraham (Matthew 1:1).

CHAPTER 3

Jesus Greater Than Moses (3:1–6)

1 **Therefore . . . fix your thoughts on Jesus.** Let us daily think about Jesus, and meditate on Him (see Hebrews 12:2–3).

Jesus is here called an APOSTLE **and high priest.** As an **apostle** He is God's representative among men. As a **high priest** He is man's representative before God. As an apostle, He was sent forth to reveal God to men. As a high priest, He has reconciled men to God.

2 Jesus was faithful to God, **who appointed him** to be an apostle and high priest. The writer of Hebrews here compares Jesus to MOSES, who was **faithful in all God's house** (Numbers 12:7). Moses was a great Jewish leader, who led the Jews out of bondage in Egypt to a new land. Moses received from God the Old Testament law, and passed it on to the Jews. Just as, in the New Testament, Jesus is the mediator between God and man, so in the Old Testament, Moses was the mediator between God and the Jews.

Why does the writer compare Jesus with Moses? The reason is that these Hebrews to whom he was writing were about to turn away from Christ. Because they had originally been Jews, they were now about to turn back to their old Jewish religion. Therefore, the writer reminds them that Jesus is far greater than their old leader Moses. The writer is, in effect, asking these Hebrews: What advantage is there in turning from what is greater to what is lesser?

3–4 Moses was like a steward in **God's house,** that is, the Jewish nation. But Jesus, because He is Himself God, is the owner and **builder** of the house. Therefore, Jesus the builder and master of the house is greater than Moses, who was only a servant in the house. Servants do not build houses. The **builder of everything** is God—that is, Jesus Christ (verse 4).

5–6 Just as Moses was a faithful **servant** in God's house, so is Jesus a faithful **son over God's house**—that is, over God's kingdom. Moses, by his own faithfulness and example, gave witness to Christ. He testified **to what would be said in the future.**

And we are [God's] **house** (verse 6). We believers in Christ are the household of God (see 1 Corinthians 3:9; Ephesians 2:19,22; 1 Peter 2:5).

We are God's household, **if we hold on to our courage and the hope of which we boast.** Here, as in many other New Testament verses (see verse 14), it is written that we will remain members of God's household only if we remain firm in the faith (see General Article: Can We Lose Our Salvation?). He who leaves the faith loses everything (see Mark 4:5–6,16–17).

Warning Against Unbelief (3:7–19)

7–11 These verse are quoted from Psalm 95:7–11. **So, as the Holy Spirit says . . .** (verse 7). These words are not merely words written in a book; they are words spoken by God's own Holy Spirit.

Moses delivered the Jews from bondage in Egypt and led them out into the Sinai desert, which lies between Egypt and Israel. Moses eventually led them up to the border of Israel, the land which God had promised to give to Abraham's descendants (the Jews). However, during the forty years they were in the Sinai desert, the Jews continually complained against God and against their leader Moses. In doing this, they **tested and tried** God (verse 9). That is, they **tested** God to find out how far they could rebel against Him before He became angry with them (Exodus 17:1–4,7). And after they had tested God a long time, the Jews finally did provoke God to anger. And God declared an oath that these rebellious and complaining Jews would **"never enter my rest"** (verse 11); that is, they would never enter the land (Israel) He had promised to give to Abraham's descendants (Numbers 14:21–23).

12 The Hebrews to whom this letter was written were about to fall into temptation, just as those rebellious Jews in the desert had fallen into temptation. Therefore, the writer gives these Hebrews a warning: Do not be like those Jews in the desert who fell into sin, who rebelled against God, and who stopped trusting in Him (see 1 Corinthians 10:1–5).

Those ancient Jews who opposed Moses and who stopped believing in God did not get to enter the land—the **rest**—that God had promised to Abraham's descendants. It is possible that this same thing could happen to us. If we, having once "believed," then leave our faith and begin to oppose Christ, we too will not get to enter our **rest**, which is heaven.

13 We need to **encourage one another daily** to stand firm in the faith. When we try to follow Christ by ourselves, it is very easy to fall into temptation, to become discouraged, to turn back. But by joining together and encouraging one another, we can together go forward in the faith (see Hebrews 10:25).

Therefore, let us encourage one another, **as long as it is called Today**. **Today** the Holy Spirit is speaking to us. **Today**, therefore, let us listen, because tomorrow the opportunity to hear may not come again. But let us remember that, today also, Satan is trying to lead us into temptation. Satan is trying to harden our hearts **by sin's deceitfulness**. **Today** we are in a struggle between spirit and flesh (Galatians 5:17). There is no **rest** today. Only "tomorrow" will our rest come—if we stand firm.

What is **sin's deceitfulness**? It is sin in disguise. When Satan tempts us to commit a particular sin, he will say to us: "That's not really a sin." He deceives us. And when we begin to commit this disguised sin, we become even more deceived, even more blind. And as we continue to sin, our hearts become **hardened**. Therefore, we must encourage and admonish one another daily, so that we will not be **hardened by sin's deceitfulness** (see 2 Timothy 4:2).

14 Here the writer again warns us to **hold firmly . . . the confidence** (faith) **we had at first**. He warns us to stand firm **till the end** (see Mark 13:13 and comment). If we remain firm in our faith and do not turn back, we will get to **share in Christ**—that is, we will be given a share in His glory and in His inheritance (Romans 8:17).

15–16 The writer again quotes from Psalm 95:7–8. Those ancient Jews who **heard and rebelled** (verse 16) against God had seen God's mighty works and miracles. Through Moses, God had led the Jews **out of Egypt** in a miraculous way. Nevertheless, they rebelled against God and stopped believing in Him.

17 God became angry with those Jews, because they had disobeyed Him. All those who opposed Him **fell** (died) **in the desert** (Numbers 14:27,29–30).

18–19 Because of the Jews' **unbelief** (verse 19), they were not allowed to enter into God's **rest**, that is, into the land (Israel) which God had promised to give them (see Hebrews 4:6 and comment). From this we can see that unbelief is the primary or root sin of man.[4] The reason is because unbelief cuts us off from God's power to save us and make us holy. Without faith, we have no power to overcome sin.

Let these above verses, then, serve as a warning for us today. Just as those ancient Jews had seen God's power and glory, so we too have seen the glory of the Lord Jesus Christ. We have begun to follow Him. Now perhaps some trial or temptation has fallen upon us, such as happened to those ancient Jews. By this our faith is being tested. Brothers and sisters, let us not be like those ancient Jews who fell away and stopped believing! There is one thing that will prevent us from entering our **rest**—and that one thing is **unbelief**. **See to it, brothers, that none of you has a sinful, unbelieving heart that turns away from the living God** (verse 12).

---

[4] For further discussion of sin, see comment on Romans 3:10–12 and footnote to comment.

CHAPTER 4

Our Rest (4:1–11)

1–2 God sent Jesus Christ into the world to lead us into **his rest**, that is, heaven. For all who believe in Christ, **the promise of entering his rest still stands.** Yet it is possible for us to "fall short of it" through unbelief; that is, it's possible for us, through unbelief, to forfeit the promise and not get to enter God's rest. It is not enough to have heard the GOSPEL **preached to us**; we must **combine it with** FAITH (verse 2). Those ancient Jews had heard the **message** of God, but they did not accept the message **with faith**. Therefore, **the message they heard was of no value to them.**

The writer of Hebrews says: **Therefore . . . let us be careful** lest any of us **be found to have fallen short**—that is, lest any of us fail to enter God's rest. Some Christians believe that we don't ever need to worry about failing to enter God's rest, or about losing our salvation. But the writer of Hebrews says we must **be careful** that it doesn't happen! It's not Christ whom we have to be concerned about; He will never fail us. It is we who can fail Christ through unbelief; that's what we must **be careful** about. We must fear unbelief (see 1 Corinthians 10:12).

3 Those who persist in faith until the end will enter God's rest. It is not our rest; it is God's rest. To show that God called it "**my rest**," the writer here quotes again from Psalm 95:11 (Hebrews 3:11). But the question arises: What is God's **rest**? Because, in a sense, God has been "resting" since the creation of the world.

4–5 God created the world in six days, and on the seventh day He rested (Genesis 2:2). His "rest" has continued ever since that time. We have been invited to share in that rest. But if we are not careful, we can forfeit our place through unbelief.

6 God's rest is still open for men and women. True believers are still entering His rest. Only those who disbelieve and disobey God are prevented from entering.

The writer here says that the ancient Jews **did not go in** (into God's rest) **because of their disobedience**. But in Hebrews 3:19, the writer says that **they were not able to enter, because of their unbelief**. We must understand here that unbelief itself is really a kind of disobedience (see Romans 14:23 and comment). Therefore, in these two verses the writer is saying the same thing.

Indeed, unbelief is the most basic form of disobedience: it is a refusal to believe. Unbelief is not only disobedience in itself, but it also leads to all other kinds of disobedience. Because of unbelief, man loses the power to overcome sin. Because of unbelief, man is separated from God. That is why unbelief prevents man from entering God's rest (see Hebrews 3:19 and comment).

7 But God says to all men and women: "It is not too late to repent; there is still time." **Today** God is giving us the opportunity to enter His rest. **Today** we can hear His **voice**; and we must hear it. **I tell you . . . now is the day of salvation** (2 Corinthians 6:2). While it is still "today," let us not lose the chance to enter God's rest, to receive salvation. Let us not **harden** our hearts (Psalm 95:7–8; Hebrews 3:13,15).

8 After those disobedient Jews died in the desert, a leader named **Joshua** led the next generation of Jews into Israel, the land which God had promised to give to Abraham's descendants (Joshua 1:1–2). Or we can say that Joshua led them into "God's rest." And just as Joshua led that generation of Jews into God's rest, so Jesus leads us into God's rest.[5] But the "rest" offered by Joshua to those ancient Jews was completely different from the rest Jesus offers to us today. The rest offered by Joshua was not permanent; because any rest in this world can never be permanent. Furthermore, many years after Joshua's time, the Psalm writer DAVID wrote about a "rest" of God that was still to come in the future. Besides the rest offered by Joshua, there is still to come another kind of rest, which Jesus will give to those who believe in Him. And the rest given by Jesus is permanent; it will never end.

9–10 **There remains, then, a Sab-**

[5] In the Greek language, the names Joshua and Jesus are the same.

bath-rest for the people of God. We, through faith, are the **people of God**. Here God's rest is called a **Sabbath-rest**, because after creating the world in six days God rested on the seventh—or **Sabbath**[6]—day. Just as God rested after creating the world, so we too shall be able to rest after our work on earth is finished.[7] We will have a share in God's rest. Indeed, we can understand that "God's rest" is the kingdom of heaven itself. Our true rest is waiting for us in heaven.

11 The writer here repeats the thought of Hebrews 3:12.

Jesus the Great High Priest (4:12–16)

12 The writer has already reminded us that we need to hear God's word (verse 7). But it is not enough to hear God's word; we must obey it (see Matthew 7:24–27). **For the word of God is living and active**. Through the prophet Isaiah, God said concerning His word: "**It will not return to me empty, but will accomplish what I desire and achieve the purpose for which I sent it**" (Isaiah 55:11). God's word is like a **double-edged sword**. To the believer it brings salvation (Romans 1:16). To the unbeliever it brings judgment (John 3:18). God's word is also sharp. Like a sword, it penetrates to a man's inner mind and conscience.[8] It judges the **thoughts and attitudes of the heart**. God's word is Christ's word. But more than that, God's word is Christ Himself (John 1:14). That **word** which brings judgment and salvation and which judges the thoughts and attitudes of the heart—that **word** is Christ Himself (see 1 Corinthians 4:5).

13 Jesus sees into our hearts. Nothing is hid from Jesus and God. We can hide our thoughts and desires from our neighbor, or from our spouse. We can even hide our inner thoughts and desires from ourselves; that is, we can deceive ourselves. But we cannot hide anything from God, nor can we deceive Him. Every man will one day have to give a complete account of himself to God; on that day, everything will be **uncovered and laid bare**.

Today the word of Jesus speaks to us: "**Come, follow me**" (Mark 1:17). What answer will we give?

14 Jesus is our **great high priest**. In Hebrews 2:17, the writer has called Jesus a **merciful and faithful high priest**. Jesus has already **gone through the heavens**—that is, He has ascended to heaven. And now He is seated at the right hand of God. He has gone before us to prepare a place for us (John 14:2). In order that we might not lose that place, **let us hold firmly to the faith we profess**.

15 Jesus knows that we are weak. He knows how great our temptations are, because He Himself **has been tempted in every way, just as we are**. Therefore, He is able to **sympathize** with us and to help us (Hebrews 2:18). We can talk to Him as a friend. He completely understands our situation.

Jesus **has been tempted . . . just as we**

---

[6] The **Sabbath** is the seventh day of the week, which by Jewish custom falls on Saturday. According to the fourth of the ten commandments, the Jews were required to rest on the Sabbath, and do no work (Exodus 20:8–11).

[7] In one sense, God did indeed rest after creating the world. However, in another sense, God never completely "rests." He continues to sustain the universe and everything in it. Without God's constant sustaining "work," everything would come to an end (see John 5:17).

[8] The writer says that the word of God penetrates **even to dividing soul and spirit, joints and marrow**. That is, the word reveals and judges the deepest parts of our being. God's word shows us what in our lives is of the flesh and what is of the spirit. God's word examines our **soul**—that is, our mind, our inner motives and desires. Sometimes we think we are doing God's will, but it's really our own selfish will that we are doing. Our **soul** naturally follows our selfish will, our **spirit** follows God's will; we often cannot tell them apart. But God's word is able to "divide," or distinguish between, these two wills. That is what the writer means when he says that the word penetrates **even to dividing soul and spirit**.

are. Jesus was made **like his brothers in every way** (Hebrews 2:17). However, He never sinned. And it was because He never sinned that He became a perfect high priest, through whom we can obtain salvation (Hebrews 5:8–9).

16 Because we have such a merciful and perfect high priest, we can now **approach the throne of GRACE**. That is, we can come directly into the presence of God Himself. And we can come **with confidence**. We can come with confidence, because we know that we shall obtain **mercy** and **grace**. Even now, Christ is at God's right hand interceding on our behalf (Romans 8:34; Hebrews 7:25–26). Therefore, when trials and temptations come upon us, let us not run and hide from God; rather, let us go at once to Jesus, and He will help us in our time of need.

CHAPTER 5

Our High Priest (5:1–10)

1 For someone to become a Jewish high priest, two things were necessary. First, the high priest was selected **from among men**; that is, he himself had to be a man. Second, the high priest was **appointed** by God. The function of the high priest was to offer to God **gifts and sacrifices for sins**. By offering these gifts and sacrifices, the high priest made atonement for the sins of the people.

2 Because the Jewish high priests were men, they themselves fell into sin from time to time. Therefore, because of their own **weakness**, they were able to **deal gently with those who** [were] **ignorant and . . . going astray**. However, they did not deal gently with those who sinned deliberately and refused to repent. According to the Jewish law, there was no forgiveness for those who sinned knowingly (see Numbers 15:27–31; Hebrews 9:7).

3 Because the Jewish high priests themselves sinned from time to time, they were required to offer a sacrifice for their own sins before they could offer sacrifices for the sins of the people (Leviticus 16:6). Only a high priest who was himself cleansed from sin could offer sacrifices for the sins of others.

4 The high priests didn't appoint themselves to the office of high priest; they were always appointed by God. Moses' brother **Aaron** was the first Jewish high priest (Exodus 28:1–2).

5 In the same way, Christ did not appoint Himself to be a high priest; He was appointed by God. God not only made Christ a high priest; He also made Him His Son. The writer here quotes from Psalm 2:7.

6 God appointed Christ to be a **priest forever**. But here a problem appears. All Jewish high priests had to be descended from Aaron, the first high priest. But Christ was descended, not from Aaron, but from David, the famous king of the Jews. Therefore, how could Christ be a true high priest?

Here the writer, quoting from Psalm 110:4, gives the answer: Christ was a high priest, not in the order of Aaron, but **in the order of Melchizedek**.

Who was **Melchizedek**? He was a priest of God long before Aaron's time. He was also the **king of Salem**—that is, Jerusalem[9] (Genesis 14:18). Thus he was both a priest and a king. Since King David later became "king of Jerusalem," it can be said that he was **in the order of Melchizedek**. And because Jesus was descended from David, He too was in the order of Melchizedek. Therefore, Jesus is both a king and a **high priest in the order of Melchizedek** (verse 10).

---

[9] Jerusalem is the most important city of the Jews. During much of the period of the Bible, Jerusalem was the Jewish capital. King David and many of the other Jewish kings reigned from Jerusalem.

7 In verse 1, the writer has said that the high priests were men. Therefore, for Jesus to serve as high priest, He had to be a man too. In this verse, the writer describes one aspect of Jesus' life as a man (see Mark 14:32–36).

Jesus was a man just like us, with all our temptations and weaknesses. Even though He was God's own Son, He endured all kinds of trials and hardships, just as we do. When He became hungry, He could have turned stones into bread; but He did not do so (Matthew 4:2–4). When He was arrested, He could have called for the help of **twelve legions of angels**, but He did not do so (Matthew 26:53). Just as we ordinary men must endure trouble and pain, so also did Christ endure trouble and pain. Thus Jesus can sympathize with us in every situation, because He Himself has experienced every kind of trouble we experience (Hebrews 2:18; 4:15).

But think for a moment: Jesus' suffering was far greater than our own. When we suffer, we know that Jesus is with us. We are never alone. But when Jesus suffered, especially when He was dying on the cross, He suffered alone. Even God, at that time, forsook Him (Mark 15:34).

The writer says that Jesus **was heard because of his reverent submission**. Jesus prayed that He might be saved from death on the cross (Mark 14:35–36), but God did not grant that prayer. God was able to **save** [Jesus] **from death**, but He chose not to. However, God certainly did hear Jesus' prayer to be saved, because three days after Jesus' death, God raised Him from the dead.

8 Although Jesus was the Son of God, He **learned obedience from what he suffered**. What does this mean? We ordinary men and women usually learn obedience through the suffering that comes upon us when we disobey. But Jesus never disobeyed. Indeed, it was because of Jesus' obedience that suffering came upon Him. Jesus learned how difficult it is to obey God fully. He experienced the suffering that comes upon those who obey God.

These Hebrew Christians, to whom this letter was written, had already begun to experience some suffering because of their obedience to Christ. But now, as a result, they were about to fall away; they were about to deny Christ. Therefore, let them remember Jesus, who Himself endured suffering in obedience until the end.

9 Jesus was made **perfect through suffering** (Hebrews 2:10). He was obedient in everything. He did not sin. Therefore, having become a perfect high priest, He is able to give **eternal salvation** to all **who obey him**. It was through His obedience that Jesus **became the source of eternal salvation**. In the same way, it is through our obedience[10] to him that we obtain that salvation.

Jesus is the source of salvation **for all who obey him**—that is, for all who believe in Him. Faith comes first; without faith, we cannot obey Christ. At the same time, without obedience, there cannot be true faith (see James 2:14–17 and comment). Both faith and obedience together are necessary for our salvation.

10 See verse 6 and comment.

Milk and Solid Food (5:11–14)

11–12 These Hebrews, to whom this letter was written, had been slow to grow

[10] We must understand here that the first and most basic form of obedience is faith itself (see Hebrews 4:6 and comment). Then, once there is true faith, that faith will always be manifested by obedience in all other matters. It is impossible to separate faith and obedience; they are like two blades of a scissors. Thus, to say that we are saved through obedience to Christ (that is, the obedience of faith) is the same as saying that we are saved through faith in Christ; both are equally true statements.

However, this is not to say that we are saved by works of obedience alone. We are not saved by works alone. Rather, we are saved by faith expressing itself in obedience (see Galatians 5:16; Ephesians 2:8–10; James 2:14,17,20–24 and comments). Furthermore, faith itself is a gift of God, a gift of God's grace. Our salvation from first to last is a work of God's grace. For further discussion, see General Article: Way of Salvation.

and mature in their faith. They were still spiritual infants (see 1 Corinthians 3:1–2). They had not fully learned even the **elementary truths of God's word** (verse 12).

God's word is made up of both **milk** and **solid food** (see Matthew 4:4). "Milk" is for new believers (1 Peter 2:2); "solid food" is for mature believers.

13 These Hebrews had been living, in a spiritual sense, on **milk** alone. Having initially grown a little in their faith, they had now stopped growing. They had found it was easier just to keep drinking milk like a baby!

In order to grow, we need **solid food.** In order to grow spiritually, we need **teaching about righteousness**. What the writer means here is that we need teaching that will prepare us to suffer for righteousness' sake (Matthew 5:10; 2 Timothy 3:12). These Hebrews weren't ready to suffer in this way. They did not know much about true righteousness.

14 Here **solid food** means the difficult and deep teachings of Jesus. When we eat such "food," we will grow in Christ. And as we grow in Christ, we shall become better able to **distinguish good from evil**. We will be able to see more clearly the sin in our own lives and the good in Jesus' life. As we grow in faith, we shall be better able to understand Jesus' righteousness and to follow Him. But, to grow in this way, we need **solid food**. We will never become mature by drinking only milk!

CHAPTER 6

Warning Against Falling Away (6:1–12)

1 Even though these Hebrews had only been drinking "milk," the writer now decides to give them some "solid food"—that is, more advanced and difficult teaching. The writer knows that only if they receive some solid food will they be able to grow further in their faith (Hebrews 5:14). **Therefore . . . let us go on to maturity,** says the writer. In the Christian life, we either go forward or we go backward; there is no standing still. We cannot remain in the same spiritual state for long. Like a tree, we either grow or die.

Once we have laid the **foundation** of our Christian faith, we don't need to lay it again. Here in verse 1, the writer mentions two parts of this **foundation** which we do not need to lay again: first, REPENTANCE **from acts that lead to death**; and second, **faith in God**. These two things are the first two steps in our Christian life (see Mark 1:15; Acts 20:21). We should not need to be taught these two things over and over.

The **acts that lead to death** are our sins; sin results in death, spiritual death (Romans 6:21,23). Here, **repentance** doesn't mean only asking for forgiveness for these **acts,** these sins; it also means to turn from these **acts**, to leave them completely.

The writer has already written above that **faith in God** is necessary to obtain salvation. Here, **faith in God** means faith in Christ, through whom we receive salvation (Hebrews 5:9).

2 In verse 1, the writer has mentioned two parts of the foundation of our Christian faith: **repentance** and **faith**. Now, in verse 2, he gives four additional parts of this foundation; once we have received **instruction** in these matters, we should not need to be instructed about them again and again.

The four additional parts to the foundation of our faith are: first, BAPTISMS; second, the **laying on of hands**; third, the RESURRECTION **of the dead**; and fourth, **eternal** (or final) JUDGMENT. These four things, in addition to the two things mentioned in verse 1, are the main doctrines of our Christian faith; these things make up the **foundation** for our lives. Once the foundation has been laid, it does not need to be laid again.

The **laying on of hands** has been a

custom in the church from New Testament times up to the present. The laying on of hands is done to impart the Holy Spirit to someone, or to appoint someone to a special task in the church, or to heal the sick (see Acts 6:6; 8:17; 9:12,17; 19:6). The laying on of hands in itself does not magically accomplish these things; rather, the laying on of hands is a confirmation of our faith that the Holy Spirit is accomplishing these works.

3 In verse 1, the writer has said that we should **leave the elementary teachings about Christ** (the six elementary teachings listed in verses 1–2), and **go on to maturity**. Having laid the foundation of our faith, let us not spend time laying it again; rather, let us now build on it. Therefore, says the writer, **God permitting, we will do so**. The writer says, **God permitting**, because everything we are and everything we do is by the permission and the grace of God.

4–6 Here the writer explains why it is pointless to lay the foundation of **elementary teachings** a second time. The reason is this: Once a person has learned these basic teachings—especially the teachings about **repentance** and **faith** (verse 1)—and then after learning them turns away from them, it is impossible for that person **to be brought back to repentance** (verse 6). It is impossible to lay the foundation a second time.

Here in verses 4–6, we see a very important doctrinal teaching. The writer here is describing certain people **who have once been enlightened** (who have seen the light of the Gospel), **who have tasted the heavenly gift** (the blessings of Christ), **who have shared in the Holy Spirit** (verse 4), and **who have tasted the goodness of the word of God and the powers of the coming age** (verse 5). In these verses, the writer certainly seems to be describing people who are true Christians. Nevertheless, the writer says here that such people can deliberately and knowingly abandon their faith. And if they do that—**if they fall away**—there is no hope for them. They cannot **be brought back to repentance**.

What does it mean here to **fall away**? The writer is obviously not talking here about committing small sins, or about wandering briefly out of God's will—which all of us do from time to time. Rather, the writer is talking here about the greatest and most fearful sin of all. That sin is this: to reject God's light after having seen it; to reject Christ after having received Christ's gifts and blessings. Those who do this are **crucifying the Son of God all over again** (verse 6). Such people no longer have a mind to repent. Their hearts have become hardened. God's grace cannot touch them.[11] Such people have committed the sin which cannot be forgiven—that is, the sin of blasphemy against the Holy Spirit, which is mentioned in Mark 3:28–29. The Apostle John calls that sin the **sin that leads to death** (1 John 5:16). Those who reject the salvation offered by Christ will find salvation nowhere else (see Hebrews 10:26–27; 2 Peter 2:20–21). Christ offers hope to the fallen; but to those who have fallen away from Him, He can offer nothing.

Here a question arises: Is it possible for a true Christian to fall away and lose his salvation? Some Christians say it is possible; they point out that the people mentioned in this section who have fallen away once **shared in the Holy Spirit** (verse 4); only true Christians can share in the Holy Spirit.

But other Christians believe that is not possible for a true Christian to lose his salvation. Those who believe this say that here in verses 4–6 the writer of Hebrews is only giving a warning; he is not saying that a true Christian actually can fall away permanently. They say that the writer of Hebrews here is simply admonishing believers who are sinning and whose faith is weak, in order that they might not fall away.

But still another question remains. How can one distinguish between a true

---

[11] Yes, God is able to touch them; He is able to bring them to repentance. God is able to do anything; **all things are possible with God** (Mark 10:27). But God will not touch them; He will not bring to repentance those who have tasted His blessings and then deliberately and knowingly rejected Him.

Christian and a false Christian? In the beginning, it is often impossible to tell them apart. Take, for example, two people who say they believe in Christ, both of whom appear to be true Christians. But then one of them falls away. No one could have known that would happen. In Jesus' parable of the sower, some seed fell **on rocky places** and some seed fell **among thorns**. Initially, just like the seed that fell on good soil, these seeds sprouted and grew rapidly (Mark 4:5–7). It was only after the sun (persecution) and thorns (temptation) came that it was possible to distinguish between the bad soil and the good soil. In the beginning the seeds grew equally well; only later did the seeds planted in the rocky and thorny soil die.

In the same way, only after trials and temptation come upon a man and he falls completely away can we then say of him, "He is not a true Christian." Before that, we must never doubt another man's faith. When times of trial and testing come, the false Christian will fall away. But the true Christian will stand firm, and at the right time (like the seed planted on good soil), he will mature and bear fruit. (see Matthew 7:24–27; 13:24–30 and comments).

It is necessary to add one further thing here. Some Christians act for a time as if they had fallen away. They fall into sin. Their faith withers. But they do not completely fall away. Their inner minds and consciences are burdened; they desire to repent. For such people there is hope. They have not totally rejected Christ. However, their situation is very dangerous; because if they refuse for long to repent, they may lose forever the chance to return to Christ.

Therefore, let us not say: "I can never fall away; I will never fall." Let us remember Paul's words: **So, if you think you are standing firm, be careful that you don't fall** (1 Corinthians 10:12). It is possible for us to reject God's grace and to deny Christ. Only God knows who will stand firm to the end.[12]

7–8 We can distinguish between true and false Christians by their fruit (see Matthew 7:17–20). These fruits are principally the fruits of the Holy Spirit (Galatians 5:22–23). Christ chose us to **bear fruit—fruit that will last** (John 15:16). He did not choose us to bear **thorns and thistles**, which in the end **will be burned** (verse 8).

Some people suppose that bearing fruit means to preach, to prophesy, and to do miracles, and that when we do these things it proves we are true Christians. But that is not so. Satan and his evil spirits can also do these things (Mark 13:22). There is only one kind of true fruit, and that is the fruit that is produced by the Holy Spirit dwelling within us (see Matthew 7:22–23 and comment).

9 The writer has just finished giving these Hebrews a terrible warning. But he now becomes gentler. Here he expresses his confidence that they will not fall away.

10 God will not fail to reward us for the "fruit" we offer to Him—in particular, the fruit of our love and faithfulness.

How did these Hebrews show love to God? They showed their love to Him by helping **his people**—that is, believers. When we do an act of love for any of God's people, we do it also for God (see Matthew 25:34–40).

11–12 The writer wants these Hebrews to continue **to show this same diligence to the very end**—that is, their **diligence** in showing love to God, which the writer mentioned in verse 10. Why does he urge the Hebrews to show their diligence **to the very end**? So that they might **make** [their] **hope sure**. Their **hope** is that they will **inherit what has been promised** (verse 12). If they continue loving God and being faithful to Him to the very end, their hope of receiving their inheritance in heaven will be **sure**; it will be guaranteed (see Mark 13:13; Galatians 6:9; 2 Peter 1:10–11). Only **through faith and patience** will we inherit **what has been promised**—namely, eternal life in heaven. To put it in Paul's words, we must **continue to work out** [our] **salvation with fear and trembling** (Philippians 2:12).

[12] For further discussion, see General Article: Can We Lose Our Salvation?

The Certainty of God's Promise (6:13–20)

13–15 God promised Abraham: "**I will make you into a great nation and I will bless you**" (Genesis 12:2). But at that time Abraham was seventy-five years old, and had no children. Without a son, how could Abraham be the father of a **great nation**?

Abraham had to wait another twenty-five years before he got a son. When he was one hundred years old, Abraham's wife gave birth to a son, Isaac. Thus, through Isaac, the promise God had given to Abraham could now be fulfilled (Genesis 17:15–17; 21:1–3). In this way, **after waiting patiently, Abraham received what was promised** (verse 15).

Then God again tested Abraham's faith. He told Abraham to offer his son Isaac as a sacrifice. That is, God told Abraham to kill this son, for whom he had patiently waited for so long! So Abraham, obeying, made preparations for the sacrifice. Then, when God had seen Abraham's faith and obedience, He at the last moment stopped Abraham from killing his son (see Genesis 22:1–14). And at that time God repeated the promise He had given to Abraham earlier (Genesis 22:15–18). But this time when God made the promise, **he swore by himself, "I will surely bless you and give you many descendants"** (verse 14). The writer here quotes from Genesis 22:16–17.

16–17 God's word is certain. But here God has **confirmed** His word or promise **with an oath** (verse 17). Therefore, God has made His promise to Abraham even more certain! Why did God confirm His promise with an oath? The reason is this: He **wanted to make . . . his purpose clear to the heirs of what was promised**. And who are the **heirs of what was promised**? It is we, who believe in Christ. We are the true spiritual heirs of Abraham through faith (Galatians 3:7,9). The promise that God gave to Abraham is now given to us. We who believe in Christ have been made God's people, God's family. And we shall obtain our full inheritance in heaven.

18 We **who have fled**—fled from evil, from Satan—can **take hold of the hope offered to us**. That **hope** is the hope we have of receiving an inheritance in heaven as Abraham's spiritual heirs. We can take hold of that hope with complete faith. That hope is **firm and secure** (verse 19), because it has been confirmed **by two unchangeable things**—namely, God's word and God's oath. Therefore, we can be **greatly encouraged**.

19 In the midst of trials and troubles—even when death is near—we can take hold of this hope. Our hope is **firm and secure** in God; it is like an **anchor**.

The writer says here that our hope enters the **inner sanctuary behind the curtain**—that is, the place where God is. This **inner sanctuary** was an inner room in the Jewish tabernacle or temple[13] (Hebrews 9:1–3), where the Jews believed God dwelled. Once each year the high priest would enter this room to make atonement for the sins of the people in the presence of God (Hebrews 9:7). Thus, when the writer of Hebrews says that our **hope enters the inner sanctuary**, he means that our hope is fixed on God Himself.

20 Jesus, on our behalf, has gone before us and entered this **inner sanctuary**—that is, heaven. He has ascended into heaven into the presence of God to make atonement for our sins. Jesus has become our true and permanent high priest **in the order of Melchizedek** (Hebrew 5:6,10). Jesus is the high priest on whom our hope is fixed. Jesus is the King, the Son of God, through whom the promise of God to Abraham has been fulfilled. Jesus is our forerunner, our leader, who has gone into heaven before us. He has opened the way for us to enter into the very presence of God (see Hebrews 10:19–22).

---

[13] Before the permanent Jewish temple was built in Jerusalem, the Jews used to worship God in a tabernacle made from a tent, which they took with them wherever they traveled. Both in the tabernacle and later in the temple, there was an **inner sanctuary** called the **Most Holy Place** (Hebrews 9:3). This is the "inner sanctuary" that the writer is referring to in this verse.

CHAPTER 7

Melchizedek the Priest (7:1–10)

1–2 Besides this letter to the Hebrews, the only other places Melchizedek is mentioned in the Bible are in Genesis 14:18–20 and Psalm 110:4. Here the writer bases his description of Melchizedek on the passage from Genesis (see Hebrews 5:6 and comment).

3 Nothing is written in the Bible about Melchizedek's mother and father, or about his birth or death. According to the writer of Hebrews, Melchizedek was never born and never died. . . . **like the Son of God he remains a priest forever**. Just as Jesus has no beginning or end, so Melchizedek has no beginning or end.

4 Melchizedek was greater than Abraham; otherwise, Abraham would not have given him a tenth part of the plunder he had gained in battle with the kings (verses 1–2).

5 **Levi** was one of the twelve sons of Jacob, Abraham's grandson. All Jewish priests were descended from Levi—including Aaron, the first high priest. According to the Jewish law, all other Jews were required every year to give a tenth part of their wealth and their produce to the priests, the descendants of Levi. In this way, the priests made their living. Therefore, the Jews gave a tenth of their income to the priests. The priests (through Levi) and all other Jews were descendants together of Abraham; thus they were all **brothers**.

6–7 But Melchizedek, the **priest of God Most High** (verse 1), was not descended from Levi or Abraham. Nevertheless, Abraham himself, the father of the Jews, gave Melchizedek a tenth part of what he had gained. Not only that, Abraham received a blessing from Melchizedek. From this, we can understand that Melchizedek was greater than Abraham. Therefore, Melchizedek is also greater than the Jewish priests descended from Abraham and Levi.

8 Furthermore, the Jewish priests all died; they were ordinary men. But Melchizedek never died; he always is **declared to be living**.

9–10 **One might even say** that Levi and his descendants, the Jewish priests, who collected a tenth from all the other Jews, had themselves, through Abraham, given a tenth of their income to Melchizedek. Because at the time Abraham met Melchizedek, Levi in a sense **was still in the body of his ancestor** (Abraham).

By writing all of this, the author of this letter has shown that Melchizedek is greater than all the Jewish priests descended from Levi.

Jesus Like Melchizedek (7:11–28)

11 At this point it is necessary to briefly review some early history of the Jewish people. Abraham was the father of Isaac, and Isaac was the father of Jacob. Jacob had twelve sons, from whom the twelve tribes of the Jews are descended.

Levi was the third of Jacob's twelve sons. About four hundred years after Levi's time, Moses was appointed by God to be the leader of the Jews. Moses received from God the Jewish law. At that time, God said that the descendants of Levi were to be the priests of the Jewish people. The writer of Hebrews, therefore, calls this the **Levitical priesthood**. The Jewish law, then, was established on the basis of this priesthood of the descendants of Levi. Moses's younger brother Aaron (also a descendant of Levi) was appointed to be the first high priest.

However, the writer of Hebrews says, this **Levitical priesthood** could not bring about the **perfection** of the Jewish people. That is, it could not make men righteous; it could not bring about their salvation. **If perfection could have been attained through the Levitical priesthood**, there would have been no need for **another priest** (Jesus Christ) **to come—one in the order of Melchizedek**.

12 Not only that, if the Levitical priesthood had to be changed, then the Jewish law also had to be changed, because the law was based on that priesthood.

13–14 **He of whom these things are said**—that is, Christ—**belonged to a different tribe**. Christ was descended from the tribe of **Judah** (Matthew 1:2; Luke 3:33). **Judah** was the fourth of Jacob's twelve sons; thus he was Levi's younger brother. When God gave Moses the law, He said nothing to Moses about priests being appointed from the tribe of **Judah**. Therefore, from these facts, we can understand that Christ's priesthood is completely different from the Levitical priesthood of the Old Testament.

15–16 Christ's priesthood is **not on the basis of a regulation as to his ancestry** or bodily descent, as the Levitical priesthood was (verse 16). Christ's priesthood is based on the **power** of His **indestructible life**. The Levitical priests lived and died in turn. But Christ lives forever. The Levitical priesthood was based on outward rules and regulations; but Christ's priesthood is based on His inner spiritual **power**.

17 The writer again quotes from Psalm 110:4 to show that Christ's priesthood will never end.

18 **The former regulation is set aside because it was weak and useless.** That **former regulation** is the Jewish ceremonial law, which consisted of many rules concerning the Levitical priesthood and such things as offerings, sacrifices, purification rites, and religious festivals. When Christ came, all these rules—that is, the ceremonial part of the Jewish law—were **set aside**, or canceled (see Matthew 5:17–18; Colossians 2:13–14 and comments).

19 Why was the Jewish law **weak and useless**—especially its ceremonial part? (verse 18). Because **the law made nothing perfect**. The law could purify the outside of the body, but it could not purify the inside of the body—that is, man's heart and conscience. The law could not make a man righteous; it could only condemn him (see Romans 8:1–3 and comment).

The **better hope** mentioned here is Jesus Christ, our true and permanent high priest, through whom we can **draw near to God**.

Unrighteous men cannot draw near to God. But through faith we can receive Christ's righteousness; and having received His righteousness, we can then come into God's presence. Therefore, men receive a **better hope** from Christ than they receive from the Old Jewish law or Levitical priesthood.

20–21 When God appointed Christ to be high priest, He made an **oath** confirming it. To show this, the writer again quotes from Psalm 110:4.

22 **Because of this oath**, Christ's priesthood is better than the Levitical priesthood. Therefore, He is the **guarantee of a better** COVENANT (see Hebrews 8:6 and comment).

23–24 From the time of the first high priest Aaron to the time of the writing of this letter, there had been eighty-three high priests. These all died in turn. But Jesus will never die; therefore, His priesthood is **permanent**.

25 Jesus **always lives to intercede** for us (see Romans 8:34). Jesus is our advocate, our lawyer, before the throne of God. And because He is a perfect high priest, God listens to Him. Not only that, Jesus has made atonement for our sins (Hebrews 2:17). God now no longer condemns us. Furthermore, Jesus gives us **mercy and . . . grace to help us in our time of need** (Hebrews 4:16). And Jesus will not stop doing all this for us, because His priesthood is never-ending. He is seated forever at the right hand of God; He is always ready to bring us into God's presence. For all these reasons, Jesus **is able to save** (us) **completely**. Let us never cease praising and thanking God for such a Savior and High Priest!

26 The writer of this letter keeps thinking of new things to say about Jesus, this wonderful high priest. Jesus is **holy, blameless, pure . . . exalted above the heavens**. Jesus' priesthood is perfect, because Jesus Himself is perfect (see Hebrews 1:3; 4:15–16).

27 Jesus never had to offer a sacrifice for His own sins, as the Jewish priests had to do (Leviticus 4:3; 16:6; Hebrews 5:1,3).

Furthermore, Jesus doesn't need to offer sacrifices for our sins over and over, as the Jewish priests did (Leviticus 16:34). Jesus' sacrifice—that is, the sacrifice of His body—was fully pleasing to God. Jesus made Himself an offering for sin. Because His sacrifice was perfect, it never has to be repeated.

What a sacrifice! Jesus sacrificed His life to give salvation to all men and women. Jesus came into the world **to give his life as a ransom for many** (Mark 10:45). And on the last night before He died, He said to His disciples: "**This is my blood of the covenant, which is poured out for many**" (Mark 14:24). This is why we testify that we have received salvation through Jesus' death, through His blood.

28 The writer here adds one final thing about Jesus. Jesus is the **Son**, God's own Son. According to the law, the Jewish high priests had to be men, men who were, of course, weak and sinful themselves. But the great high priest appointed by God's **oath** (verse 21) is God's own Son, **who has been made perfect forever**.

CHAPTER 8

The High Priest of a New Covenant (8:1–13)

1–2 The Jewish priests ministered in a **sanctuary** made by men. But Jesus serves in the **true tabernacle set up by the Lord**—a tabernacle which is in heaven at the right hand of God. The Jewish priesthood was of the world; Jesus' priesthood is of heaven. It is a spiritual priesthood.

3 Priests of the world are appointed **to offer both gifts and sacrifices**. In order to come into the presence of God, the Jewish high priest had to present an offering to God. Jesus also needed to offer something to God. Therefore, He offered up His own body.

4 According to the Jewish law and according to His ancestry, Jesus could never have been a Jewish priest. He was not of the tribe of Levi, from which all Jewish priests came. But Jesus' priesthood is not of this world; it is of heaven.

5 The Jewish priests ministered in a **sanctuary**[14] made by men. However, that earthly sanctuary was not the true sanctuary; it was only the **copy and shadow** of the true sanctuary which is in heaven.

At the time the ancient Jews were building the first sanctuary in the Sinai desert, God gave this command to their leader Moses: "**. . . make everything according to the pattern shown you on the mountain**"—that is, according to the pattern of the heavenly sanctuary. The writer quotes this command from Exodus 25:40.

Worldly men suppose that the only real and true things are the things which they can see or feel. They think that heavenly things are only imaginary and don't really exist. But the man who is spiritual knows that this world is passing away. He knows that only heavenly and spiritual things are ulitmately real and lasting. This is why the writer says here that the earthly sanctuary built by the

---

[14] The first Jewish **sanctuary**—or **tabernacle**—was a tent, which the ancient Jews moved from place to place wherever they went. Only after the Jews entered the promised land of Israel did they build a permanent tabernacle—that is, the great temple in Jerusalem.

Jews is only a **copy and shadow** of the heavenly sanctuary built by Jesus.

6 In Chapter 7 and in the first five verses of this chapter, the writer has shown that Jesus' priesthood is superior to the Jewish priesthood. Now the writer adds something new to his thoughts above. He says that Jesus is the **mediator** of a new **covenant**, a covenant which is **founded on better promises**. Just as Jesus' ministry is superior to the ministry of the Jewish priests, so the new covenant is superior to the old covenant.

What is that old covenant? A covenant is a formal agreement between two parties. According to the old covenant, God agreed to make the descendants of Abraham (the Jews) His own special people and to bless them (Genesis 12:1–3). That was God's part of the agreement. The Jews' part was to obey God's law (Exodus 19:5; Jeremiah 7:23). If the Jews did not obey, the covenant would be canceled.

The old covenant was not successful, because the Jews stopped obeying God (Jeremiah 7:24–26). The Jews did not remain faithful to their agreement; therefore, God **turned away from them** (verse 9). Under the old covenant, the Jews had neither the strength nor the will to obey God. They were unable to find freedom from the bondage of sin. Even though the Jewish priests every year offered sacrifices for the sins of the people, the people could not become pure and righteous in their hearts. Therefore, as a result of their impurity and unholiness, they could not come into the presence of God.

The new covenant between man and God is the covenant of Jesus Christ. The writer calls Jesus the **mediator** of this new covenant. Jesus stands between man and God. It is through Jesus that we receive the new covenant promises given by God. God says: "If you believe in Jesus, I will give you salvation, eternal life" (see John 3:16). God has promised to give us salvation, eternal life, the Holy Spirit, and adoption into His family; that's His part. Our part is only this: to believe in His Son Jesus.

The writer here says that the new covenant is **founded on better promises**, promises given by God to those who believe in Jesus. The writer mentions three of these **better promises** below, in a quotation from the prophet Jeremiah. The first of these promises of God is this: **"I will put my laws in their minds and write them on their hearts"** (verse 10). The second promise is: **". . . they will all know me, from the least of them to the greatest"** (verse 11). The third promise is: **"I will forgive their wickedness and will remember their sins no more"** (verse 12). In brief, the meaning of these three promises taken together is this: God makes each believer in Christ a **new creation** (2 Corinthians 5:17). He sends His Holy Spirit to dwell within each believer's heart. God said: **"I will give them an undivided heart and put a new spirit in them; I will remove from them their heart of stone and give them a heart of flesh. Then they will follow my decrees and be careful to keep my laws. They will be my people, and I will be their God"** (Ezekiel 11:19–20).

Therefore, the "new covenant" between man and God is as follows. God gives us the promise of eternal life in heaven. Together with that, He gives us a new spirit, by which we are enabled to overcome sin and to recognize Him and to love and obey Him. For the covenant to be fulfilled, only one thing is necessary: a person must believe in Christ. Truly, this new covenant is far superior to the old covenant!

7 If nothing had been **wrong** with that **first covenant** (old covenant), there would have been no need to make a new covenant.

8 But there was something "wrong" with that first covenant:[15] the Jews did not remain faithful; they did not fulfill their part of the covenant.

In verses 8–12, the writer of Hebrews quotes God's words as written down by the prophet Jeremiah in Jeremiah 31:31–

[15] It wasn't actually the covenant itself that was "wrong"; it was the Jews who were wrong. In verse 8, the writer says: **God found fault with the people**.

34. God says: **"I will make a new covenant with the house of ISRAEL and with the house of Judah."** In Jeremiah's time, the nation of Israel (the Jewish nation) was divided into two kingdoms: **Israel** in the north, and **Judah** in the south. Thus from this verse we can understand that God's new covenant is meant for "both kingdoms"—that is, for all true descendants of Abraham through faith. The true descendants of Abraham are all those who put their faith in Jesus Christ (see Galatians 3:7–9 and comment).

9–10 The new covenant is not like the old covenant. The old covenant was written on two stone tablets (Exodus 31:18). The new covenant is written on men's hearts. Men did not have the power to obey and remain faithful to the old covenant. But under the new covenant, men receive the Holy Spirit, who gives them the power and the desire to obey God. We can now say with the Psalmist: **"I desire to do your will, O my God; your law is within my heart"** (Psalm 40:8).

11 The Jews taught one another about God and His word according to what was written in the Old Testament. But under the new covenant, each believer knows God personally through the Holy Spirit dwelling within him. Just as children know their human fathers, so we believers can know our heavenly Father. Jesus Himself said that to know God in this way is to have eternal life (John 17:3).

12 Under the new covenant, our sins are forgiven; they are erased completely. Through Christ's perfect sacrifice of His own body, we have been made pure. Having been made pure, we can now enter God's presence. Only through Christ can man be made holy and acceptable in God's sight. In this way Christ is the **mediator** of the new covenant (Hebrews 9:15).

13 Thus, from what is written in verses 8–12, we can now see what this new covenant is like. It is a covenant of the Holy Spirit written on men's hearts. This is why Paul calls himself and his fellow apostles **ministers of a new covenant—not of the letter but of the Spirit** (2 Corinthians 3:6). And if a new covenant has come, the old covenant is now **obsolete** and will soon pass away. The old covenant is like the light of a candle; when the sun rises, it is no longer needed.

The old covenant was confirmed by the shedding of blood (Exodus 24:8). In the same way, the new covenant was also confirmed by the shedding of blood—Jesus' blood. This is why Jesus, at His last supper, took the cup and said to His disciples: **"This is my blood of the covenant, which is poured out for many. . . . This cup is the new covenant in my blood"** (Mark 14:24; Luke 22:20).

CHAPTER 9

Worship in the Earthly Tabernacle (9:1–10)

1–3 After God had delivered the Jews from bondage in Egypt, He established His first covenant with them (Exodus 24:7–8). Then He commanded them to build a **sanctuary** or **tabernacle** (Exodus 25:8–9). This tabernacle was a large tent; the tent contained two rooms which were divided by a curtain. One room was called the **Holy Place**, and the other was called the **Most Holy Place** (Exodus 26:33). In the Holy Place was placed the **lampstand** (Exodus 25:31), the **table** (Exodus 25:23), and the **consecrated bread** (Exodus 25:30).

4–5 In these verses, the writer describes the second room, the **Most Holy Place**. In this room was the **golden altar of incense** (Exodus 30:1) and the **ark of the covenant** (Exodus 25:10). Inside the **ark** was placed the **gold jar of manna** (Exodus 16:31–33), **Aaron's rod that had budded** (Numbers 17:1–5,8,10–11), and the two **stone tablets of the covenant**, on which God had written His law and commandments (Exodus 24:12; 25:16;

31:18). Above the ark were the **cherubim of the Glory** (Exodus 25:18), which were symbols of God's glory. The **place of atonement** was actually the lid of the ark, on which the high priest sprinkled the blood of the sacrificed animals offered to atone for the people's sins (Exodus 25:17,22).

6–7 God appeared in the Most Holy Place once a year to meet with the high priest. Only the high priest could enter into the presence of God, and then only on one special day each year, the day of atonement (Leviticus 16:2). At that time the high priest had to first offer a sacrifice to atone for his own sins (Leviticus 16:6). After that he offered a second sacrifice to atone for the sins of all the people (Leviticus 16:9). Thus, each time the high priest entered the Most Holy Place to meet with God, he brought with him the blood of sacrificed animals (Leviticus 16:14–15). The sacrifices of the high priest were not permanently effective, because they had to be repeated every year.

The high priest offered sacrifices only for the **sins the people had committed in ignorance** (verse 7). According to the Old Testament, there was no sacrifice or forgiveness possible for sins committed knowingly (see Hebrews 10:26 and comment).

8 From what is written above we can see that, except for the high priest, the way into the Most Holy Place—into God's presence—was closed to the Jews. As long as the **first tabernacle was still standing**—that is, as long as the old covenant was still in effect—the way into God's presence remained closed. But when Christ came into the world, He sacrificed His own body and entered God's presence bringing His own blood (verse 12). By doing this, He atoned for the sins of all believers, and opened the way for them to enter directly into God's presence.

9–10 The sacrifices and offerings of the old covenant could not purify the heart or **clear the conscience** of the worshiper. Without a clear conscience, no one can draw near to God. Only through Christ's sacrifice and through the Holy Spirit dwelling within us can our consciences be cleared, cleansed.

Therefore, these **external regulations** of the old covenant remained in effect only **until the time of the new order** (verse 10)—that is, until the time of the new covenant mediated by Jesus Christ. When the new covenant came, the old covenant was no longer needed (see Hebrews 8:13).

The Blood of Christ (9:11–22)

11 Christ came to this world to be the high priest of the **good things that are already here**—that is, the new covenant (see Hebrews 8:1,6 and comment).

God does not dwell in a sanctuary made by men (Acts 7:48; 17:24). He dwells in a **greater and more perfect tabernacle** in heaven. Jesus is the high priest of that heavenly tabernacle. When Jesus came to earth He, in a sense, destroyed the man-made Old Testament tabernacle, and in its place prepared a true heavenly tabernacle, where men worship God **in spirit and truth** (see Mark 14:58; John 4:21,23–24).

12 To enter God's presence, it is necessary to sprinkle the blood of animals, which have been sacrificed to atone for sin. Therefore, the Jewish high priest brought the **blood of goats and calves** into the Most Holy Place with him (verse 7). But Jesus entered God's presence bringing His own blood. Jesus' sacrifice was perfect; thus it never needs to be repeated. And through His sacrifice, we believers obtain **eternal** REDEMPTION, or salvation.

13 The blood and ashes of animals cleanse a person only **outwardly**, or **ceremonially**. The **ashes of a heifer** mentioned in this verse is a reference to Numbers 19:9.

The Jews placed great importance on outward cleanliness. But Jesus taught that inward cleanliness was much more important (see Mark 7:20–23). The blood and ashes of animals can never make a person inwardly clean and pure.

14 The blood of Christ, however, can do what the blood of animals could never do; it can cleanse our consciences from **acts that lead to death**—that is, from sins.

And the reason Christ cleanses us is so that we can **serve the living God**.

Under the old covenant, God said that the animals sacrificed had to be **unblemished**. Now under the new covenant, Jesus Christ Himself is the sinless, **unblemished** sacrifice.

15 Through Christ's death, believers have been set free from their former sins; they have been forgiven. Because Christ has died, He has become the **mediator of a new covenant**, through which we who are called **may receive the promised eternal inheritance**. That "eternal inheritance" is forgiveness of sins, salvation, eternal life (see Hebrews 7:27; 8:6 and comments). The old covenant could not set men free from sin. Now through Jesus' death, we have been set free (see Romans 8:1–2).

16–17 In order for a **will**[16] to go into effect, the person who made the will has to die. In the same way, it was only after Christ's death that the new "will" or covenant could go into effect.

18–20 For the old "will" or covenant to go into effect, there also had to be death—the death of an animal (see Exodus 24:8).

The **scarlet wool and branches of hyssop**[17] mentioned in verse 19 are also mentioned in Numbers 19:6.

21–22 Only by shedding blood could the Jewish high priest make atonement for his own sins and the sins of the people. Thus God had instructed that everything inside the tabernacle be sprinkled with blood (see Leviticus 16:14–16,18–19).

In the same way, under the new covenant, men can receive forgiveness only through the shedding of blood. That is why Christ had to shed His own blood and die in order to cleanse us from sins.

Christ's Incomparable Sacrifice (9:23–28)

23 The **copies of the heavenly things**—that is, the earthly tabernacle—were purified **with these** (animal) **sacrifices**. But the heavenly tabernacle has been purified **with better sacrifices**—namely, Christ Himself.

In one way, we believers are this heavenly tabernacle (see Ephesians 2:22; 1 Peter 2:5). We too, being God's dwelling place, must be purified **with better sacrifices**. And indeed, we have been purified by Christ's perfect sacrifice. We have been set free from sin; we have been redeemed **with the precious blood of Christ** (1 Peter 1:18–19).

24 Here the writer repeats the thoughts of Hebrews 8:1–2.

25–26 Christ's sacrifice never needs to be repeated. Through His death, Christ has once for all atoned for our sins (verse 26).

27–28 A man dies only once; therefore, it is impossible for Christ to be sacrificed again and again. His one-time sacrifice is sufficient **to take away the sins of many people** (see John 1:29 and comment).

Man's death is followed by **judgment**. Jesus' death is followed, not by judgment, but by eternal salvation for all **who are waiting for him**—that is, all believers. Jesus will come again. On that day we shall obtain our full inheritance in heaven, which He has promised to us. Therefore, let us not grow weary, but let us continue to persevere with patience and faith (see Hebrews 6:12).

---

[16] In the Greek language, the same word is used for both **will** and covenant.

[17] Hyssop is a type of plant. It was used to sprinkle blood or water.

CHAPTER 10

Christ's Sacrifice Once for All (10:1–18)

1 The Jewish **law** together with the old covenant are only the **shadow of the good things that are coming** (see Hebrews 8:5). These **good things** are Christ's sacrifice, His priesthood, and the salvation and eternal life He has provided for us.

The Jewish law and its **sacrifices repeated endlessly**, which are "shadows" of the new covenant, could not **make perfect** or inwardly cleanse the **worshipers**—that is, those drawing near to God to worship (see Hebrews 9:9).

2 The proof that the law and its sacrifices couldn't cleanse the worshipers is this: after offering a sacrifice, the worshipers still **felt guilty for their sins**; their consciences continued to accuse them. Their consciences could not be cleansed. Therefore, these sacrifices had to be repeated over and over.

An unclean or guilty conscience keeps a person from coming to God. The psalmist has written: **If I had cherished sin in my heart, the Lord would not have listened** (Psalm 66:18).

Through the sacrifice of Christ's body, the consciences of those who believe in Him have been cleansed once for all. Jesus said to His disciples: "**A person who has had a bath needs only to wash his feet; his whole body is clean. And you are clean**" (John 13:10). Paul wrote to the Corinthians: **But you were washed, you were sanctified, you were justified in the name of the Lord Jesus Christ and by the Spirit of our God** (1 Corinthians 6:11). This washing or cleansing takes place at the beginning of our Christian lives. The sign of this cleansing is our baptism.

3–4 The sacrifices of the old covenant could not **take away sins** (verse 4). Such sacrifices only reminded the Jews of their sins. But under the new covenant God says: "**I . . . will remember their sins no more**" (Jeremiah 31:34; Hebrews 8:12). When our sins are taken away and forgotten, then our consciences will be truly clean.

King David knew that sacrifices and offerings could not cleanse the conscience. He cried out to God: "**Have mercy on me, O God . . . blot out my transgressions. Wash away all my iniquity and cleanse me from my sin. . . . Create in me a pure heart, O God. . . . You do not delight in sacrifice . . . you do not take pleasure in burnt offerings. The sacrifices of God are a broken spirit; a broken and contrite heart, O God, you will not despise**" (Psalm 51:1–2,10,16–17).

5–7 The writer of Hebrews here quotes from Psalm 40:6–8. Here we again read that God did not desire sacrifices and offerings. What He desired was a body—not the body of a dumb animal, but the body of a man offered to God in complete obedience. Therefore, God **prepared** a body for Christ (verse 5). When Christ in complete obedience offered up His own body as a living sacrifice, God was pleased. Christ said, "**I have come to do your will, O God**" (verse 7). Christ's obedience was what God desired most of all. The Old Testament prophet Samuel said: "**Does the Lord delight in burnt offerings and sacrifices as much as in obeying the voice of the Lord? To obey is better than sacrifice, and to heed is better than the fat of rams**" (1 Samuel 15:22).

The **scroll** mentioned in verse 7 is the Old Testament, which contains many prophecies concerning Christ. Christ Himself was the fulfillment of all these prophecies. In the Old Testament, God's will is explained. And in Christ's life, God's will was perfectly fulfilled.

8–9 When Christ came to offer Himself as the perfect and final sacrifice, He "set aside" the **first** covenant in order to establish the **second** covenant (verse 9).

10 **And by that will**—that is, by fulfilling God's will—Christ, through the sacrifice of His body, has made us holy both inside and out. God's will was that Christ should offer His own body to atone for our sins, and that through His sacrifice we might be presented before God having been made **holy in his sight, without blemish and free from accusation** (Colossians 1:21–22).

11–12 The writer here repeats the thoughts of Hebrews 1:3; 7:27; 9:25–26. The priests of the old covenant had to offer sacrifices again and again. They could never come and sit down in the presence of God. Their work was never finished. But Christ has not only sat down in God's presence; He has sat down on a throne at God's right hand. God has raised Jesus up from a shameful death on the cross and has exalted Him to the **highest place** of glory (see Philippians 2:8–9).

13 See Hebrews 1:13 and comment.

14 In verse 10, the writer says that **we have been made holy through the sacrifice of the body of Jesus Christ**. Here in verse 14, the writer says that **by one sacrifice he has made perfect forever those who are being made holy**. The writer's meaning is this: We have been justified (declared righteous) in God's sight (Romans 5:1); Christ's work is finished. All who believe in Him have been made perfect forever.

Why, then, does the writer say in verse 14 that we are still **being made holy**? The reason is this. Even though all that has been written above is completely true, we in this present life have not yet become fully holy or perfect. From time to time we sin. God wants us to increase in holiness. He wants to make us holy in this life. Therefore, we can understand that in one way we have already been made holy and perfect for all eternity; but, in another way, we must continue growing in holiness in our daily behavior here on earth (see Philippians 1:6; 2:12–13 and comments).

15–18 The writer here again quotes from Jeremiah 31:33–34 (see Hebrews 8:10,12–13 and comment). Notice that now the **Holy Spirit** is speaking through Jeremiah (verse 15). We must understand that every word in the Bible is God's word spoken through the Holy Spirit.

In repeating these verses from Jeremiah, the writer of Hebrews wants to show that the new covenant is final and complete. God's law is now written in men's minds and on their hearts. Their sins are remembered no more. And where sins are forgotten, there is no longer any need for sacrifices (verse 18).

A New and Living Way (10:19–25)

19 Now a very important part of this letter has come. In the first nine chapters, the writer of Hebrews has described the old and new covenants, the old and new priesthoods, the old sacrifices of animals and the new sacrifice of Jesus' body. Now what are we to understand from all this?

Therefore—because of all that is written above—**since we have confidence to enter the Most Holy Place**[18] **. . . let us draw near to God with a sincere heart in full assurance of faith** (verse 22). We don't have to wait until after we die to draw near to God; through faith we can come into His presence right now.

Let us think for a moment about the first word in this verse: **Therefore**. In the New Testament, many important statements follow the word "therefore." (Good examples are found in Romans 5:1 and 8:1.) God is holy; "therefore," He will render judgment against sin. God is merciful; "therefore," He is ready to forgive our sins. Christ is our righteousness; "therefore," through faith we have been declared righteous. Christ has freed us from the law of sin and death; "therefore," we are no longer under condemnation (Romans 8:1). Christ is our great high priest, through whose perfect sacrifice of Himself we are made perfect forever; "therefore," we can now **enter the Most Holy Place by** [His] **blood**. We have become God's children; "therefore," just as children can go to

[18] In place of the words **Most Holy Place**, some translations of the Bible say "sanctuary." But here we must understand that the writer is talking about the Most Holy Place, because the way into that room goes **through the curtain**—that is, the curtain dividing the "Most Holy Place" from the "Holy Place" (see Hebrews 9:3).

their earthly fathers with **confidence**, so we believers can draw near to our heavenly Father with **confidence** (see Hebrews 4:16).

In what other religion, through what other priesthood, through what other Savior, can weak and sinful men be made righteous and come into God's presence as His children? There is no way this is possible except through faith in Jesus Christ.

In verse 10, the writer says that **we have been made holy through the sacrifice of the body of Jesus Christ**. Here and in verse 29, he says that we are made holy **by the blood of Jesus**. In both instances, the writer is saying the same thing: namely, that through Jesus' death and sacrifice we are made holy and righteous. At the time Jesus offered Himself as a sacrifice, His body was broken and His blood was shed. Both Jesus' body and His blood are important for us. At the last supper, Jesus said to His disciples: "**This is my body given for you. . . . This cup is the new covenant in my blood** (Luke 22:19–20). On another occasion, Jesus said to His followers: ". . . **unless you eat the flesh of the Son of Man and drink his blood, you have no life in you. Whoever eats my flesh and drinks my blood has eternal life**" (John 6:53–54). Just as under the old covenant there was no forgiveness **without the shedding of blood** (Hebrews 9:22), so under the new covenant it was necessary for Jesus not only to die but also to shed His blood in order to make us holy.

20 How can we enter the **Most Holy Place**? Jesus has opened up for us a **new and living way** into God's presence. This way is **living**, because Jesus Himself is **living**. Jesus said: "**I am the way and the truth and the life. No one comes to the Father except through me**" (John 14:6). Jesus' body was like the curtain that hung between the Holy Place and the Most Holy Place (Hebrews 9:3). We can say that Jesus stood between man and God—between men outside the curtain and God inside the curtain. Thus, when Jesus died, **the curtain of the temple was torn in two from top to bottom** (Mark 15:37–38). The way into God's presence was now fully opened. Not only did Jesus enter into God's presence (Hebrews 6:19–20), but we also, having been cleansed by His sacrifice and having received His righteousness through faith, can now enter God's presence.

21–22 Here the heavenly sanctuary or tabernacle is called the **house of God**. We believers are God's house (Hebrews 3:6). Christ is both the Son and the **great priest** in God's house.

Through faith in Christ, we have received full rights as children of God. We also have become sons and heirs (Galatians 4:4–5,7). Therefore, we can draw near to God. But even though we are God's children, we must go to God **with a sincere heart** and **in full assurance of faith**. Without faith, even God's children cannot please their Father (see Hebrews 11:6).

A **sincere heart** is a heart that has been cleansed and purified. Only the **pure in heart** will get to see God (Matthew 5:8). Jesus our high priest has cleansed us **from a guilty conscience** (see Hebrews 9:14). Our hearts have been **sprinkled** (verse 22); that is, our hearts have been cleansed through the blood of Jesus.

Not only our hearts have been cleansed; **our bodies**, too, have been washed—**washed with pure water** (see 1 Corinthians 6:11). This bodily or outward "washing" occurs at our baptism.[19] Thus, through Christ, we have been made clean both outwardly (ceremonially) and also inwardly (spiritually).

23 Again the writer of Hebrews exhorts us to **hold unswervingly to the hope we profess**—that is, to stand firm in the faith we profess (see Hebrews 3:14). Let us not waver. God never wavers. Man's promises may fail, but God's promises are sure. God is **faithful** to fulfill His word. Therefore, since our **hope** is placed on the sure promises of a faithful God, we have no reason to waver.

24 If anyone begins to waver

[19] Baptism is not only a "washing" of the body with water; it is also a spiritual cleansing. For further discussion, see General Article: Water Bap

be quick to encourage and strengthen him. Let us **spur** each other toward **love and good deeds**. Let us see that no one among us falls back. Together we are strong, but alone we are weak.

25 Some of these Hebrew believers had stopped meeting together. Let this not happen among us. Only by meeting together in fellowship can we encourage and strengthen one another.

There are many reasons why Christians stop meeting together. In some countries, it may be fear of government authorities that keeps Christians from meeting. Others may stop meeting because of ill feelings toward other believers. Some may refuse to meet together because of pride; they think they don't need the fellowship and support of others. Sometimes we don't go to church because of some sin in our lives. We know that we cannot continue in sin and at the same time have true fellowship with other believers, so we choose to give up the fellowship instead of our sin. Our conscience is unclean; we find it hard to look into our brother's face. All these reasons for avoiding fellowship are wrong reasons, sinful reasons. Therefore, we should never give up meeting together for any of these reasons.

. . . **but let us encourage one another—and all the more as you see the Day approaching**. The **Day** is the day of Christ's second coming. The Hebrews expected that **Day** to come quickly. They were suffering persecution; but they hoped that their suffering would not last long, and that Christ would return soon. Therefore, the writer says to them: Do not be discouraged; in a little while your suffering will end.

Let us also have that same mind. We do not know what day Christ will return; but we must remain firm in faith until He comes, so that we will not lose our inheritance in heaven (see verses 35–36).

Sin Committed Knowingly (10:26–31)

26–27 If we **deliberately keep on sinning**,[20] Christ's sacrifice is no longer of any benefit to us; **no sacrifice for sins is left** (verse 26). Because, according to verse 29, when we keep on sinning in this way without repentance, we trample the **Son of God under foot**; we **treat as an unholy thing the blood of the covenant**—that is, we despise His sacrifice for us; we **insult the** (Holy) **Spirit of grace**, through whom we have received all the blessings of Christ (see Mark 3:29 and comment). If we do all this, we have, in fact, completely given up our faith in Christ. And if we give up our faith in Christ, our salvation is lost. But it's possible that anyone who does all this never had true faith to begin with (see 1 John 3:6).

The writer of Hebrews is not talking here about those sins we do from time to time, and afterwards repent of. Because this kind of sin God is ready to forgive quickly and erase from memory (see 1 John 1:9 and comment). Instead, the writer is here talking about those sins which we continue doing deliberately without repentance (see Hebrew 6:4–6 and comment). The man who sins in this way surely has no true faith.

28 According to the Old Testament, those who rejected the **law of Moses** (the Jewish law) received the death sentence (Deuteronomy 17:2–7). Their physical bodies were put to death.

29 But how much more severe will be the punishment of those who reject Christ after having **received a knowledge of the truth**! (verse 26). If after having "accepted" Christ we then reject Him, we shall receive not only physical death but also spiritual death for all eternity.

30 The writer here quotes from Deuteronomy 32:35–36. If in the course of deliberately sinning we cease to believe, our "faith" will no longer protect us. God will **repay** us. **The Lord will judge his people**. He will separate true

---

[20] In place of the words **keep on sinning**, some versions of the Bible only say "sin." However, the meaning of the Greek text is **keep on sinning**. The writer of Hebrews is talking here about a person who knowingly continues in sin without repentance.

believers from false believers. If we, having once been counted among His people, afterward fall away, we shall in no way escape God's judgment (Hebrews 3:12).

31 **It is a dreadful thing to fall into the hands of the living God.** This verse is not written primarily for non-believers; rather, it is written primarily for those who first "believe" and then later fall away. We always like to talk about the love and mercy of God. But we must also keep in mind that God shows no love or mercy to those who deliberately keep sinning against Him and who persist in rejecting His Son Jesus.

A Call to Persevere (10:32–39)

32 When we first become Christians, we are usually filled with enthusiasm, zeal, and courage. If trouble comes on us because of our faith, we are ready to bear it with joy. We happily stand our ground in the **great contest** with Satan. These Hebrews were like that (see Matthew 5:11–12; Acts 5:41).

33 These Hebrews had been **publicly exposed to insult and persecution**. When some of them suffered, the others came and stood with them; they didn't run away and hide. If one brother was persecuted, they were all ready to be persecuted (see 1 Corinthians 12:26).

34 In New Testament times, prisoners in jail often starved to death. They relied on the help of friends and relatives to survive. But it was very risky for a believer to go and visit another Christian in jail, because frequently the visiting believer was also put in jail. Nevertheless, these Hebrews had not abandoned their brothers in prison. They remembered the words of Jesus: "**I was in prison, and you came to visit me. . . . I tell you the truth, whatever you did for one of the least of these brothers of mine, you did for me**" (Matthew 25:34–40).

Because their enemies were numerous and powerful, some of these Hebrew Christians had lost their land, their possessions, their family inheritance. Yet they had joyfully accepted this loss because they knew that they had **better and lasting possessions** in heaven (see Romans 8:18; 2 Corinthians 4:17–18).

But now what had happened to these Hebrews? Their initial zeal was beginning to cool. Now they had started to run from suffering. They had begun again to love their possessions. They were no longer so willing to suffer for Jesus' sake.

Is this situation also true in our church today? Has our initial love for Jesus cooled off? Brothers and sisters, let this not be! Listen to the words of Jesus: "**You have persevered and have endured hardships for my name, and have not grown weary. Yet I hold this against you: You have forsaken your first love. Remember the height from which you have fallen! Repent and do the things you did at first. If you do not repent, I will come to you and remove your lampstand from its place**" (Revelation 2:3–5).

35 Therefore, says the writer: **Remember those earlier days** (verse 32). In those days you showed courage. **So do not throw away your confidence.**

36 God has promised to reward us. But we must persevere, and we must continue to do the will of God with perseverance until the end; otherwise, we shall lose our reward. We shall lose **what he has promised.**

37–38 The writer here quotes from Habakkuk 2:3–4. **He who is coming**—that is, Christ—**will come and will not delay** (see 2 Peter 3:8–9). In verse 38, **my righteous one** is the believer in Christ who remains firm in persecution, who lives **by faith**. But **if he shrinks back**, God will not be pleased with him.

39 Therefore, let us not shrink back. Because if we do, we not only will lose our reward (verse 36); we will also be **destroyed** (see Mark 8:35; 13:13; Luke 21:19).

CHAPTER 11

Men of Faith—Abel to Abraham (11:1–16)

1–2 Men have faith in two kinds of things: things **we hope for**—that is, future things; and things **we do not see**. The main invisible thing that men put faith in is, of course, God Himself. And the main thing we hope for is the fulfillment of God's promises.

If we see something with our eyes, we are sure that thing is true. In the same way, through faith we can be sure that something is true even though we cannot see it. It is the same with future things, like promises. These also are invisible things. Yet, through faith, we can know that a particular promise will be fulfilled.

Therefore, faith is the assurance and certainty that invisible things are true and that future things will come true.

But that is not all. The proof of true faith is its fruit, that is, good works and obedience. If we say we have faith in God, we must do what He says. All the men of faith that are listed below showed proof of their faith by their actions. Faith without works is a dead faith, a false faith (see James 2:14,17,20–24 and comment).

The men of faith listed in this chapter are mentioned in the order they appeared in history. In each case, the faith these men had was faith in God. God promised, and they believed. God commanded, and they obeyed. Through these men of faith, God fulfilled His purposes for Israel, the Jewish nation. Therefore, in this chapter, the writer of Hebrews gives us a brief history of the Jews from the beginning right up until the time of Christ. In this way, the writer has given us an outline of the Old Testament.

By the examples of the faithful men mentioned in this chapter, the writer wants to show us that in order to receive God's promises and God's power there is one thing necessary above all: namely, faith.

3 But before the writer begins talking about these men of faith, he thinks about God and His creation. Just as we can "see" through faith what cannot be seen with our eyes, so God created the **universe** (or world) from what is invisible. God did not create the universe from any material substance; He created everything by His **command** alone. Before God spoke, there was nothing. He spoke, and the creation came into being (Genesis 1:3,9,11,24).

When we look at the earth and the heavens, we cannot understand everything about them. Our eyes cannot tell who made the earth and sun and stars. But by faith we can tell. By faith we know that everything visible was made by an invisible God.

4 **Abel** and **Cain** were the sons of the first man Adam (Genesis 4:1–2). Abel's sacrifice was better than Cain's, because Abel was righteous and Cain was not (Genesis 4:3–7; 1 John 3:12). **The Lord detests the sacrifice of the wicked, but the prayer of the upright pleases him** (Proverbs 15:8).

By faith [Abel] **was commended as a righteous man**; that is, because of Abel's faith in God, God declared him to be righteous. In the Bible, faith and righteousness always go together; they can never be separated. By faith Abel was declared righteous; therefore, his sacrifice was acceptable and pleasing to God.

Cain then killed his brother Abel out of anger and jealousy. But Abel, in a way, is still speaking. His blood **cries out . . . from the ground** for vindication (Genesis 4:10). And by his example of righteousness, Abel is still speaking to us today.

5 **Enoch** belonged to the sixth generation after Adam (Genesis 5:21–24). According to Genesis 5:24, **Enoch walked with God**; that is, he obeyed God's will. Therefore, the writer of Hebrews says here that Enoch **was commended as one who pleased God. By faith** Enoch pleased God, because **without faith it is impossible to please God** (verse 6). How can we please God if we don't believe in Him?

By faith Enoch was taken from this

life into heaven. Because of Enoch's faith, God saved him from death.

6 In order to have true faith, we must first believe that God **exists**. We must also have faith in His word, in His promises (see verse 1 and comment). If we **earnestly seek him**, God will reward us. That is, if we seek God, we will find Him; and when we find Him, He will bless us. God said: "**You will seek me and find me when you seek me with all your heart**" (Jeremiah 29:13). James wrote: **Come near to God and he will come near to you** (James 4:8). Enoch and all the other men of faith mentioned in this chapter **earnestly** sought God by faith, and they had the sure hope that He would reward them.

7 **Noah** was in the ninth generation after Adam. At that time, all the men in the world except Noah had begun to follow evil ways. Therefore, God determined to destroy all men (except Noah and his family) and every other living thing by causing a flood to come over the earth. Noah was a righteous man (Genesis 6:9); therefore, God commanded Noah to build a large boat so that he and his family might be spared.

As Noah was building the boat, his neighbors undoubtedly mocked him. To them, building a boat so far away from any sea was utterly foolish. But Noah had faith in God's word. By his faith, therefore, Noah **condemned the world**.[21] By faith Noah was saved. But because of unbelief and wickedness, the world was condemned and destroyed (Genesis 6:13–22; 7:12–24).

8 God commanded **Abraham** to leave his own country and go far away to a land he didn't know. And God promised Abraham that He would bless him and make him **into a great nation** (Genesis 12:1–2).

By faith Abraham . . . obeyed. Obedience is the proof of one's faith. That is why Abraham's faith was real. **Abraham believed the Lord, and he credited it to him as righteousness** (Genesis 15:6).

9 Abraham himself never received the land that God had promised to him as an inheritance. He lived in that **promised land** like a traveler, a foreigner. But Abraham knew by faith that God would give the land to his descendants. And about four hundred years later, Abraham's descendants (the Jews) under the leadership of Joshua finally took possession of the promised land (Joshua 1:1–3).

10 How could Abraham be so patient? He had left his own home and country. He had come to a strange and unknown land. But that land was not given to him. Why didn't Abraham complain against God? The answer is that Abraham was not seeking any land in this world. He was looking for a **city with foundations**—a permanent city that can never be destroyed—that is, a heavenly city (see Hebrews 12:22; 13:14).

11 God had promised to make from Abraham's descendants a **great nation** (Genesis 12:2). For that promise to be fulfilled, it was necessary for Abraham to have a son (Genesis 15:2–4). But Abraham and his wife Sarah were already very old, and had no children. It was physically impossible for them to have a child at their age. Nevertheless, Abraham and his wife believed God's promise. And when Abraham was one hundred years old and Sarah was ninety, they had a son Isaac (Genesis 17:15–17,19; 21:1–3).

12 For fathering a son, Abraham's body was **as good as dead**. Nevertheless, he had a son; and from that son, Abraham's descendants began to increase in ever and ever greater numbers (Genesis 15:5; 22:17; Romans 4:18–22).

13 **All these people**—Abraham, Sarah, Isaac and Jacob (verses 8–12)—did not themselves receive the **things promised**. They did not receive the promised land, and they did not see their descendants become a great nation. But they had faith that in the future God would bring to pass all that He had promised. By faith, they saw these things

---

[21] Noah himself didn't condemn the world; only God can do that. But in a sense Noah, by simply being righteous, condemned the unrighteousness of the world. Noah "condemned" the world in the same way light "condemns" darkness. Unrighteous men always appear worse in the presence of a righteous man.

from a distance—that is, far in the future. And they died still living by that faith.

It is well for us to remember that in this life even those with great faith do not always get what they hope for.

14–16 Abraham, Isaac, and Jacob **admitted that they were aliens and strangers on earth** (verse 13). Their true dwelling and true citizenship was in heaven (see Philippians 3:20). The country they sought was a **heavenly one**, a country that would last forever.

Because they sought God's country, God's heavenly city, God was **not ashamed to be called their God** (verse 16). God says: "**Those who honor me I will honor**" (1 Samuel 2:30). By believing in God, Abraham, Isaac, and Jacob honored God. And God honored them by calling Himself **the God of Abraham, the God of Isaac, and the God of Jacob** (Exodus 3:6). What higher honor can any man have than that?

Men of Faith—Abraham to Christ (11:17–40)

17–19 The story of how Abraham, at God's command, took **Isaac** to the top of a mountain to sacrifice him is written in Genesis 22:1–18.

To believe in God's promise is a great thing. But, having received a promise, to then give it up is an even greater test of a person's faith. And that is what God commanded Abraham to do—to give up the son that God had given to him. In doing this, God **tested** Abraham (verse 17). According to Genesis 21:12, God had said to Abraham, "**It is through Isaac that your offspring will be reckoned**" (verse 18). Nevertheless, God now commanded Abraham to kill his son Isaac as a sacrifice. If Abraham did that, how then could God fulfill His promise to **make** [Abraham] **into a great nation**? (Genesis 12:2).

Abraham did not question God. Abraham knew that God had the power to raise the dead to life. It was God's responsibility to fulfill His promises. It was Abraham's responsibility to obey.

At the very last moment, God stopped Abraham's hand from killing Isaac. In a way, Isaac was as good as dead; therefore, the writer says here that, **figuratively speaking**, Abraham received Isaac **back from death** (verse 19).

Then the angel of the Lord said to Abraham: "**Now I know that you fear God, because you have not withheld from me your son, your only son**" (Genesis 22:12). Then the Lord said, "**. . . because you have done this and have not withheld your son, your only son, I will surely bless you and make your descendants as numerous as the stars in the sky and as the sand on the seashore . . . through your offspring all nations on earth will be blessed, because you have obeyed me**" (Genesis 22:16–18).

One day God will surely test each of us in a similar manner. Perhaps He will test us many times. He will test us in different ways. But always He will test us where our faith is weakest, where our obedience is shakiest. He will ask us to offer to Him that thing which we love most of all. That thing which He asks us to offer to Him could be our possessions, our skills, our time, our honor, our family, or our own life. When God calls us, as He called Abraham, let us be ready to obey whatever He says (see Mark 10:17–21,29–30).

20 The story of how Isaac blessed his two sons, **Jacob** and **Esau**, is written in Genesis 27:1–40. It was the custom among the Jews for the father to give a blessing to his sons. The oldest son always received the greatest blessing. But Isaac had become blind in his old age. His younger son Jacob deceived Isaac by pretending to be Esau, and so Jacob received the greater blessing that was meant for his brother. But when Isaac discovered that he had been deceived, he did not take back the blessing he had given to Jacob. Instead, accepting it as God's will (Genesis 25:23), Isaac confirmed Jacob's blessing (Genesis 27:33).

Isaac had faith that, through Jacob, God would fulfill His promise to make Abraham into a great nation.

21 Isaac's son Jacob (also called Israel in the Old Testament) had twelve sons. Jacob gave the highest blessing to his eleventh son, **Joseph**[22] (Genesis 49:26). And Jacob (or Israel) also blessed Joseph's two sons; but he deliberately gave the higher blessing to Joseph's younger son, just as he himself had received the higher blessing from his father Isaac. And Jacob gave his blessing by faith, knowing that God would fulfill His promise to the descendants of Abraham (Genesis 48:11–20).

22 Joseph had been sold by his own brothers into slavery in **Egypt** (Genesis 37:12–36). He was later given authority over the entire land of Egypt (Genesis 41:41–43). Even though Joseph spent the rest of his life in Egypt, he continued to have complete faith that God would give to his descendants the land He had promised to Abraham, Isaac, and Jacob. And according to that faith, Jospeh instructed his sons to carry his bones to the promised land and bury them there (Genesis 50:24–26; Exodus 13:19).

23 The Jews remained in Egypt 430 years (Exodus 12:40). As they grew in numbers, the people of Egypt began to persecute them. The Jews were put into bondage and made slaves (Exodus 1:6–14). Then Pharaoh[23] ordered that all Jewish male babies were to be killed as soon as they were born (Exodus 1:22). But when **Moses** was born, his Jewish parents hid him (Exodus 2:1–3). By faith, the parents knew that God had somehow specially blessed Moses.

24–25 Pharaoh's daughter found Moses, and brought him up as her own son (Exodus 2:5–10). When Moses grew up, he became a ruler of Egypt. However, he gave up all the authority and wealth of Egypt in order to suffer with his fellow Jews (Exodus 2:11–12).

26 Moses gave up the **treasures of Egypt**. Moses considered **disgrace for the sake of Christ** to be of greater value than all the wealth of Egypt (see Philippians 3:7). Moses didn't know about Christ, but by giving up everything for God and for His people (the Jews), Moses was acting just as Christ later acted. Therefore, just as **disgrace** fell upon Christ and His followers, so the same kind of disgrace fell upon Moses (see Psalm 69:9; 89:50–51; Romans 15:3; 1 Peter 4:12–14). But in spite of such disgrace, Moses persisted in faith to the end, being confident that God would one day reward him.

Therefore, let these Hebrews, to whom this letter was written, follow the example of Moses. Moses, who never knew Christ, was ready to suffer disgrace for His sake. Thus these Hebrews, who knew Christ and had received His Spirit, should all the more be ready to suffer for Christ's sake.

27 Even though Pharaoh tried to kill Moses, Moses didn't fear him; instead, he feared God. Therefore, by faith Moses left Egypt, and for forty years lived in the land of Midian (Exodus 2:15). And he **persevered** there, because by faith he could see the invisible God. In this, Moses is an example and encouragement for all believers; for we too, like Moses, will be enabled to persevere as we look to the invisible God through the eyes of faith.

One day, toward the end of his stay in Midian, Moses saw the invisible God with his physical eyes! God appeared to Moses in a burning bush, and told Moses to return to Pharaoh and bring the Jews (Israelites) out of Egypt (Exodus 3:1–10).

28 By faith Moses delivered the Jews from bondage in Egypt. Through Moses God brought many plagues on Egypt, but in spite of the plagues, Pharaoh at first would not let the Jews go. Finally God sent an angel to kill all the firstborn of Egypt (Exodus 11:1; 12:29–30). By faith Moses commanded the Jews to put the blood of a sacrificed lamb on the door-frames of their houses as a sign; by this means the destroying angel, seeing the blood, would pass over their houses and

---

[22] God does not choose men according to their birth. As with Jacob and Esau, God often chooses the one who is last physically to be first spiritually (see Mark 10:31).

[23] During that period, all kings of Egypt were called Pharaoh.

spare their firstborn (Exodus 12:21–23). Thus, because of the sprinkled blood, the angel passed over the Jewish homes; and from this event the **Passover** festival of the Jews originated (Exodus 12:24–27).

In the same way, through the blood of Christ, we too can be delivered from the judgment and condemnation of God. Christ Himself is our Passover sacrifice, our **Passover lamb** (1 Corinthians 5:7). He is the **Lamb of God**, who makes atonement for the sins of the world (John 1:29). We are saved not by our own righteousness but by the **sprinkling of blood**, Jesus' blood.

29 When Pharaoh saw the firstborn of Egypt killed by the destroying angel, he decided to let the Jews (Israelites) go. But when the Jews had gone only a little way from Egypt, Pharaoh changed his mind and sent the Egyptian army to capture them (Exodus 14:5–9). When the Jews saw Pharaoh's huge army coming after them, they were afraid and began to rebuke Moses. Ahead of them was the **Red Sea**; behind them was the Egyptian army. They thought they would surely perish (Exodus 14:10–12).

But by faith Moses said to the Jews: "**Do not be afraid. Stand firm and you will see the deliverance the Lord will bring you today**" (Exodus 14:13). Then, through Moses, God separated the waters of the sea, and the Jews by faith **passed through the Red Sea as on dry land**. But when the pursuing Egyptians tried to cross the sea, **they were drowned** (Exodus 14:21–28).

30 Forty years after being delivered from Egypt, the Jews entered the promised land, Israel. But first it was necessary to conquer the people who had been living there. The first thing the Jews had to do was to overcome the city of **Jericho**. God told the Jewish leader Joshua how to capture the city. Jericho was surrounded by a great wall. The Jews were to march around the city for seven days blowing their trumpets. On the seventh day all the Jews were to give a great shout, and the wall would fall down. Then they would be able to enter the city and capture it. And it happened just as God had said (Joshua 6:1–5,12–16,20).

Who ever thought of capturing a big city in such a way? Joshua's faith in God surely must have been great. But God often works in such unusual ways. **'Not by might nor by power, but by my Spirit,' says the Lord Almighty** (Zechariah 4:6).

We can take Joshua's faith as an example for ourselves. In our lives there are many "Jerichos" which must be overcome. Like Joshua, we too can overcome them through faith. Paul said: **The weapons we fight with are not the weapons of the world. On the contrary, they have divine power to demolish strongholds** (2 Corinthians 10:4).

31 Joshua had first sent **spies** to Jericho, and the prostitute **Rahab** had hidden them in her house. She had believed in the God of Israel, the God of the Jews. She knew through faith that the Jews would destroy Jericho. Therefore, she gave help to the spies sent by Joshua, and thereby saved her life (Joshua 2:1–3,6,8–14; 6:24–25).

Notice that Rahab was both a Gentile (non-Jew) and a sinner; yet she was saved by faith. Furthermore, though she was a despised prostitute, God used her to accomplish His purposes.

32–34 In these verses, the writer gives examples of some other Jewish leaders in the Old Testament, who through faith accomplished great works for God (Judges 7:19–21; 15:14–16; Daniel 3:16–28; 6:16–22).

35 The two women whose sons were raised from the dead are mentioned in 1 Kings 17:17–24 and 2 Kings 4:32–37. Other men of faith **refused to be released** from death, because they didn't desire to be "resurrected" in this world, but preferred a **better resurrection** in heaven.

36–38 Here we read of Old Testament heroes who suffered severely because of their faith. But they all remained firm to the end.

. . . the world was not worthy of them (verse 38). In worldly men's eyes these heroes of faith were unworthy; but in God's eyes they were worthy. They were fully worthy to inherit the heavenly city of God (verses 10,16).

39 None of these Old Testament

heroes of faith **received what had been promised**. A number of them obtained some promises, but none of them received the one great promise—that is, the promise of a Savior. None of them saw that day when God's Son Jesus came to earth. God's greatest promise to mankind is the promise of salvation in Jesus Christ. But in their own lives on earth, none of these Old Testament heroes obtained that promise.

40 However, these Old Testament men of faith will one day **be made perfect**; that is, they will receive full salvation just as we will. When Christ comes again, these Old Testament heroes, together with us who have believed in Christ, will be resurrected and receive eternal life.

CHAPTER 12

Jesus the Supreme Example of Faith (12:1–3)

1 **Therefore**, having just learned in Chapter 11 of many great heroes of faith, let us follow their example and **run with perseverance the race marked out for us**. These Old Testament heroes are here called **witnesses**, because through their lives they gave witness to their faith.

The life of a follower of Christ is like a **race**. In a race all the runners run as fast as they can. Before the race begins, they take off all unnecessary clothing. No one runs a race wearing fine clothes and jewelry. There is nothing wrong with good clothes in themselves, but it is wrong to run a race in them! Such clothes will hinder the runner.

In the same way, there are many things in our Christian lives which are not wrong in themselves, but which hinder us in our spiritual race. We must **throw off everything that hinders** in order to run more quickly. These hindrances may even be good things, but they take time from our service to God. We all must examine ourselves to see if there are any such hindrances in our lives. And we must remember as we do so that what is a hindrance in one person's life may not be a hindrance in another's. Hindrances are not the same for everyone.

But **sin**, on the other hand, always slows everyone down. If we want to finish the race, we must throw off the **sin that so easily entangles**. We must throw off every sin, no matter how small. Small sins, if not thrown off, will grow large and soon entangle us.

In one way, however, our Christian life is different from a race. In a race only one runner wins and gets first prize. But in the "race" of our Christian lives, everyone who finishes the race gets the same prize—eternal life. Even though this is true, however, we should all run as if only one person was going to win. If we run like that, then we will be sure to run fast! We will be sure of running a good race for Jesus Christ (see 1 Corinthians 9:24–26).

2 **Let us fix our eyes on Jesus**. Let us not be distracted. Let us not gaze at all the pleasing things of the world. For if we do, we shall not be able to run in a straight line, but shall wander from side to side. And maybe we shall not even reach the finish line.

Jesus is the **author** (or pioneer) **of our faith**. He went before us into heaven. Jesus is also the **author** of the Old Testament heroes' faith. Jesus was with them from the beginning (see 1 Corinthians 10:3–4). They did not know Jesus as we know Him; nevertheless, He was their leader. The Old Testament prophets also spoke of Jesus; therefore, He was the **author** of their faith too.

Jesus is also the **perfecter of our faith**. That is, He Himself is the supreme example of faith. In the garden of Gethsemane on the last day of His earthly life, Jesus with complete faith surrendered Himself to God. He said to God, "**Take this cup from me. Yet not what I will, but what you will**" (Mark 14:36). On that day there was no sign that God was with Jesus. There was no one to comfort Him. He had been rejected by all men; even His own followers had deserted Him at the last moment. It even seemed as if God had rejected Him (Mark 15:34). Nevertheless, He **endured the CROSS, scorning its shame**. During the time of the Roman Empire, only the worst and most despised criminals were put to death on a cross. There was nothing more shameful than dying on a cross. Therefore, by enduring such terrible shame and suffering, Jesus has given us an example of faith that is above all others.

As Jesus was hanging on the cross, many stood around mocking Him. They said, "**Let this Christ, this King of Israel, come down now from the cross, that we may see and believe**" (Mark 15:32). But if Jesus by some supernatural means had come down from the cross, He could not have been the **perfecter of our faith**. Nor could He have given us such a perfect example to follow. On the contrary, Jesus was Himself made perfect by the suffering He endured (Hebrews 2:10). And we too, following His example, shall be made perfect through suffering.

If we persevere in faith until the end, we too will be exalted with Jesus (Hebrews 3:14). We too will share in the **joy** that was set before Him (see John 15:11; 16:22). And we too shall reign with Him in heaven. "**To him who overcomes, I will give the right to sit with me on my throne, just as I overcame and sat down with my Father on his throne**" (Revelation 3:21). In this way, Jesus not only perfected His own faith, but He will perfect our faith also. Jesus is not only the **author**, the creator, of our faith; He is also the **perfecter** of our faith. That work of faith which Jesus has started within us He will also bring to perfection (Philippians 1:6).

3 Is there anyone among us who is growing weary, who is losing heart? If there is, let that person consider Jesus. **Consider him**. When we consider Jesus—that is, when we meditate and reflect on Him—we shall receive from Him strength and grace to help us in our time of need (Hebrews 4:16).

God Disciplines His Sons (12:4–13)

4 The writer says here that the Hebrews have suffered persecution for Christ's sake, but they have not yet shed their blood—that is, died—for Christ. They have not yet had to suffer what some of the Old Testament heroes of the faith suffered. The Hebrews shouldn't let themselves be discouraged so quickly; their trials are just beginning! If they are discouraged by small troubles, what will happen to them when big troubles come?

But the Hebrews need to remember that God is merciful and will never allow a trial to come upon them that they cannot endure (1 Corinthians 10:13). They also need to remember that whatever trial comes upon them, it comes as DISCIPLINE from God. God's discipline is a sign, not of anger, but of His love toward us (verse 6).

5–6 The writer here quotes from Proverbs 3:11–12. When trouble and sorrow come upon us, let us not complain against God. Let us remember that in allowing such trouble and sorrow to come upon us, God is disciplining us as children for our own good. Whatever trouble and persecution comes to us has been allowed by God. Men persecute us because of our obedience to Christ, but God uses that persecution to discipline us so that we might obey Christ all the more.

7–8 Every son needs discipline. Even Christ **learned obedience from what he suffered** (Hebrews 5:8).

No one cares about disciplining illegitimate children. They will not inherit anything. But a father cares about his own son. A father wants to train his son well, because he knows that one day the son will be given great responsibility. It is the same with God. If we are being disciplined by God, let us rejoice, because we know that He is treating us as sons and is preparing a place of responsibility for us. If we have not experienced any kind of trouble in our life, then we have cause to wonder whether or not we really are God's children.

9–10 When God disciplines us, He never makes a mistake. God's discipline is always just; it is always beneficial. Our human fathers tried to discipline us as well as they could, but they made mistakes. Nevertheless, we respected them. If we respected our human fathers, how much more should we respect our heavenly Father, the **Father of our spirits** (verse 9).

Why does God discipline us? He disciplines us so that **we may share in his holiness** (verse 10). This is God's purpose. In one way, we have already been made holy by Christ's sacrifice (Hebrews 10:10). But that is only the first step in our salvation. That first holiness is the righteousness of Christ, which we receive when we first believe, and on the basis of which we are declared righteous (Romans 5:1). But there is a second kind of holiness—the full holiness or perfection of God—which is the final goal of our lives. It takes time to obtain this second kind of holiness, and we shall fully obtain it only after we get to heaven (see Hebrews 10:14 and comment). In the meantime, God is continually making us more and more holy here on earth by allowing various kinds of trouble and persecution to come upon us in the form of discipline. Paul said, "**We must go through many hardships to enter the kingdom of God**" (Acts 14:22).

11 We can respond to God's discipline in two ways. First, we can reject His discipline; we can become angry and begin to complain against God. Or second, we can thankfully accept God's discipline and let Him train us by it. If we reject His discipline, it will do us no good. If we accept His discipline, our lives will increase in **righteousness** (holiness) and PEACE. We will be turned from sin to righteousness and obedience. And the fruit of righteousness is peace with God. **Before I was afflicted I went astray, but now I obey your word. . . . It was good for me to be afflicted so that I might learn your decrees** (Psalm 119:67,71).

12 When we are being disciplined by God, let us not be discouraged. His discipline is not meant to cast us down; it is meant to make us mature and equipped for God's service. When discipline comes we must not run from it, but rather we must welcome it and allow ourselves to be trained by it. **Therefore, strengthen your feeble arms and weak knees,** says the writer (Isaiah 35:3).

13 If anyone in the church is being disciplined by God—if anyone is spiritually **lame**—let us give that person help and encouragement (Galatians 6:1–2). Let us make **level paths** for his feet (Proverbs 4:26). Let us not put any hindrance in his way, lest he stumble and fall and be unable to finish his race.

Instructions and Warnings (12:14–17)

14 **Make every effort to live in peace with all men** (see Romans 12:18). It is not possible to live in peace with everyone, because some people will oppose us simply because of our faith in Christ. But we must try as far as possible to remain at peace with everyone. And if we are supposed to remain at peace with non-believers, how much more should we strive to remain at peace with our fellow believers! (see Ephesians 4:3).

Make every effort . . . to be holy. Through the grace given to us by Christ and His Holy Spirit, God is continually making us more and more holy. But, in addition to that, we ourselves must strive to be holy. We can become holy only by being obedient to God (see Philippians 2:12–13 and comment).

"**Be holy, because I am holy,**" says God (Leviticus 11:45; 1 Peter 1:15–16). **It is God's will that you should be holy** (1 Thessalonians 4:3). . . . **without holiness no one will see the Lord** (see Matthew 5:8 and comment).

When we look at ourselves and at our church, what do we see? Holiness, or unholiness. Peace, or strife. Let each person examine himself.

15 **See to it that no one misses the grace of God** (see Hebrews 4:1). God's grace is always available to us (Hebrews 4:16). But sometimes we don't take it or appropriate it. Instead, we reject it. And when we do this, we have **fallen away from grace** (Galatians 5:4).

Why do we so often refuse to accept God's grace? Because of sin. As long as we continue in sin, we cannot receive

God's grace. Sin is like a **bitter root,** which makes the whole tree bitter. Sin in our life makes our whole life impure. Sin in the church makes the whole church impure; and in so doing, it will **defile many**. Let us take care that no "bitter root" like this grows up among us. And if it does, let us be quick to root it out (see 1 Corinthians 5:9–11,13).

16 The writer here gives two examples of sin: sexual immorality and godlessness. Sexual immorality was a very common sin in New Testament times, and new believers and new churches were always in danger of being defiled by it (see 1 Corinthians 5:1).

The second example is godlessness. Isaac's son **Esau** was **godless,** because in exchange for a small earthly benefit he gave up his God-given **inheritance rights,** his rights as the oldest son. One day Esau was very hungry, and asked his younger brother Jacob for something to eat. Jacob, being crafty, agreed to give Esau some food in exchange for Esau's **inheritance rights**. Because of his great hunger, Esau agreed (Genesis 25:29–33). **So Esau despised his birthright** (Genesis 25:34). In this way, Esau missed God's grace (verse 15). His sin was this: He desired the pleasure of this world more than the blessing of God.

Esau was like a small child who prefers a piece of candy to a thousand dollar bill. And we also are like that, when we value the things of the world more than the things of God. How many there are who in trying to gain earthly wealth lose their heavenly inheritance (see Matthew 6:19–20 and comment).

After Esau had given up his birthright, he tried to get it back but could not. And it will be so with us. If we knowingly reject God's grace, we, like Esau, will lose our inheritance in heaven (see Hebrews 10:35).

17 The story of Isaac blessing Esau is told in Genesis 27:30–40 (see Hebrews 11:20 and comment). Esau never truly repented of his sin of rejecting God's grace. Yes, he later regretted it, and wept with sorrow over the blessing he had lost; but he never wept over his sin. Because when a man rejects God's grace, his heart becomes hardened, and he loses all inclination to repent (Hebrews 3:12–13).

The Heavenly Jerusalem (12:18–29)

18–19 Here the writer of Hebrews describes how God gave His law to the Jews. God came down on Mount Sinai in fire to speak with Moses; the mountain was **burning with fire**. A great cloud covered the mountain; there was **darkness, gloom and storm** (verse 18). The whole mountain trembled violently. There was a **trumpet blast** as God descended onto the mountain. And then God spoke out of the cloud. All the Jews were filled with fear (Exodus 19:16–19; 20:18–21).

20–21 If any man or animal touched Mount Sinai during the time God was on the mountain, that man or animal was to be put to death; this was God's command. Because of God's presence, the whole mountain was filled with His holiness. God's holiness was so awesome and fearful that even an animal that strayed near the mountain had to be killed because it had come too close to that holiness. The animal itself couldn't even be touched; it had to be stoned to death from a distance (verse 20). When the Jews heard such commands and felt the terror of God's presence, they could not bear it. No one could survive who came close to God's holiness (Exodus 19:12–13). According to Deuteronomy 9:19, even Moses was **trembling with fear** (verse 21).

22 Under the old covenant men were afraid in God's presence. But under the new covenant, every believer can come into God's presence without fear. We don't have to be afraid, as the Jews were, because we are coming into the presence of our loving and merciful heavenly Father.

Mount Zion is the place where King David established the city of Jerusalem. This earthly **Mount Zion**—that is, Jerusalem—was the main center of the Jewish religion. It was here that David's son Solomon built the great Jewish temple.

Just as the earthly sanctuary of the old

covenant was merely a **copy** of the heavenly sanctuary of the new covenant (Hebrews 9:24), so the earthly Jerusalem is merely a copy of the **heavenly Jerusalem**. The "heavenly Jerusalem" is the **city of the living God**. It is God's heavenly sanctuary, where He dwells with His angels. It is that **better country**, which Abraham, Isaac, and Jacob were seeking (Hebrews 11:16).

23 Here the heavenly Jerusalem is called the **church of the firstborn**. The **firstborn** is Jesus Christ Himself; in the kingdom of God Jesus is the first, the oldest, (Romans 8:29; Colossians 1:15; Hebrews 1:6). But through faith in Him, we too become **firstborn** in a spiritual sense. We are the "firstborn" who will inherit the kingdom of God. We are members of the **joyful assembly**—Christ's church. Our **names are written in heaven** (see Luke 10:20; Revelation 21:27).

The **righteous men made perfect** are the Old Testament heroes of faith, many of whom are mentioned in Chapter 11. They also will be included in the **church of the firstborn**.

Based on what is written in this verse, many people think that as soon as believers die their **spirits** are **made perfect** and they at once enter heaven, the "heavenly Jerusalem" (see Luke 23:42–43). Then later, after Christ comes to earth again, their bodies will be resurrected, and they will receive a new, redeemed spiritual body (Romans 8:23).

God is the **judge of all men**. He will take vengeance on His enemies, and He will vindicate His people. But He will also judge His own people; none of us will escape the judgment of God. If we obey Him, we will have nothing to fear. But if we deliberately disobey Him, we will have much to fear (see Matthew 7:21; Hebrews 10:30–31).

24 When we enter the heavenly Jerusalem, we shall meet Jesus, the **mediator of a new covenant** (see Hebrews 8:6; 9:15 and comments). Through His **sprinkled blood**—that is, through His shed blood—our consciences are cleansed (Hebrews 9:14). Thus we are able to enter the heavenly sanctuary and draw near to God (Hebrews 10:19,22). Jesus' blood **speaks a better word** than Abel's blood. The **blood of Abel** cries out for vengeance against sinful Cain (see Genesis 4:8–10; Hebrews 11:4). But the blood of Jesus cries out for mercy for sinful men. Jesus' blood speaks of forgiveness and reconciliation with God. Therefore, Jesus' blood speaks a **better word** than Abel's blood.

25 **See to it that you do not refuse him who speaks**—that is, God. God warned the Jews **on earth**. He came down onto Mount Sinai to speak with them (see verses 18–19). But in the end the Jews did not heed God, and they were punished.

Today God continues to speak to us. Even now He is warning us **from heaven**. If the Jews did not escape punishment when they rejected God's warning on earth, those of us today who reject His warning from heaven will certainly not escape punishment (see Hebrews 3:7–12; 10:28–29).

26 When God spoke to the Jews from Mount Sinai, the **whole mountain trembled violently** (Exodus 19:18). Later God spoke through the Old Testament prophets, saying that He would again shake the earth—and **not only the earth but also the heavens** (Isaiah 13:13; Haggai 2:6). The meaning is this: God will one day destroy both heaven and earth, and in their place He will establish a **new heaven and a new earth** (Revelation 21:1).

27 God is going to remove **what can be shaken—that is, created things**. These **created things** are heaven and earth. God is going to remove them. That is, heaven and earth will be destroyed; they will pass away (Mark 13:31). But the kingdom of God—the **heavenly Jerusalem** (verse 22)—cannot be shaken; it will remain forever.

28–29 We believers are citizens and heirs of that **kingdom that cannot be shaken** (the kingdom of God). Therefore, let us always be thankful to God for the great grace He has shown to us. At the same time, we must **worship God acceptably**—that is, we must worship Him **with reverance and awe**. God is a loving and merciful heavenly Father, but He is also a **consuming fire** (Deuteronomy

4:24; Isaiah 33:14; 1 Corinthians 3:13–15; Hebrews 10:26–27; 2 Peter 3:10–13). Those who deliberately reject Him will never know Him as a loving Father; they will know Him only as a **consuming fire,** a "fire" of judgment and punishment. Therefore, all men must come to God with **reverance and awe**; He is mighty to save, but He is also mighty to punish.

CHAPTER 13

Concluding Exhortations (13:1–17)

1 Jesus said to His disciples, "**A new command I give you: Love one another**" (John 13:34). Such love is not just a warm and happy feeling that comes on us when everything is going well. To love **each other as brothers** is costly. To His command above, Jesus added these words: "**As I have loved you, so you must love one another**" (John 13:34). How did Jesus love us? He gave up His own life for us (1 John 3:16–17).

Keep on loving each other. Even in times of trouble and persecution, our love for each other must continue to grow (see Romans 12:10; 1 Thessalonians 4:9–10). In this way we shall be able to stand firm in the face of difficulties.

The Hebrews were facing persecution. The writer's word to them is that in order to stand firm they must keep on loving one another.

2 Here the writer recalls an Old Testament story in which Abraham entertained three angels, and one of them turned out to be God Himself (Genesis 18:1–10). The other two angels then went to Lot, Abraham's nephew, and saved him from destruction (Genesis 19:1–16). Perhaps an actual angel will never come to our home; but strangers will come, and we should not turn them away. Like the angels who went to Lot, these strangers might one day bring us great blessing.

However, we should not entertain strangers in order to get a blessing but rather to give a blessing! To show hospitality is an important Christian duty (Matthew 25:34–40; Romans 12:13; 1 Peter 4:9).

3 In this verse the writer gives us an important principle: namely, in order to adequately love those who are in trouble, we must put ourselves in their place; we must try to imagine ourselves in their circumstances. If we do this, we will be better able to love them and to sympathize with them. When we remember those in prison, let us at the same time imagine ourselves there in prison with them. When we think of those who are being mistreated or dishonored or afflicted in any way, let us imagine it is we who are enduring these sufferings instead of them.

Remember those who suffer, says the writer, **as if you yourself were suffering.**[24] We have bodies just like theirs; we experience the same sorrows and joys they do. And tomorrow our turn to suffer will surely come. At that time, we will be needing their love and sympathy! (see Hebrews 10:33–34 and comment).

4 God Himself established marriage (Genesis 2:24). Therefore, the joining of a man and woman together in marriage is honorable and pleasing to God. And if marriage is honorable and pleasing to God, that means the **marriage bed** (sexual intercourse in marriage) is also honorable and pleasing to God, because sexual intercourse is an essential part of marriage.

An **adulterer** is a person already married who then has intercourse with someone else. The **sexually immoral** are all those—either married or unmarried—

---

[24] In place of the words **as if you yourselves were suffering,** some versions of the Bible say, "since you also are in the body," which is a literal translation of the Greek text. The meaning is the same.

who engage in any kind of unlawful sexual activity, including adultery.

To marry a second wife while the first wife is still living is to commit adultery—unless the first wife herself committed adultery to begin with (see Matthew 5:32; Mark 10:11–12 and comments). If a married man goes to a prostitute, he is likewise committing adultery. God will judge all adulterers and all the sexually immoral; those who do not repent will not enter heaven (1 Corinthians 6:9–10; 1 Thessalonians 4:3–6).

5 God does not want us to lack any essential thing. God is ready to provide us with everything we need, but He usually does not provide us with more than we need. To seek for more than we need is to be greedy; and a greedy man is an idolator, because he puts wealth and possessions in the place of God (see Ephesians 5:5; Colossians 3:5). Such a man worships his possessions instead of God.

Paul wrote to Timothy: **For the love of money is a root of all kinds of evil. Some people, eager for money, have wandered from the faith and pierced themselves with many griefs** (Timothy 6:10). The person who has a **love of money** begins to love God less and less, and his worldly possessions more and more. No one can love both God and money at once (see Matthew 6:24 and comment). Not only that, those who love money end up piercing themselves **with many griefs**. These **griefs** are worry and anxiety. The lover of money is always afraid of losing his money. He is never at peace; he is never happy. He is never content with what he has; he always wants more.

Let us not be like that. Rather, let us learn to be content with what we have (Philippians 4:11–12). Paul wrote: ... **godliness with contentment is great gain. For we brought nothing into the world, and we can take nothing out of it. But if we have food and clothing, we will be content with that** (Timothy 6:6–8).

On this subject, Jesus Himself gave the main teaching: "... **do not worry, saying, 'What shall we eat ' or 'What shall we drink ' or 'What shall we wear '... But seek first** [God's] **kingdom and his righteousness, and all these things will be given to you as well**" (Matthew 6:31–33).

The writer here quotes from Deuteronomy 31:6. God will never leave us, nor forsake us! Why should we be anxious?

6 Here the writer quotes from Psalm 118:6. Believers are under the protection of almighty God. We need not be afraid.

7 In this verse, the writer is speaking about past leaders. If we honored them while they were alive, we should continue to honor them after they have gone. They brought us the word of God, and they set a good example for us to follow.

8 Our former leaders have gone, but Jesus never goes (Psalm 102:27; Hebrews 1:12). And because Jesus abides forever, His priesthood is eternal and unchangeable (Hebrews 7:24). Jesus **always lives to intercede** for us (Hebrews 7:25).

Jesus said: **"I am the First and the Last. I am the Living One; I was dead, and behold I am alive for ever and ever!"** (Revelation 1:17–18).

9 Some false teachers were trying to teach the Hebrews that in order to gain extra spiritual strength it was necessary to eat certain **ceremonial foods**. But here the writer tells the Hebrews that it is not by ceremonial foods that a person's heart is strengthened, but by God's grace (see Romans 14:17; 1 Corinthians 8:8).

10 Some Jews taught that it was spiritually beneficial to eat meat that had been sacrificed on the altar. But we Christians have a different altar, not where the bodies of animals are sacrificed but where the body of Christ was sacrificed. That altar is the spiritual altar of the new covenant, **from which those who minister at the** (old covenant) **tabernacle have no right to eat.**[25] Only eating at Christ's altar gives spiritual benefit; when we eat from Christ's altar we partake of Christ Himself (John 6:53–56).

11 Jesus Christ is our **sin offering;** He is our sacrifice of atonement for sins (Romans 3:23–25). Under the old

[25] See comment on verse 11 and footnote to comment.

covenant, the Jewish high priest each year offered a **sin offering**, or sacrifice of atonement, for the sins of the people. The priests could eat the meat of all other sacrifices, but they were not allowed to eat the meat of the sin offering.[26] The bodies of the animals sacrificed as sin offerings were **burned outside the camp** (Leviticus 16:27).

12 Jesus also died **outside the camp** (verse 11)—that is, **outside the city gate** of Jerusalem. John says that the **place where Jesus was crucified was near the city** (John 19:20). Through the sacrifice of His body on the cross—that is, **through his own blood**—Jesus has made believers **holy** (see Hebrews 10:10,14).

13 **Let us, then, go to him outside the camp**. For Jewish Christians, to "go outside the camp" meant leaving Jerusalem, leaving their old religion, their possessions, their security—everything. In the same way, all who want to follow Christ must **go to him outside the camp**; that is, they must leave their old religion, their old customs, their old life. In his day, Moses left the **treasures of Egypt** and endured **disgrace for the sake of Christ** (Hebrews 11:26). Jesus said: "**If anyone would come after me, he must deny himself and take up his cross and follow me**" (Mark 8:34) "**. . . and anyone who does not take his cross and follow me is not worthy of me**" (Matthew 10:37–38). Let us remember how disgraceful the cross was in Jesus' time. But God's only Son took up His own cross and carried it **outside the camp** (John 19:17). Therefore, let us likewise take up our cross and **go to him outside the camp, bearing the disgrace he bore.**

14 None of us likes to leave his own "camp," his own city, his old customs, his old life. But we must not put any reliance on these old things; they will not benefit us. All these things will pass away. **For here we do not have an enduring city.** Indeed, these words were soon to come true for the Jews: forty years after Jesus' death, the city of Jerusalem was totally destroyed by the Romans.

We who put our reliance in Christ do not seek an earthly city; rather, we seek a heavenly city, a **heavenly Jerusalem**, a **kingdom that cannot be shaken** (see Hebrews 11:10,16; 12:22,28).

15 The animal sacrifices of the old covenant have been done away with. The sacrifice of Christ is sufficient; it remains in effect forever. However, we Christians have a new kind of sacrifice to offer to God: namely, a spiritual sacrifice. Peter wrote that we are a **holy priesthood, offering spiritual sacrifices acceptable to God through Jesus Christ** (1 Peter 2:5).

What are these **spiritual sacrifices**? One of them is mentioned in this verse: the **sacrifice of praise**. Praise and thanksgiving are "sacrifices" which are always acceptable to God.

16 But it is not enough to offer sacrifices only with our lips. We must also offer sacrifices to God by performing works of love. True religion does not consist in offering animal sacrifices but rather in doing good and helping others (see James 1:27). Our sacrifices are love, mercy, faithfulness. But more than these, we must offer our **bodies as living sacrifices** (Romans 12:1). This is the sacrifice most pleasing to God, because if we have offered our bodies to God, then we have offered Him everything.

17 At the present time, there are many who do not like to obey their leaders. These people do not show respect for their leaders. Young people criticize their elders. But this situation should not exist among Christians. Our leaders have faults and weaknesses, but that is not our business. Our responsibility is to respect and obey them (see 1 Thessalonians 5:12–13 and comment).

God has appointed leaders to watch over us. They will have to give an account to God of how well they have served as shepherds of their flocks. If we have disobeyed them or rebelled against them, they will have great sorrow when

---

[26] This is why those who ministered under the old covenant **had no right to eat** from Christ's altar (verse 10). Christ Himself was a sin offering, and it was forbidden to eat the meat of sin offerings.

they give account of us to Christ. And if they have sorrow because of our disobedience, then surely we too shall have sorrow when it is our turn to stand before Christ. Those who oppose their leaders bring great spiritual harm upon themselves.[27]

Final Prayer and Greetings (13:18–25)

18–19 **Pray for us**. The more we pray for our leaders, the more they will be able to benefit us spiritually (see Romans 15:30–32; 2 Corinthians 1:12).

20 We can learn much about how to pray for ourselves and for others by studying the prayers written in the New Testament. Here the writer prays to the **God of peace**, the God who through Jesus Christ has made **peace** with believers. This same God, **through the blood of the eternal covenant**, has raised Christ from the dead. That is, by shedding His **blood**, Christ offered a sacrifice that was completely acceptable and pleasing to God; therefore, God brought Him back from the dead and made Him the high priest of the **eternal covenant**—the new covenant between man and God (Ezekiel 37:26).

But Christ is not only our high priest; He is also our **great Shepherd**. And we are His sheep.

21 Here the writer prays that God will equip the Hebrews **with everything good for doing his will**. What else could we ever need? "Everything good" includes God's grace, God's power, God's Holy Spirit. Besides these things, there is nothing more we need.

But one thing more is needed. Even though we have received **everything good for doing his will**, it is still necessary that God **work in us what is pleasing to him** (see Philippians 2:13). Alone we can do nothing (John 15:5). God works in our lives through the power of His Holy Spirit. **Now to him who is able to do immeasurably more than all we ask or imagine, according to his power that is at work within us, to him be glory in the church and in Christ Jesus throughout all generations, for ever and ever** (Ephesians 3:20–21).

22–25 **Timothy** (verse 23) was Paul's colleague, to whom Paul wrote two New Testament letters. This is the only place in the New Testament where it says that Timothy was in prison.

Those from Italy[28] are mentioned in verse 24. It is not known who these people were, or whether they were living inside or outside Italy when this letter was written. The only thing that can be said is that they were some Italian brothers who sent their greetings to the Hebrews.

---

27 A frightening example of what can happen when people oppose their legitimate leaders is found in Numbers Chapter 16.

28 **Italy** is an important country of Europe, whose capital is Rome. In New Testament times, Rome was the capital and center of the Roman Empire.

James

INTRODUCTION

Most Bible scholars believe that this letter was written by James, the younger brother of Jesus (Galatians 1:19). James was a leader in the church in Jerusalem (Galatians 2:9). Many scholars think that this letter was written before 50 A.D. If this is so, then it was one of the first New Testament letters to be written. The letter could not have been written later than 62 A.D., because in that year James was put to death.

James wrote this letter to Christians to teach them the duties of being a disciple of Jesus Christ. In James' time, many Christians had stopped doing good works. They said: "We are not saved by works, but only by faith; therefore, there is no need to do good works." In saying that they were saved by faith alone, these Christians were correct. But in saying that they no longer needed to do good works, they were badly mistaken. It was mainly to correct that mistaken belief that James wrote this letter.

OUTLINE

A. Trials and Temptations (1:1–18).
   1. The Testing of Faith (1:1–11).
   2. The Source of Temptation (1:12–18).
B. General Teachings (1:19–3:18).
   1. The Practice of the Word (1:19–27).
   2. Condemnation of Partiality (2:1–13).
   3. Faith and Deeds (2:14–26).
   4. Control of the Tongue (3:1–12).
   5. Two Kinds of Wisdom (3:13–18).

C. Various Exhortations (4:1–5:20).
   1. The Worldly Attitude (4:1–17).
   2. The Wicked Rich (5:1–6).
   3. Patience (5:7–12).
   4. The Prayer of Faith (5:13-20).

CHAPTER 1

Faith and Wisdom (1:1–8)

1 James calls himself a **servant of God and of the Lord Jesus Christ**. Every Christian—including the chief leaders—are God's servants (see Romans 1:1 and comment). A servant lives in complete dependence on his master and remains obedient to him in everything. We too should live as God's servants. No matter how much authority we are given in this life, we are still servants. For whatever authority we have belongs not to us but to God.

We are servants not only of God but also of the **Lord Jesus Christ**. Notice that James uses Jesus' full title here. The name **Jesus** is a man's name, the name of the man who lived here on earth, who taught and performed miracles, who died and was raised from the dead. The name **Christ** means "anointed one" (Psalm 2:2; Acts 4:26). In the Hebrew language[1] the word for "anointed one" is Messiah (John 4:25). Christ was "anointed" to be our Savior and to be the mediator to reconcile us to God. The third part of Jesus' title is **Lord**, which in the Greek language[2] means God. It is the name given to God throughout the Old Testament. Therefore, we must understand from this that Jesus is both man and God. This is why He is the one true mediator between man and God.

James wrote this letter mainly to Jewish Christians—that is, to Jews who believed in Christ.[3] These believers had been scattered about because of the persecution against Christians by non-believing Jews and also by the Romans.

James addresses these believers as the **twelve tribes**—that is, the twelve tribes of Israel, the Jewish nation. These twelve tribes were descended from the twelve sons of Jacob, Abraham's grandson. But James has not written this letter only for these Jewish Christians; he has written it for all believers everywhere. Therefore, whether we are Jewish believers or Gentile believers, this letter has been written for us.

2 The **trials** mentioned in this section are the troubles and persecution that we suffer for Christ's sake. James is not talking here about the troubles that come on us because of our own mistakes and sins.

James does not say that trials are themselves a joy. Rather, he says we are to "consider" them a joy. Why should we consider trials a joy? Because from this kind of trial we receive much spiritual benefit (see verses 3–4). The followers of other religions are able to endure trials, but only Christians are able to rejoice in their trials.

3 Here James calls these trials a **testing** of our FAITH. What benefits do these trials bring to us? Such trials produce in us **perseverance**. God allows trials to come upon us in order to test and strengthen our faith (see 1 Peter 1:6–7). To persevere means to be firm and strong in faith. It means to be brave and courageous, and not to whine and howl like a dog when it's beaten. As a man perseveres in trials, he becomes stronger. But his strength is not in himself; rather, he receives his strength from Christ through faith.

Another word for **perseverance** is

[1] Hebrew was the main language of the Jews. It was almost the same as Aramaic, which was the language spoken by most common people of the Middle East, including Jesus.

[2] Greek was the language of Greece, an important country in southern Europe. In New Testament times most educated people in the countries around the Mediterranean sea spoke Greek. The New Testament was originally written in Greek.

[3] It is not necessary to stop being a Jew in order to become a Christian. Christ Himself was a Jew. It is only necessary that a Jew stop putting his trust in the law and in his own works; he must put his trust in Christ alone.

patience. Patience is one of the fruits of the Holy Spirit (Galatians 5:22). Such spiritual patience or perseverance is essential for us; our salvation depends on it. Jesus said, "... **he who stands firm to the end will be saved**" (Mark 13:13; Luke 21:19).

There is a second reason why God allows trials to come upon us, and that is in order to discipline us. Perhaps we have wandered from God's path; or perhaps we have stopped walking according to His will. God by means of various trials will try to bring us back onto the right path. When such discipline comes upon us, we must not lose heart (Hebrews 12:5–6). Rather, we should accept such trials with joy, knowing this, that they have come upon us for our own good and in accordance with God's will.

4 The fruit of perseverance is maturity. Trials come upon us so that we might be **mature and complete**. The mature Christian is one who is patient, who perseveres. The character of a mature Christian lacks nothing; it is **complete**. All the fruits of the Holy Spirit are evident in his life. Such a person is like a fully ripened fruit.

Fruit ripens unevenly; first only one side ripens. But as the sun shines and the rain falls upon the fruit, it begins to ripen on all sides. Christians are like that.

5 All Christians are continually growing in maturity. We each still lack certain things. One thing we often lack is **wisdom**. In this verse, we are given a tremendous promise: if any of us lacks wisdom, all he has to do is ask and **it will be given to him**. We will receive all the wisdom we need; God gives His gifts **generously**. God does not find fault with us because we lack wisdom; He does not rebuke us. He is our loving heavenly Father; we can go to Him without fear.

Wisdom is different from knowledge. We gain knowledge by our own effort. We gain knowledge by studying in school. But true wisdom is a gift of God.[4] Wisdom is greater than knowledge, because wisdom includes the gift of using knowledge. Knowledge is of no benefit unless it is used wisely.

6–8 In order to receive anything from God we must ask in faith. If we pray without faith, God will not give us what we ask. This rule applies not only to wisdom, but to anything we ask for.

The man who doubts is a **double-minded** man (verse 8). With one part of his mind he hopes to receive what he asks for; but with the other part of his mind he doubts that he will receive it. Such a man's faith is not firm; it is **unstable**. Such a man is tossed back and forth like the waves of the sea.

The Poor and the Rich (1:9–11)

9 The brother **in humble circumstances** is a believer who is a slave, a servant, a prisoner, a man of low caste, or one who has fallen into some kind of difficulty. Such a man's worldly position is indeed humble and lowly. But, through faith, his spiritual position—that is, his **high position**—is good, and he can **take pride** in it.[5] He is God's child and Christ's fellow heir (Romans 8:14,16–17). The world is the opposite of the kingdom of God. Those who are lowly in the world will be exalted in the kingdom of God (see Matthew 5:3–5; 23:11–12; Mark 10:43–44).

10–11 The **one who is rich** refers here to a wealthy Christian brother. The rich brother must not take pride in his wealth; his wealth will soon perish (Matthew 6:19–21). His business will not remain forever, but in time will **fade away** (verse 11). The rich brother must not pile up his wealth; instead, he should give it to the poor and use it for Christ's work (see Mark 10:21–23). He must not consider his wealth his own; it belongs to God. Let him put himself in a **low**

---

[4] There are also special supernatural gifts of **wisdom** and **knowledge**, which are gifts of the Holy Spirit (see 1 Corinthians 12:8 and comment). However, James is not talking about these special gifts of the Spirit in this verse. He is talking about wisdom in a general sense.

[5] He must not **take pride** in himself, but rather in God. He has not obtained his **high** (spiritual) **position** because of his own worthiness; he has received it by God's grace alone.

position (verse 10); then he will **take pride** in God and not in his wealth (1 Timothy 6:17–19).

Who are the **rich**? Whoever has land and possessions should consider himself **rich**. James is not speaking here only of the very rich; he is speaking also of Christians with just a small amount of wealth. Such people don't like to think of themselves as "rich"; but compared with the poor, they are indeed rich.

Riches perish; God's word remains forever. The man who puts his trust in riches instead of in God will perish with his riches. He is like a flower that will wither and pass away (see Isaiah 40:6–8; 1 Peter 1:23–25). No one can trust both in riches and in God at the same time (see Matthew 6:24).

Trials and Temptations (1:12–18)

12 The believer who perseveres will receive the **crown of life**. The "crown of life" is the crown of victory over sin, or the crown of victory in our life's race (see 1 Corinthians 9:25; 2 Timothy 4:7–8). The main meaning of the **crown of life**, however, is salvation, or eternal life. . . . **he who stands firm to the end will be saved** (Mark 13:13). We need to bear our cross only for a short time; but we shall wear our crown forever.

God has promised to give the crown of life **to those who love him**. Those who love God are those who believe in Him and obey Him. Love, obedience, and faith can never be separated.

We must think about the word **trial** in this verse. Trials are various kinds of troubles and difficult circumstances which come upon us at different times in our lives.[6] God allows such trials to come on us in order to test and to strengthen our faith (verse 2). But when trials come, it is possible for us to fall into sin. For example, if we are suffering persecution because of our faith, we may be tempted to give up our faith. To give up our faith is a great sin. Or, for example, if by God's grace we have been given the chance to gain some wealth, we may be tempted to use that wealth for ourselves; we may begin loving our wealth and stop loving God. If we do this, we will have fallen into sin. Or, for another example, we may begin to fall in love with some man or woman, even though we are already married. In such a circumstance the temptation to sin will be very great; our faith will indeed be tested.

These are all examples of trials that can lead us into temptation to sin. If we do not stand firm and persevere in such situations, we shall fall into sin. The **trial** itself does not cause us to sin; rather, it is our inner desires and lusts that cause us to sin (verse 14). Sin arises in our sinful nature. We cannot blame our trials for our sin; we can only blame ourselves.

13–14 In these verses, James uses the word **tempted**. Here he is not talking about the kind of trials that he mentioned in verses 2 and 12. He is talking here about the TEMPTATION or desire to sin. God, according to His will, may allow trials to come upon us for the testing and strengthening of our faith. But it is never God's will that we be tempted to sin. The temptation to sin never comes from God; it comes only from our own sinful desires.

Sometimes Christians are overcome by temptation and fall into sin. Often they try to blame God for their sin; they say, "God tempted me, and I fell." But we must never think such a thing. God never tempts anyone to sin.

Therefore, as we read this chapter, we must keep in mind that James is talking about two different things. First, he talks about trials, which arise from our outward circumstances (verses 2–3,12). Second, here in verses 13–14, he talks about temptations to sin, which arise from evil desires within us. God allows the outward trials to come in order to test and strengthen our faith. The inward temptations, however, never come from God. **For God cannot be tempted by evil, nor does he tempt anyone** (verse 13). The outward

---

[6] Trials, in this sense, are not only bad things that happen to us; they can also be pleasant things. Such pleasant things can be called "trials" because they test our faith and obedience just as much as painful trials do. In this verse, then, the word **trial** means "test of faith."

trials we must endure; the inward temptations we must overcome.

15 All Christians from time to time experience various temptations, that is, evil thoughts and desires (see 2 Corinthians 10:5 and comment). If we immediately throw them off, we will not fall into sin. But if we allow any one of these evil thoughts and desires to take root and grow, it will quickly result in sin—that is, **it gives birth to sin**. Even if these thoughts and desires do not lead to actual evil behavior, the thoughts and desires themselves will become sins if they remain in our minds and hearts. And the result of sin is death. Sin leads men to eternal death (see Romans 6:23; Galatians 6:7–8).

16–17 **Don't be deceived**. God never draws men to do evil. He only draws men to do good. For those who love God, everything He does is for their benefit (Romans 8:28). Every gift that God gives is **good and perfect**. And every good and perfect gift is from God.

James here calls God the **Father of heavenly lights**. He means that God is the creator of the sun, moon, and stars. But God Himself is not like these "heavenly lights," which keep changing between day and night. God's light always shines; in Him there is no darkness (John 8:12; 1 John 1:5).

18 **He** (God) **chose to give us birth**. That is, by His will He created us. By His will He chose us to be in His family (see Ephesians 1:4–5). To be a Christian—that is, to have faith in Jesus—means to be born anew into God's family (see John 1:12; 3:3). In other words, it means to become a **new creation** (2 Corinthians 5:17).

God created us **through the word of truth**. The **word of truth** can mean Jesus Christ Himself (John 1:1–3); or it can mean the Gospel of Christ (1 Peter 1:23). Both meanings are true.

Why did God give us birth into His family? He did this so that we might be a **kind of firstfruits**. Christ Himself was the **firstfruits** among believers (1 Corinthians 15:20,23). Believers, by the same analogy, are the firstfruits of all that God created. According to the Old Testament law, the Jews were required to offer to God the firstfruits of their harvest each year (Numbers 18:12). That fruit was considered to be best of all. Therefore, among men, Christians are to be like firstfruits offered to God—the best of the harvest. Such an offering is pleasing to God.

Listening and Doing (1:19–27)

19 We should be always **quick**—ready and eager—to listen to God, to His word, and to each other. The man who is always talking and seldom listening is a proud man. He gives no regard to the thoughts of others.

We should be **slow to speak**; that is, before we speak we should first think about what we are going to say. Before speaking we should ask ourselves three questions: Is what we are about to say true? Is it kind? Is it necessary? If it's true, kind, and necessary, then let us say it. If not, then let us keep silent.

In addition to being slow to speak, we should also be **slow to become angry**. To be angry is not always a sin (Ephesians 4:26). For example, it is not a sin to be angry against wrongdoing (see Mark 11:15–17). However, it is a sin to "blow up," to lose one's temper. We must not become angry quickly. Before we allow our anger to rise up, we must be sure whether what we are getting angry at is truly evil or not. Our anger must be God's anger, not our own human anger. Our anger must never be personal; we must never desire vengeance. We must be angry with sin, but never with the sinner; otherwise, we ourselves will be sinning.

20 Human anger is never righteous. Human anger is directed against people, not against their actions. Human anger is selfish. Human anger arises because man's interests are being threatened, not because God's interests are being threatened. Human anger is for man's sake, not for God's sake. That is why **man's anger does not bring about the righteous life that God desires.**

21 **Therefore, get rid of all moral filth and the evil that is so prevalent.** Here James repeats the admonitions that Paul and Peter have frequently given in their letters (see Ephesians 4:22,31; 5:3; 1 Peter 2:1 and comments).

The word of God has been **planted** in us (see 1 Peter 1:23). We need to believe it, accept it, study it, nurture it. If God's word grows within us, it will **save** us. However, if we allow God's word in us to die, it will not save us (see Mark 4:14–20).

22 In verse 19, James wrote: **Everyone should be quick to listen**. But it is not enough only to **listen** to God's word. We must also obey it. We are not saved by listening; we are saved by believing. And true believing always includes obedience (see James 2:14,17).

Many people hear God's word and say, "What a pleasing word!" But even though they read God's word and like it, if they don't obey it, it will do them no good. In fact, they will be judged by it. People who don't obey God's word do not have true faith; they only **deceive** themselves.

23–24 Here God's word is compared to a **mirror**. When we look in a mirror, we see our true face, our true self; that is, we see our sinful nature. God's word, like a mirror, shows us our sin. But if we only listen to His word without heeding it, we will be like a man who looks into a mirror, sees his sin, and then immediately turns away and forgets about it. Let us not turn away from the "mirror" quickly. Rather let us heed what the mirror shows us—and then do something about it. We will need to wash our face! We will need to get rid of the sin that we see in the mirror.

25 Here James talks about the man who looks intently into the mirror—that is, **who looks intently into the perfect law**. The **perfect law** is Christ's word, Christ's GOSPEL. The Gospel is the power of God for man's salvation (Romans 1:16). Therefore, the **perfect law**, Christ's Gospel, gives **freedom**, because it frees us from sin and its punishment, which is death.

The man who looks intently into the **perfect law**—God's word, the Gospel—does not forget it; rather, he heeds it and obeys it. Such a man **will be blessed** not only in this life but also in the next.

26 Many people suppose that they are religious; but, in fact, they are religious only outwardly. Inwardly there is much evil in their hearts; therefore, when they speak, evil comes out in their words. Such people are not truly religious.

One of the main signs of a truly religious person is that he can control his tongue. True religion gives one the power to control one's tongue; false or outward religion cannot give that power. Such a religion is **worthless**.

Among Christians the commonest and most destructive sins are sins of the tongue, especially when we use our tongues to criticize and judge each other (see James 3:6,8). Jesus Himself taught how important our words are to God. Jesus said: **"I tell you that men will have to give account on the day of judgment for every careless word they have spoken. For by your words you will be acquitted, and by your words you will be condemned"** (Matthew 12:36–37).

27 A **pure and faultless** religion—that is, true religion—is this: first, to do works of love, such as caring for orphans and widows; and second, to keep oneself pure, to keep oneself from being **polluted by the world** (see James 4:4). In short, a pure life and a loving heart is proof that our religion is true.

CHAPTER 2

Favoritism Forbidden (2:1–13)

1 **My brothers . . . don't show favoritism**. That is, do not take into account differences in men's position and wealth. Do not look on a person's outer appearance. In our minds, we are not to divide people into rich and poor, high caste and low caste, high rank and low rank. The light of the glory of Christ makes the glory of this world fade into nothing. Therefore, let us not look at a person's worldly position or circumstances. Rather, we should look only at how much the light of Christ shines in his life. Instead of looking at man's outward appearance, let us look rather at his inward spiritual qualities.

2–4 James here illustrates his teaching on favoritism by giving the example of a rich man and a poor man coming into a Christian meeting.

But it's not only in public meetings that we must show no favoritism. We must also treat all those who come to our homes equally. At all times and in all places we must show the same love and respect to all—from the highest government official to the lowest laborer, from the highest caste to the lowest, from the richest to the poorest. If we do not do this, we make ourselves a judge between men (verse 9). God does not show favoritism; therefore, we must not show favoritism either (Romans 2:11; Ephesians 6:9).

5 In James' time, most believers were poor, and many were slaves. Because of their poverty and affliction in this world, these believers looked on the Gospel of Christ as a word of great hope, a promise of liberation from their suffering.

It is the same in our time. The rich usually do not come to Christ (Mark 10:23–25). In every generation God has chosen mainly the poor, the lower classes, the ordinary people to be the ones to **inherit the kingdom**—the KINGDOM OF GOD. In the world they are poor; but in heaven they will be rich. But in this life they will be "rich" also—that is, **rich in faith**. They will be rich in faith because they have put their trust in God and not in earthly riches.

6–7 Most rich people don't like to hear the Gospel, because the Gospel tells them to spend their money for the poor (Mark 10:21–22). Most rich people love their possessions rather than God (Matthew 6:24). Men with authority don't like to hear the Gospel either, because the Gospel says that all authority belongs to Christ (Matthew 28:18). For this reason, most rich and powerful men oppose Christ and His followers. They slander the **noble name** of Christ, and they exploit His followers and drag them into court.

And yet these believers, to whom James is writing, were disregarding the poor and showing great honor to the rich and powerful people who were persecuting them!

8–9 The second greatest commandment says: **Love your neighbor as yourself** (Leviticus 19:18; Mark 12:31). This means that we must love all people equally—whether rich or poor. But if we **show favoritism**, we are breaking the law—that is, the second commandment. And in breaking the law, we become **lawbreakers** (verse 9).

James here calls the second commandment the **royal law**, because it is the commandment of the King of kings. On earth the law of a king is the highest law. The two great commandments of Christ are like that; no other law is higher than these (Mark 12:29-31).

10 In any country there are many laws. If a person breaks just one of these laws, he is considered a criminal. It is the same with God's LAW. Included in the Old Testament law are many rules and regulations. Even if a person obeys every rule but one, it does him no good. If just one rule is broken, the person is considered a lawbreaker; he is guilty of breaking the whole law (see Galatians 3:10). Therefore, James tells us, we must not show favoritism; or else we too shall become lawbreakers, guilty of breaking the whole law.

11 Using two of the ten commandments as examples (Exodus 20:13–14), James again shows that if one does not obey the law completely, he will be considered a lawbreaker. But here James' main point is that it is impossible for anyone to obey the law completely; it is impossible for a person to obey perfectly every rule all the time. This is why in God's sight no one can be justified by the law (see Galatians 2:15–16 and comment).

12 We Christians must walk according to the **law that gives freedom,** because we will be judged by God according to that law. What is the **law that gives freedom**? It is Christ's law. The two greatest commandments and the ten commandments are included in Christ's law. But why is it called the "law that gives freedom"? The reason is because we don't follow this law by compulsion, like slaves; we follow it freely by our own desire, like children. Christ gives us a new desire, a new mind, a new life. He also gives us the power to obey His law. But that is not all; if we break His law in any respect, He will forgive us. We are no longer in bondage to sin. We are now free to follow Christ and to obey Him (see John 8:31–32,36). This is why James calls Christ's law the **law that gives freedom**.

13 James said in verse 12 that we must speak and act **as those who are going to be judged by the law that gives freedom**—that is, Christ's law. The Jewish law of the Old Testament showed no mercy (Deuteronomy 17:2–7). But Christ's law is a merciful law. If we show mercy to others, God will show mercy to us. But if we do not show mercy to others, we shall obtain no mercy (Matthew 5:7: 6:12,14–15). If we do not show mercy to others, we shall be judged according to the Old Testament law. However, if we show mercy, we shall be judged according to Christ's merciful law. So James tells us to be sure to speak and act mercifully, so that we will be judged by the merciful law.

Mercy is greater that JUDGMENT. If judgment was greater than mercy, none of us would escape condemnation. If judgment were greater than mercy, God would never have sent Christ to save the world. But God has placed mercy above judgment. Therefore, we must do the same in our dealings with others. We must show love and mercy to all people—high and low, rich and poor—without favoritism. To the extent we show mercy to others, to that same extent God will show mercy to us.

Faith and Deeds (2:14–26)

14 It is easy to say, "I believe"; but only saying it means nothing. We must ask ourselves: "Is my faith real or not?". Because we are saved only through true faith, not through false faith.[7]

How can we tell if our faith is true or not? We can tell by our **deeds**. Our **deeds**—that is, our deeds of love, our deeds of obedience—are the proof of our faith. If there are no deeds accompanying our faith, then such a "faith" will not save us (see Matthew 7:21 and comment). Such a faith is not true faith; it is **dead** faith (verse 17).

15–16 Here James says that false faith is like love that is expressed in words but not in action. We can easily say to our poor brother or sister that we love them, but if we do nothing to help them, our love is false, worthless (1 John 3:17–18). This kind of "love" benefits no one. In the same way, unless our faith is manifested by deeds, it is worthless.

17 This is one of the most important verses in the New Testament, because it keeps us from misinterpreting some of Paul's teaching. In Ephesians 2:8–9, Paul wrote that man is saved not by works but through faith. Many people misunderstand Paul, and begin to think that they no longer have to do any good works. They suppose that because man is saved through faith, good works are no longer necessary. They forget that Paul taught in other verses that good works are indeed necessary. Paul wrote in Ephesians 2:10 that we were **created in Christ Jesus to do good works**. He also wrote: **The only thing that counts is faith expressing itself through love** (Galatians 5:6).

James here seeks to correct the mistaken idea that Christians don't have to do good works. Yes, it is true that we are saved through faith, not through works. No one can obtain salvation by doing works—no matter how many or how good the works are. This is true. But we must ask: What is faith? True faith is faith that is expressed by works. Works must always accompany faith; works are included in true faith. There is no such thing as true faith without works; true faith always gives rise to good works.

What good works? The works of obedience. The work that God wants us to do is to obey Jesus' commands (John 14:15). And Jesus' main command is:

---

[7] It is important to remember throughout this discussion of faith that faith itself does not save us. We are saved **by grace**; it is God who saves us (see Ephesians 2:8–9 and comment).

Love each other as I have loved you (John 15:12).

Therefore, true faith always manifests itself by love (Galatians 5:6). If a man shows as much love for his neighbor as he does for himself, then we can be sure his faith is genuine.

First (before deeds) comes faith. Then, when we have believed, we become new people. True faith then causes a change in our behavior. God fills our life with His love through the Holy Spirit (Romans 5:5). We receive new power to love our neighbor and to obey all of Christ's other commands. And this new love and new obedience is the proof that our faith is indeed true.

Therefore, in summary, the New Testament teaches that we cannot obtain salvation by our own work and effort; rather, we obtain salvation through true faith. But true faith is always demonstrated by our love and obedience; if there is no love and obedience, then there is no faith. Deeds—that is, love and obedience[8]—are the proof of our faith. Without love and obedience our faith will not save us; it is **dead**.

One of the two criminals who was crucified with Jesus believed just before he died (Luke 23:39–43). After believing, he had no chance to do any good works. From this, we know that he was saved through faith, and not through any works. But for those who do not die immediately after believing, their faith must be manifested by works of love and obedience as long as they live.

18 James here describes an imaginary conversation between two people. The first person says that only faith is necessary, not works. The second person says that both faith and works together are necessary. The second person (James) says to the first: "You have faith, you say? **Show me your faith**. You can't show it, because your faith is without works. But **I will show you my faith by what I do**. My works are the proof of my faith."

19 Here the imaginary conversation continues. The second person (James) says to the first person, **"You believe that there is one God**, do you? You think that by saying, 'I believe there is one God,' you can show you have true faith. But you're wrong; that doesn't show anything. Even DEMONS say that. Demons also believe there is a God; but their faith is false, because their works are evil."

20–21 As the imaginary conversation continues, the second person (James) reminds the first person about Abraham. God told Abraham to sacrifice his only son Isaac on the altar (see Genesis 22:1–13; Hebrews 11:17–19). Abraham had true faith in God; therefore, he obeyed God. Why was Abraham **considered** RIGHTEOUS (verse 21)? Because he believed? Or because he obeyed? The answer is both. Abraham was considered righteous both because he believed and also because he obeyed.

22 Abraham's **faith and actions** (obedience) **were working together**. Without obedience, faith is dead (verse 17). Without faith, obedience is worthless; it can never please God. Because **without faith, it is impossible to please God** (Hebrews 11:6).

Abraham's faith came first. But only by obedience was his faith **made complete** or perfect. Faith without obedience is like a fruit tree without fruit; it is useless. A tree is "made complete" by its fruit. In the same way, our faith is made complete by our works, by our obedience. Men will recognize us by our **fruit**, by our obedience (Matthew 7:20).

23 James here quotes from Genesis 15:6. **Abraham believed God, and it was credited to him as** RIGHTEOUSNESS (see Romans 4:1–3). Again we must understand from this that man is **considered righteous** by faith. But that faith must be true faith—that is, faith that is expessed in love and obedience.

Here it is necessary to add to what was said earlier. Just as we cannot be saved by a faith without works, so we cannot be

[8] Love and obedience always go together; to obey is to love, and to love is to obey (see John 14:15). In the same way, faith and deeds always go together; you can't have one without the other.

saved by works without faith. No man's works—even his most noble religious works—can be perfect. Every person makes mistakes and sins from time to time. Therefore, on the basis of our works we can never be considered righteous in God's sight; and if we are not considered righteous by God, we will not be saved. It is only by putting our faith in the perfect work and righteousness of Jesus Christ that we ourselves can be considered righteous (see Romans 3:22–24 and comment). We can never make ourselves righteous or obtain salvation by our own labor and effort. Only by receiving Christ's righteousness through faith can we be considered righteous in God's sight.

24 Paul has said in Galatians 2:15–16 and Ephesians 2:8–9 that man is **justified** (declared righteous) and saved through faith. This is true, and James agrees with it completely. James' only point is that this faith must be true faith—that is, a faith manifested by love and obedience. Therefore, James says here that a **person is justified by what he does and not by faith alone**. James' meaning is that we will be justified only by a "working faith"—a faith that is manifested by works.

25 Here James gives a second illustration from the Old Testament, that of **Rahab the prostitute** (see Joshua 2:1–16; Hebrews 11:31). Rahab gave help to the **spies** sent by Joshua. How do we know that her faith was real? We know because of what she did. Rahab helped the Jewish spies to escape; that was the proof of her faith. And, as a result, Rahab herself escaped death; when Joshua and his army destroyed Jericho, he ordered that Rahab be spared (Joshua 6:24–25).

26 Again James repeats his main point: **faith without deeds is dead** (see verse 17 and comment). Faith without deeds is like a body without a spirit; such a body is spiritually dead. It is no better than a corpse.

CHAPTER 3

Taming the Tongue (3:1–12)

1 **Not many of you should presume to be teachers**. Why does James say this? Because in James' time (and in our time too), many people were trying to be teachers and leaders. They were seeking honor and high positions for themselves. James is saying here: "Don't seek to be a teacher in order to gain honor and position, or you may regret it." To be a teacher can be a great disadvantage. Since teachers and leaders are given greater knowledge and responsibility than others, they will be **judged more strictly** on the day of judgment (see Luke 12:47–48).

Therefore, **many** should not seek to be teachers. But it is necessary for some to be teachers. To be a teacher or leader is a good thing (1 Timothy 3:1). In this case, what kind of people should be teachers? To be a teacher or leader, there are two requirements. First, to be a teacher a person must have a special gift from the Lord, because teachers are themselves a gift from the Lord to the church (Ephesians 4:7,11–12). Second, to be a teacher or preacher a person must have a special calling or appointment from the Lord (see 1 Corinthians 9:16).

2 We all stumble and sin in many ways, but the most common way we sin is in our speech. This is a special danger for teachers, because their work involves much speaking. But speaking is not only a danger for teachers! It is a danger for all Christians; countless opportunities to sin come to all of us through our speaking.

James says that if we could perfectly control what we say—if we could control our tongue—we would be perfect people. If we could keep our tongue **in check** (under control), we could keep our whole body **in check**. Among all the members of our body, the tongue is the most difficult to keep under control. The person who can control his tongue will certainly be able to control all the other evil desires of his body also.

But we know that no one is perfect; and one reason is that no one is able to perfectly control his tongue.

3 One can control a big horse with a small **bit**. Our tongue is like a bit. If we could control our tongue, we could then control our whole body.

4 Our tongue is also like the **rudder** of a large ship. A rudder is a very small thing attached to the back of a ship, by which the ship can be steered. In the same way, our tongue is a very small member of our body, but it has a big effect.

5 Our tongue is also like a **small spark** of fire, or like a match. Such a small thing can set a huge forest on fire!

From these three examples—the bit, the rudder, and the spark—we can see that the tongue is a very important member of our body. One small word of slander can split a church and bring dishonor to its leaders. Or one small word of false teaching can cause many to go astray.

6 The tongue itself is like a **fire**. Satan uses our tongue more than any other of our members. Our tongue is **set on fire by hell**; that is, Satan sets our tongue on fire. If we do not control our tongue, our tongue will corrupt our whole person and set the **whole course of** [our] **life on fire**. That is, if not controlled, our tongue will lead us to destruction.

Among Christians, the tongue does the most evil. A Christian may lead a very devout and godly life in all other ways, but if his tongue is evil, it will ruin his life. The commonest sins among Christians are sins of the tongue.

7–8 **. . . no man can tame the tongue** (verse 8). If this is so, is there no help for us? Yes, God will help us "tame" our tongue. However, in this life we cannot expect to perfectly control our tongues all the time in every situation.

Our tongue is a **restless evil**; it is always looking for an occasion to speak evil. The tongue is **full of deadly poison**. Some kinds of poison can't be recognized when they are first tasted; some poison may even taste sweet. Only later does the poison do its deadly work. Our tongue is like that (Psalm 140:3).

9–10 Many people (including Christians) are "double-tongued." In prayer meetings they praise God with sweet words. But then they go out later and speak evil of their brother. **Out of the same mouth come praise and cursing.**[9] **My brothers, this should not be.**

11–12 Here James uses illustrations from nature to show that being double-tongued is, in fact, impossible. Because the sweet sounding prayers of the double-tongued person are not really sweet at all; they are like the sweet-tasting poison mentioned above. They are not sweet in God's ears; He will not listen to them (Psalm 66:18). The "double-tongued" person, then, is really a poison-tongued person who sounds sweet from time to time.

In nature, only one kind of water comes out of any one spring. From a fresh-water spring comes fresh water; from a salt-water spring comes salt water. Similarly, only one kind of fruit comes from any one tree. From a fig tree come figs; from a grapevine come grapes. We can recognize the spring by its water and the tree by its fruit.

In the same way, we can recognize men by their speech. If a man's speech is evil and bitter, his heart will also be evil and bitter. An evil person may fool us for a time by speaking sweet words, but we will not be fooled for long; soon the evil in his heart will be manifest by evil words.

Let no one deceive himself: God will not accept the sweet prayers of someone who speaks evil of his brother. God knows such prayers are false. **If anyone says, "I love God," yet hates his brother, he is a liar** (1 John 4:20–21).

Two Kinds of Wisdom (3:13–18)

13 If we say we are **wise and understanding**, then let us show proof of it! If we say we have love, let us show

[9] In these verses, the word **cursing** and **curse** (verse 9) refer not only to cursing itself but also to critical talk in general.

it. If we say we have faith, let us show it. How can we show it? We can show it by our **good life**, by our **deeds**.

Our teaching, our preaching—whatever work we do—must be done **in the humility that comes from wisdom**. There are two kinds of wisdom: God's wisdom (heavenly wisdom) and man's wisdom (worldly wisdom). God's wisdom always leads to humility. Man's wisdom always leads to pride—that is, to **bitter envy and selfish ambition** (verse 14).

14 The person with worldly wisdom may boast that he does God's work, but in fact he does only what is for his own benefit. Such a person should not boast about what he does for God. If he does so, it will be a lie; he will be denying the truth.

15 Just as we can recognize a spring by tasting its water, so we can recognize what kind of wisdom a man has by observing its fruit. The fruit of heavenly wisdom is humility. The fruit of worldly or natural wisdom is **envy** and **ambition**. Worldly wisdom is **of the devil**—that is, of SATAN—who is the **prince of this world** (John 16:11).

16 What is the cause of division in the church and fighting among brothers? The main cause is **envy and selfish ambition** (verse 14). And this occurs not only among ordinary brothers in the church, but also among the leaders! Let each believer examine himself.

17 The **wisdom that comes from heaven** is God's wisdom. We must ask God for this wisdom (James 1:5).

What is God's wisdom like? How can we recognize it? First, it is **pure**, because God is pure. Our wisdom must be pure, or else it cannot lead to peace and other good fruit.

Second, God's wisdom is **peace loving**. A wise man (one with God's wisdom) does not cause strife. A wise man is quick to listen and slow to speak (James 1:19). He always tries to do what leads to peace (Romans 14:19).

The wise man is **considerate**. He cares about others. He doesn't speak hurtful words. Unwise men debate in a harsh manner; they are only interested in winning the argument. Such men may win the argument, but they lose their friends. The wise man does not act in this way.

The wise man is **submissive**; he is willing to remain in submission to others (Ephesians 5:21). The wise man does not try to control other people; rather, he respects their thoughts and desires.

The wise man is **full of mercy**. He does not judge others. He is always ready to forgive others. He never tries to take revenge.

The wise man is also full of **good fruit**—that is, the fruit of the Holy Spirit (Galatians 5:22–23). He is **impartial**; he does not take sides or show favoritism.

And finally, the wise man is **sincere**. He is worthy of trust. He never tries to deceive someone for his own gain. He always speaks the truth in love (Ephesians 4:15).

Is our wisdom and our speech **sincere**? That is a deep question. Sometimes when we talk to each other our speech is not completely honest and open. We hide things. Our speech is devious, crooked, insincere. Our words are sweet, but our thoughts are not sweet! We don't speak an outright lie, of course; we all know that is a sin. But we often keep back part of the truth in order to create a false impression—and that also is a sin.[10] However, the wise man is always **sincere**; he always speaks with complete sincerity and honesty.

18 The **peacemakers** mentioned in this verse are those who are wise, those who have God's wisdom. They sow seeds of righteousness and they reap a **harvest of righteousness** (see Galatians 6:7). Peacemakers have learned to control their tongue.

---

[10] There are things, of course, about which we must not talk. (We must not talk about the faults of others, for example.) But our silence must never be for the purpose of deceiving other people.

CHAPTER 4

Submission to God (4:1–10)

1 What causes **fights and quarrels** in the church? They are caused by our **desires**. What kind of desires? Evil and selfish desires. Everyone can recognize evil desires; these are the desires to commit obvious sins. But here James is not talking only about evil desires. He is also talking about selfish desires. Selfish desires are desires for good things, but they are desired for selfish reasons. For example, we may desire good things like an education, a scholarship, or a job; but it is possible to desire these things for purely selfish reasons.

Why does our desire for these good things so often cause strife and envy among us? Because we desire these things for selfish reasons. We desire them in order to benefit ourselves, not to benefit God or others. We are interested only in our own welfare, our own advantage. This is selfishness. And all selfish desires are sinful—whether they are for a good thing or an evil thing. And these selfish desires are the main cause of fights and quarrels among Christians (1 Peter 2:11).

Some Christians who fight and quarrel among themselves even say they are doing it for God's sake. When we look at human history, we see that many evil things have been done in God's name. Jesus warned His disciples that men would persecute and kill them, and think that they were thereby offering a service to God (John 16:2). Let us not deceive ourselves. It is with Satan we must fight, not with other believers. Such fighting and quarreling among believers is never pleasing to God. Such behavior is not for God's sake; it is for one's own sake.

2 In this life no man can have all he wants. Therefore, men are always greedy to get more. As soon as we receive some gift or have some desire fulfilled, we begin again to desire something else. We are never satisfied.

Instead of our always seeking, seeking, we should rather ask God for the things we need. He knows everything we need. God will give us what is necessary for our well-being. If there is some good thing we desire, let us not strive and struggle to get it ourselves, but rather in faith let us ask God for it.

3 But some people will say: "I have asked God, but I haven't received what I asked for." Why have they not received? Because they have asked **with wrong motives**. That is, they have asked for selfish reasons. They have asked God for things for their own pleasure and contentment. They have asked God to grant them help and success in their work—not for the sake of God or others—but only for their own sake, for their own benefit.

Whenever we ask God for anything, we should always say, as Jesus did: **"Yet not what I will, but what you will"** (Mark 14:36). We must examine ourselves; we must ask ourselves: "For whose sake am I making this request to God? For my sake, or His sake?" We must say to God that whatever He gives us we will use in His service and in the service of others. This is a difficult teaching, but it is the example that Jesus Himself gave us. If we want to receive anything from God, we must ask unselfishly. And let us remember that we can never fool God. He knows our hearts. He will know whether we are asking selfishly or unselfishly.

4 **You adulterous people . . .** James here is talking to believers. Why does he call them **adulterous**? Because they have deserted Christ, their bridegroom, and gone off with the world. They have loved the pleasures of the world more than Christ (see 2 Corinthians 11:2–3; Ephesians 5:23). It is not possible to love God and the world at the same time (Matthew 6:24; 1 John 2:15).

5 **. . . the spirit he caused to live in us tends to envy.**[11] God (or Christ) is like a faithful and longing husband, and we believers are like His bride. But we have often been unfaithful. We have left our true husband and followed after other "gods"—such as, selfish ambition and money. And so God is jealous (Exodus 20:4–5).

6 But even though we stray far from God, He continues to call us by His grace and mercy. No matter how great our sin, His GRACE is greater. He **gives us more grace**, so that we might return to Him and begin to love Him again.

But God does not give grace to all—only to the **humble**. James here quotes Proverbs 3:34 (see 1 Peter 5:5). **God opposes the proud**. Let the proud beware. To be an enemy of almighty God is a fearful thing.

7 We must turn from the world and its pleasures and submit to God. Together with that, we must resist the devil. Satan is always trying to draw us away from God through worldly pleasures and enticements. Therefore, we must resist him; we must resist the temptations he sends us (1 Peter 5:8–9).

Many ask: "How can I resist Satan? How can I overcome him? A temptation comes, but no matter how hard I try to resist it, I quickly fall into it" (see Romans 7:15,18–19).

How do we resist the devil? We resist him through Christ's power. The first step is to remember that whenever we follow the devil's wishes, we betray our Lord Jesus. The second step is to **stand** in Christ's power (Ephesians 6:10–11,13). Christ's power is always available. But we must "put on" His power, His armor. Christ's power is like electricity. Electricity is always available, but we must turn on the switch.

Therefore, when the devil tempts us, we must tell him simply: **"Away from me, Satan"** (Matthew 4:10).

8 Do we want God to come near to us? If so, then we must draw near to Him. If God seems to have drawn away from us, the reason always is that we have first drawn away from Him. Why have we drawn away from God? It is always because of some sin in our lives which we are not willing to give up.

How can we again draw near to God? James gives the answer: **Wash your hands, you sinners**. That is, we must cleanse ourselves from all sinful work and behavior. Not only that, James also adds: **. . . purify your hearts, you double-minded**. We must cleanse ourselves not only from outward sins, but also from the hidden inward sins of our hearts. God sees our inner heart and mind (1 Chronicles 28:9). He knows if we are being **double-minded** or not. The double-minded man tries to love God and the world at the same time. Therefore, such a man's love for God is impure; his heart is unholy. Such a man will not be accepted by God; for only with clean hands and pure heart can we draw near to God (Psalm 24:3–4; Matthew 5:8; Hebrews 12:14).

How can our hearts be purified? We must repent and come to Jesus; that is, we must confess our sins and turn from them. We must humble ourselves, and He will give us grace (verse 6) and come near to us. Let us thank and praise Him for showing such mercy to sinners such as us!

9 Paul says: **Rejoice!** (Philippians 4:4). **Be joyful always** (1 Thessalonians 5:16). But James says here: **Grieve, mourn and wail**. Why should we grieve, mourn, and wail? Because of our sin. Here are two truths. Paul tells us, "Rejoice," because God loves us so much. James tells us, "Grieve," because we love Him so little. We must rejoice in God's goodness and in His grace. We must grieve for our sin and unholiness. Jesus said, **"Blessed are those who mourn"**—that is, blessed are those who mourn for their sins (Matthew 5:4).

---

[11] It is not certain what the exact translation of these words should be; different versions of the Bible give different translations. It is not certain whether the **spirit** mentioned here is the Holy Spirit or man's spirit. Whichever translation is chosen, the general meaning of the passage seems to be that God looks on us with jealous longing, and when we begin to love the world more than Him, He becomes very upset with us.

10 Therefore, let us humble ourselves before God. . . . **a broken and contrite heart, O God, you will not despise** (Psalm 51:17). And when we humble ourselves, God will draw near to us. He will give us grace (verse 6). And **he will lift** [us] **up** (see Matthew 5:3; Luke 18:9–14; 1 Peter 5:6).

Warning Against Slander (4:11–17)

11 James has been talking about our evil tongue (James 3:8) and about **fights and quarrels** among brothers (verse 1). Now he says: **Brothers, do not slander one another**. What is **slander**? Slander is showing our brother's faults and weaknesses to another person. Since everyone has faults and weaknesses, slander is often true or partly true. When slander is false, it becomes false witness. But whether what we say is true or false, to talk about our brother's faults to another is slander, and slander is a very great sin in God's eyes.

To slander our brother and to judge him are very similar. In our heart and mind, we judge our brother; with our tongue and lips we slander him (see Matthew 7:1 and comment).

When we judge our brother, we **judge the law**, Christ's law. To "judge" the law means to disobey it. When we do that, we make ourselves greater than the law. When we judge the law, we are saying that some commandments of the law are good and others are bad. We are, in effect, saying: "I will obey this command, but not that one." We are saying: "If I want to slander or judge my brother, I'll do so." In this way, we make ourselves "judges" of the law.

12 But there is **only one Lawgiver and Judge**. When we judge the law, we are putting ourselves in God's place, and that is the greatest sin of all. To seek to be like God is the greatest form of pride. It was for this sin that Adam and Eve were driven out of the Garden of Eden (Genesis 3:5–6). Instead of humbling ourselves before God as we ought to be doing (verse 10), we are making ourselves lord and judge. What a mistake! What a sin! Because there is only one Lord and one Judge. There is only one who is able to **save and destroy**, namely God Himself. Only He can give men salvation or condemn them to hell. No matter how much we exalt ourselves, we cannot **save** ourselves. No matter how much we judge our brother, we cannot **destroy** or condemn him. Only God can save and destroy. Therefore, let us not dare to judge our Christian brother. Not only that, we must not even dare to judge our non-Christian **neighbor**.

13–15 Now James looks at another subject: the future. Does James say here that we should never plan ahead? No. We must, of course, make plans; we must look ahead. The farmer, when he plants, must look ahead to the harvest. Paul and the other apostles planned where they would go and how long they would stay there. But as we plan we must always say in our hearts: "If it is God's will, I will do such and such" (see Acts 18:21; 1 Corinthians 4:19). Because our entire life is in God's hands. We don't know what will happen tomorrow. All is uncertain. We are like a **mist** of water: today we are here; tomorrow we are gone. Therefore, we must never put our trust in plans; we must trust only in God. Only He is certain and never-changing. Yes, we must plan and plant the seed; but God gives the harvest (1 Corinthians 3:7). We must plan and work, but God gives us success according to His will. In Him only must we put our confidence.

16 Therefore, let us not boast in our work, in our success. All our boasting must be in God. If we take for ourselves the praise that belongs to God, we sin against God. To give ourselves the praise for what God has done is a very great evil!

17 In this verse there are two very important teachings. The first is this: God will judge us according to what we know. If a small child breaks a law in ignorance, he is not punished for it; he has not sinned. On the other hand, if a grown man knowingly breaks a law, for him it is a great sin. The more a person knows, the greater will be his punishment if he disobeys God (see Luke 12:47–48; James 3:1 and comments).

The second teaching in this verse

concerns sin. Many people think that sin is only doing something bad. But here James teaches that sin is also failing to do something we ought to do. Not doing something we know we should do is just as much a sin as doing something we know we shouldn't do. If we do not help our brother when he is in need, we sin against him. Likewise, if we do not believe in Jesus, we sin against Him.

CHAPTER 5

Warning to Rich Oppressors (5:1–6)

1–3 In this section, James mainly addresses wealthy people who oppress the poor. Those Christians who are well off should pay special heed to these verses.

Here James speaks like a prophet. He says that **misery** is about to come upon the rich people who oppress the poor. Then James says that the wealth and the clothing of the rich is already ruined. The coming destruction of the rich is so certain that James speaks of it as if it had already happened.[12] The corroded wealth of the rich will **testify** against them on the final day of judgment. Instead of using their riches to serve Christ and others, these rich people have stored up their riches for themselves. They have done this **in the last days**, says James. The **last days** are the days of Jesus Christ, that is, the period between Christ's first coming (His birth) and His second coming. The world is passing away; soon the rich will not be able to use their hoarded wealth. They will lose not only their wealth, but also their souls (see Matthew 6:19–21; Mark 8:36–37; Luke 6:24; 16:19–31).

In 70 A.D., not many years after this letter was written, the Roman army utterly destroyed the city of Jerusalem. All the Jews of that city perished, together with their wealth. Thus James' "prophecy" came true, and quicker than anyone thought!

4 James accuses the rich of having cheated their workers. Such injustice cries up to heaven. **The cries of the harvesters have reached the ears of the Lord Almighty.**[13] And God hears. God will avenge all injustice.

5 The rich have lived **in luxury and self-indulgence**. Before men kill animals for food, they fatten them. In the same way, the rich have been fattening themselves for the **day of slaughter**. The "day of slaughter" is the day of judgment, which will be coming soon (see Luke 12:15–21).

6 The rich and powerful, because of their greed, have killed **innocent men**. They have killed prophets and apostles (Matthew 23:37). James himself was killed in 62 A.D. But the greatest crime of the rich was to kill Jesus Christ (Acts 7:52). The **innocent men** that James mentions here can refer to many innocent men (the poor, the prophets, etc.) **who were not opposing** the rich, or it can refer to Jesus alone. Jesus did not oppose the rich. Even when they conspired to put Him to death, Jesus did not oppose them (see 1 Peter 2:23). On the day of judgment, God Himself will oppose all rich oppressors.

Patience in Suffering (5:7–12)

7–8 In this section, James again talks to believers. He writes: **Be patient . . . and stand firm**. Great tribulation was about to come, not only on the wealthy Jews, but also on the Christians of James' time. Not only was Jerusalem soon to be

---

[12] Paul has also written of future things as if they had already happened (see Romans 8:30 and comment).

[13] In place of the words **Lord Almighty**, some translations of the Bible say "Lord of hosts." The meaning is the same. The "hosts" are armies of angels.

destroyed; but even before that, the believers in Jerusalem would be facing severe persecution. Furthermore, the second coming of Christ was not far away. Therefore, let them not give up their faith; let them not fall away (see Mark 13:13; Hebrews 3:6,14; 10:36).

We cannot make ourselves **firm** and **patient** by our own strength. But God, through His Holy Spirit, is ready to help us. Patience is a fruit of the Holy Spirit (Galatians 5:22). God Himself will make us **strong, firm and steadfast** (1 Peter 5:10).

A farmer waits patiently for the rain. In Israel the rains fall mainly in the **autumn** and the **spring**. The autumn rain is called the "early rain," and the spring rain is called the "late rain." After the autumn rain, the farmer is able to plow his fields. After the spring rain, the harvest is ready to be cut. Just as the farmer waits patiently for the rain, so must believers wait patiently for the second coming of Jesus. If a farmer can wait patiently for an ordinary harvest, can we not wait patiently for the inheritance stored up for us in heaven?

9 Here again James warns Christians not to speak against each other. **Don't grumble against each other**, he writes.

When trials and persecution come upon us, how quick we are to blame each other for our troubles! Just as the ancient Jews grumbled against Moses and Aaron in the desert, so we too grumble against others—especially against our leaders (Exodus 16:1–3; 17:1–4). Let this not be!

Trials come upon us according to God's will, so that our faith might be tested (James 1:2–3). God is watching how we stand up under these trials. If under trial we grumble against others, we are actually grumbling against God (Exodus 16:8). He will judge us. Let us beware, lest He punish us as He punished the ancient Jews in the desert (Numbers 11:1; 14:1–4, 26–29). The **Judge** (Christ) **is standing at the door** (Revelation 3:20). He hears our grumbling. Christ is ready to return to earth as Judge; and He will judge not only non-believers, but believers also (1 Peter 4:17).

10–11 Those who persevere to the end are considered **blessed** (see James 1:4). James gives the Old Testament example of **Job**, who was an important man in his time. God tested Job by allowing terrible afflictions to come upon him. Job lost everything—his land, his house, his wealth, his children, his honor. Then he lost his health. But even in the face of such severe trials, Job never grumbled against God. And **finally**, in the end, God greatly blessed Job, and his final situation was better than his first. All this the Lord brought about; it was His plan and purpose from the beginning (Job 1:1–22; 2:1–10; 42:12–17).

God allows suffering and tribulation to come upon us for our good. In the end, because of His great mercy and love, He will always turn our sorrow and pain into joy and blessing (Psalm 103:8; Isaiah 61:1–3, 7). **Come, let us return to the Lord. He has torn us to pieces but he will heal us; he has injured us but he will bind up our wounds . . . he will restore us, that we may live in his presence** (Hosea 6:1–3).

12 **. . . do not swear**. James is here talking about swearing in ordinary conversations. We must speak plainly and honestly. **Let your "Yes" be yes, and your "No," no**. Whatever we say, it should be the truth. An honest person never needs to swear in order to prove that what he says is true. Such swearing is useless. Worse than that, when we swear unnecessarily, we use the Lord's name in vain (see Matthew 5:34–37). Let us beware; the Lord will judge us for every vain and careless word we speak (Matthew 12:36).

James does not mean that we should never swear an oath under any circumstances. In law courts in every country, it is customary to swear before giving testimony; this is not a sin. In important matters, it is suitable to swear an oath (Hebrews 6:16–17). The Apostle Paul many times called on the Lord to be a witness to what he was saying (2 Corinthians 1:23; Galatians 1:20; Philippians 1:8). James is not talking here about such situations. Rather, he is talking about the unnecessary and vain swearing that goes on in ordinary conversation.

The Prayer of Faith (5:13–20)

13 We must pray in every situation (Philippians 4:6). In this verse, James says that we should sing songs of praise when we are happy. That's true; but we should also sing songs of praise when we are in trouble! (see Acts 16:23–25).

14 Those who are sick should call the **elders of the church** to pray for their healing. The **elders** are the leaders in any local church (see 1 Timothy 5:17; Titus 1:5–6 and comments). They are to **anoint**[14] [the sick person] **with oil**. In New Testament times, **oil** was used as a medicine (see Mark 6:13; Luke 10:34). In this verse, James is referring to **oil** mainly as a medicine.[15] Therefore, we can see from this that in ordinary circumstances the sick need both medicine and prayer. Both medical treatment and prayer must be done **in the name of the Lord**. "In the name of the Lord" is not just some sort of saying or mantra. It means that we are praying and giving medicine as Christ's ambassadors, according to His will and for His glory, and with full faith in His healing power.

15 **And the prayer offered in faith will make the sick person well**. That is, the prayer of faith will heal the person's physical sickness. All healing power comes from Christ.[16] Christ can heal people through medicine alone, through prayer alone, or through both together. The farmer waters the seed, but God makes it grow (1 Corinthians 3:7). In the same way, the doctor and nurse give medicine, but Christ heals. James is not talking in this verse about the special healing gift of the Holy Spirit (1 Corinthians 12:9). That gift is given to only a few members of the church. But every Christian can pray the prayer of faith. Not only the elders must pray for the sick; the sick person himself along with his family must pray for his healing (verse 13). If the elders, however, agree together and pray in faith, Jesus will answer their prayer (Matthew 18:19–20; 21:22).

If he (the sick person) **has sinned, he will be forgiven**. Many diseases are not directly caused by sin (John 9:1–3). But some diseases do arise as the direct result of sin; and it is this kind of disease that James has in mind in this verse. The person with such a disease needs not only physical healing for his body but also spiritual healing for his soul. Through the **prayer offered in faith**, the sick person's sins will be forgiven and his soul healed. When He was on earth, Christ had the power both to heal the body and also to forgive sins (Psalm 103:2–3; Mark 2:3–12). And, through faith, all believers in Christ can receive that same power.

James does not mean to say in this verse that every sick person we pray for will be physically healed. That is obviously impossible, because all men must die sometime. But even though a sick person's body is not healed, if he repents and believes in Jesus, his sins will be forgiven and his soul will be saved. Salvation is the most important kind of "healing." It is complete healing, and it lasts forever.

16 All Christians agree that fellowship is important. We have house fellowships, we have prayer meetings, we have retreats, we have church services. And all these are important—indeed, essential.

But true fellowship involves more than attending meetings. To have true fellowship means that we **confess** [our] **sins to each other**. It means that we know each other, and love each other. It means that we trust each other, and pray for each other. Everyone of us has sins; everyone of us has something to confess. We must not hide things from one another.

---

14 In the Greek text of this verse, the word **anoint** which James uses refers to the application of medicine. It does not refer to sacramental anointing; for that, a different Greek word is used.

15 However, **oil** can also mean the Holy Spirit; oil is a sign of the Holy Spirit. Both meanings of oil are possible here, and they both fit together. Because even when we use medicine to heal a person, it is actually the Holy Spirit who does the healing.

16 Christ heals through the Holy Spirit.

Therefore, let us confess our sins to each other, and then let us pray for each other. When we do this, we shall all receive spiritual healing. And, at the same time, our fellowship will grow all the more close and joyful.

The prayer of a righteous man is powerful and effective. Who is the **righteous man**? We are the "righteous man." Through faith in Christ, we have been declared righteous in God's sight. Our prayers, then, are **powerful and effective**. Therefore, let us **pray continually** (1 Thessalonians 5:17).

17–18 The Old Testament prophet **Elijah** was a man just like us. His prayers were certainly **powerful and effective**! He prayed, and no rain fell on Israel for three and a half years. Then he prayed again, and the rain came. Elijah is an example for us (1 Kings 17:1; 18:1,41–45).

19–20 James here addresses Christian **brothers**. If a brother should **wander from the truth**, he is in danger of **death** (verse 20). Therefore, let us always try to **bring him back**. Only God can save, but He uses us to turn a sinning brother **from the error of his way**. If the sinning brother turns back from his error—that is, if he repents—all of his sins will be "covered over," forgiven, erased. Only through repentance can our sins be "covered over," or forgiven; there is no other way.

1 Peter

INTRODUCTION

This letter was written by the Apostle Peter in about 64 A.D. Most Bible scholars believe that Peter was in ROME when he wrote it. The letter was written to the churches in several provinces of the Roman Empire located in what is now modern Turkey; it was written to encourage the believers there to follow in Christ's steps and to stand firm in their faith during trials.

Peter was the chief of Jesus' twelve original disciples. His life is described in detail in the four Gospels and in the book of Acts.

OUTLINE

A. The Privileges and Responsibilities of Salvation (1:1–2:10).
   1. God's Plan of Salvation (1:1–12).
   2. The Lifestyle of Salvation (1:13–25).
   3. Growth in Salvation (2:1–10).
B. Christian Submission and God's Honor (2:11–3:7).
   1. Duty of Christian Submission (2:11–2:25).
   2. Husbands and Wives (3:1–7).
C. The Suffering and Persecution of Christians (3:8–5:14).
   1. The Blessing of Suffering for Righteousness (3:8–22).
   2. Living for God (4:1–11).
   3. Consolations in Suffering (4:12–19).
   4. Exhortations to Elders and Young Men (5:1–14).

CHAPTER 1

A Living Hope (1:1–12)

1 Peter wrote this letter to **God's elect**—that is, to Christians—living in several provinces of the ROMAN EMPIRE, located in what is now modern Turkey. Because of persecution by the Romans,[1] these Christians had been **scattered** from their original homes, and had fled to these provinces. Probably they included both Jewish and Gentile believers.

Peter calls himself an APOSTLE. He had been the chief of Jesus' original twelve disciples. Except for Judas, all of these disciples became known as apostles after Jesus' death.

2 Peter addresses his readers as those **who have been chosen according to the foreknowledge of God**—that is, believers in Christ. All Christians have been **chosen according to the foreknowledge of God** from before the creation of the world (see Romans 8:29–30; Ephesians 1:4–5 and comments). We have been chosen **for obedience to Jesus Christ**. That is, God has chosen us to be **conformed to the likeness of His Son** (Romans 8:29), and to be **holy and blameless in his sight** (Ephesians 1:4). To be holy is to obey God; holiness and obedience always go together (see verse 22).

We have been chosen **through the sanctifying work of the** (Holy) **Spirit**. God chooses us; His HOLY SPIRIT sanctifies us—that is, makes us holy. Only through the help of the Holy Spirit dwelling within us can we become holy in God's sight.

To become holy, we first must be cleansed of our sins. And we are cleansed through Jesus' sacrifice—that is, through His death, through the **sprinkling of his blood** (see Hebrews 9:13–14). The old covenant that God made with the ancient Jews was confirmed by the sprinkling of blood (Exodus 24:8). In the same way, the new covenant mediated by Jesus Christ was confirmed by the sprinkling of blood, Christ's blood (Mark 14:24; Hebrews 9:18–22). Through the **sprinkling of** [Christ's] **blood** we are cleansed from our sins, and receive forgiveness not only for past sins but also for new sins committed day by day. The **blood of Jesus . . . purifies us from all sin** (1 John 1:7).

Therefore, in this verse, we can see the saving work of our triune God: God chooses us, Jesus Christ redeems us with His blood, and the Holy Spirit makes us holy.

Here Peter prays for these scattered Christians: **GRACE and PEACE be yours in abundance** (see Romans 1:7; Ephesians 1:2 and comments). First grace; then peace. Through grace we have peace with God, with each other, and with ourselves.

3–4 In these verses, Peter describes the believer's SALVATION from beginning to end. Our salvation begins in the **great mercy** of God. His mercy is so great that He saved even such undeserving sinners as us (Romans 5:8). In His **great mercy** God also gave us a **new birth** and a **living hope** (see John 3:3,5; Romans 8:24; Titus 3:7).

We receive this living hope **through the RESURRECTION of Jesus Christ from the dead**. Peter himself had seen Jesus die. His own hope had been destroyed. But then he saw Jesus risen from the dead! Peter's hope was restored to life **through the resurrection of Jesus**.

Because Jesus rose from the dead, all Christians will also rise from the dead. They will gain victory over death, and they will receive an **inheritance that can never perish, spoil or fade**—namely, eternal life (verse 4). This **inheritance** is kept for us **in heaven**. God gives good gifts to all men, but He gives an **inheritance** only to His children (Romans 8:16-17; Galatians 4:4–7).

---

[1] At the time this letter was written, the Romans had begun to persecute Christians severely. At that time, all the countries around the Mediterranean Sea were under the control of the Roman Empire.

5 From the first day we believe to the day when we receive our full salvation in heaven, we are **shielded by God's power** (see 1 Corinthians 1:8; Philippians 1:6 and comments). But to receive salvation, we must also do our part: namely, we must believe. Without FAITH we receive no salvation, no inheritance.

Our salvation will be revealed **in the last time**—that is, when Christ comes again. At that time He will **gather his elect from the four winds, from the ends of the earth to the ends of the heavens** (Mark 13:27). Our salvation begins on earth now (2 Corinthians 6:2); but only in heaven will it be completed.

6–7 God allows **all kinds of trials** to come upon us in order to test and strengthen our faith. Just as gold is **refined by fire**, so our faith is "refined" or purified by trials. By means of trials, God can tell whether our faith is genuine or not. Because of our hope of eternal life, we are able to rejoice in these brief trials. These trials are not for our harm but for our good (see Matthew 5:11–12; Romans 5:3–4; James 1:2–4; 1 Peter 4:12–14 and comments). If, after we have been tested, our faith has proved to be genuine, we will receive **praise, glory and honor**. We will receive this praise, glory, and honor **when Jesus Christ is revealed**—that is, when He comes again.

If our faith fails under testing, then everything we do is in vain. Satan especially attacks our faith. Jesus said to Peter: "**Simon, Simon, Satan has asked to sift you as wheat. But I have prayed for you, Simon, that your faith may not fail**" (Luke 22:31–32). If our faith remains firm, we will remain firm.

8–9 Those to whom this letter was sent had never seen Jesus with their eyes. Nevertheless, they had fully believed in Him and placed their confidence in Him, and loved Him (John 20:29). They had also experienced joyful fellowship with Him through the Holy Spirit. True faith always gives rise to love and joy in this way. And each day they were coming nearer to the **goal** of their faith: namely, the **salvation** of their souls, or eternal life (verse 9).

10–11 The Old Testament PROPHETS had prophesied that **grace**—that is, salvation through Christ—would come to all who believe in Him, both Jew and Gentile (see Mark 13:10; Romans 9:25–26; 15:12 and comments). The **Spirit of Christ** (verse 11)—that is, the Holy Spirit—spoke through these Old Testament prophets (see 2 Peter 1:20–21). The Holy Spirit pointed out through the prophets that Jesus would first have to suffer and then He would be glorified (Isaiah 53:3–7,10–12; Luke 24:25–27,45–47).

12 The things that the Old Testament prophets spoke about Christ were not spoken for their benefit but for our benefit. They longed to find out more about Christ, but they all died before Christ came. The grace and the blessing they pointed to are for us who believe in Christ. The **Spirit of Christ** who inspired the Old Testament prophets is the same Holy Spirit who inspired Christ's twelve disciples (John 20:22), after which they became apostles—meaning "inspired or impelled ones." He is the same Spirit who came upon the disciples on the day of Pentecost (Acts 2:1–4). That is why Paul says that the church is **built on the foundation of the prophets and apostles** (Ephesians 2:20–22). Through that same Holy Spirit the church has been built. And now through the power of that same Holy Spirit, the GOSPEL of Christ has been preached to the ends of the earth (Acts 1:8).

So wonderful is the Gospel of Christ, and so amazing has been the work of the Holy Spirit, that even ANGELS **long to look into these things**.

Be Holy (1:13–25)

13 **Therefore, prepare your minds for action**. In view of the glorious salvation that God has arranged for us (verses 3–9), we must respond. We must do our part. God has given us **grace**; therefore, we must **prepare** [our] **minds** to serve and obey Him. We must be **made new in the attitude of** [our] **minds** (Ephesians 4:23); that is, we must "put on" a new mind (see Romans 12:2; Ephesians 4:22–24 and comments). Together with that, we must be **prepared**

. . . for action.[2] Any man prepared for action must be in complete control of himself; every part of him must be ready to act. Thus he must be self-controlled. Self-control is one the gifts of the Holy Spirit (Galatians 5:23). Paul in his letters has admonished us many times to be self-controlled (1 Corinthians 9:25; 1 Timothy 3:2; Titus 2:2,5–6).

Christians must set their hope fully **on the grace to be given** [them] **when Jesus Christ is revealed**. This **grace** has already been brought to us through Jesus Christ when He first came to earth (see Titus 2:11). Furthermore, that grace is now available to us daily through Christ's Holy Spirit dwelling within us. And finally, when **Jesus Christ is revealed** at His second coming, we shall receive the full measure of His grace for all eternity. Therefore, let us set our hope fully on this grace.

14 God has given us a great blessing: He has made us His **children**. But along with this blessing, He has also given us a great responsibility: We must obey Him. Just as a child desires to please his human father, so must we try to please our heavenly Father by being obedient. Therefore, we must no longer **conform to the evil desires** we had before we became Christians (see Romans 12:2; Ephesians 2:1–3; 4:17–18; Titus 3:3 and comments).

15 Having turned from our old sinful desires, let us be **holy**. To be holy, two things are necessary: first, we must put off unholiness; second, we must put on holiness (see Ephesians 4:22–24; 1 Thessalonians 4:7; Titus 2:11–12 and comments).

16 **Be holy, because I am holy.** Peter quotes here from Leviticus 11:45; 19:2. We must imitate our heavenly Father (Ephesians 5:1). Jesus said: "**Be perfect, therefore, as your heavenly Father is perfect**" (Matthew 5:48). We have been called to be God's children (Galatians 3:26; Ephesians 1:5). Therefore, we must lead lives worthy of that calling (Ephesians 4:1).

Our supreme goal is to be like our Lord Jesus (Romans 8:29; 2 Corinthians 3:18). Our standard is God Himself. All Christian moral teaching in the Bible is based on the character and qualities of God.

17 God is a loving Father. But we must remember that God is also a judge, who **judges each man's work impartially** (see Romans 14:12; 1 Corinthians 5:10; Ephesians 6:8 and comments). Therefore, let us live our lives **in reverent fear** (see Matthew 10:28; Acts 10:34–35).

Peter says that we must live our lives here **as strangers**. Our true home is in heaven. On earth, we are only **strangers** (John 15:18–19). Therefore, let us not be proud; let us not put our confidence in earthly things. The earth will pass away (1 John 2:17). Rather, let us fear God and obey Him alone.

18–19 We were once prisoners of Satan in this world. But now Christ has **redeemed** us; that is, He has paid a price to win our freedom from Satan (Mark 10:45). The price He paid was much more valuable than **silver or gold**; the price was His own **precious blood**—His life! Christ gave up His own life as a sacrifice for our sins. He was a lamb **without defect or blemish** (Leviticus 22:19–21). John the Baptist called Him the **Lamb of God, who takes away the sin of the world** (John 1:29). Jesus Himself was **without blemish or defect**—that is, He was without sin (Hebrews 4:15; 7:26). Only a sinless person can make ATONEMENT for the sins of others. If Christ had had sins of His own, His death would have atoned only for His own sins, not for the sins of others.

20 Christ was with God before the creation of the world (John 1:1–2). At that time, God made a plan for our salvation (Ephesians 1:4). Now that plan—salvation through Christ—has been **revealed in these last times**. "These last times" are the period between Christ's first coming and His second coming (see Hebrews 1:2).

---

[2] In place of the words **prepare . . . for action**, some versions of the Bible say, "be sober," or "be self-controlled," which is a more literal translation of the Greek text. The meaning is essentially the same.

21 God has redeemed us from the punishment of sin by the sacrifice of His Son Jesus; He has **raised** Jesus from the dead and **glorified** Him in heaven. Because of this amazing work of God, we can fully place our **faith and hope** in Him. We have been set free from bondage to sin by Jesus' death. And because of Jesus' resurrection from the dead, we too will be glorified and receive eternal life with Him in heaven (Romans 6:5,8; 8:23–24).

22–23 Christians are purified **by obeying the truth**—that is, by obeying Christ's word (see John 15:3; 17:17). If we do not obey His word, it will not purify us. To obey Christ's word means to love our brother (John 13:34). We must love our brother with a **sincere love . . . deeply, from the heart**. We must love our brother without selfishness. This is how Christ loved us; and so this is how we must love our brother. We believers are all children of our heavenly Father. If we love our natural brothers and sisters, how much more should we love our spiritual brothers and sisters!

Not only have we been **purified**; we have also been **born again**. We have been spiritually born again, not by **perishable seed** (human seed) but by spiritual seed—that is, by the **living and enduring word of God** (see Luke 8:11; John 3:3; 1 John 3:9).

Here we see that two things are necessary to be a Christian. First, we must be **purified** (verse 22); that is, our sins must be washed away and forgiven. Our baptism in water signifies that this has taken place. Second, we must be **born again** (verse 23); that is, we must receive the Holy Spirit, from whom we obtain new spiritual life. Jesus said: "**. . . no one can enter the Kingdom of God unless he is born of water and the Spirit**" (John 3:5). In the same way, in his sermon on the day of Pentecost Peter spoke of these same two things—forgiveness of sins and the gift of the Holy Spirit. He said: **"Repent and be baptized, every one of you, in the name of Jesus Christ so that your sins may be forgiven. And you will receive the gift of the Holy Spirit"** (Acts 2:38).

24–25 Peter quotes here from Isaiah 40:6–8. . . . **the word of the Lord stands forever** (verse 25). Jesus said, "**Heaven and earth will pass away, but my words will never pass away**" (Mark 13:31). Men are like **grass**, but Christ's word (God's word) is **living and enduring** (verse 23). This is the word Peter has preached. This is the word that is written fully in our Bible. If anyone is seeking forgiveness, new life, and fellowship with God—that is, if anyone is seeking salvation—the way to find these things is written clearly in God's word, the Bible.

CHAPTER 2

The Living Stone and a Chosen People (2:1–10)

1 Most Christians do not murder, steal, or fornicate. These sins are found relatively infrequently among Christians. But there are other sins, which sadly are very common among Christians, such as **malice . . . deceit, hypocrisy, envy, and slander**. Indeed, among Christian workers, the most common and destructive sins are envy and slander (criticism behind another's back). If one Christian gets a high post or is successful in some endeavor, others in the church frequently become envious and begin to speak against him. Satan uses these two sins more than any other to divide the church and destroy our fellowship.

Peter warns his readers about the five sins mentioned in this verse. These sins are hidden in our hearts. Often Christians are not even aware they are committing these sins. Many deny that they have committed them. That is why it is so important to always ask the Holy Spirit to reveal to us these hidden sins. There are sins like these in each one of us, and we daily need to confess them before God (1 John 1:8–9).

However, the two most basic sins of all are pride and selfishness (or self-love). These two sins give rise to all other sins.[3] It is very difficult to uproot these two sins, because they are buried deeply within our hearts. The prophet Jeremiah wrote: **The heart is deceitful above all things and beyond cure. Who can understand it?** (Jeremiah 17:9). But God fully understands our heart; He sees all our sins. The psalmist wrote: **You have set our iniquities before you, our secret sins in the light of your presence** (Psalm 90:8).

2 Having put away the poisonous sins mentioned in verse 1, let us **crave pure spiritual milk**—that is, God's word. Just as a newborn infant eagerly desires his mother's milk, so should we eagerly desire to read and understand God's word and live according to it. Only by doing this can we **grow up in our salvation**—that is, become mature Christians and receive the full blessing of our salvation.

But first it is necessary to rid ourselves of the poisonous sins mentioned in verse 1 (and other sins too). If our stomach is filled with evil, we will have no appetite for spiritual milk.

3 As we read God's word, we can "taste" the goodness of His mercy and His other blessings. Through reading and obeying His word, we come to know God Himself and receive His grace. Therefore, when we open our Bible and read, let us not just seek to know God's word, but through His word to know, to "taste," to love, God Himself (Psalm 34:8).

4–5 Peter here calls Christ the **living Stone.** Christ is the **cornerstone** (verse 6) or **capstone**[4] (verse 7) of the church. If one were to remove this stone from a building, the building would fall down. Christ is a **living** stone, because God brought Him to life from the dead (Romans 6:9). Paul called Christ a **life-giving spirit** (1 Corinthians 15:45). But it is not only Christ Himself who is alive; He also makes alive all who come to Him. Thus we too, who believe in Jesus, become **living stones** like Him (verse 4). God takes us and builds us into a **spiritual house** or temple (verse 5), in which God Himself can live (see Ephesians 2:18–22 and comment). We ourselves are God's house!

Not only that, we are also God's priests; we are a **holy priesthood.** Among the twelve tribes of Israel, only the Levites could be appointed priests. But among Christians, every believer is a priest. And, as priests of Christ, we must offer **spiritual sacrifices acceptable to God.** These **sacrifices** include the sacrifice of obedience—that is, the sacrifice of our own bodies (Romans 12:1), the sacrifice of praise (Hebrews 13:15), and the sacrifice of service to others (Hebrews 13:16). We must never think that there are two kinds of Christians—one kind who are priests and pastors, and another kind who are just ordinary believers. We must never think that some Christians are called to be holy and others are not. All Christians are equally called to be holy; all Christians are equally called to be priests. Thus it is the duty of every Christian to offer these **spiritual sacrifices.**

Peter says here that Christ the living Stone was **rejected by men**—that is, by the Jewish leaders and their followers (see Mark 8:31). But Christ was **chosen by God** and was **precious** to Him. Notice how opposite God's thoughts are from man's thoughts. What man values, God detests (Luke 16:15). What man despises, God honors (1 Corinthians 1:27–30). Men rejected Christ, but God honored Him by raising Him from the dead and seating Him at His right hand in heaven (Ephesians 1:20–21). Peter had preached

---

[3] There is a sin that is even more basic than pride and selfishness, and that is unbelief. It is so basic that it is not usually listed along with other sins. Unbelief is the real root of all man's sins. For further discussion, see comment on Romans 3:10–12 and footnote to comment.

[4] In place of the word **capstone**, some translations of the Bible say "cornerstone." The point is the same; Christ is the most important "stone" in the church. Without Him, the church would fall down.

this very thing many times before (see Acts 2:23–24,32–33; 5:30–31).

6 To illustrate the rejection of Christ by men, Peter here in verses 6–8 quotes three passages from the Old Testament: Isaiah 28:16; Psalm 118:22; Isaiah 8:14. In verse 6, Christ is called a **precious cornerstone** (see Ephesians 2:20–21). All who trust in Christ will never be ashamed before God; they will be accepted by God (see Romans 10:11–13 and comment). Christ the cornerstone is laid in **Zion**—that is, in heaven, in the **heavenly Jerusalem** (see Hebrews 12:22–23).

7–8 For believers, Christ is a **precious** stone (verse 7). But for non-believers, Christ is a **stone that causes men to stumble** (verse 8). Paul calls Him a **stumbling block** (1 Corinthians 1:23–24). For believers, Christ is Savior; for non-believers, He is Judge (John 5:22; Romans 14:10).

The Jews rejected Christ. They refused to believe in Him. They threw out the "cornerstone." But then they stumbled on it (see Romans 9:30–32 and comment). In the same way, if we reject Christ and **disobey his message**, we too will stumble and be condemned.

All man's sins have their origin in unbelief, which is basically a refusal to acknowledge that God is greater than we are. Always associated with unbelief is disobedience; to disbelieve God and to disobey God always go together (Hebrews 3:18–19; 11:6). When we refuse to believe, we are, in effect, disobeying God (John 6:29). The destiny or end of every person is determined by whether or not he or she has believed in Jesus Christ (see John 1:10–12; 3:18,36; Romans 2:8; 10:9; 1 John 5:11–12). Those who reject and disobey Christ are **destined** to stumble; that is, they are destined to be condemned.

9 Here Peter describes Christians by quoting some expressions from the Old Testament about Israel, the Jewish nation. Indeed, Christians are the new and true "Israel." They are a **chosen people** (Isaiah 43:20), a **royal priesthood** and a **holy nation** (Exodus 19:5–6), a **people belonging to God** (see Titus 2:14). God has made us His people so that we might **declare** [His] **praises** (Isaiah 43:21). God has called us **out of darkness**—out of the world of sin and unbelief—and brought us into **his wonderful light**—that is, into the kingdom of heaven (see Acts 26:17–18; Ephesians 5:8; Colossians 1:13–14).

10 We were once unbelieving Gentiles (non-Jews). We did not belong to God's people, the Jews; we were not part of Israel, the Jewish nation. But now we have become the **people of God**; we have received God's mercy, God's salvation, through Christ (see Romans 9:23–25 and comment). But we are not merely God's people; we are His sons—**sons of the living God** (Romans 9:26).

Servants of God (2:11–17)

11 Because we are God's children, members of His holy household, we must **abstain from sinful desires** (see 1 Peter 1:14). Such sinful desires **war against our soul** (see Romans 7:21–23; Galatians 5:16–17,19–21). We are not citizens of this world; we are only passing through, like **aliens and strangers**. Therefore, let us not become entrapped by the sinful desires of the world; let us not partake of its sins.

12 Instead, let us live in the world as God's holy children, so that men will honor God because of our good deeds (Matthew 5:16). People will certainly slander and abuse us, as they slandered and abused Christ (see John 15:18–20). But we do not need to answer back. Rather, we need only to continue doing good, and in the end those who speak against us will be silenced (verse 15).

The **day** [God] **visits us** is that day when God draws near to us and calls us to repent. May men and women, because of our good deeds, be led to repent and glorify God on the **day he visits** them.

13–14 Every law and every authority among men is instituted by God. A ruler may be evil, but his authority has still been given to him by God. All authority comes from God; there is no other authority (John 19:10–11; Romans 13:1).

God has appointed rulers to punish evildoers and to reward welldoers. It is His will that we submit to these rulers and obey them. We must submit to them **for the Lord's sake**—that is, we must submit to them in order to show our submission to God's authority and to set an example of righteous living for others to follow. However, if the earthly authority or ruler commands us to do anything clearly opposed to God's word, we must not obey that command; rather, we must obey God's word (see Acts 4:18–20; 5:29; Romans 13:1–5; Titus 3:1 and comments).

15 When people oppose and slander us, let us not argue with them, let us not defend ourselves. We must never try to get even, or take revenge. Instead, we must show them love and continue to do good (verse 12). In the end their evil and foolish talk will be silenced (see Matthew 5:44; Romans 12:14,17–21; Titus 2:7–8; 1 Peter 3:9,16).

In Peter's time, Christians were considered to be outlaws and rebels, because they worshiped only Christ and refused to worship the Roman emperor. The Jews also opposed the Christians. Therefore, to avoid bringing upon themselves unnecessary accusations, it was important for Christians, as far as possible, to obey all civil laws and to submit to their rulers.

16 Christians are **free men**. They have been freed from sin, from selfish desires, and from Satan's power. They have been freed from the Jewish law and its condemnation (see John 8:31–32,34–36; Romans 8:1–2; Galatians 5:1 and comments). However, Christians are not free from God! They are **servants of God** (see 1 Corinthians 7:22–23 and comment). Christians are free from sin, but they are not free to commit sin. Therefore, Christians must **not use their freedom as a cover-up for evil**. They must never say: "I am free from the law; therefore, I don't have to obey God" (see Galatians 5:13 and comment).

We believers submit to other men, not because we are their servants but because we are God's servants. We submit to others not out of compulsion but out of love, desiring thereby to serve both them and God (see 1 Corinthians 9:19). For this reason Jesus taught that if anyone forces us to go one mile, we should go with him two miles (Matthew 5:41). Only a person who is **free**—free of sin and pride—is ready and willing to do more than is required (see Matthew 5:39–41 and comment).

17 We must show respect to everyone—whether believer or non-believer, whether good or evil; because all men are made in God's image (Genesis 1:27).

We must especially love our Christian brothers and sisters. Here Peter says that we must love the **brotherhood of believers**—that is, the church. It is possible to misinterpret this verse. Some Christians claim to love the church, but they show little love to the members of the church! Such people seek to purify the church, but in so doing they mistreat their brothers and sisters. Let us never think that we can love the church and at the same time oppose other Christians. To love the church means to love each and every brother and sister in the church.

Christ the Example of Suffering (2:18–25)

18 Just as we must all submit to our rulers (verse 13), so must slaves (or employees) submit to their masters (or employers). Even if a master is **harsh**, the slave must willingly submit to him (see Ephesians 6:5–8; 1 Timothy 6:1; Titus 2:9–10 and comments).

19–20 In these verses, Peter gives us a difficult but very important teaching: It is **commendable** in God's sight when we bear **unjust suffering**—that is, when we **suffer for doing good** (see Matthew 5:10–11,44,46–47; Luke 6:32–35). This teaching is the opposite of the world's teaching! Even Christians have difficulty accepting this teaching. The moment we suffer some small injustice or hurt from our employer, we cry out; we at once begin to oppose our employer, to talk against him. When we do this, we lose the commendation of God.

21 Instead, when we suffer unjustly, let us endure it patiently and quietly, because to this we were called. Christ was called to suffer for us (Mark 8:31; 10:45; 14:24; Luke 24:25–27,46). And those who follow Christ are called to suffer also (Mark 8:34–35; John 15:20; 2 Timothy 3:12).

22 Here Peter quotes from Isaiah

53:9. Christ was completely innocent in word and deed. **He committed no sin**; nevertheless, men despised and mocked Him, and in the end, they put Him to death as a criminal.

23 When He was abused, Christ **did not retaliate**. He did not behave badly to any man; He did not seek revenge. He suffered quietly (Isaiah 53:7; Mark 14:61,65). He entrusted Himself to God (see 1 Peter 4:19). In this world, men may judge and condemn us, but it is God who is the final judge. And God always judges justly; we can entrust ourselves to Him.

24 Christ suffered for us (verse 21). He suffered not for His own sins but for ours. Because Christ, being sinless, did not have to bear His own punishment, He was able to bear our punishment. **He himself bore our sins in his body**; that is, He bore the punishment for our sins (Isaiah 53:12). That punishment was death (Romans 4:25). Christ was put to death **on the tree**—that is, the CROSS. Christ died **so that we might die to sins and live for righteousness**. Christ not only erased our sins and delivered us from the power of Satan, but He also turned our lives completely toward God and gave us a new mind and a new power to live righteous lives (see Romans 6:2,6,11–13,18,22–23 and comment).

. . . by his wounds you have been healed (Isaiah 53:5). Christ was wounded at the hands of Roman soldiers (Mark 15:15; John 19:1). Here we see a deep and important spiritual principle: By suffering we are healed. Not only that, by our suffering others also are healed. If we suffer for God's sake and in accordance with His will, then tremendous healing power will be released through our suffering (see 1 Peter 4:14–16). When we suffer for Christ's sake, people will see that our faith is genuine, and they will turn to God. When we suffer for Christ, strife and divisions between us will be healed. Through our suffering God can accomplish great things.

25 We are like sheep who have gone astray (Isaiah 53:6). But our **Shepherd** has called us back to Him. We are one flock, because we have one shepherd, Jesus Christ (John 10:14–16).

CHAPTER 3

Husbands and Wives (3:1–7)

1–2 Just as all Christians should submit to their rulers, and all workers to their employers, so in the same way should wives be subject to their husbands. In a family, the husband is the head of the wife (see 1 Corinthians 11:3,7–9; Ephesians 5:22–24 and comments; General Article: Christian Marriage).

If a husband is an unbeliever—one who does **not believe the word**—he may oppose the Gospel. He may be harsh with his Christian wife. But let the believing wife of such a man not quarrel or complain against her husband. Rather, let her live quietly in purity and reverence, showing respect for both her husband and for God. In this way her unbelieving husband, seeing her good behavior, may in time be led to repent and believe in the Lord. Behavior is always more effective than words in winning people to our side. Indeed, the best way to bring people to Christ is through our good behavior.[5]

3–4 There are two kinds of **beauty** (or adornment): outer or physical beauty, and inner or spiritual beauty. True beauty is inner beauty, the beauty of the **inner self**; this is the beauty that God sees. Inner beauty is the **unfading beauty of a gentle and quiet spirit** (verse 4). This kind of beauty is **of great worth in God's**

---

[5] However, our good behavior by itself is never sufficient to lead people to Christ. At some point, in some way, a person must hear or read God's **word**, the Gospel, in order to be saved (see Romans 10:13–14).

sight. Let the **beauty** or adornment of the believing wife be like that.

However, to dress attractively is not a sin. A Christian woman doesn't have to wear tattered, worn-out clothes. Let the believing wife dress suitably and modestly (see 1 Timothy 2:9–10 and comment).

In New Testament times, ungodly and worldly women customarily braided their hair and wore expensive clothes and jewelry. Therefore, it was unsuitable for Christian wives in Peter's time to dress and wear their hair in this manner. To do so would give the appearance that they too were ungodly and worldly, and this would bring dishonor to God.

But in other countries, it is customary for ordinary godly people to braid their hair and wear gold jewelry. In these countries, then, it would be suitable for Christian wives to do the same. The main rule is this: whatever a woman wears must be pleasing and honoring to God. Let the Christian wife's main concern be to adorn herself spiritually, to adorn her **inner self**. Let her remember God's words to Samuel: "**Man looks at the outward appearance, but the Lord looks at the heart**" (1 Samuel 16:7).

5–6 To illustrate his teaching, Peter cites the example of godly Old Testament wives, whose beauty consisted in their submissive and obedient spirits. Peter's main example is **Sarah**, Abraham's wife, who called her husband **master**. In calling Abraham "master," Sarah showed that she submitted to her husband. Just as Abraham is called the "father" of those who believe, so Sarah can be called the "mother" of those who obey.

7 Now Peter gives some instructions to Christian husbands. Husbands must be **considerate** as they live with their wives (see Ephesians 5:25,28 and comment). Husbands must treat their wives **with respect**. Because women are physically **weaker** than men, husbands must protect their wives, and be kind and gentle with them.

However, in spiritual things, wives are not behind their husbands. The husband may be stronger than his wife physically, but spiritually they are equal. The wife receives the same grace her husband does; she receives the same salvation her husband does. Husband and wife are **heirs** together of the **gracious gift of life**.

If a husband treats his wife harshly or if a wife refuses to submit to her husband, the spiritual fellowship between them is broken. When this happens, their prayers are hindered. Let this not happen. A husband and wife must remember the words of Jesus: "**. . . if two of you on earth agree about anything you ask for, it will be done for you by my Father in heaven**" (Matthew 18:19). Think of the prayer power that a husband and wife possess together! Let nothing **hinder** it!

There is something else the husband and wife (and all of us) must remember. When the husband and wife pray together, they can know that Jesus is present with them. Jesus said: "**For where two or three come together in my name, there am I with them**" (Matthew 18:20). When the fellowship between husband and wife is broken, their fellowship with Jesus is also broken. Husbands and wives, let this not happen!

Suffering for Doing Good (3:8–22)

8 **Finally, all of you, live in harmony with one another** (see 1 Corinthians 1:10). This doesn't only mean that we should avoid arguing with each other; it also means that we should think and care deeply about the same things together, the things of Christ (Colossians 3:1–2). As Christ's mind was, so should our mind be (see Philippians 2:5).

In order to be of one mind and live in harmony together, we need to be **sympathetic** toward one another, and love each other **as brothers**; we need to be **compassionate** with one another. This means that we must share each other's joy and sorrow. It means that we must always be trying to please our brother (Romans 12:15; 15:2).

In addition, we must be **humble**. If some in the church think that they are better or more worthy than others, then there can be no harmony or unity of mind in that church (see Romans 12:3,16; Ephesians 4:2–3; Philippians 2:1–4 and comments).

9 Christians must never take revenge.[6] Rather, we must repay evil with good (see Luke 6:27–31; Romans 12:14,17–21; 1 Corinthians 4:12–13; 1 Peter 2:23). God gives blessings[7] to the evil as well as to the good (Matthew 5:44–45); therefore, so should we. As much as we show mercy and forgiveness to others, that much will God show mercy and forgiveness to us (see Matthew 5:44–45; 6:12,14–15; 18:32–35; Mark 11:25; Luke 6:35–38; Ephesians 4:32).

. . . because to this you were called. We were called to endure injustice and to do good to those who wrong us. If we do this, we will **inherit a blessing**—namely, our inheritance in heaven (see Romans 8:17–18; 1 Peter 2:21).

10–12 To show that God blesses those who do good and opposes those who do evil, Peter here quotes from Psalm 34:12–16. Notice in verse 11 that we must not only **turn from evil**, but we must also **do good**. We must not only seek peace; we must also **pursue** it (see Romans 12:18; 14:19; Hebrews 12:14).

13 If we do good, no one can really harm us, because the **eyes of the Lord are on the righteous** (verse 12). Yes, men can give us trouble in this life—they can even kill our body. But in the end they can do us no spiritual harm. We do not need to fear those who can only kill the body (Matthew 10:28; Romans 8:31,35–39).

14 In the world, believers must expect to face suffering (2 Timothy 3:12); but for those who love God and walk in His will, such suffering will in the end be for the believer's benefit (Romans 8:28; 1 Peter 1:6–7). If we suffer for the Lord's sake, we will be blessed (Matthew 5:10–12).

"Do not fear what they fear" is a quotation from Isaiah 8:12. Peter's meaning is that we believers should not fear the things that other people fear. Other people fear the loss of their wealth. Or they fear the loss of health—they fear death. These are things that believers in Christ do not need to fear.

15 **But in your hearts set apart Christ as Lord.** In our hearts Christ must be the Lord. It must not be we who reign in our hearts, but Christ. No longer can we Christians do what we want; we must do only what He wants. We are no longer the ruler of our lives: He is.

Christ is the ruler, and we are His messengers or ambassadors. In a sense, we are His lips and tongue here on earth. Therefore, we must always be ready to witness to Christ. Peter says here that we must give people the **reason for the hope** that we have. Christ is our **hope** (1 Timothy 1:1). Paul writes: **Christ in you, the hope of glory** (Colossians 1:27). If anyone asks us about our **hope**, about our Lord, let us be ready at once to give that person an answer. If someone shows even a little interest, let us be ready to share our faith with him. Most Christians remain silent. Why? Are we ashamed of our Lord? Are we afraid of man?

But when we witness to others, let us do so **with gentleness and respect**. We do not need to speak forcefully. We must never put others down. We must never argue, or give offense. Because if a person is offended by our manner of speaking, he will not listen to the words we speak.

Surely, as Peter wrote this verse, he remembered his own experience. Three times Peter had denied His Lord. He had been afraid then. He certainly had not been ready to witness to Christ. He answered those who questioned him neither with **gentleness** nor with **respect**—nor with truth! (see Mark 14:66–72). Therefore, let us not be discouraged when we fall; if Peter could overcome his early sins and weaknesses, so can we.

16 We must keep a **clear conscience**. If our conscience is unclean—that is, if sin is hidden in our hearts—we will not be able to witness to others. All Christians

---

[6] Here Peter is talking only about personal revenge. Rulers, administrators, and others in authority must punish wrongdoers.

[7] The blessings that God gives to evildoers are natural blessings, such as sunshine and rain, food and family. Apart from these natural blessings, which come to all men equally, God does not bless evildoers; rather, He opposes them.

have had this experience (see Acts 24:16; 1 Timothy 1:5,19 and comments).

If our conscience is clean—if we have repented of our sins and are obeying God's will—then those who speak against us will in the end be ashamed (see Titus 2:7–8; 1 Peter 2:12,15 and comments).

17 Suffering will come to us; but let it come because we've done good, not because we've done evil. If we are punished for doing evil, there is nothing praiseworthy about that. Only when we suffer **for doing good** will we receive praise from God (see 1 Peter 2:19–20 and comment).

18 Whenever we suffer for doing good, let us remember that Christ Himself walked the road of suffering before us. He is for us an example (1 Peter 2:21). Christ suffered for doing good. He did not deserve the suffering He received. But God had appointed Him first to suffer, and only after that to enter into glory (Luke 24:26). Christ's suffering was completely in accordance with God's will; the Old Testament prophets had written about it (Luke 24:45–46). Thus when we suffer for doing good we can rejoice, because we know we are following in Christ's footsteps and will enter into His glory (Romans 8:17–18; 2 Corinthians 4:17; Philippians 3:10–11).

In one way, Christ's suffering and our suffering are similar. But in another way, Christ's suffering was special and unique, because He was the sinless Son of God. Through His suffering Christ brought men to God; that is, through His suffering He saved them. **Christ died for sins once for all.** The RIGHTEOUS man died in the place of **unrighteous** men (see 1 Peter 2:24 and comment). The innocent Christ offered Himself as a perfect and unblemished sacrifice for our sins (Hebrews 9:14; 1 John 2:2; 4:10). His sacrifice will never have to be repeated (see Hebrews 9:26–28; 10:10–14 and comments). Christ took upon Himself the punishment for our sins. Now we are free forever from the condemnation of sin (see Romans 8:1 and comment).

As soon as Christ died, He was made alive again by the Spirit. He conquered death (Romans 6:9–10). But not only that, He also delivers us from death, the punishment for sin (Romans 6:23; Hebrews 2:14–15).

19 From this verse (and from Ephesians 4:9) comes the section in the Apostles' Creed where it says: "He descended into hell." After Jesus died and was made alive in spirit, three days passed before His body was resurrected. During that time he **went and preached to the spirits in prison**. It is not certain what **spirits** Peter is talking about here. Some Bible scholars believe that they are the spirits of men who died in the flood in Noah's time without ever hearing about Jesus. Other scholars believe that these spirits are fallen angels (see 2 Peter 2:4–5; Jude 6).

20 The flood in Noah's time was a sign both of judgment and salvation. **God waited patiently** while the ark was being built. That is, He gave the evil men of Noah's time a chance to repent. But when they did not repent, God destroyed them all by sending a flood upon the earth (2 Peter 3:5–7,9). But Noah and his family—eight people—were saved by the flood (Genesis 7:11–12,17–23). They were **saved through water**. They were saved not only from the water but also **through** the water, because the water lifted up the boat Noah had built and thus enabled Noah and his family to escape drowning.

Except for those eight people, every other person on earth was destroyed by that flood. Consider this: To follow the majority of people is neither good, nor wise, nor safe. It's better to follow the eight people in the boat! (see Matthew 7:13–14 and comment).

21 The water of the flood is an illustration or symbol of our BAPTISM into Christ. Just as those eight people who entered the boat were saved from judgment and death, so those who enter into Christ through faith are saved from judgment and death. The ceremony of baptism in itself does not save us; it is Christ who saves us. Christ saves us from death, because He Himself overcame death through His resurrection. In order to receive this salvation, all we have to do is to believe in Christ (Romans 10:9).

The meaning of baptism is this: When we are baptized, we die with Christ. . . .

all of us who were baptized into Christ Jesus were baptized into his death[8] (Romans 6:3). With Christ we die to sin (see Romans 6:6,10–11 and comment). True baptism is not an outer washing; it is an inner spiritual washing. In baptism our sins are washed away, our consciences are cleansed, and we are raised with Christ (Romans 6:5).

22 How great and deep is the meaning of baptism! How great is our Savior Christ! Christ **has gone into heaven and is at God's right hand**. All things have been placed under His authority (see Romans 14:9; Ephesians 1:20–22).

CHAPTER 4

Living for God (4:1–6)

1 When Christ suffered and died for us, He died to sin once for all (Romans 6:10). In the same way, we too must suffer with Christ; our old sinful self with its sinful nature must be crucified (see Romans 6:6; 8:13; Galatians 5:24 and comments). We must also count ourselves dead to sin (see Romans 6:11 and comment). This is the meaning of Peter's command here: **. . . arm yourselves also with the same attitude**—that is, with Christ's attitude. He who suffers—who has died to sin—has put away sin. Sin no longer has any power over him (Romans 6:7). He **is done with sin**.

2 Therefore, having died to sin, we must no longer live **for evil human desires, but rather for the will of God**. Paul writes: **Therefore do not let sin reign in your mortal body so that you obey its evil desires. Do not offer the parts of your body to sin, as instruments of wickedness** (Romans 6:12–13). This is why Christ died for us, so that we might **offer** ourselves to God (Romans 6:13; 12:1), so that we might live the **rest of** [our] **earthly life . . . for the will of God.**

3 Therefore, we must stop doing what we used to do—that is, we must stop doing **what pagans**[9] **choose to do** (see 1 Corinthians 6:9–11; Ephesians 4:17–19). Rather, we must make new our minds, goals, and desires. We must put on the mind of Christ (see Romans 12:2; Ephesians 4:22–24 and comments).

4 When we stop participating in the evil activities of our former friends, they will naturally be upset. They will be angry with us and revile us, because by our good life their evil will be exposed and condemned (see Ephesians 5:11).

5 Every evildoer will have to give an account to Christ, who is the judge of all men, both living and dead (John 5:22,27; Acts 10:42; Romans 2:16). Whoever does not accept Christ as Savior will in the end have to face Him as Judge.

6 The **gospel was preached** to men so that their sin might be judged in this life, and so that the penalty for their sin might be removed through faith in Christ—that is, so that their punishment might fall on Christ. This is Peter's meaning when he says here: **so that they** (men) **might be judged according to men in regard to the body**. The bodies of believers die like the bodies of other men (because the judgment of sin is death), but their spirits do not die. Through faith in Christ, believers receive new spiritual life, which begins now in this life and lasts forever. That is, they **live according to God in regard to the spirit**.

Therefore, even though their bodies die, believers in Christ receive eternal life (John 5:24; 11:25–26). But those who do not accept Christ will, after death, receive the eternal judgment of God. They will receive eternal punishment.

---

[8] Christ Himself called His death a "baptism" (Mark 10:38–39; Luke 12:50).

[9] The **pagans** are non-believing Gentiles.

The Gifts of God (4:7–11)

7 **The end of all things**—that is, the second coming of Christ—**is near.** We must each live our lives as if Jesus was going to come tomorrow (see Mark 13:33–37; Luke 12:35–36; 17:26–27).

We must remain **clear minded and self-controlled**, so that we can pray more effectively. As Peter wrote this, he surely had in mind the time when the disciples were in the garden of Gethsemane with Jesus, and because of sleepiness they could not stay awake to pray (Mark 14:37–40). Perhaps it was because Peter failed to pray in the garden that he later fell into temptation and denied His Lord (Mark 14:66–72).

8 **Above all, love each other deeply.** The commandments to love God and to love man are the first and greatest commandments (Mark 12:30–31). All other commands are included in these commandments to love (Romans 13:8–10; Galatians 5:14; Colossians 3:4). By our love for each other, we show the world that we are disciples of Christ and children of God (John 13:34–35; 1 John 4:7).

. . . love covers over a multitude of sins. This means that love does not look at other people's faults and weaknesses. Love **keeps no record of wrongs** (1 Corinthians 13:5). Love not only **covers** our brother's sin but it also "covers" our own sin; because to the extent we forgive our brother's sins in love, to that same extent God will "cover," or forgive, our sins (Matthew 6:12,14–15; Mark 11:25–26).

9 Christians must offer **hospitality** to all people, but especially to other believers. Not only that, they must do it **without grumbling** (Romans 12:13; Hebrews 13:2; 3 John 5–8). The more of our goods we share with others, the more God will give to us in return (2 Corinthians 9:6–8). And let us not forget that when we show hospitality to others, we are at the same time showing hospitality to Christ Himself (see Matthew 25:35,37–40). . . . **whatever you did for one of the least of these brothers of mine, you did for me** (Matthew 25:40).

10 Every Christian has received one or more gifts from God. These gifts can be both natural and spiritual gifts (see Romans 12:6–8; 1 Corinthians 12:7–11 and comments). Every gift is given **for the common good** of the members of the church (1 Corinthians 12:7). Whatever gift we have received, we have received it as stewards; we are to use it for others, not for ourselves.

No Christian can say: "I have no gift." Every Christian has received at least one gift from God, and along with it, the grace and strength to use it. If we do not use the gifts we have been given in God's service, He will punish us for it (see Matthew 25:14–30).

11 Here Peter mentions the two main kinds of Christian ministry: first, the ministry of the word—**speaking the very words of God**; and second, the ministry of service (see Acts 6:2–4). The first ministry is carried out mainly by pastors, elders, and evangelists.[10] Those who teach and preach the word of God must do so as if God Himself were speaking. They must act as God's spokesmen.

All Christians can take part in the second ministry, the ministry of serving and helping others. God will provide the means and strength—everything that is needed—for carrying out this ministry. If money is needed, God will provide it. But we can't just wait around and expect God to do everything. We must use all of our abilities, our strength, our time, and our wealth in God's service. When we do this, we will bring glory to God. All our labors and efforts in this world have but one ultimate purpose, and that purpose is to glorify God.

Suffering for Being a Christian (4:12–19)

12 Some of the believers to whom Peter wrote this letter were suffering various kinds of trouble and persecution. Perhaps they were surprised and

---

[10] All Christians, however, are called to share their faith with their friends and acquaintances (1 Peter 3:15).

shocked and disillusioned by the troubles that had come upon them. They had thought that after believing in Christ they would receive blessing, joy, and prosperity. But instead of these good things, they had received trouble from their friends and persecution from the Romans. Some of them may have thought: "We have been betrayed."

But Peter reminds his readers that just as gold is **refined by fire**, so their faith is being refined by the "fiery" or **painful trial** that has come upon them (see Mark 4:5–6,16–17; 1 Peter 1:6–7).

13 **But rejoice**[11] **that you participate in the sufferings of Christ**. For Christ, suffering was the road to glory; and it is the same for us. If we suffer for Christ now, we will share in His glory later (Matthew 5:10–12; Romans 8:17). When Christ comes to earth again, we will all the more rejoice with Him (Romans 8:18; 2 Thessalonians 1:4–5). Therefore, during times of suffering, let us turn our thoughts to the glory and the joy of Christ, in which we shall one day share—if we stand firm. Paul wrote: . . . **we rejoice in the hope of the glory of God. Not only so, but we also rejoice in our sufferings, because we know that suffering produces perseverance; perseverance, character; and character, hope. And hope does not disappoint us** (Romans 5:2–5). . . . **if we endure, we will also reign with him** (2 Timothy 2:12).

14 Anyone who faithfully follows Christ will from time to time be **insulted because of the name of Christ** (Psalm 69:7–9; 89:50–51; Matthew 10:22; John 15:18–21). To bear reproach and abuse for Christ's sake is not a disgrace but an honor and privilege (see Matthew 5:11; Acts 5:41; Hebrews 11:26; 13:13; 1 Peter 4:16). If we bear Christ's reproach, His Spirit—the **Spirit of glory**—and God Himself will come to us and remain with us (see John 14:23).

15 If we suffer for doing wrong, however, we bring no honor to Christ or to ourselves. There is no joy in suffering punishment we deserve. Therefore, let us make sure that any trouble we suffer is for Christ's sake—that is, for doing good. Only in this way will we glorify God (see 1 Peter 2:19–20; 3:17 and comments).

16 In Peter's time, the name **Christian** was despised by almost everyone. Many Christians were poor; some were slaves or servants. Some had been former Jews. Therefore, the Romans despised the Christians. To be called a "Christian" was a shameful thing. However, Peter says here, **if you suffer as a Christian, do not be ashamed**. Rather, praise God that you bear that name, because that is the name of the King of kings and Lord of lords (see verse 14 and comment).

17 God's judgment against sin begins **with the family of God**—that is, with believers. God will judge Christians, and He will give a punishment for their sins. The punishment God gives for sin is spiritual death; this is the punishment that Jesus bore in our place (see verse 6 and comment). But think: if God's judgment against the sins of believers is so great that He gave His only Son to pay the price for those sins, then how much worse will be God's judgment against the sins of those **who do not obey the gospel of God**—who do not accept Christ as their Savior.[12] The judgment of God against unbelievers will be fearful and terrible (2 Thessalonians 1:6–10).

18 Here Peter quotes Proverbs 11:31. If the **righteous** must be judged and their faith tested by fire and painful trials, what will the end of the unrighteous be like! It is better by far to come to Christ and face His judgment against sin in this life, than to wait and face God's final and terrible judgment in the next life.

19 Therefore, let us not be angry with God or man when suffering comes upon us. Because through such suffering we are being made holy. Through suffering our faith is being tested and

---

[11] In the Greek text, the word **rejoice** means "keep on rejoicing."

[12] The punishment God gives to unbelievers is eternal spiritual death. This is sometimes called the **second death** (see Revelation 20:14–15). Through Christ, believers are saved from this death. The only death that believers face is the "first death," that is, physical death.

strengthened. And through suffering we are being prepared to receive a place in God's kingdom (Romans 8:17; Hebrews 12:5–7,10). We must commit ourselves, therefore, to God; He is **faithful**. Paul writes: . . . **he** (God) **who began a good work in you will carry it on to completion until the day of Christ Jesus** (Philippians 1:6). And he also writes: **He** (God) **will keep you strong to the end, so that you will be blameless on the day of our Lord Jesus Christ. God, who has called you into fellowship with his Son Jesus Christ our Lord, is faithful** (1 Corinthians 1:8–9).

Therefore, let us commit ourselves to God, the righteous Judge (see 1 Peter 2:23). On the cross, Jesus' last words were: **"Father, into your hands I commit my spirit"** (Luke 23:46). Peter heard Jesus speak those words. He surely remembered them as he wrote this verse.

CHAPTER 5

To Elders and Young Men (5:1–11)

1 Even though Peter was the chief among Jesus' original twelve disciples, he here calls himself only a **fellow elder**. From this, we can see Peter's humility. He did not "lord it over" others (verse 3), but rather he exhorted them as a fellow believer. Peter writes this letter as a **witness of Christ's sufferings** (see Luke 24:45–48; Acts 1:8), and as **one who also will share in the glory to be revealed** (see Romans 8:17–18).

2 In the New Testament, church leaders are commonly called **elders** (Acts 14:23; 20:17; Titus 1:5), or **overseers**[13] (1 Timothy 3:1). Nowadays, we also call such church leaders ministers or pastors. In the Greek language, the word "pastor" means shepherd; thus Peter here instructs the elders of the church to be **shepherds**. From this, then, we can see the two main responsibilities of a church leader: first, as an "overseer" or supervisor, he must teach and exhort and discipline the members of the church (see 2 Timothy 4:2); second, as a "pastor" or "shepherd," he must feed and nurture the **flock** and protect the sheep from "wolves," that is, false teachers (see Matthew 7:15; Acts 20:28–29).

Peter fully understood that leaders had to be more than just rulers or **overseers**; they also had to be **shepherds**. Three times Jesus, after His resurrection, commanded Peter to take care of His sheep (John 21:15–17). The sheep belong to **God's flock**, and the **Chief Shepherd** (verse 4) is Jesus Christ Himself. Church leaders must serve God and His flock not because of compulsion but because of love. They must exercise their leadership not in order to gain money or honor but in order to serve the sheep (Mark 10:45; John 10:11).

3 A good leader leads mainly by example. Yes, a leader has authority, and he must exercise his authority in the right way and at the right times—especially when he must discipline those who oppose the truth and disobey God. But as far as possible, the leader should lead by his own good example (1 Corinthians 11:1). If the shepherd is good, the sheep will be eager to follow (John 10:14,27). The leader must not lead by force or by threats; he must not use his authority to push others down; rather, he must make himself the servant of others (Mark 10:42–45).

4 If church leaders serve well, they will receive a reward, a **crown of glory that will never fade away**. In Peter's time, the winner of a race received a crown made of leaves; the leaves, of course, quickly dried out. But the Christian's **crown of glory** will never dry out or **fade away** (see 1 Corinthians 9:25; 2 Timothy 4:8; James 1:12 and comments).

---

[13] In the Greek language, **overseer** means one who supervises. Such a person is also called a "bishop."

5 Peter has already said that Christians must remain subject to others (1 Peter 2:13,18; 3:1). Paul wrote the same thing in several of his letters (Romans 13:1; 1 Corinthians 16:16; Ephesians 5:21–22; 6:1,5). Here in this verse, Peter especially exhorts the young men of the church to **be submissive** to those who are older. Most young people do not like to remain subject to anyone; they want to be free to go their own way. But most young people are lacking in humility and wisdom. Therefore, for their own sake and for the church's sake, it is essential that young people be submissive to their elders.

All members of the church must "clothe" themselves with **humility**. Humility doesn't just mean behavior that is outwardly humble. True humility arises in our inner mind. The humble person knows he is unworthy in God's sight. He knows that all his **righteous acts are like filthy rags** (Isaiah 64:6). The humble person knows that all he is and all he does is by the grace of God alone (1 Corinthians 4:6–7; 15:10).

In the experience of most Christians, humility is the hardest virtue to maintain. The reason is because pride (the opposite of humility) is man's deepest sin and the hardest to remove.[14] Pride was Satan's chief sin; he sought to make himself equal with God (Isaiah 14:12–14). Pride was also the main sin of Adam and Eve in the Garden of Eden; they too wanted to be like God (Genesis 3:4–6). This is why **God opposes the proud but gives grace to the humble** (see Proverbs 3:34; Luke 1:51–52; James 4:6). This is why the New Testament in so many places teaches us to be humble (see Romans 12:3; Ephesians 4:2; Philippians 2:3).

6 If we humble ourselves, God will lift us up. If we try to exalt ourselves, God will humble us (see Matthew 23:12; James 4:10 and comments).

Peter says here: **Humble yourselves**. We must humble ourselves; we must put ourselves down. No one likes to do that. But it is better for us to put ourselves down than to have someone else do it!

We are to humble ourselves **under God's mighty hand**. All things are under God's mighty hand; God controls everything. His hand is mighty to punish the unrighteous and to defend the righteous. We can place ourselves under His mighty hand, because He cares for us (verse 7). We can trust God that every trial He allows to come upon us is for our ultimate good (see Romans 8:28; Hebrews 12:7–9 and comments). Such trials are for our improvement in this life and for our glory in the next.

God will lift us up **in due time**. We don't like to wait to be lifted up; rather, we want to be lifted up immediately. But God knows best what is needed for our spiritual welfare. As long as we need discipline, God will continue to give it. When we have learned to be humble, then He will lift us up.

7 When we are cast down because of trials and troubles, let us not be anxious. We may not be able to get rid of our trials and troubles, but we can get rid of our anxiety. We can give our anxiety to God (Psalm 55:22). We can have complete confidence that God will sustain and protect us (Matthew 6:25–34). And when we give our anxiety to God, then He will give us His peace, which transcends all understanding (see Philippians 4:6–7 and comment).

8 **Be self-controlled and alert**. In order to serve Christ we must be self-controlled and prepared for action (1 Peter 1:13). In order to pray effectively, we must be self-controlled and clear minded (1 Peter 4:7). And here Peter says that in order to keep the **devil**—SATAN—from devouring us, we need to remain **self-controlled and alert**.

The devil tries to **devour** or destroy us by leading us into sin and disobedience. The devil tries to destroy our fellowship by creating conflict among us, and especially by inciting us to slander and backbiting[15] (see Galatians 5:15). Above

---

[14] It has been said that pride is an even deeper sin than selfishness, or self-love. For even if we could remove all selfishness from our lives, we would still be proud that we had done so!

[15] In the Greek language, the name Satan means "slanderer" or "false accuser." (Satan is the Hebrew name for the devil.) In Revelation 12:10, Satan is called the **accuser of our brothers**.

all, the devil tries to destroy our faith by producing doubt and fear in our minds. If he can destroy our faith, we are lost. Satan is a powerful enemy (Ephesians 6:12). Let us never think that we can defeat him by our own strength.

But God and Christ are stronger than the devil and all his evil forces (Ephesians 6:10–11; 1 John 4:4). The devil may be a **roaring lion**, but God has tied a rope around his neck. Because of this "rope," the devil cannot do anything or go anywhere without God's permission. The devil can only create as much trouble as God allows. God uses Satan to accomplish His own purposes. God will never allow Satan to devour His faithful children.

But we believers must do our part. Without our cooperation, God cannot protect us. First, we must remain **self-controlled and alert**. Second, we must remain in obedience to God's will. Third, we must continually pray, so that we do not fall into temptation (Matthew 6:13; Mark 14:38). Fourth, we must put on the armor of God (Ephesians 6:13–18). And finally, having done all the above things, we must resist Satan, by standing firm in the faith (verse 9). And when we resist Satan, he will flee (James 4:7).

9 Resist him, standing firm in the faith. On one occasion, Peter did not resist Satan. His faith failed. Jesus had said to Peter: **"I have prayed for you, Simon, that your faith may not fail. And when you have turned back, strengthen your brothers"** (Luke 22:32). Now, in this verse, Peter (Simon) is doing what Jesus said: He is strengthening his brothers. All Christians throughout the world are experiencing the same kind of sufferings because of the devil's schemes. We are not suffering alone. Let us strengthen each other.

In the end, believers can overcome the devil **by the blood of the lamb** (Christ) **and by the word of their testimony**; in particular, those who overcome the devil are those who do **not love their lives so much as to shrink from death** (Revelation 12:11). Peter did not shrink from death. Indeed, because of his faithful testimony to Christ, he was put to death by the Romans. Perhaps some of those to whom Peter sent this letter were at that time facing death. Let their faith not fail! Let them be **strong in the Lord and in his mighty power** (Ephesians 6:10). Let them, too, overcome the devil (1 John 4:4).

10–11 Now, at the end of his letter, Peter gives us one of the greatest promises in the Bible: **And the God of all grace, who called you to his eternal glory in Christ, after you have suffered a little while, will himself restore you and make you strong, firm and steadfast**. Our God is a **God of all grace**. No matter what our situation, no matter what our need, God's grace is sufficient for us. Our troubles are **light and momentary** (2 Corinthians 4:17). God has called us **to his eternal glory** IN CHRIST. Paul wrote: **The one who calls you is faithful and he will do it** (1 Thessalonians 5:24).

Final Greetings (5:12–14)

12 Silas (also called Silvanus) is mentioned in 1 Thessalonians 1:1 and 2 Thessalonians 1:1. This same Silas was Paul's companion on his second missionary journey (Acts 15:40; 16:1–40; 17:1–5).

13 She who is in Babylon refers to the church in Rome. In Old Testament times, Babylon was the capital of a great kingdom (now modern Iraq); the city was known for its evil and ungodliness. Therefore, in New Testament times, Christians gave the name Babylon to Rome, because Rome was the evil capital of the Roman Empire.

Just as Timothy was Paul's spiritual son (1 Timothy 1:2), so **Mark** was Peter's spiritual son. Mark was the writer of the New Testament Gospel of Mark. Mark had learned all about Christ from Peter, and thus he wrote his Gospel according to what Peter told him. Mark is also mentioned in Acts 12:12,25; 15:36–40; Colossians 4:10; 2 Timothy 4:11.

14 In New Testament times, it was the customary greeting among Christians to give each other a kiss (Romans 16:16; 1 Corinthians 16:20).

Peace to all of you who are in Christ.

In this world we shall have suffering. But **in Christ** we will have peace. Jesus said: **"Peace I leave with you; my peace I give you. I do not give to you as the world gives. Do not let your hearts be troubled and do not be afraid"** (John 14:27).

2 Peter

INTRODUCTION

The Apostle Peter, the chief of Jesus' original twelve disciples, wrote this letter in about 65 A.D., near the end of his life. Peter wrote this letter to refute a false teaching that was spreading among Christians throughout the Middle East. There were many false teachers who were teaching that it was necessary to obtain a special knowledge of Christ to be saved, but that it was not necessary to obey Him or to lead a holy life. Peter's main teaching in this letter is that without godly behavior, such "knowledge" of Christ is false knowledge, not real knowledge.

OUTLINE

A. The Christian Virtues (1:1–21).
   1. Challenge to Go Forward in Grace (1:1–15).
   2. The Glory of Christ (1:16–21).
B. False Teachers (2:1–22).
   1. Judgments Against False Teachers (2:1–9).
   2. Characteristics of False Teachers (2:10–22).
C. Christ's Second Coming (3:1–18).
   1. The Certainty of Christ's Coming (3:1–10).
   2. The Moral Implications of Christ's Coming (3:11–18).

CHAPTER 1

God's Calling and Election (1:1–15)

1 Peter calls himself **Simon Peter.** Simon was his Jewish name; and Peter was his Christian name, which Jesus Himself gave to him (Matthew 16:17–18; Mark 3:16).

Peter was both a **servant** and an APOSTLE of Jesus Christ (see Romans 1:1). He is writing to fellow believers, to those who **through the righteousness of our God and Savior Jesus Christ** have received FAITH. From this we can understand that faith is a gift. God gives faith to those whom He calls (see John 6:44; Ephesians 2:8–9; 2 Thessalonians 2:13 and comments). But once we have received faith, we must use it—that is, we must accept Christ; otherwise, we shall receive no benefit from it (John 3:16,18,36).

Peter writes: **. . . our God and Savior Jesus Christ**. Here Peter calls Jesus **God**. And that is who Jesus is, because God, Jesus, and the Holy Spirit are all one triune God (see John 10:30 and comment).

2 Peter here repeats what he has written in 1 Peter 1:2 (see Romans 1:7; Ephesians 1:2 and comments). In this greeting, Peter adds the words: **through the knowledge of God and Jesus our Lord**. This **knowledge** that Peter is referring to is the true personal knowledge of God and Jesus, from which we receive new life, new strength, and a new mind (see John 17:3; Philippians 3:10). This **knowledge** is not like the false knowledge of the false teachers, in opposition to whom Peter is writing this letter. To receive the knowledge of Christ is to know Christ; and to know Christ is to obey Him (1 John 2:3). **The man who says, "I know him," but does not do what he commands is a liar, and the truth is not in him** (1 John 2:4). To truly know Christ is to **gain** Christ (Philippians 3:8), and to gain along with Him grace, peace, and all other blessings (Romans 8:32; Ephesians 1:3).

3 Just as Christ called Peter and the other apostles, so He also calls us. We have been called and drawn to Him **by his own glory and goodness** (see John 1:14). And having called us, Christ by His **divine power** gives us everything we need to walk according to His calling (see Ephesians 3:20–21; 4:1; Philippians 2:13; 4:13 and comments). He has given us everything we need for **life** (see John 10:10), and for **godliness** (see 1 Thessalonians 4:7).

4 **Through these**—that is, through Christ's **glory and goodness** (verse 3)—Christ has given us promises, promises of grace, forgiveness of sin, the Holy Spirit, new life, and adoption as children of God. We have been given these gifts, so that we might **participate in the divine nature** (see John 1:12; 1 John 3:2). We participate in the **sufferings** of Christ (1 Peter 4:13); we participate in the **glory** of Christ (Colossians 3:4; 1 Peter 5:1,10); and we also participate in the **divine nature** of Christ (see Romans 8:9; Galatians 2:20; 1 John 3:9 and comments).

Because we now participate in Christ's divine nature, we must act as Christ would act. We must leave the **corruption** of the world with its **evil desires** and put on the qualities of Christ (see Ephesians 4:20–24 and comment).

5–7 If we are children of God and participators in Christ's nature, then we should be growing more like Christ day by day. We should not remain satisfied with our spiritual state, but should constantly **press on** (Philippians 3:12–14) until we attain to the **whole measure of the fullness of Christ** (Ephesians 4:13).

In verses 5–7, Peter describes some of the qualities of Christ that should be increasing in our lives. The first he mentions is **faith**. Faith is always the first step of our Christian lives; faith is the foundation of all other Christian virtues. Next comes **goodness**, which Peter has already mentioned in verse 3 as being one of Christ's qualities. Next is **knowledge**, by which we can distinguish between good and evil (Hebrews 5:11–14). Through a knowledge of Christ we obtain grace and peace (verse 2), and everything we need for **life and godliness** (verse 3). We must constantly grow in our knowledge of God and Christ (Colossians 1:10).

Next, in verse 6, Peter mentions **self-control** (see Galatians 5:23; 1 Peter 1:13; 4:7; 5:8 and comments). Next comes **perseverance,** which is the outward proof of our faith (see Mark 13:13; Galatians 5:22; Romans 5:3; Hebrews 12:2; James 1:2–4; 1 Peter 1:6–7 and comments). Next Peter mentions **godliness.**

Together with godliness, there must be **brotherly kindness** (verse 7). Anyone who says "I love God," and mistreats his brother is a liar (1 John 4:20). Brotherly kindness or love is the main sign, the main proof, that we are indeed disciples of Christ (John 13:35). Brotherly love means that we carry each other's burdens (Galatians 6:2), and that we bear with one another in love (Ephesians 4:2). Before we can love those outside the church, it is necessary to first love our fellow believers within the church (John 13:34; Romans 12:10; 1 Thessalonians 4:9–10; Hebrews 13:1; 1 Peter 1:22).

Finally, the greatest of all these virtues is **love**—love for God and for all people. This love is not only for fellow believers; it is for everyone, even evildoers, even our own enemies (Matthew 5:44; Mark 12:30–31; 1 Corinthians 13:13; Colossians 3:14). This **love** is completely unselfish; it is a spiritual love. This love is not shown to another person according to that person's worthiness or according to what that person can do for us. This love is freely shown to another person for that other person's sake alone. This is the kind of love that God first showed to us (John 3:16), and it is this kind of love, therefore, that we should show to others (1 John 3:16).

8–9 The qualities that Peter has mentioned in verses 5–7 must continue to grow in us. If we do not keep growing spiritually, we will die spiritually. A plant either grows or it dies; it cannot remain the same. So it is with Christians. A plant can also be choked by weeds; in the same way, Christians can be spiritually choked by the cares and desires of the world, and thus become **unproductive** (Mark 4:7,18–19).

Therefore, let us strive to increase these virtues in our lives, so that we might bear much fruit for God. Because we glorify God most by bearing fruit for Him (John 15:8).

The Christian who does not have these qualities is spiritually blind. He is **nearsighted**; he can see only the nearby things of the world, but not the things of heaven. Such a Christian has forgotten that he is a **new creation** (2 Corinthians 5:17); he has forgotten that he has been **cleansed from his past sins** (see 1 Corinthians 6:9–11).

10–11 **Therefore . . . be all the more eager to make your calling and election sure.** In the work of our salvation, God has a part and we have a part. God must first choose us and call us (see John 6:44; Romans 8:29–30; 9:18; Ephesians 1:4–5 and comments). But after that, we ourselves must make our **calling and election sure**. God gives us faith (verse 1); but we must take that faith and place it on Jesus. God calls us; but we must then **live a life worthy** of that calling (Ephesians 4:1). We must **continue to work out** [our] **salvation with fear and trembling** (Philippians 2:12–13). If we do these things, we shall **never fall**; that is, we shall not lose our salvation. We may stumble and lose the way from time to time (James 3:2), but we shall not completely fall away. Not only that, if we do these things, we will **receive a rich welcome into the eternal kingdom of our Lord** (verse 11). We won't just barely enter God's kingdom—like the man Paul mentions in 1 Corinthians 3:14–15, whose work was burned up but he himself escaped through the flames. No, we will receive a **rich welcome** into God's kingdom; we will enter with **praise, glory and honor** (1 Peter 1:7).

12–14 Christians need constant reminding of the great truths and doctrines of the Bible. Therefore, as long as he lives, Peter will continue to strengthen his brothers and to remind them of the things of Christ. But, as he writes this letter, Peter's death is near. He calls his body a **tent**, which is about to be taken down (see 2 Corinthians 5:1). Even though Jesus told Peter that he would be put to death on a cross just as Jesus had been (John 21:18–19), Peter shows no fear of death. Because for Peter death is the doorway through which he will enter into God's **eternal kingdom**.

15 Peter told what he knew about Christ to Mark. Then, according to what he had learned from Peter, Mark wrote the New Testament Gospel called Mark's Gospel. Thus, through Mark's Gospel (and Peter's own two letters), Peter provided a means for Christians to **always be able to remember these things**.

The Glory of Christ (1:16–21)

16 When Peter wrote this letter, false teachers had arisen who were claiming that they had received special knowledge of Christ. But, according to Peter, their "knowledge" consisted of **cleverly invented stories**. But Peter's knowledge was not **invented**; the things Peter spoke about he had seen with his own eyes and heard with his own ears. Peter had seen Jesus' **majesty** when Jesus was transfigured on the mountain (Mark 9:2–8). He had heard God speak from heaven saying that Jesus was His Son.

When Peter mentions here the **power and coming of our Lord Jesus Christ**, he could be referring either to Jesus' transfiguration on the mountain, or to His second coming at the end of the world, or to both. In Peter's mind, Jesus would appear at His second coming just as He had appeared transfigured before Peter, James, and John on the mountain. In Mark's Gospel, Jesus' second coming is mentioned immediately before Mark's account of Jesus' transfiguration (Mark 9:1); thus in the minds of both Peter and Mark, the two events seem to be connected.

17–18 God descended in a cloud onto the mountain, and gave **honor and glory** to Christ (see Mark 9:7). Peter never forgot what he saw and heard at that time. It was then that Peter gained the certain knowledge that Jesus was indeed the Son of God, the King whose kingdom would last forever (Psalm 2:7; Daniel 7:13–14).

19 The Old Testament PROPHETS had spoken many prophecies concerning Christ. During His time on earth, Christ fulfilled all of these prophecies. Thus Christ, through His life, **made more certain** the word of the prophets; that is, He confirmed everything the prophets had written about Him. The prophets had prophesied about the coming of a Messiah,[1] a Savior; and Jesus was that Messiah and Savior.

Therefore, we need to pay close attention to both the Old and New Testaments of the Bible. We are only **aliens and strangers** on this dark earth (1 Peter 1:1; 2:11), and the Bible is like a **light shining in a dark place** (Psalm 119:105). Therefore, **until the day dawns and the morning star rises in** [our] **hearts**—that is, until Christ comes again—we must diligently obey what is written in the Bible (see Romans 13:12). In Revelation 2:28 and 22:16, Christ is called the **morning star**. Christ will "rise in our hearts"; and when this happens, we shall be transformed into His likeness (see 2 Corinthians 3:18; 1 John 3:2).

20–21 We can trust the Old Testament prophets, because they did not write according to their own thoughts and understanding, as the false prophets did. The Old Testament PROPHECIES did not come about by the prophet's own interpretation. Rather, the prophets wrote down what God spoke to them. The prophets **were carried along** or moved by God's HOLY SPIRIT. The Greek word for **carried along** was commonly used in connection with sailing ships; such ships were "carried along" by the wind (see Acts 27:17). The sailors would put up the sails, and the wind carried the ship along. In the same way, the Old Testament prophets put up their "sails," and the Holy Spirit carried them along. The prophets opened their mouths, and the

---

[1] Messiah means "anointed one" in the Hebrew language. The equivalent word in the Greek language is "Christ."

Holy Spirit guided their thoughts and their tongues. For this reason, we can have complete confidence that every verse in the Bible is God's own word, written by the direction of His Holy Spirit (see 2 Timothy 3:16 and comment; General Article: How We Got Our Bible).

CHAPTER 2

False Teachers (2:1–22)

1 Even in Old Testament times, there were false prophets (Deuteronomy 13:1–5; Jeremiah 5:30–31). From that time up until the present there have been false prophets and false teachers in every generation. They **secretly introduce destructive heresies**. They secretly bring false teachings into the church and deceive many (see 1 Timothy 4:1). Their teaching is **destructive**, because it destroys not only their own faith but also the faith of those who are deceived by it. By their false teaching, these teachers deny the lordship of Christ.

Concerning these false teachers, Peter says that Christ **bought** them with His own blood; therefore, they belong to Him (1 Corinthians 6:19–20; 7:23). Nevertheless, they have rebelled against Him. From this we can understand that these false teachers at one time followed Christ. But now they have wandered from the truth; they oppose the truth. Such false teachers always deny Christ, because Christ Himself is the truth (John 14:6). And when they deny Him, they bring destruction upon themselves (Matthew 10:33).

2 The **way of truth**—that is, the Gospel of Christ—is brought into disrepute not so much by those outside the church as by those inside the church, by so-called Christians. When believers follow after false teachers and false prophets and imitate their shameful behavior, then Christ is especially dishonored. In Peter's time, the main teaching of the false teachers was this: No matter how a person behaves, he is saved through grace and through a knowledge of Christ; therefore, one doesn't need to give any thought to his daily behavior. This false teaching is refuted by many passages in the New Testament (see Romans 6:1–2,15; 1 Thessalonians 4:7; 1 Peter 1:14–15).

In every church in every generation there are always some believers who are ready to listen to some new way or some false teaching (2 Timothy 4:3–4). Let us not boast that false teaching could never pass into our church; rather, let us remain on guard. **So, if you think you are standing firm, be careful that you don't fall!** (1 Corinthians 10:12).

3 False teachers are interested not in helping others but in getting their payment. They do not seek the benefit of others; they seek only their own benefit and honor (see 1 Timothy 6:3–5). Such teachers will not escape condemnation; their destruction is near. God's judgment is especially severe for those who lead others astray (Mark 9:42).

4 In verses 4–8, Peter gives three examples from the Old Testament to show that God saves the righteous and punishes the unrighteous.

The first example concerns ANGELS who sinned by rebelling against God. These angels are mentioned in Genesis 6:1–4, where they are called **sons of God**. God **sent them to hell**, where they are now being held **for** JUDGMENT. On the great day of judgment, God will give them their final punishment (see Jude 6).

5 The second example Peter gives is the example of the flood, which is described in Genesis Chapters 6–8. At that time God destroyed all the unrighteous people of the world, but He saved **Noah** and his wife, together with their three sons and their wives. Noah was a **preacher of righteousness**. According to Genesis 6:9, **Noah was a righteous man, blameless among the people of his time, and he walked with God** (see Hebrews 11:7).

6–8 Peter's third example is the destruction of the evil cities of **Sodom and Gomorrah**, which is described in Genesis 19:1–29 (see Matthew 10:15). God utterly destroyed those two cities by fire, together with all their wicked inhabitants (Genesis 19:24–25). But first God rescued one of the inhabitants, **Lot**, because Lot was righteous in God's sight.

9 By these three Old Testament examples, Peter shows that God knows how to punish those who are wicked and unrighteous. In the same way, says Peter, God will surely punish the false teachers and those who follow them.

At the same time, God **knows how to rescue godly men** like Noah and Lot, and He is fully able to do so. In the same way, if a person remains obedient to God and stands firm in the faith, God will rescue him **from trials**. In Peter's time, such trials had already begun to come upon Christians, but they will especially come just before Christ's second coming (Revelation 3:10). . . . **he who stands firm to the end will be saved** (Mark 13:13).

10 Here Peter again says that the false teachers will be punished. These teachers **follow the corrupt desire of the sinful nature**; that is, they teach that men can do whatever they want. They despise the authority of Christ and His apostles.

These false teachers are bold and arrogant. They are not afraid to slander **celestial beings**. When Peter says "celestial beings," he can be referring to angels, or to church leaders; the Greek text can be translated both ways. In either case, these false teachers refuse to submit to anyone's authority.

11 Nevertheless, even **angels** (presumably the "celestial beings" of verse 10) do not slander the false teachers in return (see Jude 9). In this we can see a common truth: evil men slander righteous men, but righteous men keep silent. The righteous do not return evil for evil. The slanderous speech of the false teachers is shameful; no righteous person would dare to speak that way **in the presence of the Lord**.

Let us remember that whenever we want to accuse someone, we will be making our accusation in the presence of the Lord. We had better be certain, therefore, that our accusation is true and acceptable to God! (see Matthew 7:1–5; 18:15–17; Romans 14:10).

12 These false teachers do not even understand the things they are blaspheming; they don't understand the people they slander. It is ignorant people such as these who oppose Christ and His followers (1 Peter 2:15). They are ignorant of spiritual things. They are **like brute beasts, creatures of instinct**, who follow only their own selfish instincts and desires. Brute beasts are born **only to be caught and destroyed**. In the same way, these false teachers will be "caught" by their own passions and destroyed by them (see Jude 10 and comment). . . . **everyone who sins is a slave to sin** (John 8:34). And the **wages of sin is death** (Romans 6:23).

13 God is always just. He who sows evil will reap evil (Galatians 6:7). **The one who sows to please his sinful nature, from that nature will reap destruction** (Galatians 6:8). Since these false teachers trade in evil, they will be paid in evil.

These teachers are not content to drink liquor only at night, but they drink it in the daytime too. One who gets drunk at night will soon begin to get drunk in the day also. Smaller sins always lead to bigger sins. These false teachers were even getting drunk at church love feasts, at which the Lord's Supper was customarily celebrated in Peter's time (see 1 Corinthians 11:20–21; Jude 12). Such men are **blots and blemishes** on the church. They have no place in Christ's church, which should be **without stain or wrinkle or any other blemish** (Ephesians 5:27). Jesus was Himself a lamb **without blemish or defect** (1 Peter 1:19), and those who follow Him should be the same (2 Peter 3:14).

14 The eyes of the false teachers are **full of adultery**. They look at every woman with lust, desiring to fulfill their evil passions (Matthew 5:28). They cannot stop sinning (see Ephesians 4:19 and comment). Evil passions are like itches; when you scratch them, they itch even more. People who seek to fulfill their evil passions are never satisfied.

These false teachers **seduce the**

unstable (see 2 Timothy 3:6–7). They are **experts in greed**; that is, they are clever and skillful in making money (see verse 3). Such teachers are truly **accursed** in God's sight. Paul called them **objects of wrath** (Ephesians 2:3). There is only one way they can escape condemnation, and that is to die to their sins and receive new life in Christ (see 1 Peter 4:1–3 and comment).

15 The false teachers are like the Old Testament prophet **Balaam**, who was tempted to prophesy for money (Numbers 22:1–21). Not only that, Balaam, through his false prophecies, led the Jews away from the Lord (Numbers 31:16; Revelation 2:14).

16 Balaam's own donkey rebuked him (Numbers 22:22–34). Notice that a dumb animal had more understanding than the prophet Balaam, whose mind had been darkened by wrongdoing (Ephesians 4:18).

17 False teachers are like **springs without water**. People come to them thirsty, but find nothing to drink. In contrast to these teachers, Jesus gives the water of life; when a person drinks of Jesus' water, he will never thirst again (John 4:13–14).

False teachers are like **mists driven by a storm**. They are blown this way and that (Ephesians 4:14). Their teaching will not last; it will be driven away like the mist.

18 False teachers pretend to be religious. They say to new believers: "It's all right to follow your **lustful desires**. It's only a man's spirit that must remain pure. God does not care what we do with our body." This same false teaching had spread to the church at Corinth. Paul taught that man's body was extremely important. He wrote: **The body is not meant for sexual immorality, but for the Lord** (1 Corinthians 6:13). Our bodies are **members of Christ** (1 Corinthians 6:15). Our body is a **temple of the Holy Spirit** (see 1 Corinthians 6:18–20 and comment).

19 Such false teachers say to new believers: "You are free from the law." But these teachers are themselves **slaves of depravity** (see Romans 6:16). Sin is their master.

Christians are indeed free, but they are not free to sin. We are slaves of Christ. Only in Christ can we obtain true **freedom** from sin and its punishment (see Galatians 5:13 and comment).

20 The main sin of these false teachers was that they deceived and led astray new Christians (see verse 3 and comment). These new believers had just **escaped the corruption of the world**, but now through the false teaching of these teachers, they had again become **entangled** in the world and been **overcome**. Thus their second state was worse than their first state (see Matthew 12:43–45).

21 It is better for a person to sin in ignorance than to sin knowingly (see Luke 12:47–48; John 15:22 and comments). Judgment will be especially severe for those who have once **known the way of righteousness** but then **turn their backs on the sacred command**—that is, Christ's commandments (see Hebrews 3:12–14; 6:4–6; 10:26–29 and comments).

22 The Jews considered dogs and pigs to be unclean (see Matthew 7:6). A dog, when it has vomited something up, will eat it again. Likewise, a person who is entangled in the corruption of the world may momentarily "vomit up" the corruption, but he soon will partake of it again.

In the same way, you can clean a pig momentarily, but it soon will go back into the mud again. Likewise, a man can be cleaned momentarily from his sin; but if he doesn't receive a new spiritual nature, he will soon go back to his sin.

Those people who taste the grace of God and experience His cleansing, but who then turn from God and return to their old sins, are like dogs and pigs. Their inner nature has not been transformed; they cannot fully free themselves from their old ways.

What terrible things Peter has to say about these false teachers! Jesus said to Peter, **"Feed my sheep"** (John 21:17). But Peter has now seen these false teachers feeding poison to Jesus' sheep—and the sheep don't even know it! Let us not say that such poisonous and false teachers can never rise up in our church. They certainly can. Jesus said: **"What I say to you, I say to everyone: 'Watch!'"** (Mark 13:37).

CHAPTER 3

Jesus' Second Coming (3:1–18)

1–2 Peter wrote both of his letters to remind Christians of the teachings of the Old Testament **prophets** and the New Testament **apostles**. Both the prophets and the apostles were inspired and **carried along** by the same Holy Spirit (2 Peter 1:21). Christ's church is built on the foundation of the prophets and apostles (Ephesians 2:19–21). The **command given by our Lord and Savior,**[2] which Peter mentions here in verse 2, refers to the main teachings of Jesus which have been passed on through the apostles.[3]

3–4 **... in the last days**[4] **scoffers will come.** These **scoffers** are the false teachers mentioned in Chapter 2. They do not believe that the world will ever come to an end. They insist that things have remained unchanged since the creation of the world. They say that from the time of their **fathers** Abraham, Isaac, and Jacob, everything has been going along the same. "Where is the end of the world?" they ask mockingly. They don't believe that Christ will come again to judge all men. People who follow their own **evil desires** don't like to think about a final judgment!

5 The scoffers who say the end of the world will never come forget that at one time God, through His word, created the earth (Genesis 1:1–2,6–10; John 1:1–3). If God could create the earth in this way, then surely He can also destroy the earth.

6 Not only that, the scoffers should remember that God once destroyed all the evil men of Noah's time by sending a flood upon the earth (Genesis 7:17–24). God cannot tolerate man's sin; He must punish man for it. And just as God punished men in the days of Noah, so will God punish men again at the end of the world, when Jesus Christ comes the second time (see Matthew 24:37–39).

7 **By the same word**—that is, by God's word—**the present heavens and earth** will be destroyed by **fire** (verses 10–12), and all ungodly men will be judged and condemned (see Isaiah 66:15–16; Malachi 4:1–2; 1 Corinthians 3:13; 2 Thessalonians 1:7–8).

8 At the time Peter wrote this letter, many believers had begun to wonder why Jesus had not yet come. And the scoffing false teachers were saying, "See, He's not going to come." Therefore, Peter says to these believers: "Do not be agitated; do not think that God has delayed Christ's coming. In God's sight, a thousand years is like one day" (Psalm 90:4). Compared with an eternity, a thousand years is but a moment.

Not only that, in God's sight one day is like a thousand years. God can do the work of a thousand years in one day. Therefore, what God does He will do in His own time, and not according to our thoughts; we need not worry. What God has promised He will fulfill. Our job is only this: to watch, to pray, and to obey.

9 Therefore, let us not think that God is delaying unnecessarily in sending Christ to earth a second time. Rather, He is being patient and merciful. He is giving men and women more time to come to REPENTANCE, before Christ returns again as judge. It is not God's desire that anyone should perish. When men perish, it is not because of God but because of their own sin. They perish because they have rejected God's son, our Savior (see Ezekiel 18:23; 1 Timothy 2:4 and comment). However, after Jesus comes again there will no longer be any chance for men to repent. And no one

---

[2] In 2 Peter 2:21, this **command** is called the "sacred command."

[3] After the apostles' teachings had been written down, they could then be passed on to all future generations in the form of the New Testament.

[4] The **last days** are the days between Jesus' first coming and His second coming. Thus we are now living in the "last days" (see 2 Timothy 3:1; Hebrews 1:2).

knows when Jesus will come (Mark 13:32; Acts 1:7). This is why men should repent now without delay, and place their faith in Christ. For if Jesus comes tomorrow and they have not repented, they will be lost (see Mark 13:33–37). **I tell you . . . now is the day of salvation** (2 Corinthians 6:2).

10 The **day of the Lord** (the day of Christ's return) **will come like a thief.** Christ will come suddenly when no one is expecting Him (see Matthew 24:43–44; 1 Thessalonians 5:2–3; Revelation 3:3; 16:15). When Christ comes again, the earth and heavens will be completely destroyed (Isaiah 34:4; Mark 13:24–25,31; Luke 21:25–26). Just as God once judged the world by water (verse 6), so He will again judge the world **by fire**; and by that fire the earth will be utterly destroyed (see 1 Corinthians 3:13–15; 2 Thessalonians 1:6–8; Hebrews 10:26–27; 12:29).

11–12 Knowing that Jesus will soon come to judge the world, we ought to **live holy and godly lives** (verse 11), lest we also be condemned with the world (see Romans 13:11–12; 1 Thessalonians 5:4–8). If we each fulfill God's will in our own lives, the **day of God**—the day of Christ's return—will come sooner; we shall **speed its coming** (see Acts 3:19–21). God is waiting for us to spread His Gospel to all nations; **then the end will come** (Matthew 24:14). We must not only repent and obey and preach the Gospel, but we must also pray this prayer: **Our Father in heaven, hallowed be your name, your kingdom come. . . .** (Matthew 6:9–10).

13 Believers do not need to fear Christ's second coming. This old earth will be destroyed, but the righteous will enter a **new heaven and a new earth** (see Isaiah 60:19–22; 65:17; 66:22; Matthew 13:40–43; Revelation 21:1–4).

14 Since only the righteous will enter this new heaven and earth, we should **make every effort** to be found righteous—that is, to be found **spotless, blameless and at peace with him** (see Hebrews 12:28 and comment). John writes: **. . .continue in him, so that when he appears we may be confident and unashamed before him at his coming** (1 John 2:28). Those who look forward to Christ's coming and also desire to lead holy lives (1 John 3:3).

Let us each ask ourselves this question: If we suddenly learned that Jesus was going to return in one year, would we live our lives any differently? Our answer should be no! If we are at present living our lives according to God's will, then learning that Jesus will return in a year should make no difference in our behavior (aside from cancelling long-range plans). We should be living each day as if the Lord were about to return.

15 As long as God waits patiently, that many more people will have the opportunity to repent and be saved (see verse 9 and comment).

Paul also wrote about Christ's second coming in many of his letters. In particular, Paul wrote many times that Christians must be holy, patient, and steadfast as they wait for the Lord to come.

16 If Paul's letters seem to us hard to understand, let us not be discouraged: even Peter found some of what Paul wrote hard to understand. But many people also **distort** Paul's meaning. In particular, they distort Paul's teaching that men are saved through faith and not through works. These **ignorant and unstable people** say that since we are saved only through faith, we no longer have to do any good works; we can do what we please. In this way, they fall into all kinds of sin.

17 **Therefore . . . be on your guard** (see Mark 13:5,22–23). Let no believer **fall from** [his] **secure position** (see Hebrews 3:12; 4:1; 10:36–38 and comments).

18 **. . . grow in the GRACE and knowledge of our Lord and Savior Jesus Christ.** In order to obtain **grace**, we need to have a **knowledge** of Christ—that is, we need to know Christ (see 2 Peter 1:2 and comment). The Christian religion does not consist in merely being happy or having good feelings. The Christian religion consists in following Christ. Christians do not follow a religion; they follow Christ. Christ Himself is our way. To be a Christian means to know Christ personally and to obey His commands. If we do this, we will certainly grow in grace (see 2 Peter 1:5–8,10–11 and comments).

To him (Christ) **be glory both now and forever!** It is not only to God we give glory but also to Christ, so that **all may honor the Son just as they honor the Father** (John 5:23). Christ is our example; Christ is also our goal. And He is coming soon. Therefore, Peter says in verse 17, **be on your guard.**

1 John

INTRODUCTION

This letter was written by the Apostle John, son of Zebedee. John was one of Jesus' original twelve disciples (Mark 1:19–20). John was called the **disciple whom Jesus loved** (John 13:23; 21:20), because Jesus loved him more deeply than He loved the other disciples. The Gospel of John, John's three New Testament letters, and the book of Revelation were all written by this same Apostle John. John lived for many years after Jesus' death. He wrote this first letter near the end of the first century A.D.

Therefore, John wrote with great authority. All Christians knew of John. In fact, John was so well-known that he didn't even need to introduce himself by name in this letter.

John wrote this first letter so that his readers might know that they had **eternal life** (1 John 5:13). He wanted to strengthen their faith.

It is not known where John was when he wrote this letter or to what church he sent it. Perhaps he intended the letter to be sent to several churches. John wrote this letter mainly to refute a false teaching that had arisen among the believers to whom he was writing. Some false teachers were teaching that Jesus never really came to earth as a man. They said that Jesus was only a spirit, or a vision. But John writes strongly in this letter that Jesus was both fully man and fully God. If Jesus was not fully a man, then His death would have no meaning. He could not have offered Himself as a sacrifice for our sins.

OUTLINE

A. Fellowship with God Who Is Light (1:1–2:29).
   1. The Word of Life (1:1–4).
   2. Walking in the Light (1:5–10).
   3. Obeying God's Commands (2:1–6).
   4. A New Command (2:7–17).
   5. Warnings against Antichrists (2:18–29).

B. Fellowship with God Who Is Righteous (3:1–4:6).
   1. Doing What Is Right (3:1–10).
   2. Loving One Another (3:11–24).
   3. Warning against False Spirits (4:1–6).

C. Fellowship with God Who Is Love (4:7–5:21).
   1. Teachings Concerning Love (4:7–21).
   2. Faith in the Son (5:1–12).
   3. Concluding Remarks (5:13–21).

CHAPTER 1

The Word of Life (1:1–4)

1 The **Word of life** is Christ Himself. In John 1:1, Christ is also called the **Word**. God's Word—that is, Christ—has been with God from the beginning. Indeed, Christ has been with God not just **from** the beginning but from before the beginning, because God has no beginning. God has always been, and so has Christ.

The Word (God's Word) **became flesh and lived for a while among us** (John 1:14). God's Word—Christ—came into the world as God's one true incarnation.[1] God's Word became "flesh"—that is, became a man. John and the other apostles saw Christ with their own eyes. They touched Him with their own hands. Christ was no vision or spirit. The apostles touched Him not only before His death but also after He had risen from the dead (Luke 24:39). Therefore, John knows without doubt that Jesus the Son of God was also fully a man.

2 **The life** (Christ) **appeared**. In this verse, John calls Christ the **eternal life**. John writes in his Gospel: **In him was life, and that life was the light of men** (John 1:4). Jesus said: **"I am the way and the truth and the life"** (John 14:6). To all who believe in Him, Jesus gives ETERNAL LIFE (John 3:16). This same Jesus was **with the Father**, and then He appeared to men. John writes here: **. . . we proclaim to you the eternal life**. In the same way, we too must proclaim eternal life to our relatives, friends, and neighbors. Have we been doing so?

3 John had seen and heard that **life** (verse 2)—that is, Christ—with his own eyes and ears. But those to whom this letter was sent had never seen and heard Christ. Therefore, John explains about Christ to his readers so that they **may have fellowship with us**—that is, so that they may have fellowship with John, with other believers, and **with the Father and with his Son, Jesus Christ**. Fellowship with the Father and Son means that God and Jesus come to us and dwell with us (John 14:23). When we have fellowship with God and Christ, then we shall also have fellowship with other believers.

4 When believers have fellowship with God, they also have **joy**. If the readers of this letter come into fellowship with God, then John will have joy and his readers will have joy too. Then **our**[2] **joy**—that is, John and the readers' joy—will be **complete**.

Christ's Gospel brings **joy**. Jesus said: **"I have told you this so that my joy may be in you and that your joy may be complete"** (John 15:11).

Walking in the Light (1:5–10)

5 **God is light**. Light stands for holiness and righteousness. Darkness stands for sin and evil.

When God's Son Jesus Christ came into the world, He was a **light** shining in the **darkness** (John 1:5,9; 3:19; 8:12; 12:46).

6 To have **fellowship** with God means to know Him, to love Him, and to be His children. If we truly have fellowship with Him, we will walk in the light. Those who walk in **darkness**—in sin—can have no fellowship with God. If they say, "We have fellowship with God," they are lying. They are not living **by the truth**.

The **truth** is not just something one speaks; truth is something one does, or lives. We must **live by the truth** (see John 3:21). We must worship God **in spirit and truth** (John 4:23). Truth is a way of life.

---

[1] Christ is not like other incarnations. He is the one and only Son of the one true living God. Christ, although He was fully God, came to earth as a man. He was both fully man and fully God (see General Article: Jesus Christ).

[2] In place of the word **our**, some versions of the Bible say "your." The general meaning is the same.

Jesus said: "**I am the way and the truth and the life**" (John 14:6).

7 When we walk **in the light**—that is, in fellowship with God—two things result: first, **we have fellowship with one another**; second, **the blood of Jesus . . . purifies**[3] **us from all sin**.

To have fellowship with one another means to love one another (1 John 4:7,11). In order to have fellowship with one another, we must be able to "see" one another; that is, we must be **in the light**. If we are living in the darkness of sin, we cannot "see" our brother. We cannot have fellowship with him.

Therefore, in order to be in fellowship with one another, we must first be in fellowship with God. In order to be in fellowship with God, we must walk in the light (verse 6), because God Himself is light (verse 5). We must walk in the light, **as he is in the light**. We must be perfect, as He is perfect (Matthew 5:48).

When we walk in the light, the **blood of Jesus** continually **purifies** us. The light of God's holiness is in our hearts. By the **blood of Jesus**—that is, by His death on the cross—we have, through faith, been cleansed from sin. Christ's blood purifies us **from all sin**—no matter how terrible our sin has been. Christ died to take away all our sins.

8 No matter how hard we try, we cannot be completely pure and sinless. There is always some sin left in our lives. God is so holy that it's impossible for man to reach His high standard. God cannot tolerate any sin or impurity; **in him there is no darkness at all** (verse 5). Therefore, we can never please Him completely, because we always have some stain, some sin, remaining in us.

In 1 John 3:9, John says: **No one who is born of God will continue to sin**. In the Greek language, the expression **continue to sin** means to continually sin without repenting, to continually live in sin. John is saying that the Christian—the one born of God—will not live in sin in this way. The Christian will not knowingly live in sin.

But here in verse 8, John says that from time to time the Christian will fall into sin. The Christian's old sinful nature occasionally causes him to stumble and fall. However, he doesn't remain fallen.

These two verses, verse 8 and 1 John 3:9, are both completely true. According to 1 John 3:9, we Christians do not live in bondage to sin. Christ is our master, not Satan. Paul says: **. . . we should no longer be slaves to sin** (Romans 6:6). Again he says: **. . . count yourselves dead to sin** (Romans 6:11). Sin has no power over Christians.

But even though all this is true, according to verse 8, we Christians do fall into sin. New temptations, new sins, keep springing up in our lives. And we must keep asking to be forgiven for these sins; we must keep on being cleansed of them. Only when we are with Christ in heaven, will we be completely sinless[4] (see 1 John 3:6,9 and comment).

9 This is an extremely important verse. All men sin, including Christians; therefore, all men need to be repeatedly purified **from all unrighteousness**—from all their sins. John has already said that Jesus' blood purifies us (verse 7), but how does it happen? Is there anything we must do? Yes, there is. We must **confess our sins**, and turn from them. And God will then erase our sins. He will **purify us from all unrighteousness**. What a wonderful promise!

Therefore, Christians do not need to despair. Yes, we must mourn for our sins (Matthew 5:4), but we must not become discouraged. For us there is always a means of being forgiven and purified.

We must understand John's meaning here when he says we must **confess our sins**. He is talking here about REPENTANCE. It is not enough to merely confess our sins with our lips. We must also "confess" them with our actions; that is, we must

---

[3] In the Greek text, the word **purifies** literally means "keeps on purifying." The New Testament was originally written in Greek.

[4] Some Christians believe that in this life also we can become sinless; but most believe that this is not possible. For further discussion, see General Article: Holy Spirit.

hate our sins and turn from them. This is true repentance.

Here it is necessary to remember something. When we confess our sins, we must confess specific sins. It is not enough just to say, "I am a sinner." That's easy to say, because everyone is a sinner. Rather, we must look at each separate sin we have committed and ask God's forgiveness for each one. This is why John says here that we must confess our **sins**—not just sin in general.

God is **faithful and just**. Why does John say that? Because God has already given the punishment for man's sin once for all. He has placed the punishment for our sins upon His own Son Jesus Christ. Therefore, He will not punish a second time those who put their faith in Jesus. To give a second punishment would not be **just**. Christ has already borne our punishment. Therefore, God will not punish us again; rather, He will forgive us and purify us. If He were to condemn us again, He would not be **faithful and just** (see Romans 3:22–26).

10 Some people say that they have no sin. In saying this, they make God out to be a **liar**, because God has said that all men are sinners (Romans 3:10–12). Because all men sin, God had to send Christ to save them. If man had no sin, there would have been no need to send Christ. Therefore, the man who says he has no sin is calling God's word false; he is denying God's Word—Christ—who came to save him from his sins. There is **no place** for God's Word, God's Son, in the life of such a man.

Every man knows in his heart that he has sinned. God speaks to us about our sins through our conscience. Let us listen to God when He speaks to us; let us not shut out His word. If we shut God's word out of our heart, we will also shut God out of our life.

CHAPTER 2

Obeying God's Commands (2:1–6)

1 John has just written that if we confess our sins God will forgive us and purify us (1 John 1:9). But some people reading this might think that sinning was not such a big thing. Some might say, "Now we can sin without worrying about it. Because if we sin, God will quickly forgive us." But John does not want the readers of this letter to have such a mistaken thought. He is writing to them, not to encourage them to sin, but to keep them from sinning!

If a believer should at any time sin, he has a spokesman, a defender, **one who speaks to God in** [the believer's] **defense**—namely, Jesus Christ. Jesus is a perfect spokesman, because He was also a man like us, and therefore He understands our weaknesses and can sympathize with us (Hebrews 2:17–18; 4:15). Also, He is the perfect spokesman because He is the **Righteous One**. Because He Himself is righteous, He is able to stand before God, the righteous Judge. Christ stands before God always, interceding for all those who put their trust in Him (Romans 8:34; Hebrews 7:25).

2 In a courtroom, the spokesman or defender takes the side of the defendant. The spokesman appeals to the judge, saying that the defendant is innocent. But our spokesman Christ does not do that. Instead, Christ says to God that we are guilty! He says to God that we are worthy of the death sentence! What kind of spokesman is that!

But then Christ says to God: "Even though men are guilty, I myself will take their punishment. Sentence me to death instead of them. I will offer myself as an **atoning sacrifice**, or ATONEMENT, for their sins" (Romans 3:23–25).

Thus John says that Christ is the **atoning sacrifice for our sins**. And Christ is the atoning sacrifice not only for our sins **but also for the sins of the whole world**. That is, His sacrifice is sufficient to atone for the sins of every believer in the whole world (John 1:29; 1 John 4:10).

All men and women in the world deserve to receive the death sentence for their sins. We must teach and preach this truth everywhere. But along with that truth, we must teach another truth: namely, that there is a spokesman, a Savior, who is able to save us from that death sentence—and that Savior is Jesus Christ.

3–4 To obey Jesus is the same thing as to walk in the light (1 John 1:7). When we are in the light, then we will see Jesus and know Him. But if we do not obey Him, we walk in darkness and cannot know Him. Some men say, "I believe in Jesus," but they do not obey Him. Such men are liars. They remain in their sins. They do not confess their sins, and they do not receive forgiveness.

5–6 If we obey God's word, His love will be **made complete** in us. God's word is this: **Love the Lord your God with all your heart and with all your soul and with all your mind and with all your strength** (Mark 12:30). Thus, to obey God's word means to love Him (see John 14:15,21; 1 John 5:3 and comments).

When we obey God, then God comes to us and makes His home with us (John 14:23). God will be in us, and we shall be in Him. If we **walk as Jesus did**, we will know that we are in Him, and we will remain in His love (John 15:10).

A New Command (2:7–17)

7 In verse 6, John says that we must **walk as Jesus did**. How did Jesus walk? In love. The **old command** that John mentions here is the two-fold commandment to love God and to love one's neighbor, which commandment the readers of this letter have had **since the beginning** of their Christian lives (Mark 12:30–31). John says: **This old command is the message you have heard**—that is, the Gospel. All other commands are based on this great two-fold commandment to love God and neighbor (Matthew 22:40).

8 But now John adds a **new command**, a command given by Jesus to His disciples: **Love each other as I have loved you** (John 15:12). Jesus Himself called this a **new command** (John 13:34).

John had seen this love in Jesus' life with his own eyes. John had seen Jesus offer up His own life for the sake of others. Jesus' love is true. And John says that the **truth** of this new command—that is, this true love—**is seen in him and you**. That is, this true love is seen not only in Jesus but also in those who believe. If the **true light** of Jesus is shining in our hearts, His love will be in us. Darkness will be gone (John 1:4–5,9).

9–11 To hate one's brother is to walk in darkness. To love one's brother is to walk in the light. When we walk in the light, we can see the way; we will not **stumble**. We will avoid the temptation to sin.

John says of the man who hates his brother that the **darkness has blinded him** (verse 11). The darkness of sin always makes men blind. Satan wants to blind us. He doesn't want us to see his schemes. Above all, he doesn't want us to see Jesus. Therefore, he tries to make us blind.

12 John calls his readers **dear children**. When John wrote this letter, he was about ninety years old. Therefore, for him it was suitable to call his readers "children."

John reminds his readers that their sins have been forgiven (1 John 1:9). Their sins have been forgiven **on account of his name**. That is, they have been forgiven in Jesus' name because of their faith in Him. Forgiveness and cleansing from sin is the first great blessing that results from our faith. Having received that blessing, we can then go forward in our Christian life.

13 The **fathers** mentioned here are mature believers. Through faith these fathers have known **him** (Christ) **who is from the beginning**. John does not mean that they have seen and heard Christ themselves; rather, they have known Christ through faith.

The **young men** are young believers. They have overcome the **evil one**—that is, SATAN. They have escaped from Satan's kingdom of darkness.

There is no need to make a great difference between the **children**, the

fathers, and the **young men** mentioned in verses 12–14. The things written in each of these verses apply to all Christians.

14 John here adds two things to what he wrote in verse 13. First, the young men here are **strong**. They are strong in the Lord; they have put on the Lord's armor (Ephesians 6:10–11). Second, they are strong because the **word of God lives** in them. The word of God is the Gospel of Christ; it is also the **sword of the Spirit**, which is used for overcoming Satan (Ephesians 6:17).

The **word of God** is also Christ Himself. Christ, the living Word, dwells in us. And because His word is in us, we can ask for anything we wish and it will be given to us (John 15:7). Therefore, let us daily ask that we might be **forgiven** of our sins (verse 12), that we might **overcome the evil one** (verse 13), that we might be made **strong** in faith (verse 14). Let us daily ask that we might be obedient, that we might be filled with God's light, His knowledge, and His love. And all these things will be granted to us!

15 **Do not love the world or anything in the world**. Here the **world** means the "kingdom of darkness." And **anything in the world** means the **cravings**, the **lust**, and the **boasting** that exists among men of the world (verse 16). It is impossible to love God and at the same time to love the world and the things in the world. **If anyone loves the world, the love of the Father is not in him**.

But there is a still deeper meaning in this verse that we need to see. In the world there are many good things, which are gifts given to us by God. These good things also we must not love. We can use these things with thanksgiving, but we must not love them. For example, money is not evil in itself, but to love money is evil. Rest is a good and necessary thing, but to love rest leads to laziness. Again, work is a good and necessary thing, but to love work in an unsuitable way gives rise to pride and worldly ambition. From these examples we must understand that instead of loving these gifts, we must love the giver of these gifts—God. Our entire love must be given to God[5] (see Matthew 10:37; Mark 12:30; Luke 14:26 and comments).

The **world** is Satan's kingdom (John 12:31; 1 John 5:19). This is the world that Jesus came to save; this is the world that God loved (John 3:16). This is the world that did not recognize Jesus and did not accept Him (John 1:10). This is the world that remains in darkness. **Light has come into the world, but men loved darkness instead of light because their deeds were evil** (John 3:19).

16 Here John gives three examples of the things of the world, the things of darkness, which we must not love. First, the **cravings of sinful man**. These include all our sinful physical desires, such as unlawful sexual desires and excessive desires for comfort, pleasure, and fine food. Second, the **lust of** [man's] **eyes**. This means man's greed and covetousness. Third, the **boasting of what** [man] **has and does**. This **boasting**, or pride, means taking pride in one's accomplishments; it means seeking a good name or high position; it means putting confidence in oneself instead of in God.

17 The world and its desires are passing away. Why put faith in things that pass away?

. . . but the man who does the will of God lives forever. God's will is this: that men believe in Christ and obey His commands—especially the two great commandments to love God and neighbor. The man or woman who believes in Christ and obeys His commands will receive eternal life and **live forever** (Matthew 7:21).

Warnings Against Antichrists (2:18–29)

18 **. . . this is the last hour**; that is, the "last hour" is now. The **last hour** began when Jesus first came into the world, and it will end when Jesus comes again at the end of the world. The entire

---

[5] We, of course, must love our neighbor too. But first of all, we must love God. Then His love will flow into us, and enable us to love our neighbor. We cannot truly love our neighbor until we have first loved God (see Mark 12:31 and comment).

history of the world can be divided into two parts: the part that took place before Christ, and the part that has taken place since Christ. Even the calendar used throughout the world is divided into B.C. (before Christ) and A.D. (the year of the Lord, meaning, after Christ). This **last hour** has now lasted almost two thousand years.

Before Christ comes again, the **antichrist**[6] will first come (see 2 Thessalonians 2:1–4,8; 1 John 4:3 and comments). But before the main antichrist comes, many other antichrists will rise up—indeed, many have already risen up (Mark 13:5–6,21–13). These are the false teachers. They entice many people to follow after them.

19 Such false teachers, or **antichrists**, come from within the church. They have gone out from the church. At first they seemed just like other believers, but John says here that they never had true faith; they never truly **belonged** to the church. These false teachers were never true Christians to begin with.

Many Christians interpret this verse to mean that anyone who falls away or leaves the faith never had true faith to start with. They say that a true believer can never really fall away; a true believer cannot lose his salvation.[7]

20 True believers have an **anointing from the Holy One**—that is, from Christ. They are anointed with the Holy Spirit. God anointed Christ with the Holy Spirit (Acts 10:38). And Christ likewise anoints all believers with the Holy Spirit. The Holy Spirit is the **Spirit of truth** (John 14:17). Therefore, through the Spirit we **know the truth**[8] (see John 14:26). Therefore, a true believer does not teach falsehood.

21 The readers of this letter know the truth already. John writes to them not because they don't know the truth, but because they do know it. This letter is written for Christians. But Christians can be deceived by false teachers. Therefore, John writes in order that they might not be deceived. False teachers teach falsehood; such teaching never comes from the truth.

22 What is the biggest lie? The biggest lie is to say that Jesus is not the Christ, that He is not the Savior, that He is not God's Son. To deny Christ is to deny God (Matthew 11:27; John 14:9–10; 2 John 7).

23 **. . . whoever acknowledges the Son has the Father also** (see 1 John 4:15). Only by knowing Christ can we truly know God (John 1:18). We cannot come to God except through Christ (John 14:6). There are many roads that run in the direction of heaven, but there is only one that reaches there. That one road is Christ. **Salvation is found in no one else, for there is no other name under heaven given to men by which we must be saved** (Acts 4:12).

24 **See that what you have heard from the beginning**—that is, God's word—**remains in you**. If God's word does not remain in us, Christ will not remain in us, and we will not remain in Him. We will become like the false teachers mentioned in verses 18–19. We will become like withered branches, fit only to be cut off and thrown away (see John 15:4–7).

But if what we have heard (God's word) remains in us, we **will remain in the Son and in the Father**. He who remains **in the Son** (Christ), will also remain in God the Father. Let us continually exhort one another not to turn away from God's word, the Gospel, that we have heard.

25 Those who remain in Christ and

---

[6] The **antichrist** is a powerful enemy of Christ, who will appear some time before Christ comes again. Many Bible scholars believe that the **antichrist** is the "man of lawlessness" that Paul refers to in 2 Thessalonians 2:1–12. The antichrist is an agent of Satan. In fact, according to John, the antichrist has his own agents, false teachers, who are already in the world. John also calls these **antichrists**.

[7] For further discussion of this subject, see General Article: Can We Lose Our Salvation?

[8] In place of the words **the truth**, some versions of the Bible say "all things." In the context of this verse, the meaning is essentially the same.

in whom Christ's word remains have the promise of **eternal life** (see John 4:14; 6:40).

26 This verse John has written to us as a warning. Let us not throw away the promise of eternal life! Let us not be led astray by false teachers.

27 The **anointing you received** is the anointing with the Holy Spirit which believers receive **from him**—Christ. John tells his readers: This anointing **remains in you**. Then he says: . . . **and you do not need anyone to teach you**. What does John mean? He means that our main teacher is the Holy Spirit. Of course, God uses Spirit-filled teachers to teach us, but these teachers themselves have been taught by the Holy Spirit. Thus all true teaching ultimately is inspired by the Holy Spirit, whether it comes directly to us from the Spirit Himself, or whether it comes through reading the Bible, or through Spirit-filled human teachers.

Jesus said: "The **Holy Spirit . . . will teach you all things**" (John 14:26) Therefore, Christians are not dependent on human wisdom. Many Christians say: "I am ignorant; I am not educated; I don't know anything." But they never need to say that! Let them read and hear God's word as much as they are able, and then let them have faith that whatever else they need to know the Holy Spirit will teach them. No believer in Christ is "ignorant" in God's sight.

Therefore, says John, let God's word remain in us, let the Holy Spirit's **anointing** remain in us, and let us **remain in him**—IN CHRIST.

28 **And now, dear children, continue in him**. There is no more important teaching in the Bible than this: Continue (or remain) in Christ. If we do not continue in Him, we shall be ashamed **when he appears** at His second coming. For He will say to us, "**I never knew you**" (Matthew 7:23).

But if we continue in Him, we shall be **confident and unashamed** when He comes again. If we continue in Him, we shall know with certainty that we are saved. We shall stand before His judgment seat, and He will say to us, "**Well done, good and faithful servant!**" (Matthew 25:21).

If Christ came today, what would He say to us? Would we be able to stand before Him **confident and unashamed**?

29 How can we recognize a true Christian—that is, one born of God? In this way: A true Christian **does**[9] **what is right**. God is **righteous**; therefore, all those who have been born of Him are also righteous. It is equally true to say that all those who do **what is right** are born of Him. Being born of God and doing what is right cannot be separated.

But what does John mean when he says that true Christians do **what is right**? What is "right"? To do "right" is to believe in Christ and to obey His commands. When one does this he is declared RIGHTEOUS, even as God is righteous (see 1 John 3:7). So then, all who believe in Christ and obey Him are righteous and are born of God.

To be **born** of God means to be born anew spiritually by the Holy Spirit (see John 3:3,5 and comment). It does not mean that a person tries to make himself "spiritual" by doing good works or by following some religious law or ritual. Man's nature cannot be made spiritual in this way. Our old sinful self cannot be born of God. In fact, there is only one thing our old sinful self can and must do: it must die. In order for a new spiritual self to be born, the old sinful self must first die (see Romans 6:6). To be born of God, then, means to put off our old sinful life, and receive a new spiritual life. It means to become a **new creation** (see 2 Corinthians 5:17). The person who is born of God will **live by the Spirit** (Galatians 5:16,25). . . . **those who are led by the Spirit of God are sons of God** (Romans 8:14).

---

[9] In the Greek text, the word **does** means "keeps on doing."

CHAPTER 3

Children of God (3:1–10)

1 How great is the love the Father has lavished on us! This is the central message of the Gospel of Christ: God loves mankind, and He desires to save men and women and make them His children (see John 3:16). In no other religion do we find this message. This is why the only hope for the world is found in the Gospel of Christ. No other religion, no other god, can offer man the sure hope of eternal life. Only the Gospel can lead man to heaven. Only the Gospel is the true word of the one true living God.

God's love is manifested in this, **that we should be called children of God.** But we are not only **called** His children—we **are** His children! (see John 1:12; Galatians 3:26; 4:7).

Let us not doubt that we are His children. Satan tries hard to make us doubt it. Satan says to us: "You are such a bad sinner that you can't possibly be a child of God." But this is a lie. We have been purified **from all sin** by the blood of Christ (1 John 1:7). We must not listen to Satan.

The **world does not know** how it's possible for low and humble believers like us to become God's own children and have an eternal inheritance in heaven. The world cannot accept it. The **world**—that is, unbelieving mankind—does not accept Christ; therefore, the world does not accept us (see John 1:10; 15:18–21).

2 But we know that when he appears—that is, when Jesus comes again at the end of the world—**we shall be like him**. Even though we are now children of God, we have not yet fully become like Christ. But when we see the glorified Christ, when we are with Him, then we shall be transformed. His glory will become manifest in us (John 17:24; 2 Corinthians 3:18).

3 What is **this hope in him** that John mentions here? This **hope** is hope in Jesus. It is the hope of meeting Jesus, of being like Jesus, of sharing in His glory. When we long and hope to be like Jesus, then we shall indeed become like Him. Our hope will be fulfilled; and **just as he is pure,** so shall we become pure also.

4 Everyone who sins breaks the law, God's law. **Everyone** includes kings, prime ministers, presidents—everyone. Anyone who sins breaks God's law.

Most people don't like the word "sin." Whenever they sin, they say, "I made a mistake." But in saying this, they deceive themselves. God sees their sin; He is not deceived.

5 Christ **appeared**—that is, came to earth—**so that he might take away our sins** (John 1:29). How did He take away our sins? He did it by taking the punishment for our sins upon Himself. He received the death penalty in our place. In this way He made atonement for our sins (see Romans 5:6,8; 1 Corinthians 15:3; 1 John 2:2). But Christ Himself did not deserve to die; He was **without sin** (Hebrews 4:15).

6 No one who lives in him keeps on sinning.[10] That is, the person who lives in Christ does not live in sin (see verse 9). He may sin from time to time, but he does not deliberately continue to sin (see 1 John 1:8 and comment). And if he does sin, he quickly repents of it and is cleansed (1 John 1:9).

If we continue to knowingly commit some sin, we are not in Christ. We do not know Him, and He does not know us. Let each one ask himself: "Is there any sin in my life which I am not willing to give up?" If there is, we must at once confess it and give it up. If we don't, we do not belong to Christ. Only those who obey Christ and are pure in heart will see Him and know Him (Matthew 5:8; 1 John 2:3–4).

7 Many false teachers will try to deceive us. But we can recognize them by their work. If a man **does** (keeps

[10] In place of the words **keeps on sinning,** some versions of the Bible say "sins." However, according to the Greek text, the correct meaning is "keeps on sinning." This is important for understanding this verse.

doing) **what is right**, then we know that he is righteous. On the other hand, if a man keeps doing what is wrong, then we know that he is a false teacher, a false Christian. Jesus said, "**By their fruit you will recognize them**" (Matthew 7:16).

8 **He who does**[11] **what is sinful is of the devil** (Satan). Satan's work is to deceive men and lead them into sin. Satan makes men slaves to sin. But Jesus came to earth **to destroy the devil's work** by freeing men from bondage to sin and delivering them out of the kingdom of darkness.

9 **No one who is born of God will continue to sin**[12] (see 1 John 1:8; 5:18 and comments).

We are **born of God**. His **seed**—His nature—is in us. His power, love, and other qualities are in us. Having received His nature, we cannot continue doing what is against His nature; we must now live according to His nature. To be a Christian is not to follow a religion or obey some law. To be a Christian is to be born anew by God's Spirit and to have a new spiritual nature (see John 3:5; Romans 8:11).

For example, oranges come from an orange tree. An orange tree does not produce sour lemons. Neither does God give birth to sinners.

But let us remember, oranges can become diseased or sucked dry by insects. But even though an orange may be diseased, it is still an orange. It is the same with us. We are children of God, but from time to time we become "diseased" or are attacked by "insects"—that is, we fall into sin. But even though we fall into sin, we still remain God's children. However, having fallen into sin, we must then confess our sin to our Father and ask forgiveness for it.

Because we are God's children, we do not want to sin. Instead, we want to do God's will; we want to please God, because He is our Father. Therefore, when we do sin, it is not our real self that is sinning; rather, it is sin living within us—our old sinful self—that is sinning (see Romans 7:18–20).

10 We can recognize the children of God and the children of the **devil** (Satan) by their works. Anyone who **does**[13] **what is right** is a child of God (1 John 2:29). Anyone who **does not do**[14] **what is right** is a child of the devil.

To not love our brother is a sin (1 John 2:9). Here John reminds us that to "do what is right" in our daily lives means above all to love others[15]—especially our **brother**[16] (John 13:34; Galatians 6:10). The entire law—all of God's commands—are summed up in the command to love others, to love our neighbor (see Romans 13:9; Galatians 5:14 and comments).

Love One Another (3:11–24)

11–12 **Cain** was the oldest son of Adam, the first man God created. Cain killed his brother Abel, because Cain was evil and his brother was righteous (Genesis 4:1–8). Evil always opposes righteousness; there can never be peace between them. John says: **Do not be like Cain**.

13 Why does the **world**[17] hate and oppose those who believe in Christ?

---

[11] In the Greek text, the word **does** means "keeps on doing."

[12] In place of the words **continue to sin**, some versions of the Bible say "sin." However, "continue to sin" is the correct meaning of the Greek text (see comment to verse 6 and footnote to comment).

[13] In the Greek language: "keeps on doing."

[14] In the Greek language: "does not keep on doing."

[15] John is speaking here in a practical sense. Of course, before we can truly love others, we must first love God and desire to do His will (Mark 12:30). His will is that we should love others.

[16] Here **brother** means fellow believer.

[17] In this context, **world** means "evil or unbelieving men."

Because believers are not of this world. They are of heaven; they have been born of God (John 1:12–13; 15:18–19). If the world hated Christ, it will also hate His followers.

14 In 1 John 2:29, John says: ... **everyone who does what is right has been born of him** (God). That is, the one who does what is right has been born anew spiritually; he has received new spiritual life. To do "what is right" means to believe and obey. To obey means to love (see verse 10 and comment). Therefore, to love means to have spiritual life. Thus, if we love our brother, we can know that **we have passed from death to life** (see John 5:24). The fruit of hatred is **death**. The fruit of love is **life**—eternal life.

15 To hate one's brother is to murder him. We murder him not with our hands; we murder him with our thoughts. Jesus taught that if we are angry at our brother we will face judgment as murderers (Matthew 5:21–22). Hatred and murder lead to spiritual death; there can be no **eternal life** for those who do such things.

16 By His own example, Jesus showed us what love is. We should follow His example. If He loved our brothers so much that He gave up His life for them, surely we should be willing to love them too. More than that, we should be willing to love them as Jesus loved them; we, too, should be willing to give up our lives for them. We must not love our own life; rather, we must be ready to lay it down for the sake of others (John 15:12–13; Romans 5:8; 1 John 4:9–11).

It is not usually necessary to die for others. What is always necessary, however, is to live for others. In fact, living for others is more difficult than dying for them!

17–18 True love arises from our hearts; it comes from within us. But true love is always manifested outwardly; it is manifested by works of love. If it is not, then it isn't true love (see James 1:22; 2:14–17).

19 **This then is how we know that we belong to the truth**. It is because of the outward manifestation of our love that we know **we belong to the truth**. This is similar to verse 14, where John says that because of our love, we know we have **life**. To "belong to the truth" and to "have life" are essentially the same thing. Jesus Himself was both the **truth** and the **life** (John 14:6). When we continue in love, the truth is in us, life is in us, Christ and God are in us. This being so, what can we fear? Those who love have nothing to fear (1 John 4:18). Therefore, we can **set our hearts at rest**; that is, we can reassure ourselves that we are indeed children of God and that we can come into His presence without fear. Therefore, if we want to put our hearts **at rest** and be able to stand before God with confidence, then we need to love our brothers.

20 Sometimes our own hearts condemn us. Our hearts say to us: "You are a sinner; you are not worthy to be a child of God." But God knows more than our hearts do. Even though our hearts condemn us in this way, God declares us innocent. **God is greater than our hearts**; and He will not condemn us (Romans 8:1).

21 According to verse 20, even if our hearts condemn us, God does not. Therefore, according to verse 21, if our hearts do not condemn us, we can have even more **confidence** that God won't condemn us either.

If our conscience is clear—that is, if our hearts have nothing to accuse us of—we will have **confidence before God** and our hearts will be at rest (see Romans 5:1; Hebrews 4:16).

22 Because we obey God's commands, we can ask Him for **anything** and we will receive it. If God does not give us exactly what we ask for, it is because we have not asked correctly (James 4:3). But God will always give us some answer to our prayers; He will always give us what is needed for our spiritual welfare.

Here we must look more closely at this subject of prayer. John says in this verse that we **receive from** [God] **anything we ask, because we obey his commands and do what pleases him**. If we do not obey His commands and do not live according to His will, then our prayers will be in vain.

Therefore, in order to receive from God the things we ask for, the first requirement or condition is that we must be obedient. The second requirement is that we must pray in faith (Matthew 21:22; Mark 11:24). The third requirement is that we must pray in Jesus' name, that is, for His sake, for His glory; we must not pray for our own sake, or for our own glory (John 14:14). The fourth requirement is that we must pray according to God's will (1 John 5:14–15). These four requirements or conditions for prayer are summed up in this one statement of Jesus: **"If you remain in me and my words remain in you, ask whatever you wish, and it will be given you"** (John 15:7).

23 What must we do to please God? Here in this important verse, John again gives us the answer to this question: To please God we must believe in Christ and obey (love) Him. True faith never exists by itself; it is always expressed through obedience, and obedience is always expressed through love (see Galatians 5:6; James 2:17 and comments). Faith is the tree; obedience (love) is the fruit.

To believe **in the name** of Christ is the same as to believe in Christ. Jesus' name tells us who He is. He is the **Christ**, the Savior, the **Son** of God. He is the **King of kings and the Lord of lords** (1 Timothy 6:15; Revelation 19:16). All these are names of Jesus.

24 Jesus said: **"If you obey my commands, you will remain in my love"** (John 15:10). Here John says: **Those who obey his commands live in him**. To live in Christ and to remain in Christ's love is the same thing. To live (or remain) in Christ is the most important thing in our lives (1 John 2:28). But in order to live in Him, we must **obey his commands.**

How do we know that Christ lives in us? We know it **by the** (Holy) **Spirit** (Romans 8:16; 1 John 4:13). The HOLY SPIRIT is Christ's Spirit. If the Holy Spirit is in us, Christ also is in us.

CHAPTER 4

True and False Spirits (4:1–6)

1 In John's time, there were many people who were teaching, preaching, and prophesying through various spirits. It is the same in these present times. We must examine every man's words. How do we examine them? We examine them by comparing them to what is written in the Bible. If what they say agrees with what is written in the Bible, then we can know that they are speaking through the Holy Spirit.

John says that we must **test the spirits to see whether they are from God**. When John says **test the spirits**, he means that we must test what the spirits are saying. We must always examine the words of anyone who claims to be speaking "through the spirit," because there are many false teachers and false prophets in the world, and they are constantly trying to deceive us (see Mark 13:22; Acts 20:29–31 and comments).

2 In John's time, the different books and letters of the New Testament had only just been written; they hadn't yet been joined together in one volume. The believers to whom John wrote this letter had not had a chance to read the entire New Testament. Therefore, John here gives them a simple rule by which they can recognize true and false spirits, or true and false teachers: **Every spirit that acknowledges that Jesus Christ has come in the flesh is from God** (see 1 Corinthians 12:3; 2 John 7). What men say about Jesus Christ is the most important thing in determining who is from God and who is not.

Who, then, is Jesus Christ? In all the world, there is no more important and urgent question than that. And the answer is this: Jesus Christ is God Himself, who **has come in the flesh**. He is both man and God. He is not simply a spirit that passed into some man and then returned to heaven. He is almighty God

Himself, who made Himself fully a man and came into the world two thousand years ago. And as a man He ascended again into heaven. And this same glorified man Jesus Christ is alive today, and sits at the right hand of God in heaven (Hebrews 1:3).

But when Jesus became a man, He did not stop being God. He was God **in the flesh**—that is, God in the form of a man; and so He remains today (see John 1:14; Philippians 2:3–8).

Therefore, all who acknowledge Christ have the true Spirit of God. They have true faith.

Thus, in summary, there is one easy way to tell what kind of spirit is in a man: Ask that man what he thinks of Jesus Christ. According to his answer, we will know whether his spirit is from God or not.[18]

3 **. . . every spirit that does not acknowledge Jesus is not from God**; it is from the devil, Satan. This is a hard saying, but it is true. There are two kinds of spirits in people: the kind that acknowledges Jesus and the kind that does not.[19] The person who acknowledges Jesus is born of God and will be saved; the person who does not acknowledge Jesus is born of the devil and will be lost. This is why it is so urgent to preach the Gospel. There is no more important work on earth than to preach the Gospel. Jesus Christ is not just another incarnation among many. He is the one true incarnation of the one true living God. All other incarnations are false; they represent false spirits, spirits of the **antichrist** (see 1 John 2:18 and comment). All such false spirits come ultimately from Satan and are under his control.

4 We, who are of God, **have overcome them**—the false spirits of the antichrist. We have already overcome them, and we will continue to overcome them.

The **one** who is in us is Jesus—or Jesus' Spirit, the Holy Spirit. Jesus lives in us through His Spirit. The **one who is in the world** is Satan, the chief of all false (evil) spirits. Jesus called Satan the **prince of this world** (John 12:31). Jesus is greater than Satan and all his evil spirits. Let us never say: "How few we are; how weak we are." Yes, perhaps we are small in number, but we are not small in strength. We have all the strength of God on our side.

5 The false spirits, the antichrists, the teachers and prophets of other religions—all these are **from the world**. They love the world, and the world loves them (John 15:19). They speak the things of the world; therefore, the world listens to them.

6 We who have the Spirit of Christ are **from God**. If a man listens to us and accepts our word, he also is from God. However, if a man rejects our word, he is not from God (John 8:47). In this way we will know who has the **Spirit of truth** (the Holy Spirit) and who has the **spirit of falsehood**.

The **Spirit of truth** is a name for the Holy Spirit (John 14:17). The world (worldly men) cannot accept the Holy Spirit, because the world cannot recognize the truth. The world has accepted a false spirit, the **spirit of falsehood**, and the men of the world have been deceived. They walk in darkness.

Peter has written: **Therefore . . . be on your guard so that you may not be carried away by the error of lawless men and fall from your secure position. But grow in the grace and knowledge of our Lord and Savior Jesus Christ** (2 Peter 3:17–18). Let us, too, through the study of God's word, grow in grace and in the knowledge of Jesus Christ.

God's Love and Ours (4:7–21)

7–8 John has written: **God is light** (1 John 1:5). He has also written: **Whoever loves his brother lives in the light** (1

[18] Of course, a man can lie in order to deceive us; but such a lie will in time be exposed by the man's actions.

[19] These two kinds of spirits influence man's own human spirit. When a spirit that acknowledges Jesus is in a man, that man will then acknowledge Jesus. When a spirit that does not acknowledge Jesus is in a man, that man will not acknowledge Jesus.

John 2:10). Now John says: **God is love** (verse 8). **Everyone who loves has been born of God** (verse 7).

God is light; therefore, we walk in light. **God is love**; therefore, we walk in love. Only those who walk in light (faith) and love are born of God (1 John 2:29; 3:10).

God is love. John doesn't just say here that God loves (which is also true). John says here that God is Himself love. His nature is love. He doesn't love us because we are worthy to be loved. Rather, He loves us because it is His nature to love.

God is love. This is the great news of the Gospel of Christ! In no other religion is this great truth taught clearly. The followers of other religions know about God. They know that God is the Creator, that He is a Spirit, that He is powerful. But they do not know that **God is love**. Why don't they know it? Because in order to know love, one has to first experience love. In order to know God, one has to first experience God—that is, one has to meet Him personally. One has to draw near to Him. One must be able to call Him Father.

Can we find out about love just by reading about it? No, we cannot. We must experience it for ourselves. We must receive love into our hearts; otherwise, we cannot know love. In the same way, we must experience God in our hearts; otherwise, we cannot know Him. But not only that, we ourselves must love. We must love God and our brother and our neighbor. It is not enough just to receive love; we must give it. To the extent that love flows out from us, to that extent love will flow in from God. God's love is like water in a pipe. If the lower end of the pipe becomes blocked, no more water will be able to flow into the top end. We are like pipes, through which God's love flows.

Notice, all true love comes from God. First, we receive God's love; and then we show it to others. We don't love others with our own human love, but with God's love. True love is spiritual; it comes not from man, but from God.

9 How is God's love manifested? God's love was manifested when He sent His only Son Jesus Christ into the world to save men and women (see John 3:16 and comment). As part of our salvation, we receive eternal life. From the first day we believe in Christ, we begin to live through Him; and through Him, we live forever. How great God's love is!

10 We did not love God first; He first loved us (see verse 19). If we had first loved God, we would have been worthy to receive His love. But we are not worthy. **God demonstrated his own love for us in this: While we were still sinners, Christ died for us** (Romans 5:8) Why did Christ die for us? He died for our sins. He offered up His own life as an **atoning sacrifice for our sins** (see 1 John 2:2 and comment).

11 Why must we love? Because God loved us. Just as Christ loved us, so must we love one another (John 15:12; 1 John 3:16). How can we refuse to love others, whom Christ loved so much?

12 We have not seen God with our eyes (John 1:18). But that is not necessary. God is in our hearts. We don't need to look for Him with our eyes.

If we love one another, God, who is love, will live in us (see John 14:23). His love will fill us (Romans 5:5). As we continue to love each other—that is, as we continue to obey His word—**his love is made complete in us** (see 1 John 2:5).

13 Here John repeats an earlier thought (see 1 John 3:24 and comment). John says here: **. . . he** (God) **has given us of his Spirit**. Other New Testament passages say simply that God has given us His Spirit (Galatians 3:2,5; 4:6). But here, says John, God has given us **of his Spirit**. However, to say, "God gives **of His Spirit**," is the same as to say, "God gives His Spirit"; the meaning is the same. God doesn't give an unlimited measure of His Spirit to men; He gives to men only a certain measure **of His Spirit**. But to Christ God gave His Spirit **without limit** (John 3:34).

14 **No one has ever seen God**[20] (verse 12). But, says John, **we have seen**

[20] In the Old Testament, God appeared in the form of an angel to a number of individuals, such as Abraham and Moses. But no man was ever allowed to fully see God Himself.

Christ (see John 1:14). And having seen Him, we **testify that the Father has sent his Son to be the Savior of the world** (see John 3:16–18).

Christ is the **Savior of the world**. But not everyone in the world is saved. To be saved, a person must acknowledge that **Jesus is the Son of God**; that is, a person must believe in Jesus (verse 15).

15 John here repeats the thoughts he has written in 1 John 2:23–24 and 4:2. To acknowledge Jesus as the Son of God—that is, to believe in Him—is to live in God. To live in God is to know God (verse 16). To know God is to have eternal life (John 17:3).

Notice that all these things—to acknowledge Jesus as God's Son, to believe in Jesus, to obey Jesus, to love God and others, to know God, to live in God, to have eternal life, to be saved—all are closely related. They always go together; they cannot be separated.

16 Because God lives in us (verse 15), **we know** the love He has for us; that is, we experience it. And having experienced God's love, we **rely on** it.

Whoever lives in love lives in God, and God in him (see 1 John 3:24; 4:12 and comments).

17 As God's love is **made complete** in us, we become more like Christ. To become like Christ—to have His love made complete in us—is the main goal of our Christian lives (Romans 8:29). When His love is **made complete** in us, then we will have **confidence** on the final **day of JUDGMENT** (see 1 John 2:28). We will not have to fear God's judgment; for us there will be no condemnation, no punishment, on that day.

We will escape punishment, **because in this world we are like him** (Christ); that is, we are like Christ in the sense that we, too, have been born of God and are no longer of the world.[21] We are like Him in the sense that His love is in us. But because of sin, we cannot be fully like Him in this life. Only at the end of the world, when Christ has come again, will we become completely like Him (2 Corinthians 3:18; 1 John 3:2)

18 What do men fear? They fear **punishment**. But because of God's great love toward us, we believers have been freed from punishment for our sins. For those who are in Christ, there is no condemnation, no punishment (Romans 8:1). Therefore, if we fear God's judgment, it means that we have not been **made perfect in love**; it means that Christ's love has not been **made complete** in us (verses 12,17). If we fear God's judgment, it means that we have not fully experienced His love.

To become a child of God, we go through four stages. In the first stage, we have no fear of God and no love for God. In the second stage, we begin to fear God, but we still have no love for Him. In the third stage, we begin to experience God's love, but fear still remains. Finally, in the fourth stage, we lose our fear; only Christ's love remains. When we reach the fourth stage, then we will have confidence before God, because we will know with certainty that we are indeed His children.

In Proverbs 1:7, it is written: **The fear of the Lord is the beginning of knowledge.** The **fear** mentioned in Proverbs is a different kind of "fear" than the fear John is talking about here. The **fear** John is talking about is a dread of God's judgment and wrath. But the **fear** mentioned in Proverbs is more a feeling of awe and respect; such "fear" comes from an awareness that God knows everything about us, and that He has the power to punish those who disobey Him. To "fear" God in this way is proper and necessary. But we who believe in Christ do not need to have the other kind of fear—that is, the fear (or dread) of God's judgment and wrath.

19 **We love because he first loved us**. Natural man has no pure spiritual love within him. We cannot truly love until God has poured out His own love into our hearts (see Romans 5:5). It is only because God first loved us and gave us

---

[21] We are **in the world,** but not **of the world** (John 15:19; 17:14–16,18).

His Holy Spirit that we can now love Him and love others[22] (see Romans 5:8; 1 John 4:10–11 and comments).

20 Love for God and love for others cannot be separated. If we truly love God, we will also love men. If we truly love men, we will also love God.

In one way, it is easy to love God. He is a Spirit. We can't see Him or hear Him. "I love God" is easy to say. But to love men is different. Men give us trouble. They oppose us. They make us angry. It is difficult for us to love them. So we say: "I love God, but I can't love men."

But to say "I love God" without loving men is a lie (see 1 John 2:4). Because our love for men is the proof of our love for God. We can only show our love for God by showing love to men. If we have no love for men, we have no love for God.

All men are made in God's image (Genesis 1:27). Therefore, there is something of God in every man. If we cannot love the image of God (man) which we can see, how can we love God Himself, whom we can't see.

From this, we can see that it is not so easy to love God! In fact, to love God is the highest and most important and most difficult work in all the world.

How, then, can we love God? We can love Him, because He has poured out His own love into our hearts (verse 19). It is only as we receive God's love that we are able to love Him and to love others. We love, not with our own love, but with His love.

21 See Mark 12:30–31; John 13:34; 1 John 3:23 and comments.

CHAPTER 5

Victory Over the World (5:1–5)

1 Here John adds to what he has written in 1 John 4:2. Every believer in Christ is born of God; that is, every believer is God's **child**. If we love the Father, we must also love His children.

2 In 1 John 4:20, John has said that if we do not love our brother, we do not love God. Here John says that if we love God, we will also love our brother. By loving our brother, we prove that we love God. By loving God, we prove that we love our brother. In fact, love for God and love for our brother is the same love. One love can't exist without the other.

3 What is **love for God**? Love for God is **to obey His commands** (see John 14:15,21). What are His commands? To love one's neighbor and one's brother (2 John 6).

God's commands are not **burdensome**, because He gives us the power to obey them (see Matthew 11:28–30).

4 God's commands are not burdensome, because we have the power to **overcome the world**—that is, overcome Satan. How do we obtain this victory? Through our FAITH in Christ. Through faith, Christ lives in us. Christ has already overcome Satan (John 16:33). Therefore, through Christ, we too can overcome Satan (see 1 John 4:4).

In 1 John 2:14, John has written: The **word of God lives in you, and you have overcome the evil one**. To have the word of God live in us is the same as to have Christ live in us. Christ Himself is God's Word (John 1:1).

5 Only those who believe in Christ can overcome the world (see 1 Corinthians 15:57).

Testimony to Christ (5:6–12)

6 Jesus **came by water and blood**—that is, He was manifested through water

---

[22] Men possess a natural human love, such as the love between family members and between close friends. This love is also pleasing to God. But this is not the kind of love that John is talking about in this section. John is talking about a totally unselfish spiritual love; only those who have the Holy Spirit will have this kind of love.

and blood. He was manifested as the Son of God **by water**—that is, at His baptism (Mark 1:10–11). He was manifested as our Savior and atoning sacrifice by **blood**—His own blood—shed for us on the cross (see John 19:34).

7 The Holy Spirit testifies that Jesus Christ is the Son of God and the Savior of the world (John 15:26). One of the works of the Holy Spirit is to testify to the truth. The testimony of the Holy Spirit is true; He is the **Spirit of truth** (John 16:13). Therefore, we can have complete confidence in His testimony.

It is through the Holy Spirit that men follow Christ. It is through the Holy Spirit that the church is established and grows. It is through the Holy Spirit that believers overcome the world (verse 4). Through all these great works, the Spirit testifies that Jesus Christ is indeed the Son of God.

8 Not only the Holy Spirit testifies, but also **water** (Jesus' baptism) and **blood** (Jesus' death) testify. The **water** "testifies" in this way: at the time of Jesus' baptism in **water**, the Holy Spirit descended upon Him, and God said, "**You are my Son, whom I love**" (Mark 1:11). The **blood** "testifies" that Jesus came to earth as a man and died for our sins. And finally the Holy **Spirit** Himself testifies in our hearts that Jesus rose from the dead and sent His Spirit (the Holy Spirit) to dwell within us. The testimony of these three—the **Spirit**, the **water**, and the **blood**—are in complete agreement. All three testify that Jesus Christ is the Son of God, the Savior of the world.

9 Man's testimony is also very important. When Jesus was baptized, the people present heard God say from heaven, "**You are my Son, whom I love**" (Mark 1:11). Men saw Jesus die on the cross, and then with their own eyes they saw Him alive again three days later! The apostles spent the rest of their lives giving witness to these things which they had seen and heard (1 John 1:1–3).

But God's own testimony is **greater** than man's testimony (John 5:32,36). God's witness is the Holy Spirit, who lives in us and through whom we experience God's presence, power, and love. Because of the testimony of the Holy Spirit in our hearts, our faith can be just as strong as the apostles' faith.

10 First we hear the Gospel—the testimony of men. Then we believe in the Son of God. And then we receive the **testimony** of the Holy Spirit in our hearts. Through the Holy Spirit our faith becomes even stronger. Through the Holy Spirit Christ lives within us as Lord.

If we reject the Gospel of Christ, we call God a liar. We have rejected the Spirit of truth.

11 And this is the **testimony**—the Gospel: **God has given us eternal life,**[23] **and this life is in his Son** (see John 1:4). God gave His Son Jesus, **that whoever believes in him . . . may have eternal life** (John 3:16).

12 Without faith in Christ, there can be no eternal life (see John 3:36 and comment). Through faith we have the Son and, together with Him, eternal life.

Concluding Remarks (5:13–21)

13 Here John states the main reason he has written this letter: namely, **so that you may know that you have eternal life**. John wrote his Gospel **that you may believe that Jesus is the Christ, the Son of God, and that by believing you may have life in his name** (John 20:31). Now, in this letter, John is writing to believers in order that their faith might become even more strong and certain—in order that they might **know** that they have eternal life.

14 If we ask God for anything **according to his will**, we can have confidence that He will hear our request. And if He hears our request, He will give us what we ask (see 1 John 3:22 and comment).

15 John says here that if God hears us, **we know that we have what we asked of him**. Even though God may not give us what we ask for immediately, we can be so sure we will receive it that we can consider that we have already received it! For example, the promise of

[23] Eternal life is the greatest and most wonderful part of our salvation.

eternal life in heaven is so certain that even though we shall receive it only in the future, in a real sense we have already received it.

16 **If anyone sees his brother commit a sin . . . he should pray and God will give him life.** James said that through our prayer for a sinning brother, that brother will be spiritually cleansed and healed (James 5:16). But not only that, says John, through our prayer **God will give him** (the sinning brother) **life.** Here **life** can mean physical life—such as the renewed life a sick person receives after recovering from an illness. Or **life** can mean spiritual life—such as the new life a sinner receives after being forgiven and cleansed from his sins (James 5:19–20; 1 John 1:9). Therefore, let us constantly pray for each other that we might be delivered from both sin and physical sickness—that we might receive both renewed spiritual life and renewed physical life.

In the first part of this verse, John has been talking about **sin that does not lead to death.** Now in the second part of the verse, he mentions a **sin that leads to death.** What sin is that? That sin is blasphemy against the Holy Spirit (Mark 3:28–29). God will not forgive this sin.

What is blasphemy against the Holy Spirit? It is the continuous and deliberate rejection of God, of Christ, of the Gospel, and of the witness of the Holy Spirit in our hearts. Or, in other words, it is to knowingly continue in sin without repentance. God is calling all men to repent, to leave their sins and turn to Christ. But if men despise God's call—if they despise His grace—then God can do nothing more for them; they have rejected His Holy Spirit. This is what it means, then, to blaspheme against the Holy Spirit.

All believers from time to time **grieve** the Holy Spirit (Ephesians 4:30). We all sin from time to time (1 John 1:10). Thus some Christians worry that perhaps they have committed this unforgivable sin, the **sin that leads to death.** But they do not need to worry! If anyone is worried that he has committed this sin, then that is proof he has not committed it. The reason is this: People who have truly committed this sin never worry about it. They don't care if they sin; they give no thought to God. Their hearts are hardened.

John does not say that we should pray for the person who commits this sin that leads to death. But how can we know for sure who has committed this sin? In one way, we might be able to recognize such a person from his evil work (Matthew 7:16). But how could we be sure he could never be forgiven? We could never be sure. Only God knows who will be forgiven and who will not be. Jesus said, **"Do not judge"** (Matthew 7:1). Therefore, we must continue to pray for all men, that they might repent of their sins and turn to Christ.

17 Here a question arises: Does not all sin lead to death? **For the wages of sin are death,** wrote Paul (Romans 6:23). Yes, for those who do not believe in Christ, all sin leads to death, eternal death. But when believers sin, their sins do not lead to death, because God forgives them and cleanses them (1 John 1:9). Therefore, for true Christians, sin does not lead to death.

18 Here John repeats what he said in 1 John 3:6,9. **. . . anyone born of God does not continue to sin.** Here again, John is not talking about the person who sins occasionally; he is talking about the person who keeps on sinning deliberately.

The **one who was born of God** (that is, Christ) **keeps him** (the believer) **safe, and the evil one** (Satan) **does not touch him.** Christ keeps believers from falling into the sin that leads to death (see John 10:28–29 and comment).

19 We believers are **children of God.** Therefore, we are not of this world. We have been moved from the kingdom of darkness (the world) into the kingdom of heaven. The world is under the control of the **evil one,** Satan (see John 17:14–16).

20 Notice how many times in this letter John says the words, **we know** (see verses 2,15,18,19). Faith in Christ is not blind faith or ignorant faith. It is true faith; it is faith in the truth. Christ is the truth (John 14:6). And we can **know** Christ, who is the true, living Son of God. Therefore, why should we worship dead idols? (verse 21).

21 We must keep ourselves from **idols** (Exodus 20:3–6). Idols are not only stones and images that people worship. Idols are anything we love more than God—such as pleasure, work, money, possessions, position, fame, family. If in our daily lives we put any of these things in a higher place than God, we make them into idols and we make ourselves idol worshipers. These things are false gods. These are things of the world. We cannot love the world and love God at the same time (see Matthew 6:24; 1 John 2:15–17). Therefore, John says: **Dear children, keep yourselves from idols**—that is, from the love of the world.

2 John

INTRODUCTION

This letter was written by the **elder**. Most Bible scholars believe that the Apostle John wrote this letter. The letter was written near the end of the first century A.D., at about the same time that John's first letter was written.

This letter is addressed to the **chosen lady and her children** (verse 1). It is not known who this woman was. Some think that the word **lady** here actually refers to the church, and that the word **children** refers to believers in the church. But it is not certain if this is John's meaning or not.

OUTLINE

A. Introduction (1–3).
B. Instructions (4–11).
  1. An Exhortation (4–6).
  2. A Warning (7–11).
C. Conclusion (12–13).

2 JOHN

To the Chosen Lady (1–13)

1 It is not known who the **chosen lady** was to whom this letter was written (see 2 John: Introduction).

All **who know the truth** are believers in Christ (John 8:31–32).

2 John and all other believers love this "chosen lady" **because of the truth**. Here the **truth** can mean the Holy Spirit, who is the **Spirit of truth** (John 15:26); or it can mean Jesus Christ, who is Himself the **truth** (John 14:6).

3 In the introductions to most of the New Testament letters, the writers ask for grace and peace for their readers (Romans 1:7; Ephesians 1:2). But here John adds **mercy** (see 1 Timothy 1:2). Mercy is one part of God's grace.

4 Some of this chosen lady's children were **walking in the truth**. That is, they were walking according to the Gospel; they were walking in obedience to Christ.

5 See John 15:7; 1 John 2:7 and comments.

6 To love is to obey Jesus. To obey Jesus is to love. Obedience is the fruit and the proof of love. We show our love by our obedience (see John 14:15; 1 John 5:3 and comments).

7–8 Even Christians can be deceived by the **antichrist** and by the **deceivers** (false teachers and false prophets) that are already in the world (see Mark 13:22–23; 1 John 2:18,22; 4:1–3 and comments).

Satan is the master of the antichrist and all deceivers and evildoers. He tries to make Christians give up their faith in Christ. He tries to create doubt and fear in their minds. He says that Christ is not really the Son of God. John gives us this warning: Don't give up your faith in Christ. **Watch out that you do not lose what you have worked for**—that is, your reward, your heavenly inheritance, your salvation (see Hebrews 10:35–36; General Article: Can We Lose Our Salvation?).

9 **Anyone who runs ahead**—who is that? The person who "runs ahead" is someone who is not satisfied with the Gospel of Christ. He "runs ahead" seeking new teachings, new philosophies, new worldly wisdom. Such a person thinks that he is wiser than other Christians.

Such a person who leaves Christ's teachings also leaves God. But the person who humbly continues in Christ's teachings has both God and Christ—and true wisdom as well (see John 14:21,23; 1 John 2:23).

10–11 The Bible teaches us that we must be hospitable (Romans 12:13; Hebrews 13:2; 1 Peter 4:9). But we are not to give any hospitality or help to false teachers. In John's time, many such teachers traveled about from village to village trying to get people to follow them. They "earned their living" from people's hospitality. That is why John says here that anyone who welcomes such a false teacher **shares in his wicked work** (verse 11).

12 Talking face to face is better than writing. John hopes to visit the "chosen lady" soon, so that their **joy might be complete** (1 John 1:4; 3 John 13–14).

In John's time there was no paper like we have today. At that time people wrote either on expensive parchment (made from the skin of sheep or goats), or on a kind of "paper" made from an Egyptian plant called papyrus.

13 Some children of the sister of the **chosen lady** were living in the same place where John was. Therefore, they also send greetings to their aunt.

3 John

INTRODUCTION

This letter was written near the end of the first century A.D., at about the same time John's other two letters were written. This third letter is a personal letter to a man named Gaius. It is not known who Gaius was.

OUTLINE

A. Personal Greeting (1–4).
B. Main Letter (5–15).
   1. Concerning Hospitality (5–8).
   2. Other Remarks (9–15).

3 JOHN

To Gaius (1–14)

1 In John's time, the name **Gaius** was very common. Three other men named Gaius are mentioned in the New Testament: one in Acts 19:29; another in Acts 20:4; and the third in Romans 16:23 and 1 Corinthians 1:14. Most scholars think that the Gaius to whom this letter was written is not one of the above three, but a fourth Gaius. Nothing else is known of this Gaius except what is written in this letter.

2–4 Pastors and preachers have great joy when they see their spiritual "children" **walking in the truth**, that is, walking in obedience to Christ. Let all church leaders and elders love and care for the members of the church as John did (see 2 John 4 and comment).

5–6 Gaius was known as a hospitable man. He repeatedly welcomed and helped traveling preachers of the Gospel. Many of them he had never even met before; they were like **strangers** to him (see Hebrews 13:2).

7–8 These traveling preachers had gone out to preach **for the sake of the Name**—that is, for the sake of Christ (see Acts 5:41; James 2:7). This is the **Name** that is above every other name (Philippians 2:9).

In John's time, traveling preachers could not afford to stay in hotels. Therefore, they relied on the hospitality of believers wherever they went. They did not stay with **pagans**—that is, unbelievers, lest they be accused by unbelievers of preaching only for the sake of food and lodging. Thus the believers who offered hospitality to these traveling preachers were providing crucial help in the spreading of the Gospel. They were workers together **for the truth**.

In the same way, we also need to be always ready to help and support those who go out in Christ's name to serve Him and to preach the Gospel (John 13:20). Some Christians are called by God to go out into the world to serve Christ; other Christians are called to stay at home and serve Christ by providing hospitality, support, and prayer for those who do go out. Thus all of us—whether we go or stay—are called to **work together for the truth**.

9 **Diotrephes** was a leader in the church that Gaius attended. Diotrephes rejected John's authority. He wanted to keep all the authority for himself. He sought **to be first**. He had forgotten what Jesus said: "**. . . many who are first will be last, and the last first**" (Mark 10:31). This desire to exalt oneself has been a common temptation among church leaders of every generation (see Matthew 23:12: Mark 10:43–44).

10 Some **brothers** (traveling preachers) had gone to Diotrephes' church, but Diotrephes had not welcomed them. Not only that, he expelled from the church those who did welcome them. Therefore, if John is able to come, he will expose Diotrephes' arrogance and evil work.

11 See Ephesians 5:1–2; 1 John 2:29; 3:6,10 and comments.

12 The **Demetrius** referred to in this verse is not mentioned elsewhere in the New Testament.[1] Perhaps it was Demetrius who delivered this letter to Gaius, in which case this verse would serve to introduce Demetrius to Gaius.

John writes here that Demetrius is well spoken of **by everyone—and even by the truth itself**. Here the **truth** means the Holy Spirit; the Holy Spirit Himself testifies that Demetrius walks in the truth (verses 3–4). And John also testifies concerning Demetrius. Because John is an apostle,[2] Gaius can have confidence that John's testimony is reliable and **true** (John 21:24).

13–14 Here John repeats what he wrote to the "chosen lady" in 2 John 12.

Then, in his final greeting, John writes:

---

[1] A man named Demetrius is mentioned in Acts 19:24, but most scholars believe that that is a different man.

[2] At the time John wrote this letter, he was the only one of the original apostles still alive.

The friends here send their greetings (verse 14). In the New Testament, the word "brothers" is usually used instead of **friends**. But John remembers the time when Jesus said to him and his fellow disciples: "**I have called you friends**" (John 15:15).

To be a friend of Jesus is the highest privilege a man or woman can have. But in order to be Jesus' friend, we must obey Him. "**You are my friends, if you do what I command**" (John 15:14).

Jude

INTRODUCTION

Jude was the brother of Jesus and James. He is mentioned in Matthew 13:55 and Mark 6:3. Before Jesus' death, His brothers had not believed that He was the Son of God. In fact, they had thought He was crazy (Mark 3:20–21; John 7:5). Only after Jesus' resurrection did they begin to believe in Him.

This letter is written to Christians, but where these Christians lived is not known. Jude wrote this letter mainly to refute some false teaching that had entered the church.

OUTLINE

A. A Warning Against False Teachers (1–16).
   1. Introduction (1–4).
   2. Description of False Teachers (5–13).
   3. The Coming Judgment (14–16).

B. A Call to Perseverance (17–25).

JUDE

False Teachers (1–16)

1–2 Jude calls himself a **servant of Jesus Christ** (Romans 1:1) and a **brother of James**. James and Jude were younger brothers of Jesus (Mark 6:3). James wrote the New Testament letter called "James," and was also the chief leader in the Jerusalem church (see James: Introduction).

From Jude's introduction to this letter, we can see that he was not trying to exalt himself. He had the right to call himself Jesus' brother, but instead he calls himself Jesus' **servant**. Neither did he try to make himself equal to James; he was content to remain in second place.

3 Jude had originally planned to write a different kind of letter to these Christians. But then, having heard that false teachers had entered their church, he decided to send this urgent letter at once to exhort them **to contend for the faith**[1]—that is, to defend the true teaching of the Gospel and to stand firm in their own faith. That **faith**—the Gospel—had been **entrusted** by the apostles to the SAINTS, that is, believers.

4 This verse is very similar to a passage written by Peter in his second letter (see 2 Peter 2:1–3 and comment).

These false teachers were teaching that it didn't matter whether a person sinned or not, because no matter how much one sinned, God's grace was sufficient to cleanse him; therefore, they said, a Christian could do whatever he pleased (see Romans 6:1–2; 2 Peter 3:16 and comments).

By their own evil behavior, these false teachers were denying Christ. Men deny Christ not only by what they say, but also by what they do (see Titus 1:16).

5 The Jews were God's specially chosen people. He delivered them from bondage in Egypt. Yet some of them stopped believing in God; therefore, God destroyed them (see 1 Corinthians 10:1–10 and comment). From this we can understand that even though we are called Christians and belong to a church, God will still destroy us if we stop believing (see 1 Corinthians 10:11–12).

6 In ancient times some of the ANGELS fell from their **positions of authority** and left **their own home** in heaven because they lusted after human women (Genesis 6:1–4) and because they arrogantly tried to make themselves like God (Isaiah 14:12–15; 24:21–22). In the same way, the lustful and arrogant false teachers of John's time will also fall, and together with the fallen angels, will be condemned **on the great Day**—that is, on the day of final JUDGMENT (see 2 Peter 2:4 and comment).

7 See 2 Peter 2:6 and comment.

8 These false teachers had impure dreams, which they claimed came from God. Using these dreams to justify their impurity and sinfulness, they went on committing greater and greater sins.

These false teachers rejected the **authority** of Christ and other church leaders. They slandered **celestial beings**, that is, angels (see 2 Peter 2:10 and comment).

9 Evil men slander others, but righteous men do not. Righteous men do not even slander evil men. Even **Michael**, the chief of all the angels (Daniel 12:1; Revelation 12:7), did not bring a **slanderous accusation** against the **devil**, SATAN (see 2 Peter 2:11 and comment).

The dispute over the **body of** MOSES is not mentioned anywhere else in the Bible; it is described in a separate Jewish book. According to this book, God sent Michael to earth to bury the body of Moses. But because Moses had killed a man,[2] Satan claimed that the body belonged to him. But Michael did not rebuke the devil; instead, he left the matter in God's hands. He said to the devil, **"The Lord rebuke**

---

[1] In this context, the word **faith** means the Gospel, or the true teachings taught by Jesus and the apostles.

[2] According to Exodus 2:12, Moses once killed an Egyptian who was mistreating a Jew.

you!" Likewise, we too should not try to struggle with the devil with our own words and with our own strength; instead, we should call upon the Lord to rebuke him.

10 The thoughts in this verse have also been written by Peter (see 2 Peter 2:12 and comment). The false teachers do not have spiritual minds. Therefore, they cannot understand spiritual things (1 Corinthians 2:14). Like animals, they only understand how to satisfy their fleshly desires.

When men continue to oppose the Holy Spirit, they soon become spiritually blind and deaf. Thus, when God calls to them, they can no longer hear; therefore, God gives them over to their sins (Romans 1:28). In the end, their sins destroy them.

11 The false teachers are like the loveless **Cain**, who killed his own brother (Genesis 4:1–10; 1 John 3:12). They are like the money-loving **Balaam** (see 2 Peter 2:15–16; Revelation 2:14 and comments). They are like **Korah** and his followers, who rebelled against Moses and were destroyed by God as a result (Numbers 16:1–35).

12 The thoughts in this verse have also been written by Peter (see 2 Peter 2:13 and comment). False teachers are like selfish shepherds, **who feed only themselves** and care nothing for the sheep (Ezekiel 34:1–10). They are like clouds which give no rain; they only shut out the light of the sun (see 2 Peter 2:17 and comment). They are like dying trees which bear no fruit; they have stopped growing (see 2 Peter 1:8 and comment). They have also been **uprooted**; thus, in a sense, such trees are **twice dead** (Psalm 52:5; Matthew 3:10).

13 False teachers are like **wild waves of the sea** (Isaiah 57:20–21). They are like stars that fall from heaven; for one moment they are bright, and then they disappear into darkness.

14–15 **Enoch** was in the seventh generation from **Adam**, the first man (Genesis 5:21–24; Hebrews 11:5). Enoch himself prophesied about the second coming of Christ, and about how Christ would be accompanied by thousands of **his holy ones**, that is, His angels (Matthew 25:31–33,41). In these verses, Jude quotes a passage from a Jewish book called the Book of Enoch.

16 Here we can again see the behavior of false teachers and false Christians. They are **grumblers and faultfinders** (see Numbers 11:1; 1 Corinthians 10:10; Philippians 2:14 and comments). Those who grumble and find fault are really finding fault with God. Whenever we grumble about anything we insult God, because God is the one who ultimately arranges everything in our lives.

Such false teachers follow their own **evil desires** (see 2 Peter 2:18). They are puffed up with pride; they **boast about themselves**. And they flatter others in order to gain some advantage for themselves (see James 2:1 and comment).

Are there any false teachers in our church? Are any of us behaving like the false teachers described in these verses? Let each person examine himself.

A Call to Persevere (17–25)

17–19 The **apostles** have given many warnings about false teachers (see Acts 20:29–30; 1 Timothy 4:1–2; 2 Peter 3:3 and comments).

The false teachers considered themselves to be superior to others. They remained separate from other believers. They went from church to church and divided the believers by accusing some of being false Christians. But it was, in fact, they who were the false Christians!

20–21 **. . . build yourselves up in your most holy faith**—that is, in the teachings and doctrines of Christ. In order to build ourselves up—to grow in faith—it is essential that we study and meditate upon the teachings of the Bible (see Hebrews 5:12–14; 1 Peter 2:2 and comments).

. . . pray in the Holy Spirit (verse 20). When Christ's Holy Spirit is in us, we shall pray "in the Spirit" (see Romans 8:9,26; Ephesians 6:18 and comments).

Keep yourselves in God's love (see Romans 11:22 and comment). Jesus said: **"As the Father has loved me, so have I loved you. Now remain in my love. If**

you obey my commands, you will remain in my love" (John 15:9–10).

22–23 Whenever a brother in the church begins to **doubt** about his faith or about Christian doctrine, we must at first admonish him gently and patiently and show him the right way. But if he has begun to follow false teaching, we must try more forcefully to turn him back to the truth. If a small child goes near the fire, we immediately grab him and forcefully pull him back. The one who begins to follow false teaching is about to fall into the fire! Let us **snatch** such a person **from the fire**!

To others who have fallen into sin we must **show mercy mixed with fear** (verse 23). The **fear** we should have is the fear that we, too, could easily fall into sin. We should remember that if it were not for the grace of God, we could have fallen into the same sin that our brother has fallen into. We must show love and mercy to the sinner, but we should hate his sin. We must remain apart from his sin (2 Corinthians 7:1). A man's clothing is **stained** by his sin (Zechariah 3:3–4). Therefore, let us be careful not to "stain" our clothing (see Revelation 3:4).

24–25 God **is able to keep you from falling**. God is **able** (see Romans 16:25; Ephesians 3:20–21). He will present us before His glorious presence **without fault**. Through faith in Christ we shall be cleansed from sin. Through our blameless Savior, we too **will be blameless on the day of our Lord Jesus Christ** (see 1 Corinthians 1:8–9). And **through Christ**, who is the **radiance of God's glory and the exact representation of his being** (Hebrews 1:3), God Himself is glorified. **To him . . . to the only God our Savior be glory, majesty, power and authority, through Jesus Christ our Lord, before all ages, now and forevermore! Amen.**

Revelation

INTRODUCTION

This book of Revelation was written by a well-known and influential elder named John. Most Bible scholars believe that this John is the beloved disciple of Jesus (John 13:23), who also wrote John's Gospel and the three New Testament letters of John. The book of Revelation was written toward the end of the first century A.D.

This entire book is the exact description of a revelation or vision that John received from God. The revelation is mainly about the last days[1] before the end of the world and about the final struggle between Christ and Satan.

In one sense, the "last days" had begun in John's time. Terrible persecution had begun to fall upon all Christians from the rulers of the ROMAN EMPIRE. This revelation, therefore, was given to John so that John might encourage the believers of his time to stand firm under this persecution. But this revelation was also given for the sake of believers in every generation, that they too might have courage to stand firm during trials and troubles. And we also, in our generation, can receive encouragement from studying this revelation.

However, even though John's revelation refers in part to events of his own time, it particularly refers to events which will take place at the end of the world. Just as in John's time the church was facing great persecution, so in the final conflict at the end of the world the church will face even greater persecution.

There are a number of different interpretations of the book of Revelation. This commentary attempts to explain only what is

[1] The expression "last days" can have two meanings. It can mean the time just before Christ comes again at the end of the world. Or it can mean the entire period of time between Christ's first coming and His second coming. The revelation of John can be interpreted according to both of these two meanings.

written in the text. The commentary tries to avoid controversial theories, as well as predictions about the future.

OUTLINE

A. Vision of the Son of Man (1:1–3:22).
   1. Introduction (1:1–8).
   2. The Son of Man Among the Lampstands (1:9–20).
   3. Letters to the Seven Churches (2:1–3:22).
B. Vision of the Scroll, Trumpets, Signs, and Bowls (4:1–19:10).
   1. The Seven-sealed Scroll (4:1–7:17).
   2. The Seven Trumpets (8:1–11:19).
   3. The Seven Signs (12:1–14:20).
   4. The Seven Bowls (15:1–19:10).
C. Vision of the Return of Christ (19:11-20:15).
   1. The Rider and the Beast (19:11–21).
   2. The Binding of Satan and the Thousand Years (20:1–6).
   3. The Release and Final End of Satan (20:7–10).
   4. The Resurrection and the Last Judgment (20:11–15).
D. Vision of the New Heaven and New Earth (21:1–22:21).
   1. The New Jerusalem (21:1–27).
   2. The River of Life (22:1–6).
   3. Conclusion (22:7–21).

CHAPTER 1

Prologue (1:1–8)

1–3 The revelation described in this book is the **revelation of Jesus Christ**. Jesus gave this revelation to John to show Christians **what must soon take place** (verse 1). Up until now, most of the events described in this revelation have not yet taken place; however, the **time is near** (verse 3). And now that almost two thousand years have passed since John wrote these things, the time is even nearer! (see 2 Peter 3:8–9 and comment).

John calls this revelation a PROPHECY (verse 3), and says that those who read it or hear it and then **take** (it) **to heart** will be blessed. The same can be said for all of God's written word, the Bible.

4–6 John wrote this book of Revelation for seven churches in particular, which were located in the Roman province of **Asia**, now modern Turkey (see verse 11). These churches were in the major cities of that province. In this way, John's book could easily be passed on to all the other churches in the province. But we must remember that this book was written not just for the churches of Asia; it was written for every church in every generation—including ours.

GRACE and PEACE to you from him (God), **who is, and who was, and who is to come** (verse 4). God has no beginning or ending. And indeed, He **is to come** again. Therefore, when the final tribulations come at the end of the world, let Christians remember that all events are ultimately under the control of God. God is the Lord of every circumstance and situation.

Grace and peace also come **from the seven spirits**. Who these seven spirits are is not certain, but many believe that they represent seven aspects or virtues of the Holy Spirit.

Grace and peace also come **from Jesus Christ** (verse 5), who is the **faithful witness**. One of Jesus' works was to be God's witness (see John 3:31–34; 18:37). Jesus here is also called the **firstborn from the dead** (see Psalm 89:27; 1 Corinthians 15:20; Colossians 1:18 and comments). There will be a resurrection of the bodies of all believers in heaven, but Jesus' resurrection has come before all the others; therefore, He is the "firstborn" (1 Corinthians 15:23). Jesus is also the **ruler of the kings of the earth**. He is the **King of kings** (Revelation 17:14). He is the supreme Lord of the universe (Philippians 2:9–11). Satan had offered Jesus **all the kingdoms of the world and their splendor** (Matthew 4:8–10). But now, through His obedience and death, Jesus has obtained not only all these kingdoms but also final victory over Satan.

Christ is our Savior. He has **freed us from our sins by his blood** (see Hebrews 9:14; 10:10 and comments). He has made us to be a **kingdom and priests** (verse 6). The Jewish nation was called a **kingdom of priests** (Exodus 19:6). Now the church of Christ has been called to be a kingdom of priests (see 1 Peter 2:5,9 and comment).

7 Christ will come **with the clouds** (Daniel 7:13; Mark 13:26; 14:62). All men, both believers and unbelievers, will see Him and know that He is the Son of God. Even those Roman soldiers who **pierced** Jesus while He was hanging on the cross will see Him (Zechariah 12:10; John 19:37). Not only that, those who today have given up their faith—who have betrayed Jesus and in effect put Him on the cross again—they too will see Jesus when they come before Him to receive judgment (Hebrews 6:4–6). On that day **all the** (unbelieving) **peoples of the earth will mourn** because of the judgment that Christ will bring upon them (see Matthew 24:30).

8 **I am the alpha and omega.** "Alpha" is the first word of the Greek alphabet, and "omega" is the last word. God is saying here that He is both the beginning and the end, that He lasts from beginning to end. God is the beginning of everything and the end of everything. But God Himself has no beginning and no end; He always was, and always will be (verse 4).

Vision of the Son of Man (1:9–20)

9 John was a **companion**, or sharer, in the **suffering** that is part of the Christian's life **in Jesus**. He was also a fellow inheritor of the **kingdom** of Jesus (Romans 8:17). All those who belong to the kingdom of Jesus will face tribulation in this world (John 16:33; Acts 14:22). Because John was a faithful witness of Christ, he had been imprisoned on the **island of Patmos.**[2]

10–11 John received this revelation on the **Lord's Day**—that is, Sunday.[3] When John received the revelation, he was **in the Spirit** (verse 10); that is, he was in a state of special spiritual awareness, which made it possible for him to receive such a revelation (see Acts 10:10; 22:17; 2 Corinthians 12:1–4).

12–15 The **seven golden lampstands** (verse 12) represent the seven churches, to which this book of Revelation was sent (see verse 20). The one **like the son of man** (verse 13) is Jesus Christ Himself (Daniel 7:13). The Old Testament prophet Daniel had seen a similar vision of the glorified Christ (Daniel 7:9; 10:5–6).

16 In the vision, Christ was holding **seven stars** in His right hand; these stars represent the spirits of the seven churches (verse 20). From His mouth came a **sharp double-edged sword,** which represents His word (Ephesians 6:17), especially His word of judgment (see Hebrew 4:12; Revelation 2:16; 19:15,21).

Christ's face was **like the sun**. John had once before seen the glorified Christ; at that time also Christ's face had **shone like the sun** (Matthew 17:2).

17–18 When John saw this vision of Christ, he fell at Christ's feet. Then Christ said to him, **"Do not be afraid"** (see Daniel 10:10–12; Matthew 17:6–7).

Christ then said that He was the **First and the Last** (the Alpha and Omega), which is the name that God gave to Himself in verse 8 (Isaiah 44:6). Christ said that he held the **keys of death and Hades;**[4] that is, He had complete authority over death.

19–20 Then Christ commanded John to write down everything he had seen and was about to see. As we study this book of Revelation, we must not forget that what we are reading is an exact account of the revelation which Christ Himself gave to John. Some parts of this revelation may be hard to understand, but regardless of that, let us remember that this revelation has come from Christ Himself, and has been written down for our benefit.

The seven stars are the ANGELS of the seven churches (verse 20). Here the word **angels** can mean the angel of each church, or it can mean a special spiritual spokesman of each church. Through such an angel or spokesman, Christ speaks to each of His churches.

The seven churches are called the **seven lampstands**. They are called lampstands because the main work of every church is to be like a lampstand showing forth the light of Christ to all the world. Christ is the lamp or light of the world (John 8:12); and we are the "lampstand" for His light (see Matthew 5:14–16 and comment).

---

[2] **Patmos** was a small island, about four miles square, located in the Mediterranean Sea south of present-day Turkey. During the time of the Roman Empire, the Romans used to send criminals and other prisoners to Patmos. The island served as a jail, from which no one could escape.

[3] At the time John wrote this book of Revelation, Christians had begun to observe the Sabbath on Sunday instead of on Saturday (the Jewish custom). They called it the **Lord's Day,** because it was on Sunday that Jesus rose from the dead.

[4] **Hades** is the place where men's departed spirits (spirits without bodies) await Christ's final judgment.

CHAPTER 2

To the Church in Ephesus (2:1–7)

1 Here we have the first of seven individual letters written to the seven churches—the letter to the church at **Ephesus.**[5] At the beginning of each of these seven letters, Christ introduces Himself in a different way. And at the end of each letter, He gives a promise to those who remain firm in their faith until the end. As we read these letters to the seven churches, we must understand that they are written by Christ not only to these seven churches but also to every church in every generation. The seven churches mentioned in Chapters 2–3 are for us examples, and the words written to them apply to all churches everywhere—including our own. These seven letters give both warning and encouragement to all believers.

Christ writes each of these letters to the **angel of the church** (see Revelation 1:20 and comment). Here in this letter to the Ephesian church, Christ introduces Himself as the one **who holds the seven stars in his right hand and walks among the seven golden lampstands** (see Revelation 1:12–13,16). Although Christ Himself is in heaven, He "walks" among His churches through the Holy Spirit, and holds them securely in His hand.

2–3 At first Christ praises the church at Ephesus. False teachers had tried to come into the church, but the Ephesian Christians had examined their teaching and rejected it (1 John 4:1). Earlier, Paul had warned the Ephesian elders about such false teachers (Acts 20:28–31). Christ praises the **hard work** and **perseverance** of the Ephesian believers (verse 2); they have **not grown weary** (verse 3). If this had been all that Christ wrote to the Ephesians, they could have been very proud of themselves!

4 However, the Ephesians had no reason to be proud. They had forsaken their **first love**. They had become so busy doing good works that they had begun to forget Christ! The great joy and love which they'd had at the beginning of their Christian lives had now begun to fade away.

Let us always remember that the first and greatest commandment is this: **Love the Lord your God with all your heart and with all your soul and with all your mind and with all your strength** (Mark 12:30). If our love for God and for our neighbor (Mark 12:31) grows cold, then all our other works are in vain (see 1 Corinthians 13:1–3 and comment). Let us never forget the love we had for Christ when we first believed. We were then filled with joy, love, zeal, and gratitude. We had just become free, after having been prisoners of Satan. We offered our entire lives to Christ. Brothers and sisters, let us ask ourselves: Has that joyful fellowship we first had with Christ grown cold? Have we, like the Ephesians, forsaken our **first love**?

5 If our love has grown cold, then Jesus has these words for us: "**Remember the height from which you have fallen!** Remember those early days when our fellowship was so rich and close, when you loved me with all your heart, when you were filled with the Holy Spirit. **Repent**[6] **and do the things**—the works of love—**you did at first**."

It is not enough just to acknowledge that we have forsaken our first love; we must begin again to do the works of love. Love must be expressed in loving works; without loving works there is no love (see 1 John 3:16–18 and comment). If we do

[5] **Ephesus** was the most important city in the province of Asia (see Ephesians: Introduction). The first Christians to live in Ephesus were Priscilla and Aquila (Acts 18:18–20). Afterwards, Paul himself lived for two years in Ephesus, and established the church there (Acts 19:1–10).

[6] Repentance is the first step in regaining our love for Christ. For further discussion, see Word List: Repentance; General Article: Revival.

not begin again to do the works of our first love, Christ will come and **remove** [our] **lampstand from its place**; that is, He will put an end to our ministry and scatter our church. A church that has forsaken its first love is of no use to Christ.

6 The **Nicolaitans** were a sect of people who pretended to be true Christians but who followed the immoral practices of the world (verse 15).

7 Notice here that the Spirit of Christ is speaking to the **churches**—not just to one church. He is speaking not only to the church at Ephesus but also to our church today. If we overcome Satan and his temptations, we shall receive the right to eat from the **tree of life, which is in the paradise**[7] (heavenly Jerusalem) **of God**; and having eaten from it, we shall receive eternal life (see Genesis 2:9: Revelation 21:10; 22:2).

To the Church in Smyrna (2:8–11)

8 Of these seven cities mentioned in Chapters 2–3, only **Smyrna** remains today. Its modern name is Izmir, and it is situated in Western Turkey about forty miles north of ancient Ephesus. The other six cities no longer exist; only their ruins remain.

Here Christ calls Himself the **First and the Last, who died and came to life again** (see Revelation 1:17–18).

9 In John's time, the church at Smyrna had suffered severe **afflictions**. Most of the inhabitants of the city worshiped the Roman emperor as a god, and a great temple in the city had been built in his name. Because the Christians refused to worship the emperor, they were persecuted by the leaders of the city and by the Roman soldiers. It was difficult for the Christians to earn a living. Their shops and houses were looted (Hebrews 10:34). As a result, they had fallen into **poverty**. Nevertheless, they had remained spiritually **rich** (see Matthew 6:19–20; James 2:5).

The **Jews** of Smyrna also opposed the Christians and slandered them. But they were false Jews, who belonged to the **synagogue of Satan**; that is, they were servants of Satan the slanderer.[8]

10 Above all, the church at Smyrna needed encouragement and strength to endure persecution. If they remained firm to the end—**to the point of death**—they would receive the **crown of life**, that is, eternal life (see Mark 13:13; 1 Corinthians 9:25; 1 Peter 5:4 and comments). The **ten days** of persecution mentioned here does not refer to the persecution coming upon all men at the end of the world (Revelation 3:10); rather, it refers to some short period of especially severe persecution that was soon to come upon the church in Smyrna.[9]

11 The **second death** mentioned here means eternal death; it is the final punishment for all evildoers. In Revelation 20:14, it is called the **lake of fire**; and in Revelation 21:8, it is called the **fiery lake of burning sulfur**.

To the Church in Pergamum (2:12–17)

12 **Pergamum** was the capital of the Roman province of Asia; it was thus the residence of the Roman governor. The governor had the authority to put people to death; that is, he had the "power of the sword." But Christ here reminds the church at Pergamum that He has a more powerful sword than the governor has: Christ has the **sharp, double-edged sword** (see Revelation 1:16); He has the final authority over both death and life. Christ not only has the power to condemn people to eternal death; He also has the power to give them eternal life.

13 Pergamum, being the capital of the province, was the center of the Roman

---

[7] In this verse, **paradise** is a name for heaven, the heavenly Jerusalem (see 2 Corinthians 12:4 and comment).

[8] In the Greek language, the name Satan means "slanderer."

[9] The persecution at the end of the world will be experienced only by those alive at that time. For those who die before then, the world "ends," in effect, when they die.

emperor's authority. Therefore, Christ says here that Pergamum is **where Satan has his throne**—that is, it was where the emperor (and his governors) sat in authority. In John's day, the Christians regarded the Roman emperor and his governors as representatives of Satan.

Antipas is not mentioned anywhere else in the Bible. He was a citizen of Pergamum, who was put to death because of his faith in Christ. Christ here gives Antipas the same name He gave Himself in Revelation 1:5—namely, **faithful witness**.

14 After praising the church at Pergamum, Christ now points out their shortcomings. They have tolerated the false teaching of **Balaam**; they have let his teaching come into their church. Balaam was an Old Testament prophet who helped Balak, king of Moab, oppose the **Israelites** (the Jews). Balaam's method of weakening the Jews was to **entice** [them] **to sin**. He advised Balak to have the women of his kingdom entice the Jewish men to eat food sacrificed to idols and to commit sexual immorality (Numbers 25:1–3; 31:15–16). Therefore, we can understand that the **teaching of Balaam** is any teaching which leads people to disobey God and to follow after the false gods and immoral desires of the world.

15 The **teaching of the Nicolaitans** was similar to the teaching of Balaam (see verse 7).

16 Christ says that He will oppose all such false teaching **with the sword of my mouth** (see Revelation 1:16 and comment). False teachers will be punished not only on the final day of judgment but in this life as well.

Although only a few members of the church at Pergamum followed such false teaching, they were nonetheless all guilty, because they had not expelled the false teachers from their midst; they had tolerated them. They had thus allowed impurity to take root in their church. Their sin was the opposite of the Ephesian church's sin. On the one hand, the Ephesian Christians did not tolerate false teaching; they were very strict and pure. But they had lost their love. On the other hand, the Pergamum Christians had not lost their love; they had lost their purity. From reading these seven letters, we can see that every church has its own special strengths and weaknesses. Let us think of our own church: What are its special strengths and weaknesses? What would Christ write to our church today?

17 To the one who **overcomes**, Christ will give the **hidden manna**[10]—that is, spiritual "bread" (see John 6:48–51 and comment). If we give up the food of idols in this world, we shall get to eat the food of Christ in heaven.

The **white stone** mentioned here refers to an Old Testament custom according to which a white stone was given to those invited to a feast or ceremony; the stone thus served as a token or proof of their invitation. Therefore, Christ's meaning here is that those who receive a white stone with their name written on it are invited to the feast of the **hidden manna** in heaven.

To the Church in Thyatira (2:18–29)

18–19 **Thyatira** was a prosperous commercial center (Acts 16:14). The situation at Thyatira was as follows. Each type of business had its own special god; in order to be successful in a particular business, one had to worship the god of that business. Thus great pressure was put upon the Christian businessmen of Thyatira to worship these gods; they were under great temptation. If they refused to worship these gods, others in the city would abuse them and, as a result, they would lose much business.

Jesus here introduces Himself according to the description given in Revelation 1:14–15. And as He has in the other letters, Jesus first praises the believers of Thyatira.

20 But now Jesus points out their fault: They have tolerated **that woman**

[10] The **manna** mentioned in this verse refers to a kind of bread, which God sent from heaven to the ancient Jews while they were in the desert (Exodus 16:4,31–35).

Jezebel. It is probable that Jezebel was a prominent woman of their church.[11] At that time, the Roman temples were filled with prostitutes; therefore, whenever the men of Thyatira went to a temple to worship, they would fornicate with the prostitutes there and partake of a feast in honor of the idol of that temple. Perhaps this **Jezebel** taught that, because idols were nothing, it was therefore all right to worship at their temples; in other words, there could be no sin in worshiping "nothing" (1 Corinthians 6:12–13,15; 8:4,7).

21–23 Because of Jezebel's refusal to repent, she will be cast upon a **bed of suffering** (verse 22). But her followers still have time to repent. Those who do not repent will be afflicted with illness and death. God often sends various diseases or death to men as a punishment for sin (see Psalm 62:12; Jeremiah 17:10; Matthew 16:27; Romans 2:6 and comments).

24–25 To those who have not followed after Jezebel and **Satan's so-called deep secrets** (verse 24), Christ gives both encouragement and a challenge: **Only hold on to what you have until I come** (see 1 Timothy 6:13–14,20; 2 Timothy 1:13–14). Christ gives the Christians of Thyatira no other **burden** or command: only this, that they remain separate from the immorality and idolatry of Jezebel (see Acts 15:28–29).

26–27 The person who **overcomes** is the one who **does** [Christ's] **will to the end**. Christ will give him **authority over the nations** (see Psalm 2:8–9; Matthew 19:28).

28–29 The meaning of the **morning star** mentioned here is uncertain. According to Revelation 22:16, the morning star is Christ Himself. If that is the meaning here, then this verse says: Those who receive the "morning star" receive Christ; that is, they receive in full measure His fellowship, His love, and His Spirit.

CHAPTER 3

To the Church in Sardis (3:1–6)

1 Christ here calls Himself the one **who holds the seven spirits . . . and the seven stars** (see Revelation 1:4,16,20 and comment). Among these seven churches, Christ's accusation against the church in Sardis is the most severe; Christ says: . . . **you are dead.**

What had happened to the Christians in Sardis? They had not received severe trials and persecution. They had not followed false teaching. They seemed spiritually alive—but they were, in fact, spiritually dead.

What had happened was this: The church had become so much like the surrounding society that it was no longer possible to distinguish between Christians and non-Christians. The Christians' witness to Christ had become dull. They tried not to be different from their non-Christian neighbors; they didn't want to oppose the customs and traditions of the people. Therefore, their church was at peace with the society around them. There was no persecution—and no life! In this world they were content; they had everything they wanted. But their spirits had become weak—as good as dead (Psalm 106:15).

2–3 But the Christians in Sardis were not completely dead. Their lives were empty, and their deeds were not **complete**; Christ was not pleased with such Christians. Nevertheless, there was still a little spiritual life left in them. Therefore Jesus tells them: **Wake up!** (see Ephesians 5:14). If they do not wake up and remain alert, Satan will devour them completely (1 Peter 5:8). Therefore, let them strengthen **what remains and is about to die**—that is, let them strengthen what remains

---

[11] Some Bible scholars believe that the name **Jezebel** does not refer to a particular person, but rather is meant to be understood as a symbol of evil (1 Kings 16:31; 21:25; 2 Kings 9:22).

of their spiritual life. Otherwise, Jesus will come at an unexpected time **like a thief,** and bring judgment upon them. Here Jesus is referring not only to the final judgment at the end of the world (Matthew 24:42–44; 1 Thessalonians 5:2), but also to the punishment He brings upon people in this life (see Revelation 2:16).

4 In every church there are true Christians and false Christians (see Matthew 13:24–30; 2 Timothy 2:20–21). In the church of Sardis there were very few true Christians—that is, very few who had kept themselves from the ways of the world. Those who follow the customs and desires of the world have **soiled their clothes** (Jude 23). But those true believers who keep themselves from the impurity of the world will be given white clothes to wear, and they will get to walk with Jesus. The color white is a sign of righteousness and purity.

5–6 In each of these seven letters, Christ gives a promise to the one who **overcomes**. The ones who overcome are those who remain firm in their faith to the end. According to this letter, they will be dressed in white clothes; that is, they will be declared righteous in God's sight. Their names will never be erased from the **book of life** (verse 5). The book of life is where the names are written of all those who will inherit eternal life (see Luke 10:20; Revelation 20:12,15; 21;27). From this we can understand that the names of those who do not remain firm in faith will be erased.

Christ will acknowledge the names of those who overcome before the Father (see Matthew 10:32–33). Christ is our spokesman, our advocate, before God (Romans 8:34; Hebrews 7:25). Therefore, let us have faith in Him without wavering.

To the Church in Philadelphia (3:7–13)

7 Christ holds the **key of DAVID**; that is, Christ has the authority to admit men into the kingdom of God (King David's spiritual kingdom); and He also has the authority to keep men out (Isaiah 22:22).

8 Christ has placed before the church in Philadelphia an **open door**. Here the word "door" can have two meanings: first, the door of heaven; or second, the door of opportunity for service to Christ. As we serve Christ, He will open some doors for us and close others. We must not try to go through the doors that Christ has closed; but we can go through those which He has opened, and no one—not even Satan—can close them against us. Let us always be ready to enter these open doors (see Acts 16:6–10; 1 Corinthians 16:8; 2 Corinthians 2:12 and comments).

9 The Jews always tried to close doors for the Christians. The Jews considered that only they were the true children of God. But because they had rejected God's Son Jesus and had slandered and opposed all those who believed in Him, they had lost the right to be God's children. Such Jews were not true Jews; they were liars (Romans 2:28–29). And their father was Satan, the **father of lies** (John 8:44; Revelation 2:9). In the end, these false Jews will be forced to acknowledge that these Christians they have despised are indeed God's true and beloved children.

10 Because the Christians of Philadelphia have kept Jesus' **command to endure patiently**, He gives them this promise: **I will also keep you from the hour of trial.** It is important to understand Jesus' meaning here. He doesn't mean that trials and troubles will not come upon Christians. Rather, His meaning is that He will preserve the spirits of Christians; that is, He will save them from Satan (see John 17:15).

The **hour of trial** mentioned here is the period of intense suffering that will come upon the world just before the return of Christ. These final trials have not yet begun (Daniel 12:1; Revelation 13:5–10). These final trials are different from the trials we are enduring now. Our present trials are sent to us in order that our faith might be tested and strengthened (see 1 Peter 1:6–7; 4:12–13; Revelation 2:10 and comments). But the final trials at the end of the world will come as judgment upon men. These final trials also will be much more terrible (Mark 13:19). The spirits of

Christians will be preserved from these trials.[12]

11 Here Jesus says to the church in Philadelphia the same thing He said to the churches of Smyrna and Thyatira (see Revelation 2:10,25 and comment). If we don't "hold on" to our faith, we will not be able to hold on to our crown; Satan will snatch it away from us.

12–13 He who overcomes Satan will become a **pillar** in God's heavenly temple, a temple that will never be destroyed. God and Christ themselves are this temple (Revelation 21:22). Therefore, those who overcome will dwell forever with God and Christ. God's name will be written on them; that is, they will be God's own people (see 1 Peter 2:9). The name of God's city, the **new Jerusalem**, will also be written on them (Revelation 21:2). That is, they will be citizens of the kingdom of God. And Christ will write His own **new name** on them, because those who overcome belong to Christ; they are His brothers and **co-heirs** (Romans 8:17,19). Therefore, they are worthy to receive His name.

To the Church in Laodicea (3:14–22)

14 The church at **Laodicea** was established during the period when Paul lived in Ephesus (Acts 19:10). Many Bible scholars believe that a Laodicean named Epaphras, having heard the Gospel from Paul in Ephesus, then went back and established the church in Laodicea (Colossians 4:12). Paul wrote a letter to the church in Laodicea, but that letter has been lost (Colossians 4:16).

Christ here calls Himself the **Amen**. In the Old Testament, the word "Amen" meant: "Yes, this is true." Here Christ gives His own meaning of "Amen": the **faithful and true witness**.

15–16 In these two verses, Christ gives all churches a frightening warning: "Do not be **lukewarm**, or I will **spit you out of my mouth**."

These verses can have two meanings, and both meanings are true. The first meaning is this. When we are cold, we like to drink something **hot**; when we are hot, we like to drink something **cold**. But no one ever likes to drink something **lukewarm**. The church in Laodicea was like a lukewarm drink: the church's ministry was neither hot nor cold—only lukewarm. Because of this, no matter what a person's need might be, the church could not satisfy it. Thus the church was fit only to be "spit out" of one's mouth.

There is an interesting historical fact about the city of Laodicea. Near the city there were some famous hot springs, from which large amounts of hot water poured out in great streams. The water was thought to have healing power, so many people came to drink the water in hopes of being healed. But as the hot water flowed down the slopes from the spring, it quickly became lukewarm and thus lost its healing power (so it was thought). Not only could it no longer heal anyone; it couldn't even quench one's thirst. It was good for nothing! Thus the Laodicean Christians surely understood what Jesus meant when He called them **lukewarm**: They were good for nothing, like the lukewarm water of their famous spring.

The second meaning of "lukewarm" is this. Jesus is saying that the Laodicean church is spiritually lukewarm. The Laodicean Christians were not **dead** like the Christians of Sardis (verse 1); they weren't cold like a corpse. But neither were they spiritually "hot"; they had no "fire" of the Holy Spirit in them. They had no spiritual energy or enthusiasm. Spiritually they were only half alive.

A "lukewarm" church is in a more dangerous situation than a "cold" church. The reason is this. Spiritually cold Christians are usually aware that they are cold, and they can repent. But

---

[12] Many Bible scholars believe this verse teaches that not only the spirits of Christians but also their bodies will be preserved from these trials. But other verses seem to say that many Christians will be martyred during these trials (see Revelation 6:9–11; 7:9–14; 13:15). One thing is certain: Our eternal souls will be preserved; God's condemnation will not fall upon believers.

spiritually lukewarm Christians usually think they are hot, and thus they feel no need to repent. They are not worried about their spiritual condition. Just like the hot water flowing out of the springs, the Laodicean Christians had gradually become lukewarm—and they hadn't even noticed it.

Therefore, whichever of these two meanings we think about, we need to make sure that we do not become lukewarm Christians; otherwise, Jesus will spit us out of His mouth (see Luke 13:24–28).

17 Jesus says to these lukewarm Laodicean Christians: "You think you are spiritually rich, but don't deceive yourselves. Because, in fact, you are spiritually **poor.**" These Laodicean Christians were **blind**; they could not see their own spiritual condition. They were **naked**; they did not have the clothing of righteousness and holiness.

Let us take warning from the example of these Laodicean Christians. How different were the thoughts they had about themselves and the thoughts Christ had about them! We must try to see ourselves the way Christ sees us. Otherwise, we shall deceive ourselves, just as these Laodicean Christians deceived themselves. There are many people in hell today who had thought they were on the road to heaven!

18 Let the Laodicean Christians buy from Christ true wealth—spiritual gold, **gold refined in the fire**. Let them buy from Christ **white clothes to wear** (see verse 4). Let them receive sight from Christ, so that they might see their spiritual poverty and nakedness. If a man can't see his condition, he can't make it better.

There is another interesting historical fact about the city of Laodicea. In John's time, Laodicea was especially famous for three things: its financial prosperity, its clothing industry, and a special, locally made eye ointment that was used all over the world. Nevertheless, in spiritual matters they were poor, naked, and blind! (verse 17).

19 See Proverbs 3:11–12; Hebrews 12:5–11 and comment.

20 These proud, blind, and lukewarm Laodicean Christians had left Christ outside their church. But Christ still loves them, and He stands knocking on the door of their church, hoping that they will open the door and invite Him to come in.

But Christ doesn't only knock on the door of a church; He knocks on the "door" of every Christian's heart. And He knocks not just on the hearts of Christians, but on the hearts of all people. This is the great and wonderful truth of the Gospel of Christ: the supreme and almighty God of the universe comes to every person and says, "Open the door of your heart, and I will come in." No other religion of the world teaches about a God who comes to men and women seeking fellowship with them.

Therefore, friend, listen to Jesus knocking, and open the door of your heart. Do not delay, or else Jesus will go away. He is patient, but He will not wait forever.

Today there is no trace left of that Laodicean church. Why? Because those Laodicean Christians did not open the door for Jesus. They did not confess their sins—their pride, their blindness, their nakedness. Jesus had said to them: "**So be earnest and repent**" (verse 19). But they had not listened to Him. **He who has an ear, let him hear**! (verse 22).

21–22 He who overcomes will not only share in Christ's inheritance and glory, but he will also reign with Christ. He will sit with Christ on His throne (Matthew 19:28). The Apostle Paul wrote to Timothy: **If we died with him, we will also live with him; if we endure, we will also reign with him** (2 Timothy 2:11 12).

CHAPTER 4

The Throne in Heaven (4:1–11)

1 When John had finished writing Christ's words to the seven churches, the voice **like a trumpet** (Revelation 1:10) spoke again to John: "**I will show you what must take place after this.**" We must understand that, from this point until the end of the book of Revelation, everything that is written is primarily a description of the events that will take place at the end of the world.

2 As John was writing the letters to the seven churches, he was in an ordinary state of consciousness. But now, once again, he is **in the Spirit** (see Revelation 1:10 and comment). He is now ready to receive the rest of the revelation.

The first thing John saw was a throne in heaven. This throne is a sign of God's power and authority to rule and to judge.

3 The precious stones mentioned in this verse indicate the glory and light of the One sitting on the throne. Except for the brilliant light, God's form itself cannot be seen. Paul wrote that God **lives in unapproachable light**; He is a God **whom no one has seen or can see** (1 Timothy 6:16).

The **rainbow** is a sign of the covenant that God made with Noah and all living things of the earth after the flood (Genesis 9:12–17; Ezekiel 1:26–28).

4 The **twenty-four elders** sitting around the throne are exalted angels, who worship God continuously. Some people think that these twenty-four elders represent the twelve tribes of Israel and the twelve apostles of Christ.

5 Then in front of the throne John saw **seven lamps**, which are the **seven spirits of God**. These seven spirits can be angels, or they can represent the "seven-part" Holy Spirit (see Revelation 1:4 and comment).

The **lightning** and **thunder** coming from the throne signify the frightening power of God (Exodus 19:16–19).

6 The **four living creatures** are special angels who guard the throne. With eyes on all sides of them, they are able to see everything.

The Old Testament prophet Ezekiel also had a vision in which he saw something like a **sea of glass** (Ezekiel 1:22).

7–8 The different appearances of these four living creatures indicate four kinds of abilities that are useful to God. The **lion** indicates strength; the **ox** indicates diligence; the **man** indicates wisdom; and the **eagle** indicates speed. The main work of these four creatures is to praise God continuously (Ezekiel 1:4–10).

God is worthy to receive praise and worship. He is the Lord God Almighty, Creator of all things, **who was, and is, and is to come** (see Revelation 1:4). God said to Moses, "**I am who I am**" (Exodus 3:14). That is, God always exists. He has existed from before the beginning, and He will exist forever (verse 9).

9–11 If the most exalted angels in heaven praise and worship God in this way, certainly we lowly humans should worship and praise Him too.

CHAPTER 5

The Scroll and the Lamb (5:1–14)

1 Then John saw in God's hand a book, or **scroll**,[13] which was sealed with seven special seals. All the events and judgments that will take place at the end of the world were written in this scroll. These things were written on both sides of the scroll.

[13] In New Testament times, books were made in the form of scrolls.

2–4 However, at first no one was found who was worthy to open the seals on the scroll; that is, no one was found in heaven or on the earth or **under the earth**[14] who was worthy to bring to pass all the events and judgments written in the scroll. It seemed to John that God's final purposes would not be fulfilled; therefore, he began to weep.

5 But there was someone who could open the seven seals of the scroll. That one was called the **Lion of the tribe of Judah** and the **Root of David**—namely, Christ Himself. **Judah** was the fourth of Jacob's twelve sons; Jacob called him a **lion's cub** (Genesis 49:9). At the time he gave the blessing to his sons, Jacob said: "**The scepter will not depart from Judah . . . until he comes to whom it belongs**"—that is, until Christ comes at the end of the world (Genesis 49:10). Christ was descended from Judah (Matthew 1:2; Luke 3:33). Therefore, Christ will receive the scepter of Judah; His kingdom will have no end.

Christ was also descended from King David (Matthew 1:6; Luke 3:31); therefore, He is called the **Root of David**. The prophet Isaiah called Christ the **Root of Jesse**[15] (Isaiah 11:1,10; Romans 15:12). This is the Christ, the Messiah, who was worthy to open the scroll and bring the world to an end. He has **triumphed** over the world, over Satan, over death (see John 16:33). Only Christ is worthy.

6 Then John saw a lamb. Perhaps he was looking for a lion, the **Lion of the tribe of Judah**; but instead, he saw a lamb! What an amazing thing! The Savior of the world, the King whose kingdom will never end, was not a lion but a lamb! Not only that, He was a lamb that looked **as if it had been slain**. Christ has received His kingdom and authority not by power and force, but rather by His suffering and dying as a sacrifice to take away our sins (see Isaiah 53:3; John 1:29; Hebrews 9:14–15,28; 1 Peter 1:18–19 and comments).

According to John's vision, this lamb had **seven horns and seven eyes**. The number "seven" has a special meaning in the Bible: it means completeness or fullness. The word "horn" in the Bible usually stands for power and authority. Therefore, the seven horns stand for complete power and authority. In the same way, the seven eyes stand for complete knowledge and wisdom. From this, we can understand that this lamb has all power and authority, and all wisdom and knowledge. The seven eyes are also seven spirits, or they represent the seven-part Holy Spirit (see Revelation 1:4; 4:5 and comments). One who has "seven spirits" has received the Holy Spirit in the fullest possible measure. We can understand, therefore, that this Lamb, Christ, has received the Holy Spirit **without limit** (see John 3:34).

7–8 When the Lamb took the scroll, the four living creatures and the twenty-four elders fell down before Him and worshiped Him. They each had a **harp**, which is a musical instrument especially used in worshiping God (Psalm 33:2). The **incense** in the golden bowls represents the prayers of believers (Psalm 141:2). Let us not doubt that God hears our prayers; our prayers constantly rise up before Him like incense.

9–10 The four living creatures and the twenty-four elders then sang a **new song** (Psalm 98:1). This song was a song of praise to the Lamb, who with His blood **purchased men for God from every tribe and language and people and nation** (see Mark 10:45; 14:24; 1 Corinthians 6:20; Ephesians 1:7 and comments). Those whom Christ has "purchased" He has made to be a **kingdom and priests** (see Revelation 1:6 and comment), and they will **reign on the earth** (verse 10). Some Bible scholars believe that this reign refers to the thousand-year reign of the saints which is to take place at the end of the world (see Revelation 20:4–6 and comment).

11–12 Then John saw over a hundred million angels worshiping the Lamb,

---

[14] The expression **under the earth** refers to Hades, where the spirits of dead men and fallen angels wait for the final judgment (Philippians 2:10; Jude 6; Revelation 1:18; 5:13).

[15] Jesse was the father of David.

Christ (Daniel 7:10). Christ not only is worthy to receive all of the things mentioned in verse 12; He has already received them. Christ has received **power** and **wisdom** (1 Corinthians 1:24), **wealth** (2 Corinthians 8:9; Ephesians 3:8), **strength** (Luke 11:22), **honor** (Philippians 2:11), **glory** (John 1:14), and **praise**[16] (Romans 15:29). And all these qualities and virtues are made complete by the last thing of all—that is, **praise**. Praise is the one thing that we who have nothing can give to Him who has everything.

What a Savior we have! Let us never stop praising Him.

13–14 Think of this amazing revelation that John was given. John saw **every creature in heaven and on earth and under the earth and on the sea** praising God and the Lamb, Christ. Here on earth not everyone praises Christ. But when He comes in glory, **every creature** will bow down before Him and worship Him (see Philippians 2:9–11).

CHAPTER 6

The Seals Opened (6:1–17)

1–2 In this chapter, the first six of the seven seals of the scroll are opened. In this way God's final judgment on the world will begin. All the dreadful events mentioned here must come to pass before Christ returns.

When the Lamb opened the first seal, one of the four living creatures said to John, "Come." Then John saw a rider on a white horse. The white horse and its rider signified the great and terrible wars that were to come upon the earth. Jesus had said, **"These are the beginning of birth pains"** (Mark 13:7–8). The rider on the white horse represented an angel or spirit, who had been appointed to bring war upon the earth.

3–4 When the second seal was opened, the second living creature called forth a rider on a red horse, who represented the angel or spirit of killing and bloodshed.

5–6 The third rider who appeared to John, the rider on the black horse, was the angel or spirit of famine. He was to bring famine upon the earth. This rider carried in his hand scales for measuring out grain; because of the lack of grain, it would be necessary to distribute (ration) the grain according to measurement (Leviticus 26:26). Only a **quart of wheat** or **three quarts of barley** would be given **for a day's wages.**[17] This price was about ten times the normal price of these grains—as would be expected in famine conditions.

One of the four living creatures said to the rider on the black horse, "**. . . do not damage the oil and wine**." This means that the rider must not damage the olive trees or the grape vines, from which the **oil and wine** comes. The rider was to bring about only a partial famine, not a complete famine.

7–8 The rider on the fourth horse, the pale horse, was the angel or spirit of death; and riding together with him was a second rider, **Hades** (see Revelation 1:18 and comment). These riders had been given the authority to kill one fourth of the earth's population.[18]

9 When the fifth seal was opened, John saw the souls of the martyrs who had died for the sake of Christ. They had taken up their crosses and followed Jesus to the death (see Mark 8:34–35 and comment). In God's sight, their deaths were like an offering sacrificed on the altar of heaven (2 Timothy 4:6).

---

[16] In place of the word **praise**, some translations of the Bible say "blessing."

[17] One quart of wheat was enough to feed a man for a day, but it was not enough to feed his family also. Barley was a cheaper grain; three quarts a day would be enough for a family.

[18] The Old Testament prophet Zechariah also had a similar vision, in which red, black, white, and dappled horses were pulling four chariots (Zechariah 6:1–6).

10 The martyrs were crying out, **"How long, Sovereign Lord . . . until you . . . avenge our blood?"** (Psalm 94:3; Habakkuk 1:2). They weren't seeking personal vengeance; they were seeking justice.

11 Then the martyrs were each given a **white robe**, which signified righteousness and holiness. They had to wait until all the others who were to become martyrs had been killed. When the number of martyrs was complete, then God would bring His final judgment against those remaining on the earth.

12–14 When the sixth seal was opened, there was a great and terrible earthquake. The sun became **black like sackcloth**[19] and the moon became **blood red**. The stars fell from the sky (Mark 13:24–25; Acts 2:20).

15–17 Then those among the earth's inhabitants who had not repented and believed in Christ were filled with terror. They begged the mountains to fall on them and kill them so they would not have to endure God's terrible wrath (Hosea 10:8). **"For the great day of their wrath has come, and who can stand?"** they said (verse 17). The prophet Malachi had also asked: **"But who can endure the day of his coming? Who can stand when he appears?"** (Malachi 3:2). On that day it will be much easier for unrepentant sinners to die than to stand in the presence of God.

Let us never forget that God is not only a God of love, but He is also a God of wrath against sin. The final day of the Lord, the day of judgment, will be a terrible day (Joel 2:11). **Who can withstand his indignation? Who can endure his fierce anger?** (Nahum 1:6). Only those who have remained faithful to Christ will be able to endure that day (Mark 13:13). Therefore, let us not delay, but let us repent at once and put our faith in Christ.

CHAPTER 7

144,000 Sealed (7:1–8)

1 Before the opening of the seventh seal (Chapter 8), John saw two other visions which are described in this chapter: first, the sealing of the 144,000 (verses 1–8); and second, the vision of the great multitude (verses 9–17).

The **four winds of the earth** mentioned in verse 1 are winds of destruction. Until all 144,000 of God's servants are sealed (verse 3), four angels are assigned to hold back these winds.

2–3 Then John saw another angel coming from the east bringing the **seal** of God. On this seal were written the names of God and the Lamb, Christ (see Revelation 14:1). All those who were sealed with this seal belonged thenceforth to God and to the Lamb. The purpose of the sealing was to protect God's **servants** from the power of Satan. The number of those sealed was 144,000 (verse 4).

These 144,000 servants of God represent those believers who will be alive at the end of the world; that is, they are the last generation of Christians. This sealing will not save them from suffering and death, but it will give them the right to enter heaven. In this life they will have to endure suffering; indeed, that entire last generation of Christians will be killed (see Revelation 13:15).

4 The number 144,00 has a special meaning in the Bible; it means completeness.[20] In other words, we can understand here that John is referring to the entire last generation of Christians, not necessarily to the exact number 144,000.

It is written here that those 144,000 will come **from all the tribes of ISRAEL**. Here the meaning of **Israel** is not the Jewish nation (its usual meaning), but rather the

---

[19] Sackcloth was made from the hair of black goats; it was worn in times of mourning.

[20] The number "seven" has the same special meaning (see Revelation 5:6).

true spiritual Israel—that is, Christ's church (see Matthew 19:28; Romans 2:28–29; Galatians 3:29; 6:16; Philippians 3:3; 1 Peter 2:9).

5–8 In this list of Jacob's twelve sons and their tribes there is something unusual: The name of Dan, one of Jacob's sons, has been omitted (Genesis 35:23–26). In its place **Manasseh,** Jacob's grandson (the son of Joseph), has been written (verse 6). Many Bible scholars believe that the tribe of Dan is omitted because from the beginning the descendants of Dan worshiped idols. Thus the name of Manasseh has been added to complete the twelve tribes.

The Great Multitude (7:9–17)

9–10 The second of John's visions described in this chapter was very different from the first vision. Instead of 144,000 servants of God, John next saw a multitude that was so great it could not be counted. They had **come out of the great tribulation** (verse 14); in other words, they had now arrived in heaven. The terrible judgments and catastrophes that had fallen on the earth were now finished. Thus John was now seeing a vision of heaven after the end of the world had taken place. All generations of believers in Christ were standing before the throne of the Lamb. They were clothed in the white robes of Christ's righteousness. They were holding **palm branches,** which are a sign of joy and victory (John 12:13).

11–12 All the angels were also standing around the throne—**ten thousand times ten thousand** of them (Revelation 5:11). Just as they worshiped the Lamb in Revelation 5:12, so in this vision they worshiped Him in almost the same words.

13–14 One of the elders asked John, "You know, don't you, where these wearing white robes have come from?" John answered, "You know; please tell me." Therefore, the elder told John that they had come out of the **great tribulation**—that is, the great calamities and afflictions associated with the end of the world (Daniel 12:1–3). They were the ones out of every generation who had remained firm in their faith to the end (Mark 13:13; Acts 14:22). Their robes, having been washed in Christ's blood, were now **white**[21] with Christ's righteousness; that is, Christ's blood had washed their sins away (see Hebrews 9:14; 1 John 1:7).

15 Because the multitude of believers were dressed in the white robes of Christ's righteousness, they were allowed to stand before God's throne. There they serve Him **day and night**[22]—that is, continuously. They serve Him **in his temple.** Here God's **temple** doesn't mean a building; rather, it means God's presence. Heaven is God's "temple." God will **spread his tent** over the believers; that is, He will protect and take care of them. Thus, in this vision, the promise written in the Old Testament that God will dwell in the midst of His people has now come to pass (Ezekiel 37:27; Zechariah 2:10).

16–17 In heaven, believers will neither hunger nor thirst (Isaiah 49:10). Jesus said: **"Blessed are those who hunger and thirst for righteousness, for they will be filled"** (Matthew 5:6). **"He who comes to me will never go hungry, and he who believes in me will never be thirsty"** (John 6:35). The Lamb of God has become the shepherd of the sheep! (John 10:11). **The Lord is my shepherd, I shall lack nothing . . . he leads me beside quiet waters** (Psalm 23:1–2). He will lead them to springs of **living water** (see John 4:14; 7:37–38). And **God will wipe away every tear from their eyes.**

Here John has shown us a vision of heaven, our eternal home. To live in heaven with God and Christ in this way is our reward. Is there anyone among us who is suffering pain or sorrow for Christ's sake? Is anyone being persecuted because of Christ? If there is, let that person remember Jesus' words:

---

[21] The color "white" is a sign of purity and righteousness (see Revelation 3:4).

[22] There is no night in heaven (Revelation 22:5).

"Rejoice and be glad, because great is your reward in heaven" (Matthew 5:12).

CHAPTER 8

The Seventh Seal and the Seven Trumpets (8:1–13)

1–2 In Chapter 6, the Lamb opened six of the seven seals that sealed the scroll, in which were written all the judgments that were to come upon the earth (Revelation 5:1). Now the time had come for the Lamb to open the seventh seal.

When the seventh seal was opened, John saw seven angels, who had been given seven trumpets. These seven angels were appointed to announce the plagues that were to come upon the unbelieving men of the world.

3–5 Another angel was given incense to add to the **prayers of all the SAINTS** (verse 3). According to Revelation 5:8, the prayers of the saints were themselves like incense. The prayers of the faithful martyrs also rose like incense to God (Revelation 6:9–10). Now all these prayers were about to be fulfilled. The angel filled the **censer** with fire from the altar, and hurled it down upon the earth. Then began the plagues of the seven trumpets.

6 According to John's revelation, God sent these seven plagues upon the earth in order to lead people to repentance. These plagues were meant to destroy only a part of the earth, not the entire earth. However, men did not repent; instead, their hearts became even harder. Just as in Egypt the heart of the Pharaoh was hardened when God sent plagues upon the Egyptians, so it will be at the end of the world. At that time, when the final tribulations come, men's hearts will become even more hardened, and they will begin to revile God. And just as God led His people, the Jews, out of Egypt and into the land He had promised them, so at the end of the world God will lead all believers out of the final tribulation and into His presence in heaven.

7 The first plague was a plague of **hail** and **fire mixed with blood**, which resulted in one third of the earth being burned up (Exodus 9:23–24).

8–9 The second plague destroyed one third of the oceans and seas of the earth (Exodus 7:20–21).

10–11 The third plague made the water of a third of the earth's rivers and springs bitter (Jeremiah 9:15). The star that fell into the water was called **Wormwood**. Wormwood is the name of a very bitter-tasting plant.

12–13 The fourth plague was a plague of darkness (Exodus 10:21–23; Mark 13:24). After this plague came, an eagle gave warning that the remaining three plagues would be even more severe.

CHAPTER 9

The Last Three Plagues, or Woes (9:1–21)

1 When the fifth trumpet sounded, John saw a **star that had fallen from the sky to the earth**. That **star** was some kind of angel, who had been appointed to bring about the fifth plague, the plague of **locusts** (verse 3).

2–3 These locusts, or demons, came out of the **Abyss** (Luke 8:31). In the Old Testament, locusts were a sign of God's judgment against men (Exodus 10:13–15; Joel 1:2–7; 2:1–11). Even now, in northern Africa large armies of locusts come from time to time; as they advance they eat everything in sight and leave the land bare. Sometimes the locusts are so numerous that their advancing column is four miles wide and three meters deep!

4 The locusts that John saw in his vision were like **scorpions**. They had been given power to torture those people **who did not have the seal of God on their foreheads** (Revelation 7:2–3)—that is, non-believers. However, they were not to harm anything else. Notice that even Satan's armies are ultimately under God's control.

5–6 The locusts were not given the power to kill people, but only to torture them for five months.[23] By this means, God was giving unbelievers still one more chance to repent and turn to Christ.

7–11 In these verses John gives a description of these locusts. The locusts were as big as horses. Their "king" was an evil angel named **Abaddon**, which means destroyer.

12 Here John calls this fifth plague the **first woe**. The sixth and seventh plagues are also called the second and third woes.

13–14 Next, in verses 13–19, John describes the sixth plague (or second woe). God commanded the sixth angel: **"Release the four angels who are bound at the great river Euphrates."**[24]

15–16 These **four angels** were generals of an army of two hundred million horsemen. This army was ordered to kill one third of all unbelievers. This army had been kept waiting until the exact time of God's final judgment against the world.

17–19 Here John gives a description of the horses and their riders. It was not the riders but the horses who did the killing; they killed men with their mouths and tails.

20–21 In spite of this terrible destruction, men still did not repent. Their hearts were hardened against God. They kept on worshiping the DEMONS and **idols**[25] that were now destroying them. Satan had indeed deluded them! (Psalm 115:4–8; Daniel 5:22–33).

CHAPTER 10

The Angel and the Little Scroll (10:1–11)

1–4 By now, six trumpets had been sounded. But before the seventh trumpet was sounded, John received two other visions: first, the vision of an angel and a small scroll (verses 1–11); and second, the vision of the two witnesses (Revelation 11:1–13).

In the first vision, John saw a **mighty angel** come down from heaven; who this angel was John doesn't tell us. When the angel shouted, John heard the **voices of the seven thunders** (verse 3). But John was told not to write down what the seven thunders said.

5–6 The mighty angel then said, **"There will be no more delay"** (verse 6). Now God's final judgment was about to come. The faithful martyrs had cried out to God: **"How long, Sovereign Lord . . . until you judge the inhabitants of the earth?"** (Revelation 6:10). Now the angel had given them their answer: "You will not have to wait any longer; the

---

[23] Ordinary locusts live for only about five months.

[24] The Euphrates River runs through the modern country of Iraq, and is 1600 miles long. In New Testament times, it served as the eastern boundary of the Roman Empire. It was also the eastern limit of the land that God had promised to give to Abraham's descendants (Genesis 15:18).

[25] To worship an idol is the same as to worship a demon. Whenever one worships an idol, he is actually worshiping the demon or demons associated with that idol (see Deuteronomy 32:17; 1 Corinthians 10:14,19–20).

defeat of Satan and the final punishment of evildoers is about to take place" (Daniel 12:5–7).

7 Then the angel announced: "When the seventh trumpet is sounded, the **mystery of God will be accomplished.**" The **mystery of God** is the establishment of the kingdom of Christ and the defeat of all evil. The mystery of God is this: **The kingdom of the world has become the kingdom of our Lord and of his Christ, and he will reign for ever and ever** (Revelation 11:15). Thus the final purpose of God is a mystery no longer. It has been revealed to the PROPHETS (Daniel 12:1–3), and now is about to be revealed to John himself.

8–11 Then John was told to **take the scroll** from the mighty angel. When John asked the angel for the scroll, the angel told him to eat it (Ezekiel 2:9–10; 3:1–4). After John had eaten the scroll, he was told that he must again prophesy. The meaning of the vision is this: In order to prophesy for God, it is necessary to take His word completely into us—as if we were eating food. From this, we can also see that the things John has recorded in this book of Revelation are indeed the truth. He has taken God's word into himself; and what he writes, therefore, is God's true word.

It is not certain what was written on the small scroll. Some Bible scholars believe that the next vision, the vision of the two witnesses (Revelation 11:1–13), was written on it. The small scroll was **as sweet as honey** in John's mouth, because it was God's word (Psalm 119:103). It turned John's stomach **sour**, because it told of the terrible tribulation that was about to come upon the world.

CHAPTER 11

The Two Witnesses (11:1–14)

1 Many Bible scholars believe the prophecy described in this section (verses 1–14) was written on the little scroll that John had just eaten (Revelation 10:10). The **temple of God** and the **worshipers** mentioned here refer to the Christian church existing at the time of God's final judgment of the world.

John is told to **measure** the temple. To measure the temple means to protect it; thus when John has measured the temple (church) and counted the worshipers there, they will be protected by God (Ezekiel Chapters 40–42).

2 According to John's vision, the **Gentiles**—that is, non-believers—will persecute the temple (church) for forty-two months. But they will only be able to overcome the **outer court**, which is the part God told John not to measure. All those within the temple—the true believers—God will protect from the attacks of the unbelievers.

The period forty-two months, or 1,260 days (verse 3), is the period of time that God will give to the unbelievers to persecute the church. The prophet Daniel had prophesied that an evil king would capture the temple for forty-two months (Daniel 8:9–14). And in 167 B.C., that prophecy was fulfilled when a Syrian king captured Jerusalem for three and a half years (forty-two months).

Therefore, at the end of the world, there will be a similar time when the non-believing Gentiles will attack the church. That time is called the **times of the Gentiles** (Luke 21:24).

3 According to John's vision, during that forty-two months (or 1,260 days) of persecution **two witnesses** will prophesy. Some Bible scholars believe that these two witnesses are the prophet Elijah (Malachi 4:5) and Moses (Deuteronomy 18:15). But other scholars think that these two witnesses are not actual people, but rather that they represent the entire church at the end of the world; in other words, they say that these two witnesses are a symbol of the witnessing church. Their word of witness is that men must repent; therefore, they will wear **sackcloth**, which is a sign of repentance.

4–6 Like Elijah and Moses, these two

witnesses (or the church) will have great power to destroy their enemies with **fire** (2 Kings 1:10), power to **shut up the sky**[26] (1 Kings 17:1), power to **turn the waters into blood** (Exodus 7:14–18), and power to **strike the earth with every kind of plague** (Exodus 8:12).

These two witnesses are called the **two olive trees** and the **two lampstands** (verse 4), which are signs of the Holy Spirit (Zechariah 4:1–6,11–14). The lamps burn by means of the oil from the olives; the oil represents the Spirit Himself. In the same way, the power and the light of these two witnesses comes from the Holy Spirit within them.

7–10 When the two witnesses (or members of the church) have finished their work of witnessing and prophesying, their bodies will no longer be protected from harm. At that time, the **beast that comes up from the Abyss** will attack them. This **beast** is also mentioned in Revelation Chapter 13. The beast is a symbol of the Roman Empire and all other evil powers of the world (Daniel 7:7; Revelation 13:1).

The bodies of the two witnesses will be left **in the street of the great city**. In the book of Revelation, the expression "great city" usually stands for the city of ROME (the capital of the Roman Empire), or the Roman Empire itself. Here in this verse, however, the **great city** probably refers to Jerusalem, because John writes that it was also the place where **their Lord was crucified**. Whichever city is in John's mind—whether Rome or Jerusalem—this **great city** is meant to be a symbol of worldly power and evil, just as **Sodom** and **Egypt** in the Old Testament were symbols of worldly power and evil.

11 But after three and a half days, God will raise up these two witnesses (or the church) from the dead. Those evil men who killed them will be filled with terror, because they will have no power over those who rise from the dead.

12–13 While their enemies watch, these two witnesses (or the church—all believers) will ascend into heaven (2 Kings 2:11; 1 Thessalonians 4:16–17). Then a great earthquake will destroy a tenth of that **great city**. Those who survive the earthquake will give **glory to God**; it is not certain whether John means that they will truly repent, or whether they will only give glory to God out of fear. This earthquake is the **second woe** (verse 14).

14 Here John says that the **second woe** (or sixth plague) **has passed**; the **third woe** (or seventh plague) is now about to come.

The Seventh Trumpet (11:15–19)

15 The seventh trumpet announces God's final judgment against the world and the establishment of Christ's kingdom. In this section (verses 15–19), John gives a summary of everything that will occur after the seventh trumpet has been sounded. That is, this short section is a summary of all the remaining chapters in the book of Revelation. Therefore, John writes here as if all these future events had already happened. The most important event of all comes here in verse 15: **The kingdom of the world has become the kingdom of our Lord and of his Christ** (Daniel 2:44; 7:13–14,27).

16–18 The **twenty-four elders** (Revelation 4:4) give thanks to God for punishing the evil nations and rewarding the prophets and all the saints (believers). The reward of the prophets and saints is to live forever in Christ's kingdom.

The nations had risen up in anger against God; they had destroyed the earth (verse 18). But now God has destroyed them (Psalm 2:2,5; Romans 2:5–6).

19 Then according to John's vision, **God's temple in heaven was opened**, and inside the temple the **ark of his covenant** was seen (Exodus 25:10–22). The **ark** is a sign of God's presence with His people. In this way, the believers enter into God's presence in heaven, which is their reward (verse 18). But on

---

[26] Elijah "shut up the sky" for three and a half years (42 months), and no rain fell during that time (Luke 4:25; James 5:17).

the earth, God's judgment is poured out in the form of **lightning**, an **earthquake**, and a **great hailstorm**.

CHAPTER 12

The Woman and the Dragon (12:1–17)

1–2 In John's vision, the seventh trumpet has just been sounded (Revelation 11:15). The seventh trumpet announces everything that is to happen from here until the end of the book of Revelation. Now God's terrible final judgment is about to fall upon the world and upon Satan. In the next two chapters, Chapters 12–13, a great conflict between Satan and Christ's church is described. In this conflict, believers suffer bodily pain and death; but they must remain firm to the end, knowing this, that Satan's final defeat is certain.

Following the sounding of the seventh trumpet, John saw in heaven a glorious woman, who was about to give birth to a child. The woman represents the true Israel—the church—the chosen people of God (1 Peter 2:9). The **twelve stars** of her crown represent the twelve tribes of Israel; they can also represent Christ's twelve apostles.

3–4 Then John saw an **enormous red dragon**, which was Satan (verse 9). On his seven heads were seven crowns; the crowns were signs of the dragon's authority. But the dragon's authority was not his own; it had been stolen from God. And just as King Herod tried to kill the infant Christ (Matthew 2:13,16), so did this dragon try to devour the newborn child of this woman (1 Peter 5:8).

5 The child of the woman is Christ, **who will rule all the nations with an iron scepter** (Psalm 2:6–9). Having learned that this child was appointed to rule all the nations, the dragon Satan became angry, because he considered that all the nations of the earth belonged to him (Matthew 4:8–9). This is why the dragon tried so hard to kill the child.

But the dragon didn't get to devour the child. The child (Christ) was **snatched up to God and to his throne**; that is, Christ was raised from the dead and taken up to heaven, where He was seated at the right hand of God.

6 The woman (the church) fled to a safe place that God had prepared for her, where the dragon Satan could not devour her. There the woman could remain safely throughout the 1,260 days of persecution (see Revelation 11:1–3 and comment).

7–9 Then John saw a great struggle between the dragon Satan and God's chief angel **Michael** (Daniel 12:1–3).

Then the dragon—that **ancient serpent called the devil**[27] (Genesis 3:1,14–15)—and all of his evil angels were hurled to the earth (see Luke 10:18).

10 At the defeat of Satan, there was great rejoicing in heaven. Satan is here called the **accuser of our brothers**. One of Satan's main evil works is to accuse believers before God and before each other (Job 1:8–11). Satan also **leads the whole world astray** (verse 9). Deception is another of Satan's main methods of bringing harm to God's people (Mark 13:22; 2 Corinthians 11:13).

Although in John's vision the hurling of Satan to earth takes place at the end of the world, there is another sense in which Satan has already been **hurled to the earth** (verse 9). He has already lost his place in heaven. He has already been defeated by Christ. He can no longer successfully accuse believers before God, because through Christ they have been declared innocent and righteous in God's sight (see Romans 8:33–34 and comment).

11 Not only angels in heaven but also believers on earth are able to overcome Satan **by the blood of the Lamb**; that is, because of Christ's death for their

[27] In the Greek language, the word **devil** means the "accuser," or "slanderer."

sins, believers are no longer in bondage to Satan. Because Christ's Holy Spirit is in them, believers are more powerful than Satan (see 1 John 4:4 and comment). Believers overcome Satan's evil power through the faithful **word of their testimony** for Christ and through their firmness in faith until death. The one who does not love his own life but offers it to Christ will surely be victorious in the end (Matthew 10:32; Mark 13:13).

12 Because he had been thrown out of heaven, Satan was furious. His remaining time was short. He began to lash out furiously in every direction, like a wild animal surrounded by hunters.

13 Having failed to kill the child, the dragon Satan then began to pursue the woman (the church). Because of Satan's anger against Christ, he also became angry at Christ's church. Jesus said to His disciples: "**If the world hates you, keep in mind that it hated me first. . . . If they persecuted me, they will persecute you also. . . . They will treat you this way because of my name**" (John 15;18,20–21). Therefore, let Christians remember that any persecution they suffer comes because of the great conflict between Christ and Satan. Because we are Christ's disciples and brothers, Satan will attack us also.

14 Before the dragon Satan could seize the woman, she was given **two wings of a great eagle**, which was a sign of God's deliverance (Isaiah 40:31). The woman then flew to the place of safety prepared for her (verse 6). There the woman remained **for a time, times and half a time**[28]—that is, for forty-two months, or 1,260 days (verse 6).

15–17 Thus Satan could not harm the woman. Therefore, he went off to make war with the **rest of her offspring** (verse 17)—that is, with other believers. Christ was this woman's oldest child; therefore, all the woman's other children were Christ's younger brothers and sisters—that is, believers (Romans 8:29). Thus Satan began to persecute them.

In this vision of the woman and the dragon, which John has related here in Chapter 12, notice how the events described can refer both to events which have already taken place and also to events that will take place at the end of the world. First, the vision can be interpreted as a commentary on the past: Christ has already been born, and has defeated Satan on the cross; and Satan, ever since, has been persecuting Christ's church. Second, the vision can be interpreted as a commentary on the future: at the end of the world, the final struggle between Satan and God will take place, and at that time Satan will again be hurled out of heaven to earth, where he will fiercely persecute Christ's church for the short time remaining to him before he is finally destroyed forever.

CHAPTER 13

The Beast out of the Sea (13:1–10)

1–2 From here on to the end of the book of Revelation, the visions that John sees refer primarily to events that will take place between now and the end of the world. However, because John believed the end of the world was going to come in his own time, he naturally interpreted these visions to refer to events that were taking place in his own day—especially in regard to the Roman Empire. It is necessary to keep this in mind as one studies the rest of this book.

In this chapter, John talks about two beasts, one from the sea (verses 1–10), and the other from the earth (verses 11–18), through which Satan will wage war with the last generation of believers.

Like the dragon Satan in the previous vision (Revelation 12:3), the beast out of

---

[28] Here **a time** means one year, **times** means two years, and **half a time** means half a year. These add up to three and a half years, which equals forty-two months, or 1,260 days.

the sea had ten horns and seven heads. In John's mind, the beast out of the sea represented the Roman Empire. Each of the seven heads represented a different emperor. A **blasphemous name**[29] was written on each head (see Revelation 17:3 and comment). The dragon Satan gave all of his power and authority to this first beast (the Roman Empire). Therefore, in Satan's name the beast at once began to persecute the church of Christ.

For John, this beast was like the Roman Empire. But we must remember that the real meaning of the beast is broader than that. The beast is a sign of every evil worldly power in every age that opposes Christ and His church.

The prophet Daniel received a vision of four beasts that came up out of the sea (Daniel 7:3–7). Here the beast in John's vision seems to be a combination of the four beasts of Daniel's vision.

3 One of the seven heads (emperors) of the beast appeared to have been fatally wounded but then to have recovered.[30] From this, we can see the great power of the beast. It was very difficult to kill this beast; it recovered from wounds that would have been fatal for anyone else.

4 Unbelieving people throughout the world followed after this beast (verse 3). Because this powerful and frightening beast had received its power from Satan (verse 2), men naturally began to worship Satan. They also worshiped the beast itself. In John's time, people were forced to worship the Roman emperors as gods. Therefore, from this verse we can learn an important truth: Whenever we worship any king or leader as a god, we are, in fact, worshiping Satan.

5 God gave this beast only three and a half years in which to exercise its authority (see Revelation 11:2; 12:6 and comments).

6–7 According to the description given here, the beast was in many ways similar to the Roman Empire of John's day (see 2 Thessalonians 2:4). The Romans did not believe in the one true God. They worshiped their emperor; they persecuted Christians. All the nations of western Europe, northern Africa, and the Middle East had fallen under the authority of the Roman Empire. This is why, in John's mind, the beast represented the Roman Empire.

Satan once had tried to give Jesus authority over all the nations of the world, but Jesus had refused his offer (Matthew 4:8–10). Now we see that Satan has given his authority to the beast instead.

8 Only believers in Christ will refuse to worship this beast; their names are written **in the book of life belonging to the Lamb** (Philippians 4:3; Revelation 3:5). John says here that this Lamb **was slain from the creation of the world**. This means that from before the creation of the world God had planned to save men through the sacrifice of Jesus' body on the cross. From before the creation of the world, our names have been written in that book! (Ephesians 1:4). According to Revelation 3:5, however, we can understand that if in this life we give up our faith, our names may be erased from that book.

9–10 Here John writes words of exhortation and encouragement to believers who are facing trouble and suffering. If any Christians have been appointed by God to be put into captivity, let them accept it. Let them not fight with the sword, or else they will be killed by the sword (see Matthew 26:50–52). Instead, let them love their enemies, and suffer all things with **patient endurance and faithfulness** (verse 10).

The Beast out of the Earth (13:11–18)

11 The second beast, which is described in this section, was another helper

---

[29] In John's time, the Roman emperors gave themselves the names of gods; in fact, they considered themselves to be gods. To call oneself a god is blasphemy against the one true God.

[30] It is not known what John is referring to here when he mentions the wounded head that recovered.

of Satan whose main work was to deceive men and lead them astray. He looked like a lamb, but he spoke like a dragon (see Matthew 7:15). In Revelation 16:13, this second beast is called the **false prophet**.

12 The particular work of this second beast was to make men worship the first beast. Therefore, we can understand that this second beast is a symbol of false religion and false priesthood.

13–14 The second beast (the false prophet) led men astray by means of signs and miracles (see Deuteronomy 13:1–4; Mark 13:22; 2 Thessalonians 2:9–10). The second beast ordered men to set up an image of the first beast.[31]

15 In John's time, many people believed that images could speak. According to John's vision, this second beast caused the image of the first beast to speak; and what the image spoke was to order the death sentence for all those who refused to worship it.

16–17 The second beast also forced all men to receive the **mark** of the first beast on their hand or forehead. This **mark** was the name of the first beast—or the **number of his name**[32] (verse 17). Just as God's faithful servants were sealed with God's name (Revelation 7:2–3), so were the followers of the beast sealed with the beast's name or number. Those who didn't have the mark of the beast couldn't buy or sell any goods; they had great difficulty in making a living. This same situation was true for Christians during the time of the Roman Empire.

18 The number of the first beast was 666. Many Bible scholars believe that this is the number of some man, but no one is sure who. Some think that 666 was the number of the Roman emperor Nero, who reigned from 54 to 68 A.D. (see Acts 18:14–16; 25:10–11 and comments).

CHAPTER 14

The Lamb and the 144,000 (14:1–5)

1 Then John saw the Lamb, Christ, standing on **Mount Zion**. Mount Zion is the heavenly Zion—that is, the heavenly Jerusalem (see Hebrews 12:22; Revelation 21:2,10). The 144,000[33] who have the name of God and of the Lamb on their foreheads represent all believers of every generation; their number is not limited just to 144,000. They are the ones who have overcome; they are the ones on whom a new name has been written (see Revelation 3:12 and comment).

Many Bible scholars believe that the 144,000 mentioned here and the 144,000 mentioned in Revelation 7:3–4 do not refer to the same group of people.[34] Here the number 144,000 stands for all Christians of every generation. None of those who have been sealed by God will be lost. The 144,000 mentioned here, therefore, corresponds to the great multitude mentioned in Revelation 7:9.

---

[31] During the time of the Roman Empire, people made many images of the different Roman emperors.

[32] In the ancient Greek and Hebrew languages, there were no symbols for numbers. Instead, regular letters of the alphabet were used for numbers. Thus every man's name also had its own "number," made from the letters of the name.

[33] Both here and in Revelation 7:3–4, the number 144,000 stands for completeness, or fullness. It does not necessarily mean the exact number 144,000.

[34] Most Bible scholars believe that the 144,000 mentioned in Revelation Chapter 7 represent only the final generation of Christians who will be alive at the end of the world (see Revelation 7:2–4 and comment). However, other Bible scholars have a different opinion: they say that these two groups of 144,000 are the same—that is, both groups represent all Christians of all generations.

2–3 Only those who have been redeemed by Christ, who have been sealed by Him, will get to sing the **new song** of victory and salvation in heaven.

4 In this verse, John says three things about this group of 144,000. First, **they did not defile themselves with women**. This can also mean that they did not defile themselves by worshiping other gods or by worshiping any king or emperor. According to Old Testament teaching, to worship anything other than the one true God was the same as to commit adultery. Whenever the Jews worshiped idols, the Jewish prophets accused them of being adulterers (Jeremiah 3:6,20). The reason was that they had left their true "husband," God, and had gone off with idols. In Revelation 17:1–2, the city of Rome is called a **great prostitute**, with whom the men of the earth committed adultery. But these 144,000 **kept themselves pure**. They were fit to be pure virgin brides of Christ (see 2 Corinthians 11:2; Revelation 21:9). They had not "committed adultery" with idols.

The second thing John says about this 144,000 is that they **follow the Lamb wherever he goes**; that is, they are Christ's faithful and obedient disciples.

Third, they were **purchased** by Christ (see Revelation 5:9 and comment), and they were **offered as firstfruits**[35]—that is, as sacrifices—**to God** (Romans 12:1).

5 The 144,000 were **blameless**. Through their faith in Christ, they had been declared righteous in God's sight (see Romans 3:22; 5:2). Their robes had been washed in the blood of the Lamb and had been made white (see Revelation 7:14 and comment).

The Three Angels (14:6–13)

6–7 The first angel then gave a final call to the people of the world to repent and turn to the living God: "**Fear God and give him glory, because the hour of his JUDGMENT has come**" (verse 7). This was mankind's last warning; it was man's last chance to find salvation. Some scholars believe that this final call to men was a fulfillment of the words spoken by Jesus: "**And the gospel must first be preached to all nations**" (Mark 13:10).

8 Then a second angel said, "**Fallen is Babylon the Great**" (Isaiah 21:9). In Old Testament times, Babylon was a famous city known for its wealth and for its evil (see Daniel 4:28–30; 1 Peter 5:13 and comment). Therefore, we can understand that the name "Babylon" signifies any evil city, kingdom, or authority. In John's time, Rome was called "Babylon."

All nations had drunk the **maddening wine of her** (Babylon's) **adulteries**; that is, they had all shared in her immorality and idolatry, and had thus brought upon themselves the wrath of God (see Jeremiah 51:7; Revelation 17:1–2).

9–11 The third angel then described the judgment that was about to come upon all those who had the mark of the beast—that is, all those who had not repented and turned to Christ (Revelation 13:16–17).

Those who had the mark of the beast would be made to drink of the **wine of God's fury** (Psalm 75:8; Jeremiah 25:15–17). The "wine of God's fury" will be **poured full strength into the cup of his wrath**; that is, it will not be mixed with water—with mercy. There will be no mercy mixed with God's final judgment against those who have the mark of the beast. They will be tormented forever **with burning sulfur** (see Genesis 19:24,28; Mark 9:44; Luke 17:29).

12 Therefore, let those who are Christians remain strong and faithful to the end, lest this judgment fall upon them also.

13 Then, in John's vision, a voice said from heaven: "**Blessed are the dead who die in the Lord.**" In John's time, many Christians who did not abandon their faith and who did not worship the emperor or other gods were put to death. But they will receive an eternal reward, an eternal rest (Hebrews 4:1). John writes

---

[35] In this verse, the word **firstfruits** means sacrifice. In other verses, the meaning of "firstfruits" is different (see Romans 8:23; James 1:18).

that **their deeds**—that is, their deeds of faith and love—**will follow them**. That means that news of their good works will reach heaven.

The Harvest and the Earth (14:14–20)

14–15 Then John saw one **like a son of man** (Daniel 7:13–14), in whose hand was a **sharp sickle** (verse 14). This, of course, is Christ. In the Bible, the sickle is a sign of judgment. The righteous will be gathered into the kingdom of God, and the wicked will be thrown into the fire of hell (Jeremiah 51:33; Matthew 13:30,36–43; Mark 4:26–29).

16 Then Christ, the one "like a son of man," swung His sickle over the earth. And when He did this, the final judgment sounded by the seventh trumpet began (see Revelation 11:15; 15:1 and comments).

17–18 Then John saw an angel, and this angel was also holding a sharp sickle. And then another angel, **who had charge of the fire** (Revelation 8:3–5), told the angel with the sickle to **gather the clusters of grapes from the earth's vine**. The **grapes** represent those who have the mark of the beast on them—that is, those who have not repented and turned to God.

19–20 In these verses we see another description of what is going to happen to the wicked. They will not only be cut down and thrown into the fire, but they will also be trampled under God's feet like grapes[36] (Isaiah 63:1–6; Joel 3:12–13; Revelation 19:15). Their blood will flow out and form a lake two meters deep and two hundred miles long!

CHAPTER 15

Seven Angels with Seven Plagues (15:1–8)

1 The last seven plagues described in this section are God's last attempt to lead men to repent and turn to Him; they are God's final warning to men. When these plagues are finished, then God's final judgment will fall.

In John's revelation, these seven last plagues begin after the seventh trumpet has been sounded[37] (Revelation 11:15; 14:16). These last seven plagues are much more severe than the earlier six plagues announced by the first six trumpets (Revelation Chapters 8–9).

2 Then in his vision, John saw all those who had been **victorious over the beast**—that is, all those who had not worshiped the image of the beast (Revelation 13:14–15), and who had not received the beast's mark (Revelation 13:16). To be victorious over the beast meant to refuse to worship and serve him. The victorious ones seen by John were those who had received salvation and had entered the kingdom of God (see Revelation 2:7,11,17,26; 3:5,12,21).

3–4 These victorious ones were singing the **song of Moses** (Exodus 15:1–18) and the **song of the Lamb** (Christ). Just as God, through Moses, delivered the Jews from bondage in Egypt, so in the same way God, through Christ the Lamb, delivers believers from bondage to Satan and gives them salvation. Because of God's great **righteous acts** of deliverance, all nations will come and worship before Him (verse 4). This does not mean that all the people of these nations will receive salvation; rather, it means that after God's final judgment is given, all

---

[36] In Bible times, in order to make wine, men put grapes into a large winepress and then trampled on them with their feet. The juice of the grapes then flowed down a little trough and was collected in a large container.

[37] One can regard these seven last plagues as one great plague—the seventh plague—announced by the seventh trumpet.

those who have gone to hell will also acknowledge the one true God (See Psalm 86:8–10; Philippians 2:9–11).

5–6 Then John saw God's temple open, and out of the temple came the seven angels with the seven last plagues. John here calls the heavenly temple the **tabernacle of Testimony** (verse 5). This was the name of the tabernacle of the ancient Jews, when they were in the desert after escaping from Egypt. It was actually a tent, and so it was also called the **Tent of the Testimony** (Numbers 9:15). The **Testimony** was the name given to the two stone tablets on which God had written the ten commandments of the Jewish law (see Exodus 32:15; Deuteronomy 10:4; Acts 7:44 and comment). The followers of the beast had disobeyed these ten commandments; therefore, it was fitting that out of the **tabernacle of Testimony** should come forth God's wrath and righteous judgment against those who had disobeyed these commandments.

7–8 One of the **four living creatures** (Revelation 4:6–8) gave the seven angels **seven golden bowls** filled with God's wrath. Then the tabernacle was filled with smoke, which was a sign of God's presence and power and glory (Exodus 19:18; 40:34–35; 1 Kings 8:10–11).

CHAPTER 16

The Seven Bowls of God's Wrath (16:1–21)

1 The seven last plagues mentioned in Revelation Chapter 15 are contained in the **seven bowls of God's wrath** mentioned in Chapter 16. These seven last plagues (or bowls) taken together constitute the final plague announced by the seventh trumpet (Revelation 11:15). These seven final "bowl-plagues" are somewhat different from the first six "trumpet-plagues" described in Revelation Chapters 8–9. The six trumpet-plagues caused only partial destruction of the earth; but these seven final bowl plagues cause utter destruction of the earth and its inhabitants.

2 The first bowl contained a plague of **sores** (Exodus 9:9–11; Job 2:7).

3 The plague in the second bowl turned the sea into blood (see Revelation 8:8–9).

4–7 The plague in the third bowl turned the rivers and springs into blood (see Exodus 7:17–21; Revelation 8:10–11). God is righteous, and His judgments are just. These men who followed Satan and the beast had shed the blood of God's **saints and prophets**—that is, believers. Therefore, it was completely just that God should give these murderers blood to drink. Blood can never quench the thirst.

8–9 The plague in the fourth bowl caused the sun to become so hot that it scorched people with fire (see Revelation 8:12). However, in heaven the sun will never scorch those who are saved (Revelation 7:16).

10–11 The plague in the fifth bowl was the plague of darkness (Exodus 10:21–23). It was poured out upon the **throne of the beast**. In John's mind, the throne of the beast represented Rome, because in his time it seemed as if Rome was the capital of Satan's kingdom. But we must understand that the "throne of the beast" can also stand for any evil kingdom or power.

12 The plague in the sixth bowl was poured out on the **great river Euphrates** (see Revelation 9:13–14 and comment). The Euphrates River formed the eastern boundary of the Roman Empire. Therefore, when the water in the river dried up, there was nothing to keep the **kings from the East** from crossing over. It is not known what kings John is referring to here. It is possible that they are the same as the ten kings mentioned in Revelation 17:12.

13 Then John saw three evil spirits that looked like frogs. One came out of the mouth of the **dragon** Satan (Revelation 12:3,9), the second came out of the mouth of the **beast** (Revelation 13:1), and the third came out of the mouth of the **false prophet.**[38]

14 According to John's vision, these three evil spirits will deceive the people of the world by means of **miraculous signs** (Mark 13:22; Revelation 13:13–14). The three spirits will gather together all the evil rulers and kings of the world to fight in the final battle against God (Revelation 19:19). That battle will occur **on the great day of God Almighty,** when Christ will finally destroy the beast and the false prophet and their followers (see Revelation 19:11–21). On that day Christ will begin His reign on earth (Revelation 11:17).

15 Here Christ warns His own followers to remain ready. **"Behold, I come like a thief"** (see Matthew 24:42–44; 1 Thessalonians 5:2). **"Blessed is he who stays awake and keeps his clothes with him."** Christians must be dressed in Christ's righteousness, and they must wear the armor of God (Ephesians 6:13–17).

16 **Armageddon** is the place where the final battle will take place between Christ and Satan and his two beasts. The meaning of the word Armageddon is not known. Neither is the location of Armageddon known.

17–18 When the plague in the seventh bowl was poured out, God said, **"It is done!"** The plagues were now finished. Now Satan's final defeat and the end of the world was about to occur. Then John saw a great and terrible earthquake (see Revelation 11:15,19).

19 Then John watched as the **great city**—that is, **Babylon the Great** (Revelation 14:8)—was split into three parts; in other words, it was totally destroyed. John considered the great city to be Rome. But Rome (that is, the Rome of John's time) has been destroyed now for 1500 years, and the end of the world has not yet come. Therefore, we can understand that the **great city—Babylon the Great—** represents all worldly authorities, kings, and countries that do not obey God. All those who disobey God will in the end drink from the **cup filled with the wine of the fury of** [God's] **wrath** (see Revelation 14:9–10 and comment).

20–21 Even after enduring such a terrible earthquake and a hailstorm with hundred-pound hailstones, men still did not repent (Exodus 9:22–26; Joshua 10:11). Instead, they cursed God. Their final judgment was now at hand.

CHAPTER 17

The Woman on the Beast (17:1–18)

1 In John's vision, the **great prostitute** is Rome. She **sits on many waters**—that is, she exercises authority over **peoples, multitudes, nations and languages** (verse 15). But the prostitute doesn't represent only Rome; she also represents all corrupt and evil powers and authorities of every age and every generation (Isaiah 23:17; Nahum 3:1–7).

2 All kings and people who share in the evil and immorality of a kingdom like the Roman Empire are like men who commit adultery with a prostitute.

3 Here John was carried away **in the Spirit** (Revelation 1:10), and he saw the great prostitute **sitting on a scarlet beast.** The scarlet beast is the same as the first beast mentioned in Revelation Chapter 13 (see Revelation 13:1–2,7 and comment).

4–6 Here we can understand that the prostitute is **Babylon the Great,** that is, Rome (see Revelation 16:19 and comment). According to the title on her forehead, she had given birth to other prostitutes and to all kinds of **abominations,** and she had spread these abominations all over the earth (verse 5). She **was drunk with the blood of the saints;** that

---

[38] This **false prophet** is the same as the second beast mentioned in Revelation 13:11–17.

is, she had murdered Christians, **those who bore testimony to Jesus** (verse 6).

7–8 Then an angel explained to John the meaning of the scarlet beast: "**The beast, which you saw, once was, now is not.**" That is, one of the beast's heads had received a **fatal wound** (see Revelation 13:3 and comment). But the beast did not die; it recovered. And it **will come up out of the Abyss** (see Revelation 9:1; 11:7 and comments). Men of the world whose names are not written in the book of life (Revelation 3:5) will fear the beast; because even though the beast has received a fatal wound, it keeps coming back to life again. That beast is a sign of all the evil empires of the world—such as Babylon, Rome, Hitler's Germany, etc. As each of these evil empires falls one by one, another rises to take its place. The beast is like that.

9–11 Just as the prostitute was a symbol of Rome, so in John's mind the beast was a symbol of the Roman Empire. The seven heads of the beast represent **seven hills on which the woman sits**[39] (verse 9). Its heads also represent **seven kings**. These seven kings can refer to seven Roman emperors or to seven kingdoms. That beast itself is an **eighth king** (verse 11), who in some way **belongs to the seven** other kings. Many Bible scholars believe that this "eighth king" is the **lawless one** or the **antichrist** mentioned elsewhere by Paul and John (see 2 Thessalonians 2:7–10; 1 John 2:18; 4:3 and comments).

Therefore, we can see that this beast represents two different things. First, it represents all evil empires and authorities in the world; and second, it represents the "eighth king," or antichrist. These two things are really the same, because every evil emperor or authority is, in a sense, an antichrist. The main antichrist is a powerful evil spirit, who is Satan's chief helper. But there are also many lesser antichrists who serve Satan[40] (see 1 John 2:18).

12–13 The ten horns of the beast represent ten kings. It is possible that these ten kings are the same as the **kings from the East** mentioned in Revelation 16:12. Or they might be the kings who give their power and authority to the beast—that is, who make themselves servants of the beast (verse 13). The reign of these kings will be very short—only one hour!

14 These kings who have given their authority to the beast will make war against Christ the Lamb. But Christ and His followers will overcome them (Revelation 2:26–27).

15–16 The prostitute, Rome, sits on many waters (verse 1); that is, she rules over many peoples and nations. But the beast with its ten horns (kings) will begin to despise the prostitute, and in the end it will destroy her. This is an amazing thing, because at first the beast and the prostitute had been partners (see verse 3). From this we can see that evil people and evil powers turn against each other in the end and destroy each other. This has happened many times in the history of the world.

17 God is the one who will cause the ten kings to give their power and authority to the beast (verse 13). God will also cause the beast and its ten kings to turn against the prostitute and destroy her. All power and authority ultimately belongs to God. God uses even evil spirits and evil powers to accomplish His purposes.

18 See verse 1 and comment.

---

39 The city of Rome was built on seven hills. Modern Rome is located on those same seven hills.

40 It is very difficult to interpret verses 7–11. Bible scholars have many different ideas about what they mean.

CHAPTER 18

The Fall of Babylon (18:1–24)

1–2 Next John received a vision of the fall of a great city, which he describes in this chapter. In John's mind, the great city was Rome, the capital of the Roman Empire, which is called **Babylon the Great** in the vision (see Revelation 14:8; 17:5 and comments). However, the great city described here represents not only Rome but also every civilization of evil, worldly men right up to this present time. Just as God brought about the destruction of ancient Rome in the 5th century A.D., so God will bring about the destruction of the world at His appointed time.

For us, therefore, John is describing in this chapter two things. First, he is describing the fall of the historic city of ancient Rome. Second, he is describing the future fall of all evil cities and kingdoms and powers in the world.[41] One day, God will destroy them all.

Then John, in his vision, heard an angel shout: "**Fallen! Fallen is Babylon the Great!**" (Isaiah 21:9; Revelation 14:8). The city—the highest and greatest work of worldly men—had become a **home for demons** (Isaiah 13:19–22).

3 The kings of all the surrounding nations had allied themselves with the city ("Babylon") and thus shared in its evil. The nations had **drunk the maddening wine of her adulteries**. The kings had **committed adultery with her**; that is, they had turned from the true God and had joined together with Babylon, the **great prostitute** (see Revelation 17:1–2 and comment). The merchants of the earth had traded with the city, and from this trade they had grown rich.

4–5 Then a voice from heaven said, "**Come out of her, my people**". Let all those who belong to God refuse to take part in the evils of Babylon; let them come out of the city (see Isaiah 52:11; Jeremiah 51:45; 2 Corinthians 6:14–18 and comment). Those who share in the sins of Babylon will also receive her plagues.

6–8 Then the voice from heaven said: "**Give back to her as she has given**" (verse 6). It's possible that this voice was speaking to the beast and its ten kings, who had been appointed to destroy Babylon, the great prostitute (Revelation 17:12,16). God will pay back evil men according to what they have done (Psalm 62:12; Jeremiah 50:29; Romans 2:5–6). Babylon had exalted herself and had puffed herself up with pride. She boasted in her heart, "**I sit as queen**" (Isaiah 47:8–9). But she will be brought low (Proverbs 29:23; Matthew 23:12). Her plagues—**death, mourning and famine**—will come upon her (verse 8). She will be destroyed **by fire** (Luke 17:28–30).

9–10 The kings of the earth who shared in Babylon's reign will mourn at her fall, because they know that now their own reigns will come to an end (Ezekiel 26:15–18).

11–13 The merchants of the earth will also mourn over Babylon's fall. Their trade with Babylon had been great. The rich and powerful people of Babylon craved all kinds of luxuries.[42] Thus, supplying Babylon with these luxuries had been very profitable for the merchants.

Among all the goods the merchants brought to Babylon, the last to be mentioned here are the **bodies and souls of men**—that is, slaves[43] (verse 13). The

[41] Some Christians believe that at the end of the world a single great and evil empire will rise up, which will be like the Roman Empire. This is possible, but no one can know this for sure. The one thing we can know, however, is that whatever empire or empires exist at that time, they will all fall—just as ancient Rome fell.

[42] As an example of such craving for luxury, one of the Roman emperors once ordered $100,000 worth of roses from Egypt for a single banquet. Another emperor spent $20,000,000 in one year for food for his family.

[43] In John's time, the slave trade was very large. It has been estimated that there were up to sixty million slaves in the Roman Empire.

slave trade not only involves selling men's **bodies**; it also involves selling their **souls**.

14–16 The merchants will mourn, because their opportunity to get rich by trading with Babylon will be lost forever. Indeed, along with the destruction of Babylon's wealth, their own wealth will be destroyed too (Ezekiel 27:1–4,12–24).

17–19 All who earn their living by the sea will also mourn, because they had earned much income by transporting goods to Babylon (Ezekiel 27:25–26).

20 All non-believing men of the world will weep at the fall of Babylon, but believers in Christ—**saints and apostles and prophets**—will rejoice. The martyrs mentioned in Revelation 6:9–10 will also rejoice, because their blood has now been avenged.

21–24 Then John saw a mighty angel throw a **boulder the size of a large millstone** into the sea (verse 21). In the same way that boulder disappeared into the sea, so will the wealth, power, and splendor of Babylon disappear also (Jeremiah 51:63–64).

By [Babylon's] **magic spell all the nations were led astray** (verse 23). These nations were bewitched by Babylon's great wealth and power. They had believed that Babylon would never fall.

Just as Babylon (or Rome) had destroyed the bodies of Christ's **prophets** and **saints**, so God will destroy Babylon (Isaiah 13:1–22).

CHAPTER 19

The Wedding of the Lamb (19:1–10)

1–5 Then John heard a great multitude in heaven shouting, "**Hallelujah!**" The great multitude consisted of all those who, having stood firm in their faith to the end, had been saved and gone to heaven (see Revelation 7:9–10 and comment). They were rejoicing in God's just and righteous judgment (Revelation 18:20).

6–8 In John's vision, the multitude shouted: "**. . . the wedding of the Lamb has come**" (verse 7). That is, the wedding was about to occur. The Lamb is Christ. The bride of the Lamb is the church—that is, the great multitude of believers in heaven (verse 1).

The bride (the church) had made herself ready; she had purified herself. She had washed her clothes in the blood of the Lamb (see Revelation 7:14 and comment). She had become a bride **without stain or wrinkle or any other blemish** (Ephesians 5:25–27). She was clothed in fine **linen, bright and clean** (verse 8); that is, she was clothed in the **righteous acts of the saints**—of believers. All believers have been created by God to perform these righteous acts (Ephesians 2:10).

9 The believers mentioned in verses 6–8 are, in one way, the bride of Christ. But in verse 9, John says that, in another way, believers are also the guests invited to Christ's wedding feast. To be a bride and to be a wedding guest are, of course, very different; but, in either case, the meaning of the two analogies is the same. In order to marry Christ, the bride must be prepared and worthy. In order to come to the wedding feast, the guests must likewise be prepared and worthy (see Matthew 22:1–14 and comment). Thus, whether as bride or guest, believers must be both prepared and worthy to take part in the wedding of the Lamb.

10 Then John fell down and began to worship the mighty angel (Revelation 18:21), mistakenly thinking that the angel was Christ. The angel immediately said: "Don't worship me. **Worship God!** I am a fellow servant, just like you" (see Acts 10:25–26; Hebrews 1:14). From this we are reminded that we must never worship any king, any priest, any angel or spirit; we must worship only the one true triune God—Father, Son, and Holy Spirit.

For the testimony of Jesus is the spirit

of prophecy. That is, the true source of revelation and testimony is not angels and prophets but rather Jesus Himself, about whom angels and prophets have spoken. Only God's one true incarnation, Jesus Christ, is worthy to be worshiped.

The Victorious Christ (19:11–16)

11 Then John saw heaven itself opened, and a rider on a white horse appeared, who was Christ (2 Thessalonians 1:7–10). Christ is here called **Faithful and True** (Psalm 96:13; Revelation 3:14).

12 Christ had a secret name written on His body (Revelation 3:12). No one knows what that name is.

13 In John's vision, Christ's robe was **dipped in blood**. That blood was the blood of His enemies (Isaiah 63:1–6). Christ is here called the **Word of God** (see John 1:1–3,14). That Word is not just an ordinary sound; it is **living and active** [and sharper] **than any double-edged sword** (Hebrews 4:12). That word is the **sword of the Spirit** (Ephesians 6:17). And that word is the weapon that Christ uses to destroy His enemies (verse 15).

14 The **armies of heaven** were following Christ. These armies were made up of both angels (Matthew 26:53) and resurrected believers (Revelation 2:26–27; 17:14). The armies in John's vision were **dressed in fine linen, white and clean** (see Revelation 7:9,14; 19:8 and comments). These armies evidently were doing no fighting themselves: there was no blood on their clothes.

15–16 Only Christ strikes down the nations—His enemies. The sword that comes out of His mouth is the sword of judgment (see Isaiah 11:4; 2 Thessalonians 2:8; Revelation 1:16 and comments). **He** (Christ) **will rule them with an iron scepter**; that is, He will strike His enemies and destroy them with a rod of iron (Psalm 2:9). Christ **treads the winepress of the fury of the wrath of God** (see Revelation 14:19–20 and comment). This, then, is our victorious Savior Christ, the **King of kings and Lord of lords** (Deuteronomy 10:17; 1 Timothy 6:15; Revelation 17:14).

The Destruction of Christ's Enemies (19:17–21)

17–18 Those who today do not accept Christ the Lamb will, on the day of the final battle, have to face Christ the King. Those who today do not accept Christ the Savior will on that last day have to face Christ the Judge. He will have the sword of judgment in His mouth and a rod of iron in his hand (verse 15). On that day, those who have not believed in Christ will become food for vultures and other birds (Ezekiel 39:17–21). And they will have no one but themselves to blame. God had offered them forgiveness and salvation, but they rejected it. Those who reject God's mercy and grace will surely receive His judgment.

19 Then John watched as the enemies of the **rider on the horse** (Christ) gathered **for the battle on the great day of God Almighty** (Revelation 16:14). The chief enemies of Christ at the battle were the **beast** and his ten **kings** (see Revelation 13:1–2; 17:7–8,12–14 and comments). The battle that John saw in this vision will one day be fought at a place called **Armageddon** (Revelation 16:16).

20 In the battle, Christ was victorious over his enemies. The **beast**, together with the **false prophet** (Revelation 13:11; 16:13), were captured, and they were both thrown into a **fiery lake of burning sulfur**. The **beast**, also known as the antichrist, represents all worldly power and authority. The beast's colleague, the **false prophet**, represents all false religion. The false prophet's work was to deceive people and entice them to follow the beast and to receive the beast's mark[44] (see Revelation 13:11–16 and comment).

The **fiery lake of burning sulfur** represents the fire of hell, where the spirits of evil men will remain forever (Matthew 5:22; Mark 9:43).

21 In John's vision, all those who

[44] We see here what happens when leaders of the church ally themselves too closely with political leaders. The church is compromised and becomes the servant of the government.

followed the beast and the false prophet were killed by the sword which came from Christ's mouth. Christ thus rendered final judgment upon them (see Revelation 14:14–16). The sword from His mouth represents the word of judgment. The judgment given to those who follow the beast is this: their bodies will be killed, and their spirits will be thrown into hell.

One of the most important teachings of the book of Revelation is that Christ has won the final victory over Satan and his two chief helpers, the beast and the false prophet. The actual battle has not yet taken place, but God has already assigned the victory to Christ. That Christ will be victorious in the final battle is absolutely certain. In this world, we believers are pressed down and severely tested by Satan's attacks. We see evil men rise to power and persecute the church. However, let us never forget John's vision of this **battle on the great day of God Almighty**. Jesus has won! Jesus said: "**In this world you will have trouble. But take heart! I have overcome the world**" (John 16:33).

CHAPTER 20

The Thousand Years (20:1–6)

1 After Satan's two helpers—the beast and the false prophet—were thrown into the fiery lake (Revelation 19:20), John saw an angel with the **key to the Abyss** (Revelation 9:1; 11:7). The **Abyss** is a huge cavern deep within the earth, where fallen angels and the spirits of the disobedient are imprisoned until the day of judgment (Jude 6).

2–3 Then the angel bound Satan with a chain and threw him into the Abyss, where he was to remain for one thousand years. After the thousand years were finished, he was to be released for a short time (see verses 7–10).

4 Then John saw some thrones, on which were sitting some who had been given authority to judge. It is not known who John is referring to here. Some think those on the thrones are the twelve apostles (Matthew 19:28). Others think that they are saints (believers) who have stood firm and overcome Satan's temptations (1 Corinthians 6:2–3; Revelation 3:21). Whoever they are, they will in some way assist Christ in the work of judging.

In addition to those sitting on the thrones, John saw the souls of martyrs **who had been beheaded**, that is, killed. They had been killed because of their faith in Christ. They had not worshiped the beast; neither had they received its mark (Revelation 13:15–17). These included not only the martyrs mentioned in Revelation 6:9, but also all those who had died after them for the sake of Christ (Revelation 6:11). In John's vision these martyrs were only **souls**, because the resurrection of their bodies had not yet taken place.

Then John saw these souls come to life; that is, he saw the resurrection of their bodies take place. They then reigned with Christ for one thousand years. This is called the thousand-year reign of Christ and His martyred saints. We know that this reign—when it actually takes place—will take place on earth; because, according to verses 7–9, after the thousand-year period is up Satan will again gather the nations of the earth and attack Christ and

His saints one last time. But while the thousand-year reign is going on, Satan will be kept bound in the Abyss.[45]

5 Then, according to John, after the thousand-year reign of Christ and His martyrs is over, the **rest of the dead**—that is, those who have not been killed for Christ's sake—will come to life (be resurrected). Here the **rest of the dead** includes two groups: first, those believers in Christ from former generations who have not been actually killed for Christ's sake; and second, all non-believers.

The **first** RESURRECTION is the resurrection of the martrys at the beginning of the thousand-year reign (verse 4). The "second resurrection" is the resurrection of all the **rest of the dead** mentioned here in verse 5.

6 Those **who have a part in the first resurrection**—that is, the martyrs—are blessed and holy. As priests of God, they will reign with Christ for one thousand years. They will not be touched by the **second death**[46] (see verse 14 and comment).

Satan's Release and Final Destruction (20:7–10)

7–8 Even after being bound in the Abyss for a thousand years, there still was no improvement in Satan's character! One last time, Satan gathered together the nations of the earth that had not already been destroyed by Christ (Revelation 19:19–21). **Gog** and **Magog** are the symbolic names for these nations (Ezekiel 38:16).

9 Here the community of martyrs which reigned for a thousand years is called the **camp of God's people**. It is called a "camp," because it was not permanent; it only lasted a thousand years. The camp was known as the city God loves. In John's vision, the armies of the nations marched against the city (or camp); but before they could attack it, they were destroyed by fire from heaven (2 Kings 1:10; Ezekiel 38:21–22; 39:6).

10 Then Satan received his final punishment: He was thrown into the **lake of burning sulfur**, where he will be tormented forever (see Revelation 19:20 and comment).

Thus we have to come to a great climax in John's revelation: the defeat of Satan and the final victory over all the evil in the universe. But there are still two great climaxes yet to come: first, John's vision of the last judgment (verses 11–15); and finally, his vision of heaven itself (Revelation Chapters 21–22).

The Resurrection and the Last Judgment (20:11–15)

11 Here John describes for us his vision of the last judgment. John saw a **great white throne**. There was one sitting on the throne, either God or Christ—John doesn't say which. The New Testament

---

[45] Some Bible scholars interpret verse 4 differently. They believe that it is not only martyrs who will reign with Christ during that thousand years; they believe that all believers who have not worshiped the beast or received its mark will also reign with Christ during that time. These scholars say that two groups are mentioned in verse 4: first, the martyrs or beheaded ones; and second, other believers who have not been put to death but who have stood firm in the faith. In other words, these scholars say that all true Christians will take part in the thousand-year reign (see Revelation 2:26–27; 5:9–10).

But according to Revelation 13:15, all believers who do not worship the beast will be put to death. Therefore, all believers who are alive at the time of the beast will become martyrs. Thus, whether we say "believers" or "martyrs," in this context it is the same group. So it seems that in verse 4, John is only talking about one group: believers who have been put to death—that is, martyrs. For the martyrs, that thousand-year reign will be a great and blessed reward.

It would appear, then, that for all other believers who have died of natural causes before the coming of the beast, their resurrection will occur after the thousand-year reign is over.

[46] Believers who take part in the "second resurrection" (the general resurrection) will also not be touched by the second death. Only unbelievers will be condemned to the second death.

teaches that God has given all work of judgment to Christ (see John 5:22; 2 Corinthians 5:10; 2 Timothy 4:1). Yet Paul has also said that we will all stand before God's judgment seat (Romans 14:10). In the book of Revelation, the one sitting on the throne is usually God Himself (Revelation 5:13; 7:10; 19:4). But whether it is God or Christ sitting on the throne makes no difference, because God and Christ are one (John 10:30).

John then saw the earth and sky flee from God's presence. The only thing remaining was the great white throne and the One sitting on it; all else had vanished. The **new heaven** and **new earth** were about to come (Revelation 21:1); but before the new could come, the old had to pass away (Isaiah 51:6; Matthew 24:35; 1 John 2:17).

12–13 Then John saw all the dead from every generation standing before the throne. Those who had drowned in the sea were also there. All those who had not believed in Christ and whose spirits had gone to Hades were there (see Revelation 1:18 and comment). And, except for the Christian martyrs[47] (verse 4), all other believers were also there. What John was seeing, therefore, was a vision of the "second resurrection," in which all the dead—both unbelievers and believers (except martyrs)—will take part (see verse 5).

As soon as the second resurrection had taken place, God's last judgment began. The **books** containing the records of each person's life on earth were opened. John writes in verse 12 that the dead were judged **according to what they had done as recorded in the books** (see Psalm 62:12; Jeremiah 17:10; Romans 2:6; 1 Peter 1:17). There was another book, too, the **book of life.** In this book were written the names of all those who were to be saved (Daniel 12:1; Revelation 3:5; 17:8). The names of all those who were true believers as recorded in the "record books" were written in the **book of life.** Thus the names in the book of life corresponded exactly to the information in the record books. Those who had not repented and believed in Christ and done the works of faith did not have their names written in the book of life. Men are not saved by their good works; they are saved only through faith. But the proof of true faith is good works. Those without good works are without true faith. Thus the faith of each person can be determined by what he or she has done on earth—**as recorded in the books** (see Ephesians 2:8–10; James 2:17,20–24,26 and comments).

14–15 Then **death and Hades** were thrown into the lake of fire (see Revelation 19:20). In a way, death and Hades are partners. Hades is the place where death sends its victims. Hades is like the "stomach" of death; it is where those "eaten" by death end up. But at the last judgment, both death and its "stomach" will be destroyed (see Isaiah 25:8; 1 Corinthians 15:54–55 and comment).

And so in John's vision, **death** and **Hades** were thrown into the **lake of fire,**[48] just as had happened to Satan and to the beast and the false prophet earlier (Revelation 19:20; 20:10). Furthermore, all those whose names were not written in the book of life were also thrown into the lake of fire. The lake of fire is called the **second death**; it lasts forever.

As it was in John's vision, so it will happen at the end of the world. John gives us a preview of what the last judgment of God will be like. After the final judgment, there will be no chance for appeal. All whose names are not written in the **book of life** will be given everlasting punishment. Therefore, there is no more important question a person can ask in this life than this: Is my name written in the book of life, or not?

---

[47] The Christian martyrs had already been resurrected in the first resurrection (see verses 4–5 and comment); therefore, they were not among the dead at the last judgment.

[48] The **lake of fire** is the same as the **fiery lake of burning sulfur** mentioned in Revelation 19:20; 20:10.

CHAPTER 21

The New Heaven and the New Earth (21:1–8)

1 God had promised the Jews through the prophet Isaiah that He would **create new heavens and a new earth** that would last forever (Isaiah 65:17; 66:22). Now in John's vision, that promise has come to pass. Peter wrote that this present heaven and earth would be destroyed, but he was looking forward to a **new heaven and a new earth, the home of righteousness** (2 Peter 3:12–13). Paul has written that the **creation itself will be liberated from its bondage to decay and brought into the glorious freedom of the children of God** (Romans 8:20–21). Now, in John's vision, the old creation has passed away (Revelation 20:11); and in its place has come a new creation, which will never decay or pass away. John adds that there will be no sea in the new creation.

2 In his vision, John saw not only a new heaven and new earth, but he also saw the **Holy City**, which is called the **new Jerusalem** (Galatians 4:26; Hebrews 11:10,16; 13:14; Revelation 3:12). In his vision, John saw the Holy City **coming down out of heaven**. This city was created by God, not by man; it was created as a gift to all believers in Christ.

At the end of the world, the **Holy City** of John's vision will indeed be created by God. This Holy City represents not only our heavenly home; it also represents Christ's church. All those whose names are written in the book of life will be in that church (Hebrews 12:22–23). That church is also Christ's **bride**, who has been **beautifully dressed for her husband** (see 2 Corinthians 11:2; Ephesians 5:25–27; Revelation 19:6–8 and comments). How great is the difference between Christ's holy bride and the great prostitute! (Revelation 17:1). How great is the difference between the heavenly Jerusalem and the worldly Babylon! (Revelation 17:5).

3 Then John heard a voice saying: **"Now the dwelling of God is with men, and he will live with them. They will be his people."** That Holy City will not only be a place for believers to live; it will also be a place for God to live! God Himself will live there, and He will make us His people, His church (see Leviticus 26:11–12; Ezekiel 37:27; 1 Peter 2:9).

4 But believers will not just simply exist in the Holy City with God; they will live there with great joy. God Himself will **wipe every tear from their eyes**. There will be no sorrow, sickness, or pain in the heavenly Jerusalem (see Isaiah 35:10; Revelation 7:16–17). And above all, there will be no more death (Isaiah 25:8; 1 Corinthians 15:54; Revelation 20:14). Death first came into the world because of sin (Romans 5:12). But in the Holy City there will be no sin; therefore, there will be no death.

5 Then John heard God say: **"I am making everything new!"**—new heavens, new earth, new city, new people. Only new people are fit to live in a new city. We believers have already begun to be made new through faith in Christ (see John 3:3; 2 Corinthians 3:18; 4:16–18; 5:17; Colossians 1:13–14 and comments). And when our bodies are resurrected, then we will be completely new. Then we shall be ready to enter the heavenly city.

6 God, who is the **Alpha and the Omega, the Beginning and the End** (Revelation 1:8), will give us to drink without cost **from the spring of the water of life**. That spring is Christ Himself (Psalm 36:7–9; John 4:14).

7 **He who overcomes**—that is, he who remains faithful to the end—**will inherit all this** (Revelation 2:7,11,17,26; 3:5,12,21). Those who overcome will be the sons of God, and because they are sons they will receive the inheritance saved up for them in heaven (see Romans 8:16–17; 1 Peter 1:3–4 and comments).

8 Here God describes those who will not receive an inheritance in heaven (see 1 Corinthians 6:9–10; Galatians 5:19–21 and comments). The **cowardly** are mentioned first. The cowardly are those who fall away when trials come. Their fear of the beast is greater than their love for Christ (see Mark 4:5–6,16–17). They have forgotten that **whoever wants to save his life will lose it** (Mark 8:35).

The **unbelieving** are not only non-Christians, but they are also those who at first come to Christ but later turn away and reject Him. They, together with the other sinners mentioned in this verse, will be thrown into the lake of fire, which is the second death (Revelation 20:14).

The Heavenly Jerusalem (21:9–27)

9–14 Then, in John's vision, an angel showed him the Holy City, the heavenly Jerusalem. What follows is a description of that city.

The city had **twelve gates** (verse 12), on which were written the names of the twelve tribes of Israel (Ezekiel 48:30–35; Revelation 7:4–8). God had chosen the ancient nation of Israel—that is, the Jews—to be His special people. The promises of God had first been given to Abraham, the first Jew, the father of the Jewish nation. Now through faith in Christ, we too have received these same promises. Therefore, for us Gentiles (non-Jews), the twelve tribes of Israel are like gateways giving us entry into the heavenly city (see Galatians 3:7–9,14,29 and comment). Through faith we now have been made citizens of the heavenly city; that is, we have become the new Israel.

The city in John's vision also had **twelve foundations** (verse 14), on which the names of Christ's twelve apostles were written. Paul wrote to the Gentile Ephesians: **Consequently, you are . . . fellow citizens with God's people** (the Jews) **and members of God's household**; that household is **built on the foundation of the apostles and prophets** (Ephesians 2:19–20).

15–21 John here further describes the city of his vision. It was **12,000 stadia** (1,400 miles) **in length**, and it was the same in width and in height (verse 16). There'd be plenty of room for all believers! (John 14:2). Thus the city was a perfect cube, 1,400 miles in each dimension. Its shape was the same as that of the inner sanctuary in the old Jewish temple in Jerusalem (1 Kings 6:20).

The wall of the city was **144 cubits** (65 meters) **thick**,[49] according to man's measurement (verse 17). That's a small wall for a city 1,400 miles high!

As we study John's description of this city, we must remember that John is trying to describe something that is beyond human experience or understanding. The city was made of **pure gold, as pure as glass** (verse 18). Its twelve gates were each made of a **single pearl** (verse 21). Such an amazing city, our eternal home!

22 John saw no temple in the city, **because the Lord God Almighty and the Lamb are its temple**. Where God is, there is our temple. God does not live in any temple built with hands (Acts 7:48–49; 17:24). In another sense, however, we believers are God's "temple," because we are a dwelling place for God's Holy Spirit (see 2 Corinthians 6:16; Ephesians 2:21–22 and comments).

23–27 The city was full of light, which came from God and Christ (Isaiah 60:19). Because there was no night in the city, it was never necessary to shut the city gates (Isaiah 60:11). **The nations will walk by its light** (verse 24). John called Jesus the **true light that gives light to every man** (John 1:9). Jesus Himself said: **"I am the light of the world. Whoever follows me will never walk in darkness, but will have the light of life"** (John 8:12).

Here a question arises: Who are the **nations** and **kings** mentioned in verses 24 and 26? (And who are the **dogs** mentioned in Revelation 22:15?) Why are these nations and kings outside the heavenly city? If they are believers, why are they not inside? If they are unbelievers, why have they not been thrown into the lake of fire? (Revelation 20:15). Bible scholars give various answers to these

---

[49] The word **thick** can also be translated "high." It is not certain here whether John is talking about thickness or height.

questions, but no one is certain what John's meaning is here. However, one thing is certain: Nothing impure will ever enter God's Holy City (verse 27). Only those can enter whose robes have been washed in the blood of Christ (Revelation 7:14), and **whose names are written in the Lamb's** (Christ's) **book of life**.

CHAPTER 22

The River of Life (22:1–6)

1 Then John was shown the **river of the water of life**, which flowed out **from the throne of God and of the Lamb**. The throne mentioned in Revelation 7:15 and 12:5 is God's throne; but here and in verse 3, the throne belongs also to the Lamb Christ. Christ is fully worthy to sit on God's throne. Jesus said: "**All authority in heaven and earth has been given to me**" (Matthew 28:18). Indeed, God and Christ are one (John 10:30).

The river of life flowed from the **spring of the water of life** (Revelation 21:6), which is Christ. There had also been a river in the Garden of Eden (Genesis 2:10). In some respects, the original Garden of Eden and the heavenly city were similar. In the beginning there had been no sin, no sickness, no sorrow, and no death in the Garden of Eden. God Himself walked in the garden (Genesis 3:8). But then those first two humans, Adam and Eve, sinned against God, and after that God expelled them from the garden (Genesis 3:23–24).

2 Together with the river of life in the heavenly city, there was a **tree of life**. There had also been a tree of life in the Garden of Eden, whose fruit gave eternal life to those who ate it (Genesis 2:9; 3:22). The tree of life in God's heavenly city was a sign of abundance and of health. Everyone in the city received spiritual food from this tree, and having eaten it, they were spiritually healed.

3–4 **No longer will there be any curse**. Because of the sin of Adam and Eve, God put a curse upon man and upon the earth (Genesis 3:14–19). But in the heavenly city there is no sin; therefore, there is no curse either.

In the heavenly city, God's servants will **see his face** (verse 4). In the Old Testament, God's greatest servant Moses was never allowed to see God's face (Exodus 33:18–23). Jesus said that only the pure in heart would be able to see God (Matthew 5:8). But we, who have been made pure by the blood of the Lamb, will see God's face. And **we shall be like him, for we shall see him as he is** (1 John 3:2). Of all the blessings of heaven, the greatest will be to see God's face, and to be with Him forever.

God's name will be written on our foreheads (Revelation 3:12; 7:3). His name on our forehead is a sign that He has made us His own people, and that He has given us His qualities and His character.

5 See Revelation 2:26; 3:21; 21:23 and comments.

6 Here John assures us that everything he has written in this book of Revelation is **trustworthy and true**. This revelation is from God, and God has sent His own angel to reveal these things to John. He is the **God of the spirits of the prophets**. Through His Holy Spirit, God has inspired and directed the spirits of all the true prophets of God. Just as the prophets have spoken by the inspiration of the Holy Spirit (2 Peter 1:21), so John has written all these things by the inspiration of that same Holy Spirit. He has written down this revelation to prepare us for the **things that must soon take place**. The time remaining is short (1 Corinthians 7:29–31). Paul wrote: . . . **our salvation is nearer now than when we first believed. The night is nearly over; the day is almost here** (Romans 13:11–12). The **bright Morning Star** will soon usher in the new day (verse 16).

Jesus Is Coming (22:7–21)

7 Jesus says: "**Behold, I am coming soon!**" (see Matthew 24:42,44; Mark

13:32–37). "**Blessed is he who keeps the words of this prophecy**"; that is, blessed is he who stands firm in his faith to the end and who does not receive the mark of the beast.

8–9 See Revelation 19:10 and comment.

10 The prophet Daniel was told to seal up the book of prophecy he had written, because his prophecy was not ready to be fulfilled (Daniel 8:26; 12:4). But here John is told not seal up this book of Revelation, because the things written in it are soon to be fulfilled.

11 Here John says that when the final tribulations at the end of the world come, those who have been doing evil will continue to do evil; they will not repent. At that time, their hearts will become even more hardened. The final tribulations at the end of the world will bring their evil into the light. But let him who has placed his faith in Christ **continue to do right** and **continue to be holy** until the end (Daniel 12:10).

12 See Jeremiah 17:10; Romans 2:6; Revelation 20:12 and comments.

13 John here repeats what is written in Revelation 1:8,17 and 2:8. In Revelation 1:8 and 21:6, God is called the **Alpha** and the **Omega**. Here Jesus gives Himself the same name.

14 Those who have washed their robes are those who have been purified from sin by the blood of Christ. Only they will be allowed to pass into the heavenly city (Revelation 7:14; 21:27).

15 See Revelation 21:8,24–26 and comment.

16 Here Jesus calls Himself the **Root and Offspring of David** (see Revelation 5:5 and comment). Next He calls Himself the **bright Morning Star**. This Morning Star is a sign of the dawning of a new day after a long night of tribulation—a sign of the new day of the kingdom of Jesus Christ (see Romans 13:12; Revelation 2:28; 22:5 and comments).

17 **The Spirit** (the Holy Spirit) **and the bride** (the church) say to all men: **"Come!" Whoever is thirsty, let him come** (see Isaiah 55:1; John 7:37–38; Revelation 21:6).

18–19 Here John gives a warning to **everyone who hears the words of prophecy of this book** of Revelation: no one in any way may change or add or take away from the words of this prophecy. If any person does so, his punishment will be severe. He may even lose his place in the heavenly city (see Deuteronomy 4:2; Galatians 1:6–9).

20–21 John here repeats the words of the One **who testifies to these things**, namely Jesus: "**Yes, I am coming soon**."

Come, Lord Jesus. We are waiting for you. Men labor and strive. They build cities and kingdoms. But what they do is all in vain. Men cannot build a better world on their own. We have failed to do so over and over again. We have only one hope, and that is in your return.

Come, Lord Jesus. Amen.

INDEX TO SUBJECTS

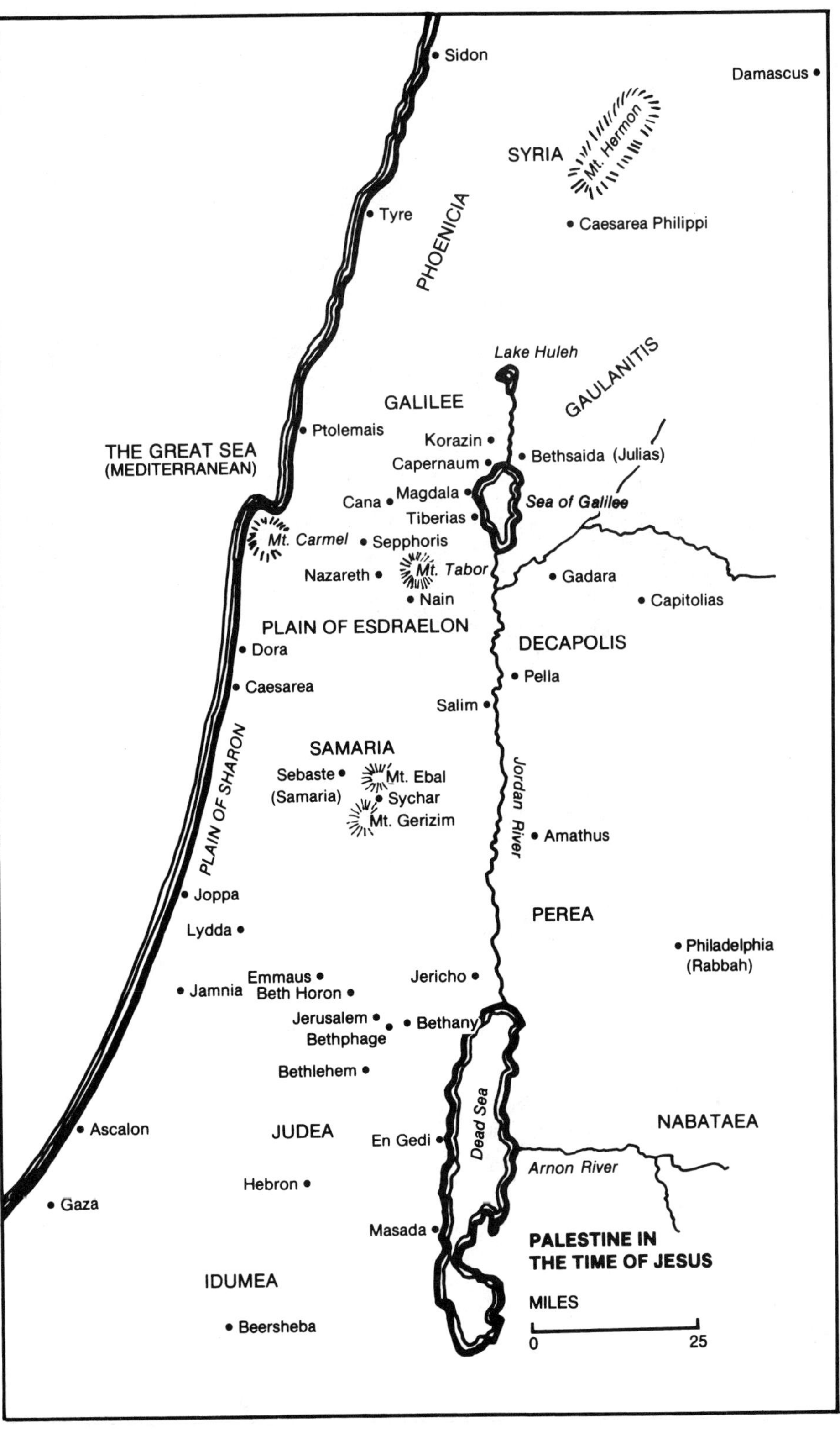
Sidon
Damascus
SYRIA
Mt. Hermon
Tyre
PHOENICIA
Caesarea Philippi
Lake Huleh
GAULANITIS
GALILEE
Ptolemais
THE GREAT SEA
(MEDITERRANEAN)
Korazin
Capernaum
Bethsaida (Julias)
Cana
Magdala
Sea of Galilee
Tiberias
Mt. Carmel
Sepphoris
Nazareth
Mt. Tabor
Gadara
Nain
Capitolias
PLAIN OF ESDRAELON
Dora
DECAPOLIS
Caesarea
Pella
Salim
PLAIN OF SHARON
SAMARIA
Sebaste
(Samaria)
Mt. Ebal
Sychar
Mt. Gerizim
Jordan River
Amathus
Joppa
Lydda
PEREA
Philadelphia
(Rabbah)
Emmaus
Jamnia
Beth Horon
Jericho
Jerusalem
Bethany
Bethphage
Bethlehem
Dead Sea
Ascalon
JUDEA
En Gedi
NABATAEA
Arnon River
Hebron
Gaza
Masada
PALESTINE IN
THE TIME OF JESUS
IDUMEA
MILES
Beersheba
0
25

ILLYRICUM
MOESIA
Black Sea
Rome
Three Taverns
Forum of Appius
Adriatic Sea
THRACE
MACEDONIA
Puteoli
ITALY
Tyrrhenian Sea
Philippi
Neapolis
Amphipolis
Thessalonica
Apollonia
Berea
BITHYNIA
GALATIA
PONTUS
Troas
Assos
Mitylene
ASIA
Pergamum
Thyatira
CAPPADOCIA
Aegean Sea
ACHAIA
Messana
Rhegium
SICILY
Syracuse
Antioch
Iconium
Lystra
Derbe
Sardis
Philadelphia
Smyrna
PISIDIA
CILICIA
Laodicea
Ephesus
Colosse
Corinth
Athens
Cenchrea
MALTA
Miletus
Perga
PAMPHYLIA
Tarsus
Cnidus
LYCIA
Attalia
Myra
Seleucia
Antioch
Patara
CRETE
CYPRUS
The Great Sea
(Mediterranean)
Lasea
Fair Havens
Salamis
Paphos
SYRIA
Damascus
Sidon
Tyre
Ptolemais
PAUL'S FIRST MISSIONARY JOURNEY
MILES
0
100
200
300
Caesarea
Joppa
Jerusalem
Gaza
LIBYA
Alexandria
EGYPT
ARABIA

PAUL'S SECOND
MISSIONARY JOURNEY
MILES
0
100
200
300
ILLYRICUM
MOESIA
Black Sea
THRACE
MACEDONIA
Rome
Three Taverns
Forum of
Appius
Adriatic Sea
Puteoli
ITALY
Tyrrhenian Sea
Philippi
Neapolis
Amphipolis
Thessalonica
Apollonia
Berea
BITHYNIA
GALATIA
PONTUS
MYSIA
Troas
Assos
ASIA
Mitylene
Pergamum
Aegean Sea
CAPPADOCIA
ACHAIA
Antioch
PHRYGIA
Thyatira
Messana
Rhegium
SICILY
Sardis
Philadelphia
Iconium
Smyrna
Lystra
Laodicea
PISIDIA
CILICIA
Athens
Corinth
Cenchrea
Ephesus
Colosse
Derbe
Syracuse
PAMPHYLIA
Tarsus
Miletus
MALTA
Cnidus
LYCIA
Antioch
Myra
Seleucia
Patara
CRETE
CYPRUS
SYRIA
The Great Sea
(Mediterranean)
Lasea
Fair Havens
Damascus
Sidon
Tyre
Ptolemais
Caesarea
Joppa
Jerusalem
Gaza
LIBYA
Alexandria
EGYPT
ARABIA

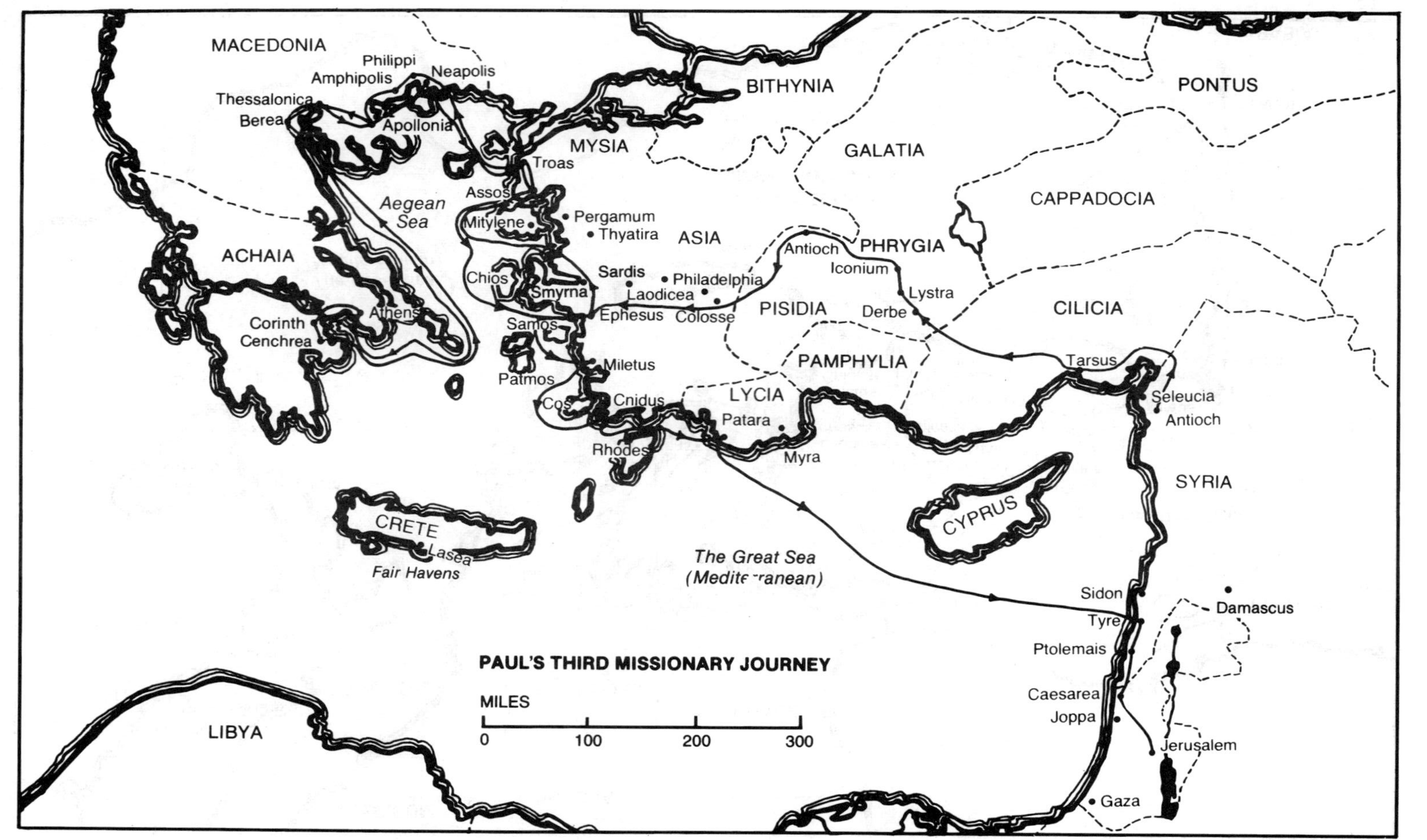
MACEDONIA
Philippi
Amphipolis
Neapolis
Thessalonica
Berea
Apollonia
BITHYNIA
PONTUS
MYSIA
GALATIA
Troas
Assos
Aegean Sea
CAPPADOCIA
Mitylene
Pergamum
Thyatira
ASIA
ACHAIA
Antioch
PHRYGIA
Iconium
Chios
Sardis
Philadelphia
Smyrna
Laodicea
Lystra
Ephesus
Colosse
PISIDIA
Derbe
CILICIA
Athens
Corinth
Cenchrea
Samos
PAMPHYLIA
Miletus
Tarsus
Patmos
Cos
Cnidus
LYCIA
Seleucia
Antioch
Patara
Rhodes
Myra
SYRIA
CYPRUS
CRETE
Lasea
Fair Havens
The Great Sea
(Medite ranean)
Sidon
Damascus
Tyre
Ptolemais
PAUL'S THIRD MISSIONARY JOURNEY
Caesarea
MILES
Joppa
0
100
200
300
LIBYA
Jerusalem
Gaza

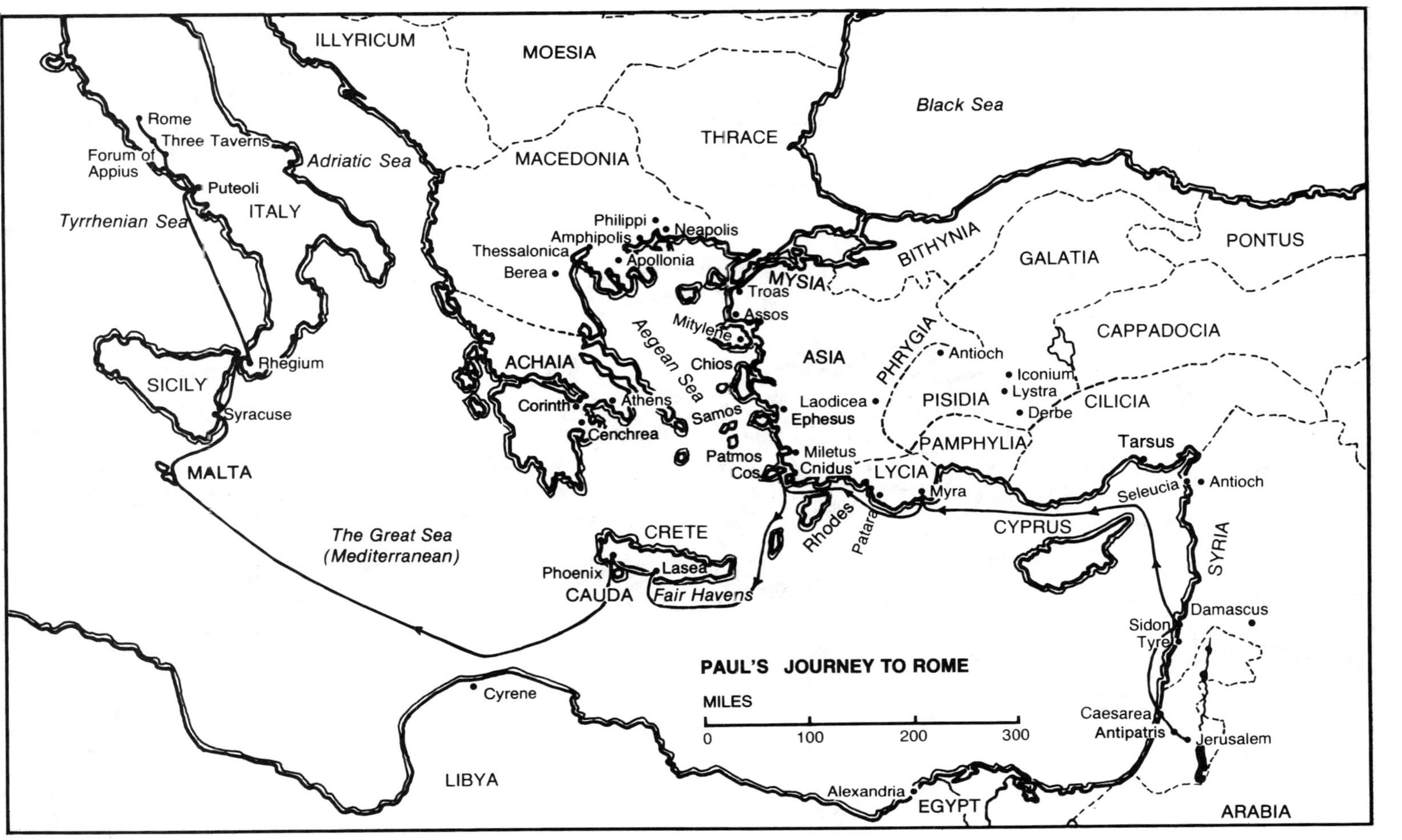
PAUL'S JOURNEY TO ROME
MILES
0
100
200
300
ILLYRICUM
MOESIA
Black Sea
THRACE
MACEDONIA
Rome
Three Taverns
Forum of Appius
Puteoli
Adriatic Sea
ITALY
Tyrrhenian Sea
Philippi
Neapolis
Amphipolis
Thessalonica
Apollonia
Berea
BITHYNIA
GALATIA
PONTUS
MYSIA
Troas
Assos
Mitylene
Aegean Sea
CAPPADOCIA
PHRYGIA
Antioch
ASIA
Chios
Iconium
Lystra
Derbe
PISIDIA
CILICIA
SICILY
Rhegium
Syracuse
ACHAIA
Corinth
Athens
Cenchrea
Samos
Laodicea
Ephesus
Patmos
Miletus
Cos
Cnidus
PAMPHYLIA
LYCIA
Myra
Tarsus
Antioch
Seleucia
MALTA
The Great Sea (Mediterranean)
CRETE
Phoenix
Lasea
CAUDA
Fair Havens
Rhodes
Patara
CYPRUS
SYRIA
Damascus
Sidon
Tyre
Caesarea
Antipatris
Jerusalem
Cyrene
LIBYA
Alexandria
EGYPT
ARABIA

THE NEW TESTAMENT WORLD
MILES
0
100
200
300
ILLYRICUM
(DALMATIA)
MOESIA
Adriatic Sea
Rome
ITALY
SICILY
MALTA
MACEDONIA
THRACE
Black Sea
Philippi
Thessalonica
ACHAIA
Corinth
Cenchrea
Athens
Aegean
Sea
Troas
BITHYNIA
PONTUS
GALATIA
CAPPADOCIA
ASIA
Antioch
Hierapolis
Laodicea
Colosse
Ephesus
Iconium
Lystra
Derbe
CILICIA
PAMPHYLIA
LYCIA
Antioch
CRETE
The Great Sea
(Mediterranean)
CYPRUS
Caesarea
Jerusalem
EGYPT